More Than Just a Textbook

Log on to ***ca.gr5math.com*** *to…*

Access your book from home

- **Online Student Edition**
- **Student Workbooks**

See mathematical concepts come to life

- **Personal Tutor**
- **Concepts in Motion**

Practice what you've learned

- **Chapter Readiness**
- **Extra Examples**
- **Self-Check Quizzes**
- **Vocabulary Review**
- **Chapter Tests**
- **Standards Practice**

Try these other activities

- **Cross-Curricular Features**
- **Game Time**

Macmillan McGraw-Hill

California Mathematics

Concepts, Skills, and Problem Solving

5

Authors

Day • Frey • Howard • Hutchens • Luchin • McClain
Molix-Bailey • Ott • Pelfrey • Price • Vielhaber • Willard

Mc Graw Hill
Macmillan
McGraw-Hill

About the Cover

California Focus A brown pelican soars high above the San Francisco Bay, which is considered the world's largest landlocked harbor, while the Golden Gate Bridge stands guard at the entrance. There are 38 painters and 17 ironworkers who work on the bridge every day. One of the distinctive features of the bridge is its color. It takes 5,000 gallons of orange vermillion paint to keep the 1.7 mile bridge looking bright. The workers paint year round, finishing at one end and starting over at the other end.

Mathematics Focus This year you will study more about geometry concepts such as parallel lines. You can recognize the Golden Gate Bridge by the hundreds of parallel lines formed by the cables. These are lines that never cross, no matter how far they are extended. What other parallel lines can you find on the cover?

Macmillan McGraw-Hill

The McGraw·Hill Companies

Printed in the United States

Send all inquiries to:
Macmillan/McGraw-Hill
8787 Orion Place
Columbus, OH 43240-4027

ISBN-13: 978-0-02-105853-2
MHID: 0-02-105853-9

1 2 3 4 5 6 7 8 9 10 027/055 15 14 13 12 11 10 09 08 07

Contents in Brief

Authors

Rhonda J. Molix-Bailey
Mathematics Consultant
Mathematics by Design
DeSoto, Texas

Roger Day, Ph.D.
Mathematics Department Chair
Pontiac Township High School
Pontiac, Illinois

Patricia Frey, Ed.D.
Math Coordinator at Westminster Community Charter School
Buffalo, New York

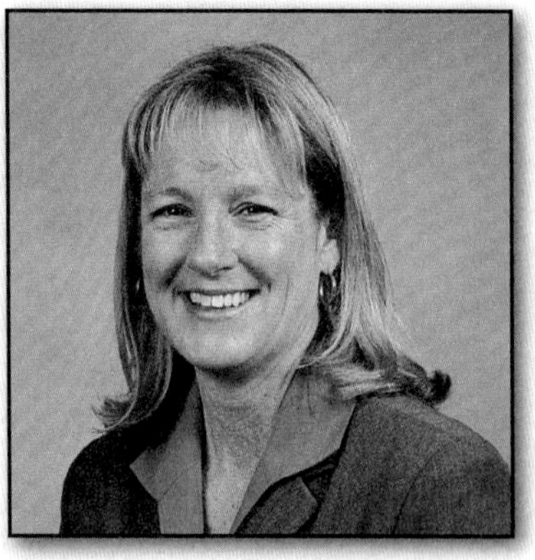

Arthur C. Howard
Mathematics Teacher
Houston Christian High School
Houston, Texas

Deborah A. Hutchens, Ed.D.
Principal
Chesapeake, Virginia

Beatrice Luchin
Mathematics Consultant
League City, Texas

Contributing Authors

Viken Hovsepian
Professor of Mathematics
Rio Hondo College
Whittier, California

Donna J. Long
Mathematics Consultant
Indianapolis, Indiana

Kay McClain, Ed.D.
Assistant Professor
Vanderbilt University
Nashville, Tennessee

Jack M. Ott, Ph.D.
Distinguished Professor
of Secondary Education
Emeritus
University of South Carolina
Columbia, South Carolina

Ronald Pelfrey, Ed.D.
Mathematics Specialist
Appalachian Rural
Systemic Initiative and
Mathematics Consultant
Lexington, Kentucky

Jack Price, Ed.D.
Professor Emeritus
California State
Polytechnic University
Pomona, California

Kathleen Vielhaber
Mathematics Consultant
St. Louis, Missouri

Teri Willard, Ed.D.
Assistant Professor
Department of Mathematics
Central Washington
University
Ellensburg, Washington

Contributing Author

FOLDABLES™ **Dinah Zike**
Educational Consultant
Dinah-Might Activities, Inc.
San Antonio, Texas

California Mathematics Advisory Board

Macmillan/McGraw-Hill wishes to thank the following professionals for their invaluable feedback during the development of the program. They reviewed a variety of instructional materials at different stages of development.

Cheryl L. Avalos
Mathematics Consultant
Hacienda Heights, California

William M. Bokesch
Rancho Bernardo High School
San Diego, California

Patty Brown
Teacher
John Muir Elementary
Fresno, California

David J. Chamberlain
Secondary Mathematics Resource Teacher
Capistrano Unified School District
San Juan Capistrano, California

Eppie Chung
K-6 Teacher
Modesto City Schools
Modesto, California

Lisa Marie Cirrincione
Middle School Teacher
Lincoln Middle School
Oceanside, California

Carol Cronk
Mathematics Program Specialist
San Bernardino City Unified School District
San Bernardino, California

Ilene Foster
Teacher Specialist–Mathematics
Pomona Unified School District
Pomona, California

Grant A. Fraser, Ph. D.
Professor of Mathematics
California State University, Los Angeles
Los Angeles, California

Suzanne Bocskai Freire
Teacher
Kingswood Elementary
Citrus Heights, California

Beth Holguin
Teacher
Graystone Elementary
San Jose, California

Donna M. Kopenski, Ed. D.
Mathematics Coordinator K-5
City Heights Educational Collaborative
San Diego, California

Kelly Mack
6th Grade Teacher
Captain Jason Dahl Elementary
San Jose, California

Juvenal Martinez
Dual Immersion/ESL Instructor
Aeolian Elementary
Whittier, California

John McGuire
Associate Principal
Pacific Union School
Arcata, California

Dr. Donald R. Price
Teacher, Adjunct Professor
Rowland Unified School District
Rowland Heights, California

Kasey St. James
Mathematics Teacher
Sunny Hills High School
Fullerton, California

Arthur K. Wayman, Ph. D.
Professor of Mathematics Emeritus
California State University, Long Beach
Long Beach, California

Beverly Wells
First Grade Teacher
Mineral King Elementary School
Visalia, California

Frances Basich Whitney
Project Director, Mathematics K-12
Santa Cruz County Office of Education
Capitola, California

Consultants

Macmillan/McGraw-Hill wishes to thank the following professionals for their feedback. They were instrumental in providing valuable input toward the development of this program in these specific areas.

Mathematical Content

Viken Hovsepian
Professor of Mathematics
Rio Hondo College
Whittier, California

Grant A. Fraser, Ph.D.
Professor of Mathematics
California State University, Los Angeles
Los Angeles, California

Arthur K. Wayman, Ph.D.
Professor of Mathematics Emeritus
California State University, Long Beach
Long Beach, California

Assessment

Jane D. Gawronski
Director of Assessment and Outreach
San Diego State University
San Diego, California

Cognitive Guided Instruction

Susan B. Empson
Associate Professor of Mathematics and Science Education
University of Texas at Austin
Austin, Texas

English Learners

Cheryl Avalos
Mathematics Consultant
Los Angeles County Office of Education, Retired
Hacienda Heights, California

Kathryn Heinze
Graduate School of Education
Hamline University
St. Paul, Minnesota

Family Involvement

Paul Giganti, Jr.
Mathematics Education Consultant
Albany, California

Literature

David M. Schwartz
Children's Author, Speaker, Storyteller
Oakland, California

Vertical Alignment

Berchie Holliday
National Educational Consultant
Silver Spring, Maryland

Deborah A. Hutchens, Ed.D.
Principal
Norfolk Highlands Elementary
Chesapeake, Virginia

California Reviewers

Each California Reviewer reviewed at least two chapters of the Student Edition, giving feedback and suggestions for improving the effectiveness of the mathematics instruction.

Sherry G. Anderson
Teacher/G.A.T.E. Coordinator
Will Rogers Elementary
Lynwood, CA

Ysaaca Axelrod
Kindergarten Teacher
El Monte Elementary
Concord, CA

Cathy Bullock
Teacher
Capri Elementary
Encinitas, CA

Michelle Callender
Teacher
Morgan/Kincaid Preparatory School of Integrated Studies
Victorville, CA

M. Olivia Campos
4th Grade Teacher
Morrison Elementary
Norwalk, CA

Malaura Page Easton, M.S.
Kindergarten Teacher
La Pluma School
La Mirada, CA

Priscilla S. Edwards
5th Grade Classroom Teacher
David Reese Elementary
Sacramento, CA

Lisa B. Friedberg
4th Grade Teacher
Alderwood Basics Plus School
Irvine, CA

Wendy Smith Hernandez
Kindergarten Teacher
Herndon-Barstow Elementary
Fresno, CA

Beth Holguin
Teacher
Graystone School
San Jose, CA

Kristi Iverson
First Grade Teacher
Village Oaks Elementary
Stockton, CA

Sheri Leiken
Teacher
Weathersfield Elementary
Thousand Oaks, CA

Sarab H. Lopes
Teacher
Anza Elementary
El Cajon, CA

Karen E. Lund
5th Grade Teacher
Meadow Park Elementary
Irvine, CA

Efrain Melendez
Teacher
Livermore Valley USD
Livermore, CA

Jean A. Nelson
Teacher
Fremont Elementary School
Alhambra, CA

Tara Pahia
Elementary Teacher
Bear Gulch Elementary
Rancho Cucamonga, CA

Dr. Donald R. Price
Teacher, Adjunct Professor
Rowland Unified School District
Rowland Heights, CA

Kitty Ritz, M.A.
Teacher
Monte Vista Elementary
Rohnert Park, CA

Corinne E. Schwartz
First Grade Teacher
Lincrest Elementary School
Yuba City, CA

Deborah Shapiro
5th Grade Teacher
Nancy Cory
Lancaster, CA

Maureen Smith
Curriculum Specialist
Fremont Unified School Dist. (retired 6/2006)
Fremont, CA

Joseph M. Snodgrass
3rd Grade Teacher
Park Elementary School
Alhambra, CA

Marie W. Stevens
Elementary Mathematics Coordinator
LAUSD
Los Angeles, CA

Jane Traut
Classroom Teacher
Lang Ranch Elementary School
Thousand Oaks, CA

Rachel C. Trowbridge
Teacher
Evergreen Elementary
San Jose, CA

Cynthia H. Vandemoortel
Educator
Alderwood Basics Plus School
Irvine, CA

Norine Yale
Teacher
Justin Elementary
Simi Valley, CA

Dr. Darlene York
Education Consultant
Associate Professor
Antioch University
Seattle, WA

Contents

Start Smart

Chapter 1 Number Sense, Algebra, and Functions

California Standards Practice

- Multiple Choice 20, 25, 30, 31, 38, 43, 49, 55, 61, 67, 68, 69
- Worked Out Example 68

H.O.T. Problems
Higher Order Thinking
20, 25, 30, 37, 38, 42, 43, 49, 55, 61

WRITING IN MATH 20, 25, 30, 31, 33, 38, 43, 45, 49, 55, 61, 67

Contents

Chapter 2 Statistics and Data Analysis

California Standards Practice

H.O.T. Problems
Higher Order Thinking

CHAPTER 3 Adding and Subtracting Decimals

Contents

Chapter 4 Fractions and Decimals

CHAPTER 5 Adding and Subtracting Fractions

California Standards Practice

H.O.T. Problems
Higher Order Thinking

CHAPTER 6 Multiplying and Dividing Decimals and Fractions

CHAPTER 7 Algebra: Integers and Equations

California Standards Practice

H.O.T. Problems
Higher Order Thinking

WRITING IN MATH

CHAPTER 8 Algebra: Ratios and Functions

Chapter 9 Percent

California Standards Practice

- Multiple Choice 470, 476, 480, 488, 489, 495, 503, 509, 516, 523, 524, 525
- Worked Out Example 524

H.O.T. Problems
Higher Order Thinking
470, 475, 480, 487, 495, 502, 508, 509, 515

WRITING IN MATH 470, 475, 480, 483, 487, 489, 495, 497, 503, 509, 515, 523

Contents

CHAPTER 10 Geometry: Angles and Polygons

Chapter 11 Measurement: Perimeter, Area, and Volume

California Standards Practice

California Standards Review

Looking Ahead to the Grade 6 Standards

Student Handbook

H.O.T. Problems
Higher Order Thinking
635, 639, 643, 647, 651

WRITING IN MATH 635, 639, 643, 647, 651

California Standards for Mathematics Grade 5

denotes key standards

Standard	Text of Standard	Primary Citations	Supporting Citations
Number Sense			
1.0	**Students compute with very large and very small numbers, positive integers, decimals, and fractions and understand the relationship between decimals, fractions, and percents. They understand the relative magnitudes of numbers:**	17–25, 113–117, 131–134, 141–145, 149–153, 182, 183, 189–192, 209–212, 349–352, 465–470, 477–480, 490–495, CA4–CA6	26, 28–30, 37, 38, 53, 57, 135, 136, 155, 157–159, 163, 176–178, 181, 184, 195–197, 200, 201, 207, 219, 231–240, 354, 355, 359, 361, 481–488, 496, 497, 499–501, 511
1.1	Estimate, round, and manipulate very large (e.g., millions) and very small (e.g., thousandths) numbers.	141–145, 149–153, CA4, CA6	155, 157–159, 163, 231–240
1.2 (key)	Interpret percents as a part of a hundred; find decimal and percent equivalents for common fractions and explain why they represent the same value; compute a given percent of a whole number.	209–212, 465–470, 477–480, 490–495	219, 481–488, 496, 497, 499–501, 511
1.3	Understand and compute positive integer powers of nonnegative integers; compute examples as repeated multiplication.	21–25, CA4–CA6	26, 28–30, 37, 38, 53, 285–287
1.4 (key)	Determine the prime factors of all numbers through 50. Write prime factors of all numbers through 50 as the product of their prime factors by using exponents to show multiples of a factor (e.g., $24 = 2 \times 2 \times 2 \times 3 = 2^3 \times 3$).	17–25, CA5	26, 57, 176–178, 181, 195–197
1.5 (key)	Identify and represent on a number line decimals, fractions, mixed numbers, and positive and negative integers.	113–117, 131–134, 182, 183, 189–192, 349–352, CA5, CA6	135, 136, 141, 142, 184, 200, 201, 207, 211, 233, 354, 355, 359, 361
2.0	**Students perform calculations and solve problems involving addition, subtraction, and simple multiplication and division of fractions and decimals:**	157–161, 241–245, 251–256, 260–269, 283–293, 296–299, 301–306, 314–331, 334–337	156, 163, 181, 184–188, 199, 210, 211, 246, 247, 249, 250, 257–259, 270, 294, 295, 300, 309–313, 332, 400, 421–424, 439, 483–488, 492, 493, 496, 497, 587, 588, 593, 594, 600–603, 610, 611, 615, 619, 620
2.1 (key)	Add, subtract, multiply, and divide with decimals; add with negative integers; subtract positive integers from negative integers; and verify the reasonableness of the results.	157–161, 283–293, 296–299, 301–306, 354–363	156, 163, 181, 199, 294, 295, 300, 309, 332, 353, 369, 376, 377, 384, 388, 391–397, 400, 421–424, 439, 492, 493, 496, 497, 587, 588, 593, 594, 601, 610, 611, 615, 619, 620
2.2 (key)	Demonstrate proficiency with division, including division with positive decimals and long division with multidigit divisors.	296–299, 303–306	210, 211, 300–302, 400
2.3 (key)	Solve simple problems, including ones arising in concrete situations, involving the addition and subtraction of fractions and mixed numbers (like and unlike denominators of 20 or less), and express answers in the simplest form.	241–245, 251–256, 260–269	184–188, 246, 247, 249, 250, 257–259, 270, 369, 421
2.4	Understand the concept of multiplication and division of fractions.	314, 315, 325, 326	316–324, 327–331, 334–337

Standard	Text of Standard	Primary Citations	Supporting Citations
2.5	Compute and perform simple multiplication and division of fractions and apply these procedures to solving problems.	316–324, 327–331, 334–337	310–315, 325, 326, 483–488, 492, 493, 587, 593, 594, 600–603, 610, 611
Algebra and Functions			
1.0	**Students use variables in simple expressions, compute the value of the expression for specific values of the variable, and plot and interpret the results:**	34–43, 46–49, 58–61, 378–382, 387–389, 394–396, 399–401, 436–447, 450–454, 512–516, CA11, CA23	52–55, 57, 153, 155, 185–187, 213–217, 285, 286, 291, 292, 295, 318, 323, 336, 357, 383–386, 391–393, 397, 398, 449, 467, 468, 485, 542, 543, 552, 554–556, 558, 560, 561, 585, 599, 600, 602, 609, 610, 620
1.1	Use information taken from a graph or equation to answer questions about a problem situation.	46–49, 437–441, 450–454	155, 295, 387–389, 394–396, 399–401, 513–516
1.2	Use a letter to represent an unknown number; write and evaluate simple algebraic expressions in one variable by substitution.	34–43, 436–447, 512–516	46–49, 52–55, 57, 60, 61, 185–187, 285, 286, 291, 292, 318, 323, 336, 383–389, 392–401, 449–454, 467, 468, 485, 542, 543, 552, 554–556, 558, 560, 561, 585, 599, 600, 602, 609, 610
1.3	Know and use the distributive property in equations and expressions with variables.	58–61	153, 620
1.4	Identify and graph ordered pairs in the four quadrants of the coordinate plane.	378–382	213–217, 391
1.5	Solve problems involving linear functions with integer values; write the equation; and graph the resulting ordered pairs of integers on a grid.	387–389, 394–396, 399–401, 442–447, 450–454, CA11, CA23	39–43, 57, 357
Measurement and Geometry			
1.0	**Students understand and compute the volumes and areas of simple objects:**	52–55, 591–595, 598–603, 608–613, 616–622, CA13	50–51, 147, 292, 309, 311–313, 323, 483, 497, 583, 584, 597, 604, 615
1.1	Derive and use the formula for the area of a triangle and of a parallelogram by comparing it with the formula for the area of a rectangle (i.e., two of the same triangles make a parallelogram with twice the area; a parallelogram is compared with a rectangle of the same area by cutting and pasting a right triangle on the parallelogram).	591–595, 598	599–603
1.2	Construct a cube and rectangular box from two-dimensional patterns and use these patterns to compute the surface area for these objects.	616–621, CA13	622
1.3	Understand the concept of volume and use the appropriate units in common measuring systems (i.e., cubic centimeter [cm^3], cubic meter [m^3], cubic inch [in^3], cubic yard [yd^3]) to compute the volume of rectangular solids.	608–613	323, 615
1.4	Differentiate between, and use appropriate units of measures for, two- and three-dimensional objects (i.e., find the perimeter, area, volume).	52–55, 585–589, 591–595, 599–603, 608–613, 622	50–51, 147, 292, 309, 311–313, 483, 497, 583, 584, 590, 597, 604, 607, 615, 617–621

Standard	Text of Standard	Primary Citations	Supporting Citations
2.0	**Students identify, describe, and classify the properties of, and the relationships between, plane and solid geometric figures:**	529–532, 537–546, 550–563, 566–570, CA16	533–535, 548, 549, 565, 583, 584, 603, 617, 618
🔑 2.1	Measure, identify, and draw angles, perpendicular and parallel lines, rectangles, and triangles by using appropriate tools (e.g., straightedge, ruler, compass, protractor, drawing software).	529–532, 537–546, 551, 553–556, 559–563, CA16	533–535, 548–550, 557, 565, 583, 584, 603
🔑 2.2	Know that the sum of the angles of any triangle is 180° and the sum of the angles of any quadrilateral is 360° and use this information to solve problems.	550, 552, 554–558, 560–563, CA16	565
2.3	Visualize and draw two-dimensional views of three-dimensional objects made from rectangular solids.	566–570	617, 618
Statistics, Data Analysis, and Probability			
1.0	**Students display, analyze, compare, and interpret different data sets, including data sets of different sizes:**	73–77, 79–91, 95–103, 106–112, 200–204, 213–217, 468–476, 504	78, 92, 93, 119, 198, 199, 219, 298, 299, 378–382, 391, 435, 511
1.1	Know the concepts of mean, median, and mode; compute and compare simple examples to show that they may differ.	95–103	119, 298, 299, 435
1.2	Organize and display single-variable data in appropriate graphs and representations (e.g., histogram, circle graphs) and explain which types of graphs are appropriate for various data sets.	73–77, 83–91, 106–112, 471–476	78, 92, 93, 119, 198, 199
1.3	Use fractions and percentages to compare data sets of different sizes.	200–204, 468–470, 473–476, 504	219, 511
🔑 1.4	Identify ordered pairs of data from a graph and interpret the meaning of the data in terms of the situation depicted by the graph.	79–82	106, 108, 109, 213–217
🔑 1.5	Know how to write ordered pairs correctly; for example, (x, y).	213–217	378–382, 391
Mathematical Reasoning			
1.0	**Students make decisions about how to approach problems:**	*Used throughout the text.* For example, 32, 33, 496, 497, 617–621	
1.1	Analyze problems by identifying relationships, distinguishing relevant from irrelevant information, sequencing and prioritizing information, and observing patterns.	32, 33, 104, 105, 180, 181, 308, 309, 368, 369, 420, 421, 496, 497, 548, 549	27–30, 39–43, 195–199, 231, 250, 258, 259, 288, 289, 332, 376, 377, 422–427, 434, 435, 505, 507, 557, 583, 584, 596, 598, 606, 607
1.2	Determine when and how to break a problem into simpler parts.	617–621	32, 33, 482, 483
2.0	**Students use strategies, skills, and concepts in finding solutions:**	*Used throughout the text.* For example, 154, 155, 482–488, 583, 584	
2.1	Use estimation to verify the reasonableness of calculated results.	265, 266, 290, 291	261, 284, 294–299, 303, 317, 334, 335, 482, 493, 593, 609, 610
2.2	Apply strategies and results from simpler problems to more complex problems.	482–488	497

Standard	Text of Standard	Primary Citations	Supporting Citations
2.3	Use a variety of methods, such as words, numbers, symbols, charts, graphs, tables, diagrams, and models, to explain mathematical reasoning.	92, 93, 156, 231, 246, 247, 249, 250, 258, 259, 353, 383, 384, 392, 422–427, 434, 435, 534, 535, 583, 584, 590, 596, 597, 606, 607	50, 51, 58, 73–77, 79–91, 95, 104–112, 131, 146, 147, 175, 176, 182, 183, 205, 206, 232–236, 241, 242, 251, 252, 260, 265, 283, 288, 289, 294–296, 301, 302, 314, 315, 325, 326, 354, 355, 359–361, 364, 371, 393, 398, 442–447, 449–454, 465–467, 490, 491, 506–509, 536, 549, 550, 563, 616
2.4	Express the solution clearly and logically by using the appropriate mathematical notation and terms and clear language; support solutions with evidence in both verbal and symbolic work.	146, 147, 376, 377	21–25, 50, 51, 73–77, 79–91, 95–98, 106–112, 139, 232–236, 259, 309, 326, 449, 473–475, 500–503, 542–544, 556, 559–563
2.5	Indicate the relative advantages of exact and approximate solutions to problems and give answers to a specified degree of accuracy.	232–240, 310–313	149, 161, 604
2.6	Make precise calculations and check the validity of the results from the context of the problem.	44, 45, 154, 155, 198, 199	46–49, 241–245, 251–256, 260–269, 284–287, 290–293, 316–324, 327–331, 334–337, 377, 385–389, 393–396, 398–401, 422–427, 436–441, 549
3.0	**Students move beyond a particular problem by generalizing to other situations:**	*Used throughout the text.* For example, 50, 51, 95–98, 296	
3.1	Evaluate the reasonableness of the solution in the context of the original situation.	294, 295	309, 611
3.2	Note the method of deriving the solution and demonstrate a conceptual understanding of the derivation by solving similar problems.	622	58–61, 95–98, 296, 353, 364, 491
3.3	Develop generalizations of the results obtained and apply them in other circumstances.	50, 51	111, 112, 156, 231, 283, 315, 353, 384, 392, 504, 550, 590–595, 598, 616

SCAVENGER HUNT

CHAPTER 1

Let's Get Started

Use the Scavenger Hunt below to learn where things are located in each chapter.

1. What is the title of Chapter 1?
2. How can you tell what you'll learn in Lesson 1-1?
3. What is the title of the feature in Lesson 1-1 that tells you to write prime factors in ascending order?
4. Suppose you're doing your homework on page 29 and you get stuck on Exercise 10. Where could you find help?
5. Sometimes you may ask "When am I ever going to use this?" Name a situation that uses the concepts from Lesson 1-3?
6. What is the key concept presented in Lesson 1-3?
7. How many examples are presented in Lesson 1-3?
8. In the margin of Lesson 1-5, there is a Vocabulary Link. What can you learn from that feature?
9. What is the Web address where you could find extra examples?
10. What problem-solving strategy is presented in the Problem-Solving Strategy in Lesson 1-7?
11. List the new vocabulary words that are presented in Lesson 1-8.
12. What is the Web address that would allow you to take a self-check quiz to be sure you understand the lesson?
13. On what pages will you find the Study Guide and Review for Chapter 1?
14. Suppose you can't figure out how to do Exercise 17 in the Study Guide on page 63. Where could you find help?

MATH? SYMBOLS!

Start Smart

Let's Review!

The Desert Tortoise
California State Reptile

Standard 4NS1.3 Round whole numbers through the millions to the nearest ten, hundred, thousand, ten thousand, or hundred thousand.

Problem Solving

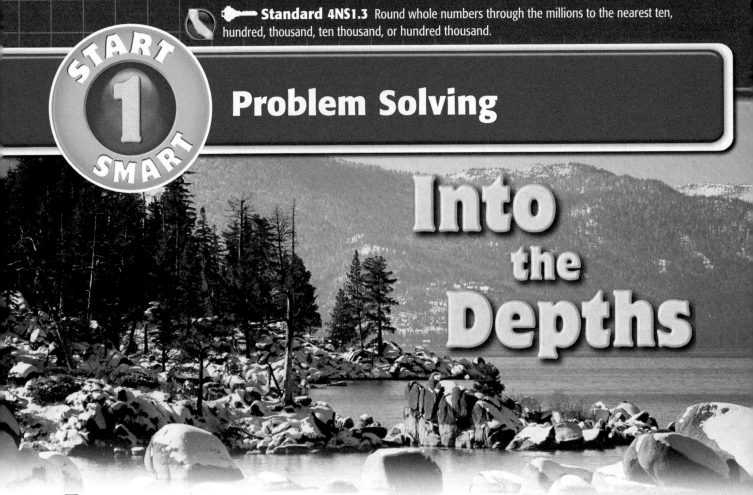

Into the Depths

Two of the most popular tourist spots in California are Big Bear Lake and Lake Tahoe. Lake Tahoe is the second deepest lake in the United States, at a maximum depth of 1,645 feet, while Big Bear Lake has a maximum depth of 72 feet.

About how much deeper is Lake Tahoe than Big Bear Lake?

You can use the four-step problem-solving plan to solve many kinds of problems. The four steps are Understand, Plan, Solve, and Check.

Understand

- **Read the problem carefully.**
- **What facts do you know?**
- **What do you need to find?**

The maximum depth of Lake Tahoe is 1,645 feet, and the maximum depth of Big Bear Lake is 72 feet. You need to find *about* how much deeper Lake Tahoe is than Big Bear Lake.

Plan

- **How do the facts relate to each other?**
- **Plan a strategy to solve the problem.**

Lake Tahoe has a maximum depth of 1,645 feet, and Big Bear Lake has a maximum depth of 72 feet. To estimate the difference between the two depths, round each number to the nearest hundred.

Solve

- **Use your plan to solve the problem.**

1,645	→	1,600	Depth of Lake Tahoe
− 72		− 100	Depth of Big Bear Lake
		1,500	

So, Lake Tahoe is about 1,500 feet deeper than Big Bear Lake.

Check

- **Look back at the problem.**
- **Does your answer make sense?**

Check by adding. Since 1,500 + 100 = 1,600, the answer makes sense.

Did you Know?

The sun shines 75% of the year at Lake Tahoe. That's about 274 days.

CHECK What You Know

1. List the steps of the four-step problem-solving plan.
2. WRITING IN ► MATH The table shows the lengths of different bridges in California. Explain how to use the four-step plan to find about how many times greater the length of the Golden Gate Bridge is than the length of the San Francisco-Oakland Bay Bridge.

Bridges in California

Bridge	Length (feet)
Antioch	9,504
Colorado Street	1,486
Golden Gate	4,200
San Francisco-Oakland Bay	2,310

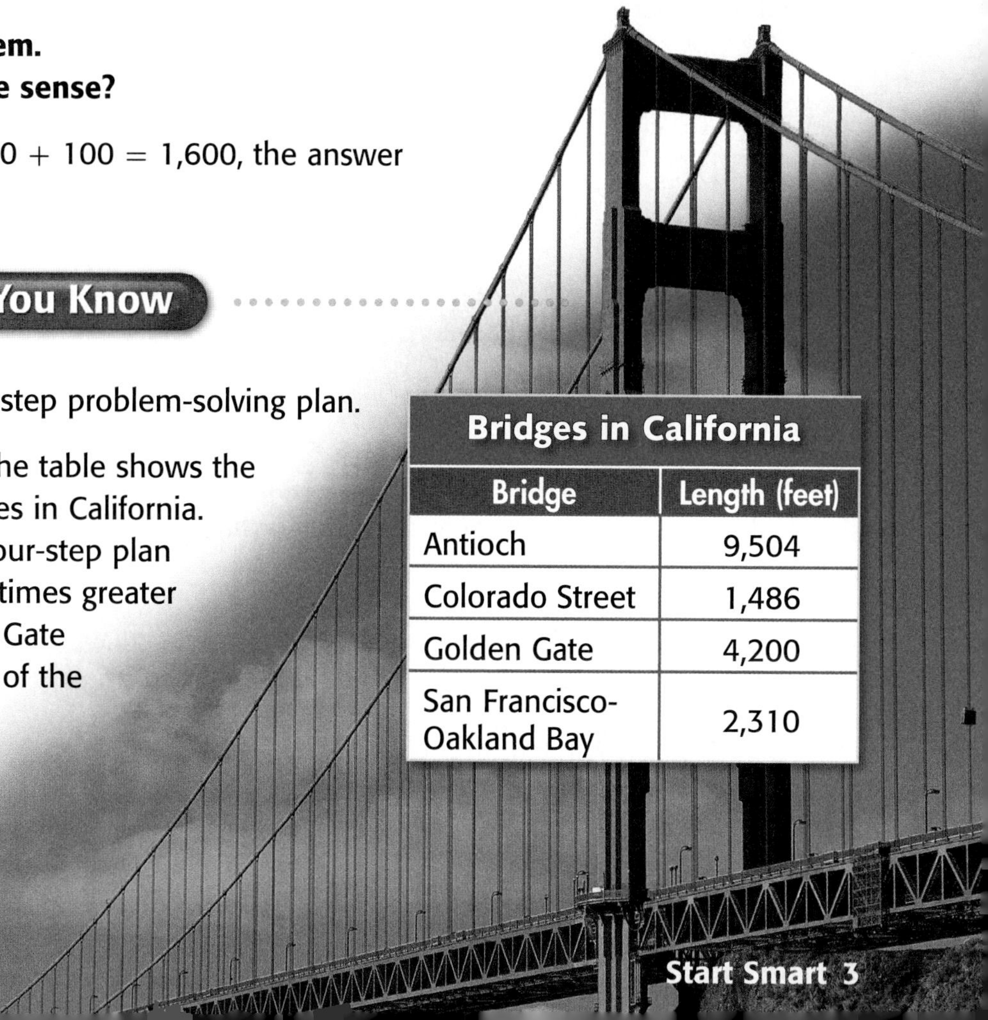

Standard 4NS2.1 Estimate and compute the sum or difference of whole numbers and positive decimals to two places.

START 2 SMART

Number Sense

High Flying Fun

California is home to many of the world's top theme parks. The table shows the approximate attendance of California's top four theme parks in a recent year.

Theme Park	Attendance
Disneyland	14,500,000
Disney's California Adventure	5,800,000
Knott's Berry Farm	3,600,000
Universal Studios Hollywood	4,700,000

Source: coastergrotto.com

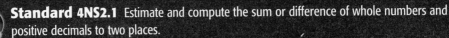

CHECK What You Know — Adding and Subtracting Whole Numbers

Did you Know?

Disneyland in Anaheim opened in 1955 and is credited with being the very first theme park in the United States.

When adding and subtracting whole numbers, always remember to add the digits in the same place-value position.

Use the table on page 4 to answer each question. First list the operation needed to solve the problem, then solve.

1. How many total people visited Knott's Berry Farm and Disney's California Adventure?
2. How many more people visited Disneyland than Universal Studios Hollywood?
3. Find the difference in the attendance between the park with the greatest attendance and the one with the least attendance.
4. Disneyland had the greatest attendance of all the theme parks listed. If the attendance for the other parks is combined, will their total attendance be greater than Disneyland's? Explain.
5. WRITING IN ▸MATH California is the leading producer of dairy products in the United States. The table shows the amount of certain dairy products produced, in tons, in California in a recent year. Use the information to write a real-world addition or subtraction problem about California dairy production.

California Dairy Production

Product	Tons Produced
Butter	203,933
Cheddar Cheese	261,312
Cottage Cheese	49,936
Monterey Jack Cheese	166,040
Yogurt	255,993

Source: cdfa.ca.gov

Standard 4AF1.1 Use letters, boxes, or other symbols to stand for any number in simple expressions or equations (e.g., demonstrate an understanding and the use of the concept of a variable).

START 3 SMART

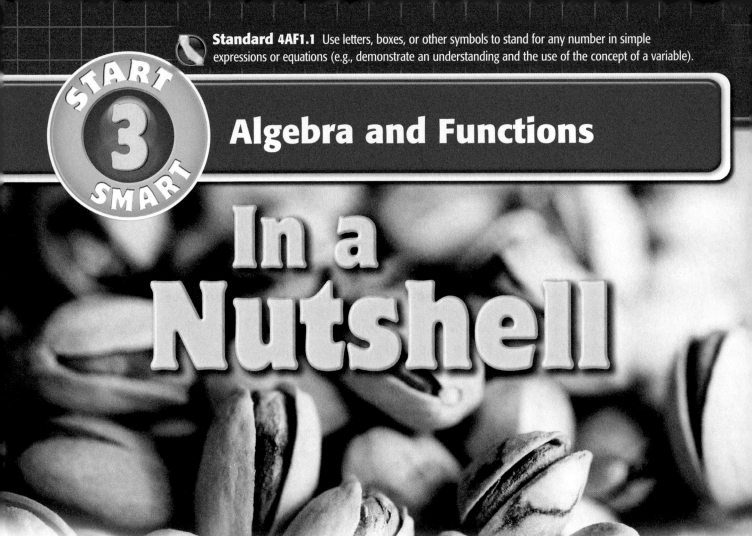

Algebra and Functions

In a Nutshell

Pistachios have been grown in Europe, Asia, and the Middle East for centuries. However, they have only been a commercial crop in California since 1976. Approximately 98% of the pistachios grown in the United States are from California.

CHECK What You Know Functions

A function is a relationship that assigns exactly one output to one input value. You can organize the input-output values in a function table.

The table shows the grams of protein per one ounce serving of pistachios.

Rule: Multiply by 6.	
Input (Servings)	Output (Grams of Protein)
1	6
2	12
3	18
4	■

1. Use the rule to find the amount of protein in four servings of pistachios.

2. Use the rule to find the amount of protein in five servings of pistachios.

3. Describe the pattern in the output column.

Did you Know?

California's population increases by 2% every year. This is nearly double the national average.

Fueled by longer life expectancies and strong birthrates, the United States reached a population of 300 million in October of 2006.

4. In the United States, there is 1 birth every 7 seconds. The function table shows the rule for finding the number of births every 7, 14, 21, and 28 seconds. Complete the function table.

Rule: Divide by 7.	
Input (Seconds)	Output (Births)
7	1
14	■
21	■
28	■

5. Use the function rule to find how many births occur in 70 seconds.

CHECK What You Know **Algebra**

Algebra is a mathematical language that uses symbols. Examples of symbols are letters and boxes. The symbols stand for numbers that are unknown.

6. WRITING IN ▸MATH Write a real-world problem in which you would use the function rule $y = 20x$.

Replace each ■ with a number to make a true sentence.

7. $(7 - 3) \times 5 = 4 \times$ ■

8. $8 + (10 \times 2) =$ ■ $+ 20$

9. $12 \div (9 - 7) = 12 \div$ ■

10. $(11 + 6) \times 3 = 17 \times$ ■

11. $(16 - 8) \times 14 =$ ■ $\times 14$

12. $(24 \div 6) + 1 =$ ■ $+ 1$

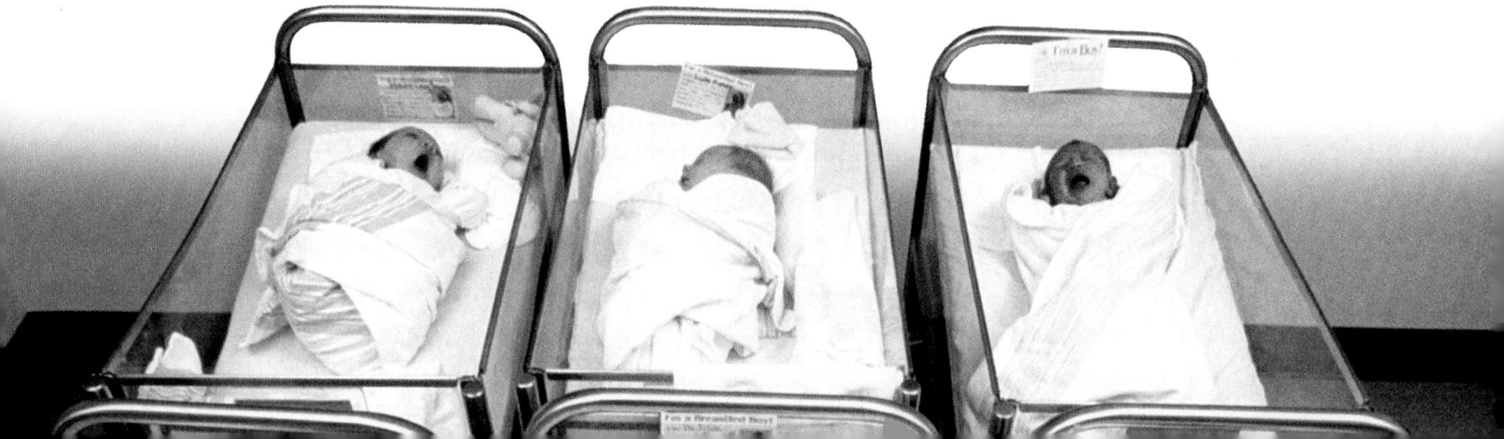

Standard 4MG1.4 Understand and use formulas to solve problems involving perimeters and areas of rectangles and squares. Use those formulas to find the areas of more complex figures by dividing the figures into basic shapes.

START SMART 4

Measurement

A Full Basket

The state of California has six professional basketball teams. Four of the teams—the Los Angeles Lakers, Sacramento Kings, Golden State Warriors, and Los Angeles Clippers—are men's teams. Two teams—the Los Angeles Sparks and the Sacramento Monarchs—are women's teams.

CHECK What You Know Area

The area of a figure refers to the number of square units needed to cover the figure. The area of a rectangle or square is found by multiplying its length by its width.

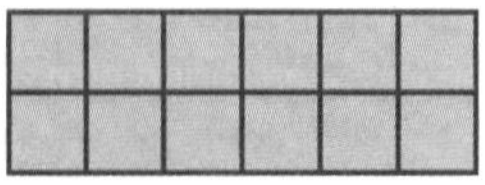

1. Find the area of the rectangle shown. Then draw two other rectangles that have the same area.

2. A regulation professional basketball court is rectangular in shape and measures 94 feet long and 50 feet wide. What is the area of a regulation professional basketball court?

3. The backboard, the board behind the net, usually measures 6 feet long by 4 feet wide. What is the area of the backboard?

CHECK What You Know Perimeter

Did you Know?

The Golden State Warriors and the Los Angeles Lakers (formerly the Minneapolis Lakers) were two of the original eight teams in the NBA.

Perimeter is the distance around a figure. To find the perimeter of a rectangle or square, find the sum of the measures of the sides.

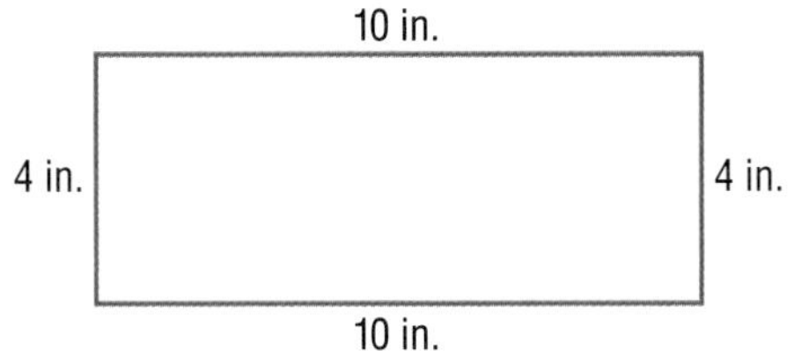

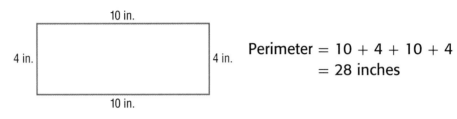

$$\text{Perimeter} = 10 + 4 + 10 + 4$$
$$= 28 \text{ inches}$$

4. Refer to the rectangle above. Draw two other rectangles or squares that have the same perimeter.

5. Using the information from Exercise 2, what is the perimeter of a regulation professional basketball court?

6. Using the information from Exercise 3, what is the perimeter of a backboard?

7. Mr. Thorne's garden is shown. The width is 5 yards less than the length. Mr. Thorne extends the length of the garden by 2 yards. What is the total distance around the new garden?

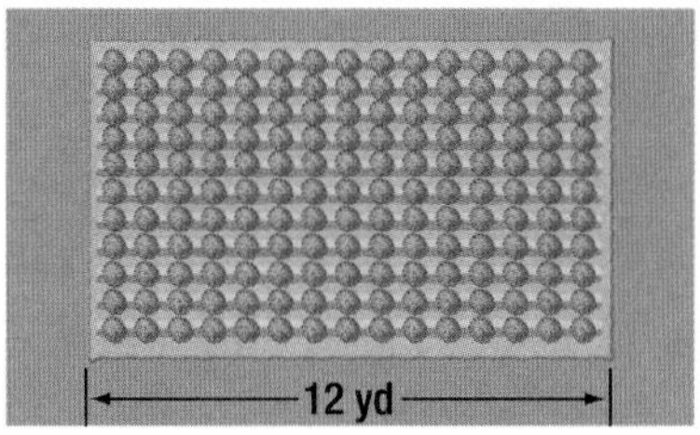

8. **WRITING IN ►MATH** Do all rectangles with the same area have the same perimeter? Explain your reasoning.

Standard 4MG3.5 Know the definitions of a right angle, an acute angle, and an obtuse angle. Understand that 90°, 180°, 270°, and 360° are associated, respectively, with $\frac{1}{4}$, $\frac{1}{2}$, $\frac{3}{4}$, and full turns.

START SMART 5

Geometry

A Capitol Idea

The California State Capitol Building in Sacramento is where the state government does its work. It was designed in 1856 by Reuben Clark, and construction was completed on the building in 1874.

CHECK What You Know Triangles and Quadrilaterals

Triangles or quadrilaterals such as squares and rectangles are commonly used in buildings.

Use the photo of the Capitol Building to solve each problem.

1. Can you see any shapes that appear to be triangles? Describe the triangles that you see.

2. Can you see any shapes that appear to be quadrilaterals? What type of quadrilaterals do they appear to be?

Start Smart

CHECK What You Know Angles

Different angles can also be found in buildings. Remember that 90°, 180°, 270°, and 360° are associated, respectively, with $\frac{1}{4}$ turn, $\frac{1}{2}$ turn, $\frac{3}{4}$ turn, and 1 full turn on a circle.

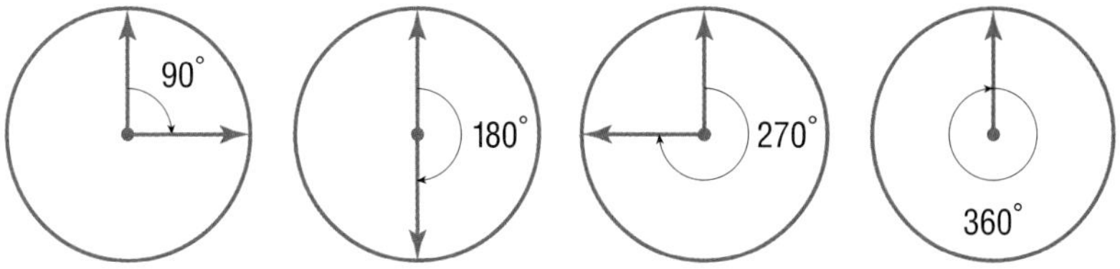

Use the photo of the Capitol Building to solve each problem.

3. Describe any angles that appear to be less than 90°.

4. Describe any angles that appear to be exactly 90°.

5. Describe any angles that appear to be greater than 90°.

Did you Know

The capital of California has not always been Sacramento. The first state capital was in San Jose, followed by Vallejo, Benicia, and finally Sacramento in 1854.

CHECK What You Know Parallel and Perpendicular Lines

Parallel and perpendicular lines can also be found in buildings. Remember that parallel lines are lines that are the same distance apart and never intersect, and perpendicular lines are lines that intersect to form right angles.

Use the photo of the Capitol Building to solve each problem.

6. Describe any lines that appear to be parallel.

7. Describe any lines that appear to be perpendicular.

8. WRITING IN ▸MATH Use the photo at the right of the Transamerica Building in San Francisco to describe any shapes, angles, and types of lines that appear to be in the building.

Standard 4SDAP1.3 Interpret one- and two-variable data graphs to answer questions about a situation.

START SMART 6

Statistics, Data Analysis, and Probability

A Real Hot Spot

Death Valley National Park is located on the eastern border of south-central California and includes a small area of Nevada. The winters in Death Valley are mild, but summers are extremely hot and dry. It is one of the hottest places on Earth.

CHECK What You Know Line Graphs

A line graph shows how a set of data changes over a period of time. The line graph at the right shows the average high temperatures in Death Valley, California.

1. What month has the highest average high temperature?

2. During which months are the average high temperatures less than 80°F?

Average High Temperatures in Death Valley

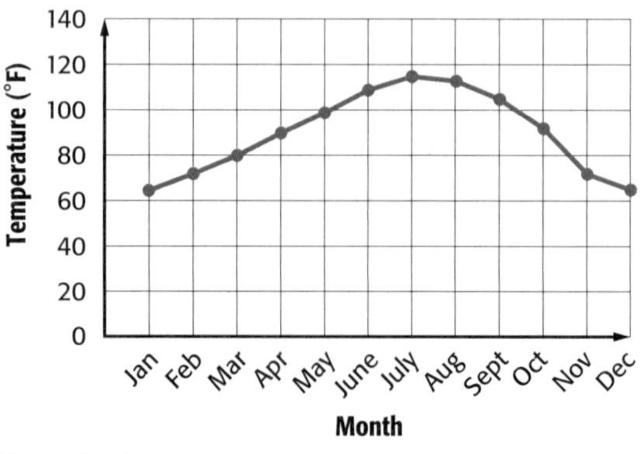

Source: desertusa.com

CHECK What You Know Interpret Line Graphs

Did you Know?

Death Valley set the record for the highest temperature ever recorded in the U.S., at 134°F on July 10, 1913.

Line graphs are often used to predict future events because they show trends over time. The line graph below shows the average rainfall for Death Valley.

Average Rainfall in Death Valley

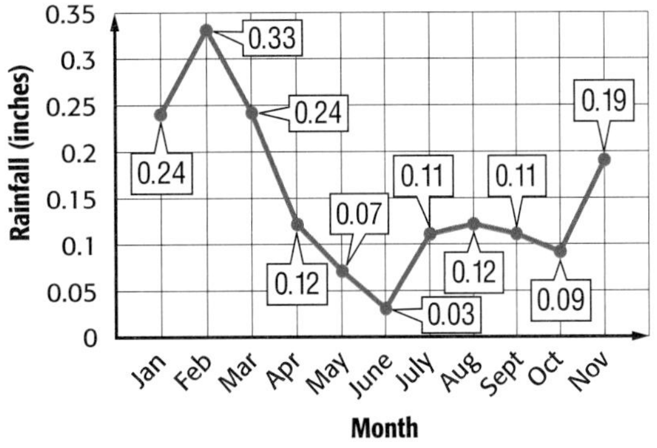

Source: desertusa.com

3. Which month has the least amount of average rainfall?

4. Is a prediction of 0.2 inch of rainfall for next March reasonable? Explain.

5. Describe the trend in average rainfall from February to June.

6. Collect the low temperatures for one week in another California national park. Then make a line graph to show the results.

7. **WRITING IN ▸MATH** Based on your graph in Exercise 6, make a prediction of what you think the low temperature might be at a future date. Explain your reasoning.

CHAPTER 1 Number Sense, Algebra, and Functions

BIG Idea What are equations?

An **equation** is a sentence that contains an equals sign.

Example The Los Angeles Memorial Coliseum, home of the University of Southern California Trojans, has a seating capacity of 92,000. Often, there is a cover on many of the seats. You can use the equation $x + 24{,}000 = 92{,}000$ to find x, the number of seats available when the cover is used.

What will I learn in this chapter?

- Find the prime factorization of a composite number.
- Use powers and exponents in expressions.
- Complete function tables and find function rules.
- Use the Distributive Property in equations and expressions.
- Solve problems using the *guess and check* strategy.

Key Vocabulary

variable
evaluate
function
equation
area

Math Online **Student Study Tools at** ca.gr5math.com

FOLDABLES™ Study Organizer

Make this Foldable to help you organize information about this chapter. Begin with six sheets of notebook paper.

1. **Stack** the pages, placing the sheets of paper $\frac{3}{4}$ inch apart.

2. **Roll** up bottom edges. All tabs should be the same size.

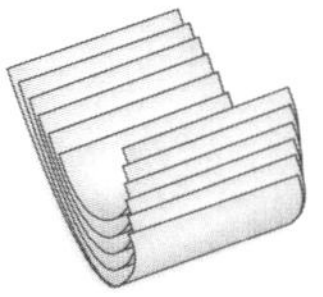

3. **Crease** and staple along the fold.

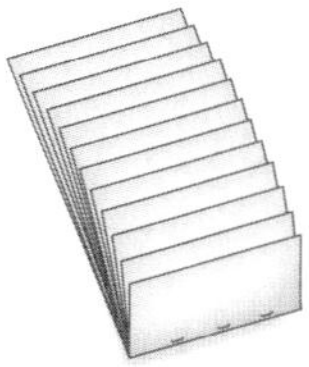

4. **Label** the tabs with the topics from the chapter.

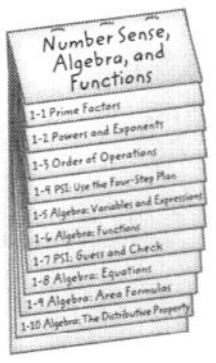

ARE YOU READY for Chapter 1?

You have two ways to check prerequisite skills for this chapter.

Option 2

Math Online Take the Chapter Readiness Quiz at ca.gr5math.com.

Option 1

Complete the Quick Check below.

QUICK Check

Add. **(Prior Grade)**

1. 83 + 129 **2.** 99 + 56 **3.** 67 + 42

4. 79 + 88 **5.** 78 + 97 **6.** 86 + 66

Subtract. **(Prior Grade)**

7. 43 − 7 **8.** 75 − 27 **9.** 128 − 34

10. 150 − 68 **11.** 102 − 76 **12.** 235 − 126

13. Ariana bought three shirts for a total of $89. If one shirt costs $24 and another costs $31, how much did the third shirt cost? **(Prior Grade)**

Multiply. **(Prior Grade)**

14. 25 × 12 **15.** 18 × 30 **16.** 42 × 15

17. 27 × 34 **18.** 50 × 16 **19.** 47 × 22

Divide. **(Prior Grade)**

20. 72 ÷ 9 **21.** 84 ÷ 6 **22.** 126 ÷ 3

23. 146 ÷ 2 **24.** 208 ÷ 4 **25.** 504 ÷ 8

26. Thirty-two students were placed into groups of four. How many groups were there? **(Prior Grade)**

1-1 Prime Factors

Concepts in Motion
Interactive Lab
ca.gr5math.com

GET READY to Learn

Hands-On Mini Lab

The table shows the different rectangles that can be made using 2, 3, 4, 5, or 6 squares.

Step 1 Copy the table.

Number of Squares	Sketch of Rectangle Formed	Dimensions of Each Rectangle
2		1×2
3		1×3
4		1×4, 2×2
5		1×5
6	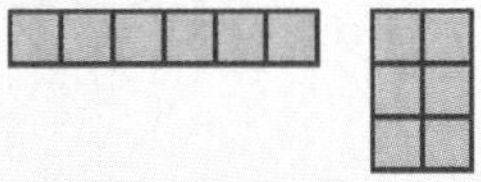	1×6, 2×3
⋮		
20		

Step 2 Use square tiles to help you complete the table.

1. For what numbers can more than one rectangle be formed?
2. For what numbers can only one rectangle be formed?
3. For the numbers in which only one rectangle is formed, what do you notice about the dimensions of the rectangle?

MAIN IDEA

I will find the prime factorization of a composite number.

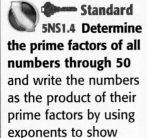

Standard 5NS1.4 Determine the prime factors of all numbers through 50 and write the numbers as the product of their prime factors by using exponents to show multiples of a factor (e.g., $24 = 2 \times 2 \times 2 \times 3 = 2^3 \times 3$).

New Vocabulary

factor
prime number
composite number
prime factorization

When two or more numbers are multiplied, each number is called a **factor** of the product.

$1 \times 7 = 7$ — The factors of 7 are 1 and 7.

$1 \times 6 = 6$ and $2 \times 3 = 6$ — The factors of 6 are 1 and 6, and 2 and 3.

A whole number that has exactly two unique factors, 1 and the number itself, is a **prime number**. A number greater than 1 with more than two factors is a **composite number**.

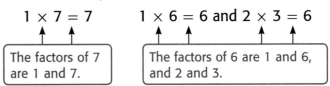

EXAMPLES Identify Prime and Composite Numbers

Tell whether each number is *prime, composite,* or *neither*.

1 **28**

Factors of 28: 1, 2, 4, 7, 14, 28
Since 28 has more than two factors, it is a composite number.

2 **11**

Factors of 11: 1, 11
Since there are exactly two factors, 11 is a prime number.

Every composite number can be expressed as a product of prime numbers. This is called a **prime factorization** of the number. A *factor tree* can be used to find the prime factorization of a number.

EXAMPLE Find Prime Factorization

3 **Find the prime factorization of 54.**

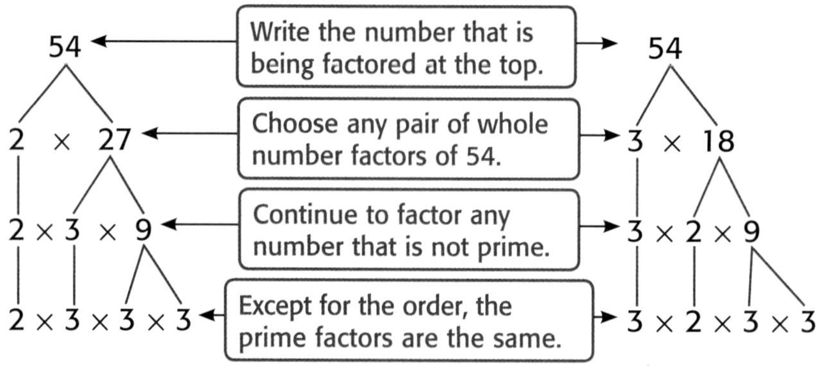

Online **Personal Tutor at** ca.gr5math.com

Remember

When writing the prime factorization, it is customary to write the prime factors in ascending order, that is, from least to greatest.

KEY CONCEPT — Prime and Composite

Number	Definition	Examples
prime	A whole number that has exactly two factors, 1 and the number itself.	11, 13, 23
composite	A number greater than 1 with more than two factors.	6, 10, 18
neither prime nor composite	1 has only one factor. 0 has an infinite number of factors.	0, 1

Reading Math

Infinite *Infinite* means *endless.*

CHECK What You Know

Tell whether each number is *prime, composite,* or *neither*.
See Examples 1, 2 (p. 18)

1. 10 **2.** 3 **3.** 1 **4.** 61

Find the prime factorization of each number. See Example 3 (p. 18)

5. 36 **6.** 81 **7.** 65 **8.** 19

9. The state of South Carolina has 46 counties. Write 46 as a product of primes.

10. Talk About It What are the factors of 12?

Practice and Problem Solving

EXTRA PRACTICE See page 654.

Tell whether each number is *prime, composite,* or *neither*.
See Examples 1, 2 (p. 18)

11. 17 **12.** 0 **13.** 15 **14.** 44

15. 23 **16.** 57 **17.** 45 **18.** 29

19. 56 **20.** 93 **21.** 53 **22.** 31

Find the prime factorization of each number. See Example 3 (p. 18)

23. 24 **24.** 18 **25.** 40 **26.** 75

27. 27 **28.** 32 **29.** 49 **30.** 25

31. 42 **32.** 104 **33.** 55 **34.** 77

Real-World PROBLEM SOLVING

Science The cheetah is the fastest land animal.

Animal	Speed (mph)	Animal	Speed (mph)
cheetah	70	rabbit	35
antelope	60	giraffe	32
lion	50	grizzly bear	30
coyote	43	elephant	25
hyena	40	squirrel	12

Source: *The World Almanac for Kids*

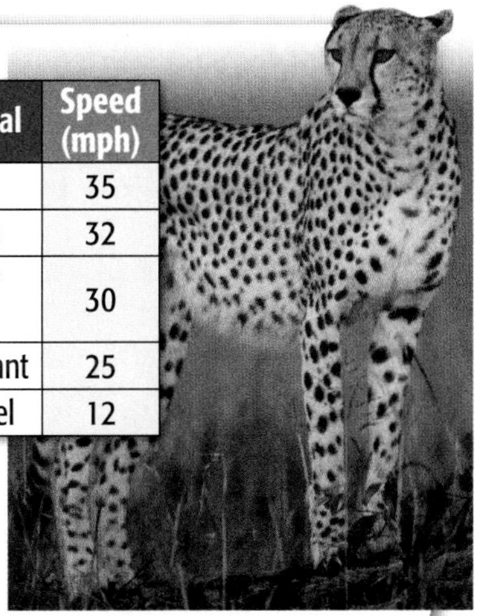

35. Which speed(s) have a prime factorization of exactly three factors?

36. Which speed(s) have a prime factorization whose factors are all equal?

37. Of the cheetah, antelope, lion, coyote, and hyena, which have speeds that are prime numbers?

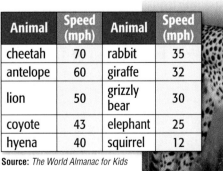

38. All odd numbers greater than or equal to 7 can be expressed as the sum of three prime numbers. Which three prime numbers have a sum of 59? Justify your answer.

39. Amanda bought bags of snacks that each cost exactly the same price. She spent a total of $30. Find three possible costs per bag and the number of bags that she could have purchased.

H.O.T. Problems

40. OPEN ENDED Select two prime numbers that are greater than 50 but less than 100.

41. NUMBER SENSE *Twin primes* are two prime numbers that are consecutive odd integers such as 3 and 5, 5 and 7, and 11 and 13. Find all of the twin primes that are less than 100.

42. CHALLENGE A *counterexample* is an example that shows a statement is not true. Find a counterexample for the statement below. Explain your reasoning.

All even numbers are composite numbers.

43. WRITING IN MATH How would you decide if a number is prime or composite? Explain by using an example.

Standards Practice

44 Which number is *not* prime?

A 7

B 31

C 39

D 47

45 Find the prime factorization of 140.

F $2 \times 2 \times 2 \times 5 \times 7$

G $2 \times 3 \times 5 \times 7$

H $2 \times 2 \times 5 \times 7$

J $3 \times 5 \times 7$

46 The volume of a rectangular prism can be found by multiplying the length, width, and height of the prism. Which of the following could be the possible dimensions of the rectangular prism below?

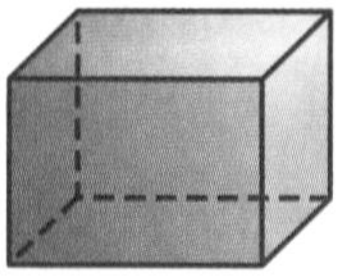

A 2 ft × 6 ft × 6 ft

B 3 ft × 5 ft × 7 ft

C 5 ft × 5 ft × 7 ft

D 3 ft × 5 ft × 5 ft

1-2 Powers and Exponents

MAIN IDEA

I will use powers and exponents in expressions.

Standard 5NS1.3 Understand and compute positive integer powers of nonnegative integers; compute examples as repeated multiplication.

Standard 5NS1.4 Determine the prime factors of all numbers through 50 and write the numbers as the product of their prime factors by using exponents to show multiples of a factor.

New Vocabulary

base
exponent
power
squared
cubed

GET READY to Learn

Hands-On Mini Lab

Any number can be written as a product of prime factors.

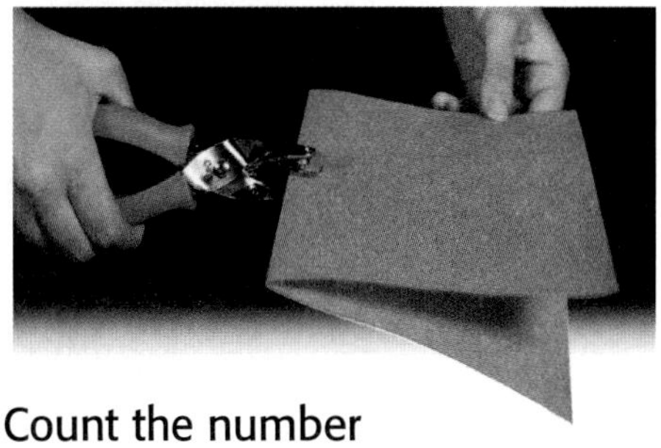

Step 1 Fold a piece of paper in half and make one hole punch. Count the number of holes and record the results.

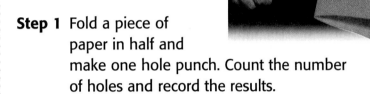

Number of Folds	Number of Holes	Prime Factorization
1 ⋮ 5		

Step 2 Find the prime factorization of the number of holes and record the results in the table.

Step 3 Fold another piece of paper in half twice. Then make one hole punch. Complete the table for two folds.

Step 4 Complete the table for three, four, and five folds.

1. What prime factors did you record?
2. How does the number of folds relate to the number of factors in the prime factorization of the number of holes?
3. Write the prime factorization of the number of holes made if you folded it eight times.

Repeated multiplication of identical factors can be written using an exponent and a base. The **base** is the number used as a factor. The **exponent** indicates how many times the base is used as a factor.

$$32 = \underbrace{2 \times 2 \times 2 \times 2 \times 2}_{5 \text{ factors}} = 2^5$$

(exponent: 5; base: 2)

When no exponent is given, it is understood to be 1. For example, $5 = 5^1$.

Numbers expressed using exponents are called **powers**.

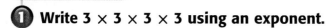

Powers	Words
2^5	2 to the fifth power
3^2	3 to the second power or 3 **squared**
10^3	10 to the third power or 10 **cubed**

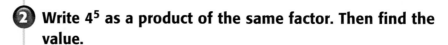

EXAMPLES Write Powers and Products

1 Write $3 \times 3 \times 3 \times 3$ using an exponent.

The base is 3. Since 3 is used as a factor four times, the exponent is 4.

$3 \times 3 \times 3 \times 3 = 3^4$ Write as a power.

Remember

4^5 does not mean 4×5.

2 Write 4^5 as a product of the same factor. Then find the value.

The base is 4. The exponent is 5. So, 4 is used as a factor five times.

$4^5 = 4 \times 4 \times 4 \times 4 \times 4$ Write 4^5 using repeated multiplication.

$= 1{,}024$ Multiply.

Real-World EXAMPLES

3 The approximate daytime surface temperature on the Moon can be written as 2^8 degrees Fahrenheit. What is this temperature?

$2^8 = 2 \times 2 \times 2 \times 2 \times 2 \times 2 \times 2 \times 2$ Write 2^8 as a product.

$= 256$ Multiply.

So, the temperature is about 256 degrees Fahrenheit.

4 A multiple choice test has 7 questions. If each question has 4 choices, there are 4^7 ways the test can be answered. What is the value of 4^7?

$4^7 = 4 \times 4 \times 4 \times 4 \times 4 \times 4 \times 4$ Write 4^7 as a product.

$= 16{,}384$ Multiply.

So, the test can be answered in 16,384 ways.

Online **Personal Tutor at** ca.gr5math.com

Exponents can be used to write the prime factorization of a number.

EXAMPLES Prime Factorization Using Exponents

Write the prime factorization of each number using exponents.

5 **72**

$72 = \underbrace{2 \times 2 \times 2} \times \underbrace{3 \times 3}$ Write the prime factorization.

$= 2^3 \times 3^2$ Write products of identical factors using exponents.

6 **135**

$135 = \underbrace{3 \times 3 \times 3} \times 5$ Write the prime factorization.

$= 3^3 \times 5$ Write products of identical factors using exponents.

7 **300**

$300 = \underbrace{2 \times 2} \times 3 \times \underbrace{5 \times 5}$ Write the prime factorization.

$= 2^2 \times 3 \times 5^2$ Write products of identical factors using exponents.

CHECK What You Know

Write each product using an exponent. See Example 1 (p. 22)

1. $2 \times 2 \times 2 \times 2$

2. $6 \times 6 \times 6$

Write each power as a product of the same factor. Then find the value. See Example 2 (p. 22)

3. 2^6

4. 3^7

5. There are nearly 3^5 species of monkeys on Earth. What is the value of 3^5? See Examples 3, 4 (p. 22)

6. An estimated 10^5 people live in Antioch, California. About how many people live in Antioch? See Examples 3, 4 (p. 22)

Write the prime factorization of each number using exponents. See Examples 5–7 (p. 23)

7. 20

8. 48

9. 90

10. Talk About It Compare 4^2 and 4×2.

Practice and Problem Solving

EXTRA PRACTICE
See page 654.

Write each product using an exponent. See Example 1 (p. 22)

11. 9×9

12. $8 \times 8 \times 8 \times 8$

13. $3 \times 3 \times 3 \times 3 \times 3 \times 3 \times 3$

14. $5 \times 5 \times 5 \times 5 \times 5$

15. $11 \times 11 \times 11$

16. $7 \times 7 \times 7 \times 7 \times 7 \times 7$

Write each power as a product of the same factor. Then find the value. See Example 2 (p. 22)

17. 2^4

18. 3^2

19. 5^3

20. 10^5

21. 9^3

22. 6^5

23. 8^1

24. 1^7

25. The number of Calories in two pancakes can be written as 7^3. What whole number does 7^3 represent?

26. An estimated 10^9 people in the world speak Mandarin Chinese. About how many people speak this language?

Write the prime factorization of each number using exponents.
See Examples 5–7 (p. 23)

27. 25

28. 56

29. 50

30. 68

31. 88

32. 98

33. 560

34. 378

Write each power as a product of the same factor. Then find the value.

35. seven squared

36. eight cubed

37. four to the fifth power

38. Mrs. Locaputo's garden is organized into 6 rows. Each row contains 6 vegetable plants. How many total vegetable plants does Mrs. Locaputo have in her garden? Write using exponents, and then find the value.

Real-World PROBLEM SOLVING

Fish To find the amount of water a cube-shaped aquarium holds, find the *cube* of the measure of one side of the aquarium.

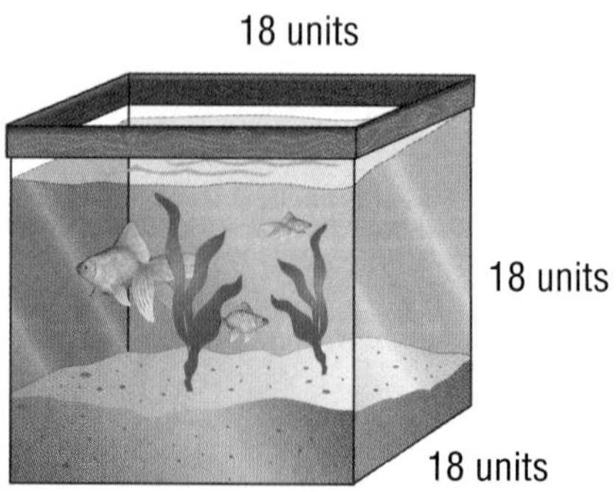

39. Express the amount of water the aquarium shown holds as a power.

40. Find the amount in cubic units.

H.O.T. Problems

41. **REASONING** What is the largest square of a whole number that divides 32? What is the largest cube of a whole number that divides 32?

42. **NUMBER SENSE** Which is greater: 3^5 or 5^3? Explain your reasoning.

43. **FIND THE ERROR** Anita and Tyree are finding the value of 6^4. Who is correct? Explain your reasoning.

Anita

$6^4 = 6 \times 6 \times 6 \times 6$
$= 1{,}296$

Tyree

$6^4 = 6 \times 4$
$= 24$

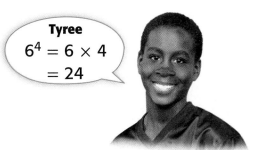

44. **CHALLENGE** Find all numbers 50 or less whose only prime factors are 2 and 5.

45. **WRITING IN ► MATH** Explain how you find the value of a power.

Standards Practice

46 $4^3 =$

A $4 + 4 + 4$

B $4 \times 4 \times 4$

C 4×3

D $3 \times 3 \times 3 \times 3$

47 Which is the prime factorization of 36?

F $2^2 \times 3$

G $2^2 \times 3^2$

H $2^2 \times 3^3$

J 2×3^2

Spiral Review

Tell whether each number is *prime, composite,* or *neither.* (Lesson 1-1)

48. 63 **49.** 0 **50.** 29 **51.** 71

52. **Measurement** The area of a rectangle can be found by multiplying its length and width. If the area of a rectangle is 30 square units, find all of its possible dimensions using only whole numbers. (Lesson 1-1)

Game Time

Facto Bingo

Finding Prime Factorizations

Get Ready!

Players: three or four

You will need: a copy of the Facto Bingo card

Get Set!

- Each player copies the Facto Bingo card shown.

Facto Bingo				
		Free Space		

- Each player selects 24 different numbers from the list below and writes them in the upper right hand corner boxes.

Facto Bingo Numbers									
6	9	10	13	15	18	20	21	24	25
28	32	37	40	43	45	48	50	52	55
59	60	62	64	66	67	69	70	72	74
75	76	79	80	85	88	89	90	96	98

Go!

- The caller reads one number at a time at random from the list above.
- If a player has the number on the card, he or she marks the space by writing the prime factorization in the larger box.
- The first player with bingo wins.

1-3 Order of Operations

GET READY to Learn

The table shows the number of Calories burned in one minute for two different activities. If you walk for 5 minutes, you will burn 5×8 Calories. If you run for 15 minutes, you will burn 15×10 Calories. So, if you walk for 5 minutes and then run for 15 minutes, you will burn $5 \times 8 + 15 \times 10$ Calories.

Activity	Calories Burned per Minute
Walking (13 min/mi)	8
Running (12 min/mi)	10

Source: The Fitness Jumpsite

MAIN IDEA

I will find the value of expressions using the order of operations.

Reinforcement of Standard 4AF1.2 Interpret and evaluate mathematical expressions that now use parentheses.

New Vocabulary

numerical expression
order of operations

A **numerical expression** like $5 \times 8 + 15 \times 10$ is a combination of numbers and operations. The **order of operations** tells you which operation to perform first so that everyone finds the same value for an expression.

KEY CONCEPT — Order of Operations

1. Simplify the expressions inside grouping symbols, like parentheses.
2. Find the value of all powers.
3. Multiply and divide in order from left to right.
4. Add and subtract in order from left to right.

EXAMPLES Use Order of Operations

1 Find the value of $4 + 3 \times 5$.

$4 + \mathbf{3 \times 5} = 4 + \mathbf{15}$ Multiply 3 and 5 first.

$= 19$ Add 4 and 15.

2 Find the value of $10 - 2 + 8$.

$\mathbf{10 - 2} + 8 = \mathbf{8} + 8$ Subtract 2 from 10 first.

$= 16$ Add 8 and 8.

EXAMPLES Parentheses and Exponents

Find the value of each expression.

3 **$20 \div 4 + 17 \times (9 - 6)$**

$20 \div 4 + 17 \times \mathbf{(9 - 6)}$	$= 20 \div 4 + 17 \times \mathbf{3}$	Subtract 6 from 9.
	$= 5 + 17 \times 3$	Divide 20 by 4.
	$= 5 + 51$	Multiply 17 by 3.
	$= 56$	Add 5 and 51.

4 **$3 \times 6^2 + 4$**

$3 \times \mathbf{6^2} + 4$	$= 3 \times \mathbf{36} + 4$	Find 6^2.
	$= 108 + 4$	Multiply 3 and 36.
	$= 112$	Add 108 and 4.

Remember

To check your answer in Example 5, find the total cost of going to the movies for one person. Then multiply by 5.

$\$7 + \$3 + \$2 = \$12$

$5 \times \$12 = \$60$ ✓

Real-World EXAMPLE

5 **Javier and four friends go to the movies. Each person buys a movie ticket, a snack, and a soda. Write an expression for the total cost of the trip to the movies. Then find the total cost.**

Cost of Going to the Movies

Item	ticket	snack	soda
Cost ($)	7	3	2

To find the total cost, write an expression and then find its value.

Words	cost of 5 tickets	plus	cost of 5 snacks	plus	cost of 5 sodas
Expression	$5 \times \$7$	+	$5 \times \$3$	+	$5 \times \$2$

$5 \times \$7 + 5 \times \$3 + 5 \times \$2$

$= \$35 + 5 \times \$3 + 5 \times \$2$	Multiply 5 and 7.
$= \$35 + \$15 + 5 \times \$2$	Multiply 5 and 3.
$= \$35 + \$15 + \$10$	Multiply 5 and 2.
$= \$60$	Add 35, 15, and 10.

The total cost of the trip to the movies is $60.

Online **Personal Tutor at** ca.gr5math.com

CHECK What You Know

Find the value of each expression. See Examples 1–4 (pp. 27–28)

1. $9 + 3 - 5$

2. $10 - 3 + 9$

3. $(26 + 5) \times 2 - 15$

4. $18 \div (2 + 7) \times 2 + 1$

5. $5^2 + 8 \div 2$

6. $19 - (3^2 + 4) + 6$

7. Tickets to a play cost $10 for members of the theater and $24 for nonmembers. Write an expression to find the total cost of 4 nonmember tickets and 2 member tickets. Then find the total cost.

8. Talk About It Tell how to solve $15 - 9 \div 3$.

Practice and Problem Solving

EXTRA PRACTICE See page 654.

Find the value of each expression. See Examples 1–4 (pp. 27–28)

9. $8 + 4 - 3$

10. $9 + 12 - 15$

11. $38 - 19 + 12$

12. $22 - 17 + 8$

13. $7 + 9 \times (3 + 8)$

14. $(9 + 2) \times 6 - 5$

15. $63 \div (10 - 3) \times 3$

16. $66 \times (6 \div 2) + 1$

17. $27 \div (3 + 6) \times 5 - 12$

18. $55 \div 11 + 7 \times (2 + 14)$

19. $5^3 - 12 \div 3$

20. $26 + 6^2 \div 4$

21. $15 - 2^3 \div 4$

22. $22 \div 2 \times 3^2$

23. Admission to a museum is $6 for adults and $3 for children. Write an expression to find the total cost of 3 adult tickets and 4 children's tickets. Then find the total cost.

24. Alexis is making chocolate covered pretzels for 15 friends. She has covered 3 dozen pretzels. If she wants each friend to receive exactly 3 pretzels and have no pretzels left over, write an expression to find how many more pretzels she should cover. Then find this number.

Write a numerical expression for each verbal expression. Then find its value.

25. the product of 7 and 6, minus 2

26. the cube of the quotient of 24 and 6

H.O.T. Problems

27. CHALLENGE Create an expression whose value is 10. It should contain four numbers and two different operations.

28. FIND THE ERROR Haley and Ryan are finding $7 - 3 + 2$. Who is correct? Explain your reasoning.

Haley

$$7 - 3 + 2 = 7 - 5$$
$$= 2$$

Ryan

$$7 - 3 + 2 = 4 + 2$$
$$= 6$$

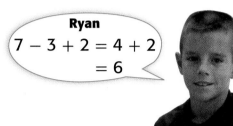

29. WRITING IN ▸MATH Write a real-world problem that can be solved using order of operations. Then solve the problem.

Standards Practice

30 Arleta is 2 years younger than Josh, and Josh is 5 years older than Marissa who is 9 years old. Which table could be used to find Arleta's age?

A

Name	Age (years)
Arleta	$9 + 5$
Josh	$9 + 5 - 2$
Marissa	9

B

Name	Age (years)
Arleta	2
Josh	5
Marissa	9

C

Name	Age (years)
Arleta	5
Josh	4
Marissa	9

D

Name	Age (years)
Arleta	$9 + 5 - 2$
Josh	$9 + 5$
Marissa	9

Spiral Review

31. Four members of a certain phone tree are each given 4 people to contact. If the phone tree is activated, the total number of calls made is 4^4. How many calls is this? **(Lesson 1-2)**

Find the prime factorization of each number. **(Lesson 1-1)**

32. 42 **33.** 75 **34.** 110 **35.** 130

CHAPTER 1

Mid-Chapter Check

Lessons 1-1 through 1-3

1. **STANDARDS PRACTICE** A principal has 144 computers for 24 classrooms. Which of the following is a factor of 24? **(Lesson 1-1)**

   A 6

   B 48

   C 120

   D 144

Tell whether each number is *prime*, *composite*, or *neither*. (Lesson 1-1)

2. 57
3. 97
4. 0

5. Can a group of 41 books be placed onto more than one shelf so that each shelf has the same number of books and has more than one book per shelf? Explain your reasoning. **(Lesson 1-1)**

Write each power as a product of the same factor. Then find the value. (Lesson 1-2)

6. 3^4
7. 6^3

Write the prime factorization of each number using exponents. (Lesson 1-2)

8. 22
9. 40
10. 75

11. The average annual cost of food for a dog is about 3^5 dollars. What is this cost? **(Lesson 1-2)**

Find the value of each expression. (Lesson 1-3)

12. $10 - 6 + 20$
13. $25 \div (15 - 10) \times 2$
14. $3^2 + 32 \div 2$
15. $12 - (4^3 \div 8) + 1$

16. **STANDARDS PRACTICE** Mr. and Mrs. Murphy and their 4 children went to the county fair. Admission to the fair was $7.75 for an adult and $5.50 for a child. Arrange the problem-solving steps below in the correct order to find the total cost of the tickets.

    Step K: Multiply the cost of a child's ticket by the number of children.

    Step L: Add the two products together.

    Step M: Multiply the cost of an adult ticket by the number of adults.

    Step N: Write down the number of adults and the number of children that are going to the county fair.

    Which list shows the steps in the correct order? **(Lesson 1-3)**

    F N, L, M, K

    G N, M, K, L

    H K, M, N, L

    J M, K, N, L

17. **WRITING IN ▸MATH** Describe how to use the order of operations to solve numerical expressions that contain more than one operation. **(Lesson 1-3)**

1-4 Problem-Solving Investigation

MAIN IDEA I will use the four-step plan to solve a problem.

Standard 5MR1.1 Analyze problems by identifying relationships, distinguishing relevant from irrelevant information, sequencing and prioritizing information, and observing patterns. **Reinforcement of Standard 4NS3.4 Solve problems involving division of multidigit numbers by one-digit numbers.**

P.S.I. TEAM +

DAVID: Today, I learned that there are 5,280 feet in one mile. I wonder how many pennies would be in one mile if I lined the pennies up side by side?

YOUR MISSION: Find how many pennies are in a row that is one mile long.

Understand

What facts do you know?

There are 5,280 feet in one mile.

What do you need to find?

You need to find how many pennies are in a row that is one mile long.

Plan

Plan a strategy for solving the problem.

Find how many pennies are in one foot. Then multiply by 5,280 to find how many pennies are in one mile.

Solve

Use your plan to solve the problem.

Line up pennies along a ruler. There are 16 pennies in one foot, and $16 \times 5{,}280 = 84{,}480$.

What is the solution?

So, a row of pennies one mile long will contain 84,480 pennies.

Check

Does the answer make sense?

Look back at the problem. Use estimation to check.
$15 \times 5{,}000 = 75{,}000$ ✓

Mixed Problem Solving

EXTRA PRACTICE
See page 655.

Use the four-step plan to solve each problem.

PROBLEM-SOLVING SKILLS
- Use the four-step plan.

1. Julian is on the swim team. The table shows the number of laps he swims in the first four days of practice. If the pattern continues, how many laps will he swim on Friday?

Day	Laps
Monday	5
Tuesday	6
Wednesday	8
Thursday	11
Friday	■

2. A bus departed at 11:45 A.M. It traveled 715 miles in 11 hours. How many miles did it travel in each hour?

3. Jupiter orbits the Sun at a rate of 8 miles per second. How far does Jupiter travel in one day?

4. An adult male walrus weighs about 2,670 pounds. An adult female walrus weighs about 1,835 pounds. How much less does an adult female walrus weigh than an adult male walrus?

5. In which corner will the circle be in the next figure in the pattern?

6. Brandon can run one mile in 7 minutes. At this rate, how long will it take him to run 8 miles?

7. After shopping at the mall, you come home with $3. You spent $4 on a snack, $8 on a movie, and $5 on arcade games. How much money did you start with?

8. The Corbetts are buying a 36-inch television for $788. They plan to pay in four equal payments. Find the amount of each payment.

9. The table shows how the number of a certain bacteria increases. At this rate, how many bacteria will there be after 2 hours? (*Hint:* There are 60 minutes in one hour.)

Time (min)	Number of Bacteria
0	5
20	10
40	20
60	40
80	80
100	■
120	■

10. English is spoken in 107 countries, and Vietnamese is spoken in 20 countries. About how many times more countries speak English than Vietnamese?

11. **WRITING IN MATH** Write a problem that you can solve using the four-step plan. Explain why it is important to compare your answer to your estimate.

1-5 Algebra: Variables and Expressions

GET READY to Learn

A box contains some crayons. There are also two crayons outside of the box. The total number of crayons is *the sum of two and some number*. The two crayons represent the known value 2, and the crayons in the box represent the unknown value.

MAIN IDEA

I will evaluate algebraic expressions.

Standard 5AF1.2 Use a letter to represent an unknown number; write and **evaluate simple algebraic expressions in one variable by substitution.**

New Vocabulary

algebra
variable
algebraic expression
evaluate

Vocabulary Link

Variable

Everyday Use able to change or vary, as in variable winds

Math Use a symbol used to represent a number

Algebra is a language of symbols. One symbol that is often used is a variable. A **variable** is a symbol, usually a letter, used to represent a number or some other unknown quantity. The expression $2 + n$ represents *the sum of two and some number.*

Algebraic expressions are combinations of variables, numbers, and at least one operation.

$2 + n$

- at least one operation → $+$
- Any letter can be used as a variable. → n
- combination of numbers and variables → $2 + n$

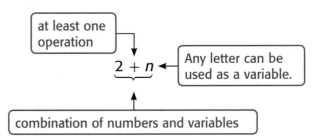

The letter *x* is often used as a variable. It is also common to use the first letter of the word describing the value you are representing.

The variables in an expression can be replaced with any number. Once the variables have been replaced, you can **evaluate**, or find the value of, the algebraic expression.

In addition to the symbol ×, there are other ways to show multiplication.

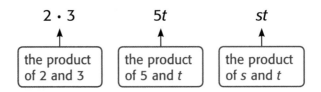

$2 \cdot 3$	$5t$	st
the product of 2 and 3	the product of 5 and *t*	the product of *s* and *t*

EXAMPLES Evaluate Algebraic Expressions

1 Evaluate $16 + b$ if $b = 25$.

$16 + b = 16 + 25$ Replace b with 25.

$= 41$ Add 16 and 25.

2 Evaluate $x - y$ if $x = 64$ and $y = 27$.

$x - y = 64 - 27$ Replace x with 64 and y with 27.

$= 37$ Subtract 27 from 64.

3 Evaluate $5t + 4$ if $t = 3$.

$5t + 4 = 5 \cdot 3 + 4$ Replace t with 3.

$= 15 + 4$ Multiply 5 and 3.

$= 19$ Add 15 and 4.

Remember

In algebra, the symbol · is often used to represent multiplication, as the symbol × may be confused with the variable *x*.

Real-World EXAMPLES

4 If admission to a fair is \$7 per person and each ride ticket costs \$2, the total cost for admission and *t* ride tickets is $7 + 2t$. Find the total cost for admission and 5 ride tickets.

$7 + 2t = 7 + 2 \cdot 5$ Replace t with 5.

$= 7 + 10$ Multiply 2 and 5.

$= 17$ Add 7 and 10.

So, the total cost for admission and 5 ride tickets is \$17.

5 Measurement An expression for finding the area of a triangle whose height is 3 units longer than its base is $(b + 3) \cdot b \div 2$, where *b* is the measure of the base. Find the area of a triangle with a base 8 units long.

You need to find the value of the expression given $b = 8$.

$(b + 3) \cdot b \div 2 = (8 + 3) \cdot 8 \div 2$ Replace b with 8.

$= 11 \cdot 8 \div 2$ Add 8 and 3.

$= 88 \div 2$ Multiply 11 and 8.

$= 44$ Divide 88 by 2.

The area of the triangle is 44 square units.

Online Personal Tutor at ca.gr5math.com

CHECK What You Know

Evaluate each expression if $m = 4$ and $z = 9$. See Examples 1–3 (p. 35)

1. $3 + m$

2. $z + 5$

3. $z - m$

4. $m - 2$

5. $4m - 2$

6. $2z + 3$

7. The amount of money that remains from a $20 dollar bill after Malina buys 4 party favors for p dollars each is $20 - 4p$. Find the amount remaining if each favor costs $3.

8. Talk About It Describe three ways to write *the product of 7 and x.*

Practice and Problem Solving

EXTRA PRACTICE See page 655.

Evaluate each expression if $m = 2$ and $n = 16$. See Examples 1, 2 (p. 35)

9. $m + 10$

10. $n + 8$

11. $9 - m$

12. $22 - n$

13. $n \div 4$

14. $12 \div m$

15. $n \cdot 3$

16. $6 \cdot m$

17. $m + n$

18. $n + m$

19. $n - 6$

20. $m - 1$

Evaluate each expression if $a = 4$, $b = 7$, and $c = 11$. See Example 3 (p. 35)

21. $b - a$

22. $c - b$

23. $5c + 6$

24. $2b + 7$

25. $3a - 4$

26. $4b - 10$

27. Distance traveled can be found using the expression rt, where r represents the speed (rate) and t represents time. How far did a hot air balloon travel at an average rate of 15 miles per hour for 6 hours?

28. To find the average speed (rate) of a racecar, use the expression $d \div t$, where d represents distance and t represents time. Find the speed s of a racecar that travels 508 miles in 4 hours.

29. The expression $500t$ can be used to find the distance in miles traveled by a DC–10 aircraft. The variable t represents time in hours. How far can a DC–10 travel in 4 hours?

30. What is the value of $st \div 6r$ if $r = 5$, $s = 32$, and $t = 45$?

Evaluate each expression if $x = 3$, $y = 12$, and $z = 8$.

31. $4z + 8 - 6$

32. $6x - 9 \div 3$

33. $15 + 9x \div 3$

34. $7z \div 4 + 5x$

35. $y^2 \div (3z)$

36. $z^2 - (5x)$

37. Measurement To find the area of a rectangle, use the expression ℓw, where ℓ represents the length, and w represents the width of the rectangle. What is the area of the rectangle shown?

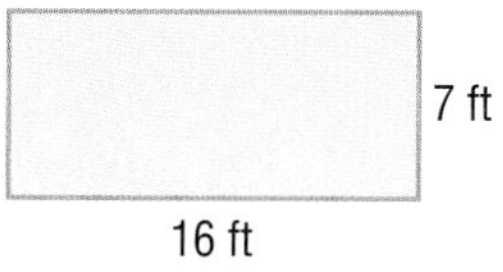

38. As a member of a music club, you can order CDs for $15 each. The music club also charges $5 for each shipment. The expression $15n + 5$ represents the cost of n CDs. Find the total cost for ordering 3 CDs.

39. Temperature To change a temperature given in degrees Celsius to degrees Fahrenheit, first multiply the Celsius temperature by 9. Next, divide the answer by 5. Finally, add 32 to the result. Write an expression that can be used to change a temperature from degrees Celsius to degrees Fahrenheit. Then use the information in the table below to find the difference in average temperatures in degrees Fahrenheit for San Antonio from January to April. (*Hint:* Convert to degrees Fahrenheit first.)

Average Monthly Temperature for San Antonio, Texas

Month	Temp. (°C)
January	10
April	20
July	29

Source: infoplease.com

H.O.T. Problems

40. OPEN ENDED Create two algebraic expressions involving multiplication that have the same meaning.

41. CHALLENGE Elan and Robin each have a calculator. Elan starts at zero and adds 3 each time. Robin starts at 100 and subtracts 7 each time. Suppose Elan and Robin press the keys at the same time. Will their displays ever show the same number? If so, what is the number? Explain your reasoning.

42. **SELECT A TECHNIQUE** Ichiro is evaluating $x^2 - z$, where $x = 3$ and $z = 8$. Which of the following techniques might Ichiro use to evaluate the expression? Justify your selection(s). Then use the technique(s) to solve the problem.

mental math	number sense	estimation

43. **Which One Doesn't Belong?** Identify the expression that does not belong with the other three. Explain your reasoning.

5x	3 + 4	ab	7x + 1

44. **WRITING IN ▸MATH** Compare and contrast numerical expressions and algebraic expressions. Use examples in your explanation.

Standards Practice

45 The expression $2r$ can be used to find the diameter of a circle, where r is the length of the radius. Find the diameter of the compact disc.

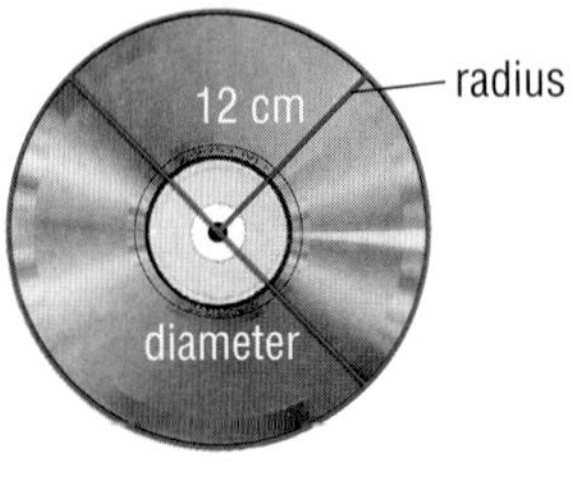

A 3 cm **C** 12 cm

B 6 cm **D** 24 cm

46 Which expression represents the product of 36 and s?

F $36 + s$ **H** $36s$

G $36 - s$ **J** $36 \div s$

47 If $S = 7$, what is the value of $8 \times S + 6$?

A 8

B 50

C 62

D 104

48 If $m = 11$, what is the value of $5m - 9$?

F 4 **H** 55

G 46 **J** 64

Spiral Review

49. On a test with 62 questions, Trey missed 4 questions. How many did he get correct? **(Lesson 1-4)**

Find the value of each expression. **(Lesson 1-3)**

50. $12 - 8 \div 2 + 1$ **51.** $5^2 + (20 \div 2) - 7$ **52.** $21 \div (3 + 4) \times 3 - 8$

53. **Measurement** The distance from Earth to the Sun is close to 10^8 miles. How many miles is this? **(Lesson 1-2)**

1-6 Algebra: Functions

MAIN IDEA

I will complete function tables and find function rules.

Standard 5AF1.2 Use a letter to represent an unknown number; write and evaluate simple algebraic expressions in one variable by substitution.

Standard 5AF1.5 Solve problems involving linear functions with integer values; write the equation; and graph the resulting ordered pairs of integers on a grid.

New Vocabulary

function
function table
function rule
defining the variable

GET READY to Learn

A brown bat can eat 600 mosquitoes an hour. At this rate, how many mosquitoes can a brown bat eat in 2 hours? 3 hours?

A **function** is a relationship that assigns exactly one output value to one input value. The number of mosquitoes eaten (output) depends on the number of hours (input). You can organize the input-output values in a **function table**.

Input	Function Rule	Output
Number of Hours (t)	$600t$	Mosquitoes Eaten
1	600(1)	600
2	600(2)	1,200
3	600(3)	1,800

The **function rule** describes the relationship between each input and output.

EXAMPLE Complete a Function Table

1 **Complete the function table below.**

Input (x)	$x + 4$	Output
10	■	■
12	■	■
14	■	■

The function rule is $x + 4$. Add 4 to each input.

Input (x)	$x + 4$	Output
10	$10 + 4$	14
12	$12 + 4$	16
14	$14 + 4$	18

EXAMPLES Find the Rule for a Function Table

Remember

To see if your function rule is correct, test more than one input value.

2 **Find the rule for the function table.**

Input (*x*)	Output (■)
2	6
5	15
7	21

Study the relationship between each input and output. Each output is three times the input.

So, the function rule is $3 \cdot x$, or $3x$.

3 **Find the rule for the function table.**

Input (*x*)	Output (■)
0	0
4	1
16	4

Study the relationship between each input and output. Each output is one-fourth the input.

So, the function rule is $x \div 4$.

Online Personal Tutor at ca.gr5math.com

When you write a function rule that represents a real-world situation, you first choose a variable to represent the input. This is called **defining the variable**.

Real-World EXAMPLE

4 **A local band charges $70 for each hour it performs. Define a variable. Then write a function rule that relates the total charge to the number of hours it performs.**

Determine the function rule. The cost of the performance depends on the number of hours. Let *h* represent the number of hours the band performs.

Words	$70 for each hour
Variable	Let *h* represent the number of hours the band performs.
Expression	$70 \cdot h$

The function rule is $70h$.

CHECK What You Know

Copy and complete each function table. See Example 1 (p. 39)

1.

Input (x)	$x + 3$	Output
0	■	■
2	■	■
4	■	■

2.

Input (x)	$4x$	Output
1	■	■
3	■	■
6	■	■

Find the rule for each function table. See Examples 2, 3 (p. 40)

3.

Input (x)	Output (■)
1	0
3	2
5	4

4.

Input (x)	Output (■)
0	0
3	6
6	12

5. Lamar is buying jelly beans for a party. He can buy them in bulk for \$3 a pound. Define a variable. Write a function rule that relates the total cost of the jelly beans to the number of pounds he buys.
See Example 4 (p. 40)

6. Talk About It A function rule is $6x$. What are the input values if the output values are 24, 30, and 36?

Practice and Problem Solving

EXTRA PRACTICE
See page 655.

Copy and complete each function table. See Example 1 (p. 39)

7.

Input (x)	$x - 4$	Output
4	■	■
8	■	■
11	■	■

8.

Input (x)	$x \div 3$	Output
0	■	■
3	■	■
9	■	■

Find the rule for each function table. See Examples 2, 3 (p. 40)

9.

Input (x)	Output (■)
0	2
1	3
6	8

10.

Input (x)	Output (■)
7	2
9	4
15	10

11.

Input (x)	Output (■)
2	4
5	10
8	16

12.

Input (x)	Output (■)
0	0
4	20
7	35

13.

Input (x)	Output (■)
5	1
15	3
25	5

14.

Input (x)	Output (■)
6	3
22	11
34	17

15. Ricardo is 8 years older than his sister. Define a variable. Write a function rule that relates Ricardo's age to his sister's age.

16. Whitney has a total of 30 sandwiches for her guests. Define a variable. Write a function rule that relates the number of sandwiches per guest to the number of guests.

For Exercises 17 and 18, define a variable and write a function rule. Then solve each problem.

17. Moose can swim up to 6 miles per hour. At this rate, find the total number of miles a moose can swim in two hours.

18. An Internet company charges $10 a year to be a member of its music program. It also charges $1 for each song you download. How much will it cost if you download 46 songs in a year?

Real-World PROBLEM SOLVING

Data File The California State Railroad Museum is located in Sacramento.

19. Write a function rule that relates the total cost of admission to the number of adult and youth (ages 6–17) tickets purchased.

20. Use the function rule to find the total cost of admission for 2 adults and 3 youth (ages 6–17).

Source: csrmf.org

Admission

Adults:
$8

Ages 6–17:
$3

Ages 5 and under:
Free

H.O.T. Problems

21. **OPEN ENDED** Create a function table. Then write a function rule. Choose three input values and find the output values.

22. **FIND THE ERROR** Olivia and Nicole are finding the function rule when each output is 5 less than the input. Who is correct? Explain.

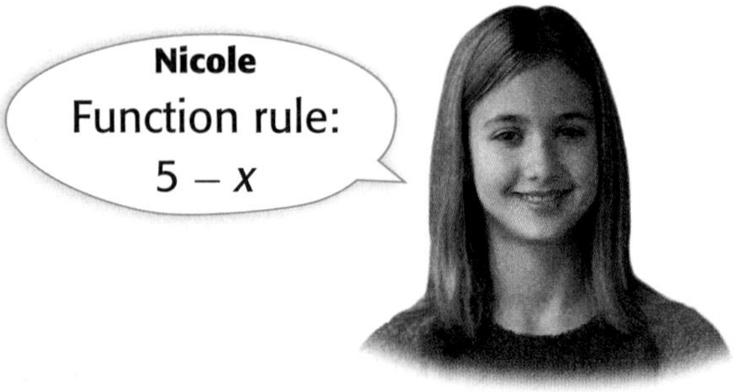

23. **CHALLENGE** Suppose the estimated 223 million Americans who have jugs or bottles of coins around their homes put coins back into circulation at a rate of $10 a year per person. Create a function table showing the amount that would be recirculated in 1, 2, and 3 years.

24. **SELECT A TOOL** Courtney is evaluating the function rule $43x - 6$ for an input of 4. Which of the following tools might Courtney use to determine the output? Justify your selection(s). Then use the tool(s) to solve the problem.

real objects | graphing calculator | paper/pencil

25. **WRITING IN ▸MATH** Explain how to find a function rule given a function table.

Standards Practice

26 Which expression represents the *y* values in terms of the *x* values?

x	1	2	3	4	5	6
y	5	7	9	11	13	15

A $2x + 3$

B $x + 3$

C $3x - 2$

D $6 - x$

27 The school store makes a profit of $5 for each sweatshirt sold. Which expression represents the profit on *n* sweatshirts?

F $5 \times n$

G $5 + n$

H $n \div 5$

J $n - 5$

Spiral Review

Algebra **Evaluate each expression if $a = 3$, $b = 6$, and $c = 10$.** **(Lesson 1-5)**

28. $b - a$

29. $3c + a$

30. $bc + 12$

31. The table represents the average amounts consumers spent on back-to-school merchandise in a recent year. How much more did consumers spend on clothing, accessories, and shoes than on school supplies? Use the four-step plan. **(Lesson 1-4)**

Back-to-School Spending

Merchandise	Amount ($)
Clothing/Accessories	219
Electronic Equipment	101
Shoes	90
School Supplies	73

Source: *USA Today*

32. A deli sells wraps for $5 and soup for $3 a bowl. Write and solve an expression for the cost of 3 wraps and 2 bowls of soup. **(Lesson 1-3)**

33. California has 5^2 area codes. What is the value of 5^2? **(Lesson 1-2)**

1-7 Problem-Solving Strategy

MAIN IDEA I will solve problems by using the *guess and check* strategy.

Standard 5MR2.6 Make precise calculations and check the validity of the results from the context of the problem.
Reinforcement of Standard 4NS2.1 Estimate and **compute the sum or difference of whole numbers** and positive decimals to two places.

A comic book store sells used comic books in packages of 5 and new comic books in packages of 3. Keisha buys a total of 16 comic books for her brother Trent for his birthday. How many packages of new and used comic books did Keisha buy for Trent?

Understand

What facts do you know?

- The comic book store sells 3-book packages and 5-book packages.
- The used comic books come in packages of 5. The new comic books come in packages of 3.
- 16 books were bought.

What do you need to find?

How many packages of new and used comic books did Keisha buy for Trent?

Plan

Plan a strategy for solving the problem.

Make a guess until you find an answer that makes sense for the problem.

Solve

Use your plan to solve the problem.

Number of 3-book packages	Number of 5-book packages	Total Number of Comic Books
1	1	1(3) + 1(5) = 8
1	2	1(3) + 2(5) = 13
2	1	2(3) + 1(5) = 11
2	2	2(3) + 2(5) = 16 ✓

So, Keisha bought two 3-book packages and two 5-book packages.

Check

Does the answer make sense?

Look back at the problem. Two 3-book packages result in 6 books. Two 5-book packages result in 10 books. Since 6 + 10 is 16, the answer is correct. ✓

ANALYZE the Strategy

Refer to the problem on the previous page.

1. Are there any other combinations of new and used packages that Keisha could have bought? Explain.

2. Suppose Keisha bought Trent 18 comic books. How many new and used packages did she buy?

3. Explain when to use the *guess and check* strategy to solve a problem.

4. Is the *guess and check* strategy always the best strategy for solving a word problem?

PRACTICE the Strategy

EXTRA PRACTICE See page 656.

Solve. Use the *guess and check* strategy.

5. Antonio is thinking of four numbers from 1 through 9 whose sum is 23. Find the numbers.

6. Each hand in the human body has 27 bones. There are 6 more bones in your fingers than in your wrist. There are 3 fewer bones in your palm than in your wrist. How many bones are in each part of your hand?

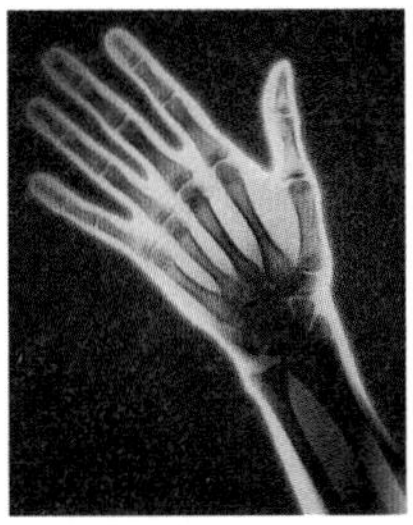

7. Mrs. Collins is buying sandwiches for the 10 students in the chess club. If she bought at least one of each type of sandwich and spent a total of $34.00, how many of each sandwich did she buy?

Sandwiches	
Type	**Price**
Italian	$4.00
Roast Beef	$3.50
Veggie	$3.00

8. Mateo has seven coins in his pocket that total $1.50. What are the coins?

9. The admission prices for a health fair are shown below. Twelve people paid a total of $50 for admission. If 8 children attended the health fair, how many adults and senior citizens attended?

Children	$4.00
Adults	$6.00
Senior Citizens	$3.00

10. Lavinia sold some wrapping paper for $7 a roll and some gift bags for $8 a set. If she sold a total of 17 items for a total of $124, how many rolls of wrapping paper and sets of gift bags did she sell?

11. A wallet contains 14 bills worth $150. If all of the money was in $5 bills, $10 bills, and $20 bills, how many of each bill was in the wallet?

12. The sum of two prime numbers is 20. Find the numbers.

13. **WRITING IN MATH** Write a problem that you can solve by the *guess and check* strategy. Then describe the steps you would take to find the solution of the problem.

1-8 Algebra: Equations

GET READY to Learn

Hands-On Mini Lab

When the amounts on each side of a scale are equal, the scale is balanced.

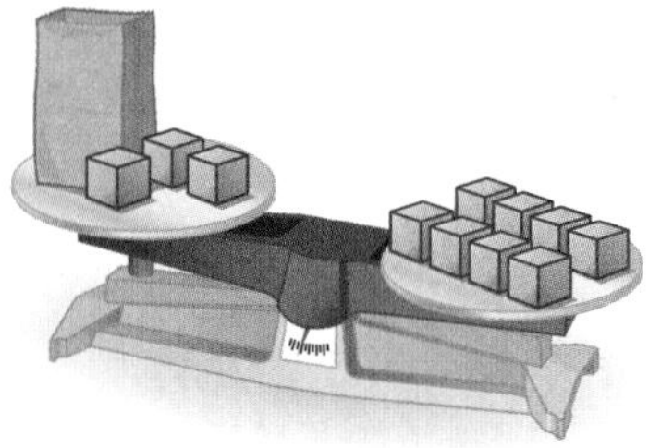

Step 1 Place three centimeter cubes and a paper bag on one side of a scale.

Step 2 Place eight centimeter cubes on the other side of the scale.

1. Suppose the variable x represents the number of cubes in the bag. What equation represents this situation?
2. Replace the bag with centimeter cubes until the scale balances. How many centimeter cubes did you need to balance the scale?

Let x represent the bag. Model each sentence on a scale. Find the number of centimeter cubes needed to balance the scale.

3. $x + 1 = 4$ **4.** $x + 3 = 5$

5. $x + 7 = 8$ **6.** $x + 2 = 2$

MAIN IDEA

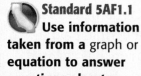

I will solve equations by using mental math and the guess and check strategy.

Standard 5AF1.1 Use information taken from a graph or **equation to answer questions about a problem situation.**

Standard 5AF1.2 Use a letter to represent an unknown number; write and evaluate simple algebraic expressions in one variable by substitution.

New Vocabulary

equation
equals sign
solve
solution

An **equation** is a number sentence that contains an **equals sign**, =, showing that two expressions are equal. A few examples are shown below.

$2 + 7 = 9$ $10 - 6 = 4$ $14 = 2 \cdot 7$

Some equations contain variables.

$2 + x = 9$ $4 = k - 6$ $15 \div m = 3$

When you replace a variable with a value that results in a true sentence, you **solve** the equation. That value for the variable is the **solution** of the equation.

$2 + \mathbf{x} = 9$ ← The equation is $2 + x = 9$.

$2 + \mathbf{7} = 9$ ← The value for the variable that results in a true sentence is 7. So, 7 is the solution.

$9 = 9$ ← This sentence is true.

EXAMPLE Find the Solution of an Equation

1 **Is 3, 4, or 5 the solution of the equation $a + 7 = 11$?**

Value of a	$a + 7 \stackrel{?}{=} 11$	Are Both Sides Equal?
3	$3 + 7 = 11$ $10 \neq 11$	no
4	$4 + 7 = 11$ $11 = 11$	yes ✓
5	$5 + 7 = 11$ $12 \neq 11$	no

The solution is 4 since replacing a with 4 results in a true sentence.

EXAMPLE Solve an Equation Mentally

2 **Solve $12 = 3h$ mentally.**

$12 = 3h$ THINK 12 equals 3 times what number?

$12 = 3 \cdot 4$ You know that $12 = 3 \cdot 4$.

So, $h = 4$. The solution is 4.

Real-World EXAMPLE

Remember

When using the *guess and check* strategy in Example 3, be sure to make reasonable guesses.

3 **An antelope can run 49 miles per hour faster than a squirrel. Let s represent the speed of a squirrel. Solve the equation $s + 49 = 61$ mentally to find the speed of a squirrel.**

Use the *guess and check* strategy.

Try 10.	Try 11.	Try 12.
$s + 49 = 61$	$s + 49 = 61$	$s + 49 = 61$
$10 + 49 \stackrel{?}{=} 61$	$11 + 49 \stackrel{?}{=} 61$	$12 + 49 \stackrel{?}{=} 61$
$59 \neq 61$	$60 \neq 61$	$61 = 61$ ✓

So, $s = 12$. The speed of the squirrel is 12 miles per hour.

Online Personal Tutor at ca.gr5math.com

CHECK What You Know

Identify the solution of each equation from the list given.
See Example 1 (p. 47)

1. $9 + w = 17$; 7, 8, 9

2. $d - 11 = 5$; 14, 15, 16

3. $4 = 2y$; 2, 3, 4

4. $8 \div c = 8$; 0, 1, 2

Solve each equation mentally. See Example 2 (p. 47)

5. $x + 6 = 18$

6. $n - 10 = 30$

7. $15k = 30$

8. The equation $b + 7 = 12$ describes the number of boxes of cereal and the number of breakfast bars in a kitchen cabinet. If b is the number of breakfast bars, how many breakfast bars are there?

9. Talk About It What is the meaning of the term *solution*?

Practice and Problem Solving

EXTRA PRACTICE See page 656.

Identify the solution of each equation from the list given. See Example 1 (p. 47)

10. $a + 15 = 23$; 6, 7, 8

11. $29 + d = 54$; 24, 25, 26

12. $35 = 45 - n$; 10, 11, 12

13. $19 = p - 12$; 29, 30, 31

14. $6w = 30$; 5, 6, 7

15. $63 = 9k$; 6, 7, 8

16. $36 \div s = 4$; 9, 10, 11

17. $x \div 7 = 3$; 20, 21, 22

Solve each equation mentally. See Example 2 (p. 47)

18. $j + 7 = 13$

19. $m + 4 = 17$

20. $22 = 30 - m$

21. $12 = 24 - y$

22. $15 - b = 12$

23. $25 - k = 20$

24. $5m = 25$

25. $10t = 90$

26. $22 \div y = 2$

27. $d \div 3 = 6$

28. $54 = 6b$

29. $24 = 12k$

30. The equation $45 + k = 63$ represents the total cost before tax of a pair of in-line skates for \$45 and a set of kneepads. If k is the cost of the set of kneepads, find the cost of the set of kneepads.

31. The equation $b \div 12 = 6$ describes the height of a grizzly bear, where b is the height of the grizzly bear in inches. What is the height of the grizzly bear in inches?

H.O.T. Problems

32. **OPEN ENDED** Give an example of an equation that has a solution of 5.

33. **REASONING** If x is a number that satisfies $4x + 3 = 18$, can x be equal to 3? Explain.

CHALLENGE For Exercises 34 and 35, tell whether each statement is *true* or *false*. Then explain your reasoning.

34. In the expression $m + 8$, the variable m can have any value.

35. In the equation $m + 8 = 12$, any value of the variable is a solution.

36. **WRITING IN MATH** Create a real-world problem in which you would solve the equation $a + 12 = 30$.

Standards Practice

37 The graph shows the life expectancy of certain mammals. Which situation could be described by $d + 35 = 80$?

A the difference between the life expectancy of a blue whale and a gorilla

B the life expectancy of a blue whale

C the total life expectancy of a blue whale and a gorilla

D the difference between the life expectancy of a gorilla and a killer whale

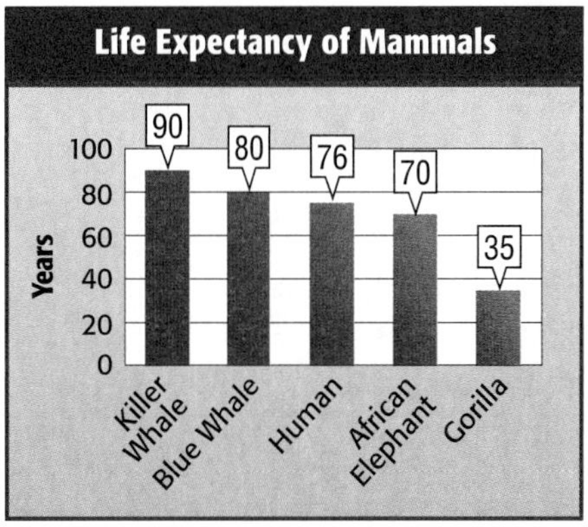

Source: *Scholastic Book of World Records*

Spiral Review

38. On a science quiz, Ivan earned 18 points. If there are 6 problems worth 2 points each and 2 problems worth 4 points each, find the number of problems of each type Ivan answered correctly. **(Lesson 1-7)**

39. Sophia earns a weekly allowance of \$4. Define a variable. Write a function rule that relates the total allowance to the number of weeks. Find the total allowance she earns in 8 weeks. **(Lesson 1-6)**

Algebra Evaluate each expression if $r = 2$, $s = 4$, and $t = 6$. **(Lesson 1-5)**

40. $3rst + 14$

41. $9 \div 3 \cdot s + t$

42. $4 + t \div r \cdot 4s$

Explore

Algebra Lab for 1-9
Writing Formulas

MAIN IDEA

I will use tables of data to generate formulas.

Standard 5MR3.3 Develop generalizations of the results obtained and apply them in other circumstances.
Preparation for Standard 5MG1.4 Differentiate between, and use appropriate units of measures for, two- and three-dimensional objects (i.e., find the perimeter, area, volume).

The number of square units needed to cover the surface of a figure is called its *area*. In this activity, you will explore how the area and side lengths of rectangles and squares are related. You will then express this relationship as an equation called a *formula*.

ACTIVITY

1 **Step 1** On centimeter grid paper, draw, label, and shade a rectangle with a length of 2 centimeters and a width of 3 centimeters.

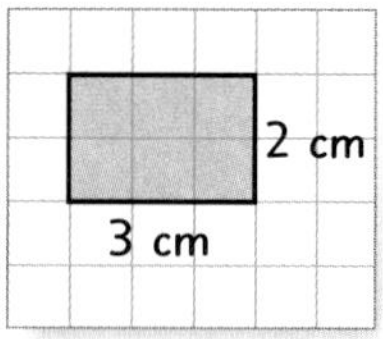

Step 2 Count the number of squares shaded to find the area of the rectangle. Then record this information in a table like the one shown.

Rectangle	Length (cm)	Width (cm)	Area (sq cm)
A	2	3	
B	2	4	
C	2	5	
D	3	4	
E	4	4	
F	5	4	

Step 3 Repeat Steps 1 and 2 for rectangles B, C, D, E, and F, whose dimensions are shown in the table.

Reading Math

Units Area is measured in square units. Read cm^2 as *square centimeters.*

Analyze the Results

1. Describe the relationship between the area of a rectangle and its length and width in words.

2. What would be the area of a rectangle with length 2 centimeters and width 8 centimeters? Test your conjecture by modeling the rectangle and counting the number of shaded squares.

3. **Algebra** If A represents the area of a rectangle, write an equation that describes the relationship between the rectangle's area A, length ℓ, and width w.

ACTIVITY

2 **For each step below, draw new rectangles on grid paper and find the areas. Organize the information in a table.**

Step 1 Using the original rectangles in Activity 1, double each length, but keep the same width.

Step 2 Using the original rectangles in Activity 1, double each width, but keep the same length.

Step 3 Using the original rectangles in Activity 1, double both the length and width.

Analyze the Results

Compare the areas you found in each step to the original areas. Write a sentence describing how the area changed. Explain.

4. Step 1

5. Step 2

6. Step 3

ACTIVITY

3 **Step 1** On centimeter grid paper, draw, label, and shade a square with a length of 2 centimeters.

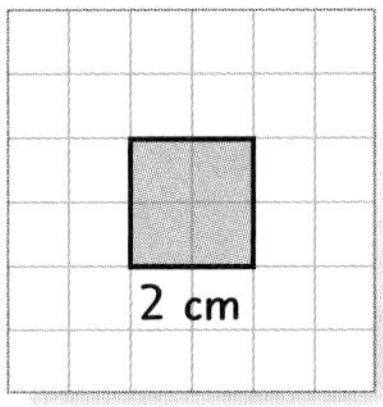

Step 2 Count the number of squares shaded to find the area of the square. Record this information in a table like the one shown.

Step 3 Repeat Steps 1 and 2 for squares B and C, whose dimensions are shown in the table.

Square	Side Length (cm)	Area (sq cm)
A	2	
B	3	
C	4	

Analyze the Results

7. What would be the area of a square with side lengths of 8 centimeters? Test your conjecture.

8. **Algebra** If A represents the area of a square, write an equation that describes the relationship between the square's area A and side length s.

1-9 Algebra: Area Formulas

GET READY to Learn

Checkered patterns can often be found on game boards and flags. What relationship exists between the length and the width, and the number of squares needed to cover the surface?

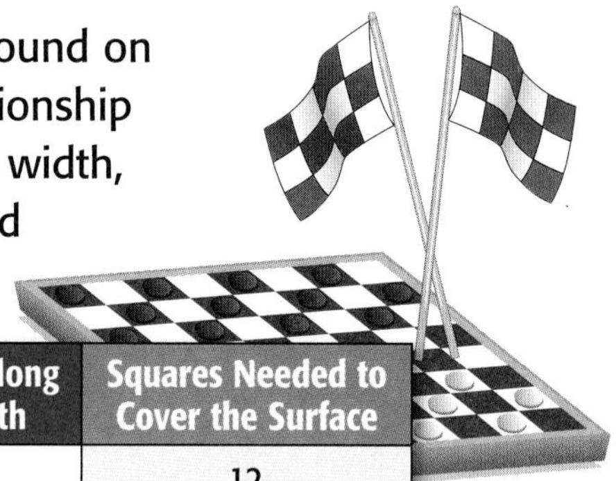

Object	Squares Along the Length	Squares Along the Width	Squares Needed to Cover the Surface
flag	4	3	12
game board	8	8	64

MAIN IDEA

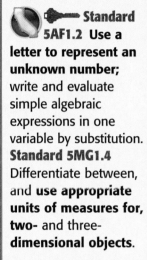

I will find the areas of rectangles and squares.

Standard 5AF1.2 Use a letter to represent an unknown number; write and evaluate simple algebraic expressions in one variable by substitution. **Standard 5MG1.4** Differentiate between, and **use appropriate units of measures for, two-** and three-**dimensional objects.**

New Vocabulary

area
formula

The **area** of a figure is the number of square units needed to cover a surface. The rectangle shown has an area of 24 square units.

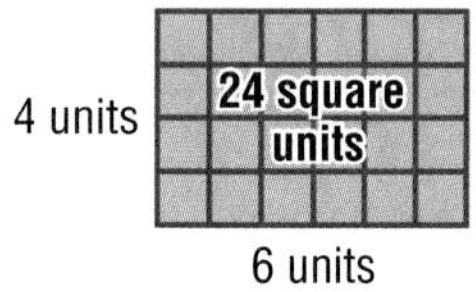

You can also use a formula to find the area of a rectangle. A **formula** is an equation that shows a relationship among certain quantities.

KEY CONCEPT — Area of a Rectangle

Words The area A of a rectangle is the product of the length ℓ and width w.

Model

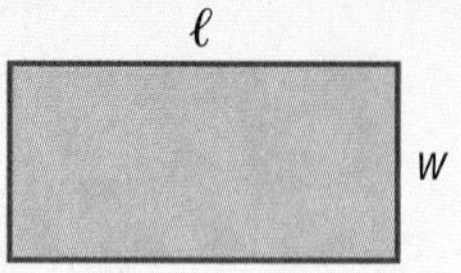

Formula $A = \ell w$

EXAMPLE Find the Area of a Rectangle

1 Find the area of a rectangle with length 12 feet and width 7 feet.

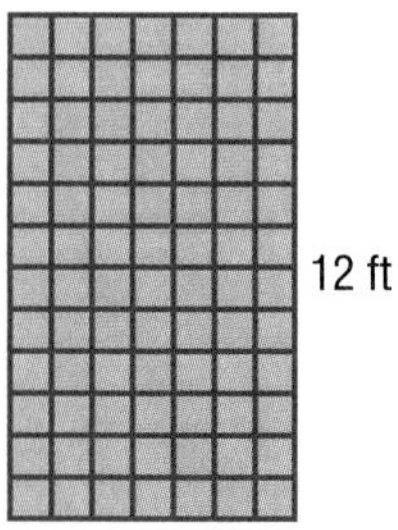

$A = \ell w$	Area of a rectangle
$A = 12 \cdot 7$	Replace ℓ with 12 and w with 7.
$A = 84$	Multiply.

The area is 84 square feet.

Remember

When finding area, the units are also multiplied. So, area is given in *square units.*

$A = 12 \text{ ft} \times 7 \text{ ft}$
$A = (12 \times 7)(\text{ft} \times \text{ft})$
$A = 84 \text{ ft}^2$

The formula for the area of a square is written with an exponent.

Concepts in Motion
Interactive Lab
ca.gr5math.com

KEY CONCEPT — Area of a Square

Words The area A of a square is the length of a side s squared.

Model

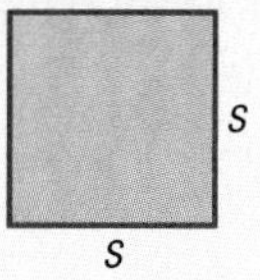

Formula $A = s^2$

EXAMPLE Find the Area of a Square

2 Find the area of a square with side length 9 inches.

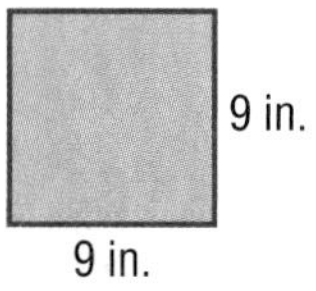

$A = \mathbf{s}^2$	Area of a square
$A = \mathbf{9}^2$	Replace s with 9.
$A = 81$	Multiply.

The area is 81 square inches.

Real-World EXAMPLES

3 A high school volleyball court is 60 feet long and 30 feet wide. What is the area of a high school volleyball court?

The length is 60 feet, and the width is 30 feet.

$A = \ell w$	Area of a rectangle
$A = \mathbf{60} \cdot \mathbf{30}$	Replace ℓ with 60 and w with 30.
$A = 1{,}800$	Multiply.

The area of a high school volleyball court is 1,800 square feet.

4 The Junkins are replacing the flooring in their kitchen with ceramic tiles. They are using 6-inch square tiles. What is the area each tile?

The length of a side is 6 inches.

$A = \mathbf{s}^2$	Area of a square
$A = \mathbf{6}^2$	Replace s with 6.
$A = 36$	Multiply.

The area of each ceramic tile is 36 square inches.

Online Personal Tutor at ca.gr5math.com

CHECK What You Know

Find the area of each rectangle or square. See Examples 1, 2 (pp. 52–53)

1. 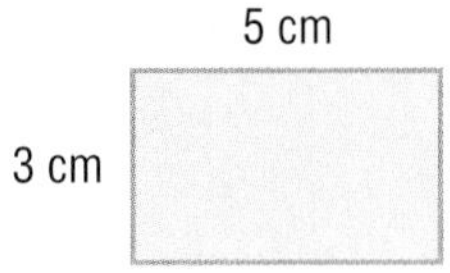

2. 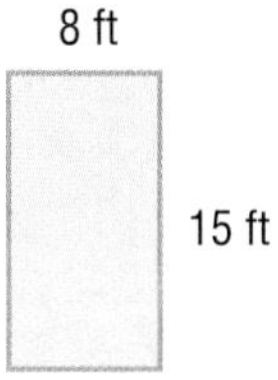

3. 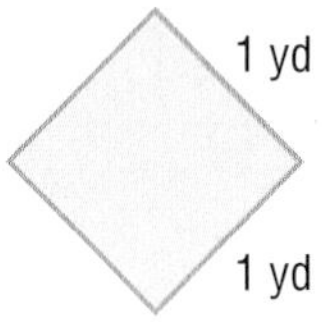

4. **Measurement** A television screen measures 9 inches by 12 inches. What is the area of the viewing screen?

5. **Talk About It** Describe two ways to find the area of a rectangle. Explain which way is the most useful.

Practice and Problem Solving

EXTRA PRACTICE
See page 656.

Find the area of each rectangle. See Example 1 (p. 52)

6. 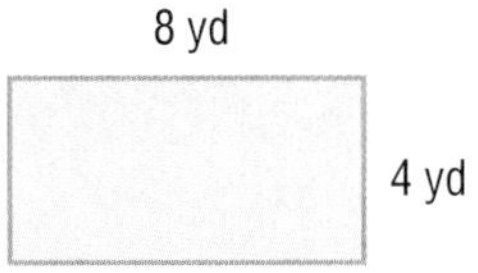

7. 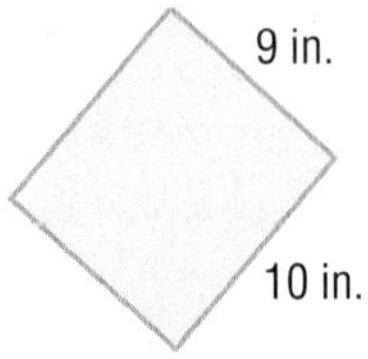

8. 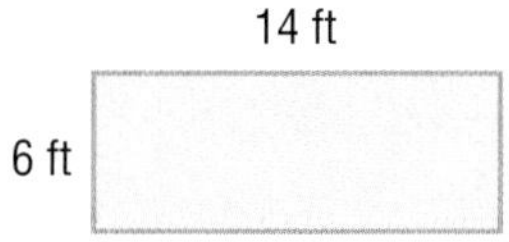

9. 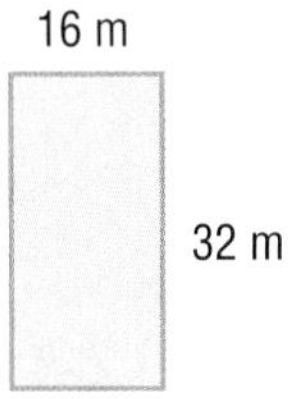

10. 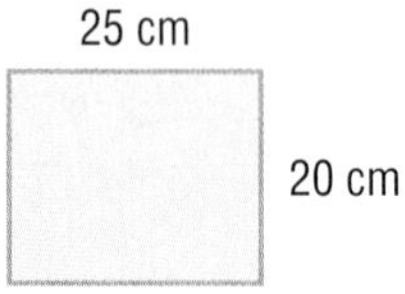

11. 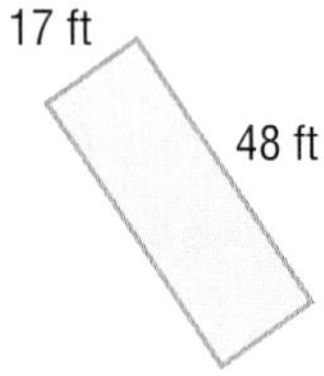

Find the area of each square. See Example 2 (p. 53)

12. 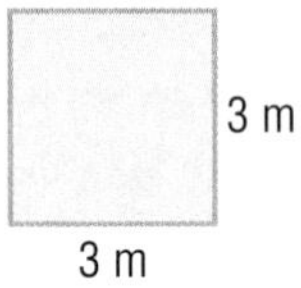

13. 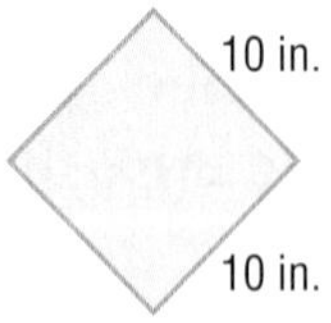

14. 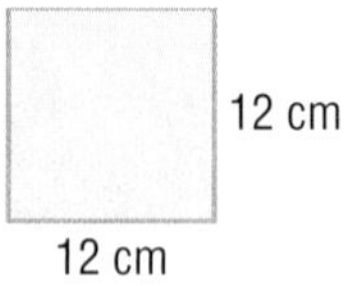

15. What is the area of a square with a side length of 22 feet?

16. **Measurement** A 3-ring binder measures 11 inches by 10 inches. What is the area of the front cover of the binder?

17. **Measurement** Meagan and her friends are knitting small squares to join together to form a blanket. The side length of each square must be 7 inches. What is the area of each square?

Find the area of each shaded region.

18.

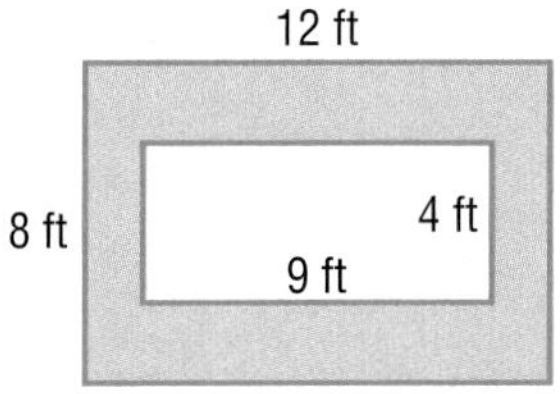

19.

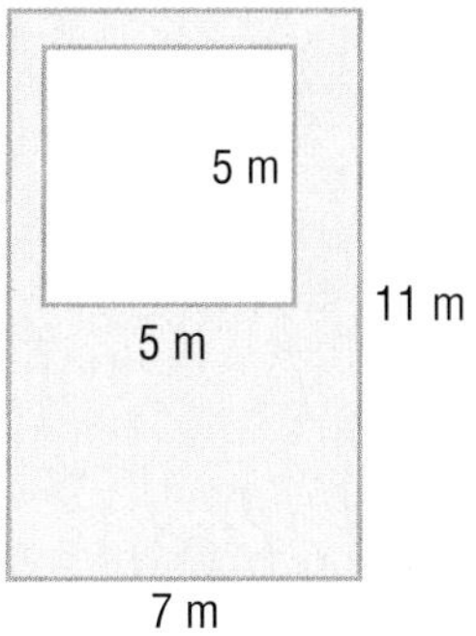

20.

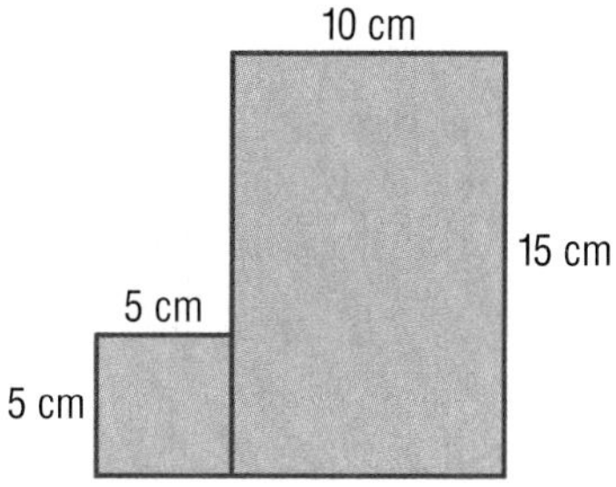

H.O.T. Problems

21. **NUMBER SENSE** Give the dimensions of two different rectangles that have the same area.

22. **CHALLENGE** Suppose opposite sides of a rectangle are increased by 3 units. Would the area of the rectangle increase by 6 square units? Use a model in your explanation.

23. **WRITING IN ▶MATH** Explain how to use the formula for the area of a square. Include the formula for the area of a square in your explanation.

Standards Practice

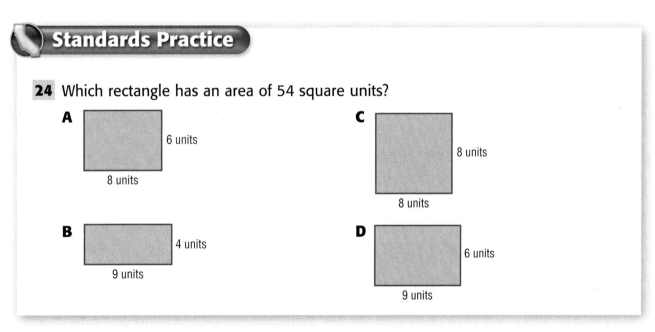

24 Which rectangle has an area of 54 square units?

A

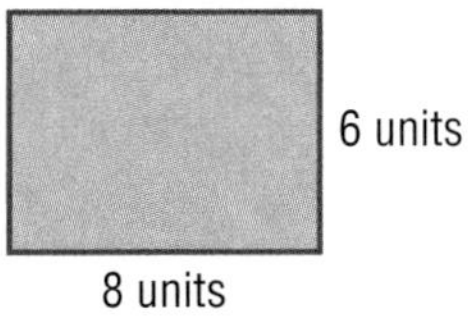

C

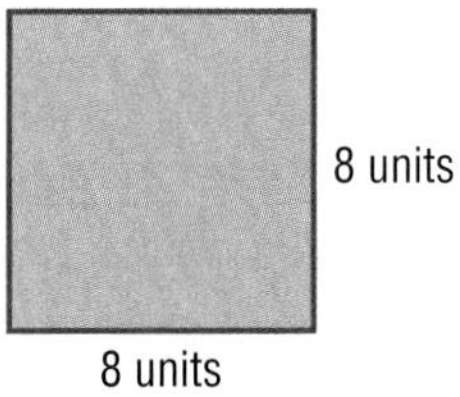

B

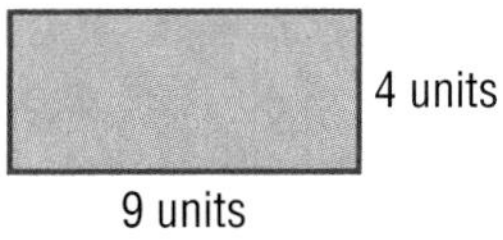

D

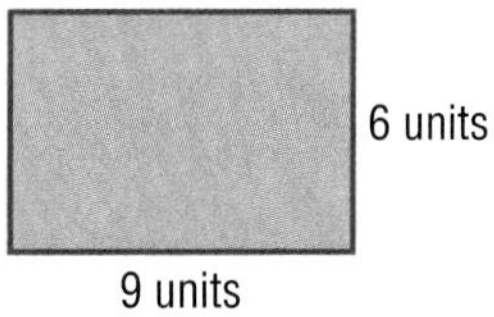

Spiral Review

Algebra Solve each equation mentally. **(Lesson 1-8)**

25. $x + 4 = 12$ **26.** $9 - m = 5$ **27.** $k - 8 = 20$

28. James is thinking of three even numbers less than 10 whose sum is 18. Find the numbers. **(Lesson 1-7)**

Problem Solving in History

SWEET DREAMS

Dreamcatchers were first made by the Chippewa people, who hung them over the beds of children to trap bad dreams. The Chippewa are one of the largest Native American groups in North America. In 1990, around 106,000 Chippewa were living throughout their original territories.

Each dreamcatcher is made with many beads and feathers. A simple dreamcatcher has 28 pony beads and is made with 7 yards of string. Today, Native Americans continue to make dreamcatchers on more than 300 reservations.

Did You Know?

The Chippewa people have signed 51 treaties with the United States government, the most of any Native American tribe.

Math Standard 5AF1.5 **Solve problems involving linear functions with integer values;** write the equation; and graph the resulting ordered pairs of integers on a grid.

Real-World Math

Use the information on page 56 to solve each problem.

1. Is the number of yards of string in a simple dreamcatcher a prime or composite number?

2. Write the number of pony beads in a simple dreamcatcher as a product of primes using exponents.

3. Each time you add a feather to a dreamcatcher, you add 3 turquoise beads. Use a function table to find out how many beads you will need if you have 2, 5, 8, or 13 feathers in your dreamcatcher.

4. Find the rule for the function table you created in Exercise 3.

5. You are making dreamcatchers that require 6 beads for every 1 feather. Let *f* represent the number of feathers. Then write a function rule that relates the total number of beads to the number of feathers.

6. Use the function rule from Exercise 5 to find the number of beads you would use if you made a dreamcatcher with 17 feathers.

7. Suppose you use 12 feathers and a certain amount of beads to make a dreamcatcher. If you had 48 feathers and beads, how many beads did you use?

1-10 Algebra: The Distributive Property

MAIN IDEA

I will use the Distributive Property in equations and expressions.

Standard 5AF1.3 Know and use the distributive property in equations and expressions with variables.

New Vocabulary

Distributive Property

GET READY to Learn

Hands-On Mini Lab

To find the area of a rectangle formed by two smaller rectangles, you can use either one of two methods.

Find the area of the blue and yellow rectangles.

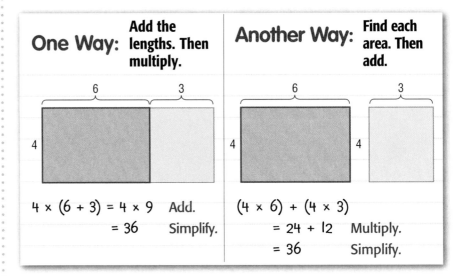

One Way: **Add the lengths. Then multiply.**

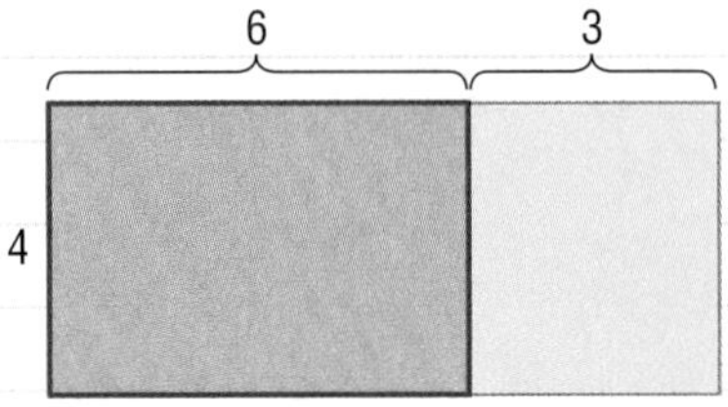

$4 \times (6 + 3) = 4 \times 9$ Add.

$= 36$ Simplify.

Another Way: **Find each area. Then add.**

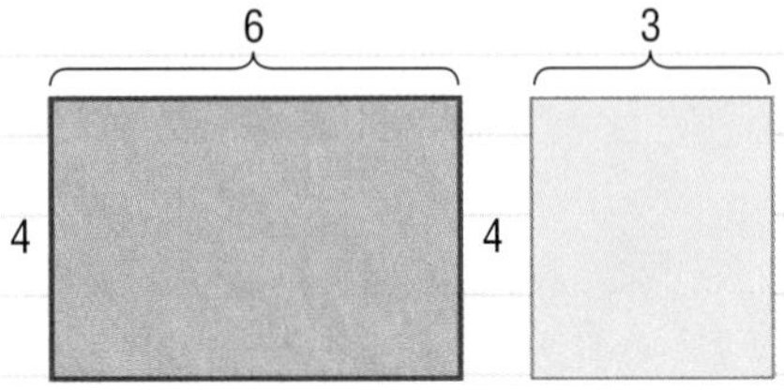

$(4 \times 6) + (4 \times 3)$

$= 24 + 12$ Multiply.

$= 36$ Simplify.

You found that $4 \times (6 + 3) = 36$. You also found that $(4 \times 6) + (4 \times 3) = 36$. So, $4 \times (6 + 3) = (4 \times 6) + (4 \times 3)$.

1. Draw a model showing $2 \times (4 + 6) = (2 \times 4) + (2 \times 6)$.
2. Write an expression that has the same value as $2 \times (5 + 7)$. Explain your reasoning.

The **Distributive Property** combines addition and multiplication.

KEY CONCEPT **Distributive Property**

Words To multiply a sum by a number, multiply each addend of the sum by the number outside the parentheses.

Symbols

Numbers	Algebra
$2(7 + 4) = (2 \times 7) + (2 \times 4)$	$a(b + c) = ab + ac$

You can use the Distributive Property to solve some multiplication problems mentally.

Vocabulary Link

Distribute

Everyday Use to divide among several people or things

Distributive

Math Use property that allows you to multiply a sum by a number

EXAMPLE Use the Distributive Property

1 Find 4 × 58 mentally using the Distributive Property.

$4 \times 58 = 4 \times (50 + 8)$	Write 58 as 50 + 8.
$= (4 \times 50) + (4 \times 8)$	Distributive Property
$= 200 + 32$	Find each product mentally.
$= 232$	Add 200 and 32 mentally.

Online Personal Tutor at ca.gr5math.com

Real-World EXAMPLE

2 More than 10 million people have visited the Wax Museum at Fisherman's Wharf in San Francisco to see wax figures like the ones shown. Suppose admission to a museum costs $5 and bus tickets are $3 per student. What is the cost for 30 students?

One Way:	Another Way:
Find the cost of 30 admissions and 30 bus tickets. Then add.	Find the cost for 1 person. Then multiply by 30.
30 × $5 + 30 × $3 (30 × $5: cost of 30 admissions; 30 × $3: cost of 30 bus tickets)	30 × ($5 + $3) ($5 + $3: cost for 1 person)

$30 \times (5 + 3) = (30 \times 5) + (30 \times 3)$	Distributive Property
$= 150 + 90$	Multiply.
$= 240$	Add.

The total cost is $240 for 30 students.

CHECK What You Know

Find each product mentally. Use the Distributive Property.
See Example 1 (p. 59)

1. 5×84

2. 10×23

3. 4×42

Rewrite each expression using the Distributive Property. Then evaluate. See Example 1 (p. 59)

4. $3 \times (20 + 4)$

5. $5 \times (60 + 5)$

6. $(12 \times 10) + (12 \times 8)$

7. Tickets to a college football game cost $21 per person and seat cushions cost $4 each. What is the total cost for 3 friends if each gets one ticket and one seat cushion? See Example 2 (p. 59)

8. Talk About It Explain why $4 \times (6 + 3) = (4 \times 6) + (4 \times 3)$.

Practice and Problem Solving

EXTRA PRACTICE See page 657.

Find each product mentally. Use the Distributive Property.
See Example 1 (p. 59)

9. 7×15

10. 3×72

11. 25×12

12. 15×11

13. 30×8

14. 60×2

Rewrite each expression using the Distributive Property. Then evaluate. See Example 1 (p. 59)

15. $7 \times (30 + 6)$

16. $12 \times (40 + 7)$

17. $2 \times (50 + 4)$

18. $13 \times (30 + 8)$

19. $(15 \times 10) + (15 \times 9)$

20. $(10 \times 100) + (10 \times 15)$

21. For a walk-a-thon, the 24 students in Mrs. Flores' class walked 12 miles each, and the 24 students in Mr. Gardner's class walked 17 miles each. Find the total number of miles walked. See Example 2 (p. 59)

22. Taylor made 15 party bags for her birthday. Each bag contained 3 chocolate chip cookies and 2 oatmeal cookies. What is the total number of cookies Taylor used? See Example 2 (p. 59)

Find the value of the variable that makes each equation true.

23. $3 \times 16 = (3 \times 10) + (3 \times y)$

24. $5 \times 85 = (5 \times z) + (5 \times 5)$

25. $10 \times 54 = (10 \times 50) + (h \times 4)$

26. $2 \times 91 = (j \times 90) + (2 \times 1)$

27. $(6 \times 10) + (6 \times k) = 6 \times 16$

28. $(4 \times m) + (4 \times 8) = 4 \times 28$

H.O.T. Problems

29. **OPEN ENDED** Create two equations that illustrate the Distributive Property.

CHALLENGE Rewrite each expression using the Distributive Property.

30. $2 \times (y + 2)$ 31. $m \times (2 + 7)$ 32. $(j \times 10) + (j \times 3)$

33. **FIND THE ERROR** Benjamin and Courtney are using the Distributive Property to simplify $5 \times (4 + 2)$. Who is correct? Explain your reasoning.

Benjamin
$(5 \times 4) + (5 \times 2)$

Courtney
$(5 + 4) \times (5 + 2)$

34. **WRITING IN MATH** Explain how to use the Distributive Property to find a product mentally.

Standards Practice

35 Which expression is equivalent to $(2 \times 4) + (6 \times 4)$?

A $4 \times (2 \times 6)$

B $6 \times (2 + 4)$

C $4 \times (2 + 6)$

D $2 \times (4 + 6)$

36 What value for y makes the following equation true?

$$2 \times 17 = (2 \times 10) + (2 \times y)$$

F 2 **H** 10

G 7 **J** 17

Spiral Review

37. **Measurement** James is mowing a rectangular lawn that measures 50 feet by 120 feet. What is the area of the lawn being mowed? (Lesson 1-9)

Algebra Solve each equation mentally. (Lesson 1-8)

38. $j + 6 = 10$ 39. $12 = 45 - m$ 40. $7m = 49$ 41. $36 \div y = 9$

42. The Milky Way galaxy is about 10^5 light years in diameter. What is the value of 10^5? (Lesson 1-2)

CHAPTER 1 Study Guide and Review

FOLDABLES Study Organizer GET READY to Study

Be sure the following Key Concepts are noted in your Foldable.

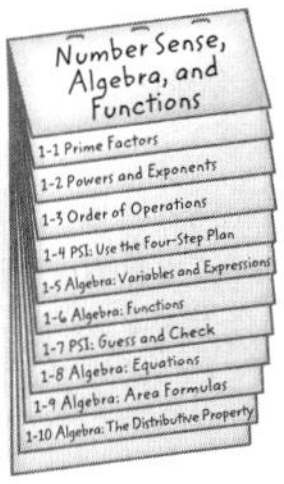

BIG Ideas

Prime and Composite Numbers (Lesson 1-1)

- A prime number has exactly two factors, 1 and the number itself.
- A composite number is a number greater than 1 with more than two factors.
- 1 has only one factor and is neither prime nor composite. 0 has an infinite number of factors and is neither prime nor composite.

Area Formulas (Lesson 1-9)

- The area *A* of a rectangle is the product of the length ℓ and width *w*.

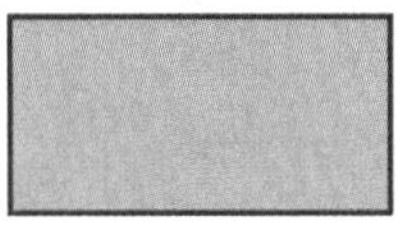

- The area *A* of a square is the length of a side *s* squared.

The Distributive Property (Lesson 1-10)

To multiply a sum by a number, multiply each addend of the sum by the number outside the parentheses.

Numbers: $2 \times (7 + 4) = (2 \times 7) + (2 \times 4)$

Algebra: $a \times (b + c) = ab + ac$

Key Vocabulary

algebra (p. 34)
algebraic expression (p. 34)
area (p. 52)
base (p. 21)
cubed (p. 22)
equation (p. 46)
evaluate (p. 34)
exponent (p. 21)
factor (p. 17)
function (p. 39)
numerical expression (p. 27)
power (p. 22)
prime factorization (p. 18)
solution (p. 46)
solve (p. 46)
squared (p. 22)
variable (p. 34)

Vocabulary Check

State whether each sentence is *true* or *false*. If *false*, replace the underlined word or number to make a true sentence.

1. A <u>formula</u> is used to find the area of a rectangle.
2. When two or more numbers are multiplied, each number is called a <u>factor</u>.
3. The <u>base</u> of a figure is the number of square units needed to cover a surface.
4. A <u>function</u> represents an unknown value.
5. A <u>variable</u> is a relationship that assigns exactly one output value to one input value.

Lesson-by-Lesson Review

1-1 Prime Factors (pp. 17–20)

Example 1
Find the prime factorization of 18.

Make a factor tree.

18	Write the number to be factored.
2×9	Choose any two factors of 18.
$2 \times 3 \times 3$	Continue to factor any number that is not prime until you have a row of prime numbers.

The prime factorization of 18 is $2 \times 3 \times 3$.

Tell whether each number is *prime*, *composite*, or *neither*.

6. 44 **7.** 67

Find the prime factorization of each number.

8. 42 **9.** 75 **10.** 96

11. Cryptography uses prime numbers to encode information. Suki's bank account was encoded with the number 273. What are the prime number factors of this code?

1-2 Powers and Exponents (pp. 21–25)

Example 2
Write $4 \times 4 \times 4 \times 4 \times 4 \times 4$ using an exponent. Then find the value of the power.

The base is 4. Since 4 is a factor 6 times, the exponent is 6.

$4 \times 4 \times 4 \times 4 \times 4 \times 4 = 4^6$ or 4,096

Write each product using an exponent. Then find the value of the power.

12. $5 \times 5 \times 5 \times 5$

13. $12 \times 12 \times 12$

14. The average brain weight in grams for a walrus is 2^{10}. Find this value.

1-3 Order of Operations (pp. 27–30)

Example 3
Find the value of $28 \div 2 - 1 \times 5$.

$28 \div 2 - 1 \times 5$	
$= 14 - 1 \times 5$	Divide 28 by 2.
$= 14 - 5$	Multiply 1 and 5.
$= 9$	Subtract 5 from 14.

The value of $28 \div 2 - 1 \times 5$ is 9.

Find the value of each expression.

15. $4 \times 6 + 2 \times 3$

16. $11^2 - 6 + 3 \times 15$

17. Maria counted 3 groups of motorcycles, each with 5 motorcycles and an additional 7 motorcycles by themselves. Write and evaluate expression for the number of motorcycles Maria saw.

1-4 Problem-Solving Investigation: Use the Four-Step Plan (pp. 32–33)

Example 4
Esteban studied 2 hours each day for 10 days. How many hours has he studied?

Explore You need to find the total number of hours.

Plan Multiply 2 by 10.

Solve $2 \times 10 = 20$
So, Esteban studied 20 hours.

Check Since $20 \div 2 = 10$, the answer makes sense.

Use the four-step plan to solve each problem.

18. Tickets to a school dance cost \$4 each. If \$352 was collected, how many tickets were sold?

19. In the 1932 presidential election, Franklin Roosevelt won 472 electoral votes while Herbert Hoover won 59. How many electoral votes were cast for these two men?

1-5 Algebra: Variables and Expressions (pp. 34–38)

Example 5
Evaluate $9 - k^3$ if $k = 2$.

$9 - k^3 = 9 - 2^3$		Replace k with 2.
$= 9 - 8$		$2^3 = 8$
$= 1$		Subtract 8 from 9.

Example 6
Evaluate $10 + mn$ if $m = 3$ and $n = 5$.

$10 + mn = 10 + (3)(5)$	$m = 3$ and $n = 5$
$= 10 + 15$	Multiply 3 and 5.
$= 25$	Add 10 and 15.

Evaluate each expression if $a = 18$ and $b = 6$.

20. $a \times b$

21. $a^2 \div b$

22. $3b^2 + a$

23. $2a - 10$

Evaluate each expression if $x = 6$, $y = 8$, and $z = 12$.

24. $2x + 4y$

25. $3z^2 + 4x$

26. $z \div 3 + xy$

27. Joe will tile a square kitchen floor with square ceramic tile. He knows the number of tiles needed is equal to $a^2 \div b^2$, where a is the floor length in inches and b is the length of the tile in inches. If $a = 96$ and $b = 8$, how many tiles are needed?

1-6 Algebra: Functions (pp. 39–43)

Example 7
Find a rule for the function table.

Input (x)	Output (■)
6	2
12	4
15	5

Study the relationship between each input and output. Divide each input by 3 to find the output.

So, the function rule is $x \div 3$.

Copy and complete each function table.

28.

Input (x)	$x - 1$	Output
1	■	■
6	■	■
8	■	■

Find the rule for each function table.

29.

Input (x)	Output (■)
2	8
7	13
12	18

30. Tina drove 60 miles per hour to Tucson. Define a variable. Write a function rule that relates the number of miles traveled to the hours driven.

31. A boy is 5 years older than his sister. Define a variable. Write a function rule that relates the age of the boy to the age of his sister.

1-7 Problem-Solving Strategy: Guess and Check (pp. 44–45)

Example 8
Owen is 8 inches taller than his sister, Lisa. If the sum of their heights is 124 inches, how tall is Owen?

Make a guess. Check to see if it is correct. Adjust the guess until it is correct.

Owen's Height		Lisa's Height		Sum of Heights	
60 in.	+	52 in.	=	112 in.	*too low*
68 in.	+	60 in.	=	128 in.	*too high*
66 in.	+	58 in.	=	124 in.	✓

Solve. Use the *guess and check* strategy.

32. A company makes toy cars. It sells red cars for $2 each and black cars for $3 each. If the company sold 44 cars total and made $105, how many red cars were sold?

33. The sum of two numbers is 22 and their product is 117. Find the numbers.

34. Alex caught 3 more catfish than he did trout. If the total number of catfish and trout was 19, how many catfish did he catch?

CHAPTER 1 Study Guide and Review

1-8 Algebra: Equations (pp. 46–49)

Example 9
Solve $x + 9 = 13$ mentally.

$x + 9 = 13$ What number plus 9 is 13?

$4 + 9 = 13$ You know that $4 + 9$ is 13.

$x = 4$

The solution is 4.

Solve each equation mentally.

35. $p + 2 = 9$

36. $20 + y = 25$

37. $40 = 15 + m$

38. $16 - n = 10$

39. $27 = x - 3$

40. $17 = 25 - h$

41. The equation $18 + p = 34$ represents the sum of Pedro's and Eva's ages, where p represents Pedro's age. How old is Pedro?

1-9 Algebra: Area Formulas (pp. 52–55)

Example 10
Find the area of the rectangle.

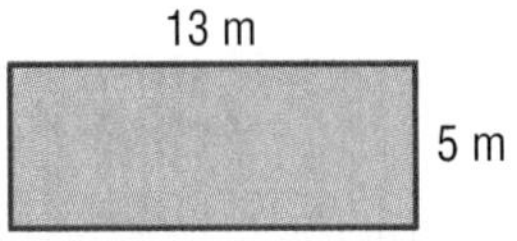

$A = \ell w$ Area of a rectangle

$= 13 \cdot 5$ Replace ℓ with 13 and w with 5.

$= 65$

The area is 65 square meters.

42. Find the area of the rectangle below.

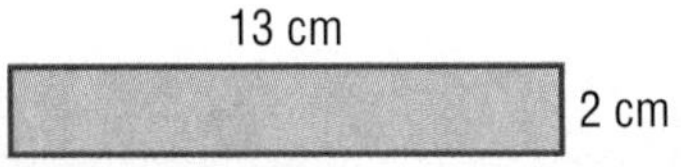

43. Measurement Find the area of a painting that measures 4 feet by 4 feet.

1-10 Algebra: The Distributive Property (pp. 58–61)

Example 11
Rewrite $4 \times (2 + 9)$ using the Distributive Property. Then evaluate.

$4 \times (2 + 9)$

$= (4 \times 2) + (4 \times 9)$ Distributive Property

$= 8 + 36$ Multiply.

$= 44$ Add.

Rewrite each expression using the Distributive Property. Then evaluate.

44. $4 \times (7 + 2)$

45. $8 \times (14 + 9)$

46. $(3 \times 8) + (3 \times 12)$

47. $(9 \times 6) + (9 \times 13)$

48. Tickets to a movie are \$7 for students and \$5 for children. What is the total cost of admission for three students and three children?

CHAPTER 1

Chapter Test

1. **STANDARDS PRACTICE** Justin earned \$308 by mowing lawns and raking leaves for a total of 43 hours. He raked leaves for 18 hours and earned \$108. Arrange the steps below in a correct order to find how much he earned per hour mowing lawns.

   Step P: Find the difference between \$308 and the amount Justin earned raking leaves.

   Step Q: Find the quotient of \$200 and the number of hours Justin spent mowing lawns.

   Step R: Find the number of hours Justin spent mowing lawns.

   Which list shows the steps in the correct order?

   A P, Q, R **C** Q, R, P

   B R, Q, P **D** R, P, Q

Tell whether each number is *prime, composite,* or *neither*.

2. 57 **3.** 1 **4.** 31

5. Find the prime factorization of 68.

6. Miranda told 3 friends that it was her birthday. Each of those 3 friends told 3 other students. By noon, 3^5 students knew it was Miranda's birthday. Write this number as a product of the same factor. Then find the value.

Find the value of each expression.

7. $12 - 3 \times 2 + 15$ **8.** $72 \div 2^3 - 4 \times 2$

Evaluate each expression if $a = 4$ and $b = 3$.

9. $a + 12$ **10.** $27 \div b$ **11.** $a^3 - 2b$

12. **STANDARDS PRACTICE** Latisha and Raquel ordered two beverages for \$1.50 each, two dinners for \$12.99 each, and a dessert for \$3.50. Which of the following expressions can be used to find the amount each should pay, not including tax?

F $1.50 + 2 \times 12.99 + 3.50 \div 2$

G $(2 \times 1.50 + 2 \times 12.99 + 3.50) \div 2$

H $2 \times (1.50 + 12.99 + 3.50)$

J $(2 \times 1.50 + 12.99) + 3.50 \div 2$

Find the rule for each function table.

13.

Input (x)	Output (■)
3	8
7	12
11	16

14.

Input (x)	Output (■)
0	0
8	1
16	2

15. A potato has 26 grams of carbohydrates. Define a variable. Write a function rule that relates the amount of carbohydrates to the number of potatoes.

16. Diego has \$1.30 in quarters, dimes, and nickels. He has the same amount of nickels as quarters, and one more dime than nickels. How many of each coin does he have?

Algebra Solve each equation mentally.

17. $d + 9 = 14$ **18.** $56 = 7k$

19. **Measurement** Find the area of the rectangle.

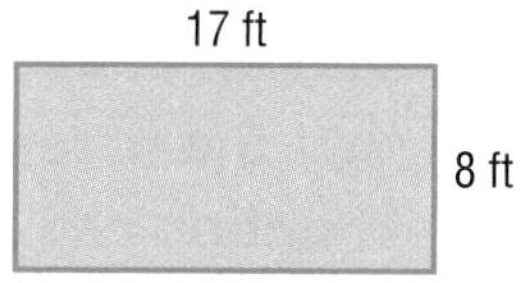

20. **WRITING IN MATH** Find the value of the variable that makes $7 \times 12 = (7 \times 10) + (7 \times y)$ true. Explain.

CHAPTER 1

California Standards Practice

Chapter 1

Standards Example

The table shows Molly's age and Max's age over 4 consecutive years.

Molly's Age, x (years)	Max's Age, y (years)
2	5
3	6
4	7
5	8

Which expression best represents Max's age in terms of Molly's age?

A $y + 3$

B $3x$

C $x + 3$

D $3y$

Read the Question

You need to find the expression that best represents Max's age in terms of Molly's age.

Solve the Question

Study the relationship between Molly's age and Max's age. Max's age is 3 more than Molly's age. Molly's age is x years. So, $x + 3$ represents Max's age. The answer is C.

Online Personal Tutor at ca.gr5math.com

Choose the best answer.

1 **The cost of renting roller blades is $4 plus an additional $3.50 for each hour that the roller blades are rented. Which equation can be used to find c, the cost in dollars of the rental for *h* hours?**

A $c = 4h + 3.50$

B $c = 3.50 - 4h$

C $c = 3.50(h + 4)$

D $c = 3.50h + 4$

2 **Which expression represents the product of *m* and 30?**

F $30m$

G $30 - m$

H $30 + m$

J $30 \div m$

3 **Which situation is described by the expression $m + 585$?**

A Samantha drove m miles on Friday and 585 miles fewer on Monday

B Samantha drove 585 miles on Friday and m miles fewer on Monday

C Samantha drove 585 miles on Friday and m times as many miles on Monday

D Samantha drove 585 miles on Friday and m miles farther on Monday

4 **A sub shop is keeping track of the number of meatball subs sold each day.**

Day	Number of Meatball Subs Sold
Monday	40
Tuesday	25
Wednesday	30
Thursday	45
Friday	65

About how many subs were sold during that week?

F 150 subs
H 300 subs
G 200 subs
J 350 subs

5 **At a large middle school, there are 18 fifth-grade homerooms and approximately 22 students in each homeroom. About how many fifth-grade students attend the middle school?**

A 250 **B** 325 **C** 400 **D** 650

6 **What value for y makes the following equation true?**

$$5 \times 13 = (5 \times 10) + (5 \times y)$$

F 3
H 10
G 5
J 13

7 **Lynette is painting a 15-foot by 10-foot rectangular wall that has a 9-foot by 5-foot rectangular window at its center. How many square feet of wall space does she need to paint?**

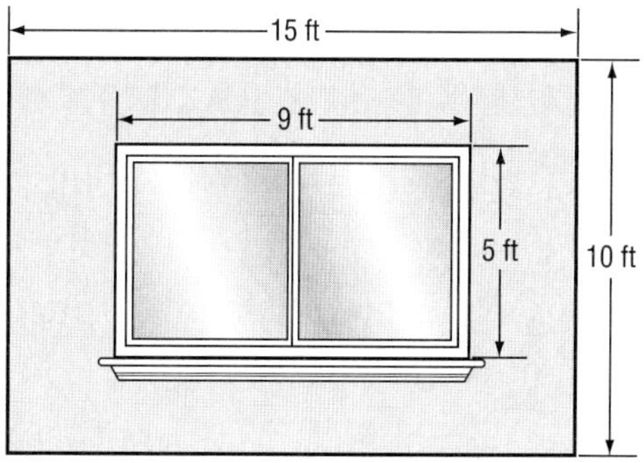

A 45 ft^2
C 150 ft^2
B 105 ft^2
D 195 ft^2

8 **Which is the prime factorization of 360?**

F 2^7
H $3^3 \times 5^2$
G $2^3 \times 3^2 \times 5$
J $3^2 \times 5 \times 7^2$

9 **Amanda planted a square garden with sides of 8 feet. Find the area.**

A 16 ft^2
C 64 ft^2
B 32 ft^2
D 80 ft^2

CHAPTER 2

Statistics and Data Analysis

BIG Idea What are data?

Data are pieces of information.

Example The flower shown is the California state flower, the Golden Poppy. The table below contains data about the Golden Poppy.

California's Golden Poppy	
Year of adoption	1903
Flower length	2.5 cm to 5 cm
Leaf length	3 cm to 10 cm

What will I learn in this chapter?

- Display and analyze data using bar graphs, line graphs, histograms, and line plots.
- Find and interpret the mean, median, mode, and range of a set of data.
- Select an appropriate display for a set of data.
- Represent integers on a number line.
- Solve problems by making a table.

Key Vocabulary

frequency

mean

integers

graph

Math Online Student Study Tools at ca.gr5math.com

FOLDABLES™
Study Organizer

Make this Foldable to help you organize information about statistics and graphs. Begin with five sheets of graph paper.

1 **Fold** each sheet of graph paper in half along the width.

2 **Unfold** each sheet and tape to form one long piece.

3 **Label** the pages with the lesson numbers as shown.

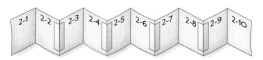

4 **Refold** the pages to form a journal.

ARE YOU READY for Chapter 2?

You have two ways to check prerequisite skills for this chapter.

Option 2

Math Online Take the Chapter Readiness Quiz at ca.gr5math.com.

Option 1

Complete the Quick Check below.

QUICK Check

Add. **(Prior Grade)**

1. 16 + 28 **2.** 39 + 25 + 11 **3.** 63 + 9 + 37

4. 74 + 14 **5.** 8 + 56 + 10 + 7 **6.** 44 + 18 + 5

7. Jeffrey mows lawns after school. He earned $46 on Monday, $24 on Tuesday, $32 on Thursday, and $18 on Friday. How much money did he earn altogether? **(Prior Grade)**

Divide. **(Prior Grade)**

8. $132 \div 11$ **9.** $96 \div 8$ **10.** $84 \div 2$

11. $102 \div 6$ **12.** $125 \div 5$ **13.** $212 \div 4$

14. A can of green beans contains 141 Calories. If there are 3 servings in the can, how many Calories does a single serving of green beans have? **(Prior Grade)**

Find the value of each expression. **(Lesson 1-3)**

15. $15 - 4 + 2$ **16.** $6 + 35 \div 7$ **17.** $30 \div (8 - 3)$

18. $(2^5 \div 4) - 5$ **19.** $5^2 \times 2 - (5 \times 4)$ **20.** $7 \times (4 \div 2) + 3^3$

21. Salma can buy pairs of earrings for $7 each and rings for $6 each. How much more do three pairs of earrings cost than two rings? **(Lesson 1-3)**

2-1 Bar Graphs and Line Graphs

GET READY to Learn

Types of roller coasters found in the United States are listed in the table. What might be an advantage of organizing data in a table? Are there any disadvantages of organizing data in a table?

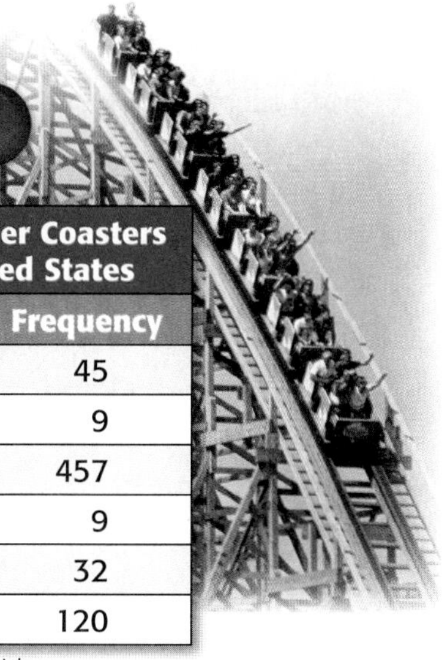

Types of Roller Coasters in the United States

Type	Frequency
inverted	45
stand up	9
steel	457
suspended	9
wild mouse	32
wood	120

Source: Roller Coaster Database

MAIN IDEA

I will display and analyze data using bar graphs and line graphs.

Standard 5SDAP1.2
Organize and display single-variable data in appropriate graphs and representations (e.g., histogram, circle graphs) and explain which types of graphs are appropriate for various data sets.

New Vocabulary

- data
- graph
- bar graph
- scale
- vertical axis
- interval
- horizontal axis
- frequency
- line graph

Data are pieces of information that are often numerical. Data are often shown in a table. A **graph** is a more visual way to display data. A **bar graph** is used to compare categories of data.

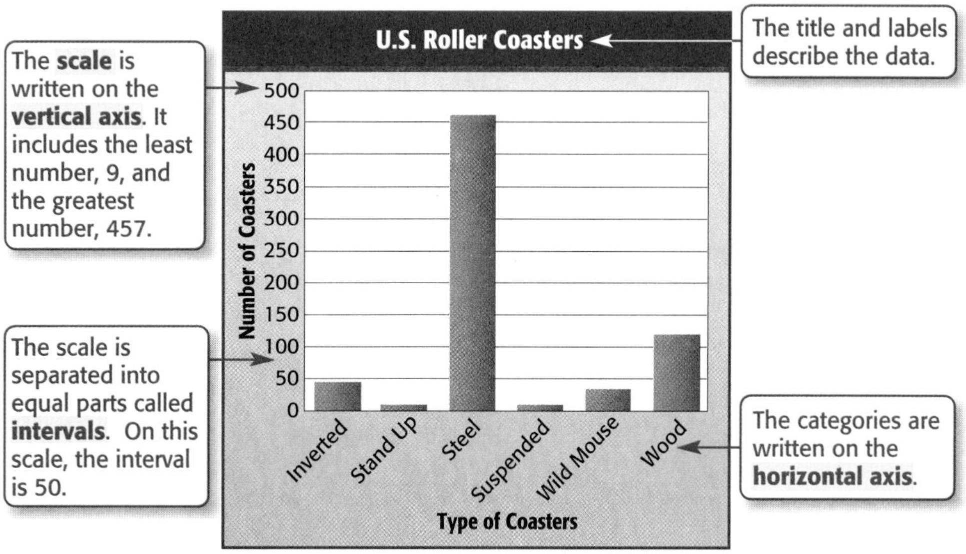
U.S. Roller Coasters
The title and labels describe the data.
The scale is written on the vertical axis. It includes the least number, 9, and the greatest number, 457.
The scale is separated into equal parts called intervals. On this scale, the interval is 50.
Number of Coasters
500
450
400
350
300
250
200
150
100
50
0
Inverted
Stand Up
Steel
Suspended
Wild Mouse
Wood
Type of Coasters
The categories are written on the horizontal axis.

Source: Roller Coaster Database

The height of each bar represents the frequency of each category of data. The **frequency** is the number of times an item occurs. For example, the frequency of inverted roller coasters in the United States is 45.

Remember

The graph shown in Example 1 is called a vertical bar graph. Bar graphs can also be horizontal.

EXAMPLE Analyze a Bar Graph

1 Make a bar graph of the data. Compare the number of students who scored a B to the number who scored a C.

Math Scores	
Grade	**Frequency**
A	10
B	13
C	7
D	2

Step 1 Decide on the scale and interval. The data include numbers from 2 to 13. So, a scale from 0 to 14 and an interval of 2 are reasonable.

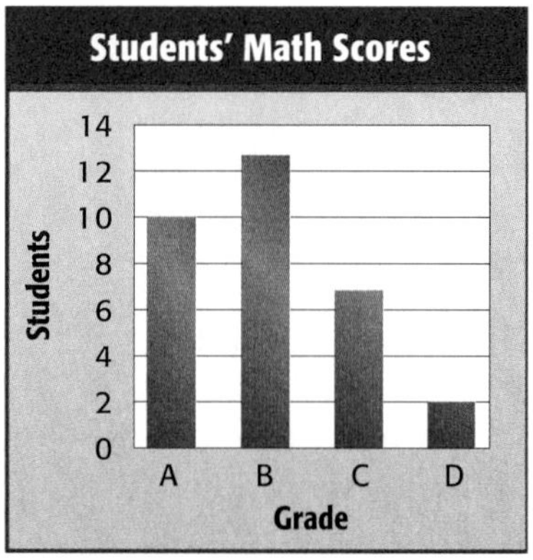

Step 2 Label the horizontal and vertical axes.

Step 3 Draw bars for each grade. The height of each bar shows the number of students earning that grade.

Step 4 Label the graph with a title.

The height of the bar for the number of students who scored a B is about twice as tall as the bar for the number of students who scored a C. So, about twice as many students scored a B than a C.

Online Personal Tutor at ca.gr5math.com

Another type of graph is a line graph. A **line graph** is used to show how a set of data changes over a period of time.

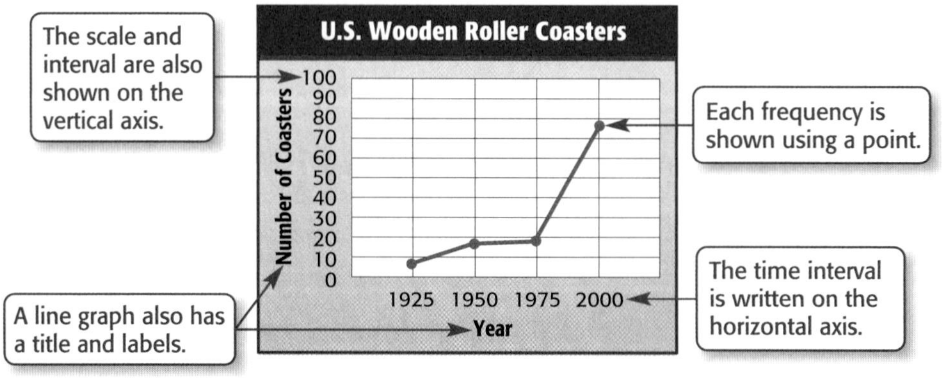

By observing the upward or downward slant of the lines connecting the points, you can describe trends in the data.

EXAMPLE Analyze a Line Graph

2 **Make a line graph of the data below. Then describe the change in the number of tornadoes from 2001 to 2004.**

U.S. Tornadoes						
Year	1999	2000	2001	2002	2003	2004
Tornadoes	1,343	1,071	1,216	941	1,246	1,819

Source: National Weather Service

Step 1 The data include numbers from 941 to 1,819. So a scale from 900 to 1,900 and an interval of 100 are reasonable. Use a break to show that numbers from 0 to 900 are left out.

Step 2 Label the horizontal and vertical axes.

Step 3 Draw and connect the points for each year.

Step 4 Label the graph with a title.

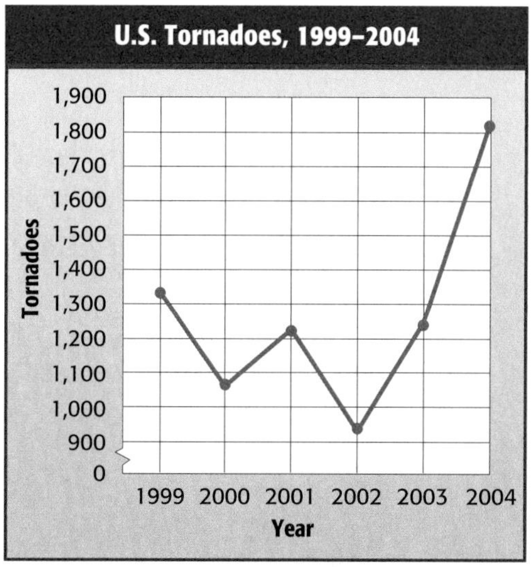

The number of tornadoes decreased from 2001 to 2002 and then increased from 2002 to 2004.

CHECK What You Know

1. Make a bar graph of the endangered species data. How do the number of endangered fish and reptiles compare? **See Example 1 (p. 74)**

U.S. Endangered Species			
Species	Fish	Amphibians	Insects
Frequency	75	13	47
Species	Reptiles	Mammals	Birds
Frequency	14	69	76

Source: Fish and Wildlife Service

2. Make a line graph of the basic cable subscribers data. Then describe the change in the number of subscribers from 1988 to 2003. **See Example 2 (p. 75)**

Subscribers (nearest million)				
Year	1988	1993	1998	2003
Frequency	49	59	67	73

Source: *The World Almanac*

3. **Talk About It** Describe a situation that would be best represented by a line graph.

Practice and Problem Solving

EXTRA PRACTICE See page 657.

4. Make a bar graph of the data below. Then compare the amount of shoreline for Louisiana and Texas. **See Example 1 (p. 74)**

U.S. Gulf Coast Shoreline	
State	**Amount (mi)**
Alabama	607
Florida	5,095
Louisiana	7,721
Mississippi	359
Texas	3,359

Source: NOAA

5. Make a bar graph of the data below. How do the number of wide-receiver winners and running-back winners compare? **See Example 1 (p. 74)**

Heisman Trophy Winners	
Position	**Frequency**
Cornerback	1
Fullback	2
Halfback	19
Quarterback	23
Running Back	20
Wide Receiver	3

Source: *The World Almanac*

6. Make a line graph of the data below. Describe the change in Australia's population from 1960 to 2000. **See Example 2 (p. 75)**

Australia's Population	
Year	**Population (millions)**
1960	10
1970	13
1980	15
1990	17
2000	19

Source: U.S. Census Bureau

7. Make a line graph of the data below. What two-year period showed the greatest increase in enrollment? **See Example 2 (p. 75)**

Public School Enrollment, K–12	
Year	**Students (thousands)**
1999	46,857
2000	47,223
2001	47,576
2002	47,613
2003	47,746

Source: National Center for Education Statistics

Real-World PROBLEM SOLVING

Weather The average monthly temperatures in Atlanta, Georgia, are shown in the table.

8. Choose an appropriate scale and interval for the data set.

9. Would these data be best represented by a bar graph or line graph? Explain your reasoning.

10. Make a graph of this data.

11. Write one question that can be answered using your graph. Then answer your question and justify your reasoning.

Average Temperatures (°F), Atlanta, Georgia			
Month	**Temp.**	**Month**	**Temp.**
Jan.	43	July	80
Feb.	47	Aug.	79
Mar.	54	Sept.	73
Apr.	62	Oct.	63
May	70	Nov.	53
June	77	Dec.	45

Source: *The World Almanac*

H.O.T. Problems

12. COLLECT THE DATA Make an appropriate display showing the amount of time you spend doing a particular activity each day for one week. Then write at least two statements that analyze your data.

13. CHALLENGE Can changes to the vertical scale or interval affect the look of a bar or line graph? Justify your reasoning with examples.

14. WRITING IN ►MATH Compare and contrast bar and line graphs.

Standards Practice

15 The table at the right shows the gross income of five of the highest-grossing country music tours in 2000. Which graph most accurately displays the information in the table?

Artist	Gross Income (millions of dollars)
A	49.6
B	46.1
C	21.0
D	10.7
E	9.0

A

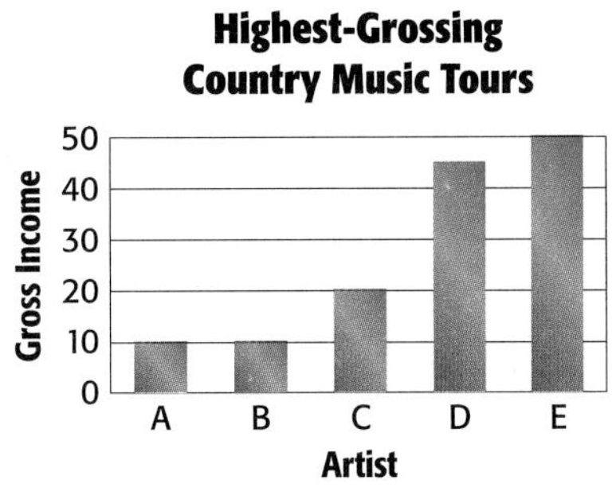

C

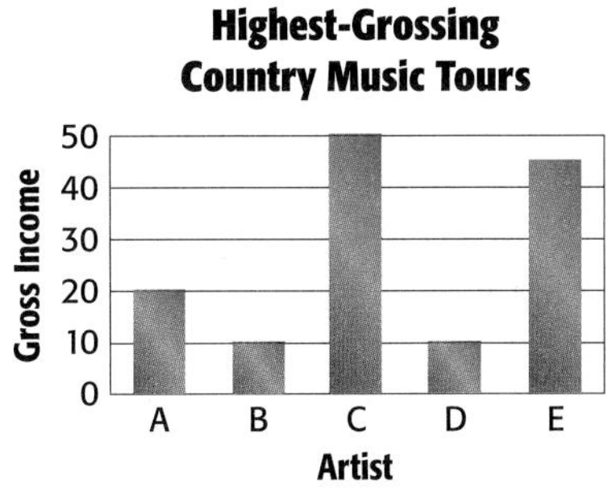

B

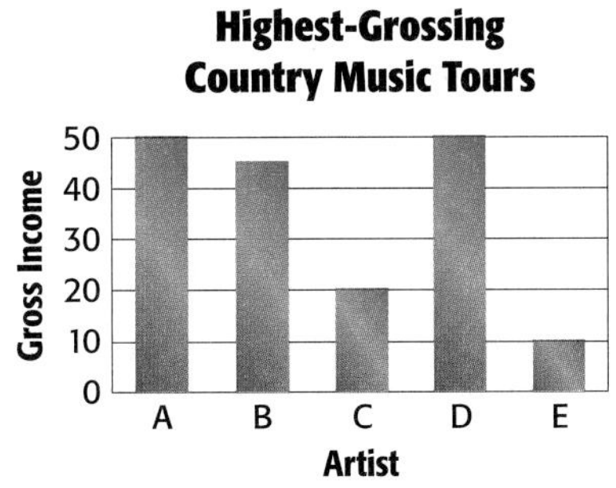

D

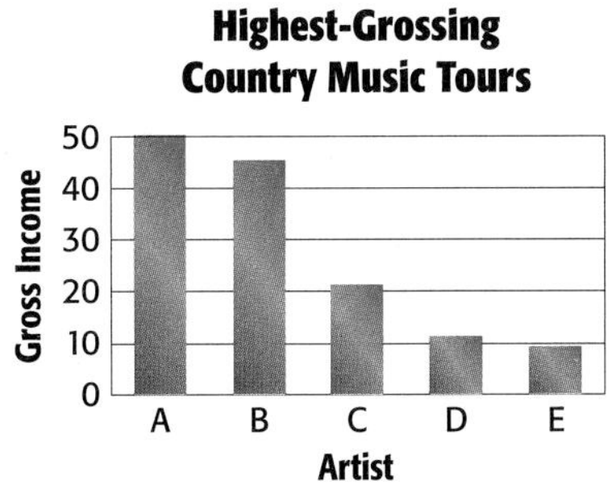

Spiral Review

Algebra Find the value of the variable that makes each equation true. (Lesson 1-10)

16. $9 \times 22 = (9 \times 20) + (9 \times y)$

17. $4 \times 36 = (4 \times z) + (4 \times 6)$

18. Measurement What is the area of a curtain that is 4 feet by 6 feet? (Lesson 1-9)

Game Time

Great Graph Race

Making Bar Graphs

Get Ready!

Players: two to seven

You will need: two spinners

Get Set!

- Label the vertical and horizontal axes of a bar graph as shown at the right.
- Each player chooses one of the products 1, 2, 3, 4, 6, 8, or 12.

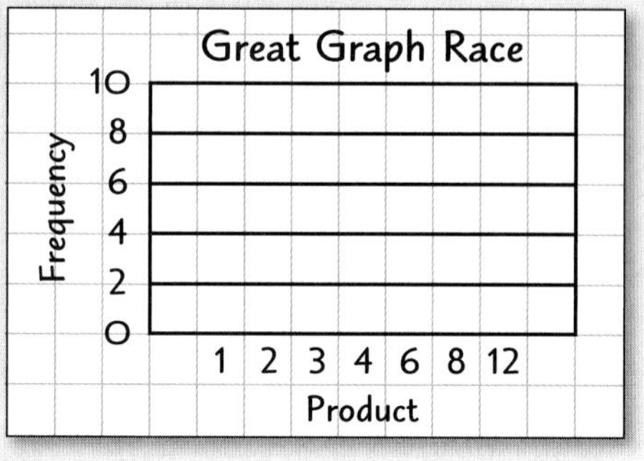

Go!

- Each player takes a turn spinning each spinner once. Then the player finds the product of the numbers on the spinners and either creates a bar or extends the bar on the graph for that product.
- The player whose bar reaches a frequency of 10 first wins.

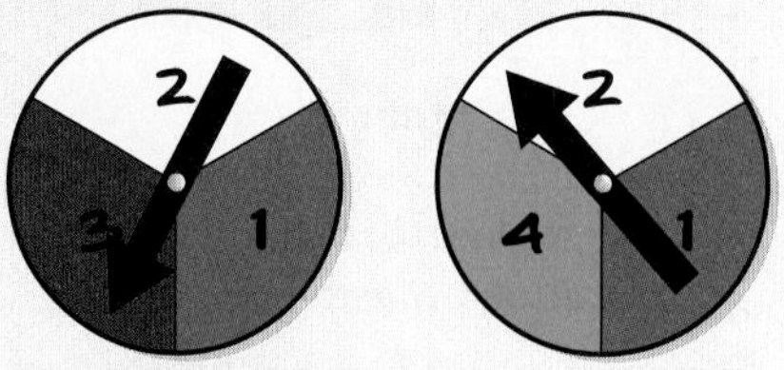

These spinners represent the product 6.

2-2 Interpret Line Graphs

GET READY to Learn

Analyze the table below. Describe the trends in the winning amounts. Predict how much money the 2010 Daytona 500 winner will receive.

Money Won by Daytona 500 Winners, 1988–2005					
Year	Amount ($)	Year	Amount ($)	Year	Amount ($)
1988	202,940	1994	258,275	2000	1,277,975
1989	184,900	1995	300,460	2001	1,331,185
1990	188,150	1996	360,775	2002	1,409,017
1991	233,000	1997	377,410	2003	1,400,406
1992	244,050	1998	1,059,805	2004	1,495,070
1993	238,200	1999	1,172,246	2005	1,497,154

Source: news-journalonline.com; daytonainternationalspeedway.com

MAIN IDEA

I will interpret line graphs.

Standard 5SDAP1.4 Identify ordered pairs of data from a graph and **interpret the meaning of the data in terms of the situation depicted by the graph.**

Line graphs are often used to predict future events because they show trends over time.

EXAMPLE Interpret Line Graphs

1 The data given in the table above are shown in the line graph below. Describe the trend. Then predict how much money the 2010 Daytona 500 winner will receive.

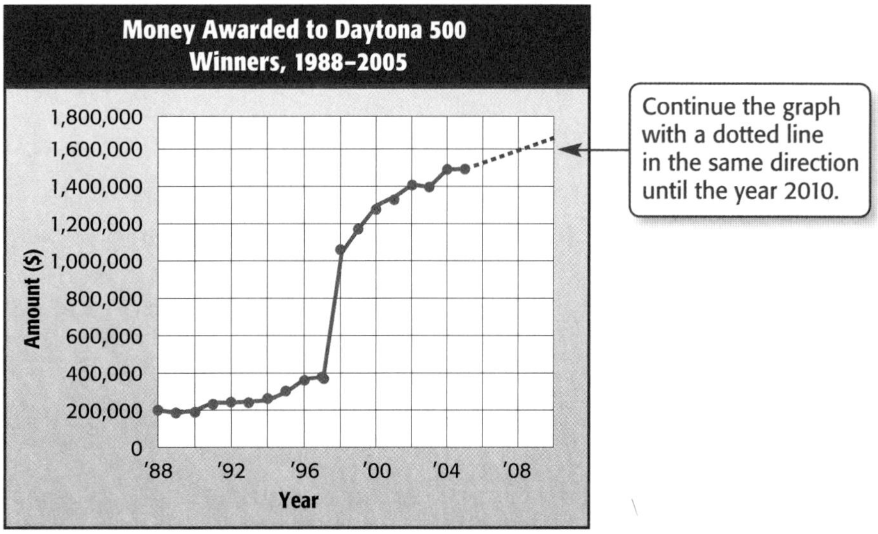

Notice that the increase since 1998 has been fairly steady. By extending the graph, you can predict that the winner of the 2010 Daytona 500 will receive about $1,650,000.

EXAMPLE Interpret Line Graphs

Concepts in Motion

Interactive Lab ca.gr5math.com

2 What does the graph tell you about the popularity of skateboarding?

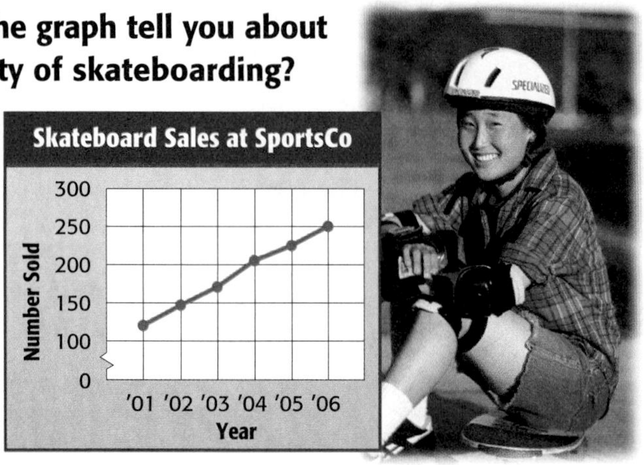

The graph shows that skateboard sales have been increasing each year. You can assume that the popularity of the sport is increasing.

Online Personal Tutor at ca.gr5math.com

CHECK What You Know

For Exercises 1–7, use the graph that shows the change in the world population from 1950 to 2000. See Examples 1, 2 (pp. 79–80)

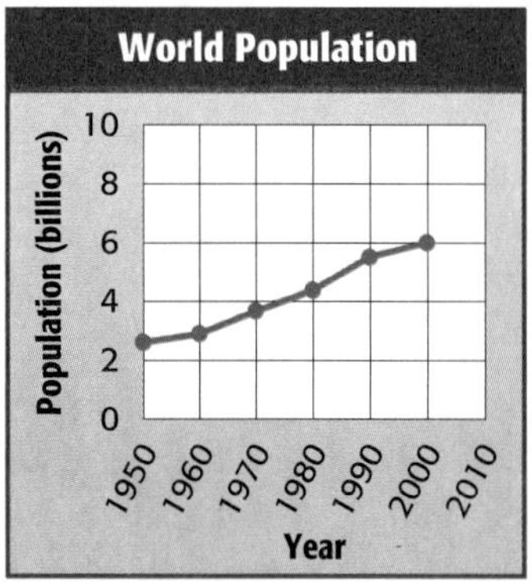

Source: U.S. Census Bureau

1. Describe the pattern or trend in the world population.
2. Predict the population in 2010.
3. What do you think will be the world population in 2030?
4. Make a prediction for the world population in 2050.
5. What does the graph tell you about future changes in the world population?
6. Use the line graph to describe the change in world population from 1950 to 2000.
7. What do you think the world population was in 1940? Explain your reasoning.
8. Talk About It Give an example of a situation when being able to make a prediction based on a line graph would be useful.

Practice and Problem Solving

EXTRA PRACTICE See page 657.

For Exercises 9 and 10, refer to Example 2 on page 80.
See Examples 1, 2 (pp. 79–80)

9. Predict the number of skateboards sold in 2009. Explain.

10. About how many skateboards were sold in 2000? Explain.

For Exercises 11–13, use the graph at the right.
See Examples 1, 2 (pp. 79–80)

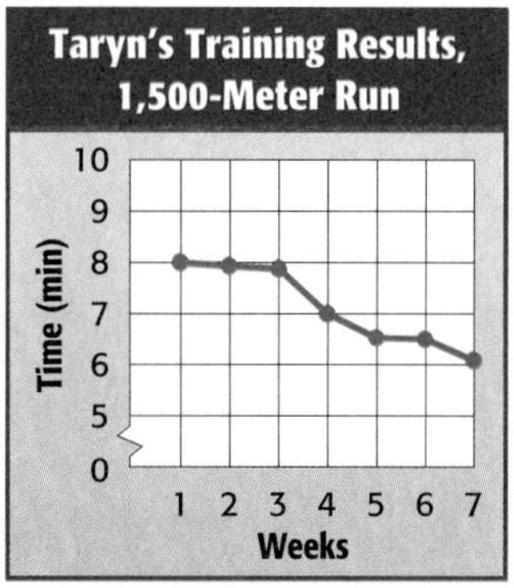

11. Describe the change in the amount of time it takes Taryn to run 1,500 meters from Week 1 to Week 7.

12. Predict when Taryn will run 1,500 meters in less than 6 minutes.

13. Predict the number of weeks it will take until Taryn runs 1,500 meters in 5 minutes.

For Exercises 14–18, use the graph at the right.
See Examples 1, 2 (pp. 79–80)

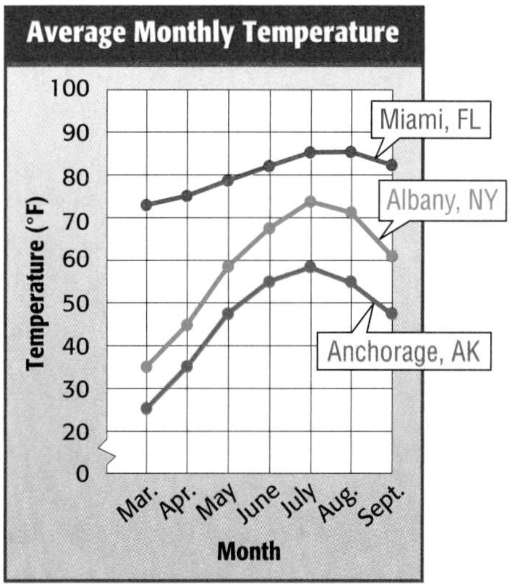

Source: *The World Almanac*

14. Predict the average temperature for Miami in February.

15. Predict the average temperature for Albany in October.

16. What do you think is the average temperature for Anchorage in October?

17. How much warmer would you expect it to be in Miami than in Albany in February?

18. How much colder would you expect it to be in Anchorage than in Miami in October?

Real-World PROBLEM SOLVING

Baseball The table below shows Reynolds Middle School's baseball wins from 2000 to 2007.

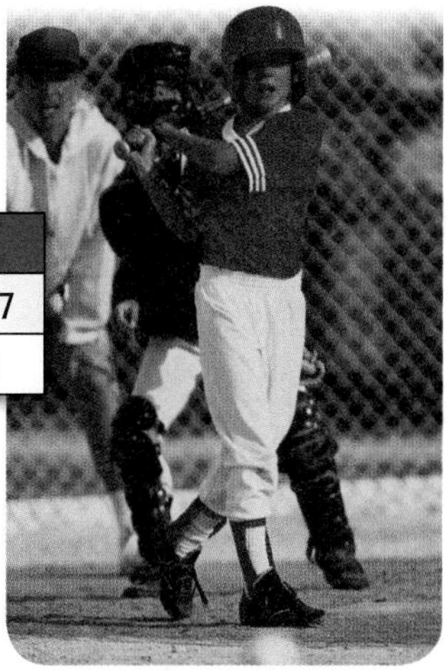

Reynolds Middle School								
Year	2000	2001	2002	2003	2004	2005	2006	2007
Games Won	46	52	25	33	35	45	42	30

19. Make a line graph of the data.

20. Explain the disadvantages of using this line graph to make a prediction about the number of games that the team will win in 2012, 2013, 2014, and 2015.

H.O.T. Problems

21. COLLECT THE DATA Use the Internet or another source to collect a set of sports data that can be displayed using a line graph. Then use your graph to make a prediction.

22. CHALLENGE Refer to the graph for Exercises 14–18. Suppose the green line for Albany and the blue line for Anchorage cross after September. What can you conclude about the point where they cross?

23. WRITING IN MATH Explain why line graphs are often used to make predictions.

Standards Practice

24 The table shows the winning times in the Olympic Women's 3,000-meter Speed Skating Relay. What is the best prediction for the winning time in 2010?

Year	Country	Time (seconds)
1992	Canada	277
1994	South Korea	267
1998	South Korea	256
2002	South Korea	253

Source: *The World Almanac*

A 228 seconds **C** 265 seconds

B 249 seconds **D** 287 seconds

25 In which years did the number of cars sold exceed 2,000?

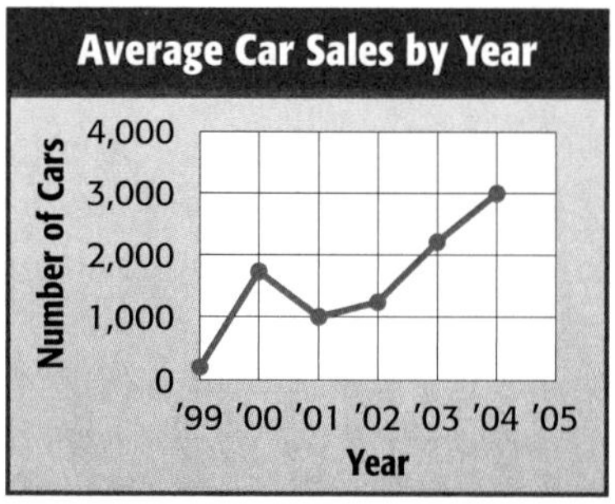

F 2003, 2004 **H** 2001, 2002

G 2002, 2003 **J** 2000, 2001

Spiral Review

26. Make a line graph of the data in the table. **(Lesson 2-1)**

27. Softballs cost $16 each, and gloves cost $30 each. What is the total cost for 2 siblings if each gets one softball and one glove? **(Lesson 1-10)**

Gasoline Prices per Gallon, 1996–2003			
Year	Cost (¢)	Year	Cost (¢)
1996	123	2000	151
1997	123	2001	146
1998	106	2002	136
1999	117	2003	159

Source: *The World Almanac*

Algebra Solve each equation mentally. (Lesson 1-8)

28. $x + 5 = 14$ **29.** $30 - y = 11$ **30.** $18 = 18m$

Tell whether each number is *prime, composite,* or *neither.* (Lesson 1-1)

31. 50 **32.** 47 **33.** 1 **34.** 37

2-3 Histograms

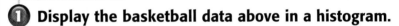

GET READY to Learn

The table shows the number of points scored by winning teams in a basketball league. How are the data in the first column organized?

Basketball Points Scored	
Points	**Frequency**
50–59	1
60–69	5
70–79	8
80–89	5
90–99	2

MAIN IDEA

I will display and analyze data using a histogram.

Standard 5SDAP1.2
Organize and display single-variable data in appropriate graphs and representations (e.g., **histogram,** circle graphs) and explain which types of graphs are appropriate for various data sets.

New Vocabulary

histogram

Vocabulary Link

Horizon
Everyday Use the line at which the sky and Earth appear to meet

Horizontal
Math Use a flat line

A **histogram** is a type of bar graph used to display numerical data that have been organized into intervals of equal size.

EXAMPLE Display Data Using a Histogram

1 Display the basketball data above in a histogram.

Step 1 Decide on a scale and interval for the vertical axis. The frequency includes numbers from 1 to 8. So a scale from 0 to 9 and an interval of 1 are reasonable. Use the intervals from the table on the horizontal axis.

Step 2 Draw and label the horizontal and vertical axes.

Step 3 Draw a bar for each interval. The height of each bar is given by its frequency.

Step 4 Label the graph with a title.

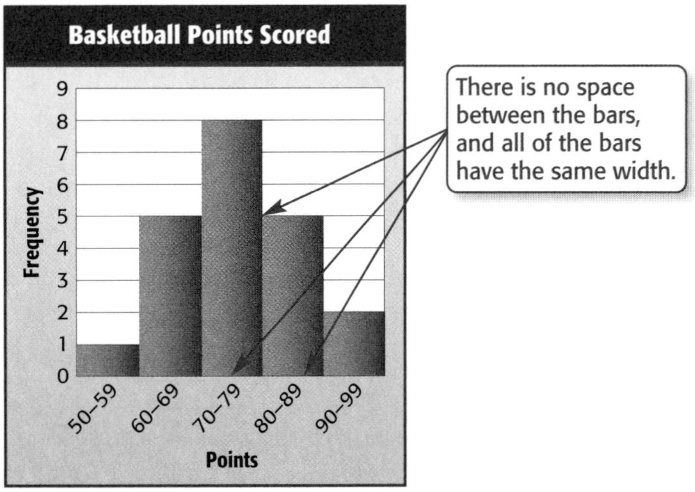

EXAMPLE Analyze Histograms

2 The histogram shows the number of monarch butterflies tagged and released by Mrs. Hudson's students for a school project. Write a few sentences that analyze the data.

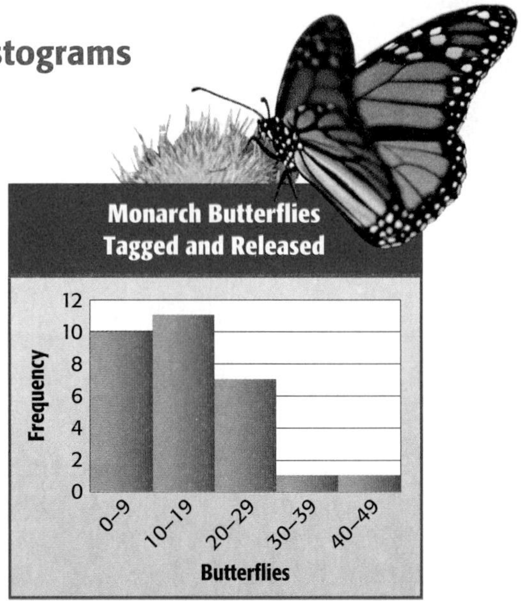

By adding the height of each bar, $10 + 11 + 7 + 1 + 1$, you can see that there are 30 students in Mrs. Hudson's class. You can also see that no students tagged and released more than 50 butterflies.

Online Personal Tutor at ca.gr5math.com

CHECK What You Know

Display each set of data in a histogram. See Example 1 (p. 83)

1.

Minutes Spent on Homework	
Minutes	**Frequency**
0–19	8
20–39	15
40–59	2
60–79	1

2.

Miles Traveled to Reach Vacation Spot	
Miles	**Frequency**
70–79	6
80–89	4
90–99	3
100–109	10

For Exercises 3 and 4, use the histogram at the right. See Example 2 (p. 84)

3. How many helmets cost $30 or less?

4. Write a few sentences that analyze the data.

5. Talk About It What is a common characteristic of the intervals in all histograms?

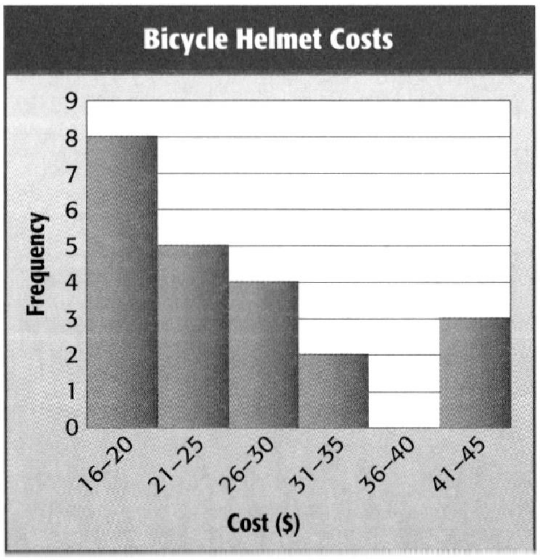

Practice and Problem Solving

EXTRA PRACTICE
See page 658.

Display each set of data in a histogram. See Example 1 (p. 83)

6.

Bus Ride	
Minutes	**Frequency**
0–9	1
10–19	4
20–29	3
30–49	4

7.

Video Game Score	
Score	**Frequency**
10–39	11
40–69	0
70–99	7
100–129	5

8.

Calories per Serving	
Calories	**Frequency**
60–69	8
70–79	5
80–89	10
90–99	3

9.

Test Scores	
Score	**Frequency**
61–70	2
71–80	13
81–90	7
91–100	6

For Exercises 10 and 11, use the histogram at the right.
See Example 2 (p. 84)

10. What is the least possible height represented in the data?

11. Write a few sentences that analyze the data.

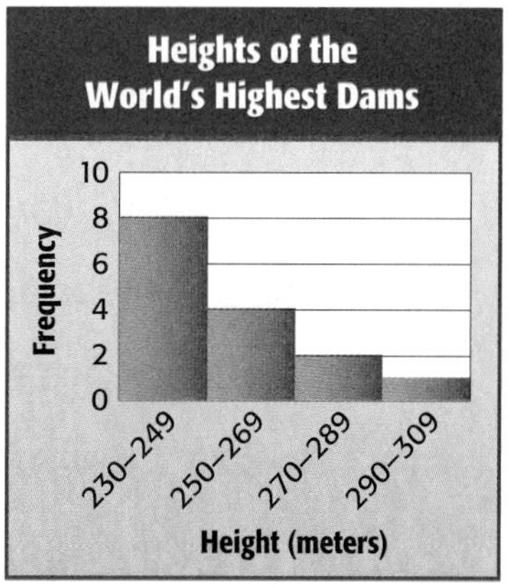

Source: *The World Almanac*

For Exercises 12 and 13, use the histogram at the right.
See Example 2 (p. 84)

12. How many tours performed more than 79 shows?

13. Write a few sentences that analyze the data.

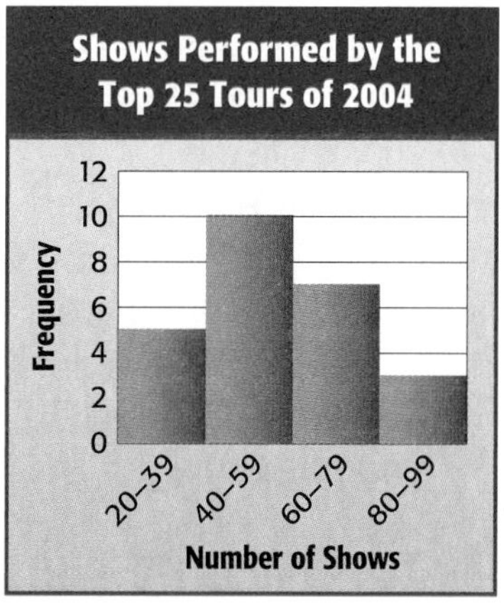

Source: billboard.com

For Exercises 14 and 15, use the table at the right.

14. Display the data in a histogram.

15. Using the histogram, write a few sentences that analyze the data.

Distance Between Checkpoints for the 2004 Iditarod Dog Sled Race (mi)							
11	39	34	45	30	48	80	48
18	25	60	112	52	52	42	90
42	48	48	28	18	55	22	

Source: iditarod.com

H.O.T. Problems

16. COLLECT THE DATA Record the height, in inches, of your classmates. Then make a histogram and a bar graph of the data. Explain why the data graphed is appropriate for the graph.

17. CHALLENGE Refer to the histogram for Exercises 12 and 13. What was the greatest number of shows performed by the top 25 tours? Explain your reasoning.

18. WRITING IN ▶MATH Describe an advantage of displaying a set of data in a histogram instead of a line graph.

Standards Practice

19 Chloe's math test scores are displayed in the histogram. Which statement is supported by the graph?

A The lowest score was 60.

B The highest score was 99.

C Three of the scores were in the 90s.

D Chloe took five math tests.

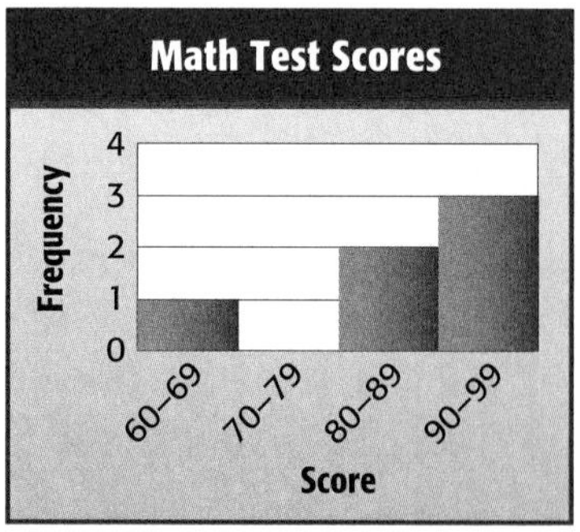

Spiral Review

For Exercises 20–23, use the graph.
(Lessons 2-1 and 2-2)

20. What was the approximate winning time in the 1908 Olympics?

21. What does the graph tell you about the winning times?

22. Between what years was the greatest decrease in the winning time?

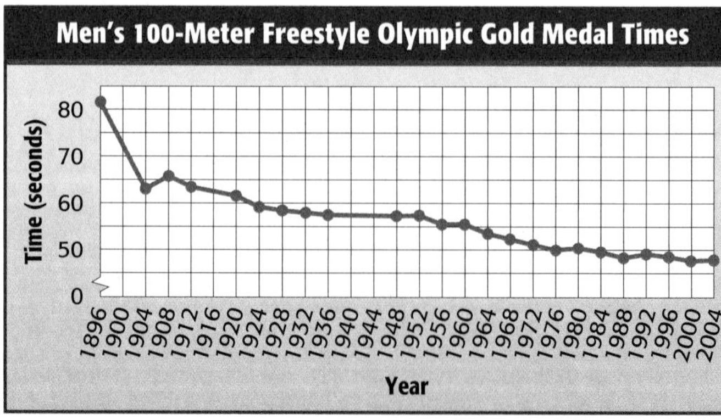

Source: *The World Almanac*

23. Make a prediction of the winning time for the 2012 Olympics in the men's 100-meter freestyle.

2-4 Line Plots

GET READY to Learn

The table shows the life expectancy of several animals. Two animals have a life expectancy of 15 years. How many animals have a life expectancy of 12 years?

Animal	Years
Black bear	18
Cat (pet)	12
Chimpanzee	20
Cow	15
Dog (pet)	12
Giraffe	10
Horse	20
Leopard	12
Lion	15
Mouse	3
Pig	10
Rabbit (pet)	5

Source: *The World Almanac*

MAIN IDEA

I will display, analyze, and interpret data using line plots.

Standard 5SDAP1.2
Organize and display single-variable data in appropriate graphs and representations (e.g., histogram, circle graphs) and explain which types of graphs are appropriate for various data sets.

New Vocabulary

line plot

A **line plot** is a diagram that shows the frequency of data on a number line. An '×' is placed above a number on a number line each time that data value occurs.

Remember

It is often easier to identify the number of data that fall in a certain category with a line plot, as opposed to counting all those values in a table.

EXAMPLE Display Data in a Line Plot

1 Make a line plot of the data above.

Step 1 Draw a number line. The smallest value is 3 years and the largest value is 20 years. So, you can use a scale of 0 to 20. Other scales could also be used.

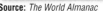

Step 2 Put an × above the number that represents the life expectancy of each animal. Add a title.

Animal Life Expectancies in Years

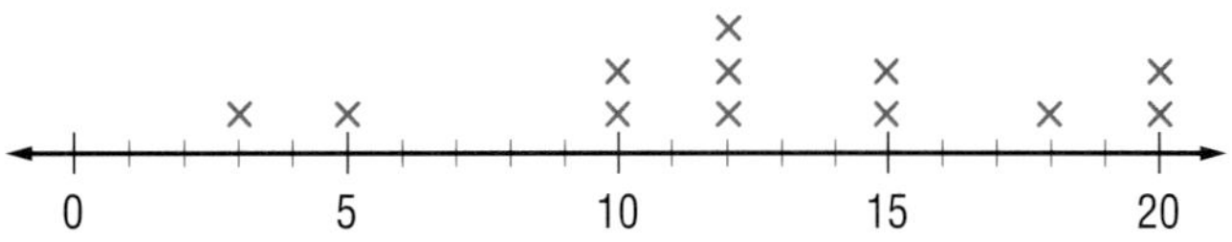

Online Personal Tutor at ca.gr5math.com

A line plot allows you to easily analyze the *distribution* of data, or how data are grouped together or spread out.

EXAMPLES Analyze a Line Plot

The line plot displays the number of Calories Justin burns per minute doing activities that he enjoys.

Calories Burned per Minute for Various Activities

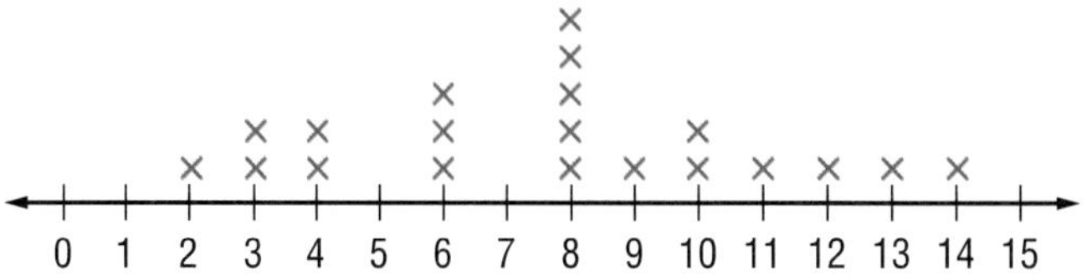

2 **How many of the activities represented on the line plot burn 8 Calories per minute?**

Locate 8 on the number line and count the number of ×'s above it. There are 5 activities that burn 8 Calories per minute.

Calories Burned per Minute for Various Activities

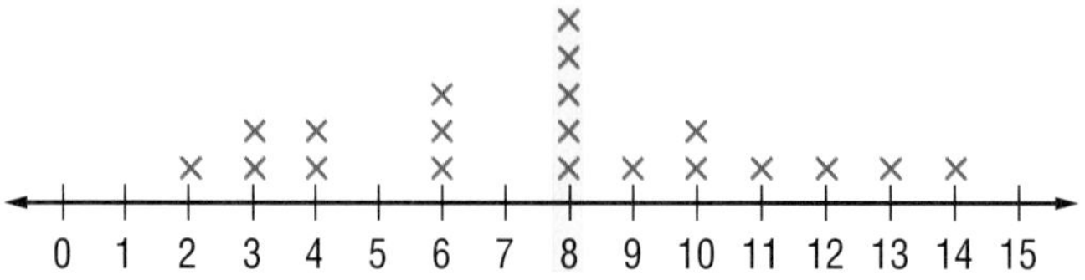

Remember

In Example 3, the numbers on the number line represent the number of Calories burned per minute.

3 **What is the difference between the least and the greatest number of Calories burned per minute by an activity represented in the line plot above?**

The least number of Calories burned per minute is 2.
The greatest number of Calories burned per minute is 14.

$14 - 2 = 12$ Subtract to find the difference.

The difference is 12 Calories per minute.

4 **If Justin exercises by doing each of these activities once a month, write one or two sentences that analyze the data.**

- Each month Justin typically burns about 6 or 8 Calories per minute exercising.
- Only one activity that Justin performs each month burns 14 Calories per minute.

 Math Online Extra Examples at ca.gr5math.com

CHECK What You Know

1. The table at the right shows the speeds of the world's fastest wooden roller coasters. Make a line plot of the data. See Example 1 (p. 87)

World's Fastest Wooden Roller Coasters (miles per hour)				
66	65	66	75	65
65	64	65	78	63

Source: coastergrotto.com

For Exercises 2–4, use the line plot at the right. See Examples 2–4 (p. 88)

Record Number of Wins by the Leading National League Pitcher, 1992–2004

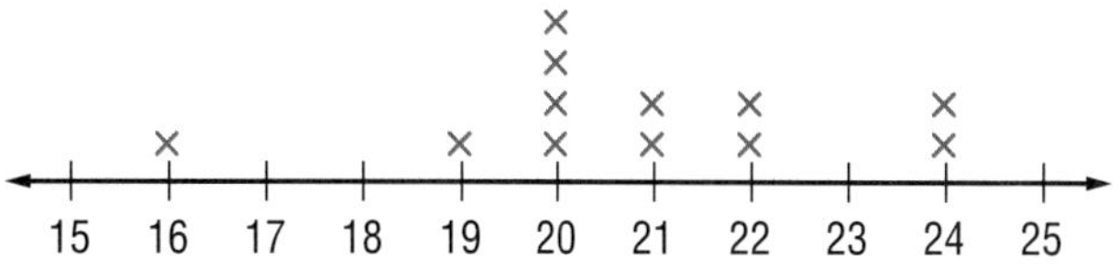

Source: mlb.com

2. What number of games was won by the most leading pitchers from 1992 to 2004?

3. How many of the leading pitchers won 22 or more games?

4. Write one or two sentences that analyze the data.

5. Talk About It Give a real-world example of a type of data that can be best represented by a line plot. Explain why.

Practice and Problem Solving

EXTRA PRACTICE See page 658.

Make a line plot of each set of data. See Example 1 (p. 87)

6.

Test Scores			
78	95	80	85
70	88	95	90
95	85	88	78
75	90	85	82
76	75	82	80

7.

Number of Stories in World's Tallest Buildings			
101	88	88	110
88	88	80	69
102	78	72	54
85	80	73	100

Source: infoplease.com

For Exercises 8–11, use the line plot at the right. See Examples 2–4 (p. 88)

Ages in Years of the 20 Oldest Astronauts on Launch Day

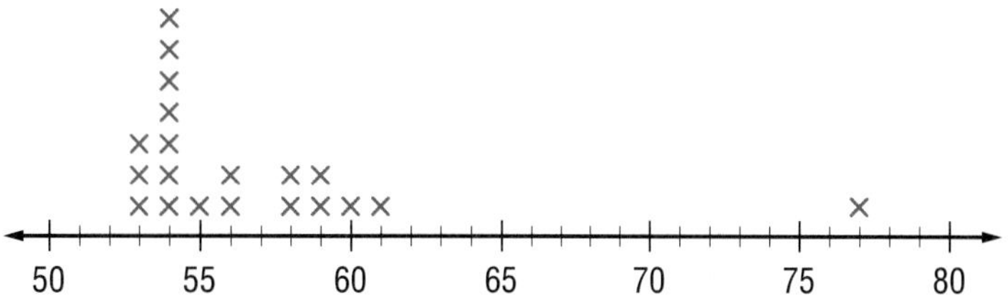

Source: space.kursknet.ru

8. How many astronauts were 56 years old on launch day?

9. Which age was most common among the oldest astronauts on launch day?

10. What is the difference between the age of the oldest and youngest astronaut represented in the line plot?

11. Write one or two sentences that analyze the data.

For Exercises 12–14, use the line plot at the right.

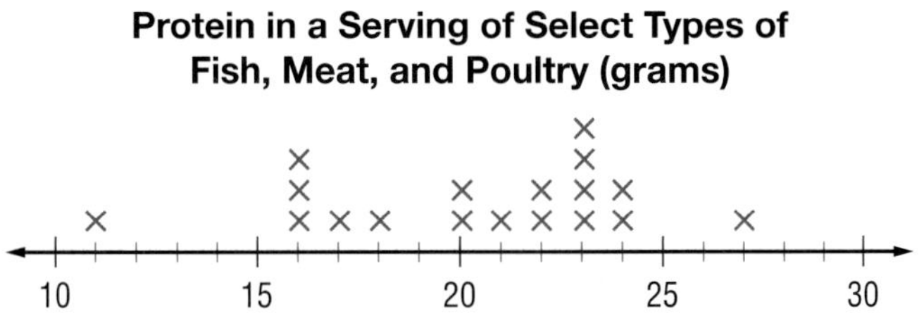

12. How many more types of fish, meat, and poultry have 23 grams of protein than 17 grams of protein?

13. How many types of fish, meat, and poultry are represented in the line plot?

14. Write one or two sentences that analyze the data.

15. Refer to the line plot you made in Exercise 6. Write one or two sentences that analyze the data.

16. Refer to the line plot you made in Exercise 7. Write one or two sentences that analyze the data.

For Exercises 17–19, use the table at the right that shows the average travel time to work for select cities.

17. Make a line plot and a bar graph of the data.

18. Which display allows you to easily determine the number of cities that have an average commute time of 29 minutes? Explain.

19. Which graph allows you to easily compare the average commute time in Atlanta with the average commute time in Omaha? Explain.

Average Travel Time to Work

City	Minutes
Anaheim, CA	24
Atlanta, GA	27
Fort Worth, TX	24
New Orleans, LA	24
New York, NY	38
Oakland, CA	29
Omaha, NE	17
Washington, D.C.	29

Source: census.gov

H.O.T. Problems

20. COLLECT THE DATA Create a line plot that displays the shoe sizes of students in your class. Then write one or two statements that analyze the data.

21. DATA SENSE The science test scores of two students are shown below. Which student is more consistent? Explain your reasoning.

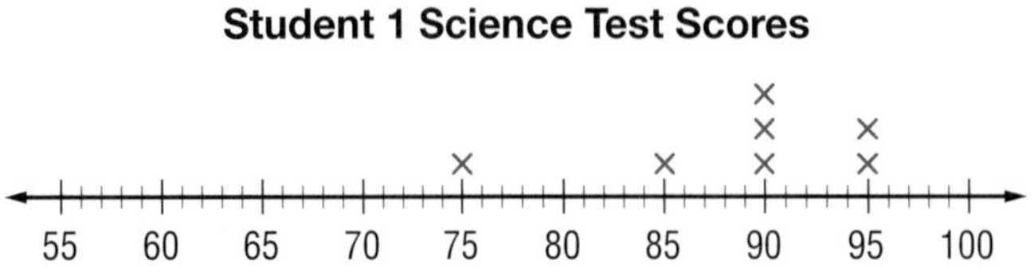

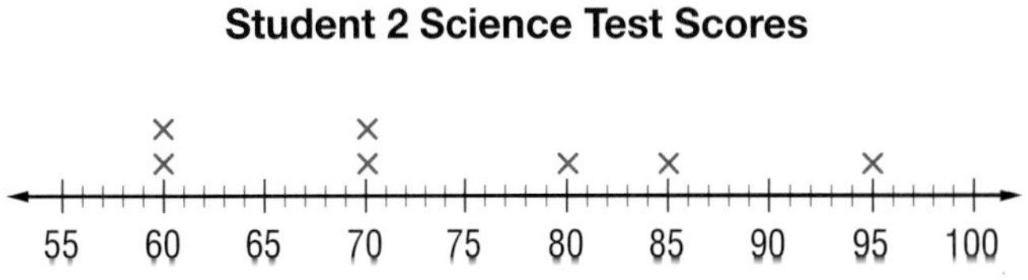

22. **CHALLENGE** *Clusters* are data that are grouped closely together. Identify the clusters in the following set of data that describe the ages of people in a movie theater.

22, 23, 11, 12, 12, 13, 12, 14, 40, 12, 30, 26

23. **WRITING IN ▸MATH** Explain the advantages of organizing data in a line plot.

Standards Practice

24 The table shows the prices, in dollars, of select DVDs. Which line plot correctly displays the data in the table?

DVD Prices ($)						
24	16	18	14	16	21	15
15	12	15	15	20	20	12

A

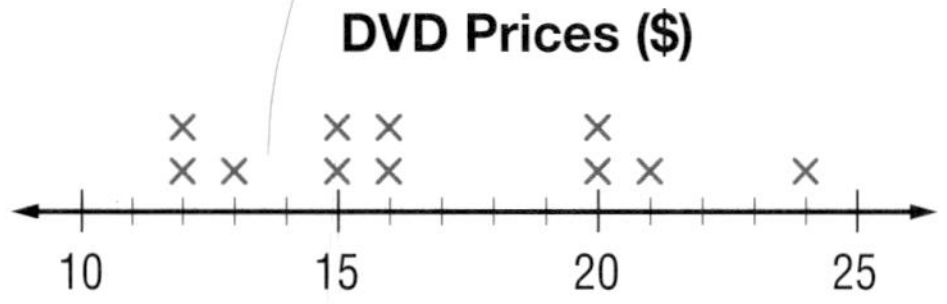

C

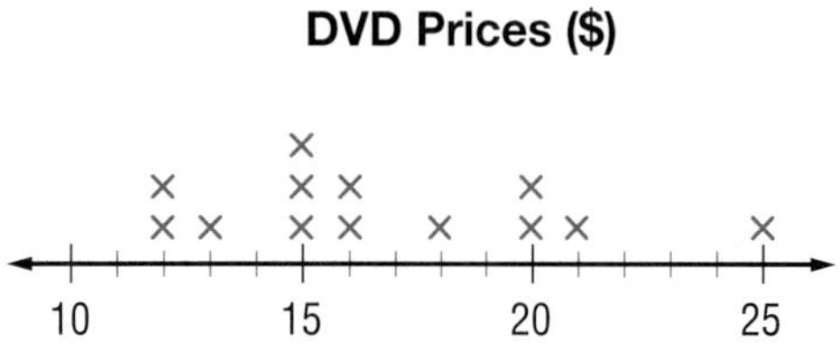

B

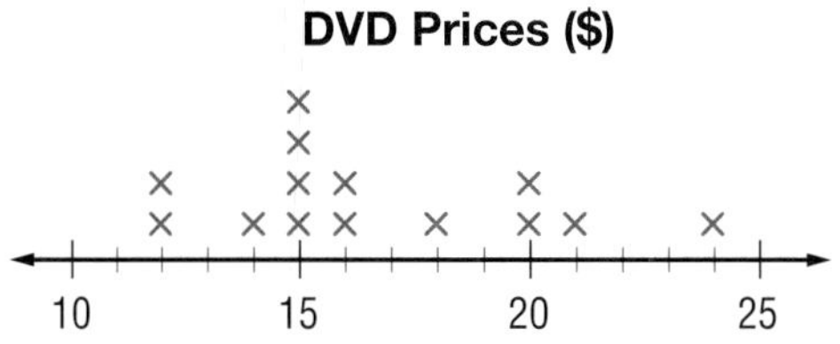

D

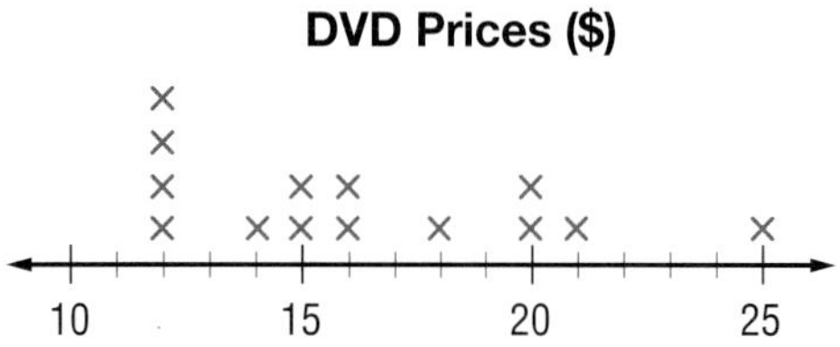

Spiral Review

25. Display the data at the right in a histogram. Then write a few sentences that analyze the data. **(Lesson 2-3)**

Study Times (min)	Frequency
10–19	2
20–29	6
30–39	4

For Exercises 26 and 27, use the line graph at the right. (Lesson 2-2)

26. Between which years did the winning time change the most? Describe the change.

27. Make a prediction of the winning time in the 2012 Olympics. Explain your reasoning.

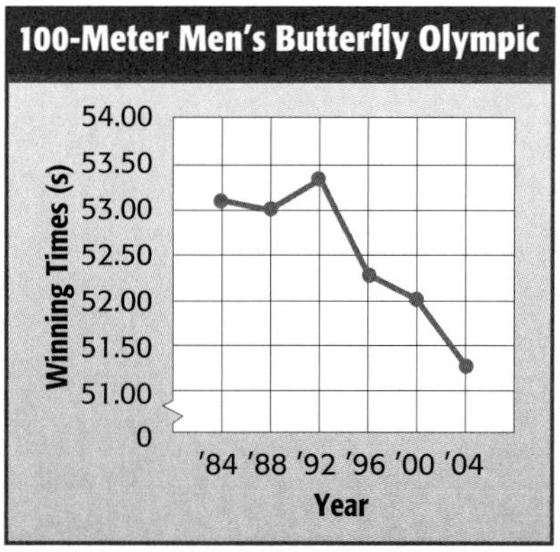

Source: *The World Almanac*

Find the value of each expression. (Lesson 1-3)

28. (15 + 17) ÷ 2

29. (4 + 8 + 3) ÷ 3

30. (10 + 23 + 5 + 18) ÷ 4

2-5 Problem-Solving Strategy

MAIN IDEA I will solve problems by making a table.

Standard 5MR2.3 **Use a variety of methods, such as** words, numbers, symbols, charts, graphs, **tables**, diagrams, and models, **to explain mathematical reasoning.** Standard 5SDAP1.2 **Organize and display single-variable data in appropriate** graphs and **representations** and explain which types of graphs are appropriate for various data sets.

Robert took a survey of all of his classmates to find out which of four food choices was their favorite. Using P for pizza, T for taco, H for hamburger, and C for chicken, the results are shown below.

C T H P P C H P T P H P P P P P H H C T

How many more people in Robert's class chose hamburger as their favorite food than chicken?

Understand

What facts do you know?

There are four food options: pizza, taco, hamburger, and chicken.

What do you need to find?

How many more people in Robert's class chose hamburger as their favorite food than chicken?

Plan

Make a frequency table to organize the data.

Solve

Draw a table with three columns and label the columns *Food*, *Tally*, and *Frequency*. In the first column, list each food. In the second column, tally the data.

Favorite Food

Food	Tally	Frequency
pizza	𝍸 ||||	9
taco	|||	3
hamburger	𝍸	5
chicken	|||	3

Then complete the table by indicating the *frequency* or number of times each food occurs.

Five people chose hamburgers and 3 chose chicken. So $5 - 3$ or 2 more students chose hamburgers than chicken.

Check

If you go back to the list, there should be 5 students who wrote an H for hamburger and 3 students who wrote a C for chicken. So, an answer of 2 students is correct.

ANALYZE the Strategy

Refer to the problem on the previous page.

1. What do the tally marks represent in the frequency table?

2. From the information given, can you determine how many students are in Robert's class? If so, find the number of students in his class. Explain your reasoning.

3. Explain when to use the *make a table* strategy to solve a problem.

4. Tell the advantages of organizing information in a table.

PRACTICE the Strategy

EXTRA PRACTICE See page 658.

Solve. Use the *make a table* strategy.

5. How many more students have a dog than a turtle?

Pets Owned by Various Students							
F	D	T	G	D	C	C	G
C	D	C	F	C	D	D	C
D	D	C	D	H	T	F	D

F = fish T = turtle D = dog G = gerbil C = cat H = hamster

6. The number of points scored by major league soccer teams in a recent season is shown. How many teams scored between 46 and 60 points in the season?

Major League Soccer Points Scored					
53	26	35	45	42	53
14	36	27	45	47	23

Source: Major League Soccer

7. How many students chose comedy or action as their favorite type of movie?

Favorite Type of Movie							
A	H	R	A	A	C	C	D
C	C	C	A	C	H	A	C
H	S	D	C	D	S	S	C
C	H	A	R	S	A	A	C

C = comedy R = romantic D = drama H = horror A = action S = science fiction

8. Mrs. Rodriguez has a list of her students' test scores. How many more students scored from 71 to 80 than from 91 to 100?

Test Scores						
71	89	65	77	79	98	84
86	70	97	93	80	91	72
100	75	73	86	99	77	68

9. Juan asked the players on his basketball team how many siblings they each had. How many team members have 3 or more siblings?

Number of Siblings						
2	0	1	1	0	0	1
3	2	1	1	2	0	2
3	3	4	1	1	1	0

10. The table shows the high temperatures of a certain city over the last two weeks. How many days were above 50°F?

High Temperature (°F)						
44	57	48	53	52	49	41
52	51	47	51	49	57	45

11. **WRITING IN MATH** Refer to Exercise 10. Write another question that can be answered by the frequency table you created.

CHAPTER 2 Mid-Chapter Check

Lessons 2-1 through 2-5

1. Make a bar graph of the data shown below. Compare the number of people who chose red to the number who chose green. **(Lesson 2-1)**

Favorite Car Color	
Color	**Frequency**
blue	12
red	19
silver	9
green	11
black	9

2. **STANDARDS PRACTICE** Kenya's total savings for seven weeks is shown in the graph.

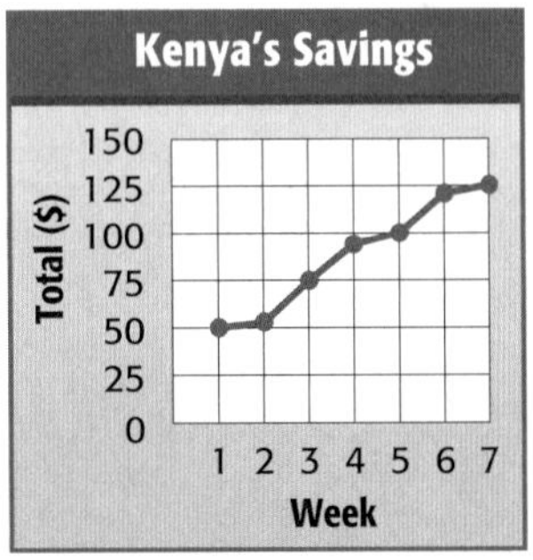

Which statement is supported by the graph? **(Lesson 2-2)**

A Kenya's total savings decreased from Week 2 to Week 5.

B By the end of Week 7, Kenya's total savings was $125.

C The total amount saved by the end of Week 8 should be about $200.

D Kenya saved more money from Week 6 to Week 7 than any other week.

3. **STANDARDS PRACTICE** The number of home runs by league leaders is shown.

Source: baseball-almanac.com

Which statement about home runs is supported by the graph? **(Lesson 2-3)**

F The least number was 30.

G The home runs of 16 players are represented in the graph.

H The greatest number was 79.

J No player made 60 home runs.

4. The ages in years of the youngest solo singers with a #1 U.S. single are listed.

15, 17, 18, 15, 17, 16, 18, 17, 17, 18, 14, 16, 16, 18, 13, 13, 14, 17, 19, 19

Make a line plot of these data. **(Lesson 2-4)**

5. Make a frequency table of the data below. How many skateboards cost between $50 and $69? **(Lesson 2-5)**

Cost ($) of Various Skateboards				
99	67	139	63	75
59	89	59	70	78
99	55	125	64	110

6. **WRITING IN ►MATH** Explain how the *make a table* strategy can help you solve problems.

2-6 Mean

MAIN IDEA

I will find the mean of a data set.

Standard 5SDAP1.1 Know the concepts of mean, median, and mode; **compute** and compare **simple examples** to show that they may differ.

New Vocabulary

average
mean
outlier

GET READY to Learn

Hands-On Mini Lab

In five days, it snowed 4 inches, 3 inches, 5 inches, 1 inch, and 2 inches.

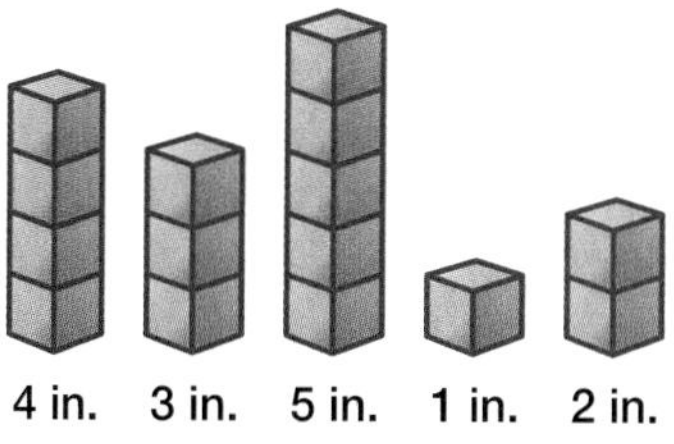

- Make a stack of centimeter cubes to represent the snowfall for each day, as shown at the right.
- Move the cubes until each stack has the same number of cubes.

1. On average, how many inches did it snow per day in five days? Explain your reasoning.

2. Suppose on the sixth day it snowed 9 inches. If you moved the cubes again, how many cubes would be in each stack?

In the Mini Lab above, the number 3 is the mean or **average** number of cubes in each stack after equally distributing all the cubes. The mean can also be calculated.

Reading Math

Division The fraction bar in the expression $\frac{4+3+5+1+2}{5}$ represents division.

KEY CONCEPT — Mean

Words The **mean** of a set of data is the sum of the data divided by the number of pieces of data.

Example Data set: 4, 3, 5, 1, 2

Mean: $\frac{4+3+5+1+2}{5} = \frac{15}{5}$ or 3

EXAMPLE Find the Mean

1 **Find the mean number of Representatives for the four states shown in the pictograph.**

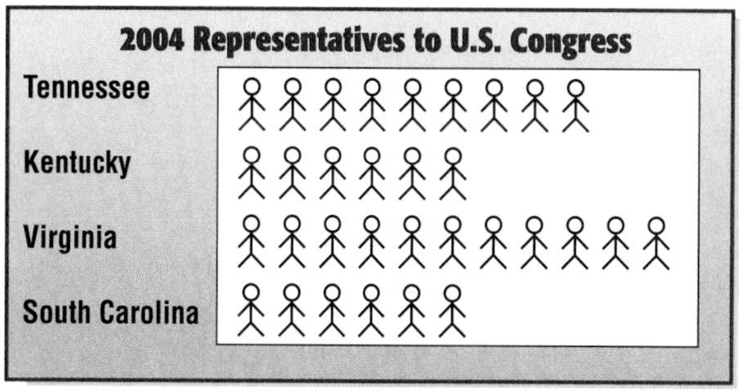

(continued on the next page)

One Way: Move the figures.

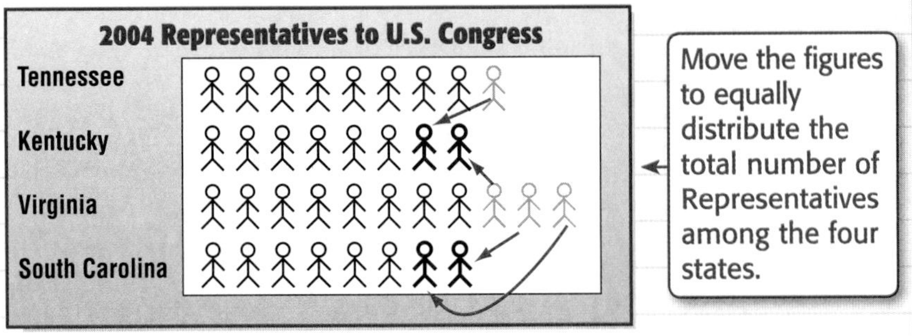
2004 Representatives to U.S. Congress
Tennessee
Kentucky
Virginia
South Carolina
Move the figures to equally distribute the total number of Representatives among the four states.

Another Way: Write and simplify an expression.

$$\text{mean} = \frac{9 + 6 + 11 + 6}{4}$$ ← sum of the data / ← number of data items

$$= \frac{32}{4} \text{ or } 8$$ Simplify.

Remember

Even if a data value is 0, it still should be counted in the total number of pieces of data.

The states have a mean, or average, of 8 representatives.

Online Personal Tutor at ca.gr5math.com

Values that are much higher or lower than others in a data set are **outliers**.

EXAMPLE Determine How Outliers Affect Mean

2 The high temperatures Monday through Friday in °F were 80, 81, 60, 77, and 82. Identify the outlier(s) in the data. Then find the mean with and without the outlier and describe how the outlier affects the mean.

Compared to the other values, 60°F is extremely low. So, it is an outlier. Find the mean with and without the outlier.

$$\text{mean} = \frac{80 + 81 + \mathbf{60} + 77 + 82}{5} = \frac{380}{5} \text{ or } 76$$

$$\text{mean} = \frac{80 + 81 + 77 + 82}{4} = \frac{320}{4} \text{ or } 80$$

With the outlier, the mean is less than all but one of the data values. Without it, the mean better represents the data.

Math Online Extra Examples at ca.gr5math.com

CHECK What You Know

Find the mean of the data represented in each model.
See Example 1 (pp. 95–96)

1.

2.

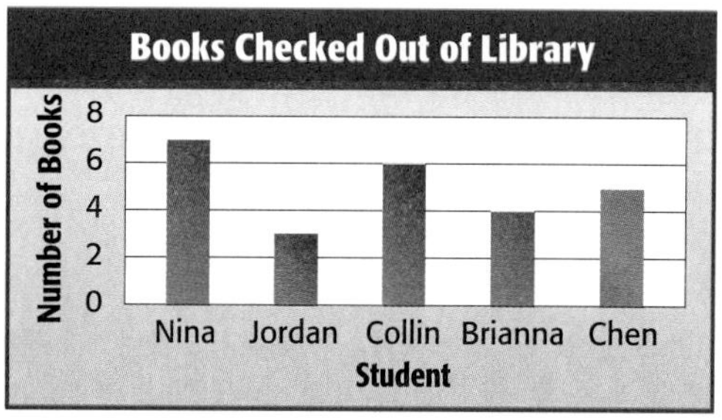

For Exercises 3–5, use the table at the right. It lists the greatest depths of the oceans. See Example 2 (p. 96)

Ocean	Depth (ft)
Pacific	15,215
Atlantic	12,881
Indian	13,002
Arctic	3,953
Southern	14,749

Source: enchantedlearning.com

3. What is the mean of the data?

4. Which depth is an outlier? Explain.

5. How does this outlier affect the mean?

6. Talk About It — Explain how to find the mean of a set of data.

Practice and Problem Solving

EXTRA PRACTICE
See page 659.

Find the mean of the data represented in each model.
See Example 1 (pp. 95–96)

7.

8.

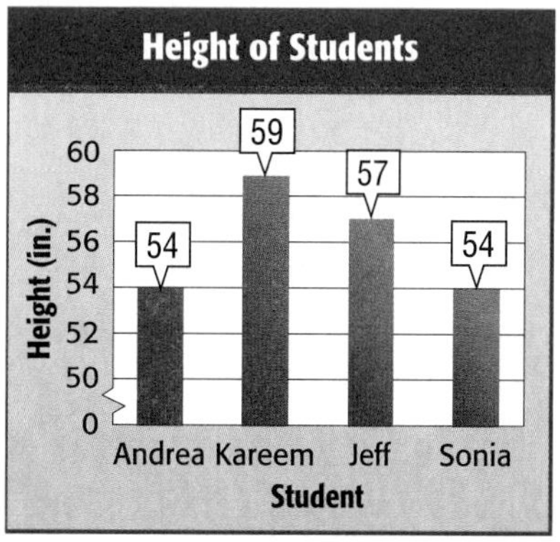

9. Jamila earned \$15, \$20, \$10, \$12, \$20, \$16, \$80, \$18, and \$25 baby-sitting. What is the mean of the amounts she earned? Identify the outlier(s). Then describe how the outlier(s) affect the mean of the data. See Example 2 (p. 96)

Real-World PROBLEM SOLVING

Nature The table shows the approximate heights of some of the tallest U.S. trees.

Tree	Height (ft)
Western Red Cedar	160
Coast Redwood	320
Monterey Cypress	100
California Laurel	110
Sitka Spruce	200
Port-Orford-Cedar	220

Source: *The World Almanac*

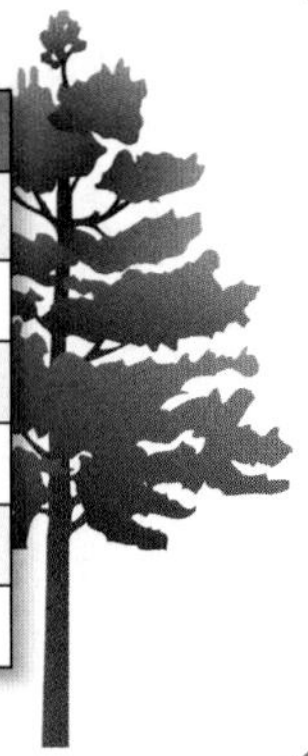

10. Find the mean of the data with and without the outlier(s).

11. How does the outlier affect the mean of the data?

H.O.T. Problems

12. **REASONING** Tell whether the following statement is *sometimes*, *always*, or *never* true. Justify your answer.

The mean of a set of data is one of the values in the data set.

13. **CHALLENGE** Find a value for n such that the mean of the ages 40, 45, 48, n, 42, and 41 is 45. Explain the method or strategy you used.

14. **WRITING IN ▸MATH** The mean amount of precipitation from January to June for a certain city was about 4 inches per month. Without doing any calculations, determine how the mean would be affected if the total precipitation for the month of July for this city is 3 inches, 5 inches, or 4 inches. Explain your reasoning.

Standards Practice

15 The bar graph shows the number of calendars David sold each year. What is the mean number of calendars David sold each year?

A 9   **C** 11

B 10   **D** 14

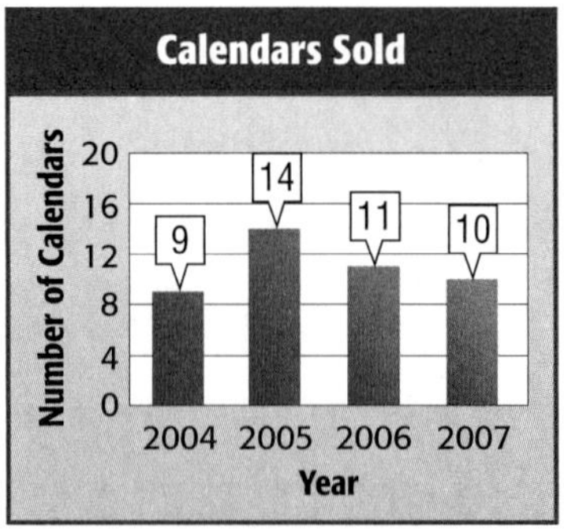

Spiral Review

16. The ages in years of Liana's friends are 10, 10, 9, 10, 12, 10, 11, 10, and 11. How many more friends are 10 years old than 11 years old? **(Lesson 2-5)**

17. The table shows the number of players on each team in a baseball league. Make a line plot of the data. **(Lesson 2-4)**

Players Per Team					
16	15	16	15	18	19
12	15	16	14	18	14

2-7 Median, Mode, and Range

GET READY to Learn

The table shows the widest wingspans of several birds. If the data were ordered from least to greatest, which number would be in the middle?

Widest Wingspans (ft)			
12	6	10	12
11	9	10	

Source: factofile.com

MAIN IDEA

I will find and interpret the median, mode, and range of a set of data.

Standard 5SDAP1.1 Know the concepts of mean, **median, and mode; compute and compare simple examples to show that they may differ.**

New Vocabulary
- **median**
- **mode**
- **range**

A data set can also be described by its median or its mode.

KEY CONCEPTS

Median

Words In a data set that has been ordered from least to greatest, the **median** is the middle number if there is an odd number of data items. If there is an even number of data items, the median is the mean of the two numbers closest to the middle.

Examples data set: 3, 4, 8, 10, 12 → median: 8

data set: 2, 4, 6, 8, 11, 12 → median: $\frac{6+8}{2}$ or 7

Mode

Words The **mode** of a set of data is the number or numbers that occur most often.

Example data set: 12, 23, 28, 28, 32, 46, 46 → modes: 28 and 46

Remember

If the set of data is not numerical, then the mode is especially useful for describing data.

EXAMPLE Find the Median and the Mode

1 The table shows the cost of nine books. Find the median and mode of the data.

Book Costs ($)				
20	7	10	15	11
20	25	15	8	

Order the data from least to greatest.

median: 7, 8, 10, 11, 15, 15, 20, 20, 25 — 15 is in the middle.

mode: 7, 8, 10, 11, 15, 15, 20, 20, 25 — 15 and 20 occur most often.

The median is $15. There are two modes, $15 and $20.

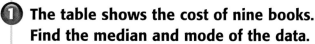

The **range** of a set of data is the difference between the greatest and the least values of the set. When compared to the values in the data set, a large range indicates that the data are spread out. A small range indicates that the data are close together.

> **Remember**
>
> The mean, median, and mode of a data set describe the center of a set of data. The range of a set of data describes how much the data vary.

EXAMPLE Find the Range

2 Ella collected 125, 45, 67, 150, 32, 45, and 12 pennies each day this week for a school fundraiser. Find the range of the data. Then write a sentence that describes how the data vary.

The greatest number of pennies is 150. The least number of pennies is 12. So, the range is 150 − 12 or 138. The range is relatively large, so the data are spread out.

You can use a line plot of the data to verify this analysis.

Pennies Collected

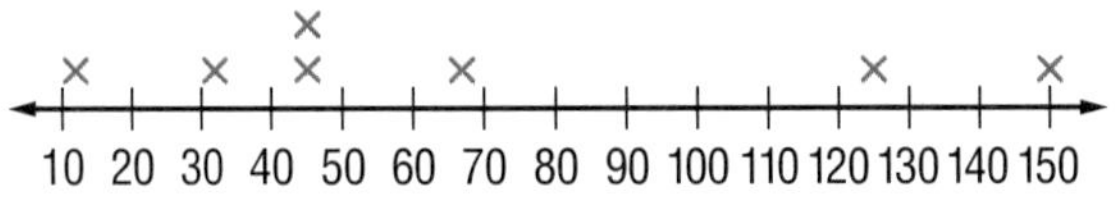

The mean, median, and mode for a set of data may differ.

Real-World EXAMPLE

3 Find the mean, median, mode, and range of the temperatures displayed in the graph.

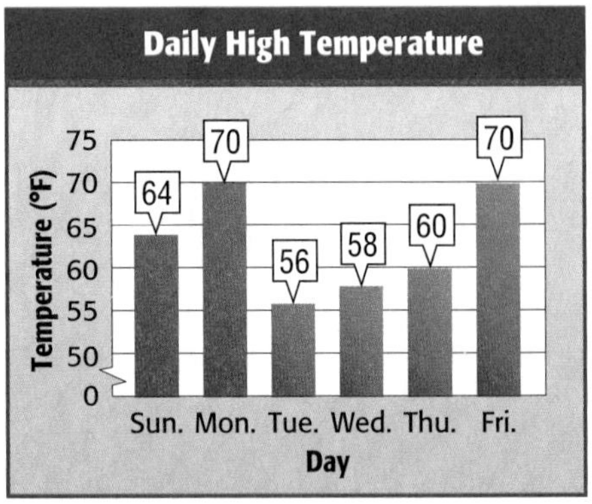

mean: $\frac{64 + 70 + 56 + 58 + 60 + 70}{6}$

$= \frac{378}{6}$

$= 63°$

median: 56, 58, $\underbrace{60, 64}$, 70, 70

$\frac{60 + 64}{2} = \frac{124}{2}$

$= 62°$

There are an even number of data values. So, to find the median, find the mean of the two middle numbers.

mode: 70°

range: 70 − 56 = 14°

Online Personal Tutor at ca.gr5math.com

CHECK What You Know

Find the median, mode, and range for each set of data.
See Examples 1, 2 (pp. 99, 100)

1. Points scored by football team: 15, 20, 23, 13, 17, 21, 17

2. Monthly spending: $46, $62, $63, $57, $50, $42, $56, $40

Find the mean, median, mode, and range of the data represented.
See Example 3 (p. 100)

3. Cost of CDs (dollars)

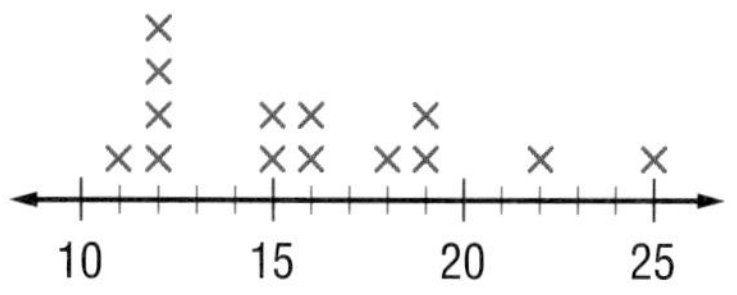

4.

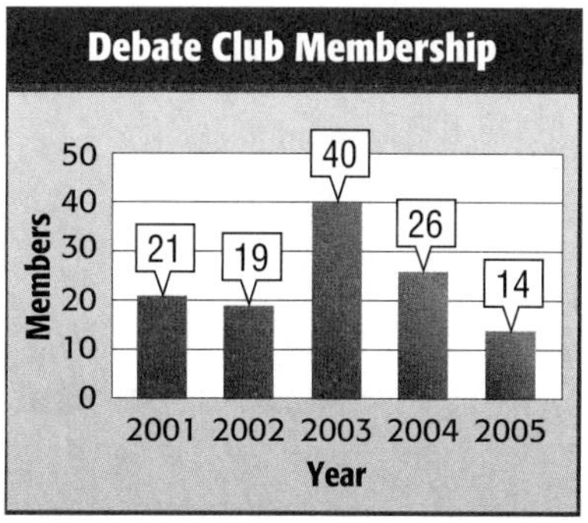

5. Talk About It — Explain how you would find the median and mode of a data set.

Practice and Problem Solving

EXTRA PRACTICE
See page 659.

Find the median, mode, and range for each set of data.
See Examples 1, 2 (pp. 99, 100)

6. Age of employees: 23, 22, 15, 36, 44

7. Minutes spent on homework: 18, 20, 22, 11, 19, 18, 18

8. Math test scores: 97, 85, 92, 86

9. Height of trees in feet: 23, 27, 24, 26, 26, 24, 26, 24

For Exercises 10 and 11, find the mean, median, mode, and range of the data represented. See Example 3 (p. 100)

10. Average Speeds (mph)

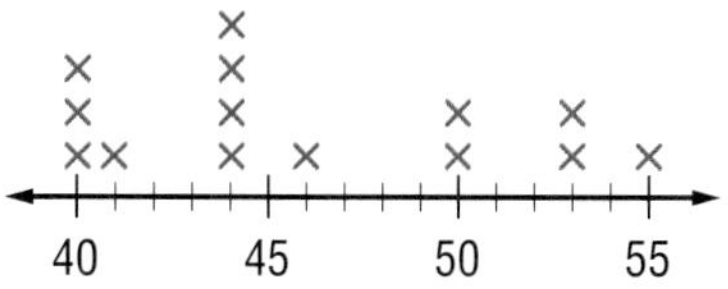

11.

Test Grades			
90	90	70	82
65	100	80	85
67	72	82	92
100	75	72	85
85	85	95	97
77	87	88	95

For Exercises 12 and 13, find the mean, median, mode, and range of the data represented. See Example 3 (p. 100)

12.

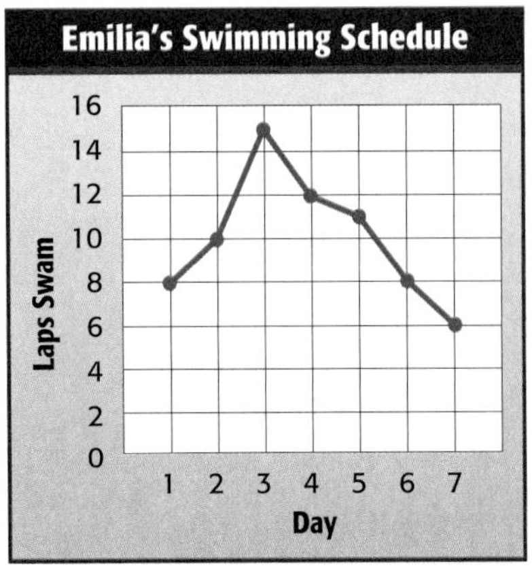

13.

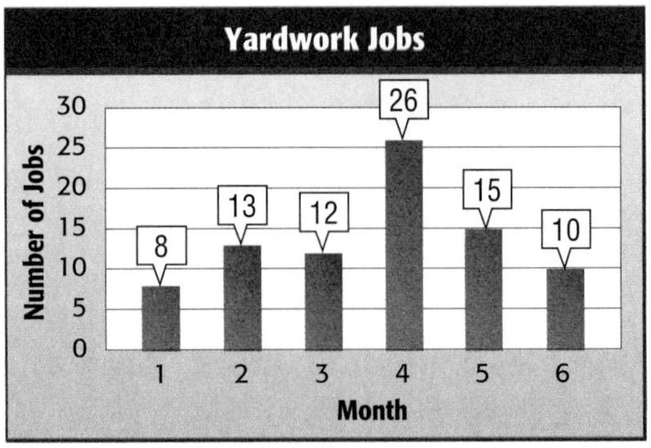

14. Marjorie's friends bought CDs for \$12, \$14, \$18, \$10, \$14, \$12, \$12, and \$12. Which measure, mean, median, or mode, best describes the cost of the CDs? Explain your reasoning.

For Exercises 15–18, create a set of data that meet the conditions indicated.

15. A set of data in which the mean, median, and mode are all different.

16. A set of data in which the median is greater than the mean.

17. Two different sets of data that have the same mean but different ranges.

18. Find the mean, median, and mode of the following 15 numbers.

$$1, 2, \underbrace{3, 3, \ldots 3,}_{11} 4, 5$$

Real-World PROBLEM SOLVING

Data File The Mighty Ducks of Anaheim officially changed its name to the Anaheim Ducks at the start of the 2006–2007 season.

19. Find the mean, median, and mode of the game attendance.

20. Which measure from Exercise 19 best describes the data? Explain.

Source: www.nhl.com

Data Card

Game Attendance 2005

November 23: 18,532

November 25: 17,174

November 27: 13,078

November 30: 12,050

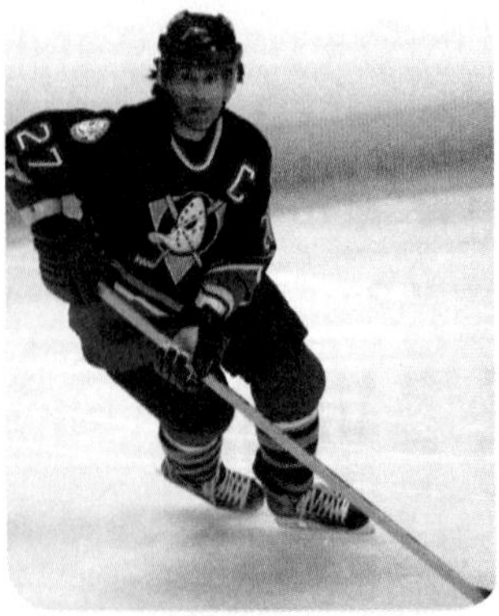

H.O.T. Problems

21. **COLLECT THE DATA** Record the number of students in your math class each day for one week. Then describe the data using the mean, median, and mode.

22. **CHALLENGE** The ticket prices in a concert series were \$12, \$37, \$45, \$18, \$8, \$25, and \$18. What was the ticket price of the eighth and final concert in this series if the set of 8 prices had a mean of \$23, a mode of \$18, a median of \$19.50, and a range of \$37?

23. **WRITING IN ▶MATH** What effect does adding a value that is much smaller than the values of the other data in a set have on the median? the mode? the range?

Standards Practice

24 The table shows the number of concerts performed by The Quest. What is the median number of concerts?

A 26 **C** 137

B 136 **D** 138

The Quest	
Year	**Number of Concerts**
2000	142
2001	142
2002	136
2003	136
2004	124
2005	138
2006	136
2007	150

Spiral Review

25. Find the mean number of cell phone minutes Samuel used each month this year. **(Lesson 2-6)**

Month	Jan.	Feb.	Mar.	Apr.	May	June	July	Aug.	Sep.	Oct.	Nov.	Dec.
Minutes Used	49	65	20	37	55	68	75	50	24	37	42	30

26. Display the following set of data in a line plot. **(Lesson 2-4)**

Number of miles biked: 27, 31, 25, 19, 31, 32, 25, 26, 33, 31

For Exercises 27–29, use the graph. **(Lesson 2-1)**

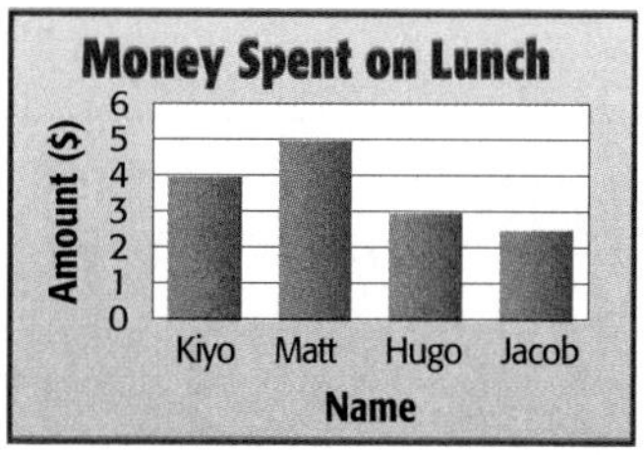

27. Who spent the most on lunch?

28. How much more did Kiyo spend than Hugo?

29. How does the amount Matt spent compare to the amount Jacob spent?

30. **Algebra** Evaluate $(2z)^2 + 3x^2 - y$ if $x = 3$, $y = 12$, and $z = 8$. **(Lesson 1-5)**

2-8 Problem-Solving Investigation

MAIN IDEA I will identify extra information or missing information to solve a problem.

Standard 5MR1.1 **Analyze problems by identifying relationships, distinguishing relevant from irrelevant information,** sequencing and prioritizing information, and observing patterns. **Reinforcement of Standard 4NS2.1** Estimate and **compute the sum or difference of whole numbers** and positive decimals to two places.

P.S.I. TEAM +

LISETA: On Monday, I was put in charge of collecting book orders. The books cost $2.50, $3.75, and $5.00. I collected 8 orders on Tuesday, 11 orders on Wednesday, and more orders on Thursday and Friday.

YOUR MISSION: Find how many book orders Liseta collected.

Understand	**What facts do you know?** You know the cost of each book, and the number of book orders that were turned in on Tuesday and Wednesday. **What do you need to find?** You need to find the total number of books ordered.
Plan	**Is there any information that is not needed?** The costs of the different books are not needed. **Is there any information that is missing?** You do not know how many book orders were turned in on Thursday and Friday.
Solve	Since you do not have enough information, the problem cannot be solved.
Check	Read the question again to see if you missed any information. If so, go back and rework the problem. If not, the problem cannot be solved.

Mixed Problem Solving

EXTRA PRACTICE
See page 659.

Solve each problem. If there is extra information, identify it. If there is not enough information, tell what information is needed.

PROBLEM-SOLVING SKILLS
- *Use the four-step plan.*
- *Identify extra or missing information.*

1. Mrs. Parry's class is having a reading challenge. Joseph reads 10 books in 8 weeks, Alison reads 7 books in 8 weeks, and Miguel reads 11 books in 8 weeks. How many more books does Joseph read than Alison?

2. How much higher is Mount Hood than Mount Marcy?

Mountain	Elevation (ft)
Mount Marcy	5,344
Mount Kea	13,796
Mount Mitchel	6,684
Mount Hood	11,239

3. Karl is collecting money for a jump-a-thon. His goal is to collect \$85. So far he has collected \$10 each from two people and \$5 each from six people. How far away is he from his goal?

4. The drama club sells 125 student tickets and 38 adult tickets for a total of \$603. How much does a student ticket cost?

5. Complete the pattern:

6, 11, 16, 21, ■, ■, ■

6. Paige studied 115 spelling words in five days. How many words did she study each day if she studied the same amount of words each day?

7. Aliana earned \$750 in May, \$656 in June, and \$912 in July, working at the grocery store. How much more did Aliana earn in July than in June?

8. Draw the next figure in the pattern.

9. Juan is downloading songs onto his digital music player. The first song is 3 minutes long, the second song is 4 minutes long, and the third song is between the lengths of the first and second song. What is the total length of all three songs?

10. Amy is slicing a loaf of Italian bread to serve with dinner. She plans to cut the loaf into slices that are 1 inch thick. How many slices can be cut?

11. The table shows the Chung family's monthly expenses.

Expense	Cost (\$)
Food	\$340
Utilities	\$112
Rent	\$675
Gasoline	\$200

In one month, how much do they spend on food and gasoline?

12. A fruit punch recipe calls for 8 cups of orange juice. How many people can be served?

13. WRITING IN ➤MATH Write a problem that has missing information. Explain how to rewrite the problem so that it can be solved.

2-9 Selecting an Appropriate Display

GET READY to Learn

The displays show the maximum speed of eight animals. Which display allows you to find a rabbit's maximum speed? In which display is it easier to find the number of animals whose speed is greater than 39 miles per hour?

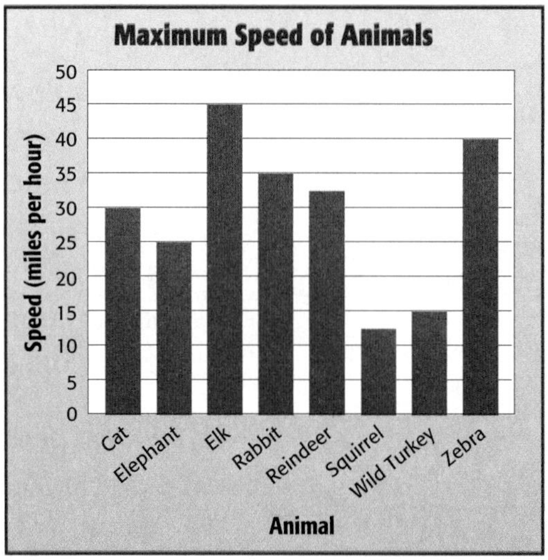

Source: *The World Almanac*

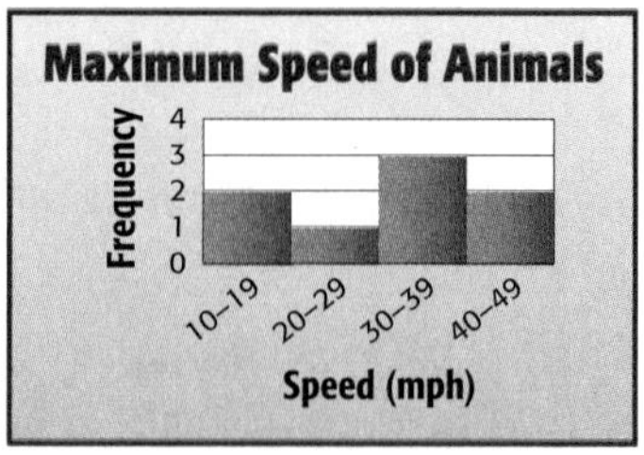

MAIN IDEA

I will select an appropriate display for a set of data.

Standard 5SDAP1.2 **Organize and display single-variable data in appropriate graphs and representations** (e.g., histogram, circle graphs) **and explain which types of graphs are appropriate for various data sets.**

Data can often be displayed in several different ways. The display you choose depends on your data and what you want to show.

EXAMPLE Choose Between Displays

1 Which display allows you to see whether the team's record of wins has steadily improved since 1998?

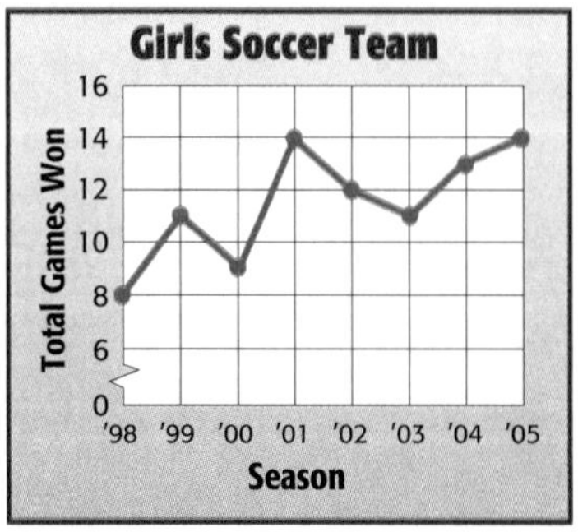

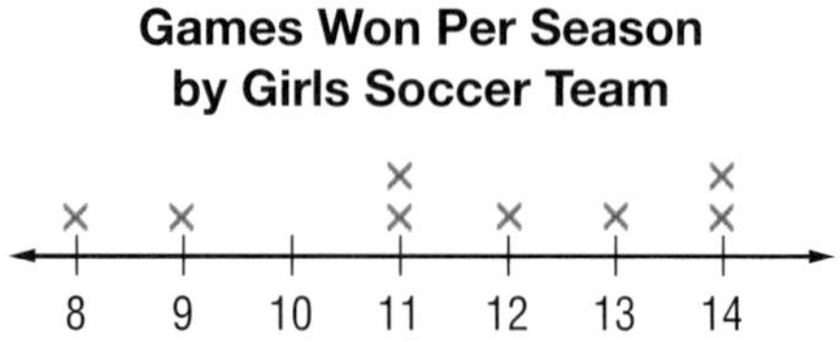

The line graph shows the change in games won from season to season, revealing some declines in the number of wins.

Real-World EXAMPLE

2 **A market researcher conducted a survey to compare different brands of shampoo. The table shows the number of first-choice responses for each brand. Select an appropriate type of display to compare the number of responses for each brand of shampoo. Explain your reasoning.**

Favorite Shampoo Survey

Brand	Responses	Brand	Responses
A	35	D	24
B	12	E	8
C	42	F	11

These data show the number of responses for each brand. A bar graph would be the best display to compare the responses.

Real-World EXAMPLE

3 **Make the appropriate display of the data in Example 2.**

Step 1 Draw and label horizontal and vertical axes. Add a title.

Step 2 Draw a bar to represent the number of responses for each brand.

Remember

Every display needs to have a title and labels on each axis.

Online Personal Tutor at ca.gr5math.com

KEY CONCEPT — Statistical Displays

Type of Display	Best Used to
Bar Graph	show the number of items in specific categories
Histogram	show frequency of data that has been divided into intervals of equal size
Line Graph	show change over a period of time
Line Plot	show how many times each number occurs in the data set

CHECK What You Know

1. Which display makes it easier to determine the change of the average price received for a hog from 1940 to 2000? See Example 1 (p. 106)

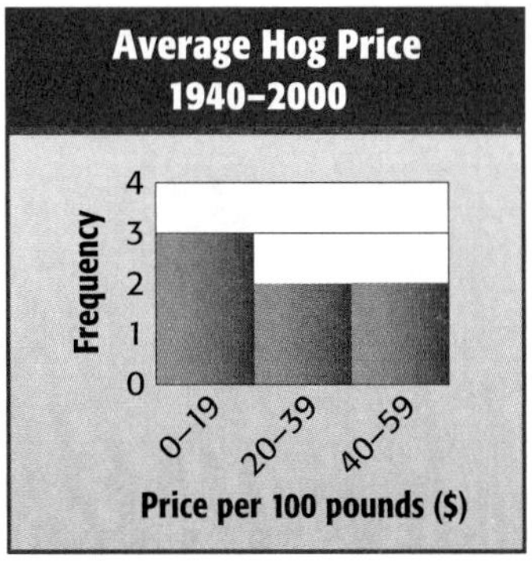

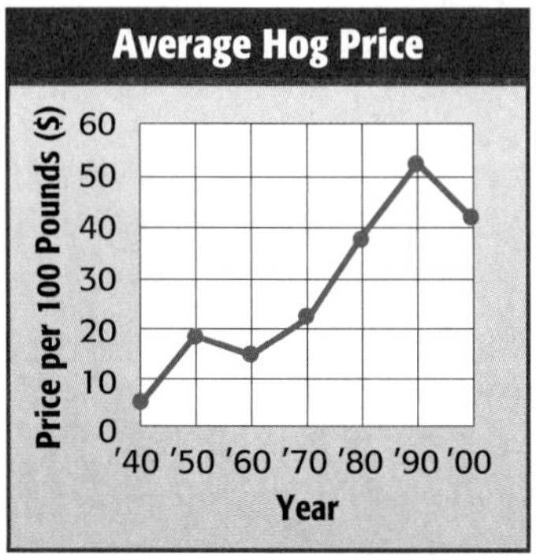

Select an appropriate type of display for data gathered about each situation. Explain your reasoning. See Example 2 (p. 107)

2. the favorite cafeteria lunch item of the fifth-grade students

3. the daily high temperature over the past seven days

4. Select and make an appropriate display for the data at the right. Justify your selection. See Example 3 (p. 107)

Number of Push-Ups Done by Each Student							
15	20	8	11	6	25	32	12
18	35	40	20	25	15	10	5
14	16	21	25	18	20	31	28

5. Talk About It Give a real-world example of data that would best be displayed in a histogram.

Practice and Problem Solving

EXTRA PRACTICE See page 660.

6. Which display makes it easier to compare the maximum speeds of Top Thrill Dragster and Millennium Force? See Example 1 (p. 106)

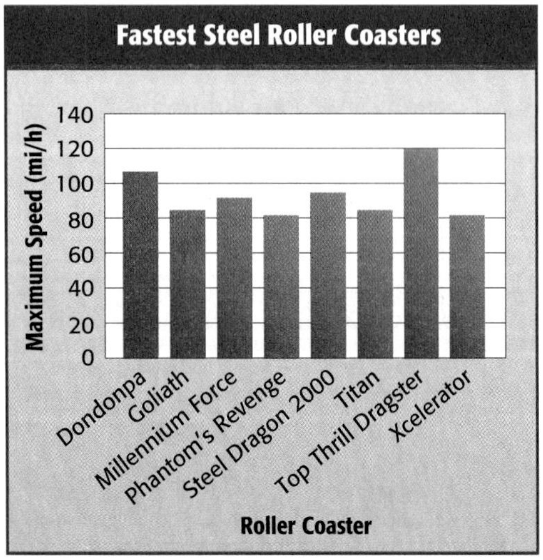

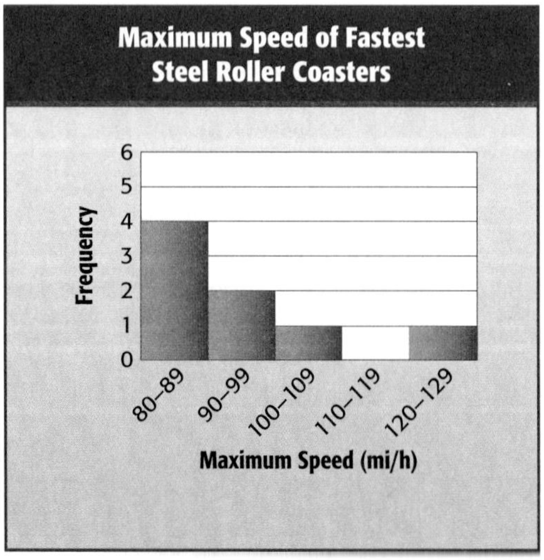

7. Which display makes it easier to see how many times the winning distance of the javelin throw was 90 meters? See Example 1 (p. 106)

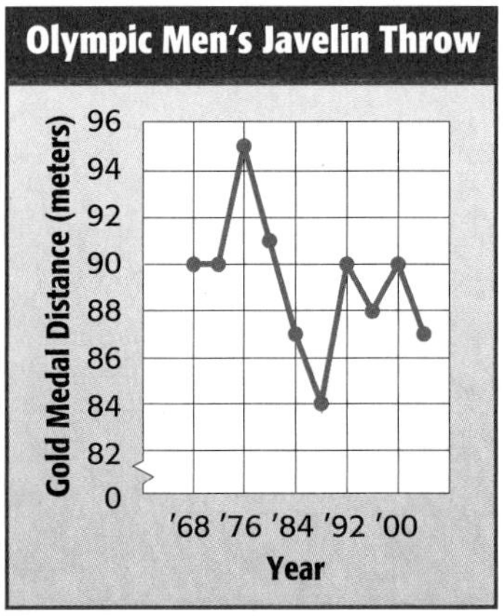

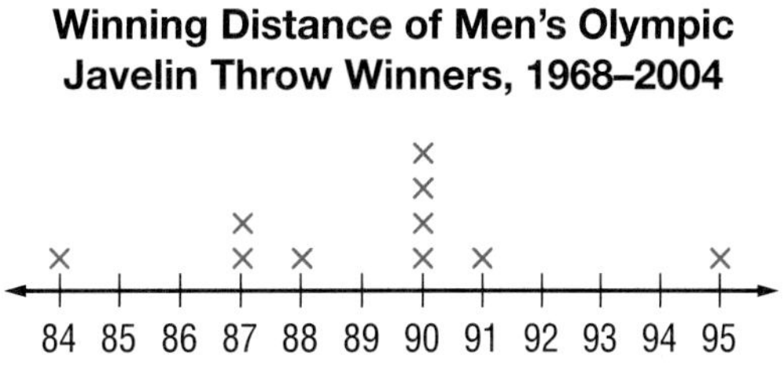

Select an appropriate type of display for data gathered about each situation. Explain your reasoning. See Example 2 (p. 107)

8. the amount of sales a company has for each of the past 6 months

9. the test scores each student had on a language arts test

10. the prices of five different brands of tennis shoes at an athletic store

Select and make an appropriate type of display for each situation. Justify your selection. See Example 3 (p. 107)

11.

Latin American Country	Year of Independence
Argentina	1816
Bolivia	1825
Chile	1818
Colombia	1819
Ecuador	1822
Mexico	1821
Peru	1824

Source: *The World Almanac*

12.

Number of Counties in Various Southern States	
67	67
95	82
33	64
63	29
46	100
75	77
95	105

Source: 50states.com

13. Display the data in the bar graph using another type of display. Compare the advantages of each display.

14. Use the Internet or another source to find a set of data that is displayed in a bar graph, line graph, histogram, or line plot. Was the most appropriate type of display used? What other ways might these same data be displayed?

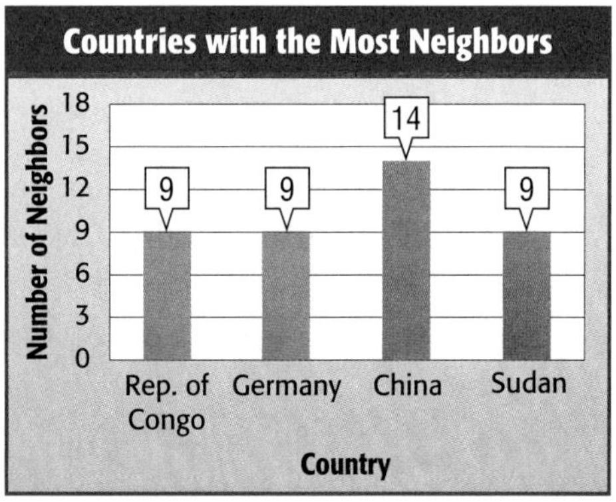

Source: *Top 10 of Everything*

H.O.T. Problems

15. **REASONING** Determine whether the following statement is *true* or *false*. If true, explain your reasoning. If false, give a counterexample.

    Any set of data can be displayed using a line graph.

16. **CHALLENGE** Which type of display allows you to easily find the mode of the data? Explain your reasoning.

17. **WRITING IN ▶MATH** Write about a real-world situation in which you would have to choose an appropriate display for a set of data.

Standards Practice

18 Which of the following situations would involve data that are best displayed in a line graph?

A the favorite subject of the students in Mrs. Ling's homeroom

B a company's yearly profit over the past 10 years

C the number of hits Dylan got in each game this baseball season

D the number of miles each student travels to school

19 The table shows the prices of the skateboards Jacy might buy.

Skateboards	
Brand	**Price**
Blackbird	\$55
Earth Bound	\$68
Element Skateboards	\$44
Venus Boards	\$61
ZoomFast	\$75

Which type of display would help Jacy best compare the prices of these skateboards?

F bar graph **H** line plot

G line graph **J** histogram

Spiral Review

20. Each class that sells 75 tickets to the school play earns an ice cream party. Mario's class has sold 42 tickets. How many more must they sell to earn an ice cream party? **(Lesson 2-8)**

21. The daily high temperatures last week in Charleston, South Carolina, were 68°, 70°, 73°, 75°, 76°, 76°, and 82°. Find the median, mode, and range of these temperatures. **(Lesson 2-7)**

Find the mean for each set of data. **(Lesson 2-6)**

22. Length of television program (in minutes): 25, 20, 19, 22, 24, 28

23. Ages of cousins (in years): 25, 14, 21, 16, 19

Extend

Statistics Lab for 2-9
Collecting Data to Solve a Problem

In this lab, you will collect, organize, display, and interpret data.

MAIN IDEA

I will solve a problem by collecting, organizing, displaying, and interpreting data.

Standard 5SDAP1.2 **Organize and display single-variable data in appropriate graphs and representations** (e.g., histogram, circle graphs) **and explain which types of graphs are appropriate for various data sets.** **Standard 5MR3.3** **Develop generalizations of the results obtained** and apply them in other circumstances.

ACTIVITY

1 *Rating scales,* like the one below, are often used on surveys to find out about people's opinions. Participants indicate how strongly they agree or disagree with a specific statement.

5	4	3	2	1
Strongly Agree	Agree	No Opinion	Disagree	Strongly Disagree

Consider each of the following topics.

- yearbooks in interactive DVD format
- voting age for presidential election
- school uniforms
- fast food in school

Step 1 **Make a data collection plan.**

- Choose one of the topics to survey.
- Write one or more survey questions that include the rating scale shown above.
- Identify an audience for your results.

Step 2 **Collect the data.**

- Conduct your survey and record the results.
- Collect responses from at least 10 people in the population you chose.
- Record your results in a frequency table.

Step 3 **Create a display of the data.**

Choose an appropriate type of display and scale for your data. Then create an accurate display.

Analyze the Results

1. What are the mean, median, mode, and range of your data?

2. Use your display to describe the distribution or shape of your data.

3. How would you summarize the opinions of those you surveyed? Include only those statements that are clearly supported by the data.

4. Based on your analysis, what course of action would you recommend to the group interested in your data?

5. Present your findings and recommendation to the whole class. Include poster-size versions of both your displays and a written report of your data analysis.

6. What other factors might influence the results of your survey?

Remember

Survey questions that favor a particular answer are biased. Be sure your survey question is worded as to avoid bias.

ACTIVITY

2 A *log* is an organized list that contains a record of events over a specified amount of time. Consider each of the following topics.

- the amount of time you spend watching television each day
- the outside air temperature over a period of 2, 4, 6, or 8 hours

Step 1 **Make a data collection plan.**

- Choose one of the topics above and a reasonable period of time over which to collect the data.
- Create a log that you can use to collect the data.

Step 2 **Collect the data and create an appropriate display.**

Record the necessary data in your log. Then choose and create an appropriate display for the data.

Analyze the Results

7. What type of display did you choose? Explain.

8. Describe the change in your data over the time period you chose.

9. If possible, use your display to make a prediction about future data. Explain your reasoning. If not possible, explain why not.

2-10 Integers and Graphing

GET READY to Learn

The bar graph shows the amount of money remaining in the clothing budgets of four students at the end of one month. A value of −\$4 means that someone overspent the budget and owes his or her parents 4 dollars.

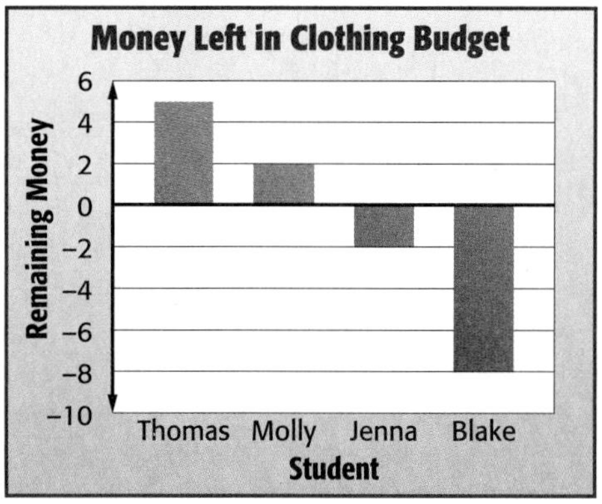

MAIN IDEA

I will represent integers on a number line.

Standard 5NS1.5 Identify and represent on a number line decimals, fractions, mixed numbers, and **positive and negative integers.**

New Vocabulary

negative numbers
positive numbers
opposites
integers
graph

To represent data that are less than a 0, you can use **negative numbers**. A negative number is written with a – sign. Data that are greater than zero are represented by **positive numbers**.

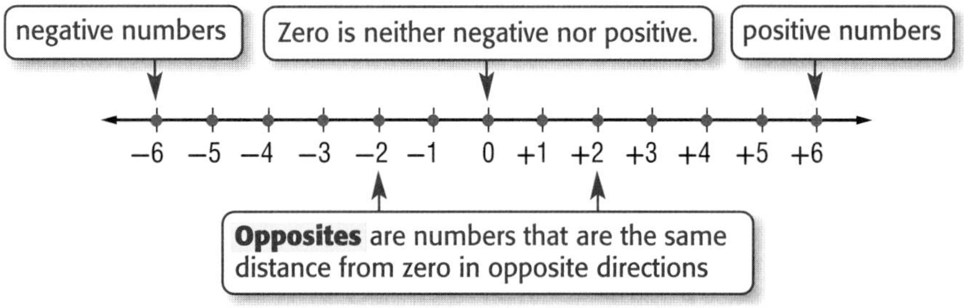

Positive whole numbers, their opposites, and zero are called **integers**.

Reading Math

Positive and Negative Signs The integer +5 is read *positive 5* or *5*. The integer −2 is read *negative two*.

EXAMPLE Use Integers to Represent Data

Write an integer to represent each piece of data.

1. **The offense had a gain of 5 yards on the first down.**

   The word *gain* represents an increase. The integer is +5 or 5.

2. **The temperature is 10 degrees below zero.**

   The word *below* here means *less than.* The integer is −10.

To **graph** a number on a number line, draw a dot at the location on the number line that corresponds to the number.

EXAMPLE Graph an Integer on a Number Line

3 Graph −3 on a number line.

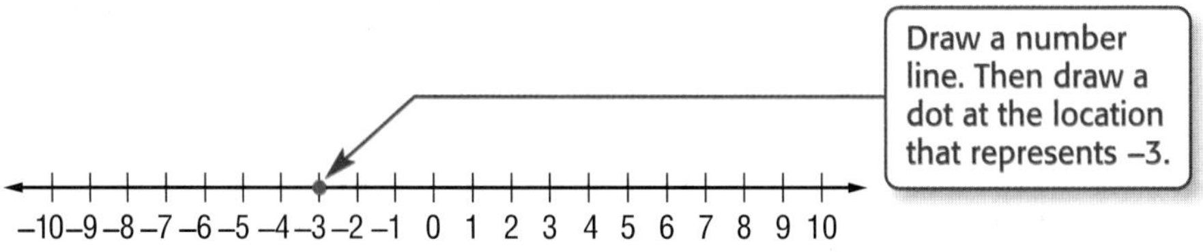

You can create line plots of data that involve positive and negative integers.

Real-World EXAMPLE

4 The table below shows the scores, in relation to par, of the top 25 leaders of the 2005 Masters Tournament in Augusta, Georgia. Make a line plot of the data.

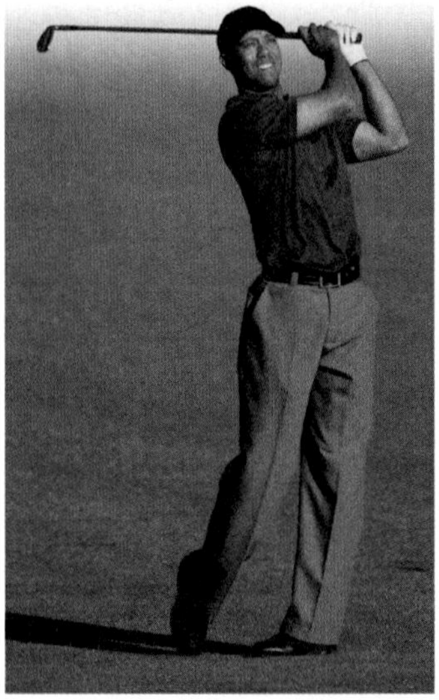

2005 Masters Tournament, Top 25 Scores (in relation to par)

0	+1	0	−12	−5
−5	−4	−2	−2	−4
+1	+1	−1	−1	−1
+1	−3	−1	−4	+2
−4	0	+1	−4	−12

Source: pgatour.com

> **Remember**
> To check your line plot in Example 4, the number of ×'s and the number of scores should be the same.

Draw a number line. −12 would be plotted farthest to the left and +2 farthest to the right. So you can use a scale of −15 to 5.

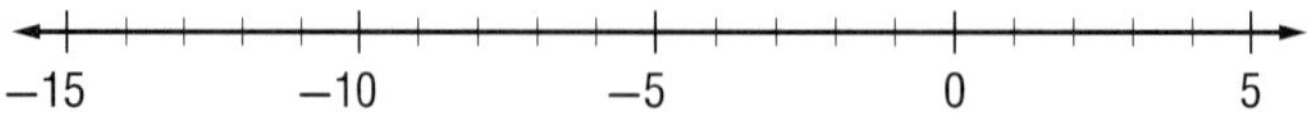

Put an × above the number that represents each score in the table.

2005 Masters Tournament, Top 25 Scores

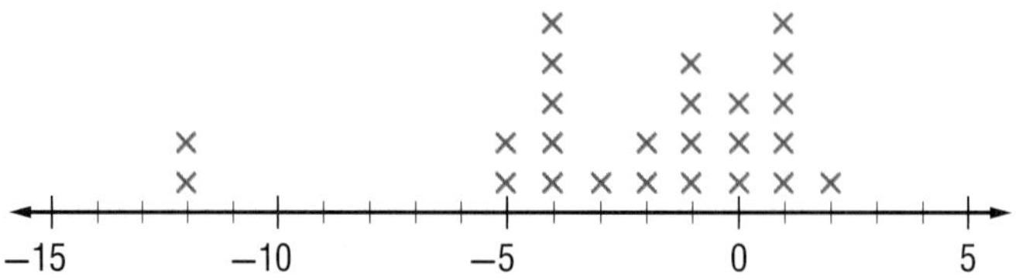

Online Personal Tutor at ca.gr5math.com

CHECK What You Know

Write an integer to represent each piece of data. See Examples 1, 2 (p. 113)

1. Mei's dog gained 3 pounds.

2. Kenji withdrew $15 from his savings account

Graph each integer on a number line. See Example 3 (p. 114)

3. −7 **4.** 10 **5.** −4 **6.** 3

7. The table at the right shows the number of points Delaney scored on each hand of a card game. Make a line plot of the data. See Example 4 (p. 114)

Points Scored			
+25	0	−15	+30
−5	+25	0	−15
+25	+20	−5	+20

8. Talk About It What is an integer? Give some examples in your definition.

Practice and Problem Solving

EXTRA PRACTICE See page 660.

Write an integer to represent each piece of data. See Examples 1, 2 (p. 113)

9. Wesley swam 5 feet below sea level.

10. Toya deposited $30 into her savings account.

11. Edmund moved ahead 4 spaces on the game board.

12. The stock market lost 6 points on Thursday.

Graph each integer on a number line. See Example 3 (p. 114)

13. 1 **14.** 5 **15.** 3 **16.** 7

17. −5 **18.** −10 **19.** −6 **20.** −8

Make a line plot of the data represented in each table. See Example 4 (p. 114)

21.

Elevations of Valleys (in relation to sea level)			
−50	25	20	−45
−15	20	0	−5
10	5	−15	25
20	−50	−15	0
20	25	−45	0

22.

Golf Scores (in relation to par)			
−1	0	5	3
−5	0	4	−6
−5	1	2	5
7	−3	−2	0
1	2	5	−2

Write the opposite of each integer.

23. −8 **24.** −3 **25.** 19 **26.** 42

Identify the integer represented by each letter on the number line below.

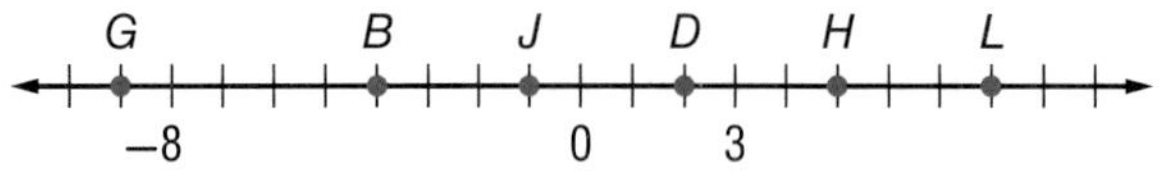

27. *B* **28.** *D* **29.** *G*

30. *H* **31.** *J* **32.** *L*

33. Death Valley, California, is 282 feet below sea level. Represent this altitude as an integer.

Real-World PROBLEM SOLVING

Animals Some sea creatures live near the surface while others live in the depths of the ocean.

34. Make a drawing showing the relative habitats of the following creatures.

- blue marlin: 0 to 600 feet below the surface
- lantern fish: 3,300 to 13,200 feet below the surface
- ribbon fish: 600 to 3,300 feet below the surface

35. The table below shows the record low temperatures for select states. Make a line plot of the data. Then explain how the line plot allows you to determine the most common record low temperature among the given states.

Record Low Temperature by State

State	AZ	CA	DE	GA	KS	KY	MD	MS	MO	NC	RI	SC	TX
Temp (°F)	−40	−45	−17	−17	−40	−37	−40	−19	−40	−34	−23	−19	−23

Source: infoplease.com

H.O.T. Problems

36. OPEN ENDED Write about a time that you used integers to describe a real-world situation.

37. REASONING Determine whether the following statement is *true* or *false*. Explain your reasoning.

The number $-2\frac{1}{4}$ is an integer.

38. CHALLENGE Two numbers, *a* and *b*, are opposites. If *a* is 4 units to the left of −6 on a number line, what is the value of *b*?

39. **REASONING** The temperature outside is 15°F. If the temperature drops 20°, will the outside temperature be represented by a positive or negative integer? Explain your reasoning.

40. **WRITING IN ▶MATH** Describe the characteristics of each set of numbers that make up the set of integers.

Standards Practice

41 The record low temperature for New Mexico is 50 degrees below zero Fahrenheit. The record low temperature for Hawaii is 12 degrees above zero Fahrenheit. What integer represents the record low temperature for New Mexico?

A 50

B 38

C −38

D −50

42 Which letter on the number line identifies the location of −3?

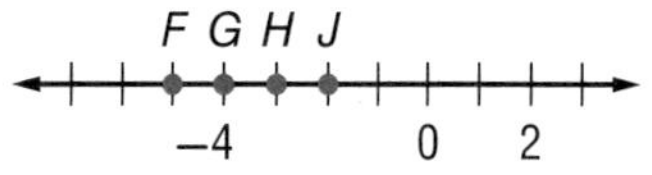

F F

G G

H H

J J

Spiral Review

43. The table shows the test grades of Mrs. Owens' science class. Select an appropriate type of statistical display for the data. Then make a display. **(Lesson 2-9)**

Science Test Scores				
83	90	74	95	80
75	92	88	85	81
98	100	70	78	85
85	90	92	76	88

Find the median, mode, and range for each set of data.
(Lesson 2-7)

44. Height of students (in inches): 55, 60, 57, 55, 58, 55, 56, 60, 59

45. Points scored in football games: 14, 24, 7, 21, 21, 14, 21, 35

Algebra Solve each equation mentally. **(Lesson 1-8)**

46. $16 + h = 24$

47. $15 = 50 - m$

48. $14t = 42$

49. The expression $d \div t$, where d represents distance and t represents time, can be used to find the speed of a plane. Find the speed of a plane that travels 3,636 miles in 9 hours. **(Lesson 1-5)**

50. New Hampshire has a total land area of about 10^4 square miles. What is the value of 10^4? **(Lesson 1-2)**

Problem Solving in Art

Art Work

Artists hold about 290,000 jobs in the United States. Some are cartoonists, sketch artists for law enforcement, or illustrators for medical and scientific publications. Many artists are involved in movie-making and theater productions. Graphic designers and animators help create videos.

About 63% of artists in the United States are self-employed. Some self-employed artists have contracts to work on individual projects for different clients. Fine artists usually sell their work when it is finished, including painters, sculptors, craft artists, and printmakers.

Art Careers Chosen by Students in a Survey

Career	Frequency
Art Museum Director	10
Book Illustrator	14
Cartoonist	16
Computer Graphic Artist	9
Craft Artist	14
Fine Art Restorer	2
Scientific Sketch Artist	12

Average Annual Salary

Profession	Salary ($)
Dancers	27,390
Fashion Designers	60,160
Film and Video Editors	44,540
Fine Artists	43,750
Graphic Designers	41,380
Interior Designers	43,770
Photographers	28,810

Source: allartschools.com

Math Standard 5SDAP1.1 **Know the concepts of mean, median, and mode; compute and compare simple examples to show that they may differ.**

Did You Know?

The oldest known paintings are in a cave in France called Grotte Chavet. The paintings were created about 32,000 years ago.

Real-World Math

Use the tables on page 118 to solve each problem.

1. Find the mean of the salary data.
2. Identify the outlier(s) of the salary data.
3. How does the outlier(s) affect the mean of the salary data?
4. Find the median of the salary data.
5. Find the mode of the salary data.
6. Find the range of the salary data.
7. Which measure, mean, median, or mode, best describes the salary data? Explain.
8. Select and make an appropriate display for the data in the frequency table. Justify your selection.
9. How does the number of students who chose cartoonist compare to the number of students who chose computer graphic artist?

CHAPTER 2

Study Guide and Review

FOLDABLES™ Study Organizer GET READY to Study

Be sure the following Key Concepts are noted in your Foldable.

BIG Ideas

Mean, Median, Mode, and Range
(Lessons 2-6, 2-7)

- The mean of a set of data is the sum of the data values divided by the number of items in the data set.
- The median of a set of data is the middle number of the ordered data, or the mean of the middle two numbers.
- The mode of a set of data is the number or numbers that occur most often.
- The range of a set of data is the difference between the greatest and the least values of the set.

Appropriate Graphs (Lesson 2-8)

- A bar graph is best used to show the number of items in specific categories.
- A histogram is best used to show frequency of data that has been divided into intervals of equal size.
- A line graph is best used to show change over a period of time.
- A line plot is best used to show how many times each number occurs in the data set.

Key Vocabulary

bar graph (p. 73)
frequency (p. 73)
graph (p. 73)
histogram (p. 83)
horizontal axis (p. 73)
integers (p. 113)
line graph (p. 74)
line plot (p. 87)
mean (p. 95)
median (p. 99)
mode (p. 99)
opposites (p. 113)
outlier (p. 96)
range (p. 100)
vertical axis (p. 73)

Vocabulary Check

State whether each sentence is *true* or *false*. If *false*, replace the underlined word or number to make a true sentence.

1. The sum of the values in a data set divided by the number of pieces of data is called the median.
2. Zero is an integer.
3. The opposite of $4\frac{3}{7}$ is $-4\frac{3}{7}$.
4. The middle number of a set of data is called the outlier.
5. Negative numbers can be written with or without a + sign.
6. The range separates the scale into equal parts.
7. A histogram shows how data changes over time.

Math Online Vocabulary Review at ca.gr5math.com

Lesson-by-Lesson Review

2-1 Bar Graphs and Line Graphs (pp. 73–77)

Example 1
The U.S. states with the five highest birth rates per 1,000 people are Utah with 20.7, Arizona with 18.0, Texas with 17.1, California with 16.9, and Alaska with 16.7. Make a bar graph of this data. Compare the birth rates in California and Arizona.

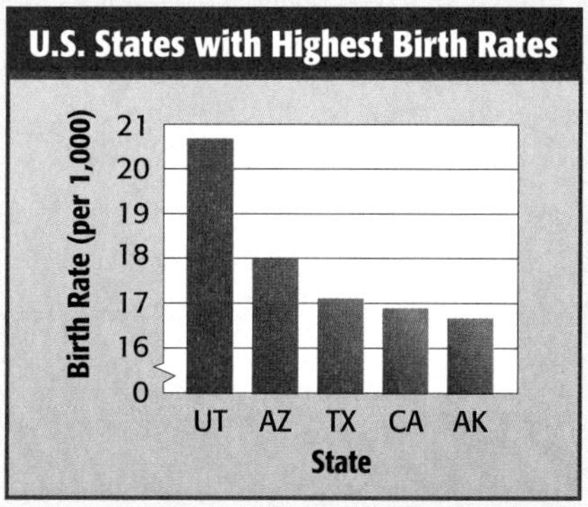

Arizona has about 1 more birth per 1,000 people than California.

8. In a recent year, U.S. produce production included 44 million tons of bananas, 60 million tons of tomatoes, 36 million tons of apples, 34 million tons of oranges, and 22 million tons of watermelon. Display this data in a bar graph. Which item was produced about half as many times as bananas?

9. Make a line graph for the set of data shown. Then describe the change in visitors from 2002 to 2004.

Zoo Visitors

Year	Visitors
2000	12,300
2001	13,400
2002	15,900
2003	15,100
2004	16,200

2-2 Interpret Line Graphs (pp. 79–82)

Example 2
Refer to the graph. Predict the number of CDs that will be sold in 2007.

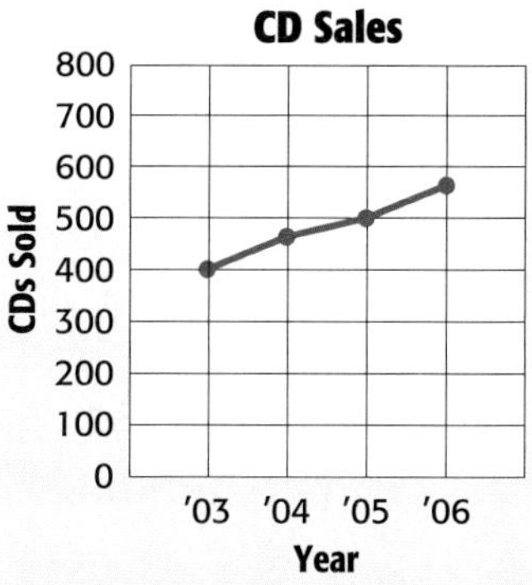

By extending the graph, it appears that about 700 CDs will be sold in 2007.

For Exercises 10–12, refer to the graph.

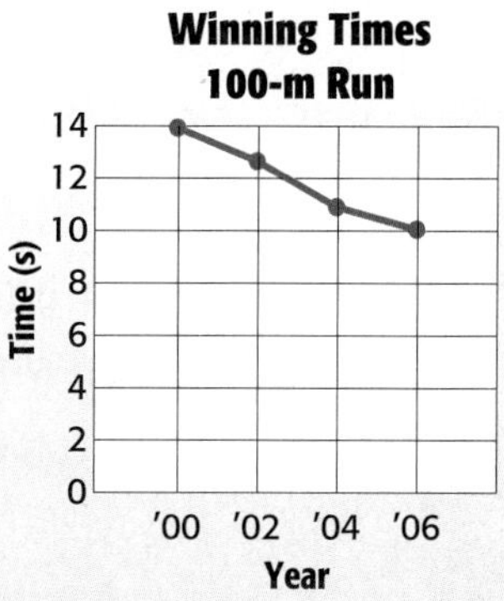

10. Describe the trend in the winning times.

11. Predict the winning time for 2008.

12. What do you think the winning time might have been in 1998?

2-3 Histograms (pp. 83–86)

Example 3

Write a few sentences that analyze the data shown in the histogram below.

By adding the heights of the bars, you can tell that data was collected for seven times spent reading. You can also see that Lucita did not read less than 61 minutes.

For Exercises 13–15, use the histogram below.

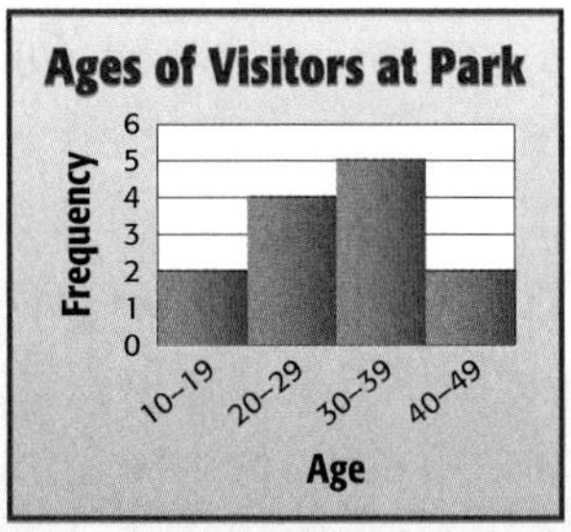

13. How many people under 20 visited the park?

14. How many people 30 and over visited the park?

15. Write a few sentences that analyze the data.

2-4 Line Plots (pp. 87–91)

Example 4

The table shows the amount Jack earned for each lawn he mowed. Make a line plot.

Jack's Earnings ($)						
15	20	10	12	10	15	20
25	15	20	15	12	15	25

Draw a number line. Place an × above each value represented in the table.

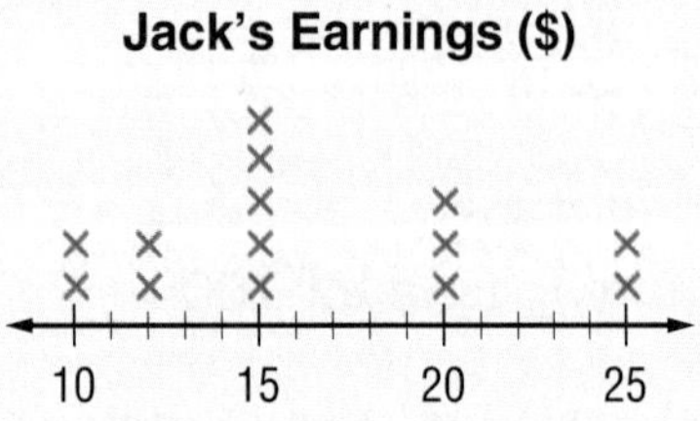

For Exercises 16–19, use the table of the number of points Patricia scored in each basketball game this season.

Patricia's Points Per Game				
5	8	10	8	6
5	14	9	8	6
8	10	10	8	5

16. Make a line plot of the data.

17. In how many games did Patricia score 8 points?

18. In how many games did Patricia score 10 or more points?

19. What is the difference between the most and the least points scored?

2-5 Problem-Solving Strategy: Make a Table (pp. 92–93)

Example 5

Make a frequency table of the data below. How many more students received a B than an A?

B A B B A B A B B

Draw a table with three columns.

Class Test Grades		
Grade	Tally	Number
A	|||	3
B	𝍸		6

So, 3 more students received a B than received an A on the test.

20. Make a frequency table of the data. How many more people have 2 than 4 siblings?

Number of Siblings								
3	1	2	1	3	1	0	4	1
0	2	1	2	1	0	3	1	0

21. Make a frequency table of the data. How many wore 3 or more ads?

Number of Ads Worn								
1	0	5+	0	4	3	0	2	0
0	1	0	3	2	0	1	5+	1

5+ = 5 or more

2-6 Mean (pp. 95–98)

Example 6

Find the mean for the set of data: 98, 117, 104, 108, 104, 111.

mean

$$= \frac{117 + 98 + 104 + 108 + 104 + 111}{6}$$

$= 107$

22. Find the mean for the set of data on hotel rooms: 103, 110, 98, 104, 110.

23. The speeds of six cheetahs were recorded as 68, 72, 74, 72, 71, and 75 miles per hour. What was the mean speed of these animals?

2-7 Median, Mode, and Range (pp. 99–103)

Example 7

Find the median, mode, and range for the set of data on points scored: 69, 56, 67, 71, 67.

median: 67 mode: 67

range: 71 − 56 or 15

Find the median, mode, and range for each set of data.

24. Number of students: 21, 23, 27, 30

25. Ages of aunts: 36, 42, 48, 36, 82

26. The minutes spent doing homework for one week were 30, 60, 77, 90, 88, 76, and 90. Find the median, mode, and range of these times.

2-8 Problem-Solving Investigation: Extra or Missing Information
(pp. 104–105)

Example 8
Allie is thinking of some integers from 1 through 10 whose sum is 12 and product is 24. What are the numbers?

There is no extra information, and since you do not know how many numbers Allie is thinking of, the problem cannot be solved.

Solve each problem. If there is extra information, identify it. If there is not enough information, tell what information is needed.

27. Find the number of seconds in a day if there are 60 seconds in a minute and 7 days in a week.

28. The length of a rectangular room is 11 feet. How many square feet of carpet is needed to carpet the room?

2-9 Selecting an Appropriate Display (pp. 106–110)

Example 9
Which type of display is most appropriate when showing how long, grouped in 5-minute intervals, it took several students to each run one mile?

These data show how long it took several students to run one mile. Since the data are grouped in 5 minute intervals, a histogram would be the best display.

Select an appropriate type of display for data gathered about each situation.

29. the change in the value of a house over a period of 30 years

30. the number of times each number turned up when a number cube was rolled ten times

2-10 Integers and Graphing (pp. 113–117)

Example 10
Graph −2 on a number line.

Draw a number line. Then draw a dot at the location that represents −2.

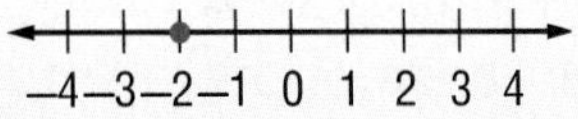

Graph each integer on a number line.

31. −6 **32.** 9

33. On a five-problem quiz, Belinda received the following points on each problem: +5, −3, −2, +5, and −2. Make a line plot of the data.

CHAPTER 2

Chapter Test

1. STANDARDS PRACTICE Mandy and her friends collected the following data during one week.

Which statement is supported by the graph?

A Gabriel watched TV three times as much as Mandy.

B Luke watched about 15 hours of TV

C Gabriel watched the most TV

D Ginger watched twice as much TV as Mandy.

2. The weights of a kitten in ounces for each week since it was born are 4, 7, 9, 13, 17, and 20. Create a line graph of this data. Make a prediction of the kitten's weight at Week 7.

3. STANDARDS PRACTICE Julio collected the following data about the number of movies his classmates saw.

Number of Movies Seen at Theater								
0	4	3	2	0	4	5	2	1
4	6	1	3	7	4	8	10	0

Which measure of the data is represented by 10 movies?

F Mean **H** Mode

G Median **J** Range

For Exercises 4–8, use data in the table below.

Number of Years the Leading Lifetime NFL Passers Played in NFL				
6	15	15	5	6
5	13	17	6	4
10	15	11	10	9
11	6	8	18	19

Source: *The World Almanac*

4. Make a histogram of the data.
5. What is the greatest number of years a leading lifetime NFL passer has played?
6. Make a line plot of the data.
7. What is the difference between the greatest and least number of years a leading lifetime NFL passer has played?
8. Write two additional sentences that analyze the data.

For Exercises 9 and 10, find the mean, median, mode, and range for each set of data.

9. Birthday money each year ($): 67, 68, 103, 65, 80, 54, 53
10. Bowling scores: 232, 200, 242, 242
11. Select an appropriate type of display for the number of digital cable subscribers each year since 2000.

For Exercises 12 and 13, write an integer to represent each piece of data.

12. He withdrew $75 from an ATM.
13. The snow level rose 4 inches.
14. WRITING IN MATH Explain how to graph −3 and its opposite on a number line. Include a graph.

CHAPTER 2

California Standards Practice

Cumulative, Chapters 1–2

Standards Example

An ice cream store collected data about ice cream sales each hour from 4 P.M. to 9 P.M. on a particular summer day. By what time had the store sold at least 50 pints?

A 5 P.M.

B 6 P.M.

C 7 P.M.

D 8 P.M.

Read the Question

You need to find when the store sold at least 50 pints of ice cream. *At least 50 pints* means *50 pints or greater.*

Solve the Question

Find the total for each hour.

4 P.M.	10 pints
5 P.M.	10 + 25 or 35 pints
6 P.M.	10 + 25 + 20 or 55 pints

By 6 P.M., the store had sold at least 50 pints of ice cream.

The answer is B.

Online Personal Tutor at ca.gr5math.com

Refer to the graph above. Choose the best answer.

1 **At 9 P.M., how many pints of ice cream were sold?**

A 10

B 20

C 30

D 50

2 **How many more pints of ice cream were sold at 8 P.M. than 6 P.M.?**

F 20

G 30

H 40

J 50

For practice by standard, see pages CA1–CA27.

3 **A shop records the number of specialty shirts sold each month. What is the mean number of T-shirts sold?**

T-Shirt Sales	
Month	**Number**
January	75
February	68
March	75
April	92
May	105

A 75 **C** 85

B 83 **D** 92

4 **Which letter on the number line identifies the location of −8?**

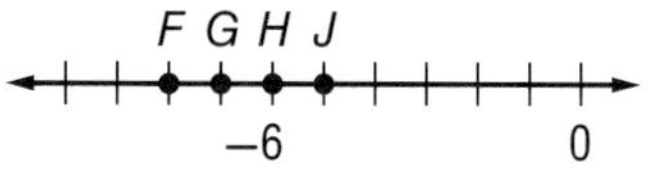

F *F* **H** *H*

G *G* **J** *J*

5 **About how many silver cars were sold?**

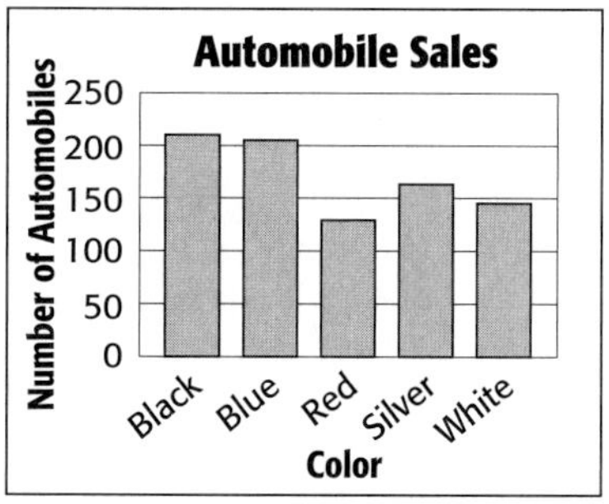

A 125 **C** 170

B 140 **D** 210

6 **Find the median of the following ages of people attending a concert: 2, 7, 41, 25, 19, 22, 28, 32, and 24.**

F 17 **G** 22 **H** 24 **J** 41

7 **If $x = 10$, what is the value of $8x - 4$?**

A 10 **B** 76 **C** 80 **D** 84

8 **The weight limit for a small boat is 1,800 pounds. Which statement is best supported by this information?**

F The boat can carry more than 25 adults.

G The boat can carry more than 30 children that weigh 75 pounds each.

H The boat can carry up to 9 people who each weigh as much as 200 pounds.

J The boat can carry twice as many children as adults.

9 **Jeremy's bill for egg and onion bagels was $12.00. He bought 12 egg bagels at $0.50 each. If an onion bagel costs $0.75, how can he determine how much money he spent on onion bagels?**

A Add $0.50 and $0.75.

B Subtract the product of 12 and $0.50 from $12.00.

C Multiply $0.75 and 12.

D Divide 12 by $0.50.

CHAPTER 3

Adding and Subtracting Decimals

BIG Idea How do you compare decimals?

One way to compare decimals is by using place value.

Example The table shows the time of two riders in the Women's Breakaway Roping event after the first round. You can compare the decimals using place value to determine which rider had the faster time.

Women's Breakaway Roping	
Rider	**Time (s)**
Whitney Gonzalez	4.334
Rachael Simms	4.357

In the hundredths place, 3 < 5. So, 4.3**3**4 < 4.3**5**7.

Whitney Gonzalez had a faster time than Rachael Simms.

What will I learn in this chapter?

- Represent decimals on a number line.
- Compare, order, and round whole numbers and decimals.
- Estimate sums and differences of decimals.
- Solve problems by estimating.
- Add and subtract decimals.

Key Vocabulary

equivalent decimals
clustering
front-end estimation

Math Online Student Study Tools at ca.gr5math.com

FOLDABLES™ Study Organizer

Make this Foldable to help you organize information about adding and subtracting decimals. Begin with two sheets of notebook paper.

1. **Fold** one sheet in half. Cut along fold from edges to margin.

2. **Fold** the other sheet in half. Cut along fold between margins.

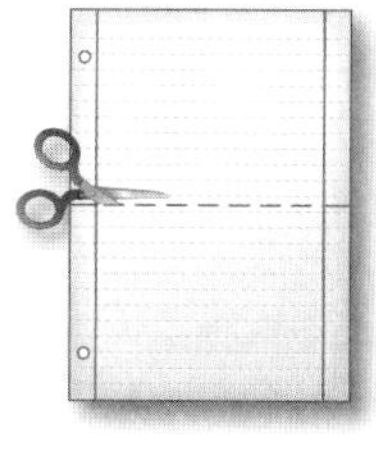

3. **Insert** first sheet through second sheet and along folds.

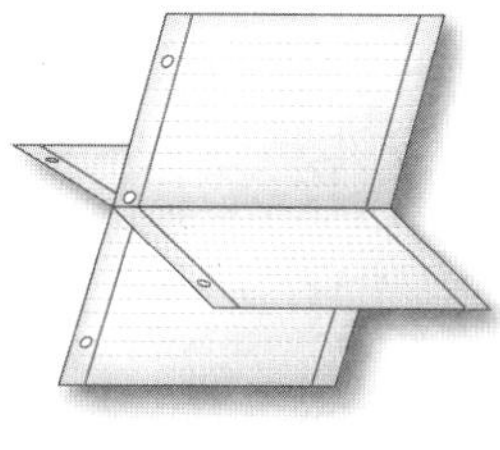

4. **Label** each side of each page with a lesson number and title.

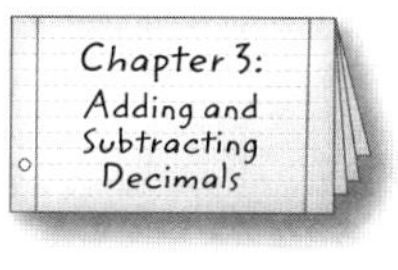

ARE YOU READY for Chapter 3?

You have two ways to check prerequisite skills for this chapter.

Option 2

Math Online Take the Chapter Readiness Quiz at ca.gr5math.com.

Option 1

Complete the Quick Check below.

QUICK Check

Evaluate each expression if $a = 3$ and $b = 4$. **(Lesson 1-5)**

1. $3a - 2b$

2. $5 + 2a$

3. $b - 1 + a$

4. $16 - b$

5. The cost of buying d DVDs and c CDs is given by the expression $17d + 12c$. What is the cost of buying 4 DVDs and 6 CDs? **(Lesson 1-5)**

Graph each integer on a number line. **(Lesson 2-10)**

6. 23

7. 17

8. −2

9. −8

Round each number to the nearest tens place. **(Prior Grade)**

10. 5

11. 75

12. 148

13. 156

Replace each ● with $<$ or $>$ to make a true sentence. **(Prior Grade)**

14. 302,788 ● 203,788

15. 54,300 ● 543,000

16. 64,935 ● 61,935

17. 892,341 ● 892,431

18. In a recent year, there were 96,834 female licensed drivers, and 97,461 male licensed drivers. Were the greater number of licensed drivers female or male? **(Prior Grade)**

3-1 Representing Decimals

MAIN IDEA

I will represent decimals on a number line.

Standard 5NS1.5 Identify and represent on a number line decimals, fractions, mixed numbers, and positive and negative integers.

Vocabulary Link

Decibel
Everyday Use a unit of sound intensity based on powers of ten

Decimal
Math Use a number system based on powers of ten

GET READY to Learn

Concepts in Motion
Interactive Lab
ca.gr5math.com

Hands-On Mini Lab

The models below show some ways to represent the decimal 1.34.

Place-Value Chart

1,000	100	10	1	0.1	0.01	0.001
thousands	hundreds	tens	ones	tenths	hundredths	thousandths
0	0	0	1.	3	4	0

Decimal Model

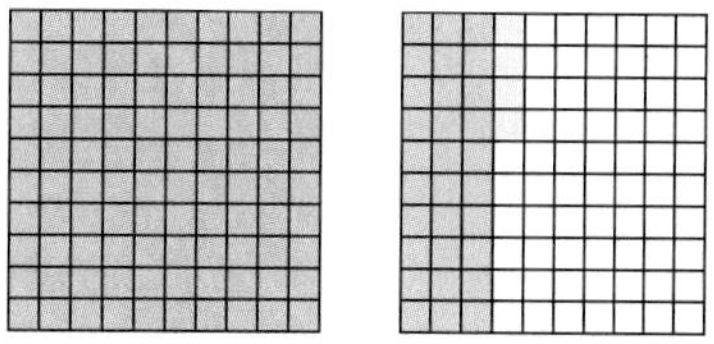

one   34 hundredths

Model each decimal using a place-value chart and a decimal model.

1. 1.56 **2.** 0.85 **3.** 0.08 **4.** $2.25

Decimals, like whole numbers, are based on the number ten. The digits and the position of each digit determine the value of a decimal. The decimal point separates the whole number part of the decimal from the part that is less than one.

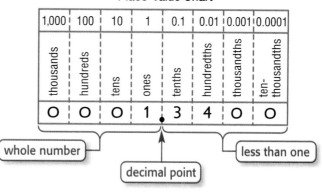

Place-Value Chart

1,000	100	10	1	0.1	0.01	0.001	0.0001
thousands	hundreds	tens	ones	tenths	hundredths	thousandths	ten-thousandths
0	0	0	1.	3	4	0	0

whole number   decimal point   less than one

In addition to representing decimals with place-value charts and decimal models, decimals can also be represented on number lines.

EXAMPLES Represent Decimals on a Number Line

1 Graph 1.7 on a number line.

Since 1.7 is between 1 and 2, draw a number line from 1 to 2. Use increments of one tenth since 1.7 is written to the tenths place value.

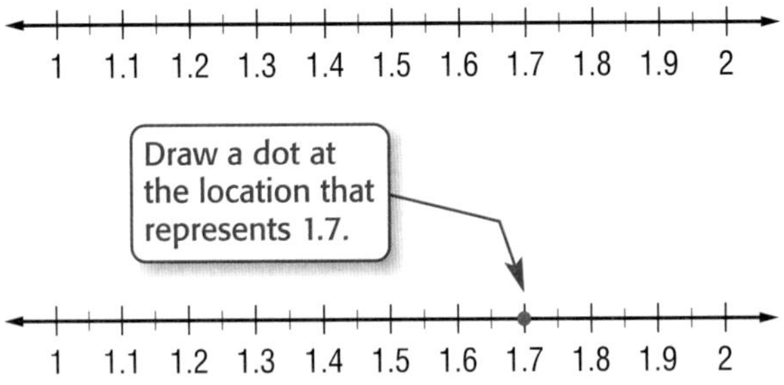

2 Graph 1.34 on a number line.

Since 1.34 is between 1.3 and 1.4, draw a number line from 1.3 to 1.4. Use increments of one hundredth since 1.34 is written to the hundredths place value.

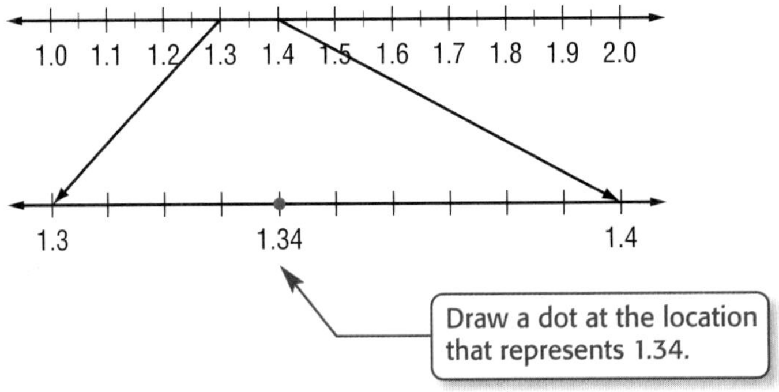

Online Personal Tutor at ca.gr5math.com

EXAMPLE Identify Decimals on a Number Line

3 Write the letter that represents 4.65 on the number line.

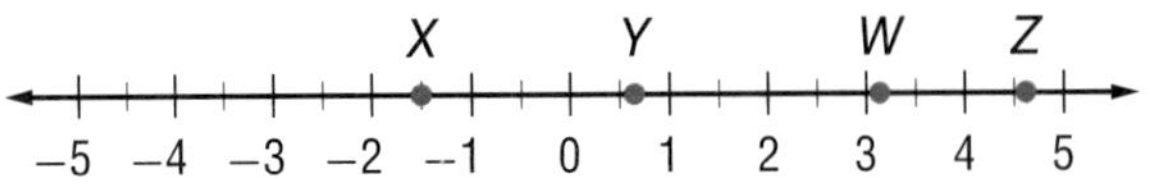

4.65 is greater than 4 and less than 5. The only letter in the interval between 4 and 5 is *Z*. So, 4.65 is represented by *Z* on the number line.

Remember

The number line in Example 3 is drawn using increments of one-half. So, you can check your answer by noting that *Z* is greater than 4.5.

CHECK What You Know

Graph each decimal in the approximate position on a number line. See Examples 1, 2 (p. 132)

1. 3.9 **2.** 1.1 **3.** 6.72 **4.** −0.5

5. A bottle of soda contains 1.25 pints. Graph this decimal on a number line.

Write the letter that represents each decimal on the number line at the right. See Example 3 (p. 132)

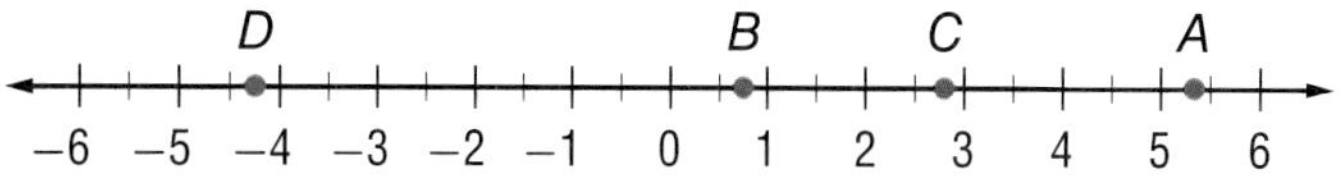

6. 0.8 **7.** 2.8 **8.** −4.25 **9.** 5.32

10. Talk About It Refer to Example 3. Which letter represents −1.5 on the number line? Explain your reasoning.

Practice and Problem Solving

EXTRA PRACTICE See page 660.

Graph each decimal in the approximate position on a number line. See Examples 1, 2 (p. 132)

11. 0.4 **12.** 0.9 **13.** 10.2 **14.** 6.8

15. 7.17 **16.** 3.56 **17.** −7.25 **18.** −5.75

19. The world's smallest vegetable is the snow pea. It measures about 0.25 inch in diameter. Graph this decimal on a number line.

20. A state park has 19.8 miles of hiking and mountain biking trails. Another state park has 20.15 miles of hiking and mountain biking trails. Graph these decimals on a number line.

Write the letter that represents each decimal on the number line below. See Example 3 (p. 132)

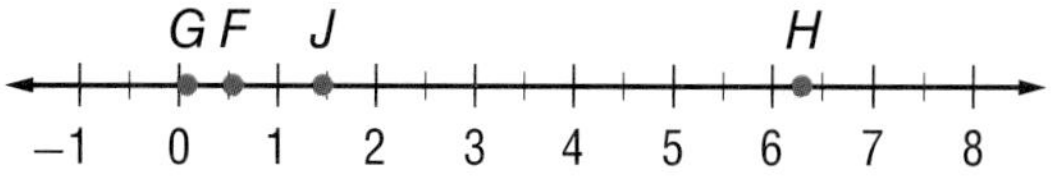

21. 0.6 **22.** 0.1 **23.** 6.32 **24.** 1.46

Write the letter that represents each decimal on the number line below. See Example 3 (p. 132)

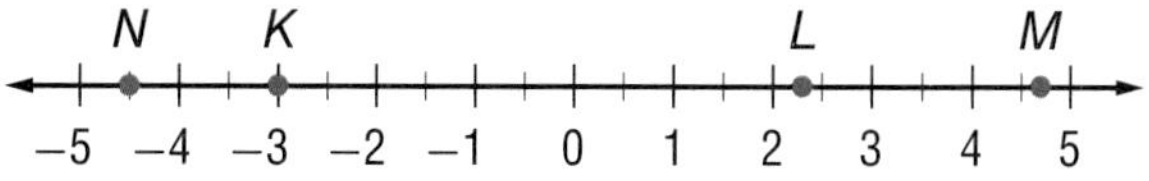

25. 4.7 **26.** 2.3 **27.** −3.0 **28.** −4.5

Write the decimal that represents each letter on the number line below.

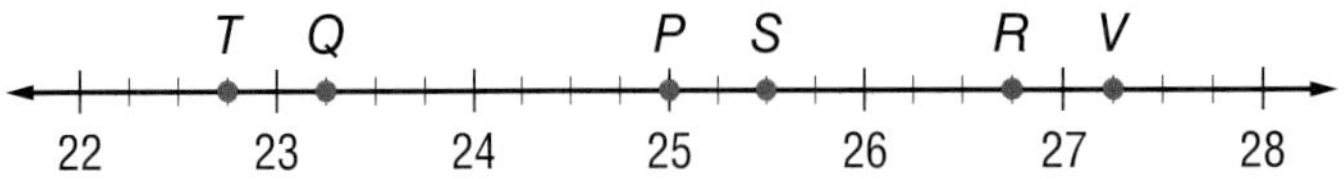

29. *P* **30.** *Q* **31.** *R* **32.** *S*

H.O.T. Problems

33. OPEN ENDED Formulate a decimal using each digit 5, 8, and 2 once. Then graph the decimal on a number line.

34. CHALLENGE The table shows the ingredients in an unpopped popcorn kernel. Place the decimals on the same number line.

35. WRITING IN ▶MATH Explain how to represent 25.4 on a number line.

Unpopped Popcorn Kernel

Ingredient	Grams
water	0.125
fat	0.03
protein	0.105
carbohydrates	0.71
mineral water	0.02

Source: popcornpopper.com

Standards Practice

36 Which point on the number line best represents 1.75?

A 

B 

C 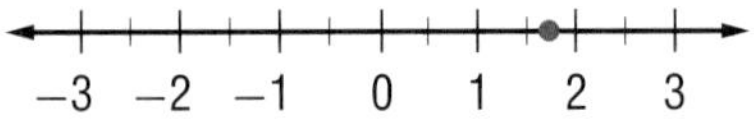

D 

Spiral Review

37. Jacksonville, Florida, is at sea level. Write this elevation as an integer. **(Lesson 2-10)**

38. Cheryl surveyed the students in her class to find their favorite type of music. What type of statistical display should Cheryl make to show the results? **(Lesson 2-9)**

39. Refugio charges $20 for each lawn he mows. Define a variable. Then write a function rule that relates the total charge to the number of lawns he mows. **(Lesson 1-6)**

Algebra Evaluate each expression if $m = 3$ and $n = 7$. (Lesson 1-5)

40. $m + 11$ **41.** $40n \div 2$ **42.** $25 - n$ **43.** $5 \times m - 15$

3-2 Comparing and Ordering Whole Numbers and Decimals

GET READY to Learn

The table lists the world's largest seas. Which sea has the smallest area? Explain.

Sea	Area (square km)
Bering	2,261,100
Caribbean	2,515,900
Mediterranean	2,509,960
Sea of Okhotsk	1,392,100
South China	2,974,600

Source: *Top Ten of Everything*

MAIN IDEA

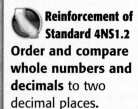

I will compare and order whole numbers and decimals.

Reinforcement of Standard 4NS1.2
Order and compare whole numbers and decimals to two decimal places.

New Vocabulary

equivalent decimals

Reading Math

$<$ **and** $>$ Recall that the symbol always points toward the lesser number.

To compare whole numbers, you can use place value or number lines.

EXAMPLE Compare Whole Numbers

1 **Refer to the table above. Use $>$ or $<$ to compare the Caribbean Sea's area with the Mediterranean Sea's area.**

One Way: Use place value.

Caribbean Sea:	2,515,900	Line up the digits at the ones place.
Mediterranean Sea:	2,509,960	Starting at the left, find the first place the digits differ. Compare the digits.

Since $1 > 0$, $2{,}515{,}900 > 2{,}509{,}960$.

Another Way: Use a number line.

Graph and then compare the numbers.

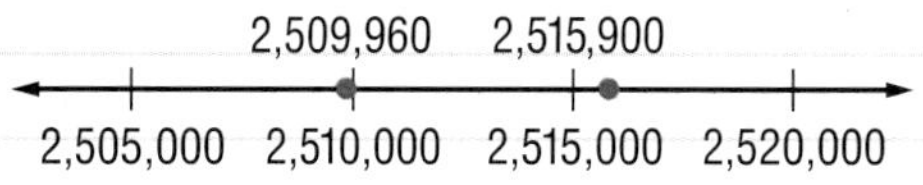

Numbers to the right are greater than numbers to the left.
So, $2{,}515{,}900 > 2{,}509{,}960$.

The Caribbean Sea has a greater area than the Mediterranean Sea.

EXAMPLE Compare Decimals

2 The table lists the top five finishers at a recent Olympic Games Men's Halfpipe. Use > or < to compare Danny Kass' score with Jarret Thomas' score.

Men's Halfpipe Results		
Snowboarders	**Country**	**Score**
Danny Kass	USA	42.5
Giacomo Kratter	Italy	42.0
Takaharu Nakai	Japan	40.7
Ross Powers	USA	46.1
Jarret Thomas	USA	42.1

Source: mountainzone.com

Remember

You can check the reasonableness of the order by using a number line.

Danny Kass: 42.**5** First, line up the decimal points.

Jarret Thomas: 42.**1** Then, starting at the left, find the first place the digits differ. Compare the digits.

Since 5 > 1, 42.5 > 42.1.
So, Danny Kass' score was higher than Jarret Thomas' score.

Online Personal Tutor at ca.gr5math.com

Decimals that name the same number are called **equivalent decimals**. They are graphed at the same place on a number line. Examples are 0.6 and 0.60.

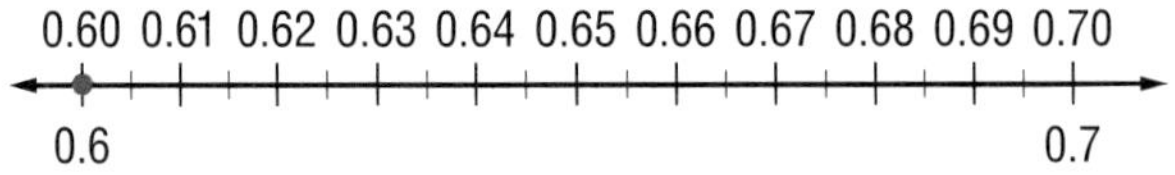

Vocabulary Link

Annex

Everyday Use a part added on to a building

Math Use to place zeros to the right of the last digit in a decimal

When you *annex*, or place zeros to the right of the last digit in a decimal, the value of the decimal does not change.

EXAMPLE Order Decimals

3 Order 15, 14.95, 15.8, and 15.01 from least to greatest.

First, line up the decimal points.		Next, annex zeros so all numbers have the same final place value.	Finally, compare and order using place value.
15	→	15.**00**	14.95
14.95	→	14.95	15.00
15.8	→	15.8**0**	15.01
15.01	→	15.01	15.80

The order from least to greatest is 14.95, 15, 15.01, and 15.8.

CHECK What You Know

Use >, <, or = to compare each pair of whole numbers.
See Example 1 (p. 135)

1. 745,017 ● 747,259

2. 623,581 ● 623,581

3. 5,491,478 ● 5,482,000

4. 12,817,001 ● 12,859,894

Use >, <, or = to compare each pair of decimals. See Example 2 (p. 136)

5. 0.4 ● 0.5

6. 0.38 ● 0.35

7. 2.7 ● 2.07

8. 25.5 ● 25.50

9. The five highest career batting averages in Major League (MLB) baseball are listed at the right. Order these averages from least to greatest.
See Example 3 (p. 136)

10. Talk About It — How are 2.05 and 2.55 alike? How are they different?

Practice and Problem Solving

EXTRA PRACTICE
See page 661.

Use >, <, or = to compare each pair of whole numbers. See Example 1 (p. 135)

11. 448,228 ● 448,251

12. 214,712 ● 215,001

13. 3,258,114 ● 3,242,000

14. 1,236,581 ● 1,131,004

15. 26,357,159 ● 26,357,159

16. 82,582,369 ● 82,582,369

17. The estimated dog population in Japan is 9,650,000 dogs. Russia has an estimated dog population of 9,600,000 dogs. Which country has the greater dog population?

18. If the production of oranges is 62,170,503 metric tons and the production of grapes is 62,150,308 metric tons, which fruit crop has the greater production?

Use >, <, or = to compare each pair of decimals. See Example 2 (p. 136)

19. 0.2 ● 2.0

20. 3.3 ● 3.30

21. 0.08 ● 0.8

22. 0.4 ● 0.004

24. 6.02 ● 6.20

24. 5.51 ● 5.15

25. 9.003 ● 9.030

26. 0.204 ● 0.214

27. 7.107 ● 7.011

28. 23.88 ● 23.880

29. 0.0624 ● 0.0264

30. 2.5634 ● 2.5364

31. In the 2004 Summer Olympics, Carly Patterson had a total score of 38.387 in the all-around gymnastics event. Svetlana Khorkina had a total score of 38.211 in the same event. Who had a higher score in this event?

32. In 1994, Sterling Marlin drove an average speed of 156.931 miles per hour to win the Daytona 500. In 2004, Dale Earnhardt Jr. won, driving an average of 156.345 miles per hour. Who was faster?

Order each set of decimals from least to greatest. See Example 3 (p. 136)

33. 16, 16.2, 16.02, 15.99

34. 44.5, 45.01, 44.11, 45

35. 5.545, 4.45, 4.9945, 5.6

36. 9.27, 9.6, 8.995, 9.0599

Order each set of decimals from greatest to least. See Example 3 (p. 136)

37. 2.1, 2.01, 2.11, 2.111

38. 7.66, 7.6, 7.666, 7.06

39. 32.32, 32.032, 32.302, 3.99

40. 57.68, 57.057, 57.507, 57.57

41. To keep track of the inventory at his store's warehouse, Akio must arrange items on shelves according to their stock numbers. Arrange the numbers in order from least to greatest.

Stock Number
321.53
321.539
321.5

42. The following table shows the amount of money Antoine spent on lunch each day this week. Order the amounts from least to greatest and then find the median amount he spent on lunch.

Day	Mon.	Tue.	Wed.	Thu.	Fri.
Amount Spent ($)	3.31	3.45	3.18	3.43	3.29

Real-World PROBLEM SOLVING

History **Use the table below that lists the number of popular votes for several presidents.**

Popular Votes		
President	**Year**	**Votes**
William J. Clinton	1996	47,401,185
Lyndon B. Johnson	1964	43,126,506
Richard M. Nixon	1972	47,165,234
Ronald W. Reagan	1980	43,899,248

Source: *Top Ten of Everything*

43. Which of these presidents had the greatest number of popular votes?

44. Which of these presidents had the least number of popular votes?

H.O.T. Problems

45. **REASONING** Explain why 0.4 is equivalent to 0.40.

46. **FIND THE ERROR** Daniel and Carlos are ordering 0.4, 0.5, and 0.49 from least to greatest. Who is correct? Explain your reasoning.

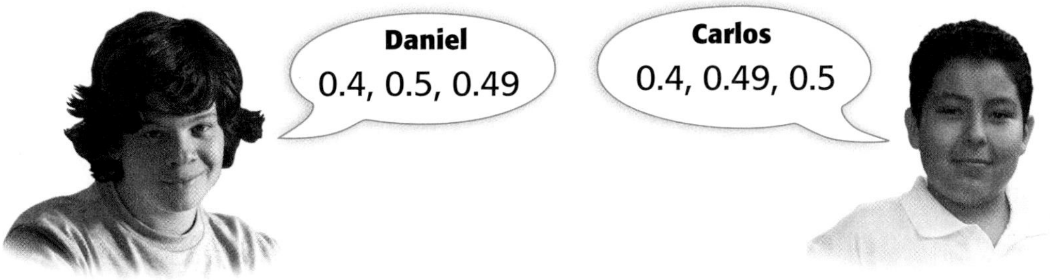

47. **CHALLENGE** Della has more money than Lindsey but less money than Nate. Camila has 10¢ more than Hector. The amounts are \$0.89, \$1.70, \$1.18, \$0.79, and \$1.07. How much money does each person have?

48. **WRITING IN MATH** Refer to the table in Exercise 49. Create a problem that involves comparing the times of two of the runners.

Standards Practice

49 The table shows the finishing times for four runners in a race. In what order did the runners cross the finish line?

Runner	Time (s)
Kara	14.31
Ariel	13.84
Mika	13.97
Nelia	13.79

A Kara, Ariel, Mika, Nelia

B Nelia, Mika, Ariel, Kara

C Mika, Nelia, Ariel, Kara

D Nelia, Ariel, Mika, Kara

50 If Cheyenne correctly marked 1.005, 0.981, 0.899, and 0.93 on a number line, which number was closest to zero?

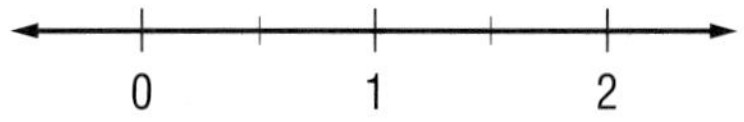

F 1.005

G 0.981

H 0.899

J 0.93

Spiral Review

51. The Andromeda Galaxy is 2.2 light years from Earth. Graph this decimal on a number line. **(Lesson 3-1)**

Graph each integer on a number line. (Lesson 2-10)

52. +3 **53.** −9 **54.** +2 **55.** −4

Decimal War

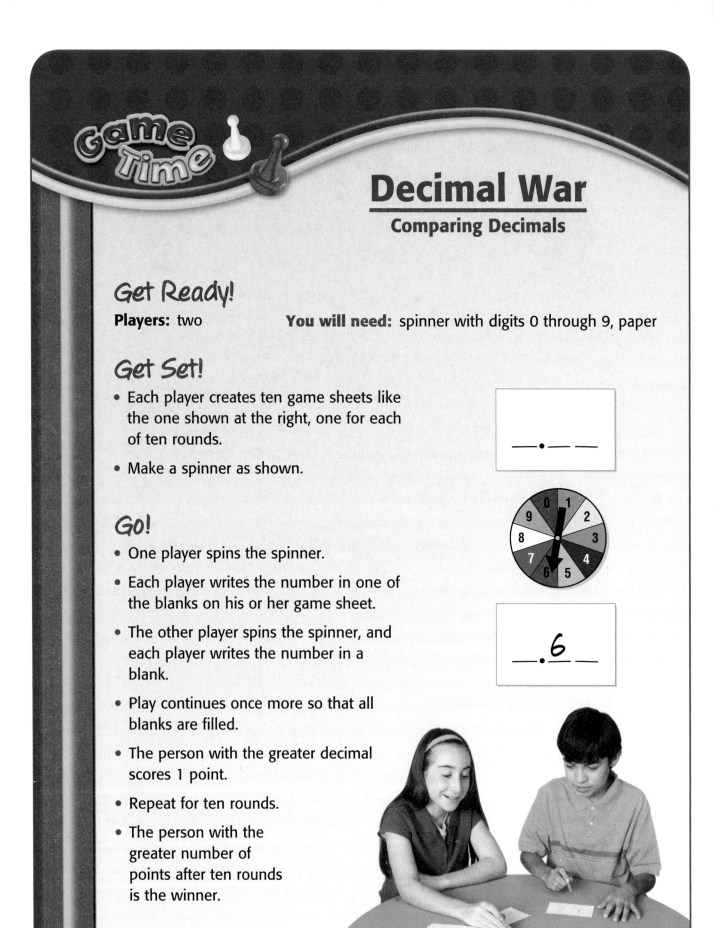

Comparing Decimals

Get Ready!

Players: two

You will need: spinner with digits 0 through 9, paper

Get Set!

- Each player creates ten game sheets like the one shown at the right, one for each of ten rounds.
- Make a spinner as shown.

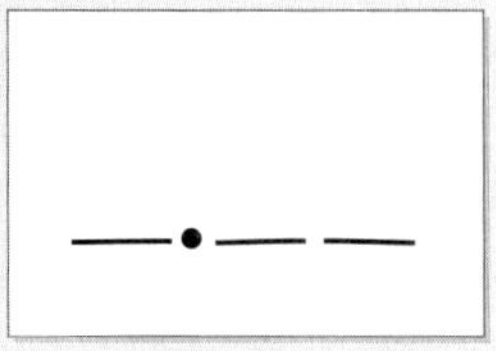

Go!

- One player spins the spinner.
- Each player writes the number in one of the blanks on his or her game sheet.
- The other player spins the spinner, and each player writes the number in a blank.
- Play continues once more so that all blanks are filled.
- The person with the greater decimal scores 1 point.
- Repeat for ten rounds.
- The person with the greater number of points after ten rounds is the winner.

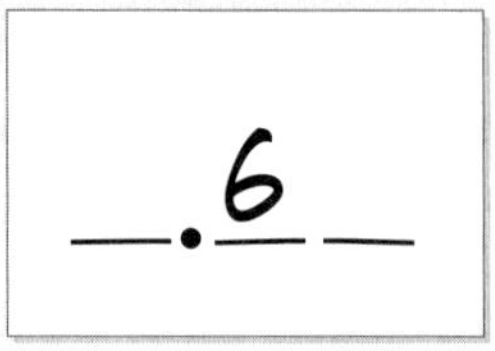

3-3 Rounding Whole Numbers and Decimals

GET READY to Learn

The number of points scored in the first round of the 2005–2006 NBA postseason is shown in the table. How could each number be rounded to the nearest hundred?

Player	Round 1 Points
LeBron James	214
Gilbert Arenas	204
Vince Carter	175

Source: nba.com

MAIN IDEA

I will round whole numbers and decimals.

Standard 5NS1.1 Estimate, **round,** and manipulate **very large (e.g., millions) and very small (e.g. thousandths) numbers.**

When rounding whole numbers, look at the digit to the right of the place value being rounded. If the digit is 4 or less, round down. If the digit is 5 or greater, round up.

EXAMPLE Round Whole Numbers

1 Round 3,741,954 to the nearest million.

Underline the digit to be rounded. In this case, the digit is in the millions place.

<u>3</u>,741,954

Then look at the digit to the right. Since the digit is 7, round up by adding 1 to the underlined digit. Then add zeros in the remaining place values.

On the number line at the right, 3,741,954 is closer to 4,000,000 than 3,000,000. To the nearest million, 3,741,954 rounds to 4,000,000.

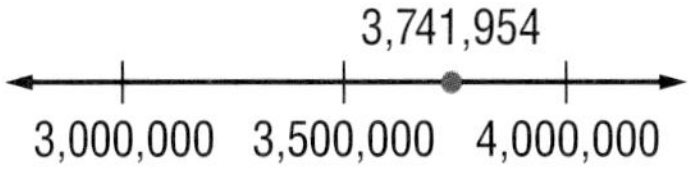

You can round decimals just as you round whole numbers.

KEY CONCEPT Round Decimals

To round a decimal, first underline the digit to be rounded. Then look at the digit to the right of the place being rounded.

- If the digit is 4 or less, the underlined digit remains the same.
- If the digit is 5 or greater, add 1 to the underlined digit.
- After rounding, drop all digits after the underlined digit.

Remember

Rounding to the nearest whole number means to round to the digit in the ones place.

EXAMPLES Round Decimals

2 Round 1.324 to the nearest whole number.

Underline the digit to be rounded. In this case, the digit is in the ones place. → 1̲.324 ← Then look at the digit to the right. Since 3 is less than 5, the digit 1 remains the same.

On the number line, 1.3 is closer to 1.0 than to 2.0. To the nearest whole number, 1.324 rounds to 1.

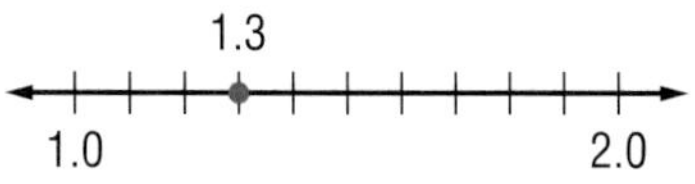

3 Round 99.96 to the nearest tenth.

Underline the digit to be rounded. In this case, the digit is in the tenths place. → 99.9̲6 ← Then look at the digit to the right. Since the digit is 6, add one to the underlined digit.

On the number line, 99.96 is closer to 100.0 than to 99.9. To the nearest tenth, 99.96 rounds to 100.0.

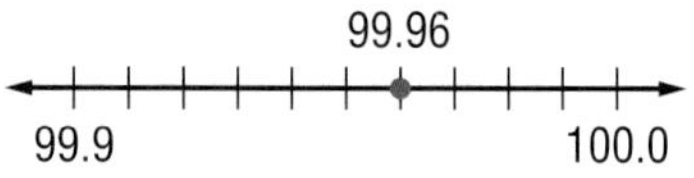

Real-World EXAMPLE

4 In a recent month, U.S. farmers received an average of $0.169 for each pound of peanuts they produced. To the nearest cent, how much did they receive for each pound?

There are 100 cents in a dollar. So, rounding to the nearest cent means to round to the nearest hundredth of a dollar.

Underline the digit in the hundredths place. → 0.16̲9 ← Then look at the digit to the right. The digit is greater than 5. So add one to the underlined digit.

To the nearest cent, the average price is $0.17.

Online Personal Tutor at ca.gr5math.com

CHECK What You Know

Round each whole number to the indicated place-value position.
See Example 1 (p. 141)

1. 9,561,210; million

2. 4,328,471; thousand

3. 36,793,182; ten million

4. 58,123,824; ten thousand

Round each decimal to the indicated place-value position.
See Examples 2, 3 (p. 142)

5. 0.329; tenths

6. 1.75; ones

7. 45.522; hundredths

8. 0.588; thousandths

9. The table shows the rate of acceleration due to gravity for a few of the planets. To the nearest tenth, what is the rate for each planet?
See Example 4 (p. 142)

Planet	Acceleration (m/s)
Jupiter	23.12
Saturn	8.96
Uranus	8.69
Mars	3.69

Source: *Science Scope*

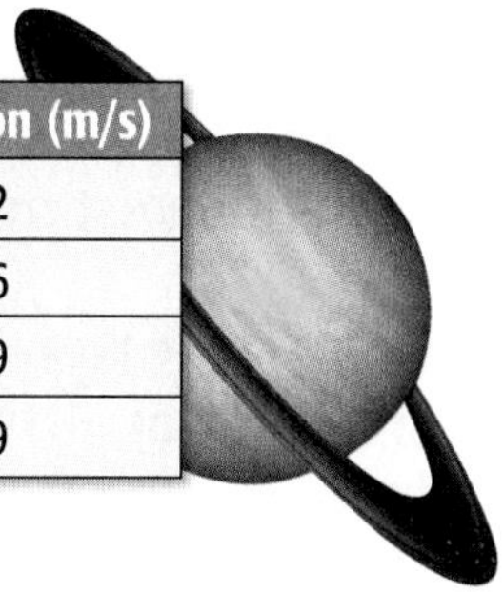

10. Talk About It Discuss why both 451 and 510 round to 500 when rounded to the nearest hundred.

Practice and Problem Solving

EXTRA PRACTICE
See page 661.

Round each whole number to the indicated place-value position. See Example 1 (p. 141)

11. 8,280,661; thousand

12. 4,961,758; thousand

13. 29,822,936; ten million

14. 13,299,872; ten million

15. 116,795,108; million

16. 899,568,363; million

17. In a recent year, the total amount of herring, sardines, and anchovies caught was 22,554,013 tons. Round 22,554,013 to the nearest ten million.

18. There are an estimated 5,310,00 hospital emergency room cases of fever per year. Round 5,310,000 to the nearest hundred thousand.

Round each decimal to the indicated place-value position.
See Examples 2, 3 (p. 142)

19. 0.445; tenths

20. 0.999; tenths

21. 5.68; ones

22. 10.49; ones

23. 0.499; hundredths

24. 0.458; hundredths

25. Each person in the United States eats an average of nearly 5.75 gallons of ice cream per year. Round 5.75 gallons to the nearest gallon.

26. In the U.S., there are 48.81 cell phones for every 100 people. Round 48.81 to the nearest whole number.

27. The table shows the average winning speeds in the Tour de France from 2000–2005. Will it help to round these average speeds before listing them in order from least to greatest? Explain.

Tour de France Average Winning Speeds		
Winner	**Year**	**Average Speed (km/h)**
Lance Armstrong	2005	41.654
Lance Armstrong	2004	40.553
Lance Armstrong	2003	40.94
Lance Armstrong	2002	39.93
Lance Armstrong	2001	40.02
Lance Armstrong	2000	38.57

Source: torelli.com

28. The price of a 12-pack of soda is $4.39. How much is this to the nearest dollar?

A calculator will often show the results of a calculation with a very long decimal. Round each of the numbers from a calculator display to the nearest thousandth.

29. .2491666667

30. 1054.677828

31. 21.25103904

Round each decimal to the indicated place-value position.

32. 9.56303; hundredths

33. 988.08055; thousandths

34. 87.092; tens

35. 1,567.893; ten-thousandths

Real-World PROBLEM SOLVING

Geography **Use the table below that lists areas of the five largest countries in the world.**

Five Largest Countries		
Country	**Area (square miles)**	**Area (square kilometers)**
Russia	6,592,850	17,075,400
Canada	3,855,103	9,984,670
China	3,600,948	9,326,411
United States	3,539,245	9,166,601
Brazil	3,265,077	8,456,511

Source: *Top Ten of Everything*

36. Find the area of Canada to the nearest thousand square miles.

37. Compare the area of China and the area of the United States when rounded to the nearest million square kilometers.

H.O.T. Problems

38. **OPEN ENDED** Select three different decimals that round to 10.0 when rounded to the nearest tenth.

39. **Which One Doesn't Belong?** Identify the decimal that does not belong with the other three. Explain your reasoning.

34.62   34.59   34.49   34.56

40. **CHALLENGE** A number rounded to the nearest tenth is 6.1. The same number rounded to the nearest hundredth is 6.08 and rounded to the nearest thousandth is 6.083. Draw a conclusion as to what the original number could be.

41. **WRITING IN ▶MATH** Draw a number line to show why 3.47 rounded to the nearest tenth is 3.5. Write a sentence explaining your reasoning.

Standards Practice

42 The atomic masses of certain elements are given in the table.

Element	Atomic Masses
Sodium	22.9898
Neon	20.180
Magnesium	24.305

Source: webelements.com

What is the atomic mass of sodium to the nearest ten?

A 20

B 22.99

C 23.0

D 23.1

43 The County of Los Angeles Public Library contains 8,796,269 books. What is this value rounded to the nearest thousand?

F 8,800,000

G 8,797,000

H 8,796,000

J 8,795,000

Spiral Review

Use >, <, or = to compare each pair of decimals. (Lesson 3-2)

44. 8.64 ● 8.065

45. 2.5038 ● 25.083

46. 12.004 ● 12.042

47. Graph 32.5 on a number line. (Lesson 3-1)

48. Admission to the San Diego Zoo is $21 for adults and $14 for children. Define variables and write an expression to find the total cost of 2 adult tickets and 3 children's tickets. Then, find the value of the expression. (Lesson 1-3)

3-4 Problem-Solving Strategy

MAIN IDEA I will solve problems by using logical reasoning.

Standard 5MR2.4 Express the solution clearly and logically by using the appropriate mathematical notation and terms and **clear language;** support solutions with evidence in both verbal and symbolic work. **Standard 5MG1.4** Differentiate between, and **use appropriate units of measures for, two-** and three-**dimensional objects** (i.e., find the perimeter, area, volume).

Mora, Sam, Aisha, and Jamal each have a different colored notebook (blue, red, purple, and green). Use the clues to determine which person owns each notebook.

1. Sam and the girl with the green notebook are in the same class.
2. The purple notebook is owned by a girl.
3. Jamal and the person with the red notebook eat lunch together.
4. Mora is not in the same class as Sam.

Understand

What facts do you know?

You know the four clues that are listed above.

What do you need to find?

Which person owns each notebook?

Plan

Use logical reasoning to find which person owns each notebook. Make a table to help sort out the information.

Solve

Place an "X" in each box that cannot be true.

	Blue	Red	Purple	Green
Mora	X	X	yes	X
Sam	X	yes	X	X
Aisha	X	X	X	yes
Jamal	yes	X	X	X

- Clue 3 shows that Jamal does not own the red notebook.
- Clues 1 and 2 show that girls own the green and purple notebooks and the boys own the blue and red notebooks.
- Clue 4 shows that Mora is not in the same class as Sam, so she does not own the green notebook.

So, Mora owns the purple notebook, Sam owns the red notebook, Aisha owns the green notebook, and Jamal owns the blue notebook.

Check

Look back. Reread the clues to see if the answers that you determined match the clues. Since all of the answers match the clues, the answers are reasonable.

ANALYZE the Strategy

Refer to the problem on the previous page.

1. If you did not know that a girl owned the purple notebook, would it be possible to determine the owners of each notebook? Explain your reasoning.

2. Suppose Clue 4 is changed so that Aisha is not in the same class as Sam. Who owns which notebook?

3. If the area of a garden is 25 square feet, and the length and width are whole numbers, is it logical to say the garden is in the shape of a square? Explain your reasoning.

4. Explain when to use the *logical reasoning* strategy to solve a problem.

PRACTICE the Strategy

EXTRA PRACTICE
See page 661.

Solve. Use the *logical reasoning* strategy.

5. Xavier is thinking of a number. It is 22 less than the number Jackie wrote on her paper. The sum of the two numbers is 96. What number did Jackie write on the paper?

6. Set up 12 toothpicks as shown below. Move 3 toothpicks so that you form 4 squares.

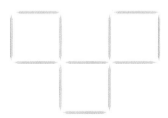

7. Charlotte, Ming, and Alexis are friends with three different professions: scientist, athlete, and doctor. Charlotte does not like sports. Ming is not the doctor or the athlete. Alexis likes to run. Who is the doctor?

8. Timothy, Connor, and Marcia are standing in line. Timothy is not last in line. Connor is in front of the tallest person in line. Marcia is standing behind Timothy. List the students in order from first to last.

9. Dolores has $1.25 in change. She has twice as many dimes as pennies, and the number of nickels is one less than the number of pennies. How many dimes, nickels, and pennies does she have?

10. There are 4 more girls in Mrs. Chang's class than Mr. Blackwell's class. Five girls moved from Mrs. Chang's class to Mr. Blackwell's class. Now there are twice as many girls in Mr. Blackwell's class as there are in Mrs. Chang's. How many girls were in Mr. Blackwell's class to begin with?

11. Thomas is making a series of figures out of pennies.

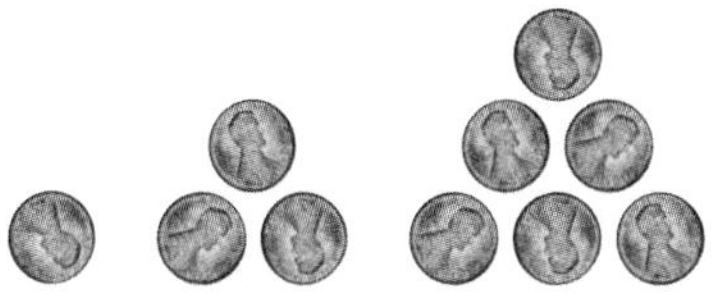

If he continues making the figures, how many pennies will be in the sixth figure?

12. **WRITING IN MATH** Refer to Exercise 7. How did you use *logical reasoning* to determine that Alexis is not the doctor?

Mid-Chapter Check

CHAPTER 3

Lessons 3-1 through 3-4

Write the letter that represents each decimal on the number line. **(Lesson 3-1)**

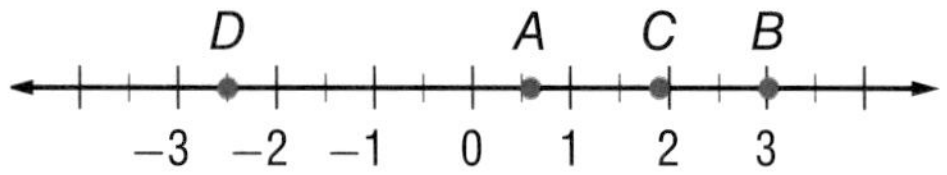

1. 1.9 **2.** 3.01 **3.** 0.6 **4.** −2.5

Graph each decimal in the approximate position on a number line. **(Lesson 3-1)**

5. 10.4 **6.** 3.72 **7.** −12.25

8. Bianca's speed while cross-country skiing was 2.8 miles per hour. Graph this decimal on a number line. **(Lesson 3-1)**

Use >, <, or = to compare each pair of numbers. **(Lesson 3-2)**

9. 632,320 ● 632,020

10. 2,150,012 ● 2,150,012

11. 0.06 ● 0.6

12. 8.04 ● 8.0004

13. Refer to the table. Which animal is shorter? **(Lesson 3-2)**

Animal	Length (inches)
Brazilian Frog	0.33
Dwarf Goby Fish	0.30

Source: *The World Almanac for Kids*

Order each set of decimals from least to greatest. **(Lesson 3-2)**

14. 8.2, 8.02, 8.025, 8.225

15. 0.101, 0.0101, 0.011, 1.00001

16. 0.002, 0.09, 0.2, 0.19

17. **STANDARDS PRACTICE** The finish times for runners are shown in the table. Order the times from least to greatest. **(Lesson 3-2)**

Runner	Finish Time (s)
1	32.02
2	31.95
3	32.2004
4	32.0029

A 32.2004, 32.02, 32.0029, 31.95

B 32.02, 32.0029, 32.2004, 31.95

C 31.95, 32.0029, 32.02, 32.2004

D 31.95, 32.2004, 32.0029, 32.02

18. **STANDARDS PRACTICE** The number of births in the United States in a recent year was 4,181,681. What is this number rounded to the nearest ten thousand? **(Lesson 3-3)**

F 4,180,000 **H** 4,182,000

G 4,181,000 **J** 4,190,000

Round each number to the indicated place-value position. **(Lesson 3-3)**

19. 2,381,410; million

20. 78,457,752; hundred

21. 0.236; tenths

22. 10.0879; thousandths

23. **WRITING IN MATH** Cassie is thinking of a decimal between 45 and 46. It contains three digits, and the sum of the digits is 12. What is the decimal? Explain. **(Lesson 3-4)**

3-5 Estimating Sums and Differences

GET READY to Learn

The graph shows about how many passengers travel through the busiest United States airports. About how many people travel through Dallas-Fort Worth and Los Angeles?

MAIN IDEA

I will estimate sums and differences of decimals.

Standard 5NS1.1 **Estimate,** round, and manipulate very large (e.g., millions) and **very small (e.g. thousandths) numbers.**

New Vocabulary

clustering

front-end estimation

To find *about* how many more people travel through these cities, you can estimate. One advantage of estimating is that the numbers are easier to compute. The answer is also close to the exact solution.

EXAMPLES Estimate with Large Numbers

1 Estimate the total number of passengers that travel through Dallas-Fort Worth and Los Angeles.

Round each number to the nearest ten for easier adding.

$$\begin{array}{rcr} 27.746 & \rightarrow & 30 \\ +\ 22.939 & \rightarrow & +\ 20 \\ \hline & & 50 \end{array}$$

27.746 rounds to 30.
22.939 rounds to 20.

About 50 million passengers travel through these two airports.

2 Estimate how many more passengers travel through Hartsfield-Atlanta than through Chicago O'Hare.

$$\begin{array}{rcr} 41.596 & \rightarrow & 40 \\ -\ 34.529 & \rightarrow & -\ 30 \\ \hline & & 10 \end{array}$$

41.596 rounds to 40.
34.529 rounds to 30.

About 10 million more passengers travel through Hartsfield-Atlanta.

Remember

There is no one correct answer when estimating. To estimate means to find an approximate value. However, reasonableness is important.

When estimating a sum in which all of the addends are close to the same number, you can use **clustering**.

EXAMPLE Estimate with Small Numbers

3 Estimate 0.566 + 1.003 + 0.782 using clustering.

The addends are clustered around 1. Round each decimal to 1.

$$\begin{array}{rcr} 0.566 & \rightarrow & 1 \\ 1.003 & \rightarrow & 1 \\ \underline{+\ 0.782} & \rightarrow & \underline{+\ 1} \\ & & 3 \end{array}$$

Using clustering, 0.566 + 1.003 + 0.782 is about 3.

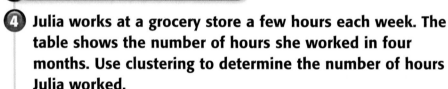

Real-World EXAMPLE

4 Julia works at a grocery store a few hours each week. The table shows the number of hours she worked in four months. Use clustering to determine the number of hours Julia worked.

Julia's Hours	
Month	**Hours Worked**
May	72.50
June	68.50
July	69.75
August	71.75

Remember

Clustering is good for problems in which the addends are close together.

The addends are clustered around 70. Round each decimal to 70.

72.50 → 70

68.50 → 70

69.75 → 70

71.75 → 70

Multiplication is repeated addition. So, a good estimate of the number of hours Julia worked in the four months is 4 × 70, or 280.

Online Personal Tutor at ca.gr5math.com

Another type of estimation is front-end estimation. When you use **front-end estimation**, add or subtract the values of the digits in the front place or left-most place-value. Front-end estimation usually gives a sum that is less than the actual sum.

EXAMPLE Use Front-End Estimation

5 **Estimate 34.6 + 55.3 using front-end estimation.**

$$\begin{array}{rcr} 34.6 & \rightarrow & 30.0 \\ +\ 55.3 & \rightarrow & +\ 50.0 \\ \hline & & 80.0 \end{array}$$

Add the leftmost digits.

Using front-end estimation, 34.6 + 55.3 is about 80.0.

CONCEPT Summary — Estimation Methods

Rounding	Estimate by rounding each decimal to the nearest whole number. Then it is easy for you to add or subtract mentally.
Clustering	Estimate by rounding a group of addends close to the same number before adding.
Front-End Estimation	Estimate by adding or subtracting the values of the digits in the leftmost place value.

CHECK What You Know

Estimate each sum using rounding. See Example 1 (p. 149)

1. 0.365 + 0.834

2. 15.24 + 32.10

Estimate each difference using rounding. See Example 2 (p. 149)

3. 4.44 – 2.79

4. 57.05 – 23.82

Estimate using clustering. See Example 3 (p. 150)

5. 5.32 + 4.78 + 5.42

6. 0.951 + 0.793 + 1.026

7. The amount Omar was charged for four phone calls is listed in the table. Estimate the total amount of the phone calls.

Phone Calls				
Minutes	8.7	9.1	9.0	8.9
Amount ($)	1.04	1.09	1.08	1.07

Estimate using front-end estimation. See Example 5 (p. 151)

8. 179.4 + 513.8

9. $442.50 – $126.73

10. Talk About It: Explain the advantages and disadvantages of finding approximate solutions.

Practice and Problem Solving

EXTRA PRACTICE
See page 662.

Estimate using rounding. See Examples 1, 2 (p. 149)

11. 49.59 + 16.22 **12.** 33.15 + 86.85 **13.** 0.575 − 0.197

14. 62.614 − 13.057 **15.** 2.33 + 4.88 + 5.5 **16.** 9.05 + 1.42 + 6.79

17. Sandra bought a pair of shoes for $24.75 and a dress for $46.55. About how much did Sandra spend on the shoes and dress?

18. Two classes are recycling paper. If one class earns $16.52 and a second class earns $28.80, about how much more did the second class earn?

Estimate using clustering. See Example 3 (p. 150)

19. 6.99 + 6.59 + 7.02 + 7.44 **20.** $3.33 + $3.45 + $2.78 + $2.99

21. 5.45 + 5.3948 + 4.7999 **22.** $55.49 + $54.99 + $55.33

23. 10.33 + 10.45 + 10.89 + 9.79 **24.** 0.998 + 1.002 + 0.995 + 0.812

Estimate using front-end estimation. See Example 5 (p. 151)

25. 75.45 − 15.23 **26.** 27.9 − 12.5 **27.** 28.65 + 71.53

28. 124.8 + 264.9 **29.** $315.65 + $130.42 **30.** $50.96 + $19.28

31. The Flathead rail tunnel in Montana is 7.78 miles long. Colorado's Moffat rail tunnel is 6.21 miles long. About how much longer is the Flathead rail tunnel than the Moffat rail tunnel using rounding? If you use front-end estimation, would the estimate be the same? Why or why not?

Real-World PROBLEM SOLVING

Sports **For Exercises 32 and 33, use the graph.**

32. Use clustering to estimate the mean ticket cost for one Houston Astros game, Atlanta Braves game, and Texas Rangers game.

33. If the average price for a soda and hot dog at a New York Yankees game is $5.75, about how much would a family pay for four tickets, four sodas and four hot dogs?

2004 Major League Baseball Ticket Prices

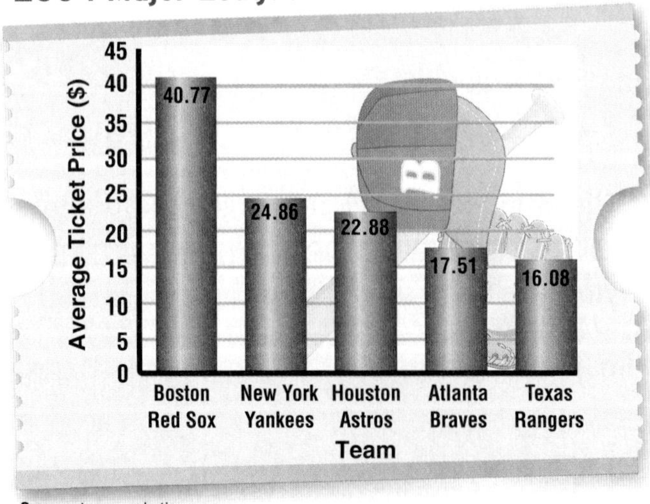

Source: teammarketing.com

H.O.T. Problems

34. **NUMBER SENSE** Explain how you know that the sum of 5.4, 6.3, and 9.6 is greater than 20.

35. **CHALLENGE** Five same-priced items are purchased. Based on rounding, the estimate of the total was $15. Decide what the maximum and minimum price of the item could be.

36. **WRITING IN ▸MATH** Explain how you would estimate 1.843 − 0.328.

Standards Practice

37 A school lunch menu is shown.

Monday
Pizza $1.10
Soda $0.85
Salad $2.65
Milk $0.75
Taco $1.30
Fruit $1.15

Estimate how much money you will need to buy a slice of pizza, a taco, and a soda.

A A little less than $2

B A little more than $2

C A little more than $3

D A little less than $3

38 Refer to the table.

Year	Acres Burned in Wildfires (millions)
2004	6.8
2000	8.4
1996	6.7
1988	7.4
1969	6.7

Source: nifc.gov

Which is the best estimate for the total number of acres of land burned by wildfires?

F 25 million

G 35 million

H 45 million

J 55 million

Spiral Review

39. Trina, Rachelle, and Isabel ate lunch together. They each had something different. One had a chicken sandwich, one had soup, and one had a peanut butter sandwich. Trina did not have bread with her meal. Rachelle is allergic to peanuts. Isabel did not use utensils. What did Rachelle eat? **(Lesson 3-4)**

40. Washington, D.C., has an average annual precipitation of 35.86 inches. Round this amount to the nearest tenth. **(Lesson 3-3)**

Algebra Find the value of the variable that makes each equation true. **(Lesson 1-10)**

41. $20 \times 44 = (20 \times 40) + (x \times 4)$

42. $5 \times 63 = (y \times 60) + (5 \times 3)$

43. $8 \times 57 = (8 \times 50) + (8 \times k)$

44. $9 \times 71 = (9 \times m) + (9 \times 1)$

3-6 Problem-Solving Investigation

MAIN IDEA I will solve problems by estimating.

Standard 5MR2.6 **Make precise calculations** and check the validity of the results from the context of the problem.
Standard 5NS1.1 **Estimate,** round, and manipulate **very large** and very small **numbers.**

P.S.I. TEAM +

PING: My family drove to North Carolina for our vacation. We drove 356.8 miles the first day, 305.2 miles the second day, and 283.1 miles the third day. We are following the same route to return home.

YOUR MISSION: Find about how far Ping's family traveled.

Understand	You know that the family drove 356.8 miles, 305.2 miles, and 283.1 miles. You need to find about how far Ping's family traveled.
Plan	Since you don't need an exact answer, you can estimate the number of miles traveled each day. Add the total for the three days and double that to account for the trip to North Carolina and then back home.
Solve	Day One → 356.8 → **400** Day Two → 305.2 → **300** Day Three → 283.1 → **+ 300** **1,000** The one-way trip was about 1,000 miles. The return trip was another 1,000 miles, for a total of 2,000 miles.
Check	Use clustering. The miles are clustered around 300. $6 \times 300 = 1{,}800$ Since $1{,}800 \approx 2{,}000$, a total of 2,000 is reasonable.

Mixed Problem Solving

EXTRA PRACTICE
See page 662.

For each problem, determine whether you need an estimate or an exact answer. Then solve it.

PROBLEM-SOLVING SKILLS
- Use the four-step plan.
- Use estimation.

1. The table shows how much time Isabelle spent working on her homework last week.

Day	Time
Monday	1 h 50 min
Tuesday	1 h 10 min
Wednesday	2 h 40 min
Thursday	2 h 5 min
Friday	45 min

About how much time did she spend working on homework last week?

2. A total of 10 sixth-grade teachers donated $25.75 each to the school orchestra. About how much money did they donate in all?

3. Mrs. Perez wants to save an average of $150 per week over six weeks. Use the graph to find how much she must save during the sixth week to meet her goal.

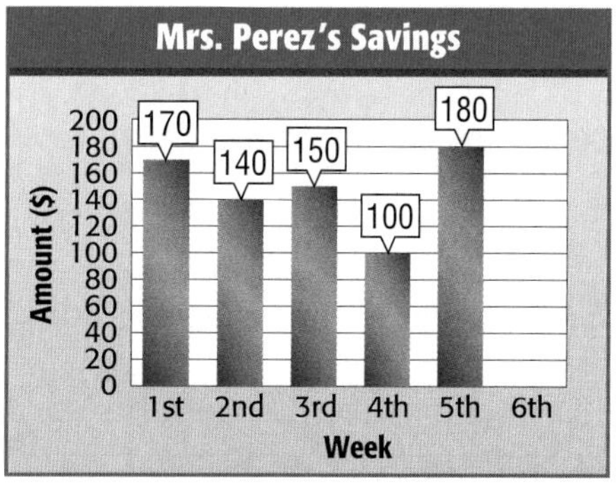

4. Ruby's lunch cost $3.64. She gave the cashier $10. How much change should Ruby receive?

5. Paolo has 11 fish in an aquarium that holds 20 gallons of water. Joanna has 5 fish in an aquarium that holds 5 gallons of water. How much larger is Paolo's aquarium than Joanna's?

6. About 1.2 million people live in Dallas, and about 2.9 million people live in Chicago. About how many more people live in Chicago than Dallas?

7. There are 33,952,003 elementary students and 13,735,868 secondary students enrolled in public schools. About how many students are enrolled in public schools?

8. Which two trimesters had the greatest difference in the number of students on the honor roll?

5th Grade Honor Roll Students	
1st trimester	40
2nd trimester	37
3rd trimester	31

9. Emma is thinking of three numbers that have a sum of 21. Find three different sets of numbers.

10. **WRITING IN ►MATH** Write a problem that you can solve by using estimation. Solve the problem. Explain an advantage of using estimation to solve your problem.

Explore

Math Lab for 3-7

Adding and Subtracting Decimals Using Models

MAIN IDEA

I will use models to add and subtract decimals.

Standard 5MR2.3 Use a variety of methods, such as words, numbers, symbols, charts, graphs, tables, diagrams, and **models, to explain mathematical reasoning.**

Standard 5NS2.1 Add, subtract, multiply, and divide **with decimals;** add with negative integers; subtract positive integers from negative integers; and verify the reasonableness of results.

Ones (1)	Tenths (0.1)	Hundredths (0.01)
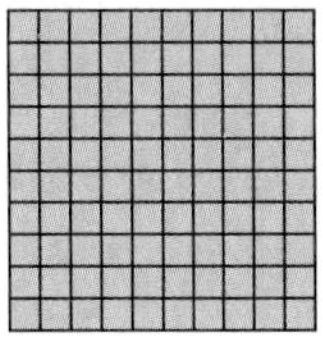	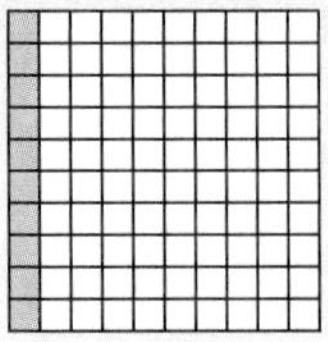	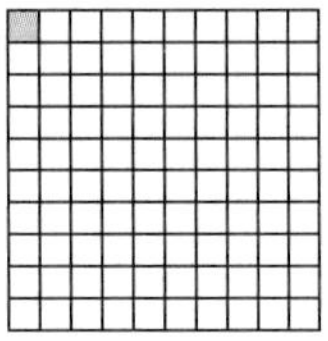
One whole 10-by-10 grid represents 1 or 1.0.	Each row or column represents one tenth or 0.1.	Each square represents one hundredth or 0.01.

ACTIVITIES Concepts in Motion Animation ca.gr5math.com

1 **Find 0.16 + 0.77 using decimal models.**

Step 1 Shade 0.16 green.

Step 2 Shade 0.77 blue. The sum is the total shaded area.

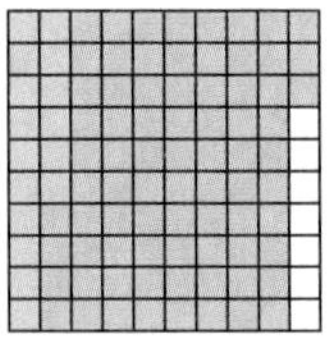

So, 0.16 + 0.77 = 0.93.

2 **Find 0.52 − 0.08 using decimal models.**

Step 1 Shade 0.52 green.

Step 2 Cross out 0.08 from the shaded area. The difference is the amount that remains.

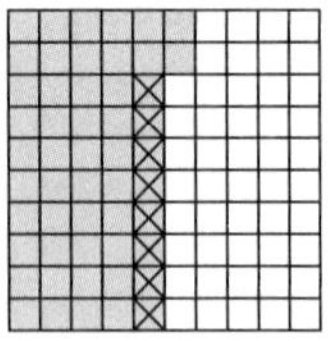

So, 0.52 − 0.08 = 0.44.

Analyze the Results

Find each sum or difference using decimal models.

1. 0.14 + 0.67 **2.** 0.35 + 0.42 **3.** 0.03 + 0.07

4. 0.75 − 0.36 **5.** 0.68 − 0.27 **6.** 0.88 − 0.49

7. Write a rule you can use to add or subtract decimals without using models.

3-7 Adding and Subtracting Decimals

GET READY to Learn

The table shows the top five consumers of carbonated soft drinks. Estimate the sum of the top two countries. How could you find the exact sum?

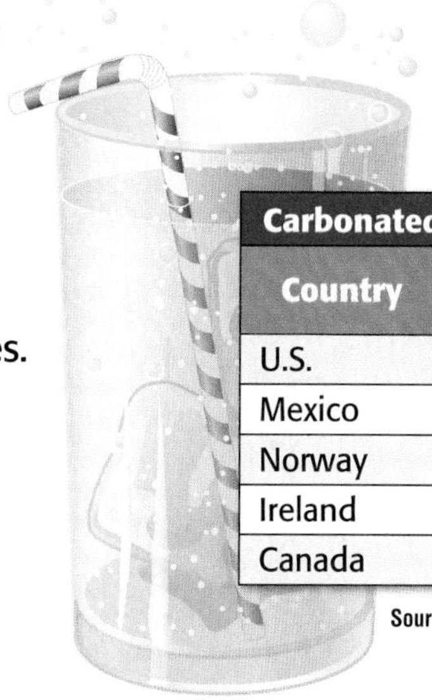

Carbonated Soft Drink Consumers	
Country	**Consumption Per Capita (gallons)**
U.S.	51.7
Mexico	33.3
Norway	32.2
Ireland	32.0
Canada	30.9

Source: Top 10 of Everything

MAIN IDEA

I will add and subtract decimals.

Standard 5NS2.1 Add, subtract, multiply, and divide **with decimals;** add with negative integers; subtract positive integers from negative integers; **and verify the reasonableness of results.**

To add or subtract decimals, add or subtract digits in the same place-value position. Line up the decimal points before you add or subtract.

Reading Math

Approximation Symbol
The symbol ≈ is read *is approximately equal to* or *is about equal to.*

EXAMPLE Add Decimals

1 Find the sum of 23.1 and 5.8.

Estimate $23.1 + 5.8 \approx 23 + 6$ or 29

$$\begin{array}{r} 23.1 \\ +\ 5.8 \\ \hline 28.9 \end{array}$$

23.1 Line up the decimal points.

28.9 Add as with whole numbers.

So, $23.1 + 5.8 = 28.9$. **Check for Reasonableness** $28.9 \approx 29$ ✓

EXAMPLE Subtract Decimals

2 Find 5.774 − 2.371.

Estimate $5.774 - 2.371 \approx 6 - 2$ or 4

$$\begin{array}{r} 5.774 \\ -\ 2.371 \\ \hline 3.403 \end{array}$$

5.774 Line up the decimal points.

3.403 Subtract as with whole numbers.

So, $5.774 - 2.371 = 3.403$. **Check for Reasonableness** $3.403 \approx 4$ ✓

Sometimes it is necessary to annex zeros before you subtract.

> **Remember**
>
> You can also check your answer in Example 3 by adding 1.219 and 4.781.

EXAMPLES Annex Zeros

3 Find 6 − 4.781.

Estimate $6 - 4.781 \approx 6 - 5$ or 1

$$\begin{array}{r} 6.000 \\ -\ 4.781 \\ \hline 1.219 \end{array}$$

Annex zeros so that both numbers have the same place value.
Subtract as with whole numbers.

So, $6 - 4.781 = 1.219$.

Check for Reasonableness $1.219 \approx 1$ ✓

4 Find 23 − 4.216.

Estimate $23 - 4.216 \approx 23 - 4$ or 19

$$\begin{array}{r} 23.000 \\ -\ 4.216 \\ \hline 18.784 \end{array}$$

Annex zeros so that both numbers have the same place value.
Subtract as with whole numbers.

So, $23 - 4.216 = 18.784$.

Check for Reasonableness $18.784 \approx 19$ ✓

Real-World EXAMPLE

5 The table shows the top three times for the women's 100-meter butterfly event in the 2004 Summer Olympics. What is the difference between Petria Thomas' time and Inge de Bruijn's time?

Women's 100-Meter Butterfly

Swimmer	Country	Time (s)
Petria Thomas	Australia	57.72
Otylia Jedrzejczak	Poland	57.84
Inge de Bruijn	Netherlands	57.99

Source: athens2004.com

Estimate $57.99 - 57.72 \approx 58 - 58$ or 0

$$\begin{array}{r} 57.99 \\ -\ 57.72 \\ \hline 0.27 \end{array}$$

Line up the decimal points.
Subtract as with whole numbers.

So, the difference between Petria Thomas' time and Inge de Bruijn's time is 0.27 second.

Check for Reasonableness $0.27 \approx 0$ ✓

Online **Personal Tutor at** ca.gr5math.com

You can also use evaluate algebraic expressions using decimal values.

EXAMPLE **Evaluate an Expression**

6 Algebra Evaluate $x + y$ if $x = 2.85$ and $y = 17.975$.

$x + y = 2.85 + 17.975$ Replace x with 2.85 and y with 17.975.

Estimate $2.85 + 17.975 \approx 3 + 18$ or 21

$$\begin{array}{r} 2.580 \\ +\ 17.975 \\ \hline 20.825 \end{array}$$

2.580 — Line up the decimal points. Annex a zero.

20.825 — Add as with whole numbers.

The value of the expression is 20.825.

Check for Reasonableness $20.825 \approx 21$ ✓

CHECK What You Know

Find each sum. See Example 1 (p. 157)

1. $5.516 + 3.245$ **2.** $72.489 + 12.503$ **3.** $9 + 29.34$

Find each difference. See Example 2 (p. 157)

4. $0.40 - 0.20$ **5.** $9.672 - 2.354$ **6.** $42.287 - 1.527$

Find each difference. See Examples 3, 4 (p. 158)

7. $8 - 5.785$ **8.** $15 - 6.249$ **9.** $36 - 7.3$

10. Use the table to find out how many more students per teacher there are in California than in Nevada. See Example 5 (p. 158)

Student-per-Teacher Ratio

State	Ratio
Washington	19.2
Oregon	20.4
New Mexico	15.1
Nevada	18.4
California	20.7

Source: *The World Almanac*

11. In a recent year, a certain magazine had an average paid circulation of 6.6 million magazines, and another magazine had an average paid circulation of 4.1 million magazines. What is the difference in circulation of these two magazines? See Example 5 (p. 158)

12. Algebra Evaluate $s - t$ if $s = 8$ and $t = 4.25$. See Example 6 (p. 159)

13. Talk About It — Explain how you would find the difference of 3 and 2.89.

Practice and Problem Solving

EXTRA PRACTICE
See page 662.

Find each sum. See Example 1 (p. 157)

14. $7.2 + 9.5$ **15.** $4.9 + 3.0$ **16.** $1.34 + 2$

17. $0.796 + 13$ **18.** $54.567 + 48.512$ **19.** $15.634 + 24.361$

Find each difference. See Examples 2–4 (pp. 157–158)

20. $5.6 - 3.5$ **21.** $19.86 - 4.94$ **22.** $97 - 16.98$

23. $82 - 67.18$ **24.** $58.673 - 28.728$ **25.** $14.395 - 12.167$

26. The table shows the top three finishers in barrel racing at a rodeo. What is the time difference between first place and second place?

Barrel Racing Results

Rider	Time (s)
Denise Jones	15.87
Angela Carter	16.00
Liz Rodriguez	16.03

27. How much change would you receive if you gave a cashier \$20 for a purchase that costs \$18.74?

Algebra Evaluate each expression if $a = 128.9$ and $d = 22.035$. See Example 6 (p. 159)

28. $a - 11.25$ **29.** $75 + a$ **30.** $a - d$ **31.** $d + a$

Find the value of each expression.

32. $2 \cdot 6 + 0.073$ **33.** $3.4 + 5 \cdot 3$ **34.** $6 - 4.304 + 2.5$

Real-World PROBLEM SOLVING

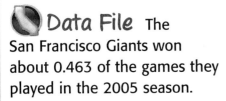

Data File The San Francisco Giants won about 0.463 of the games they played in the 2005 season.

35. Estimate the difference beween Omar Vizquel's batting average and Jason Schmidt's batting average. Then find the exact difference.

36. Of the players listed, which two had the highest batting average? What is the difference of their batting averages?

Data Card

San Francisco Giants
2005 Regular Season Batting Averages

Moises Alou: 0.321
Ray Durham: 0.290
Pedro Feliz: 0.250
Jason Schmidt: 0.094
Omar Vizquel: 0.271

Source: espn.com

H.O.T. Problems

37. CHALLENGE Arrange the digits 1, 2, 3, 4, 5, 6, 7, and 8 into two decimals so that their difference is as close to 0 as possible. Use each digit once.

38. REASONING Find a counterexample for the following statement.

If two decimals each have their last nonzero digit in the hundredths place, their sum also has its last nonzero digit in the hundredths place.

39. WRITING IN ►MATH Write a problem involving decimals in which you need to find an exact solution rather than an approximate solution. Explain your reasoning.

Standards Practice

40 Tavon has $15.00. Baseball cards cost $1.75 per pack, and hockey cards cost $0.99 per pack. If Tavon buys 6 packs of baseball cards for $10.50, how can he determine how much money he has left?

A Subtract $10.50 from $15.00

B Add $1.75 and $0.99

C Subtract $0.99 from $1.75

D Add $0.99 and $10.50

41 Over a 24-hour period, it rained 1.13 inches in Fresno, California. Over the same time, Jackson, Mississippi, received 8.5 inches of rain. How many more inches of rain did Jackson receive than Fresno?

F 6.37

G 6.08

H 7.37

J 7.08

Spiral Review

42. In a recent year, there were 45,033 beagles registered with the American Kennel Club. In the same year, there were 32,176 poodles registered. About how many were registered? **(Lesson 3-6)**

Estimate. (Lesson 3-5)

43. 4.231 + 3.98

44. 3.945 + 1.92 + 3.55

45. 9.345 − 6.625

46. Round 28.561 to the nearest tenth. **(Lesson 3-3)**

47. The table shows the number of pages of a book Elias read during the past 4 days. Find how many pages Elias will read on Friday if he continues at this rate. **(Lesson 1-4)**

Day	Pages Read
Monday	5
Tuesday	11
Wednesday	19
Thursday	29
Friday	■

Problem Solving in Science

Fun in the Sun

The Sun is amazing. It is a star that is 4.5 billion years old. At its center, the temperature is 27 million degrees Fahrenheit. That's about 67,000 times hotter than an oven! The sun is not only incredibly hot, but also very large. If it were hollow, 100 Earths could fit inside of it. Because the Sun is so big, it has a lot of gravity. This gravity pulls on the 8 planets and keeps them in orbit.

Each planet's orbit is a different shape. Orbital eccentricity describes the shape of a planet's orbit. Scientists use decimals to measure orbital eccentricity. If a planet's orbit is perfectly circular, its orbital eccentricity is 0.0. The more oval-shaped the planet's orbit, the closer the decimal is to 1.0. Because each orbit is different, the planets are not all the same distance from the sun. Scientists describe these distances from the sun as averages.

Planet	Average Distance from Sun (miles)	Orbital Eccentricity
Mercury	35,983,093	0.205
Venus	67,237,910	0.007
Earth	92,955,820	0.017
Mars	141,633,330	0.055
Jupiter	483,682,810	0.094
Saturn	886,526,100	0.057
Uranus	1,783,935,996	0.046
Neptune	2,795,084,800	0.011

Math Standard 5NS1.1 **Estimate, round, and manipulate very large (e.g., millions) and very small (e.g. thousandths) numbers.**

Real-World Math

Use the information on page 162 to solve each problem.

1. Round Saturn's orbital eccentricity to the nearest tenth.

2. Estimate the difference between Mercury's orbital eccentricity and Mars' orbital eccentricity. Then find the exact difference.

3. Which planet's orbit is closest to a circle? an oval?

4. About how much farther from the Sun is Saturn than Mars?

5. Jupiter is 402,843,290 miles away from Saturn. Is Uranus or Jupiter farther away from Saturn? Use > or < to explain.

6. Is Neptune's orbit more circular than Earth's orbit? Use > or < to explain.

7. Which four planets have orbits that are the most circular? Order these four planets from most circular to least circular.

Did You Know?

If you drove 60 miles per hour, it would take you 176 years to get to the Sun.

CHAPTER 3

Study Guide and Review

FOLDABLES™ Study Organizer — GET READY to Study

Be sure the following Key Concepts are noted in your Foldable.

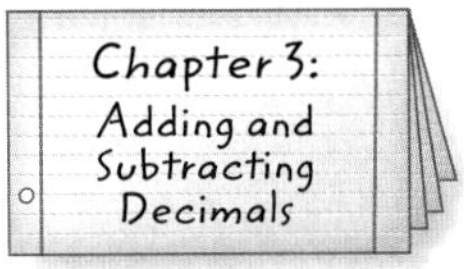

BIG Ideas

Rounding Whole Numbers and Decimals (Lesson 3-3)

First underline the digit to be rounded. Then look at the digit to the right of the place being rounded.

- If the digit is 4 or less, the underlined digit remains the same.
- If the digit is 5 or greater, add 1 to the underlined digit.

Estimation (Lesson 3-5)

- Rounding: Round each decimal to the nearest whole number that is easy for you to add or subtract mentally.
- Clustering: Round a group of close numbers to the same number.
- Front-End Estimation: Add or subtract the values of the digits in the front place or left-most place-value.

Adding and Subtracting Decimals (Lesson 3-7)

- To add decimals, line up the decimal points then add as with whole numbers.
- To subtract decimals, line up the decimal points, annex zeros if needed, and then subtract as with whole numbers.

Key Vocabulary

clustering (p. 150)
equivalent decimals (p. 136)
front-end estimation (p. 150)

Vocabulary Check

State whether each sentence is *true* or *false*. If *false*, replace the underlined word or number to make a true sentence.

1. 11,424,330 rounded to the nearest million is 11,000,000.
2. Decimals that name the same number are called equivalent decimals.
3. In 643.082, the digit 2 names the number two hundredths.
4. The sum of 45.6 and 5.1 is 40.5.
5. Estimation in which all of the decimals are close to the same number is called front-end estimation.
6. The number 3.014 is greater than 3.0014.
7. The number 245 is greater than 2,450.
8. The number 1.0487 rounded to the nearest hundredth is 1.049.
9. The symbol > means less than.

Math Online Vocabulary Review at ca.gr5math.com

Lesson-by-Lesson Review

3-1 Representing Decimals (pp. 131–134)

Example 1
Write the letter that represents 21.62 on the number line below.

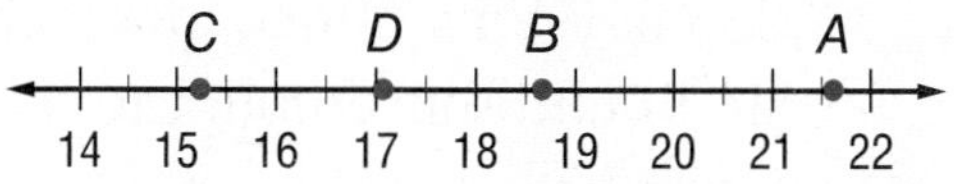

21.62 is greater than 21 and less than 22. So, 21.62 is represented by *A* on the number line.

Write the letter that represents each decimal on the number line in Example 1.

10. 18.7

11. 17.09

12. 15.3

13. A giant pumpkin weighed 53.17 pounds. Graph this decimal on a number line.

3-2 Comparing and Ordering Whole Numbers and Decimals (pp. 135–139)

Example 2
Use $<$, $>$, or $=$ to compare 4,153,677 and 4,159,300.

4,15<u>3</u>,677	Line up the ones place.
4,15<u>9</u>,300	Starting at the left, find the first place the digits differ.

Since $3 < 9$, $4{,}153{,}677 < 4{,}159{,}300$.

Example 3
Order 17.89, 0.17, 1.879, 10.789 from least to greatest.

17.89	⟶	17.890	Line up the decimal points and annex zeros so that each has the same number of decimal places.
0.17	⟶	0.170	
1.879	⟶	1.879	
10.789	⟶	10.789	

Starting at the left, use place value to compare the decimals.

The order from least to greatest is 0.17, 1.879, 10.789, and 17.89.

Use $>$, $<$, or $=$ to compare each pair of numbers.

14. 3,500,324 ● 3,500,160

15. 6,024,327 ● 6,204,986

16. 0.10 ● 0.1 **17.** 8.34 ● 9.3

18. The land area of Cottle County is 901,596 square miles. Crosby County has a land area of 901,693 square miles. Which has the greater land area?

Order each set of decimals from least to greatest.

19. 9.501, 0.9051, 90.51, 0.0951

20. 7.403, 0.0743, 7.743, 74.43

21. 0.314, 3.14, 0.0341, 34.1

22. 22.56, 2.265, 0.226, 2.562

23. The cost of four items on a menu are \$9, \$0.99, \$9.99, and \$19.99. Order these costs from greatest to least.

3-3 Rounding Whole Numbers and Decimals (pp. 141–145)

Example 4
Round 7,870,011 to the nearest million.

7,870,011 Underline the digit to be rounded.

7,870,011 ↑ Then look at the digit to the right. Since 8 is greater than 5, add one to the underlined digit.

So, 7,870,011 rounds to 8,000,000.

Example 5
Round 8.0314 to the hundredths place.

8.0314 Underline the digit to be rounded.

8.0314 ↑ Then look at the digit to the right. Since 1 is less than 5, the digit 3 stays the same.

So, 8.0314 rounds to 8.03.

Round each number to the indicated place-value position.

24. 22,964,135; million

25. The United States produced 9,033,610 tons of rice in a recent year. Round this amount to the nearest million.

26. 5.031; hundredths

27. 0.00042; ten-thousandths

28. The area of Long Beach, California, is 50.4 square miles. Round 50.4 to the nearest square mile.

3-4 Problem-Solving Strategy: Use Logical Reasoning (pp. 146–147)

Example 6
Jorge, Angela, and David play trumpet, clarinet, and trombone in the band, but not necessarily in that order. Jorge and the clarinet player ate lunch with Angela. Jorge does not play the trumpet. Who plays the trumpet?

Jorge and Angela ate lunch with the clarinet player, so David must play the clarinet.

Jorge is not the trumpet player, so he is the trombone player.

Since David plays the clarinet and Jorge plays the trombone, Angela must play the trumpet.

Solve. Use the *logical reasoning* strategy.

29. Lori has $1.85 in quarters, dimes, and nickels. She has the same number of quarters and dimes. She also has $0.40 more in dimes than nickels. How many of each coin does she have?

30. Ruben, Jerry, and Ethan are friends with different birth months: May, June, and November. It snowed on Ruben's birthday. The temperature was above 90° Fahrenheit on Jerry's birthday. There are 31 days in Ethan's birth month. List each person's birth month.

3-5 Estimating Sums and Differences (pp. 149–153)

Example 7
Estimate 38.61 − 14.25 using rounding.

38.61	⟶	39	Round to the nearest
− 14.25	⟶	− 14	whole number.
		25	

Example 8
Estimate 8.12 + 7.65 + 8.31 + 8.08 using clustering.

All addends of the sum are close to 8. So, an estimate is 4 × 8 or 32.

Example 9
Estimate 24.6 + 35.1 using front-end estimation.

24.6 + **3**5.1 Add the leftmost digits to get 5.

An estimate is 50.

Estimate using rounding.

31. 37.82 + 14.24 **32.** $72.18 − $29.93

33. 6.8 + 4.2 + 3.5 **34.** 129.6 − 9.7

Estimate using clustering.

35. 12.045 + 11.81 + 12.3 + 11.56

36. $6.45 + $5.88 + $5.61 + $6.03

Estimate using front-end estimation.

37. 31.29 + 58.07 **38.** 93.65 − 62.13

39. 145.91 + 131.65 **40.** 87.25 − 63.97

41. Jodie buys a sweater for $24.35, a bracelet for $17.62, and a pair of earrings for $11.19. If she uses front-end estimation to estimate the sum of her purchases, about how much does she spend?

3-6 Problem-Solving Investigation: Use Estimation (pp. 154–155)

Example 10
Kylee did 50 sit ups each day for one week. How many sit ups did she do in one week?

Since an exact answer is needed, first multiply 50 by 7.

50 × 7 = 350

Kylee did 350 sit ups in one week.

Check for Reasonableness
Since 350 ÷ 50 = 7, the answer is reasonable. ✓

For each problem, determine whether you need an estimate or an exact answer. Then solve it.

42. Alita, Alisa, and Alano are sharing the cost of their mother's birthday gift, which costs $60.25. About how much will each child need to contribute?

43. The road distance from Boston to Portland is 3,046 miles. The road distance from Boston to Omaha is 1,412 miles. How much further is Boston to Portland than to Omaha?

3-7 Adding and Subtracting Decimals (pp. 157–161)

Example 11
Find the sum of 48.23 and 11.65.

Estimate $48.23 + 11.65 \approx 48 + 12 = 60$

$$\begin{array}{r} 48.23 \\ +\ 11.65 \\ \hline 59.88 \end{array}$$

Line up the decimals.
Add as with whole numbers.

The sum is 59.88.

Check for Reasonableness $59.88 \approx 60$ ✓

Example 12
Find the difference between 57.68 and 34.64.

Estimate $57.68 - 34.64 \approx 23$

$$\begin{array}{r} 57.68 \\ -\ 34.64 \\ \hline 23.04 \end{array}$$

Line up the decimals.
Subtract as with whole numbers.

The difference is 23.04.

Check for Reasonableness $23.04 \approx 23$ ✓

Find each sum or difference.

44. $\begin{array}{r} 18.35 \\ +\ 23.61 \\ \hline \end{array}$

45. $\begin{array}{r} 148.93 \\ -\ 121.36 \\ \hline \end{array}$

46. $\begin{array}{r} 1.325 \\ +\ 0.081 \\ \hline \end{array}$

47. $248 - 131.28$

48. Mr. Becker drove 11.3 miles to the dentist, 7.5 miles to the library, and 5.8 miles back home. How far did he travel?

49. Coral has $40 to buy a backpack. If the backpack costs $35.99, how much money will she have left?

Chapter 3 Chapter Test

Write the letter that represents each decimal on the number line below.

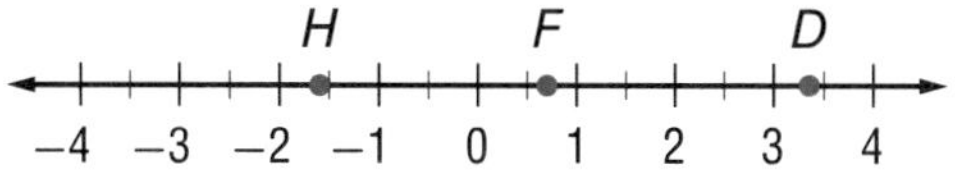

1. 3.35 **2.** −1.6 **3.** 0.7

Graph each decimal in the approximate position on a number line.

4. 1.54 **5.** 2.21 **6.** −8.0

7. The mass of a particular chemical sample is given as 4.02 grams. Graph this decimal on a number line.

Use >, <, or = to compare each pair of numbers.

8. 0.05 ● 0.50 **9.** 4.888 ● 4.880

10. 2.03 ● 2.030 **11.** 7,960 ● 7,906

12. **STANDARDS PRACTICE** Dion recorded the daily high temperatures for Phoenix over five days in the table below.

Day	Temperature (°F)
Monday	109.8
Tuesday	108.9
Wednesday	111.08
Thursday	108.92
Friday	111.0

Which of the following shows the daily high temperatures in order from least to greatest?

A 108.9, 108.92, 109.8, 111.0, 111.08

B 108.92, 108.9, 109.8, 111.0, 111.08

C 108.9, 108.92, 109.8, 111.08, 111.0

D 108.92, 108.9, 109.8, 111.08, 111.0

Round each number to the indicated place-value position.

13. 2.059; hundredths

14. 27.35; tens

15. 4,862,730; million

16. 34,556,112; thousand

17. On July 21, 2005, one U.S. dollar was equal to 0.825606 Euro. Round this exchange rate to the nearest hundredth.

Estimate each sum or difference using the indicated method.

18. 38.23 + 11.84; rounding

19. \$75.38 − \$22.04; front-end estimation

20. 6.72 + 7.09 + 6.6; clustering

21. **STANDARDS PRACTICE** Which of the following is the most reasonable total amount for the items purchased?

School Supplies	
Pens	\$2.09
Ruler	\$0.99
Paper	\$1.49
Book	\$14.99
Candy	\$0.49
Glue	\$0.89
Folder	\$1.19
Erasers	\$1.99
Pencils	\$1.87

F \$17

G \$20

H \$26

J \$30

Find each sum or difference.

22. 43.28 + 31.45

23. 392.802 − 173.521

24. Evaluate the expression $a + 17.31 - b$ if $a = 41.9$ and $b = 38.025$.

25. **WRITING IN ▶MATH** Soledad spent \$7.98 on a book, \$12.44 on dinner, and \$3.87 on ice cream. About how much money did she spend altogether?

CHAPTER 3

California Standards Practice

Cumulative, Chapters 1–3

Standards Example

Shawnda had a rope 6.22 meters long. She cut off 3.7 meters. How long was the piece of rope that was left?

A 3.15 meters

B 2.62 meters

C 2.52 meters

D 2.5 meters

Read the Question

You need to subtract in order to find the length of the piece of rope that was left.

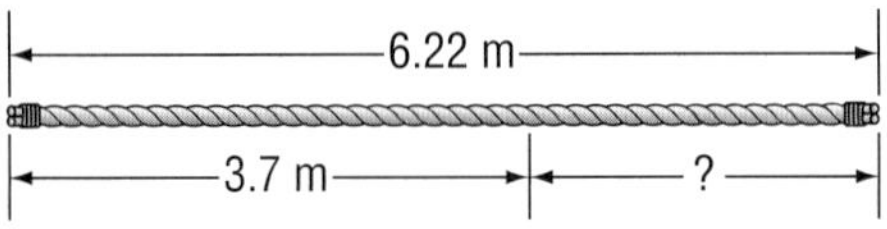

Solve the Question

Estimate $6.22 - 3.7 \approx 6 - 4$ or 2

$$\begin{array}{r} \overset{5\,1}{\not{6}.22} \\ -\ 3.70 \\ \hline 2.52 \end{array}$$

Line up the decimal points.

Annex zeros so that both numbers have the same place value.

Subtract as with whole numbers.

So, $6.22 - 3.7 = 2.52$.

Check for Reasonableness $2.52 \approx 2$ ✓

The answer is C.

Online **Personal Tutor at** ca.gr5math.com

Choose the best answer.

1 **Sharon's mom had $7,420.60 in her checkbook. After buying some furniture, the balance was $4,684.90. How much did Sharon's mom spend on furniture?**

A $2,735.70

B $2,846.70

C $3,735.70

D $3,846.70

2 **The temperature at 6:30 A.M. was 58.7°F. By 1:00 P.M., it was 92.6°F. Find the difference between the two temperatures in degrees Fahrenheit.**

F 33.8

G 33.9

H 34.9

J 43.9

More California Standards Practice

For practice by standard, see pages CA1–CA27.

3 **Round 5,230.157 to the nearest ten.**

A 5,000

B 5,230

C 5,230.16

D 5,230.2

---

4 **The table shows Mr. Coughlin's monthly heating bills for November through February. He estimates that he spent a total of $800 over these 4 months. Which best describes his estimate?**

Monthly Heating Bill	
Month	**Bill ($)**
November	196.43
December	214.89
January	204.58
February	222.76

F More than the actual amount because he rounded to the nearest $10.

G Less than the actual amount because he rounded to the nearest $10.

H More than the actual amount because he rounded to the nearest $100.

J Less than the actual amount because he rounded to the nearest $100.

---

5 **Which letter on the number line best identifies the location of 8.4?**

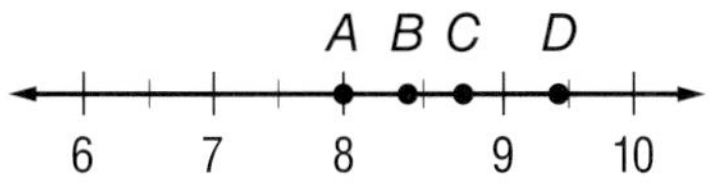

A *A* **C** *C*

B *B* **D** *D*

---

6 **The table shows the maximum wind speeds in the U.S. for certain states. What is the mean of the data?**

Place	Maximum Wind Speed (mph)
Atlanta, GA	60
Houston, TX	51
Miami, FL	86
Mobile, AL	63
New York, NY	40

F 46 mph **H** 60 mph

G 58 mph **J** 86 mph

---

7 **Danielle purchased 4 concert tickets. Each ticket was on sale for $5.95 off the original price. If the original price of each ticket was $29.95, which equation can be used to find *t*, the total price of the 4 tickets?**

A $t = 4(5.95) - 4(29.95)$

B $t = (29.95) - 5.95$

C $t = 5.95 - 29.95$

D $t = 4(29.95) - 4(5.95)$

---

8 **Karen studied the following numbers of hours for her Spanish tests.**

3, 2, 1, 0, 2, 1, 3, 5, 3, 4

What is the mode of these hours?

F 5 **H** 2

G 3 **J** 1

CHAPTER 4 Fractions and Decimals

BIG Idea **How do you express decimals as fractions?**

To write decimals as fractions, use the place value of the last decimal place as the denominator.

Example In the United States, the consumption of dairy products in a recent year was 587.125 pounds per person. What is this amount as a mixed number in simplest form?

$587.125 = 587\frac{125}{1{,}000}$ Say *five hundred eighty-seven and one hundred twenty-five thousandths.*

$= 587\frac{1}{8}$ Simplify.

What will I learn in this chapter?

- Express fractions in simplest form.
- Compare fractions.
- Write decimals as fractions and fractions as decimals.
- Use ordered pairs to locate points and organize data.
- Solve problems by making an organized list.

Key Vocabulary

greatest common factor
equivalent fractions
simplest form
mixed number
least common multiple

Math Online Student Study Tools at ca.gr5math.com

FOLDABLES™ Study Organizer

Make this Foldable to help you organize information about fractions and decimals. Begin with one sheet of $8\frac{1}{2}'' \times 11''$ paper.

1. **Fold** top of paper down and bottom of paper up as shown.

2. **Label** the top fold Fractions and the bottom fold Decimals.

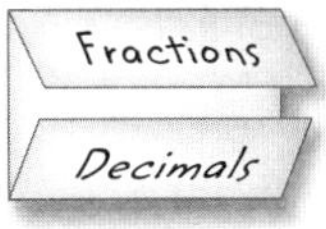

3. **Unfold** the paper and draw a number line in the middle of the paper.

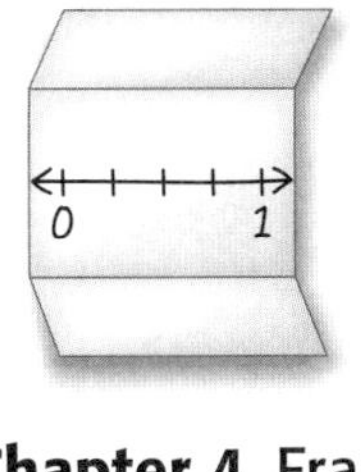

4. **Label** the fractions and decimals as shown.

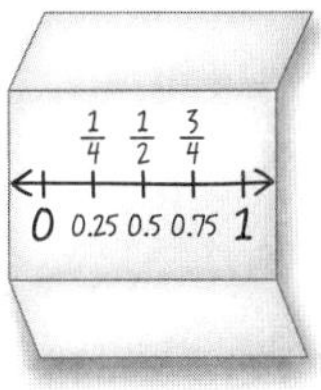

ARE YOU READY for Chapter 4?

You have two ways to check prerequisite skills for this chapter.

Option 2

Math Online Take the Chapter Readiness Quiz at ca.gr5math.com.

Option 1

Complete the Quick Check below.

QUICK Check

Tell whether each number is divisible by 2, 3, 4, 5, 6, 9, or 10. (Prior Grade)

1. 67 **2.** 891 **3.** 186

4. 145 **5.** 202 **6.** 70

7. Is it possible to divide 78 marbles evenly among 6 players? Justify your response. (Prior Grade)

Find the prime factorization of each number. (Lesson 1-2)

8. 315 **9.** 264 **10.** 50

11. 120 **12.** 28 **13.** 42

14. Mary drove 225 miles in one day. Find the prime factorization of this number. (Lesson 1-2)

Write each decimal in standard form. (Lesson 3-1)

15. five and three tenths **16.** two tenths

17. ten and three tenths **18.** seventy-four hundredths

19. sixteen thousandths **20.** nine tenths

21. The average speed at the 2006 Auto Club 500 was *one hundred forty-seven and eight hundred fifty-two thousandths* miles per hour. Write this decimal in standard form. (Lesson 3-1)

4-1 Greatest Common Factor

MAIN IDEA

I will find the greatest common factor of two or more numbers.

Preparation for Standard 6NS2.4
Determine the least common multiple and **the greatest common divisor of whole numbers;** use them to solve problems with fractions (e.g., to find a common denominator to add two fractions or to find the reduced form for a fraction).

New Vocabulary

common factor

greatest common factor (GCF)

GET READY to Learn

The Venn diagram below shows which water slides Curtis and his friends rode. *Venn diagrams* use overlapping circles to show common elements. What do Ana and Bret have in common?

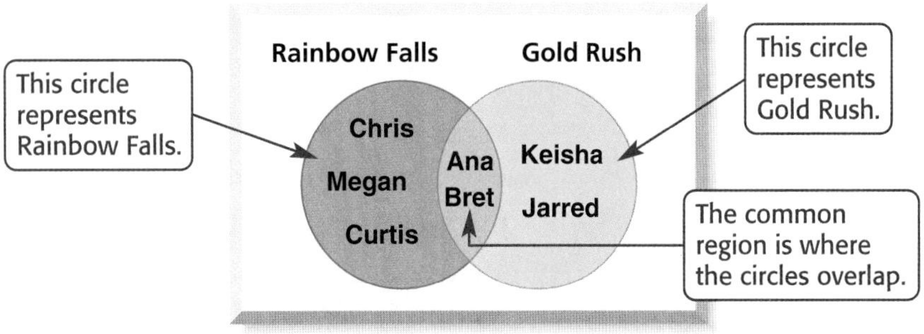

Factors that are shared by two or more numbers are called **common factors**. The greatest of the common factors of two or more numbers is the **greatest common factor (GCF)** of the numbers.

To find common factors, you can make a list.

EXAMPLE Identify Common Factors

1 Identify the common factors of 16 and 24.

First, list the factors by pairs for each number.

Factors of 16
① × 16
② × ⑧
④ × 4

Factors of 24
① × 24
② × 12
3 × ⑧
④ × 6

Circle the common factors.

The common factors of 16 and 24 are 1, 2, 4, and 8.

EXAMPLE Find the GCF by Listing Factors

2 Find the GCF of 16 and 24.

Refer to Example 1. The common factors are 1, 2, 4, and 8, and the greatest of these is 8. So, the greatest common factor or GCF of 16 and 24 is 8.

EXAMPLE Find the GCF by Using Prime Factors

3 Find the GCF of 42 and 56.

Write the prime factorization.

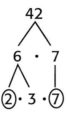

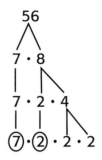

The GCF of 42 and 56 is 2 · 7 or 14.

Check

Use a Venn diagram to show the factors. Notice that the factors 1, 2, 7, and 14 are the common factors of 42 and 56 and the GCF is 14.

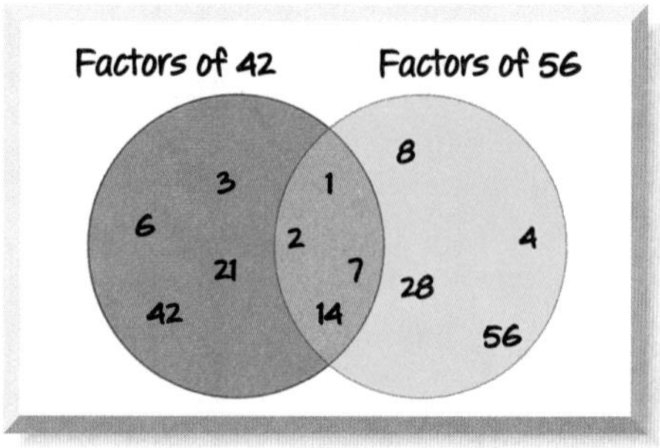

Review Vocabulary

prime number a whole number that has exactly two factors, 1 and the number itself; *Example:* 7 **(Lesson 1-1)**

prime factorization a composite number expressed as a product of prime numbers; *Example:* $12 = 2 \times 2 \times 3$ **(Lesson 1-1)**

Concepts in Motion

Interactive Lab
ca.gr5math.com

Real-World EXAMPLES

4 Ms. Taylor recorded the amount of money collected from her fifth-grade class for a field trip. Each student paid the same amount. What is the most the field trip could cost per student?

Ms. Taylor's Class Field Trip Money	
Monday	$48
Tuesday	$40
Thursday	$24

factors of 48: 1, 2, 3, 4, 6, 8, 12, 16, 24, 48

factors of 40: 1, 2, 4, 5, 8, 10, 20, 40

factors of 24: 1, 2, 3, 4, 6, 8, 12, 24

List all the factors of each number. Then find the greatest common factor.

The GCF of 48, 40, and 24 is 8. So, the most the field trip could cost is $8 per student.

5 Refer to Example 4. How many students have paid to attend the class trip if the cost is $8 per student?

There is a total of $48 + $40 + $24 or $112. So, the number of students that have paid for a ticket is $112 ÷ $8 or 14.

Online **Personal Tutor at** ca.gr5math.com

CHECK What You Know

Identify the common factors of each set of numbers. See Example 1 (p. 175)

1. 11, 44

2. 12, 21, 30

Find the GCF of each set of numbers. See Examples 2, 3 (pp. 175–176)

3. 8, 32

4. 24, 60

5. 3, 12, 18

6. 4, 10, 14

For Exercises 7 and 8, use the following information. See Examples 4, 5 (p. 176)

Oliver has 14 energy bars and 21 granola bars.

7. If Oliver gives each friend an equal number of each type of bar, what is the greatest number of friends with whom he can share the bars?

8. How many bars did each friend receive?

9. Talk About It Name all of the factors of 24 and 32. Then identify the common factors.

Practice and Problem Solving

EXTRA PRACTICE See page 663.

Identify the common factors of each set of numbers. See Example 1 (p. 175)

10. 45, 75

11. 36, 90

12. 6, 21, 30

13. 16, 24, 40

Find the GCF of each set of numbers. See Examples 2, 3 (pp. 175–176)

14. 12, 18

15. 18, 42

16. 48, 60

17. 30, 72

18. 14, 35, 84

19. 9, 18, 42

20. 16, 52, 76

21. 12, 30, 72

For Exercises 22 and 23, use the following information.
See Examples 4, 5 (p. 176)

Elizabeth has three CD storage cases that can hold 16, 24, and 32 CDs. The cases have sections holding the same number of CDs.

22. What is the greatest number of CDs in a section?

23. How many sections does she have in all?

For Exercises 24 and 25, use the following information.
See Examples 4, 5 (p. 176)

A grocery store sells boxes of juice in equal-size packs. Carla bought 18 boxes, Rico bought 36 boxes, and Winston bought 45 boxes.

24. What is the greatest number of boxes in each pack?

25. How many packs did each person buy?

H.O.T. Problems

26. **REASONING** When is the GCF of two or more numbers equal to one of the numbers? Explain your reasoning.

CHALLENGE **Determine whether each statement is *true* or *false.* If true, explain why. If false, give a counterexample.**

27. The GCF of any two even numbers is always even.

28. The GCF of any two odd numbers is always odd.

29. The GCF of an odd number and an even number is always even.

30. **WRITING IN MATH** Explain the three ways to find the GCF of two or more numbers.

Standards Practice

31 What is the greatest common factor of 28, 42, and 70?

A 2 **C** 28

B 14 **D** 42

32 Which number is *not* a common factor of 24 and 36?

F 2 **H** 12

G 6 **J** 24

33 Adam and Jocelyn are decorating the gym for the school dance. They want to cut all of the streamers the same length. One roll is 72 feet long, and the other is 64 feet long. What is the greatest length they should cut each streamer?

A 6 ft **C** 12 ft

B 8 ft **D** 16 ft

Spiral Review

34. Madison bought 5 packs of game trading cards for $16.83. How much change did she get back if she gave the cashier $20.00? **(Lesson 3-7)**

35. It costs $28 to rent a campsite for one night. About how much will it cost to rent the campsite for a week? **(Lesson 3-6)**

36. Order 7, 9.85, 8.3, and 3.9 from least to greatest. **(Lesson 3-2)**

Game Time

GCF Spin-Off

Greatest Common Factors

Get Ready!

Players: four

You will need: two spinners

Get Set!

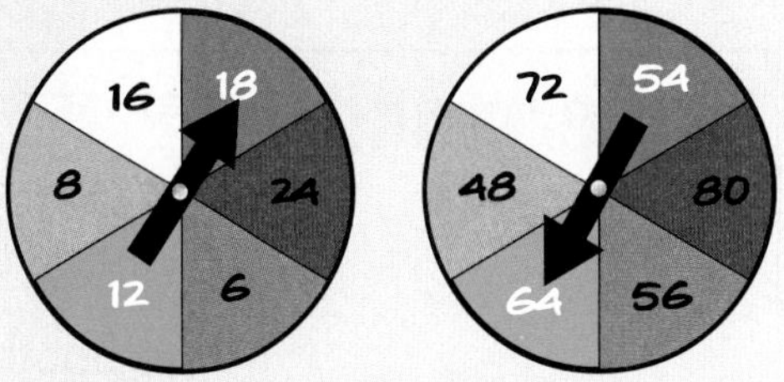

- Divide into teams of two players.
- One team labels the six equal sections of one spinner 6, 8, 12, 16, 18, and 24 as shown.
- The other team labels the six equal sections of another spinner 48, 54, 56, 64, 72, and 80 as shown.

Go!

- One player from each team spins their spinner.
- The other player on each team tries to be the first to name the GCF of the two numbers.
- The first person to correctly name the GCF gets 5 points for their team. Players must agree that the GCF is correct.
- Players take turns spinning the spinners and naming the GCF.
- The first team to get 25 points wins.

4-2 Problem-Solving Strategy

MAIN IDEA I will solve problems by making an organized list.

Standard 5MR1.1 Analyze problems by identifying relationships, distinguishing relevant from irrelevant information, **sequencing** and prioritizing **information,** and observing patterns. **Standard 5NS1.4 Determine the prime factors of all numbers through 50** and write the numbers as the product of their prime factors ... .

Jessica is setting up four booths in a row for the school carnival. There will be a dart game booth, a ring toss booth, a face-painting booth, and a virtual football booth. In how many ways can the four booths be arranged for the school carnival?

Understand

What facts do you know?

- There are four different booths: dart game, ring toss, face-painting, and virtual football.
- The booths will be set up in a row.

What do you need to find?

How many different ways can the four booths be arranged?

Plan

Make a list of all of the different possible arrangements. Use D for darts, R for ring toss, F for face-painting, and V for virtual football. Organize your list by listing each booth first as shown below.

D __ __ __   R __ __ __   F __ __ __   V __ __ __

Then fill in the remaining three positions with the other booths. Continue this process until all the different arrangements are listed in the second, third, and fourth positions.

Solve

Listing D first:	Listing R first:	Listing F first:	Listing V first:
D R F V	R F V D	F V D R	V D R F
D R V F	R F D V	F V R D	V D F R
D F R V	R V D F	F D R V	V R F D
D F V R	R V F D	F D V R	V R D F
D V R F	R D F V	F R V D	V F D R
D V F R	R D V F	F R D V	V F R D

There are 24 different ways the booths can be arranged.

Check

Look back. Is each booth accounted for six times in the first, second, third, and fourth positions?

ANALYZE the Strategy

Refer to the problem on the previous page.

1. Analyze the patterns in the 24 possible arrangements shown on page 180.

2. Explain how making an organized list helps you to solve a problem.

3. Give a real-world situation in which you might need to make an organized list.

4. What are some advantages and disadvantages of making an organized list?

PRACTICE the Strategy

EXTRA PRACTICE See page 663.

Solve. Use the *make an organized list* strategy.

5. Lourdes is having a birthday party. She wants to sit with her three best friends. How many arrangements are there for all of them to sit along one side of a rectangular table?

6. Michael needs to go to the library, the grocery store, and the video store. How many different ways can Michael make the stops?

7. A shoe store has the following options for shoes:

Shoe	Color
tennis	white
loafers	black
sandals	brown
boots	

How many combinations of style and color are possible?

8. How many different arrangements are possible for the prime factors of 30?

9. Arrange the digits 1, 5, 8, and 9 in the diagram below to find all the possible sums.

$$\begin{array}{r} \blacksquare.\blacksquare \\ +\ \blacksquare.\blacksquare \\ \hline \end{array}$$

10. Tansy's Pizzeria has the following menu options.

If you can choose one type of crust and three different toppings on each pizza, how many different pizzas can you make from the choices shown?

11. Mr. and Mrs. Glover have four children, Antoine, Rita, Monica, and Trevor. They would like to take a family portrait to hang above their fireplace. If Mr. and Mrs. Glover sit on each end, how many different ways can their children sit in between them?

12. **WRITING IN MATH** The school choir received three trophies in their last three competitions. When finding the number of ways the three trophies can be arranged in the trophy case, explain why it is important that the list be organized.

Explore

Math Lab for 4-3
Fractions on a Number Line

MAIN IDEA

I will represent fractions and mixed numbers on a number line.

Standard 5NS1.5 Identify and **represent on a number line** decimals, **fractions, mixed numbers,** and positive and negative integers.
Standard 5MR2.3 Use a variety of methods, such as words, **numbers,** symbols, charts, graphs, tables, diagrams, **and models, to explain mathematical reasoning.**

To graph a number on a number line, draw a dot at the location on the number line that corresponds to that number. You have already graphed integers on a number line. Now you will graph fractions on a number line.

ACTIVITIES

1 Use models to graph $\frac{3}{4}$ on a number line.

Step 1 Model $\frac{3}{4}$ using a fraction strip.

Step 2 Draw a number line with arrows on each end, and place the fraction strip above the number line. Mark a 0 on the left side and a 1 on the right side.

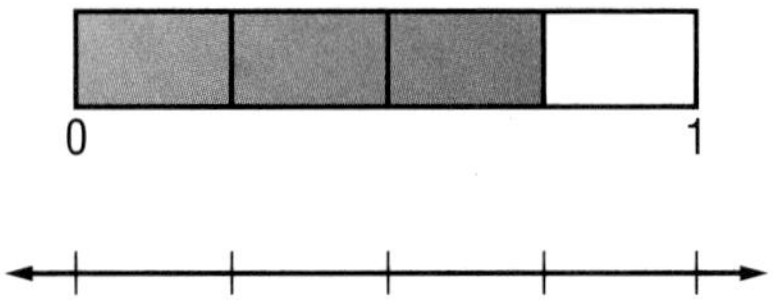

Step 3 Since the fraction is $\frac{3}{4}$, there are four sections in the fraction strip—each representing one fourth. Label the number line with $\frac{1}{4}$, $\frac{2}{4}$, and $\frac{3}{4}$.

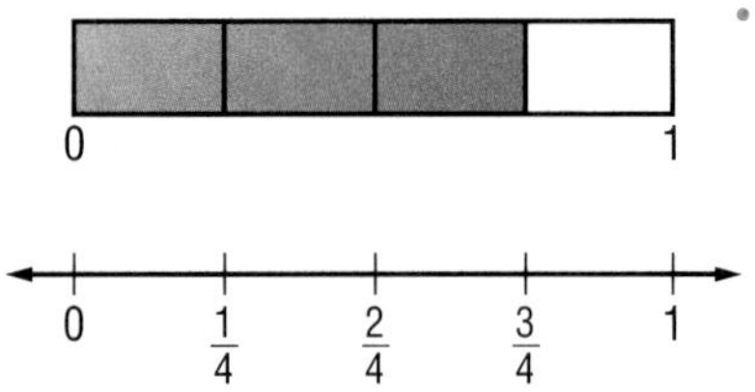

Step 4 Draw a dot on the number line above the $\frac{3}{4}$ mark.

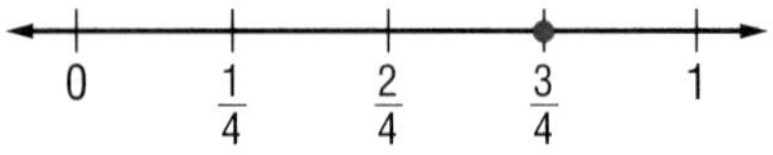

2 Use models to graph $1\frac{1}{4}$ on a number line.

Step 1 Use two fraction strips to show $1\frac{1}{4}$.

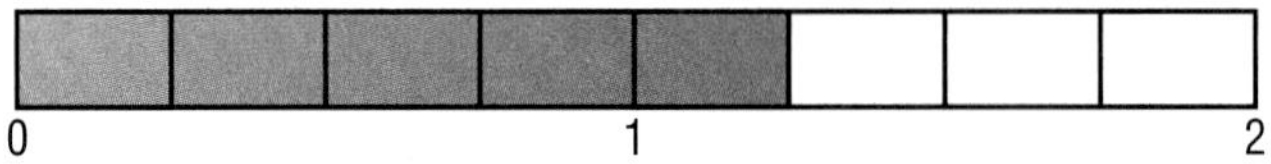

Step 2 Draw a number line from 0 to 2 using increments of $\frac{1}{4}$, and draw a dot on the number line above the $1\frac{1}{4}$ mark.

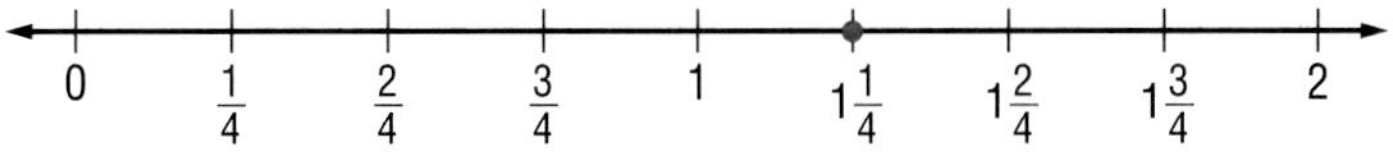

CHECK What You Know **Graph each fraction on a number line. Use a fraction strip if needed.**

a. $\frac{3}{8}$ **b.** $\frac{1}{3}$ **c.** $1\frac{2}{5}$ **d.** $2\frac{5}{6}$

Fractions that share the same relationship between part and whole are called *equivalent fractions*.

ACTIVITY

3 Use models to generate and graph equivalent fractions.

Step 1 Make a fraction strip for $\frac{6}{8}$.

Step 2 Place the fraction strip above the number line from Activity 1.

Step 3 Draw another number line and label it with $\frac{1}{8}$, $\frac{2}{8}$, and so on. Since $\frac{3}{4}$ and $\frac{6}{8}$ are graphed at the same location, they are equivalent fractions.

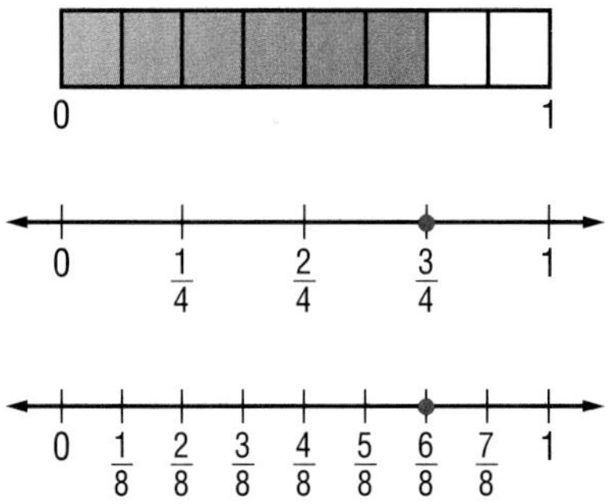

CHECK What You Know **Generate an equivalent fraction for each fraction. Show your reasoning on a number line.**

e. $\frac{5}{8}$ **f.** $\frac{3}{7}$ **g.** $\frac{2}{3}$ **h.** $\frac{4}{5}$

Analyze the Results

1. In Activity 1, you graphed $\frac{3}{4}$ on a number line using a fraction strip. Describe how you would graph $\frac{9}{11}$ on a number line.
2. The *mixed number* $1\frac{1}{4}$ can also be written as $\frac{5}{4}$. Show this on a number line.
3. Write a rule that you could use to find an equivalent fraction.

4-3 Simplifying Fractions

MAIN IDEA

I will express fractions in simplest form.

Preparation for Standard

5NS2.3 Solve simple problems, including ones arising in concrete situations, involving the addition and subtraction of fractions and mixed numbers (like and unlike denominators of 20 or less), and express answers in the simplest form.

New Vocabulary

ratio
equivalent fractions
simplest form

Vocabulary Link

Equivalent
Everyday Use equal in amount or value
Math Use equal in number or value

GET READY to Learn

The results of a favorite magazine survey are shown. According to the graph, 15 out of 50 students prefer music magazines.

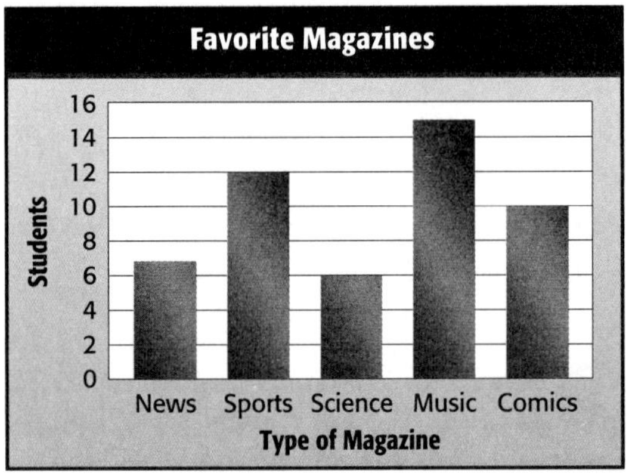

In the graph above, you can compare the students who prefer music magazines to the total number of students by using a **ratio**. A ratio is a comparison of two numbers by division. Ratios can be expressed as fractions.

$\frac{15}{50}$ ← students who prefer music magazines (numerator); ← total number of students (denominator)

Equivalent fractions are fractions that have the same value. The number lines below show that $\frac{15}{30}$ and $\frac{3}{10}$ are graphed at the same location. So, the fractions are equivalent. That is, $\frac{15}{50} = \frac{3}{10}$.

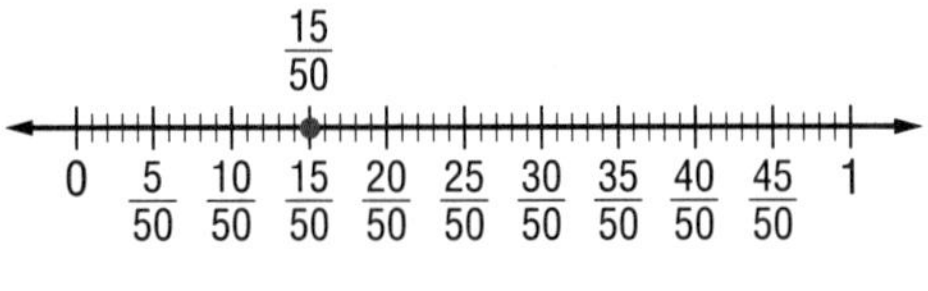

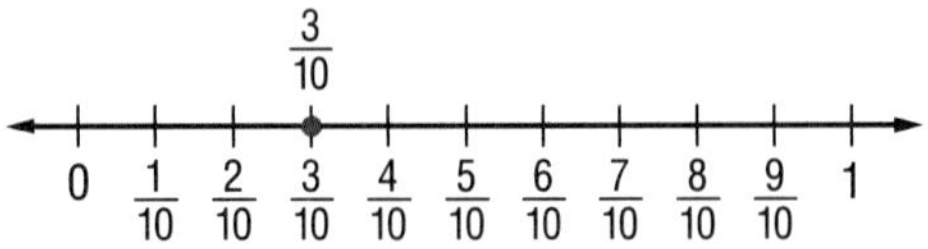

To find equivalent fractions, you can multiply or divide the numerator and denominator by the same nonzero number.

$$\frac{15}{50} = \frac{15 \div 5}{50 \div 5} \text{ or } \frac{3}{10}$$

3 out of every 10 students prefer music magazines.

Remember

You can check the answer to Example 2 by graphing each fraction on the same number line. The fractions should be graphed at the same point.

EXAMPLES Write Equivalent Fractions

Replace each *x* with a number so the fractions are equivalent.

1 $\frac{5}{7} = \frac{x}{21}$

$$\frac{5}{7} \underset{\times 3}{\overset{\times 3}{=}} \frac{15}{21}$$

Since $7 \times 3 = 21$, multiply the numerator and denominator by 3.

2 $\frac{12}{16} = \frac{6}{x}$

$$\frac{12}{16} \underset{\div 2}{\overset{\div 2}{=}} \frac{6}{8}$$

Since $12 \div 2 = 6$, divide the numerator and denominator by 2.

A fraction is in **simplest form** when the GCF of the numerator and denominator is 1.

EXAMPLE Write Fractions in Simplest Form

3 **Write $\frac{18}{24}$ in simplest form.**

One Way: **Divide by common factors.**

$$\frac{18}{24} \underset{\div 2}{\overset{\div 2}{=}} \frac{9}{12} \underset{\div 3}{\overset{\div 3}{=}} \frac{3}{4}$$

A common factor of 18 and 24 is 2

A common factor of 9 and 12 is 3.

Another Way: **Divide by the GCF.**

factors of 18: 1, 2, 3, 6, 9, 18

factors of 24: 1, 2, 3, 4, 6, 8, 12, 24

The GCF of 18 and 24 is 6.

$$\frac{18}{24} \underset{\div 6}{\overset{\div 6}{=}} \frac{3}{4}$$

Divide the numerator and denominator by the GCF, 6.

Since the GCF of 3 and 4 is 1, the fraction $\frac{3}{4}$ is in simplest form.

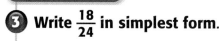

Online Personal Tutor at ca.gr5math.com

You can use mental math to simplifiy some fractions.

Real-World EXAMPLE

4 Approximately 36 out of every 40 firefighters work in city or county fire departments. Express the fraction $\frac{36}{40}$ in simplest form.

The GCF of 36 and 40 is 4.

$\frac{\overset{9}{\cancel{36}}}{\underset{10}{\cancel{40}}} = \frac{9}{10}$ Mentally divide both the numerator and denominator by 4.

So, $\frac{9}{10}$ or 9 out of every 10 firefighters work in city or county fire departments.

CHECK What You Know

Replace each *x* with a number so the fractions are equivalent.
See Examples 1, 2 (p. 185)

1. $\frac{3}{8} = \frac{x}{24}$
2. $\frac{4}{5} = \frac{40}{x}$
3. $\frac{15}{25} = \frac{3}{x}$
4. $\frac{21}{28} = \frac{x}{4}$

Write each fraction in simplest form. If the fraction is already in simplest form, write *simplest form*. See Example 3 (p. 185)

5. $\frac{2}{10}$
6. $\frac{8}{25}$
7. $\frac{10}{38}$
8. $\frac{15}{45}$

9. The table shows the fraction of each type of baked good to be sold out of the total number of baked goods at the school bake sale. Express the fraction of baked goods that were muffins in simplest form. See Example 4 (p. 186)

School Bake Sale	
breads	$\frac{6}{50}$
cakes	$\frac{6}{20}$
cookies	$\frac{26}{100}$
muffins	$\frac{24}{100}$
pies	$\frac{4}{50}$

10. Talk About It Name two fractions that are equivalent to $\frac{2}{8}$. Explain your reasoning.

Practice and Problem Solving

EXTRA PRACTICE
See page 663.

Replace each x with a number so the fractions are equivalent.
See Examples 1, 2 (p. 185)

11. $\frac{1}{2} = \frac{x}{8}$ **12.** $\frac{1}{3} = \frac{x}{27}$ **13.** $\frac{x}{5} = \frac{9}{15}$ **14.** $\frac{x}{6} = \frac{20}{24}$

15. $\frac{7}{9} = \frac{14}{x}$ **16.** $\frac{12}{16} = \frac{3}{x}$ **17.** $\frac{30}{35} = \frac{x}{7}$ **18.** $\frac{36}{45} = \frac{x}{5}$

Write each fraction in simplest form. If the fraction is already in simplest form, write *simplest form*. See Example 3 (p. 185)

19. $\frac{6}{9}$ **20.** $\frac{4}{10}$ **21.** $\frac{10}{38}$ **22.** $\frac{27}{54}$

23. $\frac{19}{37}$ **24.** $\frac{32}{85}$ **25.** $\frac{28}{77}$ **26.** $\frac{15}{100}$

27. In Mr. Rowland's class, 24 out of every 32 students own a scooter. Express the fraction of the class that owns a scooter in simplest form.

28. In a typical symphony orchestra, 16 out of every 100 musicians are first and second violin players. Express the fraction of the orchestra that are violinists in simplest form.

Write two fractions that are equivalent to the given fraction.

29. $\frac{4}{10}$ **30.** $\frac{5}{12}$ **31.** $\frac{12}{20}$ **32.** $\frac{16}{44}$

33. In a pet survey, 3 out of every 10 students chose dogs as their favorite pet. If 30 students were surveyed, how many chose dogs as their favorite pet?

Real-World PROBLEM SOLVING

Data File UCLA is well-known for its Health Sciences College.

34. What fraction in simplest form compares the number of students enrolled in dentistry to the total number of students?

35. In simplest form, what fraction of the students were enrolled in nursing?

Source: aim.ucla.edu

UCLA

Health Sciences Enrollment, Fall 2005

Dentistry: 392

Medicine: 950

Nursing: 304

Public Health: 640

H.O.T. Problems

36. Which One Doesn't Belong? Identify the fraction that does not belong with the other three. Explain your reasoning.

$\frac{8}{12}$ $\frac{12}{18}$ $\frac{9}{12}$ $\frac{32}{48}$

37. CHALLENGE A fraction is equivalent to $\frac{3}{4}$, and the sum of the numerator and denominator is 84. Analyze this information to determine the fraction.

38. WRITING IN MATH Explain in your own words how to find a fraction that is equivalent to a given fraction.

Standards Practice

39 Tyler has read $\frac{4}{5}$ of his novel for reading class. Which student has also read the same amount as Tyler?

Student	Amount Read
Abby	$\frac{1}{2}$
Gustavo	$\frac{12}{15}$
Tonisha	$\frac{4}{10}$
Lance	$\frac{16}{15}$

A Abby

B Gustavo

C Tonisha

D Lance

40 The fractions $\frac{2}{6}$, $\frac{3}{9}$, $\frac{4}{12}$, and $\frac{5}{15}$ are each equivalent to $\frac{1}{3}$. What is the relationship between the numerator and the denominator in each fraction that is equivalent to $\frac{1}{3}$?

F The numerator is three times the denominator.

G The numerator is three more than the denominator.

H The denominator is three times the numerator.

J The denominator is three more than the numerator.

Spiral Review

41. Tama needs to study for a math test, read a chapter in her novel, and write a social studies report tonight. In how many different orders can Tama do these three activities? **(Lesson 4-2)**

Find the GCF of each set of numbers. **(Lesson 4-1)**

42. 40, 36 **43.** 45, 75 **44.** 120, 150

45. In the 2005 World Figure Skating Championship, Sasha Cohen of the U.S. scored 89.78 in the short program and 124.61 in the free skate. What was Sasha's total score for the competition? **(Lesson 3-7)**

4-4 Mixed Numbers and Improper Fractions

MAIN IDEA

I will write mixed numbers as improper fractions and vice versa.

Standard 5NS1.5 Identify and represent on a number line decimals, **fractions, mixed numbers,** and positive and negative integers.

New Vocabulary

mixed number
proper fraction
improper fraction

GET READY to Learn

Hands-On Mini Lab

Step 1 Shade one index card to represent the whole number 1.

Step 2 Fold a second index card into three equal parts to show thirds. Shade one part to represent $\frac{1}{3}$.

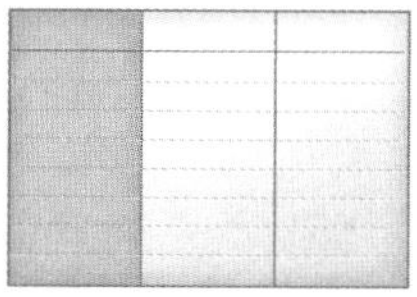

Step 3 Fold the whole number index card into thirds.

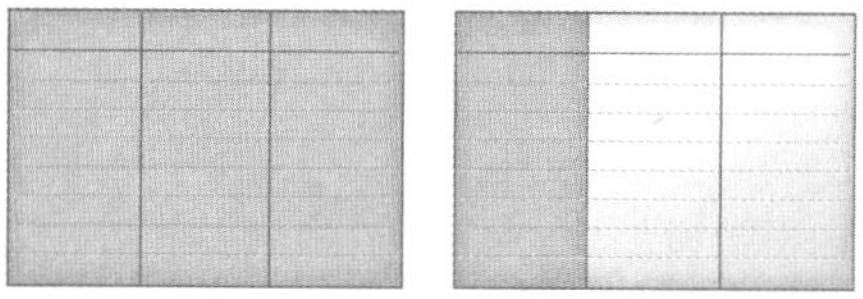

1. How many shaded $\frac{1}{3}$s are there?

2. What fraction is equivalent to $1\frac{1}{3}$?

Make a model to show each number.

3. the number of fourths in $2\frac{3}{4}$ **4.** the number of halves in $4\frac{1}{2}$

A number like $1\frac{1}{3}$ is an example of a mixed number. A **mixed number** indicates the sum of a whole number and a fraction.

$$1\frac{1}{3} = 1 + \frac{1}{3}$$

The numbers below the number line show two groups of fractions.

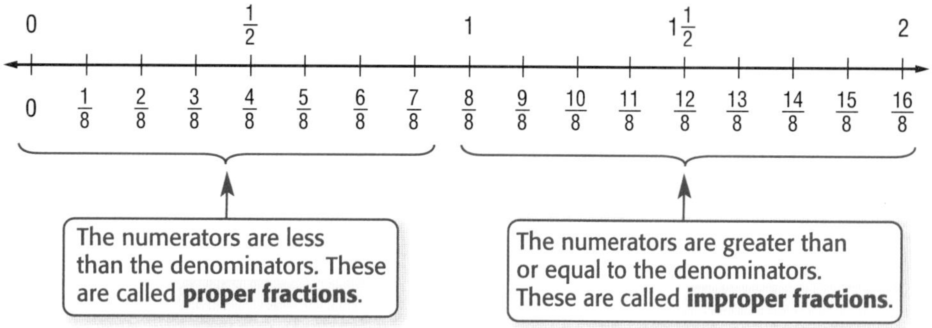

Improper fractions have values that are greater than or equal to 1.

EXAMPLE Mixed Numbers as Improper Fractions

1 Male bald eagles generally measure 3 feet from head to tail, weigh 7 to 10 pounds, and have a wingspan of about $6\frac{1}{2}$ feet. Write the length of the male bald eagle's wingspan as an improper fraction. Then graph the improper fraction on a number line.

$$6\frac{1}{2} = \frac{(6 \times 2) + 1}{2} = \frac{13}{2}$$

Multiply the whole number by the denominator. Then add the numerator. This is the numerator of the improper fraction.

So, $6\frac{1}{2} = \frac{13}{2}$.

Since $\frac{13}{2}$ is halfway between 6 and 7, draw a number line using increments of one half. Then, draw a dot at $\frac{13}{2}$.

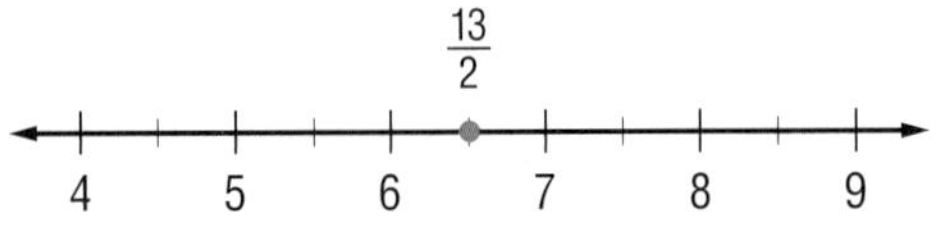

Improper fractions can also be written as mixed numbers or whole numbers. Divide the numerator by the denominator.

Remember

Number lines using scales other than the ones shown in Examples 1 and 2 can also be drawn.

EXAMPLE Improper Fractions as Mixed Numbers

2 Write $\frac{17}{5}$ as a mixed number. Then graph the mixed number on a number line.

Divide 17 by 5.

$$\begin{array}{r} 3\frac{2}{5} \\ 5\overline{)17} \\ -15 \\ \hline 2 \end{array}$$

Use the remainder as the numerator and the divisor as the denominator of the fraction.

So, $\frac{17}{5} = 3\frac{2}{5}$.

Since $3\frac{2}{5}$ is between 3 and 4, draw a number line from 3 to 4 using increments of one fifth. Then, draw a dot at $3\frac{2}{5}$.

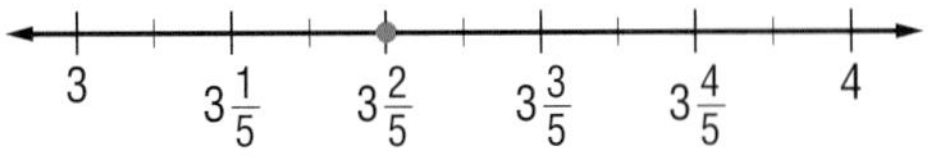

Online Personal Tutor at ca.gr5math.com

 Math Online **Extra Examples at** ca.gr5math.com

CHECK What You Know

Write each mixed number as an improper fraction. Graph the result on a number line. See Example 1 (p. 190)

1. $4\frac{1}{8}$ **2.** $2\frac{4}{5}$ **3.** $5\frac{2}{3}$

Write each improper fraction as a mixed number or a whole number. Graph the result on a number line. See Example 2 (p. 190)

4. $\frac{31}{6}$ **5.** $\frac{15}{4}$ **6.** $\frac{8}{8}$

7. Talk About It: Is $\frac{8}{5}$ a mixed number, a proper fraction, or an improper fraction? Explain how you know.

Practice and Problem Solving

EXTRA PRACTICE See page 664.

Write each mixed number as an improper fraction. Graph the result on a number line. See Example 1 (p. 190)

8. $6\frac{1}{3}$ **9.** $8\frac{2}{3}$ **10.** $7\frac{4}{5}$ **11.** $1\frac{5}{8}$

12. $7\frac{1}{4}$ **13.** $5\frac{3}{4}$ **14.** $3\frac{5}{6}$ **15.** $4\frac{1}{6}$

16. Measurement The width of a piece of paper is $8\frac{1}{2}$ inches. Write $8\frac{1}{2}$ as an improper fraction.

17. The table shows the area of three tropical rainforests. Express the area of the Congo River Basin rainforest as an improper fraction.

Rainforest	Area (square km)
Amazon	7 million
Congo River Basin	$1\frac{4}{5}$ million
Madagascar	110,000

Source: answers.com

Write each improper fraction as a mixed number or a whole number. Graph the result on a number line. See Example 2 (p. 190)

18. $\frac{16}{5}$ **19.** $\frac{27}{5}$ **20.** $\frac{9}{8}$ **21.** $\frac{19}{8}$

22. $\frac{15}{3}$ **23.** $\frac{28}{4}$ **24.** $\frac{10}{10}$ **25.** $\frac{9}{9}$

Write the letter that represents each quantity on the number line.

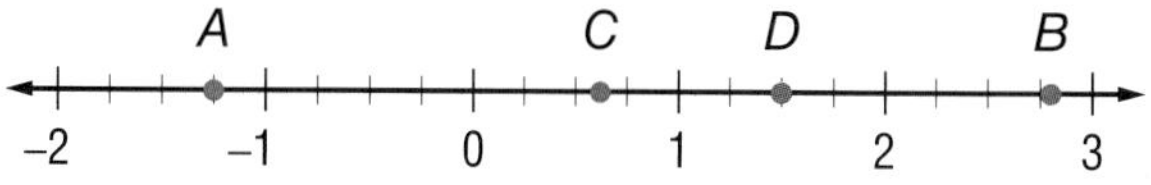

26. $2\frac{4}{5}$ **27.** $-1\frac{1}{4}$ **28.** $\frac{3}{2}$ **29.** $\frac{65}{100}$

H.O.T. Problems

30. OPEN ENDED Select a mixed number that is between $6\frac{3}{5}$ and $\frac{36}{5}$.

31. SELECT A TOOL Which of the following tools might you use to write $4\frac{1}{6}$ as an improper fraction? Justify your selection(s). Then use the tool(s) to solve the problem.

draw a model | calculator | paper/pencil

32. CHALLENGE Write $2\frac{7}{4}$ and $3\frac{15}{15}$ in simplest form so that it does not contain an improper fraction. Explain your reasoning.

33. WRITING IN ▸MATH Explain how you know whether a fraction is less than, equal to, or greater than 1.

Standards Practice

34 Which improper fraction is *not* equivalent to any of the mixed numbers listed in the table?

Ingredient	Amount
flour	$2\frac{5}{6}$ cups
butter	$1\frac{4}{5}$ cups
chocolate chips	$3\frac{1}{2}$ bags

A $\frac{9}{5}$

B $\frac{11}{5}$

C $\frac{17}{6}$

D $\frac{7}{2}$

35 Serena bought 30 oranges. How many dozen oranges did she buy?

F $1\frac{3}{4}$

G $2\frac{1}{4}$

H $2\frac{1}{2}$

J $2\frac{2}{3}$

Spiral Review

Write each fraction in simplest form. (Lesson 4-3)

36. $\frac{35}{42}$

37. $\frac{11}{12}$

38. $\frac{5}{20}$

Find the GCF of each set of numbers. (Lesson 4-1)

39. 9, 39

40. 33, 88

41. 24, 48, 63

42. Mallory spent $27.05, $26.50, $27.90, and $26.45 on her last four trips to the grocery store. Order these amounts from least to greatest. (Lesson 3-2)

Math Online Self-Check Quiz at ca.gr5math.com

CHAPTER 4

Mid-Chapter Check

Lessons 4-1 through 4-4

Identify the common factors of each set of numbers. **(Lesson 4-1)**

1. 3, 9

2. 11, 33, 55

Find the GCF of each set of numbers. **(Lesson 4-1)**

3. 27, 45

4. 24, 40, 72

5. **STANDARDS PRACTICE** The table shows the number of shrimp a restaurant ordered for three days.

Day	Shrimp
Monday	56
Tuesday	21
Wednesday	42

The shrimp come in bags, and each bag contains the same number of shrimp. What is the greatest possible number of shrimp in a bag? **(Lesson 4-1)**

A 8

B 7

C 6

D 3

6. Marta tosses two dimes. How many head-tail combinations are possible? **(Lesson 4-2)**

Replace each *x* with a number so the fractions are equivalent. **(Lesson 4-3)**

7. $\frac{2}{9} = \frac{x}{45}$

8. $\frac{5}{12} = \frac{25}{x}$

9. $\frac{27}{36} = \frac{x}{4}$

Write each fraction in simplest form. If the fraction is already in simplest form, write *simplest form*. **(Lesson 4-3)**

10. $\frac{15}{24}$

11. $\frac{12}{42}$

12. $\frac{9}{14}$

13. The world's driest city is Aswan, Egypt, which only receives an average of $\frac{32}{1,600}$ inches of rain each year. Write this fraction in simplest form. **(Lesson 4-3)**

Write each mixed number as an improper fraction. Graph the result on a number line. **(Lesson 4-4)**

14. $3\frac{5}{6}$

15. $7\frac{3}{5}$

16. **STANDARDS PRACTICE** A local newspaper is reducing the width of its paper by $1\frac{3}{4}$ inches. What is this width as an improper fraction? **(Lesson 4-4)**

F $\frac{4}{3}$

G $\frac{8}{4}$

H $\frac{7}{3}$

J $\frac{7}{4}$

17. Express the fraction of California's median age as an improper fraction. **(Lesson 4-4)**

State	Median Age (years)
California	$34\frac{3}{10}$
Illinois	$35\frac{1}{2}$
New York	$37\frac{3}{10}$

Source: census.gov

18. Write $\frac{76}{9}$ as a mixed number. Then graph the mixed number on a number line. **(Lesson 4-4)**

19. **WRITING IN MATH** The Fin Whale weighs $\frac{248}{5}$ tons. Explain how to write this weight as a mixed number or a whole number. **(Lesson 4-4)**

4-5 Least Common Multiple

GET READY to Learn

The multiplication table shown below lists the products of any two numbers from 1 to 10. Study the products of any number and the numbers from 1 to 10. What patterns did you find?

×	1	2	3	4	5	6	7	8	9	10
1	1	2	3	4	5	6	7	8	9	10
2	2	4	6	8	10	12	14	16	18	20
3	3	6	9	12	15	18	21	24	27	30
4	4	8	12	16	20	24	28	32	36	40
5	5	10	15	20	25	30	35	40	45	50
6	6	12	18	24	30	36	42	48	54	60
7	7	14	21	28	35	42	49	56	63	70
8	8	16	24	32	40	48	56	64	72	80
9	9	18	27	36	45	54	63	72	81	90
10	10	20	30	40	50	60	70	80	90	100

MAIN IDEA

I will find the least common multiple of two or more numbers.

Preparation for Standard 5SDAP1.3 Use fractions and percentages to compare data sets of different sizes.

New Vocabulary

multiple
common multiples
least common multiple (LCM)

A **multiple** of a number is the product of the number and any whole number (0, 1, 2, 3, 4, ...). Multiples that are shared by two or more numbers are **common multiples**.

EXAMPLE Identify Common Multiples

1 Identify the first three common multiples of 4 and 8.

First, list the multiples of each number.

multiples of 4: 4, 8, 12, 16, 20, 24, ... $1 \times 4, 2 \times 4, 3 \times 4, \ldots$

multiples of 8: 8, 16, 24, 32, 40, 48, ... $1 \times 8, 2 \times 8, 3 \times 8, \ldots$

Notice that 8, 16, and 24 are multiples common to both 4 and 8. So, the first three common multiples of 4 and 8 are 8, 16, and 24.

The first common multiple of 4 and 8 is actually 0, since $4 \times 0 = 0$ and $8 \times 0 = 0$. In this book, we will consider only nonzero multiples.

The least number that is a multiple of two or more whole numbers is called the **least common multiple (LCM)** of the numbers. In Example 1, the least common multiple of 4 and 8 is 8.

In addition to listing the multiples, you can also use prime factors to find the least common multiple.

> **Remember**
>
> Continue to factor any number that is not prime in the factor tree.

EXAMPLE Find the LCM

2 Find the LCM of 40 and 75.

Write the prime factorization of each number.

40 → 4×10 → $2 \times 2 \times 2 \times 5$

75 → 3×25 → $3 \times 5 \times 5$

Identify all common prime factors.

$40 = 2 \times 2 \times 2 \times 5$ or $2^3 \times 5$

$75 = 3 \times 5 \times 5$ or 3×5^2

Find the product of the prime factors using each common prime factor only once and any remaining factors.

The LCM is $2 \times 2 \times 2 \times 3 \times 5 \times 5$ or $2^3 \times 3 \times 5^2$ or 600.

Online Personal Tutor at ca.gr5math.com

Real-World EXAMPLE

3 The weight in pounds of each fish is shown on the scale readout. Suppose more of each type of fish weighing the same amount is added to each scale. At what weight will the scales have the same readout?

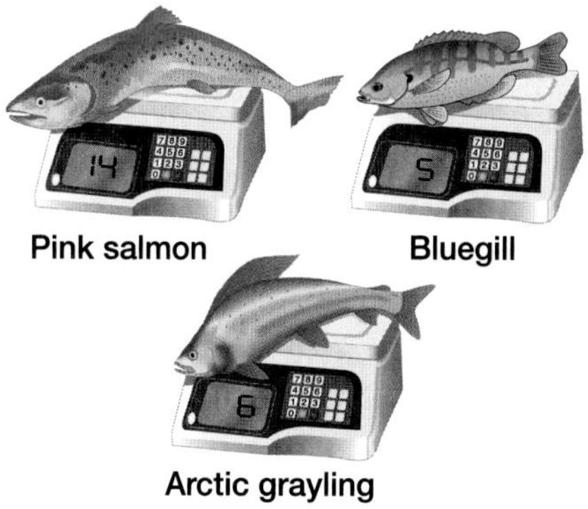

Find the LCM using prime factors.

14 → $(2) \times (7)$ 5 → $(5) \times 1$ 6 → $2 \times (3)$

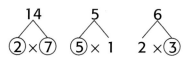

The scales will show the same weight at $2 \times 7 \times 5 \times 3$ or 210 pounds.

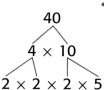

CHECK What You Know

Identify the first three common multiples of each set of numbers.
See Example 1 (p. 194)

1. 7, 14

2. 2, 8, 12

Find the LCM of each set of numbers. See Example 2 (p. 195)

3. 6, 10

4. 2, 3, 13

5. Marco gets an allergy shot every 3 weeks. Percy gets an allergy shot every 5 weeks. If Marco and Percy meet while getting an allergy shot, how many weeks will it be before they see each other again? See Example 3 (p. 195)

6. Talk About It Is 27 a multiple of 4? Explain your reasoning.

Practice and Problem Solving

EXTRA PRACTICE See page 664.

Identify the first three common multiples of each set of numbers.
See Example 1 (p. 194)

7. 2, 10

8. 1, 7

9. 6, 9

10. 3, 8

11. 4, 8, 10

12. 3, 9, 18

Find the LCM of each set of numbers. See Example 2 (p. 195)

13. 3, 4

14. 7, 9

15. 16, 20

16. 15, 12

17. 15, 25, 75

18. 9, 12, 15

Real-World PROBLEM SOLVING

Science The approximate cycles for the appearance of cicadas and tent caterpillars are shown.

Cicadas vs. Caterpillars

Insect	Life Cycle (yr)
13-year Cicada	13
17-year Cicada	17
Tent Caterpillar	6

Source: USDA Forest Service

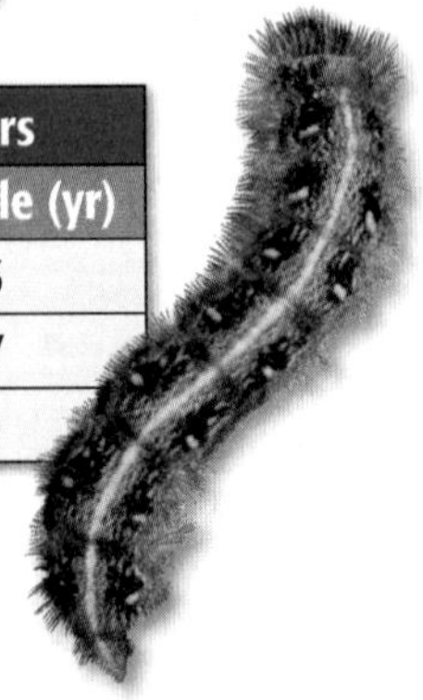

19. Suppose the peak cycles of the 17-year cicada and the tent caterpillar coincided in 1998. What is the next year in which they will coincide?

20. Suppose the peak cycles of all three insects coincided last year. How many years will pass before they will coincide again?

H.O.T. Problems

21. **FIND THE ERROR** Kurt and Alma are finding the LCM of 6 and 8. Who is correct? Explain your reasoning.

Kurt

$6 = 2 \times 3$
$8 = 2 \times 2 \times 2$
The LCM of 6 and 8 is 2.

Alma

$6 = 2 \times 3$
$8 = 2 \times 2 \times 2$
The LCM of 6 and 8 is $2 \times 2 \times 2 \times 3$ or 24.

22. **CHALLENGE** The winning number in a raffle with 119 tickets was a multiple of 2, 5, and 8. It was greater than 50. What was the winning number? Explain.

23. **WRITING IN MATH** Create a problem about a real-world situation in which it would be helpful to find the least common multiple.

Standards Practice

24 If train A and train B both leave the station at 9:00 A.M., at what time will they next leave the station together?

Train Schedule

Train	Departs
A	every 8 minutes
B	every 6 minutes

A 9:24 A.M.

B 9:48 A.M.

C 10:48 A.M.

D 12:00 P.M.

25 What is the least common multiple of 5, 9, and 15?

F 3

G 29

H 45

J 60

Spiral Review

26. A state park has $5\frac{1}{5}$ miles of beach shoreline. Write $5\frac{1}{5}$ as an improper fraction. **(Lesson 4-4)**

Algebra Replace each *x* with a number so the fractions are equivalent. (Lesson 4-3)

27. $\frac{1}{5} = \frac{x}{25}$

28. $\frac{3}{17} = \frac{9}{x}$

29. $\frac{42}{48} = \frac{x}{8}$

30. $\frac{33}{55} = \frac{3}{x}$

4-6 Problem-Solving Investigation

MAIN IDEA I will choose the best strategy to solve a problem.

Standard 5MR2.6 Make precise calculations and check the validity of the results from the context of the problem.
Standard 5SDAP1.2 Organize and display single-variable data in appropriate graphs and **representations** (e.g., histogram, circle graphs) and explain which types of graphs are appropriate for various data sets.

P.S.I. TEAM +

TROY: This weekend, my family went to the zoo. We spent a total of $42 on admission tickets. We purchased at least 2 adult tickets for $9 each and no more than three children's tickets for $5 each.

YOUR MISSION: Find how many adult and children's tickets Troy's family purchased.

Understand You know that the family spent a total of $42. Also, at least 2 adult tickets were purchased for $9 each and no more than three children's tickets were purchased for $5 each. You need to find how many of each ticket Troy's family purchased.

Plan Guess and check to find the number of adult and children's tickets purchased.

Solve

Adult Tickets	Children's Tickets	Total Cost
2	2	$2(9) + 2(5) = 28$
2	3	$2(9) + 3(5) = 33$
3	2	$3(9) + 2(5) = 37$
3	3	$3(9) + 3(5) = 42$ ✓

So, Troy's family bought 3 adult and 3 children's tickets.

Check Look back. Three adult tickets cost $3 \times \$9$, or $27 and three children's tickets cost $3 \times \$5$ or $15. Since $\$27 + \$15 = \$42$, the answer is correct.

Mixed Problem Solving

EXTRA PRACTICE
See page 664.

Use any strategy shown below to solve each problem.

PROBLEM-SOLVING STRATEGIES

- Guess and check.
- Make a table.
- Make an organized list.

1. The table shows the number of monthly trips to the mall for several fifth-grade students. How many students went to the mall six or more times in the month?

Students' Monthly Trips to the Mall					
5	10	0	1	11	4
12	4	3	6	8	5
8	9	6	2	13	2

2. Use the symbols +, −, ×, ÷ to make the following math sentence true. Use each symbol only once.

$$3 \blacksquare 4 \blacksquare 6 \blacksquare 1 = 18$$

3. A sandwich shop offers 4 different kinds of bread and 6 different kinds of meat. How many different sandwiches can be made using one kind of bread and two different kinds of meat?

4. The denominator of a fraction is 3 more than the numerator. If you add 1 to the numerator, the fraction is equivalent to $\frac{4}{5}$. What is the original fraction?

5. Mario caught two trout while fishing. The first trout weighed 7 pounds and the second trout weighed 4.125 pounds. How many more pounds did the first trout weigh than the second trout?

6. The list shows how many times each of 18 students rode a roller coaster at an amusement park one day. How many more students rode a roller coaster 5 to 9 times than 10 to 14 times?

Number of Times Rode Roller Coaster					
5	10	12	8	7	2
6	4	9	13	8	6
3	0	14	3	11	5

7. A sweater company offers 6 different styles of sweaters in 5 different colors. How many combinations of style and color are possible?

8. The difference between two whole numbers is 14. Their product is 1,800. Find the two numbers.

9. The graphic below shows the lengths in miles of the longest rivers in the world. About how many total miles long would these three rivers be if they were laid end to end?

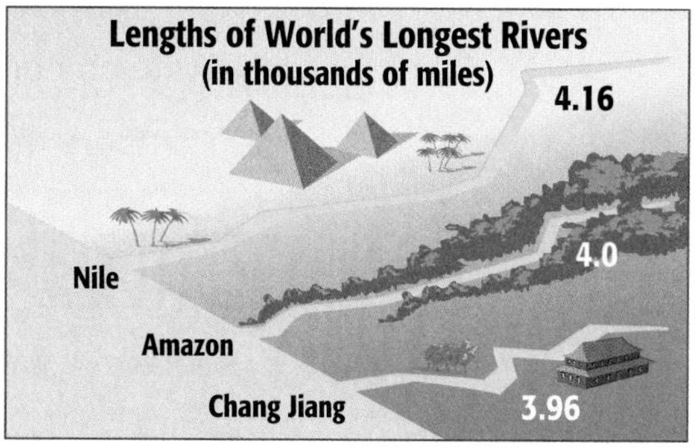

Source: *The World Almanac*

10. WRITING IN ▸MATH Write a problem that you can solve using one of the listed strategies. What strategy did you choose? Explain how to solve the problem using that strategy.

4-7 Comparing Fractions

GET READY to Learn

Hands-On Mini Lab

Use number lines to determine which is greater, $\frac{3}{5}$ or $\frac{7}{10}$.

Step 1 Graph the fractions on number lines with equal units.

Step 2 Compare the fractions. Since $\frac{7}{10}$ is to the right of $\frac{3}{5}$ on the number line, $\frac{7}{10}$ is greater than $\frac{3}{5}$.

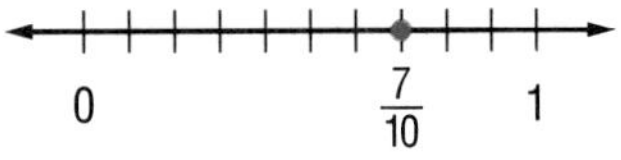

Use number lines to determine which fraction is greater.

1. $\frac{1}{2}$ or $\frac{3}{7}$ **2.** $\frac{1}{6}$ or $\frac{2}{9}$ **3.** $\frac{3}{8}$ or $\frac{4}{7}$

MAIN IDEA

I will compare fractions.

Standard 5SDAP1.3 Use fractions and percentages **to compare data sets of different sizes.**

New Vocabulary

least common denominator (LCD)

To compare two fractions without using number lines, you can follow the steps below.

KEY CONCEPT Compare Two Fractions

1. Find the **least common denominator (LCD)** of the fractions. That is, find the least common multiple of the denominators.
2. Write an equivalent fraction for each fraction using the LCD.
3. Compare the numerators.

EXAMPLE Compare Fractions

1 Replace ● with <, >, or = in $\frac{5}{8}$ ● $\frac{7}{12}$ to make a true sentence.

Step 1 The LCM of the denominators is 24. So, the LCD is 24.

Step 2 Write an equivalent fraction with a denominator of 24 for each fraction.

$$\frac{5}{8} = \frac{15}{24} \ (\times 3) \qquad \frac{7}{12} = \frac{14}{24} \ (\times 2)$$

Step 3 $\frac{15}{24} > \frac{14}{24}$, since 15 > 14. So, $\frac{5}{8} > \frac{7}{12}$.

Remember

When comparing mixed numbers like $5\frac{1}{8}$ and $3\frac{7}{10}$, it is not necessary to find a common denominator. Since $5 > 3$, $5\frac{1}{8} > 3\frac{7}{10}$.

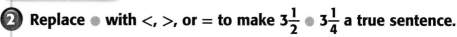

EXAMPLE Compare Mixed Numbers

2 Replace ● with <, >, or = to make $3\frac{1}{2}$ ● $3\frac{1}{4}$ a true sentence.

Since the whole numbers are the same, compare $\frac{1}{2}$ and $\frac{1}{4}$.

Step 1 The LCM of the denominators is 4. So, the LCD is 4.

Step 2 Write an equivalent fraction with a denominator of 4 for each fraction.

$$\frac{1}{2} \overset{\times 2}{=} \frac{2}{4} \qquad \frac{1}{4} \overset{\times 1}{=} \frac{1}{4}$$

Step 3 $\frac{2}{4} > \frac{1}{4}$, since $2 > 1$. So, $3\frac{1}{2} > 3\frac{1}{4}$.

Check Graph $3\frac{1}{2}$ and $3\frac{1}{4}$ on a number line. Since 4 is the LCD, separate the number line from 3 to 4 into four equal parts. Then graph $3\frac{2}{4}$ and $3\frac{1}{4}$.

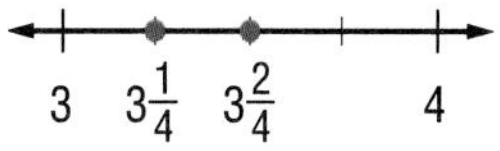

Since $3\frac{2}{4}$ is to the right of $3\frac{1}{4}$, the answer is correct.

You can compare data sets of different sizes using fractions.

EXAMPLE Compare Data Sets

3 Five out of 6 boys in a particular class play a musical instrument, and 3 out of 5 girls in the same class play a musical instrument. Which group has the greater fraction who play a musical instrument: boys or girls?

Step 1 Write each quantity as a fraction.

Boys: $\frac{5}{6}$ Girls: $\frac{3}{5}$

Step 2 The LCD of the fractions is 30. So, rewrite each fraction with a denominator of 30.

$$\frac{5}{6} \overset{\times 5}{=} \frac{25}{30} \qquad \frac{3}{5} \overset{\times 6}{=} \frac{18}{30}$$

Since $\frac{25}{30} > \frac{18}{30}$, the fraction of boys who play a musical instrument is greater than the fraction of girls who play a musical instrument.

Remember

You can also use mental math to answer the question in Example 4. $\frac{8}{25}$ is less than $\frac{1}{2}$, $\frac{3}{100}$ is less than $\frac{1}{2}$, and $\frac{13}{20}$ is greater than $\frac{1}{2}$. So, the answer is $\frac{13}{20}$.

Real-World EXAMPLE

4 According to the survey data, what did most people say should be done with the penny?

Do We Need the Penny?	
Get rid of the penny	$\frac{8}{25}$
Undecided	$\frac{3}{100}$
Keep the penny	$\frac{13}{20}$

Source: Coinstar

You need to compare the fractions. The LCD of the fractions is 100.

$$\frac{8}{25} = \frac{8 \times 4}{25 \times 4} = \frac{32}{100} \qquad \frac{3}{100} = \frac{3 \times 1}{100 \times 1} = \frac{3}{100} \qquad \frac{13}{20} = \frac{13 \times 5}{20 \times 5} = \frac{65}{100}$$

Rewrite the fractions with the LCD, 100.

Since $\frac{13}{20}$ is the greatest fraction, most people said we should keep the penny.

Online **Personal Tutor at** ca.gr5math.com

CHECK What You Know

Replace each ● with <, >, or = to make a true sentence. **See Examples 1, 2 (pp. 200–201)**

1. $\frac{3}{7}$ ● $\frac{1}{4}$ **2.** $\frac{5}{7}$ ● $\frac{15}{21}$ **3.** $8\frac{9}{16}$ ● $8\frac{5}{8}$

4. $\frac{2}{3}$ ● $\frac{4}{9}$ **5.** $\frac{15}{12}$ ● $\frac{7}{8}$ **6.** $4\frac{1}{6}$ ● $4\frac{5}{18}$

7. On Friday, 3 out of 4 customers at a pet store indicated that they have a puppy. On Saturday, 18 out of 20 customers indicated that they have a puppy. On which day was there a greater fraction of customers who said they have a puppy? **See Example 3 (p. 201)**

8. Nine out of 14 students in a math class said their least favorite chore was cleaning their room. In a science class, 5 out of 7 students voted for the same chore. Which class had the greater fraction of students who said their least favorite chore was cleaning their room? **See Example 3 (p. 201)**

9. The number of miles three friends walk each day is shown in the table at the right. Which girl walks the farthest? **See Example 4 (p. 202)**

Miles Walked	
Kayla	$\frac{3}{9}$
Nora	$\frac{1}{6}$
Mercedes	$\frac{4}{5}$

10. In a survey about household odors, $\frac{7}{20}$ of the people said pet odors were the smelliest, $\frac{1}{10}$ voted for cooking odors, and $\frac{2}{5}$ chose tobacco smoke. Which odor did people choose the most? **See Example 4 (p. 202)**

11. Talk About It Identify the least common denominator of $\frac{3}{5}$ and $\frac{3}{4}$. Explain your reasoning.

Practice and Problem Solving

EXTRA PRACTICE
See page 665.

Replace each ● with <, >, or = to make a true statement.

See Examples 1, 2 (pp. 200–201)

12. $\frac{1}{3}$ ● $\frac{3}{5}$ **13.** $\frac{7}{8}$ ● $\frac{5}{6}$ **14.** $5\frac{6}{9}$ ● $5\frac{2}{3}$ **15.** $7\frac{3}{4}$ ● $7\frac{9}{16}$

16. $\frac{7}{12}$ ● $\frac{1}{2}$ **17.** $\frac{14}{18}$ ● $\frac{7}{9}$ **18.** $2\frac{4}{5}$ ● $2\frac{13}{15}$ **19.** $10\frac{5}{8}$ ● $10\frac{20}{32}$

20. Which is shorter, $\frac{2}{3}$ of an hour or $\frac{8}{15}$ of an hour?

21. Which is more, $\frac{3}{5}$ of a dollar or $\frac{3}{4}$ of a dollar?

22. Ten out of 35 residents exercise every day in Springtown, and 3 out of 7 Pine Valley residents exercise every day. In which town do the greater fraction of the residents exercise?

23. Two out of 3 students in sixth grade said they have a web log, and 4 out of 16 students in fifth grade said they have a web log. In which grade is there a greater fraction of students who have a web log?

24. **Measurement** Three paint brushes have widths of $\frac{3}{8}$ inch, $\frac{1}{2}$ inch, and $\frac{3}{4}$ inch. What is the measure of the brush with the greatest width?

25. **Measurement** Kate is using three different-sized wood screws to build a cabinet. The sizes are $1\frac{1}{4}$ inch, $1\frac{5}{8}$ inch, and $1\frac{1}{2}$ inch. Which of these sizes is the longest?

Replace each ● with <, >, or = to make a true statement.

26. $\frac{3}{5}$ ● $\frac{3}{20}$ **27.** $5\frac{1}{3}$ ● $6\frac{1}{3}$ **28.** $\frac{15}{24}$ ● $1\frac{5}{8}$ **29.** $\frac{18}{4}$ ● $3\frac{1}{2}$

Real-World PROBLEM SOLVING

Geography The world's five largest deserts are shown in the table.

30. Which desert is the smallest?

31. Which desert is closest to 2 million square miles?

Desert	Area (millions of square miles)
Sahara	$\frac{7}{2}$
Kalahari	$\frac{2}{10}$
Gobi	$\frac{2}{5}$
Australian	$1\frac{4}{10}$
Arabian	$\frac{1}{2}$

Source: *Scholastic Book of World Records 2005*

H.O.T. Problems

32. OPEN ENDED List three fractions with different denominators that have an LCD of 24. Then arrange the fractions in order from least to greatest.

33. CHALLENGE Compare $\frac{3}{8}$, $\frac{3}{7}$, and $\frac{3}{9}$ without writing equivalent fractions with a common denominator. Explain your strategy.

34. WRITING IN MATH Explain how you can compare $\frac{1}{5}$ and $\frac{7}{8}$ without using their LCD.

Standards Practice

35 Which statement about the mixed number $2\frac{3}{4}$ is true?

A $2\frac{3}{4} > 2\frac{2}{3}$

B $3 < 2\frac{3}{4}$

C $2\frac{3}{4} < 2\frac{2}{3}$

D $2\frac{1}{4} > 2\frac{3}{4}$

36 A plumber needs to drill a hole that is just slightly larger than $\frac{3}{16}$ inch in diameter. Which measure is the smallest but still larger than $\frac{3}{16}$ inch?

F $\frac{3}{32}$ inch

G $\frac{5}{16}$ inch

H $\frac{13}{64}$ inch

J $\frac{17}{32}$ inch

37 The table shows the fraction of teenage drivers that wear seat belts in four states.

State	Teenage Drivers that Wear Seat Belts
Arizona	$\frac{3}{4}$
Georgia	$\frac{37}{50}$
California	$\frac{89}{100}$
Texas	$\frac{77}{100}$

Source: National Safety Council

Which state has the greatest fraction of drivers that wear seat belts?

A Arizona

B Georgia

C California

D Texas

Spiral Review

38. Lydia has four rabbits, three cats, and two dogs. It takes her 1 hour to clean the rabbits' cages, 20 minutes to groom each cat, and 30 minutes to wash each dog. How long does it take her to do all of these chores? **(Lesson 4-6)**

Find the LCM of each set of numbers. **(Lesson 4-5)**

39. 5, 13

40. 4, 6

41. 6, 9, 21

42. 8, 12, 27

43. Express $5\frac{3}{8}$ as an improper fraction. Graph the result on a number line. **(Lesson 4-4)**

4-8 Writing Decimals as Fractions

GET READY to Learn

The table shows the data results of a favorite summer treat survey. You can write the portion of those surveyed who prefer Italian ice as a fraction.

$0.15 = \frac{15}{100}$

Favorite Summer Treats

Treat	Portion Who Prefer the Treat
Ice Cream	0.64
Italian Ice	0.15
Ice Pop	0.14
Other	0.07

Source: Opinion Research Corporation

MAIN IDEA

I will write decimals as fractions or mixed numbers in simplest form.

Preparation for Standard

5NS1.5 Identify and represent on a number line decimals, fractions, mixed numbers, and positive and negative integers.

New Vocabulary

rational number

Decimals like 0.64, 0.15, 0.14, and 0.07 can be written as fractions with denominators of 10, 100, 1,000, and so on. Any number that can be written as a fraction is a **rational number**.

EXAMPLES Write Decimals as Fractions

1 Write 0.6 as a fraction in simplest form.

In the place-value chart, the last nonzero digit, 6, is in the tenths place. Say *six tenths*.

$0.6 = \frac{6}{10}$ Write as a fraction.

$= \frac{\overset{3}{\cancel{6}}}{\underset{5}{\cancel{10}}}$ Simplify. Divide the numerator and denominator by the GCF, 2.

$= \frac{3}{5}$

1,000	100	10	1	0.1	0.01	0.001	0.0001
thousands	hundreds	tens	ones	tenths	hundredths	thousandths	ten-thousandths
0	0	0	0.	6	0	0	0

2 Write 0.45 as a fraction in simplest form.

In the place-value chart, the last nonzero digit, 5, is in the hundredths place. Say *forty-five hundredths*.

$0.45 = \frac{45}{100}$ Write as a fraction.

$= \frac{\overset{9}{\cancel{45}}}{\underset{20}{\cancel{100}}}$ Simplify. Divide by the GCF, 5.

$= \frac{9}{20}$

1,000	100	10	1	0.1	0.01	0.001	0.0001
thousands	hundreds	tens	ones	tenths	hundredths	thousandths	ten-thousandths
0	0	0	0.	4	5	0	0

Remember

Here are some commonly used decimal fraction equivalencies:

$0.2 = \frac{1}{5}$

$0.25 = \frac{1}{4}$

$0.5 = \frac{1}{2}$

$0.75 = \frac{3}{4}$

It is helpful to memorize these.

EXAMPLES Write Decimals as Fractions

3 Write 0.05 as a fraction in simplest form.

In the place-value chart, the last nonzero digit, 5, is in the hundredths place. Say *five-hundredths.*

$0.05 = \frac{5}{100}$ Write as a fraction.

$= \frac{\overset{1}{\cancel{5}}}{\underset{20}{\cancel{100}}}$ Simplify. Divide by the GCF, 5.

$= \frac{1}{20}$

1,000	100	10	1	0.1	0.01	0.001	0.0001
thousands	hundreds	tens	ones	tenths	hundredths	thousandths	ten-thousandths
0	0	0	0.	0	5	0	0

4 Write 0.375 as a fraction in simplest form.

In the place-value chart, the last nonzero digit, 5, is in the thousandths place. Say *three hundred seventy-five thousandths.*

$0.375 = \frac{375}{1{,}000}$ Write as a fraction.

$= \frac{\overset{3}{\cancel{375}}}{\underset{8}{\cancel{1{,}000}}}$ Simplify. Divide by the GCF, 125.

$= \frac{3}{8}$

1,000	100	10	1	0.1	0.01	0.001	0.0001
thousands	hundreds	tens	ones	tenths	hundredths	thousandths	ten-thousandths
0	0	0	0.	3	7	5	0

Decimals like 3.25, 26.82, and 125.54 can be written as mixed numbers in simplest form.

EXAMPLE Write Decimals as Mixed Numbers

5 In a recent year, 3.88 million metric tons of cheese were produced in the United States. Express this amount as a mixed number in simplest form.

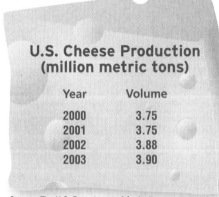

U.S. Cheese Production (million metric tons)

Year	Volume
2000	3.75
2001	3.75
2002	3.88
2003	3.90

Source: The U.S. Department of Agriculture

$3.88 = 3\frac{88}{100}$ Write as a fraction.

$= 3\frac{\overset{22}{\cancel{88}}}{\underset{25}{\cancel{100}}}$ Simplify.

$= 3\frac{22}{25}$

Online Personal Tutor at ca.gr5math.com

✓ CHECK What You Know

Write each decimal as a fraction or mixed number in simplest form. See Examples 1–5 (pp. 205–206)

1. 0.4 **2.** 0.64 **3.** 0.75 **4.** 0.07

5. 0.525 **6.** 0.375 **7.** 2.75 **8.** 5.12

9. **Measurement** The newspaper reported that it rained 1.25 inches last month. Express this amount as a mixed number in simplest form. See Example 5 (p. 206)

10. Talk About It What fraction is equivalent to 0.04? Explain how you know they are equivalent.

Practice and Problem Solving

EXTRA PRACTICE See page 665.

Write each decimal as a fraction in simplest form. See Examples 1–4 (pp. 205–206)

11. 0.3 **12.** 0.7 **13.** 0.2 **14.** 0.5

15. 0.33 **16.** 0.21 **17.** 0.06 **18.** 0.09

19. 0.875 **20.** 0.425 **21.** 0.018 **22.** 0.004

Write each decimal as a mixed number in simplest form. See Example 5 (p. 206)

23. 8.9 **24.** 12.1 **25.** 14.06 **26.** 17.03

27. 9.35 **28.** 42.96 **29.** 7.425 **30.** 50.605

Measurement For Exercises 31 and 32, use the road sign.

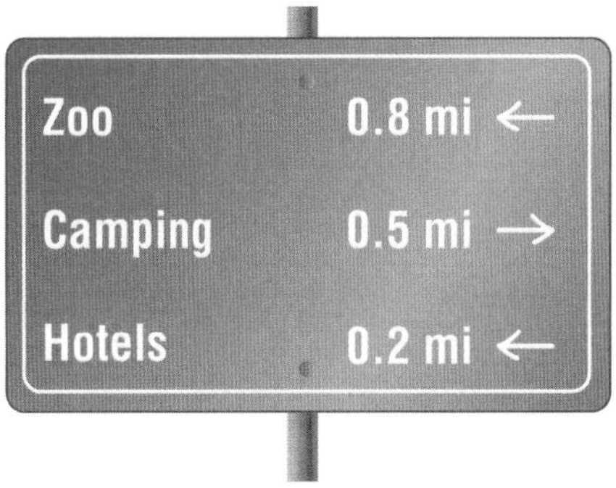

31. What fraction of a mile is each landmark from the exit?

32. How much farther is the zoo than the hotels? Write the distance as a fraction in simplest form.

Write the letter that represents each quantity on the number line.

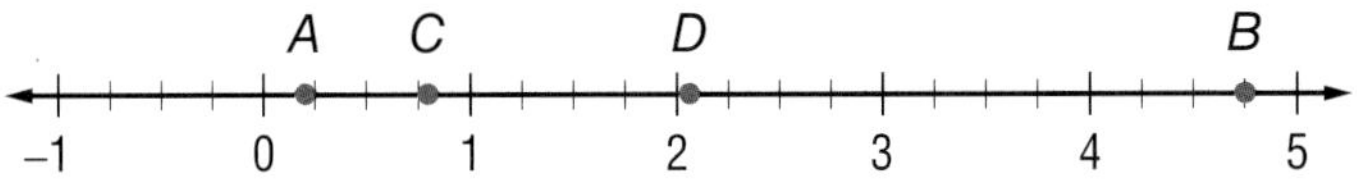

33. $\frac{1}{5}$ **34.** 4.78 **35.** $2\frac{3}{50}$ **36.** 0.8

H.O.T. Problems

37. CHALLENGE Decide whether the following statement is *true* or *false.* Explain your reasoning.

Decimals like 0.8, 0.75, and 3.852 can be written as a fraction with a denominator that is divisible by 2 and 5.

38. FIND THE ERROR Miguel and Halley are writing 3.72 as a mixed number. Who is correct? Explain your reasoning.

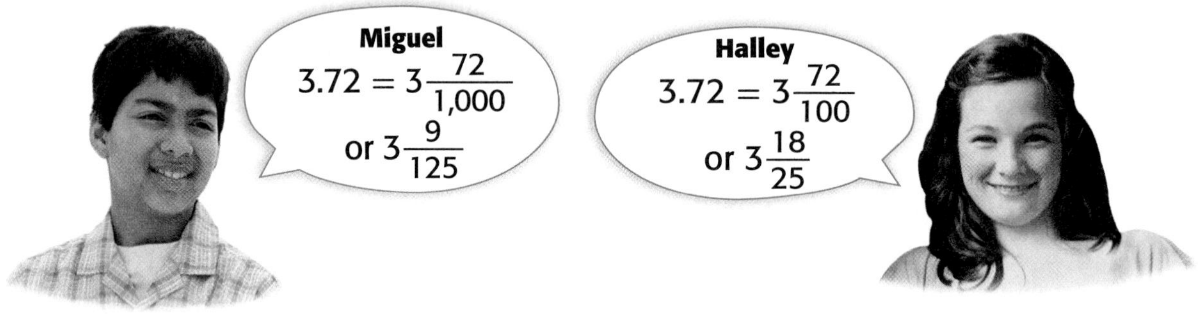

Miguel
$3.72 = 3\frac{72}{1,000}$ or $3\frac{9}{125}$
Halley
$3.72 = 3\frac{72}{100}$ or $3\frac{18}{25}$

39. WRITING IN ▸MATH Explain how to express 0.36 as a fraction.

Standards Practice

40 Rafael shaded 0.25 of the design.

Which fraction in simplest form represents the shaded part of the design?

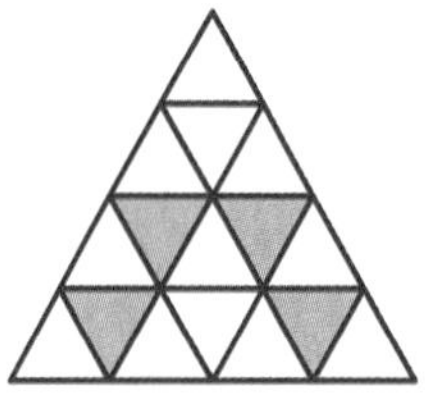

A $\frac{1}{2}$

B $\frac{25}{100}$

C $\frac{4}{16}$

D $\frac{1}{4}$

41 Write 0.9 as a fraction.

F $\frac{1}{9}$

G $\frac{3}{5}$

H $\frac{9}{10}$

J $\frac{10}{9}$

Spiral Review

Replace each ● with <, >, or = to make a true sentence. (Lesson 4-7)

42. $\frac{1}{3}$ ● $\frac{2}{7}$

43. $7\frac{5}{9}$ ● $7\frac{6}{11}$

44. $\frac{3}{5}$ ● $\frac{12}{20}$

45. $8\frac{4}{15}$ ● $9\frac{8}{27}$

46. The number of students at Aurora Junior High is half the number it was twenty years ago. If there were 758 students twenty years ago, how many students are there now? (Lesson 4-6)

47. Algebra Solve $x \div 3 = 5$ mentally. (Lesson 1-8)

4-9 Writing Fractions as Decimals

GET READY to Learn

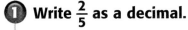

The table shows the responses to a survey of birth order. You can write the decimal for $\frac{3}{10}$ by using place value.

What is Your Birth Order?	Response
Oldest Child	$\frac{1}{20}$
Middle Child	$\frac{1}{2}$
Youngest Child	$\frac{3}{10}$
Only Child	$\frac{3}{20}$

MAIN IDEA

I will write fractions as decimals.

Standard 5NS1.2 Interpret percents as a part of a hundred; **find decimal** and percent **equivalents for common fractions and explain why they represent the same value;** compute a given percent of a whole number.

Remember

When graphed on a number line, equivalent fractions and decimals will be at the same location.

Fractions with denominators of 10, 100, or 1,000 can be written as a decimal using place value. For fractions whose denominators are *factors* of 10, 100, or 1,000, you can write equivalent fractions with these denominators.

EXAMPLES Write Fractions as Decimals

1 Write $\frac{2}{5}$ as a decimal.

Since 5 is a factor of 10, write an equivalent fraction with a denominator of 10.

$$\frac{2}{5} = \frac{4}{10}$$ (×2 numerator and denominator) Since 5 × 2 = 10, multiply the numerator and denominator by 2.

$= 0.4$ Read 0.4 as four tenths.

So, $\frac{2}{5} = 0.4$.

2 Write $\frac{3}{4}$ as a decimal.

Since 4 is a factor of 100, write an equivalent fraction with a denominator of 100.

$$\frac{3}{4} = \frac{75}{100}$$ (×25 numerator and denominator) Since 4 × 25 = 100, multiply the numerator and denominator by 25.

$= 0.75$ Read 0.75 as seventy-five hundredths.

So, $\frac{3}{4} = 0.75$.

In Example 2, you found that $\frac{3}{4} = 0.75$ by writing equivalent fractions. Another way to write a fraction as a decimal is to divide.

$$\begin{array}{r} 0.75 \\ 4\overline{)3.00} \\ -28 \\ \hline 20 \\ -20 \\ \hline 0 \end{array}$$

Divide 3 by 4.

Any fraction can be written as a decimal by dividing the numerator by the denominator.

Remember

When dividing the numerator by the denominator, division ends when the remainder is zero.

EXAMPLE Fractions as Decimals

3 Write $\frac{7}{8}$ as a decimal.

Divide 7 by 8.

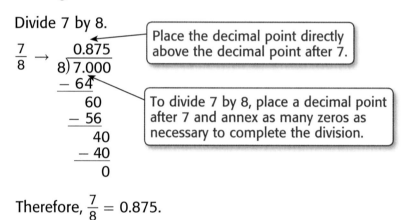

$$\frac{7}{8} \rightarrow \begin{array}{r} 0.875 \\ 8\overline{)7.000} \\ -64 \\ \hline 60 \\ -56 \\ \hline 40 \\ -40 \\ \hline 0 \end{array}$$

Place the decimal point directly above the decimal point after 7.

To divide 7 by 8, place a decimal point after 7 and annex as many zeros as necessary to complete the division.

Therefore, $\frac{7}{8} = 0.875$.

Mixed numbers can also be written as decimals.

Real-World EXAMPLE Mixed Numbers

4 In the United States, there are $55\frac{7}{50}$ Internet users per 100 people. Write the number of Internet users per 100 people as a decimal.

$55\frac{7}{50} = 55 + \frac{7}{50}$	Definition of a mixed number
$= 55 + \frac{14}{100}$	Since $50 \times 2 = 100$, multiply the numerator and the denominator by 2.
$= 55 + 0.14$ or 55.14	Read 55.14 as *fifty-five and fourteen hundredths*.

The number of Internet users per 100 people is 55.14.

Online Personal Tutor at ca.gr5math.com

CHECK What You Know

Write each fraction or mixed number as a decimal.

See Examples 1–4 (pp. 209–210)

1. $\frac{9}{10}$ **2.** $\frac{7}{2}$ **3.** $\frac{1}{8}$

4. $\frac{9}{25}$ **5.** $6\frac{4}{25}$ **6.** $4\frac{9}{40}$

7. A tiger is $10\frac{4}{5}$ feet in length. Express this length as a decimal.

8. Talk About It Name two methods for expressing fractions as decimals.

Practice and Problem Solving

EXTRA PRACTICE See page 665.

Write each fraction or mixed number as a decimal.

See Examples 1–4 (pp. 209–210)

9. $\frac{1}{20}$ **10.** $\frac{19}{25}$ **11.** $\frac{77}{200}$ **12.** $\frac{311}{500}$

13. $\frac{5}{8}$ **14.** $\frac{12}{75}$ **15.** $\frac{9}{16}$ **16.** $\frac{5}{32}$

17. $6\frac{1}{16}$ **18.** $8\frac{21}{40}$ **19.** $12\frac{43}{80}$ **20.** $9\frac{9}{32}$

21. **Measurement** Oleta ran $3\frac{2}{5}$ miles. Express this distance as a decimal.

22. Rancho Middle School has an average of $23\frac{3}{8}$ students per teacher. Write this fraction as a decimal.

Graph each pair of numbers on a number line. Then replace each ● with <, >, or = to make a true sentence.

23. $\frac{3}{4}$ ● 0.8 **24.** $\frac{17}{40}$ ● 0.4 **25.** 0.72 ● $\frac{3}{4}$

26. Paloma can run the 100-meter dash in $16\frac{1}{5}$ seconds. Savannah's best time is 19.8 seconds. How much faster is Paloma than Savannah in the 100-meter dash?

Real-World PROBLEM SOLVING

Science The table shows the sizes for different seashells.

Seashell	Minimum Size (in.)	Maximum Size (in.)
Rose Petal Tellin	$\frac{5}{8}$	$1\frac{1}{2}$
Scotch Bonnet	1	$3\frac{5}{8}$
Striate Bubble	$\frac{1}{2}$	$1\frac{1}{8}$

27. Using decimals, name the seashell having the smallest maximum size.

28. Which seashell has the greatest minimum size?

H.O.T. Problems

Express each fraction as a decimal.

29. $\frac{1}{3}$ **30.** $\frac{2}{3}$ **31.** $\frac{4}{9}$

32. **CHALLENGE** Explain why the decimals in Exercises 29–31 are called *repeating decimals.* Write a fraction that can be expressed as a repeating decimal when two digits repeat.

33. **OPEN ENDED** Write a fraction whose decimal value is between $\frac{1}{2}$ and $\frac{3}{4}$. Write both the fraction and the equivalent decimal.

34. **WRITING IN ▸MATH** Find the decimal equivalent of $\frac{8}{25}$. Explain why it has the same value as the fraction.

Standards Practice

35 Which decimal represents the fraction graphed on the number line below?

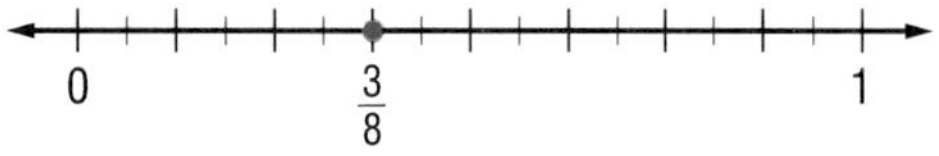

A 0.25 **C** 0.375

B 0.333 **D** 0.4

36 The formula $d = v + \frac{1}{20}v^2$ can be used to find the distance d required to stop a certain model car traveling at v miles per hour. Which of the following best represents $\frac{1}{20}$?

F 0.05 **H** 0.4

G 0.21 **J** 1.2

Spiral Review

Write each decimal as a fraction or mixed number in simplest form. (Lesson 4-8)

37. 0.25 **38.** 0.73 **39.** 8.118 **40.** 11.14

41. Which fraction is greater, $\frac{13}{40}$ or $\frac{3}{7}$? (Lesson 4-7)

42. Twenty out of two dozen tortillas are whole wheat. Write this amount as a fraction in simplest form. (*Hint:* 1 dozen = 12) (Lesson 4-3)

Round each decimal or whole number to the indicated place-value position. (Lesson 3-3)

43. 0.122; hundredths **44.** 0.899; tenths

45. 13,404,689; millions **46.** 7,965,170; ten thousands

4-10 Algebra: Ordered Pairs and Functions

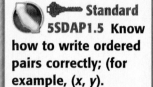

GET READY to Learn

A street map is shown. The map is labeled with letters and numbers so that the streets are easy to locate.

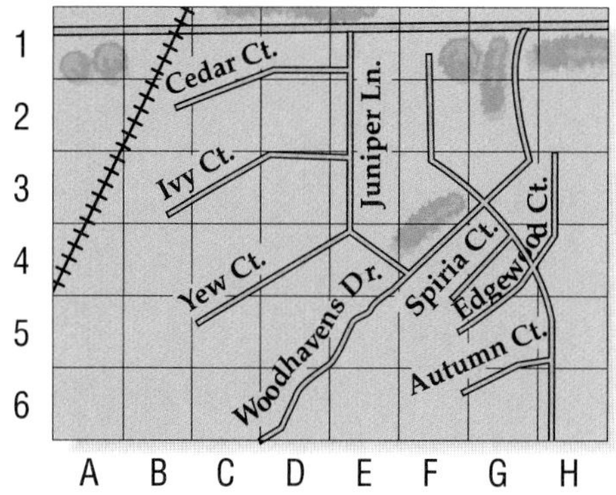

MAIN IDEA

I will use ordered pairs to locate points and organize data.

Standard 5SDAP1.5 Know how to write ordered pairs correctly; (for example, (*x*, *y*).

New Vocabulary

- coordinate plane
- origin
- *x*-axis
- *y*-axis
- ordered pair
- *x*-coordinate
- *y*-coordinate
- graph

In mathematics, points are located on a coordinate plane.

The **coordinate plane** is formed when two number lines intersect at right angles at their zero points. This point is called the **origin**. The horizontal number line is called the ***x*-axis**, and the vertical number line is called the ***y*-axis**.

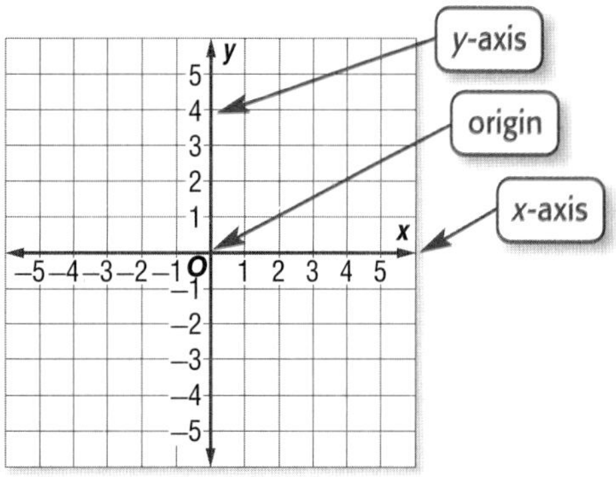

You can use an **ordered pair** to name any point on the coordinate plane. The first number in an ordered pair is the ***x*-coordinate**, and the second number is the ***y*-coordinate**.

The *x*-coordinate corresponds to a number on the *x*-axis. (3, 6) The *y*-coordinate corresponds to a number on the *y*-axis.

A point located on the *x*-axis will have a *y*-coordinate of 0. A point located on the *y*-axis will have an *x*-coordinate of 0.

In this lesson, you will name and graph ordered pairs with positive *x*- and *y*-coordinates.

Remember

A coordinate plane is also called a coordinate grid.

EXAMPLE Naming Points Using Ordered Pairs

1 Write the ordered pair that names point *L*.

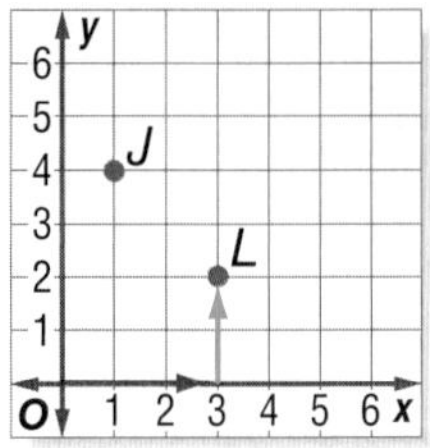

Step 1 Start at the origin. Move right along the *x*-axis until you are under point *L*. The *x*-coordinate of the ordered pair is 3.

Step 2 Now move up until you reach point *L*. The *y*-coordinate is 2.

So, point *L* is named by the ordered pair (3, 2).

You can also graph a point on a coordinate plane. To **graph** a point means to place a dot at the point named by an ordered pair.

EXAMPLES Graphing Ordered Pairs

2 Graph the point *M*(5, 6).

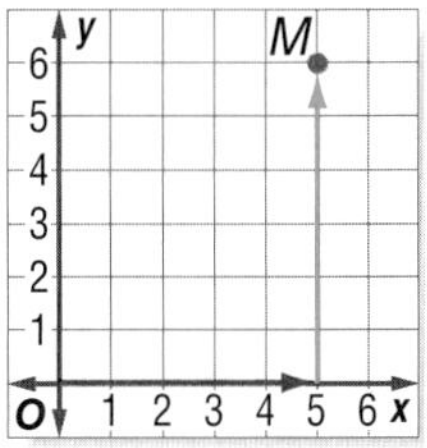

- Start at the origin.
- Move 5 units to the right on the *x*-axis.
- Then move 6 units up to locate the point.
- Draw a dot and label the dot *M*.

3 Graph the point $N\left(2\frac{1}{2}, 2\right)$.

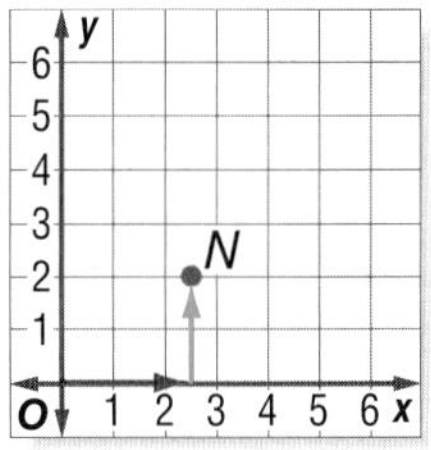

- Start at the origin.
- The value $2\frac{1}{2}$ is halfway between 2 and 3. So, on the *x*-axis move halfway between 2 and 3.
- Then move 2 units up to locate the point.
- Draw a dot and label the dot *N*.

Remember

To graph a fraction or a decimal, you can also draw the coordinate plane so that the axes are separated into halves, thirds, and so on.

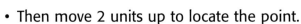

Online Personal Tutor at ca.gr5math.com

Ordered pairs can also be used to show how data are related.

Real-World EXAMPLE

4 The cheerleaders at South Middle School are selling bracelets for a fund-raiser. List this information as ordered pairs (number of bracelets, cost).

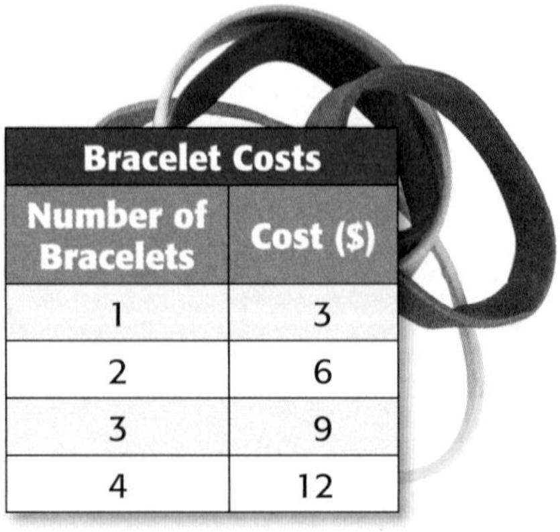

Bracelet Costs

Number of Bracelets	Cost ($)
1	3
2	6
3	9
4	12

The ordered pairs are (1, 3), (2, 6), (3, 9), and (4, 12).

Math Online Extra Examples at ca.gr5math.com

Concepts in Motion
Animation
ca.gr5math.com

Real-World EXAMPLE

5 Graph the ordered pairs from Example 4. Then describe the graph.

The ordered pairs (1, 3), (2, 6), (3, 9) and (4, 12), correspond to the points *A*, *B*, *C*, and *D* in the coordinate plane.

The points appear to lie on a line.

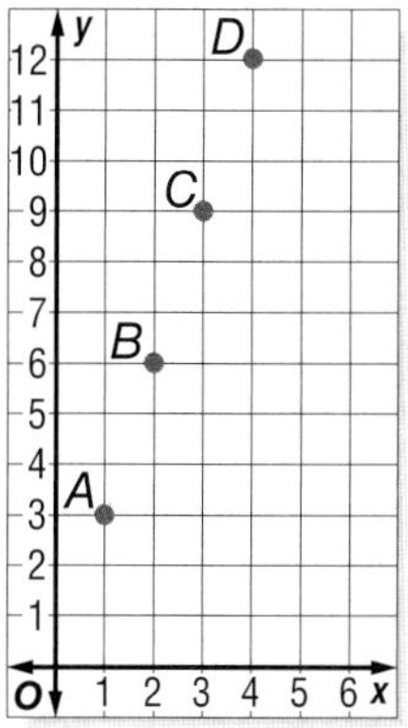

CHECK What You Know

Use the coordinate plane at the right to name the ordered pair for each point. See Example 1 (p. 214)

1. *G* **2.** *D*

3. *C* **4.** *F*

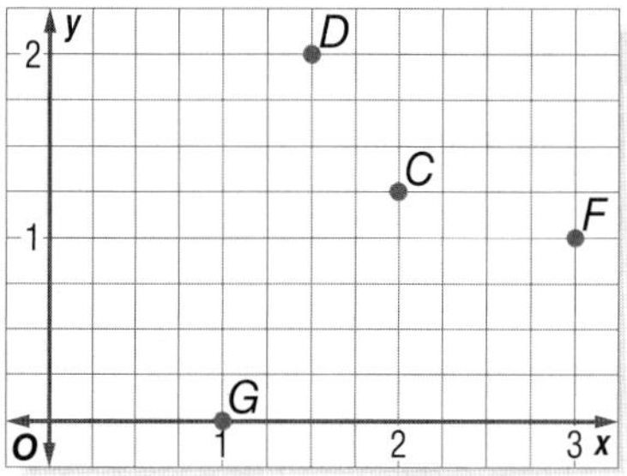

Graph and label each point on a coordinate plane.
See Examples 2, 3 (p. 214)

5. *A*(3, 7) **6.** *B*(0, 4)

7. *C*(1.5, 6) **8.** $D\left(2, 4\frac{3}{4}\right)$

For Exercises 9 and 10, use the following information.
See Examples 4, 5 (pp. 214–215)

In basketball, each shot made from outside the 3-point line scores 3 points. The total points for 0, 1, 2, and 3 shots made are shown in the table at the right.

3-Point Shots Made	Total Points
0	0
1	3
2	6
3	9

9. List this information as ordered pairs (3-point shots made, total number of points).

10. Graph the ordered pairs. Then describe the graph.

11. Talk About It Name the *x*-coordinate and the *y*-coordinate of the ordered pair (7, 5).

Practice and Problem Solving

EXTRA PRACTICE
See page 666.

Use the coordinate plane at the right to name the ordered pair for each point. See Example 1 (p. 214)

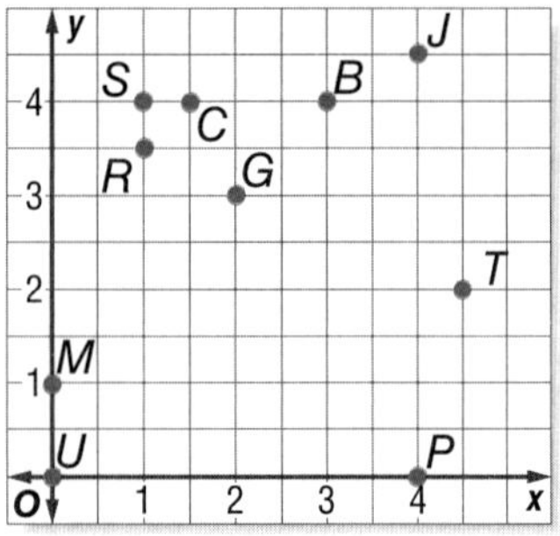

12. *P*

13. *G*

14. *B*

15. *M*

16. *S*

17. *U*

18. *T*

19. *R*

20. *J*

21. *C*

Graph and label each point on a coordinate plane.
See Examples 2, 3 (p. 214)

22. $L(6, 1)$ **23.** $M(3, 0)$ **24.** $N\left(3\frac{1}{2}, 5\right)$ **25.** $Q\left(0, 5\frac{1}{4}\right)$

26. $R(1.5, 7)$ **27.** $P(4, 1.75)$ **28.** $A\left(2\frac{3}{4}, 2\right)$ **29.** $B\left(5, 4\frac{1}{4}\right)$

Measurement For Exercises 30 and 31, use the following information. See Examples 4, 5 (pp. 214–215)

The table gives the amount of fencing needed to create square pens.

Side Length (ft)	5	$5\frac{1}{4}$	$5\frac{1}{2}$	$5\frac{3}{4}$
Amount of Fencing (ft)	20	21	22	23

30. List this information as ordered pairs (side length, amount of fencing).

31. Graph the ordered pairs. Then describe the graph.

For Exercises 32 and 33, use the following information.
See Examples 4–5 (pp. 214–215)

It takes Rashid 5 minutes to ride his scooter once around a bike path. The table at the right shows this relationship.

Times Around Path	Total Time (min)
0	0
1	5
2	10
3	15

32. List this information as ordered pairs (times around the path, total time).

33. Graph the ordered pairs. Then describe the graph.

34. Geometry Three of the corners of a square drawn on a coordinate plane are located at (3.5, 8), (3.5, 3), and (8.5, 8). What is the ordered pair of the fourth corner?

Math Online **Self-Check Quiz at** ca.gr5math.com

H.O.T. Problems

35. OPEN ENDED Give the coordinates of a point located on the *y*-axis.

36. CHALLENGE Give the coordinates of the point located halfway between (2, 1) and (2, 4).

37. WRITING IN ► MATH Explain how to graph an ordered pair.

Standards Practice

38 Which ordered pair represents a point located inside both the square and the circle?

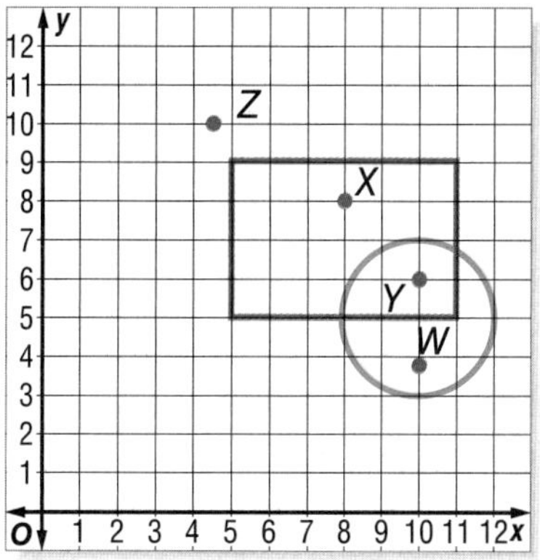

A (9, 4)

B (10, 6)

C (8, 7)

D (11, 8)

39 What point on the grid below represents $\left(9, 3\frac{1}{2}\right)$?

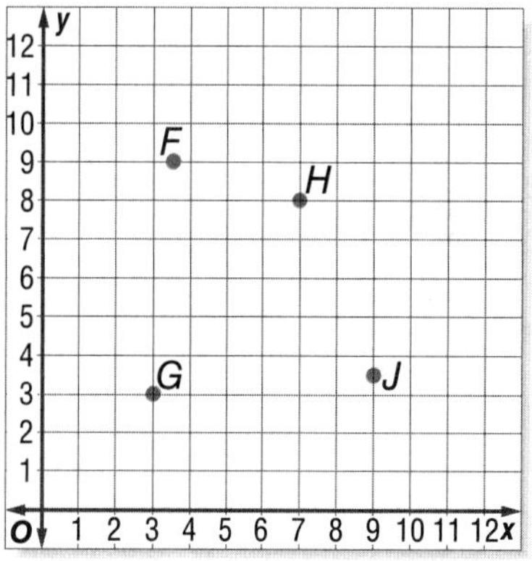

F Point *F*

G Point *G*

H Point *H*

J Point *J*

Spiral Review

40. Algebra The formula $A = \frac{1}{2}(b_1 + b_2)h$ can be used to find the area *A* of a trapezoid given the length of the bases b_1 and b_2 and the height *h*. Express $\frac{1}{2}$ as a decimal. **(Lesson 4-9)**

Write each decimal as a fraction or mixed number in simplest form. (Lesson 4-8)

41. 1.34 **42.** 0.052 **43.** 13.008

44. The manager of a shoe store wants to post a display of the number of shoes sold by each sales associate over each of the past 6 months. What type of statistical display would be most appropriate for this situation? **(Lesson 2-9)**

Problem Solving in Geography

The Great United States

How big is the United States? It depends on what you're comparing it to. In total land area, the U.S. is about three times as large as India and about one and one-third times as large as Australia. However, the U.S. is only about two-thirds the size of Russia and only accounts for about one-fifteenth of the world's land area.

Source: worldatlas.com

Did You Know?

About one-fifth of the area of the United States is water.

Math Standard 5SDAP1.3 Use fractions and percentages **to compare data sets of different sizes.**

Real-World Math

Use the information on page 218 to solve each problem.

1. Write a fraction equivalent to the United States' fraction of the world's land area.
2. Are the fractions shown in the graphic *proper fractions* or *improper fractions*?
3. Rewrite the United States' and Australia's fraction of the world's land area using their least common denominator.
4. Which countries shown in the graphic have a land area as large as or larger than the United States?
5. Which country has the greater land area, Brazil or Australia?
6. Which country makes up 0.05 of the world's land area?
7. Express India's fraction of the world's land area as a decimal.

CHAPTER 4 Study Guide and Review

FOLDABLES™ Study Organizer GET READY to Study

Be sure the following Key Concepts are noted in your Foldable.

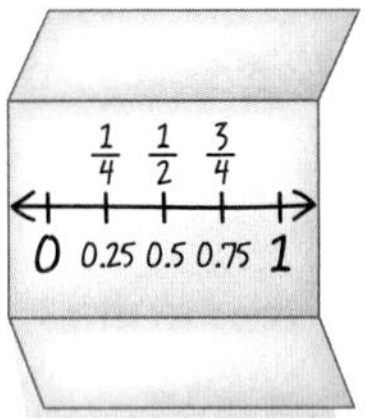

BIG Ideas

Simplest Form (Lesson 4-3)

To write a fraction in simplest form, either

- divide the numerator and denominator by common factors until the only common factor is 1, or
- divide the numerator and denominator by the GCF.

Comparing Fractions (Lesson 4-7)

To compare two fractions, follow these steps.

Step 1 Find the least common denominator (LCD) of the fractions. That is, find the least common multiple of the denominators.

Step 2 Write an equivalent fraction for each fraction using the LCD.

Step 3 Compare the numerators.

Key Vocabulary

equivalent fractions (p. 184)
greatest common factor (p. 175)
improper fraction (p. 189)
least common denominator (p. 200)
least common multiple (p. 195)
mixed number (p. 189)
multiple (p. 194)
ratio (p. 184)
simplest form (p. 185)

Vocabulary Check

State whether each sentence is *true* or *false*. If *false*, replace the underlined word or number to make a true sentence.

1. Fractions that have the same value are called multiples.
2. To write a fraction in simplest form, divide the numerator and denominator by the GCF.
3. The least common multiple of the denominators of two fractions is called the greatest common factor.
4. The LCM of 2 and 4 is less than the GCF of 2 and 4.
5. A fraction is in simplest form when the LCD of the numerator and denominator is 1.
6. $\frac{4}{5}$ and $\frac{12}{15}$ are common multiples.
7. The GCF of 5 and 3 is 1.

Lesson-by-Lesson Review

4-1 Greatest Common Factor (pp. 175–178)

Example 1
Find the GCF of 36 and 54.

To find the GCF, you can use prime factors.

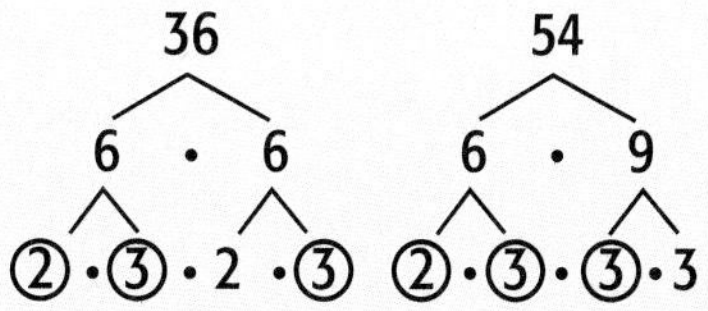

The common prime factors are 2, 3, and 3.
The GCF of 36 and 54 is $2 \times 3 \times 3$ or 18.

Find the GCF of each set of numbers.

8. 15, 18 **9.** 30, 36

10. 28, 70 **11.** 26, 52, 65

12. For a class field trip, 45 boys and 72 girls will be placed into several groups. Each group will have the same number of boys and girls. What is the greatest number of boys and girls that can be in each group?

4-2 Problem-Solving Strategy: Make an Organized List (pp. 180–181)

Example 2
A true-false test contains three questions. How many different ways are there to complete the test?

Make a list of all possible arrangements. Use T for a *true* answer to a question and F for a *false* answer.

TTT answering *false* for none of the three questions

TTF, TFT, FTT } answering *false* for one question

TFF, FTF, FFT } answering *false* for two questions

FFF answering *false* for all three questions

There are 8 ways to complete the test.

Solve. Use the *make an organized list* strategy.

13. When Rosa tossed a coin four times, she noticed that tails came up three times. In how many different ways could this have happened?

14. Shaunae has 4 stuffed animals: a tiger, teddy bear, bunny, and frog. In how many ways can she arrange these animals on her shelf?

15. A couple has 4 children, 2 of whom are boys. How many different birth orders are possible if the boys were born in consecutive years?

16. Antonio has a white shirt and a blue shirt, a pair of jeans and a pair of khakis, and a brown hat and a red hat. How many different outfits can he make if he always wears a shirt, pants, and a hat?

Study Guide and Review

4-3 Simplifying Fractions (pp. 184–188)

Example 3

Replace the x with a number so that $\frac{4}{9}$ and $\frac{x}{27}$ are equivalent.

Since $9 \times 3 = 27$, multiply the numerator and denominator by 3.

$$\frac{4}{9} \overset{\times 3}{=} \frac{12}{27}$$

Replace each x with a number so the fractions are equivalent.

17. $\frac{x}{6} = \frac{12}{24}$ **18.** $\frac{7}{x} = \frac{63}{81}$

Write each fraction in simplest form. If the fraction is already in simplest form, write *simplest form*.

19. $\frac{21}{24}$ **20.** $\frac{15}{80}$

21. Out of a dozen bagels, nine were plain. Write this fraction in simplest form.

4-4 Mixed Numbers and Improper Fractions (pp. 189–192)

Example 4

Write $4\frac{2}{5}$ as an improper fraction. Then graph the improper fraction on a number line.

$$4\frac{2}{5} = \frac{(4 \times 5) + 2}{5} = \frac{22}{5}$$

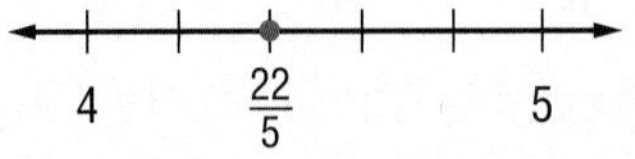

Write each mixed number as an improper fraction. Graph the result on a number line.

22. $3\frac{1}{4}$ **23.** $5\frac{3}{8}$

24. $5\frac{3}{4}$ **25.** $9\frac{4}{5}$

26. Akia bought six $\frac{1}{4}$-cup packages of peanuts. How many cups of peanuts does she have?

4-5 Least Common Multiple (pp. 194–197)

Example 5

Find the LCM of 9 and 24.

Write the prime factorization of each number.

$9 = 3 \times 3$
$24 = 2 \times 2 \times 2 \times 3$

3 is a common prime factor

So, the LCM of 9 and 24 is $2 \times 2 \times 2 \times 3 \times 3$ or 72.

Find the LCM of each set of numbers.

27. 10, 25 **28.** 8, 12, 16

29. Mr. Kwan mows his lawn every 2 days. Mr. Kwan's neighbor mows his lawn every 5 days. If both men mowed their lawn today, how many days will it be until they both mow their lawn on the same day?

4-6 Problem-Solving Investigation: Choose the Best Strategy (pp. 198–199)

Example 6

California's Mount Whitney has an elevation of 14,505 feet, and Granite Peak in Colorado has an elevation of 12,147 feet. About how much greater is Mount Whitney's elevation?

$$\begin{array}{lr l} 14{,}505 \rightarrow & 14{,}500 & \text{Estimate.} \\ 12{,}147 \rightarrow & \underline{-\ 12{,}000} & \\ & 2{,}500 & \end{array}$$

So, Mount Whitney's elevation is about 2,500 feet greater.

Choose the best strategy to solve each problem.

30. To make muffins, Kelly needs to buy almonds, flour, and butter. In how many ways can she pick up the items at the grocery store?

31. A newspaper subscription costs \$150 per year. How much does the subscription cost per month?

4-7 Comparing Fractions (pp. 200–204)

Example 7

Replace ● with <, >, or = to make $\frac{2}{5}$ ● $\frac{3}{8}$ a true sentence.

Rewrite the fractions with the LCD, 40.

$$\frac{2}{5} = \frac{16}{40} \ (\times 8) \quad \text{and} \quad \frac{3}{8} = \frac{15}{40} \ (\times 5)$$

Since $16 > 15$, $\frac{16}{40} > \frac{15}{40}$. So, $\frac{2}{5} > \frac{3}{8}$.

Replace each ● with <, >, or = to make a true sentence.

32. $\frac{2}{5}$ ● $\frac{4}{9}$

33. $2\frac{12}{15}$ ● $2\frac{4}{5}$

34. $7\frac{3}{8}$ ● $7\frac{4}{10}$

35. $\frac{7}{12}$ ● $\frac{5}{9}$

36. Four out of 6 fifth graders saw a movie last weekend. Seven out of 12 fourth graders saw a movie last weekend. In which grade did the greater fraction of students see a movie last weekend?

4-8 Writing Decimals as Fractions (pp. 205–208)

Example 8

Write 0.85 as a fraction in simplest form.

$0.85 = \frac{85}{100}$ Say *eighty-five hundredths.*

$= \frac{17}{20}$ Simplify. Divide the numerator and denominator by the GCF, 5.

Write each decimal as a fraction or mixed number in simplest form.

37. 0.9

38. 0.72

39. 0.125

40. 9.315

41. Peter's dog weighs 8.75 pounds. Write 8.75 as a mixed number in simplest form.

4-9 Writing Fractions as Decimals (pp. 209–212)

Example 9

Write $\frac{5}{8}$ as a decimal.

$$\begin{array}{r} 0.625 \\ 8\overline{)5.000} \\ -48 \\ \hline 20 \\ -16 \\ \hline 40 \\ -40 \\ \hline 0 \end{array}$$

Divide 5 by 8.

So, $\frac{5}{8} = 0.625$.

Write each fraction or mixed number as a decimal.

42. $\frac{7}{8}$

43. $\frac{9}{15}$

44. $12\frac{3}{4}$

45. $8\frac{9}{16}$

46. Measurement Carpenter bees generally measure $\frac{3}{4}$ inch long. Write this length as a decimal.

4-10 Algebra: Ordered Pairs and Functions (pp. 213–217)

Example 10

Name the ordered pair for point *A*.

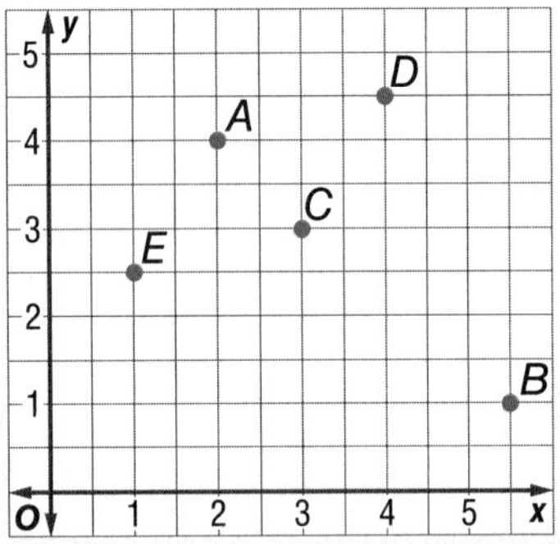

Point *A* is named by the ordered pair (2, 4).

Example 11

Graph the point $M\left(3, 2\frac{1}{4}\right)$.

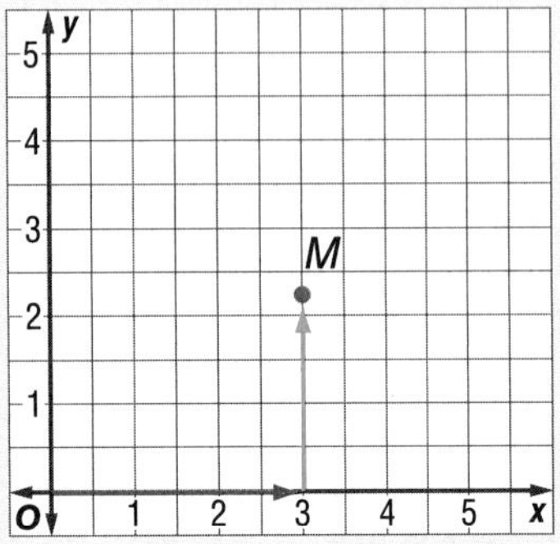

Use the coordinate plane at the left to name the ordered pair for each point.

47. *B*

48. *C*

49. *D*

50. *E*

Graph and label each point on a coordinate plane.

51. $X(5, 0)$

52. $Y(4.75, 6)$

53. $Z\left(2, 8\frac{1}{2}\right)$

54. Measurement The table gives the ages and heights, in feet, of four students in Mr. Cole's science class.

Age	11	12	11.5	12.5
Height	5	5.5	5.25	5.75

List this information as ordered pairs. Graph the ordered pairs. Then describe the graph.

CHAPTER 4

Chapter Test

1. **STANDARDS PRACTICE** Find the GCF of 24, 48, and 84.

   A 24 **C** 8

   B 12 **D** 6

Replace each *x* with a number so the fractions are equivalent.

2. $\frac{12}{18} = \frac{x}{6}$
3. $\frac{7}{9} = \frac{35}{x}$

4. Danny has 6 red marbles, 5 yellow marbles, and 4 blue marbles. Write a fraction in simplest form that compares the number of red marbles to the total number of marbles.

Write each mixed number as an improper fraction. Then graph each improper fraction on a number line.

5. $2\frac{5}{7}$
6. $4\frac{2}{3}$
7. $1\frac{4}{7}$

8. The speed of sound is about $\frac{3,806}{5}$ miles per hour. Write this speed as a mixed number.

9. In how many different ways can four friends sit next to each other in one row of a movie theater?

10. **STANDARDS PRACTICE** Hilary swims every 6 days, runs every 4 days, and cycles every 16 days. If she did all three activities today, in how many days will she do all three activities again on the same day?

    F 24 days **H** 48 days

    G 26 days **J** 64 days

Find the LCM of each set of numbers.

11. 6, 15
12. 4, 9, 18

Replace each ● with <, >, or = to make a true sentence.

13. $\frac{4}{7}$ ● $\frac{3}{5}$
14. $6\frac{1}{4}$ ● $6\frac{4}{18}$
15. $\frac{2}{9}$ ● $\frac{6}{27}$
16. $1\frac{5}{6}$ ● $1\frac{3}{4}$

17. $\frac{19}{20}$ of all bills that are printed by the U.S. Treasury Department are used to replace worn-out money. Write this fraction as a decimal.

Write each decimal as a fraction or mixed number in simplest form.

18. 0.84
19. 7.015
20. 1.3

Use the coordinate plane to name the ordered pair for each point.

21. *A*
22. *B*
23. *C*
24. *D*

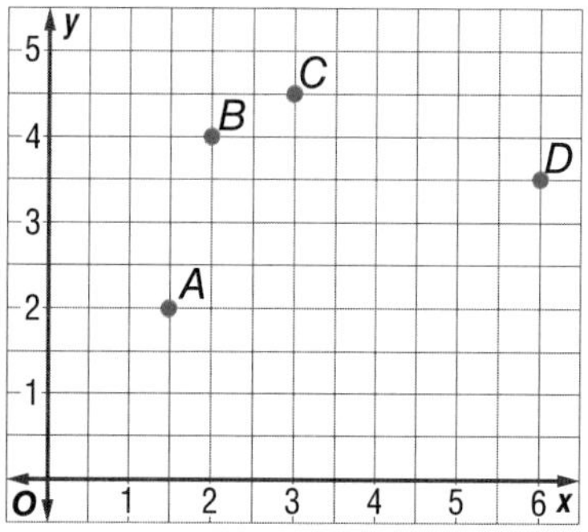

25. **WRITING IN MATH** The table shows the amount of money Andrew saved in November.

Week	Total Saved ($)
1	6
2	12
3	18
4	24

Graph this data on a coordinate plane and then describe the graph.

CHAPTER 4

California Standards Practice

Cumulative, Chapters 1–4

Standards Example

The formula $C = \frac{5}{9}(F - 32)$ can be used to convert a temperature from degrees Fahrenheit to degrees Celsius. Which of the following best represents $\frac{5}{9}$?

A 5.9

B 1.8

C 0.59

D 0.56

Read the Question

You need to convert $\frac{5}{9}$ to a decimal.

Solve the Question

Divide the numerator by the denominator.

$$\frac{5}{9} \rightarrow \begin{array}{r} 0.555\ldots \\ 9\overline{)5.0000} \\ -\,45 \\ \hline 50 \\ -\,45 \\ \hline 50 \\ -\,45 \\ \hline 5\ldots \end{array}$$

0.555... is approximately 0.56.

The answer is D.

Online Personal Tutor at ca.gr5math.com

Choose the best answer.

1 **What is the decimal 0.9 written as a fraction?**

A $\frac{9}{100}$

B $\frac{1}{9}$

C $\frac{2}{9}$

D $\frac{9}{10}$

2 **What is the fraction $\frac{5}{8}$ written as a decimal?**

F 6.25

G 1.6

H 0.625

J 0.16

3 **Find the greatest common factor of 16, 24, and 40.**

A 2
B 4
C 8
D 40

4 **Taylor, Anna, Carol, and Kaylee each walked from their houses to the public swimming pool. Taylor walked $\frac{5}{6}$ mile, Anna walked $\frac{3}{8}$ mile, Carol walked $\frac{3}{4}$ mile, and Kaylee walked $\frac{1}{2}$ mile. Who lives closest to the pool?**

F Taylor
G Anna
H Carol
J Kaylee

5 **What point corresponds to the ordered pair (7, 5)?**

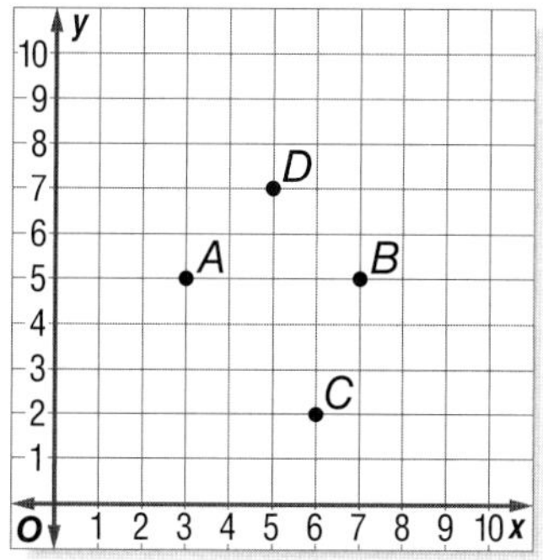

A Point *A*
B Point *B*
C Point *C*
D Point *D*

6 **What is 18,579.236 rounded to the nearest hundred?**

F 18,579
G 18,579.2
H 18,579.24
J 18,600

7 **Which situation could be described by the expression $b + \$1.25$?**

A Jill spent $1.25 for lunch and *b* dollars less for breakfast.
B Jill spent *b* dollars for breakfast and $1.25 more for lunch.
C Jill spent *b* dollars for breakfast and $1.25 times as much for lunch.
D Jill spent *b* dollars for breakfast and $1.25 less for lunch

8 **The ages of people eating at a restaurant are shown.**

12, 7, 31, 15, 9, 12, 18, 22, 14

What is the median of these ages?

F 7
G 12
H 14
J 31

9 **Alma spent 21 minutes dusting, 19 minutes vacuuming, and 28 minutes folding laundry. How much time did Alma spend on her chores?**

A 1.08 h
B 1 h 8 min
C 1.10 h
D 1 h 10 min

CHAPTER 5

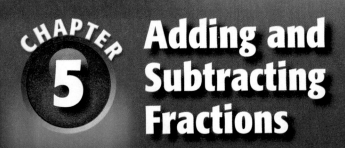

Adding and Subtracting Fractions

BIG Idea What are unlike fractions?

Unlike fractions are fractions with different denominators.

Example The waterfall shown is the Yosemite waterfall located in Yosemite National Park. It is the highest waterfall in the United States with a total drop of $808\frac{1}{3}$ yards. The Sentinel waterfall, also located in Yosemite National Park, has a total drop of $667\frac{1}{10}$ yards.

$\frac{1}{3}$ and $\frac{1}{10}$ are unlike fractions since they have different denominators.

What will I learn in this chapter?

- Round fractions and mixed numbers.
- Estimate sums and differences of fractions and mixed numbers.
- Add and subtract fractions and mixed numbers.
- Solve problems by acting them out.

Key Vocabulary

like fractions

unlike fractions

Math Online Student Study Tools at ca.gr5math.com

FOLDABLES™ Study Organizer

Make this Foldable to help you organize information about adding and subtracting fractions. Begin with two sheets of plain 11″ × 17″ paper, four index cards, and glue.

1. **Fold** one sheet in half widthwise.

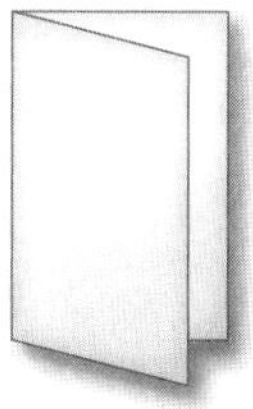

2. **Open** and fold the bottom to form a pocket. Glue edges.

3. **Repeat** steps 1 and 2. Glue the back of one piece to the front of the other to form a booklet.

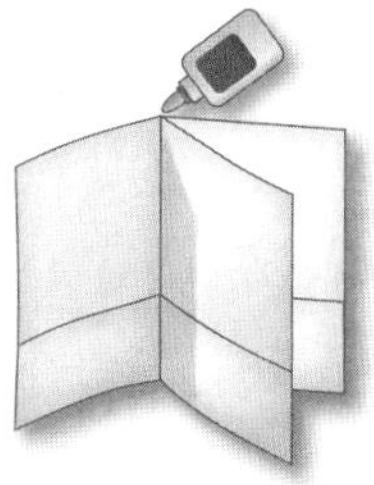

4. **Label** each left-hand pocket *What I Know* and each right-hand pocket *What I Need to Know.* Place an index card in each pocket.

ARE YOU READY for Chapter 5?

You have two ways to check prerequisite skills for this chapter.

Option 2

Math Online Take the Chapter Readiness Quiz at ca.gr5math.com.

Option 1

Complete the Quick Check below.

QUICK Check

Estimate using rounding. **(Lesson 3-5)**

1. $1.2 + 6.6$ **2.** $9.6 - 2.3$ **3.** $3.7 + 10.1$

4. $8.25 - 4.8$ **5.** $5.85 + 7.1$ **6.** $11.32 - 6.7$

7. Braden spent $17.88 on a hat and $4.22 on lunch. About how much did he spend altogether? **(Lesson 3-5)**

Write each fraction in simplest form. **(Lesson 4-3)**

8. $\frac{3}{18}$ **9.** $\frac{21}{28}$ **10.** $\frac{11}{33}$

11. $\frac{16}{40}$ **12.** $\frac{6}{38}$ **13.** $\frac{26}{52}$

14. Sandra finished 21 out of 39 problems. Write the fraction, in simplest form, of homework that she completed. **(Lesson 4-3)**

Write each improper fraction as a mixed number. **(Lesson 4-4)**

15. $\frac{11}{10}$ **16.** $\frac{14}{5}$ **17.** $\frac{9}{2}$

18. $\frac{7}{5}$ **19.** $\frac{15}{9}$ **20.** $\frac{31}{8}$

21. A recipe for a loaf of banana bread calls for $\frac{7}{3}$ cups of bananas. Write this fraction as a mixed number in simplest form. **(Lesson 4-4)**

Explore

Math Lab for 5-1
Rounding Fractions

MAIN IDEA

I will use models to round fractions to the nearest half.

Standard 5MR2.3 Use a variety of methods, such as words, numbers, symbols, charts, graphs, tables, diagrams, and **models, to explain mathematical reasoning.**

Standard 5NS1.1 Estimate, **round**, and manipulate very large (e.g., millions) and **very small** (e.g. thousandths) **numbers.**

Just as you round decimals, you can also round fractions.

ACTIVITY

Draw and shade a model to represent each fraction. Then use the model to round each fraction to the nearest half.

1 $\frac{4}{20}$

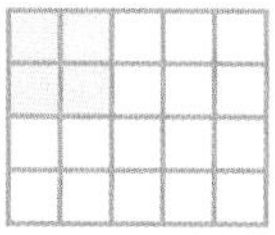

Shade 4 out of 20.

Very few sections are shaded. So, $\frac{4}{20}$ rounds to 0.

2 $\frac{4}{10}$

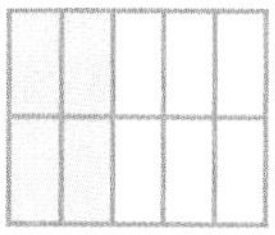

Shade 4 out of 10.

About one half of the sections are shaded. So, $\frac{4}{10}$ rounds to $\frac{1}{2}$.

3 $\frac{4}{5}$

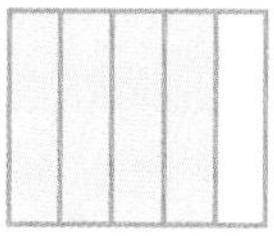

Shade 4 out of 5.

Almost all of the sections are shaded. So, $\frac{4}{5}$ rounds to 1.

CHECK What You Know

Draw and shade a model to represent each fraction. Then use the model to round each fraction to the nearest half.

a. $\frac{13}{20}$ **b.** $\frac{7}{8}$ **c.** $\frac{9}{10}$ **d.** $\frac{1}{5}$ **e.** $\frac{11}{15}$

f. $\frac{2}{25}$ **g.** $\frac{6}{10}$ **h.** $\frac{17}{20}$ **i.** $\frac{1}{8}$ **j.** $\frac{7}{16}$

Analyze the Results

1. Sort the fractions in Exercises a–j into three groups: those that round to 0, those that round to $\frac{1}{2}$, and those that round to 1.
2. Compare the numerators and denominators of the fractions in each group. Explain how to round any fraction to the nearest half without using a model.
3. Test your conjecture by repeating the activity and Exercise 1 using the fractions $\frac{3}{5}$, $\frac{3}{17}$, $\frac{16}{20}$, $\frac{2}{13}$, $\frac{5}{24}$, $\frac{7}{15}$, $\frac{7}{9}$, and $\frac{9}{11}$.

5-1 Rounding Fractions and Mixed Numbers

MAIN IDEA

I will round fractions and mixed numbers.

Standard 5MR2.5 Indicate the relative advantages of exact and approximate solutions to problems and **give answers to a specified degree of accuracy.**
Standard 5NS1.1 Estimate, **round**, and manipulate very large (e.g., millions) and **very small** (e.g. thousandths) **numbers.**

GET READY to Learn

Hands-On Mini Lab

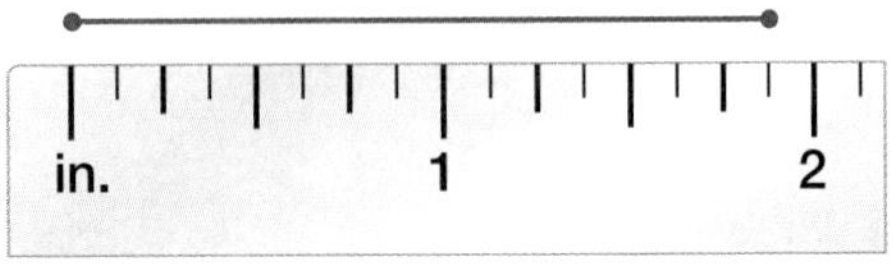

The line segment is about $1\frac{7}{8}$ inches long. The segment is between $1\frac{1}{2}$ and 2 inches long. It is closer to 2 inches.
So, to the nearest half inch, the length of the segment is 2 inches.

Step 1 Draw five short line segments. Exchange segments with your partner.

Step 2 Measure each segment in eighths and record its length. Then measure to the nearest half inch and record.

Step 3 Sort the measures into three parts: those that round up to the next greater whole number, round to a half inch, and round down to the smaller whole number.

1. Compare the numerators and denominators of the fractions in each list. How do they compare?

2. Write a rule about how to round to the nearest half inch.

Review Vocabulary

mixed number the sum of a whole number and a fraction; *Example:* $2\frac{3}{8}$ (Lesson 4-4)

KEY CONCEPT — Rounding to the Nearest Half

Round Up	**Round to $\frac{1}{2}$**	**Round Down**
If the fraction is $\frac{3}{4}$ or greater, round the number up to the next whole number.	If the fraction is greater than or equal to $\frac{1}{4}$ and less than $\frac{3}{4}$, round the fraction to $\frac{1}{2}$.	If the fraction is less than $\frac{1}{4}$, round the number down to the previous whole number.
$\frac{7}{8}$ rounds to 1.	$2\frac{3}{8}$ rounds to $2\frac{1}{2}$.	$\frac{1}{8}$ rounds to 0.
7 is almost as large as 8.	3 is about half of 8.	1 is much smaller than 8.

Remember

$\frac{1}{3}$ and $\frac{2}{3}$ each round to $\frac{1}{2}$.

EXAMPLES Round to the Nearest Half

1 Round $3\frac{1}{6}$ to the nearest half.

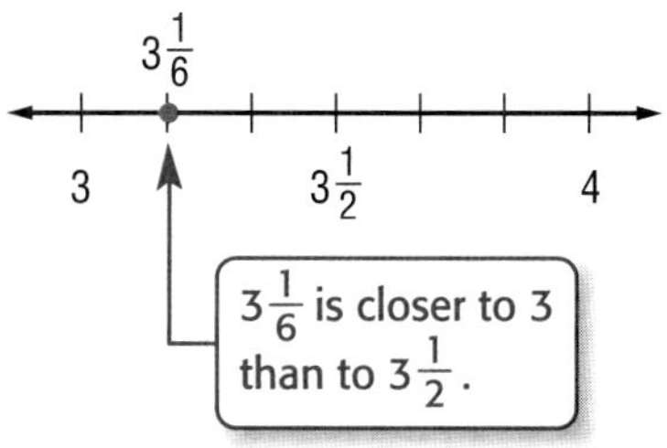

The numerator of $\frac{1}{6}$ is much smaller than the denominator, and $\frac{1}{6}$ is less than $\frac{1}{4}$. So, $3\frac{1}{6}$ rounds to 3.

2 Round $5\frac{7}{8}$ to the nearest half.

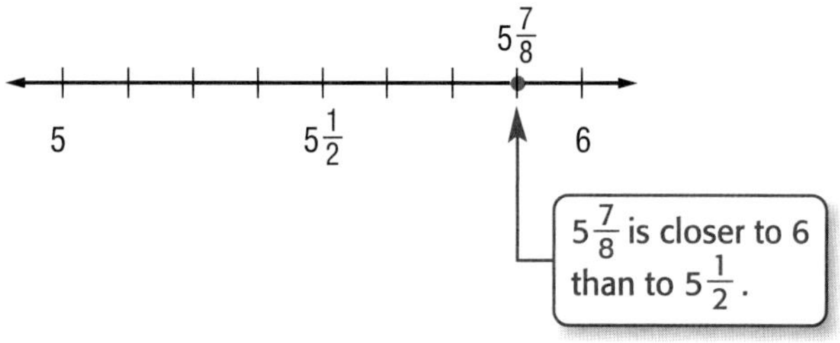

The numerator of $\frac{7}{8}$ is almost as large as the denominator, and $\frac{7}{8}$ is greater than $\frac{3}{4}$. So, $5\frac{7}{8}$ rounds to 6.

Online Personal Tutor at ca.gr5math.com

EXAMPLE Measure to the Nearest Half

3 Find the length of the leaf to the nearest half inch.

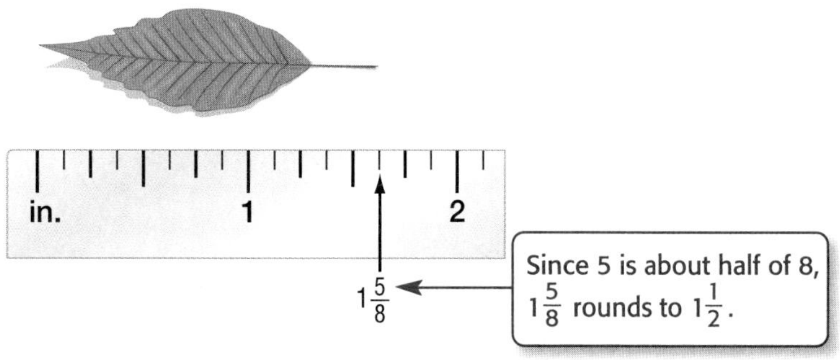

To the nearest half inch, the leaf is $1\frac{1}{2}$ inches long.

Remember

$\frac{5}{8}$ is greater than $\frac{1}{4}$ and less than $\frac{3}{4}$.

Sometimes you should round a number down when it is better for a measure to be too small than too large. Other times you should round up despite what the rule says.

Real-World EXAMPLE

4 **A recipe for tacos calls for $1\frac{1}{4}$ pounds of ground beef. Should you buy a $1\frac{1}{2}$-pound package or a 1-pound package? Explain your reasoning.**

One pound is less than $1\frac{1}{4}$ pounds. So, in order to have enough ground beef, you should round $1\frac{1}{4}$ up and buy the $1\frac{1}{2}$-pound package.

CHECK What You Know

Round each number to the nearest half. **See Examples 1, 2 (p. 233)**

1. $\frac{7}{8}$

2. $3\frac{1}{10}$

3. $\frac{3}{8}$

4. $6\frac{2}{3}$

5. $\frac{1}{5}$

6. $5\frac{11}{12}$

Round the length of each item to the nearest half inch. **See Example 3 (p. 233)**

7.

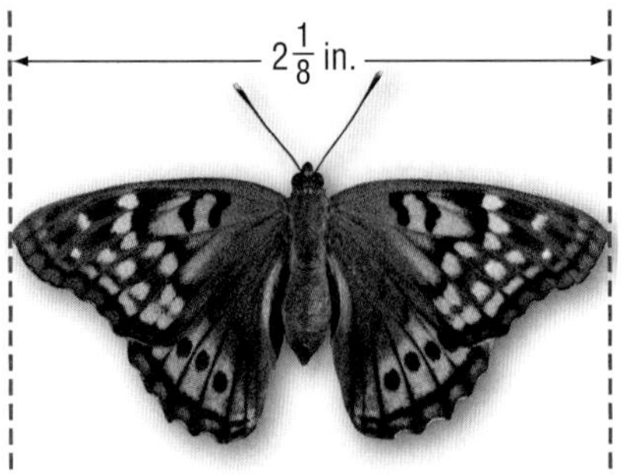

8.

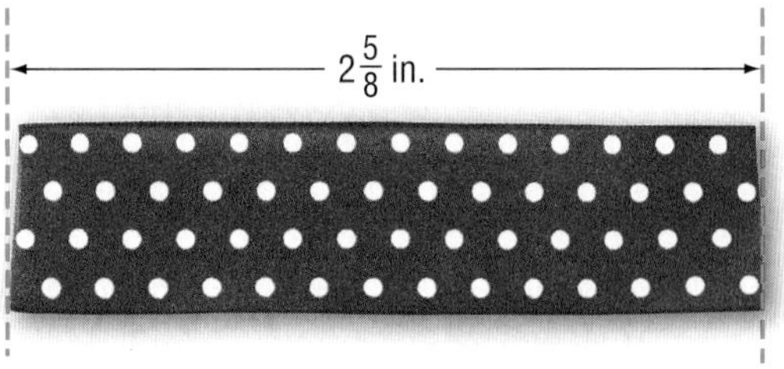

9. In order to carry her drawings home from school, Sara wants to make them small enough to fit into an $8\frac{1}{2}$-inch wide binder pocket. When deciding on the width of the drawings she will make, should she round $8\frac{1}{2}$ inches up or down? Explain your reasoning.
See Example 4 (p. 234)

10. Measurement Based on the area of his flowerbed, a gardener calculates that he needs to dilute $4\frac{3}{8}$ gallons of fertilizer with water. Should he round $4\frac{3}{8}$ gallons up or down when deciding on the amount of fertilizer to purchase? Explain your reasoning.
See Example 4 (p. 234)

11. **Talk About It** Describe a situation where it would make sense to round a fraction up to the nearest unit.

Practice and Problem Solving

EXTRA PRACTICE See page 666.

Round each number to the nearest half. See Examples 1, 2 (p. 233)

12. $\frac{5}{6}$ **13.** $2\frac{4}{5}$ **14.** $4\frac{2}{9}$ **15.** $9\frac{1}{6}$ **16.** $3\frac{2}{9}$

17. $3\frac{1}{12}$ **18.** $\frac{1}{3}$ **19.** $5\frac{3}{10}$ **20.** $\frac{7}{12}$ **21.** $3\frac{2}{3}$

Round the length of each item to the nearest half inch. See Example 3 (p. 233)

22.

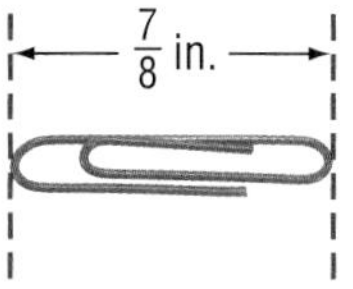

23.

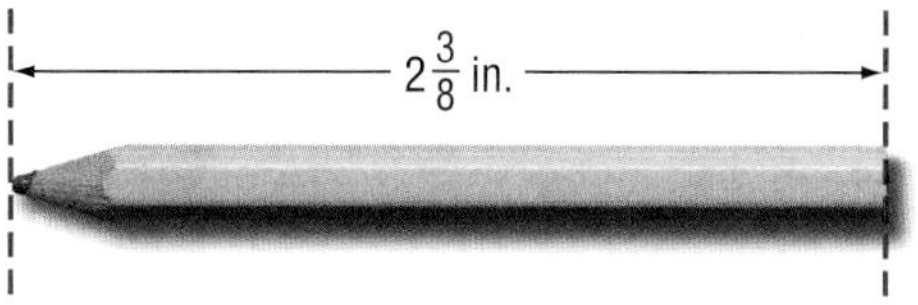

24.

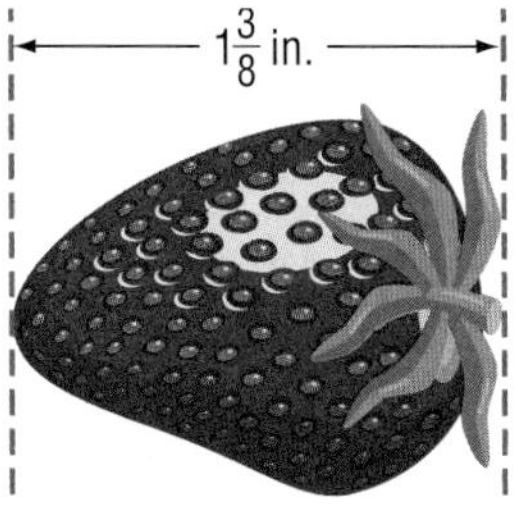

25.

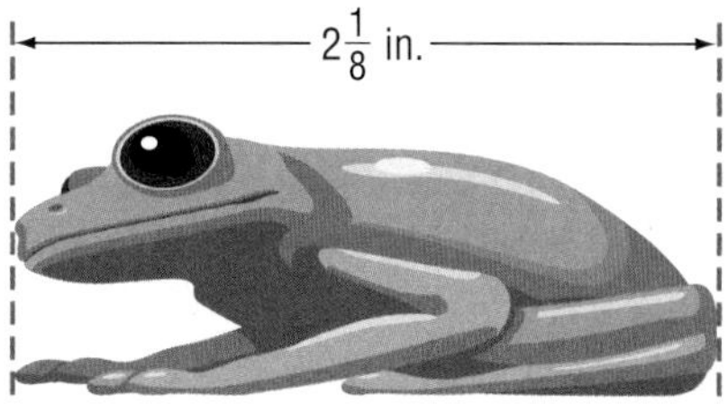

26. The Santiagos are buying blinds to fit in a window opening that is $24\frac{3}{4}$ inches wide. Should they round $24\frac{3}{4}$ inches up or down when deciding on the size of blinds to purchase? Explain your reasoning.

27. Martin is mailing a gift that is $14\frac{3}{8}$ inches tall. He can choose from several shipping boxes. Should he round $14\frac{3}{8}$ inches up or down when selecting a shipping box? Explain your reasoning.

28. Measurement Marina is making birthday cards. She is using envelopes that are $6\frac{3}{4}$ inches by $4\frac{5}{8}$ inches. To the nearest half inch, how large can she make her cards?

Use rounding to order each set of numbers from least to greatest.

29. $\frac{7}{8}, \frac{2}{11}, \frac{4}{7}$ **30.** $3\frac{5}{9}, 3\frac{3}{14}, 3\frac{6}{7}$ **31.** $7\frac{6}{11}, 7\frac{9}{10}, 7\frac{1}{7}$

32. Statistics Several students were asked to name their favorite free time activity. Are more than half the students represented by any one category? Explain your reasoning.

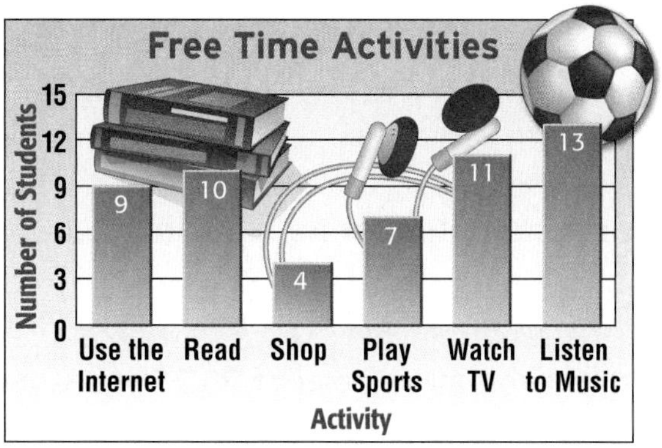

H.O.T. Problems

CHALLENGE Round each number to the nearest fourth. Explain your reasoning.

33. $\frac{3}{16}$ **34.** $\frac{79}{100}$ **35.** $\frac{21}{40}$

36. Which One Doesn't Belong? Identify the number that does not belong with the other three. Explain your reasoning.

$5\frac{1}{5}$ $4\frac{5}{5}$ $5\frac{6}{7}$ $4\frac{11}{12}$

37. OPEN ENDED Select three mixed numbers each with different denominators that each round down to $4\frac{1}{2}$.

38. WRITING IN MATH Give a situation in which rounding would be appropriate to use and a situation in which rounding would not be appropriate. What is an advantage to rounding instead of using the exact number?

Standards Practice

39 What is the length of the eraser to the nearest half inch?

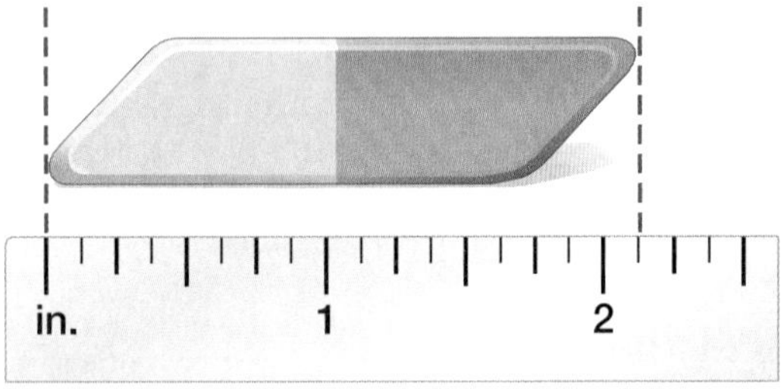

A $1\frac{1}{5}$

B 2

C $2\frac{1}{2}$

D 3

40 Brooke bought a scrapbook in which the pages are $9\frac{3}{4}$ inches by $10\frac{3}{8}$ inches. To the nearest half inch, what is the size of the largest photograph she can place on one page?

F 9 inches by 10 inches

G $9\frac{1}{2}$ inches by 10 inches

H 9 inches by $10\frac{1}{2}$ inches

J $9\frac{1}{2}$ inches by $10\frac{1}{2}$ inches

Spiral Review

41. Algebra Graph and label each point in the table at the right on a coordinate plane. **(Lesson 4-10)**

Point	x	y
A	3	1
B	2.5	4
C	4.25	0
D	1	2

Write each fraction or mixed number as a decimal. (Lesson 4-9)

42. $\frac{1}{8}$ **43.** $4\frac{4}{5}$ **44.** $\frac{2}{5}$ **45.** $2\frac{3}{16}$

46. Mercury moves in its orbit at a speed of 29.75 miles per second. Write this speed as a mixed number in simplest form. **(Lesson 4-8)**

5-2 Estimating Sums and Differences

MAIN IDEA

I will estimate sums and differences of fractions and mixed numbers.

Standard 5MR2.5 Indicate the relative advantages of exact and approximate solutions to problems and **give answers to a specified degree of accuracy.**

Standard 5NS1.1 Estimate, **round**, and manipulate very large (e.g., millions) and **very small** (e.g. thousandths) **numbers**.

GET READY to Learn

The table lists a few world records. About how much taller is the snowman than the cowboy boots? Explain.

World Records	
tallest snowman	$113\frac{2}{3}$ ft
largest cowboy boots	$4\frac{7}{12}$ ft
largest tricycle wheel	$15\frac{1}{4}$ ft

Source: guinessworldrecords.com

You can estimate sums and differences of fractions by rounding each fraction to the nearest half. Then add or subtract.

EXAMPLES Fraction Sums and Differences

1 Estimate $\frac{5}{8} + \frac{11}{12}$.

$\frac{5}{8}$ rounds to $\frac{1}{2}$. $\frac{11}{12}$ rounds to 1.

So, $\frac{5}{8} + \frac{11}{12}$ is about $\frac{1}{2} + 1$ or $1\frac{1}{2}$.

2 Estimate $\frac{7}{12} - \frac{1}{6}$.

$\frac{7}{12}$ rounds to $\frac{1}{2}$. $\frac{1}{6}$ rounds to 0.

So, $\frac{7}{12} - \frac{1}{6}$ is about $\frac{1}{2} - 0$ or $\frac{1}{2}$.

You can also estimate sums and differences of mixed numbers by rounding each number to the nearest half.

EXAMPLE Mixed Number Sums

3 Estimate $4\frac{5}{6} + 2\frac{1}{5}$.

$4\frac{5}{6}$ rounds to 5. $2\frac{1}{5}$ rounds to 2.

So, $4\frac{5}{6} + 2\frac{1}{5}$ is about 5 + 2 or 7.

EXAMPLE Mixed Number Differences

4 Estimate $2\frac{5}{8} - \frac{2}{5}$.

Round $2\frac{5}{8}$ to $2\frac{1}{2}$. Round $\frac{2}{5}$ to $\frac{1}{2}$.

So, $2\frac{5}{8} - \frac{2}{5}$ is about $2\frac{1}{2} - \frac{1}{2}$ or 2.

Remember

Sometimes you need to round all fractions up, as in Example 5, despite what the rule says.

Real-World EXAMPLE

5 Measurement Carmen plans to put a wallpaper border around the top of her room. About how much border does she need?

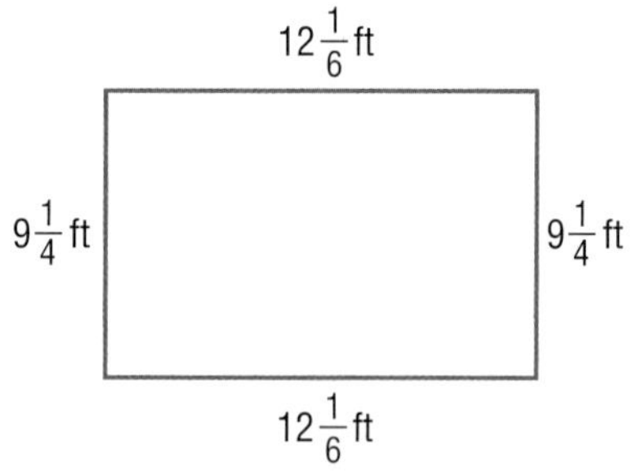

Carmen wants to make sure she buys enough border. So, she rounds up.

Round $9\frac{1}{4}$ to 10 and $12\frac{1}{6}$ to 13.

Estimate $10 + 13 + 10 + 13 = 46$ Add the lengths of all sides.

So, Carmen needs about 46 feet of border.

Online **Personal Tutor at** ca.gr5math.com

CHECK What You Know

Estimate. See Examples 1–5 (pp. 237–238)

1. $\frac{9}{10} + \frac{3}{5}$

2. $\frac{3}{7} + \frac{5}{9}$

3. $\frac{7}{8} - \frac{2}{5}$

4. $\frac{2}{5} - \frac{1}{7}$

5. $4\frac{1}{8} + 5\frac{11}{12}$

6. $8\frac{2}{3} + \frac{3}{5}$

7. $6\frac{5}{8} - 2\frac{1}{3}$

8. $6\frac{1}{3} - \frac{8}{11}$

9. Luis spent $2\frac{1}{2}$ hours watching a movie and $1\frac{1}{4}$ hours online. About how much time did he spend on these two activities?

10. Talk About It Would you round $1\frac{3}{4}$ to 1 or to 2? Explain your reasoning.

Practice and Problem Solving

EXTRA PRACTICE See page 666.

Estimate. See Examples 1–5 (pp. 237–238)

11. $\frac{6}{11} + \frac{4}{7}$ **12.** $\frac{9}{10} + \frac{1}{2}$ **13.** $\frac{3}{8} - \frac{1}{9}$ **14.** $\frac{5}{6} - \frac{3}{8}$

15. $8\frac{7}{8} + 2\frac{1}{3}$ **16.** $4\frac{1}{3} + 1\frac{5}{6}$ **17.** $3\frac{2}{3} + \frac{5}{8}$ **18.** $\frac{8}{9} + 6\frac{3}{5}$

19. $1\frac{6}{7} - 1\frac{5}{9}$ **20.** $1\frac{9}{10} - 1\frac{1}{8}$ **21.** $7\frac{1}{6} - \frac{7}{9}$ **22.** $9\frac{7}{12} - \frac{7}{15}$

23. Statistics The table lists the number of years of performance experience of four band students. The students are performing as a quartet and wish to advertise their combined number of years of experience. What total could they give by rounding up?

Musician	Years Experience
Fernando	$5\frac{3}{4}$
Linda	$4\frac{2}{3}$
Lawana	$8\frac{1}{2}$
Matthew	$2\frac{1}{3}$

24. Statistics A painting that is $24\frac{3}{4}$ inches long is enclosed in a glass case that is $26\frac{2}{5}$ inches long. What is the approximate difference in lengths of the painting and the glass case?

Estimate.

25. $\frac{3}{7} + \frac{1}{9} + \frac{5}{6}$ **26.** $4\frac{1}{10} + 3\frac{4}{5} + 7\frac{2}{3}$ **27.** $6\frac{1}{4} - \left(\frac{5}{6} + \frac{3}{8}\right)$

28. Odina needs $1\frac{1}{4}$ yards of ribbon to trim a pillow and $4\frac{5}{8}$ yards of the same ribbon for curtain trim. Is 5 yards of ribbon enough? If not, about how much more is needed? Explain.

Use estimation to determine if the answers given are reasonable.

29. $\frac{11}{12} + \frac{1}{2} = 1\frac{5}{12}$ **30.** $5\frac{1}{8} + 5\frac{5}{8} = 10\frac{3}{4}$ **31.** $4\frac{7}{9} - \frac{1}{3} = 3$

Real-World PROBLEM SOLVING

Data File California has a population of about 35,484,453 and a land area of 155,959 square miles.

32. About how much greater is the population per square mile in Pennsylvania than in California?

33. Use estimation to determine which two states have the greatest difference in their population per square mile. Explain your reasoning.

Population

Population per Square Mile

California: $227\frac{1}{2}$

Ohio: $279\frac{3}{10}$

Pennsylvania: $275\frac{9}{10}$

Source: *The World Almanac*

H.O.T. Problems

34. **OPEN ENDED** Lawrence has $20 to spend at the bookstore. He wants to purchase 3 books that cost $5.50 each, including tax. Should he use computation or estimation to determine whether or not he has enough money to purchase all 3 books? Suppose the books cost $6.30 each, including tax, should he use computation or estimation to determine whether or not he has enough money?

NUMBER SENSE **Without calculating, replace ● with < or > to make a true sentence. Explain your reasoning.**

35. $\frac{3}{8} + \frac{9}{10}$ ● 1

36. $2\frac{1}{6} + 4\frac{7}{8}$ ● 6

37. 2 ● $3\frac{9}{10} - 1\frac{1}{5}$

38. **CHALLENGE** The estimate for the sum of two fractions is 1. If 2 is added to each fraction, the estimate for the sum of the two mixed numbers is 5. Select two fractions that fit this description.

39. **WRITING IN ► MATH** Explain how to estimate the difference between $4\frac{3}{4}$ and $2\frac{1}{6}$.

Standards Practice

40 About how much taller did Rose 1 grow than Rose 3?

Height of Nicole's Roses		
Rose 1	Rose 2	Rose 3
$12\frac{5}{6}$ in.	$10\frac{1}{3}$ in.	$9\frac{5}{8}$ in.

A $1\frac{1}{2}$ in.

B $2\frac{1}{2}$ in.

C 3 in.

D 23 in.

41 Joe walks between $3\frac{1}{2}$ and $4\frac{7}{8}$ miles each week. If he plans on increasing this distance by $1\frac{1}{4}$ miles, which will be is new distance walked each week?

F Less than 4 miles

G Between 4 and 6 miles

H Between 5 and 6 miles

J More than 6 miles

Spiral Review

42. Tell whether the amount of money you expect to need for dinner at a fast-food restaurant should be rounded up or down. Explain. **(Lesson 5-1)**

43. **Algebra** Use the coordinate plane at the right to name the ordered pair for each point. **(Lesson 4-10)**

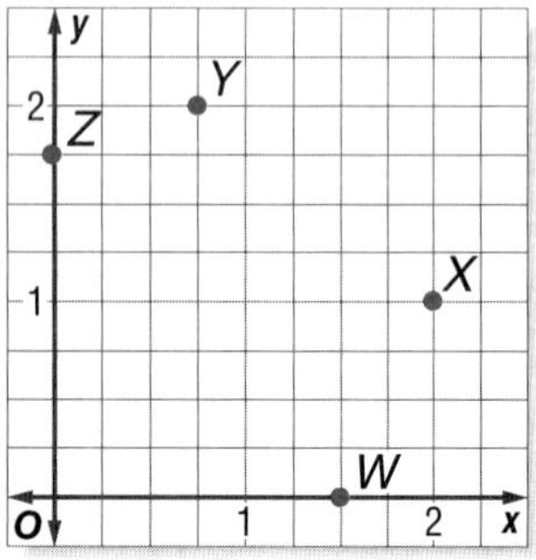

44. **Statistics** The following lists the ages of the athletes in one group at a summer hockey camp. Find the median, mode, and range of the data set. **(Lesson 2-7)**

11, 13, 14, 12, 13, 12, 11, 10, 11, 11, 10, 12

5-3 Adding and Subtracting Fractions with Like Denominators

MAIN IDEA

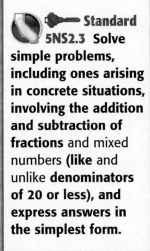

I will add and subtract fractions with like denominators.

Standard 5NS2.3 Solve simple problems, including ones arising in concrete situations, involving the addition and subtraction of fractions and mixed numbers **(like** and unlike **denominators of 20 or less), and express answers in the simplest form.**

New Vocabulary

like fractions

GET READY to Learn

Hands-On Mini Lab

You can use grid paper to model adding fractions such as $\frac{3}{12}$ and $\frac{2}{12}$.

Step 1 On grid paper, draw a rectangle like the one shown. Since the grid has 12 squares, each square represents $\frac{1}{12}$.

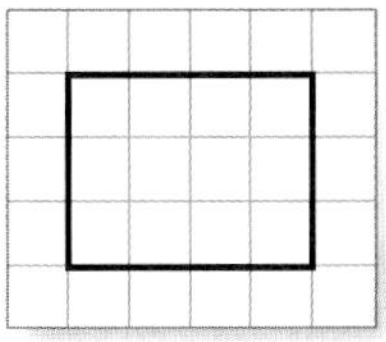

Step 2 With a marker, color three squares to represent $\frac{3}{12}$. With a different marker, color two more squares to represent $\frac{2}{12}$.

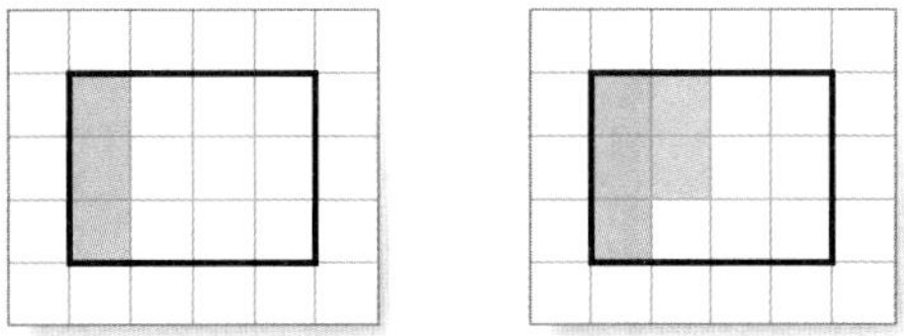

Step 3 Five of the 12 squares are colored. So, the sum of $\frac{3}{12}$ and $\frac{2}{12}$ is $\frac{5}{12}$.

Find each sum using grid paper.

1. $\frac{4}{12} + \frac{3}{12}$ **2.** $\frac{1}{6} + \frac{1}{6}$ **3.** $\frac{3}{10} + \frac{5}{10}$

4. What patterns do you notice with the numerators?

5. What patterns do you notice with the denominators?

6. How could you find the sum $\frac{3}{8} + \frac{1}{8}$ without using grid paper?

Fractions with the same denominator are called **like fractions**. When you add and subtract like fractions, the denominator names the units being added or subtracted.

$$\underbrace{\frac{3}{12}}_{\text{3 twelfths}} \underbrace{+}_{\text{plus}} \underbrace{\frac{2}{12}}_{\text{2 twelfths}} \underbrace{=}_{\text{equals}} \underbrace{\frac{5}{12}}_{\text{5 twelfths.}}$$

KEY CONCEPT — Add Like Fractions

Words To add fractions with the same denominators, add the numerators. Use the same denominator in the sum. For example, *2 fifths plus 1 fifth equals 3 fifths.*

Examples

Model

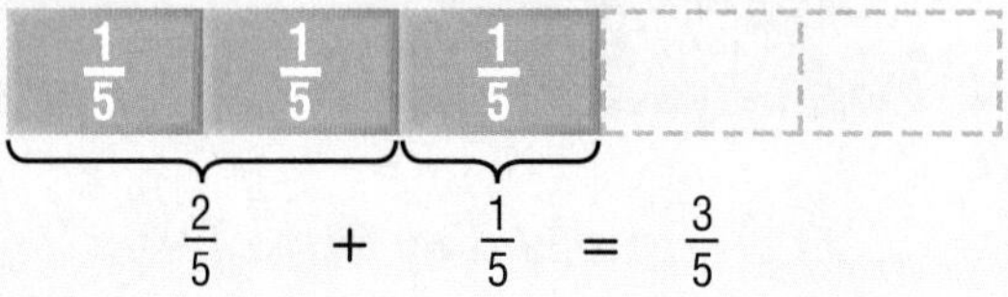

Numbers

$$\frac{2}{5} + \frac{1}{5} = \frac{2+1}{5}$$
$$= \frac{3}{5}$$

EXAMPLE — Add Like Fractions

1 **Find the sum of $\frac{3}{4}$ and $\frac{1}{4}$.**

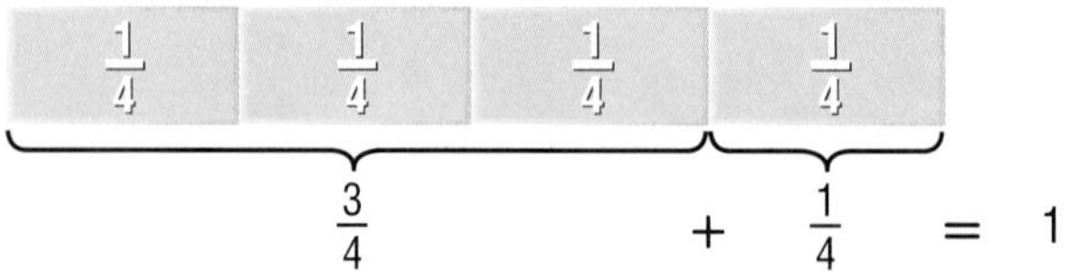

Estimate $1 + \frac{1}{2} = 1\frac{1}{2}$

$\frac{3}{4} + \frac{1}{4} = \frac{3+1}{4}$ Add the numerators.

$= \frac{4}{4}$ Simplify.

$= 1$ Write as a whole number.

Check for Reasonableness Compare 1 to the estimate. $1 \approx 1\frac{1}{2}$ ✓

The rule for subtracting fractions is similar to the rule for adding fractions.

Concepts in Motion

Interactive Lab
ca.gr5math.com

KEY CONCEPT — Subtract Like Fractions

Words To subtract fractions with the same denominators, subtract the numerators. Use the same denominator in the difference. For example, *3 fifths minus 1 fifth equals 2 fifths.*

Examples

Model

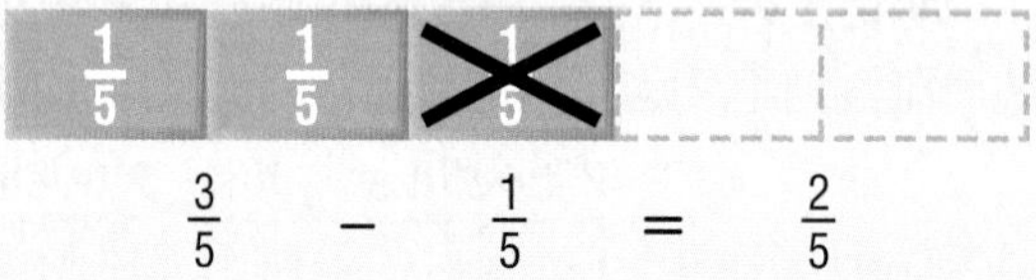

Numbers

$$\frac{3}{5} - \frac{1}{5} = \frac{3-1}{5}$$
$$= \frac{2}{5}$$

EXAMPLE Subtract Like Fractions

Review Vocabulary

simplest form the form of a fraction when the GCF of the numerator and denominator is 1; *Example:* $\frac{3}{4}$ **(Lesson 4-3)**

2 **Find $\frac{7}{8} - \frac{5}{8}$. Write in simplest form.**

$$\frac{7}{8} - \frac{5}{8} = \frac{2}{8}$$

$\frac{7}{8} - \frac{5}{8} = \frac{7-5}{8}$ Subtract the numerators.

$= \frac{2}{8}$ or $\frac{1}{4}$ Simplify.

Check *7 eighths minus 5 eighths equals 2 eighths.* ✓

Real-World EXAMPLE

3 **About $\frac{1}{20}$ of the population of California lives in San Bernardino County. Another $\frac{1}{20}$ lives in Riverside County. What fraction of the population of California lives in these two counties?**

$\frac{1}{20} + \frac{1}{20} = \frac{1+1}{20}$ Add the numerators.

$= \frac{2}{20}$ or $\frac{1}{10}$ Simplify.

About $\frac{1}{10}$ of the population of California lives in San Bernardino County and Riverside County.

Check *1 twentieth plus 1 twentieth equals 2 twentieths.* ✓

Online **Personal Tutor at** ca.gr5math.com

CHECK What You Know

Add or subtract. Write in simplest form. **See Examples 1–3 (pp. 242–243)**

1. $\frac{3}{5} + \frac{1}{5}$

2. $\frac{2}{7} + \frac{1}{7}$

3. $\frac{3}{4} + \frac{3}{4}$

4. $\frac{3}{8} - \frac{1}{8}$

5. $\frac{4}{5} - \frac{1}{5}$

6. $\frac{6}{7} - \frac{2}{7}$

7. A cornbread recipe calls for $\frac{3}{4}$ cup of cornmeal. Ali has only $\frac{1}{4}$ cup. How much more cornmeal does she need?

8. **Talk About It** When $\frac{9}{16}$ and $\frac{5}{16}$ are added together, do they equal $\frac{7}{8}$? Explain your reasoning.

Practice and Problem Solving

EXTRA PRACTICE See page 667.

Add or subtract. Write in simplest form. See Examples 1–3 (pp. 242–243)

9. $\frac{4}{5} + \frac{3}{5}$ **10.** $\frac{5}{7} + \frac{6}{7}$ **11.** $\frac{3}{8} + \frac{7}{8}$ **12.** $\frac{1}{9} + \frac{5}{9}$

13. $\frac{5}{6} + \frac{5}{6}$ **14.** $\frac{15}{16} + \frac{7}{16}$ **15.** $\frac{9}{10} - \frac{3}{10}$ **16.** $\frac{5}{8} - \frac{3}{8}$

17. $\frac{5}{14} - \frac{1}{14}$ **18.** $\frac{5}{9} - \frac{2}{9}$ **19.** $\frac{7}{12} - \frac{2}{12}$ **20.** $\frac{15}{18} - \frac{13}{18}$

21. In Mr. Navarro's first period class, $\frac{17}{20}$ of the students got an 'A' on their math test. In his second period class, $\frac{11}{20}$ of the students got an 'A.' How many more of the students got an 'A' in Mr. Navarro's first period class than his second period class?

22. Measurement The rainfall for Monday through Saturday was $\frac{3}{8}$ inch. By Sunday evening, the total rainfall for the week was $\frac{7}{8}$ inch. How much rain fell on Sunday?

23. Statistics The table shows the Instant Messenger abbreviations that students use the most at Hillside Middle School. What fraction of these students use LOL or CUL8R when using Instant Messenger?
See Example 3 (p. 243)

Instant Messenger Abbreviations	
L8R (Later)	$\frac{9}{18}$
LOL (Laughing out loud)	$\frac{5}{18}$
BRB (Be right back)	$\frac{3}{18}$
CUL8R (See you later)	$\frac{1}{18}$

Write an addition or subtraction expression for each model. Then add or subtract.

24. 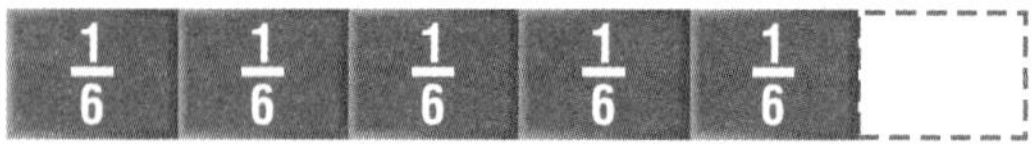

25. 

Real-World PROBLEM SOLVING

Statistics The graphic shows the results of a survey about Genoa Middle School's favorite bagels.

26. What part of the school's favorite is cinnamon, blueberry, or onion bagels?

27. How much larger is the part of the school that prefers blueberry and onion bagels than the part whose favorite is plain bagels?

Genoa Middle School's Favorite Bagels

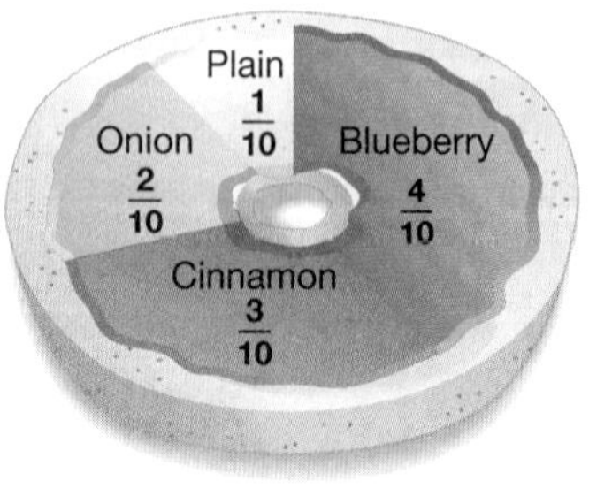

H.O.T. Problems

CHALLENGE **Replace each x to make a true sentence.**

28. $\frac{3}{11} + \frac{x}{11} = \frac{9}{11}$

29. $\frac{3}{4} - \frac{x}{4} = \frac{1}{2}$

30. $\frac{4}{9} + \frac{x}{9} = 1\frac{2}{9}$

31. **OPEN ENDED** Select two like fractions whose difference is $\frac{1}{3}$ and whose denominators are not 3. Justify your selection.

32. **CHALLENGE** Examine the following expression to determine its sum.

$$\frac{1}{20} + \frac{19}{20} + \frac{2}{20} + \frac{18}{20} + \frac{3}{20} + \frac{17}{20} + \dots + \frac{10}{20} + \frac{10}{20}$$

33. **WRITING IN ► MATH** Write a simple rule for adding and subtracting like fractions.

Standards Practice

34 A group of friends bought two large pizzas and ate only part of each pizza. The pictures show how much of the pizzas were left.

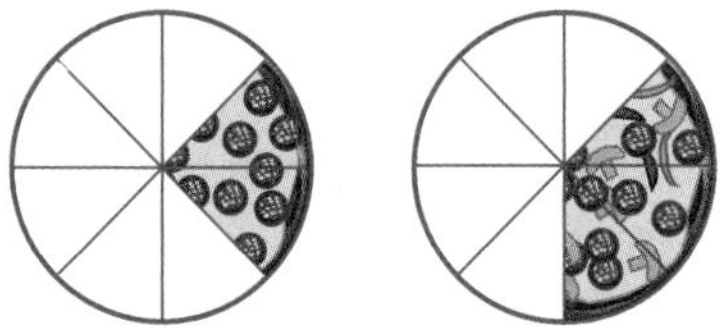

How many pizzas did they eat?

A $\frac{3}{8}$ **B** $\frac{5}{8}$ **C** $1\frac{1}{4}$ **D** $1\frac{3}{8}$

35 At a school carnival, homemade pies were cut into 8 equal-sized pieces. Eric sold $\frac{7}{8}$ of a pie, Elena sold $\frac{5}{8}$ of a pie, and Tanya sold $\frac{3}{8}$ of a pie. Find the total number of pies sold by Eric, Elena, and Tanya.

F $1\frac{3}{8}$

G $1\frac{7}{8}$

H 2

J $2\frac{1}{8}$

Spiral Review

Estimate. **(Lesson 5-2)**

36. $\frac{11}{13} - \frac{1}{2}$

37. $4\frac{4}{15} + \frac{4}{5}$

38. $18\frac{3}{11} + 4\frac{1}{9}$

39. **Measurement** A carport is $10\frac{1}{4}$ feet tall. To the nearest half foot, what is the tallest boat that can be stored in the carport? **(Lesson 5-1)**

40. **Measurement** Find the area of a rectangular game board that is 25 inches long and 11 inches wide. **(Lesson 1-9)**

5-4 Problem-Solving Strategy

MAIN IDEA I will solve problems by acting them out.

Standard 5MR2.3 Use a variety of methods, such as words, numbers, symbols, charts, graphs, tables, **diagrams, and models, to explain mathematical reasoning.** **Standard 5NS2.3 Solve simple problems, including ones arising in concrete situations, involving the addition and subtraction of fractions and mixed numbers . . . .**

Jacqui is using a roll of craft paper to make five art projects. Each project uses the same amount of paper. The roll of craft paper had $11\frac{1}{4}$ yards on it. She already used $2\frac{5}{8}$ yards for one project. Is Jacqui going to have enough paper for four more projects?

Understand

What facts do you know?

- The roll of paper had $11\frac{1}{4}$ yards on it.
- $2\frac{5}{8}$ of the roll of paper was used for one art project.
- Each project uses the same amount of paper.

What do you need to find?

Does Jacqui have enough craft paper for four more art projects?

Plan

Act out the problem by marking the floor to show a length of $11\frac{1}{4}$ yards. Then mark off the amount used in the first project and continue until there are a total of five projects marked.

Solve

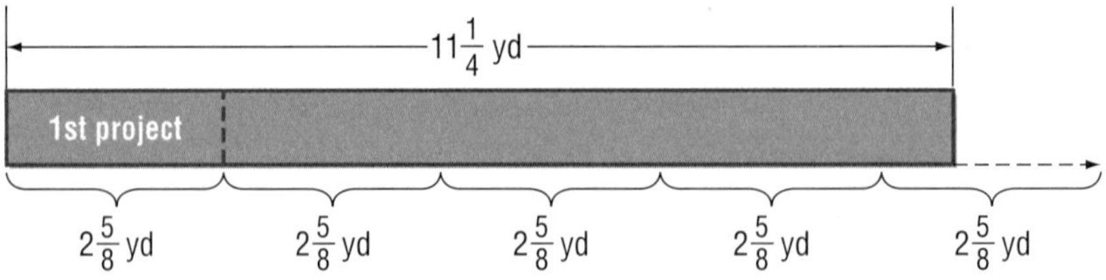

There is not enough paper for 4 additional projects.

Check

Look back. You can estimate.

Round $2\frac{5}{8}$ to $2\frac{1}{2}$.

$2\frac{1}{2} + 2\frac{1}{2} + 2\frac{1}{2} + 2\frac{1}{2} + 2\frac{1}{2} = 12\frac{1}{2}$

So, $11\frac{1}{4}$ yards will not be enough for five projects.

ANALYZE the Strategy

Refer to the problem on the previous page.

1. Suppose each of Jacqui's projects only used $2\frac{1}{3}$ yards of paper. Would the roll of craft paper be long enough for all five projects?

2. Explain an advantage of using the *act it out* strategy to solve a problem.

3. Explain how this strategy can help determine the reasonableness of your answer after the calculations are completed.

4. Give a real-world situation in which you could use the *act it out* strategy.

PRACTICE the Strategy

EXTRA PRACTICE See page 667.

Solve. Use the *act it out* strategy.

5. The members of the spirit club are making a banner using three sheets of paper. How many different banners can they make using their school colors of green, gold, and white one time each? Show the possible arrangements.

6. Dante is running drills for football practice on the field shown. He starts at the goal line on the left side of the field and runs 10 yards forward and then 5 yards backward. How many sets will he need to run in order to finish on the goal line on the right side of the field?

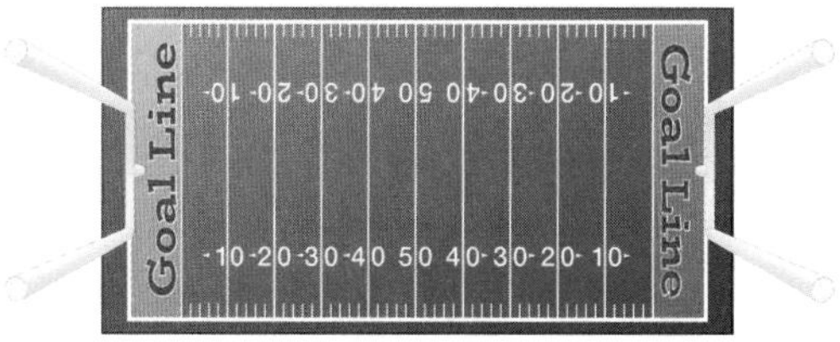

7. Of the students in class, $\frac{5}{16}$ handed in their report on Monday, and $\frac{7}{16}$ handed their report in on Tuesday. What fraction of the class had not completed the work after two days?

8. Jessica takes the change from her pocket and places it on the table. The number of each coin she has is shown below.

Coin	Number
Quarter	2
Dime	2
Nickel	4
Penny	5

How many different combinations of coins can she make to have $0.65?

9. Pablo and Elaine are painting each side of a fence. After one hour, Pablo has painted $\frac{1}{4}$ of his side and Elaine has painted $\frac{1}{3}$ of her side. How much longer than Elaine will it take Pablo to paint his side of the fence?

10. **WRITING IN MATH** Suppose you have $4.65 and you need to buy school supplies costing $1.29, $0.89, and $2.99. Explain how you could use the *act it out* strategy to determine whether or not you have enough money.

CHAPTER 5 Mid-Chapter Check

Lessons 5-1 through 5-4

Round each number to the nearest half. **(Lesson 5-1)**

1. $\frac{7}{8}$ **2.** $3\frac{2}{7}$ **3.** $6\frac{3}{4}$

4. Measurement Round the length of the sticker to the nearest half inch. **(Lesson 5-1)**

5. It takes Monica $1\frac{3}{4}$ minutes to walk to the bus stop. Should she leave her house $1\frac{1}{2}$ minutes or 2 minutes before the bus arrives? **(Lesson 5-1)**

Estimate. **(Lesson 5-2)**

6. $\frac{5}{9} + \frac{6}{7}$ **7.** $4\frac{1}{8} - 1\frac{11}{12}$ **8.** $6\frac{3}{4} + 2\frac{8}{10}$

9. Measurement A board that is $63\frac{5}{8}$ inches long is about how much longer than a board that is $62\frac{1}{4}$ inches long? **(Lesson 5-2)**

10. About what fraction of the pants ordered from an online catalog were navy blue or khaki? **(Lesson 5-2)**

Color of Pants	Fraction Ordered
Navy Blue	$\frac{1}{2}$
Khaki	$\frac{3}{8}$
Black	$\frac{1}{8}$

Add or subtract. Write in simplest form. **(Lesson 5-3)**

11. $\frac{5}{9} + \frac{7}{9}$ **12.** $\frac{9}{11} - \frac{5}{11}$ **13.** $\frac{1}{6} + \frac{5}{6}$

14. **STANDARDS PRACTICE** Malinda is making a punch mixture that calls for $\frac{3}{4}$ quart of grapefruit juice, $\frac{3}{4}$ quart of orange juice, and $\frac{3}{4}$ quart of pineapple juice. How much punch does the recipe make? **(Lesson 5-3)**

A $1\frac{3}{4}$ quarts **C** $2\frac{3}{4}$ quarts

B $2\frac{1}{4}$ quarts **D** $3\frac{1}{4}$ quarts

15. **STANDARDS PRACTICE** Sean lives $\frac{9}{10}$ mile from school. He has jogged $\frac{4}{10}$ mile from home toward the school. Which procedure can Sean use to find how much farther he has to jog? **(Lesson 5-3)**

F Add the numerators and write the sum as a mixed number.

G Subtract the numerators and simplify the difference.

H Add the numerators, add the denominators, and write the sum as a mixed number.

J Subtract the numerators, add the denominators, and simplify the result.

16. **WRITING IN MATH** Tia is making a sign with her name to hang in her bedroom. She wants each letter of her name to be a different color. How many different ways can she write her name using red, green, and yellow markers? Explain how you can use the *act it out* strategy to solve this problem. **(Lesson 5-4)**

Explore

Math Lab for 5-5
Unlike Denominators

MAIN IDEA

I will use models to add and subtract fractions with unlike denominators.

Standard 5MR2.3 Use a variety of methods, such as words, numbers, symbols, charts, graphs, tables, diagrams, and **models, to explain mathematical reasoning.**

Standard 5NS2.3 Solve simple problems, including ones arising in concrete situations, **involving the addition and subtraction of fractions** and mixed numbers, and express answers in the simplest form.

In this lab, you will use fraction tiles to add and subtract fractions with *unlike* denominators.

Concepts in Motion

Animation ca.gr5math.com

ACTIVITY

1 Use fraction tiles to find $\frac{1}{2} + \frac{1}{5}$.

Step 1 Model each fraction.

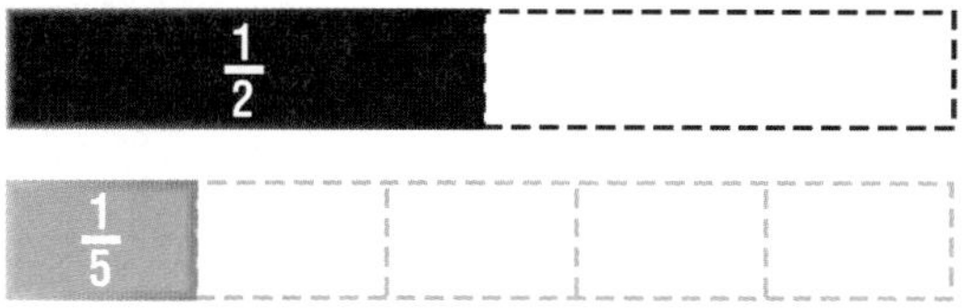

Step 2 To add, line up the end of the first tile with the beginning of the second tile.

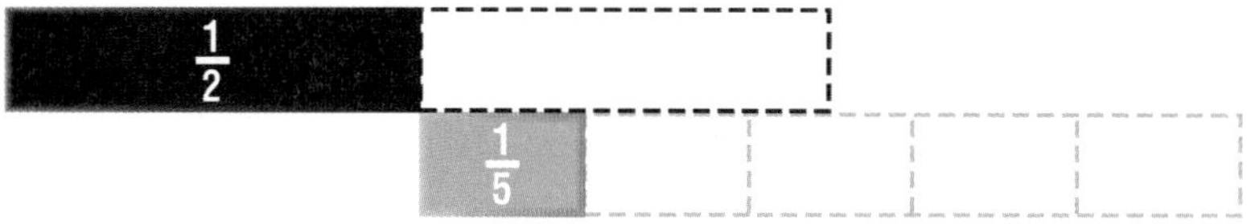

Step 3 Test different fraction tiles below the model, lining up each with the beginning of the first tile. Do the tiles line up? If not, try another tile.

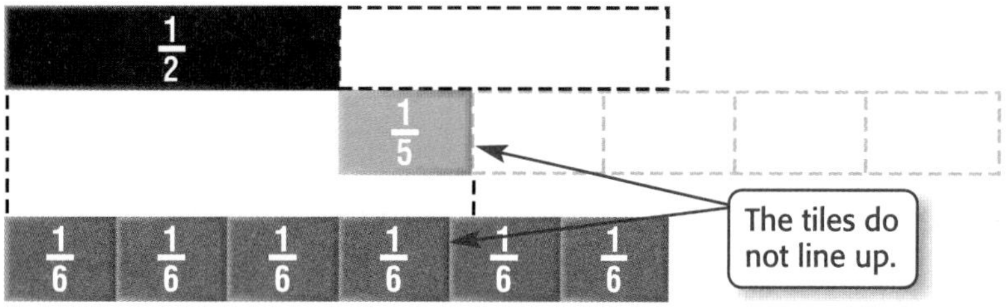

Step 4 Once the correct tile is found, add the tiles.

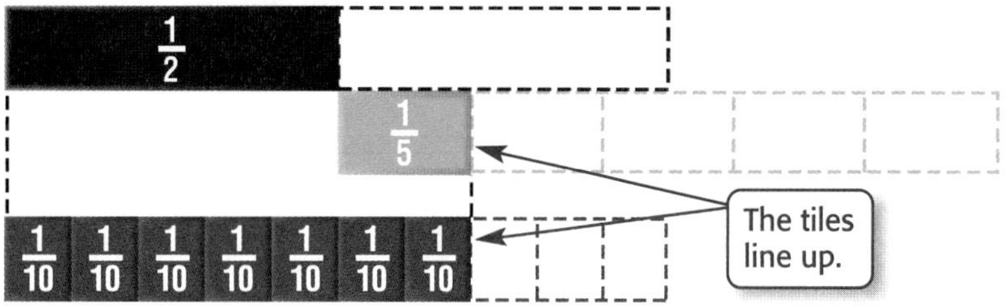

So, $\frac{1}{2} + \frac{1}{5} = \frac{7}{10}$.

ACTIVITY

2 **Use fraction tiles to find $\frac{7}{8} - \frac{3}{4}$.**

Step 1 Model each fraction.

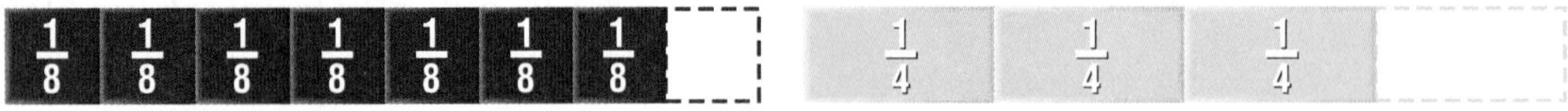

Step 2 To subtract, line up the ends of the tiles.

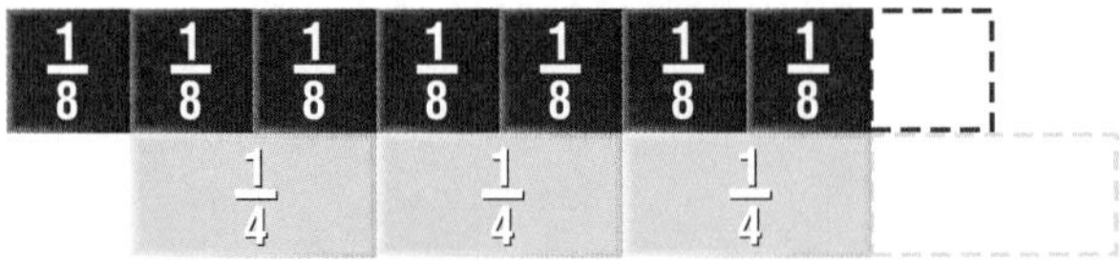

Step 3 Test different fraction tiles below the model, checking to see if the tiles line up.

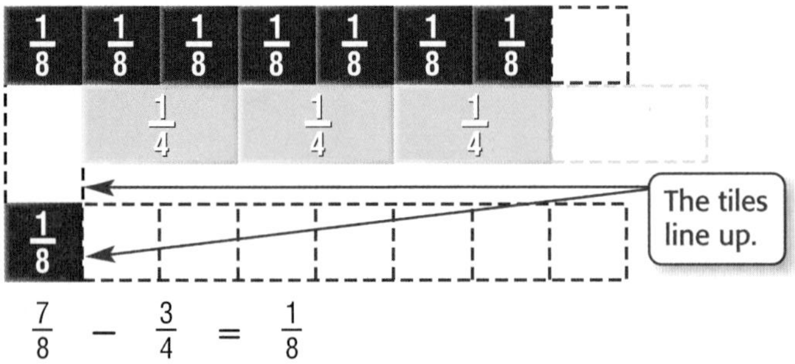

So, $\frac{7}{8} - \frac{3}{4} = \frac{1}{8}$.

CHECK What You Know

Use fraction tiles to add or subtract.

1. $\frac{1}{10} + \frac{2}{5}$ **2.** $\frac{1}{2} + \frac{3}{4}$ **3.** $\frac{3}{8} - \frac{1}{4}$ **4.** $\frac{8}{9} - \frac{1}{3}$

Analyze the Results

Use the models from Activities 1 and 2 to complete the following.

5. $\frac{1}{2} + \frac{1}{5} = \frac{\blacksquare}{10} + \frac{\blacksquare}{10}$ **6.** $\frac{7}{8} - \frac{3}{4} = \frac{\blacksquare}{8} - \frac{\blacksquare}{8}$

Write an addition or subtraction expression for each model. Then add or subtract.

7.

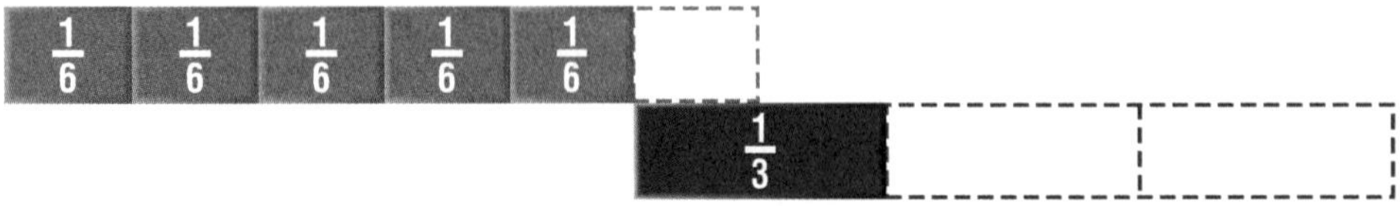

8.

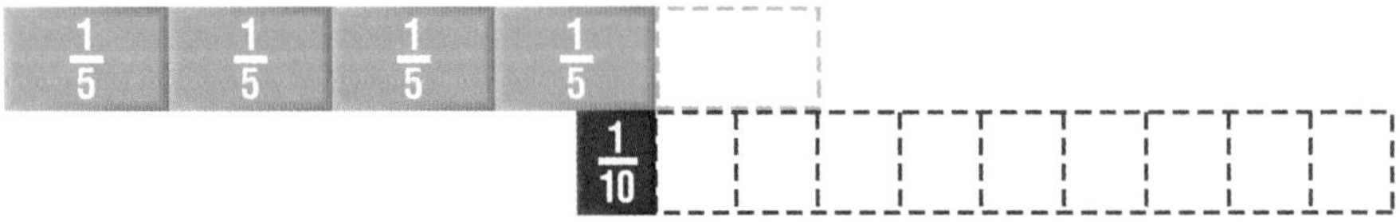

9. What is the relationship between the number of tiles on the answer fraction tile and the denominators of the fractions?

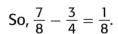

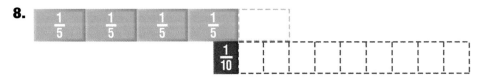

5-5 Adding and Subtracting Fractions with Unlike Denominators

MAIN IDEA

I will add and subtract fractions with unlike denominators.

Standard 5NS2.3 Solve simple problems, including ones arising in concrete situations, involving the addition and subtraction of fractions and mixed numbers (like and **unlike denominators of 20 or less), and express answers in the simplest form.**

New Vocabulary

unlike fractions

GET READY to Learn

To find the total value of different coins, rename the coins using a common unit such as dollars.

2 quarters $= \frac{1}{2}$ dollar   2 dimes $= \frac{1}{5}$ dollar

So, the total value of the coins shown is $\frac{1}{2}$ dollar $+ \frac{1}{5}$ dollar or $\frac{7}{10}$ dollar.

Before you can add two **unlike fractions**, or fractions with different denominators, one or both of the fractions must be renamed so that they have a common denominator.

KEY CONCEPT **Add or Subtract Unlike Fractions**

To add or subtract fractions with different denominators,

- Rename the fractions using the LCD.
- Add or subtract as with like fractions. Simplify.

EXAMPLE **Add Unlike Fractions**

1 **Find $\frac{1}{2} + \frac{1}{4}$.**

One Way: **Use a model.**

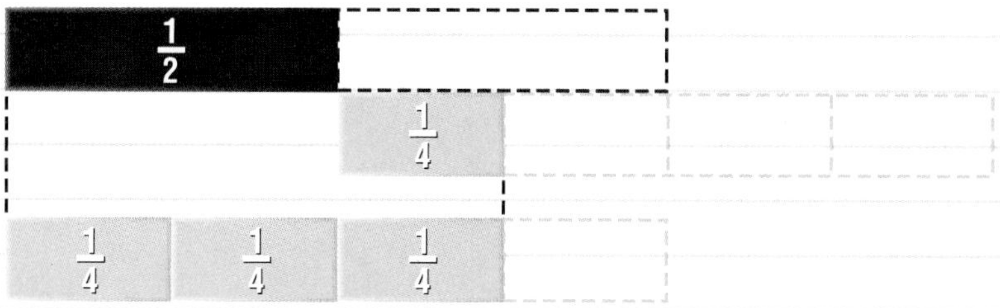

$\frac{1}{2} + \frac{1}{4} = \frac{3}{4}$

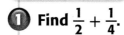

Review Vocabulary

least common denominator (LCD) the least common multiple (LCM) of the denominators of two or more fractions; *Example:* the LCD of $\frac{1}{2}$ and $\frac{1}{4}$ is 4. **(Lesson 4-5)**

Another Way: Use the LCD.

The least common denominator of $\frac{1}{2}$ and $\frac{1}{4}$ is 4.

Write the problem.		Rename using the LCD, 4.		Add the fractions.
$\frac{1}{2}$	$\longrightarrow$	$\frac{1 \times 2}{2 \times 2} = \frac{2}{4}$	$\longrightarrow$	$\frac{2}{4}$
$+\frac{1}{4}$	$\longrightarrow$	$+\frac{1 \times 1}{4 \times 1} = +\frac{1}{4}$	$\longrightarrow$	$+\frac{1}{4}$
				$\frac{3}{4}$

EXAMPLE Subtract Unlike Fractions

2 Find $\frac{2}{3} - \frac{1}{2}$.

One Way: Use a model.

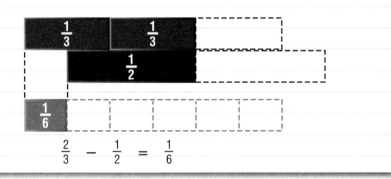

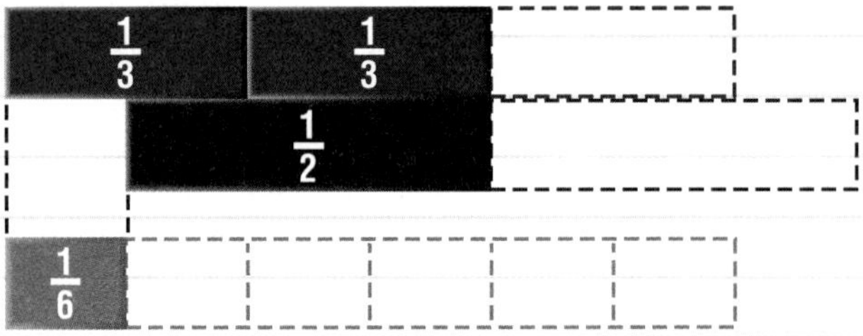

$$\frac{2}{3} - \frac{1}{2} = \frac{1}{6}$$

Another Way: Use the LCD.

The least common denominator of $\frac{2}{3}$ and $\frac{1}{2}$ is 6.

Write the problem.		Rename using the LCD, 6.		Subtract the fractions.
$\frac{2}{3}$	$\longrightarrow$	$\frac{2 \times 2}{3 \times 2} = \frac{4}{6}$	$\longrightarrow$	$\frac{4}{6}$
$-\frac{1}{2}$	$\longrightarrow$	$-\frac{1 \times 3}{2 \times 3} = -\frac{3}{6}$	$\longrightarrow$	$-\frac{3}{6}$
				$\frac{1}{6}$

Remember

Estimate the difference in Example 2.
$\frac{2}{3} - \frac{1}{2} \approx \frac{1}{2} - \frac{1}{2}$ or 0.
Compare $\frac{1}{6}$ to the estimate. $\frac{1}{6} \approx 0$.
So, the answer is reasonable.

Online **Personal Tutor at** ca.gr5math.com

 Math Online **Extra Examples at** ca.gr5math.com

Real-World EXAMPLE

3 The table lists the fraction of the total market share of five popular toys. Find the fraction of the total market share that is dolls or plush toys.

Type of Toy	Fraction of Total Market Share
Video Games	$\frac{7}{25}$
Dolls	$\frac{1}{10}$
Plush Toys	$\frac{1}{20}$
Games/puzzles	$\frac{1}{10}$
Action Figures	$\frac{1}{25}$

Source: *Top Ten of Everything*

Find $\frac{1}{10} + \frac{1}{20}$.

The least common denominator of $\frac{1}{10}$ and $\frac{1}{20}$ is 20.

Write the problem.		Rename using the LCD, 20.				Add the fractions.
$\frac{1}{10}$	$\longrightarrow$	$\frac{1 \times 2}{10 \times 2}$	$=$	$\frac{2}{20}$	$\longrightarrow$	$\frac{2}{20}$
$+\frac{1}{20}$	$\longrightarrow$	$+\frac{1 \times 1}{20 \times 1}$	$=$	$+\frac{1}{20}$	$\longrightarrow$	$+\frac{1}{20}$
						$\frac{3}{20}$

So, $\frac{3}{20}$ of the total market share is dolls or plush toys.

You can also evaluate algebraic expressions with values that are fractions.

EXAMPLE Evaluate an Expression with Fractions

Remember

You can review **evaluating expressions** in Lesson 1-5.

4 Algebra Evaluate $a - b$ if $a = \frac{3}{4}$ and $b = \frac{1}{6}$.

The least common denominator of $\frac{3}{4}$ and $\frac{1}{6}$ is 12.

$a - b = \frac{3}{4} - \frac{1}{6}$ Replace a with $\frac{3}{4}$ and b with $\frac{1}{6}$.

$= \frac{3 \times 3}{4 \times 3} - \frac{1 \times 2}{6 \times 2}$ Rename $\frac{3}{4}$ and $\frac{1}{6}$ using the LCD, 12.

$= \frac{9}{12} - \frac{2}{12}$ Simplify.

$= \frac{7}{12}$ Subtract the numerators.

CHECK What You Know

Add or subtract. Write in simplest form. See Examples 1, 2 (pp. 251–252)

1. $\frac{2}{3} + \frac{2}{9}$

2. $\frac{1}{4} + \frac{5}{8}$

3. $\frac{2}{3} - \frac{1}{2}$

4. $\frac{3}{5} - \frac{1}{2}$

5. $\frac{3}{10} + \frac{1}{5}$

6. $\frac{2}{3} + \frac{1}{4}$

7. $\frac{3}{4} - \frac{1}{8}$

8. $\frac{5}{7} - \frac{1}{2}$

9. Measurement A certain drill set includes drill bits ranging from $\frac{1}{16}$ inch to $\frac{1}{4}$ inch. What is the range of drill bits in this set?
See Example 3 (p. 253)

Algebra Evaluate each expression. See Example 4 (p. 253)

10. $x + y$ if $x = \frac{5}{6}$ and $y = \frac{7}{12}$

11. $r - s$ if $r = \frac{7}{10}$ and $s = \frac{1}{4}$

12. Talk About It Choose two fractions with unlike denominators then rewrite them as equivalent fractions using their least common denominator.

Practice and Problem Solving

EXTRA PRACTICE
See page 667.

Add or subtract. Write in simplest form. See Examples 1, 2 (pp. 251–252)

13. $\frac{3}{8} + \frac{1}{4}$

14. $\frac{2}{5} + \frac{1}{2}$

15. $\frac{9}{10} - \frac{1}{2}$

16. $\frac{5}{8} - \frac{1}{4}$

17. $\frac{1}{6} + \frac{3}{4}$

18. $\frac{1}{4} + \frac{2}{3}$

19. $\frac{5}{6} - \frac{7}{10}$

20. $\frac{3}{4} - \frac{2}{5}$

21. $\frac{8}{9} + \frac{1}{2}$

22. $\frac{5}{7} + \frac{1}{2}$

23. $\frac{9}{10} - \frac{2}{5}$

24. $\frac{7}{8} - \frac{3}{4}$

25. $\frac{7}{8} + \frac{3}{4}$

26. $\frac{7}{12} + \frac{2}{3}$

27. $\frac{3}{4} - \frac{2}{7}$

28. $\frac{9}{11} - \frac{1}{2}$

Statistics For Exercises 29 and 30, use the table showing the fraction of total coupon book sales of four students in a class. See Example 3 (p. 253)

29. What is the difference between Jabar's and Corey's fraction of total sales?

30. What part of the total sales did both Billy and Domanick have?

Coupon Book Sales

Student	Fraction of Total Sales
Corey	$\frac{1}{12}$
Billy	$\frac{3}{20}$
Domanick	$\frac{1}{3}$
Jabar	$\frac{2}{15}$

Algebra Evaluate each expression. See Example 4 (p. 253)

31. $a + b$ if $a = \frac{7}{10}$ and $b = \frac{5}{6}$

32. $x - y$ if $x = \frac{4}{5}$ and $y = \frac{1}{2}$

Add or subtract. Write in simplest form.

33. $\frac{9}{10} + \frac{2}{3} - \frac{11}{15}$

34. $\frac{7}{12} + \frac{5}{8} + \frac{5}{6}$

35. $\frac{15}{16} - \frac{1}{3} - \frac{1}{12}$

36. Write an addition or subtraction sentence for the model. Then add or subtract.

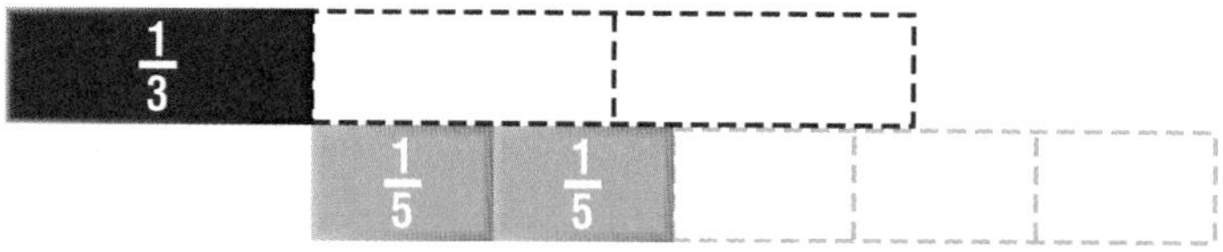

Real-World PROBLEM SOLVING

Geography For Exercises 37–39, use the table that shows the portion of Earth's landmass by continent or island group.

37. What portion of the Earth's landmass is Asia and Africa?

38. How much more is the landmass of North America than South America?

39. What portion of Earth's landmass is Antarctica, Europe, Australia, and Oceania?

Continent or Island Group	Portion of Earth's Landmass
Antarctica, Europe, Australia, and Oceania	■
Asia	$\frac{3}{10}$
Africa	$\frac{1}{5}$
North America	$\frac{1}{6}$
South America	$\frac{1}{8}$

Source: *Oxford Atlas of the World*

H.O.T. Problems

40. OPEN ENDED Create and use a model to represent the sum of two fractions with unlike denominators.

41. FIND THE ERROR Victor and Seki are finding $\frac{3}{4} + \frac{1}{2}$. Who is correct? Explain your reasoning.

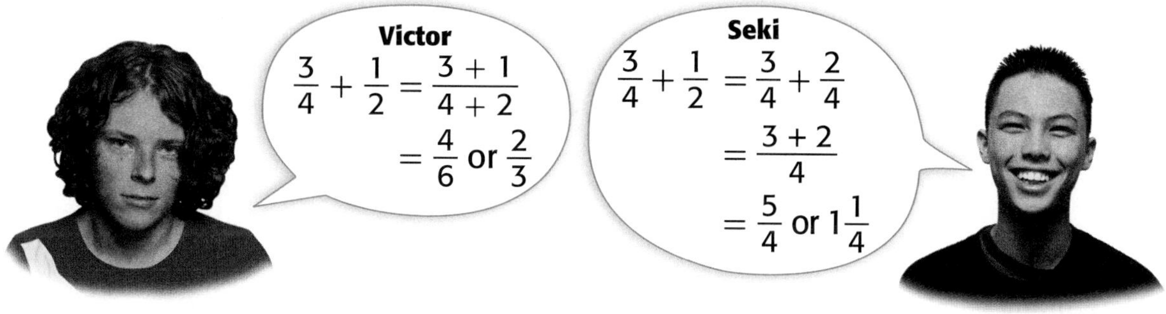

Victor
$\frac{3}{4} + \frac{1}{2} = \frac{3+1}{4+2}$
$= \frac{4}{6}$ or $\frac{2}{3}$
Seki
$\frac{3}{4} + \frac{1}{2} = \frac{3}{4} + \frac{2}{4}$
$= \frac{3+2}{4}$
$= \frac{5}{4}$ or $1\frac{1}{4}$

CHALLENGE Replace each *x* to make a true sentence.

42. $\frac{7}{9} - \frac{x}{3} = \frac{4}{9}$

43. $\frac{1}{3} + \frac{x}{6} = \frac{1}{2}$

44. $\frac{5}{6} + \frac{x}{3} = 1\frac{1}{2}$

CHALLENGE **Decide whether each sentence is *sometimes, always,* or *never* true. Explain your reasoning.**

45. The sum of two fractions that are less than 1 is less than 1.

46. The difference of two fractions is less than both fractions.

47. WRITING IN ▶MATH Write a problem about a real-world situation in which you would subtract $\frac{4}{5}$ and $\frac{3}{4}$.

Standards Practice

48 Hernando made a drawing of his bedroom. The length of his drawing is $\frac{3}{4}$ foot, and the width is $\frac{1}{3}$ foot less than the length. Find the width of the drawing.

A $\frac{1}{4}$ ft

B $\frac{5}{12}$ ft

C $\frac{7}{12}$ ft

D $1\frac{1}{12}$ ft

49 On a camping trip, it took Rebecca $\frac{1}{6}$ hour to hike to a cave and $\frac{3}{4}$ hour to hike inside the cave. How long did Rebecca hike?

F $\frac{1}{2}$ hour

G $\frac{3}{4}$ hour

H $\frac{11}{12}$ hour

J 1 hour

Spiral Review

50. Three students need to give their presentations in science class. How many different ways can the teacher arrange the presentations? Use the *act it out* strategy. **(Lesson 5-4)**

51. Measurement Ian finished filling a $\frac{7}{8}$-gallon watering can by pouring $\frac{5}{8}$ of a gallon of water into the can. How much water was already in the can? **(Lesson 5-3)**

Estimate. (Lesson 5-2)

52. $4\frac{3}{7} + \frac{1}{8}$

53. $3\frac{4}{5} + 1\frac{1}{7}$

54. $8\frac{7}{8} - 3\frac{5}{6}$

55. $13\frac{2}{5} - 9\frac{6}{7}$

Statistics For Exercises 56–58, use the histogram. (Lesson 2-3)

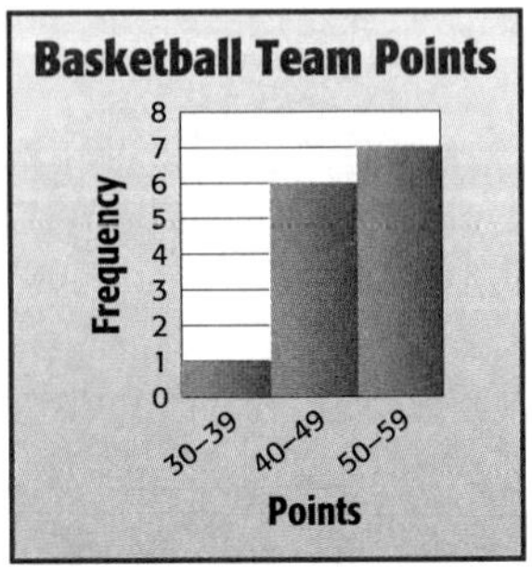

56. What is the fewest possible number of points the team scored?

57. How many games did the team score more than 49 points?

58. Write a few sentences that analyze the data.

Fraction Rummy

Adding Fractions

Get Ready!

Players: two

You will need: 27 index cards

Get Set!

Cut the index cards in half. Then label the cards.

- 4 cards each: $\frac{1}{2}, \frac{1}{3}, \frac{1}{4}$
- 3 cards each: $\frac{1}{5}, \frac{2}{5}, \frac{3}{5}, \frac{4}{5}, \frac{1}{6}, \frac{5}{6}, \frac{1}{10}, \frac{3}{10}, \frac{7}{10}, \frac{9}{10}, \frac{1}{12}, \frac{5}{12}, \frac{7}{12}, \frac{11}{12}$

Go!

- Choose one person to be the dealer.
- The dealer shuffles the cards and deals seven cards to each person, one card at a time, facedown.
- The dealer places the remaining cards facedown, turns the top card faceup, and places it next to the deck to start a discard pile.
- The players look at their cards and try to form sets of two or more cards whose sum is one. For example, $\frac{3}{10} + \frac{7}{10} = \frac{10}{10}$ or 1. Cards forming sums of one are placed in front of the player.
- Players take turns drawing the top card from the facedown deck, or the discard pile, and trying to find sums of one, which they place in front of them. To finish a turn, the player discards one card face up on the discard pile.
- The first person to discard his or her last card wins.

5-6 Problem-Solving Investigation

MAIN IDEA I will choose the best strategy to solve a problem.

Standard 5MR2.3 Use a variety of methods, such as words, numbers, symbols, charts, graphs, **tables**, diagrams, and models, **to explain mathematical reasoning.** **Standard 5NS2.3 Solve simple problems, including ones arising in concrete situations, involving the addition and subtraction of fractions** and mixed numbers (like and **unlike denominators of 20 or less),** and express answers in the simplest form.

P.S.I. TEAM +

STACY: My teacher asked me to find the average monthly precipitation for Redding, California. I found a chart that shows the averages during certain months.

Month	June	July	August
Precipitation (in.)	$\frac{7}{10}$	$\frac{1}{20}$	$\frac{1}{5}$

YOUR MISSION: Find the difference between the average precipitation for the month with the greatest average and the month with the lowest average.

Understand	You know the precipitation averages for 3 months. You need to find the difference between the average precipitation for the month with the greatest average and the month with the lowest average.
Plan	You can use logical reasoning to solve the problem.
Solve	Rewrite each fraction using the LCD, 20. $\frac{7}{10} \rightarrow \frac{14}{20}, \frac{1}{20}, \frac{1}{5} \rightarrow \frac{4}{20}$ Order the fractions from least to greatest: $\frac{1}{20}, \frac{4}{20}, \frac{14}{20}$. Subtract the lowest average from the greatest average. $\frac{14}{20} - \frac{1}{20} = \frac{13}{20}$ So, the difference between the greatest average and the lowest average is $\frac{13}{20}$ in.
Check	Look back at the problem. Estimate $\frac{7}{10} - \frac{1}{20} \approx \frac{1}{2} - 0$ or $\frac{1}{2}$. Since $\frac{1}{2} \approx \frac{13}{20}$, the answer is reasonable. ✓

Mixed Problem Solving

EXTRA PRACTICE
See page 668.

Use any strategy shown below to solve each problem.

PROBLEM-SOLVING STRATEGIES

- Act it out.
- Make a table.
- Use logical reasoning.

1. Tetsuo bought a clock radio for $9 less than the regular price. If he paid $32, what was the regular price?

2. A list of test scores is shown.

English Test Scores						
68	77	99	86	73	75	100
86	70	97	93	80	91	72
85	98	79	77	65	89	71

How many more scored 71 to 80 than 91 to 100?

3. Cesar needs to visit three Web sites for a homework assignment. In how many orders can he visit the Web sites?

4. Carlota bought three packages of ground turkey that weighed $\frac{3}{4}$ pound, $\frac{7}{8}$ pound, and $\frac{2}{3}$ pound. How much ground turkey did she buy?

5. Steve, Joseph, Alyca, and Candace all have a different favorite sport. Alyca does not like baseball or football. Joseph's favorite sport is not played with a round ball. Candace does not care for basketball or soccer. Steve's favorite sport is soccer. Find the favorite sport of each person.

6. Of the 150 students at Lincoln Middle School, 55 are in the orchestra, and 75 are in the marching band. Of these students, 25 are in both orchestra and marching band. How many students are neither in orchestra nor in the marching band?

7. How many triangles are in the bottom row of the fifth figure of this series?

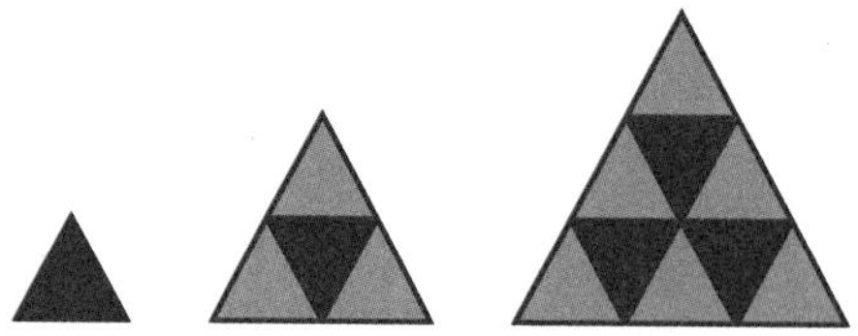

8. **Measurement** Over the last month, Sabrina grew $\frac{5}{8}$ inch more than Derrick. If Derrick grew $\frac{1}{4}$ inch, how many inches did Sabrina grow?

9. Zu-Wang surveyed his classmates to find out what type of TV program they like. He used D for drama, C for comedy, R for reality, and G for game show. How many people chose game show and reality programs?

Favorite TV Programming							
D	G	C	C	R	R	G	D
C	R	D	D	G	C	R	C
C	D	G	C	R	C	G	G

10. **WRITING IN MATH** Eight people attend an end of the year banquet. Small square tables are placed end-to-end to make one long table. Only one person can sit on a side. Is the *act it out* strategy the best problem-solving strategy to find the number of tables needed? Explain why or why not.

5-7

Adding and Subtracting Mixed Numbers

GET READY to Learn

Hands-On Mini Lab

You can use paper plates to add and subtract mixed numbers.

Step 1 Cut a paper plate into fourths and another plate into halves.

Step 2 Use one whole plate and three fourths of a plate to show the mixed number $1\frac{3}{4}$.

Step 3 Use two whole plates and one half of a plate to show $2\frac{1}{2}$.

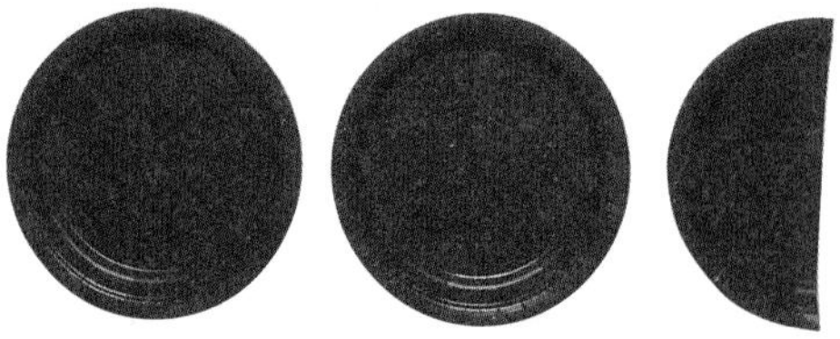

Step 4 Make as many whole paper plates as you can.

1. How many whole paper plates can you make?

2. What fraction is represented by the leftover pieces?

Use paper plate models to find each sum or difference.

3. $1\frac{3}{4} + 2\frac{1}{2}$ **4.** $2\frac{3}{4} - 1\frac{1}{4}$ **5.** $1\frac{2}{3} + 2\frac{1}{6}$

MAIN IDEA

I will add and subtract mixed numbers.

Standard 5NS2.3 Solve simple problems, including ones arising in concrete situations, involving the addition and subtraction of fractions and **mixed numbers (like and unlike denominators of 20 or less), and express answers in the simplest form.**

The Mini Lab suggests the following rule.

KEY CONCEPT **Add and Subtract Mixed Numbers**

- Add or subtract the fractions.
- Then add or subtract the whole numbers.
- Rename and simplify if necessary.

EXAMPLE Subtract Mixed Numbers

1 **Find $4\frac{5}{6} - 2\frac{1}{6}$.** **Estimate** $5 - 2 = 3$

Subtract the fractions. Subtract the whole numbers.

$$\begin{array}{r} 4\frac{5}{6} \\ -\ 2\frac{1}{6} \\ \hline \frac{4}{6} \end{array} \quad \rightarrow \quad \begin{array}{r} 4\frac{5}{6} \\ -\ 2\frac{1}{6} \\ \hline 2\frac{4}{6} \text{ or } 2\frac{2}{3} \end{array}$$

Check for Reasonableness $2\frac{2}{3} \approx 3$ ✓

EXAMPLE Add Mixed Numbers

2 **Find $5\frac{1}{4} + 10\frac{2}{3}$.** **Estimate** $5 + 11 = 16$

The LCD of $\frac{1}{4}$ and $\frac{2}{3}$ is 12.

Write the problem. Rename the fractions using the LCD, 12. Add the fractions. Then add the whole numbers.

$$\begin{array}{r} 5\frac{1}{4} \\ +\ 10\frac{2}{3} \\ \hline \end{array} \rightarrow \begin{array}{c} \frac{1 \times 3}{4 \times 3} \\ \frac{2 \times 4}{3 \times 4} \end{array} \rightarrow \begin{array}{r} 5\frac{3}{12} \\ +\ 10\frac{8}{12} \\ \hline \end{array} \rightarrow \begin{array}{r} 5\frac{3}{12} \\ +\ 10\frac{8}{12} \\ \hline 15\frac{11}{12} \end{array}$$

Check for Reasonableness $15\frac{11}{12} \approx 16$ ✓

Real-World EXAMPLE

3 **What is the overall height of the TV and stand shown?**

First use the LCD to rename the fractions. Then add.

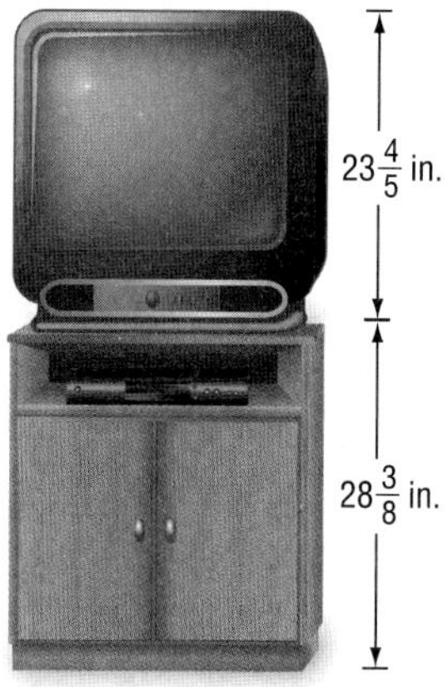

$$23\frac{4}{5} + 28\frac{3}{8} = 23\frac{32}{40} + 28\frac{15}{40}$$
$$= 51\frac{47}{40}$$
$$= 51 + \frac{47}{40}$$
$$= 51 + 1\frac{7}{40} \text{ or } 52\frac{7}{40}$$

The overall height of the TV and stand is $52\frac{7}{40}$ inches.

Remember

By estimating $23\frac{4}{5} + 28\frac{3}{8}$, you know the height must be greater than 52 inches and less than 53 inches.

Online **Personal Tutor at** ca.gr5math.com

You can also evaluate algebraic expressions with mixed numbers.

EXAMPLES Evaluate an Expression

4 Algebra Evaluate $x - y$ if $x = 4\frac{2}{3}$ and $y = 2\frac{1}{6}$.

$x - y = 4\frac{2}{3} - 2\frac{1}{6}$ Replace x with $4\frac{2}{3}$ and y with $2\frac{1}{6}$.

$= 4\frac{4}{6} - 2\frac{1}{6}$ Rename $4\frac{2}{3}$ as $4\frac{4}{6}$.

$= 2\frac{3}{6}$ Subtract.

$= 2\frac{1}{2}$ Simplify.

5 Algebra Evaluate $c + d$ if $c = 1\frac{2}{5}$ and $d = 7\frac{3}{4}$.

$c + d = 1\frac{2}{5} + 7\frac{3}{4}$ Replace c with $1\frac{2}{5}$ and d with $7\frac{3}{4}$.

$= 1\frac{8}{20} + 7\frac{15}{20}$ Rename $1\frac{2}{5}$ as $1\frac{8}{20}$ and $7\frac{3}{4}$ as $7\frac{15}{20}$.

$= 8\frac{23}{20}$ Add.

$= 8 + \frac{23}{20}$ Add.

$= 8 + 1\frac{3}{20}$ or $9\frac{3}{20}$ Write $\frac{23}{20}$ as a mixed number. Simplify.

CHECK What You Know

Add or subtract. Write in simplest form. **See Examples 1, 2 (p. 261)**

1. $5\frac{3}{4} - 1\frac{1}{4}$

2. $2\frac{3}{8} + 4\frac{1}{8}$

3. $14\frac{3}{5} - 6\frac{3}{10}$

4. $6\frac{9}{10} + 8\frac{1}{4}$

5. $3\frac{2}{3} - \frac{3}{5}$

6. $4\frac{5}{6} + 3\frac{3}{4}$

7. A g-force is a unit of measurement for an object being accelerated. The Great White rollercoaster has a g-force of $4\frac{3}{5}$. The Joker's Revenge rollercoaster has a g-force of $3\frac{1}{2}$. How much greater is the g-force of Great White than Joker's Revenge? **See Example 3 (p. 261)**

8. Algebra Evaluate $e - f$ if $e = 5\frac{9}{10}$ and $f = 4\frac{1}{2}$. **See Example 4 (p. 262)**

9. Algebra Evaluate $m + n$ if $m = 2\frac{3}{4}$ and $n = 3\frac{3}{5}$. **See Example 5 (p. 262)**

10. **Talk About It** Give a real-world example of when you would add mixed numbers.

Practice and Problem Solving

EXTRA PRACTICE
See page 668.

Add or subtract. Write in simplest form. See Examples 1–3 (p. 261)

11. $3\frac{5}{6} + 4\frac{1}{6}$

12. $4\frac{5}{12} + 6\frac{7}{12}$

13. $4\frac{5}{8} - 2\frac{3}{8}$

14. $9\frac{4}{5} - 4\frac{2}{5}$

15. $10\frac{3}{4} - 3\frac{1}{2}$

16. $8\frac{1}{3} - 3\frac{1}{6}$

17. $3\frac{1}{2} + 2\frac{2}{3}$

18. $11\frac{3}{10} + 9\frac{1}{4}$

19. $6\frac{3}{5} + \frac{4}{5}$ **20.** $3\frac{3}{8} + 6\frac{5}{8}$ **21.** $7\frac{7}{9} - 4\frac{1}{3}$ **22.** $6\frac{6}{7} - 4\frac{5}{14}$

23. $6\frac{5}{8} + 7\frac{1}{4}$ **24.** $4\frac{5}{6} + 15\frac{3}{8}$ **25.** $9\frac{5}{6} - 2\frac{1}{6}$ **26.** $5\frac{3}{4} - 3\frac{1}{3}$

27. The table shows the standings in the American League East. How many more games behind 1st place is Baltimore than Tampa Bay?

— Daily Sports Review —

Team	W	L	GB*
Boston	8	4	–
New York	8	7	$1\frac{1}{2}$
Toronto	6	7	$2\frac{1}{2}$
Tampa Bay	5	7	3
Baltimore	4	9	$4\frac{1}{2}$

*games behind 1st place

28. Measurement Pamela is going to paint three different rooms. She will need $2\frac{1}{2}$ gallons of paint for the first room, $4\frac{1}{3}$ gallons of paint for the second room, and $3\frac{3}{4}$ gallons of paint for the third room. How much paint does Pamela need for all three rooms?

Algebra Evaluate each expression if $a = 2\frac{1}{6}$, $b = 4\frac{3}{4}$, and $c = 5\frac{2}{3}$.

See Examples 4, 5 (p. 262)

29. $a + b$ **30.** $c - a$ **31.** $b + c$ **32.** $b - a$

33. Neil lives $3\frac{1}{2}$ blocks from Dario's house. Dario lives $2\frac{1}{4}$ blocks from the library, and the video store is $1\frac{1}{8}$ blocks from the library. How far will Neil travel if he walks from his home to Dario's house, the library, and then the video store?

Write an addition or subtraction expression for each model. Then add or subtract.

34. 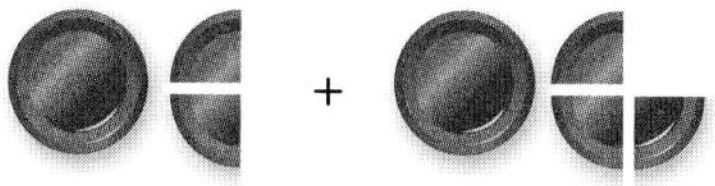

35. 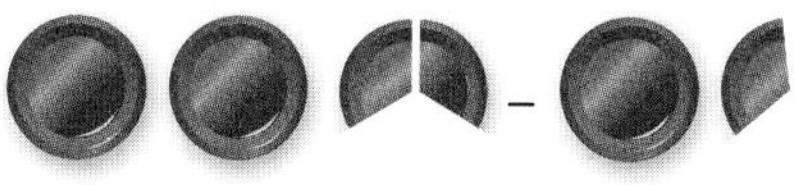

36. Measurement To win horse racing's Triple Crown, a horse must win the Kentucky Derby, Preakness Stakes, and Belmont Stakes. The lengths of the tracks are shown. How much longer is the longest race than the shortest? Justify your solution.

Triple Crown	
Race	**Length (mi)**
Kentucky Derby	$1\frac{1}{4}$
Preakness Stakes	$1\frac{3}{16}$
Belmont Stakes	$1\frac{1}{2}$

H.O.T. Problems

37. OPEN ENDED Create a problem involving the addition or subtraction of mixed numbers in which the result is $4\frac{3}{8}$.

38. CHALLENGE Use the digits 1, 1, 2, 2, 3, and 4 to create two mixed numbers whose sum is $4\frac{1}{4}$.

39. WRITING IN MATH *True* or *false*? The sum of two mixed numbers is always a mixed number. If true, explain your reasoning. If false, provide a counterexample.

Standards Practice

40 Mrs. Matthews bought $3\frac{1}{4}$ pounds of fish, $2\frac{1}{2}$ pounds of chicken, and $2\frac{3}{4}$ pounds of beef. How many pounds of meat did she buy altogether?

A $8\frac{1}{2}$ lb

B $8\frac{1}{4}$ lb

C 8 lb

D $7\frac{9}{10}$ lb

41 Travis Middle School recycled $89\frac{3}{8}$ pounds of paper this year. They recycled $77\frac{1}{3}$ pounds last year. How many more pounds did they recycle this year than last year?

F $11\frac{1}{8}$ lb

G $11\frac{11}{24}$ lb

H $12\frac{1}{24}$ lb

J $166\frac{17}{24}$ lb

Spiral Review

42. Corey bought a video game that cost $37.55, including tax. If he gave the cashier $40.00, how much change did he receive? **(Lesson 5-6)**

Add or subtract. Write in simplest form. **(Lessons 5-3 and 5-5)**

43. $\frac{1}{3} + \frac{1}{3}$ **44.** $\frac{9}{10} - \frac{3}{10}$ **45.** $\frac{4}{5} - \frac{3}{4}$ **46.** $\frac{7}{9} + \frac{5}{12}$

5-8 Subtracting Mixed Numbers with Renaming

MAIN IDEA

I will subtract mixed numbers involving renaming.

Standard 5NS2.3 Solve simple problems, including ones arising in concrete situations, involving the addition and **subtraction of** fractions and **mixed numbers (like and unlike denominators of 20 or less), and express answers in the simplest form. Standard 5MR2.1 Use estimation to verify the reasonableness of calculated results.**

GET READY to Learn

Hands-On Mini Lab

Use fraction tiles to find $3 - 1\frac{1}{4}$.

Step 1 Model 3 and $1\frac{1}{4}$.

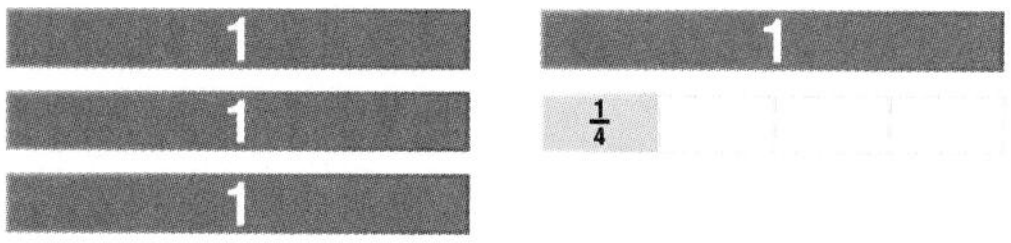

Step 2 Rename 3 as $2\frac{4}{4}$.

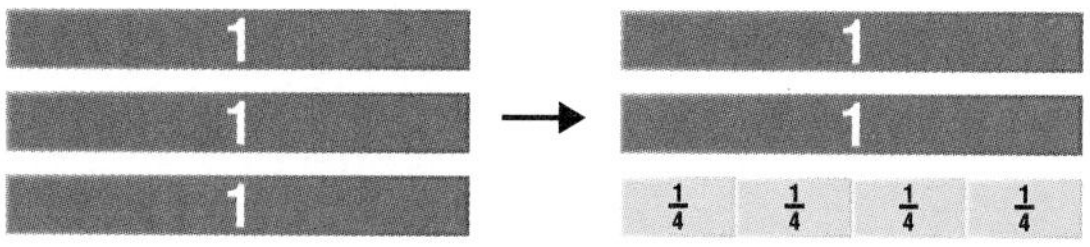

$3 = 2\frac{4}{4}$

Step 3 Subtract.

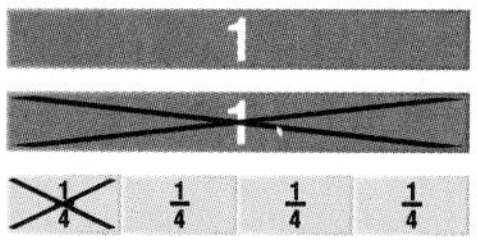

$2\frac{4}{4} - 1\frac{1}{4} = 1\frac{3}{4}$

Subtract. Use fraction tiles.

1. $5 - 2\frac{7}{8}$ **2.** $2 - 1\frac{4}{5}$ **3.** $4 - 2\frac{1}{3}$

Sometimes it is necessary to rename a whole number or a mixed number as an improper fraction in order to subtract.

EXAMPLE Rename Mixed Number to Subtract

1 **Find $4\frac{1}{3} - 1\frac{2}{3}$.** **Estimate** $4\frac{1}{2} - 1\frac{1}{2} = 3$

$4\frac{1}{3} \rightarrow 3\frac{4}{3}$ Rename $4\frac{1}{3}$ as $3\frac{4}{3}$.

$-1\frac{2}{3} \rightarrow -1\frac{2}{3}$

$2\frac{2}{3}$ Subtract.

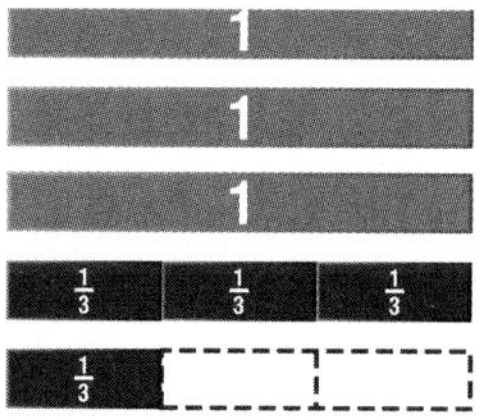

$4\frac{1}{3} = 3\frac{4}{3}$

Check for Reasonableness $2\frac{2}{3} \approx 3$ ✓

Remember

You can check your answer in Example 3 by adding $2\frac{7}{8}$ and $9\frac{1}{4}$. The answer should be $12\frac{1}{8}$.

EXAMPLE Rename Mixed Number to Subtract

2 **Find $12\frac{1}{8} - 9\frac{1}{4}$.** **Estimate** $12 - 9 = 3$

Step 1

$$\begin{array}{r} 12\frac{1}{8} \\ -\ 9\frac{1}{4} \\ \hline \end{array} \rightarrow \begin{array}{r} 12\frac{1}{8} \\ -\ 9\frac{2}{8} \\ \hline \end{array}$$

Rename $\frac{1}{8}$ and $\frac{1}{4}$ using their LCD, 8.

Step 2

$$\begin{array}{r} 12\frac{1}{8} \\ -\ 9\frac{2}{8} \\ \hline \end{array} \rightarrow \begin{array}{r} 11\frac{9}{8} \\ -\ 9\frac{2}{8} \\ \hline 2\frac{7}{8} \end{array}$$

Rename $12\frac{1}{8}$ as $11\frac{8}{8} + \frac{1}{8}$ or $11\frac{9}{8}$.

Check for Reasonableness $2\frac{7}{8} \approx 3$ ✓

Real-World EXAMPLE

3 **The height of Mt. Rainier, near Seattle, Washington, is $2\frac{3}{4}$ miles. Compare the height of Mt. Rainier to the height of the highest mountain in the world. Find the difference between the heights of the two mountains.**

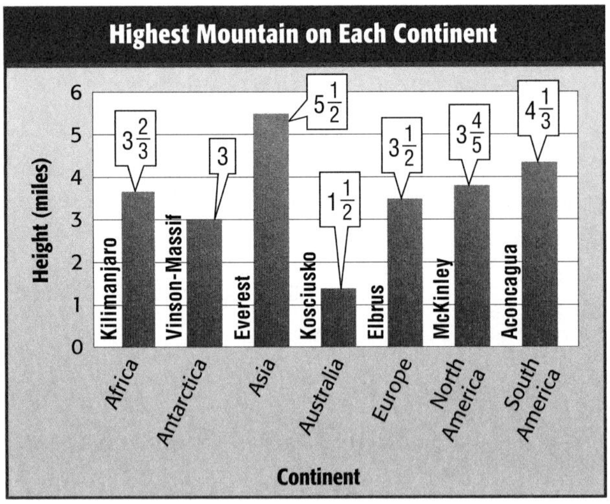

Source: *Oxford Atlas of the World*

Find $5\frac{1}{2} - 2\frac{3}{4}$. **Estimate** $6 - 3 = 3$

$$\begin{array}{r} 5\frac{1}{2} \\ -\ 2\frac{3}{4} \\ \hline \end{array} \rightarrow \begin{array}{r} 5\frac{2}{4} \\ -\ 2\frac{3}{4} \\ \hline \end{array} \rightarrow \begin{array}{r} 4\frac{6}{4} \\ -\ 2\frac{3}{4} \\ \hline 2\frac{3}{4} \end{array}$$

Rename $5\frac{2}{4}$ as $4\frac{6}{4}$.

Check for Reasonableness $2\frac{3}{4} \approx 3$ ✓

So, Mt. Everest is $2\frac{3}{4}$ miles higher than Mt. Rainier.

Online **Personal Tutor at** ca.gr5math.com

CHECK What You Know

Subtract. Write in simplest form. See Examples 1–3 (pp. 265–266)

1. $4 - 3\frac{1}{6}$

2. $6 - 3\frac{1}{4}$

3. $3 - 2\frac{2}{5}$

4. $3\frac{1}{8} - 1\frac{3}{8}$

5. $6\frac{1}{2} - 2\frac{3}{4}$

6. $5\frac{1}{4} - 3\frac{3}{5}$

7. The pilot said it will take $2\frac{1}{2}$ hours to reach your destination. You have been in flight for $1\frac{3}{4}$ hours. How much longer is your flight?

8. Talk About It Name two fractions that are equivalent to 10.

Practice and Problem Solving

EXTRA PRACTICE See page 668.

Subtract. Write in simplest form. See Examples 1–3 (pp. 265–266)

9. $7 - 5\frac{1}{2}$

10. $9 - 3\frac{3}{5}$

11. $4\frac{1}{4} - 2\frac{3}{4}$

12. $9\frac{3}{8} - 6\frac{5}{8}$

13. $12\frac{1}{5} - 5\frac{3}{10}$

14. $8\frac{1}{3} - 1\frac{5}{6}$

15. $14\frac{3}{8} - 5\frac{3}{4}$

16. $10\frac{5}{9} - 3\frac{2}{3}$

17. $7\frac{1}{3} - 3\frac{1}{2}$

18. $5\frac{1}{6} - 1\frac{3}{8}$

19. $12\frac{3}{4} - \frac{4}{5}$

20. $9\frac{5}{9} - \frac{5}{6}$

21. Measurement How much longer is $1\frac{1}{2}$ inches than $\frac{3}{4}$ inch?

22. Caroline bought $2\frac{1}{4}$ pounds of turkey and $1\frac{2}{3}$ pounds of roast beef. How much more turkey than roast beef did Caroline buy?

23. The U.S. Department of Transportation prohibits a truck driver from driving more than 70 hours in any 8-day period. Mr. Galvez has driven $53\frac{3}{4}$ hours in the last 6 days. How many more hours is he allowed to drive during the next 2 days?

24. Measurement How much more is 8 quarts than $5\frac{1}{2}$ quarts?

25. Statistics Sei ("say") whales can reach different sizes based on their location. Find the difference between the longest and shortest sei whales according to their location. Justify your solution.

Sei Whale Lengths

Location	Length (feet)
Southern hemisphere	$65\frac{3}{5}$
North Pacific	61
North Atlantic	$56\frac{4}{5}$

Source: seaworld.org

Measurement **The sum of the measures of the sides of each figure are given. Find the length of each missing measure. Justify your answers.**

26.

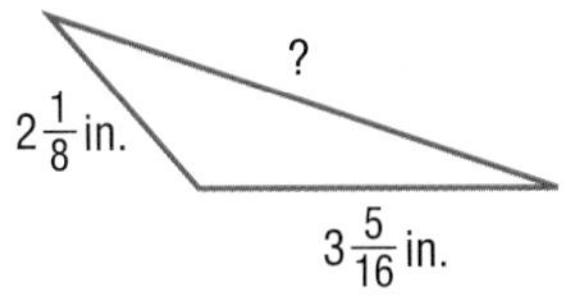

Sum of measures = $10\frac{5}{16}$ in.

27.

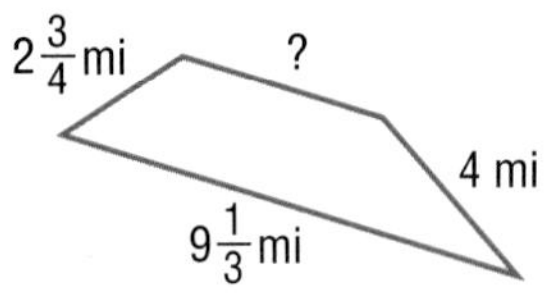

Sum of measures = 20 mi

Real-World PROBLEM SOLVING

Measurement **The table shows the Men's Olympic Long Jump winners from 1988–2004.**

28. How much farther did Carl Lewis jump in 1992 than Ivan Pedroso in 2000?

29. How much farther did Dwight Phillips jump in 2004 than Ivan Pedroso in 2000?

Men's Olympic Long Jump Winners

Year	Athlete, Country	Distance
1988	Carl Lewis, U.S.	28 ft $7\frac{1}{2}$ in.
1992	Carl Lewis, U.S.	28 ft $5\frac{1}{2}$ in.
1996	Carl Lewis, U.S.	27 ft $10\frac{3}{4}$ in.
2000	Ivan Pedroso, Cuba	28 ft $\frac{3}{4}$ in.
2004	Dwight Phillips, U.S.	28 ft $2\frac{1}{4}$ in.

Source: *The World Almanac*

H.O.T. Problems

30. FIND THE ERROR Lareina and Tabitha are finding $9\frac{1}{2} - 3$. Who is correct? Explain your reasoning.

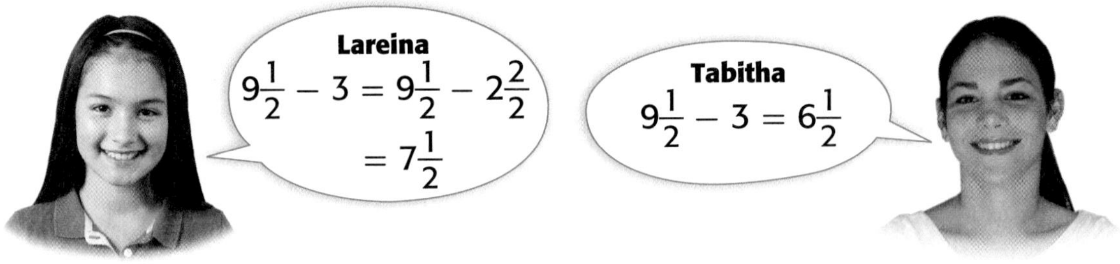

Lareina
$9\frac{1}{2} - 3 = 9\frac{1}{2} - 2\frac{2}{2}$
$= 7\frac{1}{2}$
Tabitha
$9\frac{1}{2} - 3 = 6\frac{1}{2}$

31. CHALLENGE Refer to the table for Exercises 28 and 29 on Olympic long jump distances. What is the difference between the shortest and longest jumps represented in the table?

32. SELECT A TOOL Alyssa lives three miles from the beach and her cousin lives $2\frac{1}{3}$ miles from the beach. Which of the following tools might Alyssa use to determine how much farther she lives from the beach than her cousin? Justify your selection(s). Then use the tool(s) to solve the problem.

draw a model | paper/pencil | real objects

33. **WRITING IN ▸MATH** Describe a method of renaming $5\frac{3}{7}$ as $4\frac{10}{7}$ that involves mental math. Explain why your method works.

Standards Practice

34 The table lists differences between the court size for basketball in the Olympics and in the National Basketball Association (NBA). How much longer is the court in the NBA than in the Olympics?

Sport	Length of Court (feet)	Width of Court (feet)
Olympic Basketball	$91\frac{5}{6}$	$49\frac{1}{6}$
NBA Basketball	94	50

A $3\frac{2}{3}$ ft

B $2\frac{5}{6}$ ft

C $2\frac{1}{6}$ ft

D $\frac{5}{6}$ ft

35 Melika was making a quilt for her room. She had $10\frac{1}{4}$ yards of material. It took $7\frac{1}{2}$ yards for the quilt. How much material was not used for the quilt?

F $2\frac{3}{4}$ yd

G $3\frac{1}{4}$ yd

H $3\frac{1}{2}$ yd

J $17\frac{3}{4}$ yd

Spiral Review

Algebra Evaluate each expression if $a = 1\frac{1}{6}$, $b = 4\frac{3}{4}$, and $c = 6\frac{5}{8}$. **(Lesson 5-7)**

36. $b + c$ **37.** $b - a$ **38.** $c - a$ **39.** $a + b$

40. Find the sum of $\frac{7}{8}$ and $\frac{5}{6}$. Write in simplest form. **(Lesson 5-5)**

41. Norfolk, Virginia, has an area of $53\frac{7}{10}$ square miles. Express this fraction as a decimal. **(Lesson 4-9)**

Replace each x with a number so the fractions are equivalent. **(Lesson 4-3)**

42. $\frac{3}{5} = \frac{x}{25}$ **43.** $\frac{18}{24} = \frac{6}{x}$ **44.** $\frac{x}{7} = \frac{20}{35}$ **45.** $\frac{x}{10} = \frac{15}{30}$

46. $\frac{1}{3} = \frac{14}{x}$ **47.** $\frac{4}{11} = \frac{12}{x}$ **48.** $\frac{3}{5} = \frac{x}{45}$ **49.** $\frac{2}{9} = \frac{x}{63}$

For Exercises 50 and 51, use the following information. **(Lesson 1-3)**

Admission to a zoo is $3 for adults and $2 for children.

50. Write an expression to find the total cost of 4 adult tickets and 5 children's tickets.

51. Find the value of the expression in Exercise 50.

Problem Solving in Science

Making Mixtures

Mixtures are all around you. Rocks, air, and ocean water are all mixtures. So are paints, clay, and chalk. The substances in mixtures are combined physically, not chemically. Although some substances seem to dissolve in others, each substance in a mixture keeps its own physical properties. This means that the substances in mixtures can be physically separated.

You can make some fun mixtures by using specific amounts of substances. For example, to make one type of invisible ink, you use $\frac{1}{2}$ as much baking soda as water. If you use $\frac{1}{2}$ of a cup of water, you use $\frac{1}{4}$ of a cup of baking soda. You can use other recipes to make mixtures such as sculpting clay and bubble-blowing liquid.

Real-World Math

Use the information on page 271 to solve each problem.

1. How much water do you need to make a batch of clay?
2. How much more salt than cornstarch do you need to make a batch of clay?
3. What amount of solid ingredients do you need to make a batch of clay?
4. How much liquid do you need to make bubble-blowing liquid?
5. If you make three batches of clay, how much food coloring will you need?
6. If you make two batches of bubble-blowing liquid, how much water will you need?
7. If you make two batches of bubble-blowing liquid, how much soap will you need?
8. How many cups of ingredients do you need to make one batch of clay?

Math Standard 5NS2.3 Solve simple problems, including ones arising in concrete situations, involving the addition and subtraction of fractions and mixed numbers (like and unlike denominators of 20 or less), and express answers in the simplest form.

Did You Know?

Hundreds of different colors of paint can be made by mixing different amounts of just three colors: yellow, magenta, and cyan.

Clay

$2\frac{1}{3}$ cups of salt

$\frac{3}{4}$ cup of cold water

$1\frac{2}{3}$ cups cornstarch

$\frac{1}{2}$ cup boiling water

$1\frac{2}{3}$ teaspoons of oil

$\frac{2}{3}$ teaspoon food coloring

Bubble-Blowing Liquid

$4\frac{1}{4}$ cups of water

$\frac{1}{4}$ cup glycerin

$1\frac{3}{4}$ ounces grated soap

CHAPTER 5 Study Guide and Review

FOLDABLES™ Study Organizer GET READY to Study

Be sure the following Key Concepts are noted in your Foldable.

BIG Ideas

Fractions with Like Denominators (Lesson 5-3)

To add or subtract fractions with the same denominators follow these steps:
1. Add or subtract the numerators.
2. Use the same denominator in the sum or difference.
3. If necessary, simplify the sum or difference.

Fractions with Unlike Denominators (Lesson 5-5)

To add or subtract fractions with different denominators, follow these steps:
1. Rename the fractions using the LCD.
2. Add or subtract as with like fractions. Simplify.

Mixed Numbers (Lesson 5-7)

To add or subtract mixed numbers, follow these steps:
1. Add or subtract the fractions.
2. Add or subtract the whole numbers.
3. Rename and simplify if necessary.

Key Vocabulary

like fractions (p. 241)
unlike fractions (p. 251)

Vocabulary Check

State whether each sentence is *true* or *false*. If *false*, replace the underlined word or number to make a true sentence.

1. In painting a wall that is $9\frac{3}{5}$- by $8\frac{1}{4}$-feet, it would make sense to round the number of gallons of paint that is needed up to the nearest gallon.

2. To the nearest half, $5\frac{1}{5}$ rounds to $5\frac{1}{2}$.

3. When adding or subtracting like fractions, use the same denominator in the sum.

4. Fractions with the same numerator are called like fractions.

5. Sometimes it is necessary to rename the fraction part of a mixed number as an improper fraction in order to subtract.

6. The mixed number $9\frac{1}{4}$ can be renamed as $8\frac{5}{4}$.

7. To add or subtract fractions with unlike denominators, first rename the fractions using the GCF.

Math Online Vocabulary Review at ca.gr5math.com

Lesson-by-Lesson Review

5-1 Rounding Fractions and Mixed Numbers (pp. 232–236)

Example 1
Round $\frac{5}{8}$ to the nearest half.

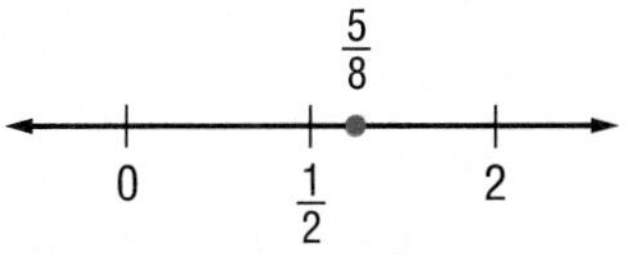

$\frac{5}{8}$ rounds to $\frac{1}{2}$.

Example 2
Round $2\frac{4}{5}$ to the nearest half.

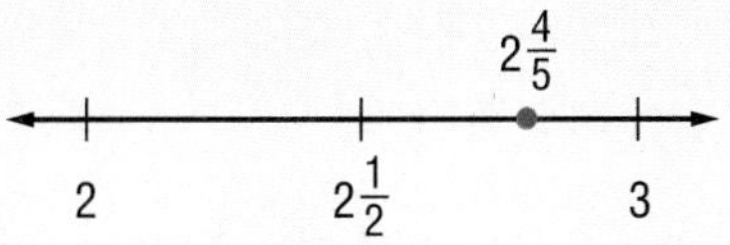

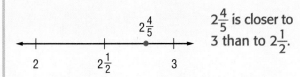

$2\frac{4}{5}$ is closer to 3 than to $2\frac{1}{2}$.

$2\frac{4}{5}$ rounds to 3.

Round each number to the nearest half.

8. $\frac{4}{5}$

9. $4\frac{1}{3}$

10. $6\frac{6}{14}$

11. $\frac{11}{20}$

12. $2\frac{2}{11}$

13. $9\frac{4}{9}$

14. Measurement Round the length of the key to the nearest half inch.

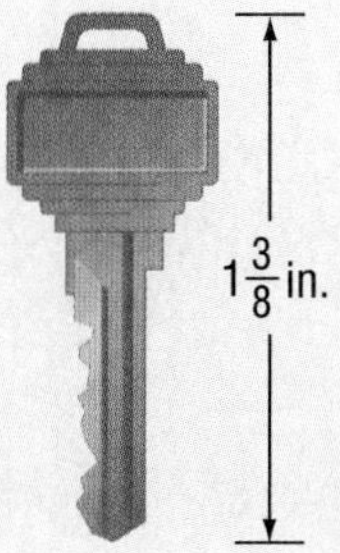

5-2 Estimating Sums and Differences (pp. 237–240)

Example 3
Estimate $\frac{5}{6} - \frac{4}{9}$.

$\frac{5}{6} - \frac{4}{9}$ is about $1 - \frac{1}{2}$ or $\frac{1}{2}$.

Example 4
Estimate $2\frac{4}{5} + 6\frac{1}{8}$.

$2\frac{4}{5} + 6\frac{1}{8}$ is about $3 + 6$ or 9.

Estimate.

15. $\frac{3}{4} + \frac{1}{3}$

16. $\frac{7}{8} - \frac{1}{5}$

17. $3\frac{1}{9} - 1\frac{6}{7}$

18. $6\frac{7}{12} - 2\frac{1}{4}$

19. $4\frac{9}{10} + 1\frac{2}{9}$

20. $3\frac{7}{8} - \frac{1}{12}$

21. Tamika is making two different kinds of jam. One jam recipe calls for $2\frac{1}{4}$ cups of sugar. The other recipe calls for $3\frac{2}{3}$ cups of sugar. About how much sugar should Tamika have so that she is sure to have enough sugar for both jam recipes?

Study Guide and Review

5-3 Adding and Subtracting Fractions with Like Denominators (pp. 241–245)

Example 5

Find $\frac{3}{8} + \frac{1}{8}$. Estimate $\frac{1}{2} + 0 = \frac{1}{2}$

$\frac{3}{8} + \frac{1}{8} = \frac{3+1}{8}$ Add the numerators.

$= \frac{4}{8}$ or $\frac{1}{2}$ Simplify.

Example 6

Find $\frac{7}{12} - \frac{5}{12}$. Estimate $\frac{1}{2} - \frac{1}{2} = 0$

$\frac{7}{12} - \frac{5}{12} = \frac{7-5}{12}$ Subtract the numerators.

$= \frac{2}{12}$ or $\frac{1}{6}$ Simplify.

Add or subtract. Write in simplest form.

22. $\frac{5}{8} + \frac{1}{8}$

23. $\frac{7}{12} + \frac{1}{12}$

24. $\frac{7}{10} + \frac{3}{10}$

25. $\frac{6}{7} - \frac{2}{7}$

26. $\frac{11}{12} - \frac{7}{12}$

27. $\frac{7}{9} + \frac{4}{9}$

28. Tori ate $\frac{4}{12}$ of a large pizza, and Ben ate $\frac{5}{12}$. How much of the pizza did they eat in all? Write in simplest form.

5-4 Problem-Solving Strategy: Act It Out (pp. 246–247)

Example 7

Drew wants to center the word *California* on a sheet of paper as shown. What should the top and side margins be?

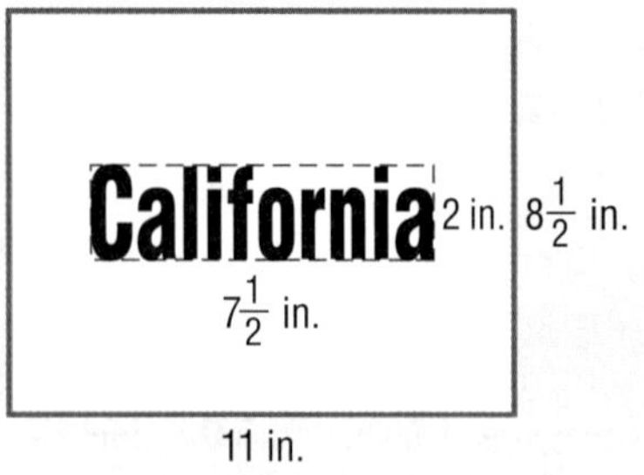

Cut a $7\frac{1}{2}$- by 2-inch piece of paper and place it roughly in the center of an $8\frac{1}{2}$- by 11-inch piece of paper. Measure the top and side margins to see if they are equal and adjust if necessary. The top top margin should be $3\frac{1}{4}$ inches. The side margin should be $1\frac{3}{4}$ inches.

Solve. Use the *act it out* strategy.

29. In how many different ways can four students be seated in a row of four seats?

30. Kenneth walks at the rate of 1 foot every five seconds while Ebony walks at the rate of 2 feet every five seconds. If Kenneth has a head start of 3 feet, after how many seconds will they be at the same spot?

31. Eight friends are seated in a circle. Juana walks around the circle and lightly taps every third person on the shoulder. How many times does she need to walk around the circle in order to have tapped each person on the shoulder at least once?

5-5 Adding and Subtracting Fractions with Unlike Denominators (pp. 251–256)

Example 8

Find $\frac{3}{8} + \frac{2}{3}$. Estimate $\frac{1}{2} + \frac{1}{2} = 1$

The LCD of $\frac{3}{8}$ and $\frac{2}{3}$ is 24.

$$\frac{3}{8} \rightarrow \frac{3 \times \mathbf{3}}{8 \times \mathbf{3}} \rightarrow \frac{\mathbf{9}}{24}$$

$$+\frac{2}{3} \rightarrow \frac{2 \times \mathbf{8}}{3 \times \mathbf{8}} \rightarrow +\frac{\mathbf{16}}{24}$$

$$\frac{\mathbf{25}}{24} \text{ or } 1\frac{1}{24}$$

Add or subtract. Write in simplest form.

32. $\frac{1}{2} + \frac{2}{3}$
33. $\frac{5}{8} + \frac{1}{4}$
34. $\frac{7}{9} - \frac{1}{12}$
35. $\frac{9}{10} - \frac{1}{4}$
36. $\frac{7}{9} - \frac{1}{6}$
37. $\frac{4}{5} + \frac{2}{10}$
38. Teresa used $\frac{5}{6}$ of her total monthly cell phone minutes while Yolanda used $\frac{1}{4}$ of her minutes. By what fraction did Teresa use more monthly minutes than Yolanda?

5-6 Problem-Solving Investigation: Choose the Best Strategy (pp. 258–259)

Example 9

Statistics Aaron surveyed his friends about the last type of music source they listened to, radio (R) or CD (C). The results are shown below. What fraction of the total friends surveyed said CD?

Last Music Source
C C R C R R C R C
C R R C C C R C C R

You can make a frequency table of the data. Draw a table with three columns.

Last Music Source		
Source	**Tally**	**Frequency**
Radio	𝍸 III	8
CD	𝍸 𝍸 I	11

8 + 11 or 19 friends were surveyed, and 11 said CD. So, $\frac{11}{19}$ of the friends said CD.

Choose the best strategy to solve each problem.

39. The Sears Tower in Chicago is 1,450 feet tall and has 110 stories. The Chrysler Building in New York has 77 stories and is 1,046 feet tall. About how many stories taller is the Sears Tower than the Chrysler Building?
40. Theodore numbered four index cards from 1–4, with one number on each card. If he rearranges the index cards, how many possible arrangements can he have?
41. A container has $\frac{13}{16}$ gallon of juice in it. If the container can hold 2 gallons of juice, how much more juice will fit into the container?

Study Guide and Review

5-7 Adding and Subtracting Mixed Numbers (pp. 260–264)

Example 10

Find $6\frac{5}{8} - 2\frac{2}{5}$. Estimate $7 - 2 = 5$

$$6\frac{5}{8} \rightarrow \frac{5 \times \mathbf{5}}{8 \times \mathbf{5}} \rightarrow 6\frac{25}{40}$$

$$-2\frac{2}{5} \rightarrow \frac{2 \times \mathbf{8}}{5 \times \mathbf{8}} \rightarrow -2\frac{16}{40}$$

$$4\frac{9}{40}$$

Add or subtract. Write in simplest form.

42. $3\frac{2}{5} + 1\frac{3}{5}$

43. $9\frac{7}{8} - 5\frac{3}{8}$

44. $7\frac{5}{6} + 9\frac{3}{4}$

45. $4\frac{3}{7} - 2\frac{5}{14}$

46. Over the weekend, Brad spent $\frac{3}{4}$ hour on his math homework and $2\frac{1}{6}$ hours on his science paper. How much time did he spend on these two subjects?

5-8 Subtracting Mixed Numbers with Renaming (pp. 265–269)

Example 11

Find $6 - 3\frac{2}{3}$. Estimate $6 - 3\frac{1}{2} = 2\frac{1}{2}$

$$6 \rightarrow 5\frac{3}{3} \quad \text{Rename 6 as } 5\frac{3}{3}.$$

$$-3\frac{2}{3} \rightarrow -3\frac{2}{3}$$

$$2\frac{1}{3} \quad \text{Subtract.}$$

Example 12

Find $3\frac{1}{5} - 1\frac{4}{5}$. Estimate $3 - 2 = 1$

$$3\frac{1}{5} \rightarrow 2\frac{6}{5} \quad \text{Rename } 3\frac{1}{5} \text{ as } 2\frac{6}{5}.$$

$$-1\frac{4}{5} \rightarrow -1\frac{4}{5}$$

$$1\frac{2}{5}$$

Subtract. Write in simplest form.

47. $5 - 3\frac{2}{3}$

48. $6\frac{3}{8} - 3\frac{5}{6}$

49. $12\frac{2}{5} - 9\frac{2}{3}$

50. $8\frac{5}{8} - 1\frac{3}{4}$

51. Measurement A board measures $9\frac{2}{3}$ feet. A piece measuring $5\frac{7}{8}$ feet is cut off. Find the length of the remaining board.

52. Kaye's goal was to read 10 hours over the past two weeks. So far, she has read $6\frac{1}{3}$ hours. How many more hours does Kaye need to read to reach her goal?

CHAPTER 5

Chapter Test

Round each number to the nearest half.

1. $4\frac{7}{8}$ **2.** $1\frac{10}{18}$ **3.** $11\frac{1}{17}$

Estimate.

4. $\frac{8}{10} + \frac{3}{5}$ **5.** $5\frac{1}{7} - 2\frac{9}{11}$

6. **Measurement** The table shows the amount of rainfall over a one week period in May. Estimate the amount of rainfall for the week.

Day of Week	Rainfall (in.)
Monday	$1\frac{1}{4}$
Tuesday	0
Wednesday	0
Thursday	$\frac{5}{8}$
Friday	0
Saturday	$1\frac{5}{16}$
Sunday	0

7. For a 3-person relay race, a coach can choose from 4 of his top runners. How many different 3-person teams can he choose? Use the *act it out* strategy.

Add or subtract. Write in simplest form.

8. $\frac{2}{9} + \frac{5}{9}$ **9.** $\frac{9}{10} - \frac{4}{10}$

10. $\frac{5}{6} - \frac{2}{6}$ **11.** $\frac{2}{9} + \frac{5}{6}$

12. $\frac{11}{12} - \frac{3}{8}$ **13.** $\frac{2}{5} + \frac{2}{4}$

14. At a party, if $\frac{1}{3}$ of one sheet cake and $\frac{1}{6}$ of another sheet cake remain uneaten, what fraction of a whole sheet cake remains uneaten?

15. **STANDARDS PRACTICE** In industrial technology class, Aiko made a plaque by gluing a piece of $\frac{3}{8}$-inch oak to a piece of $\frac{5}{8}$-inch poplar, as shown below. What was the total thickness of the plaque?

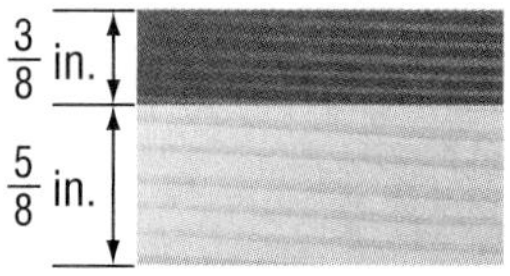

A $\frac{3}{8}$ inch **C** $\frac{1}{2}$ inch

B $\frac{5}{8}$ inch **D** 1 inch

Add or subtract. Write in simplest form.

16. $2\frac{1}{5} + 4\frac{2}{5}$ **17.** $6\frac{5}{8} - 4\frac{1}{2}$ **18.** $11\frac{1}{2} - 7\frac{3}{5}$

19. **STANDARDS PRACTICE** Emily has $4\frac{1}{4}$ cups of flour. She is making cookies using a recipe that calls for $2\frac{5}{8}$ cups of flour. How much flour will she have left?

F $6\frac{7}{8}$ cups **H** $2\frac{3}{8}$ cups

G $2\frac{1}{2}$ cups **J** $1\frac{5}{8}$ cups

20. **WRITING IN MATH** Refer to the grocery shopping list below. If you use $1\frac{1}{4}$ pounds of the ground beef you purchased for a meatloaf and freeze the rest, how much ground beef do you freeze? Explain your answer.

Shopping List
3 pounds ground beef
2 small onions
1 dozen eggs
bread crumbs

CHAPTER 5

California Standards Practice

Cumulative, Chapters 1–5

Standards Example

Ted is going to make three different picture frames. He will need the following amounts of wood for each frame. How much wood does Ted need for all three picture frames?

Frame 1	Frame 2	Frame 3
$3\frac{1}{4}$ feet	$1\frac{2}{3}$ feet	$2\frac{1}{2}$ feet

A $6\frac{3}{4}$ feet

B $7\frac{5}{12}$ feet

C $7\frac{7}{8}$ feet

D $8\frac{1}{2}$ feet

Read the Question

You need to find how much wood Ted needs.

Solve the Question

First use the LCD to rename the fractions. Then add. The total amount of wood needed is $7\frac{5}{12}$ feet.

The answer is B.

$$\begin{array}{rcr} 3\frac{1}{4} & \rightarrow & 3\frac{3}{12} \\ 1\frac{2}{3} & \rightarrow & 1\frac{8}{12} \\ +\ 2\frac{1}{2} & \rightarrow & +\ 2\frac{6}{12} \\ \hline & & 6\frac{17}{12} \text{ or } 7\frac{5}{12} \end{array}$$

Online Personal Tutor at ca.gr5math.com

Choose the best answer.

1 **Trevor plans to buy rope for two projects. One project requires $\frac{5}{8}$ yard of rope, and the other requires $\frac{1}{4}$ yard of rope. Find the total amount of rope Trevor will need for both projects.**

A 1 yard

B $\frac{7}{8}$ yard

C $\frac{5}{8}$ yard

D $\frac{3}{8}$ yard

2 **It takes Lee $\frac{1}{4}$ hour to walk to the playground and $\frac{1}{5}$ hour to walk from the playground to school. How much time does it take Lee to walk to the playground and then to school?**

F $\frac{1}{9}$ hour

G $\frac{9}{20}$ hour

H $\frac{1}{2}$ hour

J $\frac{3}{5}$ hour

3 **It took Javier $\frac{3}{4}$ of an hour to clean his room and $\frac{1}{6}$ of an hour to make a snack. How much time did it take Javier to clean his room and make a snack?**

A $\frac{1}{4}$ hour

B $\frac{2}{5}$ hour

C $\frac{2}{3}$ hour

D $\frac{11}{12}$ hour

---

4 $4\frac{2}{3} - 2\frac{1}{2} =$

F $2\frac{1}{6}$ **H** $2\frac{1}{2}$

G $2\frac{1}{3}$ **J** $2\frac{2}{3}$

---

5 **The Sonoma family and the Canini family each brought a pie to the picnic. Only a portion of each pie was eaten. The pictures below show how much of the pies were left. What portion of the pies was eaten altogether?**

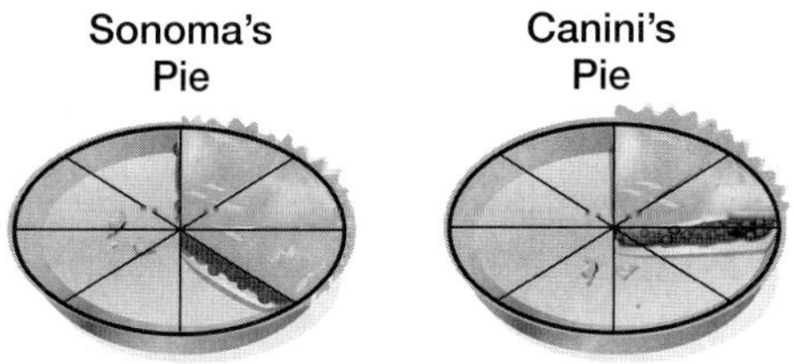

A $\frac{5}{8}$

B $1\frac{1}{4}$

C $1\frac{3}{8}$

D $1\frac{3}{4}$

6 **Which letter on the number line identifies the location of −9?**

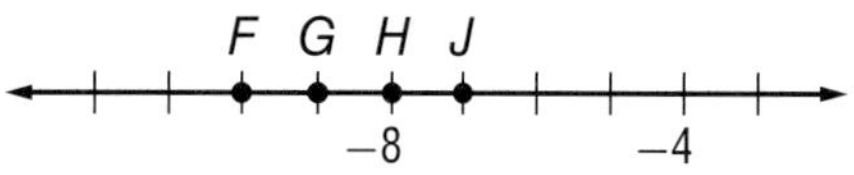

F *F* **G** *G* **H** *H* **J** *J*

---

7 **Drew read 120 pages of his book last night, which was $\frac{3}{5}$ of the book. What decimal represents the fraction of the book that he has read?**

A 0.12 **C** 0.60

B 0.35 **D** 0.80

---

8 **If $S = 8$, what is the value of $11 \times S - 7$?**

F 8 **H** 81

G 11 **J** 95

---

9 **Find the prime factorization of 72.**

A $2^3 \times 10$ **C** 2×3^4

B $2^2 \times 5^2$ **D** $2^3 \times 3^2$

---

10 **At Medina Middle School there are 53 homerooms. If 922 students attend Medina Middle School, about how many students are in each homeroom?**

F 17 **H** 19

G 18 **J** 20

CHAPTER 6 Multiplying and Dividing Decimals and Fractions

BIG Idea **How do you multiply decimals by whole numbers?**

When multiplying decimals by whole numbers, multiply as with whole numbers, and then use estimation to place the decimal point in the product.

Example Blue whales eat 3.6 metric tons of krill per day. To find the amount of krill blue whales can eat in a week, you can **multiply 3.6 by 7**.

Estimate: $3.6 \times 7 \approx 4 \times 7$ or 28

$3.6 \times 7 = 25.2$ Since the estimate is 28, place the decimal point after the 5.

So, blue whales can eat 25.2 metric tons of krill per week.

What will I learn in this chapter?

- Estimate and find the product of decimals and whole numbers.
- Multiply and divide decimals.
- Estimate products of fractions using compatible numbers and rounding.
- Multiply and divide fractions and mixed numbers.
- Solve problems by determining reasonable answers.

Key Vocabulary

scientific notation

compatible numbers

reciprocal

Math Online Student Study Tools at ca.gr5math.com

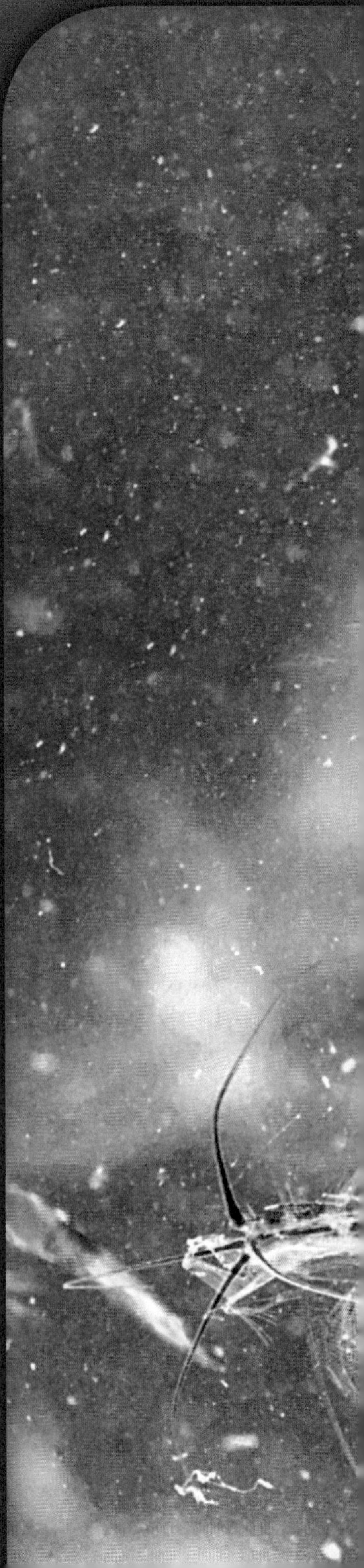

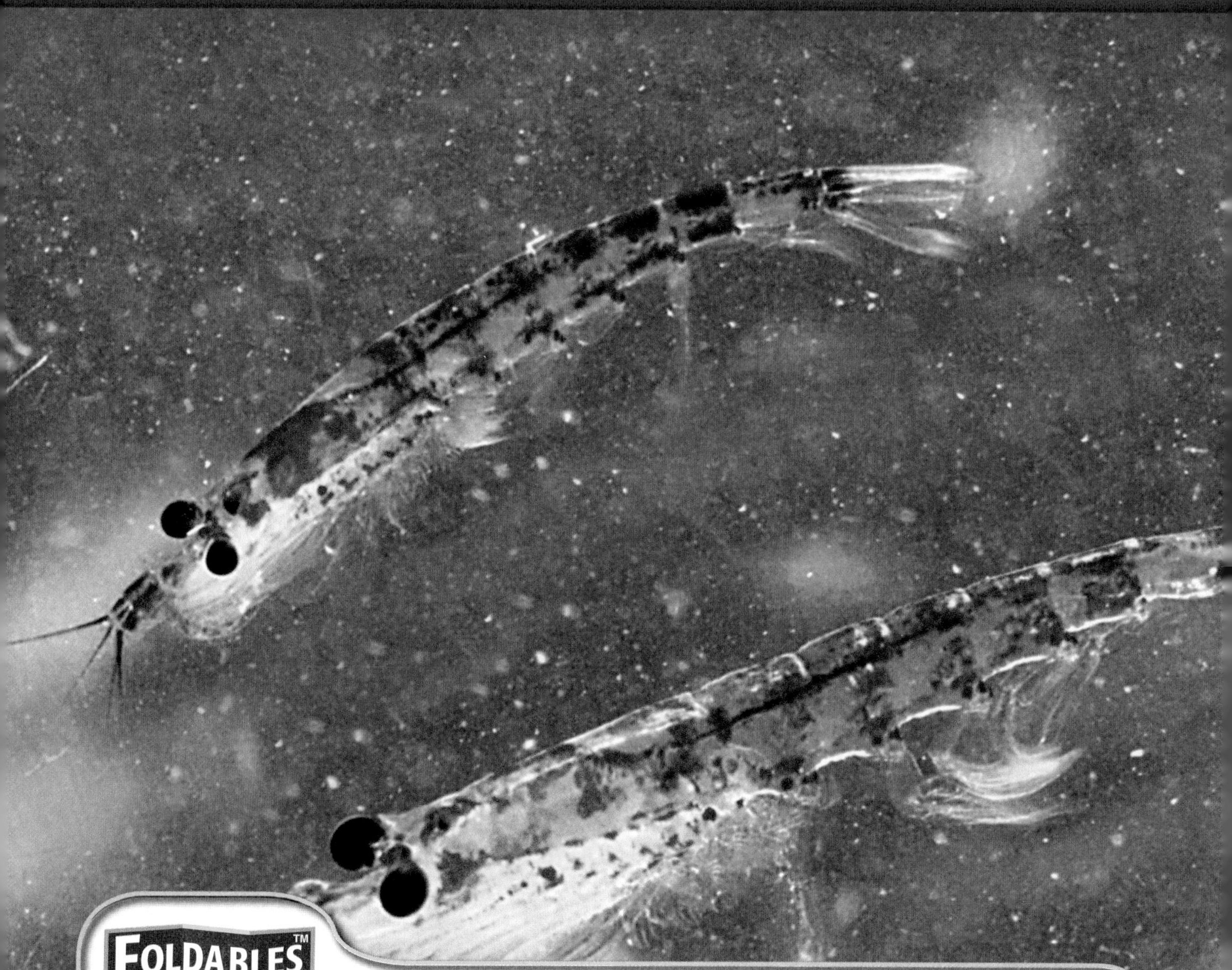

FOLDABLES™ Study Organizer

Make this Foldable to help you organize information about multiplying and dividing decimals and fractions. Begin with twelve sheets of notebook paper.

1. **Staple** the twelve sheets together to form a booklet.

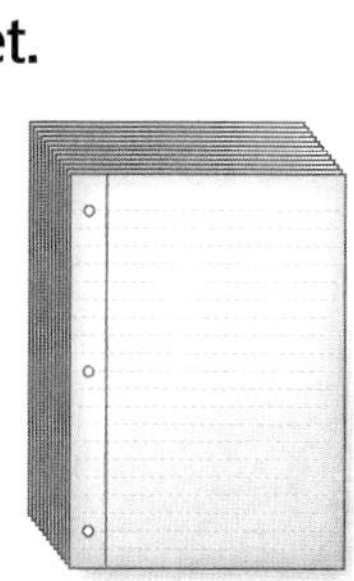

2. **Cut** a tab on the second page the width of the white space. On the third page, make the tab 2 lines longer, and so on.

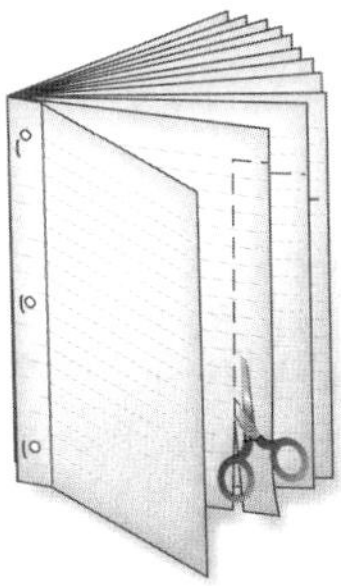

3. **Write** the chapter title on the cover and label each tab with the lesson number.

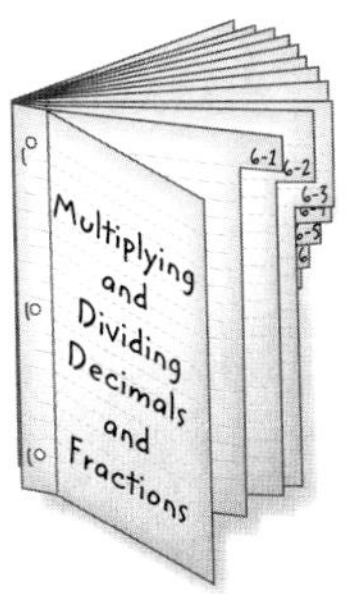

ARE YOU READY for Chapter 6?

You have two ways to check prerequisite skills for this chapter.

Option 2

Math Online Take the Chapter Readiness Quiz at ca.gr5math.com.

Option 1

Complete the Quick Check below.

QUICK Check

Multiply. **(Prior Grade)**

1. 17×28

2. 31×6

3. 109×14

4. 212×62

5. 228×19

6. 547×31

7. The average adult gets 8 hours of sleep each night. How many total hours of sleep does the average adult get in one year (365 days)? **(Prior Grade)**

Divide. **(Prior Grade)**

8. $186 \div 3$

9. $171 \div 9$

10. $238 \div 14$

11. $832 \div 26$

12. $4{,}356 \div 36$

13. $1{,}728 \div 6$

14. Four friends drove from Chicago to Florida and spent $188 on gasoline. If they split the cost evenly, how much does each owe? **(Prior Grade)**

Write each number as an improper fraction. **(Lesson 4-4)**

15. $2\frac{3}{4}$

16. $1\frac{6}{7}$

17. $5\frac{7}{9}$

18. $3\frac{1}{8}$

19. $4\frac{2}{5}$

20. $6\frac{5}{6}$

21. Trent practiced the piano for $3\frac{5}{6}$ hours last week. Write this time as an improper fraction. **(Lesson 4-4)**

Explore

Math Lab for 6-1
Multiplying Decimals by Whole Numbers

MAIN IDEA

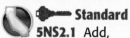

I will use models to multiply a decimal by a whole number.

Standard 5NS2.1 Add, subtract, **multiply,** and divide **with decimals;** add with negative integers; subtract positive integers from negative integers; and verify the reasonableness of results.
Standard 5MR2.3 Use a variety of methods, such as words, numbers, symbols, charts, graphs, tables, diagrams, and **models, to explain mathematical reasoning.**

You can use decimal models to multiply a decimal by a whole number. Recall that a 10-by-10 grid represents the number one.

ACTIVITY

Model 0.5 × 3 using decimal models.

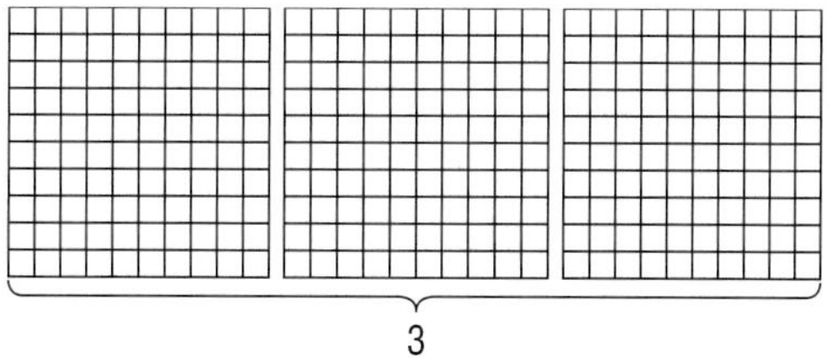

Draw three 10-by-10 decimal models to show the factor 3.

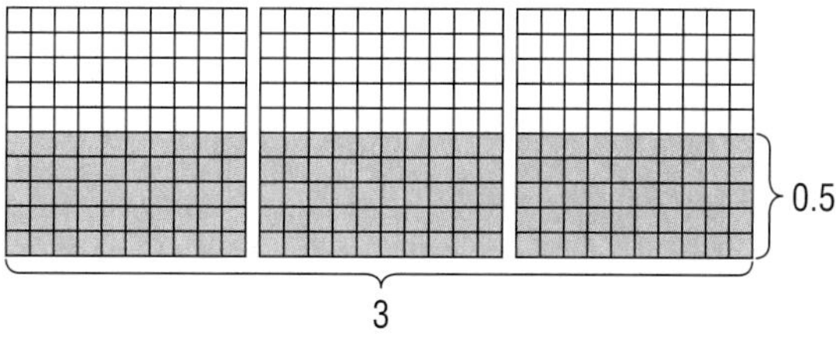

Shade five rows of each decimal model to represent 0.5.

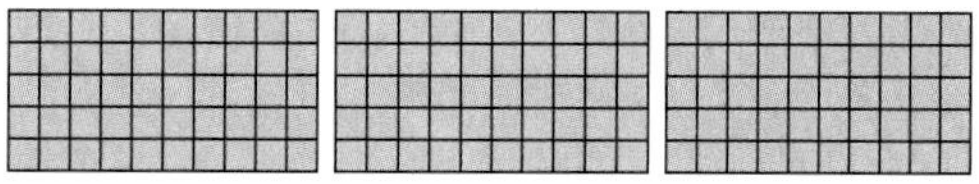

Cut off the shaded rows and rearrange them to form as many 10-by-10 grids as possible.

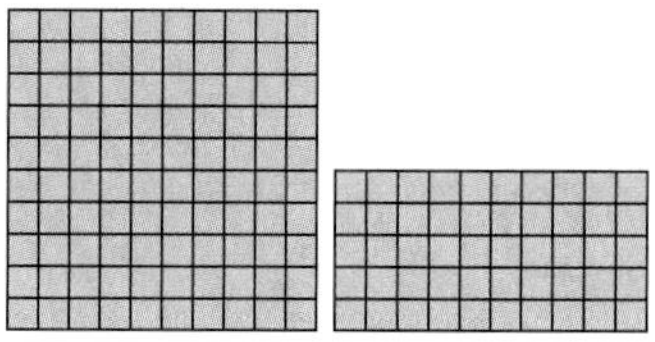

The product is *one and five tenths.*

So, 0.5 × 3 = 1.5.

CHECK What You Know

Use decimal models to show each product.

a. 3 × 0.5 **b.** 2 × 0.7 **c.** 0.8 × 4

Analyze the Results

1. Is the product of a whole number and a decimal greater than the whole number or less than the whole number? Explain.

2. Test your conjecture on 7 × 0.3. Check your answer by making a model.

6-1 Multiplying Decimals by Whole Numbers

MAIN IDEA

I will estimate and find the product of decimals and whole numbers.

Standard 5NS2.1 Add, subtract, **multiply,** and divide **with decimals;** add with negative integers; subtract positive integers from negative integers; and verify the reasonableness of results.

New Vocabulary

scientific notation

GET READY to Learn

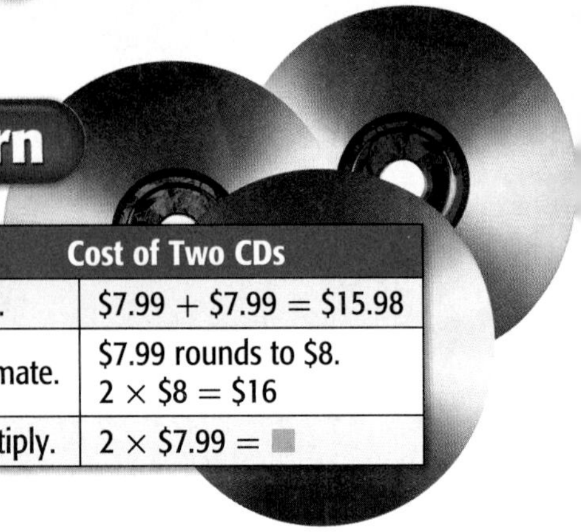

CDs are on sale for $7.99. Tia wants to buy two. The table shows different ways to find the total cost.

Cost of Two CDs	
Add.	$7.99 + $7.99 = $15.98
Estimate.	$7.99 rounds to $8. 2 × $8 = $16
Multiply.	2 × $7.99 = ■

When multiplying a decimal by a whole number, multiply as with whole numbers. Then use estimation to place the decimal point in the product. You can also count the number of decimal places.

EXAMPLES Multiply Decimals

1 Find 14.2 × 6.

One Way: Use estimation.

Round 14.2 to 14.

14.2 × 6 ⟶ 14 × 6 or 84

```
 21
 14.2
×  6
 85.2
```

Since the estimate is 84, place the decimal point after the 5.

Another Way: Count decimal places.

```
 21
 14.2  ← one decimal place
×  6
 85.2
```

Count one decimal place from the right.

2 Find 9 × 0.83.

One Way: Use estimation.

Round 0.83 to 1.

9 × 0.83 ⟶ 9 × 1 or 9

```
   2
 0.83
×   9
 7.47
```

Since the estimate is 9, place the decimal point after the 7.

Another Way: Count decimal places.

```
   2
 0.83  ← two decimal places
×   9
 7.47
```

Count two decimal places from the right.

If there are not enough decimal places in the product, you need to annex zeros to the left.

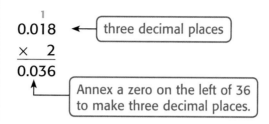

EXAMPLES Annex Zeros in the Product

Vocabulary Link

Annex

Everyday Use to add something

Math Use to annex a zero means to add a zero at the beginning or end of a decimal

3 **Find 2×0.018.**

$$\begin{array}{r} \overset{1}{0.018} \\ \times \quad 2 \\ \hline 0.036 \end{array}$$

0.018 ← three decimal places

0.036 ← Annex a zero on the left of 36 to make three decimal places.

4 **Algebra** **Evaluate $4c$ if $c = 0.0027$.**

$4c = 4 \times 0.0027$ Replace c with 0.0027.

$$\begin{array}{r} 0.00\overset{2}{2}7 \\ \times \quad 4 \\ \hline 0.0108 \end{array}$$

0.0027 ← four decimal places

0.0108 Annex a zero to make four decimal places.

Online **Personal Tutor at** ca.gr5math.com

When the number 450 is expressed as the product of 4.5 and 10^2, the number is written in **scientific notation**. You can use order of operations or mental math to write these numbers in standard form.

EXAMPLE Scientific Notation

5 **Dinosaurs roamed Earth until about 6.5×10^7 years ago. Write 6.5×10^7 in standard form.**

One Way: Use order of operations.	Another Way: Use mental math.
Evaluate 10^7 first. Then multiply.	Move the decimal point to the right the same number of places as the exponent of 10, or 7 places.
$6.5 \times 10^7 = 6.5 \times 10{,}000{,}000$ $= 65{,}000{,}000$	$6.5 \times 10^7 = 6.5000000$ $= 65{,}000{,}000$

CHECK What You Know

Multiply. See Examples 1–3 (pp. 284–285)

1. 2.7×6 **2.** 0.52×3 **3.** 4×0.012 **4.** 0.065×18

5. Algebra Evaluate $14t$ if $t = 2.9$. See Example 4 (p. 285)

6. Measurement The distance from Earth to the Moon is approximately 3.84×10^5 kilometers. Write this number in standard form. See Example 5 (p. 285)

7. Talk About It What are two methods of placing the decimal point in the product of a decimal and a whole number?

Practice and Problem Solving

EXTRA PRACTICE See page 669.

Multiply. See Examples 1–3 (pp. 284–285)

8. 1.2×7 **9.** 1.7×5 **10.** 0.7×9 **11.** 0.9×4

12. 2×1.3 **13.** 2.4×8 **14.** 0.8×9 **15.** 3×0.5

16. 3×0.02 **17.** 7×0.012 **18.** 0.0036×19 **19.** 0.0198×75

20. Algebra Evaluate $3.05n$ if $n = 27$. See Example 4 (p. 285)

21. Algebra Evaluate $80.44w$ if $w = 2$. See Example 4 (p. 285)

Write each number in standard form. See Example 5 (p. 285)

22. 5×10^4 **23.** 4×10^6 **24.** 1.5×10^3 **25.** 9.3×10^5

26. 2.5×10^3 **27.** 1.26×10^2 **28.** 3.45×10^3 **29.** 2.17×10^6

30. Measurement Find the area of a poster that is 4 feet by 3.2 feet.

31. Sharon buys 14 folders for \$0.75 each. How much do they cost?

Real-World PROBLEM SOLVING

Health The table shows the average number of blood vessels in the human body and the approximate number of skin cells lost per minute from the surface of the skin.

The Human Body	
Blood Vessels	2.5×10^{11}
Skin Cells Lost per Minute	3.5×10^4

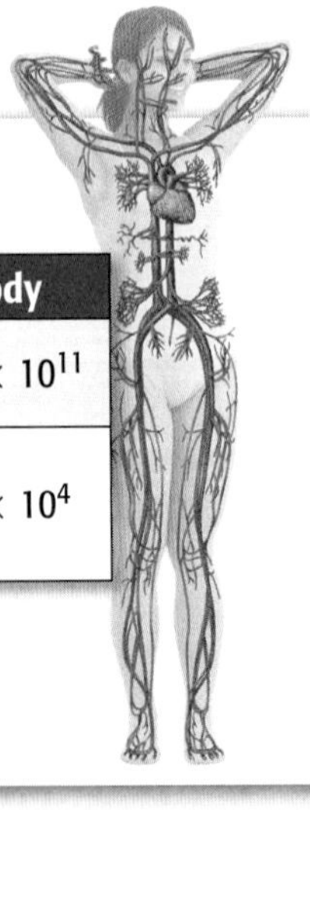

32. Write the average number of blood vessels in standard form.

33. In standard form, how many skin cells are lost per minute?

H.O.T. Problems

34. OPEN ENDED Create a problem about a real-world situation involving multiplication by a decimal factor. Then solve the problem.

35. CHALLENGE Discuss two different ways to find the value of the expression $5.4 \times 1.17 \times 10^2$ that do not require you to first multiply 5.4×1.17.

36. WRITING IN MATH Summarize how to convert a number in scientific notation to standard form.

Standards Practice

37 A recipe for a batch of cookies calls for one 5.75-ounce package of coconut. How many ounces of coconut are needed for 5 batches of cookies?

A 20.50 oz

B 25.25 oz

C 28.75 oz

D 29.75 oz

38 Admission to an amusement park is $30.59 per child. At this rate, what is the cost of admission for 3 children?

F $30.59

G $62.20

H $91.77

J $93.97

Spiral Review

Subtract. Write in simplest form. **(Lesson 5-8)**

39. $10\frac{3}{8} - 7\frac{1}{8}$

40. $5\frac{1}{6} - 3\frac{8}{9}$

41. $8\frac{2}{3} - 3\frac{6}{7}$

42. $6\frac{3}{5} - 4\frac{2}{3}$

43. Measurement Viho needs $2\frac{1}{4}$ cups of flour for cookies, $1\frac{2}{3}$ cups for almond bars, and $3\frac{1}{2}$ cups for cinnamon rolls. How much flour does he need in all? **(Lesson 5-7)**

44. Janie is arranging a bookshelf, a chair, and a dresser along one wall of her bedroom. Use the *make a list* strategy to find the number of ways Janie can arrange the furniture. **(Lesson 4-2)**

45. In a recent year, a popular teen magazine had a paid circulation of 1,571,272. What is this value rounded to the nearest thousand? **(Lesson 3-3)**

Explore

Math Lab for 6-2
Multiplying Decimals

In the lab on page 283, you used decimal models to multiply a decimal by a whole number. You can use similar models to multiply a decimal by a decimal.

MAIN IDEA

I will use decimal models to multiply decimals.

Standard 5NS2.1 Add, subtract, **multiply,** and divide **with decimals;** add with negative integers; subtract positive integers from negative integers; and verify the reasonableness of results.
Standard 5MR2.3 Use a variety of methods, such as words, numbers, symbols, charts, graphs, tables, diagrams, and **models, to explain mathematical reasoning.**

ACTIVITY

1 Model 0.8 × 0.4 using decimal models.

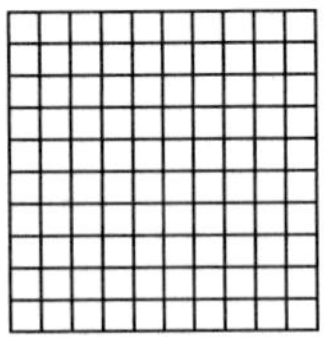

Draw a 10-by-10 decimal model. Recall that each small square represents 0.01.

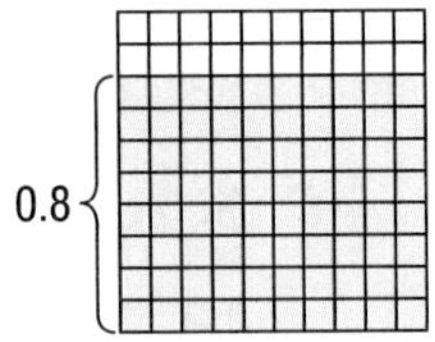

Shade eight rows of the model yellow to represent the first factor, 0.8.

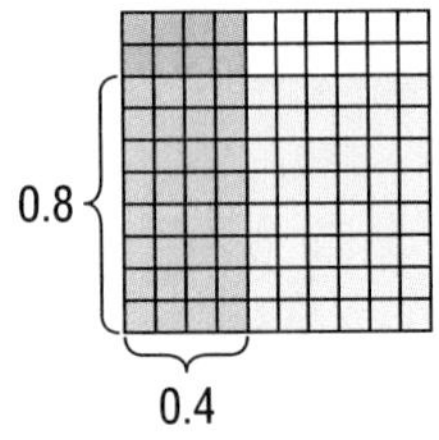

Shade four columns of the model blue to represent the second factor, 0.4. The green region has been shaded twice. It represents the product.

There are *thirty-two hundredths* in the region that is shaded green. So, 0.8 × 0.4 = 0.32.

CHECK What You Know

Use decimal models to show each product.

a. 0.3 × 0.3 **b.** 0.4 × 0.9 **c.** 0.9 × 0.5

Analyze the Results

1. Tell how many decimal places are in each factor and in each product of Exercises a–c above.
2. Use the pattern you discovered in Exercise 1 to find 0.6 × 0.2. Check your conjecture with a model.
3. Find two decimals with a product of 0.24.

ACTIVITY

2 Model 0.7 × 2.5 using decimal models.

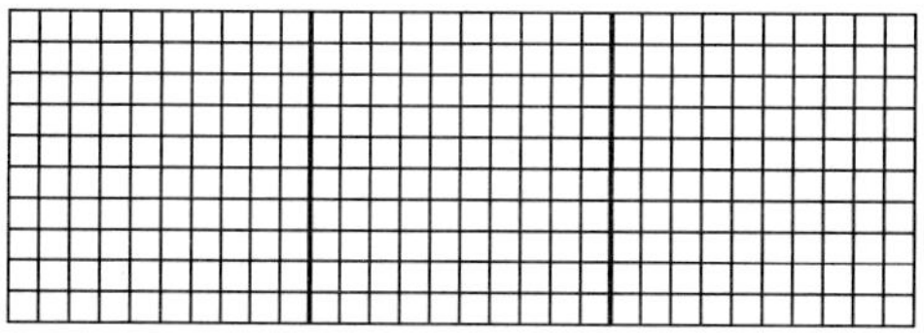

Draw three 10-by-10 decimal models.

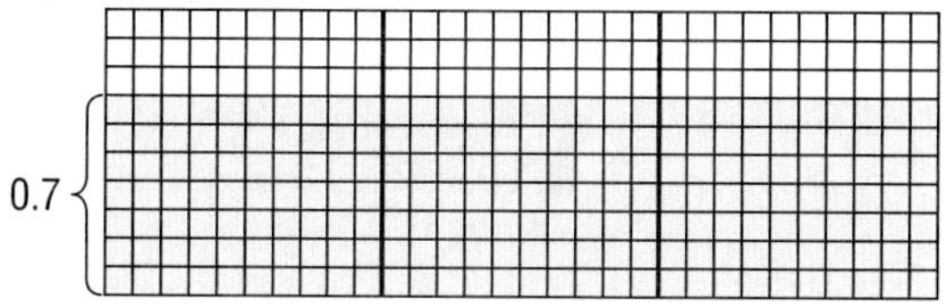

Shade 7 rows yellow to represent 0.7.

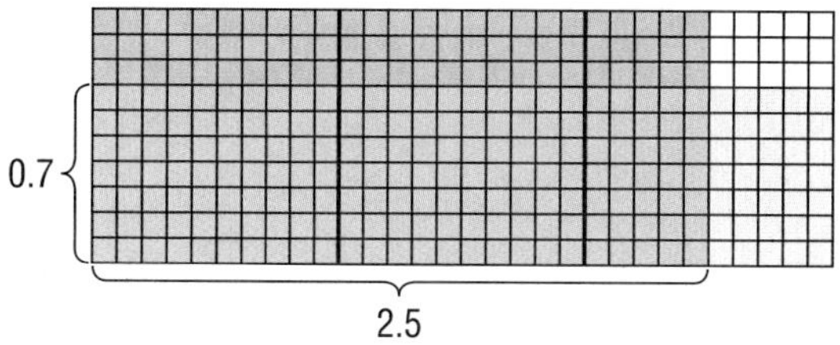

Shade 2 large squares and 5 columns of the next large square blue to represent 2.5.

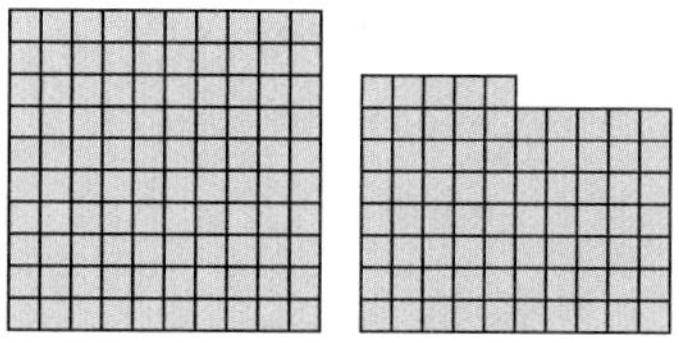

Cut off the squares that are shaded green and rearrange them to form 10-by-10 grids.

There are *one and seventy-five hundredths* in the region that is shaded green. So, 0.7 × 2.5 = 1.75.

Remember

Arrange the squares to form as many whole decimal models as possible. Then arrange the remaining squares into as many rows of 10 as possible to make counting them easier.

CHECK What You Know

Use decimal models to show each product.

d. 1.5 × 0.7 **e.** 0.8 × 2.4 **f.** 1.3 × 0.3

Analyze the Results

4. How does the number of decimal places in the product relate to the number of decimal places in the factors?

5. Use the table below to analyze each product.

First Factor		Second Factor		Product
0.9	×	0.6	=	0.54
1.0	×	0.6	=	0.60
1.5	×	0.6	=	0.90

a. Explain why the first product is less than 0.6.

b. Explain why the second product is equal to 0.6.

c. Explain why the third product is greater than 0.6.

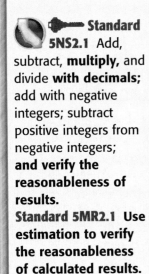

6-2 Multiplying Decimals

MAIN IDEA

I will multiply decimals by decimals.

Standard 5NS2.1 Add, subtract, **multiply,** and divide **with decimals;** add with negative integers; subtract positive integers from negative integers; **and verify the reasonableness of results.**
Standard 5MR2.1 Use estimation to verify the reasonableness of calculated results.

GET READY to Learn

A nut store is having a sale. The sale prices are shown in the table. Suppose you fill a bag with 1.3 pounds of cashews. The product of 5×1.3 can be used to estimate the total cost. How could you find the actual cost of 1.3 pounds of cashews?

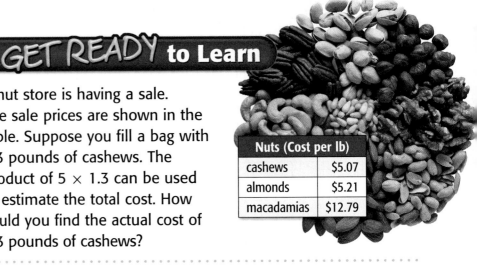

Nuts (Cost per lb)	
cashews	$5.07
almonds	$5.21
macadamias	$12.79

When multiplying a decimal by a decimal, multiply as with whole numbers. To place the decimal point, find the sum of the number of decimal places in each factor. The product has the same number of decimal places.

EXAMPLES Multiply Decimals

1 Find 4.2×6.7.

Estimate $4.2 \times 6.7 \rightarrow 4 \times 7$ or 28

$$\begin{array}{rl} 4.2 & \leftarrow \text{one decimal place} \\ \times\ 6.7 & \leftarrow \text{one decimal place} \\ \hline 294 & \\ +\ 252 & \\ \hline 28.14 & \leftarrow \text{two decimal places} \end{array}$$

The product is 28.14.

Check for Reasonableness Compare 28.14 to the estimate. $28.14 \approx 28$ ✓

2 Find 1.6×0.09.

Estimate $1.6 \times 0.09 \rightarrow 2 \times 0$ or 0

$$\begin{array}{rl} 1.6 & \leftarrow \text{one decimal place} \\ \times\ 0.09 & \leftarrow \text{two decimal places} \\ \hline 0.144 & \leftarrow \text{three decimal places} \end{array}$$

The product is 0.144.

Check for Reasonableness Compare 0.144 to the estimate. $0.144 \approx 0$ ✓

EXAMPLE Evaluate an Expression

3 **Algebra Evaluate $1.4n$ if $n = 0.067$.**

$1.4n = 1.4 \times \mathbf{0.067}$ Replace n with 0.067.

$$\begin{array}{r l} 0.067 & \leftarrow \text{three decimal places} \\ \times\ 1.4 & \leftarrow \text{one decimal place} \\ \hline 268 & \\ +\ 67 & \\ \hline 0.0938 & \leftarrow \text{Annex a zero to make four decimal places.} \end{array}$$

Real-World EXAMPLE

4 **Tariq is traveling to Mexico. One U.S. dollar is worth 11.3 pesos. How many pesos would he receive for $75.50?**

Estimate $11.3 \times 75.50 \rightarrow 11 \times 80$ or 880

$$\begin{array}{r l} 75.50 & \leftarrow \text{two decimal places} \\ \times\ 11.3 & \leftarrow \text{one decimal place} \\ \hline 22650 & \\ 7550 & \\ +\ 7550 & \\ \hline 853.150 & \end{array}$$

← The product has three decimal places. You can drop the zero at the end because 853.150 = 853.15.

Tariq would receive 853.15 pesos.

Check for Reasonableness Compare 853.15 to the estimate. $853.15 \approx 880$ ✓

Online Personal Tutor at ca.gr5math.com

CHECK What You Know

Multiply. See Examples 1, 2 (p. 290)

1. 0.6×0.5
2. 1.4×2.56
3. 27.43×1.089
4. 0.3×2.4
5. 0.52×2.1
6. 0.45×0.053

Algebra Evaluate each expression if $n = 1.35$. See Example 3 (p. 291)

7. $2.7n$
8. $5.343 + 0.5n$
9. $0.02n + 0.016$

10. Juanita is buying a video game that costs $32.99. The sales tax is found by multiplying the cost of the video game by 0.06. How much is sales tax for the video game? See Example 4 (p. 291)

11. Talk About It Without calculating, determine how many decimal places are in the product of 22.251 and 0.014. Explain.

Practice and Problem Solving

EXTRA PRACTICE
See page 669.

Multiply. See Examples 1, 2 (p. 290)

12. 0.7×0.4 **13.** 1.5×2.7 **14.** 0.4×3.7

15. 3.1×0.8 **16.** 0.98×7.3 **17.** 2.4×3.48

18. 6.2×0.03 **19.** 5.04×3.2 **20.** 14.7×11.36

21. 27.4×33.68 **22.** 0.28×0.08 **23.** 0.45×0.05

Algebra Evaluate each expression if $x = 8.6$, $y = 0.54$, and $z = 1.18$. See Example 3 (p. 291)

24. $2.7x$ **25.** $6.34y$ **26.** $3.45x + 7.015$

27. $1.8y + 0.6z$ **28.** $9.1x - 4.7y$ **29.** $0.096 + 2.28y$

30. A steamboat travels 36.5 miles each day. How far will it travel in 6.5 days?

31. Katelyn earns $5.80 an hour. If she works 16.75 hours in a week, how much will she earn for the week?

Evaluate.

32. 25.04×3.005 **33.** 1.03×1.005

Algebra Evaluate each expression if $a = 1.3$, $b = 0.042$, and $c = 2.01$.

34. $ab + c$ **35.** $a \times 6.023 - c$

36. $3.25c + b$ **37.** abc

38. **Measurement** Find the area of the figure at the right. Justify your answer.

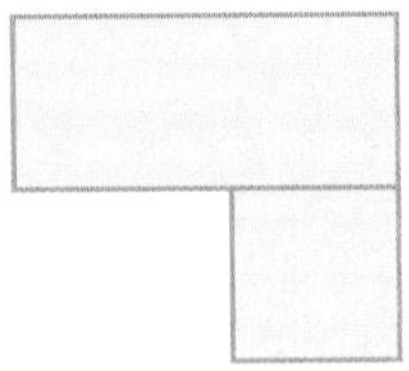

39. Pears cost $0.98 per pound, and apples cost $1.05 per pound. Mr. Bonilla bought 3.75 pounds of pears and 2.1 pounds of apples. How much did he pay for the pears and apples?

Tell whether each sentence is *sometimes, always,* or *never* true. Explain your reasoning.

40. The product of two decimals that are each less than one is also less than one.

41. The product of a decimal greater than one and a decimal less than one is greater than one.

H.O.T. Problems

CHALLENGE Evaluate each expression.

42. $0.3 \times (3 - 0.5)$ **43.** $0.16 \times (7 - 2.8)$ **44.** $1.06 \times (2 + 0.58)$

45. OPEN ENDED Write a multiplication problem in which the product is between 0.05 and 0.75.

46. NUMBER SENSE Place the decimal point in the answer to make it correct. Explain your reasoning. $3.9853 \times 8.032856 = 320133410168$

47. WRITING IN MATH Describe two methods for determining where to place the decimal point in the product of two decimals.

Standards Practice

48 What is the area of the rectangle?

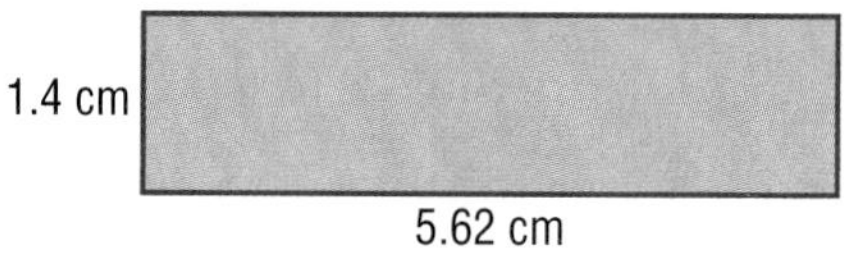

A $14.04\ cm^2$ **C** $8.992\ cm^2$

B $10.248\ cm^2$ **D** $7.868\ cm^2$

49 $14.6 \times 4.8 =$

F 70.08 **H** 71.08

G 70.28 **J** 71.28

50 72.01×0.5

A 35.005 **C** 36.005

B 35.105 **D** 36.105

Spiral Review

Multiply. **(Lesson 6-1)**

51. 45×0.27 **52.** 3.2×109 **53.** 27×0.45 **54.** 2.94×16

Subtract. Write in simplest form. **(Lesson 5-8)**

55. $6\frac{5}{8} - 3\frac{3}{4}$ **56.** $5 - 2\frac{1}{3}$ **57.** $2\frac{1}{2} - 1\frac{4}{5}$

58. List the next five common multiples after the LCM of 6 and 9. **(Lesson 4-5)**

59. Josefina took her grandmother to lunch. Josefina's lunch was $6.70, her grandmother's lunch was $7.25, and they split a dessert that cost $3.50. Find the total amount of the lunch before tax. **(Lesson 3-7)**

Use >, <, or = to compare each pair of decimals. **(Lesson 3-2)**

60. 0.5 ● 5.0 **61.** 9.90 ● 0.990 **62.** 0.007 ● 0.007

63. 0.516 ● 0.506 **64.** 0.0771 ● 0.771 **65.** 8.834 ● 8.832

6-3 Problem-Solving Strategy

MAIN IDEA I will solve problems by determining reasonable answers.

Standard 5MR3.1 Evaluate the reasonableness of the solution in the context of the original situation.
Standard 5NS2.1 Add, subtract, **multiply,** and divide **with decimals**; add with negative integers; subtract positive integers from negative integers; and verify the reasonableness of results.

For their science project, Stephanie and Angel need to know about how much more a blue whale weighs in pounds than a humpback whale.

They have learned that there are 2,000 pounds in one ton. While doing research, they found a table that shows the weights of whales in tons.

Whale	Weight (tons)
Blue	151.0
Bowhead	95.0
Fin	69.9
Gray	38.5
Humpback	38.1

Source: *Top 10 of Everything*

Understand

What facts do you know?

- There are 2,000 pounds in one ton.
- A blue whale weighs 151.0 tons.
- A humpback whale weighs 38.1 tons.

What do you need to find?

- A reasonable estimate of the difference in the weight of a blue whale and a humpback whale.

Plan

Estimate to find the weight of each whale in pounds and then subtract to find a reasonable estimate of the difference.

Solve

Blue whale:

$$2{,}000 \times 151 \rightarrow 2{,}000 \times 150 = 300{,}000$$

Humpback whale:

$$2{,}000 \times 38.1 \rightarrow 2{,}000 \times 40 = 80{,}000$$

$300{,}000 - 80{,}000 = 220{,}000$

A reasonable estimate for the difference in the weight of a blue whale and a humpback whale is 220,000 pounds.

Check

Look back at the problem. A blue whale weighs about $150 - 40$ or 110 more tons than a humpback whale. This is equal to $110 \times 2{,}000$ or 220,000 pounds. So the answer is reasonable. ✓

ANALYZE the Strategy

Refer to the problem on the previous page.

1. Is 200,000 pounds a reasonable answer for the weight of a fin whale? Use the table on page 294. Explain.

2. Which two whales together weigh about 500,000 pounds? Explain how you know.

3. Explain when you would use the strategy of determining reasonable answers to solve a problem.

4. Explain why estimation is often the best way to determine whether an answer is reasonable.

PRACTICE the Strategy

EXTRA PRACTICE See page 669.

Solve. Determine which answer is reasonable.

5. In a recent year, a total of 820,590 people attended 25 of the Atlanta Braves home games. Which is a more reasonable estimate for the number of people that attended each game: 30,000 or 40,000?

6. Use the graph below to determine whether 1,000, 1,300, or 1,500 is a reasonable prediction of the population of Dorsey Intermediate School in 2008.

Dorsey Intermediate Enrollment

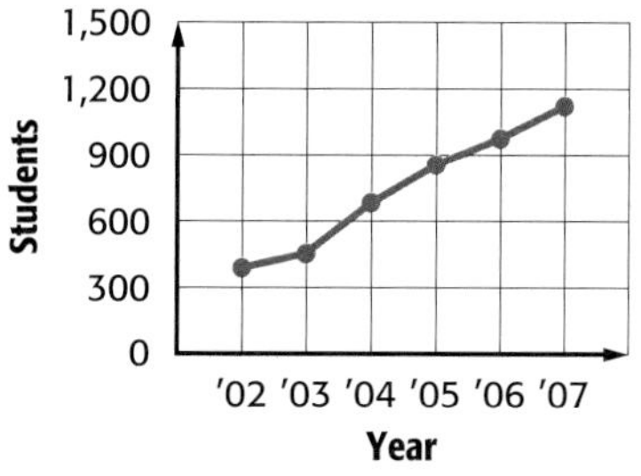

7. Brandy wants to buy 2 science fiction books for \$3.95 each, 3 magazines for \$2.95 each, and 1 bookmark for \$0.39 at the book fair. Does she need to bring \$20 or will \$15 be enough? Explain your reasoning.

8. A high school gym will hold 2,800 guests and the 721 seniors who are graduating. Is it reasonable to offer each graduate three, four, or five tickets for family and friends? Explain your reasoning.

9. The table shows the number of CD singles that were shipped for sale from 2001 to 2005. Is 25 million, 30 million, or 35 million a more reasonable estimate for the total number of CD singles shipped from 2001 to 2005? Explain.

Year	CD Singles Shipped (millions)
2001	17.3
2002	4.5
2003	8.3
2004	3.1
2005	2.8

Source: www.riaa.com

10. WRITING IN ▸MATH In 1977, there were 12,168,450 basic cable television subscribers. By 2005, there were 73,219,360 subscribers. Explain why 61,000,000 is a reasonable estimate for how many more subscribers there were in 2005 than in 1977.

6-4 Dividing Decimals by Whole Numbers

MAIN IDEA

I will divide decimals by whole numbers.

Standard 5NS2.1 Add, subtract, multiply, and **divide with decimals;** add with negative integers; subtract positive integers from negative integers; **and verify the reasonableness of results.**

Standard 5NS2.2 Demonstrate proficiency with division, including division with positive decimals and long division with multidigit divisors.

GET READY to Learn

Hands-On Mini Lab

To find 2.4 ÷ 2 using base-ten blocks, model 2.4 as 2 wholes and 4 tenths. Then separate into two equal groups.

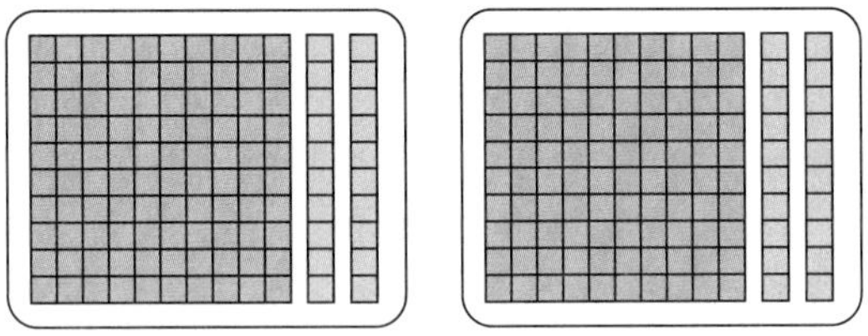

There is one whole and two tenths in each group.

So, 2.4 ÷ 2 = 1.2.

Use base-ten blocks to show each quotient.

1. 3.4 ÷ 2 **2.** 4.2 ÷ 3 **3.** 5.6 ÷ 4

Find each whole number quotient.

4. 34 ÷ 2 **5.** 42 ÷ 3 **6.** 56 ÷ 4

7. Compare and contrast the quotients in Exercises 1–3 with the quotients in Exercises 4–6.

8. Write a rule for dividing a decimal by a whole number.

Review Vocabulary

quotient the solution in division; *Example:* the quotient of 16 and 8 is 2

Dividing a decimal by a whole number is similar to dividing whole numbers.

EXAMPLE Divide a Decimal by a 1-Digit Number

1 Find 6.8 ÷ 2. **Estimate** 6 ÷ 2 = 3

```
   3.4   ← Place the decimal point directly above
2)6.8      the decimal point in the dividend.
 − 6
   08
 − 8
    0
```

6.8 ÷ 2 = 3.4 Compared to the estimate, the quotient is reasonable.

Math Online Extra Examples at ca.gr5math.com

EXAMPLE Divide a Decimal by a 2-Digit Number

Remember

To check that the answer is correct, multiply the quotient by the divisor. In Example 2, $0.55 \times 14 = 7.7$.

2 Find $7.7 \div 14$.

Estimate $10 \div 10 = 1$

```
     0.55  ← Place the decimal point.
 14)7.70
   -7 0
     70   ← Annex a zero and continue dividing.
    -70
      0
```

$7.7 \div 14 = 0.55$ Compared to the estimate, the quotient is reasonable.

If the answer does not come out evenly, round the quotient to a specified place-value position.

Real-World EXAMPLE

3 Seth purchased 3 video games for \$51.79. If each game costs the same amount, find the price of each game in dollars.

Estimate $\$51 \div 3 = \$17$

To find the price of one game, divide the total cost by the number of games. Round to the nearest cent, or hundredths place.

```
   17.263   Place the decimal point.
 3)51.790
  -3
   21
  -21
   07
   -06
     19
    -18
      10   Divide until you have a digit
      -9   in the thousandths place.
       1
```

To the nearest cent, the cost in dollars is 17.26.

$51.79 \div 3 \approx 17.26$ Compared to the estimate, the quotient is reasonable.

Online Personal Tutor at ca.gr5math.com

CHECK What You Know

Divide. Round to the nearest tenth if necessary. **See Examples 1–3 (pp. 296–297)**

1. 3.6 ÷ 4

2. 9.6 ÷ 2

3. 8.53 ÷ 6

4. 1,087.9 ÷ 46

5. 12.32 ÷ 22

6. 69.904 ÷ 34

7. Four girls on a track team ran the 4-by-100 meter relay in a total of 46.9 seconds. What was the average time for each runner to the nearest tenth?

8. Talk About It Is the quotient 8.3 ÷ 10 greater than one or less than one? Explain your reasoning.

Practice and Problem Solving

EXTRA PRACTICE See page 670.

Divide. Round to the nearest tenth if necessary.

See Examples 1–3 (pp. 296–297)

9. 39.39 ÷ 3

10. 36.8 ÷ 2

11. 118.5 ÷ 5

12. 124.2 ÷ 9

13. 7.24 ÷ 7

14. 6.27 ÷ 4

15. 11.4 ÷ 19

16. 10.22 ÷ 14

17. 55.2 ÷ 46

18. 59.84 ÷ 32

19. 336.75 ÷ 31

20. 751.2 ÷ 25

21. Jackson's father has budgeted $64.50 for his three children's monthly allowance. Assuming they each earn the same amount, how much allowance will Jackson receive?

22. Find the average time of a track on a CD from the times in the table.

Time of Track (minutes)				
4.73	3.97	2.93	2.83	3.44

23. Each story in an office building is about 4 meters tall. The Eiffel Tower in Paris, France, is 300.51 meters tall. To the nearest whole number, about how many stories tall is the Eiffel Tower?

24. A class set of 30 calculators would have cost $4,498.50 in the early 1970s. However, in 2005, 30 calculators could be purchased for $284.70. How much less was the average price of one calculator in 2005 than in 1970?

Statistics Find the mean for each set of data.

25. 22.6, 24.8, 25.4, 26.9

26. 1.43, 1.78, 2.45, 2.78, 3.25

H.O.T. Problems

27. OPEN ENDED Create a set of data for which the mean is 5.5.

28. CHALLENGE **Create a division problem that meets all of the following conditions.**
- The divisor is a whole number, and the dividend is a decimal.
- The quotient is 1.265 when rounded to the nearest thousandth.
- The quotient is 1.26 when rounded to the nearest hundredth.

29. FIND THE ERROR Felisa and Tom are finding 11.2 ÷ 14. Who is correct? Explain your reasoning.

Felisa

$$\begin{array}{r} 8. \\ 14\overline{)11.2} \\ -\ 112 \\ \hline 0 \end{array}$$

Tom

$$\begin{array}{r} 0.8 \\ 14\overline{)11.2} \\ -\ 112 \\ \hline 0 \end{array}$$

30. WRITING IN ▶MATH Explain how you can use estimation to place the decimal point in the quotient 42.56 ÷ 22.

Standards Practice

31 22,409.6 ÷ 40 =

A 560.02

B 560.225

C 560.24

D 562.24

32 What was Ursalina's approximate average pay for these three jobs?

Jobs	Weekly Pay
baby-sitting	$50.00
pet-sitting	$10.50
lawn work	$22.50

F $28.00

G $35.00

H $55.00

J $80.00

Spiral Review

33. The whale shark is the world's biggest fish at $41\frac{1}{4}$ feet long. The largest reptile is the saltwater crocodile, which can grow up to 16 feet long. Which is the more reasonable estimate for the difference in length of the whale shark and the saltwater crocodile: 20 feet or 25 feet? **(Lesson 6-3)**

Multiply. **(Lesson 6-2)**

34. 2.4 × 5.7 **35.** 1.6 × 2.3 **36.** 0.32 × (8.1) **37.** 2.68 × (0.84)

Game Time

Decimos

Dividing Decimals by Whole Numbers

Get Ready!

Players: two, three, or four

You will need: spinner, index cards

Get Set!

- Each player makes game sheets like the one shown at the right.
- Make a spinner as shown.

___ . ___ ÷ ___

Go!

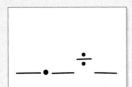

- The first person spins the spinner. Each player writes the number in one of the blanks on his or her game sheet.

  The second person spins and each player writes that number in a blank.

  The next person spins and players fill in their game sheets. A zero cannot be placed as the divisor.

- All players find their quotients. Round to the nearest hundredth if necessary. The player with the greatest quotient earns one point. In case of a tie, those players each earn one point.
- The first person to earn 5 points wins.

Explore

Math Lab for 6-5
Dividing by Decimals

MAIN IDEA

I will use models to divide a decimal by a decimal.

Standard 5NS2.1 Add, subtract, multiply, and **divide with decimals**; add with negative integers; subtract positive integers from negative integers; and verify the reasonableness of results.
Standard 5MR2.3 Use a variety of methods, such as words, numbers, symbols, charts, graphs, tables, diagrams, and **models, to explain mathematical reasoning.**

The model below shows 15 ÷ 3.

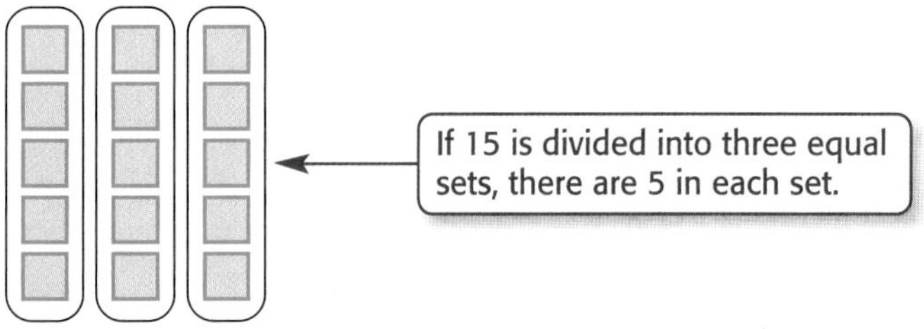
If 15 is divided into three equal sets, there are 5 in each set.

Dividing decimals is similar to dividing whole numbers. In the Activity below, 1.5 is the *dividend* and 0.3 is the *divisor*.

- Use base-ten blocks to model the dividend.
- Replace any ones block with tenths.
- Separate the tenths into groups represented by the divisor.
- The quotient is the number of groups.

ACTIVITY

1 Model 1.5 ÷ 0.3.

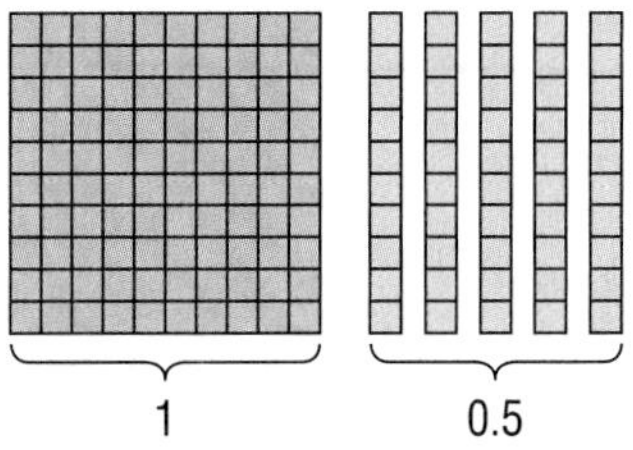

Place one and 5 tenths to show 1.5.

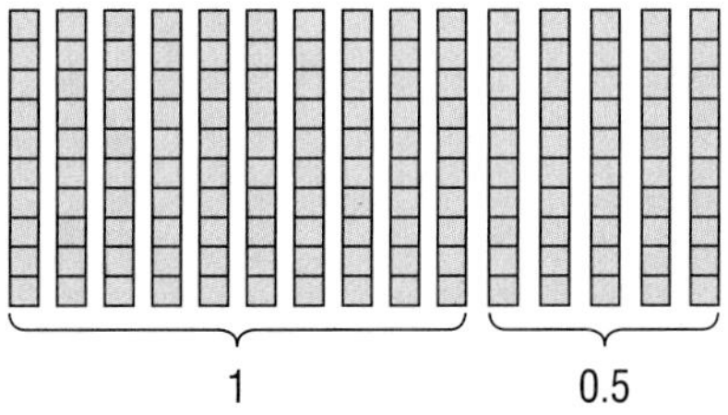

Replace the ones block with tenths. You should have a total of 15 tenths.

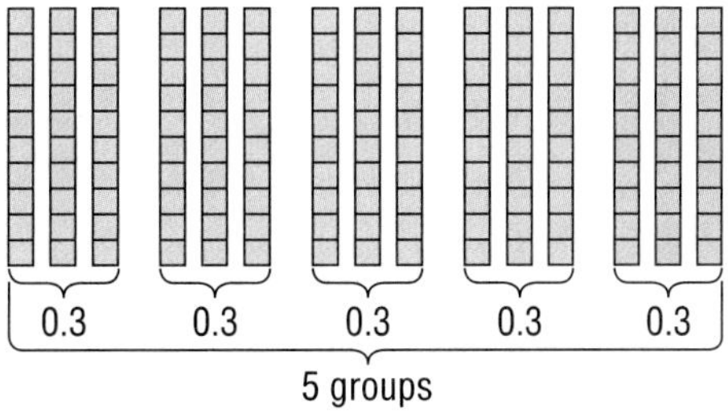

Separate the tenths into groups of three tenths to show dividing by 0.3.

There are five groups of three tenths in 1.5. So, 1.5 ÷ 0.3 = 5.

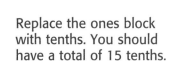

You can use a similar model to divide by hundredths.

ACTIVITY

2 Model 0.4 ÷ 0.05.

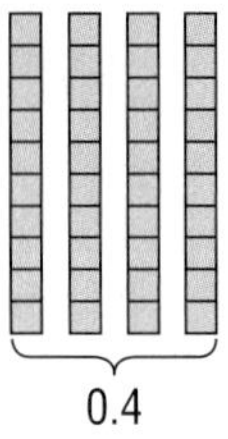

Model 0.4 with base-ten blocks.

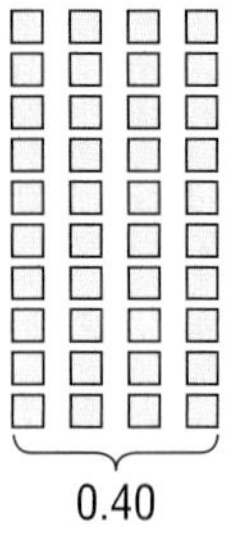

Replace the tenths with hundredths since you are dividing by hundredths.

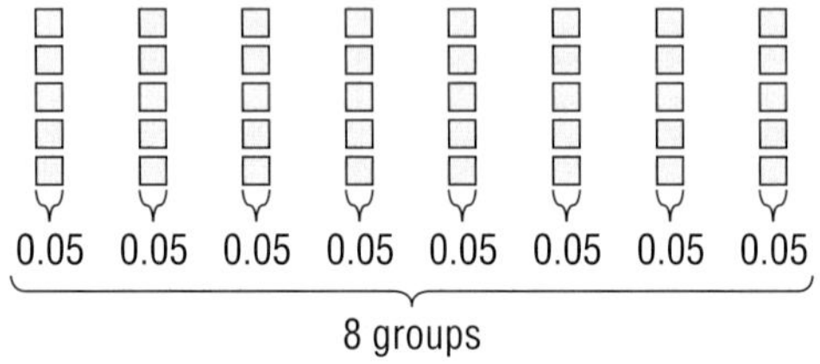

Separate the hundredths into groups of five hundredths to show dividing by 0.05.

There are eight groups of five hundredths in 0.4.

So, 0.4 ÷ 0.05 = 8.

CHECK What You Know

Use base-ten blocks to find each quotient.

a. 2.4 ÷ 0.6 **b.** 1.2 ÷ 0.4 **c.** 1.8 ÷ 0.6

d. 0.9 ÷ 0.09 **e.** 0.8 ÷ 0.04 **f.** 0.6 ÷ 0.05

Analyze the Results

1. Explain why the base-ten blocks representing the dividend must be replaced or separated into the smallest place value of the divisor.

2. Tell why the quotient 0.4 ÷ 0.05 is a whole number. What does the quotient represent?

3. Determine the missing divisor in the sentence 0.8 ÷ ■ = 20. Explain.

4. Tell whether 1.2 ÷ 0.03 is *less than, equal to,* or *greater than* 1.2. Explain your reasoning.

6-5 Dividing by Decimals

Concepts in Motion
Interactive Lab
ca.gr5math.com

GET READY to Learn

The table below shows the daily admission rates to Knott's Berry Farm in Buena Park, California. Mr. and Mrs. Lindley paid a total of \$59.80 for their children to enter the park. If their children are between the ages of 3 and 11, use estimation to find the number of children's tickets they purchased.

Knott's Berry Farm Daily Admission Rates

Tickets	Adults	Children (3–11)	Seniors (62+)
Southern California Residents	\$31.95	\$14.95	\$14.95
Full-Day Prices	\$39.95	\$14.95	\$14.95
After 4 P.M. Admission	\$25.00	\$14.95	\$14.95

Source: knotts.com

MAIN IDEA

I will divide decimals by decimals.

Standard 5NS2.1 Add, subtract, multiply, and **divide with decimals;** add with negative integers; subtract positive integers from negative integers; **and verify the reasonableness of results.**

Standard 5NS2.2 Demonstrate proficiency with division, including division with positive decimals and long division with multidigit divisors.

Review Vocabulary

power a number expressed using exponents: *Example:* 10^2 **(Lesson 1-2)**

When dividing by decimals, change the divisor into a whole number. To do this, multiply both the divisor and the dividend by the same power of 10. Then divide as with whole numbers. In the example above, to find 59.80 ÷ 14.95, you would multiply by 100.

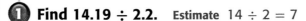

$$14.95\overline{)59.80} \rightarrow 1495\overline{)5980}$$

EXAMPLE Divide by Decimals

1 Find 14.19 ÷ 2.2. **Estimate** 14 ÷ 2 = 7

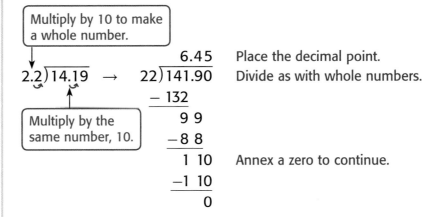

Multiply by 10 to make a whole number.

Multiply by the same number, 10.

$$2.2\overline{)14.19} \rightarrow 22\overline{)141.90}$$

```
      6.45     Place the decimal point.
 22)141.90     Divide as with whole numbers.
  - 132
      9 9
     -8 8
      1 10     Annex a zero to continue.
     -1 10
         0
```

14.19 divided by 2.2 is 6.45. Compare to the estimate.

Check 6.45 × 2.2 = 14.19 ✓

EXAMPLES Zeros in the Quotient and Dividend

2 **Find 52 ÷ 0.4.**

$0.4\overline{)52.0}$ → Multiply each by 10.

```
   130.     Place the decimal point.
 4)520.
 - 4
   12
 - 12
   00       Write a zero in the ones
            place of the quotient
            because 0 ÷ 4 = 0.
```

So, 52 ÷ 0.4 = 130.

Check 130 × 0.4 = 52 ✓

3 **Find 0.09 ÷ 1.8.**

$1.8\overline{)0.09}$ → Multiply each by 10.

```
    0.05    Place the decimal point.
 18)0.90    18 does not go into 9, so
  - 0       write a 0 in the tenths place.
    09
  - 00
     90     Annex a 0 in the dividend
   - 90     and continue to divide.
      0
```

So, 0.09 ÷ 1.8 is 0.05.

Check 0.05 × 1.8 = 0.09 ✓

Online Personal Tutor at ca.gr5math.com

EXAMPLE Round Quotients

4 **How many times more DSL subscribers are there in China than in France? Round to the nearest tenth.**

DSL Broadband Subscribers in 2004 (millions)	
China	13.7
Japan	12.7
U.S.	12.6
South Korea	6.7
Germany	6.0
France	5.3

Source: internetworldstats.com

Find 13.7 ÷ 5.3.

```
                   2.58
5.3)13.7  →  53)137.00
              - 106
                 310
               - 265
                  450
                - 424
                   26
```

Remember

When rounding to the nearest tenth, you can stop dividing when there is a digit in the hundredths place.

To the nearest tenth, 13.7 ÷ 5.3 = 2.6. So, there are about 2.6 times more DSL subscribers in China than in France.

CHECK What You Know

Divide. See Examples 1–4 (pp. 303–304)

1. 3.69 ÷ 0.3
2. 9.92 ÷ 0.8
3. 0.45 ÷ 0.3
4. 13.95 ÷ 3.1
5. 0.6 ÷ 0.0024
6. 0.462 ÷ 0.06
7. 0.321 ÷ 0.4
8. 2.943 ÷ 2.7
9. Alicia bought 5.75 yards of fleece fabric to make blankets for a charity. She needs 1.85 yards of fabric for each blanket. How many blankets can Alicia make with the fabric she bought?
10. Talk About It Explain why 1.92 ÷ 0.51 should be about 4.

Practice and Problem Solving

EXTRA PRACTICE See page 670.

Divide. See Examples 1–4 (pp. 303–304)

11. 1.44 ÷ 0.4
12. 0.68 ÷ 3.4
13. 16.24 ÷ 0.14
14. 2.07 ÷ 0.9
15. 0.0338 ÷ 1.3
16. 0.16728 ÷ 3.4
17. 96.6 ÷ 0.42
18. 1.08 ÷ 2.7
19. 13.5 ÷ 0.03
20. 8.4 ÷ 0.02
21. 0.12 ÷ 0.15
22. 0.242 ÷ 0.4
23. If a board 4.5 feet long is cut into 0.75-foot pieces, how many pieces will there be?
24. The average person's step length is approximately 2.5 feet long. How many steps would the average person take to travel 50 feet?
25. Refer to the table. How many times more people attended Big Bend National Park than Lyndon B. Johnson National Park? Round to the nearest tenth if necessary.
26. The Vielhaber family drove 315.5 miles for a soccer tournament and used 11.4 gallons of gas. How many miles did they get per gallon of gas to the nearest hundredth? Estimate the answer before calculating.

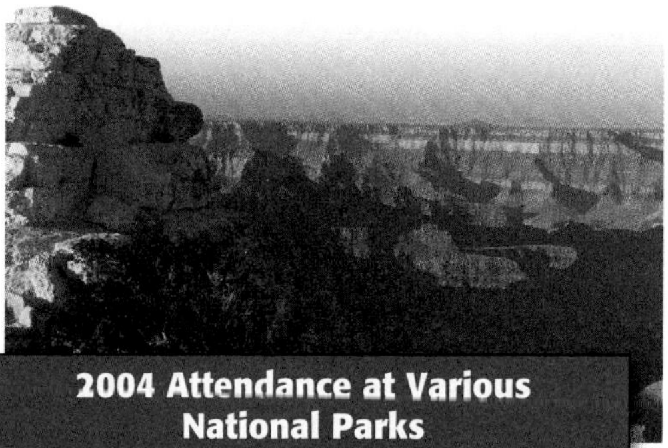

2004 Attendance at Various National Parks

National Park	Attendance (thousands)
Big Bend (TX)	357.7
Grand Canyon (AZ)	4,326.2
Lyndon B. Johnson (TX)	80.7
Yosemite (CA)	3,280.9
Zion (UT)	2,677.3

Source: National Parks Service

H.O.T. Problems

27. CHALLENGE Replace each ■ below with different digits in order to make a true sentence. ■.8 ■ 3 ÷ 0.82 = 4.6 ■

28. NUMBER SENSE Use the number line to determine if the quotient of 1.92 ÷ 0.5 is closest to 2, 3, or 4. Do not calculate. Explain.

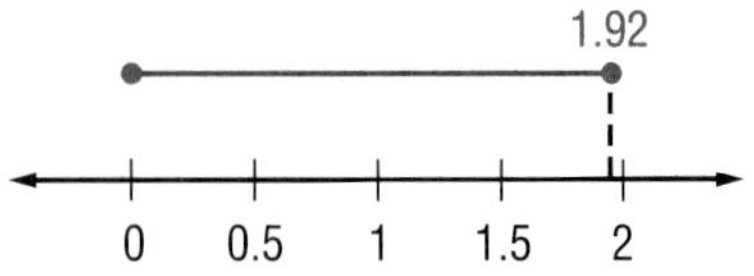

29. Which One Doesn't Belong? Identify the problem that does not have the same quotient as the other three. Explain your reasoning.

0.35 ÷ 0.5	3.5 ÷ 5	0.035 ÷ 0.05	35 ÷ 5

30. WRITING IN ▸MATH Refer to the table in Exercise 25 on 2004 national park attendance. Write and solve a problem in which you would divide decimals. Include instructions for rounding in your problem.

Standards Practice

31 17.24 ÷ 2.5 =

A 0.6896

B 0.708

C 6.896

D 7.08

32 To the nearest tenth, how many times greater was the average gasoline price on January 9, 2006 than on January 9, 2005?

Date	Average Price (per gal)
January 9, 2005	$1.79
January 9, 2006	$2.33

Source: Energy Information Administration

F 0.5

G 1.3

H 1.5

J 1.8

Spiral Review

33. Find the quotient when 68.52 is divided by 12. **(Lesson 6-4)**

Multiply. (Lesson 6-2)

34. 19.2 × 2.45

35. 8.25 × 12.42

36. 9.016 × 51.9

37. The Sears Tower in Chicago has 30 stories more than the Aon Centre in Chicago. Together, both buildings have 190 stories. Find the number of stories in each building. Use the *guess and check* strategy. **(Lesson 1-7)**

CHAPTER 6

Mid-Chapter Check

Lessons 6-1 through 6-5

Multiply. **(Lesson 6-1)**

1. 4.3×5 **2.** 0.78×9

3. 3×0.006 **4.** 44×0.035

Algebra Evaluate each expression if $p = 5.7$, $m = 0.08$, and $n = 1.7$. **(Lesson 6-1)**

5. $26p$ **6.** $15m$ **7.** $9n$

8. **STANDARDS PRACTICE** Yoko wants to buy 3 necklaces that cost \$12.99 each and 4 T-shirts that are on sale for \$11.95 each. Which of the following is the total amount Yoko will pay? **(Lesson 6-1)**

A \$24.94 **C** \$86.77

B \$50.92 **D** \$87.81

Write each number in standard form. **(Lesson 6-1)**

9. 3×10^4 **10.** 7.7×10^6

11. 1.21×10^5 **12.** 4.09×10^2

13. The distance from Earth to the Moon is about 3.83×10^5 kilometers. Write this distance in standard form. **(Lesson 6-1)**

Multiply. **(Lesson 6-2)**

14. 5.72×6.9 **15.** 18.55×0.002

16. 0.08×1.26 **17.** 33.71×1.9

18. **Measurement** Find the area of the rectangle. **(Lesson 6-2)**

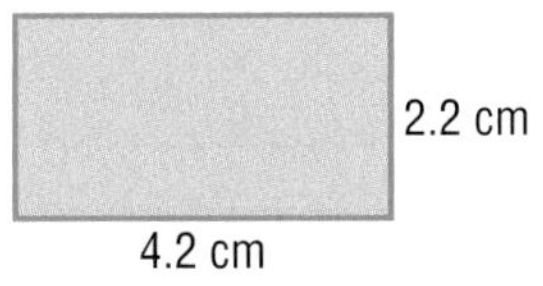

19. Six friends will split the cost of 2 large pizzas. If each pizza costs \$14.99, is \$4, \$5, or \$6 a reasonable answer for the amount that each friend will pay? **(Lesson 6-3)**

Divide. Round to the nearest tenth if necessary. **(Lesson 6-4)**

20. $19.752 \div 24$ **21.** $48.6 \div 6$

22. $54.45 \div 55$ **23.** $2.08 \div 5$

24. **STANDARDS PRACTICE** Mr. Dillon will pay a total of \$9,100.08 for his car lease over 36 months. Which of the following is his monthly payment? **(Lesson 6-4)**

F \$200.96 **H** \$602.88

G \$252.78 **J** \$758.34

Algebra Evaluate each expression if $w = 26.8$, $y = 0.01$, and $z = 3.4$. Round to the nearest tenth if necessary. **(Lesson 6-5)**

25. $\frac{w}{y}$ **26.** $\frac{5.1w}{z}$ **27.** $\frac{wy}{z}$

Divide. Round to the nearest tenth if necessary. **(Lesson 6-5)**

28. $3.29 \div 1.4$ **29.** $93.912 \div 4.3$

30. $0.015 \div 0.02$ **31.** $0.008 \div 0.01$

32. **WRITING IN MATH** At the 1996 Olympics, Michael Johnson set a world record of 19.32 seconds for the 200-meter dash. A bee can fly 200 meters in 40.752 seconds. About how many times faster was Michael Johnson? Explain. **(Lesson 6-5)**

6-6 Problem-Solving Investigation

MAIN IDEA I will choose the best strategy to solve a problem.

Standard 5MR1.1 Analyze problems by identifying relationships, distinguishing relevant from irrelevant information, **sequencing** and prioritizing **information,** and observing patterns. **Standard 5NS2.1 Add,** subtract, **multiply,** and divide **with decimals;** . . . and verify the reasonableness of results.

P.S.I. TEAM +

MIGUEL: **At the store, I saw the following items: a batting glove for \$8.95, roller blades for \$39.75, a can of tennis balls for \$2.75, and weights for \$5.50. I have \$15 and I would like to buy more than one item.**

YOUR MISSION: **Find which items Miguel can buy and spend about \$15.**

Understand	You know the cost of the items and that Miguel has \$15 to spend. You need to find which items Miguel can buy.
Plan	Make an organized list to see the different possibilities and use estimation to be sure he spends about \$15.
Solve	Since the roller blades cost more than \$15, you can eliminate the roller blades. The batting glove is about \$9, the weights are about \$6, and the can of tennis balls is about \$3. Start with the batting glove: • 1 glove + 1 weights ≈ \$9 + \$6 or \$15 • 1 glove + 2 cans of tennis balls ≈ \$9 + \$6 or \$15 List other combinations that contain the weights: • 2 weights + 1 can of tennis balls ≈ \$12 + \$3 or \$15 • 1 weights + 3 cans of tennis balls ≈ \$6 + \$9 or \$15 List the remaining combinations that contain only tennis balls: • 5 cans of tennis balls ≈ \$15
Check	Check the list to be sure that all of the possible combinations of sporting good items that total no more than \$15 are included. ✓

Mixed Problem Solving

EXTRA PRACTICE
See page 670.

Use any strategy shown below to solve each problem.

PROBLEM-SOLVING STRATEGIES
- *Make an organized list.*
- *Determine reasonable answers.*
- *Use logical reasoning.*

1. Refer to page 308. What sporting good items can Miguel buy and spend between \$20 and \$25?

2. The admission prices for a local water park are shown below.

Admission Rates	
Adult	\$39.75
Child	\$29.25

What is the total price for two adult and three children passes?

3. How many different products as shown below are possible using the digits 1, 3, 5, and 7?

$$\begin{array}{r} \blacksquare.\blacksquare \\ \times\ \blacksquare.\blacksquare \\ \hline \end{array}$$

4. A red, a blue, a green, and a yellow marble are placed in a brown paper bag. If you take one marble out of the bag at a time, in how many different orders can all four marbles be removed from the bag? List all possibilities.

5. Guillermo bought a new baseball glove for \$49.95. The sales tax is found by multiplying the price of the glove by 0.075. Is about \$3, \$4, or \$5 a reasonable answer for the amount of sales tax that Guillermo paid?

6. Marisol would like to buy gifts that cost \$12.80, \$10.85, \$11.15, and \$9.75. Should she take \$40 or \$50 with her to the store?

7. **Measurement** Find the area of the sixth figure in the pattern shown.

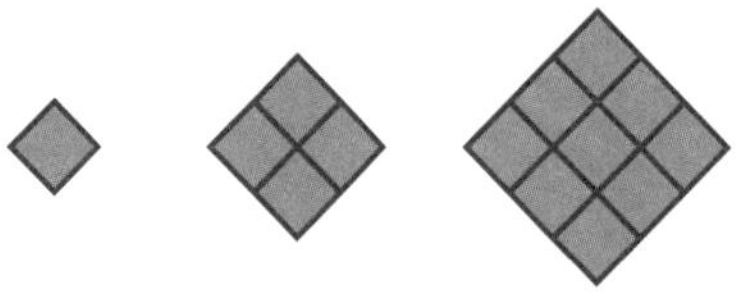

8. Dylan, Sydney, and Gabriel went shopping. Each bought a different type of clothing: a hat, a shirt, and a pair of shoes. Dylan did not buy something to put on his feet. Sydney bought her item before the person bought the shoes. Either Gabriel or Sydney bought the hat. What item did each person buy?

9. The table shows the passing yards of the winning Super Bowl quarterbacks. Which is a more reasonable estimate for the difference that Brady passed the ball in the 2004 Super Bowl than in the 2005 Super Bowl: 90 yards, 110 yards, or 200 yards?

Passing Yards of Winning QBs		
Player	Year	Yards
Tom Brady	2004	354
Tom Brady	2005	236
Ben Roethlisberger	2006	123

Source: superbowl.com

10. **WRITING IN ▸MATH** Can the *make an organized list* strategy be used to answer the following problem? Explain. *Mrs. Wright has 4 pictures to display in a row on her desk. In how many different ways can she display the pictures?*

6-7 Estimating Products of Fractions

GET READY to Learn

Gracia made about $\frac{1}{4}$ of the 13 shots she attempted in a basketball game. About how many shots did Gracia make?

MAIN IDEA

I will estimate products of fractions using compatible numbers and rounding.

Standard 5MR2.5 Indicate the relative advantages of exact and approximate solutions to problems and **give answers to a specified degree of accuracy.**

Standard 5NS2.5 **Compute** and perform **simple multiplication** and division **of fractions** and apply these procedures to solving problems.

New Vocabulary

compatible numbers

Review Vocabulary

multiple of a number the product of the number and any whole number; *Example:* 6, 9, and 12 are all multiples of 3 **(Lesson 4-4)**

One way to estimate products involving fractions is to use **compatible numbers**, or numbers that are easy to divide mentally. For example, to estimate $16 \div 3$, find a multiple of 3 close to 16.

$15 \div 3 = 5$ 15 and 3 are compatible numbers.

So, $16 \div 3$ is about 5.

EXAMPLES Estimate Using Compatible Numbers

1 Estimate $\frac{1}{4} \times 13$.

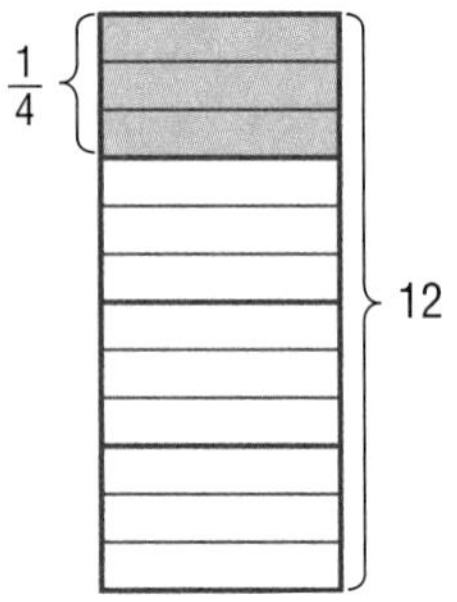

$\frac{1}{4} \times 13$ means $\frac{1}{4}$ of 13.

Find a multiple of 4 that is close to 13.

$\frac{1}{4} \times 13 \rightarrow \frac{1}{4} \times 12$ 12 and 4 are compatible numbers since $12 \div 4 = 3$

$\frac{1}{4} \times 12 = 3$ $12 \div 4 = 3$.

So, $\frac{1}{4} \times 13$ is *about* 3.

2 Estimate $\frac{2}{5}$ of 11.

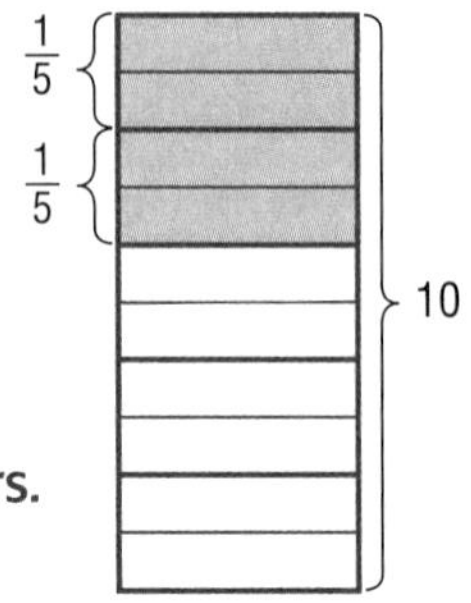

Estimate $\frac{1}{5} \times 11$ first.

Find a multiple of 5 that is close to 11.

$\frac{1}{5} \times 11 \rightarrow \frac{1}{5} \times 10$ Use 10 since 10 and 5 are compatible numbers.

$\frac{1}{5} \times 10 = 2$ $10 \div 5 = 2$

If $\frac{1}{5}$ of 10 is 2, then $\frac{2}{5}$ of 10 is 2×2 or 4.

So, $\frac{2}{5}$ of 11 is *about* 4.

EXAMPLE Estimate by Rounding to 0, $\frac{1}{2}$, or 1

3 **Estimate $\frac{1}{3} \times \frac{7}{8}$.**

$\frac{1}{3} \times \frac{7}{8} \rightarrow \frac{1}{2} \times 1$

$\frac{1}{2} \times 1 = \frac{1}{2}$

So, $\frac{1}{3} \times \frac{7}{8}$ is *about* $\frac{1}{2}$.

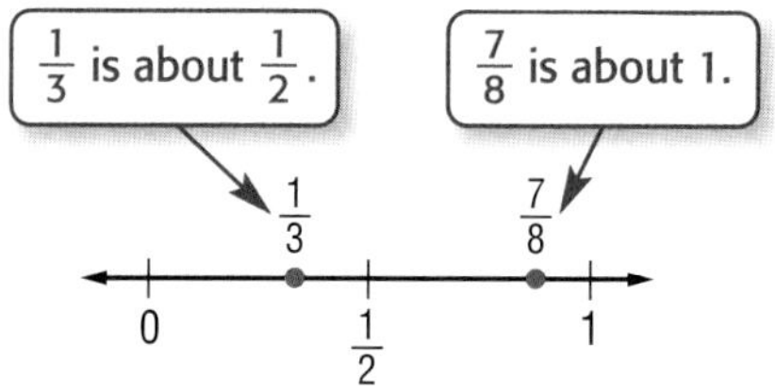

Online Personal Tutor at ca.gr5math.com

EXAMPLE Estimate With Mixed Numbers

4 **Estimate the area of the flower bed.**

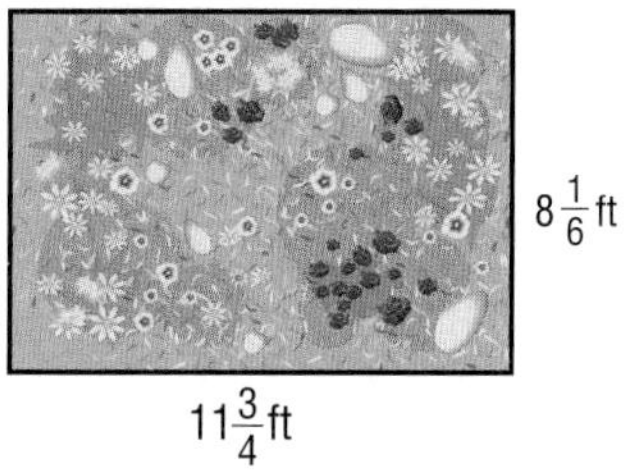

Remember

You can review **rounding fractions** in Lesson 5-1.

Round each mixed number to the nearest whole number.

$11\frac{3}{4} \times 8\frac{1}{6} \rightarrow 12 \times 8 = 96$

Round $11\frac{3}{4}$ to 12.

Round $8\frac{1}{6}$ to 8.

So, the area is *about* 96 square feet.

CHECK What You Know

Estimate each product. See Examples 1–4 (pp. 310–311)

1. $\frac{1}{8} \times 15$
2. $\frac{3}{4} \times 21$
3. $\frac{2}{5}$ of 26
4. $\frac{1}{10}$ of 68
5. $\frac{1}{4} \times \frac{8}{9}$
6. $\frac{5}{8} \times \frac{1}{9}$
7. $6\frac{2}{3} \times 4\frac{1}{5}$
8. $\frac{9}{10} \times 10\frac{3}{4}$
9. Hakeem's front porch measures $9\frac{3}{4}$ feet by 4 feet. Estimate the area of his front porch.
10. A kitchen measures $24\frac{1}{6}$ feet by $9\frac{2}{3}$ feet. Estimate the area of the kitchen.
11. **Talk About It** Is $\frac{2}{3} \times 20$ greater than 14 or less than 14? Explain your reasoning.

Practice and Problem Solving

EXTRA PRACTICE See page 671.

Estimate each product. See Examples 1, 2 (p. 310)

12. $\frac{1}{4} \times 21$ **13.** $\frac{1}{5} \times 26$ **14.** $\frac{1}{3}$ of 41 **15.** $\frac{1}{6}$ of 17

16. $\frac{5}{7}$ of 22 **17.** $\frac{2}{9}$ of 88 **18.** $\frac{2}{3} \times 10$ **19.** $\frac{3}{8} \times 4$

20. Cyrus is inviting 11 friends over for pizza. He would like to have enough pizza so each friend can have $\frac{1}{4}$ of a pizza. About how many pizzas should he order?

21. Tara would like to finish $\frac{2}{5}$ of her book by next Friday. If the book has 203 pages, about how many pages does she need to read?

Estimate each product. See Example 3 (p. 311)

22. $\frac{5}{7} \times \frac{1}{9}$ **23.** $\frac{1}{10} \times \frac{7}{8}$ **24.** $\frac{11}{12} \times \frac{3}{8}$ **25.** $\frac{2}{5} \times \frac{9}{10}$

26. $4\frac{1}{3} \times 2\frac{3}{4}$ **27.** $6\frac{4}{5} \times 4\frac{1}{9}$ **28.** $5\frac{1}{8} \times 9\frac{1}{12}$ **29.** $2\frac{9}{10} \times 8\frac{5}{6}$

Measurement **Estimate the area of each rectangle.** See Example 4 (p. 311)

30.

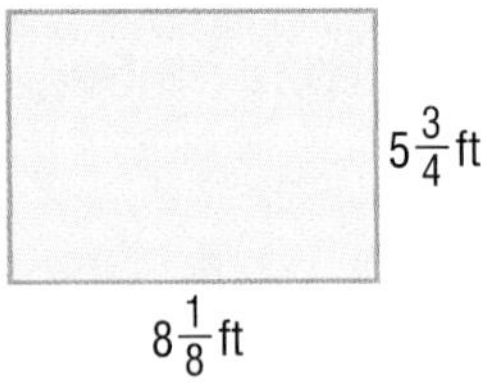

31.

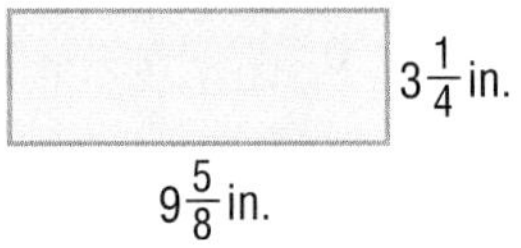

32. **Measurement** A wall measures $8\frac{1}{2}$ feet by $12\frac{3}{4}$ feet. If a gallon of paint covers about 150 square feet, will one gallon of paint be enough to cover the wall? Explain.

Real-World PROBLEM SOLVING

Data File San Diego County is the Avocado Capital of the United States.

33. A cup of white goat cheese weighs about 8 ounces. About how many ounces are called for in the recipe?

34. If you want to double the recipe, about how many garlic cloves will you need?

Source: avocado.org

Guacamole

$1\frac{1}{3}$ California avocados

$\frac{1}{3}$ cup white goat cheese

$\frac{1}{6}$ cup cilantro

$1\frac{1}{3}$ Tbsp pistachio nuts

$\frac{1}{6}$ tsp red pepper flakes

$1\frac{1}{3}$ garlic cloves

H.O.T. Problems

35. SELECT A TECHNIQUE Which of the following techniques could you use to easily determine whether an answer is reasonable to the multiplication of $4\frac{10}{11}$ by $7\frac{1}{13}$? Justify your response.

mental math | number sense | estimation

36. CHALLENGE Determine which point on the number line could be the graph of the product of the numbers graphed at *C* and *D*. Explain your reasoning.

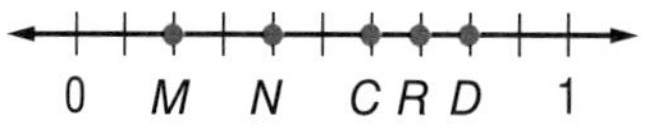

37. WRITING IN ▶MATH Summarize how you would use compatible numbers to estimate $\frac{2}{3}$ of 8.

Standards Practice

38 Which is the best estimate of the area of the rectangle?

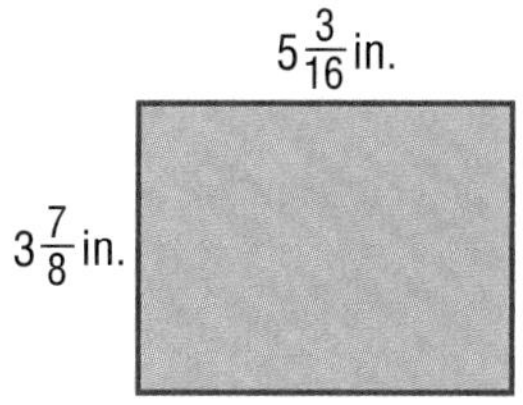

A 24 in^2

B 20 in^2

C 16 in^2

D 15 in^2

39 A total of 133 sixth-grade students went to a local museum. Of these, between one half and three fourths packed their lunch. Which of the following ranges could represent the number of students who packed their lunch?

F Less than 65

G Between 65 and 100

H Between 100 and 130

J More than 130

Spiral Review

40. After 5 performances, the total attendance of a play was 39,963. Which is a more reasonable estimate for the number of people that attended each performance: 7,000 or 8,000? **(Lesson 6-6)**

Divide. Round to the nearest hundredth, if necessary. (Lesson 6-5)

41. 94.3 ÷ 16.4 **42.** 14.798 ÷ 4.9 **43.** 95.5 ÷ 0.05 **44.** 112 ÷ 5.2

45. Three people equally share 7.5 ounces of juice. How much juice does each receive? **(Lesson 6-4)**

46. Measurement Anoki's bedroom is 8.25 feet long. Write this length as a fraction in simplest form. **(Lesson 4-8)**

Explore

Math Lab for 6-8
Multiplying Fractions

MAIN IDEA

I will multiply fractions using models.

Standard 5NS2.4 Understand the concept of multiplication and division **of fractions.**
Standard 5MR2.3 Use a variety of methods, such as words, numbers, symbols, charts, graphs, tables, diagrams, and **models, to explain mathematical reasoning.**

In the lab on pages 288 and 289, you used decimal models to multiply decimals. You can use a similar model to multiply fractions.

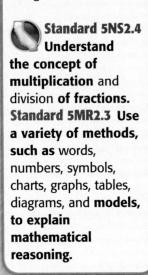

ACTIVITY

1 Find $\frac{1}{3} \times \frac{1}{2}$ using a model.

To find $\frac{1}{3} \times \frac{1}{2}$, find $\frac{1}{3}$ of $\frac{1}{2}$.

Begin with a square to represent 1.

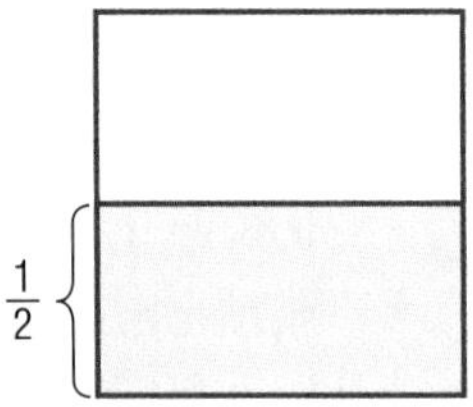

Shade $\frac{1}{2}$ of the square yellow.

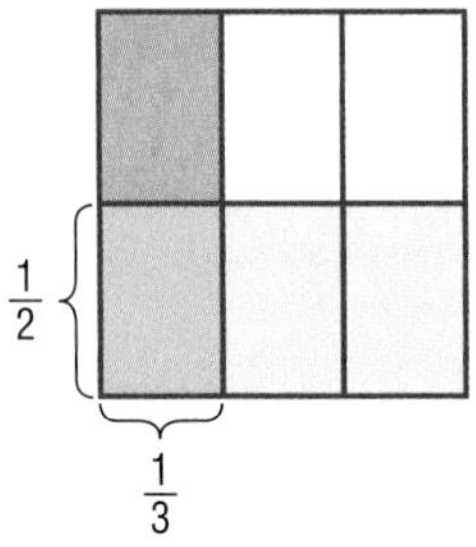

Shade $\frac{1}{3}$ of the square blue. The green region has been shaded twice. It represents the product.

One sixth of the square is shaded green. So, $\frac{1}{3} \times \frac{1}{2} = \frac{1}{6}$.

CHECK What You Know

Find each product using a model.

a. $\frac{1}{4} \times \frac{1}{2}$ **b.** $\frac{1}{3} \times \frac{1}{4}$ **c.** $\frac{1}{2} \times \frac{1}{5}$

Analyze the Results

1. Describe how you would change the model to find $\frac{1}{2} \times \frac{1}{3}$. Is the product the same as $\frac{1}{3} \times \frac{1}{2}$? Explain.

ACTIVITY

2 **Find $\frac{3}{5} \times \frac{2}{3}$ using a model. Write in simplest form.**

To find $\frac{3}{5} \times \frac{2}{3}$, find $\frac{3}{5}$ of $\frac{2}{3}$.

Begin with a square to represent 1.

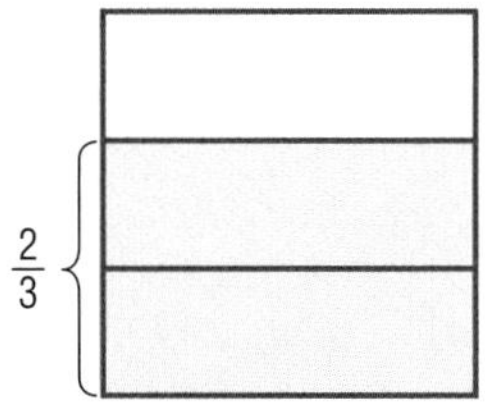

Shade $\frac{2}{3}$ of the square yellow.

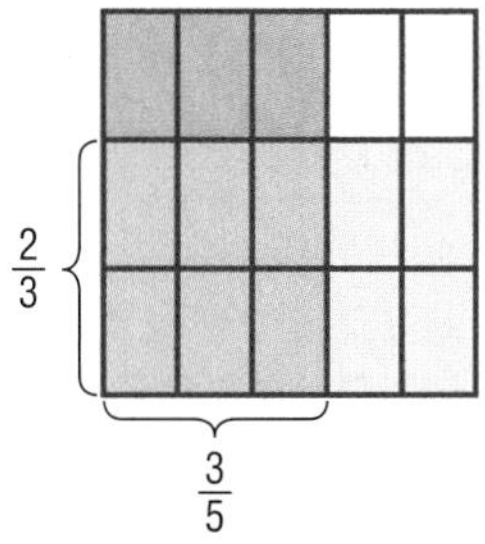

Shade $\frac{3}{5}$ of the square blue.

Six out of 15 parts are shaded green. So, $\frac{3}{5} \times \frac{2}{3} = \frac{6}{15}$ or $\frac{2}{5}$.

CHECK What You Know

Find each product using a model. Then write in simplest form.

d. $\frac{3}{4} \times \frac{2}{3}$ **e.** $\frac{2}{5} \times \frac{5}{6}$ **f.** $\frac{4}{5} \times \frac{3}{8}$

Analyze the Results

2. Draw a model to show that $\frac{2}{3} \times \frac{5}{6} = \frac{10}{18}$. Then explain how the model shows that $\frac{10}{18}$ simplifies to $\frac{5}{9}$.

3. Explain the relationship between the numerators of the problem and the numerator of the product. What do you notice about the denominators of the problem and the denominator of the product?

4. Write a rule you can use to multiply fractions.

5. **Algebra** Find the value of y in $\frac{7}{10} \times \frac{4}{9} = \frac{y}{90}$ without using models. Justify your answer.

6-8 Multiplying Fractions

MAIN IDEA

I will multiply fractions.

Standard 5NS2.5 Compute and perform simple multiplication and division **of fractions and apply these procedures to solving problems.**

GET READY to Learn

About $\frac{7}{10}$ of Earth is covered by water. Of that part, about $\frac{1}{2}$ is covered by the Pacific Ocean. The overlapping area of the model below represents the part covered by the Pacific Ocean, which is $\frac{1}{2}$ of $\frac{7}{10}$ or $\frac{1}{2} \times \frac{7}{10}$. What part of Earth's surface is covered by the Pacific Ocean?

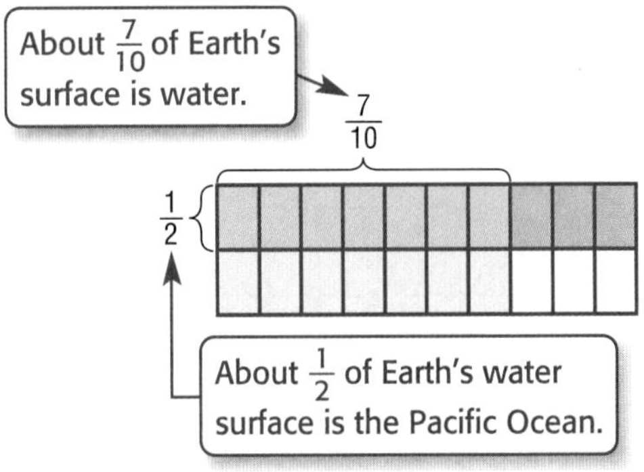

About $\frac{7}{10}$ of Earth's surface is water.
$\frac{7}{10}$
$\frac{1}{2}$
About $\frac{1}{2}$ of Earth's water surface is the Pacific Ocean.

KEY CONCEPT — Multiply Fractions

Words To multiply fractions, multiply the numerators and multiply the denominators.

Examples

Numbers

$$\frac{2}{5} \times \frac{1}{2} = \frac{2 \times 1}{5 \times 2}$$

Algebra

$$\frac{a}{b} \times \frac{c}{d} = \frac{a \times c}{b \times d},$$

where b and d are not 0.

EXAMPLE Multiply Fractions

1 Find $\frac{1}{3} \times \frac{1}{4}$.

$\frac{1}{3} \times \frac{1}{4} = \frac{1 \times 1}{3 \times 4}$ Multiply the numerators. Multiply the denominators.

$= \frac{1}{12}$ Simplify.

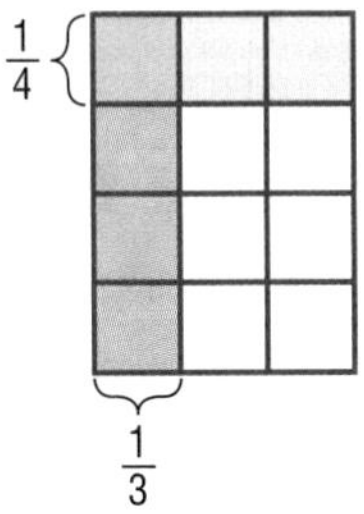

$\frac{1}{4}$
$\frac{1}{3}$

Concepts in Motion

Interactive Lab
ca.gr5math.com

To multiply a fraction and a whole number, first write the whole number as a fraction.

EXAMPLE Multiply Fractions and Whole Numbers

2 **Find $\frac{3}{5} \times 4$.**

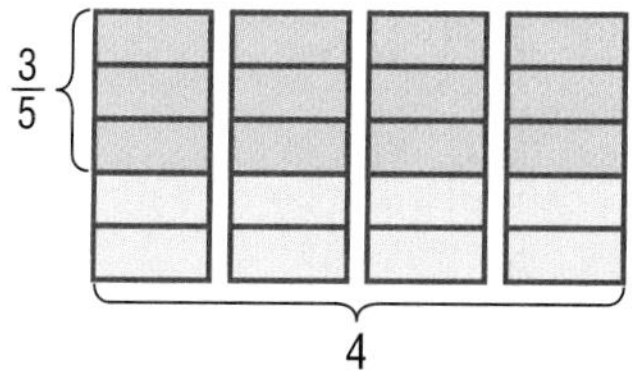

Estimate $\frac{1}{2} \times 4 = 2$

$\frac{3}{5} \times 4 = \frac{3}{5} \times \frac{4}{1}$ Write 4 as $\frac{4}{1}$.

$= \frac{3 \times 4}{5 \times 1}$ Multiply.

$= \frac{12}{5}$ or $2\frac{2}{5}$ Simplify.

Check for Reasonableness $2\frac{2}{5} \approx 2$ ✓

Review Vocabulary

factor two or more numbers that are multiplied together to form a product; *Example:* 1, 2, 3, and 6 are all factors of 6 **(Lesson 1-2)**

If the numerators and the denominators have a common factor, you can simplify *before* you multiply.

EXAMPLE Simplify Before Multiplying

3 **Find $\frac{3}{4} \times \frac{5}{6}$.**

Estimate $\frac{1}{2} \times 1 = \frac{1}{2}$

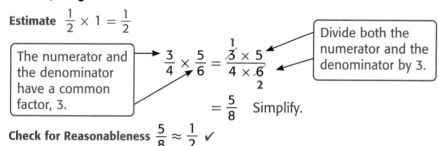

The numerator and the denominator have a common factor, 3.

$\frac{3}{4} \times \frac{5}{6} = \frac{\overset{1}{\cancel{3}} \times 5}{4 \times \underset{2}{\cancel{6}}}$

Divide both the numerator and the denominator by 3.

$= \frac{5}{8}$ Simplify.

Check for Reasonableness $\frac{5}{8} \approx \frac{1}{2}$ ✓

Online Personal Tutor at ca.gr5math.com

EXAMPLE Evaluate Expressions

4 **Algebra Evaluate ab if $a = \frac{2}{3}$ and $b = \frac{3}{8}$.**

$ab = \frac{2}{3} \times \frac{3}{8}$ Replace a with $\frac{2}{3}$ and b with $\frac{3}{8}$.

$= \frac{\overset{1}{\cancel{2}} \times \overset{1}{\cancel{3}}}{\underset{1}{\cancel{3}} \times \underset{4}{\cancel{8}}}$ The GCF of 2 and 8 is 2. The GCF of 3 and 3 is 3. Divide both the numerator and the denominator by 2 and then by 3.

$= \frac{1}{4}$ Simplify.

Check $\frac{1}{3}$ of $\frac{3}{8} = \frac{1}{8}$

So, $\frac{2}{3}$ of $\frac{3}{8} = \frac{2}{8}$ or $\frac{1}{4}$. ✓

CHECK What You Know

Multiply. Write in simplest form. **See Examples 1–3 (pp. 316–317)**

1. $\frac{1}{8} \times \frac{1}{2}$

2. $\frac{2}{3} \times \frac{4}{5}$

3. $\frac{4}{5} \times 10$

4. $\frac{3}{4} \times 12$

5. $\frac{3}{10} \times \frac{5}{6}$

6. $\frac{3}{5} \times \frac{5}{6}$

7. Suppose you are building a model car that is $\frac{1}{12}$ the size of the actual car. How long is the model if the actual car is shown at the right?

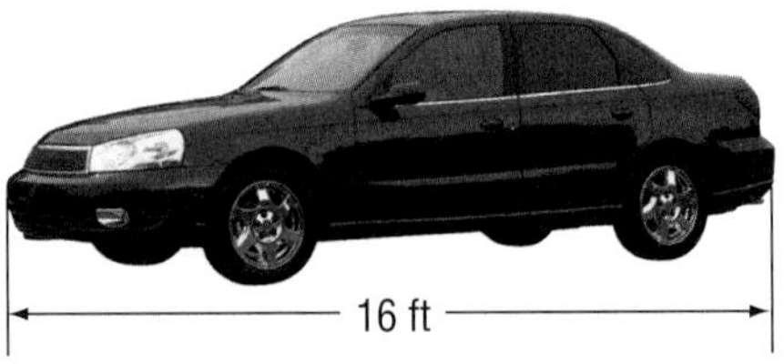

8. Algebra Evaluate xy if $x = \frac{1}{4}$ and $y = \frac{5}{6}$.
See Example 4 (p. 317)

9. **Talk About It** When multiplying $\frac{3}{4}$ and $\frac{2}{9}$, can you simplify before you multiply? Explain your reasoning.

Practice and Problem Solving

EXTRA PRACTICE
See page 671.

Multiply. Write in simplest form. **See Examples 1–3 (pp. 316–317)**

10. $\frac{1}{3} \times \frac{2}{5}$

11. $\frac{1}{8} \times \frac{3}{4}$

12. $\frac{3}{4} \times \frac{5}{8}$

13. $\frac{2}{5} \times \frac{3}{7}$

14. $\frac{3}{4} \times 2$

15. $\frac{2}{3} \times 4$

16. $\frac{5}{6} \times 15$

17. $\frac{3}{8} \times 11$

18. $\frac{2}{3} \times \frac{1}{4}$

19. $\frac{3}{5} \times \frac{5}{7}$

20. $\frac{4}{9} \times \frac{3}{8}$

21. $\frac{2}{5} \times \frac{5}{6}$

Algebra Evaluate each expression if $a = \frac{3}{5}$, $b = \frac{1}{2}$, and $c = \frac{1}{3}$.
See Example 4 (p. 317)

22. ab

23. bc

24. $\frac{1}{3}a$

25. $\frac{6}{7}c$

26. About $\frac{7}{10}$ of the human body is water. How many pounds of water are in a person who weighs 120 pounds?

27. The South Coast Plaza in Orange County, California, is one of the largest shopping malls in the U.S. It has an area of about 2,700,000 square feet. If $\frac{1}{9}$ of the area is for stores that are food-related, about how many square feet in the mall are for food-related stores?

28. Alvin ate $\frac{5}{8}$ of a pizza. If there were 16 slices of pizza, how many slices did Alvin eat?

6-10 Dividing Fractions

MAIN IDEA

I will divide fractions.

Standard 5NS2.5 Compute and perform simple multiplication and **division of fractions and apply these procedures to solving problems.**

New Vocabulary

reciprocal

GET READY to Learn

Hands-On Mini Lab

Kenji and his friend Malik ordered three one-foot submarine sandwiches. They estimate that $\frac{1}{2}$ of a sandwich will serve one person.

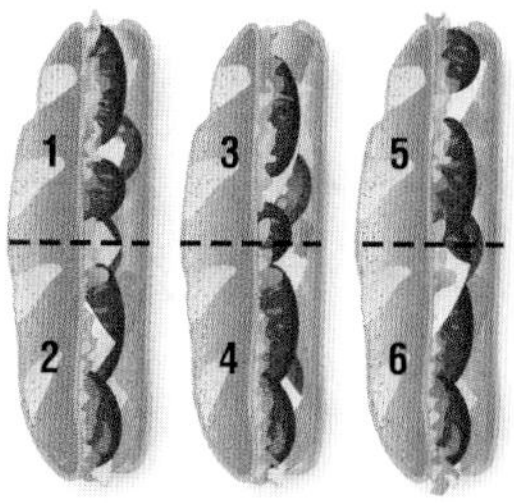

1. How many $\frac{1}{2}$-sandwich servings are there?

2. The model shows $3 \div \frac{1}{2}$. What is $3 \div \frac{1}{2}$?

Draw a model to find each quotient.

3. $3 \div \frac{1}{4}$ **4.** $2 \div \frac{1}{6}$ **5.** $4 \div \frac{1}{2}$

The Mini Lab shows that $3 \div \frac{1}{2} = 6$. Notice that dividing by $\frac{1}{2}$ gives the same result as multiplying by 2.

$$3 \div \frac{1}{2} = 6 \qquad 3 \times 2 = 6$$

Notice that $\frac{1}{2} \times 2 = 1$.

The numbers $\frac{1}{2}$ and 2 have a special relationship. Their product is 1. Any two numbers whose product is 1 are called **reciprocals** of each other.

EXAMPLES Find Reciprocals

1 Find the reciprocal of 5.

Since $5 \times \frac{1}{5} = 1$, the reciprocal of 5 is $\frac{1}{5}$.

2 Find the reciprocal of $\frac{2}{3}$.

Since $\frac{2}{3} \times \frac{3}{2} = 1$, the reciprocal of $\frac{2}{3}$ is $\frac{3}{2}$.

You can use reciprocals to divide fractions.

Remember

To find the reciprocal of a fraction, *invert* the fraction. That is, switch the numerator and denominator.

KEY CONCEPT — Divide Fractions

Words To divide by a fraction, multiply by its reciprocal.

Examples

Numbers

$\frac{1}{2} \div \frac{2}{3} = \frac{1}{2} \times \frac{3}{2}$

Algebra

$\frac{a}{b} \div \frac{c}{d} = \frac{a}{b} \times \frac{d}{c}$, where b, c, and $d \neq 0$

EXAMPLES Divide by a Fraction

3 **Find $\frac{1}{8} \div \frac{3}{4}$.**

$\frac{1}{8} \div \frac{3}{4} = \frac{1}{8} \times \frac{4}{3}$ Multiply by the reciprocal, $\frac{4}{3}$.

$= \frac{1 \times \overset{1}{\cancel{4}}}{\underset{2}{\cancel{8}} \times 3}$ Divide 8 and 4 by the GCF, 4.

$= \frac{1}{6}$ Multiply numerators. Multiply demonimators.

4 **Find $3 \div \frac{1}{2}$.**

$3 \div \frac{1}{2} = \frac{3}{1} \times \frac{2}{1}$ Multiply by the reciprocal of $\frac{1}{2}$.

$= \frac{6}{1}$ or 6 Simplify.

Real-World EXAMPLE

5 **At a summer day camp, $\frac{3}{4}$ of each day is spent in group activities. There are 6 camp counselors who split their time equally as the activity leaders. What fraction of the day is each counselor the activity leader?**

Divide $\frac{3}{4}$ into 6 equal parts.

$\frac{3}{4} \div 6 = \frac{3}{4} \times \frac{1}{6}$ Multiply by the reciprocal.

$= \frac{\overset{1}{\cancel{3}}}{4} \times \frac{1}{\underset{2}{\cancel{6}}}$ Divide 3 and 6 by the GCF, 3.

$= \frac{1}{8}$ Simplify.

Each camp counselor spends $\frac{1}{8}$ of his or her day at camp as the activity leader.

Online Personal Tutor at ca.gr5math.com

CHECK What You Know

Find the reciprocal of each number. See Examples 1, 2 (p. 327)

1. $\frac{2}{3}$ **2.** $\frac{1}{7}$ **3.** $\frac{2}{5}$ **4.** 4

Divide. Write in simplest form. See Examples 3–5 (p. 328)

5. $\frac{1}{4} \div \frac{1}{2}$ **6.** $\frac{5}{6} \div \frac{1}{3}$ **7.** $2 \div \frac{1}{3}$

8. $5 \div \frac{2}{7}$ **9.** $\frac{4}{5} \div 2$ **10.** $\frac{5}{6} \div 3$

11. Mrs. Perkins has $\frac{2}{3}$ of a pan of lasagna left for dinner. She wants to divide the lasagna into 6 equal pieces for her family. What part of the original pan of lasagna will each person get?

12. Talk About It What is the reciprocal of $\frac{2}{5}$? Explain.

Practice and Problem Solving

EXTRA PRACTICE See page 672.

Find the reciprocal of each number. See Examples 1, 2 (p. 327)

13. $\frac{1}{4}$ **14.** $\frac{1}{10}$ **15.** $\frac{2}{5}$

16. $\frac{7}{9}$ **17.** 8 **18.** 1

Divide. Write in simplest form. See Examples 3–5 (p. 328)

19. $\frac{1}{8} \div \frac{1}{2}$ **20.** $\frac{1}{2} \div \frac{2}{3}$ **21.** $\frac{3}{4} \div \frac{2}{3}$ **22.** $\frac{3}{4} \div \frac{9}{10}$

23. $3 \div \frac{3}{4}$ **24.** $2 \div \frac{3}{5}$ **25.** $5 \div \frac{3}{4}$ **26.** $8 \div \frac{4}{7}$

27. $\frac{3}{5} \div 6$ **28.** $\frac{5}{6} \div 5$ **29.** $\frac{5}{8} \div 2$ **30.** $\frac{8}{9} \div 4$

31. Aida works at a kennel and uses 30-pound bags of dog food to feed the dogs. If each dog gets $\frac{2}{5}$ pound of food each day, how many dogs can she feed with one bag?

32. Measurement Jamar has a piece of plywood that is $\frac{8}{9}$ yard long. He wants to cut this into 3 equal-size pieces to use as small shelves. What is the length of each shelf?

33. Chelsea devoted $\frac{3}{8}$ of her day to run errands, exercise, visit with her friends, and go shopping. If she devotes an equal amount of time to each of these four activities, what fraction of her day is spent on each activity?

Algebra **Find the value of each expression if $a = \frac{2}{3}$, $b = \frac{3}{4}$, and $c = \frac{1}{2}$.**

34. $a \div b$

35. $b \div c - a$

36. $a \div c$

37. $c \div b + a$

Real-World PROBLEM SOLVING

Geography The table shows the approximate fraction of the total United States coastline for each coast.

United States Coastlines	
Coast	**Fraction of Total U.S. Coastline**
Arctic	$\frac{1}{10}$
Atlantic	$\frac{9}{50}$
Gulf	$\frac{3}{25}$
Pacific	$\frac{3}{5}$

Source: *The World Almanac*

38. How many times longer is the Pacific coastline than the Atlantic coastline?

39. How many times longer is the Gulf coastline than the Arctic coastline?

H.O.T. Problems

40. OPEN ENDED Create a model to explain why $\frac{1}{2} \div \frac{2}{3} = \frac{1}{2} \times \frac{3}{2} = \frac{3}{4}$.

41. FIND THE ERROR Jason and Max are solving $\frac{2}{3} \div 4$. Who is correct? Explain your reasoning.

Jason
$\frac{2}{3} \div 4 = \frac{2}{3} \times \frac{4}{1}$
$= \frac{8}{3}$ or $2\frac{2}{3}$

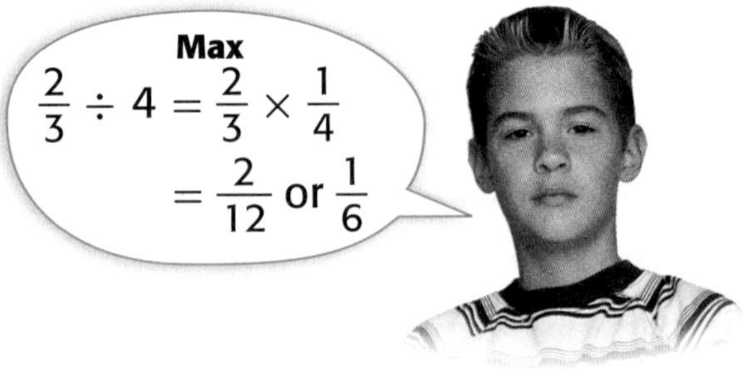

Max
$\frac{2}{3} \div 4 = \frac{2}{3} \times \frac{1}{4}$
$= \frac{2}{12}$ or $\frac{1}{6}$

CHALLENGE **Analyze each expression to find the solution mentally.**

42. $\left(\frac{2{,}345}{1{,}015} \times \frac{12}{11}\right) \div \frac{2{,}345}{1{,}015}$

43. $\left(\frac{2{,}345}{11} \times \frac{12}{1{,}015}\right) \div \frac{2{,}345}{1{,}015}$

44. WRITING IN MATH Create two real-world problems that involve the fraction $\frac{1}{2}$ and the whole number 3. One problem should involve multiplication, and the other should involve division.

Standards Practice

45 The table shows the weight factors of other planets relative to Earth. For example, an object on Jupiter is 3 times heavier than on Earth.

Planets' Weight Factors	
Planet	**Weight Factor**
Mercury	$\frac{1}{3}$
Venus	$\frac{9}{10}$
Jupiter	3

Source: factmonster.com

About how many times heavier is an object on Venus than on Mercury?

A $1\frac{3}{5}$

B $2\frac{1}{16}$

C $2\frac{7}{10}$

D $3\frac{1}{8}$

46 $\frac{5}{24} \div \frac{5}{6} =$

F 4

G $2\frac{1}{6}$

H $\frac{1}{4}$

J $\frac{25}{144}$

47 A piece of string is to be cut into equal size pieces. If the length of the string is $\frac{11}{12}$ foot long and each piece is to be $\frac{1}{24}$ foot long, how many pieces can be cut?

A 11

B 15

C 22

D 28

Spiral Review

Multiply. Write in simplest form. **(Lesson 6-9)**

48. $2\frac{2}{5} \times 3\frac{1}{3}$

49. $1\frac{5}{6} \times 2\frac{3}{4}$

50. $3\frac{3}{7} \times 2\frac{3}{8}$

51. $4\frac{4}{9} \times 5\frac{1}{4}$

52. According to a survey, 9 in 10 teens volunteer at least once a year. Of these, about $\frac{1}{3}$ help clean up their communities. What fraction of teens volunteer by helping to clean up their communities? **(Lesson 6-8)**

53. Three out of the 20 students in first period were absent today. In third period, 4 out of the 25 students were absent. In which class was there a greater fraction of the students who were absent? **(Lesson 4-7)**

For Exercises 54 and 55, refer to the table. **(Lesson 2-2)**

54. Make a line graph of the data.

55. Describe the change in the average number of tornadoes per month from January to December.

Average Number of Tornadoes per Month in the United States			
Month	**Number**	**Month**	**Number**
January	40	July	135
February	23	August	82
March	62	September	81
April	141	October	62
May	300	November	55
June	231	December	22

Source: *USA Today*

Problem Solving in History

The Statue of Liberty

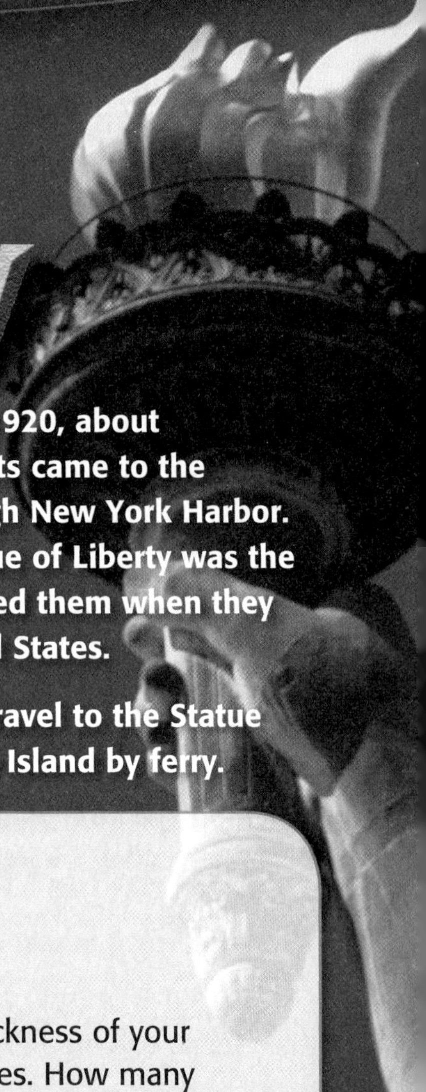

In 1886, the people of France presented the Statue of Liberty to the people of the United States. The French people gave this statue to the United States in order to honor the friendship between the two nations. This statue has become a world-wide symbol of freedom.

Between 1860 and 1920, about 25 million immigrants came to the United States through New York Harbor. After 1886, the Statue of Liberty was the first sight that greeted them when they arrived in the United States.

Today, visitors can travel to the Statue of Liberty on Liberty Island by ferry.

Real-World Math

Use the table on page 333 to solve each problem.

1. Write the total weight of the foundation in standard form.

2. How many times longer is the length of the tablet than its width? Round to the nearest hundredth.

3. The distance of the Statue of Liberty from the ground to the top of the torch is about twice as great as the distance from the top of the base to the top of the torch. How tall is the Statue from the ground to the top of the torch?

4. Measure the thickness of your textbook in inches. How many times greater is the thickness of the Statue's tablet than your textbook?

5. Ferry ticket prices for children are \$4.50 each and \$11.50 for adults. What is the total cost for a class of 20 students and 3 adults?

6. The total cost of ferry tickets for 5 senior citizens is \$47.50. How much more does an adult ferry ticket cost than a senior citizen ferry ticket?

Math Standard 5NS2.1 **Add, subtract, multiply, and divide with decimals;** add with negative integers; subtract positive integers from negative integers; and verify the reasonableness of results.

Did You Know?

When the Statue of Liberty was completed in France, it was dismantled into 350 pieces. Then it was shipped to the United States and rebuilt.

Statue of Liberty Measurements

Total Weight of the Concrete Foundation	**2.7×10^4 tons**
Length of Tablet	**7.19 meters**
Width of Tablet	**4.14 meters**
Thickness of Tablet	**24 inches**
Height from Top of Base to Top of Torch	**$151\frac{1}{12}$ feet**

Source: The National Park Service

6-11 Dividing Mixed Numbers

GET READY to Learn

Measurement Suppose you are going to cut pieces of fabric $1\frac{3}{4}$ yards long from a bolt containing $5\frac{1}{2}$ yards of fabric. The model shows that $5\frac{1}{2} \div 1\frac{3}{4}$ is about 3.

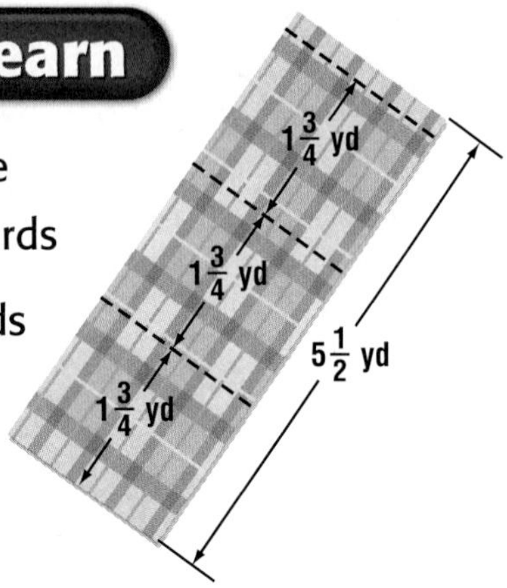

MAIN IDEA

I will divide mixed numbers.

Standard 5NS2.5 Compute and perform simple multiplication and **division of fractions and apply these procedures to solving problems.**

Dividing mixed numbers is similar to dividing fractions.

KEY CONCEPT — Dividing by Mixed Numbers

To divide by mixed numbers,

- Write the mixed numbers as improper fractions.
- Multiply by the reciprocal.
- Simplify.

EXAMPLE Divide by a Mixed Number

1 Find $5\frac{1}{2} \div 1\frac{3}{4}$.

Estimate $6 \div 2 = 3$

$5\frac{1}{2} \div 1\frac{3}{4} = \frac{11}{2} \div \frac{7}{4}$ Write mixed numbers as improper fractions.

$= \frac{11}{2} \times \frac{4}{7}$ Multiply by the reciprocal.

$= \frac{11}{\cancel{2}_1} \times \frac{\cancel{4}^2}{7}$ Divide 2 and 4 by the GCF, 2.

$= \frac{22}{7}$ or $3\frac{1}{7}$ Simplify.

Check for Reasonableness $3\frac{1}{7} \approx 3$ ✓

Online **Personal Tutor at** ca.gr5math.com

EXAMPLE Evaluate Expressions

2 Algebra **Find $m \div n$ if $m = 1\frac{3}{4}$ and $n = \frac{2}{5}$.**

$m \div n = 1\frac{3}{4} \div \frac{2}{5}$ Replace m with $1\frac{3}{4}$ and n with $\frac{2}{5}$.

$= \frac{7}{4} \div \frac{2}{5}$ Write the mixed number as an improper fraction.

$= \frac{7}{4} \times \frac{5}{2}$ Multiply by the reciprocal.

$= \frac{35}{8}$ or $4\frac{3}{8}$ Simplify.

Real-World EXAMPLE

3 A tornado traveled 100 miles in $1\frac{1}{2}$ hours. How many miles per hour did it travel? **Estimate** $100 \div 2 = 50$

$100 \div 1\frac{1}{2} = \frac{100}{1} \div \frac{3}{2}$ Write the mixed number as an improper fraction.

$= \frac{100}{1} \times \frac{2}{3}$ Multiply by the reciprocal.

$= \frac{200}{3}$ Simplify.

$= 66\frac{2}{3}$ Compare to the estimate.

So, the tornado traveled $66\frac{2}{3}$ miles per hour.

CHECK What You Know

Divide. Write in simplest form. **See Example 1 (p. 334)**

1. $3\frac{1}{2} \div 2$

2. $8 \div 1\frac{1}{3}$

3. $3\frac{1}{5} \div \frac{2}{7}$

4. Algebra What is the value of $c \div d$ if $c = \frac{3}{8}$ and $d = 1\frac{1}{2}$?
See Example 2 (p. 335)

5. Jay is cutting a roll of biscuit dough into slices that are $\frac{3}{8}$ inch thick. If the roll is $10\frac{1}{2}$ inches long, how many slices can he cut?
See Example 3 (p. 335)

6. The soccer team has $16\frac{1}{2}$ boxes of wrapping paper to sell. If selling the wrapping paper is split equally among the 12 players, how many boxes should each player sell?

7. **Talk About It** Explain how to find $6\frac{3}{4}$ divided by $\frac{1}{4}$.

Practice and Problem Solving

EXTRA PRACTICE
See page 672.

Divide. Write in simplest form. See Example 1 (p. 334)

8. $5\frac{1}{2} \div 2$ **9.** $4\frac{1}{6} \div 10$ **10.** $3 \div 4\frac{1}{2}$

11. $6 \div 2\frac{1}{4}$ **12.** $6\frac{1}{2} \div \frac{3}{4}$ **13.** $7\frac{4}{5} \div \frac{1}{5}$

14. $6\frac{1}{2} \div 3\frac{1}{4}$ **15.** $8\frac{3}{4} \div 2\frac{1}{6}$ **16.** $3\frac{3}{5} \div 1\frac{4}{5}$

17. $3\frac{3}{4} \div 5\frac{5}{8}$ **18.** $4\frac{2}{3} \div 2\frac{2}{9}$ **19.** $6\frac{3}{5} \div 2\frac{3}{4}$

Algebra Evaluate each expression if $a = 4\frac{4}{5}$, $b = \frac{2}{3}$, $c = 6$, and $d = 1\frac{1}{2}$. See Example 2 (p. 335)

20. $12 \div a$ **21.** $b \div 1\frac{2}{9}$ **22.** $a \div b$

23. $a \div c$ **24.** $c \div d$ **25.** $c \div (ab)$

26. How many $\frac{1}{4}$-pound hamburgers can be made from $2\frac{1}{2}$ pounds of ground beef?

27. Measurement Suppose you are designing the layout for your school yearbook. If a student photograph is $1\frac{3}{8}$ inches wide, how many photographs will fit across a page that is $6\frac{7}{8}$ inches wide? Assume there is no spacing between photographs.

28. How many $\frac{3}{8}$-pound bags of cashews can be made from $6\frac{3}{8}$ pounds of cashews?

29. Measurement The length of a kitchen wall is $24\frac{2}{3}$ feet long. A border will be placed along the wall of the kitchen. If the border comes in strips that are each $1\frac{3}{4}$ feet long, how many strips of border are needed?

30. In 2005, Robert Sorlie won the Iditarod Trail Sled Dog Race for the second time. He completed the 1,100-mile course in $9\frac{3}{4}$ days. How many miles did he average each day?

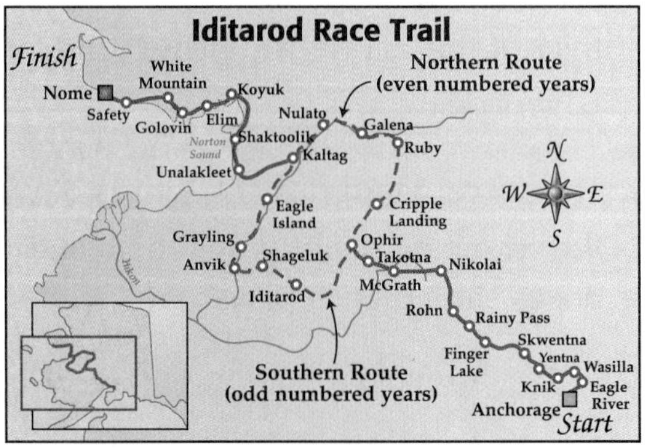

H.O.T. Problems

31. Which One Doesn't Belong? Select the expression that has a quotient less than 1. Explain your reasoning.

$2\frac{1}{2} \div 1\frac{1}{3}$ | $4\frac{1}{3} \div 2\frac{2}{5}$ | $2\frac{1}{8} \div 3\frac{1}{3}$ | $3\frac{1}{2} \div 1\frac{3}{5}$

32. CHALLENGE Decide whether $\frac{8}{10} \div 1\frac{2}{3}$ is greater than or less than $\frac{8}{10} \div 1\frac{3}{4}$. Write a convincing explanation to support your decision.

33. WRITING IN ▶MATH Explain why $2\frac{2}{3} \div \frac{1}{12} = 32$.

Standards Practice

34 The widths of 10 blooms in a test of a new marigold variety are given.

Marigold Bloom Width (in.)				
$3\frac{1}{4}$	$2\frac{3}{4}$	$2\frac{1}{2}$	$2\frac{3}{4}$	3
$3\frac{1}{4}$	$3\frac{1}{2}$	$3\frac{1}{4}$	$3\frac{1}{4}$	3

What is the average (mean) bloom width?

A $2\frac{3}{4}$ in.

B $3\frac{1}{20}$ in.

C $3\frac{1}{4}$ in.

D $3\frac{2}{5}$ in.

35 Lola used $1\frac{1}{2}$ cups of dried apricots to make $\frac{5}{6}$ of her trail mix. How many more cups of dried apricots does she need to finish making her trail mix?

F $\frac{3}{10}$ c

G $\frac{1}{2}$ c

H $\frac{5}{9}$ c

J $\frac{2}{3}$ c

Spiral Review

Measurement For Exercises 36 and 37, use the graphic at the right and the information below. **(Lesson 6-10)**

One U.S. ton equals $\frac{9}{10}$ metric ton. So, you can use $t \div \frac{9}{10}$ to convert t metric tons to U.S. tons.

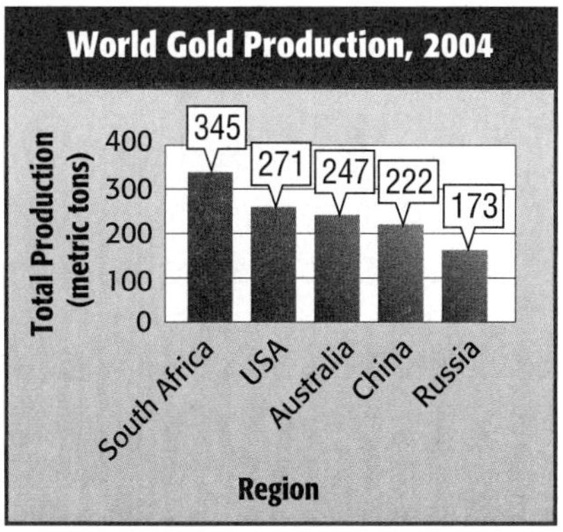

Source: World Gold Council

36. Write a division expression to represent the U.S. tons of gold that were produced in South Africa. Then simplify.

37. How many U.S. tons of gold were produced in Russia?

Multiply. Write in simplest form. **(Lesson 6-9)**

38. $\frac{4}{5} \times 1\frac{3}{4}$

39. $2\frac{5}{8} \times \frac{2}{7}$

40. $1\frac{1}{8} \times 5\frac{1}{3}$

Chapter 6 Study Guide and Review

FOLDABLES™ Study Organizer GET READY to Study

Be sure the following Key Concepts are noted in your Foldable.

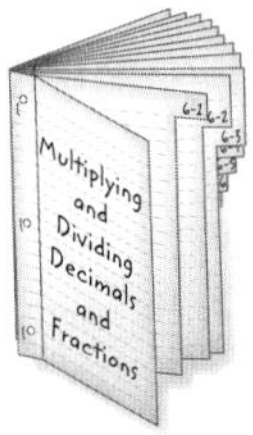

BIG Ideas

Multiplying Decimals (Lessons 6-1 and 6-2)

- When multiplying decimals, multiply with whole numbers. The product has the same number of decimal places as the sum of the number of decimal places in each factor.

Dividing Decimals (Lessons 6-4 and 6-5)

- When dividing a decimal by a decimal, change the divisor into a whole number by multiplying both the dividend and the divisor by the same power of ten. Then divide as with dividing a decimal by a whole number.

Multiplying Fractions (Lessons 6-7 to 6-9)

- To multiply fractions, multiply the numerators and multiply the denominators.
- To multiply mixed numbers, write the mixed numbers as improper fractions and then multiply as with fractions.

Dividing Fractions (Lessons 6-10 to 6-11)

- To divide by a fraction, multiply by its reciprocal.
- To divide mixed numbers, write the mixed numbers as improper fractions. Then divide as with fractions.

Key Vocabulary

compatible numbers (p. 310)
reciprocal (p. 327)
scientific notation (p. 285)

Vocabulary Check

State whether each sentence is *true* or *false*. If *false*, replace the underlined word or number to make a true sentence.

1. Any two numbers whose product is 1 are called compatible numbers.
2. Reciprocals can be used when estimating products and are numbers that are easy to divide mentally.
3. The number 3.85×10^2 is written in scientific notation.
4. The product of 9.12×0.8 will have two decimal places.
5. When rounding the quotient of a division problem to the nearest tenth, stop dividing when there is a digit in the hundredths place.
6. The reciprocal of $\frac{1}{4}$ is 4.
7. When dividing fractions, multiply the reciprocal of the first fraction.

Lesson-by-Lesson Review

6-1 Multiplying Decimals by Whole Numbers (pp. 284–287)

Example 1

Find 6.45 × 7. **Estimate** 6.45 × 7 → 6 × 7 or 42

```
 3 3
 6.45   There are two decimal places to the
×   7   right of the decimal in 6.45.
45.15   Count the same number of places
        from right to left in the product.
```

Multiply.

8. 0.082 × 17 **9.** 12.09 × 19

10. 5 × 0.048 **11.** 24.7 × 31

12. 16 × 6.65 **13.** 2.6 × 38

14. If you work 6 hours at $6.35 an hour, how much would you make?

6-2 Multiplying Decimals (pp. 290–293)

Example 2

Find 38.76 × 4.2.

```
   38.76   ← two decimal places
 ×   4.2   ← one decimal place
    7752
 + 15504
 162.792   ← three decimal places
```

Multiply.

15. 8.74 × 2.23 **16.** 0.04 × 5.1

17. 0.002 × 50 **18.** 0.04 × 0.0063

19. Measurement Find the area of the rectangle.

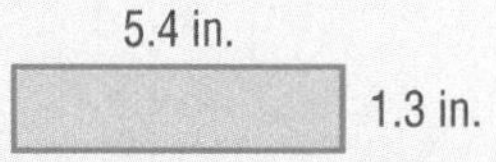

6-3 Problem-Solving Strategy: Reasonable Answers (pp. 294–295)

Example 3

There are 24 students in the Spanish club. If the number of students in the school is $19\frac{7}{8}$ times this amount, would about 400, 500, or 600 be a reasonable number of students in the school?

$24 \times 19\frac{7}{8}$ is about 25 × 20 or 500. So, 500 is a reasonable number of students in the school.

Solve. Determine which answer is reasonable.

20. Evan is $5\frac{11}{12}$ feet tall. His sister, Cindy, is $\frac{4}{5}$ of his height. Which is a reasonable height for Cindy: about 4 feet, 5 feet, or 6 feet? Explain.

21. Derek has $23.80 in his pocket. He spent about $\frac{2}{3}$ of this amount on a CD. Would $8, $16, or $20 be a reasonable price of the CD?

Study Guide and Review

6-4 Dividing Decimals by Whole Numbers (pp. 296–299)

Example 4
Find the quotient of 16.1 ÷ 7.

$$\begin{array}{r} 2.3 \\ 7\overline{)16.1} \\ -\,14 \\ \hline 2\,1 \\ -\,2\,1 \\ \hline 0 \end{array}$$

Place the decimal point.
Divide as with whole numbers.

Divide.

22. 12.24 ÷ 36 **23.** 203.84 ÷ 32

24. The cost of a banquet is to be divided equally among the 62 people attending. If the cost is $542.50, find the cost per person.

6-5 Dividing by Decimals (pp. 303–306)

Example 5
Find 11.48 ÷ 8.2.

$$8.2\overline{)11.48} \longrightarrow \begin{array}{r} 1.4 \\ 82\overline{)114.8} \\ -\,82 \\ \hline 32\,8 \\ -\,32\,8 \\ \hline 0 \end{array}$$

Divide.

25. 0.96 ÷ 0.6 **26.** 11.16 ÷ 6.2

27. The Aero Spacelines Super Guppy, a converted Boeing C-97, can carry 87.5 tons of cargo. Tanks that weigh 4.5 tons each are loaded onto the Super Guppy. What is the most number of tanks it can transport?

6-6 Problem-Solving Investigation: Choose the Best Strategy (pp. 308–309)

Example 6
Luanda is arranging three trophies on a shelf. How many ways can she arrange the trophies on the shelf?

To solve the problem, make an organized list. Use 1, 2, and 3 for the trophies.

123	132	Listing 1 first
213	231	Listing 2 first
312	321	Listing 3 first

So, there are 6 ways Luanda can arrange the trophies on a shelf.

Choose the best strategy to solve each problem.

28. Belinda has $2\frac{5}{6}$ yards of red ribbon, $4\frac{3}{4}$ yards of blue ribbon, and $1\frac{2}{3}$ yards of white ribbon. If she needs a total of 10 yards of ribbon for a project, will she have enough? Explain.

29. The sum of two even numbers is 18. Their product is 56. What are the numbers?

6-7 Estimating Products of Fractions (pp. 310–311)

Example 7

Estimate $\frac{1}{7} \times 41$.

$\frac{1}{7} \times 41 \longrightarrow \frac{1}{7} \times 42$ 42 and 7 are compatible numbers since $42 \div 7 = 6$.

$\frac{1}{7} \times 42 = 6$ $\frac{1}{7}$ of 42 is 6.

So, $\frac{1}{7} \times 41$ is *about* 6.

Estimate each product.

30. $\frac{1}{5} \times 21$

31. $10 \times 2\frac{3}{4}$

32. $\frac{5}{6} \times 13$

33. $7\frac{3}{4} \times \frac{1}{4}$

34. $4\frac{5}{6} \times 8\frac{3}{10}$

35. $\frac{3}{7} \times \frac{11}{12}$

36. The average wait time to ride the Super Coaster is 55 minutes. If Joy and her friends have waited $\frac{5}{6}$ of that time, estimate how long they have waited.

6-8 Multiplying Fractions (pp. 316–320)

Example 8

Find $\frac{3}{10} \times \frac{4}{9}$.

$\frac{3}{10} \times \frac{4}{9} = \frac{\overset{1}{\cancel{3}} \cdot \overset{2}{\cancel{4}}}{\underset{5}{\cancel{10}} \cdot \underset{3}{\cancel{9}}}$ Divide the numerator and denominator by the GCF.

$= \frac{2}{15}$ Simplify.

Multiply. Write in simplest form.

37. $\frac{1}{3} \times \frac{1}{4}$ **38.** $\frac{7}{8} \times \frac{4}{21}$ **39.** $\frac{5}{6} \times 9$

40. Half of Mr. Carson's class play a sport. Of these, two-thirds are male. What fraction of the class is male and play a sport?

6-9 Multiplying Mixed Numbers (pp. 321–324)

Example 9

Find $3\frac{1}{2} \times 4\frac{2}{3}$.

$3\frac{1}{2} \times 4\frac{2}{3} = \frac{7}{2} \times \frac{14}{3}$ Write the numbers as improper fractions.

$= \frac{7}{\underset{1}{\cancel{2}}} \times \frac{\overset{7}{\cancel{14}}}{3}$ Divide 2 and 14 by their GFC, 2.

$= \frac{49}{3}$ or $16\frac{1}{3}$ Simplify.

Multiply. Write in simplest form.

41. $\frac{2}{3} \times 4\frac{1}{2}$ **42.** $6\frac{5}{8} \times 4$ **43.** $2\frac{1}{4} \times 6\frac{2}{3}$

44. Find the area of the painting.

Study Guide and Review

6-10 Dividing Fractions (pp. 327–331)

Example 10

Find $\frac{3}{8} \div \frac{2}{3}$.

$\frac{3}{8} \div \frac{2}{3} = \frac{3}{8} \times \frac{3}{2}$ Multiply by the reciprocal of $\frac{2}{3}$.

$= \frac{9}{16}$ Multiply the numerators and multiply the denominators.

Divide. Write in simplest form.

45. $\frac{2}{3} \div \frac{4}{5}$

46. $\frac{1}{8} \div \frac{3}{4}$

47. $5 \div \frac{4}{9}$

48. $\frac{3}{8} \div 6$

49. Ashanti uses $\frac{3}{4}$ cup of oats to make cookies. This is $\frac{1}{3}$ the amount called for in the recipe. How many cups of oats are called for in the recipe?

6-11 Dividing Mixed Numbers (pp. 334–337)

Example 11

Find $5\frac{1}{2} \div 1\frac{5}{6}$.

$5\frac{1}{2} \div 1\frac{5}{6} = \frac{11}{2} \div \frac{11}{6}$ Rewrite as improper fractions.

$= \frac{11}{2} \times \frac{6}{11}$ Multiply by the reciprocal.

$= \frac{\overset{1}{\cancel{11}}}{\underset{1}{\cancel{2}}} \times \frac{\overset{3}{\cancel{6}}}{\underset{1}{\cancel{11}}}$ Divide by the GCF.

$= \frac{3}{1}$ or 3 Simplify.

Divide. Write in simplest form.

50. $2\frac{4}{5} \div 5\frac{3}{5}$

51. $8 \div 2\frac{1}{2}$

52. $4\frac{2}{3} \div 7$

53. $1\frac{1}{6} \div 3\frac{3}{4}$

54. Daniela has $1\frac{1}{2}$ pizzas to divide evenly among 6 friends. How much of a pizza will each friend get?

Chapter 6 Chapter Test

Multiply.

1. 7.8×6

2. 0.92×4

3. 12×0.034

4. 4.56×9.7

5. **STANDARDS PRACTICE** Armando and his 3 friends ordered a 4-foot sub for $25.99, 4 large drinks for $1.79 each, and a salad for $5.89. Which of the following represents the total cost, not including tax?

A $134.68

B $39.04

C $37.25

D $33.67

6. **Measurement** The speed of light is 1.86×10^5 miles per second. Write this speed in standard form.

Write in standard form.

7. 3.24×10^3

8. 0.175×10^5

Divide. Round to the nearest tenth if necessary.

9. $7.2 \div 3$

10. $0.45 \div 15$

11. $36.08 \div 8.2$

12. $10.79 \div 4.15$

13. **Algebra** Evaluate $a \div b$ if $a = 8.62$ and $b = 3.79$. Round to the nearest tenth if necessary.

14. The greyhound dog can run as fast as 39.35 miles per hour. Without calculating, would about 12, 14, or 16 be a reasonable answer for the number of miles a greyhound could run at this rate in 0.4 hour? Explain.

Estimate each product.

15. $\frac{1}{3} \times 22$

16. $3\frac{2}{3} \times 5\frac{1}{9}$

17. $\frac{7}{8} \times 39$

18. $6\frac{4}{5} \times 8\frac{1}{7}$

19. A recipe calls for $2\frac{2}{3}$ cups of flour. If Tremayne triples the recipe, how many cups of flour does he need?

Multiply. Write in simplest form.

20. $\frac{1}{4} \times \frac{4}{9}$

21. $\frac{3}{5} \times \frac{2}{9}$

22. $\frac{3}{8} \times 2\frac{2}{3}$

23. $7\frac{7}{8} \times 5\frac{1}{3}$

24. **Algebra** Evaluate $2\frac{1}{3}m$ if $m = 4\frac{5}{6}$. Write in simplest form.

25. **Measurement** To find the area of a parallelogram, use the formula $A = bh$, where b is the length of the base and h is the height. Find the area of the parallelogram.

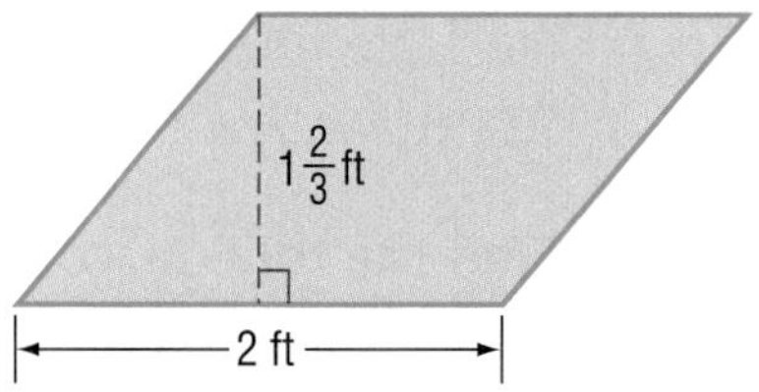

26. **STANDARDS PRACTICE** Pearl works at a kite store. To make a kite tail, she needs $2\frac{1}{4}$ feet of fabric. If Pearl has $29\frac{1}{4}$ feet of fabric, how many kite tails can she make?

F 26

G 15

H 14

J 13

Divide. Write in simplest form.

27. $\frac{1}{8} \div \frac{3}{4}$

28. $\frac{2}{5} \div 4$

29. $6 \div 1\frac{4}{5}$

30. $5\frac{3}{4} \div 1\frac{1}{2}$

31. **WRITING IN MATH** If you walk $3\frac{1}{2}$ miles per hour, how long will it take you to walk 7 miles? Explain.

CHAPTER 6 California Standards Practice

Cumulative, Chapters 1–6

Standards Example

Carlos bought 2 pairs of pants that were originally priced at \$31.50 each. Each pair of pants was on sale for \$2.97 off the original price when Carlos bought them. How much did Carlos pay for both pairs of pants?

A \$28.53 **C** \$60.03

B \$57.06 **D** \$68.94

Read the Question

You need to find how much Carlos paid for both pairs of pants.

Solve the Question

Step 1 Find the total original cost of both pants.
$\$31.50 \times 2 = \$63.00$

Step 2 Find the total discount.
$\$2.97 \times 2 = \$5.94$

Step 3 Subtract the total discount from the original cost.
$\$63.00 - \$5.94 = \$57.06$

The answer is B.

Online Personal Tutor at ca.gr5math.com

Choose the best answer.

1 **Todd bought 8 pounds of ground pork. He saved \$3.92 by using a store coupon. How much did he save per pound of pork?**

A \$0.49 **C** \$4.90

B \$3.12 **D** \$31.36

2 **A recipe calls for $1\frac{2}{3}$ cups of pumpkin. If Amy doubles the recipe, how many cups of pumpkin does she need?**

F $2\frac{1}{3}$ c **H** $3\frac{2}{3}$ c

G $3\frac{1}{3}$ c **J** $4\frac{1}{3}$ c

More California Standards Practice
For practice by standard, see pages CA1–CA27.

3 $\frac{2}{5} \div \frac{3}{4} =$

A $\frac{3}{10}$ **C** $\frac{8}{15}$

B $\frac{6}{15}$ **D** $\frac{5}{9}$

---

4 **Mr. Williams teaches science to 50 students. Two-fifths of Mr. Williams' students signed up for a field trip to the museum. About how many of Mr. Williams' students signed up to go to the museum?**

F 20 students **H** 30 students

G 25 students **J** 35 students

---

5 **Find the area of the rectangle.**

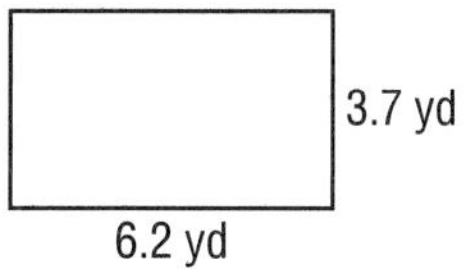

A 6.5 yd^2

B 9.4 yd^2

C 19.8 yd^2

D 22.94 yd^2

---

6 **Callie has a piece of ribbon that is 6.75 feet long. She wants to cut it into pieces that are 2.25 feet long. How many pieces of ribbon will she have?**

F 3 **H** 5

G 4 **J** 6

---

7 **Which point on the number line best represents 2.76?**

A

B
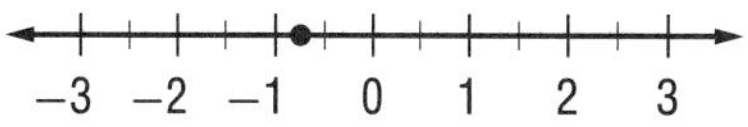

C

D
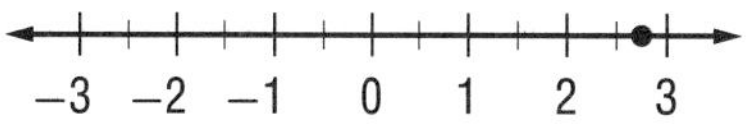

---

8 **On Monday, Jake ran $3\frac{2}{3}$ miles. Then on Wednesday, he ran $1\frac{1}{2}$ miles, and on Friday, he ran $2\frac{1}{4}$ miles. Find the total number of miles Jake ran.**

F $6\frac{1}{2}$

G $7\frac{5}{12}$

H $7\frac{1}{2}$

J $8\frac{1}{12}$

---

9 **For lunch today, Kaneesha bought a hamburger for \$2.75, a fruit cup for \$1.10, and milk for \$0.55. What was the total cost of Kaneesha's meal?**

A \$3.30

B \$3.85

C \$4.40

D \$9.35

CHAPTER 7

Algebra: Integers and Equations

BIG Idea How do you compare integers?

You can use a number line to compare integers.

Example The total height of the Empire State Building is 1,454 feet, including the lightning rod. The foundation is 55 feet below ground, which can be represented by -55. The lobby is 47 feet above ground, which can be represented by $+47$.

Since -55 is left of $+47$ on the number line, $-55 < 47$.

What will I learn in this chapter?

- Compare and order integers.
- Add, subtract, multiply, and divide integers.
- Locate and graph ordered pairs on a coordinate plane.
- Solve and write addition, subtraction, and multiplication equations.
- Solve problems by working backward.

Key Vocabulary

quadrants
inverse operations
coefficient

Math Online Student Study Tools at ca.gr5math.com

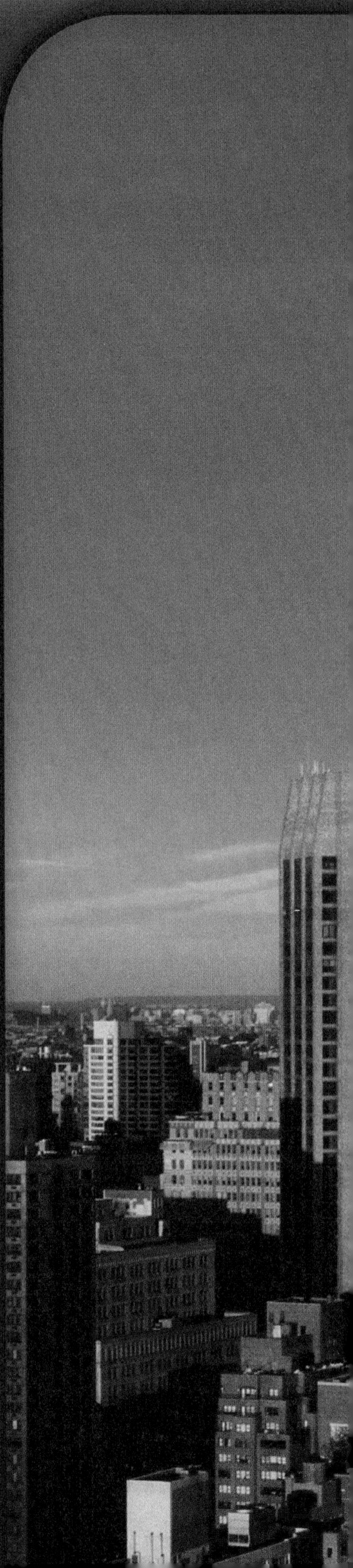

FOLDABLES™ Study Organizer

Make this Foldable to help you organize information about integers. Begin with a sheet of 11″ × 17″ paper.

1. **Fold** the short sides so they meet in the middle.

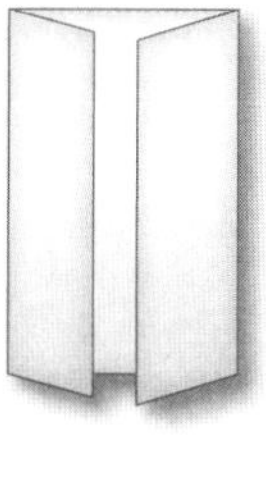

2. **Fold** the top to the bottom.

3. **Unfold** and cut along the second fold to make tabs.

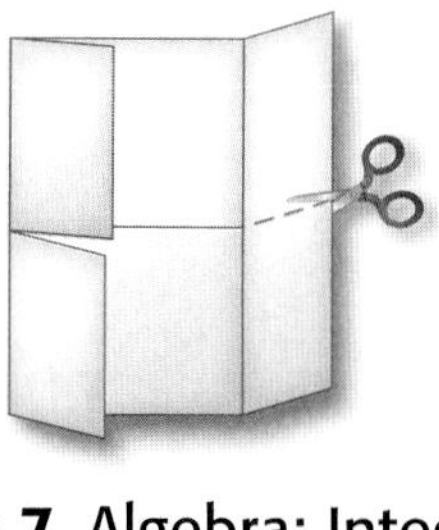

4. **Label** each tab as shown.

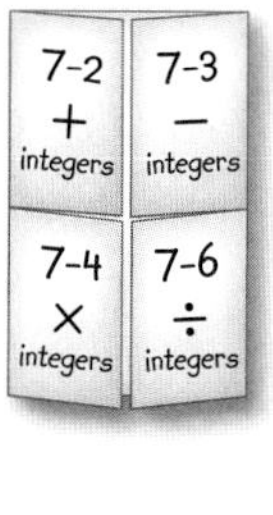

ARE YOU READY for Chapter 7?

You have two ways to check prerequisite skills for this chapter.

Option 2

Math Online Take the Chapter Readiness Quiz at ca.gr5math.com.

Option 1

Complete the Quick Check below.

QUICK Check

Add. **(Prior Grade)**

1. 12 + 15

2. 3 + 4

3. 5 + 7

4. 16 + 9

5. Kalib scored 15 points. Andrea scored 21 points. How many points did they score altogether? **(Prior Grade)**

Subtract. **(Prior Grade)**

6. 14 − 6

7. 9 − 4

8. 11 − 5

9. 8 − 3

10. Stan exercises 3 days a week. How many days during the week does he *not* exercise? **(Prior Grade)**

Multiply. **(Prior Grade)**

11. 7 × 6

12. 10 × 2

13. 5 × 9

14. 8 × 3

15. 4 × 4

16. 6 × 8

17. Marty studied 3 hours a day for five days. How many hours total did he study? **(Prior Grade)**

Divide. **(Prior Grade)**

18. 32 ÷ 4

19. 63 ÷ 7

20. 21 ÷ 3

21. 18 ÷ 9

22. 72 ÷ 9

23. 45 ÷ 3

7-1 Ordering Integers

MAIN IDEA

I will compare and order integers.

Standard 5NS1.5 Identify and **represent on a number line** decimals, fractions, mixed numbers, and **positive and negative integers.**

GET READY to Learn

Lynn, Chi, and Todd are reviewing their accounts at the school's Snack Emporium. Lynn has \$7 left in her account, Chi has \$10 left in his account, and Todd owes the Snack Emporium \$3. Who has the least money in his or her Snack Emporium account?

In Lesson 2-9, you learned that an integer is any number from the set {…−4, −3, −2, −1, 0, 1, 2, 3, 4…}. You can use a number line to compare and order integers.

Reading Math

Inequality symbols

< is less than

> is greater than

EXAMPLE Compare Integers

1 Replace ● with < or > in 12 ● −4 to make a true sentence.

Graph 12 and −4 on a number line. Then compare.

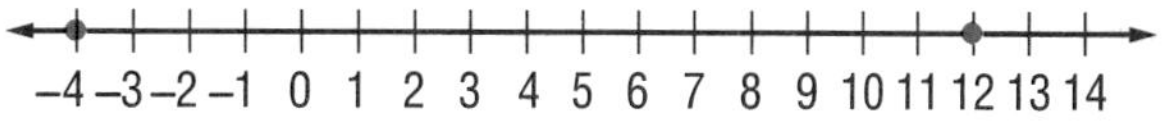

Since 12 is to the right of −4, 12 > −4.

EXAMPLES Order Integers

2 Order −9, 6, −3, and 0 from least to greatest.

Graph the numbers on a number line.

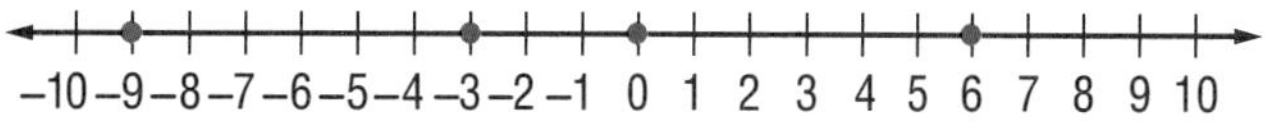

The order from least to greatest is −9, −3, 0, and 6.

Remember

When ordering integers from greatest to least, write the integers as they appear from right to left.

3 Order 8, −3, 4, and −7 from greatest to least.

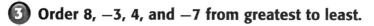

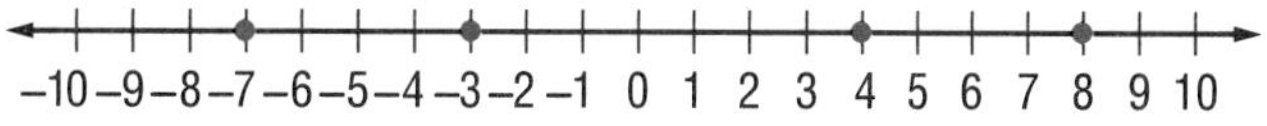

The order from greatest to least is 8, 4, −3, and −7.

Real-World EXAMPLE

4 **The average surface temperatures of Jupiter, Mars, Earth, and the Moon are given in the table. Order the temperatures from least to greatest.**

Name	Average Surface Temperature (°F)
Jupiter	−162
Moon	−10
Mars	−81
Earth	59

Source: *The World Almanac*

First, graph each integer. Then, write the integers as they appear on the number line from left to right.

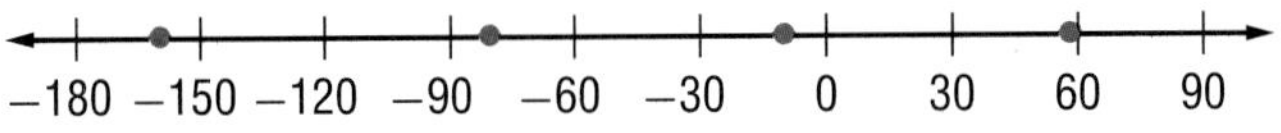

The order from least to greatest is −162°F, −81°F, −10°F, and 59°F.

Online **Personal Tutor at** ca.gr5math.com

CHECK What You Know

Replace each ● with < or > to make a true sentence. **See Example 1 (p. 349)**

1. 17 ● 31 **2.** −6 ● −10 **3.** 9 ● −8 **4.** −83 ● −38

Order each set of integers from least to greatest. **See Example 2 (p. 349)**

5. 9, −5, −13, −8, 1 **6.** 22, 4, 14, −2, 5

Order each set of integers from greatest to least. **See Example 3 (p. 349)**

7. −54, 7, −8, −14, 9, −33 **8.** −17, −16, 12, 24, −7

9. The timeline shows the years various cities were established. Which city was established after Rome, but before London? **See Example 4 (p. 350)**

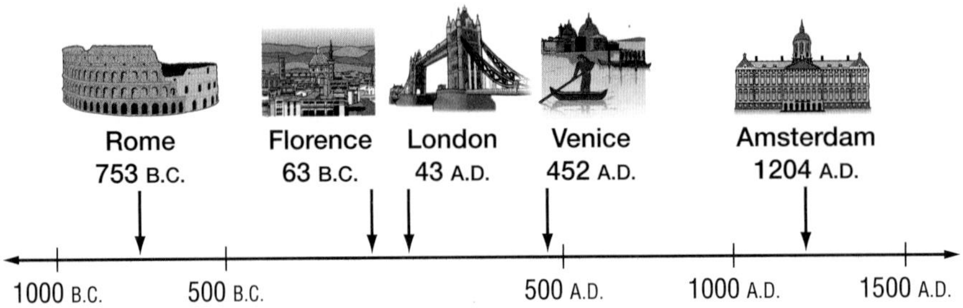

10. Talk About It Explain how you would determine that −5 is less than −1.

Practice and Problem Solving

EXTRA PRACTICE
See page 672.

Replace each ● with < or > to make a true sentence.
See Example 1 (p. 349)

11. −2 ● −4 **12.** −2 ● 4 **13.** 1 ● −3

14. −6 ● 3 **15.** 5 ● 0 **16.** −3 ● 2

Order each set of integers from least to greatest. See Example 2 (p. 349)

17. 15, 17, 21, 6, 3

18. 14, 1, 6, 23, 14, 5

19. −55, 143, 18, −79, 44, 101

20. −221, 63, 54, −89, −71, −10

21. Order 5, 33, 24, 17, and 6 from greatest to least.

22. Gary, Sindhu, and Beth are all waiting for their trains to arrive. Gary's train leaves at 5 minutes before noon, Sindhu's leaves at 25 minutes after noon, and Beth's leaves 5 minutes before Sindhu's train. Order the three by who will leave first.

23. The table indicates Xavier's cell phone use over the last four months. Positive values indicate the number of minutes he went over his allotted time, and negative values indicate the number of minutes he was under. Arrange the months from least to most minutes used.

Month	Time (min)
February	−156
March	12
April	0
May	−45

24. At the end of a round of miniature golf, James, Ravi, Cody, and Santiago had scores of 2 over par, 4 under par, 3 under par, and 6 over par, respectively. In miniature golf, the lowest score is the best score. Order the scores on a number line. Which player had the worst score? Explain your answer.

Real-World PROBLEM SOLVING

Weather **For Exercises 25–27, refer to the table.**

25. Which state had the lowest temperature?

26. Arrange the given states from least to greatest temperature.

27. What is the median coldest recorded temperature for the states listed in the table?

Coldest Temperature on Record (°F)

Alaska	−80
California	−45
Florida	−2
Ohio	−39
Montana	−70
Texas	−23

Source: *The World Almanac*

H.O.T. Problems

28. OPEN ENDED Describe a real–world situation in which integers are compared or ordered.

29. NUMBER SENSE Explain why any negative number is less than any positive number.

30. CHALLENGE Order the fractions $-\frac{1}{2}, \frac{5}{2}, -\frac{12}{4}, \frac{1}{6}$, and $\frac{7}{8}$ from least to greatest.

31. WRITING IN ▶MATH In your own words, explain how to list integers from greatest to least.

Standards Practice

32 The table shows the temperatures for a four-day period.

Temperature (°F)	
Monday	−7
Tuesday	8
Wednesday	−2
Thursday	−1

Which list shows the temperatures from least to greatest?

A 8, −2, −1, −7

B 8, −1, −2, −7

C −7, −2, −1, 8

D −7, −1, −2, 8

33 Verónica (V) was 12 minutes early to class, Deshawn (D) was right on time, and Kendis (K) was 3 minutes late. Which time line represents the students' arrival to class?

F

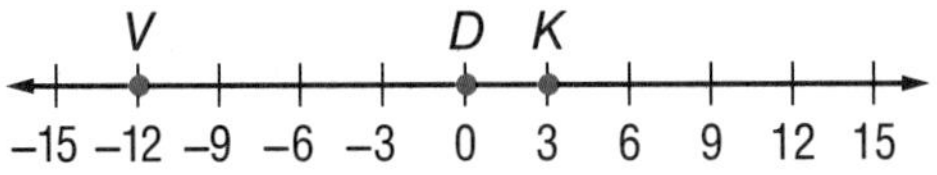

G

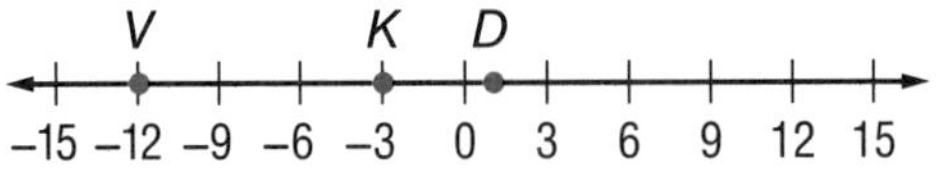

H

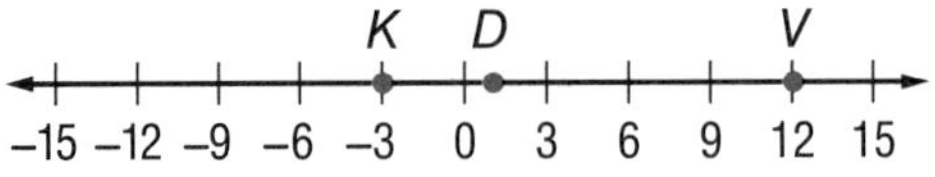

J

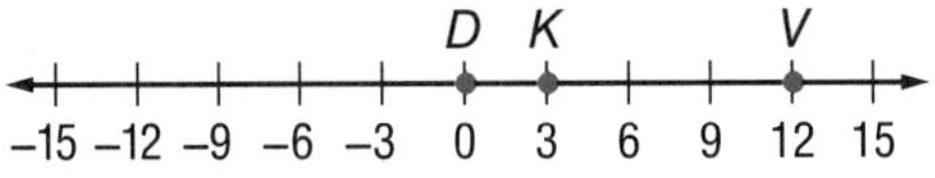

Spiral Review

Divide. Write in simplest form. **(Lesson 6-11)**

34. $6\frac{3}{4} \div \frac{1}{8}$

35. $8\frac{2}{3} \div \frac{6}{4}$

36. $\frac{4}{5} \div \frac{2}{3}$

37. $3\frac{2}{3} \div 7$

38. Dayna is making bows to decorate for the fall dance. If she has 10 yards of ribbon and each bow requires $\frac{3}{8}$ of a yard of ribbon, how many ribbons can she make? **(Lesson 6-10)**

Add or subtract. Write in simplest form. **(Lesson 5-7)**

39. $2\frac{1}{4} + \frac{3}{4}$

40. $5\frac{2}{3} - 3\frac{1}{3}$

41. $2\frac{2}{5} - \frac{3}{5}$

42. $3\frac{3}{8} + 1\frac{6}{8}$

Explore

Math Lab for 7-2
Zero Pairs

MAIN IDEA

I will use models to understand zero pairs.

Standard 5MR2.3 Use a variety of methods, such as words, numbers, symbols, charts, graphs, tables, diagrams, and **models, to explain mathematical reasoning.**

Standard 5NS2.1 Add, subtract, multiply, and divide with decimals; **add with negative integers**; subtract positive integers from negative integers; and verify the reasonableness of results.

New Vocabulary

zero pair

Counters can be used to help you understand integers. A yellow counter represents the integer +1. A red counter represents the integer −1. When one yellow counter is paired with one red counter, the result is zero. This pair of counters is called a **zero pair**.

ACTIVITY

1 Use counters to model +4 and −4. Then form as many zero pairs as possible to find the sum +4 + (−4).

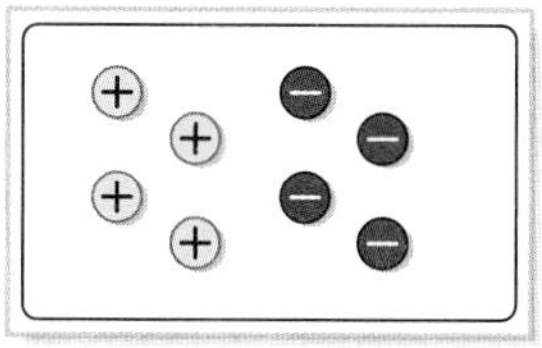

Place four yellow counters on the mat to represent +4. Then place four red counters on the mat to represent −4.

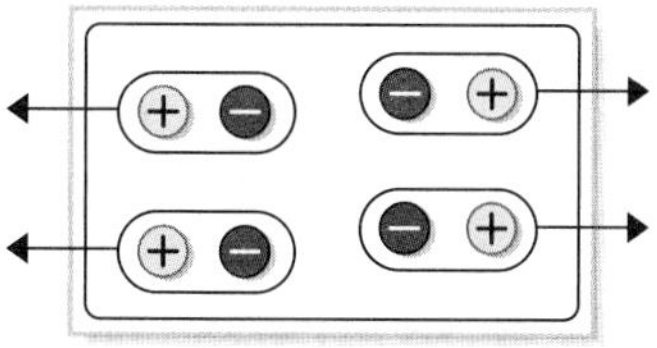

Pair the positive and negative counters. Then remove all zero pairs.

There are no counters on the mat. So, +4 + (−4) = 0.

CHECK What You Know

Use counters to model each pair of integers. Then form zero pairs to find the sum of the integers.

a. +3, −3 **b.** +5, −5 **c.** −7, +7

Analyze the Results

1. What is the value of a zero pair? Explain your reasoning.

2. Suppose there are 5 zero pairs on an integer mat. What is the value of these zero pairs? Explain.

3. Explain the effect of removing a zero pair from the mat. What effect does this have on the remaining counters?

4. Integers like +4 and −4 are called opposites. What is the sum of any pair of opposites?

5. How do you think you could find +5 + (−2) using counters?

7-2 Adding Integers

GET READY to Learn

Viviana and Conner are playing a board game. The cards Viviana selected on each of her first three turns are shown in order from left to right. After Viviana's third turn, her game piece is $+5 + (+6) + (-3)$ spaces from the start.

MAIN IDEA

I will add integers.

Standard 5NS2.1 Add, subtract, multiply, and divide with decimals; **add with negative integers;** subtract positive integers from negative integers; and verify the reasonableness of results.

To add integers, you can use counters or a number line.

EXAMPLES Add Integers with the Same Sign

1 Find $+3 + (+2)$.

One Way: Use counters.	**Another Way:** Use a number line.
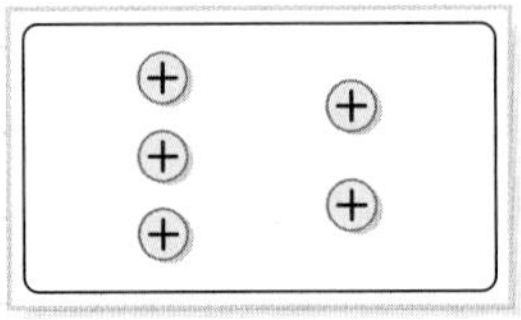	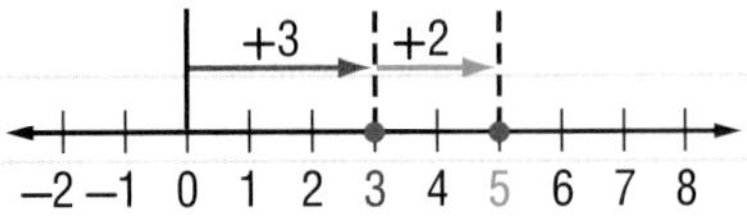

So, $+3 + (+2) = +5$ or 5.

2 Find $-2 + (-4)$.

One Way: Use counters.	**Another Way:** Use a number line.
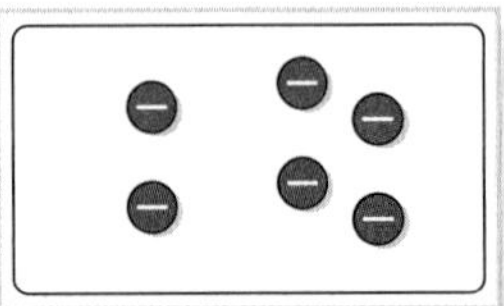	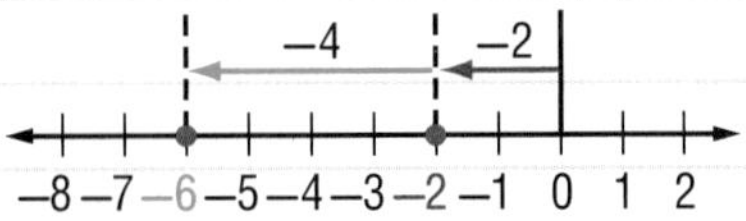

So, $-2 + (-4) = -6$.

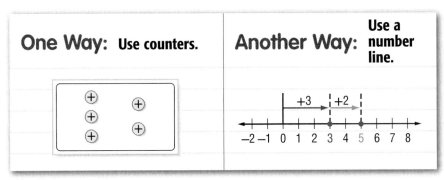

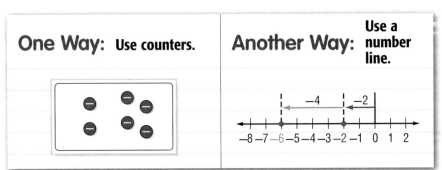

Online Personal Tutor at ca.gr5math.com

To add two integers with different signs, it is necessary to remove any zero pairs. A *zero pair* is a pair of counters that includes one positive counter and one negative counter.

EXAMPLE **Add Integers with Different Signs**

3 **Find −8 + 6.**

Remember

A number without a sign is assumed to be positive.

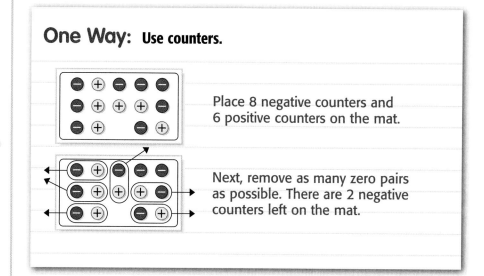

One Way: **Use counters.**

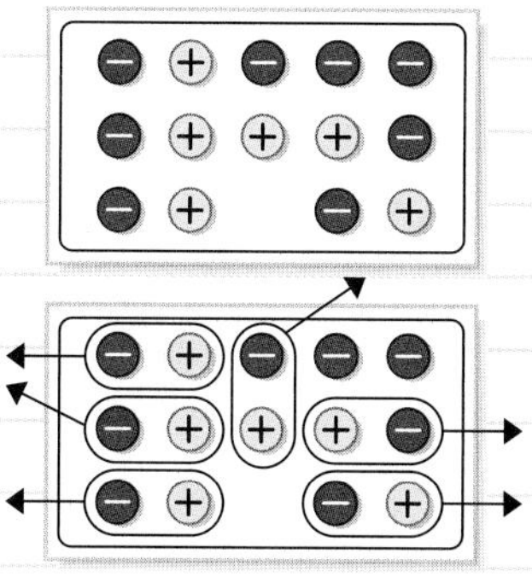

Place 8 negative counters and 6 positive counters on the mat.

Next, remove as many zero pairs as possible. There are 2 negative counters left on the mat.

Another Way: **Use a number line.**

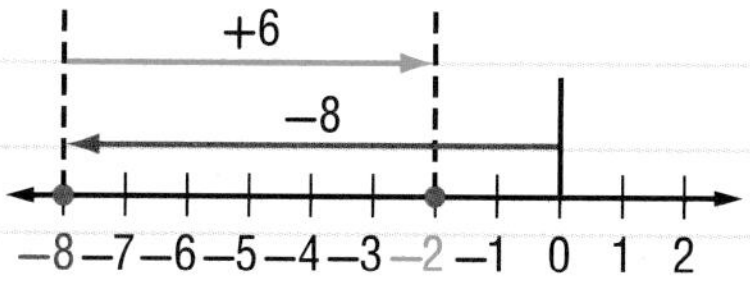

Start at 0. Move 8 units to the left to show −8. From there, move 6 units right to show +6. You end at −2.

So, $-8 + 6 = -2$.

The following rules are often helpful when adding integers.

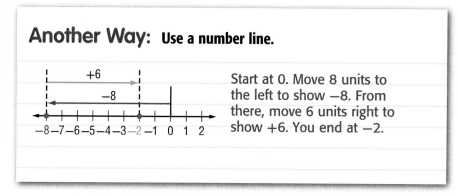

KEY CONCEPT — **Add Integers**

Words	The sum of two positive integers is always positive. The sum of two negative integers is always negative.		
Examples	$5 + 1 = 6$	$-5 + (-1) = -6$	
Words	The sum of a positive integer and a negative integer is sometimes positive, sometimes negative, and sometimes zero.		
Examples	$5 + (-1) = 4$	$-5 + 1 = -4$	$-5 + 5 = 0$

CHECK What You Know

Add. See Examples 1–3 (pp. 354–355)

1. $+3 + (+1)$

2. $4 + (+2)$

3. $-3 + (-5)$

4. $-6 + (-4)$

5. $+2 + (-5)$

6. $-4 + 9$

7. You and a friend are playing a game. The scores for the games played so far are shown at the right. If the player with the most points wins, who is winning? See Example 3 (p. 355)

Game	You	Friend
1	+10	+8
2	−5	−10
3	+15	+13

8. Talk About It Does $-3 + 6$ have a positive or a negative sum? Explain.

Practice and Problem Solving

EXTRA PRACTICE
See page 673.

Add. See Examples 1–3 (pp. 354–355)

9. $+2 + (+1)$

10. $+5 + (+1)$

11. $6 + (+2)$

12. $3 + (+4)$

13. $+8 + 3$

14. $+9 + 4$

15. $-4 + (-1)$

16. $-5 + (-4)$

17. $-2 + (-4)$

18. $-3 + (-3)$

19. $-2 + (-3)$

20. $-6 + (-10)$

21. $-7 + (+5)$

22. $-3 + (+3)$

23. $-2 + 6$

24. $-12 + 7$

25. $15 + (-6)$

26. $8 + (-18)$

For Exercises 27 and 28, write an addition problem that represents the situation. Then solve. See Examples 2, 3 (pp. 354–355)

27. The temperature outside is −5°F. If the temperature drops 4 degrees, what temperature will it be?

28. A scuba diver descends 25 feet below the surface of the water and then swims 12 feet up toward the surface. What is the location of the diver?

29. Algebra Evaluate $a + b$ if $a = 7$ and $b = -3$.

30. Algebra Evaluate $a + b$ if $a = -9$ and $b = 4$.

Add.

31. $12 + 13 + (-4)$

32. $5 + (-8) + (-7) + 11$

33. $5 + 2 + (-8) + (-3) + 9$

34. $3 + (-5) + 7 + 0 + (-2)$

35. Jeff's golf score was 5 strokes less than Mike's golf score. Mike's score was 2 strokes more than Sam's. If Sam's score relative to par was +2, what was Jeff's golf score relative to par?

36. The table shows the yards gained or yards lost on each of the first three plays of a football game. What is the total number of yards gained or lost on the three plays?

Play	Yards Lost or Gained
1	+8
2	−3
3	+2

37. Lakin is painting his grandmother's house. He climbs 10 feet up the ladder. Then he climbs down 8 feet and then ascends another 7 feet. What is Lakin's location?

Copy and complete each function table.

38.

x	$y = x + 3$
−5	■
−2	■
0	■

39.

x	$y = x + 7$
−10	■
−1	■
8	■

40.

x	$y = x + (-4)$
−3	■
0	■
12	■

H.O.T. Problems

41. OPEN ENDED Write two different addition sentences with sums that are each −10.

NUMBER SENSE Tell whether each sum is *positive, negative,* or *zero* without adding.

42. −8 + (−8)

43. −2 + 2

44. 6 + (+6)

45. −5 + 2

46. −3 + 8

47. −2 + (−6)

CHALLENGE For Exercises 48 and 49, write an addition sentence that satisfies each statement.

48. All addends are negative integers, and the sum is −7.

49. At least one addend is a positive integer, and the sum is −7.

50. **WRITING IN MATH** Explain how a number line can be used to model adding positive and negative integers. Relate this to a real-world situation.

Standards Practice

51 Which expression is represented by the model?

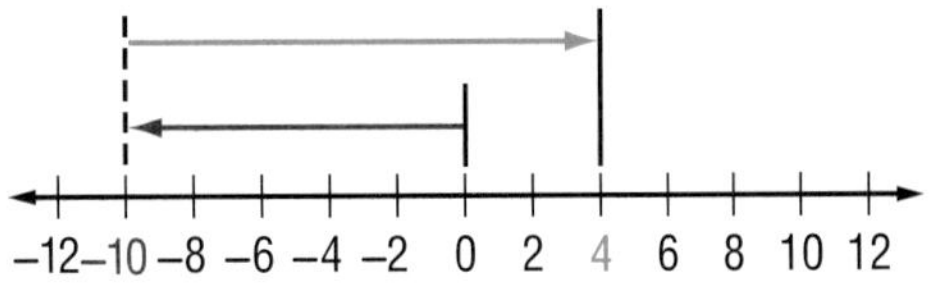

A $0 + (-4)$

B $-10 + 4$

C $-14 + 10$

D $-10 + 14$

52 Find the sum of 7 and (−3).

F 10 **H** −4

G 4 **J** −10

53 Which table represents x and y values in which $y = x + 25$?

A

x	y
−15	40
0	25

B

x	y
−10	15
0	25

C

x	y
5	20
8	33

D

x	y
10	20
20	5

Spiral Review

54. Jacqui's score on the biology test was the average score for her class. Marquez's score was three points above the average, Melanie's score was 10 points below the average, and Len's score was 5 points above the average. Write the scores as integers and order them from least to greatest. **(Lesson 7-1)**

Divide. (Lesson 6-11)

55. $3\frac{3}{4} \div 4\frac{1}{2}$ **56.** $1\frac{2}{5} \div 1\frac{3}{8}$ **57.** $5\frac{4}{3} \div \frac{4}{5}$ **58.** $6\frac{1}{6} \div 2\frac{1}{3}$

Replace each ● with <, > or = to make a true sentence. (Lesson 4-7)

59. $\frac{3}{24}$ ● $\frac{2}{8}$ **60.** $\frac{5}{7}$ ● $\frac{4}{20}$ **61.** $\frac{13}{11}$ ● $1\frac{1}{3}$ **62.** $2\frac{3}{10}$ ● $\frac{21}{4}$

63. Hunter likes to make sandwiches for his lunch. He can choose among ham, turkey, salami, and roast beef and white, rye, or wheat bread. If he makes a different sandwich everyday, how many days will it be before he makes the same sandwich? **(Lesson 4-2)**

64. LaTasha is going on a rappelling trip with some friends. They're going to rappel down a 50-foot cliff, a 180-foot cliff, a 90-foot tower, and a 200-foot canyon. What is the average height they are going to rappel? **(Lesson 2-6)**

7-3 Subtracting Integers

MAIN IDEA

I will subtract integers.

Standard 5NS2.1 Add, subtract, multiply, and divide with decimals; add with negative integers; **subtract positive integers from negative integers;** and verify the reasonableness of results.

GET READY to Learn

Hands-On Mini Lab

The number line below models the subtraction problem $-3 - 4$.

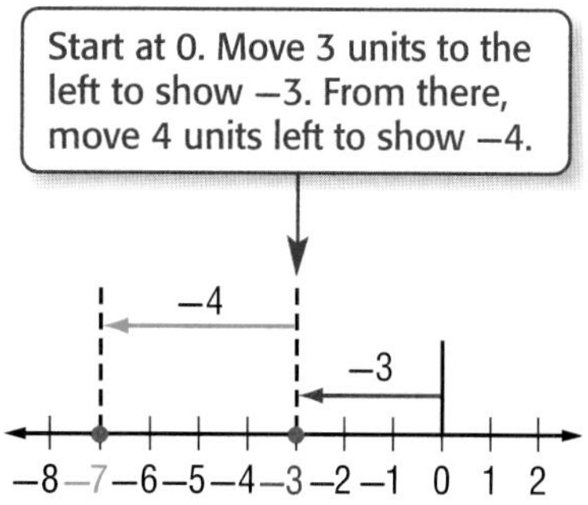

Start at 0. Move 3 units to the left to show −3. From there, move 4 units left to show −4.
−4
−3
−8 −7 −6 −5 −4 −3 −2 −1 0 1 2

$$-3 - 4 = -7$$

1. Use a number line to model $-3 + (-4)$.

2. Compare this model to the model for $-3 - 4$. How is $-3 - 4$ related to $-3 + (-4)$?

The Mini Lab shows that when you subtract a number, the result is the same as adding the opposite of the number.

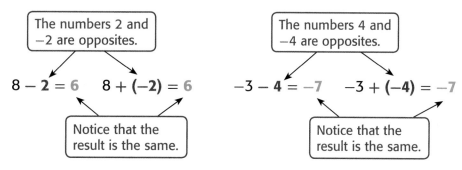

The numbers 2 and −2 are opposites.

$8 - \mathbf{2} = 6$ $\quad$ $8 + \mathbf{(-2)} = 6$

Notice that the result is the same.

The numbers 4 and −4 are opposites.

$-3 - \mathbf{4} = -7$ $\quad$ $-3 + \mathbf{(-4)} = -7$

Notice that the result is the same.

Review Vocabulary

Opposites numbers that are the same distance from zero in opposite directions; *Example:* 4 and −4 **(Lesson 2-10)**

To subtract integers, you can use counters or the following rule.

KEY CONCEPT — **Subtract Integers**

Words To subtract an integer, add its opposite.

Examples
$5 - 2 = 5 + (-2)$
$-3 - 4 = -3 + (-4)$
$-1 - (-2) = -1 + 2$

Remember

In Example 1, you can check $3 - 1 = 2$ by adding. $2 + 1 = 3$ ✓
In Example 2, you can check $-2 - 3 = -5$ by adding. $-5 + 3 = -2$ ✓

EXAMPLE Subtract Positive Integers

1 Find $3 - 1$.

One Way: **Use counters.**

Place 3 positive counters on the mat to show +3. Then, remove 1 counter.

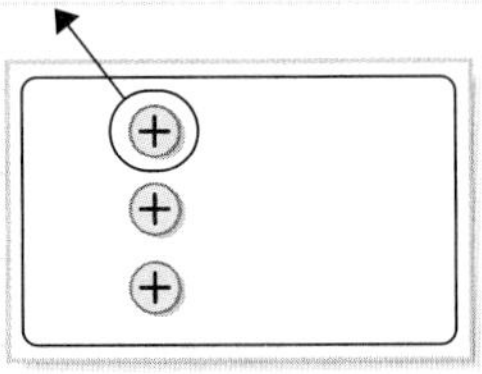

Another Way: **Add the opposite.**

To subtract 1, add -1.

$3 - 1 = 3 + (-1)$

$= 2$

So, $3 - 1 = 2$.

Remember

When you add zero pairs, the value represented by the counters on the mat does not change.

Sometimes you need to add zero pairs before you can subtract.

EXAMPLE Subtract Integers

2 Find $-2 - 3$.

One Way: **Use counters and zero pairs.**

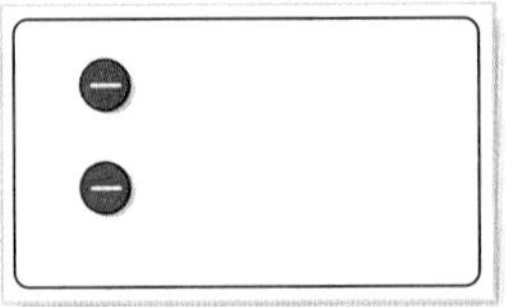

Place 2 negative counters on the mat to show -2.

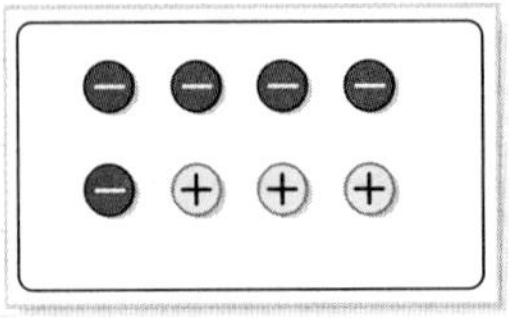

There are no positive counters on the mat. Add 3 zero pairs to get some positive counters on the mat.

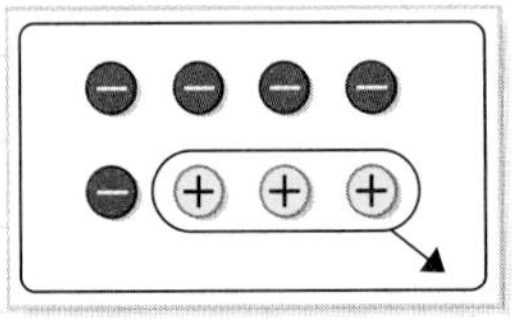

Now to subtract 3, remove 3 positive counters. This leaves 5 negative counters.

Remember

The number line shows that $-2 - 3 = -5$.

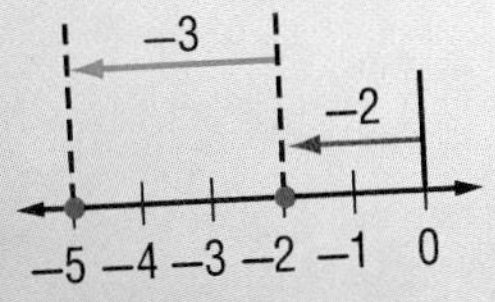

Another Way: **Add the opposite.**

$-2 - 3 = -2 + (-3)$ *To subtract 3, add -3.*
$= -5$

So, $-2 - 3 = -5$.

EXAMPLE Subtract Negative Integers

3 **Find $-5 - (-3)$.**

One Way: **Use counters.**

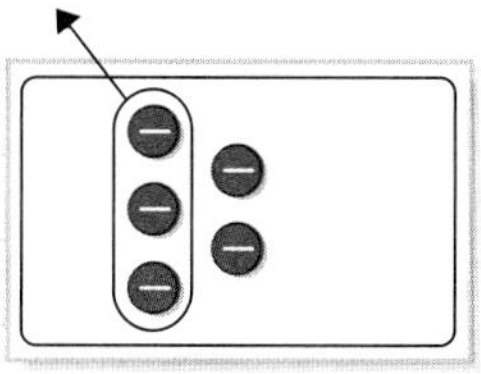

Place 5 negative counters on the mat to show -5. Then, remove 3 of the negative counters. This leaves 2 negative counters.

Another Way: **Add the opposite.**

$-5 - (-3) = -5 + 3$ *To subtract -3, add 3.*
$= -2$

So, $-5 - (-3) = -2$.

Math Online **Personal Tutor at** ca.gr5math.com

Real-World EXAMPLE

4 **Matt and Isabel are contestants on a game show. Currently, Isabel has 13 points and Matt has −7 points. How many more points does Isabel have than Matt?**

Subtract Matt's score from Isabel's.

$13 - (-7) = 13 + 7$ To subtract −7, add 7.
$= 20$ Simplify.

Isabel has 20 more points than Matt.

CHECK What You Know

Subtract. See Examples 1–3 (pp. 360–361)

1. $7 - 5$ **2.** $+4 - 1$ **3.** $-1 - 5$

4. $-2 - (-3)$ **5.** $-9 - (-4)$ **6.** $-6 - (-6)$

7. Rodney receives \$20 every month for his allowance. He owes his brother \$13. After Rodney pays back his brother, how much of his allowance will he have left? See Example 4 (p. 361)

8. Talk About It Is the value of $7 - (-6)$ the same as the value of $7 + 6$? Explain.

Practice and Problem Solving

EXTRA PRACTICE See page 673.

Subtract. See Examples 1–3 (pp. 360–361)

9. $8 - 3$ **10.** $6 - 5$ **11.** $11 - 7$

12. $15 - 8$ **13.** $+6 - 2$ **14.** $+8 - 1$

15. $-7 - 9$ **16.** $-6 - 2$ **17.** $-4 - 2$

18. $-5 - 4$ **19.** $-12 - 3$ **20.** $-15 - 5$

21. $-7 - (-5)$ **22.** $-8 - (-4)$ **23.** $-10 - (-5)$

24. $-9 - (-6)$ **25.** $-9 - (-9)$ **26.** $-2 - (-2)$

27. Time zones all over the world base their standard time on their distance from Greenwich, England. Any time zone east of Greenwich is behind GMT (Greenwich Mean Time). Any time zone west of Greenwich is ahead. The table shows certain cities' time in relation to GMT. What is the difference in time between Paris and Los Angeles?

City	Time (hours)
New York	−5
Tokyo	+8
Los Angeles	−5
Paris	+1

28. Statistics For a class project, Mykia recorded the outside temperature for five nights. Find the range of his data: −5°F, 12°F, −11°F, 4°F, and 0°F.

29. Colleen's bank subtracts a positive number from her account balance when she makes a withdrawal and adds a positive number when she deposits money. The table shows her account activity over the last month. If she started the month with \$500, how much does she have now?

Week	Deposits	Withdrawals
1		\$45
2		\$75
3	\$200	
4		\$115

H.O.T. Problems

30. OPEN ENDED Write a subtraction sentence that contains two integers in which the result is -3.

31. Which One Doesn't Belong? Identify the expression that does not belong with the other three. Explain your reasoning.

$-6 - (-4)$ $-6 + 4$ $4 - 6$ $-4 + 6$

CHALLENGE For Exercises 32–35, tell whether each statement is *sometimes, always,* or *never* true. Give an example or a counterexample for each.

32. positive − positive = positive

33. negative − negative = negative

34. negative − positive = negative

35. positive − negative = negative

36. WRITING IN ▸MATH Explain how $6 - 3$ is related to $6 + (-3)$.

Standards Practice

37 Which equation represents the relationship of the *x* and *y* values in the table below?

x	*y*
−7	−14
−5	−12
0	−7
8	1

A $x = y - 7$

B $y = x - 7$

C $x = y + 7$

D $y = x + 7$

38 If $t = 12$, what is the value of $9 - t$?

F 21

G 3

H −3

J −21

Spiral Review

Add. **(Lesson 7-2)**

39. $3 + (-4)$

40. $4 + (-4)$

41. $-2 + (-3)$

42. Order −6, 2, 0, −2, and 4 on the same number line. **(Lesson 7-1)**

43. Cristiano and four of his friends are going to play paintball this weekend. The total cost of their trip will be $118.75. If they split the total evenly, how much will the trip cost each person? **(Lesson 6-4)**

44. Statistics Find the mean of the following shoe sizes: 11, 10, 15, 9, 17, 12, and 10. **(Lesson 2-6)**

7-4 Multiplying Integers

MAIN IDEA

I will multiply integers.

Preparation for Standard

6NS2.3 Solve addition, subtraction, **multiplication,** and division **problems, including those arising in concrete situations, that use positive and negative integers and combinations of these operations.**

GET READY to Learn

Concepts in Motion

Interactive Lab
ca.gr5math.com

Hands-On Mini Lab

Just as 3×2 means 3 groups of 2, $3 \times (-2)$ means 3 groups of (-2). Place 3 sets of 2 negative counters on the mat.

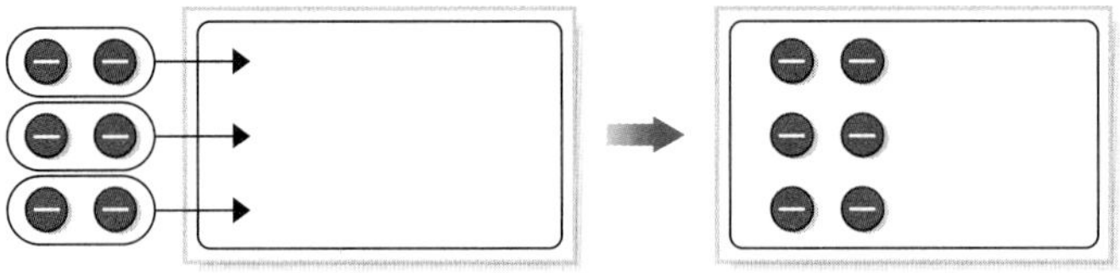

$3 \times (-2) = -6$

1. Use counters to find $4 \times (-3)$ and $5 \times (-2)$.
2. What is the sign of the product of a positive and negative integer?

To find the sign of products like -3×2 and $-3 \times (-2)$, you can use patterns.

$3 \times 2 = 6$
$2 \times 2 = 4$
$1 \times 2 = 2$
$0 \times 2 = 0$
$-1 \times 2 = -2$
$-2 \times 2 = -4$
$-3 \times 2 = \blacksquare$

By extending the number pattern, you find that $-3 \times 2 = -6$.

$3 \times (-2) = -6$
$2 \times (-2) = -4$
$1 \times (-2) = -2$
$0 \times (-2) = 0$
$-1 \times (-2) = 2$
$-2 \times (-2) = 4$
$-3 \times (-2) = \blacksquare$

By extending the number pattern, you find that $-3 \times (-2) = 6$.

To multiply integers, the following rules apply.

KEY CONCEPT — **Multiply Integers**

Words	The product of two integers with different signs is negative.	
Examples	$3 \times (-2) = -6$	$-3 \times 2 = -6$
Words	The product of two integers with the same sign is positive.	
Examples	$3 \times 2 = 6$	$-3 \times (-2) = 6$

Remember

When multiplying by a negative integer, you can check your answer by using repeated addition. For example:
$4 \times (-2) = (-2) + (-2) + (-2) + (-2) = -8$

EXAMPLES Multiply Integers with Different Signs

Multiply.

1 $4 \times (-2)$

$4 \times (-2) = -8$ The integers have different signs. The product is negative.

2 -8×3

$-8 \times 3 = -24$ The integers have different signs. The product is negative.

EXAMPLES Multiply Integers with Same Signs

Multiply.

3 4×8

$4 \times 8 = 32$ The integers have the same sign. The product is positive.

4 $-5 \times (-6)$

$-5 \times (-6) = 30$ The integers have the same sign. The product is positive.

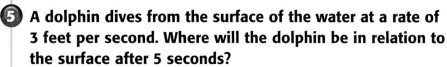

Real-World EXAMPLE

5 **A dolphin dives from the surface of the water at a rate of 3 feet per second. Where will the dolphin be in relation to the surface after 5 seconds?**

To find the location of the dolphin after 5 seconds, you can multiply 5 by the amount of change per second, −3 feet.

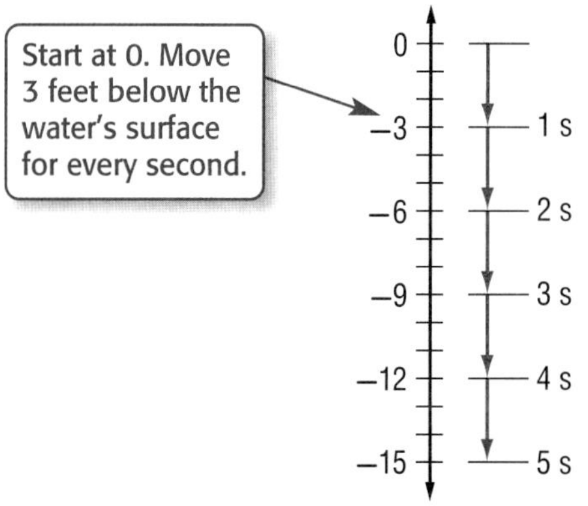

$5 \times (-3) = -15$

So, after 5 seconds, the dolphin will be −15 feet from the surface or 15 feet *below* the surface.

Online Personal Tutor at ca.gr5math.com

CHECK What You Know

Multiply. See Examples 1–4 (p. 365)

1. $4 \times (-7)$ **2.** $8(-7)$ **3.** 4×4

4. $9(3)$ **5.** $-1 \times (-7)$ **6.** $-7(-6)$

7. For each kilometer above Earth's surface, the temperature decreases 7°C. If the temperature at Earth's surface is 0°C, what will the temperature be 2 kilometers above the surface? See Example 5 (p. 365)

8. Talk About It: What are two integers that would have a negative product?

Practice and Problem Solving

EXTRA PRACTICE See page 673.

Multiply. See Examples 1–4 (p. 365)

9. $6 \times (-6)$ **10.** $9 \times (-1)$ **11.** $7(-3)$ **12.** $2(-10)$

13. -7×5 **14.** -2×9 **15.** $-5(6)$ **16.** $-6(9)$

17. 8×7 **18.** $9(4)$ **19.** $-5 \times (-8)$ **20.** $-9 \times (-7)$

21. 12×7 **22.** 9×5 **23.** $-6(-10)$ **24.** $-1(-9)$

25. A school district loses 30 students per year due to student transfers. If this pattern continues for the next 4 years, what will be the loss in relation to the original enrollment?

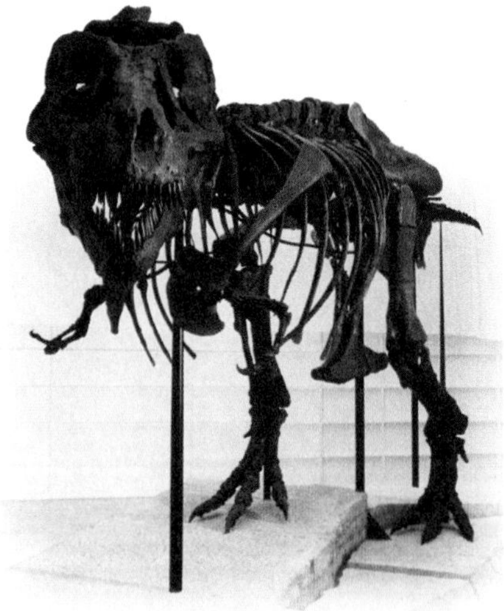

26. In 1990, Sue Hendrickson found the T-Rex fossil that now bears her name. To excavate the fossil, her team had to remove about 3 cubic meters of dirt each day from the site. Write an integer to represent the change in the amount of soil at the site at the end of 5 days.

Algebra For Exercises 27 and 28, find the next two numbers in the pattern. Then describe the pattern.

27. 2, –4, 8, –16, … **28.** –2, –6, –18, –54, …

Multiply.

29. $3(-4 - 7)$ **30.** $-2(3)(-4)$ **31.** $-4[5 + (-9)]$

32. On Wednesday morning, the temperature dropped 4°F every hour for 5 hours. If the temperature was 11°F before it started dropping, what was the temperature after 5 hours?

H.O.T. Problems

33. **OPEN ENDED** Write two sets of integers that have the same negative product.

REASONING **Decide whether each sentence is *sometimes, always,* or *never* true. Provide an example or counterexample for each.**

34. The product of two positive integers is negative.

35. A negative integer multiplied by a negative integer is positive.

36. **CHALLENGE** What is the sign of the product of three negative numbers? What is the sign of the product of four negative numbers? Justify your reasoning.

37. **WRITING IN MATH** Write a problem about a real-world situation in which you would multiply integers.

Standards Practice

38 A rock climber descended from the top of a rock at a rate of 4 meters per minute. Where will the rock climber be in relation to the top of the rock after 8 minutes?

A -8 m

B -12 m

C -32 m

D -48 m

39 Which equation was used to create the function table below?

x	y
−2	−8
−6	−24
10	40
15	60

F $y = x + 10$

G $y = x - 10$

H $y = -4x$

J $y = 4x$

Spiral Review

Subtract. **(Lesson 7-3)**

40. $9 - 2$ **41.** $+3 - 1$ **42.** $-5 - 10$ **43.** $-7 - 6$

Add. **(Lesson 7-2)**

44. $-7 + 2$ **45.** $+4 + (-3)$ **46.** $-2 + (-2)$ **47.** $7 + (-8)$

48. **Statistics** The table shows the scores for the last day for the top five players of a recent LPGA Championship. Find the median of the data. **(Lessons 7-1 and 2-7)**

Players	Score
Annika Sorenstam	+1
Shi Hyun Ahn	−5
Grace Park	−3
Angela Stanford	0
Gloria Park	0

Source: womenssportsnet.com

49. Estimate the product of $\frac{3}{4}$ and 37. **(Lesson 6-7)**

7-5 Problem-Solving Strategy

MAIN IDEA I will solve problems by working backward.

Standard 5MR1.1 Analyze problems by identifying relationships, ... and observing patterns. **Standard 5NS2.1 Add, subtract,** multiply, and divide **with decimals; add with negative integers;** subtract positive integers from negative integers; and verify the reasonableness of results.

Paco's favorite board game has many different colored squares. He has written some clues about the squares.

There are:
- 224 squares total.
- 8 more light blue than pink.
- twice as many light blue as dark blue.
- 6 times as many red as dark blue.
- 28 fewer red than gray.
- 100 gray squares.

How many pink squares are there?

Understand	**What facts do you know?** The clues that are listed above. **What do you need to find?** How many pink squares there are.
Plan	Start with the last clue and work backward.
Solve	There are 100 gray squares. $100 - 28 = 72$ ⟶ number of red squares $72 \div 6 = 12$ ⟶ number of dark blue squares $12 \times 2 = 24$ ⟶ number of light blue squares $24 - 8 = 16$ ⟶ number of pink squares So, there are 16 pink squares.
Check	Look back at the clues. Start with 16 pink squares and follow the clues to be sure you end with 100 gray squares. $16 + 8 = 24$ ⟶ number of light blue squares $24 \div 2 = 12$ ⟶ number of dark blue squares $6 \times 12 = 72$ ⟶ number of red squares $72 + 28 = 100$ ⟶ number of gray squares ✓

ANALYZE the Strategy

Refer to the problem on the previous page.

1. Compare and contrast the words from the game clues with the operations Paco used to find the number of pink squares.

2. Explain how using the *work backward* strategy helped Paco find the number of pink squares.

3. What is the best way to check your solution when using the *work backward* strategy?

4. Explain when you would use the *work backward* strategy to solve a problem.

PRACTICE the Strategy

EXTRA PRACTICE See page 674.

Solve. Use the *work backward* strategy.

5. A number is divided by 5. Next, 4 is subtracted from the quotient. Then, 6 is added to the difference. If the result is 10, what is the number?

6. Marta and Scott volunteer at the food bank at 9:00 A.M. on Saturday. It takes 30 minutes to get from Scott's house to the food bank. It takes Marta 15 minutes to get to Scott's house. If it takes Marta 45 minutes to get ready in the morning, what is the latest time she should wake up?

7. Chet has $4.50 in change after purchasing a skateboard for $62.50 and a helmet for $32. How much money did Chet have originally?

8. A number is multiplied by 4, and then −6 is added to the product. The result is 18. What is the number?

9. Fernando is 2 inches taller than Jason. Jason is $1\frac{1}{2}$ inches shorter than Kendra and 1 inch taller than Nicole. Hao, who is 5 feet 10 inches tall, is $2\frac{1}{2}$ inches taller than Fernando. How tall is Nicole?

10. Mr. Numkena used the point system below to grade a 10 question multiple-choice test. Meg scored 23 points on the test. She answered all but one of the questions. How many did she answer correctly? How many did she answer incorrectly?

Response	Points
Correct	+3
Incorrect	−1
No answer given	0

11. At the end of the day, you have the amount shown. How much money was in your account at the beginning of the day?

	CREDITS	DEBITS	BALANCE
Balance			?
Check #1175		$21.78	
Check #1176		$7.08	
Deposit	$43.00		$114.89

12. **WRITING IN ►MATH** Teresa is 4 years older than her brother Omar. Omar is 2 years older than their sister Cristina. Cristina is 10 years younger than their brother Ruben. If Ruben is 19 years old, explain how you could use the *work backward* strategy to find Teresa's age.

CHAPTER 7

Mid-Chapter Check

Lessons 7-1 through 7-5

Replace each ● with <, >, or = to make a true sentence. (Lesson 7-1)

1. −7 ● −3 **2.** 4 ● −2

3. −8 ● 6 **4.** 78 ● 76

5. Order −5, −7, 4, −3, and −2 from greatest to least. (Lesson 7-1)

6. Order 0, −9, 6, −1, and 5 from least to greatest. (Lesson 7-1)

7. In golf, the lowest score wins. The table shows the scores relative to par of the winners of the U.S. Open from 1999 to 2005. What was the lowest winning score? (Lesson 7-1)

Year	Winner	Score
2005	Michael Campbell	even
2004	Retief Goosen	−4
2003	Jim Furyk	−8
2002	Tiger Woods	−3
2001	Retief Goosen	−4
2000	Tiger Woods	−12
1999	Payne Stewart	−1

Source: golfonline.com

Add. (Lesson 7-2)

8. +8 + (−3) **9.** −6 + 2

10. −4 + (−7) **11.** −2 + (−5)

12. Algebra Evaluate $x + y$ if $x = 7$ and $y = -12$. (Lesson 7-2)

13. STANDARDS PRACTICE A mole is in a burrow 12 inches below ground. It digs down 2 more inches. Which addition sentence represents the situation? (Lesson 7-2)

A 12 + (−2) **C** −12 + (−2)

B −12 + 2 **D** 12 + 2

Subtract. (Lesson 7-3)

14. 9 − (+3) **15.** −3 − 5

16. 8 − (−2) **17.** −4 − (−7)

18. STANDARDS PRACTICE Which equation represents the relationship of the x and y values in the table below? (Lesson 7-3)

x	y
−20	4
−9	15
−4	20
0	24

F $x = y - 24$ **H** $y = x - 24$

G $x = y + 24$ **J** $x = 24 - y$

Multiply. (Lesson 7-4)

19. −4 × (−7) **20.** 6(−9)

21. 8 × 2 **22.** −7(10)

23. The table shows the distance a cyclist traveled. If the cyclist continues at the same rate, how many yards will she have traveled after four minutes? (Lesson 7-4)

Time (min)	Distance (yd)
1	360
2	720
3	1,080
4	■

24. WRITING IN MATH Theo ordered juice for \$0.89, scrambled eggs for \$3.69, and milk for \$0.59. How much money did he have if he received \$3.50 in change? Explain your reasoning. (Lesson 7-5)

7-6 Dividing Integers

MAIN IDEA

I will divide integers.

Preparation for Standard 6NS2.3
Solve addition, subtraction, multiplication, and **division problems, including those arising in concrete situations, that use positive and negative integers and combinations of these operations.**

GET READY to Learn

Hands-On Mini Lab

You can use counters to model $-12 \div 3$.

Step 1 Place 12 negative counters on the mat to represent -12.

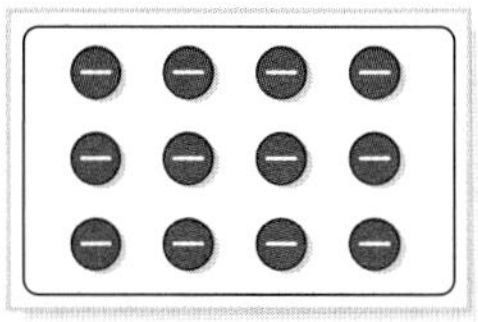

Step 2 Separate the 12 negative counters into three equal-size groups. There are 3 groups of 4 negative counters.

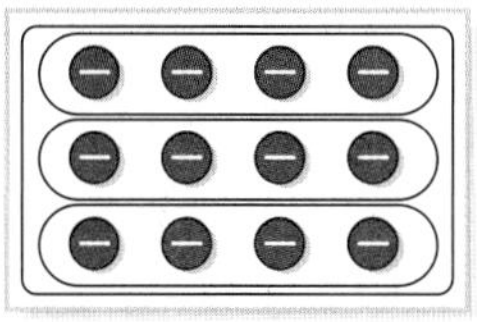

So, $-12 \div 3 = -4$.

1. Explain how you would model $-9 \div 3$.

2. What would you do differently to model $8 \div 2$?

Division means to separate the number into groups of equal size.

EXAMPLES Divide Integers

1 Divide $-8 \div 4$.

Separate 8 negative counters into 4 groups of equal size.

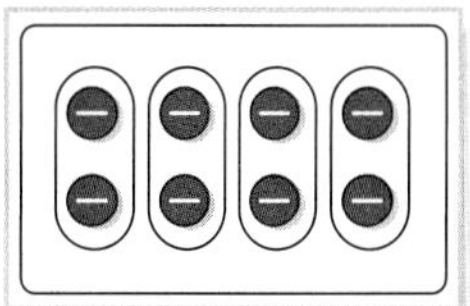

There are 4 groups of 2 negative counters.

So, $-8 \div 4 = -2$.

2 Divide $15 \div 3$.

Separate 15 positive counters into 3 groups of equal size.

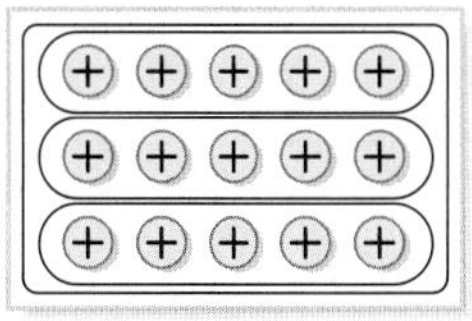

There are 3 groups of 5 positive counters.

So, $15 \div 3 = 5$.

EXAMPLES Divide Integers

> **Remember**
>
> For Examples 3–5, use the *work backward* strategy to find each quotient. In Example 3, to find $-10 \div 2$, think: 2 times what integer equals -10?

3 **Find $-10 \div 2$.**

Since $-5 \times 2 = -10$, it follows that $-10 \div 2 = -5$. ← negative quotient

4 **Find $14 \div (-7)$.**

Since $-2 \times (-7) = 14$, it follows that $14 \div (-7) = -2$. ← negative quotient

5 **Find $-24 \div (-6)$.**

Since $4 \times (-6) = -24$, it follows that $-24 \div (-6) = 4$. ← positive quotient

KEY CONCEPT — Divide Integers

Words	The quotient of two integers with different signs is negative.
Examples	$8 \div (-2) = -4$ $\quad$ $-8 \div 2 = -4$
Words	The quotient of two integers with the same sign is positive.
Examples	$8 \div 2 = 4$ $\quad$ $-8 \div (-2) = 4$

Real-World EXAMPLE

6 **Over 5 years, the number of registered Beagles declined by 4,525. If the decline in the numbers was the same each year, what was the change per year?**

You need to find the change per year. Represent the total decline by $-4{,}525$.

Since $-4{,}525 \div 5 = -905$, the change per year in the number of registered Beagles was -905.

Check

Since $-905 \times 5 = -4{,}525$, it follows that $-4{,}525 \div 5 = -905$.

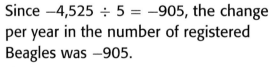

Online Personal Tutor at ca.gr5math.com

CHECK What You Know

Divide. See Examples 1–5 (pp. 371–372)

1. $-6 \div 2$ **2.** $-12 \div 3$ **3.** $15 \div 3$

4. $-25 \div 5$ **5.** $72 \div (-9)$ **6.** $-36 \div (-4)$

7. In 1996, there were 431 endangered plants in the U.S. By 2004, the number of endangered plants in the U.S. had increased by 168. If the increase in endangered plants was equal each year from 1996 to 2004, which integer represents the change for each year? See Example 6 (p. 372)

8. Talk About It In the equation $-24 \div h = 6$, is h a positive or negative integer?

Practice and Problem Solving

EXTRA PRACTICE See page 674.

Divide. See Examples 1–5 (pp. 371–372)

9. $-8 \div 2$ **10.** $-12 \div 4$ **11.** $-18 \div 6$

12. $-32 \div 4$ **13.** $21 \div 7$ **14.** $35 \div 7$

15. $-40 \div 8$ **16.** $-45 \div 5$ **17.** $63 \div (-9)$

18. $81 \div (-9)$ **19.** $-48 \div (-6)$ **20.** $-54 \div (-6)$

21. Anando lost a total of 28 points over the last 2 rounds of a game. If he lost the same number of points each round, what integer represents the change in his score each round?

22. A submarine starts at the surface of the water and then travels 95 meters below sea level in 19 seconds. If the submarine traveled an equal distance each second, what integer gives the distance and direction traveled relative to the surface each second?

23. **Algebra** Find the value of $c \div d$ if $c = -22$ and $d = 11$.

24. **Algebra** What value of m makes $48 \div m = -16$ true?

Find the value of each expression.

25. $\dfrac{-3 + (-7)}{2}$ **26.** $\dfrac{-10 + (-6)}{4}$

27. $\dfrac{[4 + (-6)] \times (-1 + 7)}{-3}$ **28.** $\dfrac{[-9 - (-5)] \times (-2 + 8)}{-8}$

29. The table shows the record low temperatures for certain cities in Arizona. What is the average record low temperature for these cities?

City	Temp (°F)	Year
Flagstaff	−30	1937
Glendale	20	1971
Grand Canyon	−23	1985
Mesa	15	1950
Tucson	8	1954

Source: weather.com

30. A study revealed that 6,540,000 acres of coastal wetlands have been lost over the past 50 years due to draining, dredging, landfills, and spoil disposal. If the loss continues at the same rate, how many acres will be lost in the next 10 years?

For Exercises 31 and 32, use the table below.

A teacher posted the sign shown below so that students would know the process of earning points to have a year-end class pizza party.

Positive Behavior	Points	Negative Behavior	Points
Complete Homework	+5	Incomplete Homework	−5
Having School Supplies	+3	Not Having School Supplies	−3
Being Quiet	+2	Talking	−2
Staying in Seat	+1	Out of Seat	−1
Paying Attention	+1	Not Paying Attention	−1
Being Cooperative	+4	Not Following Directions	−4

31. After 5 days, a student has −15 points. On average, how many points is the student losing each day?

32. Suppose a student averages −2 points every day for 4 days. How many positive points would the student need to earn on the fifth day to have a +5?

H.O.T. Problems

33. **OPEN ENDED** Write a division sentence whose quotient is −4. Then describe a real-world situation that this division sentence could represent.

34. **FIND THE ERROR** Emily and Mateo are finding $-42 \div 6$. Who is correct? Explain your reasoning.

Emily
$-42 \div 6 = -7$

Mateo
$-42 \div 6 = 7$

35. **SELECT A TOOL** Melissa wants to show her brother how to divide -15 by 3. Which of the following tools might Melissa use to show this division problem? Justify your selection(s). Then use the tool(s) to demonstrate this division problem.

paper/pencil | counters | paper plates

36. **NUMBER SENSE** Determine if $-24 \div 4$ is greater than, less than, or equal to $-24 \div (-4)$.

37. **CHALLENGE** List all the integers by which -24 is divisible.

38. **WRITING IN MATH** Without calculating, explain how you know whether the quotient $432 \div (-18)$ is greater than or less than 0.

Standards Practice

39 Which equation was used to create the function table below?

x	y
−20	−4
−5	−1
10	2
30	6

A $y = \frac{x}{5}$

B $y = -5x$

C $y = x + 10$

D $y = x - 10$

40 The table shows the number of points each student earned on the first math test. Each question on the test was worth an equal number of points.

Student	Points
Charlie	76
Serefina	84
Kaneesha	96

If Charlie answered 19 questions correctly, how many questions did Serefina answer correctly?

F −4

G −3

H 21

J 22

Spiral Review

41. Brianna and 5 of her friends bought a pack of six fruit juices after their lacrosse game. If the pack costs $3.29, how much does each person owe to the nearest cent if the cost is divided equally? Use the *work backward* strategy. **(Lesson 7-5)**

42. Find the product of -3 and -7. **(Lesson 7-4)**

Subtract. **(Lesson 7-3)**

43. $-45 - 20$ **44.** $-18 - (-5)$ **45.** $-9 - 10$ **46.** $14 - 15$

7-7 Problem-Solving Investigation

MAIN IDEA I will choose the best strategy to solve a problem.

Standard 5MR2.4 Express the solution clearly and logically by using the appropriate mathematical notation and terms and **clear language.** **Standard 5NS2.1** Add, subtract, multiply, and divide with decimals; **add with negative integers;** subtract positive integers from negative integers; **and verify the reasonableness of results.**

P.S.I. TEAM +

REBECCA: I love solving number puzzles! In the magic square shown, each row, column, and diagonal have the same sum.

−2	■	■
−3	−1	1
■	■	■

YOUR MISSION: Complete the magic square.

Understand You know that each row, column, and diagonal in the magic square has the same sum. You need to find the missing integers.

Plan You can use logical reasoning to find the missing integers.

Solve Evaluate the middle row. Since $-3 + (-1) + 1 = -3$, each row, column, and diagonal must have a sum of -3. So, in the first column, the missing integer is 2 since $-2 + (-3) + 2 = -3$.
Next, find the missing integer for each diagonal.
$2 + (-1) + (-4) = -3$ and $-2 + (-1) + 0 = -3$
Finally, find the last two missing integers.
$-2 + (3) + (-4) = -3$ and $2 + (-5) + 0 = -3$

−2	■	■
−3	−1	1
2	■	■

−2	■	−4
−3	−1	1
2	■	0

−2	3	−4
−3	−1	1
2	−5	0

Check Check the sum in each row, column, and diagonal. If each sum is -3, then the answers are correct. ✓

Mixed Problem Solving

EXTRA PRACTICE
See page 674.

Use any strategy shown below to solve each problem.

PROBLEM-SOLVING STRATEGIES
- *Use logical reasoning.*
- *Work backward.*
- *Guess and check.*

1. Copy and complete the magic square below.

■	■	3
■	2	■
1	■	−1

2. **Algebra** Find the missing term in the pattern below.

   …, ■, −3, −1, 1, 3, …

3. Jasmine and Carla run every day. Jasmine runs 6 kilometers in the time that it takes Carla to run 4 kilometers. On Saturday, they run the 9-kilometer course at Woodland Park. If they want to finish at the same time, how many kilometers should Carla run before Jasmine begins running?

4. On Monday, 86 science fiction books were sold at a book sale. This is 8 more than twice the amount sold on Thursday. How many science fiction books were sold on Thursday?

5. **Algebra** Find the missing term in the pattern below.

   …, ■, 1, 2, 3, 5, 8, 13 …

6. A relative gives you twice as many dollars as your age on each birthday. You are 13 years old. How much money have you been given over the years by this relative?

7. **Algebra** Find the missing term in the pattern below.

   $\ldots, ■, -\frac{1}{4}, \frac{1}{2}, -1, 2, \ldots$

8. Salvador needs to arrive at school at 9:15 A.M. It takes him 0.5 hours to walk to school, 0.25 hours to eat breakfast, and 1 hour to get ready. What time does he need to set his alarm clock in order to get to school on time?

9. The North Shore Fish Market reported the following sales each day during the first half of April. Which is greater, the mean or the median sales during this time?

April

	1 $700	2 $720	3 $790	4 $650	5 $950	6 $1,100
7	8 $750	9 $900	10 $850	11 $625	12 $930	13 $1,030
14	15 $800	16	17	18	19	20
21	22	23	24	25	26	27

10. Halley's Comet is visible from Earth approximately every 76 years. If the next scheduled appearance is in 2062, in what years were the last two appearances of Halley's Comet?

11. **WRITING IN MATH** Compare and contrast the *guess-and-check* strategy and the *logical reasoning* strategy. How are they alike? How do they differ?

7-8 The Coordinate Plane

GET READY to Learn

The map shows the layout of a small town. The locations of buildings are described with respect to the Town Hall. Each unit on the grid represents one block.

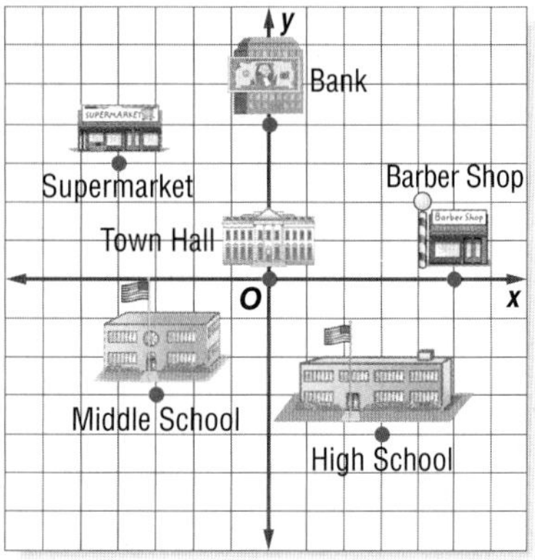

Let north and east directions be represented by positive integers. Let west and south directions be represented by negative integers. Describe the location of the high school as an ordered pair using integers.

MAIN IDEA

I will locate and graph ordered pairs on a coordinate plane.

Standard 5AF1.4 Identify and graph ordered pairs in the four quadrants of the coordinate plane.

New Vocabulary

quadrants

Vocabulary Link

Quadruplet
Everyday Use one of four babies born at one birth

Quadrant
Math Use four regions of the coordinate plane

Recall that a coordinate plane is formed when the *x*-axis and *y*-axis intersect at right angles at their zero points. The *x*-axis and *y*-axis separate the coordinate plane into four regions called **quadrants**. In Lesson 4-9, you graphed and named ordered pairs in Quadrant I.

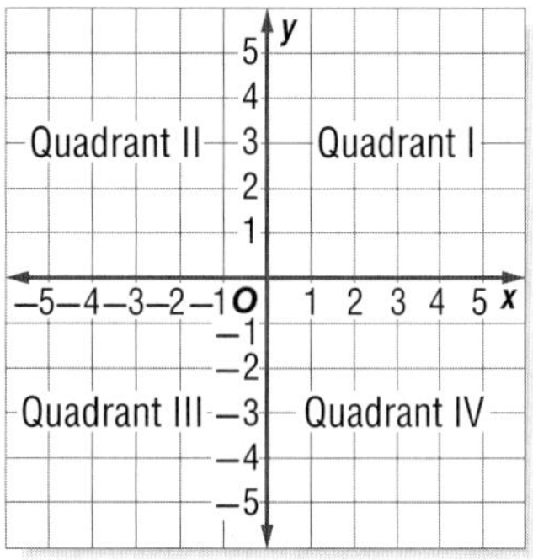

EXAMPLES Identify Ordered Pairs

Identify the ordered pair that names each point. Then identify the quadrant in which each point is located.

1 point *B*

Step 1 Start at the origin. Move right on the *x*-axis to find the *x*-coordinate of point *B*, which is 4.

Step 2 Move up the *y*-axis to find the *y*-coordinate, which is 3.

Point *B* is named by (4, 3). Point *B* is in the first quadrant.

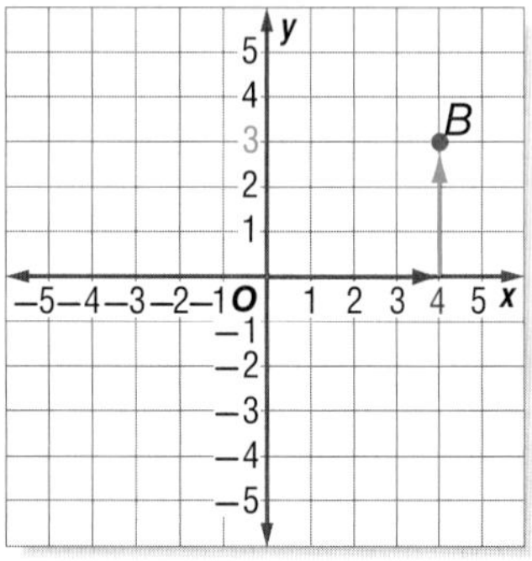

Remember

A point located on the x-axis will have a y-coordinate of 0. A point located on the y-axis will have an x-coordinate of 0. Points located on an axis are not in any quadrant.

2 point *D*

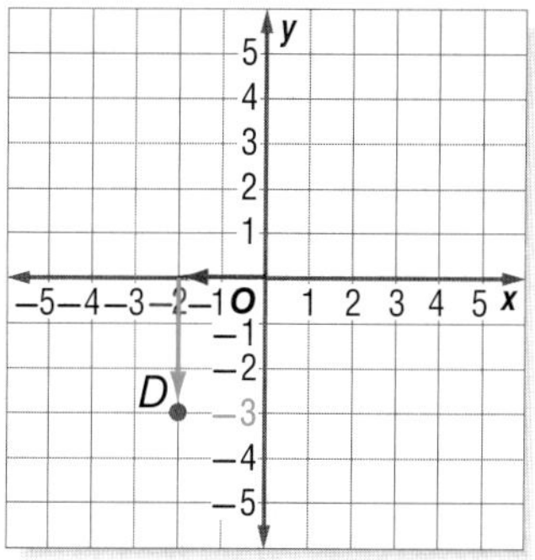

Step 1 Start at the origin. Move left on the x-axis to find the x-coordinate of point D, which is -2.

Step 2 Move down the y-axis to find the y-coordinate, which is -3.

Point D is named by $(-2, -3)$. Point D is in the third quadrant.

3 point *C*

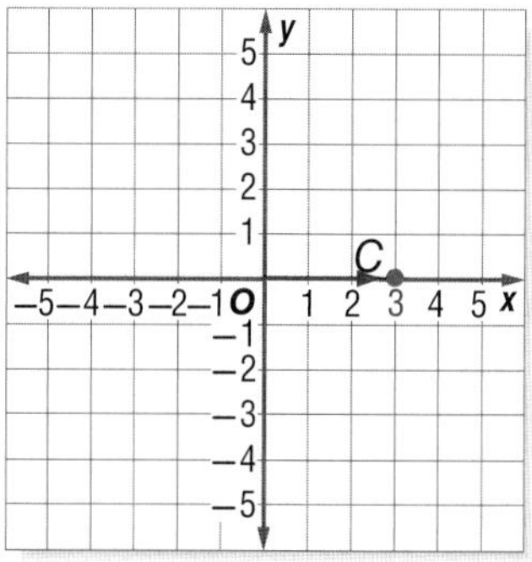

Step 1 Start at the origin. Move right on the x-axis to find the x-coordinate of point C, which is 3.

Step 2 Since no movement up or down is needed, the y-coordinate is 0.

Point C is named by $(3, 0)$. Point C is on the x-axis.

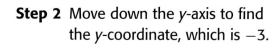

Online Personal Tutor at ca.gr5math.com

To graph an ordered pair, draw a dot at the point that corresponds to the coordinates.

EXAMPLES Graph Ordered Pairs

4 Graph point *M* at (−3, 5).

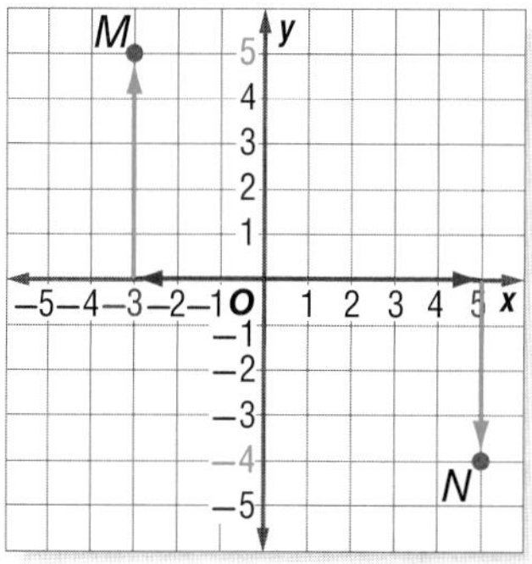

Step 1 Start at the origin. The x-coordinate is -3. So, move 3 units to the left.

Step 2 Next, since the y-coordinate is 5, move 5 units up. Draw a dot.

5 Graph point *N* at (5, −4).

Step 1 Start at the origin. The x-coordinate is 5. So, move 5 units to the right.

Step 2 Next, since the y-coordinate is -4, move 4 units down. Draw a dot.

CHECK What You Know

For Exercises 1–6, use the coordinate plane at the right. Identify the point for each ordered pair. See Examples 1–3 (pp. 378–379)

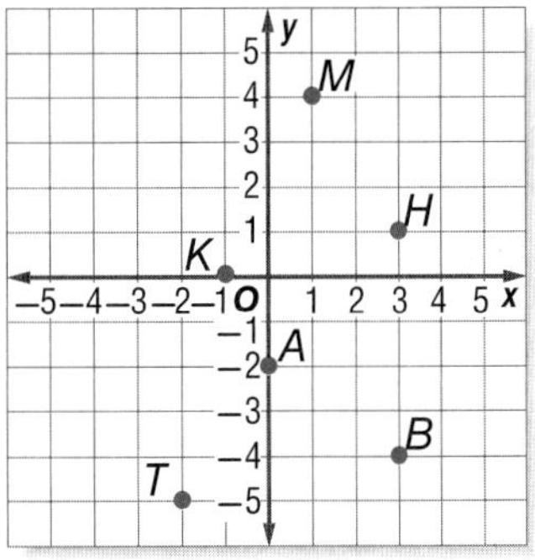

1. (3, 1) **2.** (−1, 0) **3.** (3, −4)

Write the ordered pair that names each point. Then identify the quadrant where each point is located. See Examples 1–3 (pp. 378–379)

4. *M* **5.** *A* **6.** *T*

For Exercises 7 and 8, refer to the diagram of a school at the right. See Examples 1–3 (pp. 378–379)

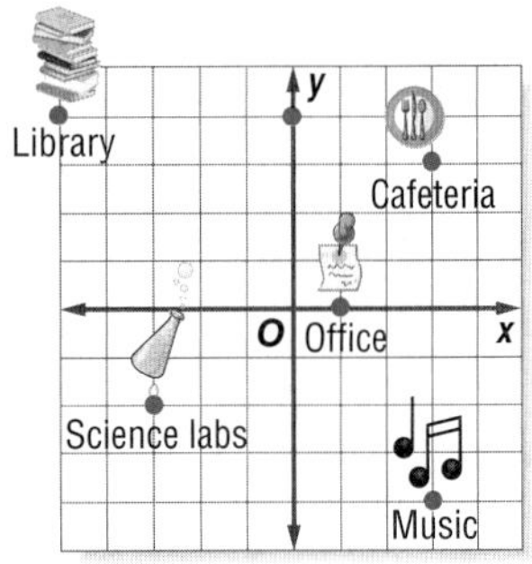

7. What part of the school is located at (3, −4)?

8. What ordered pair represents the location of the science labs?

Graph and label each point on a coordinate plane.
See Examples 4, 5 (p. 379)

9. *D*(2, 1) **10.** *K*(−3, 3) **11.** *N*(0, −1)

12. Talk About It How do you graph a point on the coordinate plane using an ordered pair?

Practice and Problem Solving

EXTRA PRACTICE
See page 675.

Use the coordinate plane at the right. Identify the point for each ordered pair. See Examples 1–3 (pp. 378–379)

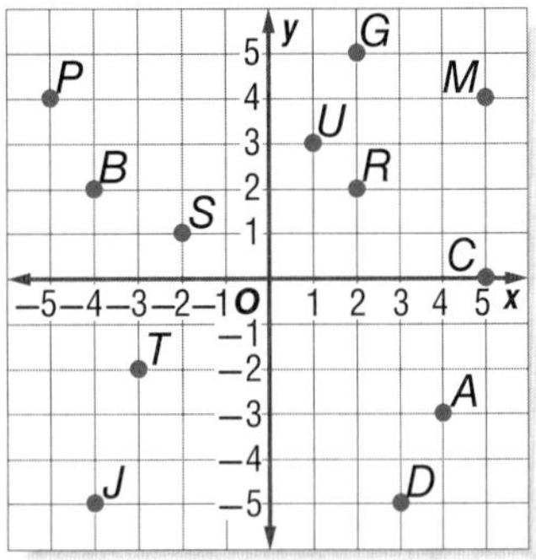

13. (2, 2) **14.** (1, 3)

15. (−4, 2) **16.** (−2, 1)

17. (−3, −2) **18.** (−4, −5)

Write the ordered pair that names each point. Then identify the quadrant where each point is located. See Examples 1–3 (pp. 378–379)

19. *G* **20.** *C* **21.** *A*

22. *D* **23.** *P* **24.** *M*

Graph and label each point on a coordinate plane. See Examples 4, 5 (p. 379)

25. *N*(1, 2) **26.** *T*(0, 0) **27.** *B*(−3, 4)

28. *F*(5, −2) **29.** *H*(−4, −1) **30.** *K*(−2, −5)

For Exercises 31–35, refer to the map of Wonderland Park. See Examples 1, 2 (pp. 378–379)

31. In which quadrant is the Wonder Wheel located?

32. What attraction is located at (−3, 3)?

33. What attraction is located at (−1.5, −3.5)?

34. What is located closest to the origin?

35. If you are standing at The Clock, how would you get to the Pipeline Plunge?

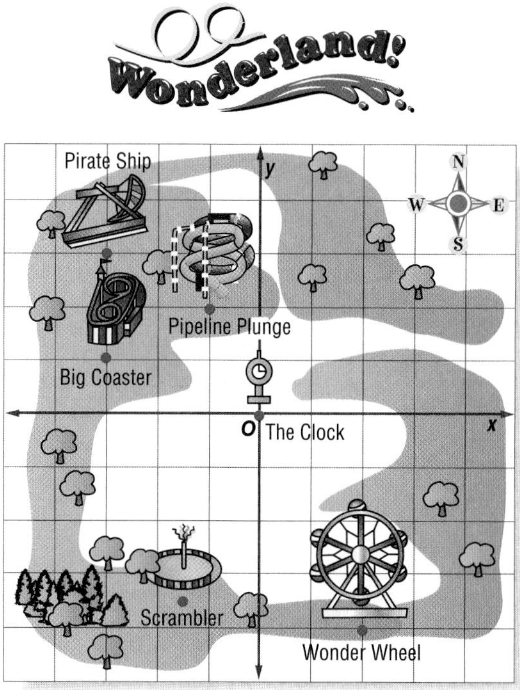

Graph and label each point on a coordinate plane.

36. $J\left(2\frac{1}{2}, -2\frac{1}{2}\right)$

37. $A\left(4\frac{3}{4}, -1\frac{1}{4}\right)$

38. $D(-1.5, 2.5)$

39. $M(-3.75, -1.25)$

Real-World PROBLEM SOLVING

Geography A map of South America is shown.

40. What country is located at (10°S latitude, 60°W longitude)?

41. Use latitude and longitude to name a location in the country Argentina as an ordered pair. (*Hint:* Refer to Exercise 40 for the format of the ordered pair.)

42. What line on a coordinate plane is similar to the line labeled 0° on the map?

43. Begin at (20°S latitude, 40°W longitude). Travel 20° west and 10° south. What country will you be in?

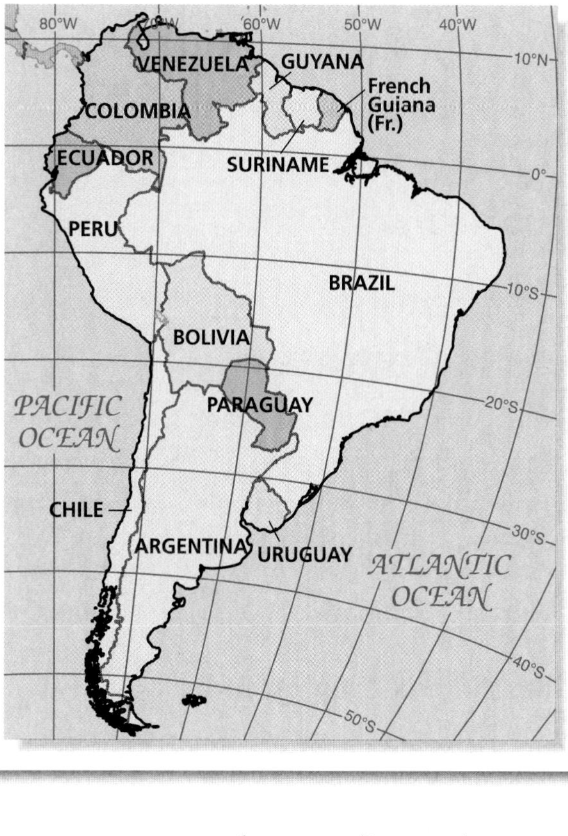

H.O.T. Problems

CHALLENGE If the graph of a set of ordered pairs forms a line, the graph is *linear*. Otherwise, the graph is *nonlinear*.

Graph each set of points on a coordinate plane. Then decide whether the graph is linear or nonlinear.

44. $(-1, -1), (2, 2), (-3, -3), (4, 4)$

45. $(-1, 1), (2, -2), (-3, 3), (-4, -4)$

46. OPEN ENDED Identify the coordinates of two points located on the y-axis, one above the origin and one below.

47. WRITING IN MATH Explain what all points located on the x-axis have in common. Then explain what points located on the y-axis have in common.

Standards Practice

48 Which of the following coordinates lie within the circle graphed below?

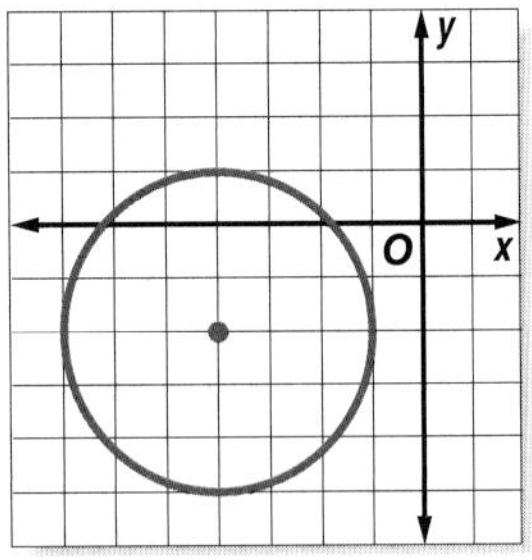

A $(-2, 3)$

B $(-3, -4)$

C $(-1, 2)$

D $(-3, 4)$

49 The map below shows the location of various classrooms.

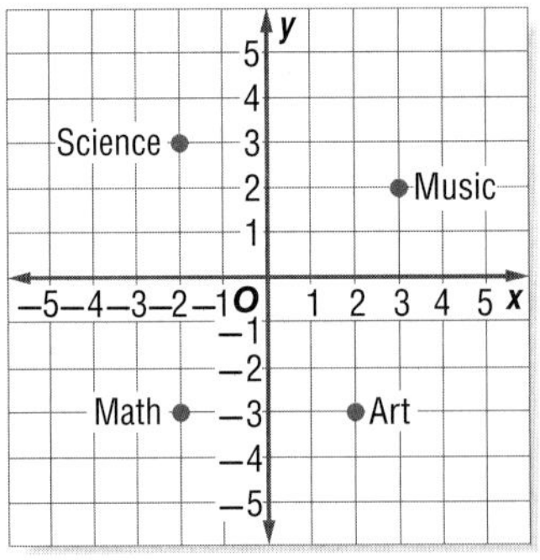

Which classroom is located at the point $(2, -3)$?

F Art

G Music

H Math

J Science

Spiral Review

50. Pia saved $55 in one week towards the purchase of a new bicycle. She continued to save at this rate for a total of six weeks and did not make any withdrawals. Find the change in her savings account at the end of the six weeks. **(Lesson 7-7)**

51. Find the value of $x \div y$ if $x = -15$ and $y = -3$. **(Lesson 7-6)**

Divide. Write in simplest form. **(Lesson 6-10)**

52. $\frac{1}{2} \div \frac{1}{8}$

53. $\frac{6}{7} \div 3$

54. $\frac{5}{8} \div \frac{1}{4}$

55. $\frac{2}{3} \div \frac{2}{5}$

Explore

Algebra Lab for 7-9
Solving Addition Equations Using Models

MAIN IDEA

I will solve addition equations using models.

Standard 5MR2.3 Use a variety of methods, such as words, numbers, symbols, charts, graphs, tables, diagrams, and **models, to explain mathematical reasoning.**

Standard 5NS2.1 Add, subtract, multiply, and divide with decimals; **add with negative integers;** subtract positive integers from negative integers; and verify the reasonableness of results.

Review Vocabulary

equation a sentence that contains an equals sign, = **(Lesson 1-8)**

An equation is like a balance scale. The quantity on the left side of the equals sign is *balanced* with the quantity on the right. When you solve an equation, you need to keep the equation *balanced.*

To solve an equation using cups and counters, remember to add or subtract the same number of counters on each side.

ACTIVITY

1 Solve $x + 5 = 9$ using models.

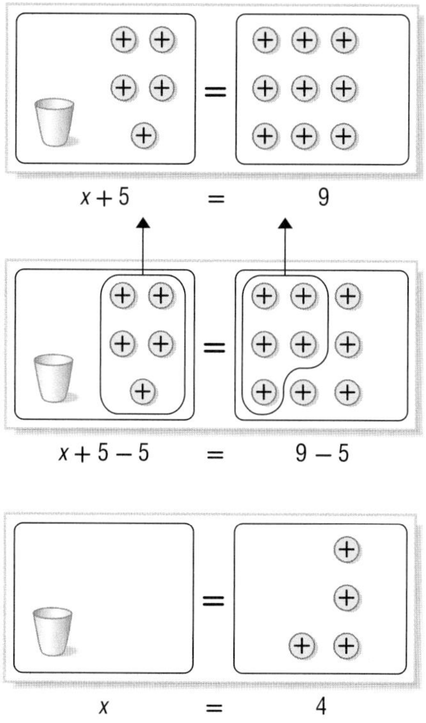

Model the equation.

Remove 5 counters from each side to get the cup by itself.

There are 4 counters remaining on the right side, so $x = 4$.

The solution is 4.

Check	$x + 5 = 9$	Write the original equation.
	$4 + 5 \stackrel{?}{=} 9$	Replace x with 4.
	$9 = 9$ ✓	This sentence is true.

CHECK What You Know

Solve each equation using models.

a. $1 + x = 8$ **b.** $x + 2 = 7$ **c.** $9 = x + 3$

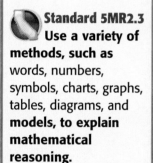

ACTIVITY

2 Solve $x + 2 = -5$ using models.

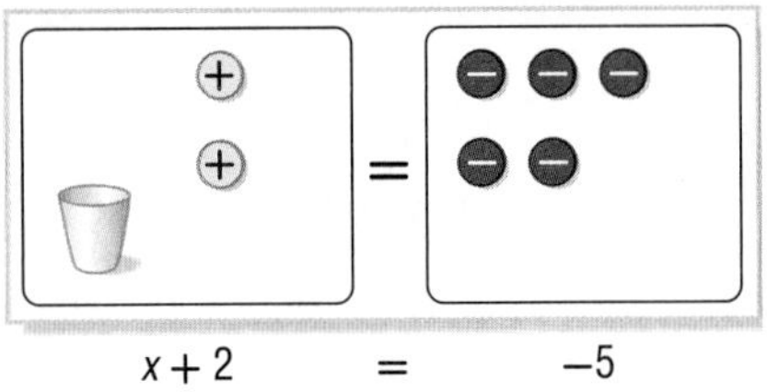

Model the equation.

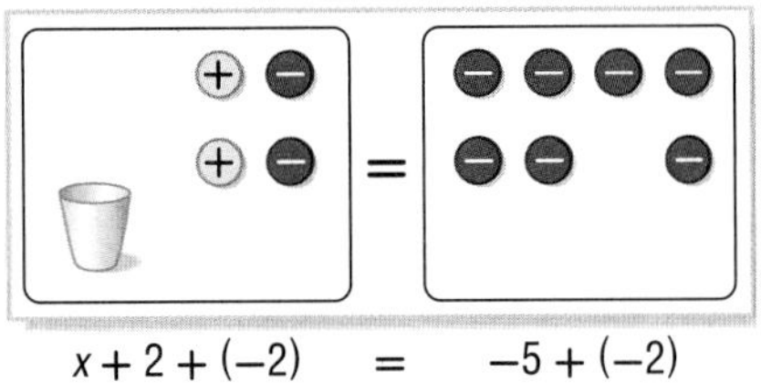

You cannot remove 2 positive counters from each side. Add 2 negative counters to each side of the mat to create two zero pairs on the left side.

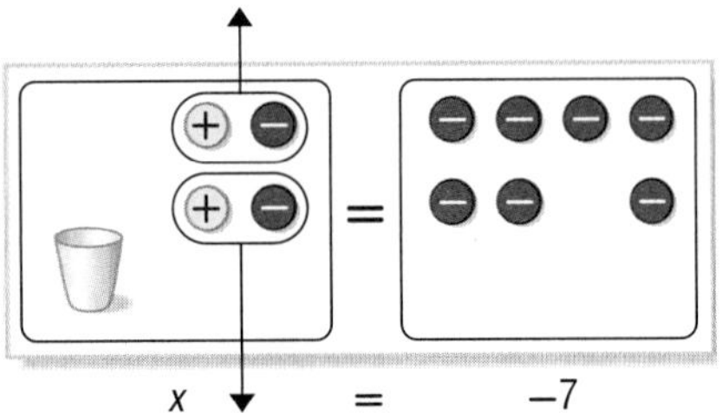

Remove the zero pairs from the left side of the mat. The cup is now by itself. There are 7 negative counters on the right side, so $x = -7$.

The solution is −7.

Check	$x + 2 = -5$	Write the original equation.
	$-7 + 2 \stackrel{?}{=} -5$	Replace *x* with −7.
	$-5 = -5$ ✓	This sentence is true.

CHECK What You Know

Solve each equation using models.

d. $x + 3 = -7$ **e.** $2 + x = -5$ **f.** $-3 = x + 3$

Remember

To review zero pairs, see Explore Math Lab for 7-2.

Analyze the Results

1. Explain how you decide how many counters to add or subtract from each side.
2. Write an equation in which you need to remove zero pairs in order to solve it.
3. Model the equation *some number plus 5 is equal to* −2. Then solve the equation.
4. Write a rule that you can use to solve an equation like $x + 3 = 6$ without using models.

7-9 Solving Addition Equations

MAIN IDEA

I will solve and write addition equations.

Standard 5AF1.5 Solve problems involving linear functions with integer values; **write the equation;** and graph the resulting ordered pairs of integers on a grid.

New Vocabulary

inverse operations

GET READY to Learn

A forecaster reported that although an additional 3 inches of rain had fallen, the total rainfall was still 9 inches below normal for the year. This is shown on the number line.

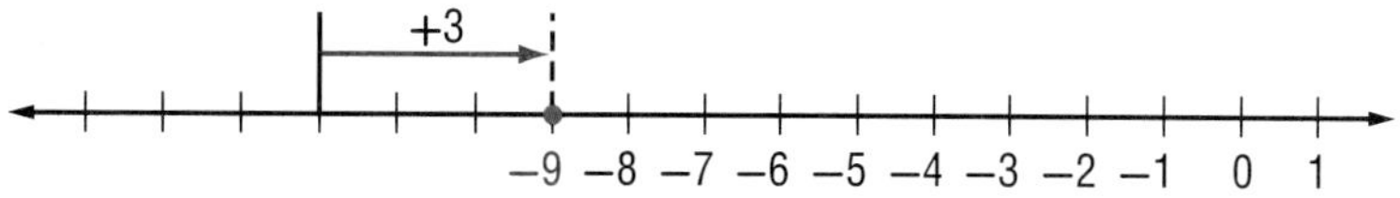

The equation $x + 3 = -9$ can be used to find the rainfall before the additional three inches. Solve the equation by counting backward. What operation did you use?

In Lesson 1-8, you solved equations mentally. Another way is to use **inverse operations**, which *undo* each other. For example, to solve an addition equation, use subtraction.

EXAMPLE **Solve an Equation By Subtracting**

1 **Solve $8 = x + 3$.**

One Way: Use models.

Model the equation.

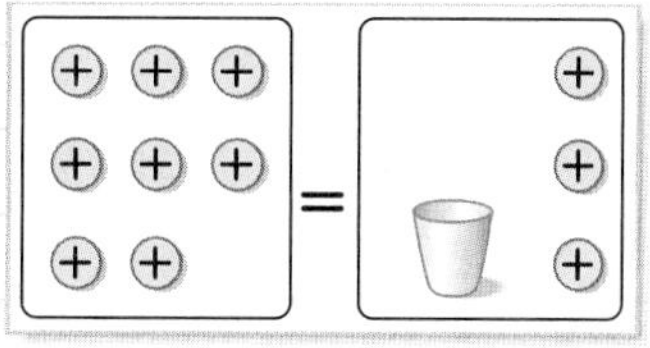

$8 = x + 3$

Remove 3 counters from each side.

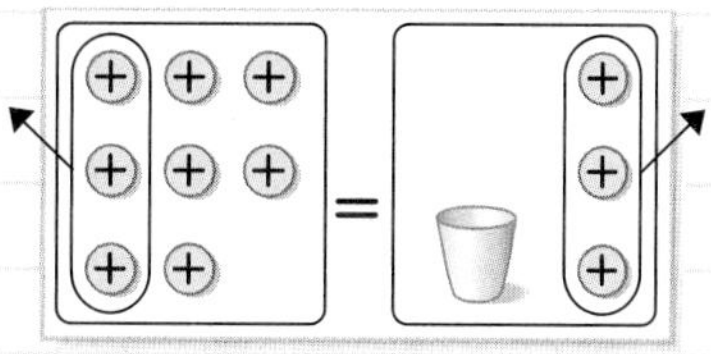

$8 - 3 = x + 3 - 3$

$5 = x$

Another Way: Use symbols.

$8 = x + 3$ Write the equation.

Subtract 3 from each side to "undo" the addition of 3 on the right.

$$\begin{array}{rcl} 8 &=& x + 3 \\ -\ 3 &=& \quad -\ 3 \\ \hline 5 &=& x \end{array}$$

$8 - 3 = 5$

The solution is 5.

EXAMPLE Solve an Equation

2 **Solve $b + 5 = 2$. Check your solution.**

One Way: Use models and zero pairs.

Model the equation.

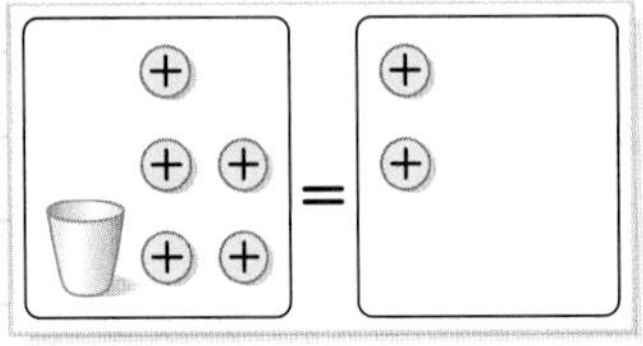

$b + 5 = 2$

Add 3 zero pairs to the right side to produce 5 positive counters.

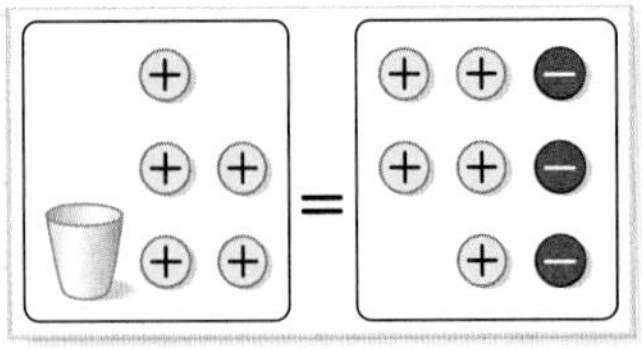

$b + 5 = 2$

Remove 5 positive counters from each side.

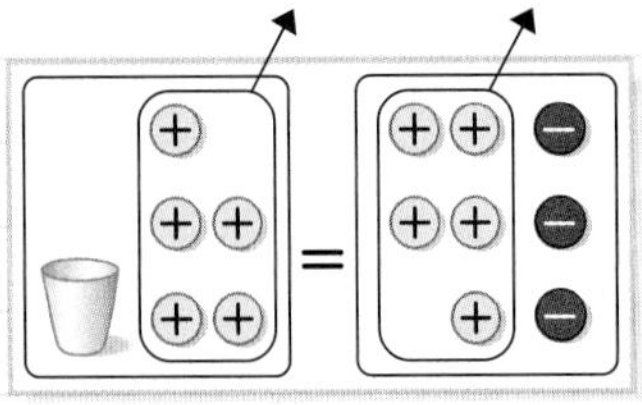

$b + 5 - 5 = 2 - 5$
$b = -3$

Remember

You should always check your solution. You will know immediately whether your solution is correct or not.

Another Way: Use symbols.

$b + 5 = 2$ Write the equation.

Subtract 5 from each side to "undo" *b* plus 5.

$b + 5 = 2$	Subtract 5 from
$\quad - 5 = -5$	each side.
$b = -3$	$2 - 5 = -3$

Check

$b + 5 = 2$	Write the equation.
$-3 + 5 \stackrel{?}{=} 2$	Replace *b* with -3.
$2 = 2$ ✓	This sentence is true.

The solution is -3.

Math Online **Extra Examples at** ca.gr5math.com

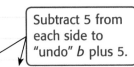

Subtracting the same number from each side of an equation shows the **Subtraction Property of Equality**.

KEY CONCEPT — Subtraction Property of Equality

Words If you subtract the same number from each side of an equation, the two sides remain equal.

Examples

Numbers	Algebra
$5 = 5$	$x + 2 = 3$
$\mathbf{-3 = -3}$	$\mathbf{-2 = -2}$
$2 = 2$	$x = 1$

Real-World EXAMPLE

3 A male gorilla weighs 379 pounds on average. This is 181 pounds more than the weight of the average female gorilla. Write and solve an addition equation to find the weight of an average female gorilla.

Words	181 pounds	plus	the weight of an average female gorilla	is 379 pounds.
Variable	Let w represent the weight of an average female gorilla.			
Equation	181	+	w	= 379

$$\begin{aligned} 181 + w &= 379 \\ \mathbf{-181} \quad &= \mathbf{-181} \\ w &= 198 \end{aligned}$$

Write the equation.
Subtract 181 from each side.
$379 - 181 = 198$

So, an average female gorilla weighs 198 pounds.

Online Personal Tutor at ca.gr5math.com

CHECK What You Know

Solve each equation. Check your solution. See Examples 1, 2 (pp. 385–386)

1. $x + 3 = 5$

2. $2 + m = 7$

3. $c + 6 = -3$

4. $-4 = 6 + e$

5. A hot air balloon is 200 feet in the air. A few minutes later it ascends to 450 feet. Write and solve an addition equation to find the change of altitude of the hot air balloon. See Example 3 (p. 387)

6. Talk About It Describe one method to solve the equation $x + 4 = 2$.

Practice and Problem Solving

EXTRA PRACTICE
See page 675.

Solve each equation. Check your solution. See Examples 1, 2 (pp. 385–386)

7. $y + 7 = 10$
8. $x + 5 = 11$
9. $9 = 2 + x$
10. $7 = 4 + y$
11. $9 + a = 7$
12. $6 + g = 5$
13. $d + 3 = -5$
14. $x + 4 = -2$
15. $-5 = 3 + f$
16. $-1 = g + 7$
17. $b + 4 = -3$
18. $h + 6 = 2$

19. Zane and his dog weigh 108 pounds. Zane weighs 89 pounds. Write and solve an addition equation to find the dog's weight.

20. On average, men burn 180 more Calories per hour running than women do. If a man burns 600 Calories per hour running, write and solve an addition equation to find how many Calories a woman burns running one hour.

21. Find the value of x if $x + 3 = 7$.

22. If $c + 6 = 2$, what is the value of c?

Solve each equation. Check your solution.

23. $t + 1.9 = 3.8$
24. $1.8 + n = -0.3$
25. $a + 6.1 = -2.3$
26. $7.8 = x + 1.5$
27. $m + \frac{1}{3} = \frac{2}{3}$
28. $t + \frac{1}{4} = -\frac{1}{2}$

29. Suppose your friend had a score of −5 in the second round of a certain game. This made her total score after two rounds equal to −2. What was her score in the first round?

Real-World PROBLEM SOLVING

Data File Visitors to the Huntington Beach International Surfing Museum can view historic hardwood surfboards.

30. The longest longboard is 4 feet longer than your surfboard. Write and solve an addition equation to find the length of your surfboard.

31. The smallest funboard is 1 foot longer than your surfboard. Write and solve an addition equation to find the length of your surfboard.

Source: www.surfingmuseum.org

Data Card

Surfboard Lengths
Shortboards:
$5\frac{1}{2}$ feet – 7 feet
Funboards:
$6\frac{1}{2}$ feet – $7\frac{2}{3}$ feet
Longboards:
9 feet – 12 feet

H.O.T. Problems

32. **CHALLENGE** In the equation $x + y = -3$, the value of x is an integer greater than 1, but less than 6. Determine the possible solutions for y in this equation.

33. **OPEN ENDED** Write a problem that can be represented by the equation $x + 2 = 7$. Explain the meaning of the equation.

34. **WRITING IN ▶MATH** Without solving, decide whether the solution to $a + 14 = -2$ will be positive or negative. Explain.

Standards Practice

35 The model represents the equation $x + 4 = 7$.

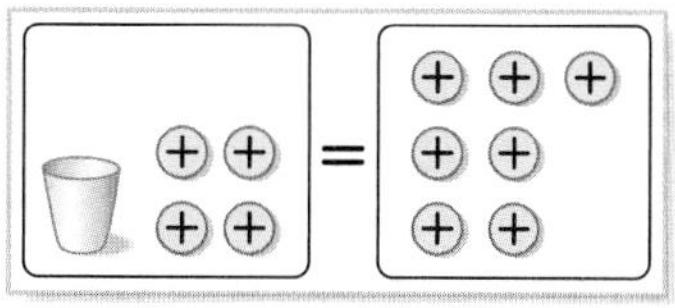

What is the first step in finding the value of x?

A Add 4 positive tiles to each side of the model.

B Subtract 7 positive tiles from each side of the model.

C Add 7 positive tiles to each side of the model.

D Subtract 4 positive tiles from each side of the model.

36 Niko wants to buy a skateboard that costs $85. He has already saved $15. Which equation represents the amount of money Niko needs to buy the skateboard?

F $t - 15 = 85$

G $t + 15 = 85$

H $15 - t = 85$

J $t = 15 + 85$

37 What is the value of x in the equation $x + 5 = -4$?

A -9

B -1

C 1

D 9

Spiral Review

Refer to the coordinate plane to identify the point for each ordered pair. **(Lesson 7-8)**

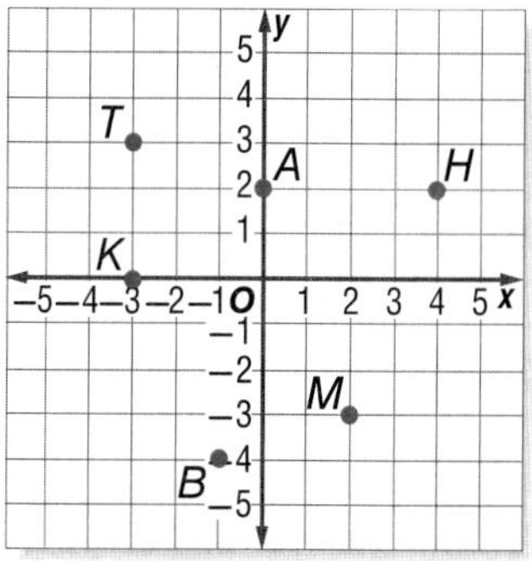

38. (4, 2)

39. (−3, 0)

40. (−1, −4)

41. On a quiz, Kedar missed a total of 10 points on two questions. If each question has the same value, which integer represents the number of points lost per question? **(Lesson 7-6)**

What's Your Latitude?

Think of your street address. You use this to describe the location of your home. How can you describe this location on Earth? Latitude and longitude are used to describe the position of any place on Earth. They are measured in degrees (°), minutes (′), and seconds (″). For example, San Diego is located at 32°42′55″N, 117°9′23″W. That is 32 degrees, 42 minutes, and 55 seconds north of the equator and 117 degrees, 9 minutes, and 23 seconds west of the Prime Meridian.

Is there a relationship between latitude and temperature? Complete the exercises on page 391 to help you decide.

Did You Know?

The longest latitude line is the equator, whose latitude is zero degrees.

Key Math Standard 5AF1.4 Identify and **graph ordered pairs in** the four quadrants of **the coordinate plane.**

City	Latitude (nearest degree)	High Temperature, 2004 (°F)	Low Temperature, 2004 (°F)
Atlanta, GA	34	95	16
Bismarck, ND	47	103	−30
Denver, CO	40	99	−11
Fairbanks, AK	65	88	−46
Honolulu, HI	21	92	60
Minneapolis, MN	45	95	−24
Nashville, TN	36	94	11
New York, NY	41	91	1
San Diego, CA	33	96	41
Seattle, WA	48	96	20

Source: *The World Almanac*

Real-World Math

Use the table above to solve each problem.

1. Which city had the highest temperature? the lowest temperature?

2. The higher the latitude number is, the farther the location is from the equator. Which city is closest to the equator? Which city is farthest from the equator?

3. Make a table listing the cities from least to greatest latitude. Include latitude and low temperatures. What do you notice about the relationship between latitudes and low temperatures?

4. Write the latitude and the low temperature of each city as an ordered pair. Graph the ordered pairs on a coordinate plane.

5. Find the difference between the high and low temperatures for each city. Write the latitude and the temperature difference of each city as an ordered pair.

6. Refer to Exercise 5. Graph the ordered pairs on a coordinate plane. Let the x-axis represent the latitude and the y-axis represent the temperature difference. Then describe the graph.

Explore

Algebra Lab for 7-10

Solving Subtraction Equations Using Models

MAIN IDEA

I will solve subtraction equations using models.

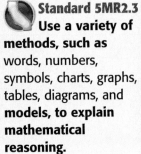

Standard 5MR2.3 Use a variety of methods, such as words, numbers, symbols, charts, graphs, tables, diagrams, and **models, to explain mathematical reasoning.**

Standard 5NS2.1 Add, subtract, multiply, and divide with decimals; **add with negative integers;** subtract positive integers from negative integers; and verify the reasonableness of results.

Recall that subtracting an integer is the same as adding its opposite. For example, $4 - 7 = 4 + (-7)$ or $x - 3 = x + (-3)$.

ACTIVITY

Solve $x - 3 = -2$ using models.

$x - 3 = -2 \longrightarrow x + (-3) = -2$ Rewrite the equation.

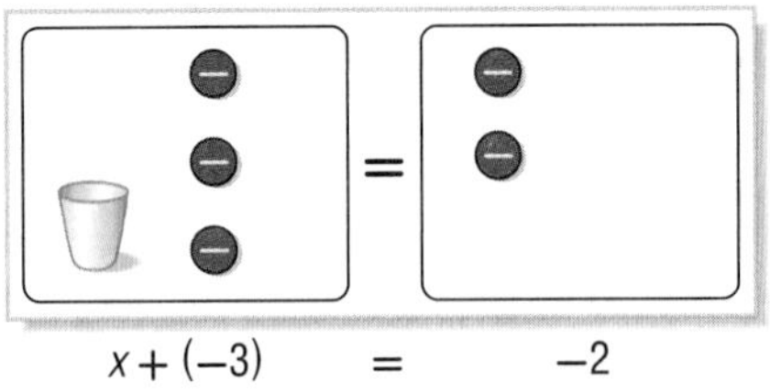

Model the addition equation.

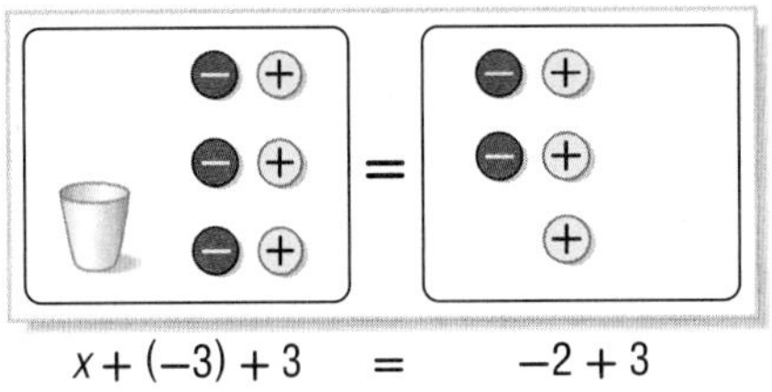

Add 3 positive counters to each side of the mat to make 3 zero pairs on the left side.

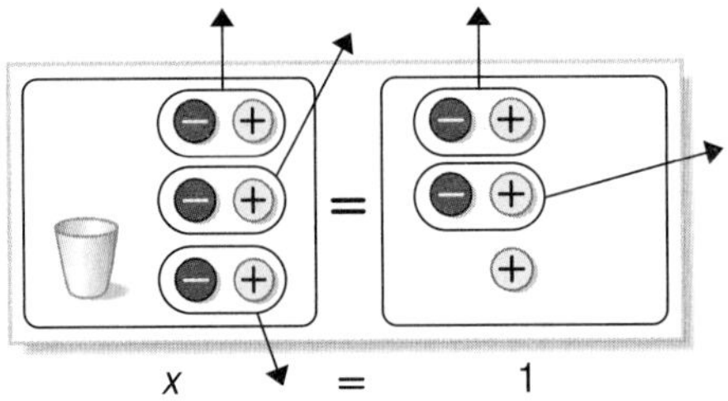

Remove 3 zero pairs from the left side and 2 zero pairs from the right side. That leaves one positive counter on the right side and the cup by itself on the left side. So, $x = 1$.

The solution is 1. **Check** $1 - 3 = 1 + (-3)$ or -2 ✓

CHECK What You Know

Solve each equation using models.

a. $x - 4 = 2$ **b.** $-3 = x - 1$ **c.** $x - 5 = -1$

Analyze the Results

1. Explain why it is helpful to rewrite a subtraction problem as an addition problem when solving equations using models.

2. Write a rule for solving equations like $x - 7 = -5$ without using models.

7-10 Solving Subtraction Equations

GET READY to Learn

Raul is 5 inches shorter than his brother Jorge. Raul is 59 inches tall. Let h represent Jorge's height.

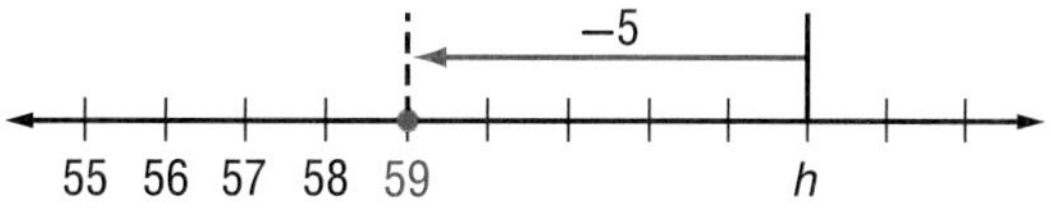

5 inches shorter than Jorge is equal to 59 inches can be represented by the equation $h - 5 = 59$. Find Jorge's height. What operation did you use?

MAIN IDEA

I will solve and write subtraction equations.

Standard 5AF1.5 Solve problems involving linear functions with integer values; **write the equation;** and graph the resulting ordered pairs of integers on a grid.

You can solve a subtraction equation by adding.

EXAMPLE Solve an Equation by Adding

1 Solve $x - 3 = 2$.

One Way: Use models.

Model the equation.

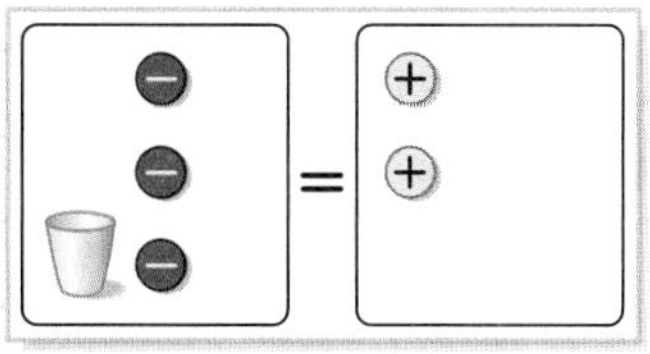

$x - 3 = 2$

Add 3 positive counters to each side of the mat. Remove the zero pairs.

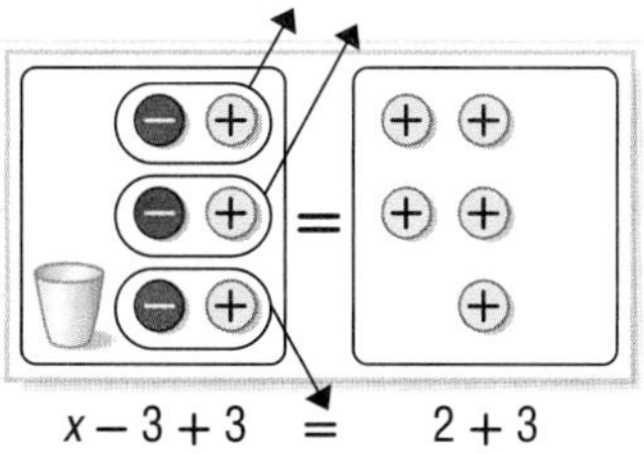

$x - 3 + 3 = 2 + 3$

$x = 5$

Another Way: Use symbols.

$x - 3 = 2$ Write the equation.

Add 3 to each side to undo the subtraction of 3 on the left.

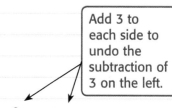

$x - 3 = 2$

$+3 = +3$ Add 3 to each side.

$x = 5$ Simplify.

The solution is 5.

Remember

The expression $x - 3$ is the same as $x + (-3)$. To model the expression, use one cup and three negative counters.

When you solve an equation by adding the same number to each side of the equation, you are using the **Addition Property of Equality**.

Concepts in Motion
Interactive Lab
ca.gr5math.com

KEY CONCEPT — Addition Property of Equality

Words If you add the same number to each side of an equation, the two sides remain equal.

Examples

Numbers	Algebra
$5 = 5$	$x - 2 = 3$
$+3 = +3$	$+2 = +2$
$8 = 8$	$x = 5$

EXAMPLE Solve a Subtraction Equation

2 Solve $-10 = y - 4$. Check your solution.

$-10 = y - 4$	Write the equation.	**Check** $-10 = y - 4$
$+4 = +4$	Add 4 to each side.	$-10 \stackrel{?}{=} -6 - 4$
$-6 = y$	Simplify.	$-10 = -10$ ✓

The solution is -6.

Real-World EXAMPLE

3 The difference between the record high and low temperatures in South Carolina is 130°F. The record low temperature is −19°F. What is the record high temperature?

Words	Record high temperature	minus	record low temperature	is	130°F.
Variable	Let h represent the record high temperature.				
Equation	h	$-$	(-19)	$=$	130

$h - (-19) = 130$	Write the equation.
$h + 19 = 130$	Definition of subtraction
$-19 = -19$	Subtract 19 from each side.
$h = 111$	Simplify.

The record high temperature is 111°F.

Online Personal Tutor at ca.gr5math.com

CHECK What You Know

Solve each equation. Check your solution. See Examples 1, 2 (pp. 393–394)

1. $a - 5 = 9$ **2.** $b - 3 = 7$ **3.** $4 = y - 8$

4. $x - 4 = -1$ **5.** $x - 2 = -7$ **6.** $-3 = n - 2$

7. Mika's cat lost 3 pounds. It now weighs 12 pounds. Write and solve a subtraction equation to find its original weight.
See Example 3 (p. 394)

8. Talk About It Tell how to check your solution to an equation.

Practice and Problem Solving

EXTRA PRACTICE See page 675.

Solve each equation. Check your solution. See Examples 1, 2 (pp. 393–394)

9. $c - 1 = 8$ **10.** $f - 1 = 5$ **11.** $2 = e - 1$

12. $1 = g - 3$ **13.** $r - 3 = -1$ **14.** $t - 2 = -2$

15. $t - 4 = -1$ **16.** $h - 2 = -9$ **17.** $-3 = u - 8$

18. $-5 = v - 6$ **19.** $x - 3 = -5$ **20.** $y - 4 = -7$

21. A diver is swimming below sea level. A few minutes later the diver descends 35 feet until she reaches a depth of 75 feet below sea level. Write and solve a subtraction equation to find the diver's original position.

22. The difference between the record high and record low temperatures for September in Bryce Canyon, Utah, is 70°F. Write and solve an equation to find the record high temperature.

Bryce Canyon, Utah Record Temperatures in September	
High	■
Low	16°F

23. Algebra Find the value of t if $t - 7 = -12$.

Solve each equation. Check your solution.

24. $-6 + a = -8$ **25.** $a - 1.1 = 2.3$ **26.** $-4.6 = e - 3.2$

27. $-4.3 = f - 7.8$ **28.** $m - \frac{1}{3} = \frac{2}{3}$ **29.** $n - \frac{1}{4} = -\frac{1}{2}$

30. Alejandra spent her birthday money on a video game that cost $24, a new controller for $13, and a memory card for $16. The tax on the purchase was $3. Write and solve a subtraction equation to find how much money Alejandra gave the cashier if she received $4 back in change.

H.O.T. Problems

31. CHALLENGE Analyze how you would solve $6 - x = -3$.

32. FIND THE ERROR Ramón and Bron are explaining how to solve the equation $d - 6 = 4$. Who is correct? Explain your reasoning.

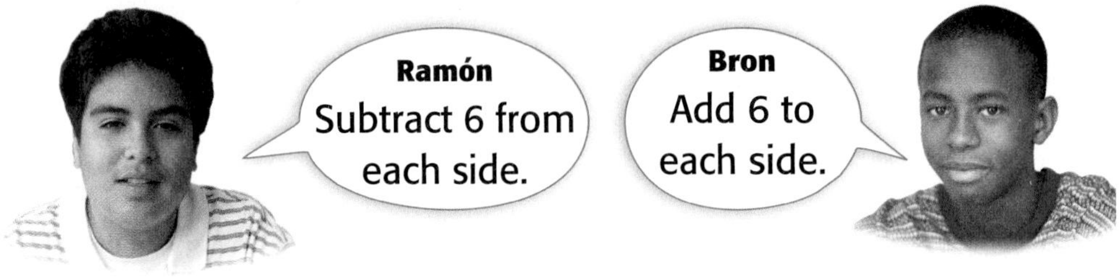

33. WRITING IN MATH Without solving the equation, what do you know about the value of x in $x - 5 = -3$? Is x greater than 5 or less than 5? Explain your reasoning.

Standards Practice

34 The model represents $x - 5 = 3$.

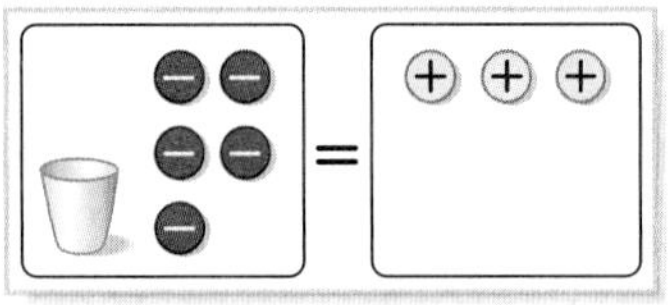

What is the value of x?

A $x = -8$

B $x = -2$

C $x = 2$

D $x = 8$

35 Alabama became a state in 1819. Texas became a state 26 years later. Which equation can be used to find the year y Texas became a state?

F $y = 1819 - 26$

G $y + 26 = 1819$

H $y - 1819 = 26$

J $1819 - y = 26$

Spiral Review

36. Refer to the graph. Write and solve an addition equation to find how many fewer people can be seated at Dodger Stadium than at Yankee Stadium. **(Lesson 7-9)**

37. Graph and label $X(2, -3)$ and $Y(-3, 2)$ on a coordinate plane. **(Lesson 7-8)**

38. Multiply $2\frac{3}{4} \times 3\frac{1}{3}$. Write in simplest form. **(Lesson 6-9)**

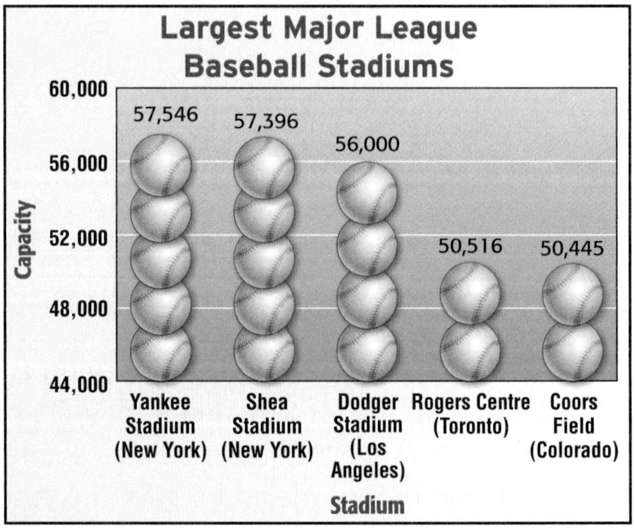

Source: ballparksofbaseball.com

Four in a Line

Solving Equations

Get Ready!

Players: two to ten

You will need: 12 index cards, scissors, poster board, beans

Get Set!

- Cut all 12 index cards in half. Your teacher will give you a list of 24 equations. Label each card with a different equation.
- Cut one 6-inch by 5-inch playing board for each player from the poster board.
- For each playing board, copy the grid shown. Complete each column by choosing from the solutions below so that no two cards are identical.

a	b	c	d
			Free
	Free		

Solutions

a: −9, −3, 4, 6, 11, 16
b: −3, −1, 1, 5, 10, 12
c: −6, 2, 3, 7, 8, 12
d: −3, −2, 0, 1, 3, 8

Go!

- Mix the equation cards and place the deck facedown.
- After an equation card is turned up, all players solve the equation.
- If a player finds a solution on the board, he or she covers it with a bean.
- The first player to cover four spaces in a row either vertically, horizontally, or diagonally is the winner.

7-11 Solving Multiplication Equations

GET READY to Learn

Kara baby-sat for 3 hours and earned $12. How much did she make each hour? Let x represent the amount Kara earns each hour.

Explain how the equation $3x = 12$ represents the situation.

MAIN IDEA

I will solve and write multiplication equations.

Standard 5AF1.5 Solve problems involving linear functions with integer values; **write the equation;** and graph the resulting ordered pairs of integers on a grid.

New Vocabulary

coefficient

The equation $3x = 12$ is a multiplication equation. In $3x$, 3 is the **coefficient** of x because it is the number by which x is multiplied. To solve a multiplication equation, use division.

EXAMPLE Solve a Multiplication Equation

1 Solve $3x = 12$. Check your solution.

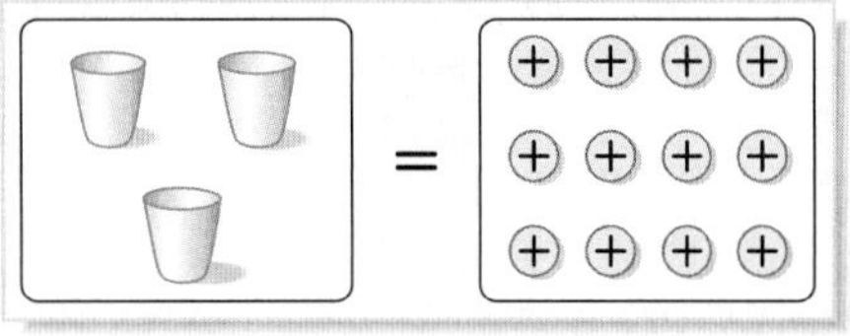

Model the equation.

$$3x = 12$$

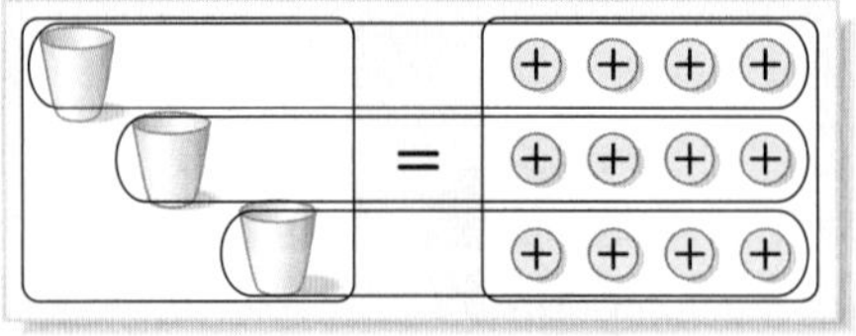

Divide the 12 counters equally into 3 groups. There are 4 counters in each group.

$$\frac{3x}{3} = \frac{12}{3}$$

$$x = 4$$

Check $3x = 12$ Write the original equation.

$3(4) \stackrel{?}{=} 12$ Replace x with 4.

$12 = 12$ This sentence is true. ✓

The solution is 4.

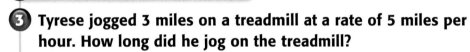

EXAMPLE Solve a Multiplication Equation

Remember

In Example 2, you can check your solution by replacing x with -5.

$-2x = 10$

$-2(-5) \stackrel{?}{=} 10$

$10 = 10$ ✓

2 **Solve $-2x = 10$.**

$-2x = 10$	Write the equation.
$\frac{-2x}{-2} = \frac{10}{-2}$	Divide each side by -2.
$1x = -5$	$-2 \div (-2) = 1$, $10 \div (-2) = -5$
$x = -5$	$1x = x$

The solution is -5.

The equation $d = r \cdot t$ or $d = rt$ shows the relationship between the variables d (distance), r (rate or speed), and t (time).

Real-World EXAMPLE

3 **Tyrese jogged 3 miles on a treadmill at a rate of 5 miles per hour. How long did he jog on the treadmill?**

Use the formula distance = rate × time.

$d = rt$	Write the equation.
$3 = 5t$	Replace d with 3 and r with 5.
$\frac{3}{5} = \frac{5t}{5}$	Divide each side by 5.
$0.6 = t$	Simplify.

Tyrese jogged on the treadmill for 0.6 hour, or 36 minutes.

Online Personal Tutor at ca.gr5math.com

CHECK What You Know

Solve each equation. Check your solution. See Examples 1, 2 (pp. 398–399)

1. $2a = 6$ **2.** $20 = 4c$ **3.** $16 = 8b$

4. $-4d = 12$ **5.** $-6c = 24$ **6.** $-3g = -21$

7. An object on Earth weighs six times what it would weigh on the moon. An object weighs 72 pounds on Earth. Write and solve a multiplication equation to find the weight of the object on the Moon. See Example 3 (p. 399)

8. Talk About It What are two different multiplication equations that have 5 as the solution?

Practice and Problem Solving

EXTRA PRACTICE See page 676.

Solve each equation. Check your solution. See Examples 1, 2 (pp. 398–399)

9. $5d = 30$ **10.** $4c = 16$ **11.** $36 = 6e$

12. $21 = 3g$ **13.** $3f = -12$ **14.** $4g = -24$

15. $-5a = 15$ **16.** $-6x = 12$ **17.** $-5t = -25$

18. $-6n = -36$ **19.** $-32 = -4s$ **20.** $-7 = -14x$

21. A jewelry store is selling a set of 4 pairs of gemstone earrings for $58, including tax. Neva and three of her friends bought the gift set so each could have one pair of earrings. Write and solve a multiplication equation to find how much each person should pay.

22. In 2004, Pen Hadow and Simon Murray walked 680 miles to the South Pole in 58 days. Write and solve a multiplication equation to find about how many miles they traveled each day.

Solve each equation. Check your solution.

23. $1.5x = 3$ **24.** $8.1 = 0.9a$ **25.** $39 = 1.3b$

26. $0.4g = -0.6$ **27.** $-0.3w = -0.12$ **28.** $-2.6 = -1.3m$

29. **Geometry** The area of a rectangle is 120 square inches, and the width is 5 inches. Write a multiplication equation to find the length of the rectangle and use it to solve the problem. Describe how you can check your answer.

30. The Raimonde family drove 1,764 miles across the United States on their vacation. If it took a total of 28 hours, what was their average speed, in miles per hour?

Real-World PROBLEM SOLVING

Football **For Exercises 31 and 32, use the table.**

31. George Blanda played in the NFL for 26 years. Write and solve an equation to find how many points he averaged each year.

32. Norm Johnson played in the NFL for 16 years. Write and solve an equation to find how many points he averaged each year.

Top NFL Kickers

Player	Career Points
Gary Anderson	2,346
Morten Andersen	2,259
George Blanda	2,002
Norm Johnson	1,736
Nick Lowery	1,711

Source: *Scholastic Book of World Records*

33. An average person's heart beats about 103,680 times a day. Write and solve an equation to find about how many times the average person's heart beats in one minute.

34. On average, a person blinks his or her eyes about 20,000 times a day. About how many times does a person blink his or her eyes per minute?

H.O.T. Problems

35. **Which One Doesn't Belong?** Identify the equation that does not belong with the other three. Explain your reasoning.

$2x = 24$ | $6a = 72$ | $3c = 4$ | $5y = 60$

36. **CHALLENGE** Without solving, decide whether $4x = 1{,}000$ or $8x = 1{,}000$ has the greater solution. Explain your reasoning.

37. **WRITING IN ▶MATH** Write a problem about a real-world situation that can be represented by the equation $4x = 24$.

Standards Practice

38 Use the formula $A = \ell w$ to find the length of the rectangle shown below.

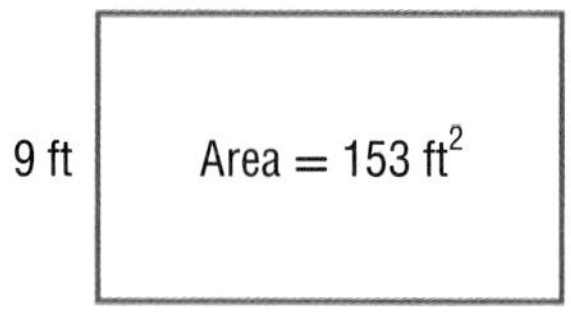

A 9 feet
B 17 feet
C 34 feet
D 153 feet

39 If Mr. Solomon bikes at a constant speed of 12 miles per hour, which method can be used to find the number of hours it will take him to bike 54 miles?

F Add 12 to 54.
G Subtract 12 from 54.
H Multiply 54 by 12.
J Divide 54 by 12.

Spiral Review

Solve each equation. **(Lessons 7-9 and 7-10)**

40. $b - 5 = -2$
41. $t - 6 = 5$
42. $g - 6 = -7$
43. $a - 2 = -2$
44. $x + 4 = 9$
45. $p + 3 = -2$
46. $6 + r = 2$
47. $7 + q = -1$

48. Eight people borrowed a total of $56. If each borrowed the same amount, how much did each person borrow? **(Lesson 7-6)**

Chapter 7 Study Guide and Review

FOLDABLES™ Study Organizer GET READY to Study

Be sure the following Key Concepts are noted in your Foldable.

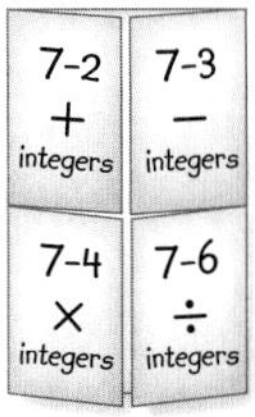

Key Concepts

Integers (Lessons 7-1 to 7-4, 7-6)

- **Add**

  The sum of two positive integers is always positive.

  The sum of two negative integers is always negative.

- **Subtract**

  To subtract an integer, add its opposite.

- **Multiply**

  The product of two integers with different signs is negative.

  The product of two integers with the same sign is positive.

- **Divide**

  The quotient of two integers with different signs is negative.

  The quotient of two integers with the same sign is positive.

Coordinate Plane (Lesson 7-8)

- The *x*-axis and *y*-axis separate the coordinate plane into four regions called quadrants.

Key Vocabulary

coefficient (p. 398)
inverse operations (p. 385)
quadrants (p. 378)

Vocabulary Check

State whether each sentence is *true* or *false*. If *false*, replace the underlined word or number to make a true sentence.

1. An integer is any number from the set {…, −3, −2, −1, 0, 1, 2, 3, …}.
2. The numerical factor of a term that contains a variable is called a quadrant. ?
3. Any integer that is less than zero is a positive integer.
4. Inverse operations *undo* each other.
5. The sign of the sum of two positive integers is negative.
6. Addition and multiplication are inverse operations.
7. The four regions into which the two perpendicular lines of a coordinate system separate the plane are called integers.
8. The *y*-coordinate is the first number in an ordered pair.

Lesson-by-Lesson Review

7-1 Ordering Integers (pp. 349–352)

Example 1
Replace the ● in –5 ● –2 with <, >, or = to make a true sentence.

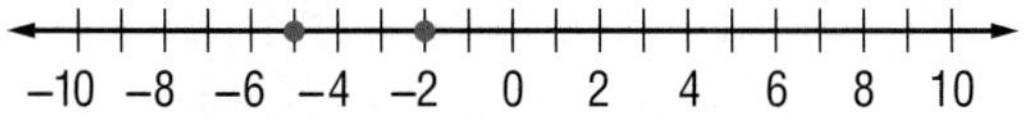

Since –5 is to the left of –2, $-5 < -2$.

Replace each ● with <, >, or = to make a true sentence.

9. –4 ● 0 **10.** 6 ● 2

11. –1 ● 1 **12.** 7 ● –6

13. Order \$8, –\$7, –\$5, and –\$12 from greatest to least.

7-2 Adding Integers (pp. 354–358)

Example 2
Find $-3 + 2$.

Use counters.

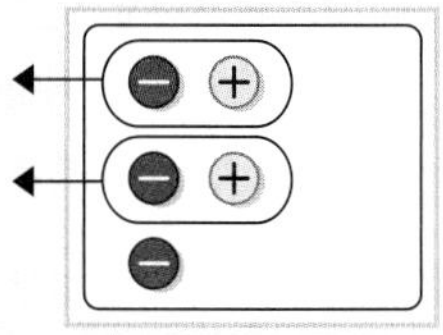

Add 3 negative counters and 2 positive counters to the mat. Then remove as many zero pairs as possible.

So, $-3 + 2 = -1$.

Add.

14. $-8 + (-5)$ **15.** $-4 + (-2)$

16. $-9 + 5$ **17.** $-6 + 6$

18. Suppose the temperature outside is 4°F. If the temperature drops 7 degrees, what temperature will it be?

7-3 Subtracting Integers (pp. 359–363)

Example 3
Find $-2 - 3$.

Add the opposite.

$-2 - 3 = -2 + (-3)$ To subtract 3, add –3.
$= -5$ Simplify.

So, $-2 - 3 = -5$.

Subtract.

19. $-4 - (-9)$ **20.** $-12 - (-8)$

21. $-8 - (-3)$ **22.** $6 - 4$

23. In Antarctica, an average temperature can be –4°F. With the wind, the windchill temperature is –19°F. Find the difference between the temperature and the windchill temperature.

CHAPTER 7

Study Guide and Review

7-4 Multiplying Integers (pp. 364–367)

Example 4
Find -4×3.

$-4 \times 3 = -12$ The integers have different signs. The product is negative.

Example 5
Find $-8 \times (-3)$.

$-8 \times (-3) = 24$ The integers have the same sign. The product is positive.

Multiply.

24. -3×5

25. $6(-4)$

26. $-2 \times (-8)$

27. $7(5)$

28. Sherita invested in the stock market. Over three months, she lost an average of \$2 each month. Write an integer that represents her loss.

7-5 Problem-Solving Strategy: Work Backward (pp. 368–369)

Example 6
A number is divided by 2. Then 5 is added to the quotient. The result is 35. What is the number?

Start with the final value. Perform the opposite operation with each resulting value until you arrive at the starting value.

$35 - 5 = 30$ Undo adding 5.
$30 \cdot 2 = 60$ Undo dividing by 2.

The number is 60.

Solve. Use the *work backward* strategy.

29. After school, Lynn watched TV for half an hour, played basketball for 45 minutes, and studied for an hour. If it is now 7:00 P.M., what time did Lynn come home from school?

30. Neil has four less than twice the number of baseball cards Marcus has. Neil has 156 baseball cards. How many does Marcus have?

7-6 Dividing Integers (pp. 371–375)

Example 7
Find $-6 \div 3$.

$-2 \times 3 = -6$. So, $-6 \div 3 = -2$.

Divide.

31. $-81 \div -9$

32. $-36 \div (-3)$

33. $-72 \div 6$

34. $42 \div (-7)$

35. Algebra Evaluate $k \div j$ if $k = -28$ and $j = 7$.

7-7 Problem-Solving Investigation: Choose the Best Strategy (pp. 376–377)

Example 8
A room is 11 feet by 14 feet. Is 125 square feet or 150 square feet a reasonable estimate of the area of the room?

Since 11×14 is about 10×15 or 150, 150 square feet is a reasonable estimate of the area of the room.

Choose the best strategy to solve each problem.

36. California contains 40.2 million acres of forest. Hawaii has 1.7 million acres of forest. About how many times more acres of forest does California have than Hawaii?

37. How many pieces of ribbon each measuring $1\frac{3}{4}$ yards can be cut from a piece of ribbon measuring $8\frac{3}{4}$ yards?

7-8 The Coordinate Plane (pp. 378–382)

Example 9
Which building is located at (3, 1)?

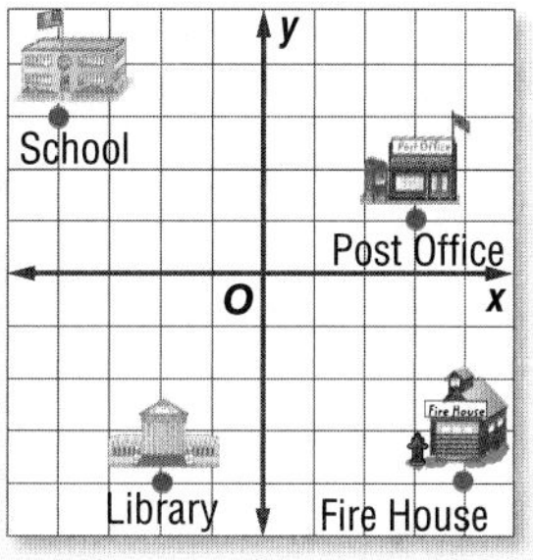

Start at the origin. Move 3 units right and 1 unit up.

The Post Office is at point (3, 1).

38. Refer to Example 9. Which building is located at $(-2, -4)$?

Graph and label each point on a coordinate plane.

39. $E(2, -1)$

40. $F(-3, -2)$

41. $G(4, 1)$

42. $H(-2, 4)$

7-9 Solving Addition Equations (pp. 385–389)

Example 10
Solve $x + 8 = 10$.

$$
\begin{aligned}
x + 8 &= 10 \\
-8 &= -8 \quad \text{Subtract 8 from each side.} \\
x &= 2 \quad \text{Simplify.}
\end{aligned}
$$

Solve each equation.

43. $c + 8 = 11$

44. $x + 15 = 14$

45. $54 = m + 9$

46. $-5 = 2 + x$

47. When Marco stands on a box, he is 10 feet tall. If the box is 4 feet tall, write and solve an addition equation to find Marco's height.

Study Guide and Review

7-10 Solving Subtraction Equations (pp. 393–396)

Example 11
Solve $a - 5 = -3$.

$$\begin{aligned} a - 5 &= -3 \\ +5 &= +5 \quad \text{Add 5 to each side.} \\ a &= 2 \quad \text{Simplify.} \end{aligned}$$

Example 12
Solve $4 = m - 9$.

$$\begin{aligned} 4 &= m - 9 \\ +9 &= \quad +9 \quad \text{Add 9 to each side.} \\ 13 &= m \quad \text{Simplify.} \end{aligned}$$

Solve each equation.

48. $z - 7 = 11$ **49.** $s - 9 = -12$

50. $14 = m - 5$ **51.** $-4 = y - 9$

52. $h - 2 = -9$ **53.** $-6 = g - 4$

54. $p - 22 = -7$ **55.** $d - 3 = -14$

56. **Algebra** Find the value of c if $c - 9 = -3$.

57. Francesca borrowed $8 from her mother. She now owes her mother $47. Write and solve a subtraction equation to find the original amount of money Francesca owed her mom.

7-11 Solving Multiplication Equations (pp. 398–401)

Example 13
Over a period of 9 days, the outside temperature dropped a total of 27°F. Write and solve an equation to find the average number of degrees the temperature changed each day.

Let d represent the average number of degrees the temperature changed each day.

$$\begin{aligned} 9d &= -27 \quad \text{Write the equation.} \\ \frac{9d}{9} &= \frac{-27}{9} \quad \text{Divide each side by } -9. \\ d &= -3 \quad \text{Simplify.} \end{aligned}$$

So, the temperature dropped 3°F each day.

Solve each equation.

58. $4b = 32$ **59.** $5y = 60$

60. $-3m = 21$ **61.** $-18 = -6c$

62. $7a = -35$ **63.** $28 = -2d$

64. $-4x = 12$ **65.** $-6y = -18$

66. **Algebra** The product of a number and 8 is -56. What is the number?

67. A store is selling blank CDs in packages of 25 for $5. Write and solve a multiplication equation to find the cost of one blank CD.

68. The band director is organizing the clarinet players into 5 rows. If there are 30 clarinet players, how many clarinet players are in each row?

CHAPTER 7

Chapter Test

Order each set of integers from least to greatest.

1. −9, 1, 4, −1, −4 **2.** −5, 3, −8, 1, 0

Add or subtract.

3. $-5 + (-7)$ **4.** $-13 + 10$

5. $-4 - (-9)$ **6.** $6 - (-5)$

7. $2 + (-8)$ **8.** $-11 - 3$

9. The temperature at 6:00 A.M. was −5°F. Find the temperature at 8:00 A.M. if it was 7 degrees warmer.

10. **STANDARDS PRACTICE** Which equation was used to create the function table below?

x	*y*
−48	−6
−16	−2
0	0
8	1

A $y = -8x$ **C** $y = \frac{x}{8}$

B $y = x + 8$ **D** $y = x - 8$

Multiply or divide.

11. $4(-9)$ **12.** $24 \div (-4)$

13. $-63 \div (-9)$ **14.** $-2(-7)$

15. $-3(8)$ **16.** $-15 \div (-5)$

17. Avery's temperature dropped 1°F each hour for 3 hours. What was the change from his original temperature?

18. A bacteria doubles its population every 12 hours. After 3 days, there are 1,600 bacteria. How many bacteria were there at the beginning of the first day? Use the *work backward* strategy.

Graph and label each point on a coordinate grid.

19. $C(-4, -2)$ **20.** $D(5, 3)$

Name the ordered pair for each point and identify its quadrant.

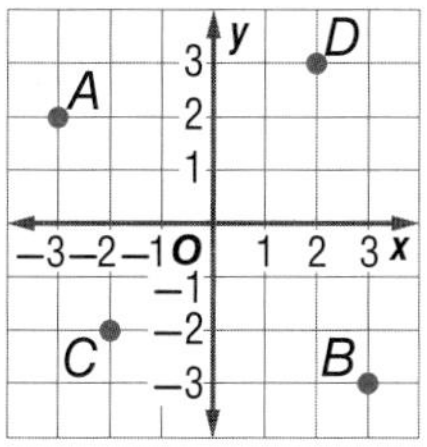

21. *A*

22. *B*

23. *C*

24. *D*

25. **STANDARDS PRACTICE** Which line contains the ordered pair (−2, 1)?

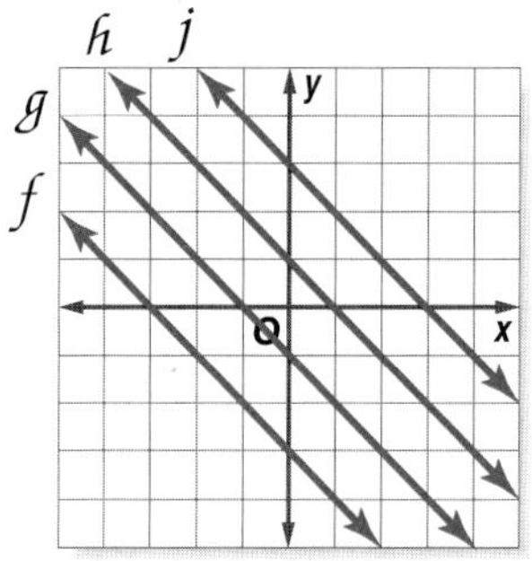

F Line *f*

G Line *g*

H Line *h*

J Line *j*

Solve each equation. Check your solution.

26. $w + 8 = 5$ **27.** $-8 = d - 9$

28. $15 = 3n$ **29.** $-3 + x = 11$

30. $z - 3 = -6$ **31.** $-5m = -30$

32. **Algebra** The product of a number and 18 is −36. Write and solve an equation to find the value of *n*.

33. **WRITING IN ►MATH** For a science project, Reynaldo and Beth are raising tadpoles. They have 12 tadpoles and some frogs. They have a total of 20 tadpoles and frogs. What type of equation could you use to find how many frogs they have?

CHAPTER 7 California Standards Practice

Cumulative, Chapters 1–7

Standards Example

The locations of the pool, horse barn, cabin, and cafeteria at a summer camp are shown on the coordinate plane. Which ordered pair names the location of the pool?

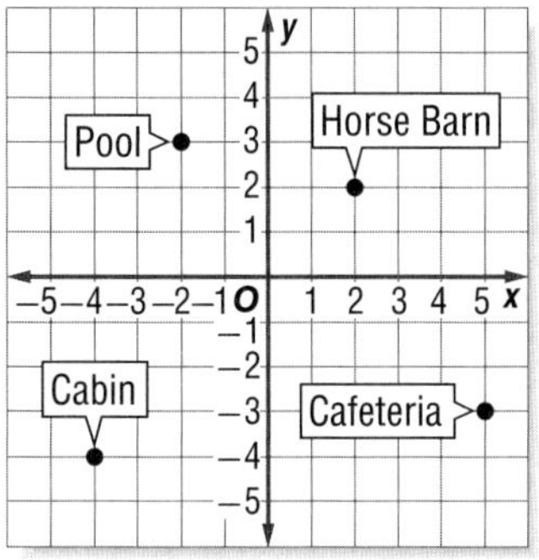

A (−2, 3)

B (−3, 2)

C (3, −2)

D (2, −3)

Read the Question

You are to find which ordered pair names the location of the pool.

Solve the Question

Start at the origin. Move right on the *x*-axis to find the *x*-coordinate of the pool, which is −2.

Move up the *y*-axis to find the *y*-coordinate, which is 3.

The pool is named by (−2, 3).

The answer is A.

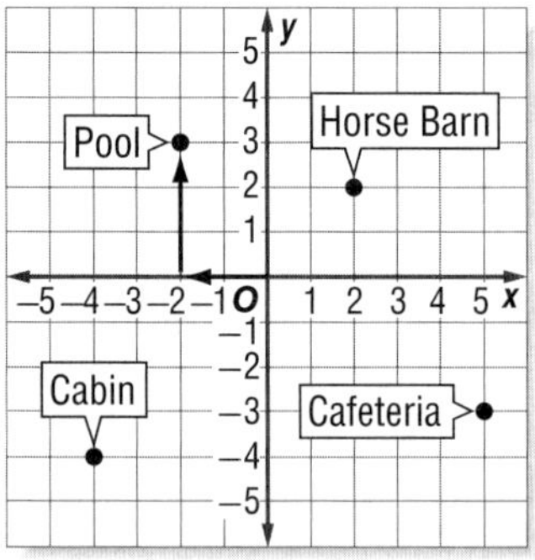

Online **Personal Tutor at** ca.gr5math.com

Refer to the coordinate plane above. Choose the best answer.

1 **An exercise facility is to be built at (−4, −2). What existing facility would be closest to the new exercise facility?**

A pool **C** horse barn

B cabin **D** cafeteria

2 **Which ordered pair gives a possible location for a new pavilion if it is to be built at a location in which *y* = 3?**

F (3, −4) **H** (2, 3)

G (3, 2) **J** (3, 1)

3 **If $d = 8$, find the value of $5d - 11$.**

A 20 **C** 39

B 29 **D** 50

---

4 **The temperature of the water in a pool was 78°F. Then, the temperature of the water drops 8°F. Which addition sentence represents this situation?**

F $78 + 8$ **H** $-78 + 8$

G $78 + (-8)$ **J** $-78 + (-8)$

---

5 **The equation of line *t* is $y = 2$.**

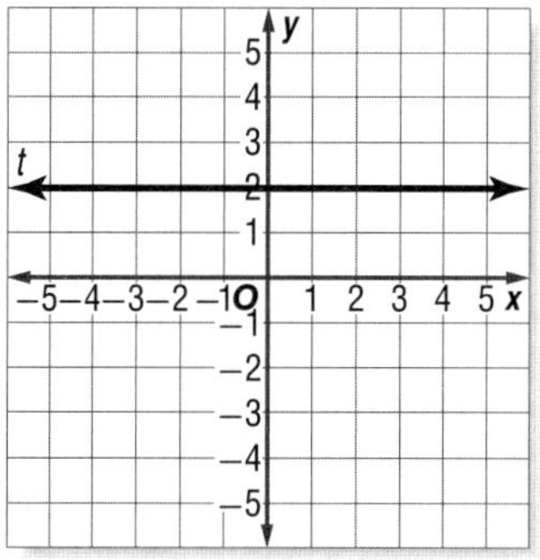

Which ordered pair is located on line *t*?

A (2, 0) **C** (−2, 2)

B (2, 3) **D** (0, −2)

---

6 **If Janice drives at a constant speed of 60 miles per hour, which equation can be used to determine the number of miles she will drive in *h* hours?**

F $60 + h$ **H** $60h$

G $60 - h$ **J** $60 \div h$

---

7 **It costs $0.25 to run a dryer at the laundromat for one fourth of an hour. How much does it cost to run the dryer for 2 hours?**

A $0.50 **B** $1.25 **C** $1.75 **D** $2.00

---

8 **What is the area of the square below?**

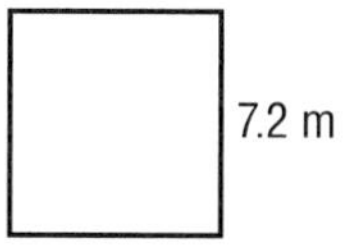

F 7.2 square meters

G 14.4 square meters

H 28.8 square meters

J 51.84 square meters

---

9 **$10.4 \times 5.8 =$**

A 59.32 **B** 60.02 **C** 60.32 **D** 61.02

---

10 **A piece of string is 5.625 inches long. If 2.5 inches are cut off, how long is the piece of string that is left?**

F 3.62 inches **H** 2.62 inches

G 3.125 inches **J** 2.125 inches

---

11 **Mary's temperature on Sunday night was 101°F. On Monday morning, her temperature was 103°F. Which integer represents Mary's temperature on Sunday night in degrees Fahrenheit?**

A −103 **B** −101 **C** 101 **D** 103

CHAPTER 8

Algebra: Ratios and Functions

BIG Idea What is a ratio?

A **ratio** is a comparison of two quantities by division.

Example Catalina Island, off the coast of southern California, has two towns. Avalon has a population of 3,500, and Two Harbors has a population of 100. The **ratio** of Avalon's population to Two Harbors' population can be written in three ways.

3,500 to 100   3,500:100 $\frac{3,500}{100}$

Read each ratio as *three thousand five hundred to one hundred.*

What will I learn in this chapter?

- Express ratios and rates in fraction form.
- Extend and describe arithmetic sequences using algebraic expressions.
- Write an equation to describe a linear situation.
- Solve problems by looking for a pattern.

Key Vocabulary

ratio
rate
unit rate
sequence

Math Online Student Study Tools at ca.gr5math.com

FOLDABLES™ Study Organizer

Make this Foldable to help you organize information about the chapter. Begin with a piece of graph paper.

1 Fold the paper in thirds lengthwise.

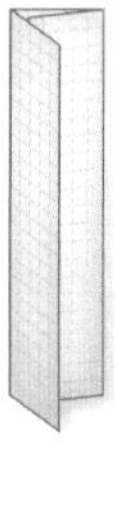

2 Fold one-fourth down. Cut to make three tabs as shown.

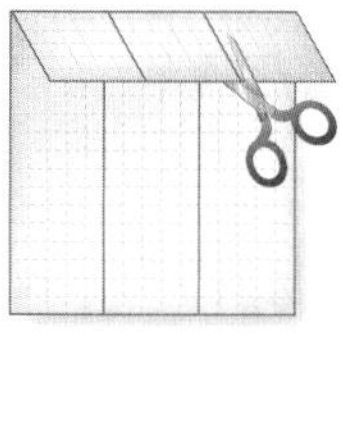

3 Unfold the tabs. Label the paper as shown.

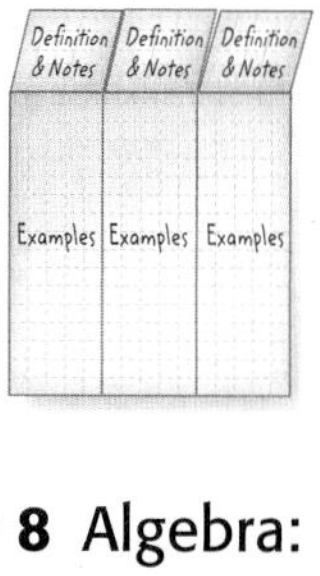

4 Refold the tabs and label as shown.

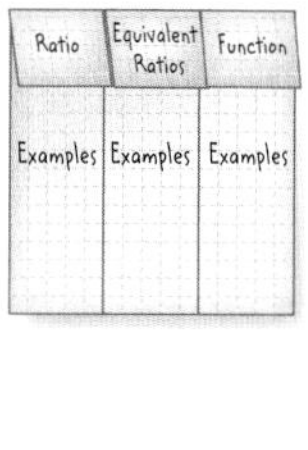

ARE YOU READY for Chapter 8?

You have two ways to check prerequisite skills for this chapter.

Option 2

Math Online Take the Chapter Readiness Quiz at ca.gr5math.com.

Option 1

Complete the Quick Check below.

QUICK Check

Write each fraction in simplest form. **(Lesson 4-3)**

1. $\frac{32}{48}$ **2.** $\frac{7}{28}$ **3.** $\frac{15}{25}$

4. $\frac{30}{35}$ **5.** $\frac{15}{18}$ **6.** $\frac{27}{36}$

7. An airplane has flown 260 miles out of a total trip of 500 miles. What fraction, in simplest form, of the trip has been completed? **(Lesson 4-3)**

Algebra Solve each equation. **(Lesson 7-11)**

8. $16m = 48$ **9.** $5x = 40$ **10.** $15p = 150$

11. $7y = 56$ **12.** $12z = 72$ **13.** $8h = 96$

14. The number of students in the fifth grade at a certain school is shown by the equation $22c = 110$, where c is the number of 5th grade classrooms. How many fifth grade classrooms are in the school? **(Lesson 7-11)**

Algebra Find the next three values in each pattern. **(Lesson 1-4)**

15. 4, 7, 10, 13, ...

16. 62, 66, 70, 74, ...

17. 1.8, 2.4, 3.0, 3.6, ...

18. Mario played the drums for 30 minutes on Tuesday, 45 minutes on Wednesday, and 60 minutes on Thursday. At this rate, how many minutes will he play on Friday? **(Lesson 1-4)**

8-1 Ratios and Rates

Concepts in Motion
Interactive Lab
ca.gr5math.com

GET READY to Learn

Hands-On Mini Lab

Consider the set of paper clips shown.

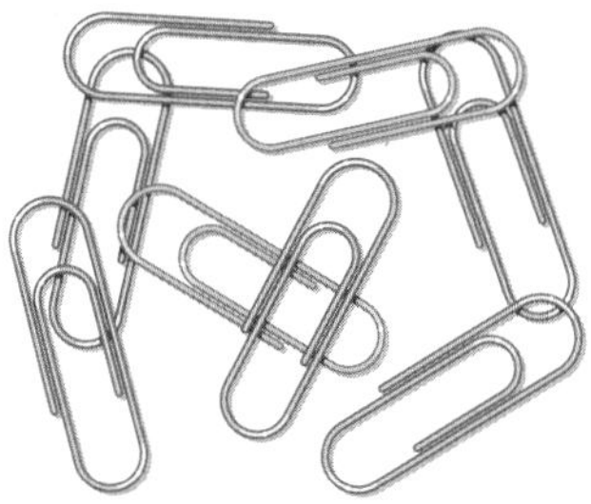

1. Compare the number of blue paper clips to the number of green paper clips using the word *more* and then using the word *times*.
2. Compare the number of green paper clips to the number of blue paper clips using the word *less* and then using a fraction.

MAIN IDEA

I will express ratios and rates in fraction form.

Preparation for Standard 6NS1.2
Interpret and use ratios in different contexts (e.g., batting averages, miles per hour) to show the relative sizes of two quantities, **using appropriate notations** $\left(\frac{a}{b}, a \text{ to } b, a{:}b\right)$.

New Vocabulary

ratio
rate
unit rate

There are many different ways to compare amounts or *quantities*. A **ratio** is a comparison of two quantities by division. A ratio of 2 green paper clips to 6 blue paper clips can be written in three ways.

Ratio	Using *to*	Using :	Using a *Fraction*
green paper clips to blue paper clips	2 to 6	2:6	$\frac{2}{6}$

Read each ratio as *two to six.*

As with fractions, ratios are often expressed in simplest form.

EXAMPLE Write a Ratio in Simplest Form

1 **Write the ratio in simplest form that compares the number of green paper clips to the number of blue paper clips. Then explain its meaning.**

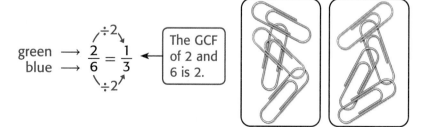

$$\begin{matrix} \text{green} \longrightarrow \\ \text{blue} \longrightarrow \end{matrix} \frac{2}{6} \overset{\div 2}{\underset{\div 2}{=}} \frac{1}{3}$$

The GCF of 2 and 6 is 2.

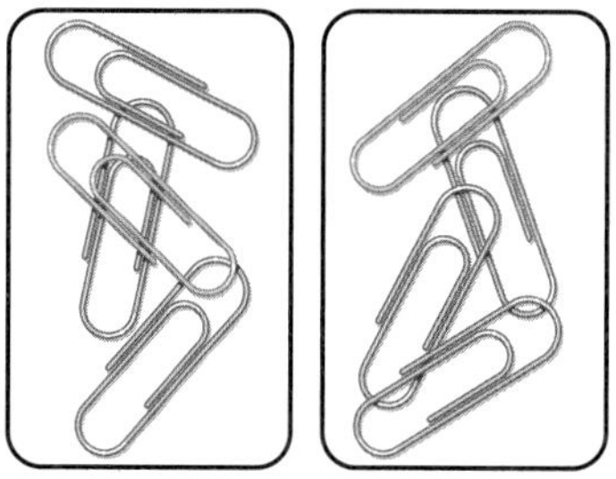

The ratio of green to blue paper clips is $\frac{1}{3}$, 1 to 3, or 1:3. This means that for every 1 green paper clip there are 3 blue paper clips.

Remember

To review **simplifying fractions**, see Lesson 4-3.

Ratios can also be used to compare a part to a whole.

EXAMPLE Use Ratios to Compare Parts to a Whole

2 **Several students were asked to name their favorite flavor of gum. Write the ratio that compares the number of students who chose fruit to the total number of students who responded.**

Favorite Flavor of Gum	
Flavor	**Number of Responses**
Peppermint	9
Cinnamon	8
Fruit	3
Spearmint	1

Three students preferred fruit out of a total of $9 + 8 + 3 + 1$ or 21 responses.

fruit flavor responses ⟶
total responses ⟶

$$\frac{3}{21} = \frac{1}{7} \quad (\div 3 \text{ numerator and denominator})$$

The GCF of 3 and 21 is 3.

The ratio in simplest form of the number of students who chose fruit to the total number of responses is $\frac{1}{7}$, 1 to 7, or 1:7.
So, one out of every 7 students preferred fruit-flavored gum.

A **rate** is a ratio comparing two quantities with different kinds of units.

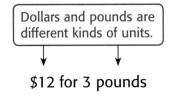

Dollars and pounds are different kinds of units.

$12 for 3 pounds

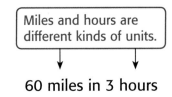

Miles and hours are different kinds of units.

60 miles in 3 hours

The rate for one unit of a given quantity is called a **unit rate**.

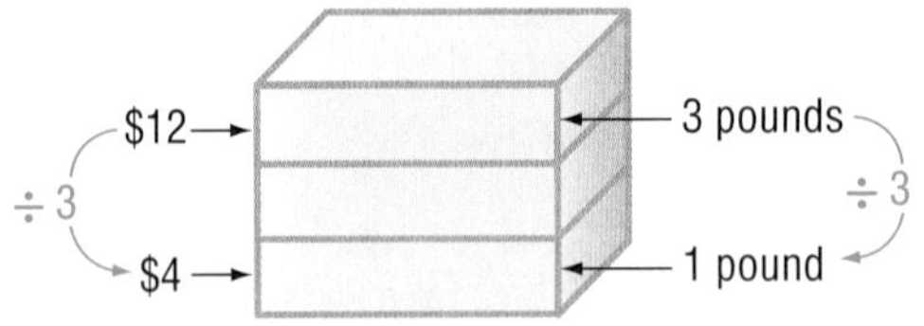

The model shows that the dollars divided by the number of pounds is the number of dollars for 1 pound.

A unit rate of $4 for 1 pound can be read as $4 per pound.

Remember

Some common unit rates are miles per hour, miles per gallon, price per pound, and dollars per hour.

When written as a fraction, a unit rate has a denominator of 1. Therefore, to write a rate as a unit rate, divide the numerator and denominator of the rate by the denominator.

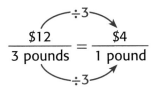

$$\frac{\$12}{3 \text{ pounds}} = \frac{\$4}{1 \text{ pound}} \quad (\div 3)$$

EXAMPLE Find a Unit Rate

3 **The roadrunner is the state bird of New Mexico. Roadrunners prefer running to flying. It would take 4 hours for a roadrunner to run about 54 miles. How many miles can a roadrunner run per hour?**

$$\frac{54 \text{ miles}}{4 \text{ hours}} = \frac{13.5 \text{ miles}}{1 \text{ hour}} \quad (\div 4)$$

So, a roadrunner can run about 13.5 miles per hour.

Online **Personal Tutor at** ca.gr5math.com

CHECK What You Know

For Exercises 1–3, write each ratio as a fraction in simplest form. Then explain its meaning. **See Example 1 (p. 413)**

1.

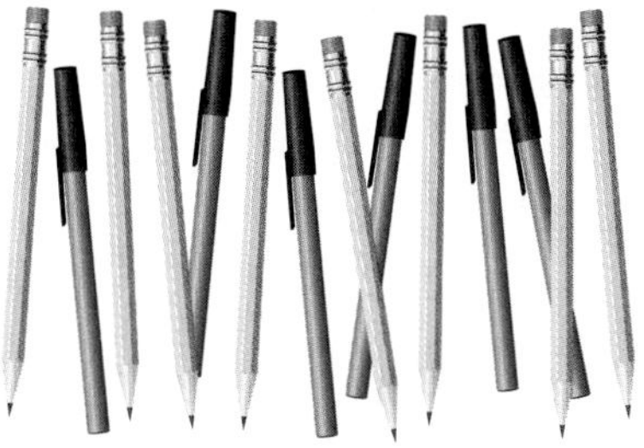

pens to pencils

2.

pennies:dimes

3. A theater is showing 8 comedies and 12 action movies. What is the ratio of action movies to comedies?

4. Last month, Amber ate 9 apples, 5 bananas, 4 peaches, and 7 oranges. Find the ratio, in simplest form, of bananas to the total number of pieces of fruit Amber ate last month. Then explain its meaning. **See Example 2 (p. 414)**

Write each rate as a unit rate. **See Example 3 (p. 415)**

5. $9 for 3 cases of soda

6. 25 meters in 2 seconds

7. Shina's heart beats 410 times in 5 minutes. At this rate, how many times does Shina's heart beat per minute?

8. **Talk About It** Give the ratio 6 geese out of 15 birds in simplest form in three different ways.

Practice and Problem Solving

EXTRA PRACTICE See page 676.

For Exercises 9–14, write each ratio as a fraction in simplest form. Then explain its meaning. See Example 1 (p. 413)

9.

flutes:drums

10.

sandwiches to milk cartons

11. A class has 6 boys and 15 girls. What is the ratio of boys to girls?

12. Audrey counted 6 motorcycles and 27 cars at the restaurant parking lot. Find the ratio of motorcycles to cars.

13. The jewelry store is having a sale on 25 emerald rings and 15 ruby rings. Find the ratio of ruby rings to emerald rings.

14. An animal shelter has 36 kittens and 12 puppies available for adoption. What is the ratio of puppies to kittens?

15. For reading class, Salvador is keeping track of the types of books he has read so far this year. Find the ratio, in simplest form, of mystery books to the total number of books Salvador has read. Then explain its meaning.

Type	Number of Books
Mystery	10
Nonfiction	7
Science Fiction/Fantasy	5
Western	2

16. Last week, a phone company sold the cell phone covers listed in the table. Find the ratio, in simplest form, of black cell phone covers to the total number of cell phone covers sold last week. Then explain its meaning.

Color	Number of Cell Phone Covers
Green	5
Silver	6
Red	3
Black	4

17. For a trip, Ramona packed 6 blouses, 5 pairs of shorts, 3 pairs of jeans, and 1 skirt. Find the ratio, in simplest form, of pairs of jeans to the total number of pieces of clothing Ramona packed. Then explain its meaning.

18. On the first day of the food drive, Mrs. Teasley's classes brought in 6 cans of fruit, 4 cans of beans, 7 boxes of noodles, and 4 cans of soup. Find the ratio, in simplest form, of cans of fruit to the total number of food items collected. Then explain its meaning.

Write each rate as a unit rate. See Example 3 (p. 415)

19. 180 words in 3 minutes

20. $36 for 4 tickets

21. $4 for 8 bottles of water

22. $3 for a dozen eggs

23. A marathon is approximately 26 miles. If Joshua ran the marathon in 4 hours at a constant rate, how far did he run per hour?

24. 340 trees are saved by recycling 20 tons of paper. How many trees are saved from 1 ton of recycled paper?

25. The 24 students in Mr. Brown's class sold 72 magazine subscriptions. The 28 students in Mrs. Garcia's class sold 98 magazine subscriptions. Whose class sold more magazine subscriptions per student? Explain your reasoning.

Real-World PROBLEM SOLVING

Insects **For Exercises 26 and 27, use the table. Mr. Bell asked each of his students to bring a live insect to school to study. The graphic shows the different insects and how many of each were brought to school. Write each ratio in simplest form. Then explain its meaning.**

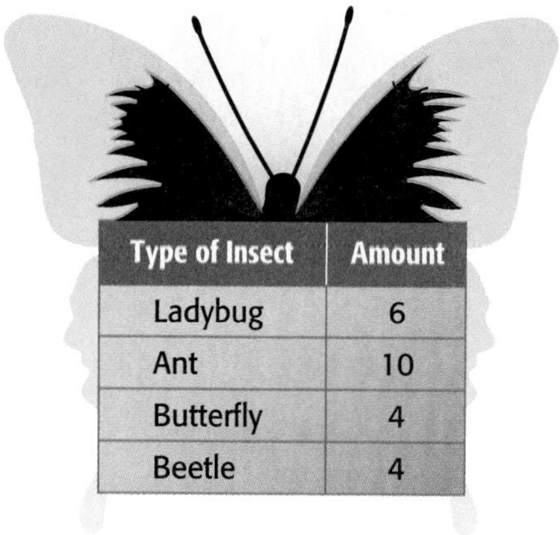

Type of Insect	Amount
Ladybug	6
Ant	10
Butterfly	4
Beetle	4

26. Write the ratio that compares the number of ladybugs to the total number of insects.

27. Write the ratio that compares the number of butterflies to the number of ants.

H.O.T. Problems

28. **OPEN ENDED** Create three different drawings showing a number of circles and triangles in which the ratio of circles to triangles is 2:3.

29. **CHALLENGE** The student store sold 8 boxes of colored pencils in 15 minutes. At this rate, how many boxes will they sell per hour?

30. FIND THE ERROR Nicole and Mirna are writing the rate $56 in 4 weeks as a unit rate. Who is correct? Explain your reasoning.

Nicole

$$\frac{\$56}{4 \text{ weeks}} = \frac{\$14}{1 \text{ week}}$$

Mirna

$$\frac{\$56}{4 \text{ weeks}} = \frac{\$28}{2 \text{ weeks}}$$

31. WRITING IN ► MATH What is the difference between a ratio and a rate? Give two examples of each.

Standards Practice

32 While working out at the gym, Rodrigo spends 25 minutes on a treadmill and 35 minutes lifting weights. What is the ratio of the time Rodrigo spends on the treadmill to the time spent lifting weights?

A 2 to 3

B 5 to 7

C 4 to 5

D 1 to 7

33 The table shows the age ranges of the guests at Margo's birthday party. Which ratio accurately compares the number of guests ages 15 to 40 to the total number of guests?

Age Range	Number of Guests
Under 15	11
15–40	6
41–65	3
Over 65	2

F 1:2 **H** 1:11

G 3:22 **J** 3:11

Spiral Review

Algebra Solve each equation. Check your solution. **(Lessons 7-10 and 7-11)**

34. $c - 7 = 54$ **35.** $24 = d - 6$ **36.** $e - 1 = -3$ **37.** $-4 = g - 14$

38. $10y = 120$ **39.** $45 = 9x$ **40.** $8f = -48$ **41.** $-2t = -36$

42. Algebra A number is multiplied by 8. Next, 4 is subtracted from the product. Then, 12 is added to the difference. If the result is 32, what is the number? Use the *work backward* strategy. **(Lesson 7-5)**

Multiply. Write in simplest form. **(Lesson 6-8)**

43. $\frac{1}{9} \times \frac{3}{4}$ **44.** $\frac{5}{8} \times 2$ **45.** $\frac{4}{7} \times \frac{1}{2}$ **46.** $\frac{3}{10} \times 5$

Game Time

Fishin' for Ratios

Equivalent Ratios

Get Ready!

Players: two or three

You will need: scissors, 18 index cards

Get Set!

- Cut all index cards in half.
- Write the ratios shown on half of the cards.
- Write a ratio equivalent to each of these ratios on the remaining cards.
- Two cards with equivalent ratios are considered matching cards.

$\frac{1}{2}$	$\frac{1}{4}$	$\frac{2}{3}$	$\frac{3}{4}$	$\frac{5}{8}$	$\frac{1}{3}$
$\frac{2}{5}$	$\frac{3}{7}$	$\frac{1}{5}$	$\frac{4}{5}$	$\frac{3}{5}$	$\frac{7}{8}$
$\frac{5}{7}$	$\frac{5}{9}$	$\frac{1}{8}$	$\frac{3}{8}$	$\frac{2}{7}$	$\frac{2}{9}$

Go!

- Shuffle the cards. Then deal 7 cards to each player. Place the remaining cards facedown in a pile. Players set aside any pairs of matching cards that they were dealt.
- The first player asks for a matching card. If a match is made, then the player sets aside the match, and it is the next player's turn. If no match is made, then the player picks up the top card from the pile. If a match is made, then the match is set aside, and it is the next player's turn. If no match is made, then it is the next player's turn.
- After all of the cards have been drawn or when a player has no more cards, the player with the most matches wins.

8-2 Problem-Solving Strategy

MAIN IDEA I will solve problems by looking for a pattern.

Standard 5MR1.1 Analyze problems by identifying relationships, distinguishing relevant from irrelevant information, sequencing and prioritizing information, and **observing patterns. Standard 5NS2.1 Add,** subtract, multiply, and divide **with decimals**; ... and verify the reasonableness of results.

Emelia is waiting for her friend Casey to arrive. It is 1:15 P.M. now, and Casey said that he would be on the first bus to arrive after 6:00 P.M. Emelia knows that buses arrive every 30 minutes, starting at 1:45 P.M. How much longer will it be before Casey arrives?

Understand

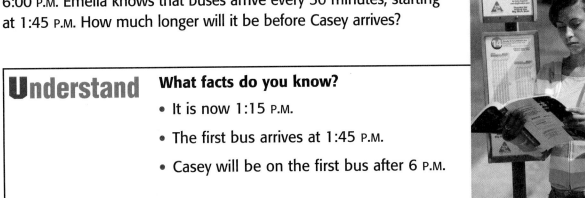

What facts do you know?

- It is now 1:15 P.M.
- The first bus arrives at 1:45 P.M.
- Casey will be on the first bus after 6 P.M.

What do you need to find?

- How much longer will it be before Casey arrives?

Plan

Start with the time the first bus arrives and look for a pattern.

Solve

Bus	Arrival Time
1	1:45 P.M.
2	1:45 P.M. + 30 minutes = 2:15 P.M.
3	2:15 P.M. + 30 minutes = 2:45 P.M.
4	2:45 P.M. + 30 minutes = 3:15 P.M.
⋮	⋮

The buses arrive every 15 and 45 minutes after the hour.

So, the first bus to arrive after 6:00 P.M. is the 6:15 P.M. bus. Since it is now 1:15 P.M., Casey will not arrive for another 5 hours.

Check

Look back at the problem. Continue adding 30 minutes to the previous arrival time until you reach 6:15 P.M.

5	3:15 P.M. + 30 minutes = 3:45 P.M.
6	3:45 P.M. + 30 minutes = 4:15 P.M.
7	4:15 P.M. + 30 minutes = 4:45 P.M.
8	4:45 P.M. + 30 minutes = 5:15 P.M.
9	5:15 P.M. + 30 minutes = 5:45 P.M.
10	5:45 P.M. + 30 minutes = 6:15 P.M.

Then add up the 30-minute periods. ✓

ANALYZE the Strategy

Refer to the problem on the previous page.

1. Suppose the buses arrive every 45 minutes instead of every 30 minutes. What time would Casey's bus arrive?

2. Explain when you would use the *look for a pattern* strategy to solve a problem.

3. Describe how to solve a problem using the *look for a pattern* strategy.

4. How could you check the solution to Exercise 1 using the *work backward* strategy?

PRACTICE the Strategy

EXTRA PRACTICE
See page 676.

Solve. Use the *look for a pattern* strategy.

5. Geometry Draw the next two figures in the pattern below.

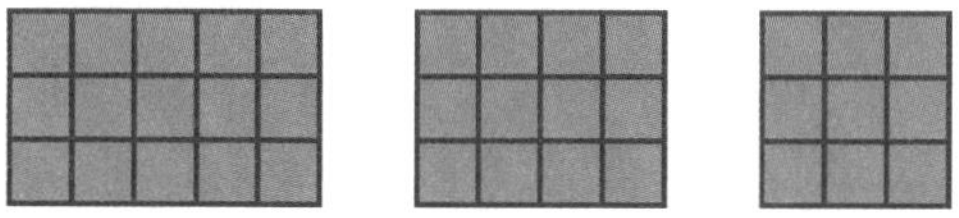

6. Algebra Describe the pattern below. Then find the missing number.

30, 300, ■, 30,000

7. In 2008, Celina earned $19,500 per year, and Roger earned $17,500. Each year Roger received a $1,000 raise, and Celina received a $500 raise. In what year will they earn the same amount of money? How much will it be?

8. Geometry The numbers below are called *triangular numbers*. Find the next two triangular numbers.

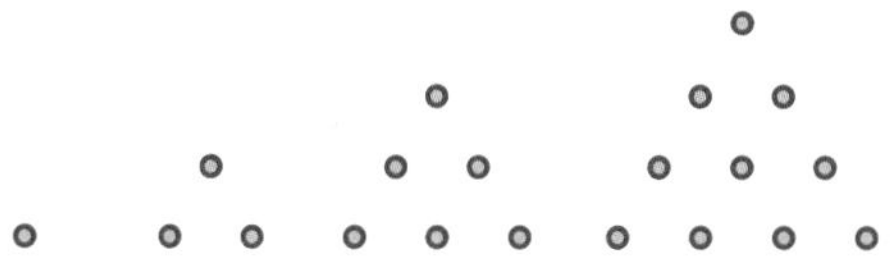

1 3 6 10

9. Algebra Find the next three numbers in the pattern below. Then describe the pattern.

2, −4, 8, −16, ■, ■, ■,

10. The price of oranges at a market is shown in the table. How much will 16 oranges cost?

Number of Oranges	Cost ($)
4	$2.75
8	$5.50
12	$8.25
16	■

11. Orlando is stacking cans of soup in a triangular form for a display at a grocery store. The top row has 1 can, the second row has 3 cans, and the third row has 5 cans. How many cans will be in the seventh row?

12. WRITING IN ▸MATH Suppose you start walking every day, beginning with 1 block. After every 2 days, you increase the amount by $1\frac{1}{2}$ blocks. How could looking for a pattern help you find the number of blocks you would walk after 2 weeks?

8-3 Ratio Tables

MAIN IDEA

I will use ratio tables to represent and solve problems involving equivalent ratios.

Standard 5MR2.3 Use a variety of methods, such as words, numbers, symbols, charts, graphs, **tables,** diagrams, and models, **to explain mathematical reasoning.**

Preparation for Standard 5AF1.5 Solve problems involving linear functions with integer values; write the equation; and graph the resulting ordered pairs of integers on a grid.

New Vocabulary

ratio table
equivalent ratio
scaling

GET READY to Learn

One can of frozen orange juice concentrate is mixed with 3 cans of water to make one batch of orange juice. How many cans of juice and how many cans of water would you need to make 2 batches that have the same taste? 3 batches? Draw a picture to support your answers.

The quantities in the activity above can be organized into a table. This is called a **ratio table** because the columns are filled with pairs of numbers that have the same ratio.

Cans of Concentrate	1	2	3
Cans of Water	3	6	9

The ratios $\frac{1}{3}$, $\frac{2}{6}$, and $\frac{3}{9}$ are equivalent since each simplifies to a ratio of $\frac{1}{3}$.

Equivalent ratios express the same relationship between two quantities. You can use a ratio table to find equivalent ratios or rates. One way is by finding the pattern in the ratio table.

EXAMPLE Equivalent Ratios of Larger Quantities

1 To make yellow icing, 6 drops of yellow food coloring are added to 1.5 cups of white icing. Use the ratio table to find how much yellow to add to 7.5 cups of white icing to get the same shade.

Cups of Icing	1.5				7.5
Drops of Yellow	6				■

One Way: Find a pattern and extend it.

For 3 cups of icing, you would need a total of 6 + 6 or 12 drops.

+1.5 +1.5 +1.5 +1.5

Cups of Icing	1.5	3	4.5	6	7.5
Drops of Yellow	6	12	18	24	30

+6 +6 +6 +6

Continue this pattern until you reach 7.5 cups.

Remember

To check your answer for Example 1, check to see if the ratio of the two new quantities is equivalent to the ratio of the original quantities.

Another Way: Multiply each quantity by the same number.

Cups of Icing	1.5	7.5
Drops of Yellow	6	**30**

×5 ×5

Since 1.5 × 5 = 7.5, multiply each quantity by 5.

So, add 30 drops of yellow food coloring to 7.5 cups of icing.

You can also divide each quantity in a ratio by the same number to produce an equivalent ratio involving smaller quantities.

EXAMPLE Equivalent Ratios of Smaller Quantities

2 **In 2006, Takeru Kobayashi won a hot dog eating contest by eating nearly 54 hot dogs in 12 minutes. If he ate at a constant rate, use the ratio table to determine about how many hot dogs he ate every 2 minutes.**

Hot Dogs Eaten	54		■
Time (min)	12		2

Divide each quantity by one or more common factors until you reach a quantity of 2 minutes.

÷2 ÷2

Hot Dogs Eaten	54	**27**	■
Time (min)	12	**6**	2

Divide each quantity by a common factor, 2.

÷3 ÷3

Hot Dogs Eaten	54	**27**	9
Time (min)	12	**6**	2

Divide each quantity by a common factor, 3.

So, Kobayashi ate about 9 hot dogs every 2 minutes.

Multiplying or dividing two related quantities by the same number is called **scaling**. Sometimes you may need to *scale back* and then *scale forward* to find an equivalent ratio.

Remember

You can check the answer to Example 3 by finding the unit rate and then multiplying by 15.

$\frac{\$4}{10 \text{ cans of corn}} = \frac{\$0.40}{1 \text{ can of corn}}$

So, 15 cans cost 0.40×15 or \$6. ✓

EXAMPLE Use Scaling

3 Cans of corn are on sale at 10 for \$4. Use the ratio table to find the cost of 15 cans.

Cans of Corn	10		15
Cost in Dollars	4		■

There is no whole number by which you can multiply 10 to get 15. So, scale back to 5 and then scale forward to 15.

÷2

Cans of Corn	10	5	15
Cost in Dollars	4	2	■

÷2

Divide each quantity by a common factor, 2.

×3

Cans of Corn	10	5	15
Cost in Dollars	4	2	6

×3

Then, since $5 \times 3 = 15$, multiply each quantity by 3.

So, 15 cans of corn would cost \$6.

Real-World EXAMPLE Use a Ratio Table

4 On her vacation, Leya exchanged \$50 American and received \$90 Canadian. Use a ratio table to find how many Canadian dollars she would receive for \$20 American.

Set up a ratio table.

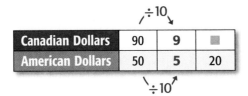

Canadian Dollars	90		■
American Dollars	50		20

Label the rows with the two quantities being compared. Then fill in what is given.

Use scaling to find the desired quantity.

÷10

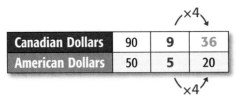

Canadian Dollars	90	9	■
American Dollars	50	5	20

÷10

Divide each quantity by a common factor, 10.

×4

Canadian Dollars	90	9	36
American Dollars	50	5	20

×4

Then, since $5 \times 4 = 20$, multiply each quantity by 4.

Leya would receive \$36 Canadian for \$20 American.

Online Personal Tutor at ca.gr5math.com

CHECK What You Know

For Exercises 1–3, use the ratio tables given to solve each problem.
See Examples 1–3 (pp. 422–424)

1. Santiago receives an allowance of $7.50 every week. How much does he receive every 4 weeks?

Allowance	7.50			■
Number of Weeks	1			4

2. Tonya runs 8 kilometers in 60 minutes. At this rate, how long would it take her to run 2 kilometers?

Distance Run (km)	8		2
Time (min)	60		■

3. A certain 12-ounce soft drink contains about 10 teaspoons of sugar. If you drink 18 ounces of this soft drink, how many teaspoons of sugar have you consumed?

Ounces of Soft Drink	12		18
Teaspoons of Sugar	10		■

4. Lamika buys 12 packs of juice boxes that are on sale and pays a total of $48. Use a ratio table to determine how much Lamika will pay to buy 8 more packs of juice boxes at the same store. See Example 4 (p. 424)

5. Talk About It What is one way to find an equivalent ratio in a ratio table?

Practice and Problem Solving

EXTRA PRACTICE See page 677.

For Exercises 6–11, use the ratio tables given to solve each problem. See Examples 1–3 (pp. 422–424)

6. To make 5 apple pies, you need about 2 pounds of apples. How many pounds of apples do you need to make 20 apple pies?

Number of Pies	5		20
Pounds of Apples	2		■

7. A zoo requires that 1 adult accompany every 7 students that visit the zoo. How many adults must accompany 28 students?

Number of Adults	1			■
Number of Students	7			28

8. Before leaving to visit Mexico, Levant traded 270 American dollars and received 3,000 Mexican pesos. When he returned from Mexico, he had 100 pesos left. How much will he receive when he exchanges these pesos for dollars?

American Dollars	270		■
Mexican Pesos	3,000		100

9. Valentina purchased 200 beads for $48 to make necklaces. If she needs to buy 25 more beads, how much will she pay if she is charged the same rate?

Number of Beads	200		25
Cost in Dollars	48		■

10. Four balls of wool will make 8 knitted caps. How many balls of wool will Malcolm need if he wants to make 6 caps?

Balls of Wool	4		■
Number of Caps	8		6

11. If a hummingbird were to get all of its food from a feeder, then a 16-ounce nectar feeder could feed about 80 hummingbirds a day. How many hummingbirds would you expect to be able to feed with a 12-ounce feeder?

Ounces of Nectar	16		12
Number of Birds Fed	80		■

12. On a bike trip across the United States, Jason notes that he covers about 190.2 miles every 4 days. If he continues at this rate, use a ratio table to determine about how many miles he could bike in 6 days. **See Example 4 (p. 424)**

13. When a photo is reduced or enlarged, its length to width ratio usually remains the same. Aurelia wants to enlarge a 4-inch by 6-inch photo so that it has a height of 15 inches. Use a ratio table to determine the new width of the photo.
See Example 4 (p. 424)

6 in.

4 in.

14. Before administering medicine, a veterinarian needs to know the animal's mass in kilograms. If 20 pounds is about 9 kilograms and a dog weighs 30 pounds, use a ratio table to find the dog's mass in kilograms. Explain your reasoning.

15. On a typical day, flights at a local airport arrive at a rate of 10 every 15 minutes. At this rate, how many flights would you expect to arrive in 1 hour?

H.O.T. Problems

16. CHALLENGE Use the ratio table to determine how many people 13 submarine sandwiches would serve. Explain your reasoning.

Number of Subs	3	5	8	13
People Served	12	20	32	■

17. NUMBER SENSE There are 10 girls and 8 boys in Mr. Augello's class. If 5 more girls and 5 more boys join the class, will the ratio of girls to boys remain the same? Justify your answer using a ratio table.

18. WRITING IN ▸MATH Explain two different methods that can be used to find the missing value in the ratio table.

Pages Read	60		80
Number of Days	9		■

Standards Practice

19 Paul buys 5 DVDs for $60. At this rate, how much would he pay for 3 DVDs?

A $10 **C** $36

B $30 **D** $58

20 Beth walks 2 blocks in 15 minutes. How many blocks would Beth walk if she walked at the same rate for an hour?

F 4 blocks **H** 9 blocks

G 8 blocks **J** 30 blocks

21 Jay Len is making biscuits using the recipe below.

Whole Wheat Biscuits

2 c	Whole wheat flour
4 tsp	Baking powder
$\frac{1}{2}$ tsp	Salt
2 tbsp	Shortening
1 c	Milk
1	Small egg

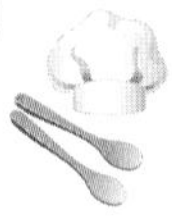

Makes 20 biscuits

How many cups of flour will he need to make 30 biscuits?

A $1\frac{1}{2}$ cups **C** 10 cups

B 3 cups **D** 15 cups

Spiral Review

22. One can of dog food costs $2.38, two cans of dog food cost $4.76, and three cans of dog food cost $7.14. If this pattern continues, how much would five cans of dog food cost? **(Lesson 8-2)**

23. A horse ranch has 6 mustangs and 18 Arabians. Write the ratio of mustangs to Arabians as a fraction in simplest form. Then explain its meaning. **(Lesson 8-1)**

Write each fraction in simplest form. (Lesson 4-3)

24. $\frac{6}{10}$ **25.** $\frac{15}{18}$ **26.** $\frac{3}{12}$ **27.** $\frac{25}{35}$

8-4 Equivalent Ratios

MAIN IDEA

I will determine if two ratios are equivalent.

Preparation for Standard 5AF1.5
Solve problems involving linear functions with integer values; write the equation; and graph the resulting ordered pairs of integers on a grid.

GET READY to Learn

Leon spent $2 to make 10 prints from his digital camera. Later, he went back to the same store and spent $6 to make 30 prints. Are these rates equivalent?

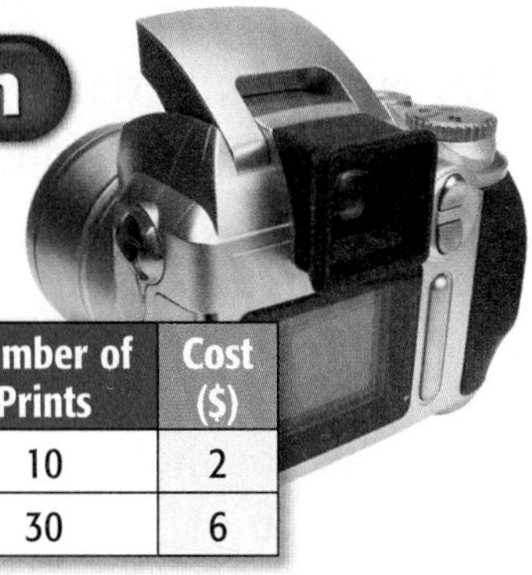

Number of Prints	Cost ($)
10	2
30	6

In the situation above, there are two related quantities: the number of prints and the cost for these prints. Notice that both quantities change, but in the same way.

Number of Prints	10	30
Cost ($)	2	6

(×3 from 10 to 30; ×3 from 2 to 6)

As the number of prints triples, the cost also triples.

By comparing these quantities as rates in simplest form, you can see that the relationship between the two quantities stays the same.

$$\frac{10 \text{ prints}}{\$2} \overset{\div 2}{=} \frac{5 \text{ prints}}{\$1} \quad \text{and} \quad \frac{30 \text{ prints}}{\$6} \overset{\div 6}{=} \frac{5 \text{ prints}}{\$1}$$

Since the rates have the same unit rate, $\frac{10 \text{ prints}}{\$2}$ is equivalent to $\frac{30 \text{ prints}}{\$6}$.

In the example above, suppose 20 prints cost $5. Is this rate equivalent to 10 prints for $2?

Number of Prints	10	20
Cost ($)	2	5

$$\frac{10 \text{ prints}}{\$2} \overset{\div 2}{=} \frac{5 \text{ prints}}{\$1} \quad \text{and} \quad \frac{20 \text{ prints}}{\$5} \overset{\div 5}{=} \frac{4 \text{ prints}}{\$1}$$

Since the two rates do not have the same unit rate, they are *not* equivalent.

There are different ways to determine if two ratios or rates are equivalent. One way is by examining unit rates.

EXAMPLES Use Unit Rates

Determine if each pair of rates are equivalent. Explain your reasoning.

1 20 miles in 5 hours; 45 miles in 9 hours

Write each rate as a fraction. Then find its unit rate.

$$\frac{20 \text{ miles}}{5 \text{ hours}} \overset{\div 5}{=} \frac{4 \text{ miles}}{1 \text{ hour}} \qquad \frac{45 \text{ miles}}{9 \text{ hours}} \overset{\div 9}{=} \frac{5 \text{ miles}}{1 \text{ hour}}$$

Since the rates do not have the same unit rate, they are not equivalent.

2 3 T-shirts for \$21; 5 T-shirts for \$35

Write each rate as a fraction. Then find its unit rate.

$$\frac{\$21}{3 \text{ T-shirts}} \overset{\div 3}{=} \frac{\$7}{1 \text{ T-shirt}} \qquad \frac{\$35}{5 \text{ T-shirts}} \overset{\div 5}{=} \frac{\$7}{1 \text{ T-shirt}}$$

Since the rates have the same unit rate, they are equivalent.

Remember

The unit rate in Example 2, $\frac{\$7}{1 \text{ T-shirt}}$ or \$7 per T-shirt, is called the *unit price* since it gives the cost per unit.

Real-World EXAMPLE

3 Felisa read the first 60 pages of a book in 3 days. She read the last 90 pages in 6 days. Are these reading rates equivalent? Explain your reasoning.

Write each rate as a fraction. Then find its unit rate.

$$\frac{60 \text{ pages}}{3 \text{ days}} \overset{\div 3}{=} \frac{20 \text{ pages}}{1 \text{ day}} \qquad \frac{90 \text{ pages}}{6 \text{ days}} \overset{\div 6}{=} \frac{15 \text{ pages}}{1 \text{ day}}$$

Since the rates do not have the same unit rate, they are not equivalent. So, Felisa's reading rates are not equivalent.

Online Personal Tutor at ca.gr5math.com

If a unit rate is not easily found, use equivalent fractions to decide whether the ratios or rates are equivalent.

EXAMPLES Use Equivalent Fractions

Determine if each pair of ratios or rates are equivalent. Explain your reasoning.

4 **3 free throws made out of 7 attempts; 9 free throws made out of 14 attempts**

Write each ratio as a fraction.

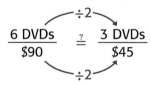

$$\frac{3 \text{ free throws}}{7 \text{ attempts}} \stackrel{?}{=} \frac{9 \text{ free throws}}{14 \text{ attempts}}$$

(numerator: ×3; denominator: ×2)

The numerator and the denominator are not multiplied by the same number. So, the fractions are not equivalent.

Since the fractions are not equivalent, the ratios are not equivalent.

5 **6 DVDs for $90; 3 DVDs for $45**

$$\frac{6 \text{ DVDs}}{\$90} \stackrel{?}{=} \frac{3 \text{ DVDs}}{\$45}$$

(numerator: ÷2; denominator: ÷2)

The numerator and the denominator are divided by the same number. So, the fractions are equivalent.

Since the fractions are equivalent, $\frac{6 \text{ DVDs}}{\$90} = \frac{3 \text{ DVDs}}{\$45}$, the rates are equivalent.

CHECK What You Know

Determine if each pair of ratios or rates are equivalent. Explain your reasoning. See Examples 1, 2, 4, 5 (pp. 429–430)

1. $24 saved after 3 weeks; $52 saved after 7 weeks

2. 270 Calories in 3 servings; 450 Calories in 5 servings

3. 3 hours worked for $12; 9 hours worked for $36

4. Micah can do 75 push-ups in 3 minutes. Eduardo can do 130 push-ups in 5 minutes. Are these rates equivalent? Explain. See Example 3 (p. 429)

5. Talk About It Describe what it means for two ratios to be equivalent.

Practice and Problem Solving

EXTRA PRACTICE
See page 677.

Determine if each pair of ratios or rates are equivalent. Explain your reasoning. See Examples 1, 2, 4, 5 (pp. 429–430)

6. \$12 for 3 paperback books; \$28 for 7 paperback books

7. 16 points scored in 4 games; 48 points scored in 8 games

8. 96 words typed in 3 minutes; 160 words typed in 5 minutes

9. \$3 for 6 bagels; \$9 for 24 bagels

10. 288 miles driven on 12 gallons of fuel; 240 miles driven on 10 gallons of fuel

11. 15 computers for 45 students; 45 computers for 135 students

12. 12 minutes to drive 30 laps; 48 minutes to drive 120 laps

13. 16 out of 28 students own pets; 240 out of 560 students own pets

14. Jade enlarged the photograph at the right to a poster. The size of the poster is 60 inches by 100 inches. Is the ratio of the poster's length and width equivalent to the ratio of the photograph's length and width? Explain your reasoning.

3 in.

5 in.

15. One school survey showed that 3 out of 5 students buy their lunch. Another survey showed that 12 out of 19 students buy their lunch. Are these ratios equivalent? Explain.

Real-World PROBLEM SOLVING

Baseball **For Exercises 16–18, refer to the table. Determine if each pair of players' ratios of hits to at bats are equivalent. Explain.**

16. Hank Blalock and Gabe Gross

17. Vinny Castilla and Hank Blalock

18. Carl Crawford and Chase Utley

2005 Spring Batting Statistics

Player	Team	At Bats	Hits
Hank Blalock	Texas Rangers	52	13
Carl Crawford	Tampa Bay Devil Rays	64	18
Vinny Castilla	San Diego Padres	30	10
Gabe Gross	Milwaukee Brewers	68	17
Chase Utley	Philadelphia Phillies	54	15

Source: espn.go.com

H.O.T. Problems

19. **OPEN ENDED** The Agriculture Club is raising animals in a ratio of 4 pigs for every 5 cows. Write two different ratios that are equivalent to this ratio.

CHALLENGE **A survey showed that 7 out of 10 youth use instant messaging. Create equivalent ratios to predict how many of the following youth you would expect to use instant messaging.**

20. 100 youth

21. 250 youth

22. 3,000 youth

23. **WRITING IN MATH** Ashley and Regina are mixing red and white fabric dye. Ashley used more red and more white dye than Regina. Which of the following statements is true? Explain.

a. Ashley mixed the darker shade of red.

b. Regina mixed the darker shade of red.

c. Their mixtures were the same shade of red.

d. There is not enough information to tell whose mixture is darker.

Standards Practice

24 The ratio of girls to boys in a band is 3 to 4. Which of these shows possible numbers of the girls and boys in the band?

A 30 girls, 44 boys

B 27 girls, 36 boys

C 22 girls, 28 boys

D 36 girls, 50 boys

25 Which of the following shows an equivalent way to show the cost of the tomatoes?

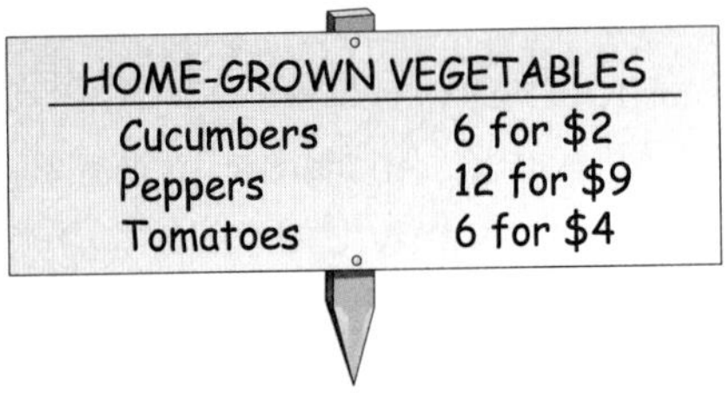

F 15 for $10

G 20 for $15

H 12 for $9

J 8 for $6

Spiral Review

26. Walter purchased 2 CDs for $26. Use a ratio table to find how much he would pay for 6 CDs. **(Lesson 8-3)**

27. Nestor makes 5 free throws for every 7 that he attempts. Find the number of free throws he will make after 14, 21, and 28 attempts. Use the *look for a pattern* strategy. **(Lesson 8-2)**

28. Write the prime factorization of 45 using exponents. **(Lesson 1-2)**

CHAPTER 8

Mid-Chapter Check

Lessons 8-1 through 8-4

1. Tyson's math class has 12 boys and 8 girls. What is the ratio of boys to girls? **(Lesson 8-1)**

2. At a bake sale, 15 cookies and 40 brownies were sold. What is the ratio of cookies sold to brownies sold? **(Lesson 8-1)**

Write each rate as a unit rate. (Lesson 8-1)

3. 171 miles in 3 hours

4. $15 for 3 pounds

5. **STANDARDS PRACTICE** A hockey team made four of their 10 attempted goals. Which ratio compares the number of goals made to the number of goals attempted? **(Lesson 8-1)**

A $\frac{4}{5}$

B $\frac{3}{5}$

C $\frac{5}{2}$

D $\frac{2}{5}$

6. Christina made 1 bracelet in 9 minutes, 3 bracelets in 27 minutes, and 5 bracelets in 45 minutes. If this pattern continues, how many bracelets will Christina make in 81 minutes? Use the *look for a pattern* strategy. **(Lesson 8-2)**

For Exercises 7 and 8, use the ratio tables given to solve each problem. (Lesson 8-3)

7. Peyton spends $15 on lunch every week. At this rate, how much money will he spend in 5 weeks?

Number of Weeks	1				5
Money Spent ($)	15				■

8. Charlee washes 10 dishes in 8 minutes. At this rate, how long will it take her to wash 25 dishes?

Number of Dishes	10		25
Number of Minutes	8		■

Determine if each pair of ratios or rates are equivalent. Explain your reasoning. (Lesson 8-4)

9. $4 for 12 doughnuts; $9 for 36 doughnuts

10. 24 pages read in 8 minutes; 72 pages read in 24 minutes

11. 48 out of 64 students own cell phones; 192 out of 258 students own cell phones

12. **STANDARDS PRACTICE** The ratio of brown tiles to tan tiles in a mosaic is 2 to 3. Which of these shows the possible numbers of brown tiles and tan tiles in the mosaic? **(Lesson 8-4)**

F 16 brown tiles, 24 tan tiles

G 14 brown tiles, 20 tan tiles

H 12 brown tiles, 19 tan tiles

J 8 brown tiles, 9 tan tiles

13. **WRITING IN MATH** Suppose a survey found that 27 out of 50 people living in one neighborhood exercise regularly. In another neighborhood, 81 out of every 150 people exercise regularly. Are these ratios equivalent? Explain your reasoning. **(Lesson 8-4)**

8-5 Problem-Solving Investigation

MAIN IDEA I will choose the best strategy to solve a problem.

Standard 5MR2.3 Use a variety of methods, such as words, numbers, symbols, charts, graphs, **tables,** diagrams, **and models, to explain mathematical reasoning. Standard 5SDAP1.1** Know the concepts of mean, median, and mode; **compute and compare simple examples to show that they may differ.**

P.S.I. TEAM +

AJAY: I took my dog to the veterinarian's office. While waiting, I noticed that there were more dogs than cats in the waiting room. The vet said that for about every 5 dogs he sees, he sees 2 cats.

YOUR MISSION: Find about how many dogs the vet will see if 21 total pets come into the office.

Understand	You know that the ratio of dogs to cats is about 5:2. You need to find about how many dogs the vet will see.
Plan	Use counters to act out how many dogs the vet will see.
Solve	Use red counters to represent the dogs and yellow counters to represent the cats. Since the ratio of dogs to cats is 5:2, place 5 red counters and 2 yellow counters in a group. Make groups of 7 counters until you have 21 counters total. 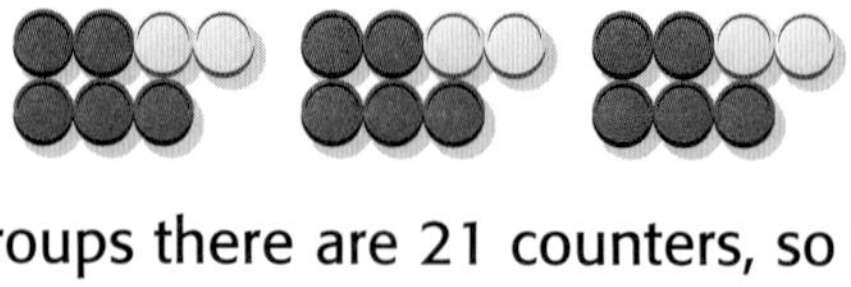 After three groups there are 21 counters, so you can stop making groups. Find the number of red counters to find how many dogs the vet will see. $5 + 5 + 5 = 15$. So, if the vet sees 21 pets, about 15 of them will be dogs.
Check	Find the ratio of red counters to yellow counters. If the ratio is equivalent to the original ratio, 5:2, then the answer is correct. ✓

Mixed Problem Solving

EXTRA PRACTICE
See page 677.

Use any strategy shown below to solve each problem.

PROBLEM-SOLVING STRATEGIES
- Act it out.
- Look for a pattern.
- Make a table.

1. The number of baskets Gina scored in her first four basketball games are shown. At this rate, how many baskets should she expect to make in her fifth game?

Year	Goals
1	4
2	5
3	7
4	10
5	■

2. To begin training for the upcoming swim meet, Rico plans to swim one lap the first day and double the number of laps he swims each day for 6 days. How many laps will he swim the sixth day?

3. Hector is taking a picture of the 5 members of the chess club. The team captain must be in the middle of the group with two team members on either side of him. How many different ways can Hector arrange the team members for the picture?

4. Draw the next two figures in the pattern.

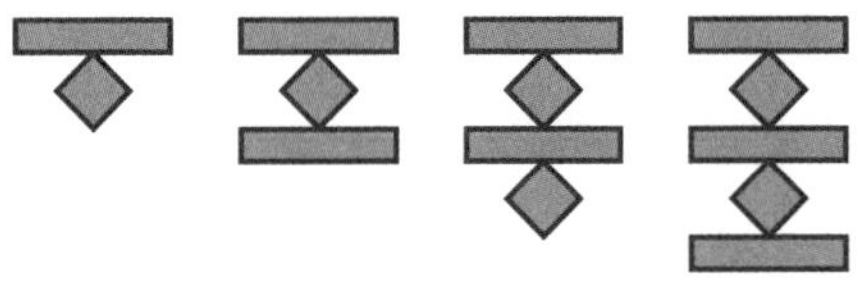

5. Jacinta took a survey of the day of the month of birthdays in her classroom. Which is greater for this set of data, the mode or the median?

Date of Birth				
2	13	5	12	18
1	5	27	23	31
11	17	1	20	9
25	18	27	3	26
8	27	30	13	25

6. The ratio of boys to girls in the fifth grade is about 3:4. If the fifth grade has a total of 245 students, how many of the students are girls?

7. Jeffrey drove a total of 285 miles to visit his sister. He drove 55 miles per hour for the first 165 miles and then 60 miles per hour for the rest of the trip. How many hours did it take him to complete the trip?

8. The table below shows hurricane wind speeds. What is the average of the minimum and maximum speeds for a level four hurricane?

Hurricanes

Category	Wind Speed (miles per hour)
one	74–95
two	96–110
three	111–130
four	131–155
five	above 155

Source: *The World Almanac*

9. **WRITING IN MATH** The 154 fifth grade students need to sit in rows of 7 for a school assembly. Is the *act it out* strategy a reasonable strategy to find how many different ways the students can sit? Explain.

8-6 Algebra: Ratios and Equations

MAIN IDEA

I will solve equations using equivalent fractions.

Standard 5AF1.1 Use information taken from a graph or **equation to answer questions about a problem situation.**

Standard 5AF1.2 Use a letter to represent an unknown number; write and evaluate simple algebraic expressions in one variable by substitution.

GET READY to Learn

A florist is using roses to make bouquets. The following equation expresses the relationship between 18 roses for 3 bouquets and *n* roses for 9 bouquets.

$$\frac{18 \text{ roses}}{3 \text{ bouquets}} = \frac{n \text{ roses}}{9 \text{ bouquets}}$$

How many roses would it take to make 9 bouquets?

Number of Bouquets	Number of Roses
3	18
4	24
5	30
6	36

Equivalent ratios form an equation. Recall from Lesson 1-8 that solving an equation means finding the value of the variable. In the example above, you found a value for the variable so that the ratios or fractions are equivalent.

EXAMPLES Solve Using Equivalent Fractions

Solve.

1 $\frac{4}{7} = \frac{m}{35}$

Find a value for *m* so the fractions are equivalent.

$\frac{4}{7} = \frac{m}{35}$ (×5 on numerator and denominator) Since 7 × 5 = 35, multiply the numerator and denominator by 5.

$\frac{4}{7} = \frac{20}{35}$ Since 4 × 5 = 20, *m* = 20.

2 $\frac{12}{15} = \frac{4}{y}$

$\frac{12}{15} = \frac{4}{y}$ (÷3 on numerator and denominator) Since 12 ÷ 3 = 4, divide the numerator and denominator by 3.

$\frac{12}{15} = \frac{4}{5}$ Since 15 ÷ 3 = 5, *y* = 5.

Remember

Write each ratio in simplest form. If they simplify to the same ratio, they are equivalent.

3 $\frac{x}{16} = \frac{7}{8}$

$\frac{x}{16} = \frac{7}{8}$ (÷2 on numerator and denominator) Since 16 ÷ 2 = 8, divide the numerator and denominator by 2.

$\frac{14}{16} = \frac{7}{8}$ THINK: What number divided by 2 is 7? The answer is 14.

So, $x = 14$.

4 $\frac{5}{d} = \frac{40}{64}$

$\frac{5}{d} = \frac{40}{64}$ (×8 on numerator and denominator) Since 5 × 8 = 40, multiply the numerator and denominator by 8.

$\frac{5}{8} = \frac{40}{64}$ THINK: What number multiplied by 8 is 64? The answer is 8.

So, $d = 8$.

Real-World EXAMPLE Make Predictions

5 **Eight of the 32 students in Mr. Mason's class prefer using gel toothpaste. Use this ratio to predict how many would prefer using gel toothpaste in the school of 500 students.**

Write and solve an equation. Let *s* represent the number of students who can be expected to prefer gel toothpaste.

	Class		School	
prefer gel toothpaste →	8	=	s	← prefer gel toothpaste
total students →	32		500	← total students

$\frac{8}{32} = \frac{s}{500}$

The denominators 32 and 500 are not easily related by multiplication, so simplify the ratio 8 out of 32. Then solve using equivalent fractions.

$\frac{8}{32} = \frac{1}{4} = \frac{125}{500}$ (÷8, then ×125) Since 4 × 125 = 500, multiply the numerator and denominator by 125.

So, about 125 out of 500 students in the school can be expected to prefer gel toothpaste.

Real-World EXAMPLE Solve Using Unit Rates

6 The Millers drove 105 miles on 3 gallons of gas. At this rate, how many miles can they drive on 10 gallons of gas?

Step 1 Set up the equation. Let *a* represent the number of miles that can be driven on 10 gallons of gas.

$$\frac{105 \text{ miles}}{3 \text{ gallons of gas}} = \frac{a \text{ miles}}{10 \text{ gallons of gas}}$$

Step 2 Find the unit rate.

$$\frac{105 \text{ miles}}{3 \text{ gallons of gas}} \overset{\div 3}{=} \frac{35 \text{ miles}}{1 \text{ gallon of gas}}$$

Find an equivalent fraction with a denominator of 1.

Step 3 Rewrite the equation using the unit rate and solve using equivalent fractions.

$$\frac{105 \text{ miles}}{3 \text{ gallons of gas}} \overset{\div 3}{=} \frac{35 \text{ miles}}{1 \text{ gallon of gas}} \overset{\times 10}{=} \frac{\mathbf{350} \text{ miles}}{10 \text{ gallons of gas}}$$

So, the value of *a* is 350. At the given rate, the Millers can drive 350 miles on 10 gallons of gas.

Online Personal Tutor at ca.gr5math.com

CHECK What You Know

Solve. See Examples 1–4 (pp. 436–437)

1. $\frac{3}{4} = \frac{x}{20}$ **2.** $\frac{5}{4} = \frac{a}{36}$ **3.** $\frac{18}{20} = \frac{9}{n}$

4. Out of 30 students surveyed, 17 have a dog. Based on these results, predict how many of the 300 students in the school have a dog. See Example 5 (p. 437)

5. If 15 out of 25 students go to bed before 10 P.M., predict how many go to bed before 10 P.M. in a school of 1,000 students. See Example 5 (p. 437)

6. Three average-size apples contain 180 Calories. How many average-size apples contain 300 Calories? See Example 6 (p. 438)

7. If 84 cookies will serve 28 students, how many cookies are needed for 30 students? See Example 6 (p. 438)

8. Talk About It Explain how you would solve $\frac{8}{12} = \frac{x}{60}$.

Practice and Problem Solving

EXTRA PRACTICE
See page 678.

Solve. See Examples 1–6 (pp. 436–438)

9. $\frac{2}{5} = \frac{w}{15}$ **10.** $\frac{3}{4} = \frac{z}{28}$ **11.** $\frac{7}{d} = \frac{35}{10}$ **12.** $\frac{4}{x} = \frac{16}{28}$

13. $\frac{p}{3} = \frac{25}{15}$ **14.** $\frac{h}{8} = \frac{6}{16}$ **15.** $\frac{6}{7} = \frac{18}{c}$ **16.** $\frac{21}{35} = \frac{3}{r}$

17. A recent survey reported that out of 50 teenagers, 9 said they get most of their news from a newspaper. At this rate, how many out of 300 teenagers would you expect to get their news from a newspaper?

18. A Clydesdale horse drinks about 120 gallons of water every 4 days. At this rate, about how many gallons of water does a Clydesdale horse drink in 28 days?

19. Nata spent $28 on 2 DVDs. At this rate, how much would 5 DVDs cost?

20. Four students spent $12 on school lunch. At this rate, find the amount 10 students would spend on the same school lunch.

21. If 15 baseballs weigh 75 ounces, how many baseballs weigh 15 ounces?

22. In 10 minutes, a heart can beat 700 times. At this rate, in how many minutes will a heart beat 140 times?

Solve.

23. $\frac{x}{27.3} = \frac{4}{9.1}$ **24.** $\frac{3.5}{128} = \frac{14}{c}$ **25.** $\frac{5.4}{12} = \frac{x}{6}$

26. Suppose 8 out of every 20 students are absent from school less than five days a year. Predict how many students would be absent from school less than five days a year in a school system of 40,000 students.

27. The table shows which physical education activities are favored by a group of students. Write and solve an equation that could be used to predict the number of students out of 300 that would pick sit-ups as their favorite physical education activity.

Favorite Physical Education Activity

Activity	Number of Responses
Jump Rope	2
Running	7
Push-ups	3
Sit-ups	8

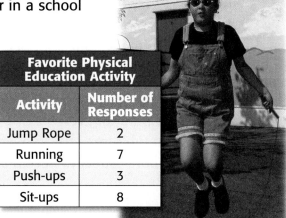

28. Liliana takes 4 breaths per 10 seconds during yoga. At this rate, about how many breaths would Liliana take in 2 minutes of yoga?

29. There were 340,000 cattle placed on feed in Texas in a recent month. Write an equation using ratios that could be used to find how many of these cattle were between 700 and 799 pounds. How many of the 340,000 cattle placed on feed were between 700 and 799 pounds?

Cattle Placed on Feed in Texas

Weight Group	Fraction of Total Cattle
Less than 600 pounds	$\frac{1}{5}$
600–699 pounds	$\frac{11}{50}$
700–799 pounds	$\frac{2}{5}$
800 pounds	$\frac{9}{50}$

Source: National Agriculture Statistics Service

H.O.T. Problems

30. **OPEN ENDED** One side of an equation is $\frac{9}{n}$. Select two other rates to form the equation, one that can be solved using equivalent fractions and the other that can be solved with unit rates. Then solve the equation using each method.

31. **FIND THE ERROR** Noah and Yoko are setting up an equation to solve the following problem. Who set up their equation correctly? Explain.

Angelina's mom teaches at a preschool. There is 1 teacher for every 12 students and 276 students total. How many teachers are there at the preschool?

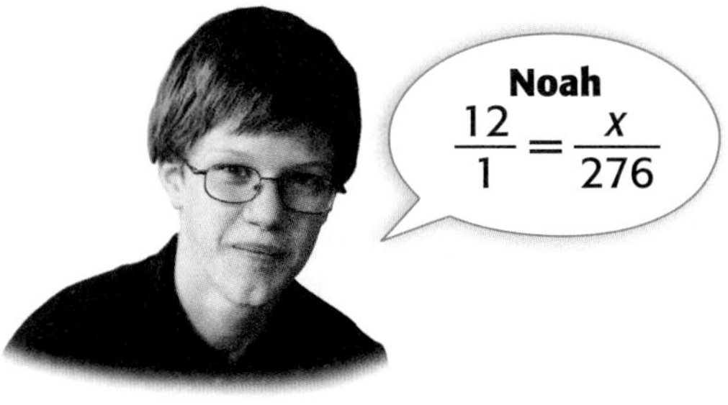

32. **REASONING** Tell whether the following statement is *sometimes*, *always*, or *never* true for numbers greater than zero. Explain.

In an equation that contains two ratios, if the numerator of the first ratio is greater than the denominator of the first ratio, then the numerator of the second ratio is greater than the denominator of the second ratio.

33. **CHALLENGE** Suppose 25 out of 175 people said they like to play disc golf and 5 out of every 12 of the players have a personalized flying disc. At the same rate, in a group of 252 people, predict how many you would expect to have a personalized flying disc.

34. **WRITING IN MATH** Jonah can run 3 laps in 24 minutes. At the same rate, about how many laps can Jonah run in 50 minutes? Explain your reasoning.

Standards Practice

35 A spinner is divided into equal sections. There are 6 green sections and 4 yellow sections. Damon spins the spinner 30 times. Which equation can be used to find y, the number of times that the spinner can be expected to land on a yellow section?

A $\frac{y}{30} = \frac{4}{6}$

B $\frac{y}{30} = \frac{6}{10}$

C $\frac{y}{30} = \frac{4}{10}$

D $\frac{y}{30} = \frac{6}{4}$

36 Which situation could be described by the equation below?

$$\frac{3 \text{ cases}}{20 \text{ minutes}} = \frac{x}{180 \text{ minutes}}$$

F The cheerleaders sold 3 cases of bottled water in 3 hours. At this rate, they can sell x cases of bottled water in 20 minutes.

G The cheerleaders sold 20 cases of bottled water in 3 hours. At this rate, they can sell x cases of bottled water in 180 minutes.

H The cheerleaders sold 3 cases of bottled water in 20 minutes. At this rate, they can sell x cases of bottled water in 2 hours.

J The cheerleaders sold 3 cases of bottled water in 20 minutes. At this rate, they can sell x cases of bottled water in 3 hours.

Spiral Review

37. A tutor charges $30 for 2 hours. Determine how much she charges for 5 hours. **(Lesson 8-5)**

Determine if each pair of rates are equivalent. Explain your reasoning. (Lesson 8-4)

38. $36 for 4 baseball hats; $56 for 7 baseball hats

39. 12 posters for 36 students; 21 posters for 63 students

For Exercises 40 and 41, refer to the table at the right. **(Lesson 2-1)**

40. Make a line graph of the data.

41. Describe the change in the daily high temperature from Tuesday to Friday.

5-Day Forecast	
Day	**High Temperature (°F)**
Monday	76
Tuesday	81
Wednesday	78
Thursday	62
Friday	53

8-7 Algebra: Sequences and Expressions

GET READY to Learn

The table shows the number of slices of pizza for different numbers of large pizzas. What pattern do you notice in the number of slices?

The Pizza Palace	
Number of Pizzas	Number of Slices
1	8
2	16
3	24
4	32

MAIN IDEA

I will extend and describe arithmetic sequences using algebraic expressions.

Standard 5AF1.2 Use a letter to represent an unknown number; write and evaluate simple algebraic expressions in one variable by substitution.

Standard 5AF1.5 Solve problems involving linear functions with integer values; write the equation; and graph the resulting ordered pairs of integers on a grid.

New Vocabulary

sequence
term
arithmetic sequence

The number of slices in the table above is an example of a sequence. A **sequence** is a list of numbers in a specific order. Each number in the list at the right is called a **term** of the sequence.

sequence

8, **16**, 24, 32, ...

term

This sequence is an **arithmetic sequence** because each term is found by adding the same number to the previous term.

8, 16, 24, 32, ...

+8 +8 +8

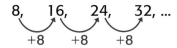

There are several ways of showing a sequence. In addition to being shown as a list, a sequence can also be shown in a table. The table gives both the position of each term in the list and the value of the term.

List 8, 16, 24, 32, ...

Table

Position	1	2	3	4
Value of Term	8	16	24	32

You can also write an algebraic expression to describe a sequence. The value of each term can be described as a function of its position in the sequence.

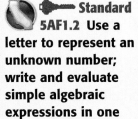

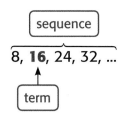

Review Vocabulary

function a relationship that assigns exactly one output value to one input value **(Lesson 1-6)**

EXAMPLES Describe Sequences

Use words and symbols to describe the value of each term as a function of its position. Then find the value of the tenth term in the sequence.

1

Position	1	2	3	4	n
Value of Term	3	6	9	12	■

Notice that the value of each term is 3 times its position number. So the value of the term in position n is $3n$.

Position	Multiply by 3	Value of Term
1	$1 \times \mathbf{3}$	3
2	$2 \times \mathbf{3}$	6
3	$3 \times \mathbf{3}$	9
4	$4 \times \mathbf{3}$	12
n	$n \times \mathbf{3}$	$\mathbf{3n}$

Now find the value of the tenth term.

$3n = 3 \cdot 10$ Replace n with 10.
$= 30$ Multiply.

The value of the tenth term in the sequence is 30.

2

Position	6	7	8	9	n
Value of Term	8	10	12	14	■

The value of each term increases by 2, so the rule contains $2n$. If the rule were simply $2n$, then the value for position 6 would be 2×6 or 12. Notice that the value of each term is 4 less than 2 times the position number. So, the value of the term in position n is $2n - 4$.

Position	Multiply by 2 and Subtract 4	Value of Term
6	$6 \times 2 - 4$	8
7	$7 \times 2 - 4$	10
8	$8 \times 2 - 4$	12
9	$9 \times 2 - 4$	14
n	$n \times 2 - 4$	$2n - 4$

Now find the value of the tenth term.

$2n - 4 = 2 \cdot 10 - 4$ Replace n with 10.
$= 20 - 4$ or 16 Multiply 2 by 10. Subtract 4 from 20.

The value of the tenth term in the sequence is 16.

Real-World EXAMPLE — Make a Table

Remember

You can review **evaluating algebraic expressions** in Lesson 1-5.

3 **Measurement There are 12 inches in 1 foot. Make a table and write an algebraic expression relating the number of feet to the number of inches. Then find Becca's height in feet if she is 60 inches tall.**

Inches	Divide by 12	Feet
12	$12 \div 12$	1
24	$24 \div 12$	2
36	$36 \div 12$	3
48	$48 \div 12$	4
n	$n \div 12$	$n \div 12$

Notice that the number of inches divided by 12 gives the number of feet. So, to find Becca's height, use the expression $n \div 12$.

$n \div 12 = 60 \div 12$ Replace n with 60.

$= 5$ Divide.

So, Becca is 5 feet tall.

Real-World EXAMPLE

4 **The cost of renting a bike is \$1, plus \$10 for each hour of use. Write an expression to find the amount charged for renting a bike for *n* hours.**

Number of Hours	Amount (\$)
1	11
2	21
3	31
4	41
n	■

The amount increases by \$10, so the rule contains $10n$. If the rule were simply $10n$, then the value for 1 hour would be \$10. Notice that adding 1 to the number of hours multiplied by 10 gives the amount charged.

Number of Hours	Multiply by 10 and Add 1	Amount (\$)
1	$1 \times 10 + 1$	11
2	$2 \times 10 + 1$	21
3	$3 \times 10 + 1$	31
4	$4 \times 10 + 1$	41
n	$n \times 10 + 1$	$10n + 1$

So, $10n + 1$ gives the cost to rent a bike for n hours.

Online Personal Tutor at ca.gr5math.com

Math Online Extra Examples at ca.gr5math.com

CHECK What You Know

Use words and symbols to describe the value of each term as a function of its position. Then find the value of the fifteenth term in the sequence. See Examples 1, 2 (p. 443)

1.

Position	1	2	3	4	n
Value of Term	2	4	6	8	■

2.

Position	3	4	5	6	n
Value of Term	22	27	32	37	■

3. Measurement There are 16 ounces in 1 pound. Make a table and write an algebraic expression relating the number of ounces to the number of pounds. Then find the number of ounces of potatoes Mr. Padilla bought if he bought a ten-pound bag of potatoes. See Example 3 (p. 444)

4. The table at the right shows the fee for overdue books at a library, based on the number of weeks the book is overdue. Write an expression to find the fee for a book that is n weeks overdue. See Example 4 (p. 444)

Weeks Overdue	Fee ($)
1	3
2	5
3	7
4	9
n	■

5. Talk About It In the sequence 3, $4\frac{1}{2}$, ____, $7\frac{1}{2}$, is the missing number $5\frac{1}{2}$ or 6? Explain.

Practice and Problem Solving

EXTRA PRACTICE See page 678.

Use words and symbols to describe the value of each term as a function of its position. Then find the value of the twelfth term in the sequence. See Examples 1, 2 (p. 443)

6.

Position	3	4	5	6	n
Value of Term	12	13	14	15	■

7.

Position	6	7	8	9	n
Value of Term	2	3	4	5	■

8.

Position	Value of Term
1	8
2	14
3	20
4	26
n	■

9.

Position	Value of Term
2	21
3	33
4	45
5	57
n	■

10. Measurement There are 60 minutes in 1 hour. Make a table and write an algebraic expression relating the number of hours to the number of minutes. Then find the duration of the movies in hours if Hannah and her friends watched two movies that together were 240 minutes long. See Example 3 (p. 444)

11. Measurement There are 12 months in 1 year. Make a table and write an algebraic expression relating the number of months to the number of years. Then find Andre's age in months if he is 12 years old. See Example 3 (p. 444)

Use the table at the right and the following information for Exercises 12 and 13. See Example 4 (p. 444)

The table shows the amount it costs to rock climb at an indoor rock climbing facility, based on the number of hours.

Time (h)	Amount ($)
1	13
2	21
3	29
4	37
n	■

12. How does the cost change with each additional hour?

13. What is the rule to find the amount charged to rock climb for n hours?

Determine how the next term in each sequence can be found. Then find the next two terms in the sequence.

14. 1, 4, 7, 10, ...

15. 4, 16, 28, 40, ...

16. 2.3, 3.2, 4.1, 5.0, ...

17. 1.5, 3.9, 6.3, 8.7, ...

18. $1\frac{1}{2}$, 3, $4\frac{1}{2}$, 6, ...

19. $2\frac{1}{4}$, $2\frac{3}{4}$, $3\frac{1}{4}$, $3\frac{3}{4}$, ...

20. Algebra Assume the pattern below continues. Write an algebraic expression to find the number of squares in Figure x. Let y represent the number of squares in each figure. Graph the ordered pairs (x, y) on a coordinate grid for Figures 1 through 5.

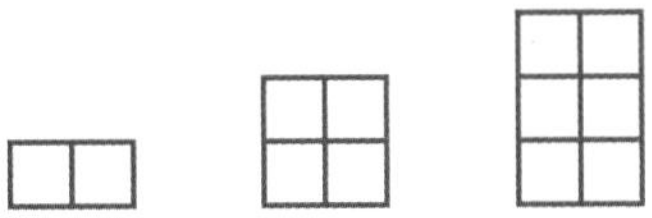

Figure 1 Figure 2 Figure 3

Real-World PROBLEM SOLVING

Data File Many recipes call for raisins. The three sizes of California raisins are select, small, and mixed.

21. Write an algebraic expression relating the grams of protein to the number of cups.

22. Find the amount of protein in seven cups of raisins.

Source: www.calraisins.org

California Raisins

Nutrition Facts
Serving Size: 1 cup

Calories: 520

Potassium: 1,240 mg

Protein: 4 g

H.O.T. Problems

23. SELECT A TECHNIQUE Gene charges a base fee of $5 for each lawn he mows plus $2 for each hour it takes to complete the job. Which of the following techniques might Gene use to determine an expression he can use to represent the total charge for mowing a lawn based on the number of hours? Justify your selection(s). Then use the technique(s) to solve the problem.

mental math | number sense | estimation

24. ANALYZE TABLES Use words and symbols to generalize the relationship of each term as a function of its position. Then determine the value of the term when $n = 100$.

Position	1	2	3	4	5	n
Value of Term	1	4	9	16	25	■

25. WRITING IN MATH Write a problem about a real-world situation in which you would use a sequence to describe a pattern.

Standards Practice

26 What is the rule to find the value of the missing term in the sequence below?

Position, x	Value of Term
1	1
2	5
3	9
4	13
5	17
x	■

A $x + 4$
B $4x - 3$
C $4x$
D $x - 3$

27 The table shows Samantha's age and Ling's age over four consecutive years.

Samantha's Age, x (years)	Ling's Age, y (years)
9	6
10	7
11	8
12	9

Which expression represents Ling's age in terms of Samantha's age?

F $y - 3$
G $3x$
H $3y$
J $x - 3$

Spiral Review

Solve. (Lesson 8-6)

28. $\frac{3}{4} = \frac{a}{28}$ **29.** $\frac{5}{x} = \frac{45}{63}$ **30.** $\frac{24}{38} = \frac{12}{m}$ **31.** $\frac{n}{75} = \frac{5}{25}$

32. Randall, Sonia, Melinda, and Diego are all standing in the school lunch line. In how many ways can they be first and last in the line? (Lesson 8-5)

UNDERWATER MAPS

Oceans cover $\frac{7}{10}$ of Earth's surface. Just as there are maps of land, there are maps of the ocean's floor. Oceanographers use sonar to measure the depths of different places in the ocean. The average depth of Earth's oceans is 12,200 feet.

Oceanographers send out sound waves from a sonar device on a ship. They measure how long it takes for sound waves to reach the bottom of the ocean and return. They use the fact that sound waves travel through sea water at about 5,000 feet per second. That's about 3,400 miles per hour!

Did You Know?

The deepest part of the ocean floor has been recorded at 36,198 feet. This distance is 7,163 feet greater than the height of Mount Everest, the highest mountain on Earth.

Math Standard 5AF1.2 Use a letter to represent an unknown number; write and evaluate **simple algebraic expressions in one variable** by substitution.

Real-World Math

Use the information from page 448 and the table below to solve each problem.

1. Make a table that relates the number of feet sound travels through sea water for 1, 2, 3, 4, and 5 seconds.

2. Use your table to estimate how long it will take a sound wave to reach the average depth of Earth's oceans.

3. Suppose your ship sends out a sound wave and it returns to the ship in 8 seconds. About how deep is the ocean where you are?

4. Suppose a thunderstorm is about 1 mile away from where you are standing. About how long will it take before you hear the thunder? (*Hint:* 1 mile = 5,280 feet)

5. **WRITING IN ▸MATH** Explain how to write an expression that gives the number of feet that sound travels through steel for any number of seconds. How would you vary your expression if the sound was traveling through diamond?

SPEED OF SOUND THROUGH DIFFERENT MEDIA (FEET PER SECOND)

Air (20°C)	1,121
Pure Water	4,882
Sea Water	5,012
Steel	16,000
Diamond	39,240

8-8 Algebra: Equations and Graphs

GET READY to Learn

The table shows Carli's earnings based on the number of hours she baby-sits. The amount Carli earns for baby-sitting h hours is represented by $5h$. If e represents the amount Carli earns, what equation can you use to represent this situation?

Hours Baby-Sitting	Earnings ($)
1	5
2	10
3	15
4	20

MAIN IDEA

I will write an equation to describe a linear situation.

Standard 5AF1.1 Use the information taken from a graph or **an equation to answer questions about a problem situation.**

Standard 5AF1.5 Solve problems involving linear functions with integer values; write the equation; and graph the resulting ordered pairs of integers on a grid.

You can use an equation to represent a function.

EXAMPLE Write an Equation for a Function

1 Write an equation to represent the function displayed in the table.

Input, x	1	2	3	4
Output, y	9	18	27	36

Each output y is equal to 9 times the input x. So, the equation that represents the function is $y = 9x$.

Input, x	Multiply by 9	Output, y
1	1×9	9
2	2×9	18
3	3×9	27
4	4×9	36

Real-World EXAMPLES

The marching band is holding a car wash to raise money. They are charging $7 for each car they wash.

2 Make a table to show the relationship between the number of cars washed *c* and the total amount earned *t*.

The total earned (output) is equal to $7 times the number of cars washed (input).

Cars Washed, c	Multiply by 7	Total Earned ($), t
1	1×7	7
2	2×7	14
3	3×7	21
4	4×7	28

3 **Write an equation to find the total amount earned *t* for washing *c* cars.**

Study the table from Example 2. The total earned equals \$7 times the number of cars washed.

Words	Total earned equals \$7 times the number of cars washed.
Variable	Let t represent the total earned and c represent the number of cars washed.
Equation	$t \quad = \quad 7 \quad \cdot \quad c$

So, the equation is $t = 7c$.

4 **How much will the marching band earn if they wash 25 cars?**

$t = 7c$ Write the equation.

$t = 7 \cdot 25$ Replace c with 25.

$t = 175$ Multiply.

The marching band will earn \$175 for washing 25 cars.

Check $t = 7c$

$$\frac{175}{7} \stackrel{?}{=} \frac{7c}{7}$$

$$25 = c \text{ or } c = 25$$

Remember

In Example 5, only whole number values are used for the number of hours, h.

Real-World EXAMPLES

5 **The cost of renting a jet ski at a local marina is shown in the table. Write a sentence and an equation to describe the data. Then find the total cost of renting a jet ski for 6 hours, 7 hours, and 8 hours.**

Number of Hours, *h*	Total Cost (\$), *t*
1	10
2	20
3	30
4	40

The cost of renting a jet ski is \$10 for each hour. The total cost t is \$10 times the number of hours h. Therefore, $t = 10h$. Use this equation to find the total cost t of renting a jet ski for 6 hours, 7 hours, and 8 hours. Organize the information in a function table. Include a column of ordered pairs in the form (h, t).

Number of Hours, *h*	$10h$	Total Cost (\$), *t*	(h, t)
6	10×6	60	(6, 60)
7	10×7	70	(7, 70)
8	10×8	80	(8, 80)

6 Graph the results from Example 5 on a coordinate grid.

Step 1 Make a coordinate plane with the *h* values along the *x*-axis and the *t* values along the *y*-axis.

Step 2 Using the (*h*, *t*) values from Example 5, plot the points on the coordinate plane.

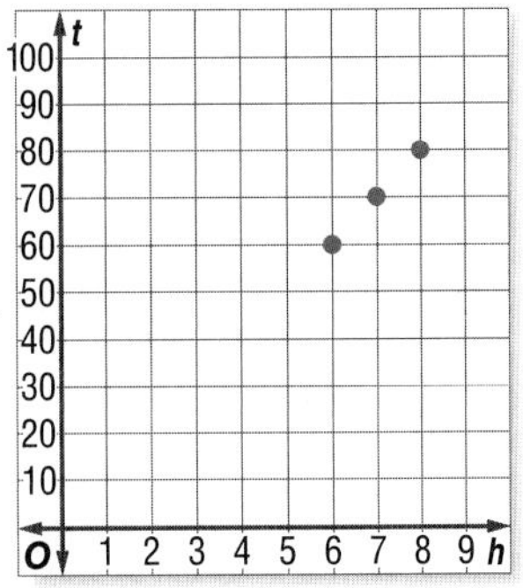

Online Personal Tutor at ca.gr5math.com

CHECK What You Know

Write an equation to represent the function displayed in each table. See Example 1 (p. 450)

1.

Input, *x*	0	1	2	3	4
Output, *y*	0	4	8	12	16

2.

Input, *x*	1	2	3	4	5
Output, *y*	8	16	24	32	40

Use the following information for Exercises 3–5. See Examples 2–4 (pp. 450–451)

The school cafeteria sells lunch passes that allow a student to purchase any number of lunches in advance for $3 each.

3. Make a table to show the relationship between the number of lunches *n* and the total cost *t*. Graph the results on a coordinate grid.

4. Write an equation to find *t*, the total cost in dollars for a lunch card with *n* lunches.

5. If Lolita buys a lunch pass for 20 lunches, how much will it cost?

6. The general admission to a local carnival is shown in the table. Write a sentence and an equation to describe the data. Then find the total cost of admission for 7 people, 8 people, and 9 people. Graph the results on a coordinate grid.
See Examples 5–6 (pp. 451–452)

Number of People, *n*	Total Admission ($), *t*
1	4
2	8
3	12
4	16

7. Talk About It How can you determine if an equation accurately represents a function displayed in a table?

Practice and Problem Solving

EXTRA PRACTICE
See page 678.

Write an equation to represent the function displayed in each table. See Example 1 (p. 450)

8.

Input, x	1	2	3	4	5
Output, y	6	12	18	24	30

9.

Input, x	0	1	2	3	4
Output, y	0	11	22	33	44

10.

Input, x	0	1	2	3	4
Output, y	0	15	30	45	60

11.

Input, x	1	2	3	4	5
Output, y	10	20	30	40	50

Use the following information for Exercises 12 and 13. See Examples 2–4 (pp. 450–451)

In a video game, each player earns 15 points for each coin they collect.

12. Make a table to show the relationship between the number of coins collected c and the total points p. Graph the results on a coordinate grid.

13. Write an equation to find p, the total points for collecting c coins. How many points will a player earn if she collects 21 coins?

Use the following information for Exercises 14 and 15. See Examples 2-4 (pp. 450–451)

An African elephant eats 400 pounds of vegetation each day.

14. Make a table to show the relationship between the number of pounds v an African elephant eats in days d. Graph the results on a coordinate grid.

15. Write an equation to find v, the number of pounds of vegetation an African elephant eats in d days. How many pounds of vegetation does an African elephant eat in 5 days?

16. The disc jockey hired for the spring dance charges the amount shown in the table. Write a sentence and an equation to describe the data. At this rate, how much will it cost to hire the disc jockey for 5 hours? 6 hours? 7 hours? Graph the results on a coordinate grid.

Number of Hours, h	Total Charge ($), t
1	35
2	70
3	105

17. A catering service provides the table shown as a guide to help its customers decide how many pans of lasagna to order for events. Write a sentence and an equation to describe the data. At this rate, how many people would 8 pans, 9 pans, and 10 pans of lasagna serve? Graph the results on a coordinate grid.

Number of Pans, p	Total Number Served, n
1	24
2	48
3	72

18. Jared withdraws \$20 from his savings account every week. Write an equation that represents the change in his savings account each week. Then find the change in his savings account for week 1, week 2, and week 3. Graph the results as ordered pairs on a coordinate grid.

H.O.T. Problems

19. **OPEN ENDED** Write about a real-world situation that can be represented by the equation $y = 5x$. Be sure to explain what the variables represent in the situation.

20. **CHALLENGE** Toothpicks were used to make the figures below.

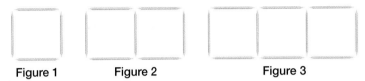

Figure 1 Figure 2 Figure 3

Explain why the equation $y = 3x + 1$ represents the number of toothpicks y needed to build each figure x. Then graph this equation on a coordinate grid.

21. **WRITING IN MATH** Choose an exercise from this lesson, and explain why the relationship is linear.

Standards Practice

22 The table shows admission prices at a local zoo based on the number of guests.

Number of Guests, x	Total Admission (\$), y
1	7
2	14
3	21
4	28

Which equation can be used to find y, the total admission for x guests?

A $x = 7y$

B $y = 7 + x$

C $y = 7x$

D $x = 7 + y$

23 The cost of snorkeling is \$5 for the equipment plus an additional \$7 for each hour that you snorkel. Which equation represents c, the cost in dollars for snorkeling for h hours?

F $c = 7h + 5$

G $c = 5h + 7$

H $c = 7(h + 5)$

J $c = 5(h + 7)$

Spiral Review

24. Find the next two terms of the sequence 3, 11, 19, 27, ... **(Lesson 8-7)**

25. At the store, DVDs are on sale 3 for \$35.00. At this rate, find the cost of 5 DVDs to the nearest cent. **(Lesson 8-6)**

CHAPTER 8 Study Guide and Review

FOLDABLES™ Study Organizer GET READY to Study

Be sure the following Key Concepts are noted in your Foldable.

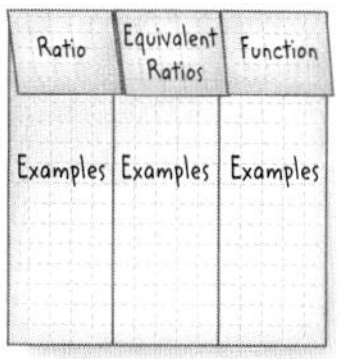

BIG Ideas

Ratios (Lessons 8-1 and 8-3)

- Ratios are a comparison of two quantities by division.
- Equivalent ratios express the same relationship between two quantities.

Rates (Lesson 8-1)

- Rates are a ratio comparing two quantities with different kinds of units.

Sequences (Lesson 8-7)

- Sequences are a list of numbers in a specific order.
- Each number listed in a sequence is called a term.
- Each term of an arithmetic sequence is found by adding the same number to the previous term.
- Algebraic expressions can be used to describe a sequence.

Equations (Lesson 8-8)

- An equation can be used to represent a function.

Key Vocabulary

arithmetic sequence (p. 442)
equivalent ratio (p. 422)
rate (p. 414)
ratio (p. 413)
ratio table (p. 422)
scaling (p. 423)
sequence (p. 442)
term (p. 442)
unit rate (p. 414)

Vocabulary Check

State whether each sentence is *true* or *false*. If *false*, replace the underlined word or number to make a true sentence.

1. A ratio is a comparison of two numbers by multiplication.
2. A rate is the ratio of two measurements that have different units.
3. Two ratios are said to be equivalent if they have the same unit rate.
4. Adding or subtracting two related quantities by the same number is called scaling.
5. A sequence is a list of numbers in a specific order.
6. In an arithmetic sequence, each term is found by multiplying the same number.

Lesson-by-Lesson Review

8-1 Ratios and Rates (pp. 413–418)

Example 1
Write the ratio 30 fifth graders out of 45 students as a fraction in simplest form.

$$\frac{30}{45} = \frac{2}{3} \quad (\div 15)$$

The GCF of 30 and 45 is 15.

Example 2
Write the rate 150 miles in 4 hours as a unit rate.

$$\frac{150 \text{ miles}}{4 \text{ hours}} = \frac{37.5 \text{ miles}}{1 \text{ hour}} \quad (\div 4)$$

Divide the numerator and the denominator by 4 to get the denominator of 1.

Write each ratio or rate as a fraction in simplest form.

7. 12 blue marbles out of 20 marbles

8. 18 boys out of 21 students

Write each rate as a unit rate.

9. 3 inches of rain in 6 hours

10. 189 pounds of garbage in 12 weeks

11. Rick has 12 action, 15 comedy, and 9 drama DVDs. Find the ratio of action DVDs to the total number of DVDs. Then explain its meaning.

8-2 Problem-Solving Strategy: Look for a Pattern (pp. 420–421)

Example 3
A display of cans is stacked in the shape of a pyramid. There are 2 cans in the top row, 4 in the second row, 6 in the third row, and so on. The display contains 7 rows. How many cans are in the display?

Make a table to see the pattern.

Row	1	2	3	4	5	6	7
Number of Cans	2	4	6	8	10	12	14

+2 +2 +2 +2 +2 +2

There are 2 + 4 + 6 + 8 + 10 + 12 + 14 or 56 cans in the display.

Solve by looking for a pattern.

12. Cheyenne ran 1 lap on day 1. She ran 2 laps on day 2, 4 laps on day 3, and 8 laps on day 4. If this pattern continues, how many laps will she run on day 7?

13. The table shows the hits at a baseball game. If the hitting pattern continues, how many hits will the Reds have in the 7th inning?

Inning	1	2	3	4	5	6	7
Cubs	0	1	2	0	1	2	0
Reds	4	3	2	4	3	2	■

8-3 Ratio Tables (pp. 422–427)

Example 4

Boston received 6 inches of rain in 24 hours. If it kept raining at a constant rate, how much rain would Boston receive in 48 hours?

Inches of Rain	6	■
Number of Hours	24	48

Since $24 \times 2 = 48$, multiply 6 by 2.

So, Boston would receive 12 inches of rain in 48 hours.

14. Arthur bought 5 notebooks for $3. How much will he spend on 10 notebooks?

Number of Notebooks	5	10
Money Spent ($)	3	■

15. Roman spent $306 for 17 baseball tickets. Use a ratio table to determine how much each ticket costs.

8-4 Equivalent Ratios (pp. 428–432)

Example 5

Are the ratios 18 weeks to 3 years and 54 weeks to 10 years equivalent? Explain your reasoning.

$\frac{18 \text{ weeks}}{3 \text{ years}} = \frac{6 \text{ weeks}}{1 \text{ year}}$ $\frac{54 \text{ weeks}}{10 \text{ years}} = \frac{5.4 \text{ weeks}}{1 \text{ year}}$

Since the ratios do not share the same unit ratio, they are not equivalent.

16. Ajay rowed 220 feet in 55 seconds and Leigh rowed 120 feet in 30 seconds. Are these rates equivalent? Explain your reasoning.

17. Stacey made 8 necklaces in 48 minutes. Nick made 4 necklaces in 24 minutes. Are these rates equivalent? Explain your reasoning.

8-5 Problem-Solving Investigation: Choose the Best Strategy (pp. 434–435)

Example 6

The area of a square window is 144 square feet. What is the length of each side?

The area of a square is the length of a side squared. Work backward. Since 12×12 is 144, the length of each side is 12 feet.

Choose the best strategy to solve each problem.

18. In how many ways can you have three friends sign your yearbook?

19. Wyoming has a land area of 97,100 square miles. If it has a population of 501,242, how many people on average live in Wyoming per square mile? Round to the nearest whole number.

8-6 Algebra: Ratios and Equations (pp. 436–441)

Example 7
Solve $\frac{9}{12} = \frac{g}{4}$.

$$\frac{9}{12} \overset{\div 3}{=} \frac{3}{4}$$

Since 12 ÷ 3 = 4, divide the numerator and denominator by 3.

So, $g = 3$.

Solve.

20. $\frac{7}{11} = \frac{m}{33}$

21. $\frac{3}{20} = \frac{15}{k}$

22. At a school, the teacher to student ratio is 3 to 42. If 504 students are enrolled at the school, how many teachers are there?

8-7 Algebra: Sequences and Expressions (pp. 442–447)

Example 8
Use words and symbols to describe the value of each term as a function of its position. Then find the value of the ninth term in the sequence.

Position	5	6	7	8	n
Value of Term	20	24	28	32	■

Notice that the value of each term is 4 times its position number.

$4n = 4 \cdot 9$ Replace n with 9.
$= 36$ Multiply.

The value of ninth term is 36.

Use words and symbols to describe the value of each term as a function of its position. Then find the value of the sixteenth term in the sequence.

23.

Position	22	23	24	25	n
Value of Term	15	16	17	18	■

24. Jennifer earns $12 for every dog she walks. Write an algebraic expression to find the amount of money she would earn for walking n number of dogs. Then find the amount of money she would earn for walking 45.

8-8 Algebra: Equations and Graphs (pp. 450–454)

Example 9
Write an equation to represent the function displayed in the table.

Input, x	1	2	3	4	5
Output, y	9	18	27	36	45

Each output is equal to 9 times the input.

So, the equation that represents the function is $y = 9x$.

Write an equation to represent the function displayed in the table.

25.

Input, x	1	2	3	4	5
Output, y	6	12	18	24	30

26. A bowling alley charges $4 per game. Write an equation to find the total cost in dollars t for the number of games bowled n. Then find the total cost for 8 games bowled.

CHAPTER 8

Chapter Test

Write each ratio as a fraction in simplest form.

1. 12 red blocks out of 20 blocks
2. 24 potato chips out of 144 chips
3. 65 rotten apples out of 520 apples
4. If 3 ostriches weigh 1,020 pounds, how many pounds does 1 ostrich weigh?

Write each rate as a unit rate.

5. $2 for 36 erasers
6. 180 pages in 90 minutes

7. **STANDARDS PRACTICE** Candace buys 12 cans of orange juice for $6. At this rate, how much would she pay for 48 cans of orange juice?

   A $20

   B $22

   C $24

   D $30

Determine if each pair of ratios or rates are equivalent. Explain your reasoning.

8. 32 pencils for $8; 16 pencils for $4
9. 72 out of 90 students have siblings; 362 out of 450 students have siblings
10. 524 Calories for 4 servings; 786 Calories for 6 servings

Solve.

11. $\frac{4}{6} = \frac{x}{12}$

12. $\frac{10}{p} = \frac{2}{8}$

13. $\frac{n}{13} = \frac{8}{52}$

14. $\frac{7}{13} = \frac{a}{52}$

15. If 7 of the 28 students in a class prefer the winter months, predict how many would prefer the winter months in a school of 400 students.

16. Ellie is using the following table to help her calculate the discount on baseball caps. Mr. Gomez would like to order 8 baseball caps. How much of a discount should Ellie give him?

Baseball caps	1	2	3
Discount ($)	2	3	4

17. **STANDARDS PRACTICE** Which expression was used to create the table?

Position, x	Value of Term
3	11
4	14
5	17
6	20
7	23
x	■

   F $x + 8$

   G $2x + 3$

   H $x - 8$

   J $3x + 2$

18. **WRITING IN MATH** Darnell reads an average of 2 hours each day. Write an equation to find *h*, the number of hours Darnell reads in *d* days. Then find the total number of hours Darnell reads in 3 days, 4 days, and 5 days. Graph the results on a coordinate grid and explain why the relationship is linear.

CHAPTER 8

California Standards Practice

Cumulative, Chapters 1–8

Standards Example

Which expression could have been used to create the table below?

Position	1	2	3	4	n
Value of Term	4	7	10	13	?

A $n + 1$

B $3n$

C $3n + 1$

D $n - 1$

Read the Question

To find the expression, determine the function.

Solve the Question

Notice that the values 4, 7, 10, 13, ... increase by 3, so the rule contains $3n$. Therefore, choices A and D can be eliminated.

If the rule were simply $3n$, then the value for position 1 would be 3×1 or 3. But this value is 4. So, choice B can be eliminated.

So, the answer is C.

Check by substituting each position number in $3n + 1$.

Is the result the value of the term?

Online Personal Tutor at ca.gr5math.com

Choose the best answer.

1 **Which expression could have been used to create the table below?**

Position	Value of Term
1	4
2	9
3	14
4	19
n	?

A $5n - 1$

B $5n$

C $n + 1$

D $n + 5$

2 **There were six buses and 150 people signed up for the field trip. What is the ratio of people to buses?**

F 1:25

G 25:1

H 6:150

J 150:6

For practice by standard, see pages CA1–CA27.

3 **The cost of renting a speed boat is \$25 plus an additional fee of \$12 for each hour that the boat is rented. Which equation can be used to find *c*, the cost in dollars for *h* hours?**

A $c = 12h + 25$

B $c = 25h + 12$

C $c = 12(h + 25)$

D $c = 25(h + 12)$

---

4 **Which equation shows the relationship of all the values in the table below?**

x	1	2	3	4
y	4	8	12	16

F $y = \frac{x}{4}$ **H** $y = x - 4$

G $y = x + 4$ **J** $y = 4x$

---

5 **At a sports camp there is 1 counselor for every 12 campers. If there are 156 campers attending the camp, which equation can be used to find *x*, the number of counselors?**

A $\frac{x}{12} = \frac{1}{156}$ **C** $\frac{1}{12} = \frac{x}{156}$

B $\frac{12}{1} = \frac{x}{156}$ **D** $\frac{x}{1} = \frac{12}{156}$

---

6 **Samantha's class was sorting books in the library. The class sorted 45 books in 90 minutes. If they continue sorting at this rate, how long will it take them to sort 120 books?**

F 5 h **H** 4 h

G $4\frac{1}{2}$ h **J** $3\frac{1}{2}$ h

---

7 **Which table represents *x* and *y* values for $9 + x = y$?**

A

x	y
−5	−4
0	9

B

x	y
−10	−1
1	10

C

x	y
−6	3
−1	−8

D

x	y
4	5
7	16

---

8 **The temperature at noon was 8 degrees below zero. At five o'clock it was 12 below zero. Which integer represents the temperature at noon in degrees?**

F −12 **G** −8 **H** 8 **J** 12

---

9 **At a school concert, free movie passes were awarded to the person sitting in the seat numbered with the least common multiple of 9, 12, and 18. Find the number of the prize-winning seat.**

A 3 **B** 12 **C** 36 **D** 45

---

10 **18.55 ÷ 3.6 =**

F 0.52 **G** 0.632 **H** 5.2 **J** 6.32

---

11 **Which letter on the number line best identifies the location of 3.68?**

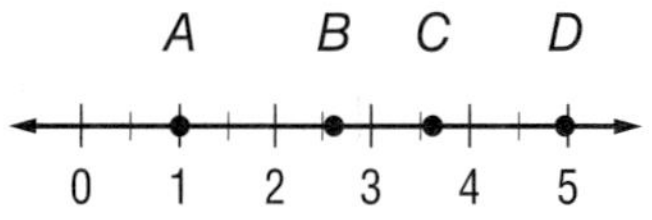

A *A* **B** *B* **C** *C* **D** *D*

CHAPTER 9 Percent

BIG Idea What is a percent?

A **percent** is a ratio that compares a number to 100.

Example Suppose a soccer player made 40% of his or her goals. Forty percent means **40 out of 100.**

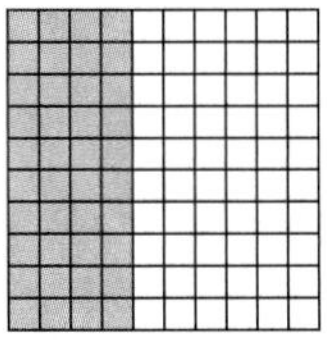

40 out of the 100 squares on the decimal model are shaded.

What will I learn in this chapter?

- Express percents as fractions and fractions as percents.
- Sketch and analyze circle graphs.
- Express percents as decimals and decimals as percents.
- Estimate and find the percent of a number.
- Solve problems by solving a simpler problem.

Key Vocabulary

percent
circle graph
outcomes
tree diagram

Math Online Student Study Tools at ca.gr5math.com

FOLDABLES™ Study Organizer

Make this Foldable to help you organize information about percents. Begin with a piece of 11″ × 17″ paper.

1. **Fold** a 2″ tab along the long side of the paper.

2. **Unfold** the paper and fold in thirds widthwise.

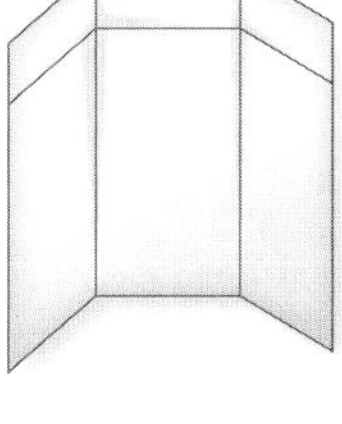

3. **Draw** lines along the folds and label the head of each column as shown. Label the front of the folded table with the chapter title.

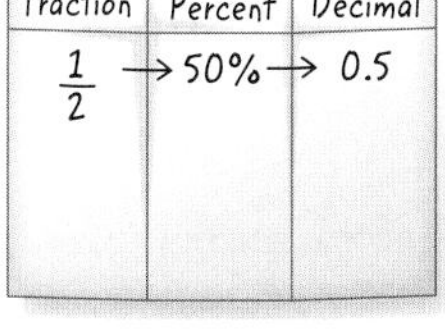

ARE YOU READY for Chapter 9?

You have two ways to check prerequisite skills for this chapter.

Option 2

Math Online Take the Chapter Readiness Quiz at ca.gr5math.com.

Option 1

Complete the Quick Check below.

QUICK Check

Write each fraction in simplest form. If the fraction is already in simplest form, write *simplest form*. (Lesson 4-3)

1. $\frac{25}{100}$ **2.** $\frac{17}{100}$ **3.** $\frac{30}{100}$

4. In a school survey, 15 out of every 100 students said they wear contact lenses. Express the fraction $\frac{15}{100}$ in simplest form. (Lesson 4-3)

Solve. (Lesson 8-6)

5. $\frac{1}{a} = \frac{3}{9}$ **6.** $\frac{7}{16} = \frac{h}{48}$ **7.** $\frac{5}{8} = \frac{30}{y}$

8. $\frac{t}{35} = \frac{6}{7}$ **9.** $\frac{s}{18} = \frac{2}{3}$ **10.** $\frac{36}{p} = \frac{2}{3}$

11. If baking 4 apple pies requires 2 pounds of apples, how many pounds of apples are needed to bake 12 apple pies? (Lesson 8-6)

Round each number to the nearest ten. (Prior Grade)

12. 42 **13.** 5 **14.** 68

15. 74 **16.** 18 **17.** 9

18. Rebekah has saved $77 toward new speakers for her computer. To the nearest ten, how much has she saved? (Prior Grade)

Explore

Math Lab for 9-1
Modeling Percents

MAIN IDEA

I will use models to illustrate the meaning of percents.

Standard 5NS1.2 Interpret percents as a part of a hundred; find decimal and percent equivalents for common fractions and explain why they represent the same value; compute a given percent of a whole number. **Standard 5MR2.3 Use a variety of methods, such as** words, **numbers, symbols,** charts, graphs, tables, diagrams, **and models, to explain mathematical reasoning.**

In Lesson 3-1, you learned that a 10 × 10 grid can be used to represent *hundredths*. The word *percent* (%) means *out of one hundred*, so you can also use a 10 × 10 grid to model percents.

ACTIVITIES

1 Model 18%.

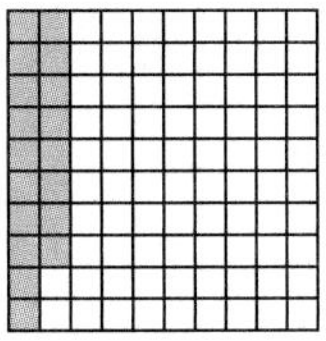

18% means 18 out of 100.

So, shade 18 of the 100 squares on the decimal model.

Identify each percent that is modeled.

2

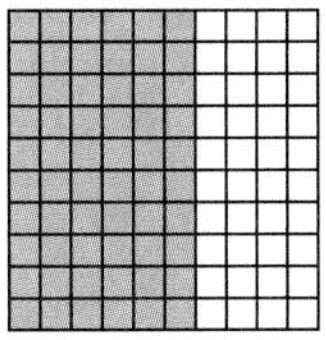

There are 60 out of 100 squares shaded.

So, the model shows 60%.

3

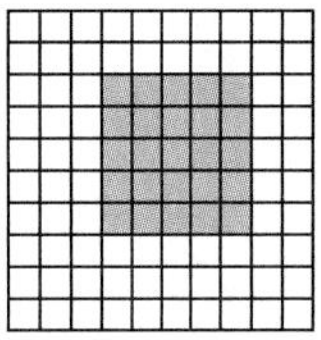

There are 25 out of 100 squares shaded.

So, the model shows 25%.

CHECK What You Know

Model each percent.

a. 30% **b.** 8% **c.** 42% **d.** 75%

Identify each percent modeled.

e.

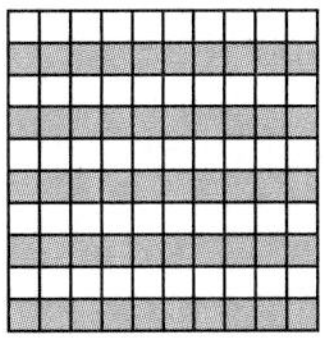

f.

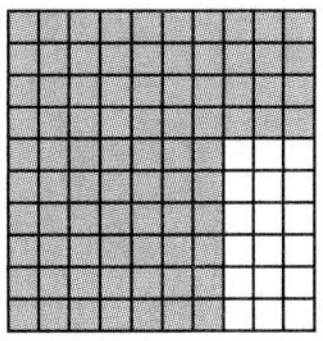

g.

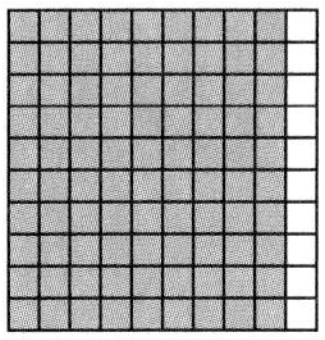

Remember

To model 100%, shade all of the squares since 100% means 100 out of 100.

Analyze the Results

1. Identify the fraction of each model in Exercises a–g that is shaded.

2. How can you write a percent as a fraction? How can you write a fraction with a denominator of 100 as a percent?

9-1 Percents and Fractions

MAIN IDEA

I will express percents as fractions and fractions as percents.

Standard 5NS1.2 Interpret percents as a part of a hundred; find decimal and **percent equivalents for common fractions and explain why they represent the same value;** compute a given percent of a whole number.
Standard 5SDAP1.3 Use fractions and **percentages to compare data sets of different sizes.**

New Vocabulary

percent

GET READY to Learn

Kimiko asked 100 students in the cafeteria what their favorite fruit bar flavor was: cherry, grape, strawberry, or blueberry. The results are shown in the bar graph. What ratio compares the number of students who prefer grape fruit bars to the total number of students?

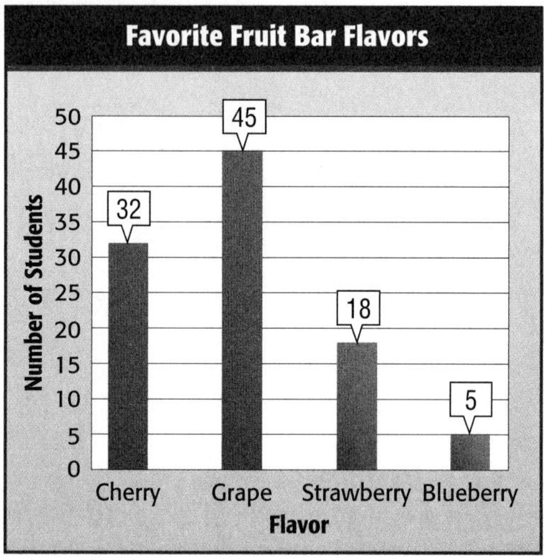

Ratios like 32 out of 100, 45 out of 100, 18 out of 100, and 5 out of 100, can be written as percents.

KEY CONCEPT — Percent

Words A **percent** is a ratio that compares a number to 100.

Examples 75% ⇒ 75 out of 100 or $\frac{75}{100}$

Model

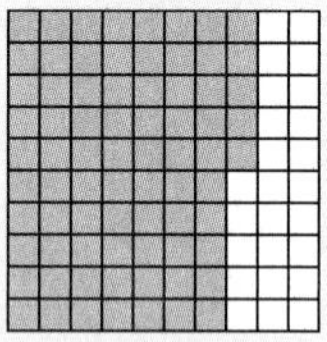

75%

EXAMPLES Write a Percent as a Fraction

1 Write 50% as a fraction in simplest form.

50% means *50 out of 100.*

$50\% = \frac{50}{100}$ Definition of percent

$= \frac{\overset{1}{\cancel{50}}}{\underset{2}{\cancel{100}}}$ or $\frac{1}{2}$ Simplify. Divide the numerator and the denominator by the GCF, 50.

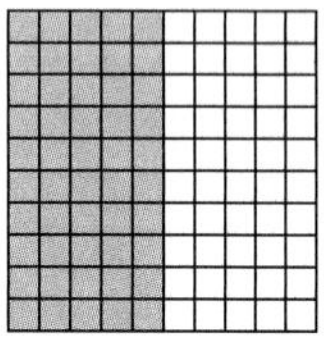

$50\% = \frac{1}{2}$

Remember

A percent can be greater than 100%. Since percent means *hundredths*, or *per 100*, a percent like 150% means 150 hundredths, or 150 per 100.

2 **Write 125% as a mixed number in simplest form.**

125% means *125 for every 100.*

$125\% = \frac{125}{100}$	Definition of percent
$= 1\frac{25}{100}$	Write as a mixed number.
$= 1\frac{\cancel{25}^{\,1}}{\cancel{100}_{\,4}}$ or $1\frac{1}{4}$	Divide the numerator and denominator by the GCF, 25.

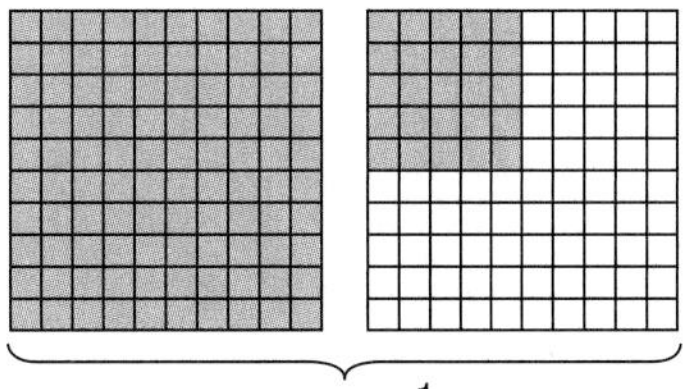

$125\% = 1\frac{1}{4}$

Real-World EXAMPLE

Remember

You can conclude that $\frac{13}{20}$ is a reasonable answer because 65% is a little more than 50%, and $\frac{13}{20}$ is a little more than $\frac{10}{20}$ or $\frac{1}{2}$.

3 **What fraction of those surveyed are extremely proud to be an American?**

The table shows that 65% of those surveyed are extremely proud to be an American.

Proud to Be an American

Answer	Percent
Extremely	65
Very	25
Moderately	6
A little/not at all	3
No opinion	1

Source: Gallup Poll

$65\% = \frac{65}{100}$	Definition of percent
$= \frac{13}{20}$	Simplify.

So, $\frac{13}{20}$ of those surveyed are extremely proud to be American.

Online **Personal Tutor at** ca.gr5math.com

EXAMPLE Write a Fraction as a Percent

4 **Write $\frac{9}{20}$ as a percent.**

$\frac{9}{20} = \frac{n}{100}$	Write an equation using ratios. One ratio is the fraction. The other is an unknown value compared to 100.
$\frac{9}{20} \overset{\times 5}{=} \frac{45}{100}$ (numerator and denominator each ×5)	Since 20 × 5 = 100, multiply 9 by 5 to find *n*.

So, $\frac{9}{20} = \frac{45}{100}$ or 45%.

Real-World EXAMPLE

5 **At Boulder Middle School, $\frac{78}{600}$ of the students speak Spanish at home, and at Foothills Middle School, $\frac{120}{480}$ of the students speak Spanish at home. Which school has the greater percent of students that speak Spanish at home?**

Write each fraction as a percent. Then compare.

Boulder MS

$$\frac{78}{600} = \frac{n}{100}$$

$$\frac{78}{600} \underset{\div 6}{\overset{\div 6}{=}} \frac{13}{100} \text{ or } 13\%$$

Foothills MS

$$\frac{120}{480} = \frac{n}{100}$$

$$\frac{120}{480} \underset{\div 4.8}{\overset{\div 4.8}{=}} \frac{25}{100} \text{ or } 25\%$$

Since 25% > 13%, Foothills Middle School has the greater percent of students that speak Spanish at home.

CHECK What You Know

Write each percent as a fraction or mixed number in simplest form. See Examples 1–3 (pp. 466–467)

1. 15% **2.** 80% **3.** 180%

4. More than 70% of the world's farm-raised catfish supply comes from Mississippi. What fraction of the world's catfish is this? See Example 3 (p. 467)

5. The graphic shows the results of a survey about recycling. What fraction of those surveyed said that they recycle at school and at home? See Example 3 (p. 467)

Students Who Recycle

Responses	Percent
Yes, just at school	14
Yes, just at home	15
Yes, at school & home	46
No, I don't recycle	23

Source: pbskids.org

Write each fraction or mixed number as a percent. See Example 4 (p. 467)

6. $\frac{1}{4}$ **7.** $\frac{2}{5}$ **8.** $2\frac{1}{4}$

9. If $\frac{6}{300}$ of the animals at the Oakland Zoo are tigers and $\frac{2}{200}$ of the animals at Zoo Boise are tigers, which zoo has the greater percent of animals that are tigers? See Example 5 (p. 468)

10. Talk About It How do you write any percent as a fraction?

Practice and Problem Solving

EXTRA PRACTICE
See page 679.

Write each percent as a fraction or mixed number in simplest form. See Examples 1–3 (pp. 466–467)

11. 14% **12.** 47% **13.** 2%

14. 20% **15.** 185% **16.** 280%

17. In 2004, 22% of e-mail users said they spent less time using e-mail because of spam. What fraction of e-mail users is this?

18. In a recent season, the Dallas Burn won or tied about 54% of their games. What fraction of their games did they win or tie?

Write each fraction or mixed number as a percent. See Example 4 (p. 467)

19. $\frac{3}{10}$ **20.** $\frac{7}{20}$ **21.** $1\frac{1}{4}$

22. $1\frac{2}{5}$ **23.** $\frac{1}{100}$ **24.** $\frac{5}{100}$

25. About $\frac{7}{10}$ of a cat's day is spent dozing. About what percent of a cat's day is spent dozing?

26. About $\frac{23}{25}$ of a watermelon is water. About what percent of a watermelon is water?

27. In Ashlee's coin jar, $\frac{28}{200}$ of the coins are dimes. In her sister's coin jar, $\frac{120}{400}$ of the coins are dimes. Which sibling has the greater percent of coins that are dimes? See Example 5 (p. 468)

28. In a certain rock band, $\frac{4}{5}$ of the members play more than one instrument. In a certain country band, $\frac{6}{10}$ of the members play more than one instrument. Which band has the greater percent of members that can play more than one instrument? See Example 5 (p. 468)

Write a percent to represent the shaded portion of each model.

29. 

30. 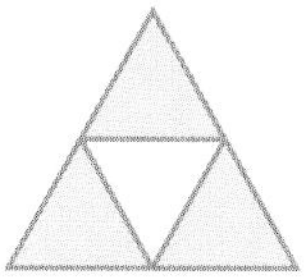

31. 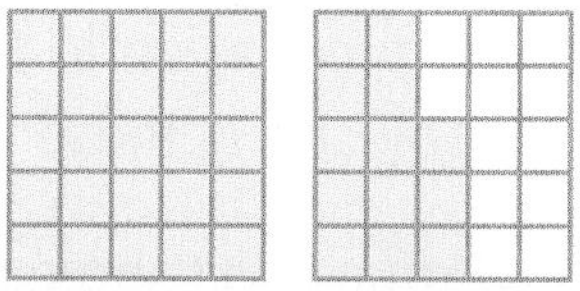

32. Use the table to determine what percent of the baskets Khaliah made and what percent she missed. What is the relationship between these two percents?

Khaliah's Basketball Chart	
Baskets Made	Baskets Missed
卌 卌 卌 III	卌 II

H.O.T. Problems

33. OPEN ENDED Write three fractions that can be written as percents between 50% and 75%. Justify your solution.

34. CHALLENGE Write $\frac{1}{200}$ as a percent.

35. Which One Doesn't Belong? Identify the number that does not belong with the other three. Explain your reasoning.

25%	$\frac{2}{8}$	$\frac{7}{25}$	$\frac{25}{100}$

36. WRITING IN ▸MATH Marita has visited $\frac{3}{5}$ of the national parks in her state. Explain why this is the same at 60%.

Standards Practice

37 On Friday, 65% of the students at Plainview Middle School bought a hot lunch in the cafeteria. What fractional part of the school did *not* buy a hot lunch in the cafeteria?

A $\frac{1}{65}$

B $\frac{13}{20}$

C $\frac{7}{20}$

D $\frac{6}{5}$

38 A certain action movie is being shown on 5 of the 25 screens at a movie theater. What percent of the movie screens are showing the action movie?

F 5%

G 15%

H 20%

J 25%

Spiral Review

Algebra Use the following information for Exercises 39 and 40. (Lesson 8-8)

Vonzell earns $7 per hour for baby-sitting twin boys.

39. Write an equation to represent the total amount t that Vonzell earns for baby-sitting these boys for h hours.

40. How much will she earn if she baby-sits them for 6 hours?

Describe how the next term in each sequence can be found. Then find the next two terms. (Lesson 8-7)

41. 5, 8, 11, 14, ...

42. $\frac{1}{2}, \frac{3}{4}, 1, 1\frac{1}{4}, \ldots$

9-2 Circle Graphs

GET READY to Learn

Concepts in Motion
Animation
ca.gr5math.com

Hands-On Mini Lab

The table below shows the number of people driving together in one vehicle during a spring break trip. These data can be displayed in a circle graph.

Step 1 For each category, let 1 centimeter equal 1%. Mark the length, in centimeters, that represents each percent on a piece of adding machine tape. Label each section.

People in Vehicle	Percent
1–3	11
4–5	35
6–7	29
8–9	11
10 or more	14

Source: carmax.com

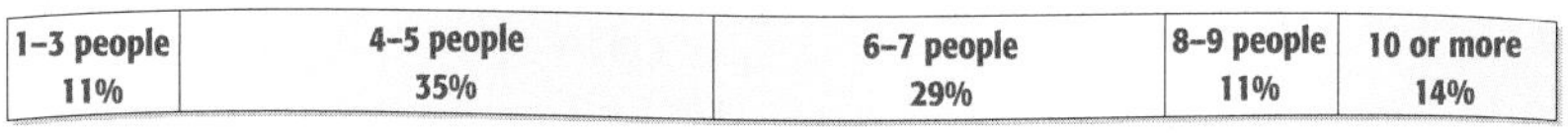

Step 2 Tape the ends together to form a circle.

Step 3 Tape one end of a piece of string to the center of the circle. Tape the other end to the point where two sections meet. Repeat with four more pieces of string.

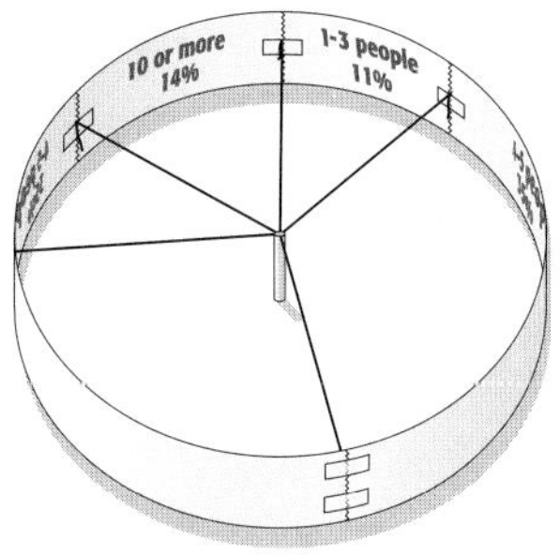

1. Make a bar graph of the data.
2. Which graph represents the data better, a circle graph or a bar graph? Explain.

MAIN IDEA

I will sketch and analyze circle graphs.

Standard 5SDAP1.2 **Organize and display single-variable data in appropriate graphs and representations** (e.g., histogram, **circle graphs**) and explain which types of graphs are appropriate for various data sets.
Standard 5SDAP1.3 **Use** fractions and **percentages to compare data sets of different sizes.**

New Vocabulary

circle graph

A **circle graph** is used to compare data that are parts of a whole.

Driving Together in One Vehicle to Spring Break

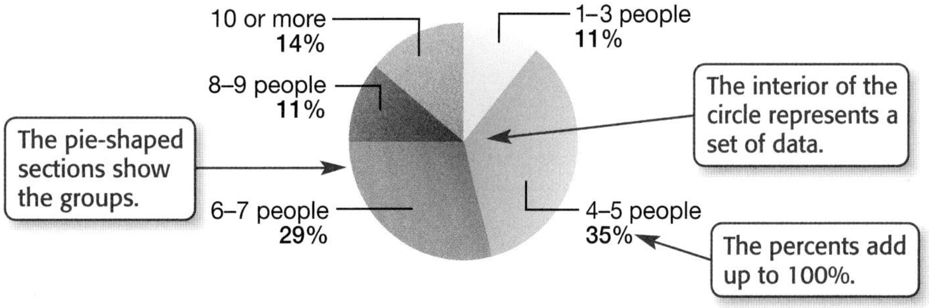

You can use number sense to sketch circle graphs.

Remember

You can review **simplifying fractions** in Lesson 4-3.

EXAMPLE Sketch Circle Graphs

1 A group of teenagers were asked to name their top priority for the school year. The results are shown below. Sketch a circle graph to display the data.

Top Priorities for School Year	
Top Priority	**Percent**
Sports	12.5
Good Grades	52
Friends	23
Boyfriend/Girlfriend	12.5

- Write a fraction to estimate each percent.

  $52\% \approx 50\%$ and $50\% = \frac{50}{100}$ or $\frac{1}{2}$

  $23\% \approx 25\%$ and $25\% = \frac{25}{100}$ or $\frac{1}{4}$

  $12.5\% \approx 10\%$ and $10\% = \frac{10}{100}$ or $\frac{1}{10}$

- Use a compass to draw a circle with at least a 1-inch radius.

- Since 52% is a little more than 50% or $\frac{1}{2}$, shade a little more than $\frac{1}{2}$ of the circle for "Good Grades."

  Since 23% is a little less than 25% or $\frac{1}{4}$, shade a little less than $\frac{1}{4}$ of the circle for "Friends."

  Since the last two sections are equal, take the remaining portion of the circle and divide it into two equal parts.

- Label each section of the circle graph. Then give the graph a title.

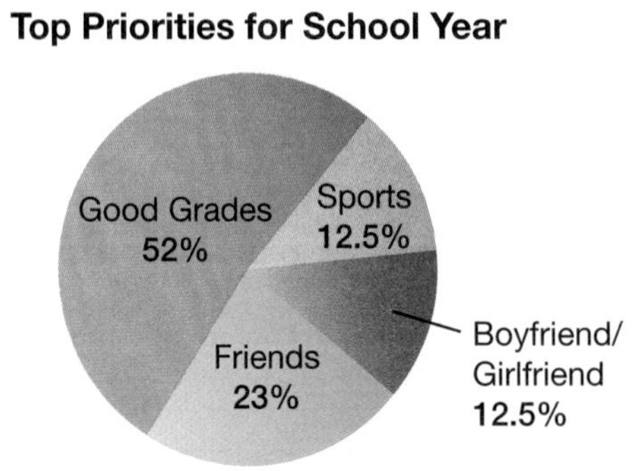

Online Personal Tutor at ca.gr5math.com

You can analyze data displayed in a circle graph. Refer to the circle graph below from Example 1.

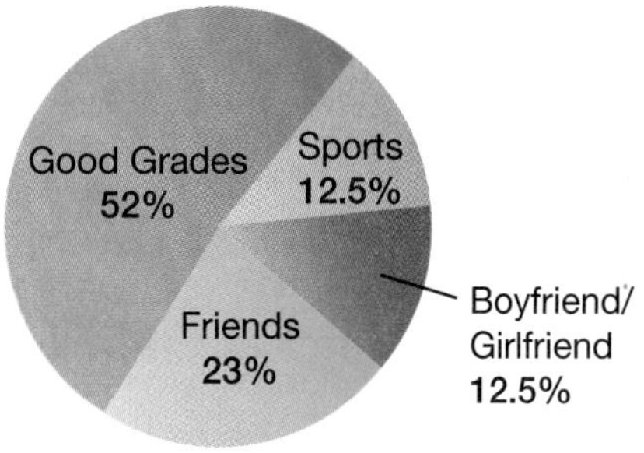

You can easily see that the largest section of the circle graph is the section labeled "Good Grades" and that it represents a little over half of the circle graph. So, you can conclude that about half of the teenagers surveyed said that getting good grades was their top priority for the school year.

EXAMPLES Analyze Circle Graphs

Karen surveyed her class to see which rooms in their homes were the messiest. The circle graph at the right shows the results of her survey.

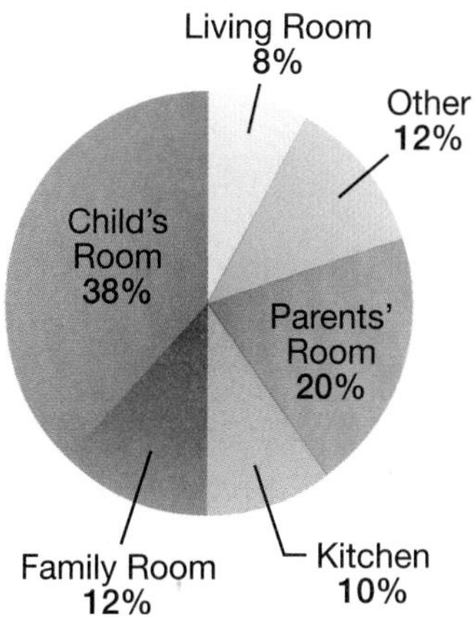

2 Which room did students say is the messiest?

The largest section of the graph is the section that represents a child's room. So, students said that a child's room is the messiest room in the home.

3 Which two sections represent the responses by the same amount of students?

By comparing the percents, the sections labeled "Other" and "Family Room" are the same size. So, the same number of students chose these two rooms.

4 How does the number of students that say their parents' room is the messiest compare to the number of students that say the family room is the messiest?

The section representing parents' room is about twice the size of the section representing family room. So, twice as many students say that the parents' room is the messiest room.

Remember

For Example 3, you can also compare the size of the sections. Since the "Other" section is the same size as the "Family Room" section, the answer seems reasonable.

CHECK What You Know

1. Marciano asked the students in his class whether or not they have a nickname. The table shows the results. Sketch a circle graph to display the data. See Example 1 (p. 472)

Do You Have a Nickname?	
No	19%
Yes, from family	55%
Yes, from friends	26%

For Exercises 2–4, use the graph at the right.
See Examples 2–4 (p. 473)

Who Influences Kids to Read

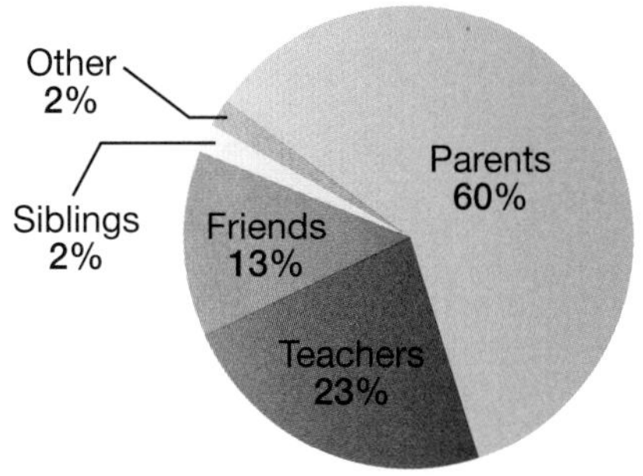

Source: SWR Worldwide for shopforschool.com

2. Who most influences kids to read?
3. Which two groups are least influential in getting kids to read?
4. About how much more do parents influence kids to read than teachers?
5. Talk About It Explain how to identify the greatest and least values of a set of data when looking at a circle graph.

Practice and Problem Solving

EXTRA PRACTICE
See page 679.

6. The table shows the results of an election for class president. Sketch a circle graph to display the data. See Example 1 (p. 472)

Class President Ballots	
Melissa	31%
Lacey	25%
Troy	25%
Omar	19%

7. In Mrs. Castro's class, 75% of the students like rock music, 10% favor country music, 5% prefer classical, and 10% chose another type of music. Sketch a circle graph to display the data. See Example 1 (p. 472)

For Exercises 8–10, use the graph below that shows the ages at which libraries in the U.S. stop requiring parental permission for children to use the Internet. See Examples 2–4 (p. 473)

Ages at Which Libraries Stop Requiring Permission to Use the Internet

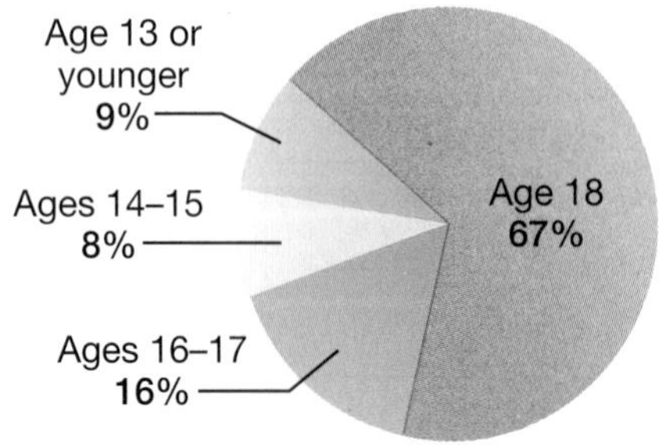

Source: University of Illinois

8. At what age do all libraries stop requiring parental permission?
9. For which two age intervals do libraries stop requiring permission to use the Internet about the same percent of the time?
10. How does the number of libraries that stop requiring parental permission at ages 14–15 compare to the number of libraries that stop requiring parental permission at ages 16–17?

For Exercises 11–13, use the graph at the right.

See Examples 2–4 (p. 473)

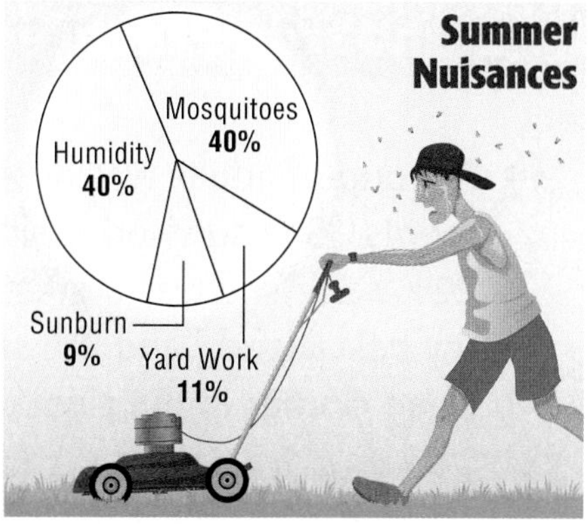

Source: Impulse Research Corporation

11. Which summer nuisance is named least often?

12. Which two sections represent the same percent of summer nuisances?

13. How does humidity compare to yard work as a summer nuisance?

14. A group of students was asked about their movie-going experience pet peeves. The table shows their responses. Sketch a circle graph to compare the students' responses. What percent of the students chose bad manners or overpriced food as their pet peeves?

Movie Pet Peeves	
Response	**Number of Students**
Bad Manners	98
Preshow Commercials	48
Overpriced Food	24
Babies/Noisy Children	24
Other	6

H.O.T. Problems

15. COLLECT THE DATA Record your activities for one 24-hour period. Sketch a circle graph to display your data. Then write a few sentences that analyze the data.

16. CHALLENGE Decide which of the following is the least appropriate data to display in a circle graph. Explain your decision.

a. data that show what age groups buy athletic shoes

b. data that show what most motivates teens to volunteer

c. data that show the average price of a hamburger every five years

d. data that show how many hours adults help their children study

17. SELECT A TECHNIQUE Carter wants to sketch a circle graph of the data in the table. Which of the following techniques might Carter use to determine how big to make each section of the circle graph? Justify your selection(s). Then use the technique(s) to sketch the circle graph.

How Students Travel to Clint Middle School	
Bicycle	5%
Bus	47%
Carpool	25%
W alk	22%

mental math | number sense | estimation

18. WRITING IN ▶MATH Write a problem that can be solved using one of the circle graphs in this lesson. Be sure to include a statement about the graph to which you are referring.

Standards Practice

19 A group of adults was asked to give a reason why they honor their moms. "She survived raising me" was given by 50% of the adults, 22% said "she was a great role model," 19% said "she has become my best friend," and 9% said "she always had dinner on the table and clean clothes in the closet." Which circle graph best displays the data?

A

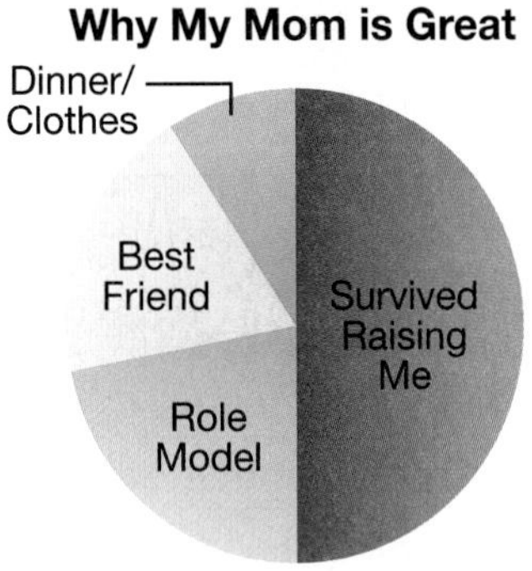

C

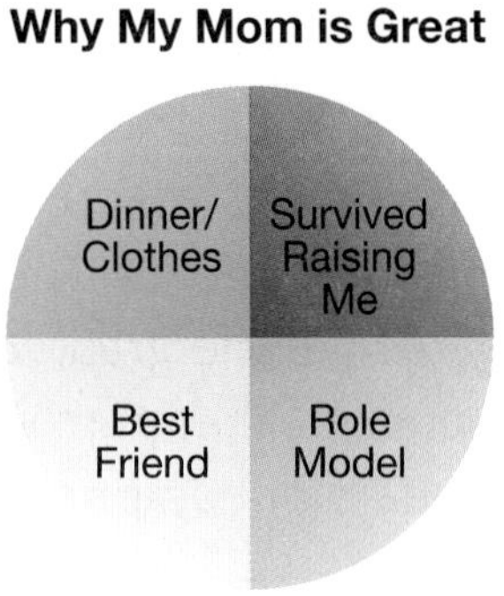

B

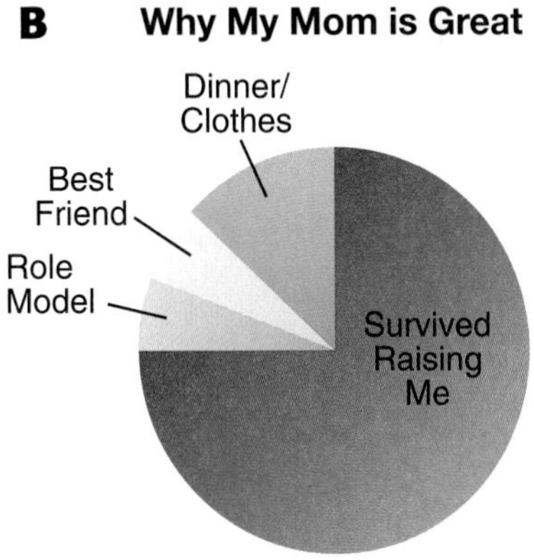

D

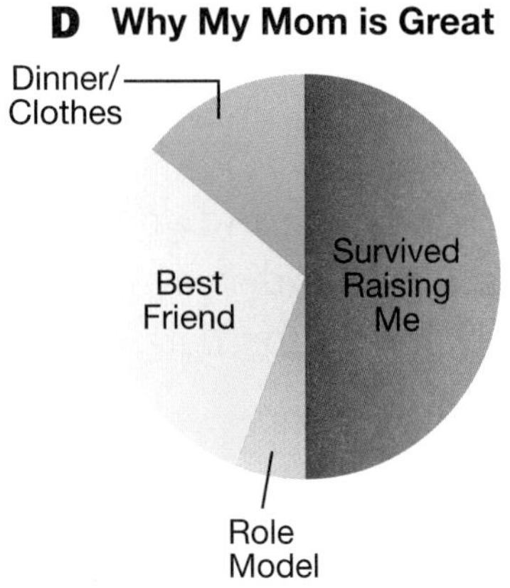

Spiral Review

Write each fraction or mixed number as a percent. **(Lesson 9-1)**

20. $\frac{43}{100}$ **21.** $\frac{9}{10}$ **22.** $1\frac{1}{5}$

Use the following information for Exercises 23 and 24. **(Lesson 8-8)**

A video store charges $3 to rent a DVD.

23. Write an equation to represent the total cost *c* for renting *d* DVDs.

24. How much will it cost to rent 4 DVDs?

25. Josh is drawing a map of his walk to school. His house is located at (3, 5). To get to school he walks one block south and three blocks west. At what coordinates on the map should Josh draw the school? **(Lesson 4-10)**

26. Order 3.8, 3.05, 0.39, and 3.5 from greatest to least. **(Lesson 3-2)**

9-3 Percents and Decimals

GET READY to Learn

The circle graph shows the favorite subjects of students in a recent survey. The fraction, $\frac{28}{100}$, represents the section of the graph labeled math. What decimal is equivalent to $\frac{28}{100}$?

Favorite Subject

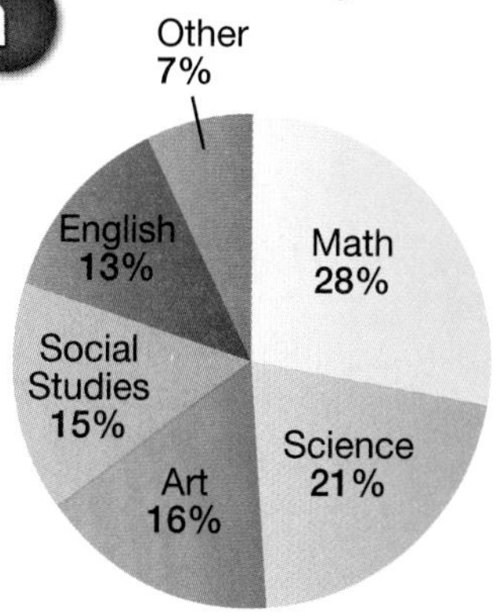

Source: *Time for Kids Almanac 2005*

MAIN IDEA

I will express percents as decimals and decimals as percents.

Standard 5NS1.2 Interpret percents as a part of a hundred; find decimal and percent equivalents for common fractions and explain why they represent the same value; compute a given percent of a whole number.

Remember

To write a percent as a decimal, move the decimal point two places to the left. This is the same as dividing by 100.

$56\% = 56\%$

$= 0.56$

Percents can be written as decimals. To write a percent as a decimal, rewrite the percent as a fraction with a denominator of 100. Then write the fraction as a decimal.

EXAMPLES Write a Percent as a Decimal

Write each percent as a decimal.

1 56%

$56\% = \frac{56}{100}$ Rewrite the percent as a fraction with a denominator of 100.

$= 0.56$ Write *56 hundredths* as a decimal.

2 8%

$8\% = \frac{8}{100}$ Rewrite the percent as a fraction with a denominator of 100.

$= 0.08$ Write *8 hundredths* as a decimal.

3 120%

$120\% = \frac{120}{100}$ Rewrite the percent as a fraction with a denominator of 100.

$= 1\frac{20}{100}$ Write as a mixed number.

$= 1.20$ Write *1 and 20 hundredths* as a decimal.

$= 1.2$

You can also write a decimal as a percent. To write a decimal as a percent, write the decimal as a fraction whose denominator is 100. Then write the fraction as a percent.

EXAMPLES Write a Decimal as a Percent

Write each decimal as a percent.

Remember

To write a decimal as a percent; move the decimal point two places to the right. This is the same as multiplying by 100.

$0.38 = 0.38$
$= 38\%$

4 **0.38**

$0.38 = \frac{38}{100}$ Write *38 hundredths* as a fraction.

$= 38\%$ Write the fraction as a percent.

5 **1.45**

$1.45 = 1\frac{45}{100}$ Write *1 and 45 hundredths* as a mixed number.

$= \frac{145}{100}$ Write the mixed number as an improper fraction.

$= 145\%$ Write the fraction as a percent.

6 **0.07**

$0.07 = \frac{7}{100}$ Write *7 hundredths* as a fraction.

$= 7\%$ Write the fraction as a percent.

Real-World EXAMPLE

7 **The United States produces more corn than any other country, producing 0.4 of the total corn crops. Write 0.4 as a percent.**

$0.4 = \frac{4}{10}$ Write *4 tenths* as a fraction.

$= \frac{4 \times \mathbf{10}}{10 \times \mathbf{10}}$ Multiply the numerator and denominator by 10 so that the denominator is 100.

$= \frac{40}{100}$ Simplify.

$= 40\%$ Write the fraction as a percent.

Check

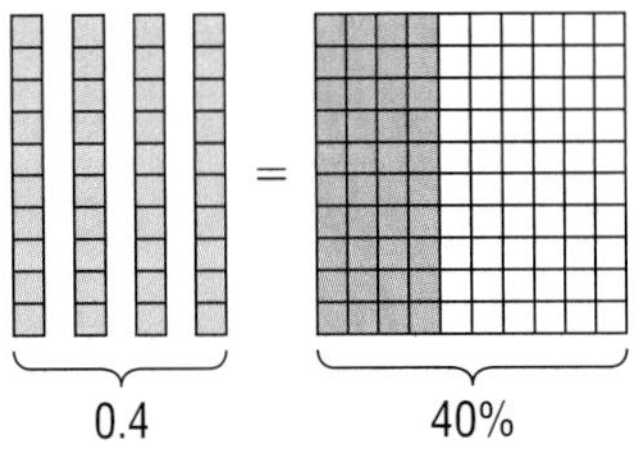

Online Personal Tutor at ca.gr5math.com

CHECK What You Know

Write each percent as a decimal. See Examples 1–3 (p. 477)

1. 27% **2.** 15% **3.** 4%

4. 9% **5.** 115% **6.** 136%

Write each decimal as a percent. See Examples 4–6 (p. 478)

7. 0.32 **8.** 0.15 **9.** 2.91

10. 1.25 **11.** 0.09 **12.** 0.03

13. About 0.7 of the human body is water. What percent is equivalent to 0.7? See Example 7 (p. 478)

14. Talk About It Describe how you would write 0.34 as a percent.

Practice and Problem Solving

EXTRA PRACTICE See page 679.

Write each percent as a decimal. See Examples 1–3 (p. 477)

15. 17% **16.** 35% **17.** 2% **18.** 3%

19. 125% **20.** 104% **21.** 11% **22.** 95%

23. Each year about 14% of the world's fruit is produced in China. Write 14% as a decimal.

24. About 95% of all species of fish have skeletons made of bone. Write 95% as a decimal.

Write each decimal as a percent. See Examples 4–6 (p. 478)

25. 0.22 **26.** 0.99 **27.** 1.75 **28.** 3.55

29. 0.5 **30.** 0.6 **31.** 0.01 **32.** 0.06

33. In 2004, the number of homes with digital cameras grew 0.44 from the previous year. Write 0.44 as a percent. See Example 7 (p. 478)

34. According to the *American Pasta Report,* 0.12 of Americans say that lasagna is their favorite pasta. What percent is equivalent to 0.12? See Example 7 (p. 478)

Replace each ● with $<$, $>$, or $=$ to make a true sentence.

35. 18% ● 0.2 **36.** 0.5 ● 5% **37.** 2.3 ● 23%

H.O.T. Problems

38. OPEN ENDED Write a decimal between 0.5 and 0.75. Then write it as a fraction in simplest form and as a percent.

39. CHALLENGE Order 23.4%, 2.34, 0.0234, and 20.34% from least to greatest.

40. CHALLENGE Order $2\frac{1}{4}$, 0.6, 2.75, 40%, and $\frac{7}{5}$ from greatest to least.

41. WRITING IN MATH Write a problem about a real-world situation in which you would either write a percent as a decimal or write a decimal as a percent.

Standards Practice

42 Each square below is divided into sections of equal size. Which square has 75% of its total area shaded?

A

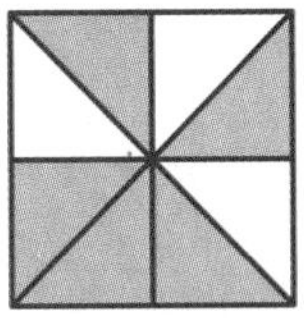

C

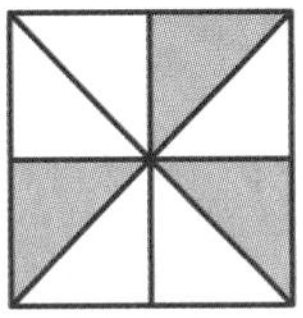

B

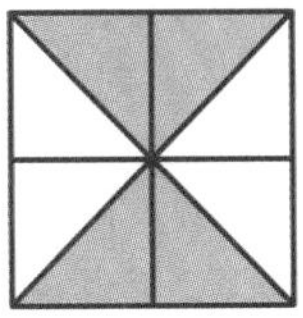

D

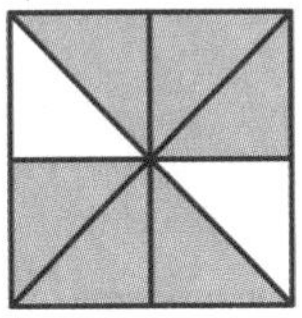

43 Which decimal is equivalent to 25%?

F 0.025

G 0.25

H 2.5

J 25.0

Spiral Review

44. The circle graph shows pie sales at a local bakery. What part of the total sales is greater, peanut butter or strawberry? **(Lesson 9-2)**

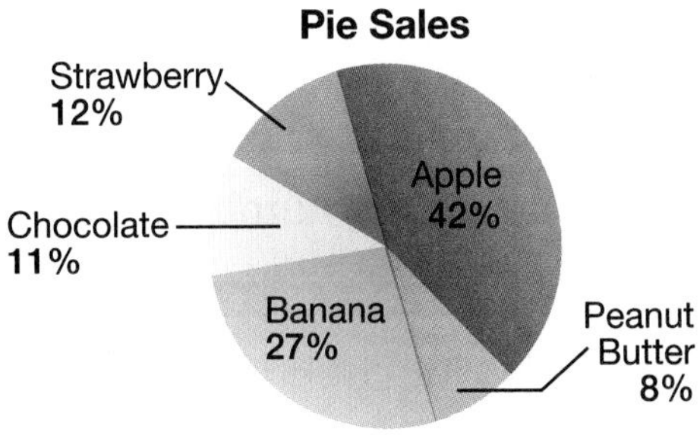

Write each percent as a fraction or mixed number in simplest form. (Lesson 9-1)

45. 24%

46. 38%

47. 125%

48. 35%

49. The equation $17 - v = 5$ gives Virginia's age, v, in years. Solve the equation mentally. **(Lesson 1-8)**

Match 'Em Up

Finding Percent Equivalents

Get Ready!

Players: two

You will need: 16 index cards

Get Set!

- Make a set of 8 percent cards using the numbers below.

25% | 30% | 95% | 56% | 125% | 62% | 19% | 75%

- Make a set of 8 fraction or decimal cards that are equivalent to the percents.

0.75 | $\frac{3}{10}$ | 1.25 | $\frac{19}{20}$

$\frac{1}{4}$ | 0.62 | $\frac{14}{25}$ | 0.19

Go!

- Mix up each set of cards and place the cards facedown as shown.

Percent Cards

Fraction or Decimal Cards

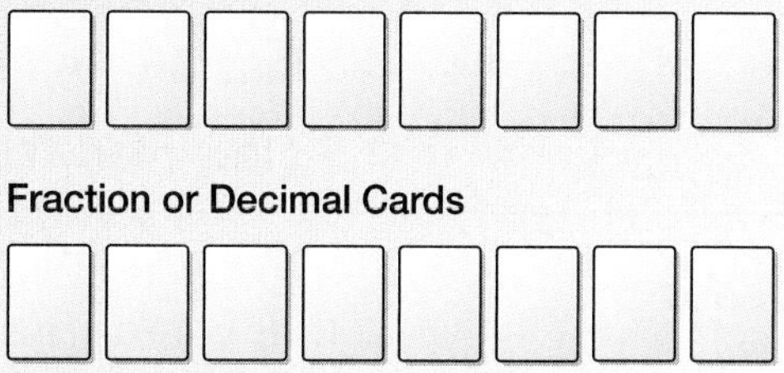

- Player 1 turns over a percent card and a fraction or decimal card. If the fraction or decimal is equivalent to the percent, the player removes the cards, a point is scored, and the player turns over two more cards.
- If the fraction or decimal is not equivalent to the percent, the player turns the cards facedown, no points are scored, and it is the next player's turn.
- Take turns until all cards are matched.
- The player with more points wins.

9-4 Problem-Solving Strategy

MAIN IDEA I will solve problems by solving a simpler problem.

Standard 5MR2.2 Apply strategies and results from simpler problems to more complex problems. **Standard 5NS1.2 Interpret percents as a part of a hundred;** find decimal and percent equivalents for common fractions and explain why they represent the same value; compute a given percent of a whole number.

A total of 400 students at Liberty Elementary voted on whether a tiger or a dolphin should be the new school's mascot. The circle graph shows the results. How many students voted for the tiger for the school mascot?

School Mascot

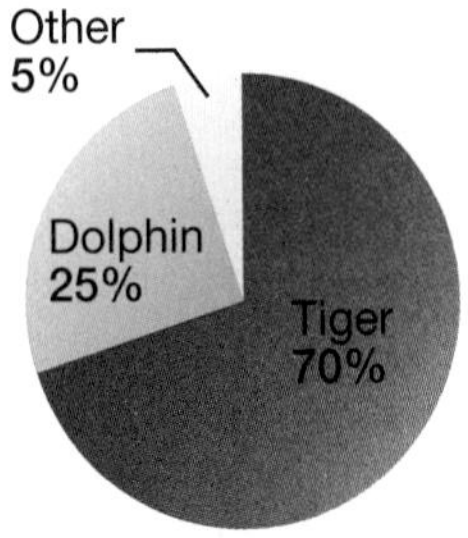

Understand

What facts do you know?

- 400 students voted.
- 70% of the students voted for the tiger.

What do you need to find?

- How many students voted for the tiger for the school mascot?

Plan

Solve a simpler problem by finding 10% of the number of students that voted. Then use that result to find 70% of the number of students that voted.

Solve

Since $10\% = \frac{10}{100}$ or $\frac{1}{10}$, 1 out of every 10 students voted for the tiger.

$$400 \div 10 = 40 \text{ students.}$$

Since 70% is equal to 7 times 10%, multiply 40 by 7.

$$40 \times 7 = 280 \text{ students.}$$

So, 280 students voted for the tiger.

Check

Look back at the problem. You know that 70% is close to 75%, which is $\frac{3}{4}$. Since $\frac{1}{4}$ of 400 is 100, $\frac{3}{4}$ of 400 is 300. So, 280 is a reasonable answer. ✓

ANALYZE the Strategy

Refer to the problem on the previous page.

1. In the example, why was it simpler to work with 10%?
2. Explain how you could use the *solve a simpler problem* strategy to find the thickness of one page of your textbook.
3. How could the *solve a simpler problem* strategy help when you are trying to solve a problem that involves large numbers?
4. Explain when you would use the *solve a simpler problem* strategy.

PRACTICE the Strategy

EXTRA PRACTICE
See page 680.

Solve. Use the *solve a simpler problem* strategy.

5. Kip's mom wants to leave a 20% tip for a $19.30 restaurant bill. About how much money should she leave?
6. Sound travels through air at a speed of 1,129 feet per second. At this rate, about how far will sound travel in 1 minute?
7. A gold album award is presented to an artist who has sold at least 500,000 units of a single album or CD. If an artist has 16 gold albums, what is the minimum number of albums that have been sold?
8. Yuma's watch beeps every hour. How many times will it beep in one week?
9. Part of a strip of border for a bulletin board is shown.

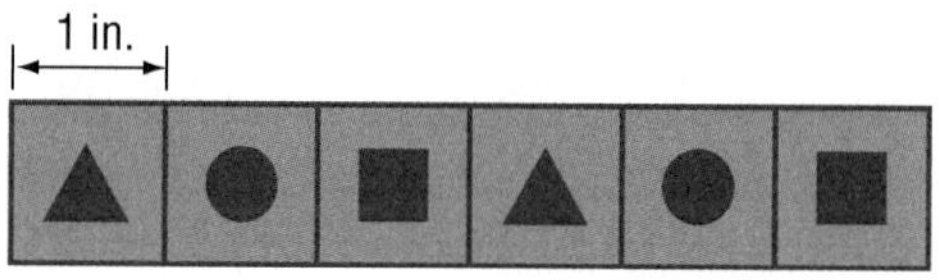

All the sections of the border are the same width. If the first shape on the strip is a triangle, and the strip is 74 inches long, what is the last shape on the strip?

10. Five farmers can plow five fields in five hours. How many fields can ten farmers plow in ten hours?
11. Find the area of the figure.

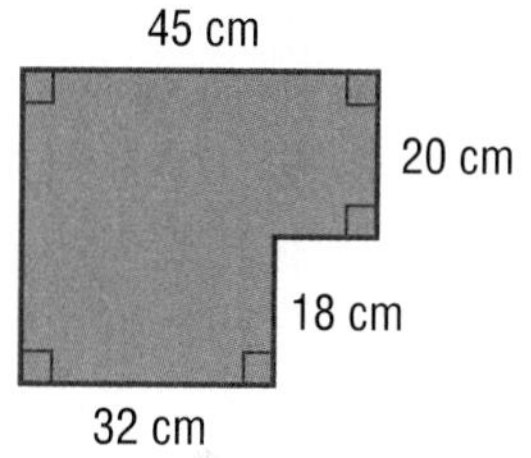

12. The total area of Minnesota is 86,939 square miles. Of that, about 90% is land area. About how much of Minnesota is not land area?
13. Debra has a string of ribbon 20 inches long. She needs to cut the ribbon into 2 inch long pieces to tie around party favors. How many cuts will she make if she uses all 20 inches?
14. In Mr. Braddock's class, $\frac{2}{5}$ of the students will volunteer at the annual fall festival. If there are 30 students in Mr. Braddock's class, how many will volunteer at the fall festival?
15. **WRITING IN MATH** How is the *solve a simpler problem* strategy similar to the *look for a pattern* strategy?

9-5 Estimating with Percents

MAIN IDEA

I will estimate the percent of a number.

Standard 5MR2.2 Apply strategies and results from simpler problems to more complex problems.
Standard 5NS2.5 Compute and perform simple multiplication and division **of fractions and apply these procedures to solving problems.**

GET READY to Learn

Concepts in Motion
Animation
ca.gr5math.com

Hands-On Mini Lab

You can use a model and find a fractional part of a number. The model below shows how to find $\frac{1}{4}$ of 20.

Step 1 Model 20 on a piece of grid paper.

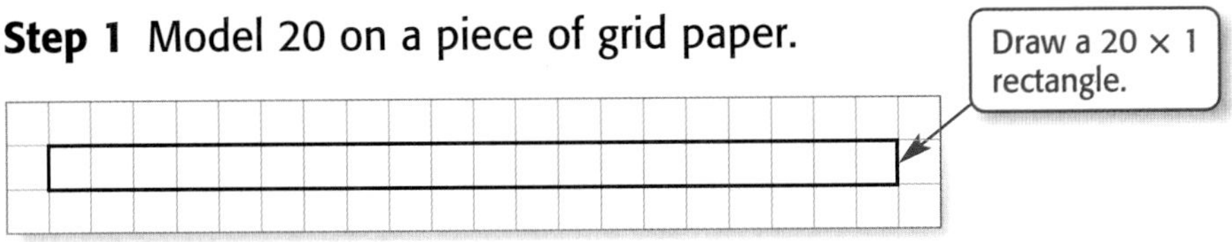
Draw a 20 × 1 rectangle.

Step 2 Divide the rectangle into 4 equal sections and shade one of them.

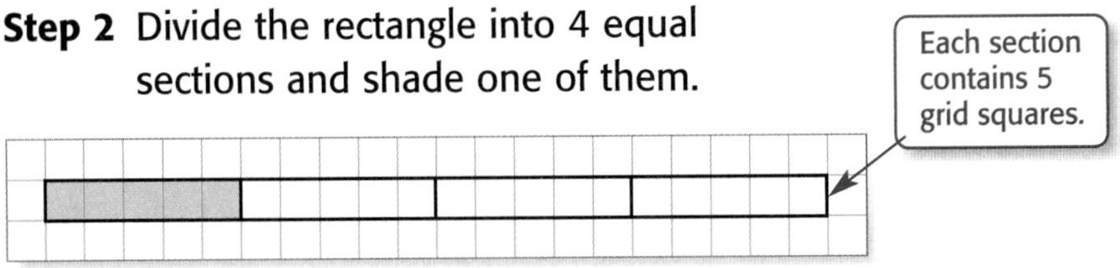
Each section contains 5 grid squares.

So, $\frac{1}{4}$ of 20 is 5.

Use grid paper to find the fractional portion of each number.

1. $\frac{1}{2}$ of 10 **2.** $\frac{1}{5}$ of 10 **3.** $\frac{2}{5}$ of 20 **4.** $\frac{5}{6}$ of 36

5. How can you find a fractional part of a number without drawing a model on grid paper?

Estimating with percents will provide a reasonable solution to many real-world problems. The table below shows some commonly used percents and their fraction equivalents. It is helpful to memorize the percent-fraction equivalencies shown in the Key Concept box.

KEY CONCEPT **Percent-Fraction Equivalents**

$20\% = \frac{1}{5}$	$50\% = \frac{1}{2}$	$80\% = \frac{4}{5}$	$25\% = \frac{1}{4}$	$33\frac{1}{3}\% = \frac{1}{3}$
$30\% = \frac{3}{10}$	$60\% = \frac{3}{5}$	$90\% = \frac{9}{10}$	$75\% = \frac{3}{4}$	$66\frac{2}{3}\% = \frac{2}{3}$
$40\% = \frac{2}{5}$	$70\% = \frac{7}{10}$	$100\% = 1$		

When you estimate the percent of a number, you are solving a simpler problem.

EXAMPLES Estimate the Percent of a Number

1 Estimate 52% of 298.

52% is close to 50% or $\frac{1}{2}$. Round 298 to 300.

$\frac{1}{2}$ of 300 is 150. $\frac{1}{2}$ or *half* means to divide by 2.

So, 52% of 298 is about 150.

2 Estimate 60% of 27.

60% is $\frac{3}{5}$. Round 27 to 25 since it is divisible by 5.

$\frac{3}{5}$ of 25 $= \frac{3}{5} \times 25$ or 15

Thus, 60% of 27 is about 15.

Remember

You can also solve Example 2 mentally. $\frac{1}{5}$ of 25 is 5, and so $\frac{3}{5}$ of 25 is 3×5 or 15.

Real-World EXAMPLE

3 A DVD that originally costs $15.99 is on sale for 50% off. If you have $9, would you have enough money to buy the DVD?

To determine whether you have enough money to buy the DVD, you need to estimate 50% of $15.99.

One Way: Use an equation.

$50\% = \frac{1}{2}$ and $\$15.99 \approx \$16$

$\frac{1}{2} = \frac{x}{16}$ Write the equation.

$\frac{1 \times 8}{2 \times 8} = \frac{x}{16}$ Since $2 \times 8 = 16$, multiply 1 by 8.

$x = 8$

Another Way: Use mental math.

$50\% = \frac{1}{2}$ and $\$15.99 \approx \$16$

$\frac{1}{2}$ of 16 is 8.

Since $8 is less than $9, you should have enough money.

Real-World EXAMPLE

4 **Yutaka surveyed the students in his health class regarding their favorite juice. Predict the number of students out of 353 that would prefer orange juice.**

Favorite Juice	Percent of Students
Mixed Fruit	34
Apple	29
Orange	22
Grape	15

You need to estimate the number of students out of 353 that would prefer orange juice. 22% of the students surveyed chose orange juice.

22% is about 20% or $\frac{1}{5}$.

Round 353 to 350 since it is divisible by 5.

$\frac{1}{5}$ of 350 = $\frac{1}{5} \times 350$ or 70.

So, about 70 students would prefer orange juice.

Online Personal Tutor at ca.gr5math.com

CHECK What You Know

Estimate each percent. See Examples 1, 2 (p. 485)

1. 19% of \$53 **2.** 34% of 62 **3.** 47% of \$118

4. 38% of \$50 **5.** 59% of 16 **6.** 75% of 33

7. Adrienne wants to give a 20% tip to a taxi driver. If the fair is \$23.78, what would be a reasonable amount to tip? See Example 3 (p. 485)

8. A group of friends went on a hiking trip. They planned to hike a total of 38 miles. They want to complete 25% of the hike by the end of the first day. About how many miles should they hike the first day? See Example 3 (p. 485)

9. Ayana surveyed several classmates about their favorite winter activity. Use the graph to predict the number of students out of 164 that prefer snowboarding. See Example 4 (p. 486)

Favorite Winter Activity

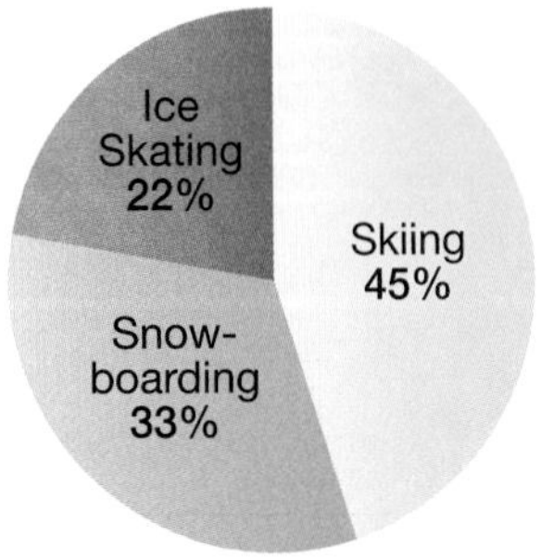

10. Talk About It Give a real-world example of when you would need to estimate the percent of a number.

Practice and Problem Solving

EXTRA PRACTICE See page 680.

Estimate each percent. See Examples 1, 2 (p. 485)

11. 21% of 96

12. 53% of 59

13. 19% of 72

14. 35% of 147

15. 26% of 125

16. 42% of 16

17. 79% of 82

18. 67% of 296

19. 89% of 195

20. Estimate seventy-four percent of forty-five.

21. Louisa deposited 25% of the money she earned baby-sitting into her savings account. If she earned $237.50, about how much did she deposit into her savings account?

22. Penguins spend as much as 75% of their lives in the sea. An Emperor Penguin living in the wild has a life span of about 18 years. About how many years does a wild Emperor Penguin spend in the sea?

23. The Atlantic coast has 2,069 miles of coastline. Of that, about 28% is located in Florida. About how many miles of coastline does Florida have?

24. A test has 28 questions. If you answered 65% of the questions correctly, about how many questions did you answer correctly?

25. A group of students were asked how they most often communicate with their grandparents. Sketch a circle graph of the results shown in the table.

Communicating with Grandparents	
Phone	43%
E-mail	32%
Letters	19%
Instant Messages	6%

Estimate the percent that is shaded in each figure.

26.

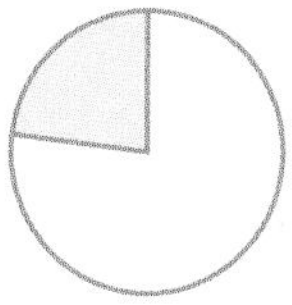

27.

28.

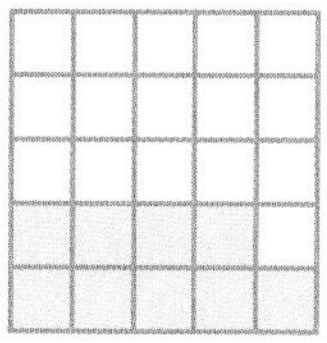

H.O.T. Problems

29. **CHALLENGE** Order from least to greatest 40% of 50, 50% of 50, and $\frac{1}{2}$% of 50.

30. **NUMBER SENSE** A shirt regularly priced at $32 is on sale for 40% off. You estimate that you will save $\frac{2}{5}$ of $30 or $12. Will the actual amount be more or less than $12? Explain.

31. **WRITING IN ▶MATH** A classmate is trying to estimate 42% of $122. Explain how your classmate should solve the problem.

Standards Practice

32 Refer to the graph. If 3,608 people were surveyed, which statement can be used to estimate the number of people that are influenced by a friend or relative when buying a CD?

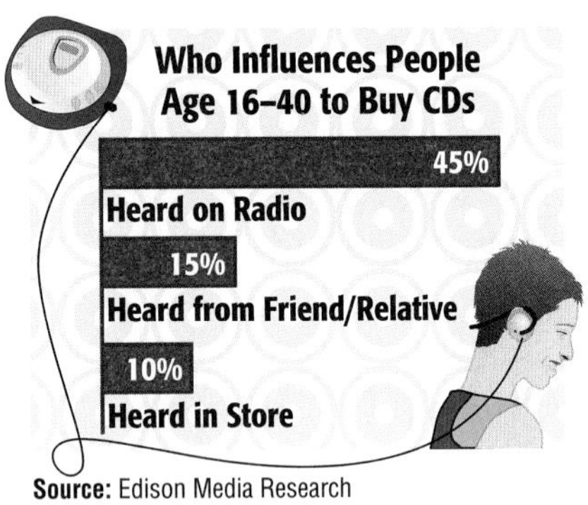

Source: Edison Media Research

A $\frac{1}{8}$ of 3,600 is 450.

B $\frac{1}{6}$ of 3,600 is 600.

C $\frac{1}{5}$ of 3,600 is 720.

D $\frac{1}{4}$ of 3,600 is 900.

33 Which of the following is the best estimate for 21% of 1,095?

F 125 **H** 350

G 200 **J** 495

34 After a group of 24 parts were tested, 5 were found to be defective. About what percent of the parts tested were defective?

A 5%

B 20%

C 25%

D 33%

35 The volleyball team played 20 games this season. If they won 78% of their games, about how many games did they win?

F 7 **H** 16

G 10 **J** 20

Spiral Review

36. Every 12th person entering the gym on Saturday will receive a free T-shirt. How many T-shirts will be given away if 190 people go to the gym on Saturday? **(Lesson 9-4)**

Express each decimal as a percent. (Lesson 9-3)

37. 0.45 **38.** 0.02 **39.** 0.362 **40.** 0.058

41. The table shows how people responded to a question about the importance of sunny weather in a vacation location. Sketch a circle graph to display the data. **(Lesson 9-2)**

Sunshine While on Vacation	
Response	**Percent**
Very important	45%
Important	30%
Not Very Important	15%
Not At All Important	10%

Source: Opinion Research Corp.

Algebra Solve. (Lesson 8-6)

42. $\frac{2}{3} = \frac{x}{6}$ **43.** $\frac{3}{5} = \frac{x}{45}$

44. $\frac{x}{9} = \frac{20}{36}$ **45.** $\frac{7}{x} = \frac{42}{48}$

CHAPTER 9 Mid-Chapter Check

Lessons 9-1 through 9-5

Write each percent as a fraction in simplest form. **(Lesson 9-1)**

1. 39% **2.** 18% **3.** 175%

4. **STANDARDS PRACTICE** At West Middle School, 48 of the 100 students ride the bus to school. What fractional part of the school does *not* ride the bus to school? **(Lesson 9-1)**

A $\frac{13}{25}$ **C** $\frac{5}{4}$

B $\frac{1}{48}$ **D** $\frac{12}{15}$

Write each fraction or mixed number as a percent. **(Lesson 9-1)**

5. $\frac{8}{20}$ **6.** $1\frac{1}{2}$ **7.** $\frac{3}{100}$

For Exercises 8 and 9, use the graph below. **(Lesson 9-2)**

Pasta Sales by Pasta Shape

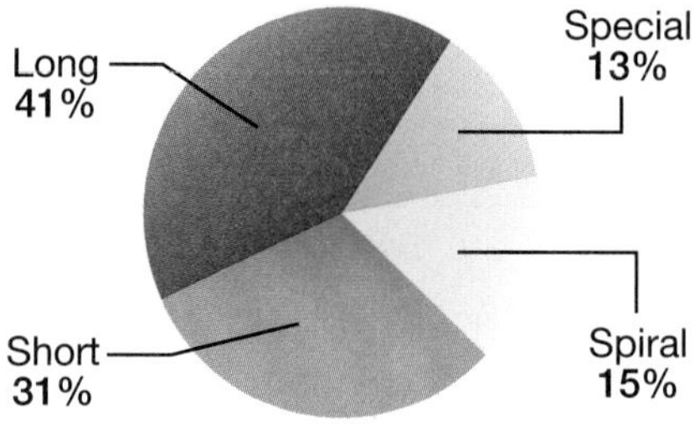

8. Which pasta had the most sales?

9. Did special pasta have a greater or lesser portion of the sales compared to spiral pasta?

10. In Ms. Thorne's class, 60% of the students like soccer, 25% favor football, and 15% choose another type of sport. Sketch a circle graph to display the data. **(Lesson 9-2)**

Write each percent as a decimal. **(Lesson 9-3)**

11. 73% **12.** 145% **13.** 9%

14. Twyla has memorized 85% of her lines for the school play. What decimal is equivalent to 85%? **(Lesson 9-3)**

Write each decimal as a percent. **(Lesson 9-3)**

15. 0.22 **16.** 6.75 **17.** 0.1

18. The number of chorus students increased by 1.2 from the previous year. Write 1.2 as a percent. **(Lesson 9-3)**

19. **STANDARDS PRACTICE** Each circle is divided into sections of equal size. Which circle has 25% of its total area shaded? **(Lesson 9-3)**

F

H

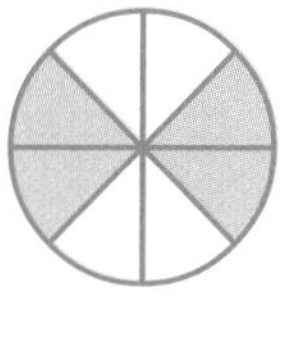

G

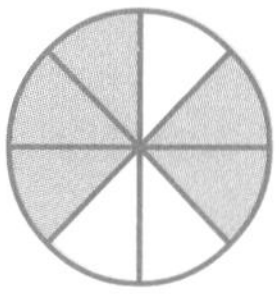

J

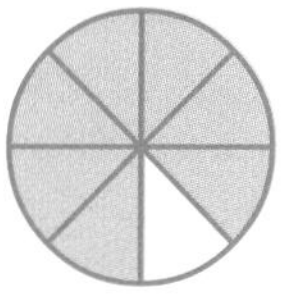

20. The world's fastest typist can type up to 212 words per minute. At this rate, how many words can she type in 2 hours? **(Lesson 9-4)**

21. **WRITING IN ▶MATH** Is 25 a reasonable estimate for 51% of 47? Explain. **(Lesson 9-5)**

Explore

Math Lab for 9-6
Percent of a Number

MAIN IDEA

I will use a model to find the percent of a number.

Standard 5NS1.2 Interpret percents as a part of a hundred; find decimal and percent equivalents for common fractions and explain why they represent the same value; **compute a given percent of a whole number.**
Standard 5MR2.3 Use a variety of methods, such as words, numbers, symbols, charts, graphs, tables, diagrams, **and models, to explain mathematical reasoning.**

A skateboard is on sale for 20% off the original price of $80. How much will you save? You know the percent of the discount. You need to find what *part* of the original price you will save. This is called *finding the percent of a number.*

ACTIVITY

1 Use a model to find 20% of $80.

Step 1 Draw a 1-by-10 rectangle on grid paper as shown. Since percent is a ratio that compares a number to 100, label the units on the top of the model from 0% to 100% as shown.

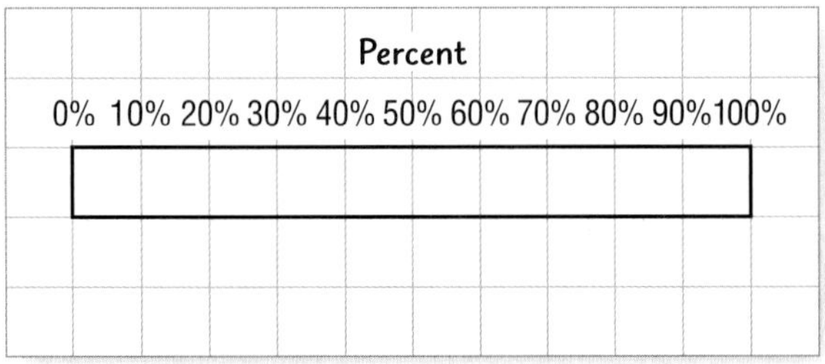

Step 2 Since $80 represents the original price, label equal units from $0 to $80 on the bottom of the model.

Step 3 Draw a line from 20% to the bottom of the model as shown. Shade to the left of this line.

The model shows that 20% of $80 is $16. So, you will save $16 off of the original price of the skateboard.

ACTIVITY

2 Adriana's parents pay for 45% of her and her sister's monthly cell phone bill. If their May phone bill is $110, how much will their parents pay?

Use a model to find 45% of $110.

Step 1 Draw a 1-by-10 rectangle on grid paper. Label the units on the top of the model from 0% to 100%.

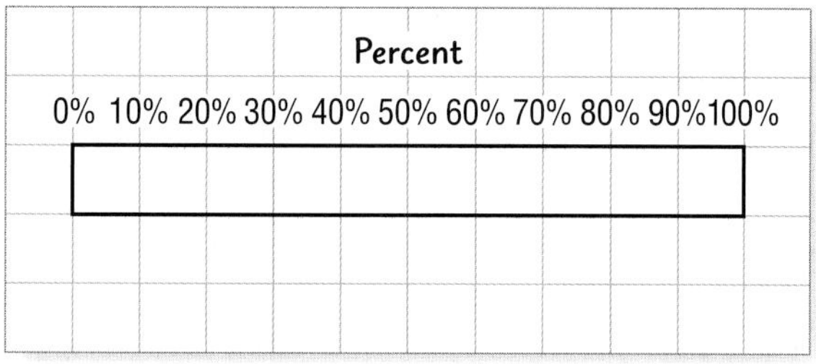

Step 2 The phone bill is $110. So, label equal units from $0 to $110 on the bottom of the model as shown. Then draw a line from 45% to the bottom of the model. Shade the portion of the rectangle to the left of this line.

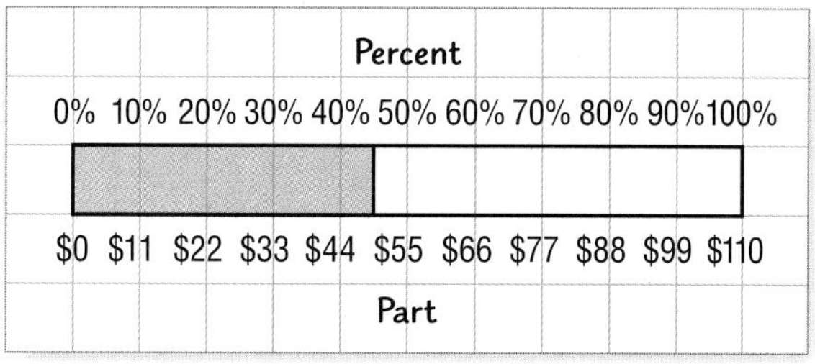

The model shows that 45% of $110 is halfway between $44 and $55, or $49.50. So, Adriana's parents will pay $49.50 of the phone bill.

Remember

To find the number halfway between two numbers, find the mean. In Activity 2, $\frac{\$44 + \$55}{2} = \$49.50$.

Analyze the Results

1. Explain why the top of the percent models were labeled from 0% to 100%.

2. How were the bottom scales on the percent models determined?

3. Draw a model to find the percent of each number.

a. 65% of 200 **b.** 30% of 90

4. Explain how you could use a model to find 8% of 50.

9-6 Percent of a Number

MAIN IDEA

I will find the percent of a number.

Standard 5NS1.2 Interpret percents as a part of a hundred; find decimal and percent equivalents for common fractions and explain why they represent the same value; **compute a given percent of a whole number.**

GET READY to Learn

A local police department wrote a report on how much cars were traveling over the speed limit in a school zone. The results are shown in the graph. If the report involves 300 cars, then the expression 5% × 300 can be used to find the number of cars traveling 20 miles per hour over the speed limit.

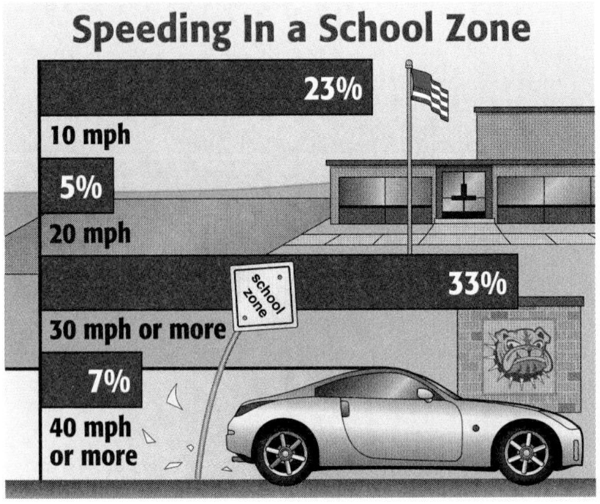

To find the percent of a number such as 23% of 300, 33% of 300, or 5% of 300, you can use one of the following methods.

- Write the percent as a fraction and then multiply, or
- Write the percent as a decimal and then multiply.

EXAMPLE Find the Percent of a Number

1 Find 5% of 300.

To find 5% of 300, you can use either method.

One Way: Write the percent as a fraction.	Another Way: Write the percent as a decimal.
$5\% = \frac{5}{100}$ or $\frac{1}{20}$	$5\% = \frac{5}{100}$ or 0.05
$\frac{1}{20}$ of $300 = \frac{1}{20} \times 300$ or 15	0.05 of $300 = 0.05 \times 300$ or 15

So, 5% of 300 is 15. Use a model to check the answer.

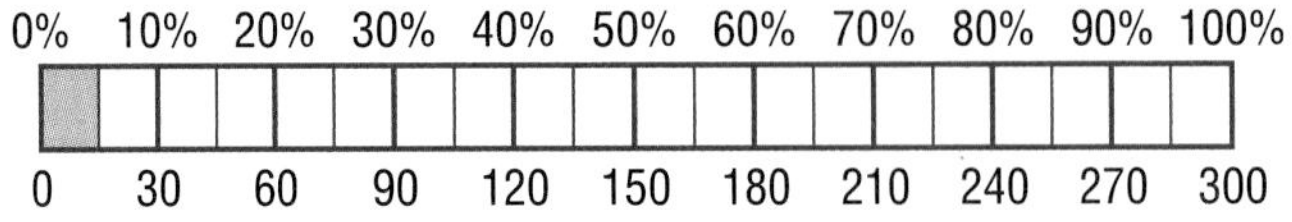

The model confirms that 5% of 300 is 15.

EXAMPLE Find the Percent of a Number

2 Find 120% of 75.

One Way: Write the percent as a fraction.	**Another Way:** Write the percent as a decimal.
$120\% = \frac{120}{100}$ or $\frac{6}{5}$	$120\% = \frac{120}{100}$ or 1.2
$\frac{6}{5}$ of $75 = \frac{6}{5} \times 75$	1.2 of $75 = 1.2 \times 75$ or 90
$= \frac{6}{5} \times \frac{75}{1}$ or 90	

Remember

120% is a little more than 100%. So, the answer should be a little more than 100% of 75 or a little more than 75.

So, 120% of 75 is 90.

Online **Personal Tutor at** ca.gr5math.com

Real-World EXAMPLE

3 The circle graph shows the results of an online survey about young people's favorite sport to watch. If 450 young people responded to the survey, how many said soccer was their favorite sport to watch?

What is Your Favorite Sport to Watch?

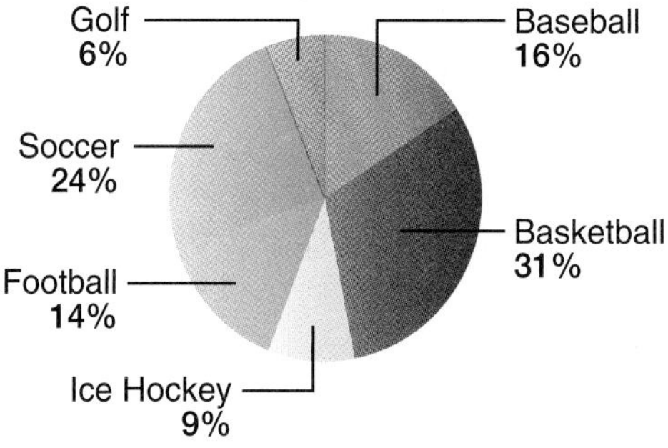

Source: pbskids.org

You need to find 24% of 450.

Estimate $24\% \approx 25\%$ or $\frac{1}{4}$ and $450 \approx 460$. $\frac{1}{4}$ of $460 = \frac{1}{4} \times 460$ or 115.

$24\% = \frac{24}{100}$ Definition of percent

$= 0.24$ Write *24 hundredths* as a decimal

0.24 of $450 = 0.24 \times 450$

$= 108$ Multiply.

So, 108 young people said soccer was their favorite sport to watch.

Check for Reasonableness $108 \approx 115$ ✓

CHECK What You Know

Find the percent of each number. See Examples 1, 2 (pp. 492–493)

1. 30% of 90

2. 4% of 65

3. 150% of 38

4. A coat is on sale for 85% of the regular price. If it is regularly priced at $40, how much is the sale price? See Example 3 (p. 493)

5. Talk About It Is 140% of 15 greater than 20? Explain.

Practice and Problem Solving

EXTRA PRACTICE See page 680.

Find the percent of each number. See Examples 1, 2 (pp. 492–493)

6. 15% of 60

7. 12% of 800

8. 75% of 120

9. 25% of 80

10. 2% of 25

11. 4% of 9

12. 7% of 85

13. 3% of 156

14. 150% of 90

15. 125% of 60

16. 140% of 85

17. 133% of 95

18. Chad and Alisa donated 30% of their book collection to a local children's hospital. If they had 180 books, how many did they donate to the hospital? See Example 3 (p. 493)

19. The Mooney High School football team won 75% of their football games. If they played 12 games, how many did they win? See Example 3 (p. 493)

Solve.

20. What is 78% of 265?

21. 24% of 549 is what number?

22. 3% of 300 is what number?

23. What is 124% of 260?

Real-World PROBLEM SOLVING

School Use the diagram at the right that shows Sarah's and Morgan's test scores.

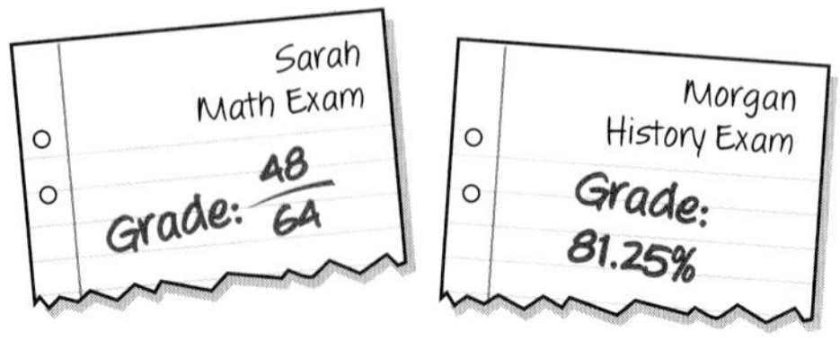

24. What percent of the questions did Sarah answer correctly?

25. What percent did Sarah answer incorrectly?

26. If there were 64 questions on the test, how many did Morgan answer correctly?

H.O.T. Problems

27. OPEN ENDED Write a problem in which the percent of the number results in a number greater than the number itself.

CHALLENGE Solve each problem.

28. 14 is what percent of 70?

29. What percent of 240 is 84?

30. 45 is 15% of what number?

31. 21 is 30% of what number?

32. CHALLENGE The sale price of a bodyboard that is 40% off is $35.70. Find the original price. If the original price is reduced by 10%, find the sale price.

33. FIND THE ERROR Gary and Belinda are finding 120% of 60. Who is correct? Explain your reasoning.

Gary

$120\% \text{ of } 60 = 1\frac{1}{5} \times 60$
$= 72$

Belinda

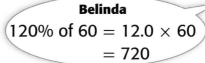

$120\% \text{ of } 60 = 12.0 \times 60$
$= 720$

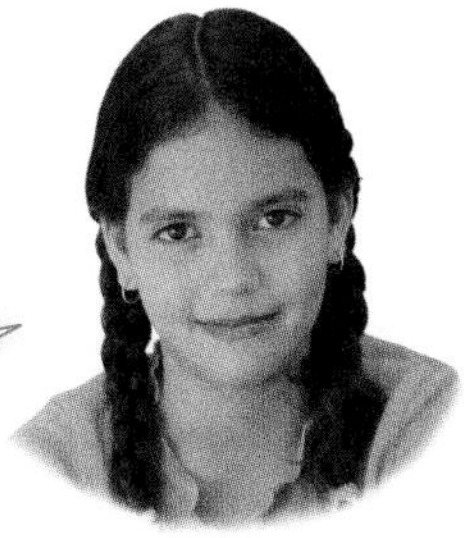

34. WRITING IN MATH Explain how to find 40% of 65 by changing the percent to a decimal.

Standards Practice

35 What is 26% of 350?

A 26

B 35

C 91

D 100

36 At Langley Elementary, 19% of the 2,200 students walk to school. How many students walk to school?

F 400

G 418

H 428

J 476

Spiral Review

Estimate each percent. **(Lesson 9-5)**

37. 21% of 100

38. 32% of 36

39. 9% of 247

40. About 93% of Nebraska's land area is occupied by 48,500 farms and ranches. Write 93% as a decimal. **(Lesson 9-3)**

9-7 Problem-Solving Investigation

MAIN IDEA I will choose the best strategy to solve a problem.

Standard 5MR1.1 Analyze problems by identifying relationships, distinguishing relevant from irrelevant information, sequencing and prioritizing information, **and observing patterns.** **Standard 5NS1.2** Interpret percents as a part of a hundred; . . . **compute a given percent of a whole number.**

P.S.I. TEAM +

TYRA: **I'm going to the mall with $75 to buy a shirt, a pair of jeans, and a hat. The hat costs $15, which is 50% of the cost of one shirt. The shirt costs $10 less than the jeans. If I spend more than $50, I get a 15% discount off of the total price.**

YOUR MISSION: **Determine if Tyra has enough money to buy all three items.**

Understand	Tyra has $75 to spend. You need to determine if Tyra has enough money to buy all three items.
Plan	You can work backward to find the amount that each item costs. Then find out how much she spent.
Solve	The hat is 50% of the cost of one shirt. So, one shirt costs $15 × 2 or $30. The cost of the jeans is $10 more than the cost of the shirt. So, the jeans cost $30 + $10 or $40. So, Tyra spent $15 + $30 + $40 or $85. Since she spent a total of $85, she gets a 15% discount. $85 \times 15\% \rightarrow 85 \times 0.15 = \$12.75$ The discount is $12.75. So, Tyra spent $85 − $12.75 or $72.25. Since $72.25 is less than $75, Tyra has enough money.
Check	Start with the cost of the jeans. The jeans cost $40. The shirt costs are $40 − $10 or $30. The hat is 50% of the cost of the shirt, so the hat is $30 ÷ 2 or $15. ✓

Mixed Problem Solving

EXTRA PRACTICE
See page 681.

Use any strategy shown below to solve each problem.

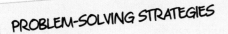

PROBLEM-SOLVING STRATEGIES
- Work backward.
- Look for a pattern.
- Solve a simpler problem.

1. Find the difference in the areas of the square and rectangle.

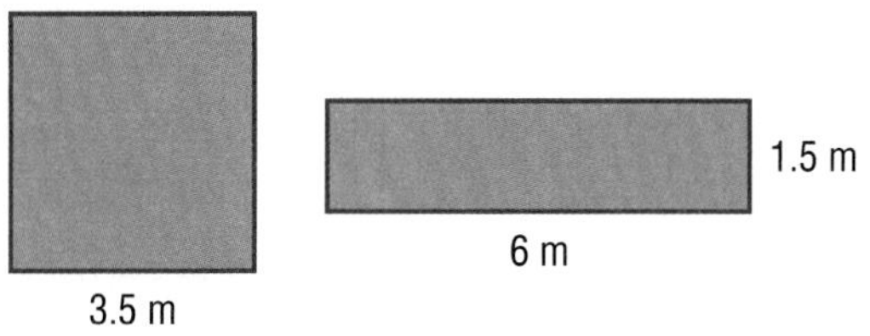

2. Jhan has $95 to spend on athletic shoes. The shoes cost $59.99. If he buys one pair, he gets a second pair for half price. Will he have about $5 or $10 left if he purchases two pairs of the shoes?

3. What is the least positive number that you can divide by 7 and get a remainder of 4, divide by 8 and get a remainder of 5, and divide by 9 and get a remainder of 6?

4. Draw the next two figures in the pattern below.

5. About how much more money is spent on strawberry and grape jelly than the other types of jelly each year?

Yearly Jelly Sales (thousands)	
Strawberry and grape	$366.2
All others	$291.5

6. The Grayson softball team won three times as many games as they lost. If they lost 5 games, how many games did they play?

7. Four people can make 8 baskets in one hour. How many baskets can 12 people working at the same rate make in $\frac{1}{2}$ hour?

8. If you purchase one, two, or three greeting cards, you can save 5%, 10%, or 15%, respectively, off the total cost of the cards. If this pattern continues, how much will you save if you purchase five greeting cards for $11?

9. Tate earns $260 each month delivering newspapers. If he saves 80%, of his earnings each month, how much does he have left to spend each month?

10. The Venn diagram shows information about the members in a scout troop.

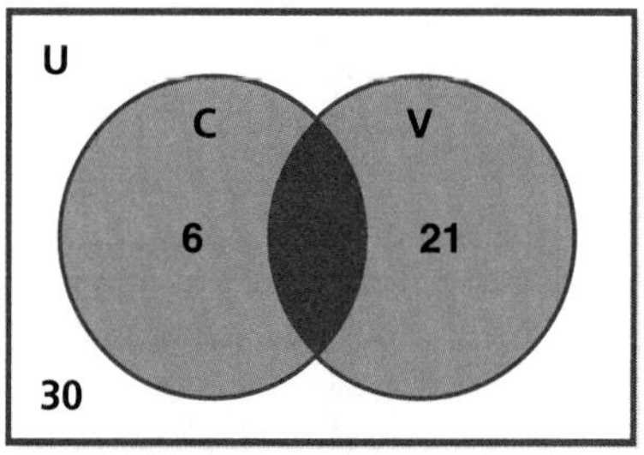

U = all members in the troop
C = members with a camping badge
V = members with a volunteer badge

How many more members have a badge than do not have a badge?

11. WRITING IN ▸MATH Three workers can make three desks in three days. Explain how you can determine how many desks nine workers working at the same rate can make in 30 days using the *solve a simpler problem* strategy.

9-8 Probability

GET READY to Learn

Duane and Morgan are playing cards. Morgan needs to draw a 3 in order to make a match and win the game. The cards shown are shuffled and placed facedown on the table. Does Morgan have a good chance of winning? Explain.

MAIN IDEA

I will find and interpret the probability of a simple event.

Preparation for Standard 6SDAP3.3 **Represent probabilities as ratios,** proportions**, decimals between 0 and 1, and percentages between 0 and 100** and verify that the probabilities computed are reasonable; **know that if *P* is the probability of an event, 1 − *P* is the probability of an event not occurring.**

New Vocabulary

- **outcomes**
- **simple event**
- **probability**
- **random**
- **complementary events**

It is equally likely to select any one of the five cards. The player hopes to select a card numbered 3. The five cards represent the possible **outcomes**. A **simple event** is a collection of one or more outcomes. For example, selecting a card numbered 3 is a simple event.

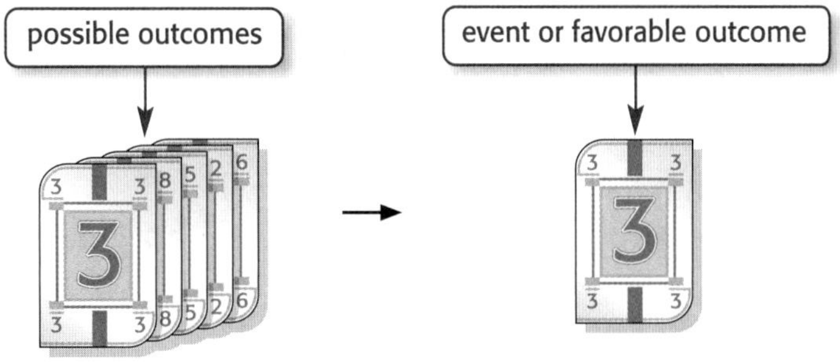

Probability is the chance that some event will occur. You can use a ratio to find probability.

KEY CONCEPT — Probability

Words The probability of an event is a ratio that compares the number of favorable outcomes to the number of possible outcomes.

Symbols $P(\text{event}) = \dfrac{\text{number of favorable outcomes}}{\text{number of possible outcomes}}$

In the example above, the probability of selecting a card numbered 3 is $\frac{1}{5}$.

$$P(3) = \frac{\text{number of favorite outcomes}}{\text{number of possible outcomes}}$$

$$= \frac{1}{5}$$

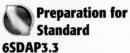

The probability that an event will occur is a number from 0 to 1, including 0 and 1. The closer a probability is to 1, the more likely it is that the event will happen.

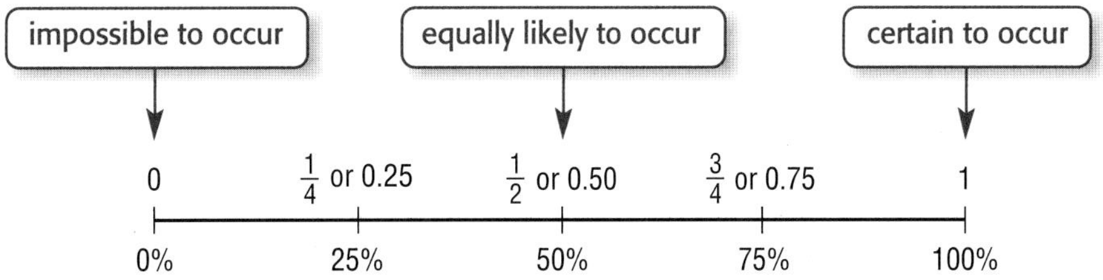

Outcomes occur at **random** if each outcome is equally likely to occur.

EXAMPLES Find Probability

There are eight equally likely outcomes on the spinner.

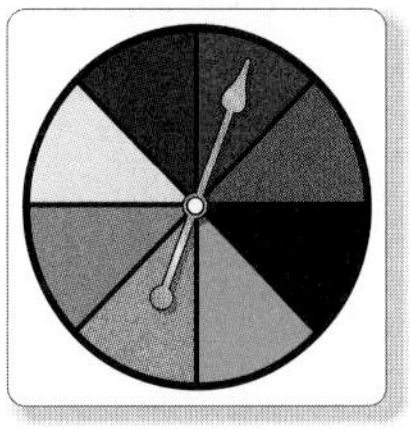

1 Find the probability of landing on red.

Reading Math

Probability The notation P(red) is read *the probability of landing on red.*

There is one section of the spinner that is red.

$$P(\text{red}) = \frac{\text{number of favorable outcomes}}{\text{number of possible outcomes}}$$
$$= \frac{1}{8}$$

The probability of landing on red is $\frac{1}{8}$, 0.125, or 12.5%.

2 Find the probability of landing on blue or yellow.

The word *or* indicates that the favorable outcomes are the blue and yellow sections. There is one section of the spinner that is blue and one section that is yellow.

$$P(\text{blue or yellow}) = \frac{\text{number of favorable outcomes}}{\text{number of possible outcomes}}$$
$$= \frac{2}{8}$$
$$= \frac{1}{4} \quad \text{Simplify.}$$

The probability of landing on blue or yellow is $\frac{1}{4}$, 0.25, or 25%.

Vocabulary Link

Complement

Everyday Use the quantity required to make something complete

Complementary Events

Math Use two events that are the only ones that can happen

If you toss a coin, it can either land on heads or *not* land on heads. These two events are complementary events. **Complementary events** are two events in which either one or the other must happen, but they cannot both happen at the same time. The sum of the probabilities of an event and its complement is 1 or 100%.

EXAMPLE Find Probability of the Complement

3 Find the probability of *not* landing on red in Example 1.

The probability of *not* landing on red and the probability of landing on red are complementary.

Remember

You can review **solving equations** in Lesson 1-8.

$P(\text{red}) + P(\text{not red}) = 1$		The sum of the probabilities is 1.
$\frac{1}{8} + P(\text{not red}) = 1$		Replace P(red) with $\frac{1}{8}$.
$-\frac{1}{8} \quad = -\frac{1}{8}$		Subtract $\frac{1}{8}$ from each side.
$P(\text{not red}) = \frac{7}{8}$		

So, the probability of *not* landing on red is $\frac{7}{8}$, 0.875, or 87.5%.

Online Personal Tutor at ca.gr5math.com

Real-World EXAMPLE

4 The morning newspaper reported a 20% chance of snow. Identify the complement. Then find its probability.

The complement of snowing is *not* snowing. The sum of the probabilities is 100%.

$P(\text{snow}) + P(\text{not snowing}) = 100\%$	
$20\% + P(\text{not snowing}) = 100\%$	Replace P(snow) with 20%.
$-\,20\% \quad = -\,20\%$	Subtract 20% from each side.
$P(\text{not snowing}) = 80\%$	

So, the probability that it will *not* snow is 80%, 0.8, or $\frac{4}{5}$.

Math Online Extra Examples at ca.gr5math.com

CHECK What You Know

A counter is chosen randomly. Find each probability. Write each answer as a fraction, a decimal, and a percent. See Examples 1–3 (pp. 499–500)

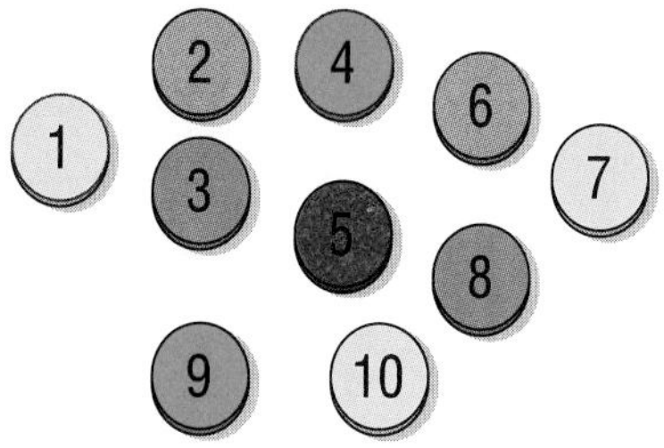

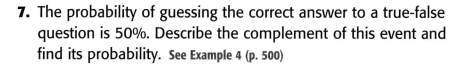

1. $P(4)$
2. $P(2 \text{ or } 5)$
3. $P(\text{less than } 8)$
4. $P(\text{prime})$
5. $P(\textit{not } 6)$
6. $P(\textit{not } 1 \text{ and } \textit{not } 10)$
7. The probability of guessing the correct answer to a true-false question is 50%. Describe the complement of this event and find its probability. See Example 4 (p. 500)
8. **Talk About It** What can you conclude about an event if its probability is 1?

Practice and Problem Solving

EXTRA PRACTICE See page 681.

The spinner shown is spun once. Find each probability. Write each answer as a fraction, a decimal, and a percent. See Examples 1–3 (pp. 499–500)

9. $P(Z)$
10. $P(U)$
11. $P(A \text{ or } M)$
12. $P(C, D \text{ or } A)$
13. $P(\textit{not} \text{ a vowel})$
14. $P(\textit{not} \text{ a consonant})$

A number cube marked with 1, 2, 3, 4, 5, and 6, one number on each face, is rolled. Find each probability. Write each answer as a fraction. See Examples 1–3 (pp. 499–500)

15. $P(3)$
16. $P(4 \text{ or } 6)$
17. $P(\text{greater than } 4)$
18. $P(\text{less than } 1)$
19. $P(\text{even})$
20. $P(\text{odd})$
21. $P(\textit{not} \text{ a multiple of } 2)$
22. $P(\textit{not } 3 \text{ and } \textit{not } 4)$

One marble is selected, without looking, from the bag shown. Write a sentence stating how likely it is for each event to happen. Justify your answer.

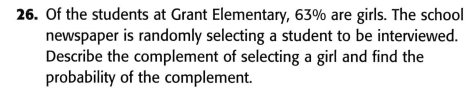

23. green
24. yellow
25. purple, yellow, or orange
26. Of the students at Grant Elementary, 63% are girls. The school newspaper is randomly selecting a student to be interviewed. Describe the complement of selecting a girl and find the probability of the complement.

For Exercises 27–29, use the information below and the bar graph.

The students at Meridian Middle School were asked how they get to school.

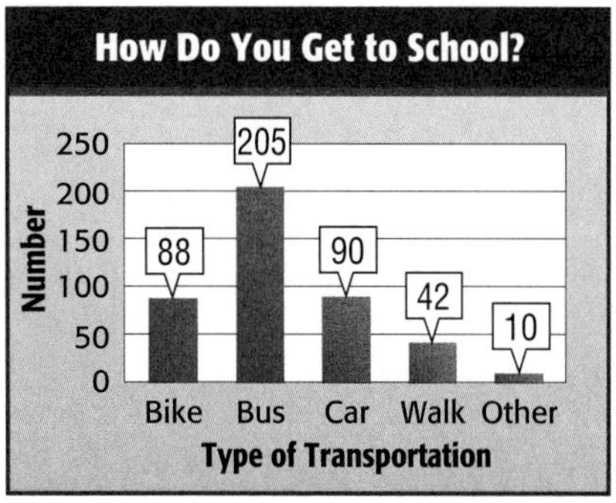

27. If a student is selected at random, what is the probability that he or she primarily rides the bus to school?

28. If a student is selected at random, is the probability that he or she primarily rides in a car more or less likely than the probability that he or she rides a bike? Explain your reasoning.

29. If a student is selected at random, what is the probability that he or she does not walk to school?

Real-World PROBLEM SOLVING

Data File The Imperial County Airport in El Centro, California, is served by only one commercial airline.

Air Travel

Airport	Arrivals (Percent on-time)
El Centro (CA)	80
Baltimore (MD)	82
Charleston (SC)	77
Islip (NY)	83
Milwaukee (WI)	76

Source: U.S. Department of Transportation

30. Suppose a flight that arrived at El Centro is selected at random. What is the probability that the flight did not arrive on time?

31. Suppose a flight that arrived at Islip is selected at random. What is the probability that the flight did arrive on time?

H.O.T. Problems

32. OPEN ENDED The number cube with sides labeled 1 through 6 is rolled. Describe an event in which the probability is $\frac{1}{3}$.

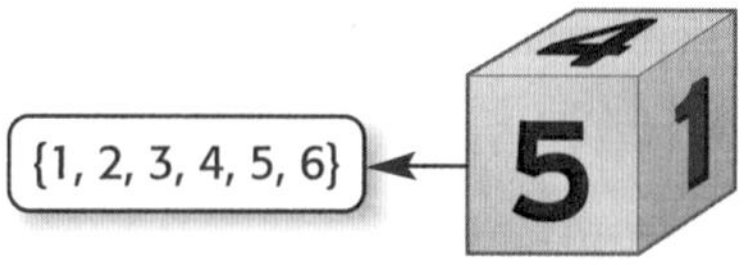

33. CHALLENGE A spinner for a board game has more than three sections, all of equal size, and the probability of the spinner stopping on blue is 0.5. Design two possible spinners for the game. Explain why each spinner drawn makes sense.

34. **FIND THE ERROR** Laura and Luisa are finding the probability of rolling a 5 on a number cube. Who is correct? Explain your reasoning.

35. **WRITING IN MATH** Explain the relationship between the probability of an event and its complement. Give an example.

Standards Practice

36 Joel has a bowl containing the mints shown in the table.

Color	Number
Red	5
Orange	3
Yellow	1
Green	6

If he randomly chooses one mint from the bowl, what is the probability that the mint will be orange?

A $\frac{1}{5}$

B $\frac{2}{3}$

C $\frac{11}{15}$

D $\frac{4}{5}$

37 A miniature golf course has a bucket with 7 yellow golf balls, 6 green golf balls, 3 blue golf balls, and 8 red golf balls. If Tamika draws a golf ball at random from the bucket, what is the probability that she will *not* draw a green golf ball?

F 25%

G $\frac{1}{3}$

H $\frac{2}{3}$

J 0.75

Spiral Review

38. Chandler collected \$2 from each student to buy a gift for their teacher. If one student contributed \$3 extra and a total of \$59 was collected, how many students contributed? **(Lesson 9-7)**

Find the percent of each number. **(Lesson 9-6)**

39. 3% of 190

40. 45% of 200

41. 110% of 65

Add or subtract. Write in simplest form. **(Lessons 5-7 and 5-8)**

42. $4\frac{3}{8} + 7\frac{1}{8}$

43. $8\frac{1}{6} - 2\frac{2}{3}$

44. $1\frac{2}{3} + 5\frac{3}{4}$

Extend

Statistics Lab for 9-8

Experimental and Theoretical Probability

MAIN IDEA

I will compare experimental probability with theoretical probability.

Standard 5SDAP1.3 **Use fractions and percentages to compare data sets of different sizes.**

Standard 5MR3.3 **Develop generalizations of the results obtained** and apply them in other circumstances.

New Vocabulary

theoretical probability

experimental probability

Reading Math

Trials A *trial* is a single part of a well-defined experiment. In this lab, a trial is the selection of a cube from the bag.

Theoretical probability is based on what *should* happen under perfect conditions. These are the probabilities you found in Lesson 9-8. **Experimental probability** is based on what *actually* happens in an experiment. In this lab, you will investigate the relationship between these two types of probability.

ACTIVITY

Step 1 Place 3 blue cubes and 5 red cubes in a paper bag.

Step 2 Without looking, draw a cube out of the bag. If the cube is blue, record a Y. If the cube is not blue, record an N.

Step 3 Replace the cube and repeat steps 1 and 2 for a total of 30 trials.

Analyze the Results

1. To find the experimental probability of selecting a blue cube, write the ratio of the number of times a blue cube was selected to the number of trials. What is the experimental probability of selecting a blue cube?
2. What is the theoretical probability of selecting a blue cube? How does this probability compare to the experimental probability found in Exercise 1? Explain any differences.
3. Compare your results to the results of other groups in your class. Why do you think the experimental probabilities usually vary when an experiment is repeated?
4. Find the experimental probability for the entire class's trials. How do the experimental and theoretical probability compare?
5. Explain why the experimental probability obtained in Exercise 4 may be closer in value to the theoretical probability than to the experimental probability in Exercise 1.

9-9 Sample Spaces

MAIN IDEA

I will construct sample spaces using tree diagrams or lists.

Preparation for Standard 6SDAP3.1 Represent all possible outcomes for compound events in an organized way (e.g. tables, grids, **tree diagrams) and express the theoretical probability of each outcome.**

New Vocabulary

sample space
tree diagram

GET READY to Learn

A movie theater's concession stand sign is shown. List all the possible ways to choose a soft drink, popcorn, and candy.

The set of all possible outcomes of an event is called the **sample space**. The sample space for rolling a number cube and the sample space for spinning the spinner shown are listed below.

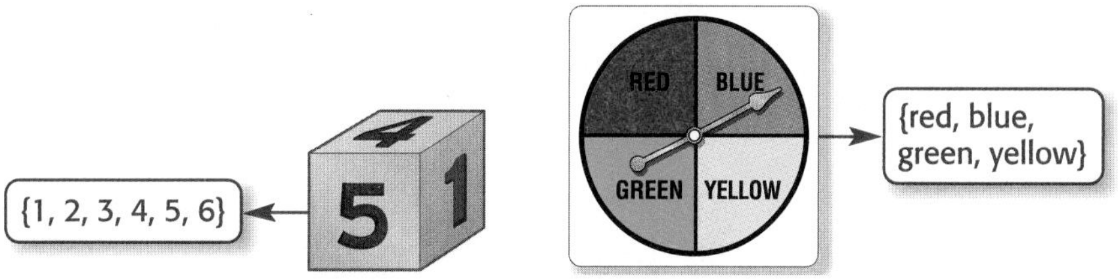

You can make a list to determine the sample space.

EXAMPLE Use a List to Find Sample Space

1 **The names of three bulldog puppies are shown. In how many different ways can the puppies be arranged in a row?**

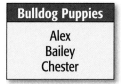

Bulldog Puppies
Alex
Bailey
Chester

Make an organized list. Use A for Alex, B for Bailey, and C for Chester. Use each letter exactly once.

ABC	BAC	CAB
ACB	BCA	CBA

There are 6 ways to arrange the three puppies in a row.

Online **Personal Tutor at** ca.gr5math.com

A tree diagram can also be used to show a sample space. A **tree diagram** is a diagram that shows all possible outcomes of an event.

EXAMPLE Use a Tree Diagram to Find Sample Space

2 **Use a tree diagram to find how many outfits are possible from a choice of jean or khaki shorts and a choice of a yellow, white, or blue shirt.**

List each shorts choice. Then pair each shorts choice with each shirt choice.

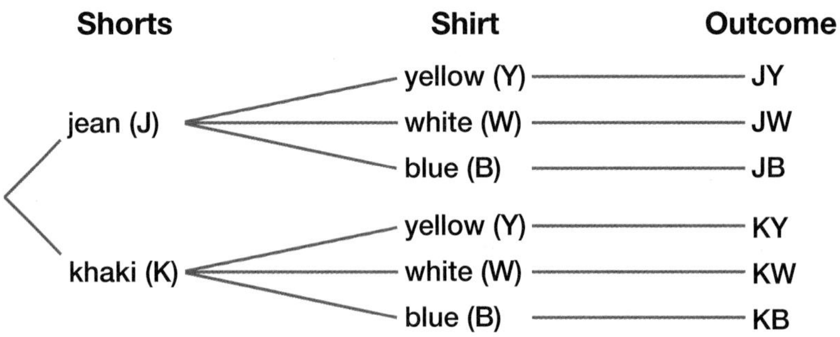

There are six possible outfits.

Reading Math

Outcomes The outcome JY means jean shorts and a yellow shirt.

EXAMPLE Use a Tree Diagram to Find Probability

3 **Lexi spins the two spinners at the right. What is the probability of spinning red on the first spinner and blue on the second spinner?**

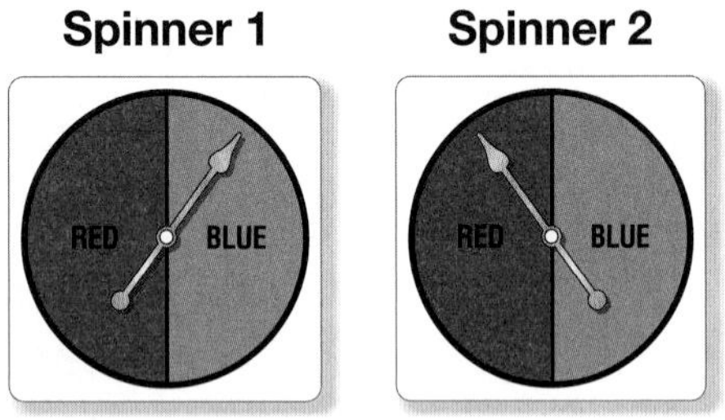

Use a tree diagram to find all of the possible outcomes.

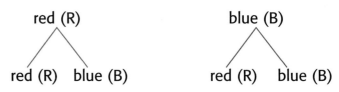

The possible outcomes are RR, RB, BR, and BB. One outcome has red first, and then blue. Since there are four possible outcomes, $P(\text{red, blue}) = \frac{1}{4}$, 0.25, or 25%. Notice that the outcome "blue first, then red" was not considered as a favorable outcome.

Reading Math

Probability Notation

P(red, blue) is read *the probability of red then blue.*

CHECK What You Know

1. How many ways can Ramiro, Garth, and Lakita line up to check out library books? Make an organized list to show the sample space. See Example 1 (p. 505)

2. Use a tree diagram to find how many sandwich and drink combinations can be made if you can choose from a hamburger or cheeseburger with a soft drink, water, or juice. See Example 2 (p. 506)

3. If each spinner shown is spun once, what is P(blue, green) in that order? See Example 3 (p. 506)

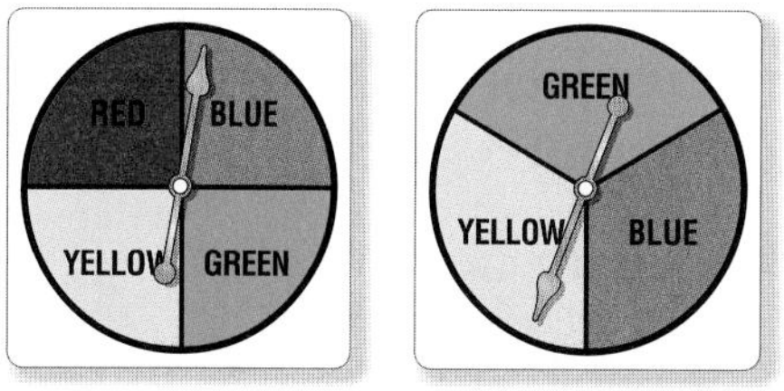

4. **Talk About It** What is a sample space?

Practice and Problem Solving

EXTRA PRACTICE See page 681.

For Exercises 5 and 6, make an organized list to show the sample space for each situation. See Example 1 (p. 505)

5. The names of three roller coasters at Six Flags Over Georgia are shown. In how many different ways can Felipe and his friend ride each of the three roller coasters, if they ride once on each?

Roller Coasters at Six Flags Over Georgia
Superman-Ultimate Flight
Deja Vu
The Georgia Cyclone

Source: sixflags.com

6. In how many ways can Kame listen to 4 CDs assuming he listens to each CD once?

Draw a tree diagram to show the sample space for each situation. Then tell how many outcomes are possible. See Example 2 (p. 506)

7. apple, peach, or cherry pie with milk, juice, or tea

8. nylon, leather, or mesh backpack in red, blue, gold, or black

9. roll two number cubes

10. toss a dime, quarter, and penny

For Exercises 11–16, a number cube is tossed, and a letter is chosen from the bag shown. Use a tree diagram to find each probability. See Example 3 (p. 506)

11. P(prime, E)

12. P(odd, M)

13. P(4, vowel)

14. P(1 or 6, Z)

15. P(> 2, consonant)

16. P(even, M or A or Y)

17. Use a tree diagram to find how many different sandwiches can be made from a choice of white or multigrain bread, a choice of ham, turkey, or roast beef, and a choice of American or provolone cheese.

18. A science quiz has one multiple-choice question with answer choices A, B, and C, and two true/false questions. Draw a tree diagram that shows all of the ways a student can answer the questions. Then find the probability of answering all three questions correctly by guessing.

For Exercises 19–21, a coin is tossed, the spinner shown is spun, and a number cube is rolled.

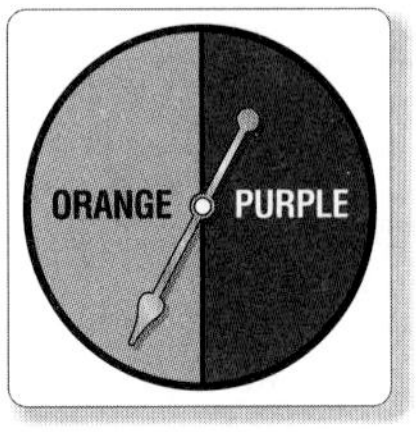

19. How many outcomes are possible?

20. What is P(heads, purple, 5)?

21. Find P(tails, orange, less than 4).

Real-World PROBLEM SOLVING

Books Over 14.8 million copies of *The Poky Little Puppy* have been sold.

22. Ms. Collins plans on buying one of the books listed for her nephew. She can also choose from yellow or green gift bags. How many book and gift bag combinations are possible?

Best-Selling Children's Hardcover Books of All Time
1. *The Poky Little Puppy* (1942)
2. *The Tale of Peter Rabbit* (1902)
3. *Tootle* (1945)
4. *Green Eggs and Ham* (1960)

Source: infoplease.com

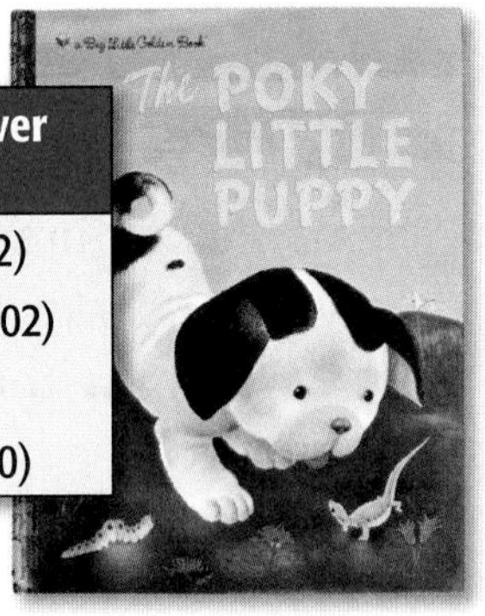

23. Use the Internet or another source to find the fifth book on the all-time best-selling list of children's hardcover books. How many book and gift bag combinations are possible if Ms. Collins can also choose from the fifth best-selling book?

H.O.T. Problems

24. **OPEN ENDED** Describe a situation in which there are 8 possible outcomes.

25. **REASONING** A video game allows you to personalize your player's vehicle. You can choose a vehicle, an exterior paint color, and an interior upholstery color. Determine the number of possible outcomes without using a tree diagram. Explain your reasoning.

Vehicle	Exterior Color	Interior Color
car	black	tan
van	red	grey
truck	blue	white
	white	black
	yellow	

Math Online Self-Check Quiz at ca.gr5math.com

26. **CHALLENGE** One of the bags shown is selected without looking, and then one marble is selected from the bag without looking. Draw a tree diagram showing all of the outcomes. Decide if each outcome is equally likely. Explain your reasoning.

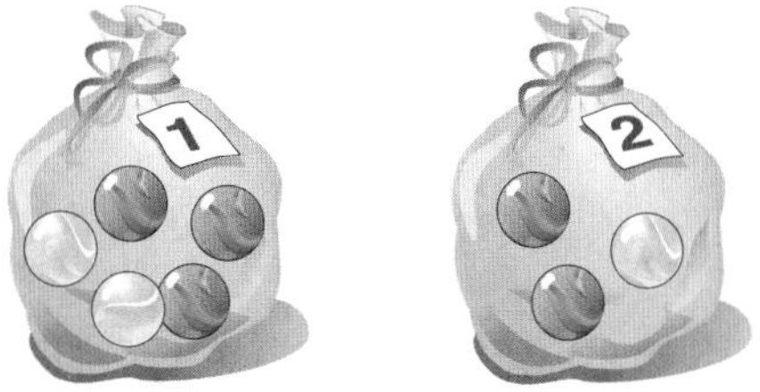

27. **WRITING IN ►MATH** Each homeroom class at your school will select one boy and one girl to be homeroom representative and alternate. Recommend a method your teacher can use to determine all the possible combinations of one boy and one girl from your homeroom.

Standards Practice

28 Claire is deciding between a red shirt and a blue shirt. The shirt also comes in small, medium, and large sizes. Which diagram shows all of the possible combinations of shirt color and size?

A
- Red
  - Small
  - Medium
  - Large
- Blue
  - Small
  - Large

B
- Red
  - Small
  - Large
- Blue
  - Medium
  - Large

C
- Red
  - Small
  - Medium
  - Large
- Blue
  - Small
  - Medium
  - Large

D
- Small
  - Red
  - Blue
- Medium
  - Red
  - Blue
- Large
  - Red

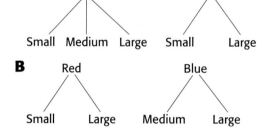

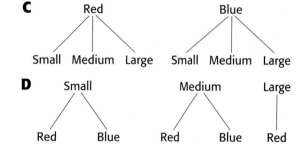

Spiral Review

A bag contains 5 red marbles, 6 green marbles, and 4 blue marbles. One marble is selected at random. Find each probability. **(Lesson 9-8)**

29. *P*(green) **30.** *P*(green or blue) **31.** *P*(red or blue)

32. At a popular ski resort, 35% of all people who buy tickets are snowboarders. If 80 people buy tickets on a particular day, how many of them snowboard? **(Lesson 9-6)**

Algebra Solve. **(Lesson 8-6)**

33. $\frac{2}{3} = \frac{8}{x}$ **34.** $\frac{k}{9} = \frac{10}{45}$ **35.** $\frac{5}{c} = \frac{30}{96}$ **36.** $\frac{15}{35} = \frac{3}{d}$

WILD ABOUT WILDFLOWER HABITATS

Many people like to grow flowers in their yards. The National Wildlife Federation encourages people to grow wildflowers and also to include plants that provide protective cover and food for another type of wildlife—animals!

A wildlife habitat for animals needs to have four essential ingredients: food, water, protective cover, and places for animals to raise their young. If you can provide these elements, you can enjoy a wildlife habitat in your own backyard!

Math Standard 5NS1.2 **Interpret percents as a part of a hundred; find decimal** and percent **equivalents for common fractions** and explain why they represent the same value; **compute a given percent of a whole number.**

Real-World Math

Use the circle graph below to solve each problem.

1. Write the percent of grains as a fraction in simplest form.
2. How does the amount of grain compare to the amount of clovers?
3. Write the percent of grass as a decimal.
4. Write the percent of clovers as a decimal.
5. If there are 700 seeds in the wildflower habitat mix, how many would be annual flowers?
6. If you pick one seed at random from the packet of wildflower habitat mix, what is the probability that you would pick a wildflower seed? Write your answer as a fraction and a decimal.
7. Describe your answer for Problem 6 as *certain, impossible,* or *equally likely.*
8. **WRITING IN ▸MATH** Explain how the percent of seeds in the wildlife habitat mix will result in a well-balanced wildlife habitat.

WILDFLOWER HABITAT MIX

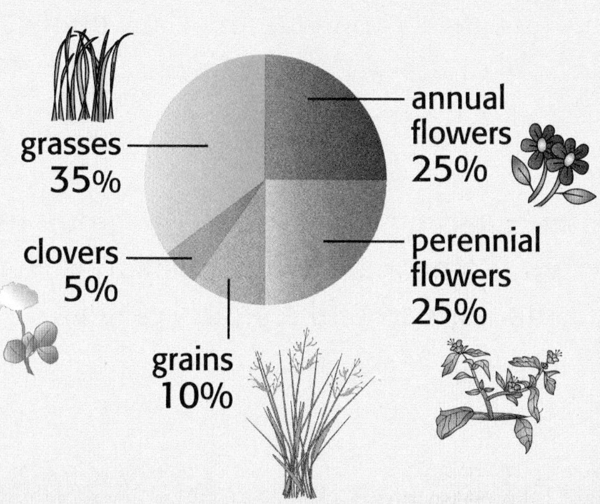

Did You Know?

To celebrate its 70th anniversary in 2006, the National Wildlife Federation certified over 70,000 sites in the United States as wildlife habitats.

9-10 Making Predictions

MAIN IDEA

I will predict the actions of a larger group using a sample.

Standard 5AF1.2 Use a letter to represent an unknown number; write and evaluate simple algebraic expressions in one variable by substitution.

New Vocabulary

survey
population
sample

GET READY to Learn

Hands-On Mini Lab

In this activity, you will make a prediction about the number of left-handed or right-handed students in your school.

Left- or Right-Handed?	
Trait	**Students**
Left-handed	
Right-handed	

Step 1 Have one student in each group copy the table shown.

Step 2 Count the number of left-handed students and right-handed students in your group. Record the results.

Step 3 Predict the number of left-handed and right-handed students in your school.

Step 4 Combine your results with the other groups in your class. Make a class prediction.

1. When working in a group, how did your group predict the number of left-handed and right-handed students in your school?
2. Compare your group's prediction with the class prediction. Which do you think is more accurate? Explain.

Remember

A survey has questions that require a response. The most common types of surveys are interviews, telephone surveys, or mailed surveys.

A **survey** is a method of collecting information. The group being studied is the **population**. Sometimes, the population is very large. To save time and money, part of the group, called a **sample**, is surveyed.

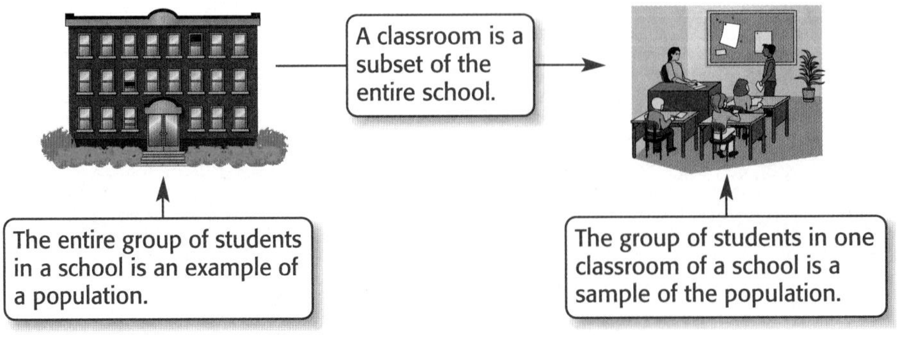
A classroom is a subset of the entire school.
The entire group of students in a school is an example of a population.
The group of students in one classroom of a school is a sample of the population.

A good sample is:

- selected at random, or without preference,
- representative of the population, and
- large enough to provide accurate data.

The responses of a good sample are equivalent to the responses of the population. So, you can use the results of a survey or past actions to predict the actions of a larger group.

EXAMPLES Make Predictions

Lorenzo asked every tenth student who walked into school to name his or her favorite pizza topping.

Favorite Pizza Topping

Topping	Students
Pepperoni	17
Cheese	6
Sausage	3
Mushroom	4

1 What was the probability that a student preferred pepperoni?

$$P(\text{pepperoni}) = \frac{\text{number of students that like pepperoni}}{\text{number of students surveyed}}$$

$$= \frac{17}{30}$$

So, the probability that a student preferred pepperoni was $\frac{17}{30}$.

Remember

You can review solving equations using equivalent fractions in Lesson 8-6.

2 There are 300 students at the school Lorenzo attends. Predict how many students prefer pepperoni.

Let s represent the number of students who prefer pepperoni.

$\frac{17}{30} = \frac{s}{300}$ Write an equation.

$\frac{17}{30} = \frac{s}{300}$ (×10 numerator, ×10 denominator) Since $30 \times 10 = 300$, multiply 17 by 10 to find s.

$\frac{17}{30} = \frac{170}{300}$ $s = 170$

Of the 300 students, about 170 will prefer pepperoni.

Math Online Personal Tutor at ca.gr5math.com

CHECK What You Know

For Exercises 1 and 2, use the following information and the table shown. See Examples 1, 2 (p. 513)

Favorite Milk Shake	People
Vanilla	30
Chocolate	15
Strawberry	10
Mint	5

Every tenth person entering a concert is asked to name his or her favorite milk shake flavor.

1. Find the probability that a person attending the concert prefers chocolate milk shakes.

2. Predict how many people out of 620 would prefer chocolate milk shakes.

3. Talk About It Tell how you would choose a random sample for a survey to find out how many students at your school ride the bus.

Practice and Problem Solving

EXTRA PRACTICE See page 682.

For Exercises 4 and 5, use the following information.
See Examples 1, 2 (p. 513)

Isabelle made 4 baskets in her last 10 attempts.

4. Find the probability of Isabelle making a basket on her next attempt.

5. Suppose Isabelle attempts 20 baskets. About how many baskets would you expect her to make?

For Exercises 6 and 7, use the following information.
See Examples 1, 2 (p. 513)

Luther won 12 of the last 20 video games he played.

6. Find the probability of Luther winning the next game he plays.

7. Suppose Luther plays a total of 60 games with his friends over the next month. Predict how many of these games Luther will win.

For Exercises 8–11, use the table to predict the number of students out of 450 that would prefer each type of music.
See Example 2 (p. 513)

Favorite Music	Students
Rock	9
Country	5
Pop	2
Rap	5
Alternative	4

8. rock

9. alternative

10. country

11. pop

12. A survey found that 6 out of every 10 students have a weblog. What is the probability that a student has a weblog? If there are 250 students at a school, about how many have a weblog?

13. The probability of Jaden making a free throw is 15%. Predict the number of free throws that he can expect to make if he attempts 40 free throws.

Real-World PROBLEM SOLVING

Volunteering In the U.S., 28.8 percent of the population volunteered at some point during 2004.

14. About 2.8 million kids ages 10–14 live in California. Predict the number of kids that volunteer a few times a year.

15. North Carolina has about 600,000 kids ages 10–14. Predict the number of kids in this age group that volunteer once a week.

16. About 300,000 kids ages 10–14 live in South Carolina. Predict the number of kids in this age group that volunteer once a year.

How Often Kids Volunteer

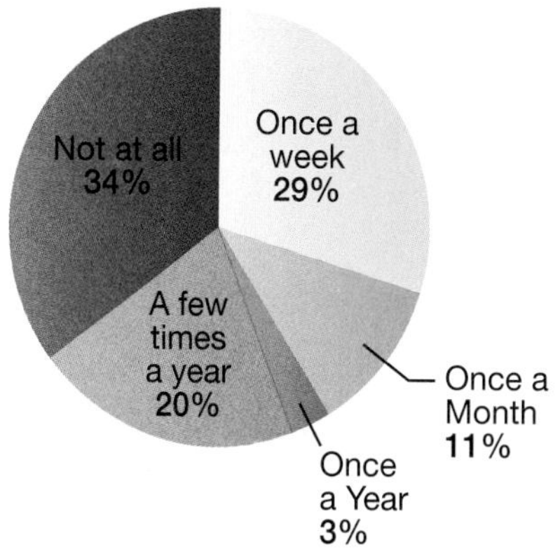

Source: pbskids.org

H.O.T. Problems

17. **FIND THE ERROR** A survey of a fifth-grade class showed that 4 out of every 10 students are taking a trip during spring break. There are 150 students in the fifth grade. Raheem and Elisa are trying to determine how many of the fifth-grade students can be expected to take a trip during spring break. Who is correct? Explain your reasoning.

Raheem

$$\frac{4}{10} = \frac{x}{150}$$
$$\frac{4}{10} = \frac{60}{150}$$
$$x = 60 \text{ students}$$

Elisa

$$\frac{4}{10} = \frac{150}{x}$$
$$\frac{4}{10} = \frac{150}{375}$$
$$x = 375 \text{ students}$$

18. **CHALLENGE** If the spinner is spun 400 times, predict how many times the spinner will stop on something other than yellow.

19. **OPEN ENDED** Give an example of a situation in which you would make a prediction.

20. **WRITING IN MATH** Three out of four of Mitch's fifth-grade friends say that they will not attend the school carnival. Based on this information, Mitch predicts that only 25 of the 100 fifth graders at his school will attend the carnival. Is this a valid prediction? Explain.

Standards Practice

21 At the fair, Jesse won the balloon dart game 1 out of every 5 times he played. If he plays the game 15 more times, about how many times can he expect to win?

A 3

B 4

C 5

D 15

22 If 7 out of 30 students are going on the ski trip, predict the number of students out of 150 that are going on the ski trip.

F 5 **H** 35

G 30 **J** 100

23 The table shows the results of a survey of fifth-grade students in the lunch line.

Favorite Drink	
Drink	**Students**
Chocolate Milk	15
Soda	12
Milk	6
Water	2

If there are 245 fifth graders in the school, how many can be expected to prefer chocolate milk?

A 45 **C** 90

B 84 **D** 105

Spiral Review

24. How many ways can a person watch 3 different videos? Make an organized list to show the sample space. **(Lesson 9-9)**

Sarah randomly turns to a page in a 12-month calendar. Find each probability. **(Lesson 9-8)**

25. *P*(April or May)

26. *P*(*not* June)

27. *P*(begins with a J)

28. *P*(begins with an M)

29. A mosquito's proboscis, the part that sucks blood, is the first $\frac{1}{3}$ of its body's length. The rest of the mosquito is made up of the head, thorax, and abdomen. How much of a mosquito is the head, thorax, and abdomen? **(Lesson 5-3)**

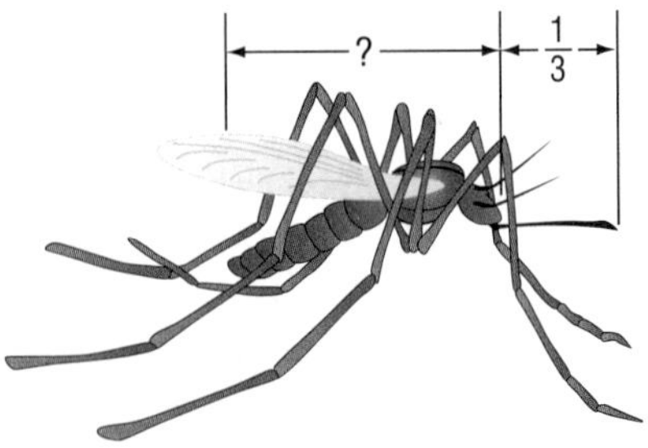

Write each improper fraction as a mixed number. Graph the result on a number line. **(Lesson 4-4)**

30. $\frac{16}{9}$

31. $\frac{22}{9}$

32. $\frac{35}{6}$

33. $\frac{50}{6}$

34. About how much more is $74.50 than $29.95? **(Lesson 3-5)**

CHAPTER 9

Study Guide and Review

FOLDABLES™ Study Organizer GET READY to Study

Be sure the following Key Concepts are noted in your Foldable.

Fraction	Percent	Decimal
$\frac{1}{2}$ →	50% →	0.5

BIG Ideas

Percent (Lesson 9-1)

- A percent is a ratio that compares a number to 100.

Percent Conversions (Lessons 9-1 and 9-3)

- To write a percent as a fraction, write the percent as a fraction with a denominator of 100. Then simplify.
- To write a percent as a decimal, rewrite the percent as a fraction with a denominator of 100. Then write the fraction as a decimal.
- To write a decimal as a percent, write the decimal as a fraction whose denominator is 100. Then write the fraction as a percent.

Percent of a Number (Lesson 9-6)

To find the percent of a number, use one of the following methods.

- Write the percent as a fraction and then multiply, or
- Write the percent as a decimal and then multiply.

Key Vocabulary

circle graph (p. 471)
outcomes (p. 498)
percent (p. 466)
probability (p. 498)
sample (p. 512)
sample space (p. 505)
simple event (p. 498)
survey (p. 512)
tree diagram (p. 506)

Vocabulary Check

State whether each sentence is *true* or *false*. If *false*, replace the underlined word or number to make a true sentence.

1. An organized list that is used to show all of the possible outcomes is called a survey.
2. A percent is a ratio that compares a number to 10.
3. A ratio that compares the number of favorable outcomes to the number of possible outcomes is the probability of an event.
4. If an event is certain to occur, the probability of that event is 0.
5. Thirty percent of 45 has the same value as 0.3×45.

Lesson-by-Lesson Review

9-1 Percents and Fractions (pp. 466–470)

Example 1

Write 24% as a fraction in simplest form.

$24\% = \frac{24}{100}$ Definition of percent

$= \frac{6}{25}$ Simplify. Divide numerator and denominator by the GCF, 4.

Example 2

Write $\frac{3}{5}$ as a percent.

$\frac{3}{5} = \frac{n}{100}$ Write an equation. Since $5 \times 20 = 100$, multiply 3 by 20 to find n.

$\frac{3}{5} = \frac{60}{100}$ (×20) $\frac{3}{5} = 60\%$

Write each percent as a fraction or mixed number in simplest form.

6. 3% **7.** 48% **8.** 120%

Write each fraction as a percent.

9. $\frac{7}{8}$ **10.** $1\frac{3}{5}$ **11.** $\frac{19}{100}$

12. One third of Earth's land surface is covered by desert and about 13% of the world's population live in a desert area. Write the percent of the world's population that live in a desert area as a fraction in simplest form.

9-2 Circle Graphs (pp. 471–476)

Example 3

In Mr. Finn's class, 54% of the students favor chocolate muffins, 23% favor blueberry, and 23% favor banana. Sketch a circle graph of the data.

Since 23% is a little less than 25% or $\frac{1}{4}$, shade a little less than $\frac{1}{4}$ of the circle for "Banana." Do the same for "Blueberry." The remaining section is "Chocolate."

Label each section of the graph. Then give the graph a title.

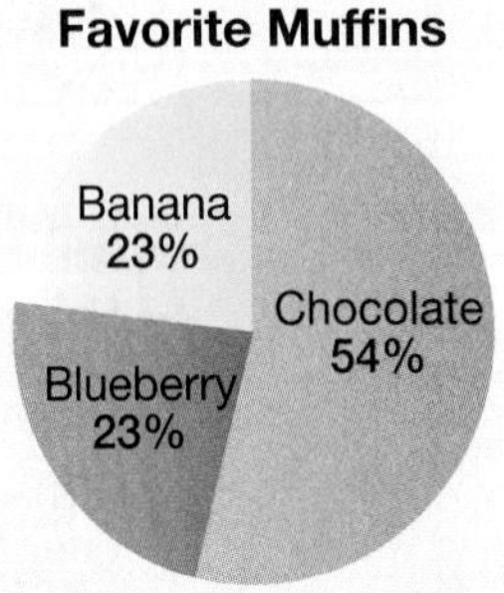

13. A group of adults were asked to name their favorite type of movie. The results are shown in the table. Sketch a circle graph of the data.

Type of Movie	Percent
Comedy	40
Action	25
Drama	25
Romance	10

For Exercises 14 and 15, refer to the circle graph from Exercise 13.

14. Which type of movie did the adults say is their favorite?

15. Which two sections represent the responses by the same amount of adults?

9-3 Percents and Decimals (pp. 477–480)

Example 4

Write 46% as a decimal.

$46\% = \frac{46}{100}$ Rewrite the percent as a fraction with a denominator of 100.

$= 0.46$ Write *46 hundredths* as a decimal.

Example 5

Write 0.85 as a percent.

$0.85 = \frac{85}{100}$ Write *85 hundredths* as a fraction.

$= 85\%$ Write the fraction as a percent.

Write each percent as a decimal.

16. 2%
17. 38%

18. 140%
19. 90%

Write each decimal as a percent.

20. 0.03
21. 1.3

22. 1.75
23. 0.51

24. A slice of bread is 30% water. Write this as a decimal.

9-4 Problem-Solving Strategy: Solve a Simpler Problem (pp. 482–483)

Example 6

In May, Marisol had earned $240 from baby-sitting. She wants to save 70% of this amount to put toward a new laptop. How much money does she need to save?

Solve a simpler problem.

10% of \$240 $= \frac{1}{10}$ of \$240 $\quad 10\% = \frac{1}{10}$

$= \$24$ $\quad \frac{1}{10}$ means divide by 10.

Since 70% is 7 · 10%, multiply $24 by 7.

So, Marisol needs to save 7 · $24 or $168.

Solve. Use the *solve a simpler problem* strategy.

25. The cafeteria has 45 square tables that can be pushed together to form one long table for the lacrosse team's banquet. Each square table can seat one person on each side. How many people can be seated at the banquet table?

26. In one year, Orlando received 62.51 inches of rain. In September, the city received 25% of that rainfall. About how much rain did Orlando receive in September?

27. In a community survey, $\frac{4}{5}$ of the people said they would use a 25-mile bike path if it were built. If 1,000 people were surveyed, how many said they would use the bike path?

9-5 Estimating with Percents (pp. 484–488)

Example 7
Estimate 33% of 60.

33% is close to $33\frac{1}{3}\%$ or $\frac{1}{3}$.

$\frac{1}{3}$ of 60 $= \frac{1}{3} \times 60$ or 20.

So, 33% of 60 is about 20.

Example 8
When the library surveyed the entire school regarding their favorite type of magazine, about 28% of the students preferred sports magazines. Predict the number of students out of 1,510 that would prefer sports magazines.

28% of the students preferred sports.

28% is about 30% or $\frac{3}{10}$.

Round 1,510 to 1,500.

$\frac{1}{10}$ of 1,500 is 150. So, $\frac{3}{10}$ of 1,500 is $3 \cdot 150$ or 450.

So, about 450 students would prefer sports magazines.

Estimate each percent.

28. 40% of 78 **29.** 73% of 20

30. 25% of 122 **31.** 19% of 99

32. 48% of 48 **33.** 41% of 243

34. According to the 2000 Census, about 27.3% of Californians were under 18 years old. If the population of California was estimated at 33,871,648, about how many Californians were under 18 years old?

35. Sofia wants to save 30% of her paycheck. If her paycheck is $347.89, what would be a reasonable amount for her to save?

36. According to a recent national survey, about 83% of teens oppose school uniforms. Predict the number of teens out of 2,979 that would *not* oppose school uniforms.

9-6 Percent of a Number (pp. 492–495)

Example 9
Find 42% of 90.

42% of 90	$= 0.42 \times 90$	Change the percent to a decimal.
	$= 37.8$	Multiply.

So, 42% of 90 is 37.8.

Find the percent of each number.

37. 40% of 150 **38.** 5% of 340

39. 18% of 90 **40.** 8% of 130

41. 170% of 30 **42.** 125% of 120

43. Brock attended 60% of his school's baseball games. How many games did Brock attend if there were 15 games?

9-7 Problem-Solving Investigation: Choose the Best Strategy
(pp. 496–497)

Example 10

What number is missing in the pattern below?

…, 234, 345, ■, 567, …

Look for a pattern. Since 234 + 111 = 345, 345 + 111 = 456, and 456 + 111 = 567, 111 is being added to the previous term.

So, the missing number is 456.

Choose the best strategy to solve each problem.

44. A recipe for cornbread calls for $\frac{1}{3}$ cup of cheese. If you have 2 cups of cheese, how much cheese will you have left?

45. Lana has a total of 12 blue pens and purple pens. She has two fewer purple pens than blue pens. How many of each type of pen does Lana have?

9-8 Probability
(pp. 498–503)

Example 11

The spinner shown is spun once. Find the probability of landing on one of the colors in the United States flag.

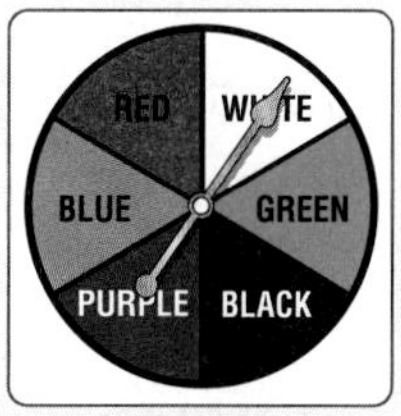

There are six equally likely outcomes on the spinner. Three of the colors appear in the United States flag. Those colors are red, white, and blue.

$P(\text{red, white, or blue}) = \frac{3}{6}$ or $\frac{1}{2}$

So, $P(\text{red, white, or blue})$ is $\frac{1}{2}$, 0.5, or 50%.

One coin shown is chosen without looking. Find each probability. Write each answer as a fraction, a decimal, and a percent.

46. *P*(nickel)

47. *P*(*not* dime)

48. *P*(quarter or penny)

A number cube is rolled. Find each probability. Write each answer as a fraction.

49. *P*(5)

50. *P*(less than 4)

51. *P*(odd)

52. *P*(at least 5)

53. There is a 78% chance of rain. Identify the complement of this event. Then find its probability.

9-9 Sample Spaces (pp. 505–509)

Example 12

Suppose you have a choice of a sugar cone (S) or a waffle cone (W) and blueberry (B), mint (M), or peach (P) yogurt. How many yogurt cones are possible?

Use a tree diagram.

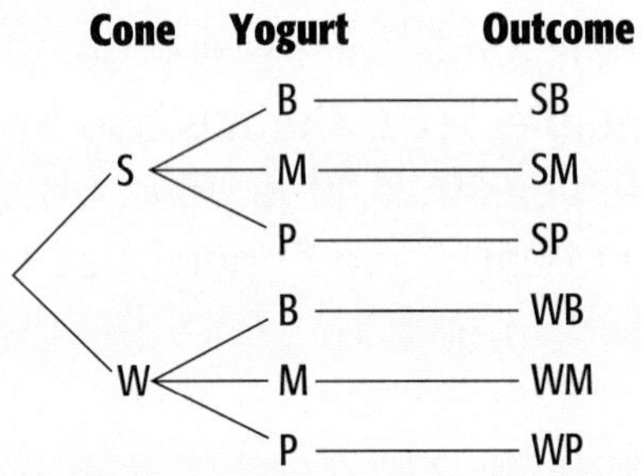

There are 6 possible cones.

For Exercises 54 and 55, make an organized list to show the sample space for the situation. Then tell how many outcomes are possible.

54. a choice of black or blue jeans in classic fit, stretch, or bootcut style

55. a choice of comedy, action, horror, or science fiction DVD in widescreen or full screen format

Draw a tree diagram to show the sample space for the situation. Then tell how many outcomes are possible.

56. a choice of going to a basketball game, an amusement park, or a concert on a Friday or a Saturday

9-10 Making Predictions (pp. 512–516)

Example 13

If 12 out of 50 people surveyed watch TV after 11 P.M., how many people out of 1,000 would you expect to watch TV after 11 P.M.?

Let p represent the number of people who watch TV after 11 P.M.

$\frac{12}{50} = \frac{p}{1{,}000}$ Write an equation.

$\frac{12}{50} = \frac{240}{1{,}000}$ (×20, ×20) Since $50 \times 20 = 1{,}000$, multiply 12 by 20 to find p.

So, of the 1,000 people, you would expect 240 to watch TV after 11 P.M.

For Exercises 57 and 58, use the following information.

Out of 40 students, 14 are interested in publishing a school newspaper.

57. What is the probability that a student at this school would be interested in publishing a school newspaper?

58. If there are 420 students, how many would you expect to be interested in publishing a school newspaper?

CHAPTER 9 Chapter Test

Write each percent as a fraction or mixed number in simplest form.

1. 42% **2.** 110% **3.** 18%

Write each fraction as a percent.

4. $\frac{2}{5}$ **5.** $\frac{11}{20}$ **6.** $1\frac{1}{2}$

7. **STANDARDS PRACTICE** $\frac{17}{20}$ of the students dressed up for spirit week. What percent of the student body did *not* dress up for spirit week?

A 15% **C** 20%

B 17% **D** 85%

For Exercises 8 and 9, refer to the circle graph.

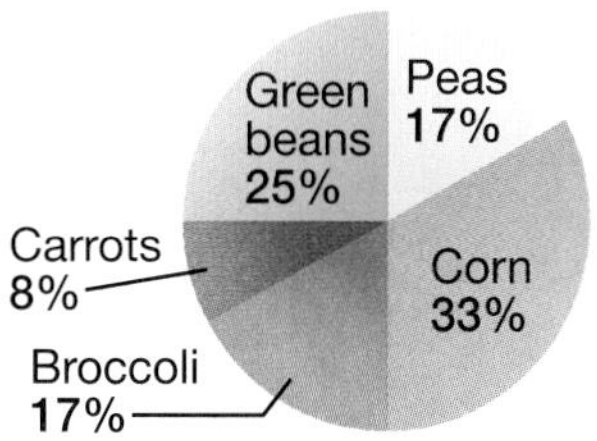

8. Which vegetable is most frequently named as favorite?

9. How do peas compare to corn as a favorite vegetable?

Express each decimal as a percent.

10. 0.3 **11.** 0.87 **12.** 1.49

Estimate each percent.

13. 19% of 51 **14.** 49% of 26

15. 77% of 51 **16.** 69% of 203

17. **STANDARDS PRACTICE** What is 30% of 140?

F 14 **G** 40 **H** 42 **J** 80

A set of 20 cards is numbered 1–20. One card is chosen without looking. Find each probability. Write each probability as a fraction, a decimal, and a percent.

18. $P(8)$

19. $P(3 \text{ or } 10)$

20. $P(\text{prime})$

21. $P(\text{not odd})$

For Exercises 22 and 23, use the following information.

A food cart offers a choice of iced tea or soda and nachos, popcorn, or pretzels.

22. Draw a tree diagram that shows all of the choices for a beverage and a snack.

23. Find the probability that the next customer who orders a beverage and a snack will choose iced tea and popcorn.

24. **WRITING IN MATH** Alonso asked every fourth sixth-grade student who walked into a school dance to name his or her favorite sport.

Favorite Sport	
Sport	Students
Football	52
Soccer	22
Baseball	16
Hockey	10

If there are 375 students in the sixth grade, how many can be expected to prefer football? Explain.

CHAPTER 9

California Standards Practice

Cumulative, Chapters 1–9

Standards Example

Twelve people at the basketball game won a T-shirt. If there were 600 people at the basketball game, what percent of the people at the basketball game won a T-shirt?

A 2% **C** 12%

B 4% **D** 24%

Read the Question

You are asked to find what percent of the people at the basketball game won a T-shirt.

Solve the Question

Since $\frac{12}{600}$ people won a T-shirt, write $\frac{12}{600}$ as a percent.

$\frac{12}{600} = \frac{n}{100}$ Write an equation.

$\frac{12}{600} = \frac{2}{100}$ (÷6 top and bottom) Since 600 ÷ 6 = 100, divide 12 by 6 to find *n*.

So, $\frac{12}{600} = \frac{2}{100}$ or 2%. The answer is A.

Online **Personal Tutor at** ca.gr5math.com

Choose the best answer.

1 **Sanford's Shoe Store received a shipment of shoes for its newest location. The manager determined that 35% of the shoes were athletic shoes. What fraction of the shoes were athletic shoes?**

A $\frac{1}{6}$ **B** $\frac{7}{20}$ **C** $\frac{3}{8}$ **D** $\frac{13}{20}$

2 **In a jar there are 4 oatmeal cookies, 9 chocolate chip cookies, 3 sugar cookies, and 4 peanut butter cookies. What percent of the cookies are oatmeal or peanut butter?**

F 15% **H** 75%

G 40% **J** 85%

3 **Each figure below is divided into sections of equal size. Which figure has 87.5% of its total area shaded?**

A 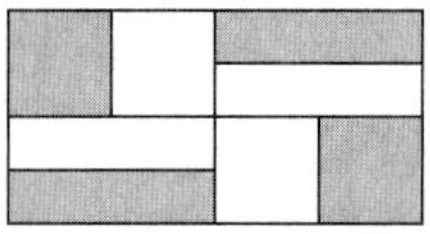

C 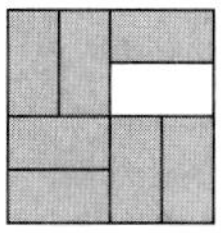

B 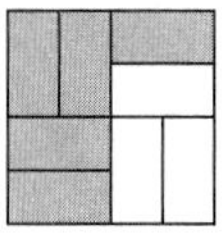

D 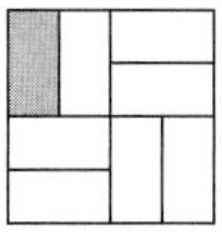

---

4 **What is 65% of 320?**

F 5 **H** 208

G 120 **J** 2,112

---

5 **Rob has the following cards on his desk. What percent of the cards are *not* vowels?**

A 27.3% **C** 63.6%

B 37.5% **D** 93.5%

---

6 **What is 45% written as a fraction in simplest form?**

F $\frac{1}{45}$ **H** $\frac{3}{10}$

G $\frac{2}{9}$ **J** $\frac{9}{20}$

7 **What is the decimal 0.55 written as a fraction?**

A $\frac{11}{20}$ **C** $\frac{3}{25}$

B $\frac{1}{2}$ **D** $\frac{1}{55}$

---

8 **The map below shows the location of 4 friends' homes.**

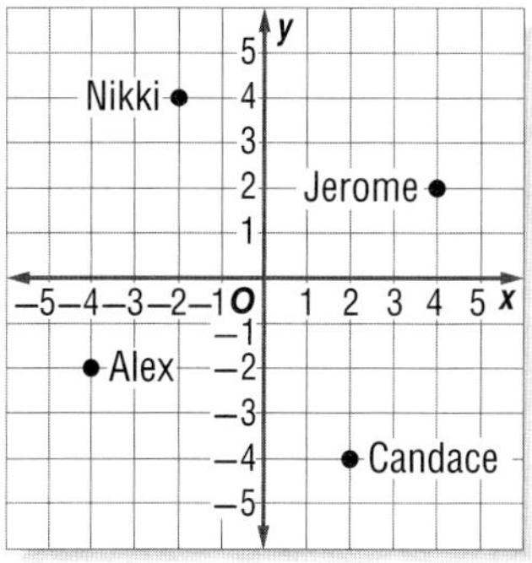

Which friends' home is represented by the point (−2, 4)?

F Alex **H** Jerome

G Candace **J** Nikki

---

9 $4\frac{1}{5} + 3\frac{1}{3} =$

A $7\frac{1}{8}$ **C** $7\frac{3}{8}$

B $7\frac{2}{15}$ **D** $7\frac{8}{15}$

---

10 **Chicago, Illinois, has a population of 2,869,121. What is this value rounded to the nearest ten thousand?**

F 2,860,000 **H** 2,870,000

G 2,869,000 **J** 2,900,000

CHAPTER 10 Geometry: Angles and Polygons

BIG Idea How do you classify angles?

Angles can be classified according to their measures. Angles can be right, acute, obtuse, or straight.

Example Riders of the Millennium Force roller coaster in Ohio travel at a 45° angle up the first hill and then down a 300-foot-long drop at an 80° angle. Since 45° and 80° are less than 90°, they are both **acute angles**.

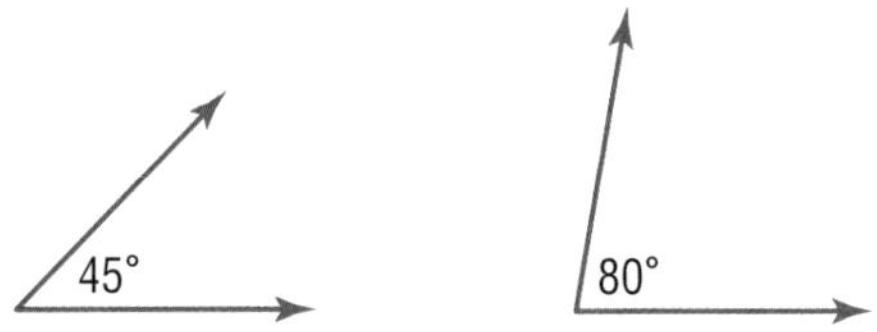

What will I learn in this chapter?

- Measure and classify angles.
- Identify and measure parallel and perpendicular lines.
- Classify quadrilaterals and find missing angle measures in quadrilaterals.
- Draw two-dimensional views of three-dimensional figures.
- Solve problems by drawing a diagram.

Key Vocabulary

angle
parallel lines
perpendicular lines
quadrilateral
three-dimensional figure

Math Online Student Study Tools at ca.gr5math.com

FOLDABLES™ Study Organizer

Make this Foldable to help organize information about angles and polygons. Begin with seven half-sheets of notebook paper.

1. **Fold** a sheet in half lengthwise. Then cut a 1″ tab along the left edge through one thickness.

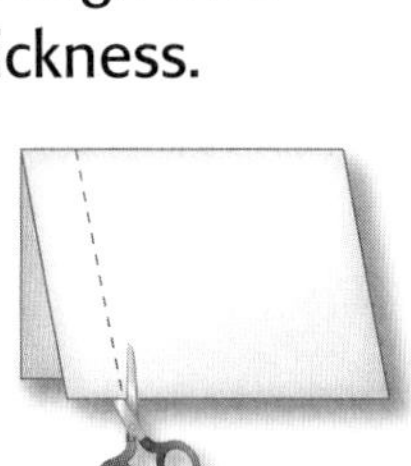

2. **Glue** the 1″ tab down. Write the word *Geometry* on this tab and the lesson title on the front tab.

3. **Write** *Definitions* and *Examples* under the tab.

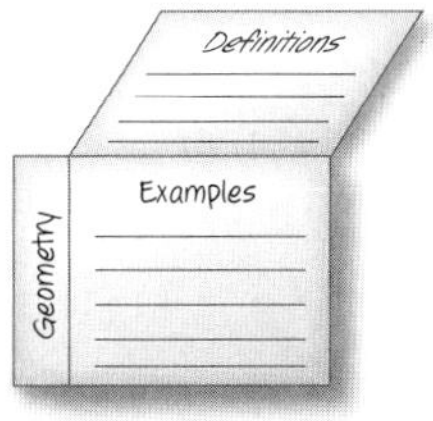

4. **Repeat** Steps 1–3 for each lesson using the remaining paper. Staple them to form a booklet.

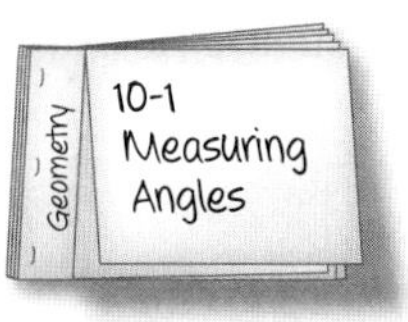

ARE YOU READY for Chapter 10?

You have two ways to check prerequisite skills for this chapter.

Option 2

Math Online Take the Chapter Readiness Quiz at ca.gr5math.com.

Option 1

Complete the Quick Check below.

QUICK Check

Use a ruler to draw a diagram that shows how the hands on a clock appear at each time. **(Prior Grade)**

1. 9:00

2. 12:10

3. 3:45

4. 6:00

5. Pete's baseball practice begins at 2:30 P.M. Draw a diagram that shows how the hands on a clock appear at this time. **(Prior Grade)**

Solve each equation. **(Lesson 7-9)**

6. $x + 44 = 180$

7. $68 + x = 180$

8. $x + 122 = 180$

9. $87 + x = 180$

10. In the first two games, Lee scored a total of 40 points. If he scored 21 points in the second game, how many points did he score in the first game? **(Lesson 7-9)**

Solve each equation. **(Lesson 7-9)**

11. $x + 120 = 360$

12. $180 + x = 360$

13. $53 + x + 108 + 82 = 360$

14. $29 + 38 + 112 + x = 360$

15. A hotel room for four people costs $360. If three people each pay $85, how much will the fourth person have to pay? **(Lesson 7-9)**

10-1 Measuring Angles

GET READY to Learn

The circle graph shows what Mai-Lin planted in her garden this spring. The percents 30%, 25%, 20%, 15%, and 10% correspond to the sections in the graph. Explain how you would match each percent with its corresponding section.

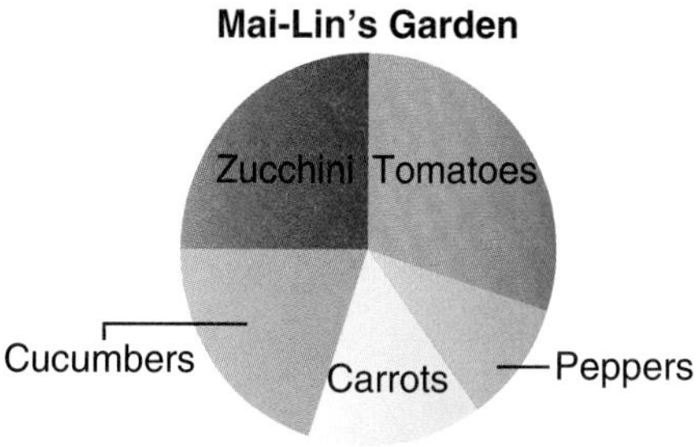

MAIN IDEA

I will measure and classify angles.

Standard 5MG2.1
Measure, identify, and draw **angles,** perpendicular and parallel lines, rectangles, and triangles **by using appropriate tools** (e.g., **straightedge,** ruler, compass, **protractor,** drawing software.)

New Vocabulary

- **angle**
- **side**
- **vertex**
- **degree**
- **right angle**
- **acute angle**
- **obtuse angle**
- **straight angle**

Each section of the circle graph above shows an angle. **Angles** have two **sides** that share a common endpoint called the **vertex** of the angle. An angle is often named by the label at the vertex. Angle *C* can be written as $\angle C$.

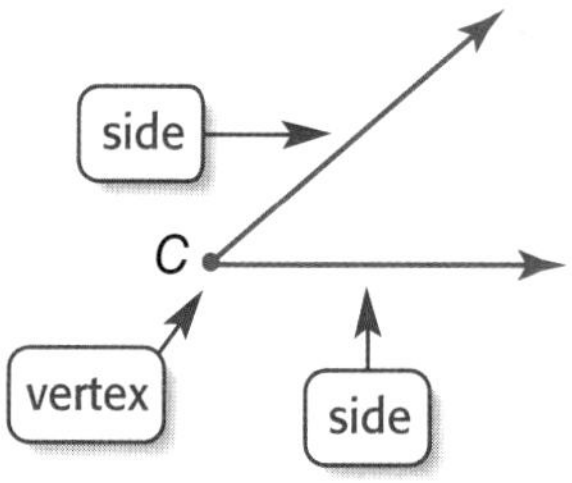

The most common unit of measure for angles is the **degree**. A circle can be separated into 360 equal-sized parts. Each part would make up a one-degree (1°) angle.

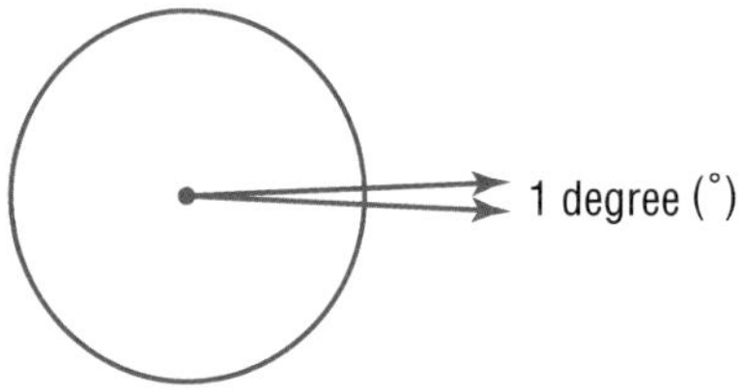

1 degree (°)

EXAMPLES Measure Angles

1 Use a protractor to find the measure of the angle.

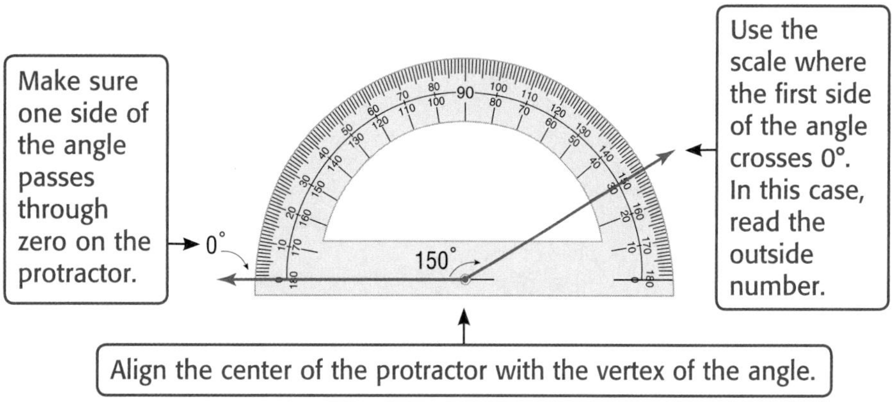

Make sure one side of the angle passes through zero on the protractor.
0°
150°
Use the scale where the first side of the angle crosses 0°. In this case, read the outside number.
Align the center of the protractor with the vertex of the angle.

The angle measures 150°.

Reading Math

Naming Angles Angles can be named using the vertex and a point along each side of the angle. In Example 2, $\angle C$ can also be named $\angle ACB$.

2 **Use a protractor to find the measure of the angle.**

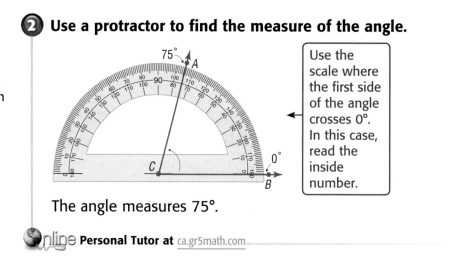

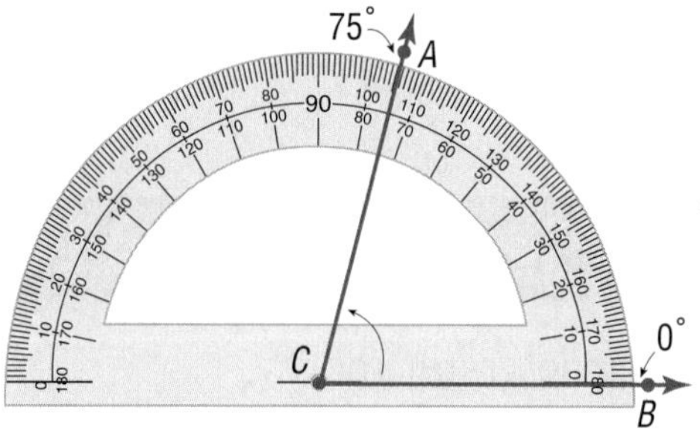
75°
A
C
0°
B
Use the scale where the first side of the angle crosses 0°. In this case, read the inside number.

The angle measures 75°.

Online **Personal Tutor at** ca.gr5math.com

Angles can be classified according to their measures.

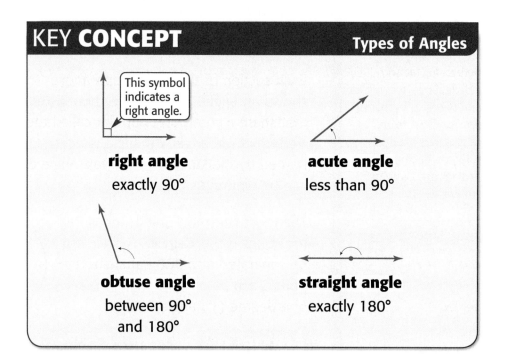

KEY CONCEPT — Types of Angles

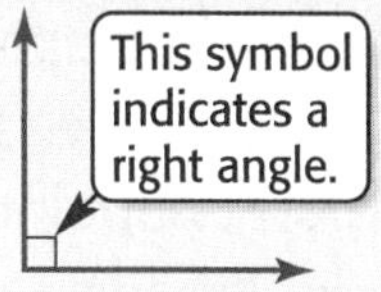
This symbol indicates a right angle.

right angle
exactly 90°

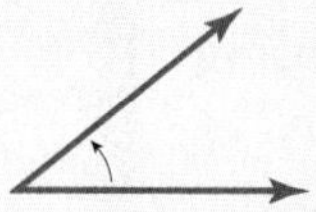

acute angle
less than 90°

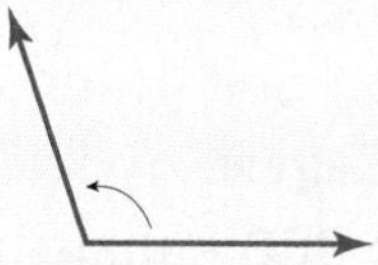

obtuse angle
between 90° and 180°

straight angle
exactly 180°

EXAMPLES Classify Angles

Classify each angle as *acute, obtuse, right,* or *straight*.

3

The angle is 90°. So, it is a right angle.

4

The angle is larger than a right angle, but smaller than a straight angle. So, it is an obtuse angle.

Math Online **Extra Examples at** ca.gr5math.com

CHECK What You Know

Use a protractor to find the measure of each angle. Then classify each angle as *acute*, *obtuse*, *right*, or *straight*. See Examples 1–4 (pp. 529–530)

1. 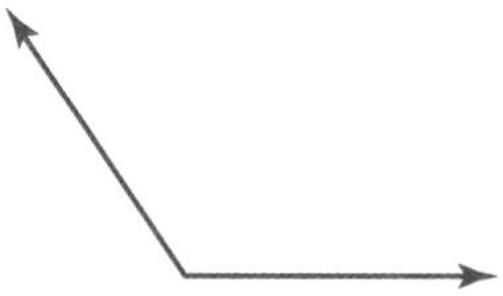

2. 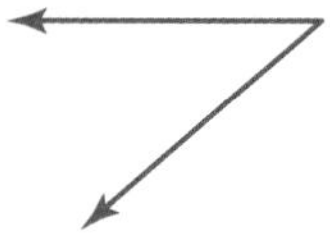

3. 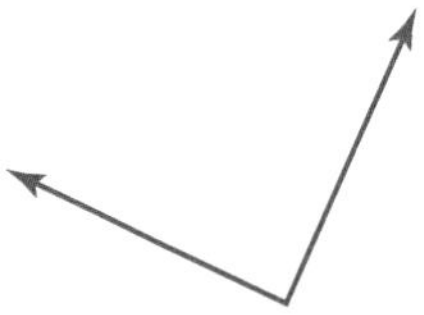

4. The *lie* of a hockey stick is the angle between the blade and the shaft. Classify this angle.
See Examples 3, 4 (p. 530)

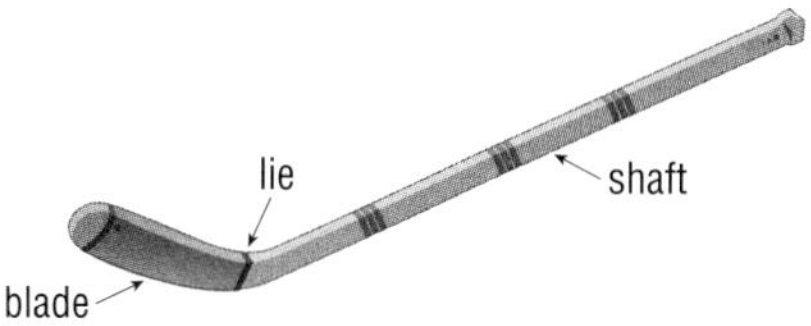

5. Talk About It: Describe how you use a protractor to measure an angle.

Practice and Problem Solving

EXTRA PRACTICE
See page 682.

Use a protractor to find the measure of each angle. Then classify each angle as *acute, obtuse, right,* or *straight*. See Examples 1–4 (pp. 529–530)

6. 

7. 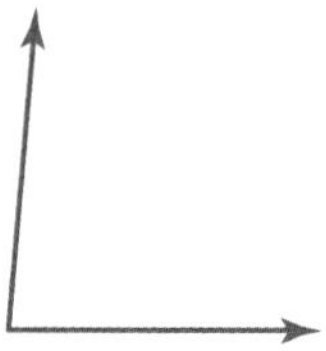

8. 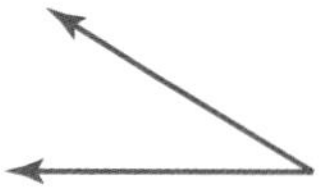

9. 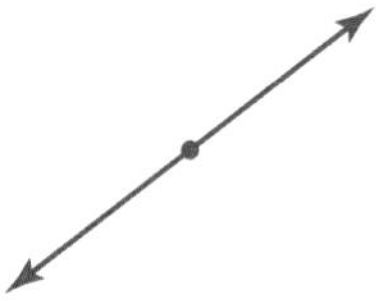

10. 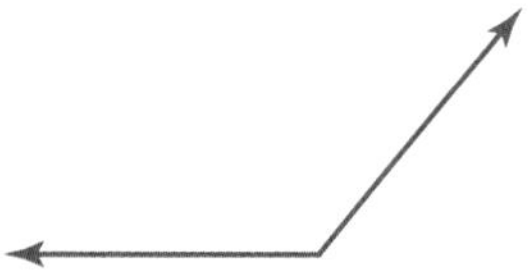

11. 

Classify the angles in each road sign. See Examples 3, 4 (p. 530)

12. 

13. 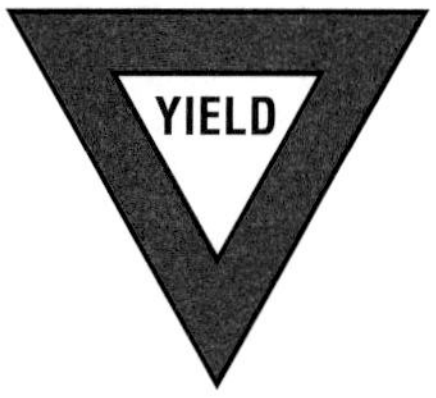

Real-World PROBLEM SOLVING

Flags The Ohio state flag is shown.

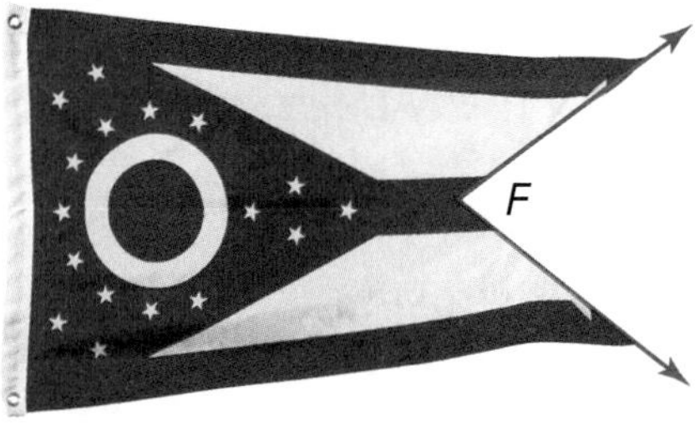

14. What is the measure of $\angle F$ on the Ohio flag?

15. Name the types of angles found on the flag.

H.O.T. Problems

16. **OPEN ENDED** Select three objects in your classroom or at home. Measure the angles found in the objects, and then classify each angle.

17. **FIND THE ERROR** Lorena and Dave are measuring angles. Who is correct? Explain your reasoning.

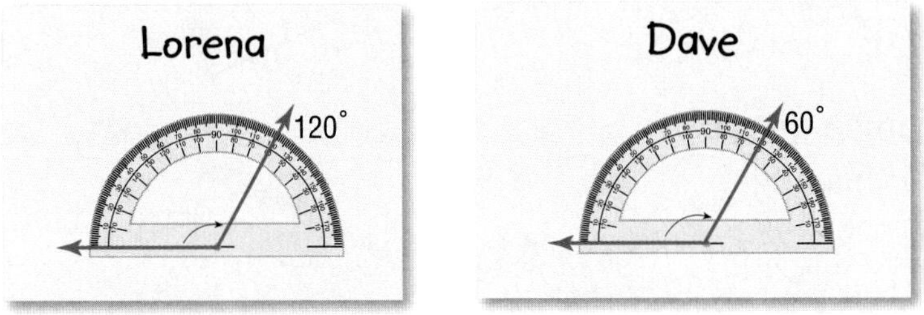

18. **CHALLENGE** Measure ∠*Z* to the nearest degree. Then describe the method you used to find the measure.

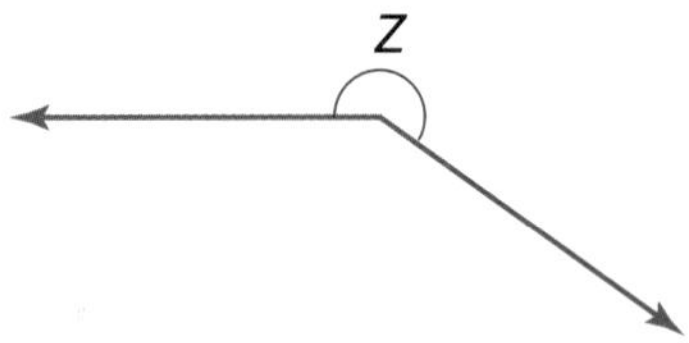

19. **WRITING IN ▸MATH** Without measuring, explain in your own words how you can classify an angle as acute, obtuse, or right.

Standards Practice

20 Find the measure of ∠*FGH* to the nearest degree.

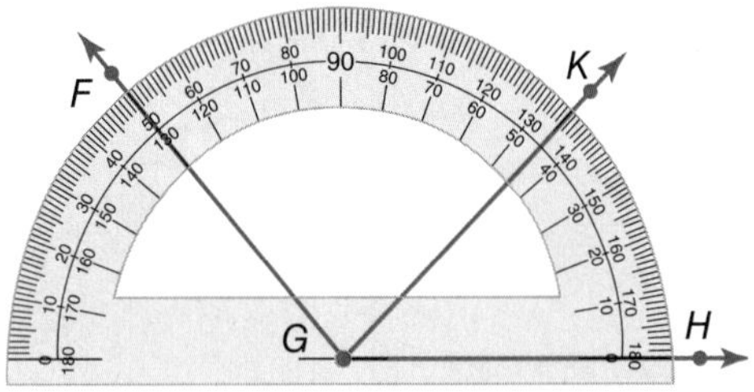

A 130° **C** 85°

B 95° **D** 45°

21 What type of angle is at each vertex of the regular hexagon below?

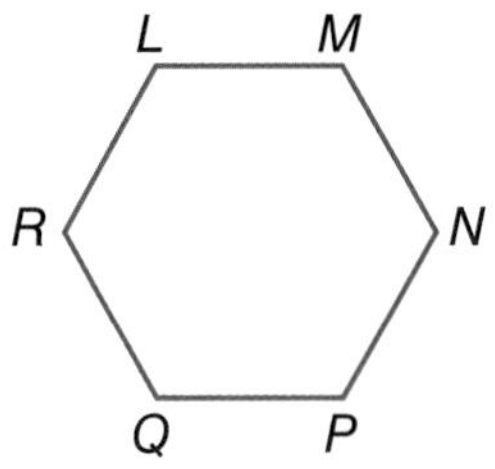

F acute **H** right

G obtuse **J** straight

Spiral Review

22. The average human heart beats 72 times per minute. At this rate, how many beats will there be in one week? **(Lesson 9-10)**

23. The bakery offers a choice of plain or onion bagels, with a topping of cream cheese or jelly, and cinnamon or nutmeg sprinkled on top. How many different ways can you choose a bagel, a topping, and spice? **(Lesson 9-9)**

Wild Angles

Classifying Angles

Get Ready!

Players: two

You will need: 27 index cards, spinner

5°	5°	10°	10°	15°	15°
20°	20°	25°	25°	30°	30°
35°	35°	40°	40°	45°	45°
50°	50°	55°	55°	60°	60°
65°	65°	70°	70°	75°	75°
80°	80°	85°	85°	90°	90°
95°	100°	105°	110°	115°	120°
125°	130°	135°	Wild	Wild	Wild
Wild	Wild	Wild	Wild	Wild	Wild

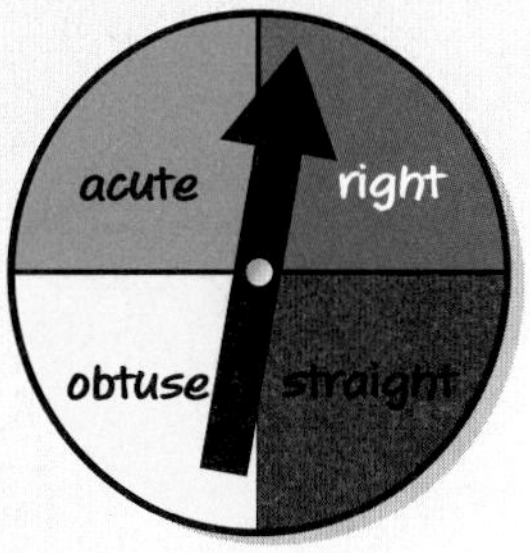

Get Set!

- Cut the index cards in half.
- Label the cards and spinner as shown.

Go!

- Shuffle the cards and then deal six cards to each player. Place the remaining cards facedown in a pile.
- A player spins the spinner.
- Using two cards, the player forms a pair whose sum results in the type of angle spun. A wild card represents any angle measure. Each pair is worth 2 points. The player draws a card from the deck. Then it is the other player's turn.
- If a pair cannot be formed, the player draws another card from the pile. If a pair is formed, the player sets aside the two cards and draws another card. Then it is the other player's turn.
- The first player to reach 20 points, or the player with the most pairs when the pile is gone wins.

10-2 Problem-Solving Strategy

MAIN IDEA I will solve problems by drawing a diagram.

Standard 5MR2.3 Use a variety of methods, such as words, numbers, symbols, charts, graphs, tables, **diagrams,** and models**, to explain mathematical reasoning.** **Standard SMG2.1** Measure, identify, and **draw angles, perpendicular and parallel lines, rectangles,** and triangles **by using appropriate tools.**

The science club is going to plant flowers in the school courtyard, which is 46 feet by 60 feet, and has walls on each side. The flower beds will be 6 feet by 6 feet and will be 8 feet apart and 6 feet from the walls. How many flower beds can the science club make to fit in the school courtyard?

Understand

What facts do you know?

- The courtyard measures 46 feet by 60 feet.
- Each flower bed will be 6 feet by 6 feet and will be 8 feet apart and 6 feet from the walls.

What do you need to find?

- How many flower beds can fit in the school courtyard?

Plan

Draw a diagram.

Solve

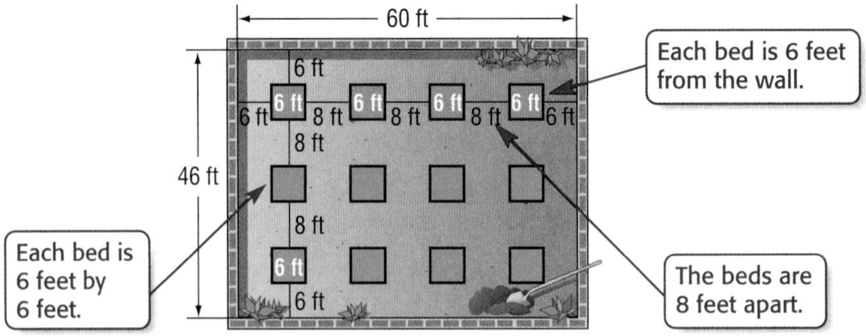

The diagram shows that 12 flower beds will fit inside the courtyard.

Check

Look back at the problem. Add the total distances along the width to check that the sum is 46 feet. $6 + 6 + 8 + 6 + 8 + 6 + 6 = 46$

Add the total distances across the length to check that the sum is 60 feet. $6 + 6 + 8 + 6 + 8 + 6 + 8 + 6 + 6 = 60$

Since the distances match the information in the problem, the answer is correct. ✓

ANALYZE the Strategy

Refer to the problem on the previous page.

1. How many flower beds could be planted if the courtyard measures 74 feet by 88 feet?

2. Explain why you think it helped to draw a diagram to solve the problem.

3. Give a real-world example of when you could solve a problem by drawing a diagram.

4. Explain why drawing a diagram can be a useful problem-solving strategy.

PRACTICE the Strategy

EXTRA PRACTICE See page 682.

Solve. Use the *draw a diagram* strategy.

5. Lauren is putting her pictures into photo album pages like the one shown.

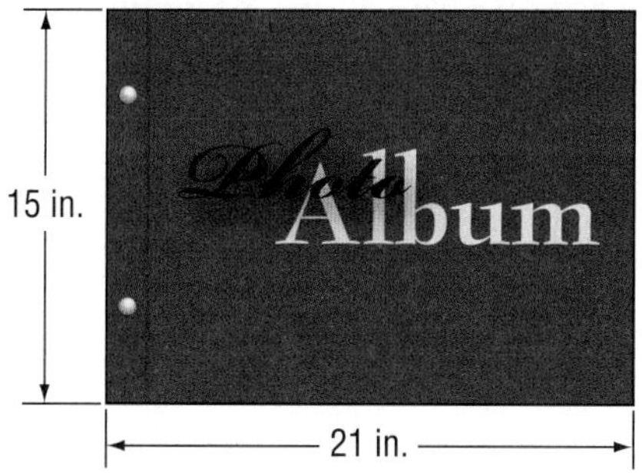

Each picture measures 4 inches by 5 inches. She wants each picture to be $\frac{1}{2}$ inch from the edge of the page and have one inch between pictures. The album has 10 pages and she uses both sides of each page. How many pictures can Lauren place in the photo album?

6. The downtown section of a city is rectangular, 4 blocks by 3 blocks. How many ways are there to drive from one corner of downtown to the opposite corner, if you can make exactly two turns?

7. Carla's house, her school, and the park are on the same road. Carla lives 2.5 miles from the school, which is 0.75 mile farther from her house than the park. How far is it from Carla's house to the park?

8. For the spring dance, there are 5 columns arranged in the shape of a pentagon. One streamer is hung from each column to every other column. How many streamers are there in all?

9. The Delgados are planting trees along each side of their driveway. The driveway is rectangular with the dimensions shown in the table below. If there is 4 feet between each tree, and the trees are planted directly across from each other on each side of the driveway, how many trees can the Delgados plant in all?

House Dimensions	
Deck	12 ft by 12 ft
Driveway	52 ft by 10 ft
Garage	20 ft by 21 ft
Porch	25 ft by 5 ft

10. Mrs. Collins is planting marigolds around the outside edge of a square garden. There will be 10 plants on each side of the garden. What is the least number of marigolds she needs to plant?

11. WRITING IN ►MATH How are the *draw a diagram* strategy and the *make an organized list* strategy similar?

10-3 Estimating and Drawing Angles

Concepts in Motion
Animation
ca.gr5math.com

GET READY to Learn

MAIN IDEA

I will estimate measures of angles and draw angles.

Standard 5MG2.1 Measure, identify, and **draw angles**, perpendicular and parallel lines, rectangles, and triangles **by using appropriate tools** (e.g., **straightedge, ruler,** compass, **protractor**, drawing software.)

Hands-On Mini Lab

To estimate the measure of an angle, use angles that measure 45°, 90°, and 180°.

Step 1 Fold a paper plate in half twice to find the center of the plate.

Step 2 Cut wedges as shown. Then measure and label each angle.

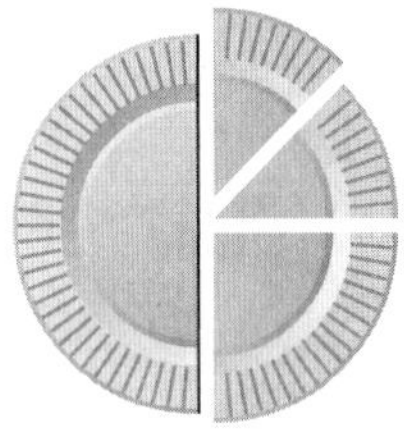

1. Use the wedges to estimate the measure of each angle shown.

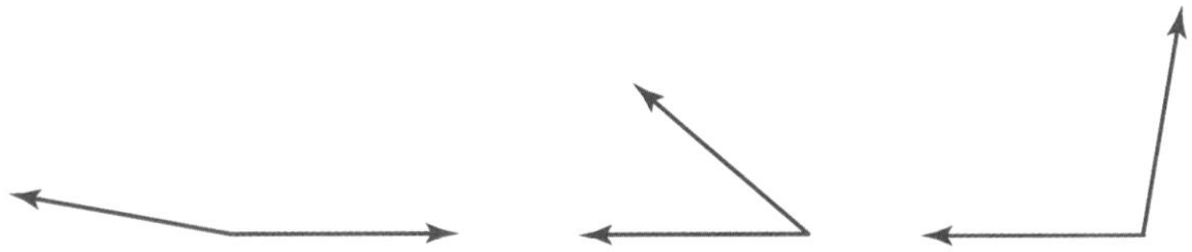

2. How did the wedges help you to estimate each angle?
3. Explain how the 90° and 45° wedges can be used to estimate the angle at the right. What is a reasonable estimate for the angle?

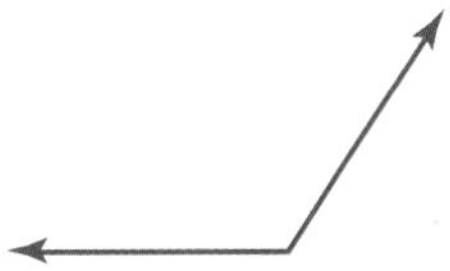

4. How would you estimate the measure of any angle without using the wedges?

To estimate the measure of an angle, compare it to an angle whose measure you know.

EXAMPLE Estimate Angle Measures

1 **Estimate the measure of the angle.**

The angle is a little less than a 90° angle. So, a reasonable estimate is about 80°.

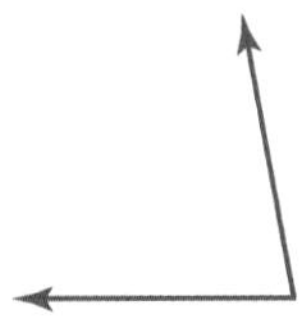

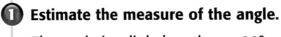

Online Personal Tutor at ca.gr5math.com

Reading Math

straightedge A straightedge is an object, like a ruler, used to draw straight lines.

Remember

You can check whether you have used the correct scale by making an estimate of its size.

EXAMPLE **Draw an Angle**

2 **Use a protractor and a straightedge to draw a 74° angle.**

Step 1 Draw one side of the angle. Then mark the vertex and draw an arrow at the opposite end.

Step 2 Place the center point of the protractor on the vertex. Align the mark labeled 0 on the protractor with the line. Count from 0° to 74° on the correct scale and make a dot.

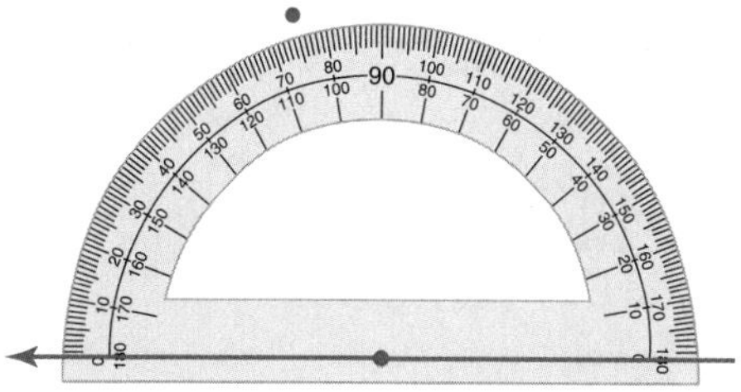

Step 3 Remove the protractor and use a straightedge to draw the side that connects the vertex and the dot.

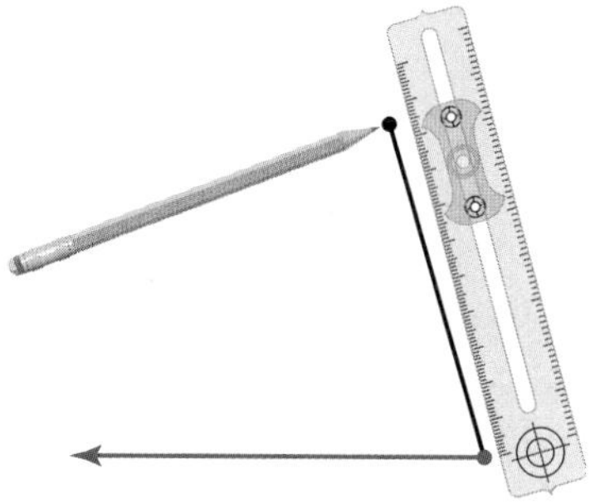

CHECK What You Know

Estimate the measure of each angle. See Example 1 (p. 536)

1.

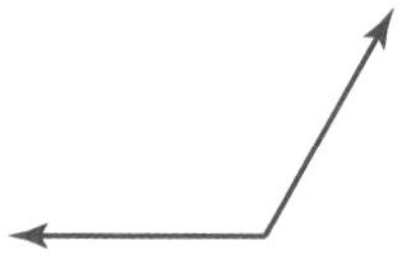

2.

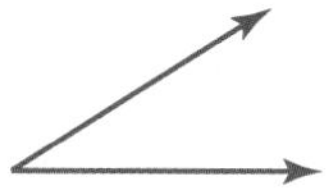

3.

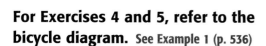

For Exercises 4 and 5, refer to the bicycle diagram. See Example 1 (p. 536)

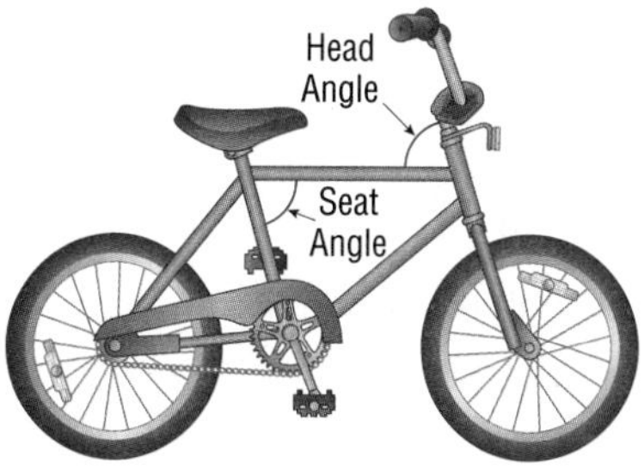

4. Estimate the measure of the head angle.

5. Estimate the measure of the seat angle.

Use a protractor and a straightedge to draw angles having the following measurements. See Example 2 (p. 537)

6. 25° **7.** 140° **8.** 60°

9. Talk About It Explain how you would draw an angle measuring 65°.

Practice and Problem Solving

EXTRA PRACTICE
See page 683.

Estimate the measure of each angle. **See Example 1 (p. 536)**

10.
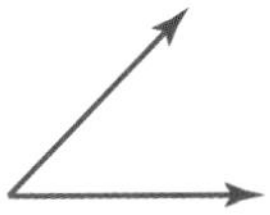

11.
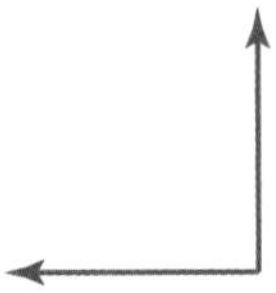

12.

13.

14.
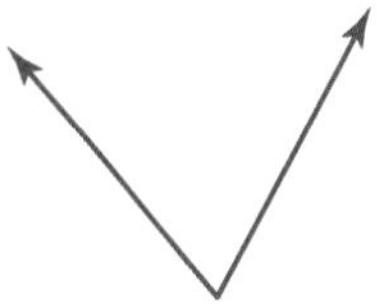

15.

Use a protractor and a straightedge to draw angles having the following measurements. **See Example 2 (p. 537)**

16. 75° **17.** 50° **18.** 45° **19.** 20°

20. 115° **21.** 175° **22.** 133° **23.** 79°

24. Estimate the measure of the smaller angle formed by the hands on the clock shown. **See Example 1 (p. 536)**

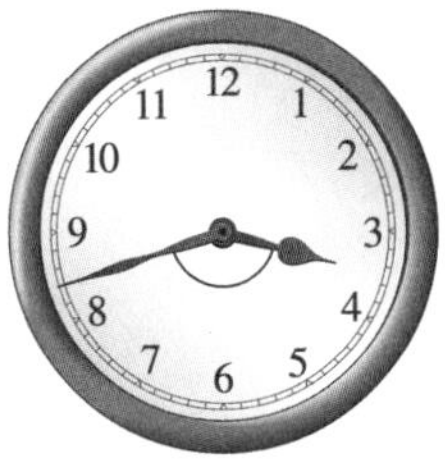

Estimate the measure of each angle. Explain your reasoning.

25.
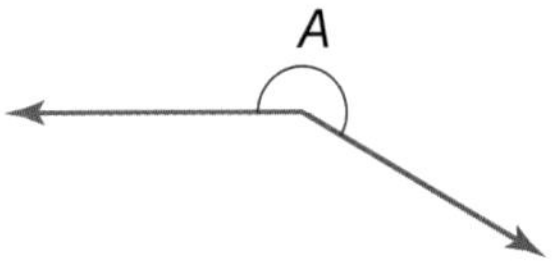

26.
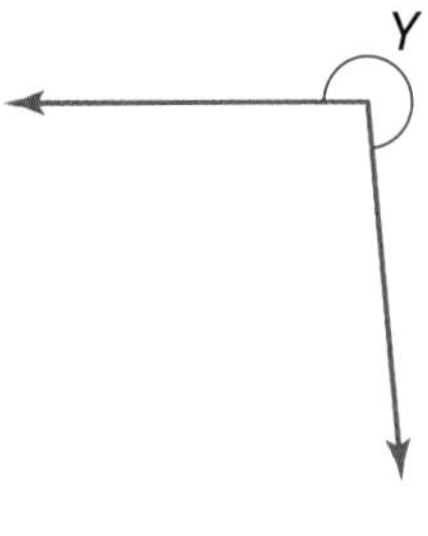

27.
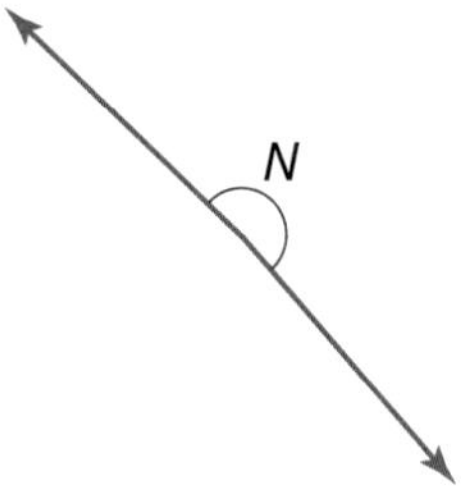

28. Use the Internet or another source to find a photo of a humpback whale. Draw an example of the angle formed by the two tail fins. Then give a reasonable estimate for the measure of this angle.

29. To be considered *safe*, a ladder should be leaned at an angle of about fifteen degrees formed by the top of the ladder and the vertical wall. Estimate the measure of the angles formed by each ladder below and determine which ladders would be considered *safe*.

a.
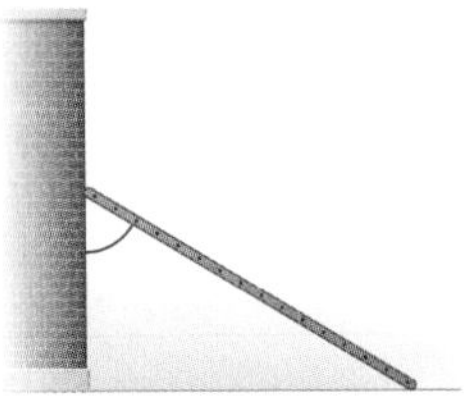

b.

c.
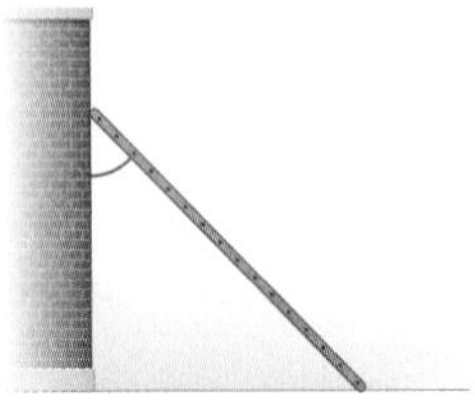

30. Most globes show that Earth's axis inclines 23.5° from vertical. Use the data below to draw diagrams that show the inclination of axis of each planet listed.

Planet	Uranus	Neptune	Jupiter	Venus
Inclination of Axis	97.9°	29.6°	3°	177.3°

31. Mr. Morales is a physical therapist. At each visit with a patient recovering from knee surgery, he determines the angle at which the patient can bend his or her knee. Do you think Mr. Morales should use estimation to track his patient's progress? Explain your reasoning.

Real-World PROBLEM SOLVING

Data File The Santa Monica Pier first opened to the public in 1909.

32. Estimate the measure of angle *A*.

33. Estimate the measure of angle *B*.

Source: santamonicapier.org

Santa Monica Pier

- The Santa Monica Pier contains many amusement rides.
- The current pier is actually two piers—the Municipal Pier and the Pleasure Pier.

H.O.T. Problems

34. CHALLENGE Estimate the measure of each angle in the figure at the right. Then analyze any relationships you observe in these angle measures.

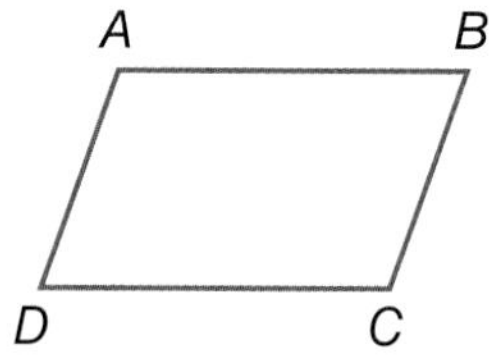

35. CHALLENGE Use a protractor and straightedge to draw a triangle with angle measures of 70°, 60°, and 50°. Label each angle with its measure.

36. OPEN ENDED Choose a capital letter that is made up of straight line segments, at least two of which meet to form an acute angle. Draw this letter using a straightedge. Label the angle ∠1. Then estimate the measure of this angle.

37. WRITING IN MATH Describe a situation in which drawing a diagram with approximate angle measures would be appropriate and useful.

Standards Practice

38 Which angle has an approximate measure of 50°?

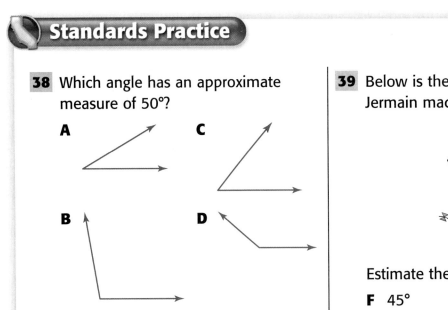

A

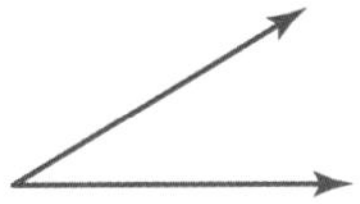

B

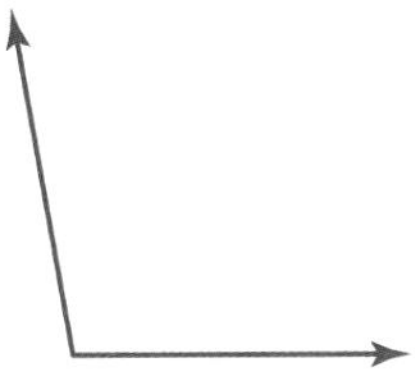

C

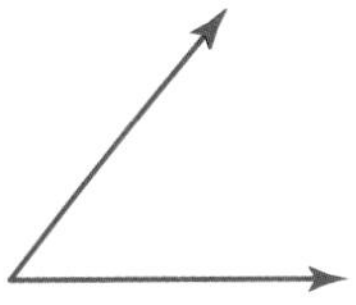

D

39 Below is the shape of a kite that Jermain made.

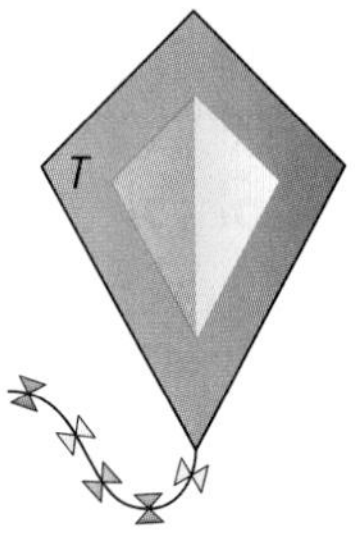

Estimate the measure of $\angle T$.

F 45° **H** 100°

G 80° **J** 140°

Spiral Review

40. A main satellite sends a signal to each of two smaller satellites. If each of those two satellites sends a signal to each other and a signal back to the main satellite, draw a diagram to determine the number of signals sent. **(Lesson 10-2)**

Use a protractor to find the measure of each angle. Then classify each angle as *acute, obtuse, right,* or *straight.* **(Lesson 10-1)**

41.

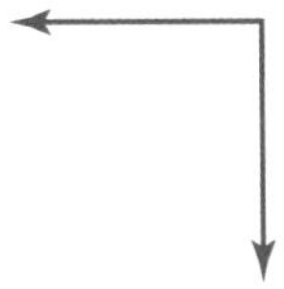

42.

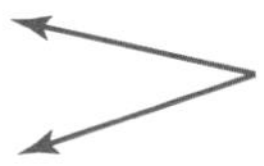

43.

For Exercises 44 and 45, refer to the graph at the right.
(Lesson 3-7)

44. What is the combined area of the two smallest oceans?

45. How many millions of square miles greater is the Pacific Ocean than the Atlantic Ocean?

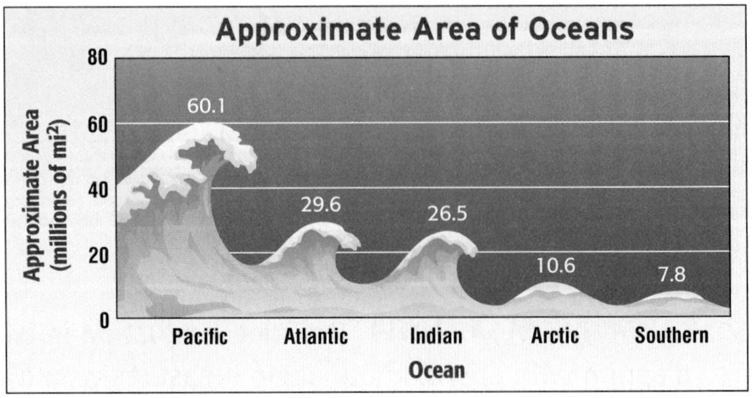

Source: *Time Almanac for Kids*

10-4 Parallel and Perpendicular Lines

GET READY to Learn

Hands-On Mini Lab

Step 1 Draw two horizontal lines on notebook paper. Then draw a line that intersects both of those lines as shown.

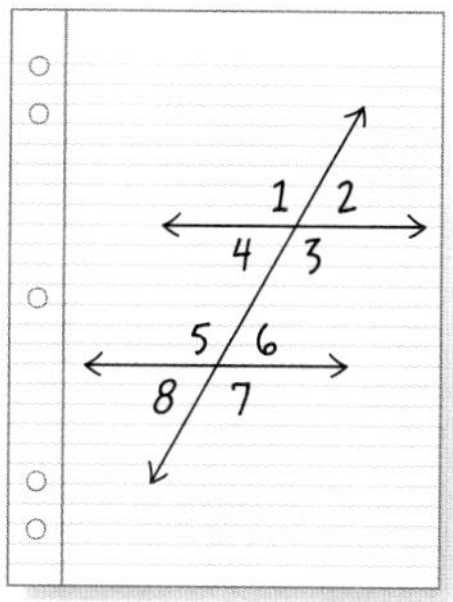

Step 2 Label the angles formed as shown.

Step 3 Use a protractor to find the measure of each numbered angle.

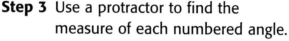

1. What is the relationship between the two horizontal lines?

2. Describe the pairs of angles that appear to have the same measure.

3. What do you notice about the measures of angles that are side by side?

4. Explain why none of the measured angles are 90°.

MAIN IDEA

I will identify and measure parallel and perpendicular lines.

Standard 5MG2.1 **Measure, identify, and draw** angles, **perpendicular and parallel lines,** rectangles, and triangles **by using appropriate tools (e.g., straightedge, ruler,** compass, **protractor,** drawing software.)

New Vocabulary

intersecting lines
parallel lines
perpendicular lines
vertical angles
congruent angles

Two lines can intersect or be parallel. **Intersecting lines** meet at a point. **Parallel lines** never intersect.

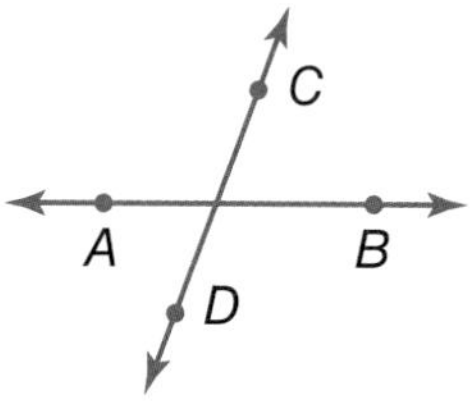

$\overleftrightarrow{CD}$ intersects $\overleftrightarrow{AB}$.

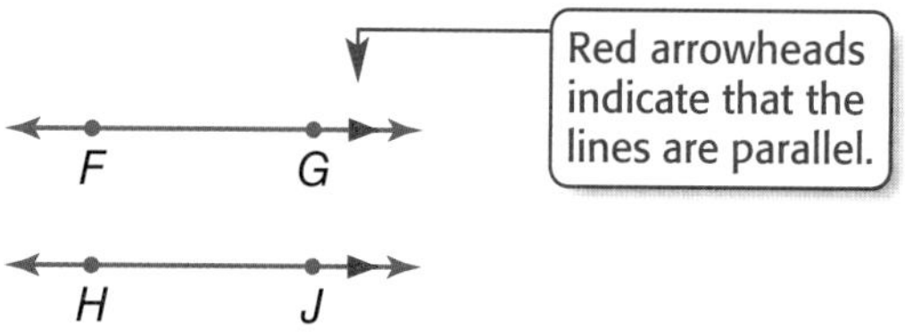

$\overleftrightarrow{FG}$ is parallel to $\overleftrightarrow{HJ}$.

Reading Math

Lines $\overleftrightarrow{CD}$ is read *line* CD.

A special case of intersecting lines is when the lines intersect to form four right angles. These are called **perpendicular lines**. In the figure at the right, $\overleftrightarrow{MN}$ is perpendicular to $\overleftrightarrow{KL}$.

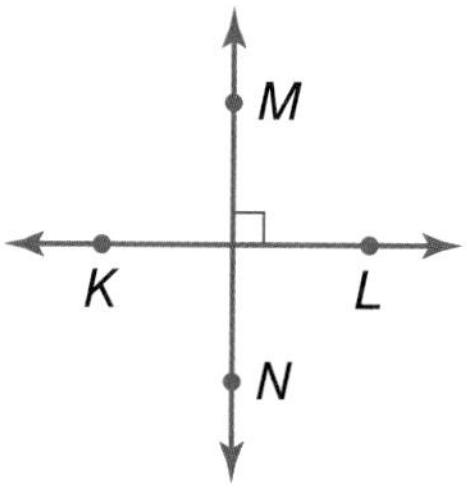

EXAMPLES Identify Parallel and Perpendicular Lines

Use the figure below to determine if each pair of lines is *parallel, perpendicular,* or *neither*.

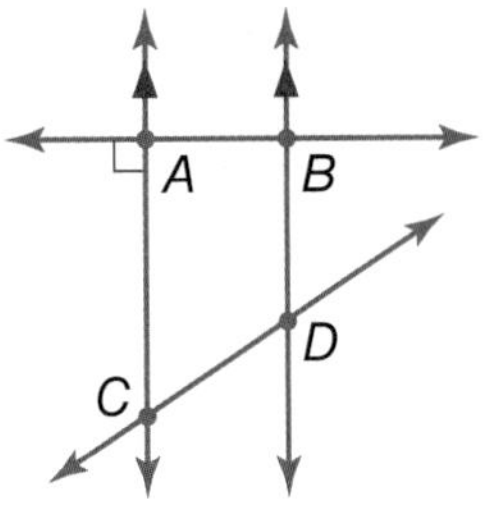

1 **$\overleftrightarrow{AC}$ and $\overleftrightarrow{AB}$**

The red square at point A indicates that $\overleftrightarrow{AC}$ and $\overleftrightarrow{AB}$ intersect at right angles. Therefore, $\overleftrightarrow{AC}$ and $\overleftrightarrow{AB}$ are perpendicular lines.

2 **$\overleftrightarrow{AC}$ and $\overleftrightarrow{BD}$**

If you extend the lengths of the lines $\overleftrightarrow{AC}$ and $\overleftrightarrow{BD}$, the lines will never intersect. Therefore, $\overleftrightarrow{AC}$ and $\overleftrightarrow{BD}$ are parallel.

3 **$\overleftrightarrow{BD}$ and $\overleftrightarrow{CD}$**

Since $\overleftrightarrow{BD}$ and $\overleftrightarrow{CD}$ intersect, they are not parallel lines. And since $\overleftrightarrow{BD}$ and $\overleftrightarrow{CD}$ do not intersect at right angles, they are not perpendicular lines either. Therefore, $\overleftrightarrow{BD}$ and $\overleftrightarrow{CD}$ are neither parallel nor perpendicular.

Online **Personal Tutor at** ca.gr5math.com

When two lines intersect, they form two pairs of opposite angles called **vertical angles**. Vertical angles have the same measure. Angles with the same measure are **congruent angles**.

Reading Math
≅ is congruent to

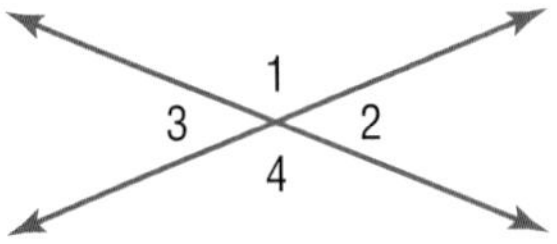

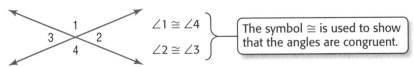

$\angle 1 \cong \angle 4$
$\angle 2 \cong \angle 3$

The symbol ≅ is used to show that the angles are congruent.

EXAMPLE Find Angle Measures

4 **Find the value of x in the figure.**

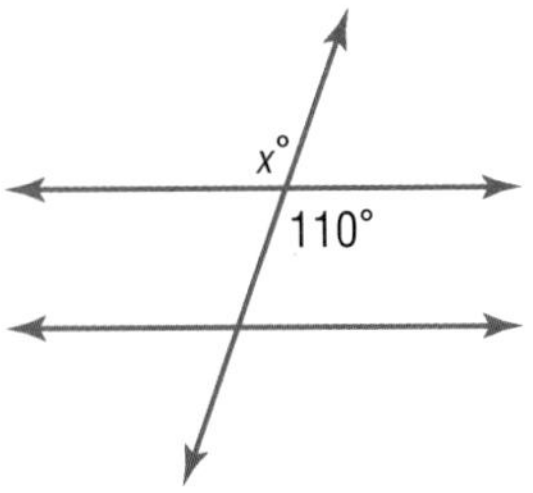

Since the two given angles are vertical angles, they are congruent.

So, the value of x is 110.

CHECK What You Know

Use the figure at the right to determine if each pair of lines is *parallel, perpendicular,* or *neither*. See Examples 1–3 (p. 542)

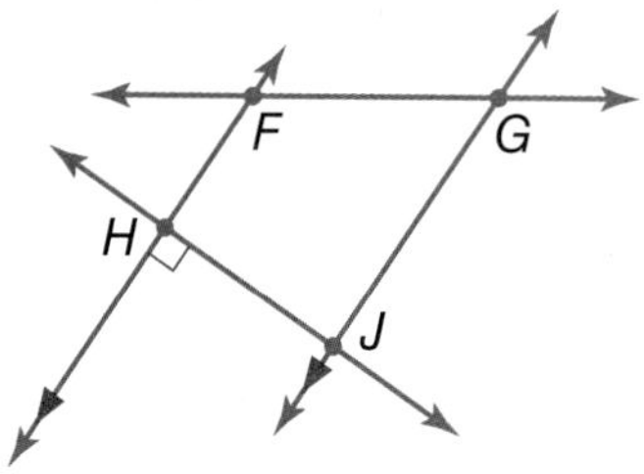

1. $\overleftrightarrow{FG}$ and $\overleftrightarrow{HJ}$

2. $\overleftrightarrow{FH}$ and $\overleftrightarrow{HJ}$

3. $\overleftrightarrow{FH}$ and $\overleftrightarrow{GJ}$

4. $\overleftrightarrow{GJ}$ and $\overleftrightarrow{FG}$

Find the value of x in each figure. See Example 4 (p. 542)

5.

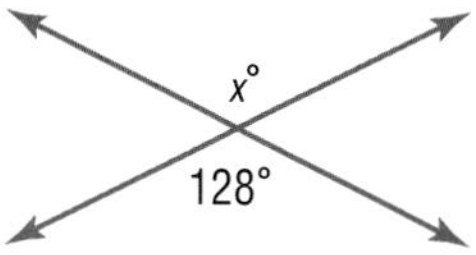

6.

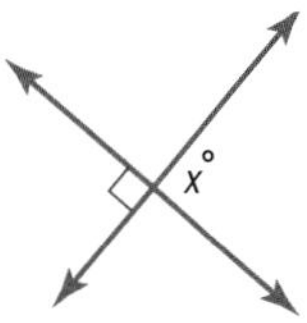

7. Are the lines marked on the picture frame best described as *parallel, perpendicular,* or *neither*? Explain your reasoning.
See Examples 1–3 (p. 542)

8. Talk About It: Give an example of a real-world situation where you would see parallel or perpendicular lines.

Practice and Problem Solving

EXTRA PRACTICE See page 683.

Use the figure at the right to determine if each pair of lines is *parallel, perpendicular,* or *neither*. See Examples 1–3 (p. 542)

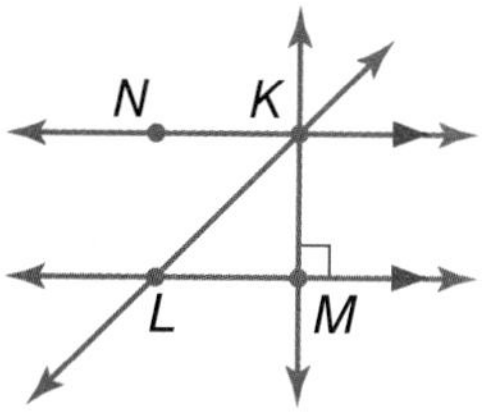

9. $\overleftrightarrow{NK}$ and $\overleftrightarrow{LM}$

10. $\overleftrightarrow{KL}$ and $\overleftrightarrow{LM}$

11. $\overleftrightarrow{KM}$ and $\overleftrightarrow{LM}$

12. $\overleftrightarrow{KL}$ and $\overleftrightarrow{NK}$

13. Are the lines marked on the photo of the stairs best described as *parallel, perpendicular,* or *neither*? Explain your reasoning. See Examples 1–3 (p. 542)

Find the value of x in each figure. See Example 4 (p. 542)

14.

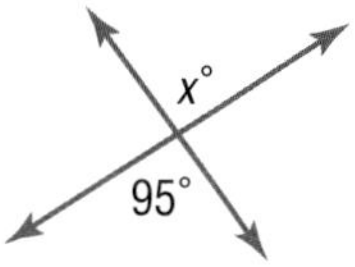

15.

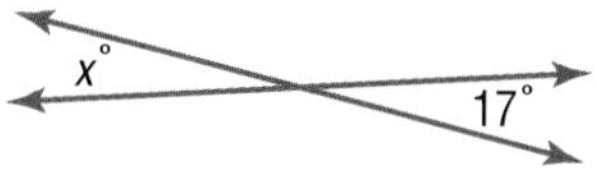

16.

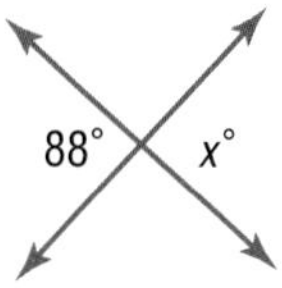

17.

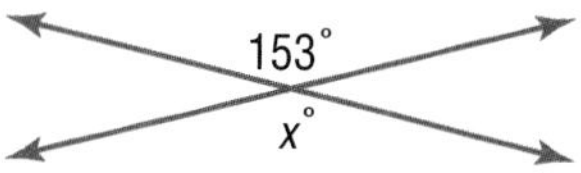

18. Are the lines marked on the map best described as *parallel*, *perpendicular*, or *neither*? Explain your reasoning.

19. Draw two parallel lines. Then draw a line that intersects both of the parallel lines. Measure each angle formed by the three lines.

H.O.T. Problems

CHALLENGE Determine whether each statement is *sometimes*, *always*, or *never* true. Explain your reasoning.

20. Parallel lines meet at exactly one point.

21. Intersecting lines are perpendicular.

22. Perpendicular lines form at least one right angle.

23. WRITING IN ▸MATH Describe the difference between parallel and perpendicular lines.

Standards Practice

24 Which of the following best describes the figure below?

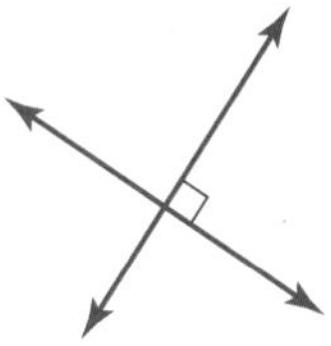

A 45° angles

B obtuse angles

C parallel lines

D perpendicular lines

25 Which of the following best describes the figure below?

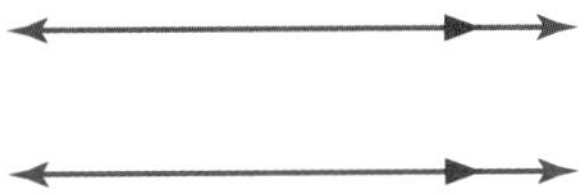

F acute angles

G parallel lines

H perpendicular lines

J right angles

Spiral Review

Use a protractor and a straightedge to draw angles having the following measurements. **(Lesson 10-3)**

26. 75° **27.** 25° **28.** 110°

29. There are 10 people at Alita's birthday party. If each person shakes hands with everyone else exactly once, how many total handshakes will be given at the party? **(Lesson 10-2)**

Extend

Geometry Lab for 10-4
Constructions

MAIN IDEA

I will draw perpendicular and parallel lines.

Standard 5MG2.1 Measure, identify, and **draw angles, perpendicular and parallel lines,** rectangles, and triangles **by using appropriate tools (e.g., straightedge,** ruler, **compass,** protractor, drawing software.**)**

In Lesson 10-4, you identified perpendicular and parallel lines. In this lab, you will construct them using a compass and straightedge.

ACTIVITY Construct Perpendicular Lines

1 **Step 1** Draw a line with point C using a straightedge.

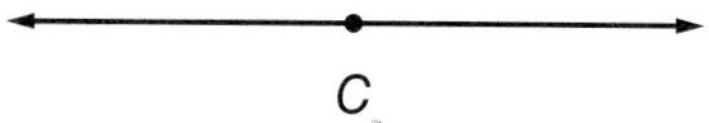

Step 2 Place the compass at point C. Using the same compass setting, draw two *arcs* as shown. Label the points of intersection A and B.

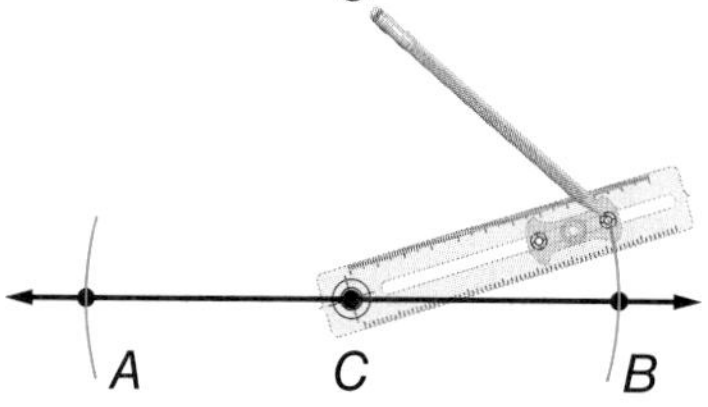

Step 3 Using a setting greater than segment AC, place the compass at point A. Draw an arc above the line as shown.

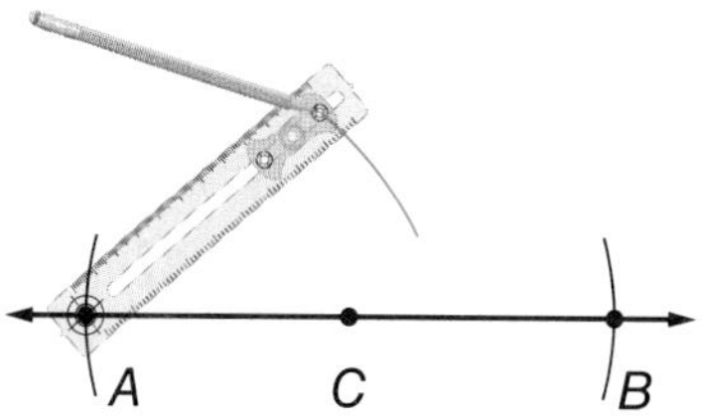

Step 4 Using the same setting, place the compass at point B. Draw an arc intersecting the arc drawn in Step 3. Label the point of intersection D.

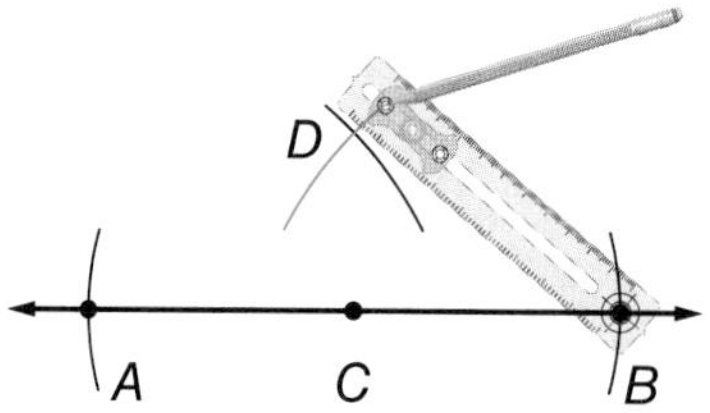

Step 5 Use a straightedge to draw $\overleftrightarrow{CD}$.

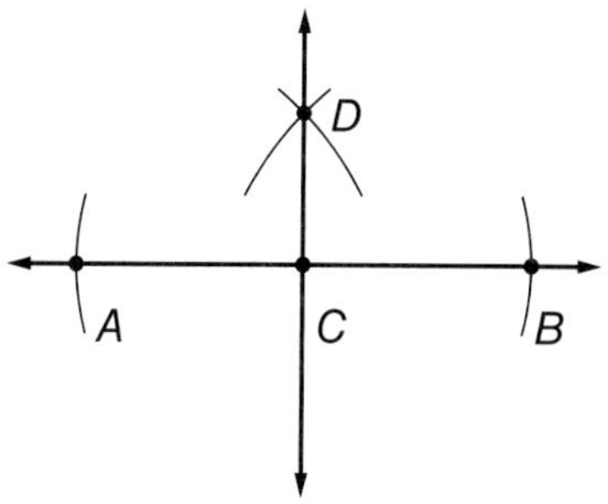

So, $\overleftrightarrow{AB}$ is perpendicular to $\overleftrightarrow{DC}$.

Reading Math

Arcs Arcs are part of a circle.

ACTIVITY Construct Parallel Lines

2 **Step 1** Use a straightedge to draw $\angle M$ as shown.

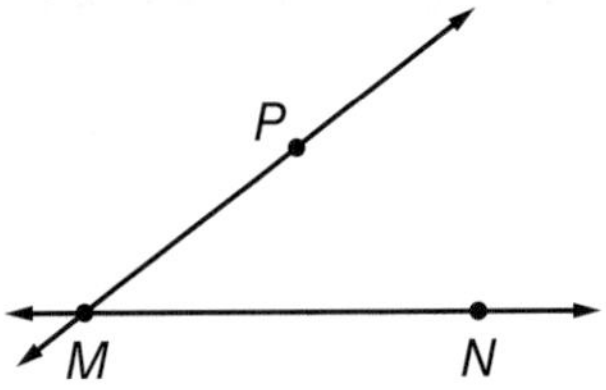

Step 2 Place the compass at point *M*. Draw an arc that intersects both sides of $\angle M$. Label the points of intersection *Q* and *R*.

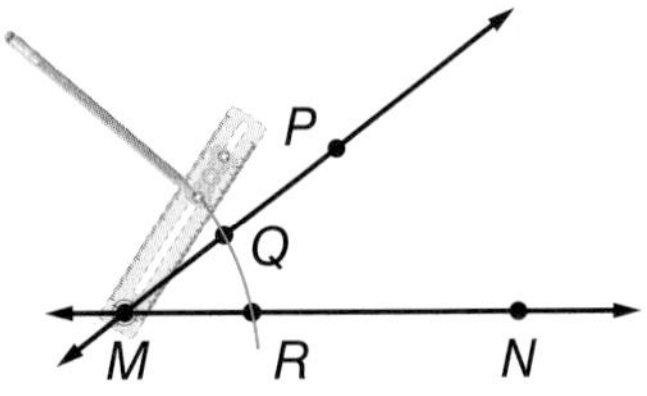

Step 3 Using the same setting, place the compass at point *P*. Draw an arc as shown. Label the point of intersection *S*.

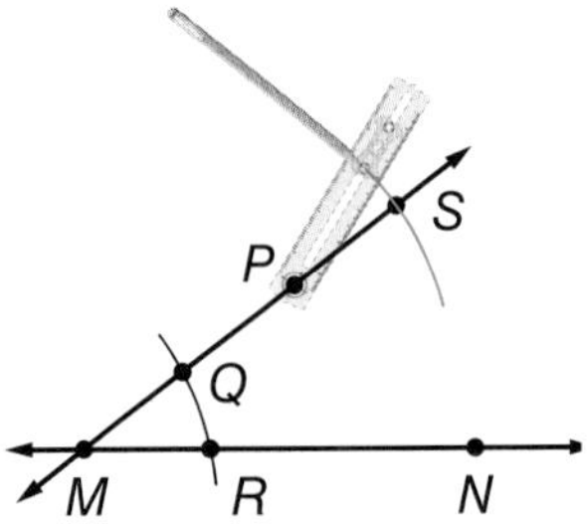

Step 4 Place the compass at point *R* and adjust so that the pencil tip is on point *Q*. Using this setting, place the compass at point *S*. Draw an arc that intersects the arc drawn in Step 3. Label the point of intersection *T*.

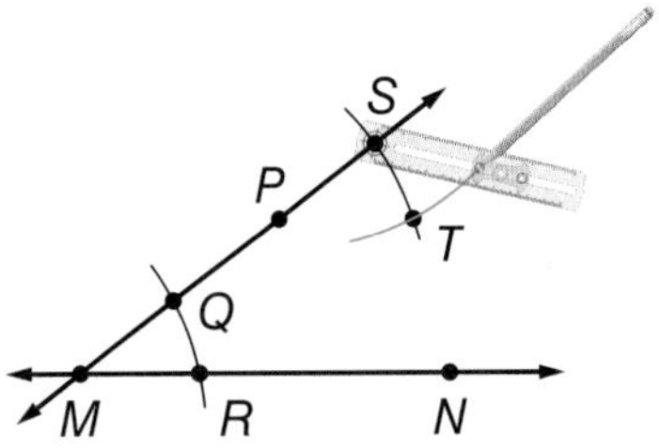

Step 5 Use a straightedge to draw $\overleftrightarrow{PT}$.

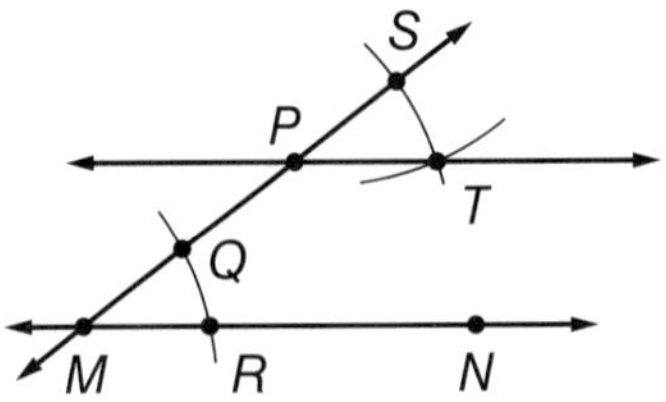

So, $\overleftrightarrow{PT}$ is parallel to $\overleftrightarrow{MN}$.

Remember

$\angle M$ is read *angle M*.

Analyze the Results

1. Draw a line segment. Then construct a square in which the segment is the length of each side.
2. A *parallelogram* is a four-sided figure with opposite sides that are parallel and congruent. Construct a parallelogram.

Mid-Chapter Check

CHAPTER 10

Lessons 10-1 through 10-4

Use a protractor to find the measure of each angle. Then classify each angle as *acute, obtuse, right,* or *straight.* **(Lesson 10-1)**

1.

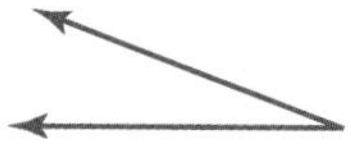

2.

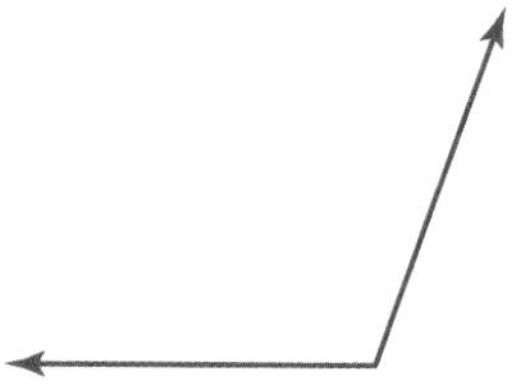

3. **STANDARDS PRACTICE** Find the measure of $\angle HJE$ to the nearest degree. **(Lesson 10-1)**

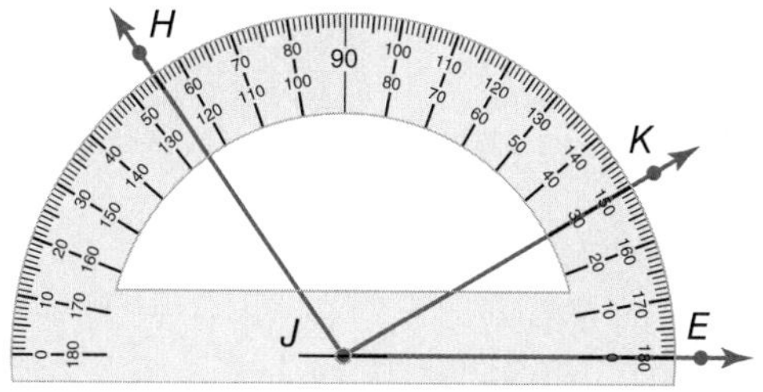

A 180° **C** 90°

B 125° **D** 30°

4. Brianna is placing a wallpaper border around her bedroom. One wall is 8 feet long. She has wallpapered $\frac{3}{4}$ of this wall. Draw a diagram to determine how much of the wall is left to wallpaper. **(Lesson 10-2)**

5. Estimate the measure of $\angle R$ on the leaf rake shown. **(Lesson 10-3)**

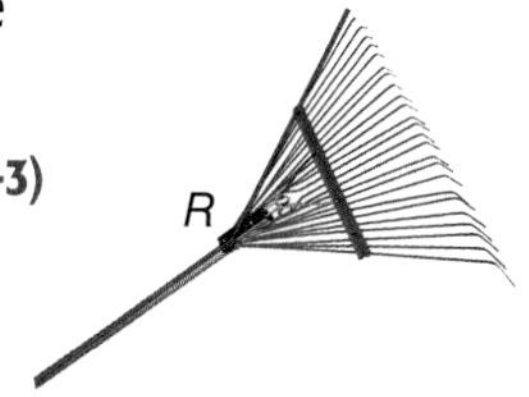

Use a protractor to draw angles having the following measurements. **(Lesson 10-3)**

6. 35° **7.** 110° **8.** 80°

9. **STANDARDS PRACTICE** Which angle measures between 45° and 90°? **(Lesson 10-3)**

F

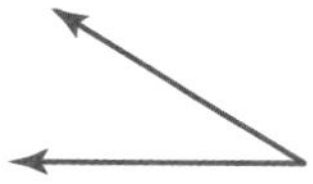

H

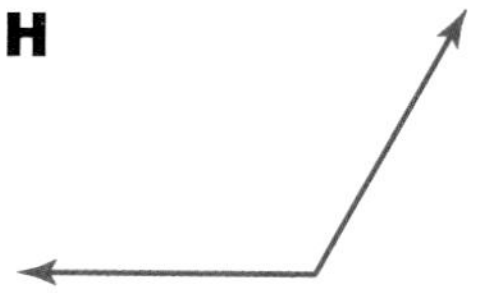

G

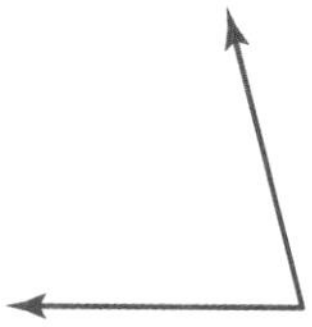

J

Use the figure below to determine if the pair of lines are *parallel, perpendicular,* or *neither.* **(Lesson 10-4)**

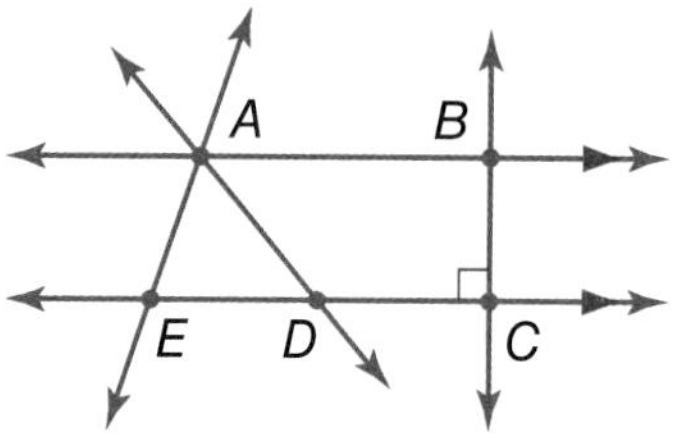

10. $\overleftrightarrow{BC}$ and $\overleftrightarrow{EC}$

11. $\overleftrightarrow{AB}$ and $\overleftrightarrow{DC}$

12. $\overleftrightarrow{AD}$ and $\overleftrightarrow{BC}$

13. Find the value of x. **(Lesson 10-4)**

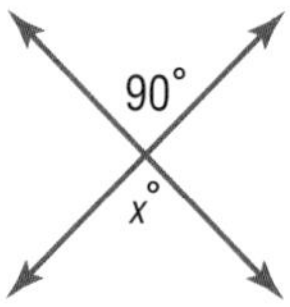

14. **WRITING IN MATH** Draw a rectangle. Then describe any sides that appear to be parallel and any sides that appear to be perpendicular. **(Lesson 10-4)**

10-5 Problem-Solving Investigation

MAIN IDEA I will choose the best strategy to solve a problem.

Standard 5MR1.1 **Analyze problems by identifying relationships,** distinguishing relevant from irrelevant information, sequencing and prioritizing information, **and observing patterns.** Standard 5MG2.1 Measure, identify, and **draw** angles, perpendicular and parallel lines, **rectangles, and triangles by using appropriate tools.**

P.S.I. TEAM +

EMELIA: I recently made my own quilt pattern. I pieced together triangles to make squares of different sizes. The first square is made from 2 triangles, the second square is made from 8 triangles, and the third square is made from 18 triangles. The quilt will have squares of 5 different sizes.

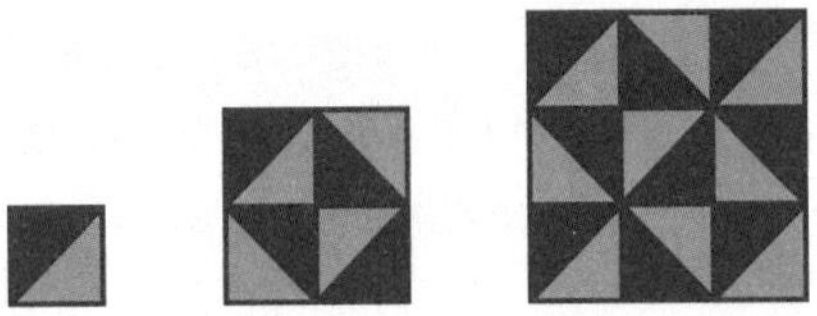

YOUR MISSION: Find how many triangles are in the fifth square.

Understand	You know how many triangles are in the first, second, and third squares. You need to find how many triangles are in the fifth square.
Plan	Look for a pattern to find the number of triangles.
Solve	Each square has twice as many triangles as small squares. First square 2×1 or 2 triangles Second square 2×4 or 8 triangles Third square 2×9 or 18 triangles Continuing the pattern, the fourth square has 2×16 or 36 triangles and the fifth square has 2×25 or 50 triangles.
Check	Draw the fifth square and count the number of triangles. Since there are 50 triangles in the fifth square, the answer is correct. ✓

Mixed Problem Solving

EXTRA PRACTICE
See page 683.

Use any strategy shown below to solve each problem.

PROBLEM-SOLVING STRATEGIES
- Look for a pattern.
- Draw a diagram.
- Guess and check.

1. Which is more, $\frac{3}{8}$ of a pizza or $\frac{1}{3}$ of the same pizza?

2. Elena has 8 different shirts and 3 pairs of pants. If she wears a different combination of shirts and pants each day, how many days will pass before she must repeat an outfit?

3. Mr. Brooks left San Diego at 3:00 P.M. and arrived in Bakersfield at 8:00 P.M., driving a distance of approximately 240 miles. During his trip, he took a one-hour dinner break. What was Mr. Brooks' average speed in miles per hour?

4. Draw the next figure.

5. In 2007, 25 parents were members of the band booster club at King Middle School. Membership increased to 40 parents in 2008 and 55 parents in 2009. If the trend continues, about how many parents can be expected to be members of the band booster club in 2010?

6. A number multiplied by itself is 676. What is the number?

7. Refer to the Venn diagram. If there are 28 students in the class, determine the number of students that are in both the safety patrol and the writing club.

Safety Patrol and Writing Club

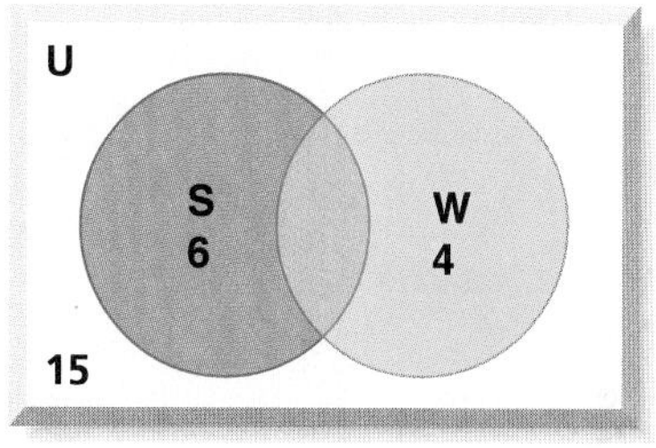

U = all students in the class
S = safety patrol W = writing club

8. Jennifer's aunt is four times as old as Jennifer. In 16 years, her aunt will be twice her age. How old is Jennifer now?

9. At a business meeting, everyone shook hands with everyone else exactly once. There were a total of 36 handshakes. How many people were at the party?

10. How many times greater is the length of the longest side in the triangle below than the length of the shortest side?

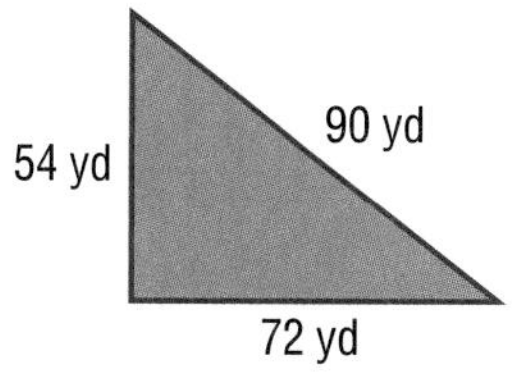

11. **WRITING IN MATH** Describe how you might use the *draw a diagram* strategy to solve Exercise 1. Are there any disadvantages of using this strategy?

Explore

Geometry Lab for 10-6
Angles in Triangles

Triangle means *three angles*. In this lab, you will explore how the three angles of a triangle are related.

MAIN IDEA

I will explore the relationship among the angles of a triangle.

Standard 5MG2.2 Know that the sum of the angles of any triangle is 180° and the sum of the angles of any quadrilateral is 360° and use this information to solve problems.
Standard 5MR3.3 Develop generalizations of the results obtained and apply them in other circumstances.

Concepts in Motion

Animation
ca.gr5math.com

ACTIVITY

Step 1 Draw a triangle similar to the one shown below on notebook or construction paper.

Step 2 Label the corners 1, 2, and 3. Then tear each corner off.

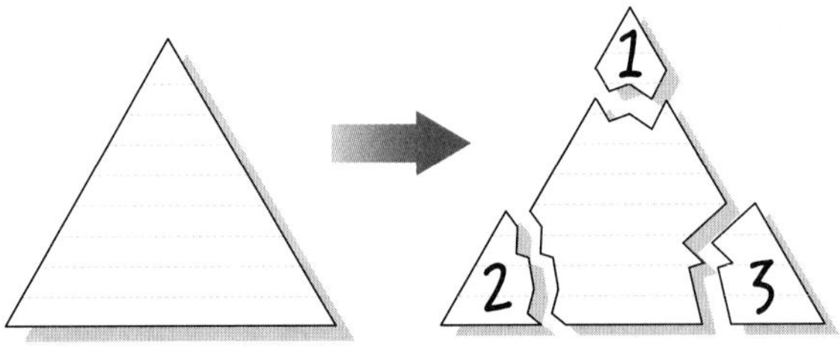

Step 3 Rearrange the torn pieces so that the corners all meet at one point as shown.

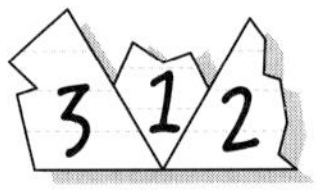

Step 4 Repeat steps 1 and 2 with two different triangles.

Analyze the Results

1. What does each torn corner represent?
2. The point where these three corners meet is the vertex of another angle as shown. Classify this angle as right, acute, obtuse, or straight. Explain.

3. What is the measure of this angle?
4. What is the sum of the measures of angles 1, 2, and 3 for each of your triangles? Verify your conjecture by measuring each angle using a protractor.
5. What can you conclude about the sum of the measures of the angles of any triangle?

10-6 Triangles

MAIN IDEA

I will classify triangles and find missing angle measures in triangles.

Standard 5MG2.1 **Measure, identify, and draw** angles, perpendicular and parallel lines, rectangles, and **triangles by using appropriate tools.**

Standard 5MG2.2 **Know that the sum of the angles of any triangle is 180°** and the sum of the angles of any quadrilateral is 360° **and use this information to solve problems.**

New Vocabulary

- acute triangle
- right triangle
- obtuse triangle
- line segment
- congruent segments
- scalene triangle
- isosceles triangle
- equilateral triangle

GET READY to Learn

Hands-On Mini Lab

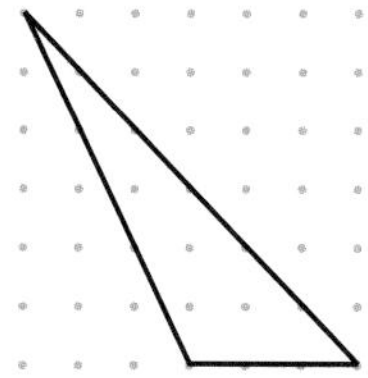

Step 1 Draw the triangle shown at the right on dot paper. Then cut it out.

Step 2 Measure each angle of the triangle and label each angle with its measure.

The triangle shown above has two acute angles. Since the third angle is obtuse, the triangle is an *obtuse triangle.*

1. Repeat the activity with nine other triangles.
2. Sort your triangles into three groups based on the measure of the largest angle in the triangles. Name the groups *acute, right,* and *obtuse.*

All triangles have at least two acute angles and can be classified according to the angle measure of its third angle.

KEY CONCEPT — Classify Triangles Using Angles

Acute Triangle	Right Triangle	Obtuse Triangle
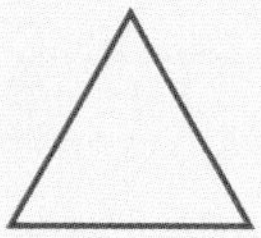	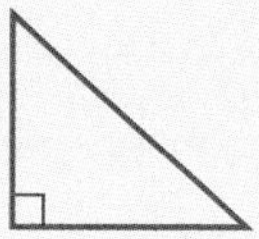	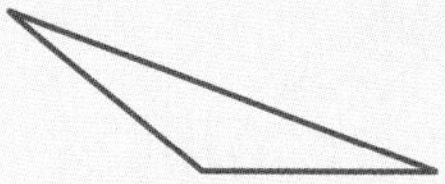
all acute angles	1 right angle	1 obtuse angle

EXAMPLE Classify a Triangle by Its Angles

Classify each triangle as *acute, right,* or *obtuse.*

1

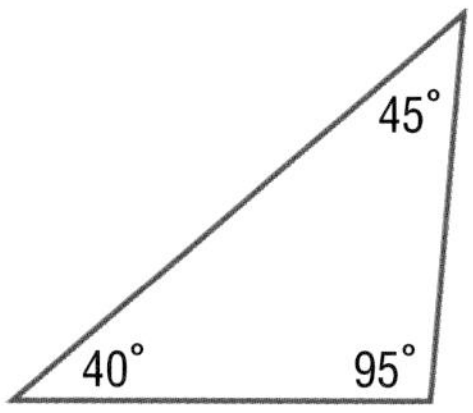

The 95° angle is obtuse. The triangle is obtuse.

2

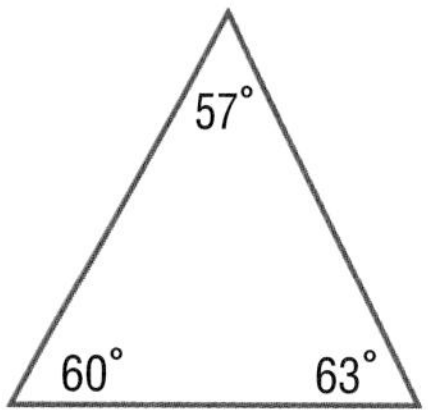

All the angles are acute. The triangle is acute.

In the Lab on page 550, you discovered the following relationship.

KEY CONCEPT **Sum of Angle Measures in a Triangle**

Words The sum of the measures of the angles in a triangle is 180°.

Model

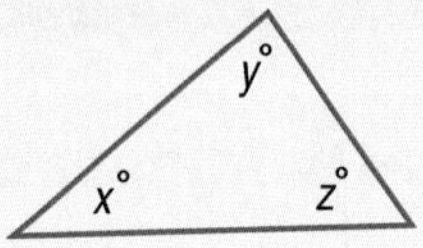

Symbols $x° + y° + z° = 180°$

You can find a missing angle measure by using the fact that the sum of the measures of the angles is 180°.

EXAMPLE **Find Angle Measures**

3 **Algebra Find the value of *x* in the triangle.**

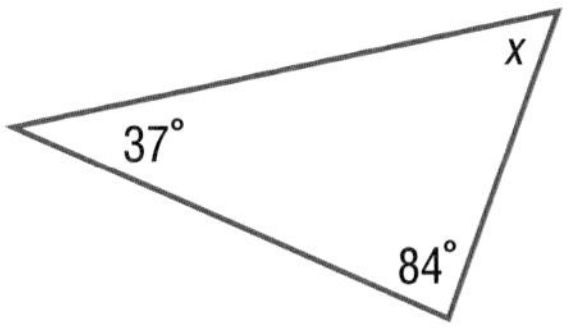

Since the sum of the angle measures in a triangle is 180°, $x + 37 + 84 = 180$.

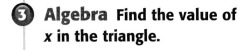

$x + 37 + 84 =$	180	Write the equation.
$x + 121 =$	180	Add 37 and 84.
$-121 =$	-121	Subtract 121 from each side.
$x =$	59	Simplify.

So, the value of x is 59.

Remember

If you know two of the angle measures in a triangle, you can find the third angle measure by subtracting the two known measures from 180°. The value of x is $180 - 55 - 90$ or 35.

Real-World EXAMPLE

4 **Algebra Find the value of *x* in the Antigua and Barbuda flag.**

The three angles marked are the angles of a triangle. Since the sum of the angle measures in a triangle is 180°, $x + 55 + 90 = 180$.

$x + 55 + 90 =$	180	Write the equation.
$x + 145 =$	180	Add 55 and 90.
$-145 =$	-145	Subtract 145 from each side.
$x =$	35	Simplify.

So, the value of x is 35.

Online **Personal Tutor at** ca.gr5math.com

Reading Math

Segments $\overline{AB}$ is read as *segment AB*.

You can also classify triangles by their sides. Each side of a triangle is a **line segment**, or a straight path between two points. Line segments are named by their endpoints. So the sides of the triangle below are $\overline{AB}$, $\overline{BC}$, and $\overline{AC}$.

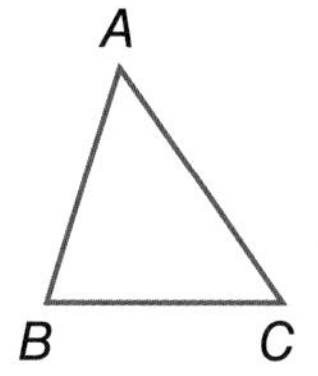

Line segments that have the same length are called **congruent segments**. On a figure, congruent sides are indicated by the tick marks on the sides of the figure.

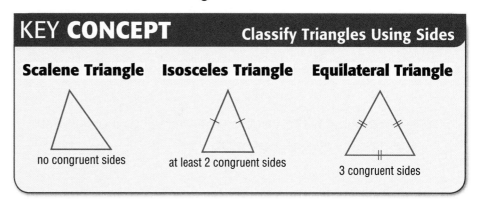

KEY CONCEPT — Classify Triangles Using Sides

Scalene Triangle

no congruent sides

Isosceles Triangle

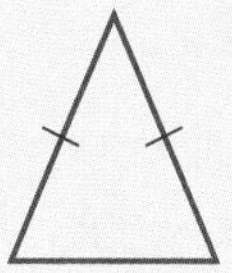

at least 2 congruent sides

Equilateral Triangle

3 congruent sides

Since an isosceles triangle is defined as having *at least* two congruent sides, all equilateral triangles are also isosceles.

EXAMPLES Classify a Triangle by Its Sides

Classify each triangle as *scalene*, *isosceles*, or *equilateral*.

5

Only two of the sides are congruent.
So, the triangle is an isosceles triangle.

6

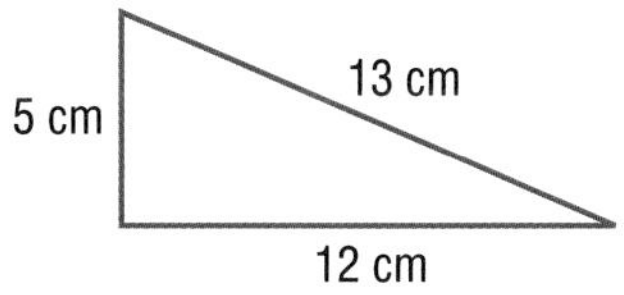

None of the sides are congruent.
So, the triangle is a scalene triangle.

CHECK What You Know

Classify each triangle as *acute, right,* or *obtuse.* See Examples 1, 2 (p. 551)

1.
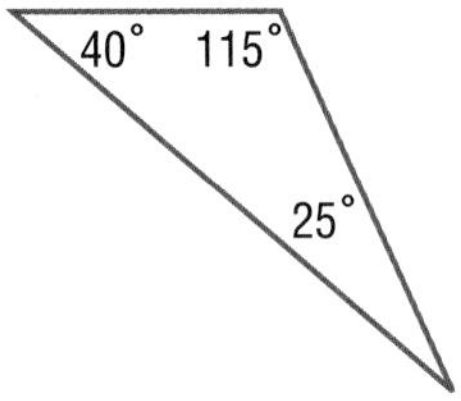

2.
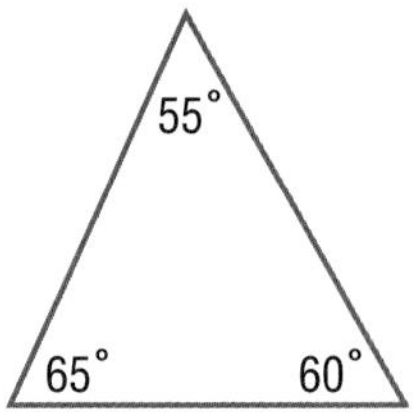

Algebra Find the value of *x* in each triangle. See Examples 3, 4 (p. 552)

3.
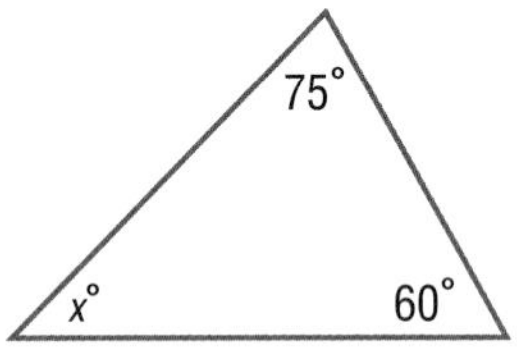

4.
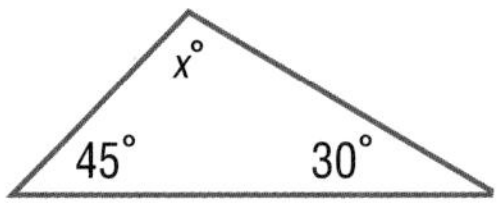

5. Algebra What is the value of *x* in the sail of the sailboat at the right? See Examples 3, 4 (p. 552)

Classify each triangle as *scalene, isosceles,* or *equilateral.* See Examples 5, 6 (p. 553)

6.
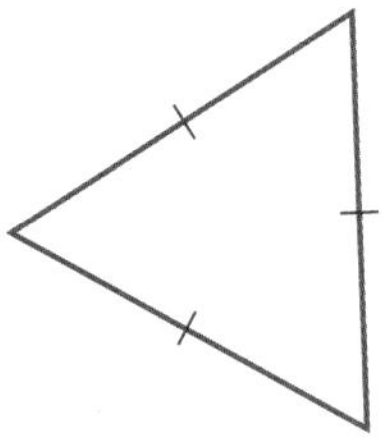

7.
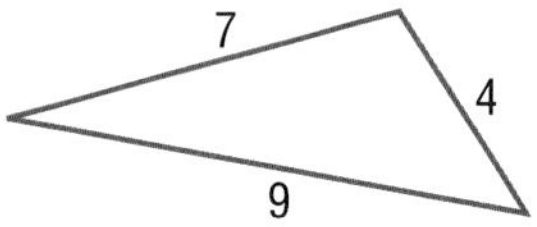

8. Talk About It Explain why a triangle must always have at least two acute angles.

Practice and Problem Solving

EXTRA PRACTICE
See page 684.

Classify each triangle drawn or having the given angle measures as *acute, right,* or *obtuse.* See Examples 1, 2 (p. 551)

9.
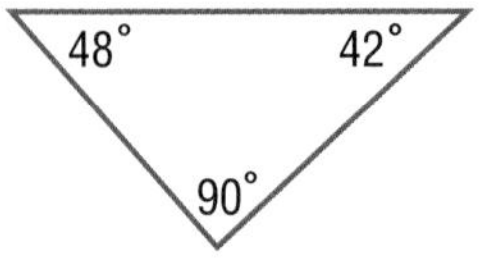

10.
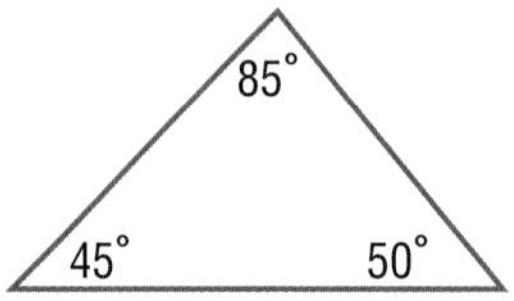

11.
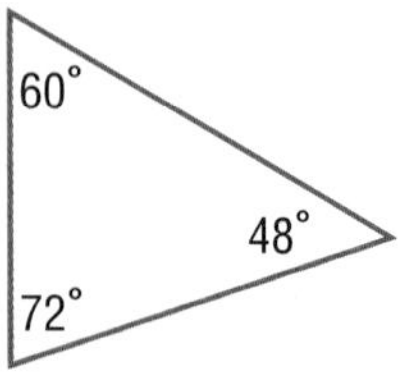

12. 100°, 45°, 35°

13. 90°, 75°, 15°

14. 114°, 33°, 33°

Algebra Find the value of x in each triangle drawn or having the given angle measures. See Examples 3, 4 (p. 552)

15.
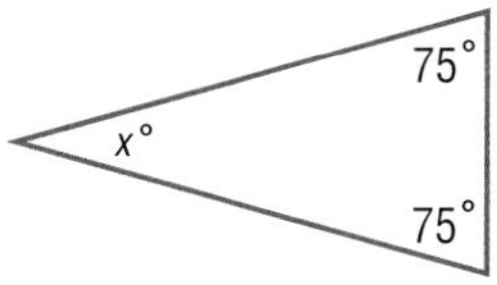

16.
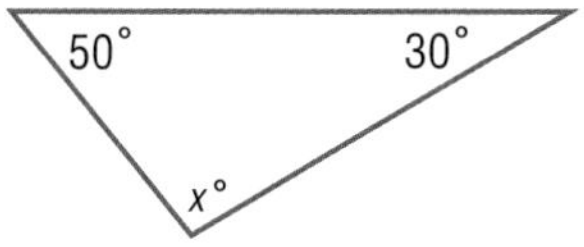

17.
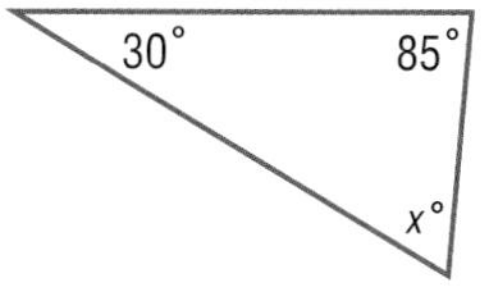

18. 70°, 60°, x°

19. x°, 60°, 25°

20. x°, 35°, 25°

21. The diagram below shows the view of the top of Fountain Place in Dallas. What is the value of x?
See Example 4 (p. 552)

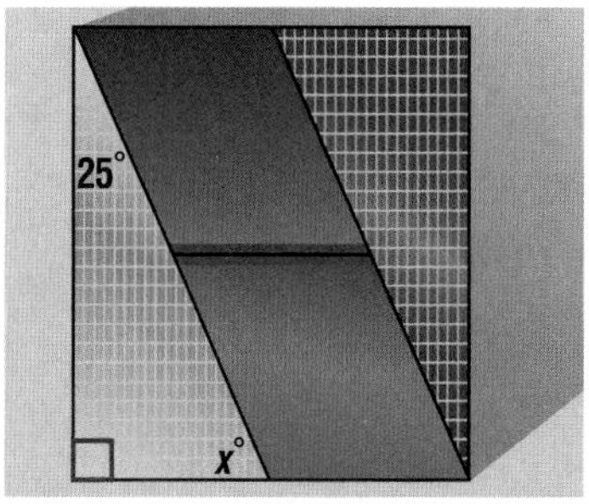

22. An A-frame picnic shelter at George Rogers Clark Historic Park in Ohio is shown below. What is the value of x?
See Example 4 (p. 552)

Classify each triangle drawn or described as *scalene, isosceles*, or *equilateral*. See Examples 5, 6 (p. 553)

23.
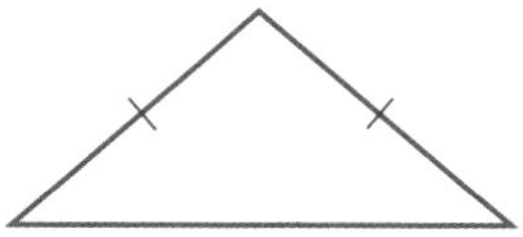

24.
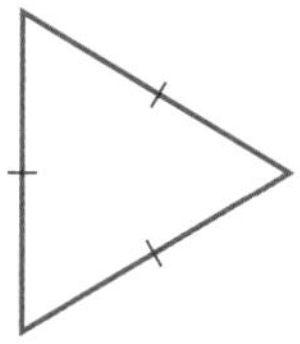

25.
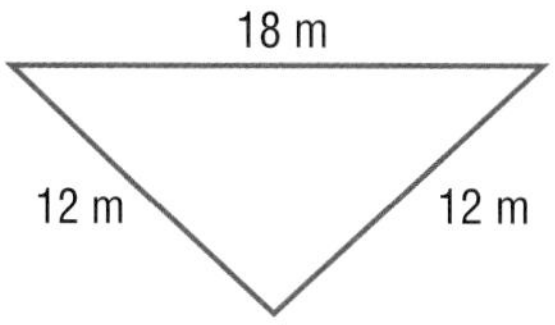

26. sides: 9 in., 11 in., 13 in.

27. sides: 5 cm, 6 cm, 5 cm

28. What is the measure of the third angle of a triangle if one angle measures 25° and the second angle measure 50°?

29. What is the measure of the third angle of a right triangle if one of the angles measures 30°?

Measure the angles and sides of each triangle. Classify each triangle as *acute, right*, or *obtuse*. Then classify each triangle as *scalene, isosceles*, or *equilateral*.

30.
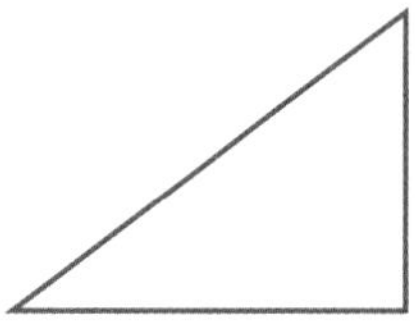

31.
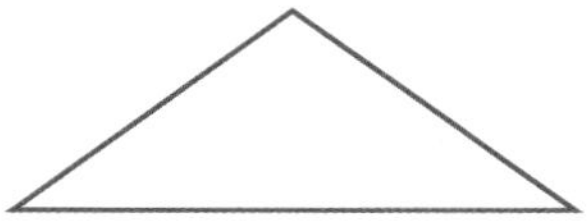

32.
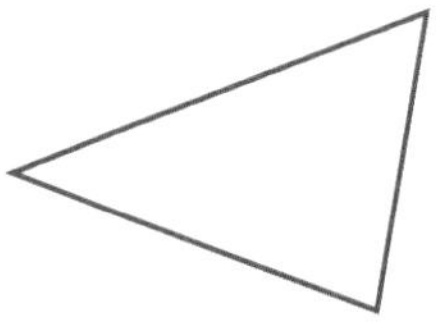

H.O.T. Problems

33. OPEN ENDED Draw an obtuse scalene triangle using a ruler and protractor. Label each side and angle with its measure.

34. CHALLENGE Apply what you know about the sum of the measures of the angles of a triangle to find the values of *x* and *y* in the figure at the right. Justify your answer.

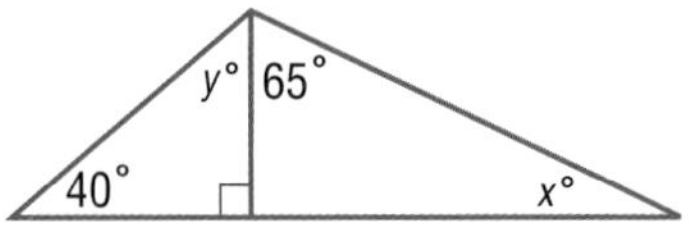

35. WRITING IN MATH Explain how to construct an equilateral triangle using a compass and a straightedge.

Standards Practice

36 What is the value of *x* in the flag frame below?

A 20° **C** 90°

B 45° **D** 100°

37 Triangle *ABC* is isosceles. If the measure of $\angle B$ is 48° and the measures of $\angle A$ and $\angle C$ are equal, what is the measure of $\angle A$?

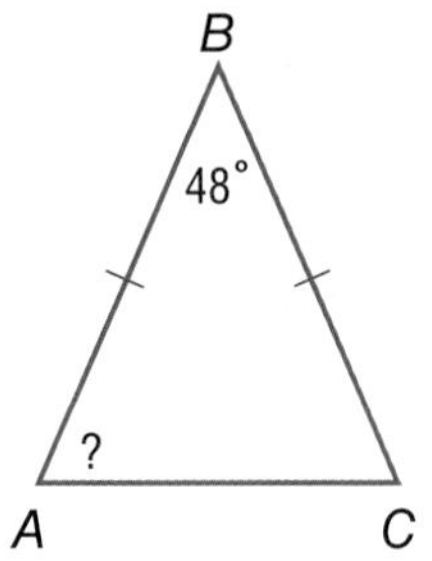

F 24° **H** 66°

G 48° **J** 90°

Spiral Review

38. Anoki is on the school swim team. His best time for the 100-meter freestyle race is 47.45 seconds. What is his speed in meters per second for this race? Round to the nearest tenth. **(Lesson 10-5)**

Use the figure at the right to determine if each pair of lines is *parallel, perpendicular,* or *neither.* **(Lesson 10-4)**

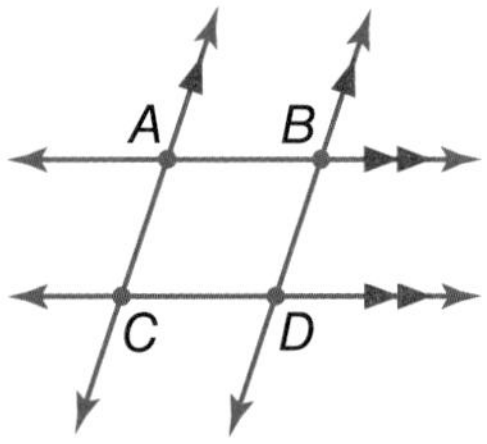

39. $\overleftrightarrow{AC}$ and $\overleftrightarrow{BD}$

40. $\overleftrightarrow{AC}$ and $\overleftrightarrow{AB}$

41. Twenty-seven percent of the students in Ms. Malan's class are female. Identify the complement of selecting a female student at random from the class. Then find its probability. **(Lesson 9-8)**

Algebra Evaluate each expression if $m = 88.2$, $n = 3$, and $p = 17.5$. Round to the nearest tenth if necessary. **(Lesson 6-5)**

42. $\frac{mp}{n}$

43. $\frac{p}{n}$

44. $\frac{m + n + p}{p}$

Explore

Geometry Lab for 10-7
Angles in Quadrilaterals

MAIN IDEA

I will explore the relationship among the angles of different quadrilaterals.

Standard 5MG2.2 Know that the sum of the angles of any triangle is 180° and **the sum of the angles of any quadrilateral is 360°** and use this information to solve problems.
Standard 5MR1.1 Analyze problems by identifying relationships, distinguishing relevant from irrelevant information, sequencing and prioritizing information, and **observing patterns.**

Quadrilateral means *four sides*. Four-sided figures also have four angles. In this lab, you will explore how the angles of different quadrilaterals are related.

ACTIVITY

Step 1 Draw the quadrilaterals shown on grid paper.

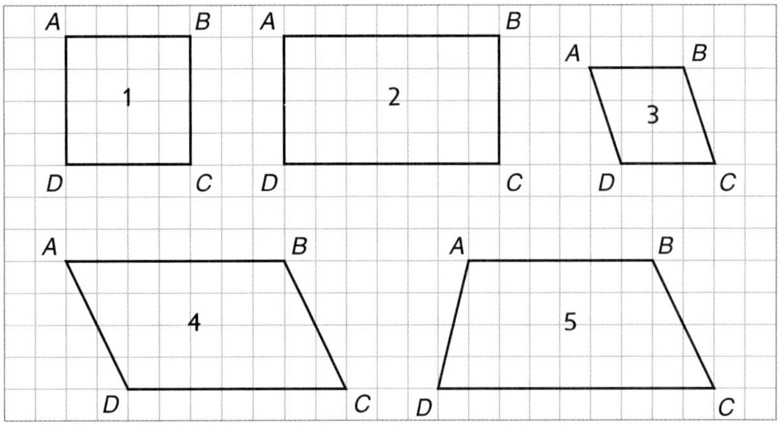

Step 2 Use a protractor to measure the angles of each figure. Record your results in a table like the one shown.

Quadrilateral	$m\angle A$	$m\angle B$	$m\angle C$	$m\angle D$	Sum of Angles
1					
2					
3					
4					
5					

Analyze the Results

1. Describe any patterns you see in the sum of the angle measurements of Quadrilaterals 1–5.

2. Describe any patterns you see in the angle measurements of opposite angles.

3. Are there any additional patterns found in Quadrilaterals 1 and 2 that are not present in Quadrilaterals 3 and 4?

10-7 Quadrilaterals

GET READY to Learn

Hands-On Mini Lab

The figure below is a **quadrilateral**, since it has four sides and four angles.

Step 1 Draw a quadrilateral.

Step 2 Pick one vertex and draw a segment to the opposite vertex.

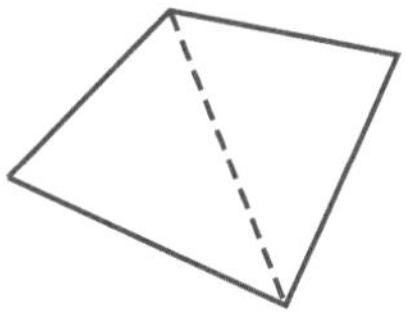

1. How many triangles were formed?
2. Use the relationship among the angle measures in a triangle to find the sum of the angle measures in a quadrilateral. Explain.

MAIN IDEA

I will classify quadrilaterals and find missing angle measures in quadrilaterals.

Standard 5MG2.1 Measure, identify, and draw angles, perpendicular and parallel lines, **rectangles,** and triangles **by using appropriate tools.**

Standard 5MG2.2 Know that the sum of the angles of any triangle is 180° and **the sum of the angles of any quadrilateral is 360° and use this information to solve problems.**

New Vocabulary

- quadrilateral
- rectangle
- square
- parallelogram
- rhombus
- trapezoid

The angles of a quadrilateral have a special relationship.

KEY CONCEPT — Angles of a Quadrilateral

Words The sum of the measures of the angles of a quadrilateral is 360°.

Model

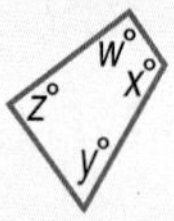

Symbols $w° + x° + y° + z° = 360°$

EXAMPLE Find Angle Measures

1 Algebra Find the value of *x* in the quadrilateral.

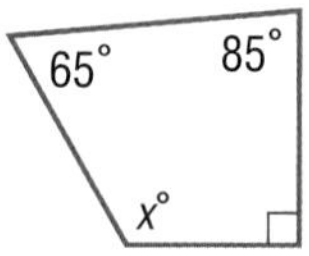

Since the sum of the angle measures in a quadrilateral is 360°, $x + 65 + 85 + 90 = 360$.

$x + 65 + 85 + 90 = 360$	Write the equation.
$x + 240 = 360$	Add 65, 85, and 90.
$-240 = -240$	Subtract 240 from each side.
$x = 120$	Simplify.

So, the value of x is 120.

Reading Math

Congruent Angles

The red arcs show congruent angles.

KEY CONCEPT — Classifying Quadrilaterals

Quadrilateral	Figure	Characteristics
Rectangle	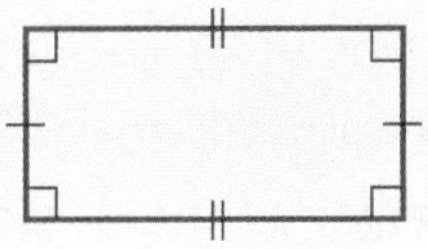	• Opposite sides congruent • All angles are right angles • Opposite sides parallel
Square	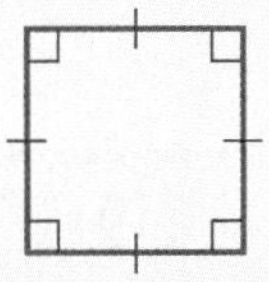	• All sides congruent • All angles are right angles • Opposite sides parallel
Parallelogram	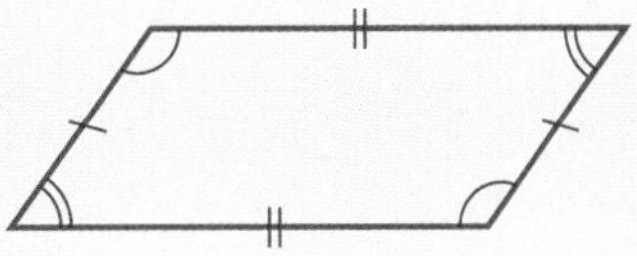	• Opposite sides congruent • Opposite sides parallel • Opposite angles congruent
Rhombus	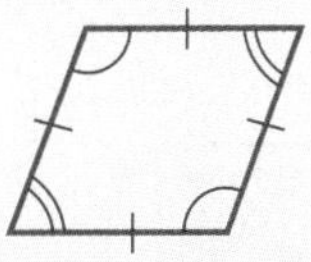	• All sides congruent • Opposite sides parallel • Opposite angles congruent
Trapezoid	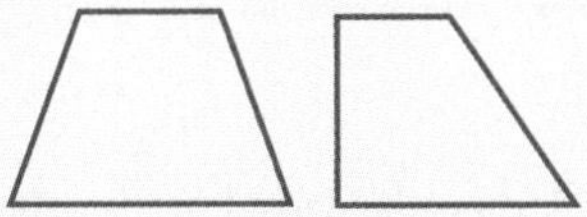	• Exactly one pair of opposite sides parallel

Real-World EXAMPLE — Classify Quadrilaterals

2 **Classify the quadrilaterals labeled 1 and 2 in the quilt piece.**

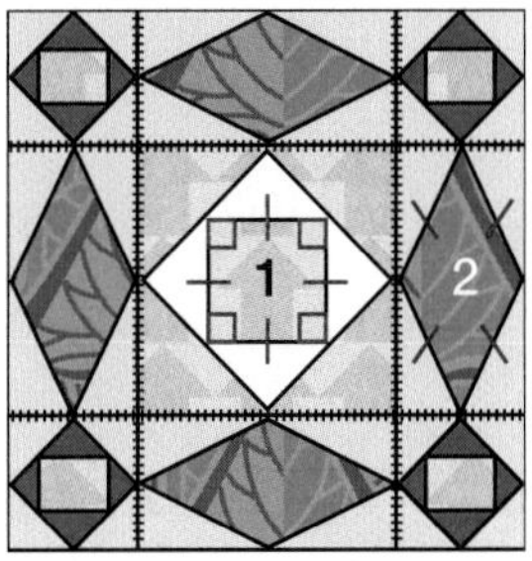

Figure 1 is a square. Figure 2 is a rhombus.

EXAMPLE Find Angle Measures

3 What is the value of x in the parallelogram at the right?

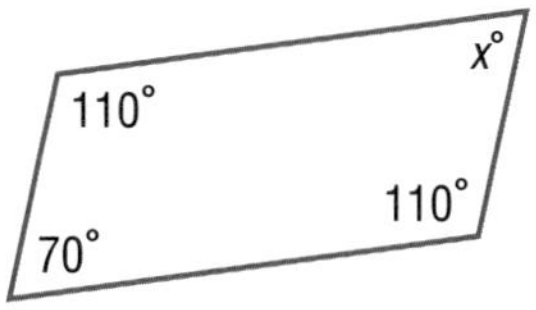

You know that in a parallelogram, opposite angles are congruent. Since the angle opposite the missing measure has a measure of 70°, $x = 70$.

Check $70° + 110° + 70° + 110° = 360°$ ✓

Online **Personal Tutor at** ca.gr5math.com

CHECK What You Know

Algebra Find the value of x in each quadrilateral. See Example 1 (p. 558)

1.

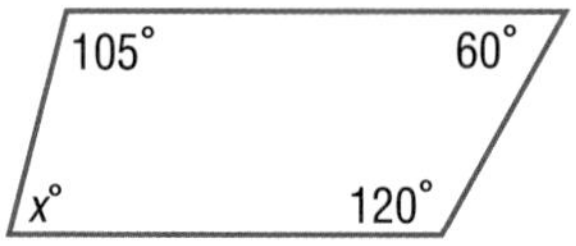

2.

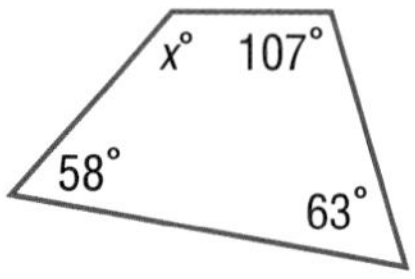

3.

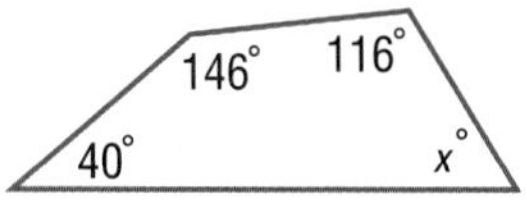

4.

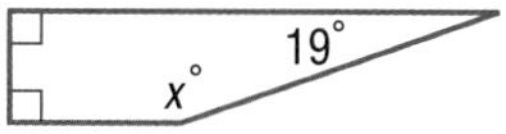

5. Classify each quadrilateral. See Example 2 (p. 559)

6. Safari Stereo created the logo shown below for use in their new advertisement. Classify the quadrilaterals used in the logo.
See Example 2 (p. 559)

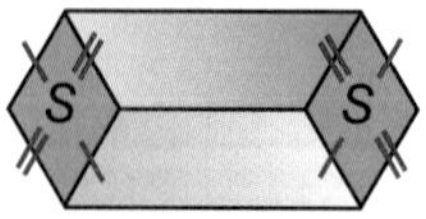

7. Algebra Find the value of x in the parallelogram at the right.
See Example 3 (p. 560)

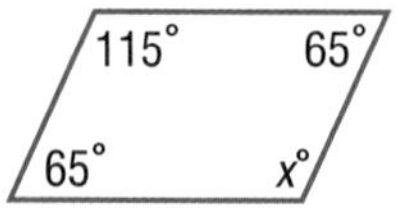

8. Talk About It Describe two different real-world items that are shaped like quadrilaterals. Then classify those quadrilaterals.

Practice and Problem Solving

EXTRA PRACTICE
See page 684.

Algebra Find the value of *x* in each quadrilateral. See Examples 1, 3 (pp. 558, 560)

9.
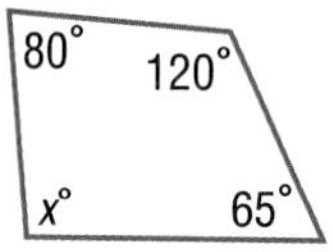

10.
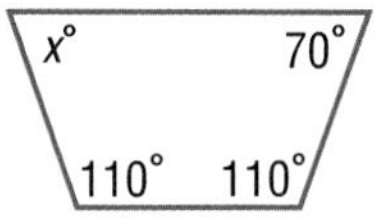

11.
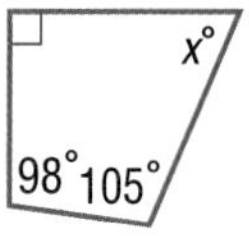

12.
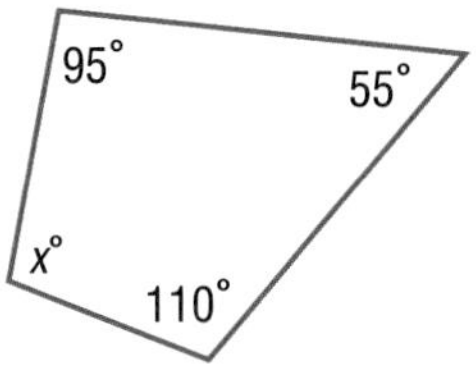

13.
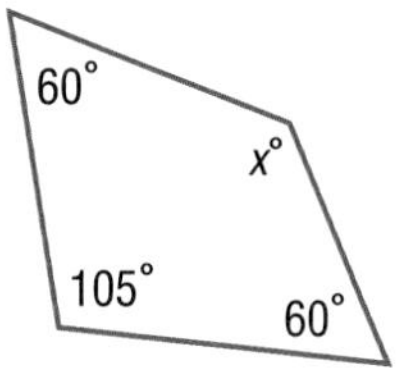

14.
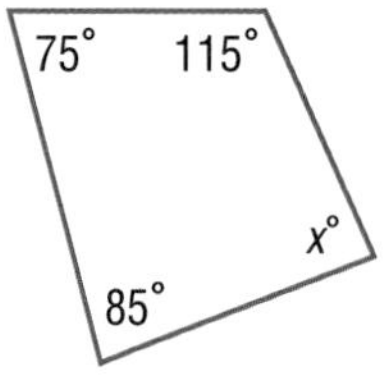

Classify each quadrilateral. See Example 2 (p. 559)

15.
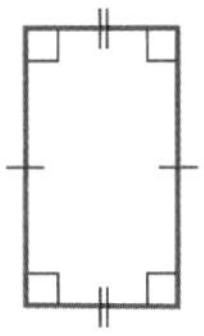

16.
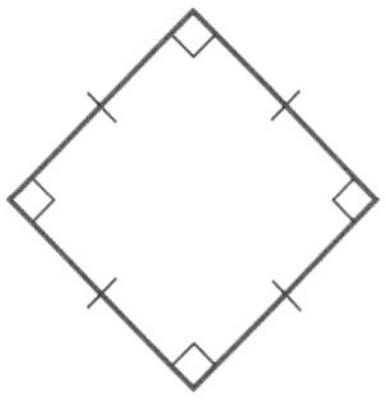

17.
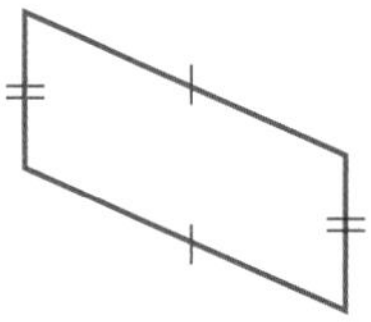

18.
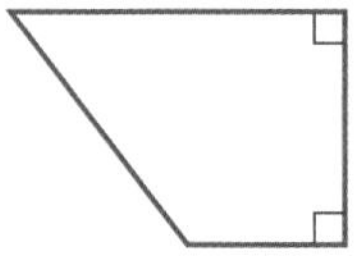

19.
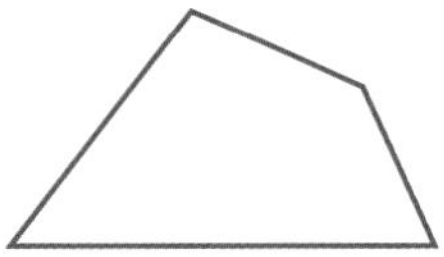

20.
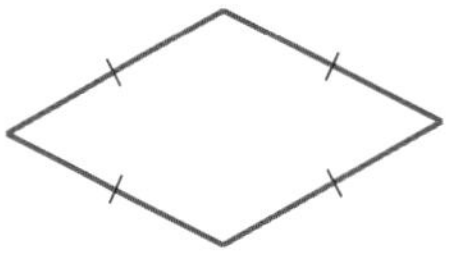

21. Many aircraft display the shape of the American flag slightly distorted to indicate motion. Classify each quadrilateral. See Example 2 (p. 559)

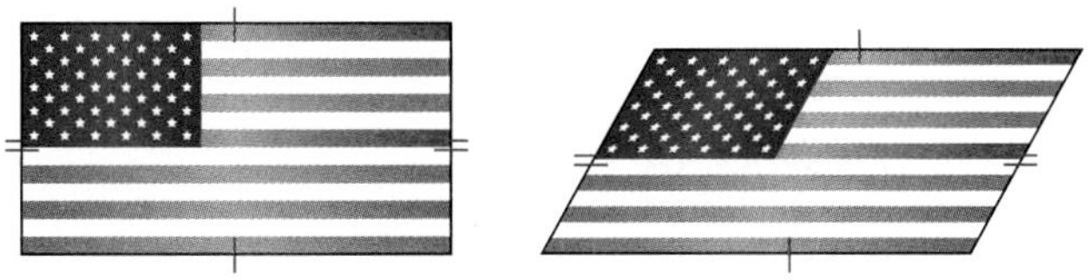

22. Classify each quadrilateral. See Example 2 (p. 559)

Measure the angles and sides of each quadrilateral. Then use this information to classify each quadrilateral.

23.

24.
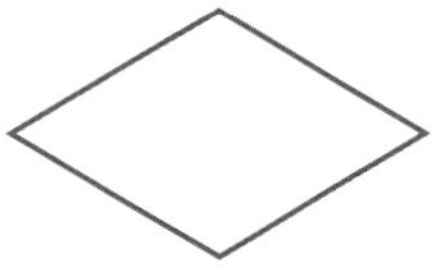

25.

26. Grace sorted a set of quadrilaterals into two categories according to a certain rule. The shapes that followed the rule were put in Set A, and the shapes that did not follow the rule were put in Set B.

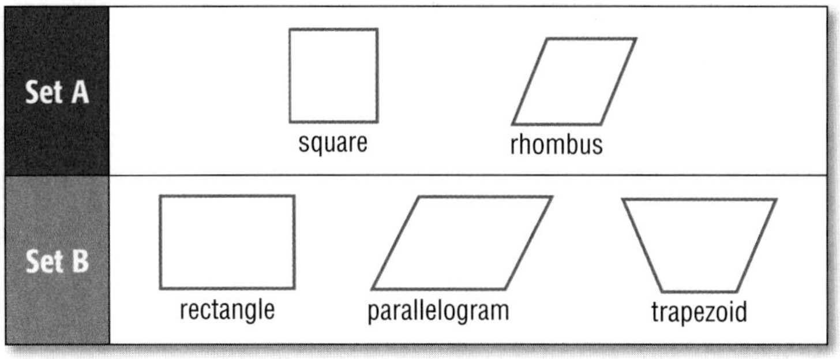

What rule did Grace use to sort the quadrilaterals?

27. Use the Internet or another source to look up the meaning of the term *isosceles trapezoid.* Explain how an isosceles trapezoid is related to an isosceles triangle. Then draw an example of an isosceles trapezoid.

H.O.T. Problems

28. **OPEN ENDED** Draw a rectangle using a ruler and protractor. Label each side and angle with its measure. Label all parallel and perpendicular lines.

29. **NUMBER SENSE** Three of the angle measures of a quadrilateral are congruent. Without calculating, determine if the measure of the fourth angle in each of the following situations is greater than, less than, or equal to 90°. Explain your reasoning.

a. The three congruent angles each measure 89°.

b. The three congruent angles each measure 90°.

c. The three congruent angles each measure 91°.

CHALLENGE **Determine whether each statement is *sometimes, always,* or *never* true. Explain your reasoning.**

30. A rhombus is a square.

31. A quadrilateral is a parallelogram.

32. A rectangle is a square.

33. A square is a rectangle.

34. **SELECT A TOOL** Quentin is designing a logo for his lawn care company. He wants to use polygons in the logo. Which of the following tools might Quentin use to design several sample logos? Justify your selection(s). Use the tool(s) to create a sample logo using polygons. Then classify each polygon you used in the sample logo.

real objects | paper/pencil | technology

35. **WRITING IN ▶MATH** Make a diagram that shows the relationship between each of the following shapes: rectangle, parallelogram, square, rhombus, quadrilateral, and trapezoid. Then write a few sentences that explain your diagram.

Standards Practice

36 The drawing below shows the shape of Hinto's patio.

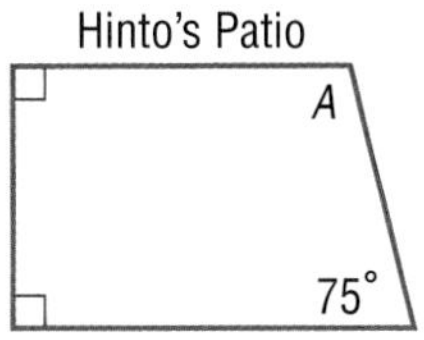

Find the measure of $\angle A$.

A 75°

B 105°

C 165°

D 195°

37 A parallelogram is shown below. Find the measure of $\angle M$ to the nearest degree.

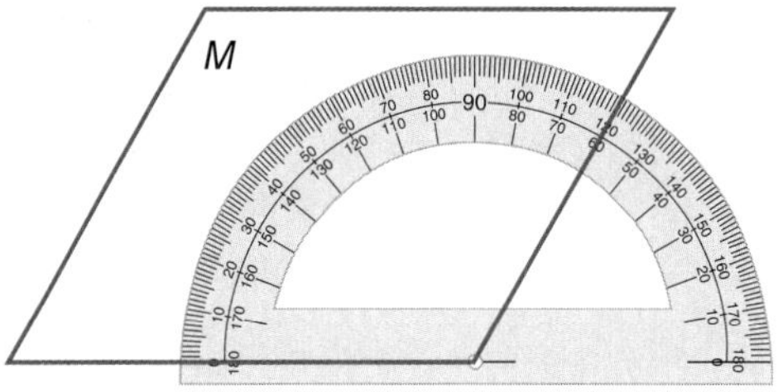

F 30° **H** 120°

G 60° **J** 150°

Spiral Review

Algebra Find the value of *x* in each triangle. **(Lesson 10-6)**

38.

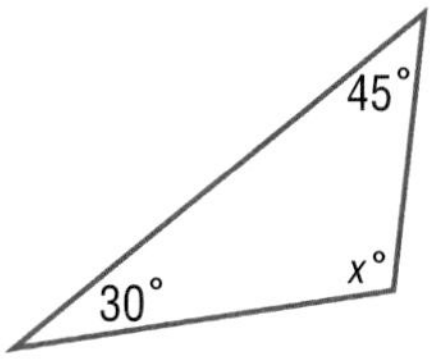

39.

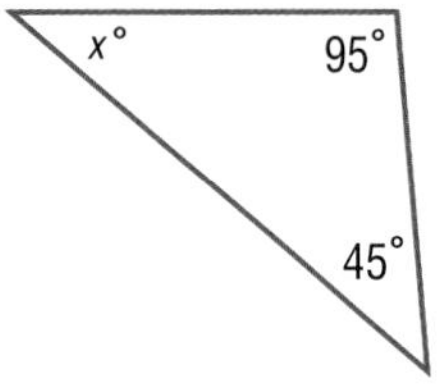

40.

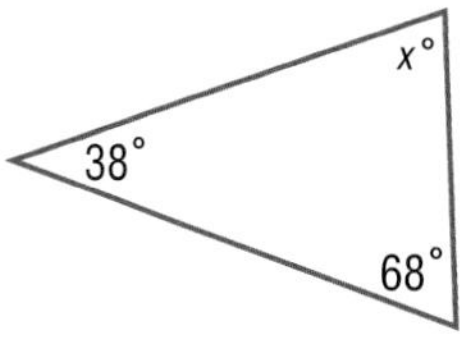

41. Tamika is working on a group project with 3 other students. They must decide who will be the researcher, the artist, the writer, and the presenter. How many ways can they choose to assign the jobs? **(Lesson 10-5)**

42. **Geometry** Determine if the pair of lines marked on the polygon is best described as *parallel*, *perpendicular*, or *neither*. **(Lesson 10-4)**

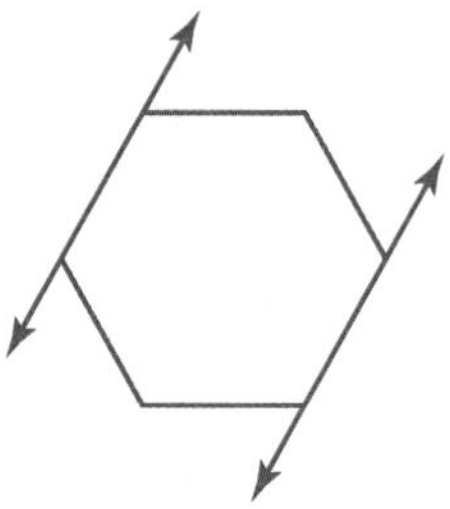

43. Mallory needs $4\frac{3}{4}$ cups of flour for a bread recipe. Write $4\frac{3}{4}$ as an improper fraction. **(Lesson 4-4)**

Problem Solving in Art

POMPEII PATTERNS

Pompeii was a popular vacation spot for wealthy members of the ancient Roman Empire. The city had houses that were designed in classic Roman style. This style was characterized by using a variety of geometrical shapes and patterns. Many of the houses included murals painted on the walls, decorative fountains, and patterned mosaic floors.

In the year 79, nearby Mount Vesuvius erupted violently, spewing lava and ash throughout Pompeii. For 1,600 years, the city and its residents were lost under Mount Vesuvius' ashes. Today, scientists continue to uncover buildings and artworks at the site.

Did You Know?

The city of Pompeii was accidentally rediscovered by an Italian architect named Fontana in 1599.

Math Standard 5MG2.1 Measure, **identify**, and draw **angles, perpendicular and parallel lines, rectangles, and triangles** by using appropriate tools (e.g., straightedge, ruler, compass, protractor, drawing software.)

Real-World Math

Use the image above of the design on a Pompeii building to solve each problem.

1. Identify all of the geometric figures in the design.

2. Where do you see acute angles in the design?

3. Where do you see obtuse angles in the design?

4. Are there any right angles in the design? If so, where?

5. Where in the design do you see parallel lines?

6. Where in the design do you see perpendicular lines?

7. What can you tell about the triangles in the design?

8. If opposite angles of the rhombi are each 55°, what are the measures of the other two angles?

10-8 Drawing Three-Dimensional Figures

GET READY to Learn

Hands-On Mini Lab

Use centimeter cubes to build the figure shown. Then make a sketch of the top, the side, and the front views.

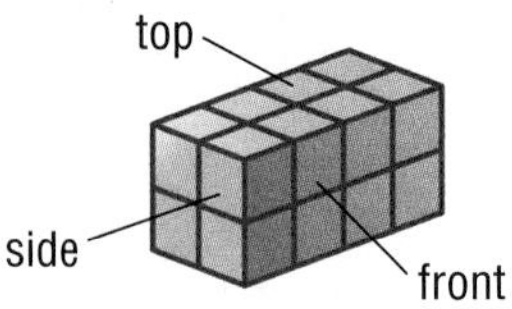
top
side
front

top view
side view
front view

Build each figure. Then make a sketch of the top, the side, and the front views of each figure.

1. 

2. 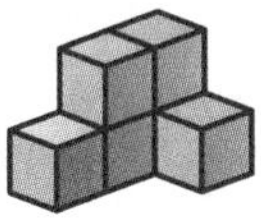

3. 

MAIN IDEA

I will draw two-dimensional views of three-dimensional figures.

Standard 5MG2.3 Visualize and draw two-dimensional views of three-dimensional objects made from rectangular solids.

New Vocabulary

- three-dimensional figure
- face
- edge
- vertex
- prism
- base

The figures in the Mini Lab are examples of **three-dimensional figures** because they have length, width, and depth.

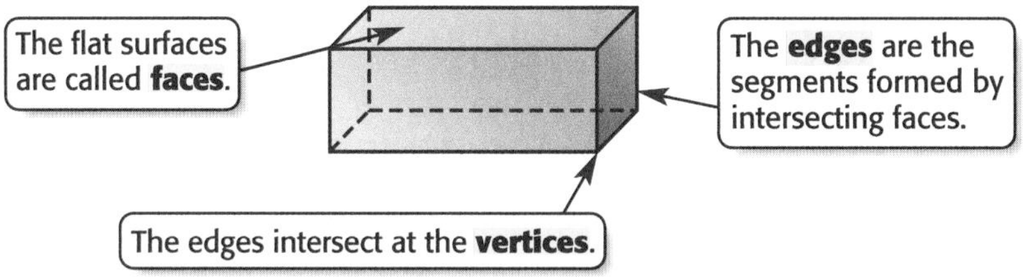
The flat surfaces are called **faces**.
The **edges** are the segments formed by intersecting faces.
The edges intersect at the **vertices**.

Prisms are one type of three-dimensional figure.

KEY CONCEPT — Prisms

- A **prism** is a three-dimensional figure with two parallel and congruent faces that are polygons.
- The two parallel and congruent faces are called the **bases**.
- The shape of the base tells the name of the prism.

Rectangular prism **Square prism or cube**

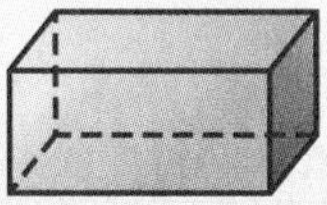

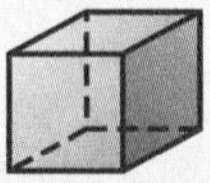

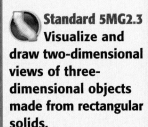

EXAMPLE Draw Two-Dimensional Views

1 Draw a top, a side, and a front view of the prism at the right.

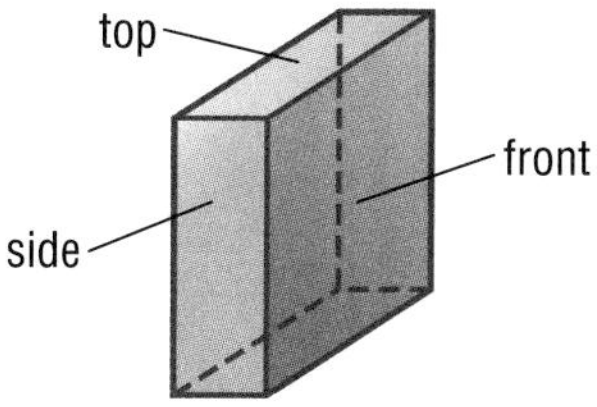

The top and side views are rectangles. The front view is a square.

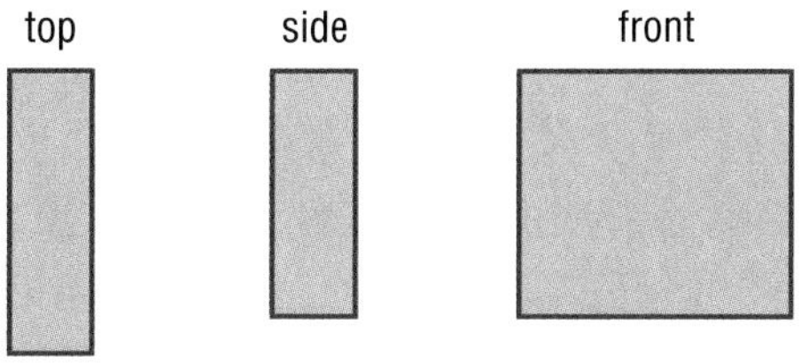

Online Personal Tutor at ca.gr5math.com

Many real-world objects are rectangular prisms. You can also draw top, side, and front views of these objects.

Real-World EXAMPLE

2 The top section of a building is shown. Draw a top, a side, and a front view of the building section.

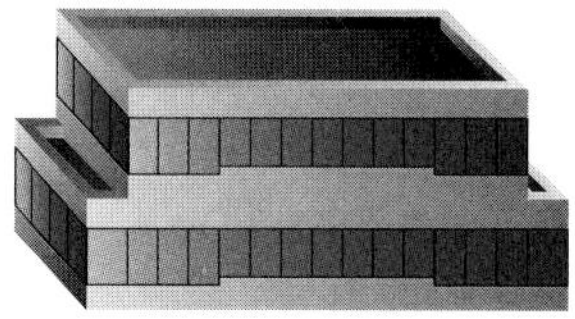

The top view is a rectangle. The side and front views are two rectangles.

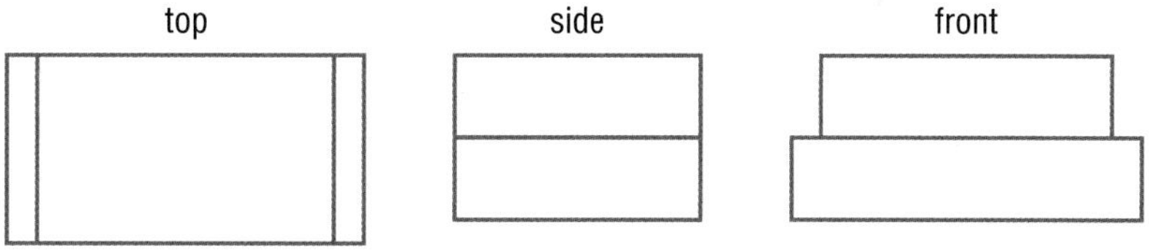

EXAMPLE Draw a Three-Dimensional Figure

3 Draw the three-dimensional figure whose top, side, and front views are shown. Use isometric dot paper.

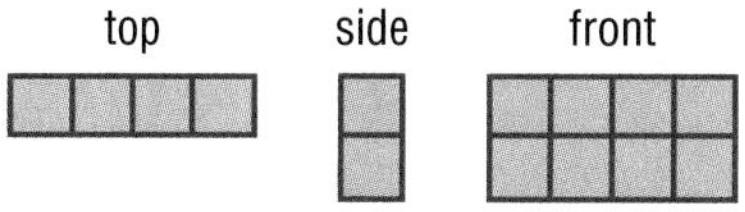

Step 1 Use the top view to draw the base of the figure, a rectangle that is 1 unit wide and 4 units long.

Step 2 Use the side and front views to complete the figure.

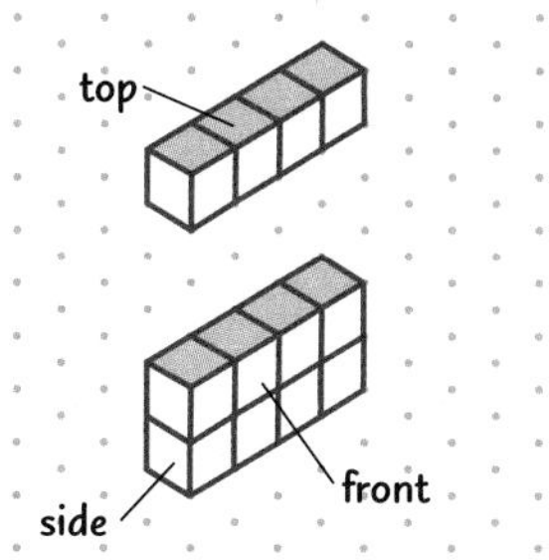

Remember

In Example 3, check your completed drawing with the top, side, and front views of the original problem.

CHECK What You Know

Draw a top, a side, and a front view of each prism. See Example 1 (p. 567)

1.

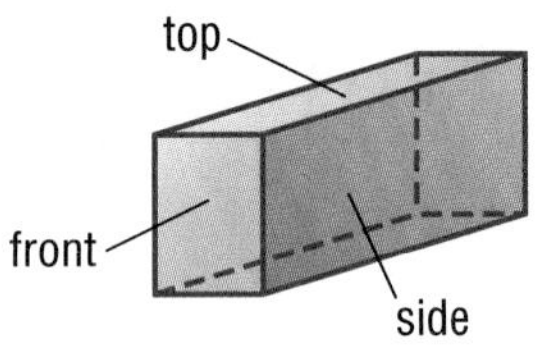

2.

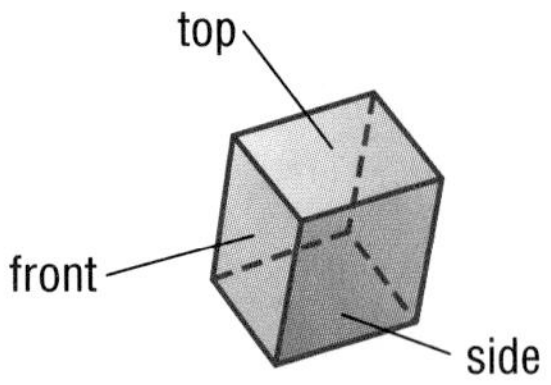

3. Draw a top, a side, and a front view of the DVDs shown. See Example 2 (p. 567)

4. Draw the three-dimensional figure whose top, side, and front views are shown. Use isometric dot paper. See Example 3 (p. 567)

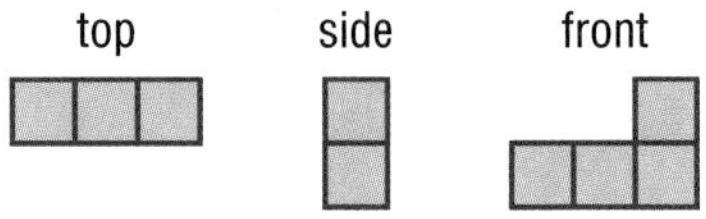

5. Talk About It: Does a top-front-side view diagram always provide enough information to draw a figure? Explain.

Practice and Problem Solving

EXTRA PRACTICE See page 684.

Draw a top, a side, and a front view of each prism. See Example 1 (p. 567)

6.

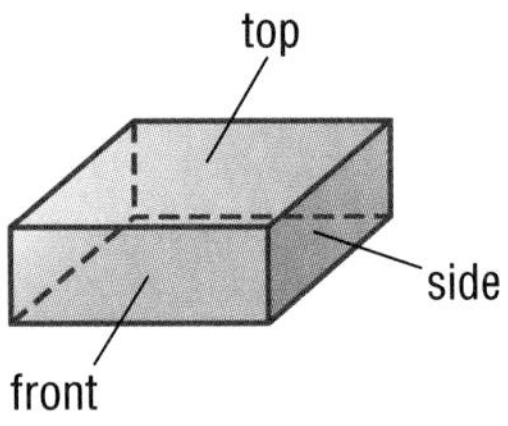

7.

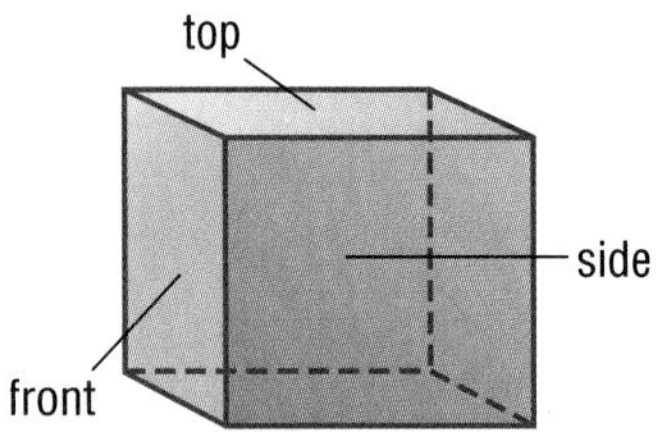

8.

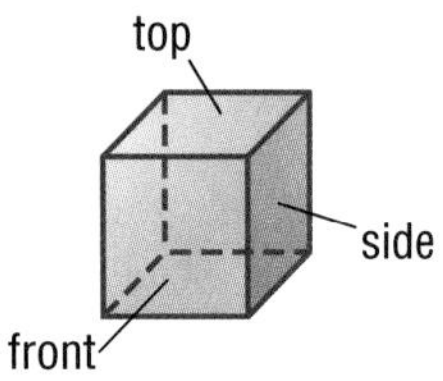

9.

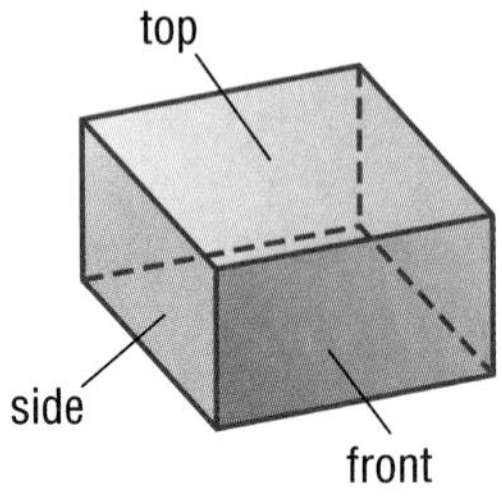

10.

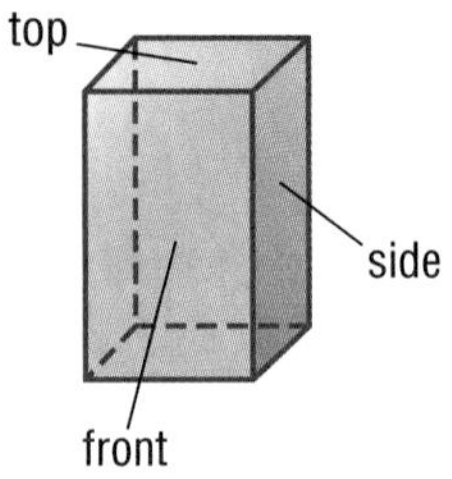

11.

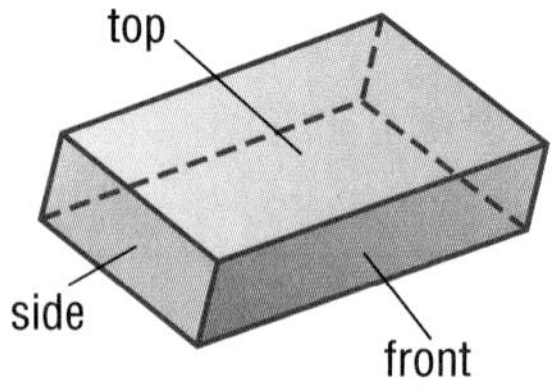

12. Two candles are shown. Draw a top, a side, and a front view of the candles. See Example 2 (p. 567)

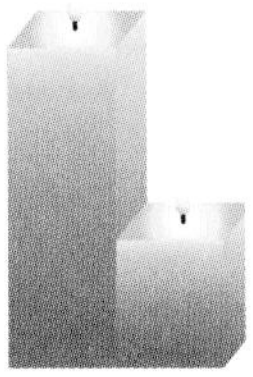

13. Draw a top, a side, and a front view of the photo box shown. See Example 2 (p. 567)

Draw the three-dimensional figure whose top, side, and front views are shown. Use isometric dot paper. See Example 3 (p. 567)

14. top side front

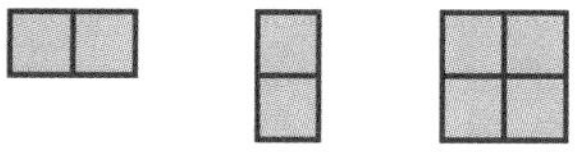

15. top side front

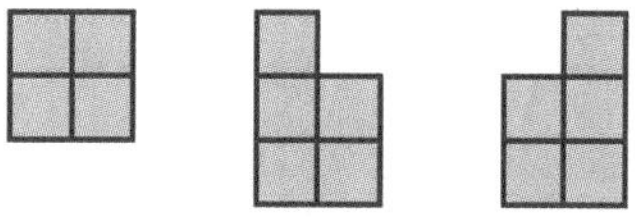

16. top side front

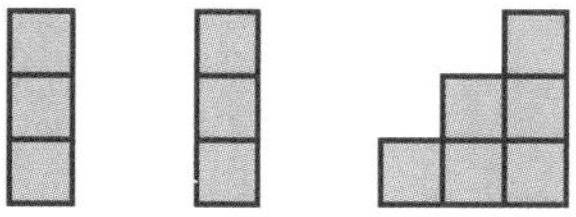

17. top side front

For Exercises 18 and 19, refer to the computer desk shown.

18. Sketch a top, a side, or a front view of the desk.

19. Explain why you chose the view.

Geometry All three-dimensional geometric figures are *solids*. Draw a top, a side, and a front view of each solid.

20.

21.

22.

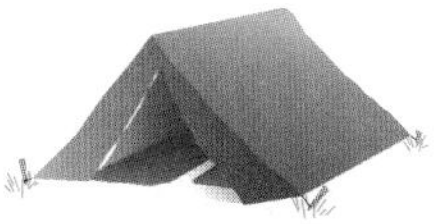

Real-World PROBLEM SOLVING

Architecture Four Embarcadero Center is a 45-story building in San Francisco's financial district.

23. Sketch a top, a side, or a front view of the building.

24. Use the Internet or another resource to find a photo of another building. Sketch the top, side, and front view of the building.

H.O.T. Problems

CHALLENGE Determine whether each statement is *always*, *sometimes*, or *never* true. Explain your reasoning.

25. Three-dimensional figures have length and depth.

26. The top, side, and front views of a rectangular prism are rectangles.

27. **WRITING IN ►MATH** Describe a real-world situation in which you would need to visualize and draw two-dimensional views of objects made from rectangular prisms.

Standards Practice

28 Which drawing best represents the top view of the prism below?

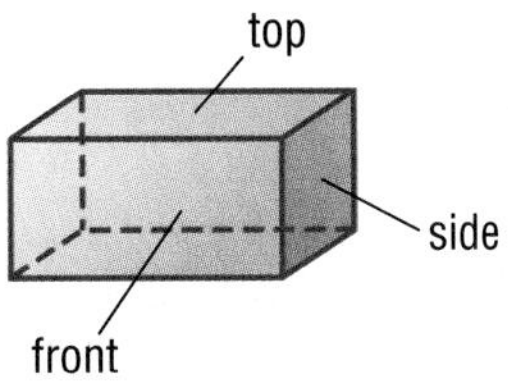

A 

B 

C 

D 

29 A three-dimensional figure made of cubes is shown.

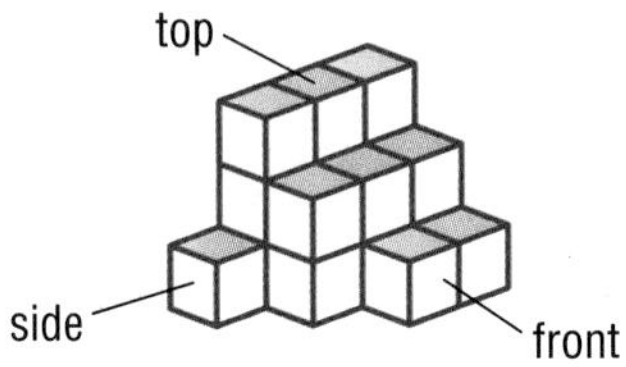

Which drawing represents the front view of the figure?

F 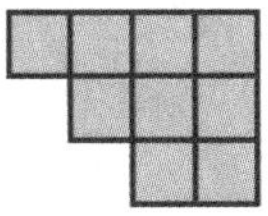

H 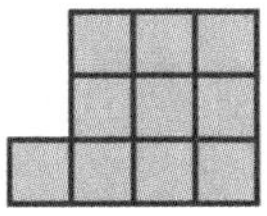

G 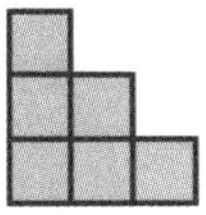

J 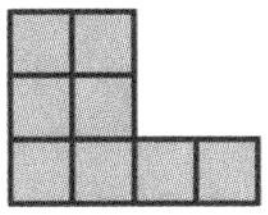

Spiral Review

Algebra Find the value of *x* in each quadrilateral. **(Lesson 10-7)**

30. 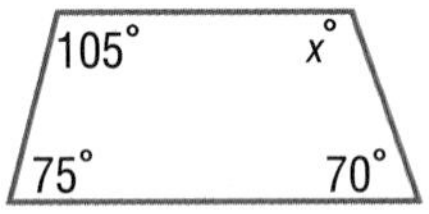

31. 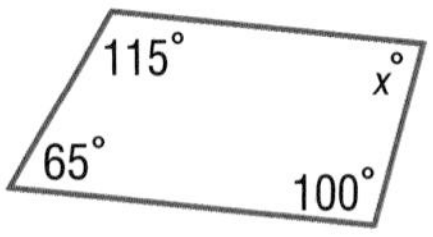

32. 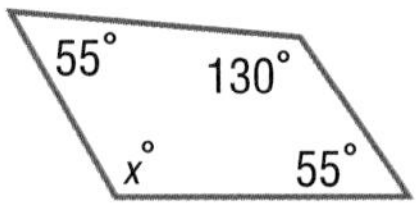

33. Classify the triangle as *acute*, *right*, or *obtuse*. **(Lesson 10-6)**

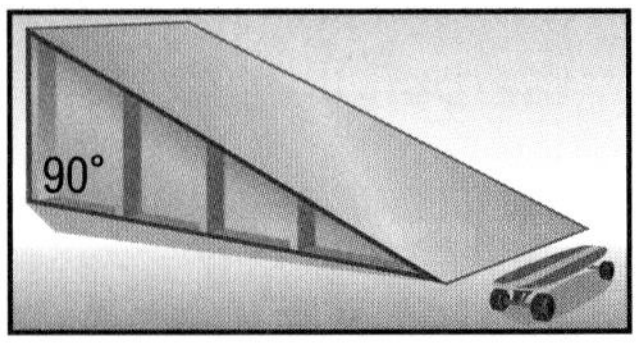

34. The probability that it will snow tomorrow is forecasted at 60%. Describe the complement of this event and find its probability. **(Lesson 9-8)**

35. The table shows the ages of children attending story hour at the library. Make a line plot of the data. Which age group was the most common? **(Lesson 2-4)**

Age of Children at Story Hour (years)

4	7	4	5	6	3	2	4	8	6
7	5	3	2	4	4	7	3	2	5

CHAPTER 10

Study Guide and Review

FOLDABLES™ Study Organizer

GET READY to Study

Be sure the following Key Concepts are noted in your Foldable.

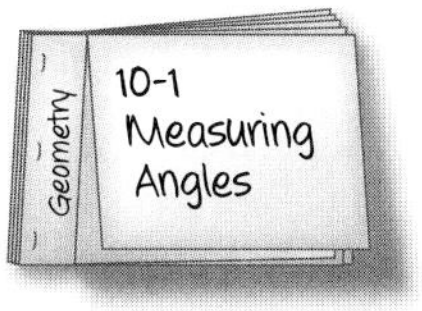

BIG Ideas

Types of Angles (Lesson 10-1)

- An acute angle measures less than 90°.
- An obtuse angle measures between 90° and 180°.
- A right angle measures exactly 90°.
- A straight angle measures exactly 180°.

Parallel and Perpendicular Lines (Lesson 10-4)

- Parallel lines are lines that never intersect.
- Perpendicular lines are lines that intersect at right angles.

Classifying Triangles (Lesson 10-6)

- An acute triangle has all acute angles.
- A right triangle has one right angle.
- An obtuse triangle has one obtuse angle.

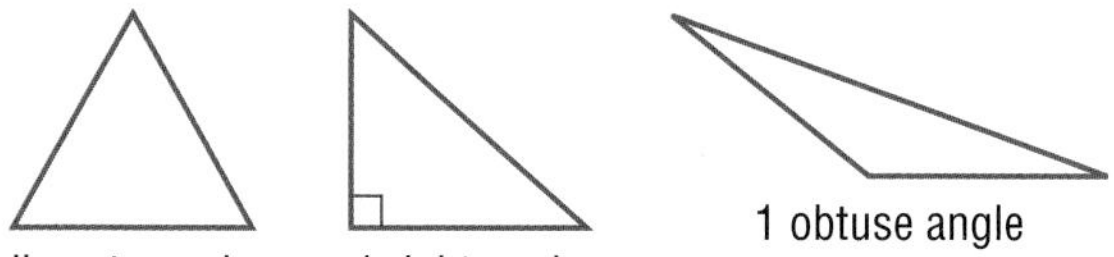

Sum of Angle Measures (Lessons 10-6 and 10-7)

- The sum of the angle measures in a triangle is 180°.
- The sum of the measures of the angles in a quadrilateral is 360°.

Key Vocabulary

acute angle (p. 530)
acute triangle (p. 551)
angle (p. 529)
equilateral triangle (p. 553)
intersecting lines (p. 541)
isosceles triangle (p. 553)
obtuse angle (p. 530)
obtuse triangle (p. 551)
parallel lines (p. 541)
perpendicular lines (p. 541)
quadrilateral (p. 558)
rectangle (p. 559)
right angle (p. 530)
right triangle (p. 551)
scalene triangle (p. 553)
straight angle (p. 530)
three-dimensional figure (p. 566)

Vocabulary Check

State whether each sentence is *true* or *false*. If *false*, replace the underlined word or number to make a true sentence.

1. When two lines intersect, they form two pairs of opposite angles called <u>right angles</u>.
2. A four-sided figure with exactly one pair of opposite sides parallel is a <u>trapezoid</u>.
3. All triangles have at least two <u>obtuse</u> angles.

Study Guide and Review

Lesson-by-Lesson Review

10-1 Measuring Angles (pp. 529–532)

Example 1

Use a protractor to find the measure of the angle. Then classify the angle as *acute, obtuse, right,* or *straight*.

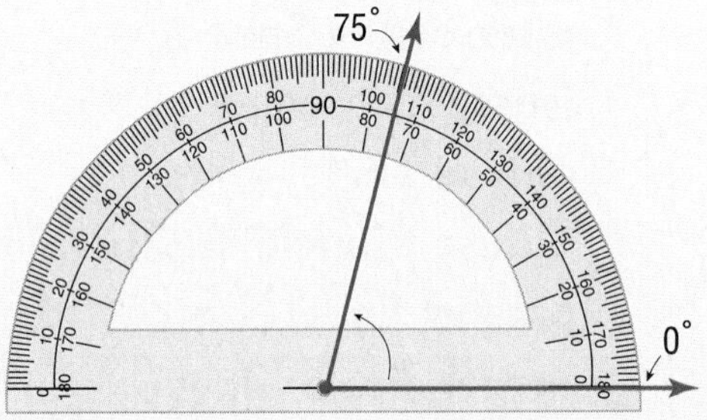

The angle measures 75°. Since it is less than 90°, it is an acute angle.

Use a protractor to find the measure of each angle. Then classify each angle as *acute, obtuse, right,* or *straight*.

4. 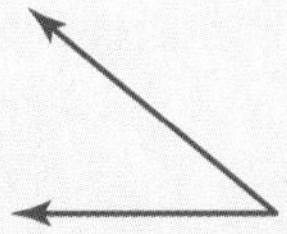

5. 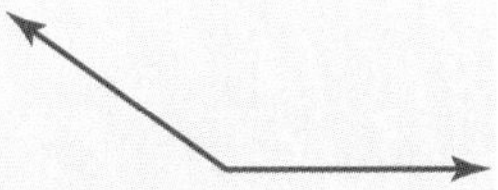

6. Use a protractor to measure the angle formed at the top of the roller coaster. Then classify it as *right, acute, obtuse,* or *straight*.

10-2 Problem-Solving Strategy: Draw a Diagram (pp. 534–535)

Example 2

Five friends are seated in a circle at a restaurant. How many ways can any two friends split a meal?

Draw five dots to represent the friends. Connect all dots to represent all possible choices for splitting a meal.

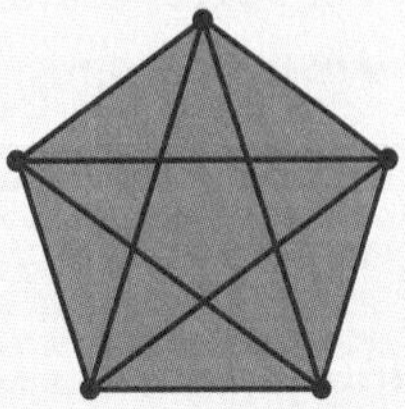

Count the number of lines that were drawn, 10. So, there are 10 ways for any two friends to split a meal.

Solve by drawing a diagram.

7. Gina is painting a design. She will paint six dots in a circle. Each dot is to be connected to every other dot by a straight line. How many straight lines will Gina need to draw?

8. A contractor is designing one side of an office building 48 feet in length. The windows are each 5 feet long, and will be placed 6 feet apart and 5 feet from the end of the building wall. How many windows can the contractor design?

10-3 Estimating and Drawing Angles (pp. 536–540)

Example 3
Use a protractor and a straightedge to draw a 47° angle.

Draw one side of the angle. Align the center of the protractor and the 0° with the line. Count from 0° to 47°. Make a mark.

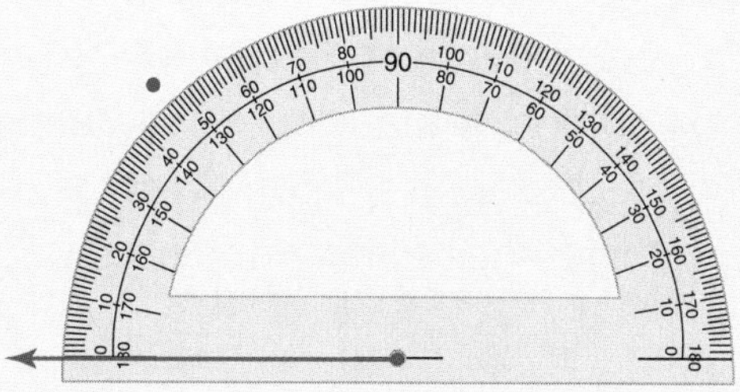

Draw the other side of the angle.

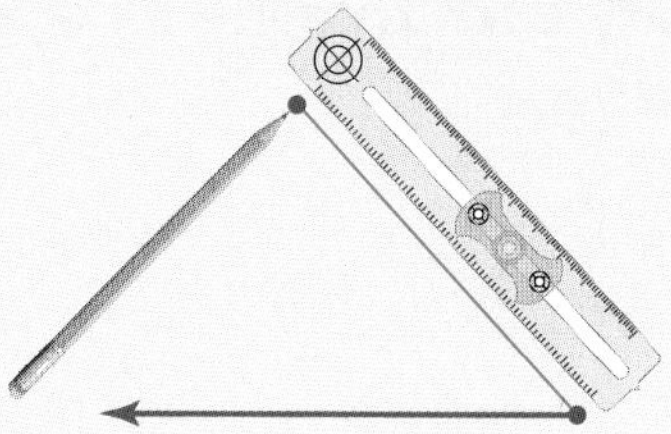

Use a protractor and a straightedge to draw angles having the following measurements.

9. 36°

10. 127°

11. 180°

12. 90°

Estimate the measure of each angle.

13.

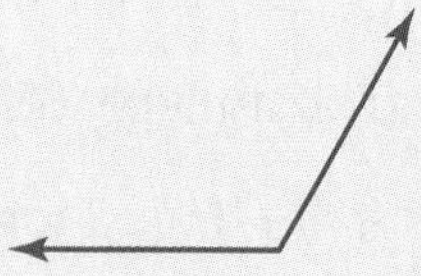

14.

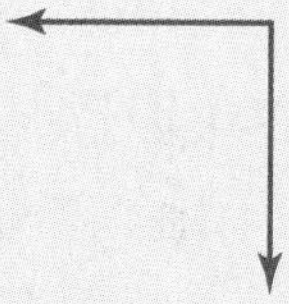

15. Estimate the measure of the angle shown below.

10-4 Parallel and Perpendicular Lines (pp. 541–544)

Example 4
Use the figure below to determine if $\overleftrightarrow{AB}$ and $\overleftrightarrow{BD}$ are *parallel, perpendicular,* or *neither*.

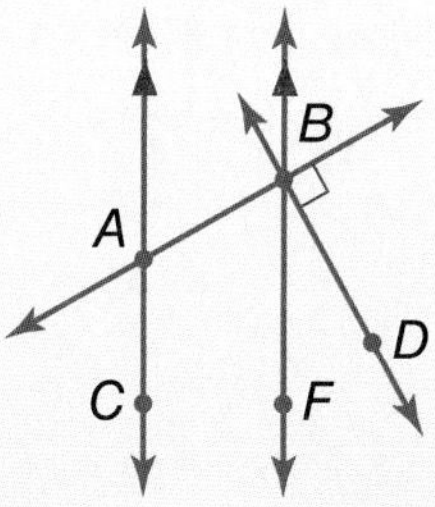

$\overleftrightarrow{AB}$ and $\overleftrightarrow{BD}$ intersect at right angles.
So, $\overleftrightarrow{AB}$ and $\overleftrightarrow{BD}$ are perpendicular lines.

Use the figure at the left to determine if each pair of lines is *parallel, perpendicular,* or *neither*.

16. $\overleftrightarrow{AC}$ and $\overleftrightarrow{BF}$

17. $\overleftrightarrow{AC}$ and $\overleftrightarrow{AB}$

18. $\overleftrightarrow{BD}$ and $\overleftrightarrow{AC}$

10-5 Problem-Solving Investigation: Choose a Strategy (pp. 548–549)

Example 5
At a clothing store, last month's total sales were $8,700. If 30% of the sales were children's clothes, how much of last month's sales were children's clothes?

Solve a simpler problem.

10% of $8,700 = $\frac{1}{10}$ × $8,700 or $870

Since 30% is 3 × 10%, multiply $870 by 3.

So, 30% of $8,700 is $870 × 3 or $2,610.

Choose the best strategy to solve each problem.

19. Eighteen teachers and 348 students are going on a field trip. If each bus holds 48 people, how many buses will they need?

20. The hottest temperature on Earth has been recorded at 134°F, and the coldest temperature has been recorded at −128°F. What is the difference between the temperatures?

10-6 Triangles (pp. 551–556)

Example 6
Classify the triangle shown as *acute, right,* or *obtuse.*

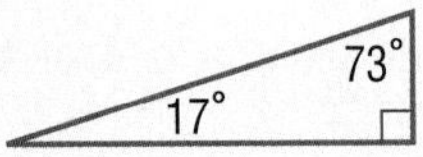

Since the triangle has one right angle, it is a right triangle.

Example 7
Algebra Find the value of x.

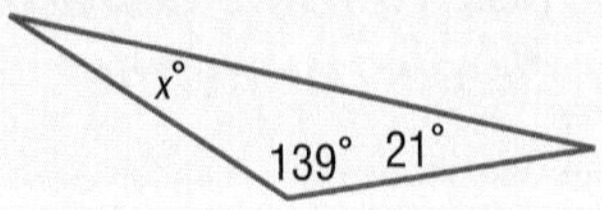

The sum of the angle measures in a triangle is 180°. So, $x + 139 + 21 = 180$.

$x + 21 + 139 =$	180	Write the equation.
$x + 160 =$	180	Add 21 and 139.
$-160 =$	-160	Subtract 160 from each side.
$x =$	20	Simplify.

So, the value of x is 20.

Classify each triangle as *acute, right,* or *obtuse.*

21.

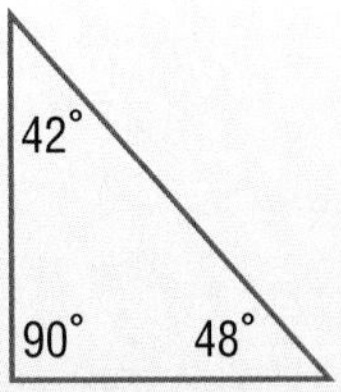

22.

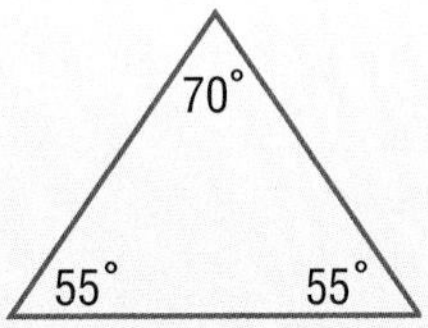

Algebra Find the value of x in each triangle.

23.

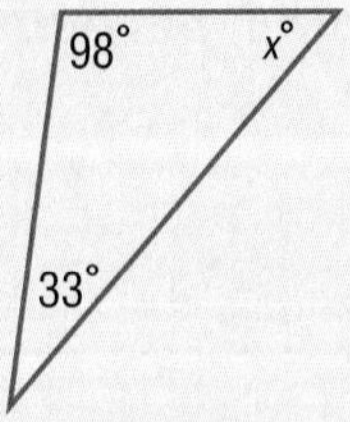

24.

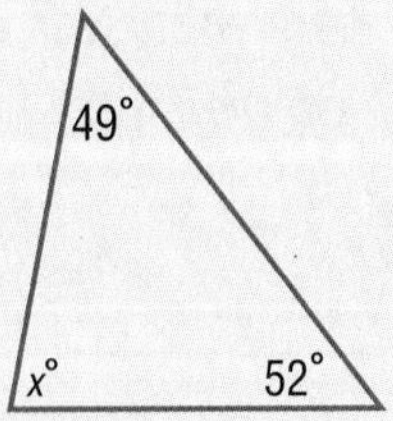

10-7 Quadrilaterals (pp. 558–563)

Example 8

Algebra Find the value of x.

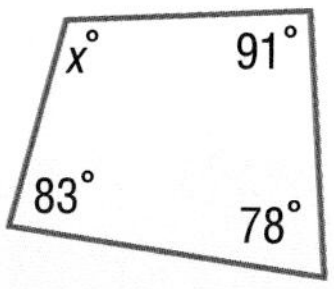

The sum of the angle measures in a quadrilateral is 360°.

So, $x + 91 + 78 + 83 = 360$.

$x + 91 + 78 + 83 =$	360	Add 91, 78, and 83.
$x + 252 =$	360	
$-252 =$	-252	Subtract 252 from each side.
$x =$	108	Simplify.

So, the value of x is 108.

Example 9

Classify the quadrilateral shown.

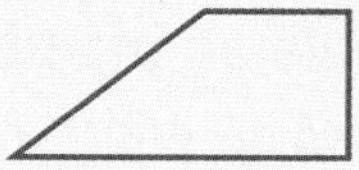

The quadrilateral has exactly one pair of parallel sides, so it is a trapezoid.

Example 10

Algebra Find the value of x.

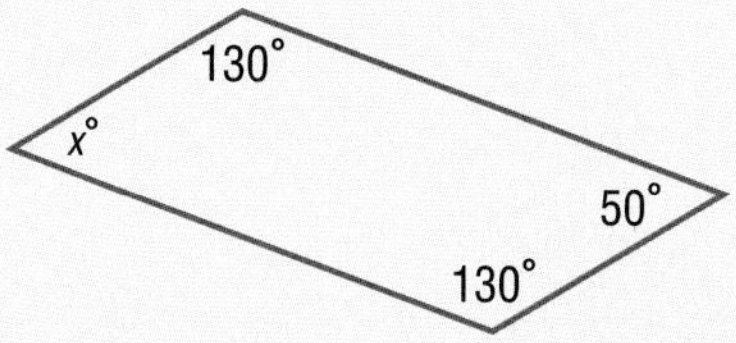

In a parallelogram, the opposite angles are congruent. Since the angle opposite the missing measure has a measure of 50°, $x = 50$.

Check $50° + 130° + 50° + 130° = 360°$ ✓

Algebra Find the value of x in each quadrilateral.

25.

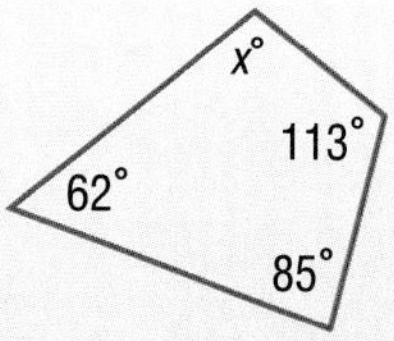

26.

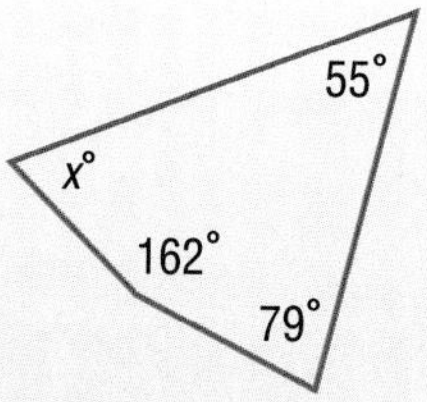

Classify each quadrilateral.

27.

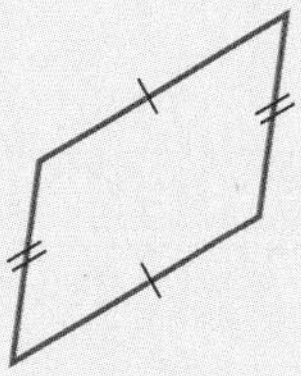

28.

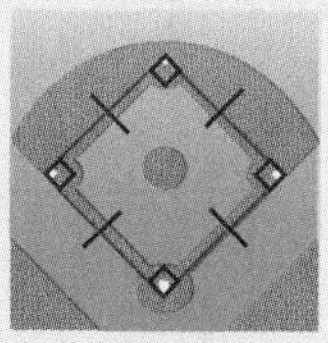

29. Identify the quadrilateral outlined.

30. Algebra Find the value of x in the rhombus shown.

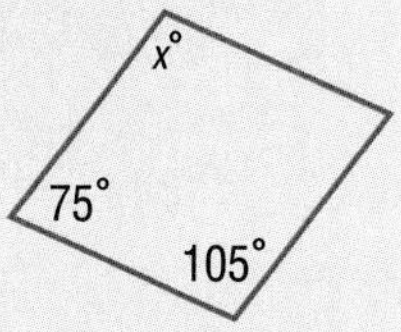

31. Algebra Find the value of x in the parallelogram shown.

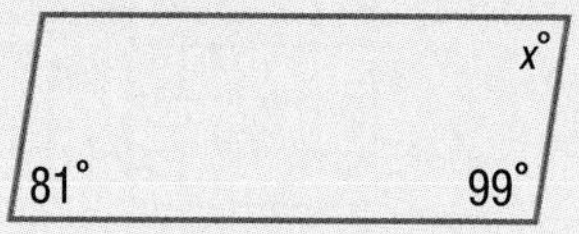

10-8 Drawing Three-Dimensional Figures (pp. 566–570)

Example 11

Draw a top, a side, and a front view of the prism below.

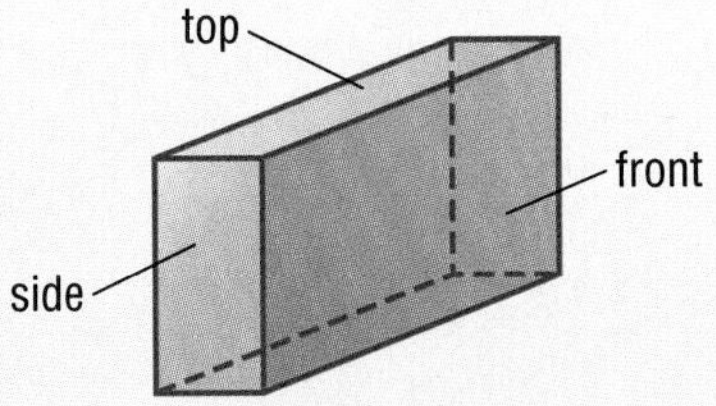

The top, side, and front views are rectangles.

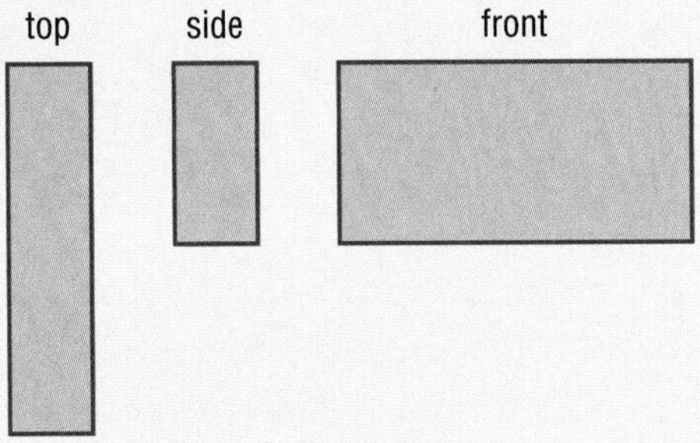

Example 12

A stack of books is shown. Draw a top, a side, and a front view of the books.

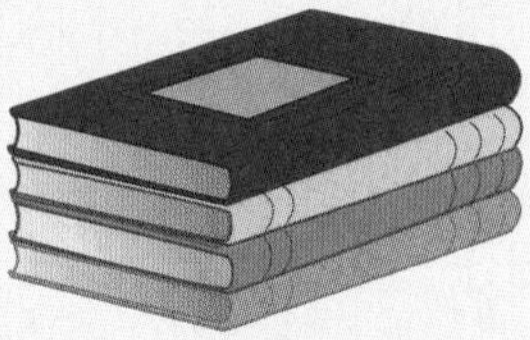

The top view is a rectangle. The side and front views are four rectangles.

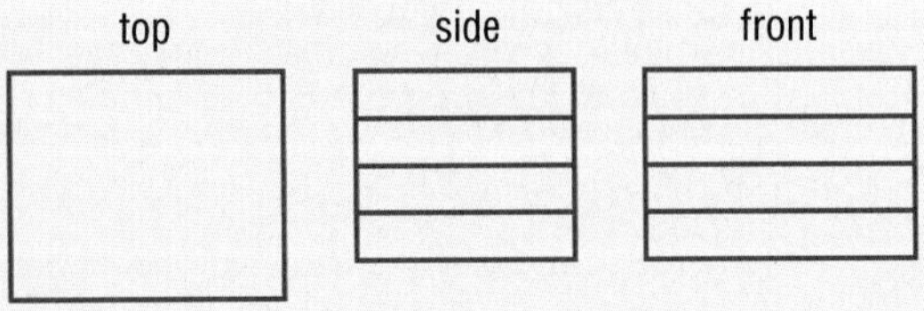

Draw a top, a side, and a front view of each prism.

32.

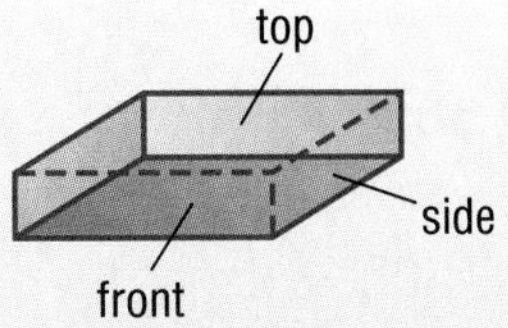

33.

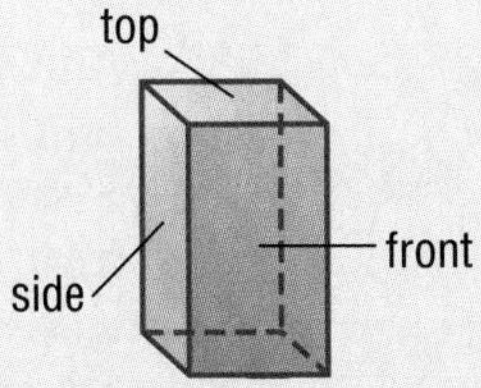

34.

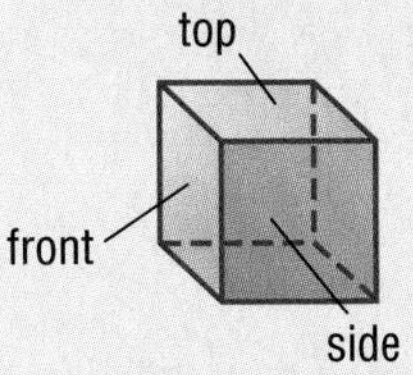

35. Manuela arranged some toy blocks as shown. Draw a top, a side, and a front view of the blocks.

CHAPTER 10 Chapter Test

Use a protractor to measure each angle and classify as *acute, obtuse, right,* or *straight*.

1.

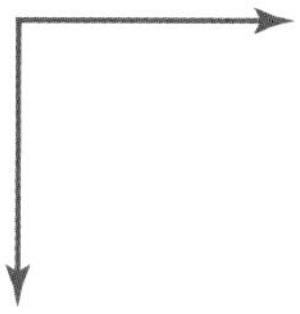

2.

3.

4. Estimate the measure of *x*.

Determine if the pair of lines are *parallel, perpendicular,* or *neither*.

5.

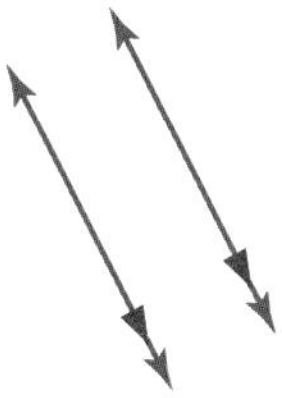

6.

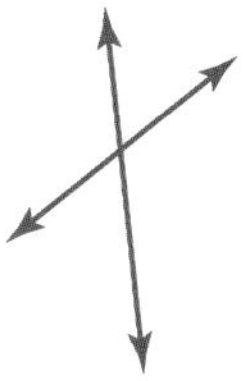

7. Algebra Find the value of *x* in the triangle at the right.

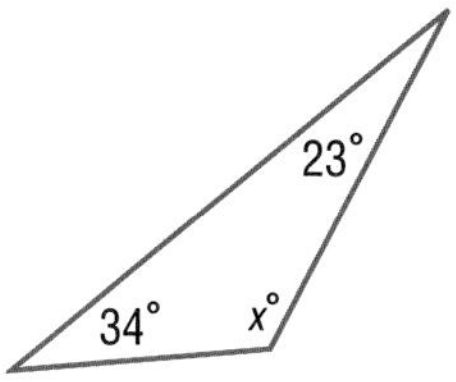

8. Classify the triangle at the right as *scalene, isosceles,* or *equilateral.*

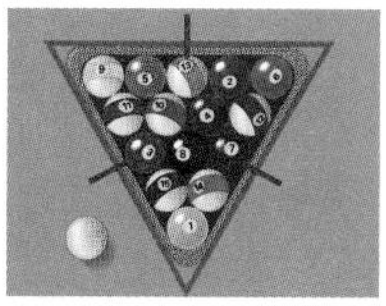

9. **STANDARDS PRACTICE** Find the measure of ∠*R* in the trapezoid below.

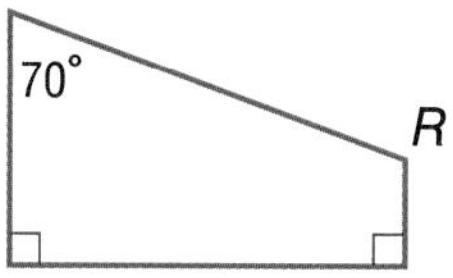

A 110° **C** 90°
B 100° **D** 20°

10. Classify the quadrilateral below.

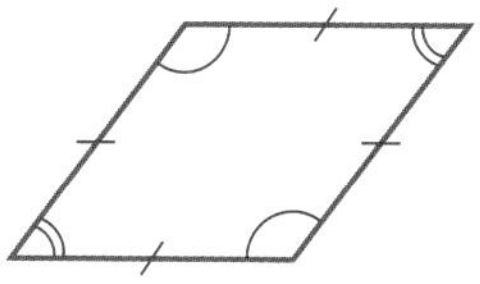

11. **STANDARDS PRACTICE** Refer to the shapes.

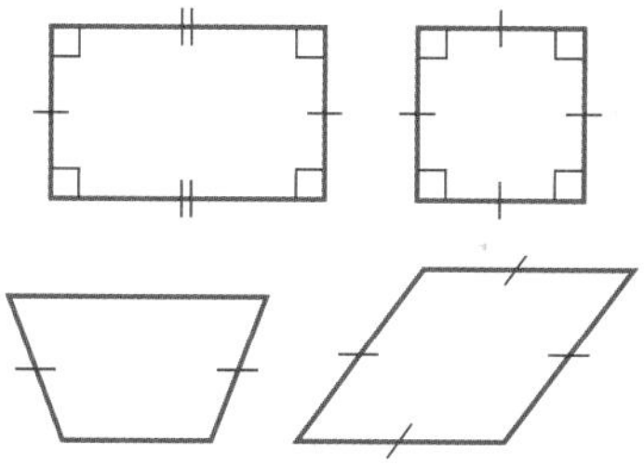

Which statement is *not* true?

F Each shape is a quadrilateral.

G Each shape has at least two congruent sides.

H Each shape is a parallelogram.

J The sum of the angle measures of each shape is 360°.

12. Draw a top, a side, and a front view of the prism.

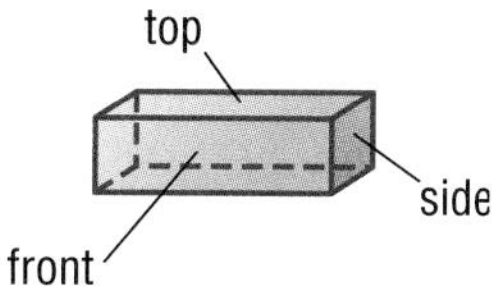

13. **WRITING IN MATH** To block off the boundaries for a game, Jonas plans to use 5 orange cones on each side of a rectangular field. This includes one cone at each corner. How many cones are needed? Describe how you solved the problem.

CHAPTER 10

California Standards Practice

Cumulative, Chapters 1–10

Standards Example

Which is *closest* to the measure of ∠*ABC*?

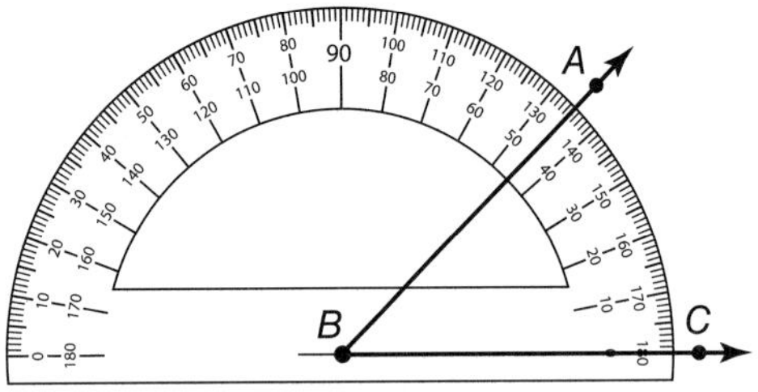

A 135° **C** 65°

B 115° **D** 45°

Read the Question

You are asked to find which angle measure is closest to the measure of ∠*ABC*.

Solve the Question

The angle is less than 90° so you can eliminate choices A and B. The top side of the angle goes between 40° and 50°. So, the measure of ∠*ABC* is 45°.

The answer is D.

Online **Personal Tutor at** ca.gr5math.com

Choose the best answer.

1 **Estimate the measure of ∠*P* of the parallelogram shown.**

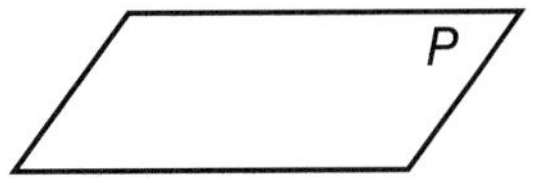

A 127°

B 96°

C 53°

D 13°

2 **Classify ∠*C* in triangle *ABC*.**

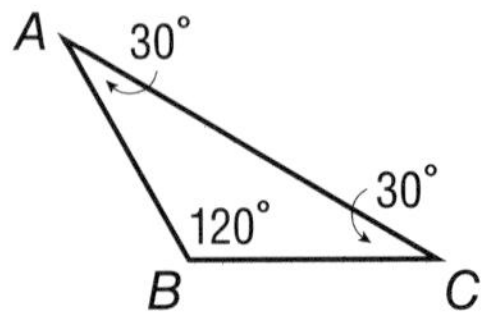

F right **H** obtuse

G acute **J** straight

More California Standards Practice
For practice by standard, see pages CA1–CA27.

3 **Find the measure of ∠*H*.**

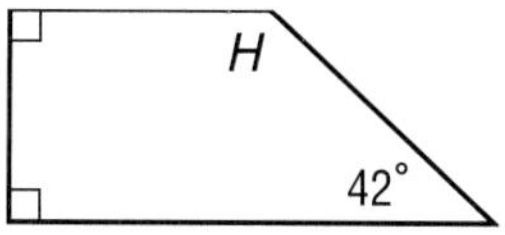

A 26° **B** 138° **C** 180° **D** 212°

---

4 **One angle of an isosceles triangle measures 40°. The other two angles in the triangle are congruent. Which method can be used to find the measure of each congruent angle?**

F Multiply 40 by 2 and then add 180.

G Subtract 40 from 180 and then divide by 2.

H Add 40 to 180 and then divide by 3.

J Divide 50 by 2 and then subtract from 180.

---

5 **Find the measure of ∠2 in rectangle *WXYZ*.**

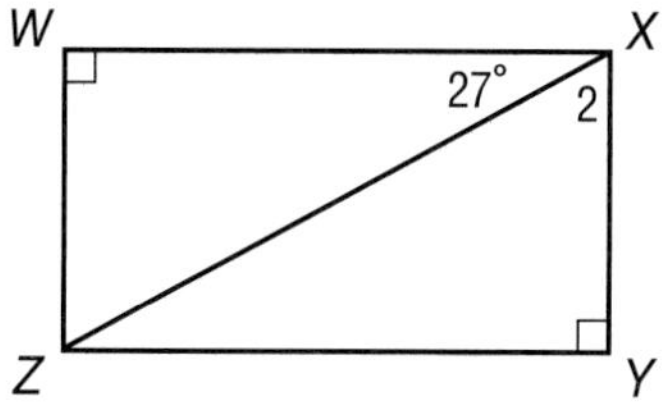

A 27° **B** 45° **C** 63° **D** 90°

---

6 **The clock shows the position of the hands at 3:10 P.M. What kind of angle is ∠*S*?**

F Straight **H** Obtuse

G Acute **J** Right

---

7 **Sarah wants to select two sweaters to take on a vacation. She has 1 red, 1 yellow, 1 green, and 1 blue sweater to choose from. Which diagram shows all the possible outcomes?**

A

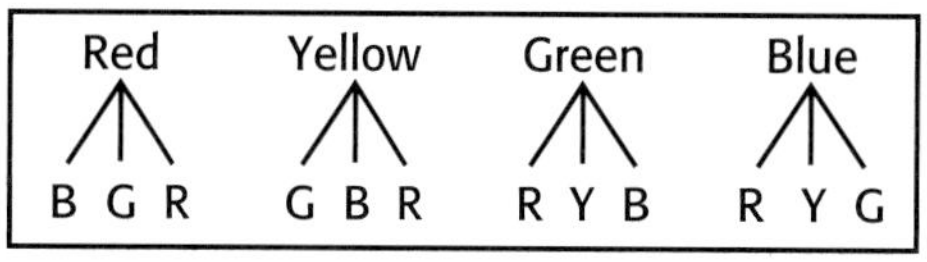

B

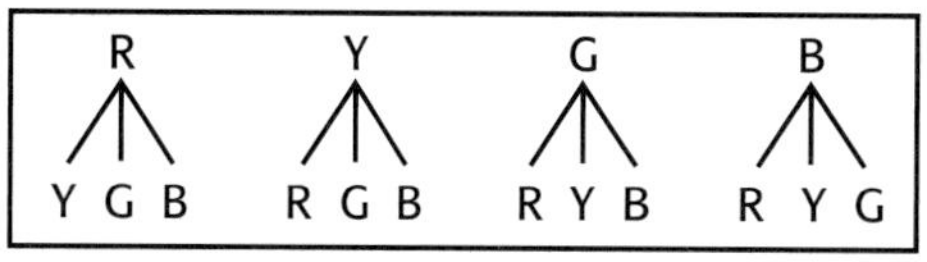

C

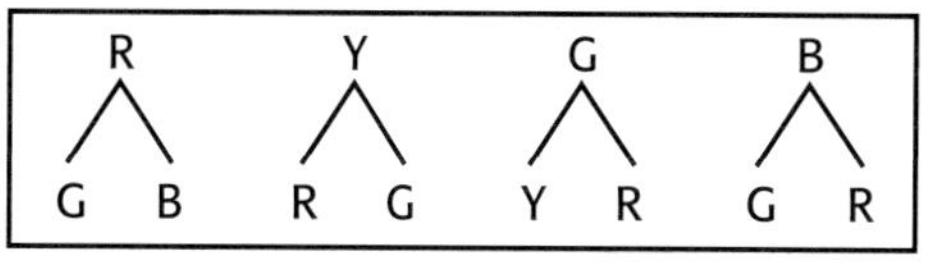

D

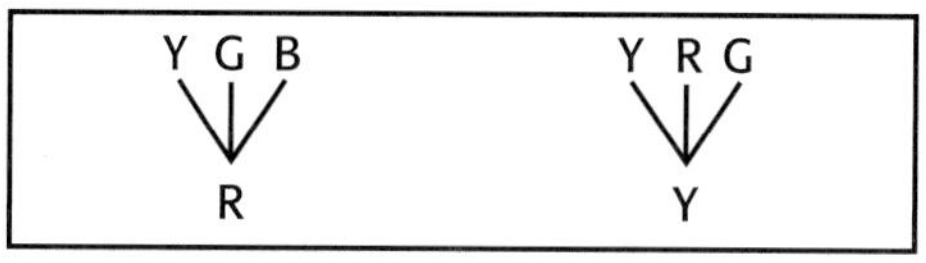

---

8 **At a concession stand, each pizza was cut into 8 equal-size pieces. Dave sold 7 pieces, Sally sold 5 pieces, and Lori sold 6 pieces. Find the total amount of pizza sold by these three people.**

F 18 **G** $2\frac{9}{10}$ **H** $2\frac{3}{4}$ **J** $2\frac{1}{4}$

---

9 **The table shows the scores at a gymnastics competition. Who had the highest overall score?**

Gymnast	Overall Score
Amber	8.95
Camille	8.82
Jacy	8.73
Luisa	8.99

A Amber **C** Jacy

B Camille **D** Luisa

CHAPTER 11 Measurement: Perimeter, Area, and Volume

BIG Idea What is volume?

Volume is the amount of space inside a three-dimensional figure. It is measured in cubic units.

Example The San Diego Zoo is one of the most visited zoos in the country. It features over 4,000 animals, including hummingbirds. Suppose the hummingbirds are kept in an aviary that is roughly the shape of a rectangular prism. The **volume** of the aviary is the product of its length, width, and height.

What will I learn in this chapter?

- Find the perimeters of squares and rectangles.
- Find the areas of parallelograms and triangles.
- Find the volume of rectangular prisms.
- Find the surface areas of rectangular prisms.
- Solve problems by making a model.

Key Vocabulary

perimeter
volume
cubic units
net
surface area

Math Online Student Study Tools at ca.gr5math.com

FOLDABLES™
Study Organizer

Make this Foldable to help you organize your notes. Begin with a sheet of 11″ × 17″ paper and six index cards.

1. **Fold** lengthwise about 3″ from the bottom.

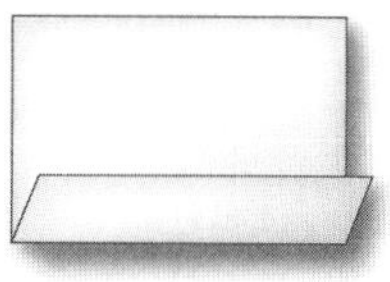

2. **Fold** the paper in thirds.

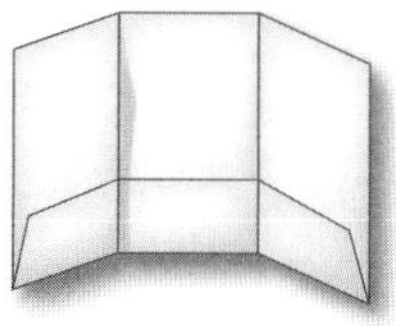

3. **Open** and staple the edges on either side to form three pockets.

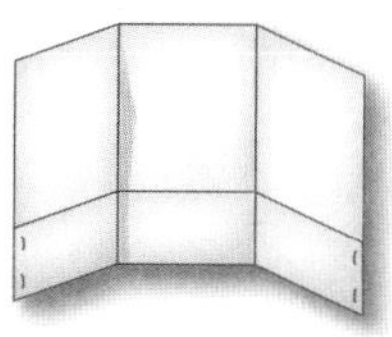

4. **Label** the pockets as shown. Place two index cards in each pocket.

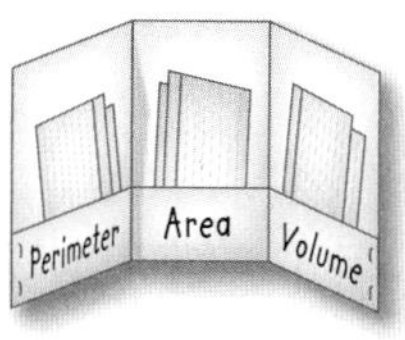

ARE YOU READY for Chapter 11?

You have two ways to check prerequisite skills for this chapter.

Option 2

Math Online Take the Chapter Readiness Quiz at ca.gr5math.com.

Option 1

Complete the Quick Check below.

QUICK Check

Evaluate each expression. **(Lesson 1-3)**

1. $4(9)$

2. $4(17)$

3. $4(5.8)$

4. $4\left(3\frac{1}{3}\right)$

5. $2(8) + 2(5)$

6. $2(16) + 2(11)$

7. $2(13.5) + 2(6.9)$

8. $2(10) + 2\left(6\frac{1}{4}\right)$

9. Renee ran four days last week. If she ran 6 miles each day, how many miles did she run last week? **(Prior Grade)**

10. Lou bought two pairs of pants and two shirts. If each pair of pants cost $22 and each shirt cost $13, how much did Lou spend? **(Lesson 1-3)**

Evaluate each expression. **(Lesson 1-3)**

11. $16 \cdot 7$

12. $23 \cdot 5$

13. $\frac{1}{2}(8 \times 9)$

14. $\frac{1}{2}(14)(11)$

15. $10 \times 12 \times 8$

16. $\frac{1}{3} \times \frac{2}{5} \times 15$

17. $(2)(3.6)(5.2) + (2)(3.6)(9) + (2)(5.2)(9)$

18. $(2)(8)(4) + (2)(8)(6) + (2)(4)(6)$

19. Lucinda bought four packages of muffin mix. Each mix makes 12 muffins. If Lucinda sells each muffin for $2, what is the most she could earn? **(Lesson 1-3)**

Explore

Measurement Lab for 11-1
Area and Perimeter

MAIN IDEA

I will explore changes in area and perimeter of rectangles and squares.

Standard 5MR2.3 Use a variety of methods, such as words, numbers, symbols, charts, graphs, **tables,** diagrams, **and models, to explain mathematical reasoning.**
Standard 5MG1.4 Differentiate between, and use appropriate units of measures for two- and three-**dimensional objects (i.e., find the perimeter, area,** volume).

If you increase the side lengths of a rectangle or square proportionally, how are the area and the perimeter affected? In this lab, you will investigate relationships between the areas and perimeters of original figures and those of the similar figures.

ACTIVITY

1 Step 1 On centimeter grid paper, draw and label a rectangle with a length of 6 centimeters and a width of 2 centimeters.

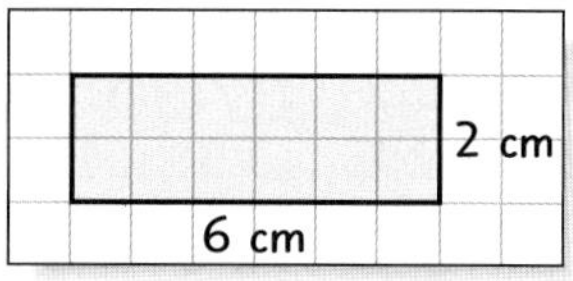

Step 2 Find the area and perimeter of this original rectangle. Then record the information in a table like the one shown.

Rectangle	Length (cm)	Width (cm)	Area (sq cm)	Perimeter (cm)
original	6	2		
A	12	4		
B	18	6		
C	24	8		

Step 3 Repeat Steps 1 and 2 for rectangles A, B, and C, whose dimensions are shown in the table.

Analyze the Results

1. Describe how the area and the perimeter of the original rectangle changed when the length and width were both doubled.
2. Describe how the area and the perimeter of the original rectangle changed when the length and width were both tripled.
3. Describe how the area and the perimeter of the original rectangle changed when the length and width were both quadrupled.

4. Draw a rectangle with a length and width that are half those of the original rectangle. Describe how the area and perimeter change.

5. How are the perimeter and area of a rectangle affected if the length and the width are changed proportionally?

ACTIVITY

2 **Step 1** On centimeter grid paper, draw and label a square with a length of 4 centimeters.

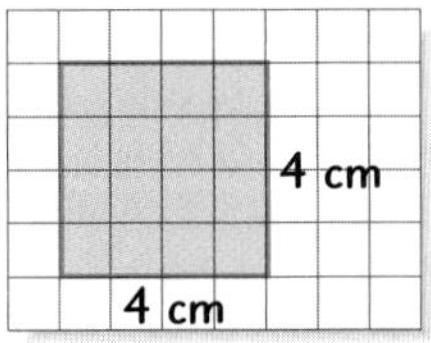

Step 2 Find the area and perimeter of this original square. Then record the information in a table like the one shown.

Square	Side Length (cm)	Area (sq cm)	Perimeter (cm)
original	4		
A	5		
B	6		
C	7		

Step 3 Repeat Steps 1 and 2 for squares A, B, and C, whose dimensions are shown in the table.

Analyze the Results

6. Describe how the dimensions of squares A, B, and C are different from the original square.

7. Describe how the perimeter of the original square changed when the side lengths increased by one centimeter.

8. Compare the ratios $\frac{\text{side length}}{\text{perimeter}}$ in the table above.

9. Suppose the perimeter of a square is 60 centimeters. Explain how you can use the ratio in Exercise 10 to find the length of its side. Then find its side length.

10. If P represents the perimeter of a square, write an equation that describes the relationship between the square's side length s and perimeter P.

11. Suppose you double the side lengths of the orginal square. Use what you learned in Activity 1 to predict the area and perimeter of the new square. Explain your reasoning.

Remember

You can review **area of squares** in Lesson 1-9.

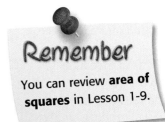

11-1 Perimeter

MAIN IDEA

I will find the perimeters of squares and rectangles.

Standard 5MG1.4 Differentiate between, and **use appropriate units of measures for two-** and three-**dimensional objects (i.e., find the perimeter,** area, volume**).**

New Vocabulary

perimeter

GET READY to Learn

Hands-On Mini Lab

Step 1 Use a centimeter ruler to measure the side length of each square shown below. Round each to the nearest centimeter.

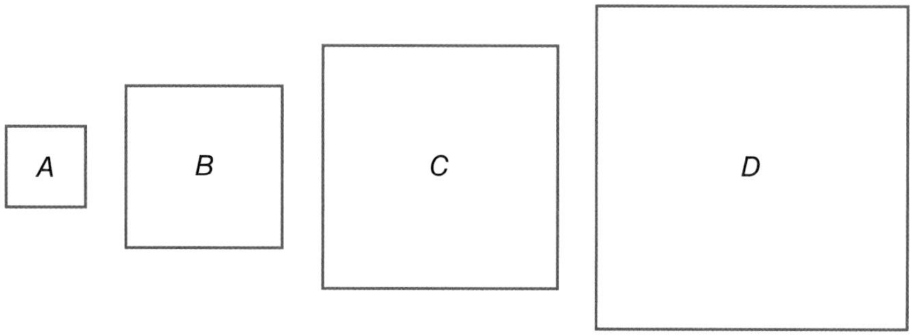

Step 2 Copy and complete the table shown. Find the distance around each square by adding the measures of its sides.

Square	Side Length	Distance Around
A		
B		
C		
D		

1. Write the ratio $\frac{\text{distance around}}{\text{side length}}$ in simplest form for squares A through D. What do you notice about these ratios?

2. Write an expression for the distance around a square that has a side length of x centimeters.

The distance around any closed figure is called its **perimeter**. As you discovered in the Mini Lab above, you can multiply the measure of any side of a square by 4 to find its perimeter.

KEY CONCEPT — **Perimeter of a Square**

Words The perimeter P of a square is four times the measure of any of its sides s.

Symbols $P = 4s$

Model

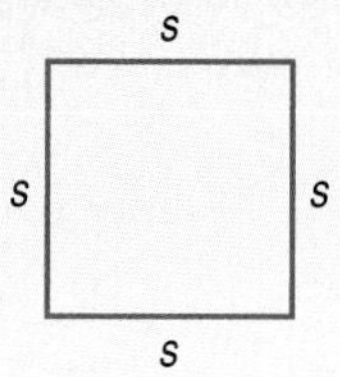

Real-World EXAMPLE — Perimeter of a Square

1 **A bear's sleeping quarters at a zoo is a square that measures 5 yards on each side. What is the perimeter of the sleeping quarters?**

$P = 4s$ Perimeter of a square

$P = 4(\mathbf{5})$ Replace s with 5.

$P = 20$ Multiply.

The perimeter of the bear's sleeping quarters is 20 yards.

Online **Personal Tutor at** ca.gr5math.com

KEY CONCEPT — Perimeter of a Rectangle

Words The perimeter P of a rectangle is the sum of the lengths and widths. It is also two times the length ℓ plus two times the width w.

Symbols $P = \ell + w + \ell + w$

$P = 2\ell + 2w$

Model

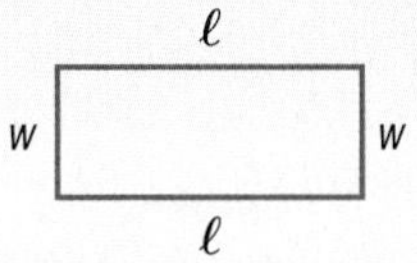

EXAMPLE — Perimeter of a Rectangle

2 **Find the perimeter of the rectangle.**

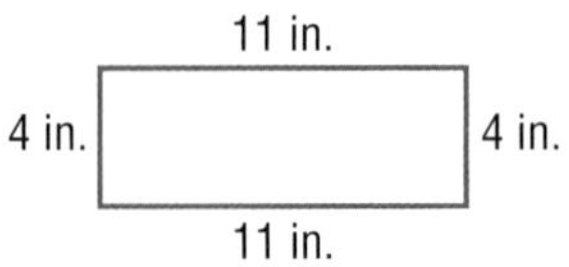

$P = 2\ell + 2w$ Write the formula.

$P = 2(\mathbf{11}) + 2(\mathbf{4})$ Replace ℓ with 11 and w with 4.

$P = 22 + 8$ Multiply.

$P = 30$ Add.

The perimeter is 30 inches.

Remember

You can check your answer in Example 2 by finding the sum of the lengths and widths of the rectangle. $P = 11 + 4 + 11 + 4$ or 30 inches. So, the answer is correct.

Math Online Extra Examples at ca.gr5math.com

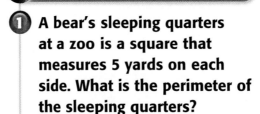

CHECK What You Know

1. The game of chess is played on a square-shaped board. What is the perimeter of the chess board shown? See Example 1 (p. 586)

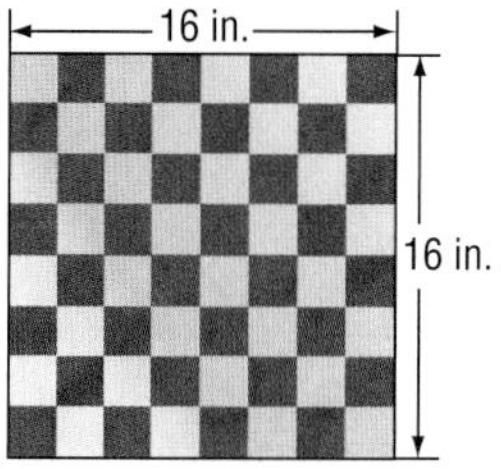

Find the perimeter of each rectangle. See Example 2 (p. 586)

2. 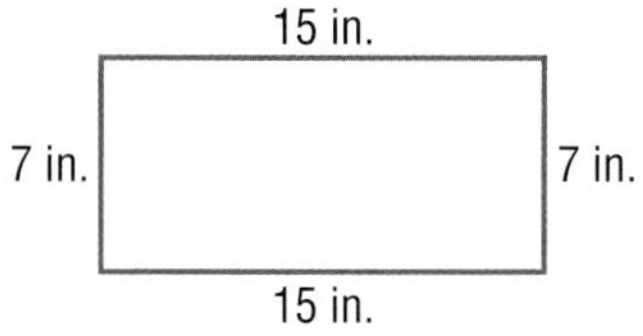

3. 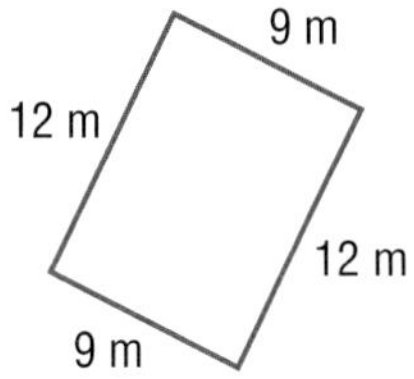

4. 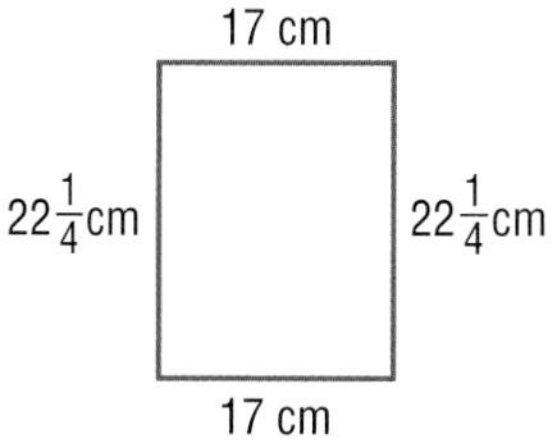

5. Talk About It Describe two ways to find the perimeter of a rectangle.

Practice and Problem Solving

EXTRA PRACTICE See page 685.

6. A typical *Do Not Enter* sign is 750 millimeters on each side. What is the perimeter of the sign? See Example 1 (p. 586)

7. Gray County is a square with each side measuring 30 miles. What is the perimeter of Gray County? See Example 1 (p. 586)

Find the perimeter of each square or rectangle. See Examples 1, 2 (p. 586)

8. 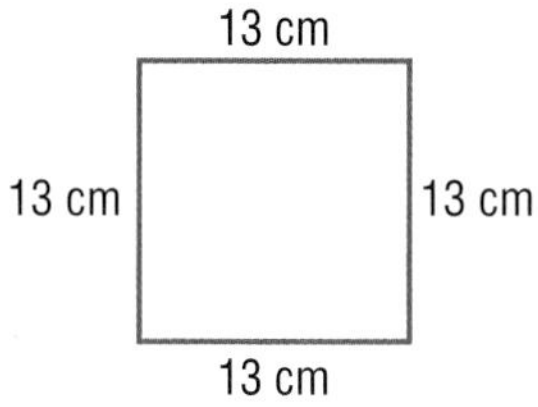

9. 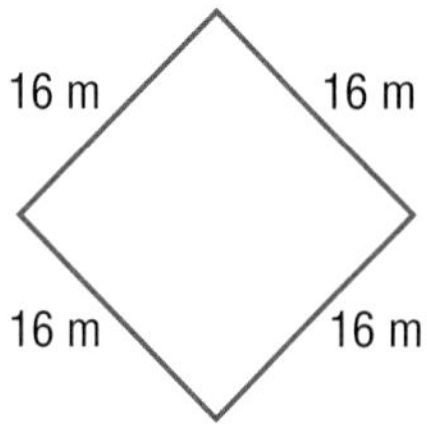

10. 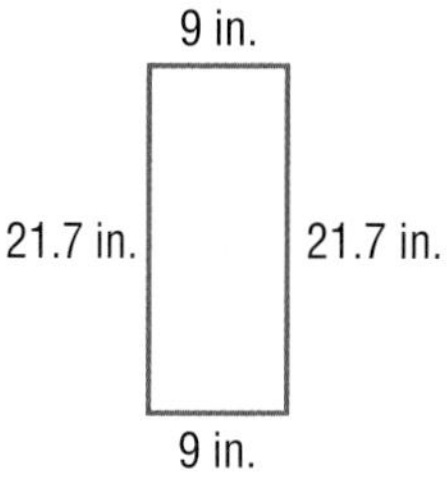

11. 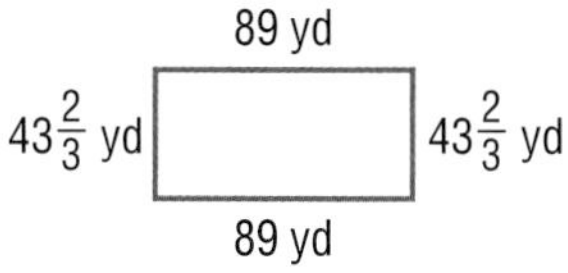

12. 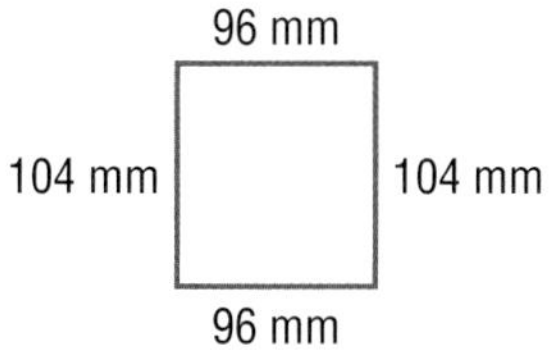

13. 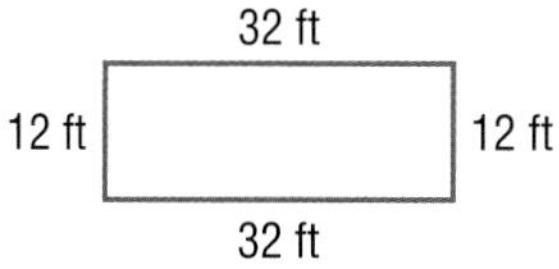

14. Nadia has a square picture frame that will hold a 5-inch by 5-inch photo. The picture frame has a border that is 1 inch thick all the way around. How much larger is the perimeter of the frame than the perimeter of the picture?

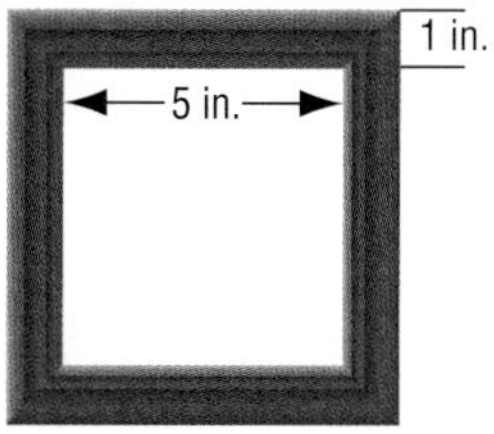

Find the perimeter of each figure.

15.

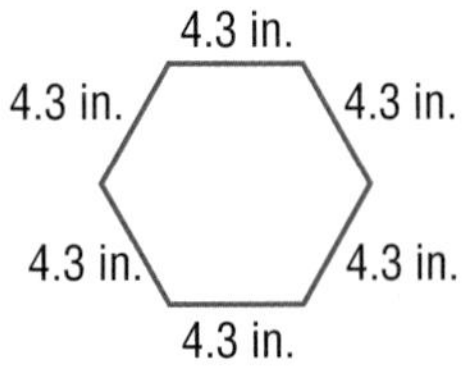

16.

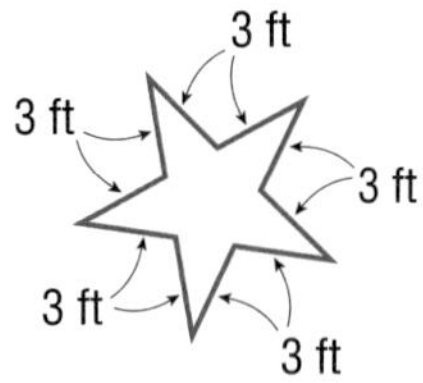

17.

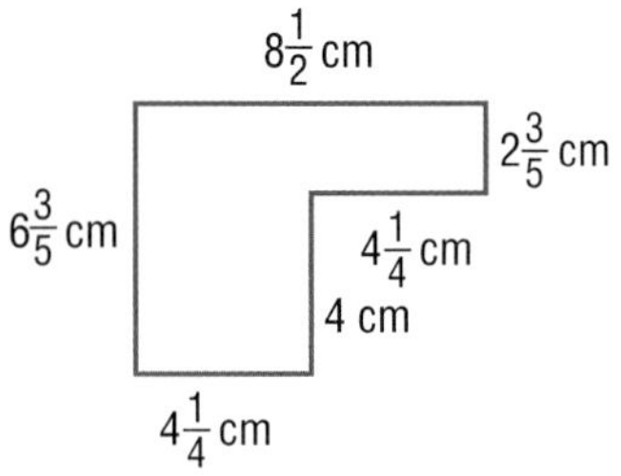

How many segments *y* units long are needed for the perimeter of each figure?

18.

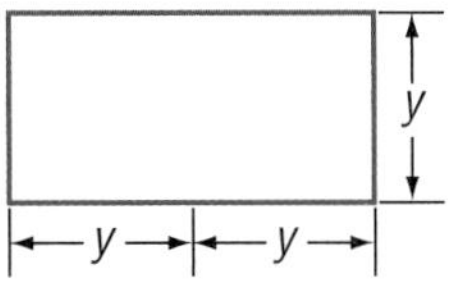

19.

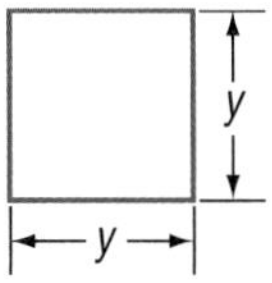

Real-World PROBLEM SOLVING

Data File The California state flag was adopted in 1911.

20. Find the perimeter of the flag.

21. If the perimeter of a certain flag is 20 feet, give a reasonable dimension for the flag.

Source: 50states.com

Data Card

California State Flag

- Designed by William Todd
- First used in 1846
- The grizzly bear represents the bears that were found in the state.
- The star imitates the lone star of Texas' state flag.

H.O.T. Problems

22. OPEN ENDED Draw a rectangle that has a perimeter of 14 inches.

23. REASONING Are two rectangles with equal perimeters always congruent? Explain your reasoning.

24. FIND THE ERROR Cassandra and Lawanda are finding the perimeter of a rectangle that is 16 inches by 11 inches. Who is correct? Explain your reasoning.

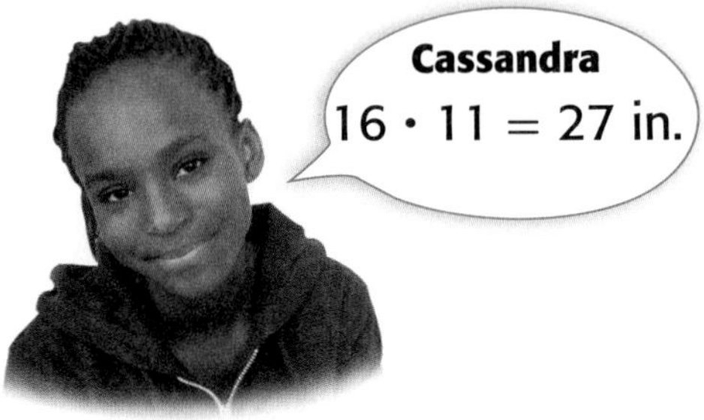

25. **CHALLENGE** Find and compare the perimeters of the rectangles whose dimensions are listed in the table. Then create another set of at least three rectangles that share a similar relationship.

Length (ft)	Width (ft)
6	1
5	2
4	3

26. **WRITING IN ▶MATH** Compare and contrast the formulas for the perimeter of squares and rectangles.

Standards Practice

27 Mr. Johnson is building a bottomless square sandbox using cedar wood.

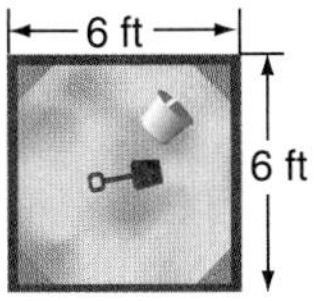

Which method can Mr. Johnson use to find the amount of cedar needed to build the sandbox?

A Multiply the length of a side by 2.

B Multiply the length of a side by 4.

C Square the length of a side.

D Multiply the length of each side by 2 and add the result.

28 Francisco cut a rectangle out of construction paper for a geometry project.

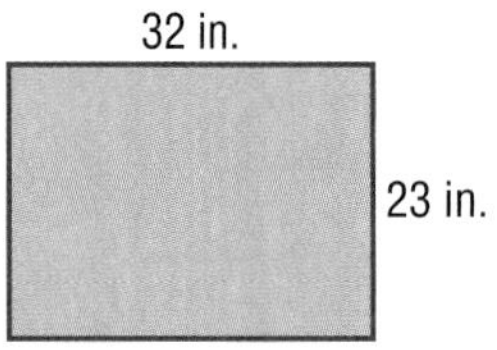

Find the perimeter of the rectangle.

F 92 inches

G 110 inches

H 128 inches

J 736 inches

Spiral Review

Geometry **Draw the three-dimensional figure whose top, side, and front views are shown. Use isometric dot paper.** (Lesson 10-8)

29.

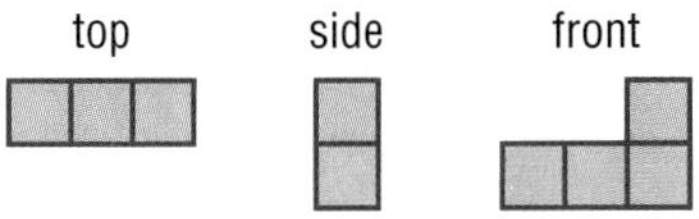

30.

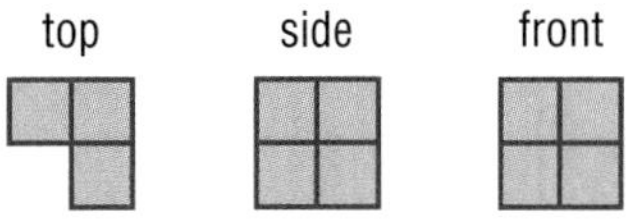

31. Chayton lives in Glacier and works in Alpine. There is no direct route from Glacier to Alpine, so Chayton drives through either Elm or Perth. How many different ways can he drive to work? Use the *draw a diagram* strategy. (Lesson 10-2)

32. The table shows the choices available when ordering a pie from the Taste-n-Tell Bakery. How many different pies are available? (Lesson 9-9)

Taste-n-Tell Bakery		
Flavor	**Crust**	**Size**
Apple Cherry Peach	Single Double	Medium Large

Extend

Measurement Lab for 11-1
Circumference

MAIN IDEA

I will describe the relationship between the diameter and circumference of a circle.

Standard 5MR2.3 Use a variety of methods, such as words, numbers, **symbols,** charts, graphs, **tables,** diagrams, and **models, to explain mathematical reasoning.**
Standard 5MG1.4 Differentiate between, and **use appropriate units of measures for two-** and three-**dimensional objects (i.e., find the perimeter,** area, volume**).**

The perimeter of a circle is called the *circumference.* In this investigation, you will discover the relationship between the circumference of a circle and its diameter—the distance across the circle through its center.

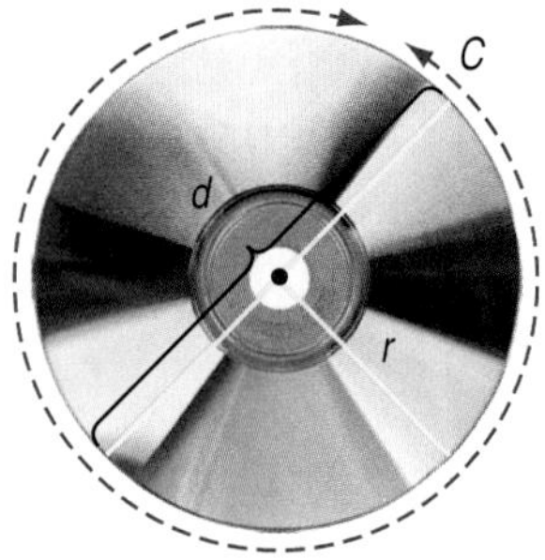

ACTIVITY

Step 1 Make a table like the one shown.

Object	C	d	$\frac{C}{d}$

Step 2 Cut a piece of string the length of the distance C around a circular object such as a jar lid. Use a centimeter ruler to measure the length of the string to the nearest tenth of a centimeter.

Step 3 Measure the distance d across the lid. Record this measurement in the table.

Step 4 Use a calculator to find the ratio of the distance around each circle to the distance across the circle.

Step 5 Repeat Steps 2 though 4 for several other circular objects.

Analyze the Results

1. If you know the diameter of a circle, how can you find the circumference?

2. What would be the approximate circumference of a circle that is 4 inches across?

3. How can you find the circumference of a circle if you know the distance from the center of the circle to the edge of the circle?

Reading Math

Perimeter The circle is the only shape that has a specific term to describe its perimeter.

11-2 Area of Parallelograms

MAIN IDEA

I will find the areas of parallelograms.

Standard 5MG1.1 Derive and use the formula for the area of a triangle and of a **parallelogram by comparing it with the formula for the area of a rectangle.**
Standard 5MG1.4 Differentiate between, and **use appropriate units of measures for two-** and three-**dimensional objects.**

New Vocabulary

base
height

GET READY to Learn

Hands-On Mini Lab

Step 1 Draw and then cut out a rectangle as shown.

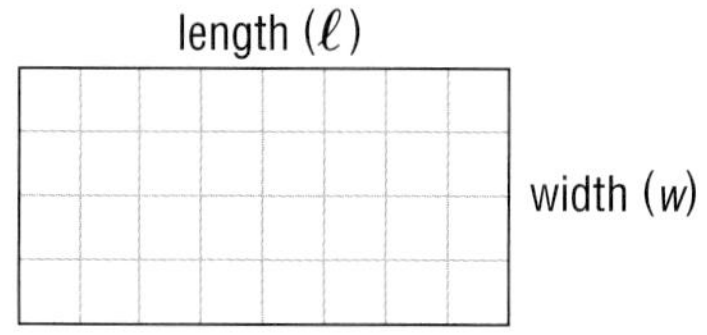

Step 2 Cut a triangle from one side of the rectangle and move it to the other side to form a parallelogram.

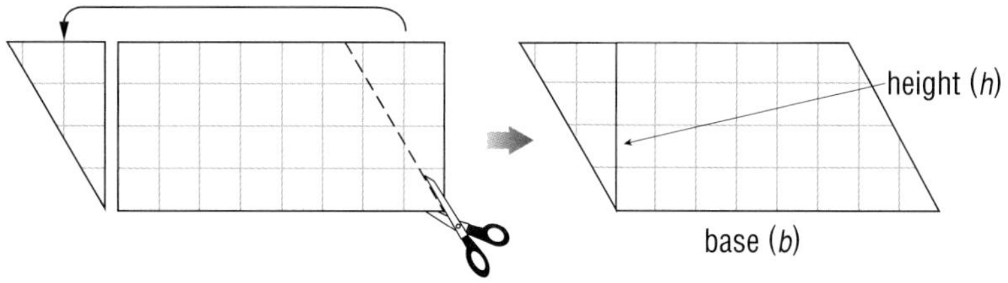

Step 3 Repeat Steps 1 and 2 with two other rectangles of different dimensions on grid paper.

Step 4 Copy and complete the table below using the three rectangles and three corresponding parallelograms you created.

	Length (ℓ)	Width (w)		Base (b)	Height (h)
Rectangle 1			Parallelogram 1		
Rectangle 2			Parallelogram 2		
Rectangle 3			Parallelogram 3		

1. How does a parallelogram relate to a rectangle?

2. What part of the parallelogram corresponds to the length of the rectangle?

3. What part corresponds to the rectangle's width?

4. What is the formula for the area of a parallelogram?

In the Mini Lab, you discovered how the area of a parallelogram is related to the area of a rectangle.

To find the area of a parallelogram, multiply the measures of the base and the height.

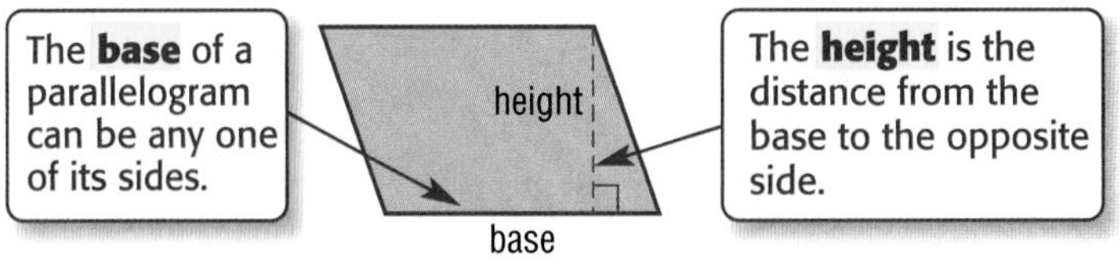

The **base** of a parallelogram can be any one of its sides.
height
base
The **height** is the distance from the base to the opposite side.

KEY CONCEPT — Area of a Parallelogram

Words The area A of a parallelogram is the product of any base b and its height h.

Model

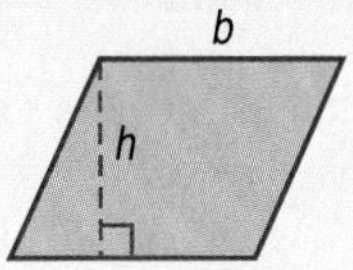

b
h

Symbols $A = bh$

EXAMPLES Find Areas of Parallelograms

Find the area of each parallelogram.

1

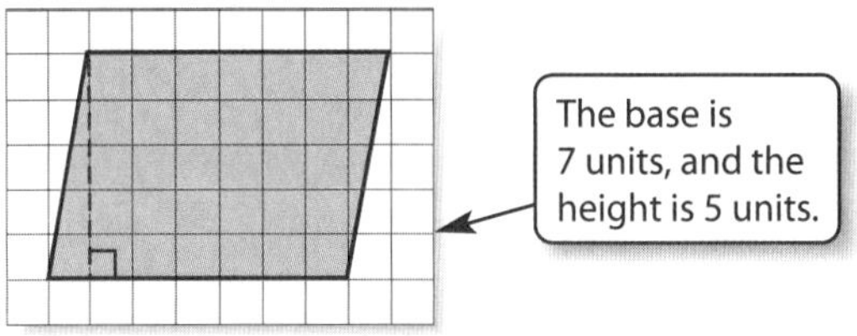

The base is 7 units, and the height is 5 units.

$A = bh$ Area of parallelogram

$A = 7 \cdot 5$ Replace b with 7 and h with 5.

$A = 35$ Multiply.

The area is 35 square units or 35 units^2.

2

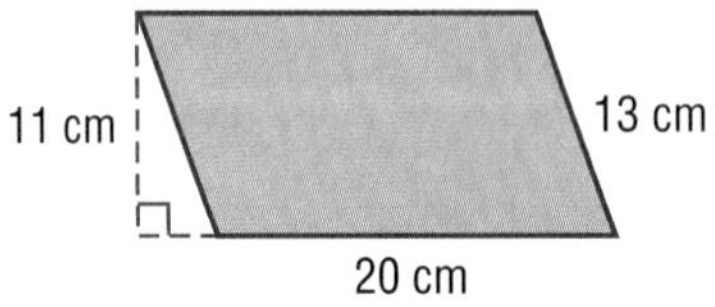

11 cm
13 cm
20 cm

$A = bh$ Area of parallelogram

$A = 20 \cdot 11$ Replace b with 20 and h with 11.

$A = 220$ Multiply.

The area is 220 square centimeters or 220 cm^2.

Reading Math

Area Measurement Area measurement can be written using abbreviations and an exponent of 2.
For example:
square units = units^2
square inches = in^2
square feet = ft^2
square meters = m^2

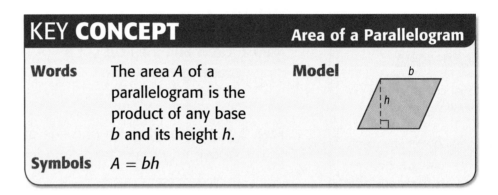

Real-World EXAMPLE

3 An architect is designing a parallelogram-shaped lobby for a small office building. Find the area of the lobby.

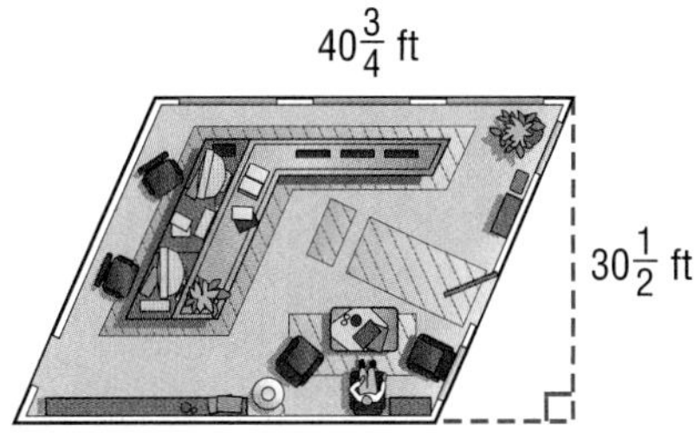

The floor plan of the lobby is a parallelogram, so use the formula $A = bh$.

Estimate $A = 40 \cdot 30$ or $1{,}200$ ft^2

$A = bh$	Area of parallelogram
$A = 40\frac{3}{4} \cdot 30\frac{1}{2}$	Replace b with $40\frac{3}{4}$ and h with $30\frac{1}{2}$.
$A = 1{,}242\frac{7}{8}$	Multiply.

The area of the lobby's floor plan is $1{,}242\frac{7}{8}$ square feet.

Check for Reasonableness Compare to the estimate.
$1{,}242\frac{7}{8} \approx 1{,}200$ ✓

Online Personal Tutor at ca.gr5math.com

CHECK What You Know

Find the area of each parallelogram. **See Examples 1, 2 (p. 592)**

1.

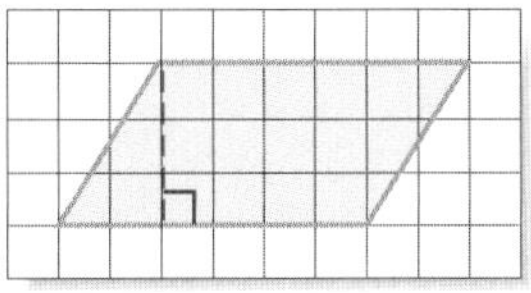

2.

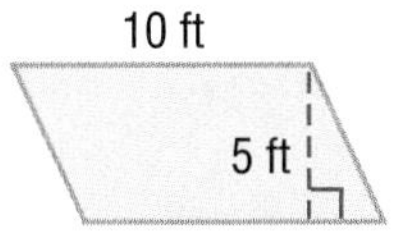

3.

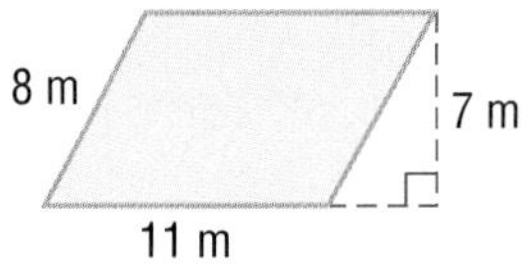

4. Find the area of a parallelogram with base $13\frac{1}{6}$ yards and height $21\frac{2}{3}$ yards.

5. The size of the parallelogram piece in a set of tangrams is shown at the right. Find the area of the piece.
See Example 3 (p. 593)

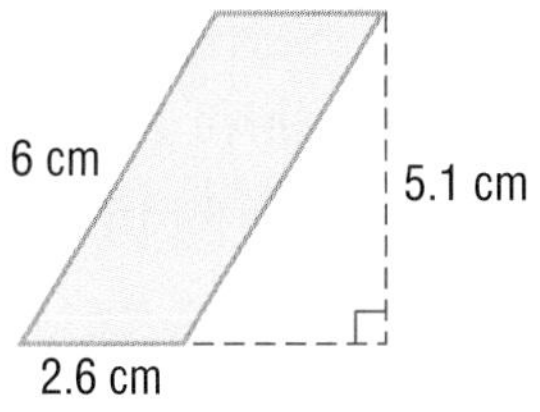

6. **Talk About It** A parallelogram has a base of 18.75 inches and a height of 11.125 inches. What is a reasonable estimate for the area of the parallelogram?

Practice and Problem Solving

EXTRA PRACTICE
See page 685.

Find the area of each parallelogram. See Examples 1, 2 (p. 592)

7.

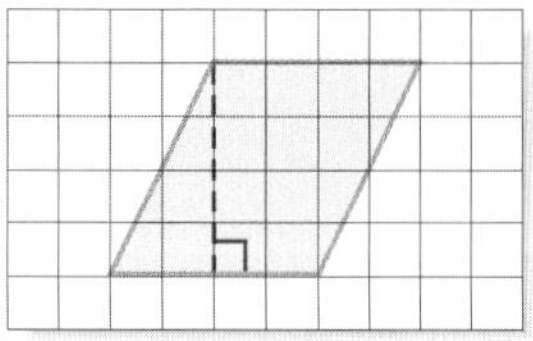

8.

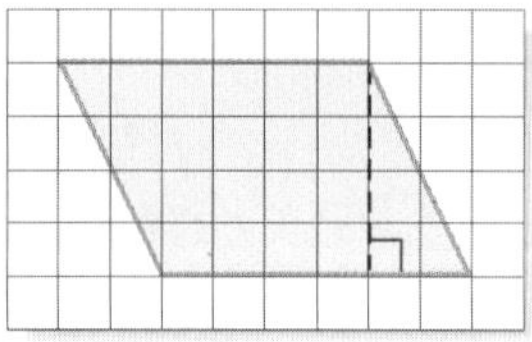

9.

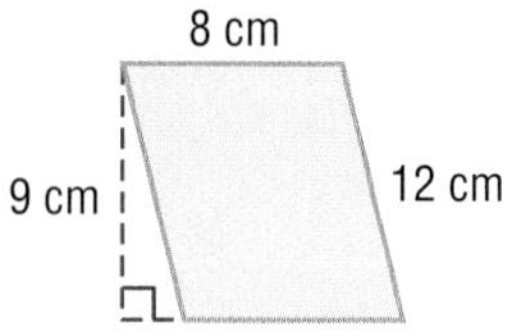

10.

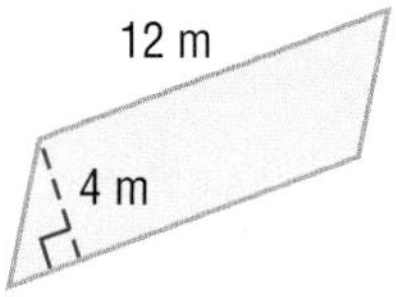

11.

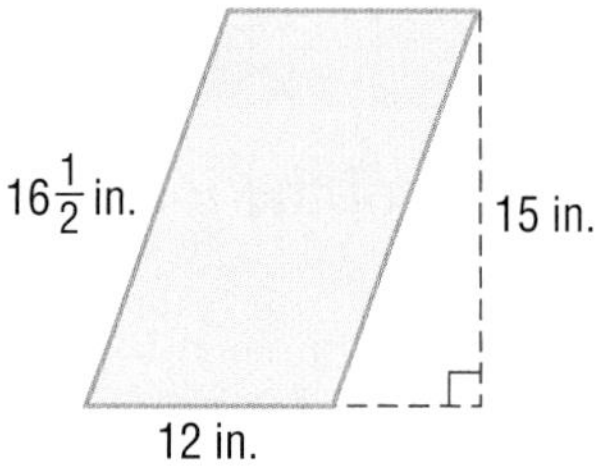

12.

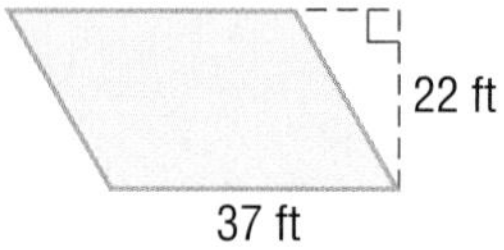

13. Find the area of a parallelogram with base $8\frac{4}{5}$ inches and height $6\frac{3}{8}$ inches.

14. Find the area of a parallelogram with base 6.75 meters and height 4.8 meters.

15. A local meteorologist alerted people to a thunderstorm warning for the region shown on the map. What is the area of the region that is under a thunderstorm warning?
See Example 3 (p. 593)

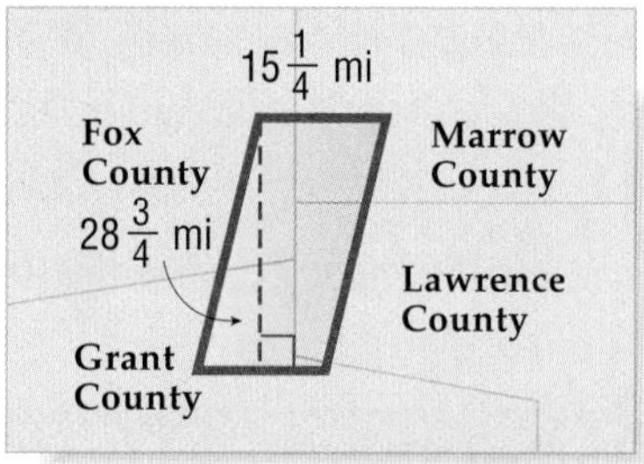

16. What is the area of the side of the eraser?
See Example 3 (p. 593)

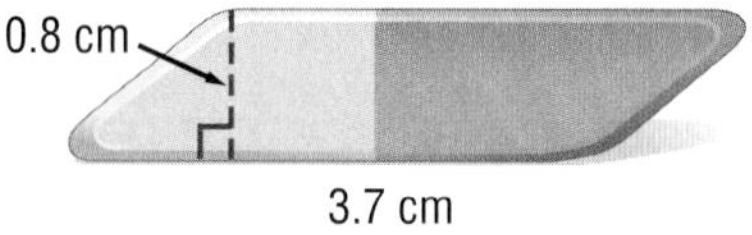

Find the area of the shaded region in each figure.

17.

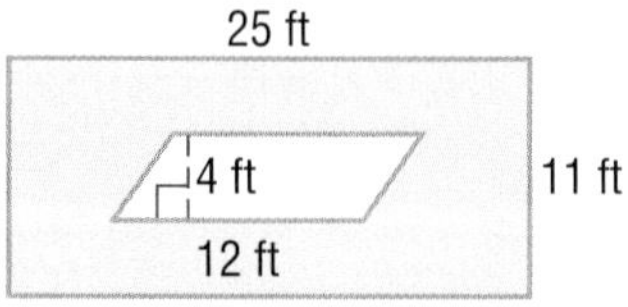

18.

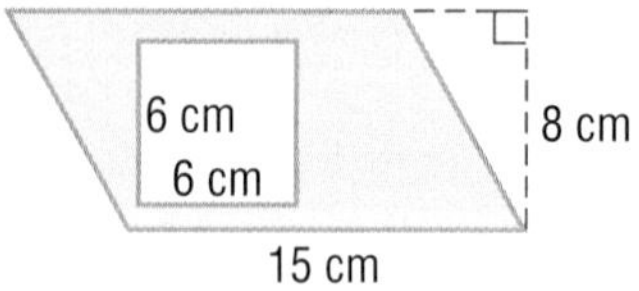

19. Guadalupe made a parallelogram-shaped picture frame to display a piece of art work. What is the area of the art work that will be visible in the picture frame?

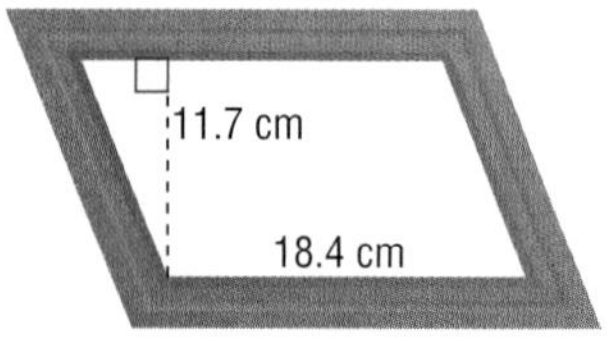

20. The base of the Wilshire Palisades building in Santa Monica is shaped like a parallelogram. The first floor has an area of 20,000 square feet. If the base of this parallelogram is 250 feet, can its height be 70 feet? Explain.

H.O.T. Problems

21. **REASONING** Refer to parallelogram *KLMN* at the right. If the area of parallelogram *KLMN* is 35 square inches, what is the area of triangle *KLN*?

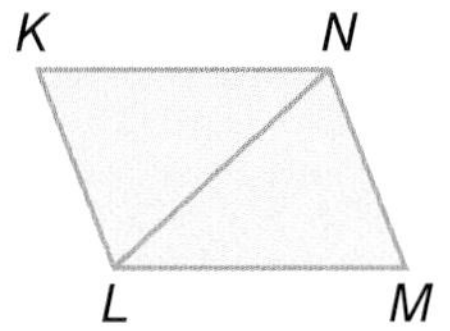

22. **OPEN ENDED** On grid paper, draw three different parallelograms with base three units and height two units. Then find the area of each parallelogram.

23. **CHALLENGE** If $x = 5$ and $y < x$, which figure has the greater area? Explain your reasoning.

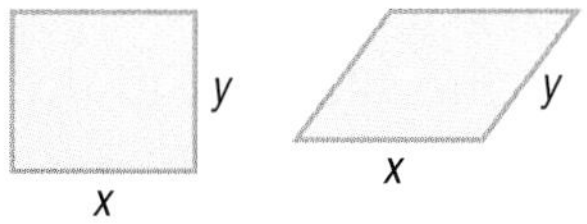

24. **WRITING IN MATH** Explain how the formula for the area of a parallelogram is related to the formula for the area of a rectangle.

Standards Practice

25 Robert used a piece of poster board shaped like a parallelogram to make a sign for his campaign as class president. The base of the poster board is 52 inches, and the height is 36 inches. Find the area of the poster board.

A 176 in^2

B 936 in^2

C 1,664 in^2

D 1,872 in^2

26 A family has a flower garden in the shape of a parallelogram in their backyard. They planted grass in the rest of the yard. What is the area of the backyard that is planted with grass?

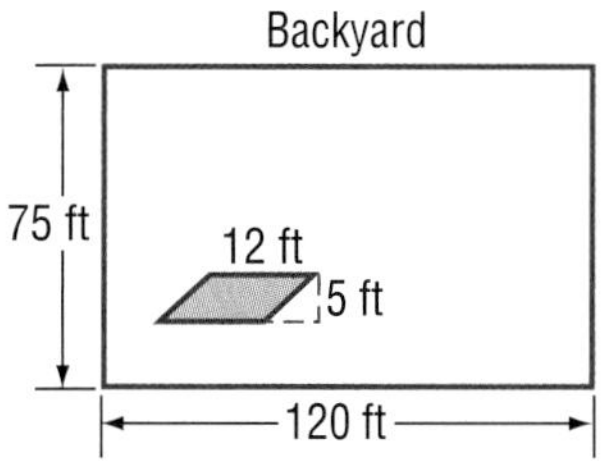

F 390 sq ft

G 8,940 sq ft

H 9,060 sq ft

J 9,144 sq ft

Spiral Review

27. **Measurement** The Lincoln Memorial is a rectangular structure whose base is 188 feet by 118 feet. What is the perimeter of the base of the Lincoln Memorial? **(Lesson 11-1)**

28. Dawn packed some moving boxes into the trunk of her car as shown. Draw a top, a side, and a front view of the boxes. **(Lesson 10-8)**

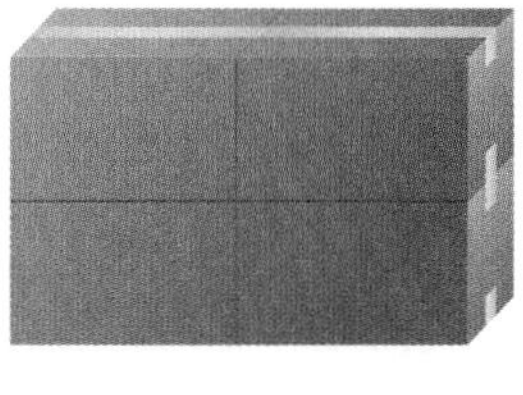

11-3 Problem-Solving Strategy

MAIN IDEA I will solve problems by making a model.

Standard 5MR2.3 Use a variety of methods, such as words, numbers, symbols, charts, graphs, tables, diagrams, and **models, to explain mathematical reasoning. Standard 5MG1.4** Differentiate between, and **use appropriate units of measures for two-** and three-**dimensional objects.**

While volunteering at the local farm market, Julia was asked to make a display for the oranges. She needs to stack the oranges in the shape of a square pyramid. The base should have 100 oranges and one orange needs to be on top. There are 400 oranges total. Are 400 oranges enough to make a square pyramid with a base of 100 oranges?

Understand

What facts do you know?

- The oranges need to be in the shape of a square pyramid with 100 oranges in the base and 1 orange on top.
- There are 400 oranges altogether.

What do you need to find?

Are 400 oranges enough to make a square pyramid with a base of 100 oranges?

Plan

Make a model using pennies to find the number of oranges needed.

Solve

Begin with 100 pennies. For each consecutive layer, place 1 penny where 4 meet.

bottom layer | second layer | third layer | fourth layer

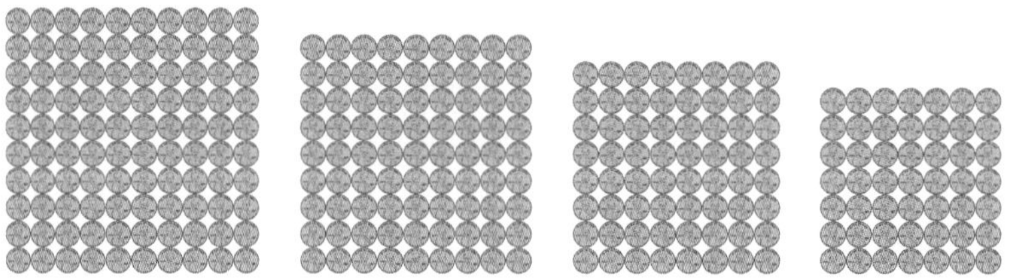

100 | 81 | 64 | 49

By continuing this pattern, 100 + 81 + 64 + 49 + 36 + 25 + 16 + 9 + 4 + 1 or 385 oranges will be needed. Since $385 < 400$, 400 oranges are enough to make a square pyramid.

Check

Look back at the problem. 400 − 100 − 81 − 64 − 49 − 36 − 25 − 16 − 9 − 4 − 1 leaves 15 oranges. ✓

ANALYZE the Strategy

Refer to the problem on the previous page.

1. If the base of the pyramid had 121 oranges, the next row would have 100 and then 81 and so on. How many more oranges would be needed to complete the pyramid?

2. Tell how making a model helped to solve the problem.

3. What is a real-world example of when you could use the *make a model* strategy?

4. How are the *draw a diagram* strategy and the *make a model* strategy similar? How do they differ?

PRACTICE the Strategy

EXTRA PRACTICE
See page 685.

Solve. Use the *make a model* strategy.

5. Kim is designing a rectangular stained glass window made of congruent pieces of glass shaped like squares. If the window frame is 3 feet by 4 feet and the square pieces are 4 inches long, how many squares are needed to fill the window?

6. Terrell is arranging boxes of rice, like the one shown, on a shelf that is 3 feet long and 11 inches deep. If he needs to place 20 boxes of rice on the shelf, describe a possible arrangement for the boxes.

7. A designer wants to arrange 12 square tiles into a rectangular shape with the least perimeter possible. How many tiles will be in each row?

8. Bruce is stacking boxes for a display. The bottom layer of the display has six boxes. There is one less box in each layer, and there are five layers in the display. How many boxes does Bruce use?

9. Rhonda folded a piece of notebook paper in half three times. Then she punched a hole through all the layers. How many holes will there be when she unfolds the paper?

10. For a school assignment, Santiago has to give three different possibilities for the dimensions of a rectangular garden that has a perimeter of 28 feet and an area greater than 30 square feet. One of the models he made is shown. What are two other possibilities for the dimensions of the garden?

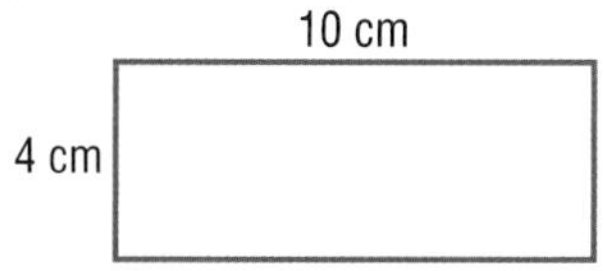

11. **WRITING IN MATH** Refer to Exercise 7. Describe what type of model you used to solve the problem.

Explore

Measurement Lab for 11-4
Area of Triangles

In this activity, you will discover the formula for the area of a triangle using the properties of parallelograms.

MAIN IDEA

I will discover the formula for the area of a triangle using the properties of parallelograms and a table of values.

Standard 5MG1.1 Derive and use the formula for the area of a triangle and of a parallelogram **by comparing it with the formula for the area of a rectangle.**
Standard 5MR3.3 Develop generalizations of the results obtained and apply them in other circumstances.

ACTIVITY

Step 1 Copy the table shown.

Parallelogram	Base, *b*	Height, *h*	Area of Parallelogram	Area of Each Triangle
A	4	6		
B	2	5		
C	3	4		
D	5	3		
E	7	5		

Step 2 Draw Parallelogram A on grid paper using the dimensions given in the table.

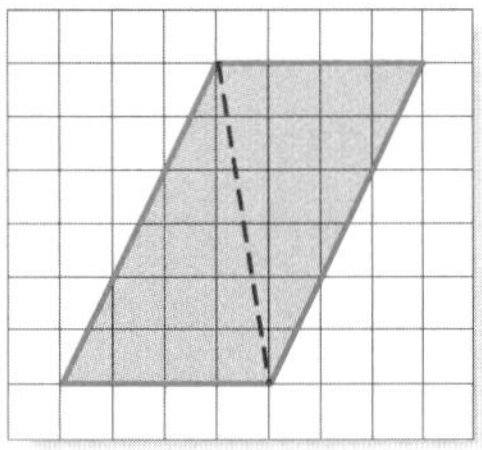

Step 3 Draw a diagonal as shown.

Step 4 Cut out the parallelogram. Then calculate its area. Record this measure in the table.

Step 5 Cut along the diagonal to form two triangles.

Analyze the Results

1. Compare the base and height of each triangle to the base and height of the original parallelogram. What do you notice?
2. Compare the two triangles formed. How are they related?
3. What is the area of each triangle? Record your answer.
4. Repeat Steps 2 through 5 for Parallelograms B through E. Calculate the area of each triangle formed and record your results in the table.
5. Study the patterns in the table. Then write a formula that relates the area A of a triangle to the length of its base b and height h.

11-4 Area of Triangles

Concepts in Motion
Interactive Lab
ca.gr5math.com

GET READY to Learn

Tri-Ominos is a game played with triangular game pieces that are all the same size. Describe the relationship that exists between the area of one triangle and the area of the figure formed by the two triangles.

MAIN IDEA

I will find the areas of triangles.

Standard 5MG1.1 Derive and use the formula for the area of a triangle and of a parallelogram **by comparing it with the formula for the area of a rectangle.**
Standard 5MG1.4 Differentiate between, and **use appropriate units of measures for two-** and three-**dimensional objects.**

A parallelogram can be formed by two congruent triangles. Since congruent triangles have the same area, the area of a triangle is one half the area of the parallelogram.

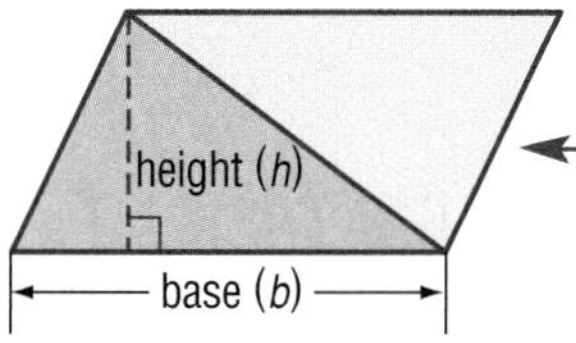

The base of a triangle can be any one of its sides. The height is the shortest distance from a base to the opposite vertex.

KEY CONCEPT — Area of a Triangle

Words The area *A* of a triangle is one half the product of the base *b*, and its height *h*.

Model

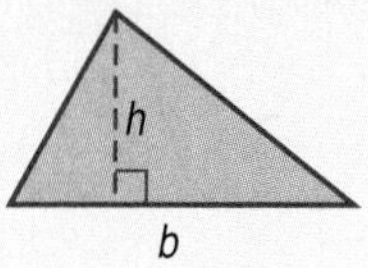

Symbols $A = \frac{1}{2}bh$

EXAMPLES Find the Area of a Triangle

Find the area of each triangle.

1

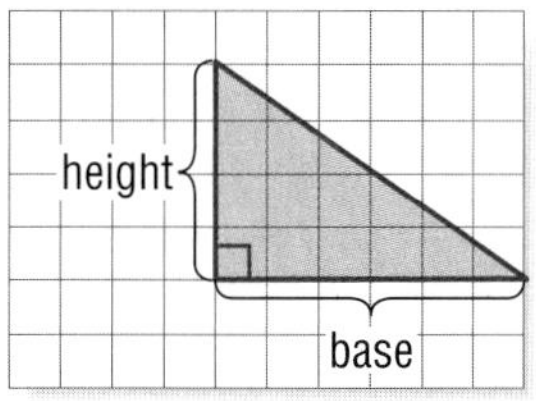

By counting, you find that the measure of the base is 6 units and the height is 4 units.

(continued on the next page)

Remember

You can use mental math to multiply $\frac{1}{2}(6)(4)$. Think: Half of 6 is 3 and 3×4 is 12.

$A = \frac{1}{2}bh$ Area of a triangle

$A = \frac{1}{2}(6)(4)$ Replace b with 6 and h with 4.

$A = \frac{1}{2}(24)$ Multiply.

$A = 12$ Multiply.

The area of the triangle is 12 square units.

Remember

To estimate the area of the triangle in Example 2, round the base to 15 meters and the height to 10 meters. The area is then $\frac{1}{2}(15)(10)$ or 75 square meters. Since 76.5 is close to 75, the answer is reasonable.

2

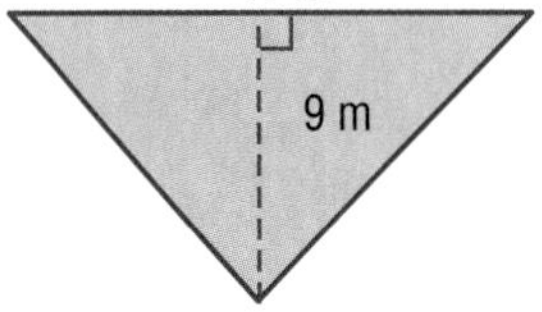

$A = \frac{1}{2}bh$ Area of a triangle

$A = \frac{1}{2}(17)(9)$ Replace b with 17 and h with 9.

$A = \frac{1}{2}(153)$ Multiply.

$A = 76.5$ Divide. $153 \div 2 = 76.5$

The area of the triangle is 76.5 square meters.

Online **Personal Tutor at** ca.gr5math.com

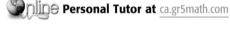

Real-World EXAMPLE

3 **The front of a two-person camping tent has the dimensions shown. How much material was used to make the front of the tent?**

$A = \frac{1}{2}bh$ Area of a triangle

$A = \frac{1}{2}(5)(3)$ Replace b with 5 and h with 3.

$A = \frac{1}{2}(15)$ Multiply.

$A = 7.5$ Divide. $15 \div 2 = 7.5$

The front of the tent has an area of 7.5 square feet.

CHECK What You Know

Find the area of each triangle. See Examples 1, 2 (pp. 599–600)

1.

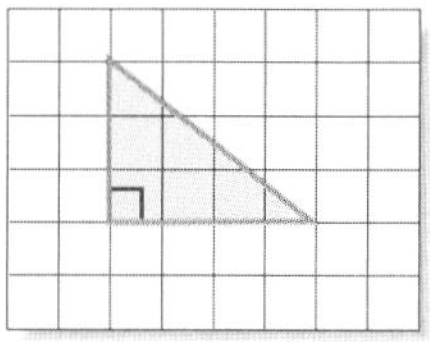

2.

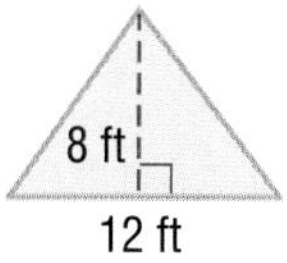

3.

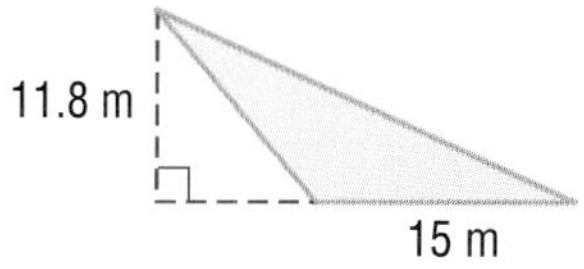

4. Consuela made an equilateral triangular paper box as shown. What is the area of the top of the box? See Example 3 (p. 600)

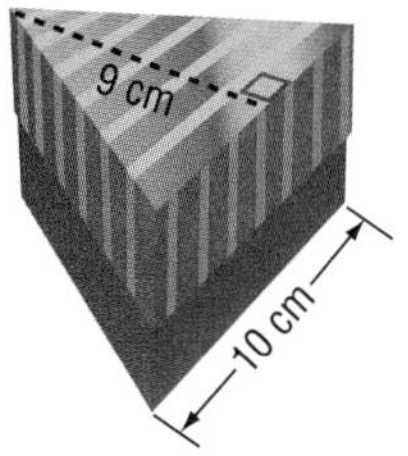

5. Talk About It In your own words, explain how to find the area of a triangle.

Practice and Problem Solving

EXTRA PRACTICE See page 686.

Find the area of each triangle. See Examples 1, 2 (pp. 599–600)

6.

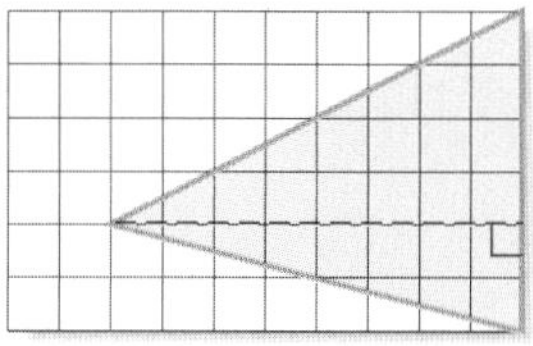

7.

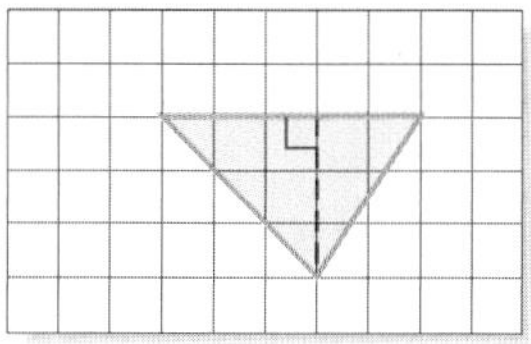

8.

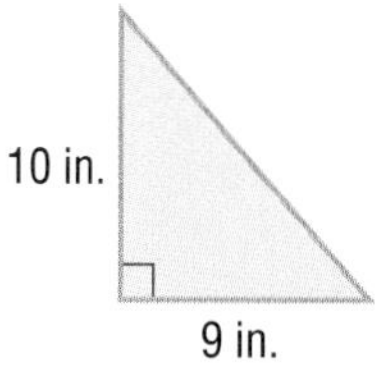

9.

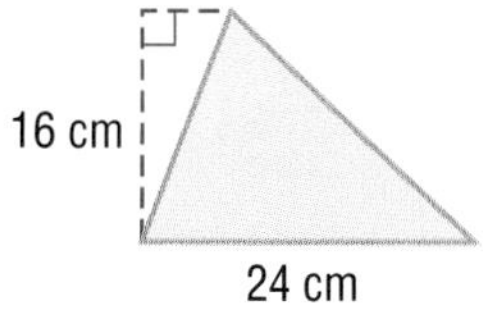

10.

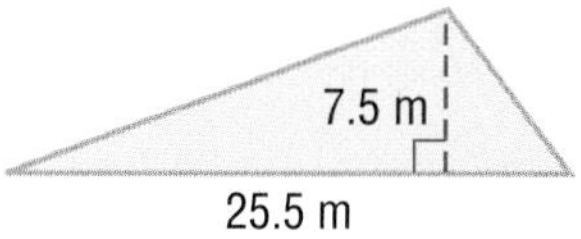

11.

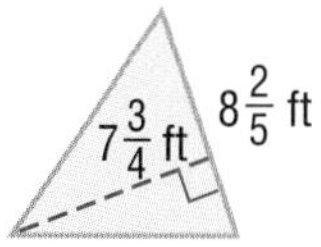

12. height: 14 in., base: 35 in.

13. height: 27 cm, base: 19 cm

14. Ansley is going to help his father shingle the roof of their house. What is the area of the triangular portion of one end of the roof to be shingled? See Example 3 (p. 600)

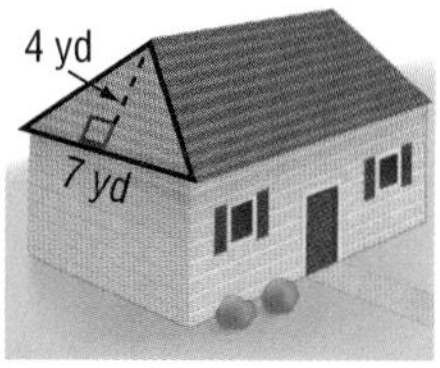

15. An architect plans on designing a building on a triangular plot of land. If the base of the triangle is 100 feet and the height is 96 feet, find the available floor area the architect has to design the building. See Example 3 (p. 600)

16. A flower bed in a parking lot is shaped like a triangle as shown. Find the area of the flower bed in square feet. If one bag of topsoil covers 10 square feet, how many bags are needed to cover this flower bed?

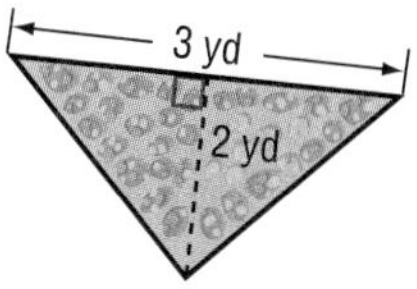

17. Algebra The table at the right shows the areas of a triangle where the base of the triangle stays the same but the height changes. Write an algebraic expression that can be used to find the area of a triangle that has a base of 5 units and a height of n units.

Area of Triangles		
Base (units)	Height (units)	Area (units^2)
5	2	5
5	4	10
5	6	15
5	8	20
5	n	■

18. Which is smaller, a triangle with an area of 1 square foot or a triangle with an area of 64 square inches?

Find the perimeter and area of each figure.

19.

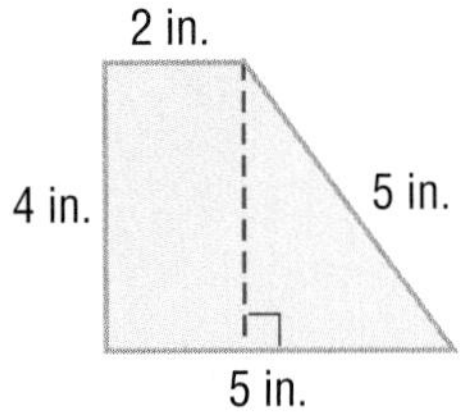

20.

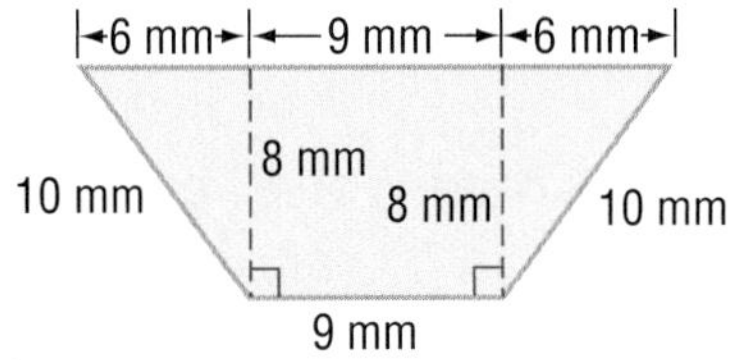

H.O.T. Problems

21. FIND THE ERROR Susana and D.J. are finding the area of the triangle. Who is correct? Explain your reasoning.

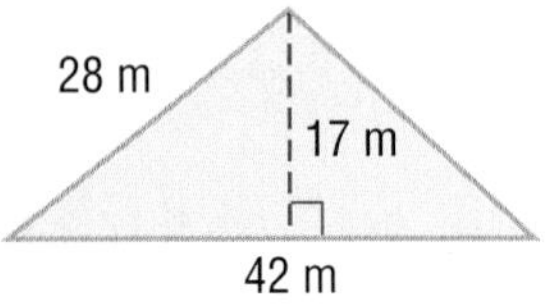

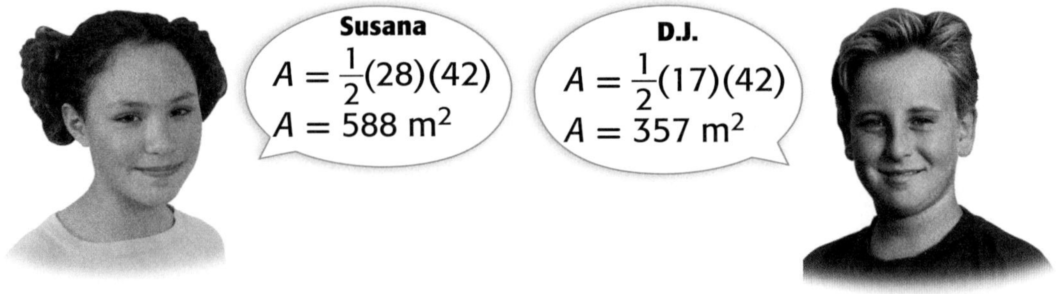

CHALLENGE For Exercises 22–24, use the information below.

The four shaded triangles in the figure shown are congruent.

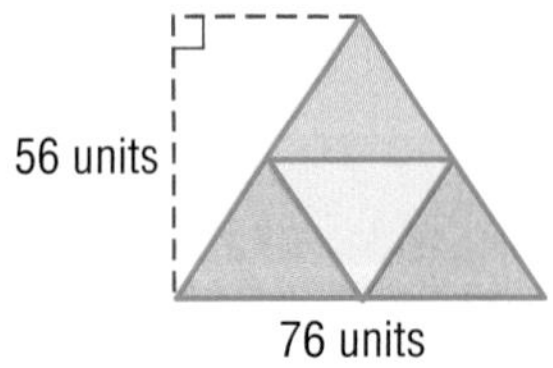

22. Calculate the area of the figure.

23. Find the measure of the base and height of the four smaller triangles.

24. Calculate the area of one small triangle. Is this answer reasonable? Explain.

25. OPEN ENDED Draw two different triangles each having an area of 24 square feet.

26. **WRITING IN ▶MATH** Draw a triangle and label its base and height. Draw another triangle that has the same base, but a height twice that of the first triangle. Find the area of each triangle. Then write a ratio that expresses the area of the first triangle to the area of the second triangle.

Standards Practice

27 If the area of parallelogram *FGHJ* is 14.2 square units, what is the area of triangle *FGH*?

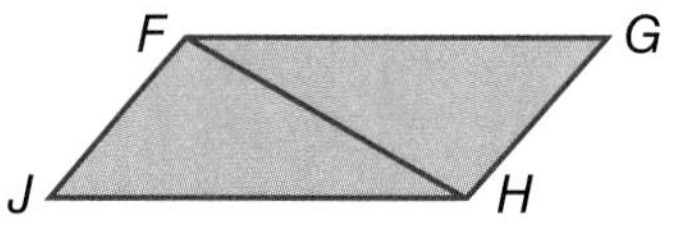

A 7.1 square units

B 14.2 square units

C 28.4 square units

D 56.8 square units

28 Norma cut a triangle out of construction paper for an art project.

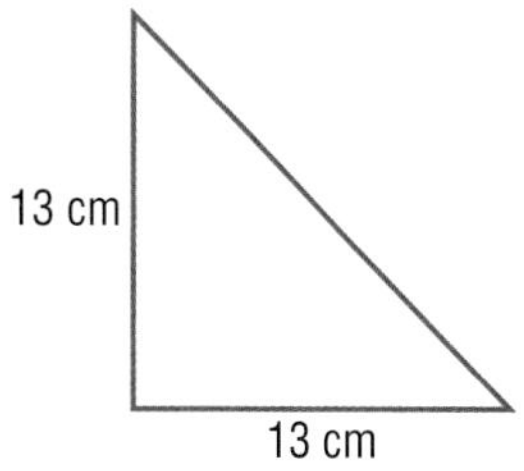

What is the area of the triangle?

F 13 cm^2 **H** 84.5 cm^2

G 26 cm^2 **J** 90.5 cm^2

Spiral Review

29. A bookstore arranges its best-seller books in the front window on three shelves. The top shelf has 2 books. Each consecutive shelf has one more book than the previous shelf. How many books can be displayed on the three shelves? Use the *make a model* strategy. **(Lesson 11-3)**

30. **Measurement** Find the area of a parallelogram with a base of 20 millimeters and a height of 16 millimeters. **(Lesson 11-2)**

31. **Measurement** Measure the length and width of a student ID card or library card to the nearest eighth inch. Then find the perimeter of the card. **(Lesson 11-1)**

32. The table shows the interest rates advertised by three different banks for a house loan. Find the difference between the highest and the lowest rate. **(Lesson 5-8)**

House Loan Rates

Bank	Interest Rate
A	$7\frac{1}{4}\%$
B	$6\frac{3}{5}\%$
C	$6\frac{5}{6}\%$

Game Time

What's the Area?

Estimate and Measure Area

Get Ready!

Players: two to four

You will need: 18 cards with diagrams of figures, centimeter ruler, paper, pencils

Get Set!

- Shuffle and turn the cards facedown.
- Give paper and pencil to each player.

Go!

- Turn the first card face up.
- Each of you estimates the area of the figure in square inches and writes that number on your paper.
- Work together to measure the figure and calculate the area.
- Each of you compares the actual area to your estimate. The player or players with the closest estimate earn one point.
- Play continues until all the cards are used. The player with the most points wins.

Mid-Chapter Check

Lessons 11-1 through 11-4

Find the perimeter of each square or rectangle. **(Lesson 11-1)**

1.

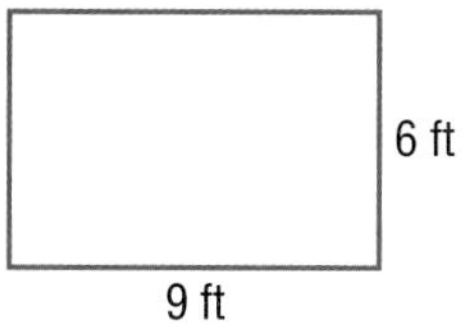

2.

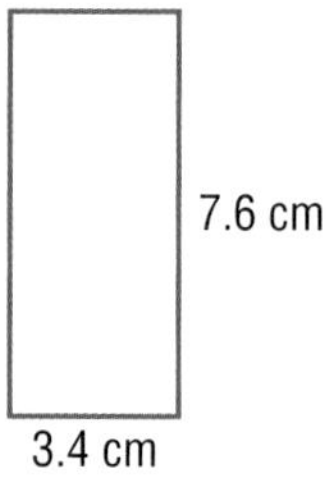

3.

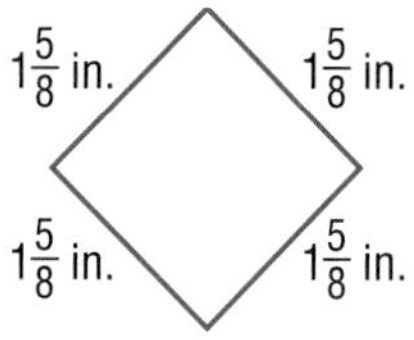

4.

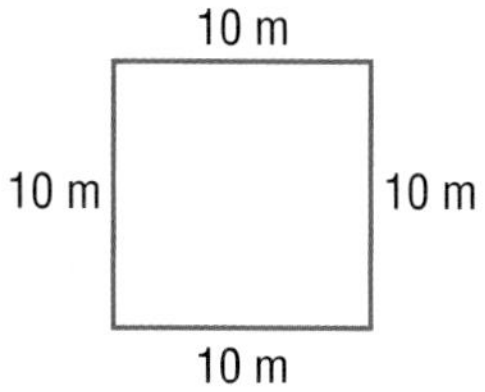

5. Ernesto rides his bike around a square path that measures 50 feet on each side. How far does Ernesto ride one time around the path? **(Lesson 11-1)**

6. How many feet of fencing is needed to fence a rectangular field 126 feet by 84 feet? **(Lesson 11-1)**

7. **STANDARDS PRACTICE** *FGHJ* is a parallelogram in the figure below. If the area of triangle *FGJ* is 42 square meters, find the area of *FGHJ*. **(Lesson 11-2)**

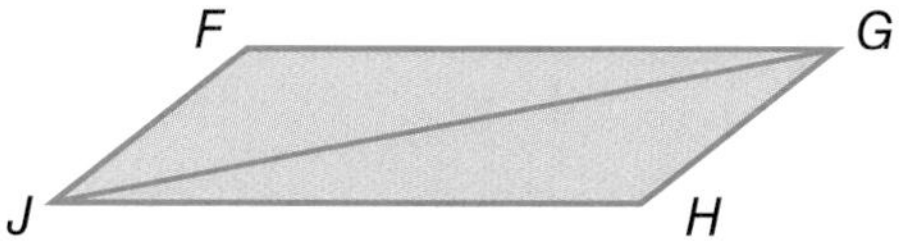

A 10 square meters

B 21 square meters

C 84 square meters

D 168 square meters

Find the area of each parallelogram. **(Lesson 11-2)**

8.

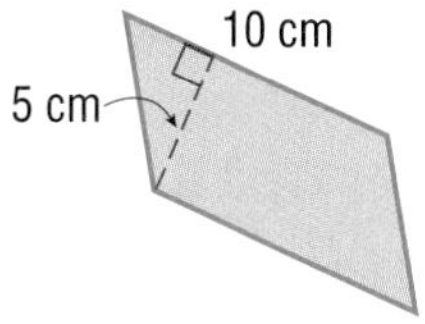

9.

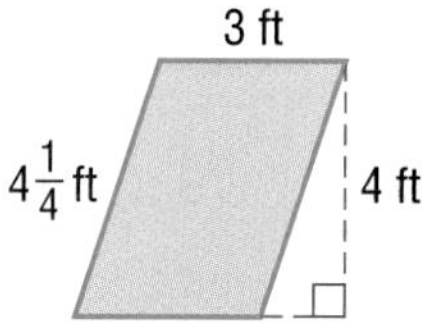

10. A kite has two pairs of congruent sides. If two sides are 56 centimeters and 34 centimeters, what is the perimeter of the kite? Use the *make a model* strategy. **(Lesson 11-3)**

11. **STANDARDS PRACTICE** Which expression can be used to find the area of a triangle that has a height of 9 units and a base of *n* units? **(Lesson 11-4)**

F $9n$ **H** $\frac{9}{2}$

G $4.5n$ **J** $0.5n$

Find the area of each triangle. **(Lesson 11-4)**

12.

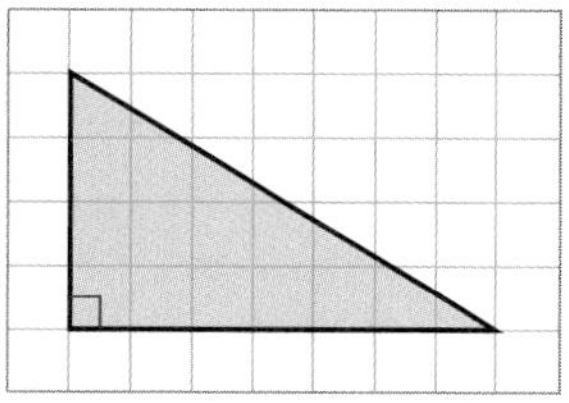

13.

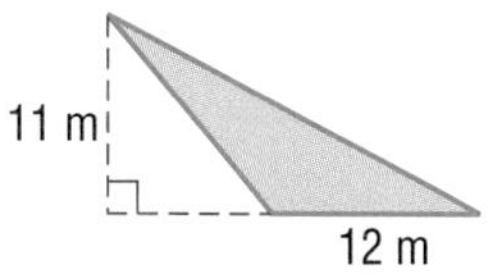

14. **WRITING IN ►MATH** A sailboat has a triangular sail with a base of 10 feet and a height of 31 feet. Is the area of the sail greater than 150 square feet? Explain. **(Lesson 11-4)**

11-5 Problem-Solving Investigation

MAIN IDEA I will choose the best strategy to solve a problem.

Standard 5MR2.3 Use a variety of methods, such as words, **numbers,** symbols, charts, graphs, tables, **diagrams, and models, to explain mathematical reasoning. Standard 5MG1.4** Differentiate between, and **use appropriate units of measures for two-** and three-**dimensional objects.**

P.S.I. TEAM +

ROSS: I want people to find out about a party I'm having, so I will tell Jamie and Cara and have each of them tell two friends, and so on. I wonder how many people would be invited to the party in three minutes if two friends tell another two friends each minute?

YOUR MISSION: Find the number of people who would be invited to the party in three minutes.

Understand — You know that Ross tells Jamie and Cara about the party, and then each friend tells two other friends each minute. You need to find the number of people who would be invited to the party in three minutes.

Plan — Draw a diagram to show the number of people who would be invited to the party.

Solve

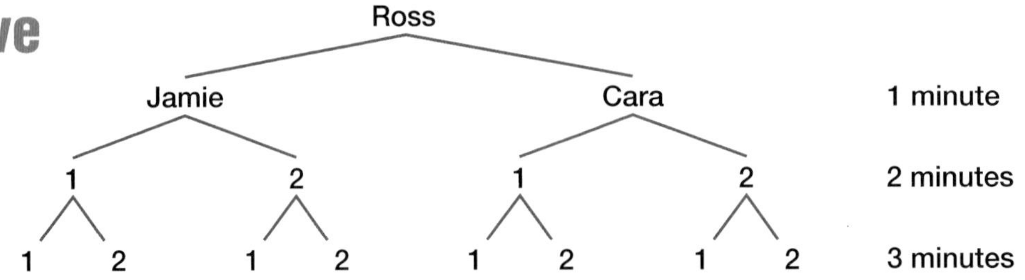

So, 14 people would be invited to the party.

Check — Look back at the problem to see if the diagram meets all of the requirements. Since the diagram is correct, the answer is correct. ✓

Mixed Problem Solving

EXTRA PRACTICE
See page 686.

Use any strategy shown below to solve each problem.

PROBLEM-SOLVING STRATEGIES

- Make a model.
- Draw a diagram.
- Look for a pattern.

1. The sides of each square in the figure are twice as long as the square on its immediate right. What is the perimeter of the entire figure?

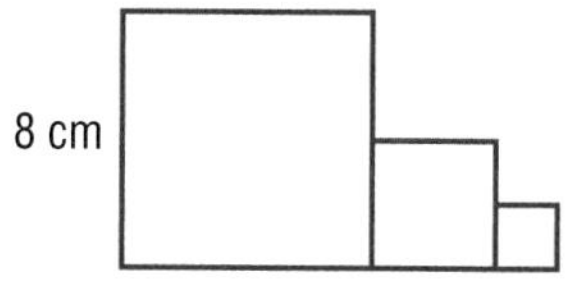

2. The fifth grade class is planning a field trip. There are 575 students in the fifth grade. If each bus holds 48 people, how many buses will they need?

3. Of 75 families surveyed, 24 have a red car, and 14 have a silver car. Of those families, 5 have both a red car and a silver car. How many have neither a red car nor a silver car?

4. Jacinta has a $31\frac{1}{2}$-inch long piece of ribbon that she needs to cut for an art project. How many cuts does she need to make if she needs 9 equal-size pieces for the project?

5. What are the next two figures in the pattern?

6. Myron sends three of his friends an e-mail. Each friend then forwards the e-mail to three other friends, and so on. If three friends can forward the e-mail to another three friends each hour, how long will it take for 39 friends to receive the e-mail?

7. The table below gives the average price of a dozen eggs in a recent year for two states.

State	Price ($)
Nebraska	0.34
Alabama	1.62

Which state was closer to the national average of $0.73?

8. Samantha's father purchased a new car. His loan, including interest, is $12,720. How much are his monthly payments if he has 12 payments per year for 5 years?

9. Mario took a piece of notebook paper and cut it in half. Then he placed the 2 pieces on top of each other and cut them in half to have 4 pieces of paper. If he could keep cutting the paper, how many pieces of paper would he have after 6 cuts?

10. WRITING IN MATH A rectangle is 2 centimeters longer than it is wide. The perimeter is 28 centimeters. Explain how you could use the *draw a diagram* strategy to find the length of the rectangle.

11-6 Volume of Rectangular Prisms

MAIN IDEA

I will find the volume of rectangular prisms.

Standard 5MG1.3 **Understand the concept of volume and use the appropriate units in common measuring systems to compute the volume of rectangular solids.**
Standard 5MG1.4 **Differentiate between, and use appropriate units of measures for two- and three-dimensional objects (i.e., find the** perimeter, area, **volume).**

New Vocabulary

rectangular prism
volume
cubic units

GET READY to Learn

Hands-On Mini Lab

Recall from Lesson 10-8 that the figures below are prisms.

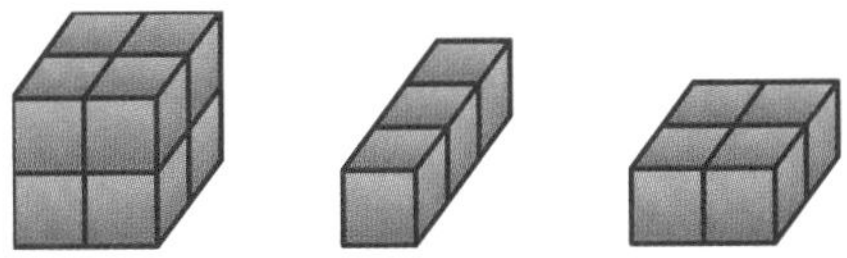

Step 1 Copy the table below.

Prism	Number of Cubes	Height of Prism	Length of Base	Width of Base	Area of Base
A					
B					
C					
D					
E					

Step 2 Using centimeter cubes, build five different prisms. For each prism, record the dimensions and the number of cubes used.

1. Examine the rows of the table. What patterns do you notice?

2. Describe the relationship between the number of cubes needed and the dimensions of the prism.

A **rectangular prism** is a three-dimensional figure with two parallel bases that are congruent rectangles.

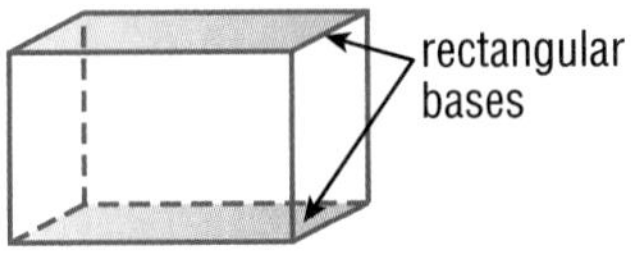

Volume is the amount of space inside a three-dimensional figure. Volume is measured in **cubic units**. This tells you the number of cubes of a given size it will take to fill the prism.

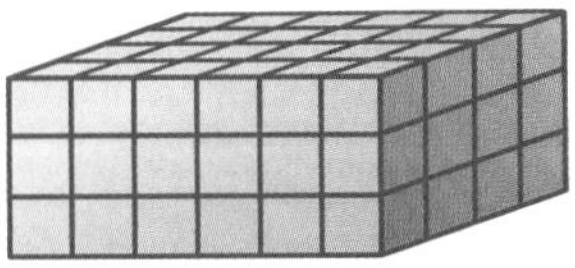

The volume of a rectangular prism is related to its dimensions.

Reading Math

A volume measurement can be written using abbreviations and an exponent of 3. For example:

cubic units = $units^3$
cubic inches = in^3
cubic feet = ft^3
cubic meters = m^3
cubic centimeters = cm^3
cubic yards = yd^3

KEY CONCEPT — Volume of a Rectangular Prism

Words The volume V of a rectangular prism is the product of its length ℓ, width w, and height h.

Model

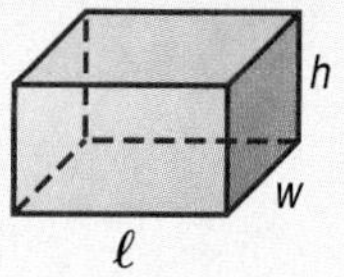

Symbols $V = \ell wh$

Another method you can use to find the volume of a rectangular prism is to multiply the area of the base (B) by the height (h).

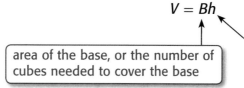

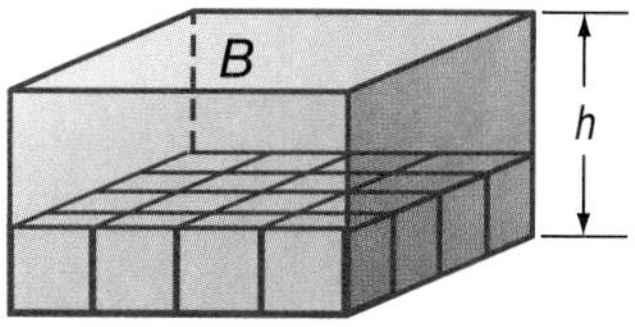

$$V = Bh$$

B: area of the base, or the number of cubes needed to cover the base

h: number of rows of cubes needed to fill the prism

EXAMPLE Find the Volume of a Rectangular Prism

1 Find the volume of the rectangular prism.

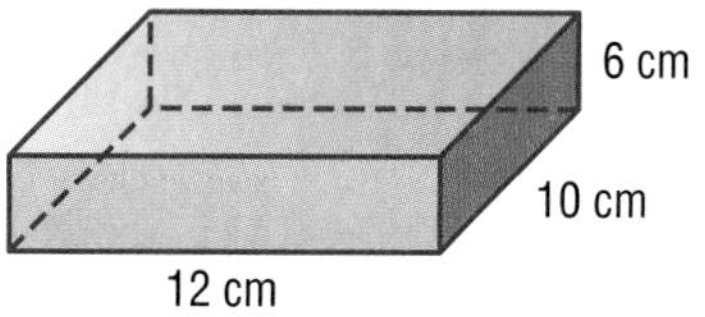

Estimate

$V \approx 10 \text{ cm} \times 10 \text{ cm} \times 6 \text{ cm}$ or 600 cm^3

In the figure, the length is 12 centimeters, the width is 10 centimeters, and the height is 6 centimeters.

Use $V = \ell wh$.

$V = \ell wh$	Volume of rectangular prism
$V = 12 \times 10 \times 6$	Replace ℓ with 12, w with 10, and h with 6.
$V = 720$	Multiply.

The volume is 720 cubic centimeters.

Check for Reasonableness Since we underestimated, the answer should be greater than the estimate. $720 > 600$ ✓

Online **Personal Tutor at** ca.gr5math.com

Real-World EXAMPLE

2 **A cereal box has the dimensions shown. What is the volume of the cereal box?**

Estimate $V \approx 8 \text{ in.} \times 3 \text{ in.} \times 13 \text{ in.}$ or 312 in^3

$V = \ell wh$	Volume of rectangular prism
$V = 8 \times 3.25 \times 12.5$	Replace ℓ with 8, w with 3.25, and h with 12.5.
$V = 325$	Multiply.

The volume of the cereal box is 325 cubic inches.

Check for Reasonableness Compare to the estimate. $325 \approx 312$ ✓

CHECK What You Know

Find the volume of each prism. **See Example 1 (p. 609)**

1. 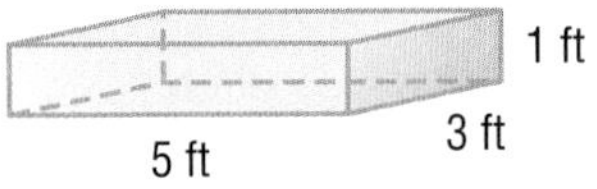

2. 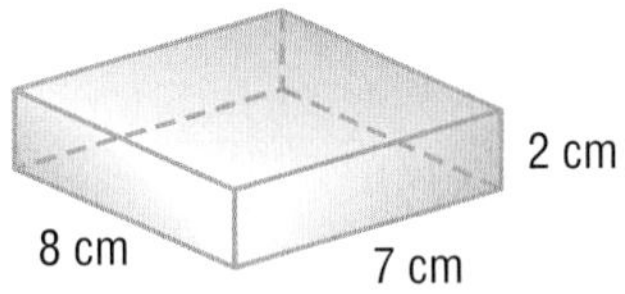

3. 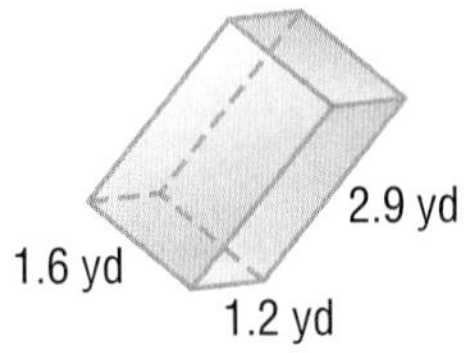

4. 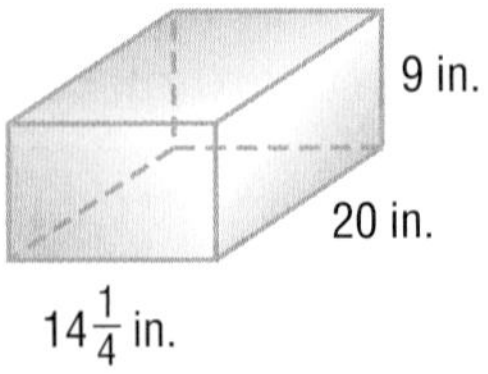

5. A rectangular kitchen sink is 25.25 inches long, 19.75 inches wide, and 10 inches deep. Find the amount of water that can be contained in the sink. **See Example 2 (p. 610)**

6. **Talk About It** Explain why the volume of a rectangular prism with a length of 13 inches, width of 6 inches, and a height of $2\frac{1}{2}$ inches has a volume of 195 cubic inches.

Practice and Problem Solving

EXTRA PRACTICE See page 687.

Find the volume of each prism. **See Example 1 (p. 609)**

7.

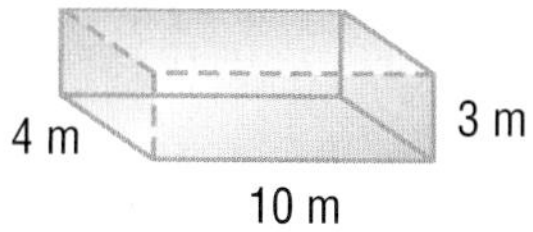

8.

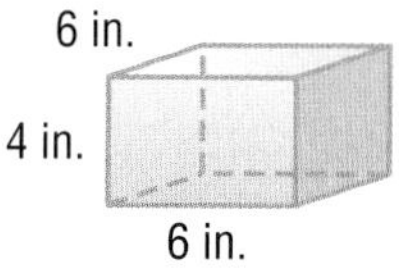

9.

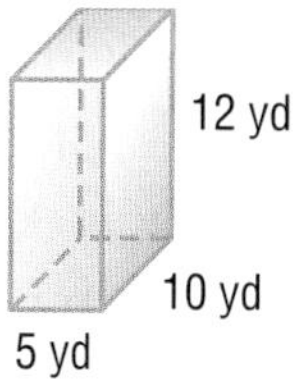

10.

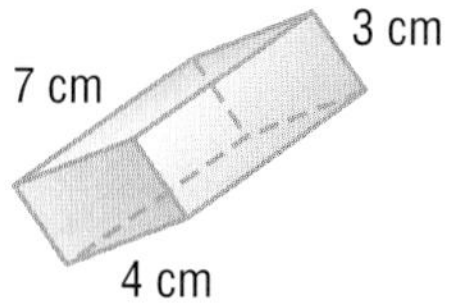

11.

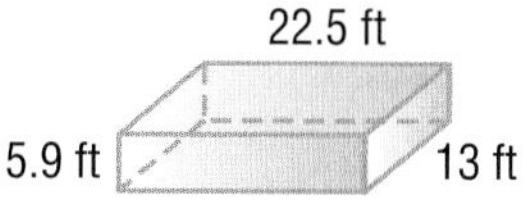

12.

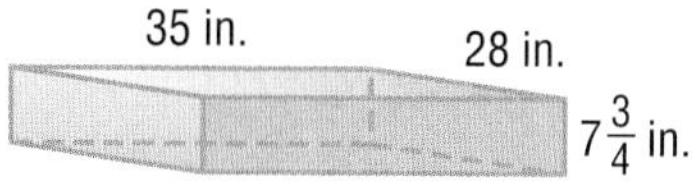

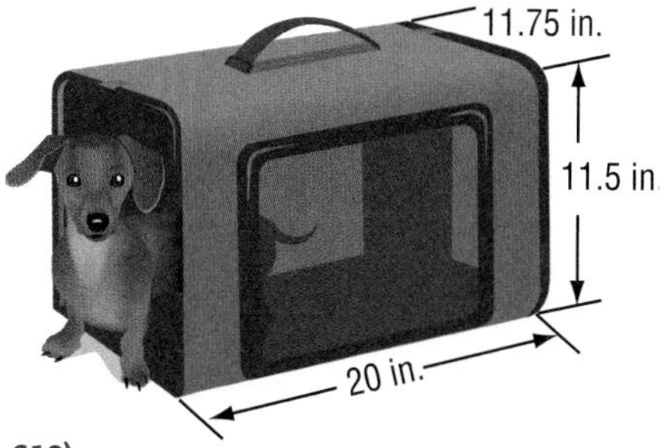

13. Find the volume of the pet carrier shown at the right. **See Example 2 (p. 610)**

14. The Palo Duro Canyon is 120 miles long, as much as 20 miles wide, and has a maximum depth of more than 0.15 mile. What is the approximate volume of this canyon? **See Example 2 (p. 610)**

15. Find the volume of a rectangular prism having a length of 7.7 meters, width of 18 meters, and height of 9.7 meters.

16. What is the volume of a rectangular prism with a length of 10.3 feet, width of 9.9 feet, and height of 5.6 feet?

For Exercises 17–19, use the table at the right.

17. What is the volume of the small truck?

18. The Davis family is moving, and they estimate that they will need a truck with about 1,300 cubic feet. Which truck would be best for them to rent?

19. About how many cubic feet greater is the volume of the Mega Moving Truck than the 2-bedroom moving truck?

Inside Dimensions of Moving Trucks

Truck	Length (ft)	Width (ft)	Height (ft)
Van	10	$6\frac{1}{2}$	6
Small Truck	$11\frac{1}{3}$	$7\frac{5}{12}$	$6\frac{3}{4}$
2-Bedroom Moving Truck	$14\frac{1}{12}$	$7\frac{7}{12}$	$7\frac{1}{6}$
3-Bedroom Moving Truck	$20\frac{5}{6}$	$7\frac{1}{2}$	$8\frac{1}{12}$
Mega Moving Truck	$22\frac{1}{4}$	$7\frac{7}{12}$	$8\frac{5}{12}$

20. Jeffrey estimates that the volume of a rectangular prism with a length of 5.8 meters, a width of 3 meters, and a height of 12.2 meters is less than 180 cubic meters. Is he correct? Explain.

21. The volume of a rectangular prism is 16 cubic feet. If the length of the prism is 4 feet and the width is 2 feet, what is the height of the prism?

22. Which has the greater volume: a prism with a length of 5 inches, a width of 4 inches, and a height of 10 inches or a prism with a length of 10 inches, a width of 5 inches, and a height of 4 inches? Justify your selection.

23. The volume of a fishing tackle box is 195 cubic inches. If the length of the tackle box is 13 inches and the width of the tackle box is 6 inches, what is the height of the tackle box?

Real-World PROBLEM SOLVING

Fish The fish tank shown is filled to a height of 15 inches.

24. How much water is currently in the tank?

25. How much more water could the tank hold before it overflowed?

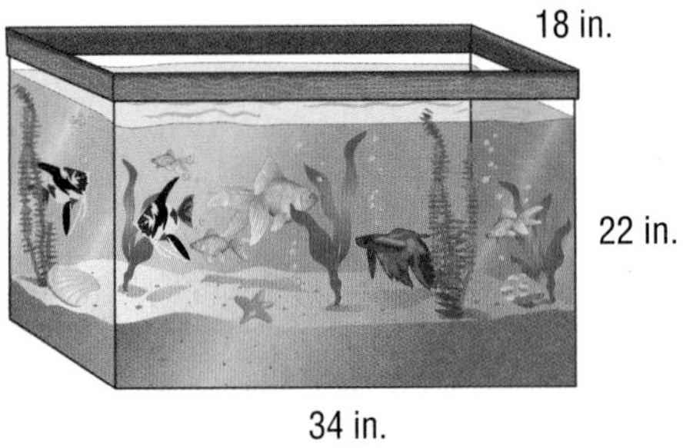

H.O.T. Problems

26. **Which One Doesn't Belong?** Identify the rectangular prism that does not belong with the other three. Explain your reasoning.

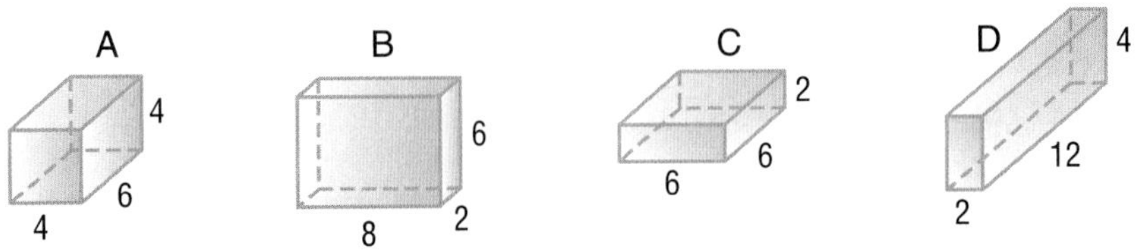

27. **OPEN ENDED** Draw and label a rectangular prism that has a volume between 200 and 400 cubic inches. Then give an example of a real-world object that is this approximate size.

28. **SELECT A TOOL** Basilio is filling his new fish tank with water. The dimensions of the fish tank are 36 inches by 13 inches by 16 inches. Basilio knows that 1 gallon equals 231 cubic inches. Which of the following tools might Basilio use to determine about how many gallons of water he needs to fill the fish tank? Justify your selection(s). Then use the tool(s) to solve the problem.

calculator | centimeter cubes | paper/pencil

29. **CHALLENGE** Refer to the prism at the right. If all the dimensions of the prism doubled, would the volume double? Explain your reasoning.

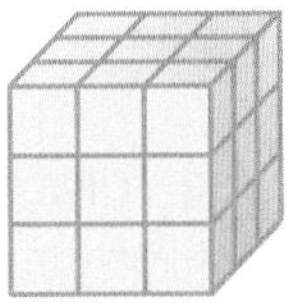

30. **WRITING IN ▸MATH** Explain why cubic units are used to measure volume instead of linear units or square units.

Standards Practice

31 Justin used the box to create a home for the toad he caught.

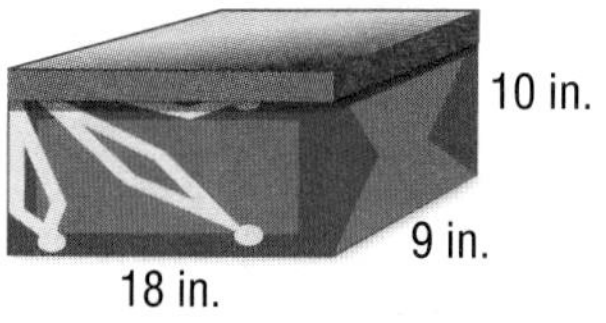

Find the volume of the box.

A 222 in^3

B 864 in^3

C 1,620 in^3

D 1,710 in^3

32 A cereal company is creating a new size box in which to package cereal. The box has a width of 27 centimeters, a length of 7 centimeters, and a height of 34 centimeters. Find the volume of the cereal box.

F 6,426 cm^3

G 6,216 cm^3

H 2,690 cm^3

J 408 cm^3

Spiral Review

33. Tiffany is using wooden cube blocks to make rectangular prisms. If she has exactly 8 wooden cube blocks, make a model to find the length, width, and height of two possible rectangular prisms. **(Lesson 11-5)**

34. Measurement What is the area of a triangle with base 52 feet and height 38 feet? **(Lesson 11-4)**

Find the value of *x* in each quadrilateral. **(Lesson 10-7)**

35.

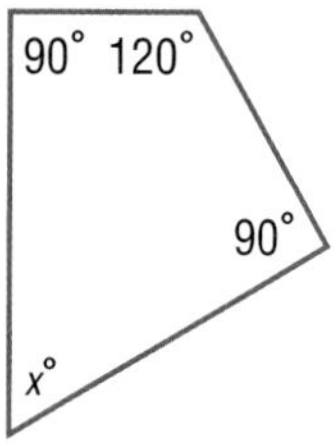

36.

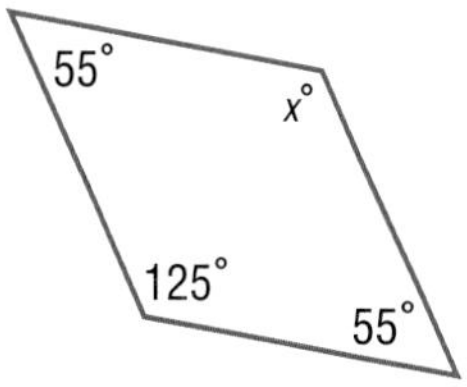

37. How many outfits can you make with two different colored sweatshirts and four types of jeans? Make an organized list to show the sample space. **(Lesson 9-9)**

38. Statistics Write the ratio that compares the number of leaves to the number of acorns in three different ways. **(Lesson 8-3)**

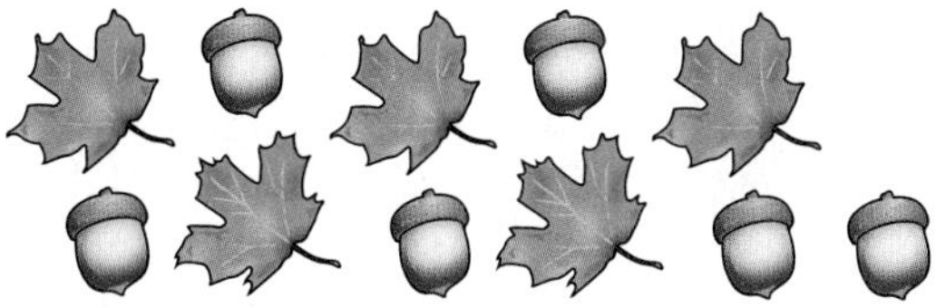

Problem Solving in Science

Birdseye View

You probably eat packaged frozen food every day. Frozen food might seem like a simple concept, but there's more to it than just putting a container of food in the freezer.

Clarence Birdseye is sometimes called "the father of frozen food" because he was the first to develop a practical way to preserve food by flash freezing.

Birdseye experimented with freezing fruits and vegetables, as well as fish and meat. His method of freezing food preserved the food's taste, texture, and appearance. He also was the first to package food in waxed cardboard packages that could be sold directly to consumers.

Did You Know?

148 patents were issued that related to Clarence Birdseye's flash-freezing method, his type of packaging, and the packaging materials he used.

Standard 5MG1.3 Understand the concept of volume and use the appropriate units in common measuring systems (i.e., cubic centimeters [cm3], cubic meter [m3], cubic inch [in.3], cubic yard [yd3]) to compute the volume of rectangular solids.

Dimensions of Frozen Food Packages in Inches

Item	Length	Width	Height
Pizza	12	12	2
Vegetables	5	6	1.5
Frozen Dinner	11	7.5	2
Fish Sticks	9	5	2.5
Hamburger Patties	8.5	10	4

Real-World Math

Use the information above to solve each problem.

1. What is the volume of a frozen pizza package?

2. How much more space does a package of frozen fish sticks occupy than a package of frozen vegetables?

3. Is 175 cubic inches a reasonable estimate for the volume of a frozen dinner package? Explain.

4. A freezer has 2,600 cubic inches of available space. What is the maximum number of frozen hamburger patty packages that could fit inside the freezer?

5. A larger package of frozen vegetables has the same length and width but twice the height. What is the volume of this package?

6. Thirty-six packages of frozen fish sticks are placed in a box to be delivered to a grocery store. Find the volume of ten of these boxes.

7. **WRITING IN MATH** Explain the differences between area and volume and the units used to represent them.

Explore

Geometry Lab for 11-7

Using a Net to Build a Cube

In this lab, you will make a two-dimensional pattern of a cube called a **net** and use it to build the three-dimensional figure.

MAIN IDEA

I will make a two-dimensional pattern for a cube and use it to build another cube.

Standard 5MG1.2 Construct a cube and rectangular box **from two-dimensional patterns and use these patterns to compute the surface area for these objects.**

Standard 5MR3.3 Develop generalizations of the results obtained and apply them in other circumstances.

New Vocabulary

net

ACTIVITY

Concepts in MOtion
Animation ca.gr5math.com

Step 1 Place the cube on paper as shown. Trace the base of the cube, which is a square.

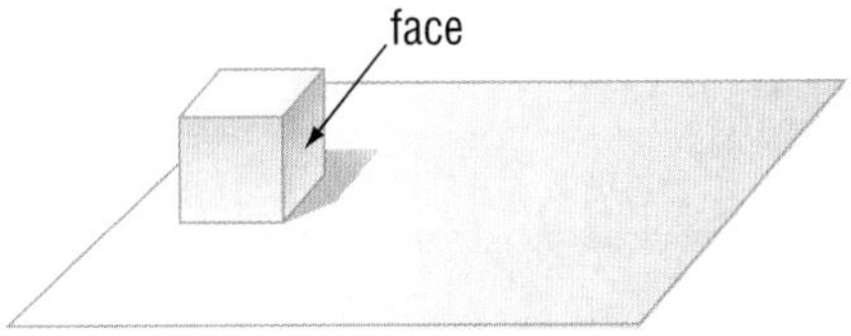

Step 2 Roll the cube onto another side. Continue tracing each side to make the figure shown. This two-dimensional figure is called a net.

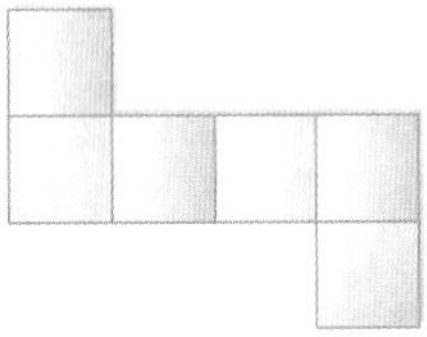

Step 3 Cut out the net. Then build the cube.

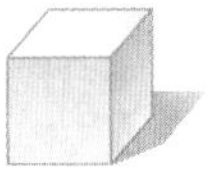

Step 4 Make a net like the one shown. Cut out the net and try to build a cube.

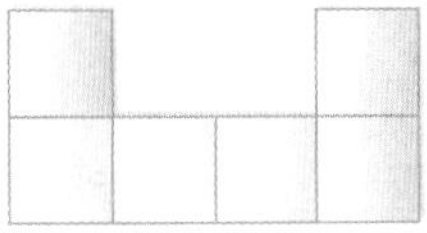

Analyze the Results

1. Explain whether both nets formed a cube. If not, describe why the net or nets did not cover the cube.
2. Draw three other nets that will form a cube and three other nets that will not form a cube. Describe a pattern in the nets that do form a cube.
3. Measure the edges of the cube in the activity above. Use this measure to find the area of one side of the cube.
4. Write an expression for the total area of all the surfaces of a cube with edge length s.
5. Draw a net for a rectangular prism. Explain the difference between this net and the nets that formed a cube.

11-7 Surface Area of Rectangular Prisms

MAIN IDEA

I will find the surface areas of rectangular prisms.

Standard 5MG1.2 **Construct a** cube and **rectangular box from two-dimensional patterns and use these patterns to compute the surface area for these objects.**
Standard 5MR1.2 **Determine when and how to break a problem into simpler parts.**

New Vocabulary

surface area

GET READY to Learn

Hands-On Mini Lab

Step 1 Draw and cut out the net below.

Step 2 Fold along the dashed lines. Tape the edges.

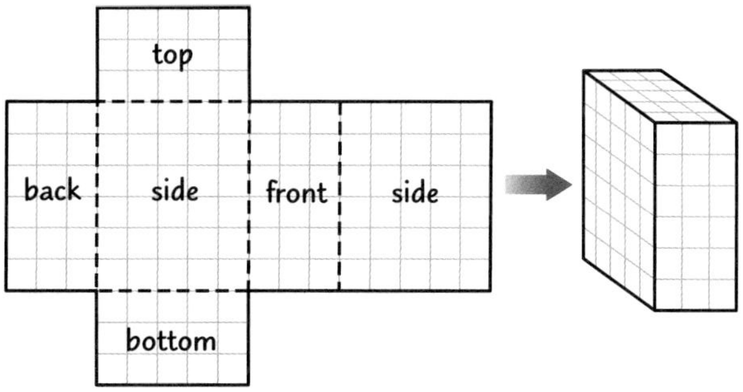

1. Find the area of each face of the prism.
2. What is the sum of the areas of the faces of the prism?

The sum of the areas of all the faces of a prism is called the **surface area** of the prism.

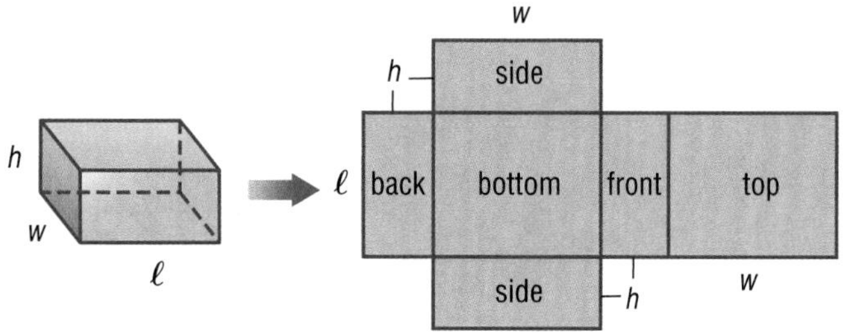

Sum of areas of faces = $2\ell w + 2\ell h + 2wh$.

KEY CONCEPT Surface Area of a Rectangular Prism

Words The surface area S of a rectangular prism with length ℓ, width w, and height h is the sum of the areas of the faces.

Model

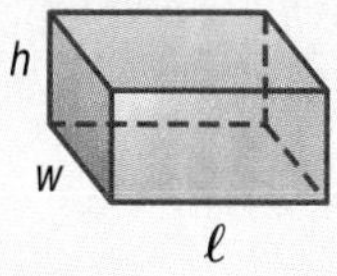

Symbols $S = 2\ell w + 2\ell h + 2wh$

EXAMPLE Find the Surface Area

1 Find the surface area of the rectangular prism.

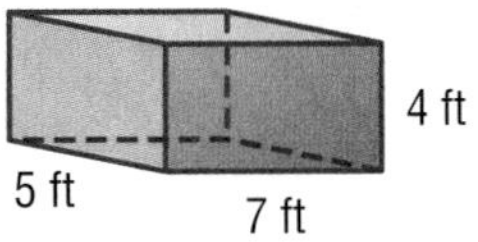

Find the area of each face.

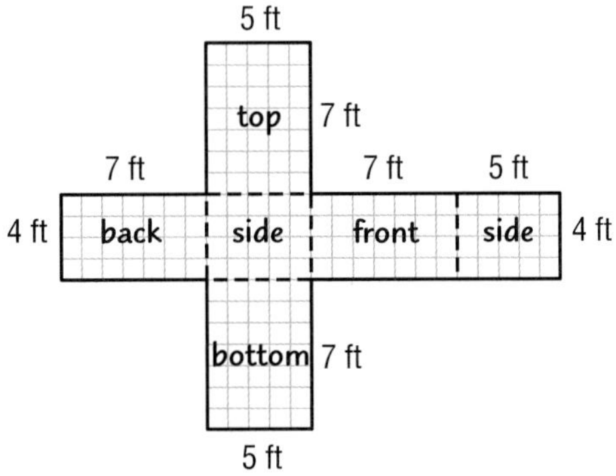

top and bottom:
$2(\ell w) = 2(7 \times 5)$ or 70

front and back:
$2(\ell h) = 2(7 \times 4)$ or 56

two sides:
$2(wh) = 2(5 \times 4)$ or 40

Add to find the surface area.

The surface area is 70 + 56 + 40 or 166 square feet.

Surface area can be applied to many real-world situations.

Real-World EXAMPLE

Remember

Check your answer for Example 2 by making a net of a prism 21 units by 8 units by 8 units.

2 An asteroid measures about 21 miles long, 8 miles wide, and 8 miles deep. Its shape resembles a rectangular prism. What is the approximate surface area of the asteroid?

$S = 2\ell w + 2\ell h + 2wh$	Surface area of a prism
$S = 2(21 \times 8) + 2(21 \times 8) + 2(8 \times 8)$	$\ell = 21, w = 8, h = 8$
$S = 2(168) + 2(168) + 2(64)$	Simplify within parentheses.
$S = 336 + 336 + 128$	Multiply.
$S = 800$	Add.

The approximate surface area of the asteroid is 800 square miles.

Online Personal Tutor at ca.gr5math.com

CHECK What You Know

Find the surface area of each rectangular prism. **See Example 1 (p. 618)**

1. 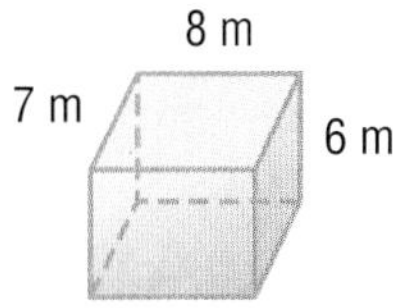

2. 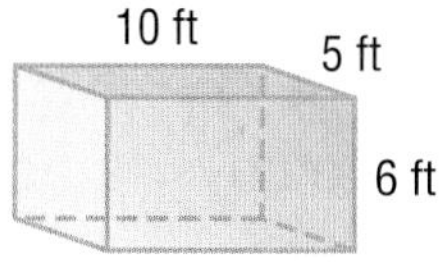

3. 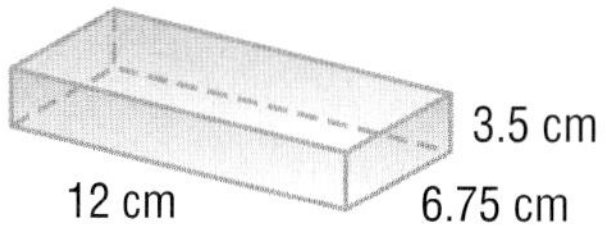

4. A game box for video games is shaped like a rectangular prism. What is the surface area of the game box? **See Example 2 (p. 618)**

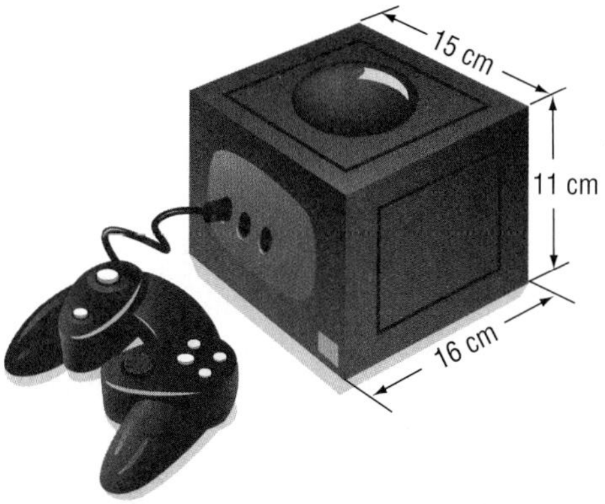

5. Talk About It: Explain how a net can help you find the surface area of a rectangular prism.

Practice and Problem Solving

EXTRA PRACTICE
See page 687.

Find the surface area of each rectangular prism. **See Example 1 (p. 618)**

6. 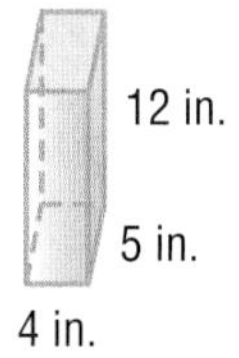

7. 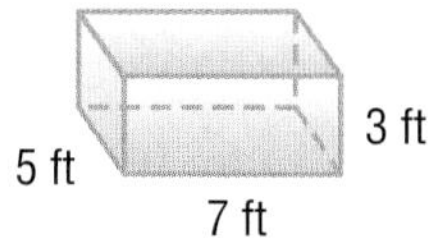

8. 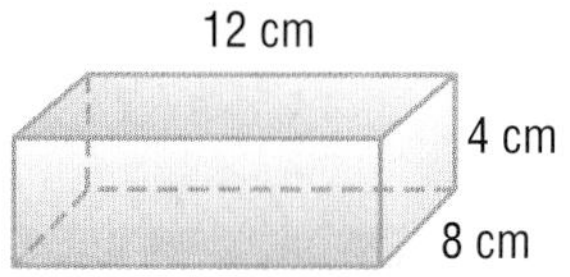

9. 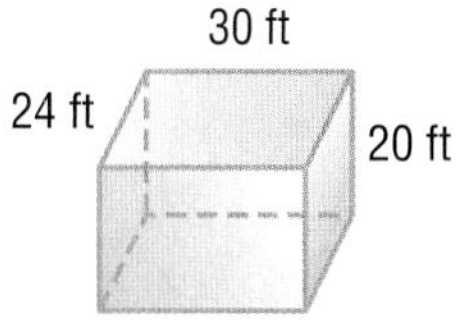

10. 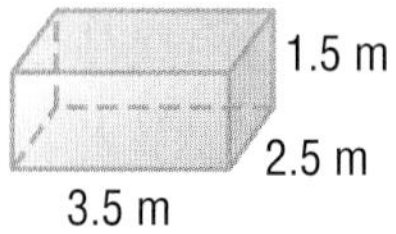

11. 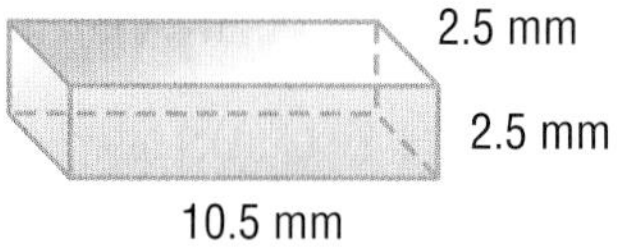

12. Tomás keeps his diecast car in a glass display case as shown. What is the surface area of the glass? **See Example 2 (p. 618)**

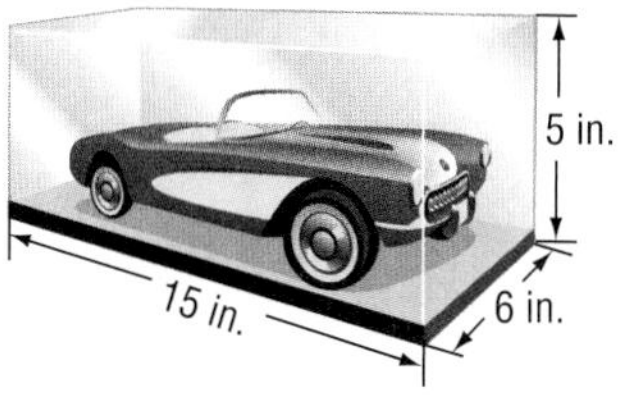

13. A full sheet cake is typically 18 inches by 24 inches by 2 inches. What is the minimum surface area of a rectangular box that will contain the cake? **See Example 2 (p. 618)**

14. Stella estimates that the surface area of a rectangular prism with a length of 13.2 feet, a width of 6 feet, and a height of 8 feet is about 460 cubic feet. Is her estimate reasonable? Explain your reasoning.

15. Nadine bought the board game shown for her friend. How many square inches of wrapping paper does she need to completely cover the box?

Classify each measure as *length, area, surface area,* or *volume*. Explain your reasoning. Include an appropriate unit of measure.

16. the amount of water in a lake

17. the amount of land available to build a house

18. the amount of wrapping paper needed to cover a box

19. the number of tiles needed to tile a bathroom floor

20. the amount of tin foil needed to cover a sandwich

21. the amount of cereal that will fit in a box

22. the height of a tree

23. Find the surface area of each shipping package. Which package has the greater surface area? Does the same package have a greater volume? Explain.

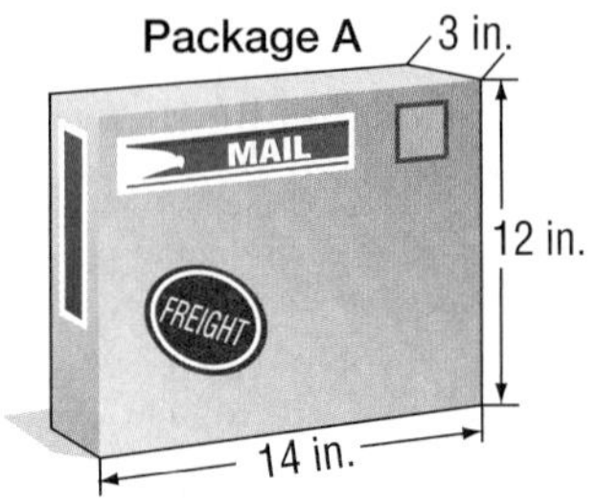

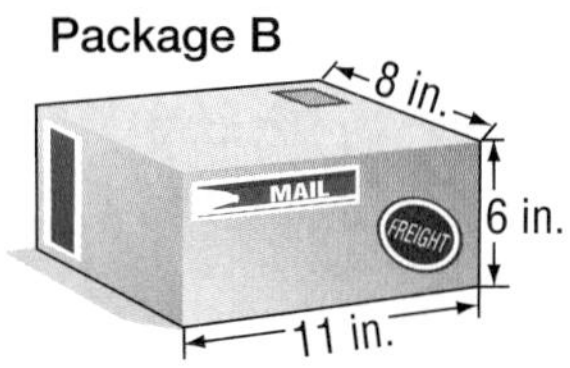

Real-World PROBLEM SOLVING

Food Pretzels are to be packaged in the box shown.

24. What is the surface area of the box?

25. What is the surface area if the height is doubled?

26. What is the surface area if the height is half as great?

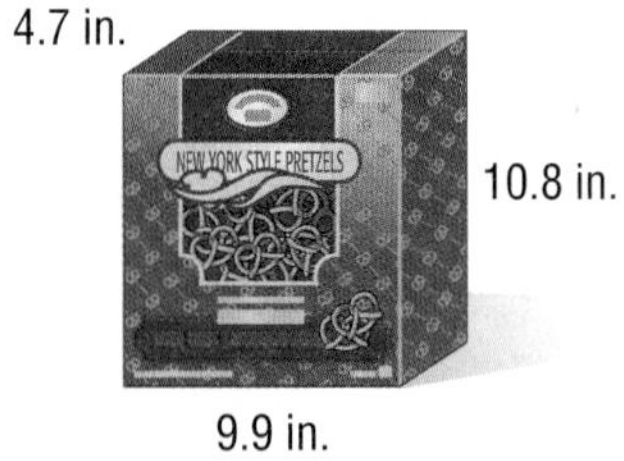

H.O.T. Problems

27. OPEN ENDED Draw and label a rectangular prism that has a surface area of 208 square feet.

CHALLENGE For Exercises 28 and 29, use the cube shown.

28. What is true about the area of the faces of a cube?

29. Rewrite the formula $S = 2\ell w + 2\ell h + 2wh$ into a simplified formula for the surface area of a cube with edge length s.

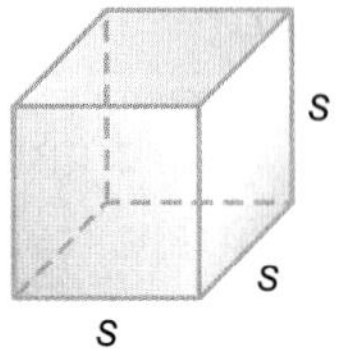

30. **REASONING** Determine whether the following statement is *sometimes*, *always*, or *never* true. Explain your reasoning.

If all the dimensions of a cube are doubled, the surface area is four times greater.

31. **WRITING IN ►MATH** Write a problem about a real-world situation in which you would need to find the surface area of a rectangular prism.

Standards Practice

32 What is the surface area of the rectangular prism formed by the net below?

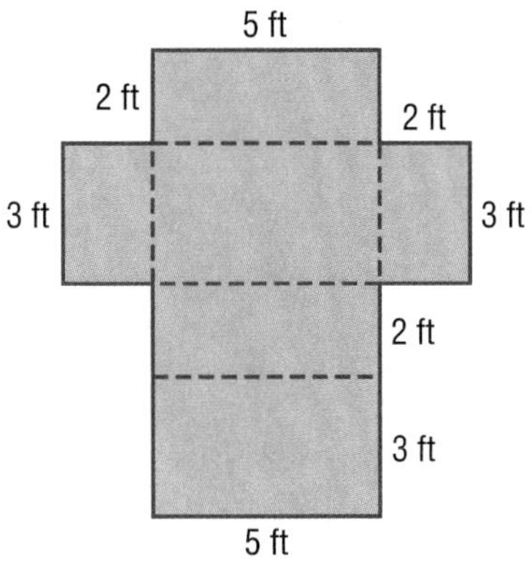

A 54 ft^2 **C** 70 ft^2

B 62 ft^2 **D** 72 ft^2

33 Horacio is going to paint a shoebox to use for storage of his trading cards. The shoebox is 23 inches long, 10 inches wide, and 8 inches high. Find the surface area of the shoebox.

F 246 in^2

G 828 in^2

H 988 in^2

J 1,840 in^2

Spiral Review

34. **Measurement** Find the volume of a rectangular prism with sides measuring 5 feet, 8 feet, and 12 feet. **(Lesson 11-6)**

35. **Measurement** A triangular cracker has a height of 4 centimeters and a base of 5 centimeters. Find the area of the cracker. **(Lesson 11-4)**

36. **Measurement** Find the perimeter and area of the football field. **(Lessons 1-9 and 11-1)**

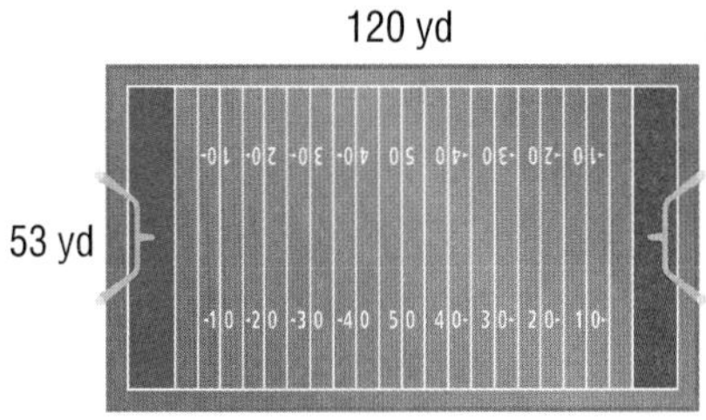

Write each decimal as a percent. **(Lesson 9-3)**

37. 0.44 **38.** 5.35 **39.** 0.6 **40.** 2.1

Extend

Measurement Lab for 11-7

Selecting Formulas and Units

MAIN IDEA

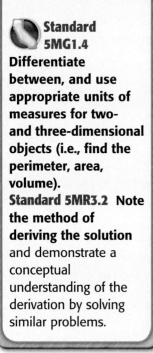

I will select appropriate units, tools, and formulas to measure objects.

Standard 5MG1.4 Differentiate between, and use appropriate units of measures for two- and three-dimensional objects (i.e., find the perimeter, area, volume).
Standard 5MR3.2 Note the method of deriving the solution and demonstrate a conceptual understanding of the derivation by solving similar problems.

An *attribute* is a characteristic of an object. Attributes, like length and width, that can be measured directly on the object are called *direct measures*. Others, like perimeter, area, and volume, can be calculated from direct measures. These are *calculated measures*.

ACTIVITY

Step 1 Copy the table below.

Object	Attribute	Formula Needed	Direct Measure(s)	Calculated Measure(s)
Shoebox				
Chalkboard				
Cereal box				
Bulletin board				

Step 2 Choose an attribute for each object that involves a calculated measure. Then determine what attributes you must measure directly in order to calculate this measure. Record this information in the table.

Step 3 Indicate what formula you need to use.

Step 4 Select a measuring tool and find the direct measure(s) for each object using the smallest unit on your measuring tool. Record each measure in the table. Be sure to include appropriate units.

Step 5 Calculate the attribute you selected using the formula and the direct measures you found. Record the result in the table. Use appropriate units.

Analyze the Results

1. **WRITING IN MATH** Write a real-world problem that could be solved using one of the objects and the measure you calculated.

CHAPTER 11 Study Guide and Review

FOLDABLES™ Study Organizer GET READY to Study

Be sure the following Key Concepts are noted in your Foldable.

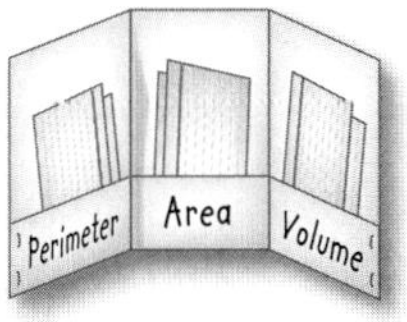

BIG Ideas

Perimeter (Lesson 11-1)

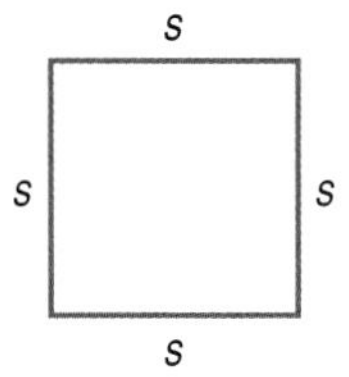

$P = 4s$

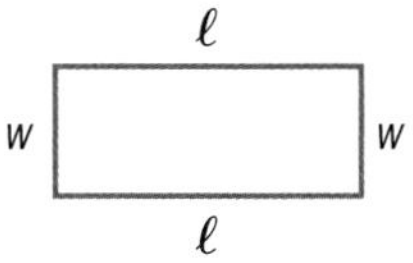

$P = 2\ell + 2w$

Area (Lessons 11-2 and 11-3)

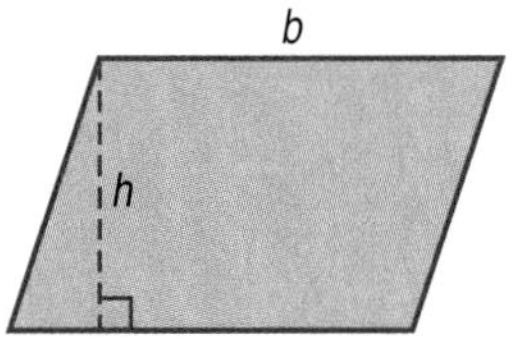

$A = bh$

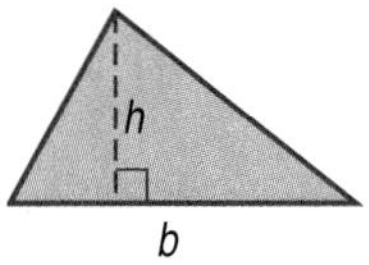

$A = \frac{1}{2}bh$

Volume and Surface Area (Lessons 11-5 and 11-6)

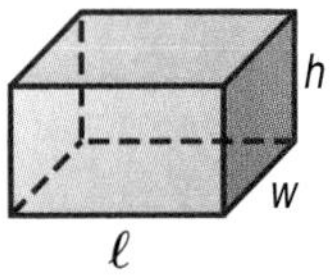

$V = \ell wh$

$S = 2\ell w + 2\ell h + 2wh$

Key Vocabulary

base (p. 591)
cubic units (p. 608)
height (p. 591)
net (p. 616)
perimeter (p. 585)
rectangular prism (p. 608)
surface area (p. 617)
volume (p. 608)

Vocabulary Check

Choose the correct term to complete each sentence.

1. The amount of space that a three-dimensional figure contains is called its (area, volume).
2. The shortest distance from the base to the opposite side of a parallelogram is called the (height, center).
3. The distance around any closed figure is called its (surface area, perimeter).
4. Cubic units are used when calculating (area, volume).
5. Two congruent triangles placed together form a (rectangular prism, parallelogam) with twice the area as one of the triangles.
6. The number of square units needed to cover a surface is called its (area, volume).

Lesson-by-Lesson Review

11-1 Perimeter (pp. 585–589)

Example 1
Find the perimeter of the rectangle.

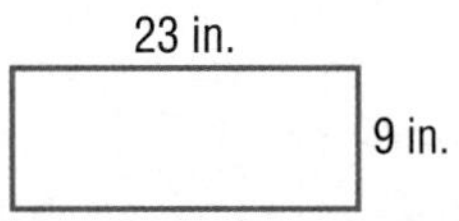

$P = 2\ell + 2w$

$P = 2(23) + 2(9)$

$P = 46 + 18$

$P = 64$ in.

The perimeter is 64 inches.

Find the perimeter of each figure.

7.

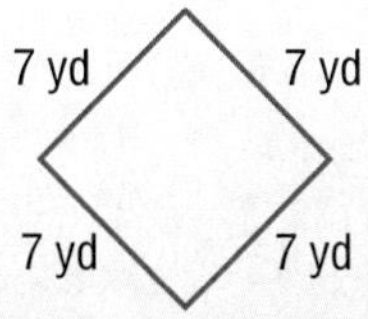

8.

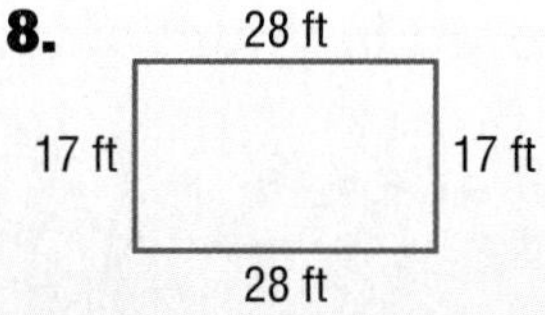

9. How many feet of wallpaper border are needed for a bedroom wall that is 11 feet long and 9 feet wide?

10. The infield of a softball field is a square that measures 60 feet on each side. What is the perimeter of the infield?

11-2 Area of Parallelograms (pp. 591–595)

Example 2
Find the area of the parallelogram.

$A = bh$

$A = 6 \cdot 5$

$A = 30 \text{ in}^2$

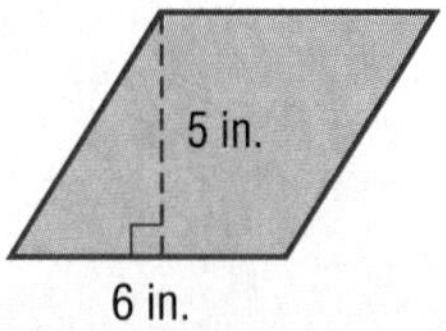

Example 3
Find the area of a parallelogram with base 4 meters and height 11.25 meters.

Estimate $4 \cdot 11 = 44$

$A = bh$

$A = 4 \cdot 11.25$

$A = 45$

The area is 45 square meters.

Check $45 \approx 44$ ✓

Find the area of each parallelogram.

11.

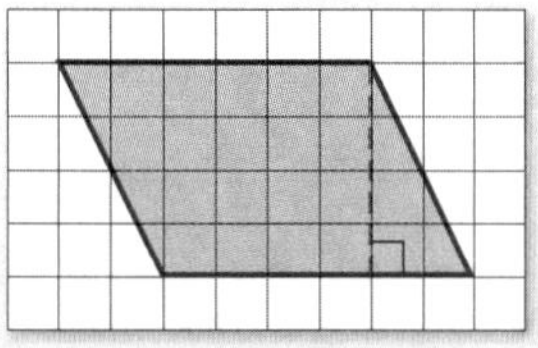

12.

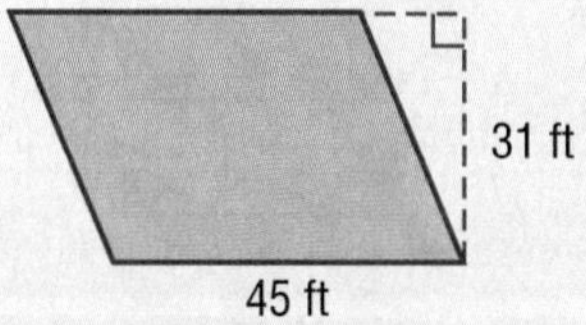

13.

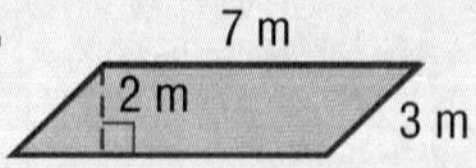

14.

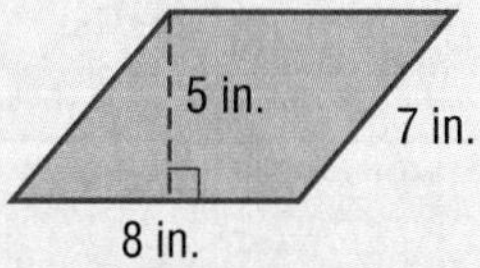

15. Find the area of a deck if it is a parallelogram with base $8\frac{1}{4}$ feet and height $6\frac{5}{6}$ feet.

11-3 Problem-Solving Strategy: Make a Model (pp. 596–597)

Example 4
A cheerleading squad formed a pyramid. There were 5 cheerleaders on the bottom and one less cheerleader in each row. How many rows were in the pyramid, if there are 12 cheerleaders?

Using 12 cubes, place 5 cubes on the bottom and one less cube in each layer as shown. There are 3 rows.

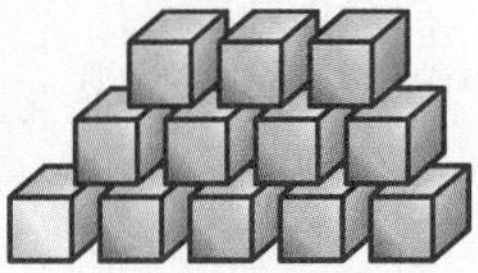

Solve. Use the *make a model* strategy.

16. A grocer is stacking cans of tomato soup into a pyramid-shaped display. The bottom layer has 8 cans. There is one less can in each layer and there are 6 layers. How many cans are in the display?

17. A brick layer wants to arrange 16 bricks into a rectangular shape with the greatest perimeter possible. How many bricks will be in each row?

11-4 Area of Triangles (pp. 599–603)

Example 5
Find the area of the triangle.

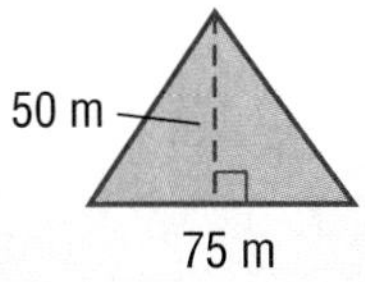

$A = \frac{1}{2}bh$

$A = \frac{1}{2}(75)(50)$

$A = 1{,}875 \text{ m}^2$

Example 6
Find the area of a triangular garden with base 8 feet and height 7 feet.

$A = \frac{1}{2}bh$

$A = \frac{1}{2}(8)(7)$

$A = \frac{1}{2}(56)$

$A = 28$

The area is 28 square feet.

Find the area of each triangle.

18.

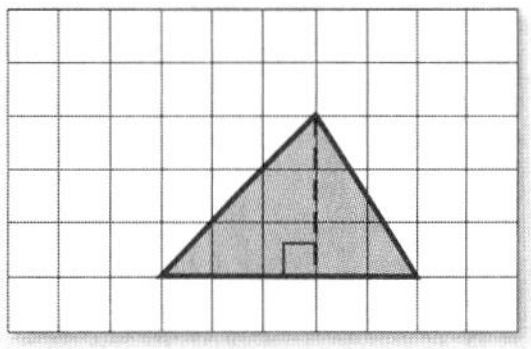

19.

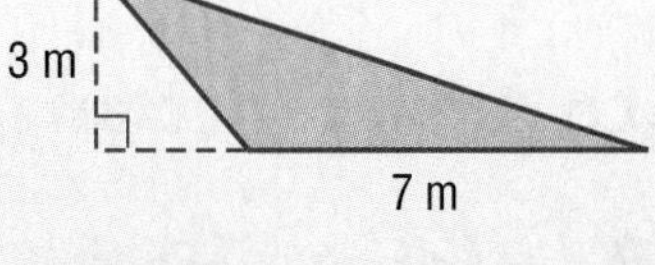

20.

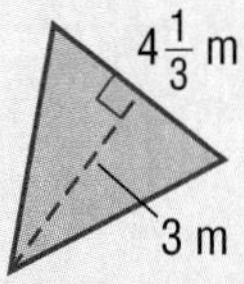

21.

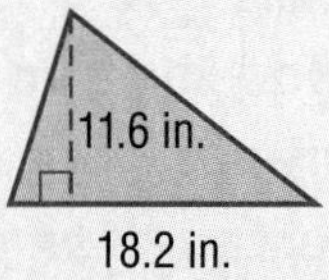

22. How much material is needed to make a triangular flag with base 2 feet and height 8 feet?

11-5 Problem-Solving Investigation: Choose the Best Strategy (pp. 606–607)

Example 7

The Turners are going to San Diego on vacation. They have traveled $\frac{2}{3}$ of the total distance or 326 miles. How far is it from their house to San Diego?

Draw a diagram.

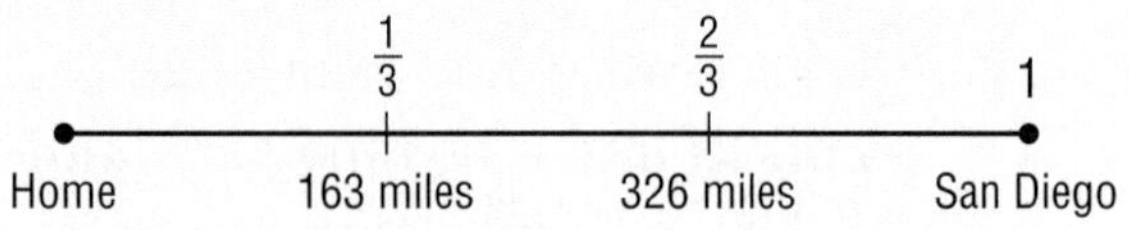

The distance is 326 + 163 or 489 miles.

Choose the best strategy to solve each problem.

23. Mrs. Rocha has a swimming pool that measures 41 feet by 11 feet. If the deck around the pool is 3 feet wide, what is the outside perimeter of the deck?

24. What are the next two numbers in the pattern listed below?

567, 189, 63, ...

11-6 Volume of Rectangular Prisms (pp. 608–613)

Example 8

Find the volume of the figure.

$V = \ell wh$

$V = 8 \times 4 \times 5$

$V = 160$

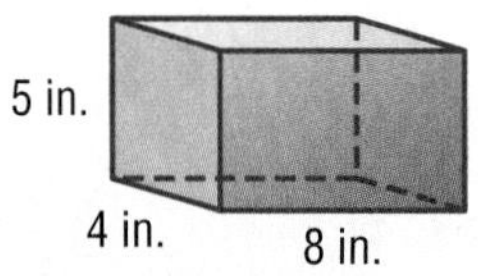

The volume is 160 cubic inches.

Find the volume of each prism.

25.

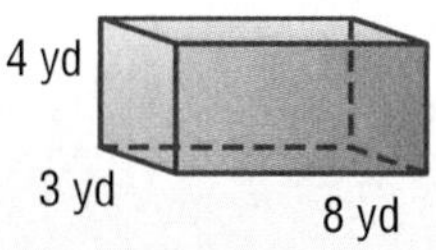

26.

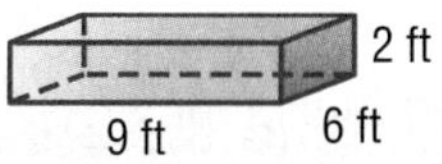

27. How much space is in a building with length 168 yards, width 115 yards, and height 96 yards?

11-7 Surface Area of Rectangular Prisms (pp. 617–621)

Example 9

Find the surface area of the rectangular prism.

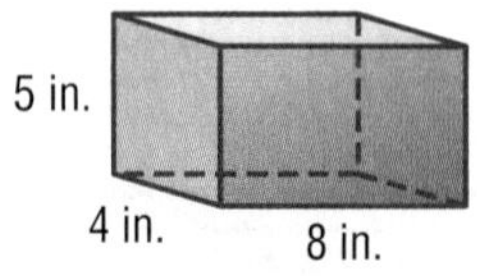

$S = 2\ell w + 2\ell h + 2wh$

$S = 2(8)(4) + 2(8)(5) + 2(4)(5)$

$S = 184$

The surface area is 184 square inches.

Find the surface area of each prism.

28.

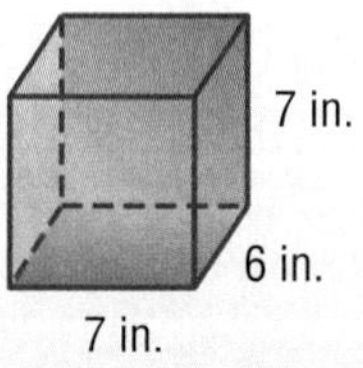

29.

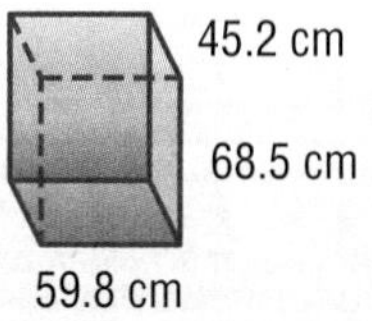

30. How much cardboard covers the outside of a box if the box is 4 inches by 3 inches by 5 inches?

CHAPTER 11

Chapter Test

Find the perimeter of each figure.

1.

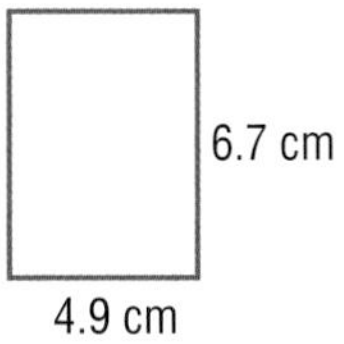

2.

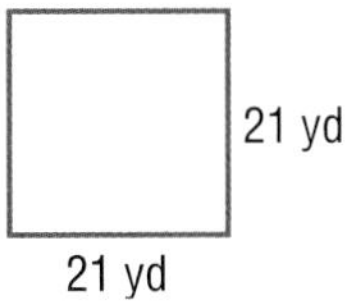

3. Paul has 24 feet of fence to make a square pen for his dog. What will be the dimensions of the dog pen?

4. **STANDARDS PRACTICE** What is the perimeter of the rectangle below?

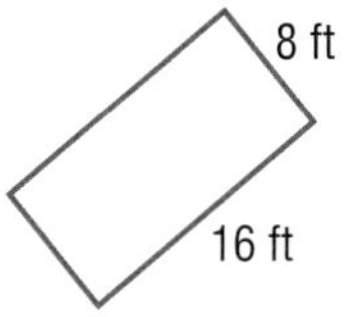

A 32 ft

B 48 ft

C 64 ft

D 128 ft

Find the area of each figure.

5.

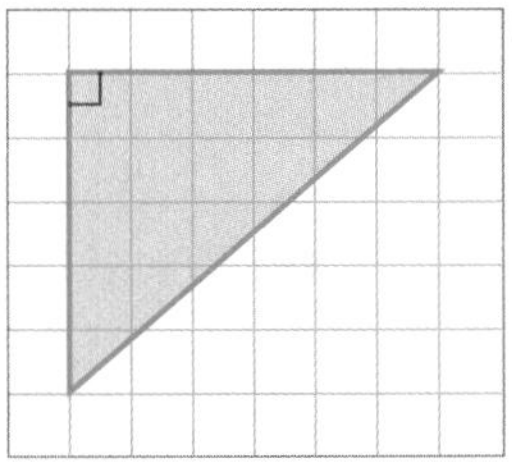

6.

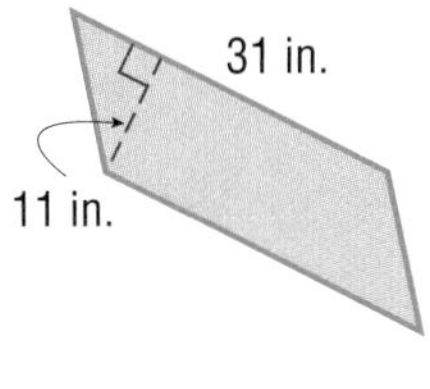

7. Which has the greater area: a triangle with a base of 8 meters and a height of 12 meters or a triangle with a base of 4 meters and a height of 16 meters? Justify your response.

8. A triangular garden has a base of 7 meters and a height of 6 meters. If one bag of fertilizer covers 25 square meters, how many bags of fertilizer are needed to fertilize the garden?

9. **Geometry** A rectangular prism is made using exactly 12 cubes. Find a possible length, width, and height of the prism. Use the *make a model* strategy.

Find the volume of each prism.

10.

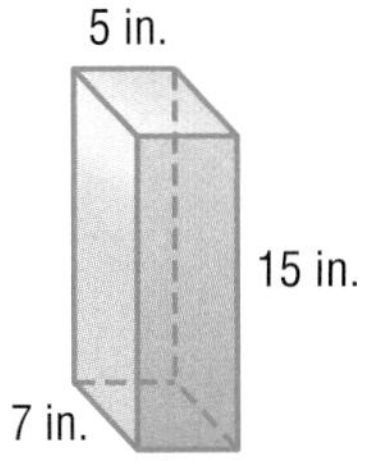

11.

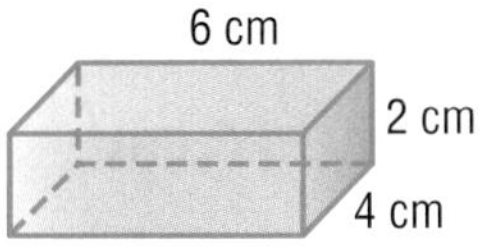

12. **STANDARDS PRACTICE** What is the volume of the rectangular prism below?

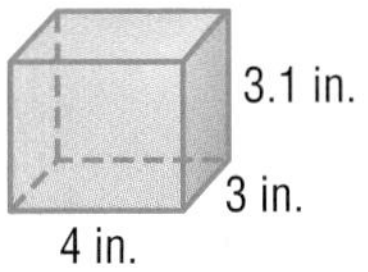

F 9.3 in^3

G 12 in^3

H 12.4 in^3

J 37.2 in^3

Find the surface area of each rectangular prism.

13.

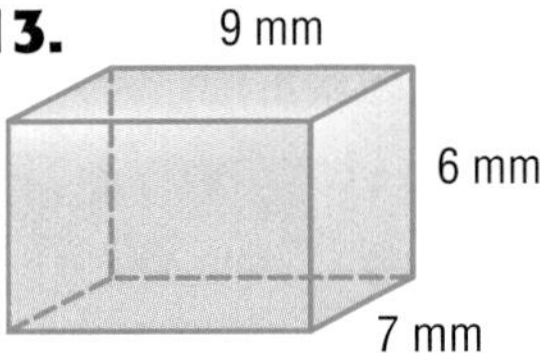

14.

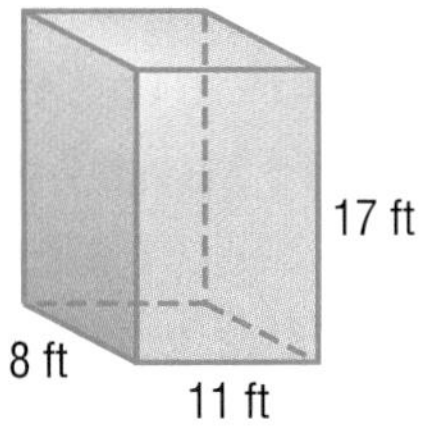

15. **WRITING IN MATH** A rectangular pool is 21 feet long by 18 feet wide. About how much water is required to fill the pool so that the water is 9 feet deep? Explain.

California Standards Practice

CHAPTER 11

Cumulative, Chapters 1–11

Standards Example

A tissue box has the dimensions shown. What is the volume of the tissue box?

A 47 cm^3

B 276 cm^3

C 299 cm^3

D 3,168 cm^3

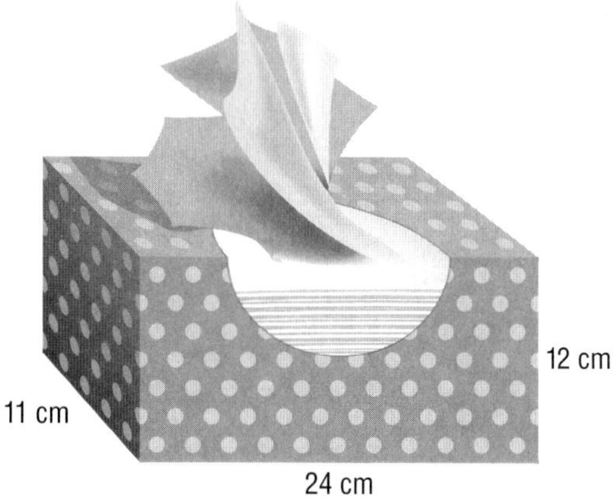

Read the Question

You need to find the volume of the tissue box.

Solve the Question

Use the formula for the volume of a rectangular prism, $V = \ell wh$.

$V = \ell wh$	Volume of a rectangular prism
$V = 24 \times 11 \times 12$	Replace ℓ with 24, w with 11, and h with 12.
$V = 3{,}168$	Multiply.

The volume of the tissue box is 3,168 cubic centimeters. The answer is D.

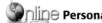

Online Personal Tutor at ca.gr5math.com

Choose the best answer.

1 **Shane built a figure using centimeter cubes. The figure is 4 cubes high and covers a 12-centimeter by 8-centimeter area of the floor. What is the volume of the figure?**

A 384 cm^3

B 160 cm^3

C 100 cm^3

D 80 cm^3

2 **The rectangular prism below has a length of 12 centimeters, a height of 6 centimeters, and a width of 4 centimeters. What is the volume?**

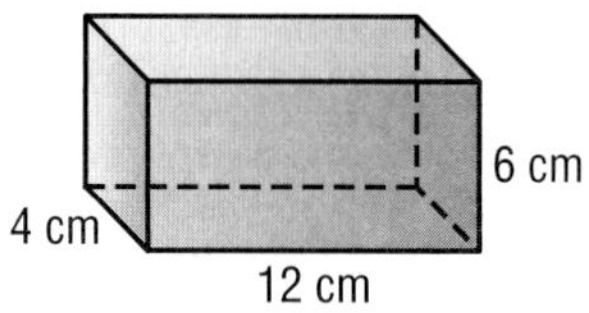

F 22 cm^3

G 96 cm^3

H 120 cm^3

J 288 cm^3

3 **The table below shows the areas of a triangle where the height of the triangle stays the same, but the base changes.**

Area of Triangles		
Height (units)	Base (units)	Area (units^2)
4	4	8
4	5	10
4	6	12
4	n	■

Which expression can be used to find the area of a triangle that has a height of 4 units and a base of *n* units?

A $\frac{n}{4}$ **B** $\frac{4n}{2}$ **C** $\frac{4}{2n}$ **D** $4n$

4 **Find the volume of a rectangular prism with sides measuring 4 feet, 5 feet, and 9 feet.**

F 18 ft^3
G 65 ft^3
H 180 ft^3
J 202 ft^3

5 **The side lengths and perimeters of regular polygons are shown in the table below. Which geometric figure is represented by the information?**

Side Length (inches)	Perimeter (inches)
3	12
5	20
8	32
10	40

A pentagon
B square
C hexagon
D triangle

6 **Mrs. Johnson designed a quilt by outlining equilateral triangles with ribbon as shown below. How much ribbon did Mrs. Johnson use to complete her quilt?**

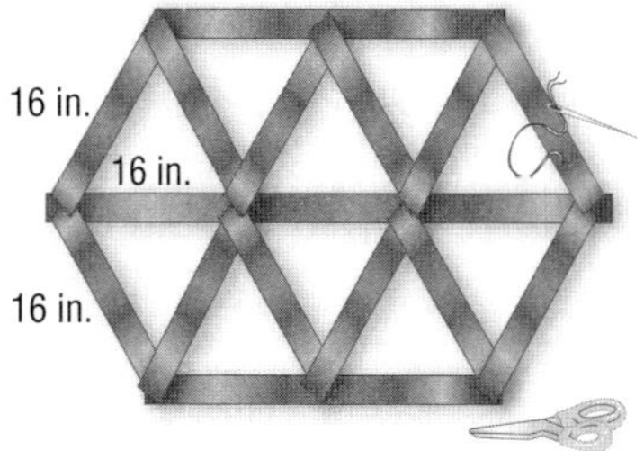

F 125 in.
G 264 in.
H 304 in.
J 320 in.

7 **Jermil bought two hockey jerseys for \$151.28. If they each cost the same, how much did he pay per jersey?**

A \$7.56
B \$75.00
C \$75.14
D \$75.64

8 **What is 55% of 520?**

F 260 **G** 286 **H** 290 **J** 300

9 **In the spreadsheet below, a formula applied to the values in columns A and B results in the values in column C. What is the formula?**

	A	B	C
1	4	0	4
2	5	1	3
3	6	2	2
4	7	3	1

A $C = A - B$
B $C = A - 2B$
C $C = A + B$
D $C = A + 2B$

Standards Review

Throughout the school year, you may be required to take several tests, and you may have many questions about them. Here are some answers to help you get ready.

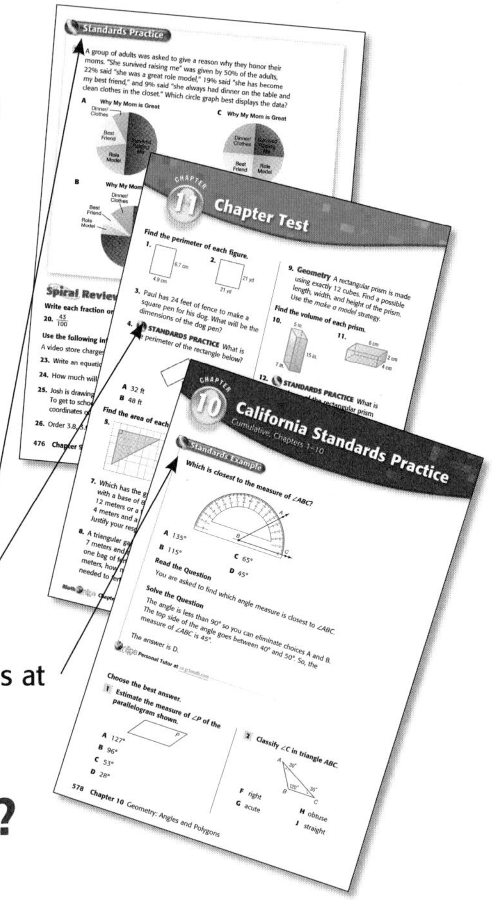

How Should I Study?

The good news is that you've been studying all along–a little bit every day. Here are some of the ways your textbook has been preparing you.

- **Every Day** Each lesson had practice questions that cover the California Standards.
- **Every Week** The Mid-Chapter Check and Chapter Test had several practice questions.
- **Every Month** The California Standards Practice pages at the end of each chapter had even more questions similar to those on tests.

Are There Other Ways to Review?

Absolutely! The following pages contain even more practice for each California Standard.

Math Online Additional California Standards Practice at ca.gr5math.com

Tips for SUCCESS

Prepare

- Go to bed early the night before the test. You will think more clearly after a good night's rest.
- Become familiar with common formulas and when they should be used.
- Think positively.

During the Test

- Read each problem carefully. Underline key words and think about different ways to solve the problem.
- Watch for key words like *not*. Also look for order words like *least*, *greatest*, *first*, and *last*.
- Answer questions you are sure about first. If you do not know the answer to a question, skip it and go back to that question later.
- Check your answer to make sure it is reasonable.
- Make sure that the number of the question on the answer sheet matches the number of the question on which you are working in your test booklet.

Whatever you do...

- Don't try to do it all in your head. If no figure is provided, draw one.
- Don't rush. Try to work at a steady pace.
- Don't give up. Some problems may seem hard to you, but you may be able to figure out what to do if you read each question carefully or try another strategy.

Multiple-Choice Questions

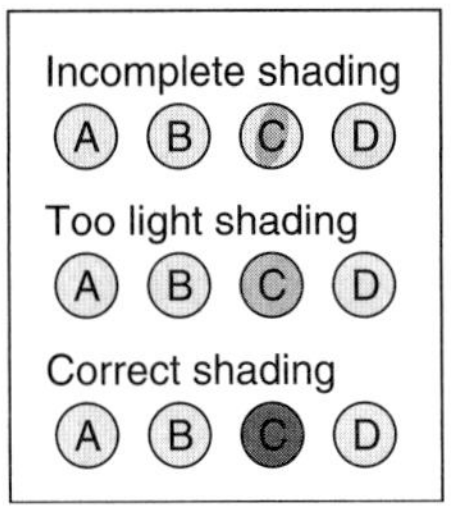

In multiple-choice questions you are asked to choose the best answer from four possible answers.

To record a multiple-choice answer, you will be asked to shade in a bubble that is a circle. Always make sure that your shading is dark enough and completely covers the bubble.

Standards Example

1 **The graph shows the maximum life span in years for five birds. Which fraction compares the life span of a bald eagle to the life span of an eletus parrot?**

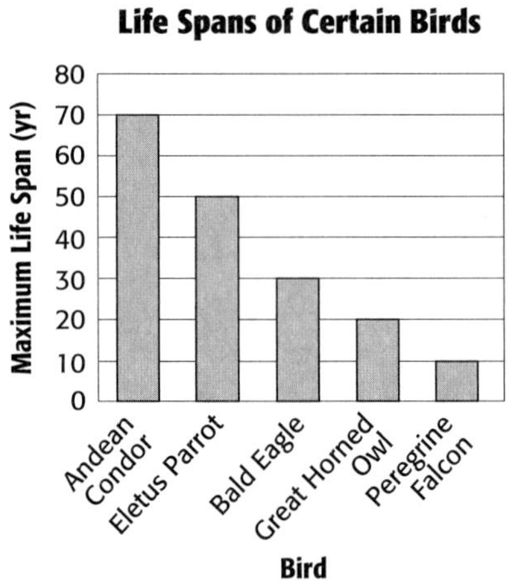

STRATEGY

Elimination Can you eliminate any of the choices?

A $\frac{5}{2}$ **B** $\frac{5}{3}$ **C** $\frac{2}{5}$ **D** $\frac{3}{5}$

Before finding the fraction, look at the answers. The bald eagle has a shorter life span than the eletus parrot, so the fraction cannot be greater than 1. Answers A and B are greater than 1. The answer must be C or D.

Compare the life span for the bald eagle to the life span for the eletus parrot. Write the fraction and simplify.

$$\frac{\text{life span of bald eagle}}{\text{life span of eletus parrot}} = \frac{30}{50}$$ Write the fraction.

$$= \frac{30 \div 10}{50 \div 10}$$ The GCF of 30 and 50 is 10.

$$= \frac{3}{5}$$ Simplify.

The correct choice is D.

Standards Example

STRATEGY

Diagrams Draw a diagram for the situation. If you cannot write in the test booklet, draw a diagram on scratch paper.

2 The Jung family is building a fence around a rectangular section of their backyard. The section measures 21 feet by 27 feet. They are going to place a post at each corner and then place posts three feet apart along each side. How many posts will they need?

F 28 **G** 32 **H** 36 **J** 63

To solve this problem, draw a diagram of the situation. Label the important information from the problem. The width of the rectangle is 21 feet, and the length of the rectangle is 27 feet.

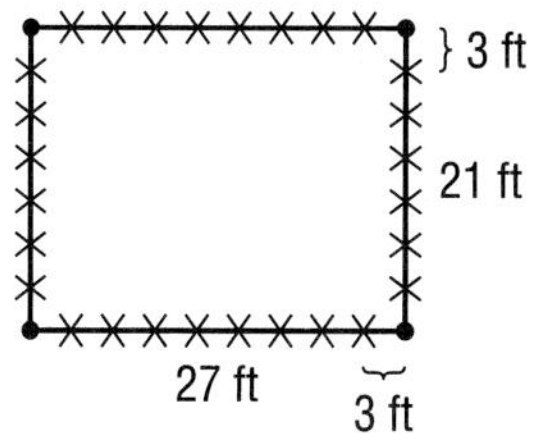

In the diagram, the corner posts are marked with points. The other posts are marked with x's and are 3 feet apart.

Add the number of posts on each side to the posts on the four corners.

4 points + 6 x's + 8 x's + 6 x's + 8 x's = 32 posts

The correct choice is G.

Often multiple-choice questions require you to convert measurements. Pay careful attention to each unit of measure in the question and the answer choices.

Standards Example

3 The Art Club is selling 12-ounce boxes of chocolate candy for a fund-raiser. There are 36 boxes of candy in a case. How many pounds of chocolate are in one case?

A 20 lb **B** 27 lb **C** 108 lb **D** 432 lb

STRATEGY

Units of Measure Do you have the correct unit of measurement?

Each box of candy weighs 12 ounces. So, 36 boxes weigh $36 \cdot 12$ or 432 ounces. However, Choice D is *not* the correct answer. The question asks for *pounds* of chocolate.

432 oz = ■ lb **THINK** 16 oz = 1 lb

$432 \div 16 = 27$ Divide to change ounces to pounds.

So, there are 27 pounds in one case. The correct choice is B.

Practice by Standard: Number Sense

Standard Set 1.0: Students compute with very large and very small numbers, positive integers, decimals, and fractions and understand the relationship between decimals, fractions, and percents. They understand the relative magnitudes of numbers.

DIRECTIONS
Choose the best answer.

QUICK Practice	QUICK Review
1 What is 4,368.375 rounded to the nearest ten? **(5NS1.1)** **A** 4,368 **B** 4,370 **C** 4,368.4 **D** 4,368.38	STRATEGY Be sure you round to the appropriate place. What digit is in the ones place? What digit is in the tens place? For more help with rounding decimals, see page 142.
2 What is 60% of 240? **(5NS1.2)** **F** 125 **G** 140 **H** 144 **J** 166	READING HINT Percent means *per hundred*. You can answer this question by finding $\frac{3}{5}$ of 240. For more help with percent of a number, see page 492.
3 $2^5 =$ **(5NS1.3)** **A** 5×5 **B** $5 + 5$ **C** $2 + 2 + 2 + 2 + 2$ **D** $2 \times 2 \times 2 \times 2 \times 2$	STRATEGY Think of a power as repeated multiplication. How many times is 2 being multiplied by itself? For more help with powers, see page 22.

QUICK Practice

4 What is the prime factorization of 24? **(5NS1.4)**

F $2^3 \times 3$

G $2^2 \times 3^2$

H $3^2 \times 4$

J $3^3 \times 4^2$

QUICK Review

STRATEGY Think: Which answers can you eliminate because they are not reasonable?

Multiply the numbers in the remaining choices.

For more help with prime factorization, see page 23.

---

5 Which letter on the number line best identifies the location of −6? **(5NS1.5)**

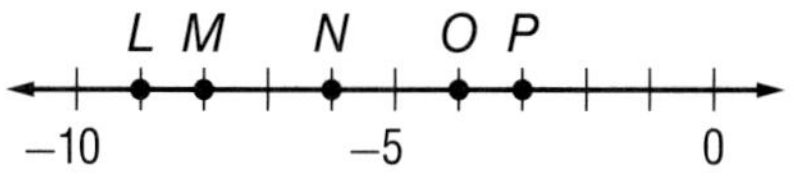

A *L**C** *N*

B *M*

C *N*

D *O*

STRATEGY Write the missing numbers on the number line.

Find the point that corresponds to −6 on the number line.

For more help with locating integers on number lines, see page 114.

---

6 What is $\frac{3}{4}$ written as a percent? **(5NS1.2)**

F 0.75%

G 34%

H 65%

J 75%

READING HINT Percent means *per hundred.* What part of 100 is equal to three-fourths?

You can answer this question by solving $\frac{3}{4} = \frac{n}{100}$.

For more help with writing fractions as percents, see page 467.

---

7 Salvador had a basket of 140 blocks. If 35% of the blocks are red, how many blocks are *not* red? **(5NS1.2)**

A 49

B 56

C 91

D 94

READING HINT When reading a question, look for key words such as *not* or *both.*

To find the percent of blocks that are not red, subtract 35% from 100%.

For more help with percent of a number, see page 492.

Practice on Your Own

Standard Set 1.0

8 What is the prime factorization of 20? **(5NS1.4)**

F $2^2 \times 3^2$ **H** $2^2 \times 5$

G $2^3 \times 5$ **J** $2^3 \times 3$

9 Which point on the number line best represents 2.65? **(5NS1.5)**

A 

B 

C 

D 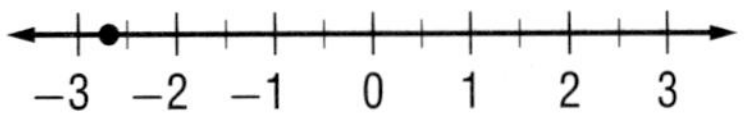

10 California is the third largest state in the United States with an area of 163,707 square miles. What is this value rounded to the nearest thousand square miles? **(5NS1.1)**

F 164,000

G 163,710

H 163,700

J 163,000

11 $3^4 =$ **(5NS1.3)**

A $3 \times 3 \times 3 \times 3$

B $3 + 3 + 3 + 3$

C $4 \times 4 \times 4$

D $4 + 4 + 4$

12 What is 7,080.362 rounded to the nearest ten? **(5NS1.1)**

F 7,100 **H** 7,080.36

G 7,080 **J** 7,080.4

13 What is $\frac{1}{8}$ written as a percent? **(5NS1.2)**

A 0.125% **C** 12.5%

B 1.25% **D** 125%

14 An electronics store sold 150 computers last month. If 105 of the computers sold came with flat panel monitors, what percent of the computers came with flat panel monitors? **(5NS1.2)**

F 80%

G 70%

H 60%

J 45%

15 What is the decimal 0.4 written as a fraction? **(5NS1.2)**

A $\frac{1}{5}$

B $\frac{1}{4}$

C $\frac{2}{5}$

D $\frac{3}{4}$

16 What is 75% of 120? **(5NS1.2)**

F 75 **H** 90

G 82 **J** 93

17 What is the prime factorization of 90? **(5NS1.4)**

A $2^2 \times 3 \times 5^2$

B $2^2 \times 3^2 \times 5$

C $2 \times 3^3 \times 5^2$

D $2 \times 3^2 \times 5$

Practice by Standard: Number Sense

Standard Set 2.0: Students perform calculations and solve problems involving addition, subtraction, and simple multiplication and division of fractions and decimals.

DIRECTIONS
Choose the best answer.

QUICK Practice | QUICK Review

1 $14.7 \times 3.9 =$ (5NS2.1)

A 57.3
B 57.33
C 59.13
D 59.33

STRATEGY Align the decimal points and then multiply the numbers.

Remember that there should be 2 digits to the right of the decimal point in the product.

For more help with multiplying decimals, see page 290.

2 $46.62 \div 6.3 =$ (5NS2.2)

F 0.67
G 0.74
H 6.7
J 7.4

STRATEGY Solve a simpler problem.

You can answer this question by multiplying the divisor and dividend by 10. Then perform the division shown below.

$$63\overline{)466.2}$$

For more help with dividing decimals, see page 303.

3 Anna bought $1\frac{1}{8}$ pounds of turkey and $3\frac{1}{4}$ pounds of roast beef. How many pounds of meat did she buy? (5NS2.3)

A $3\frac{1}{4}$
B $3\frac{7}{8}$
C $4\frac{3}{8}$
D $4\frac{3}{4}$

STRATEGY Find a common denominator for the fractions.

Write each mixed number using the common denominator of 8. Then add.

For more help with adding mixed numbers, see page 260.

QUICK Practice

4 $\frac{2}{5} \div \frac{4}{9} =$ **(5NS2.4)**

F $\frac{8}{45}$

G $\frac{4}{5}$

H $\frac{9}{10}$

J $\frac{7}{20}$

QUICK Review

STRATEGY Rewrite the division problem as a multiplication problem by multiplying the dividend by the reciprocal of the divisor.

The division problem $\frac{2}{5} \div \frac{4}{9}$ is equivalent to the multiplication problem $\frac{2}{5} \times \frac{9}{4}$.

For more help with dividing fractions, see page 328.

5 $\frac{1}{7} \cdot \frac{1}{3} =$ **(5NS2.5)**

A $\frac{1}{21}$

B $\frac{1}{15}$

C $\frac{1}{10}$

D $\frac{1}{4}$

STRATEGY When multiplying fractions, multiply the numerators. Then multiply the denominators.

What is the product of 7 and 3?

For more help with multiplying fractions, see page 316.

6 Cindy can type 34 words per minute. At this rate, how many words can Cindy type in 8.5 minutes? **(5NS2.1)**

F 275

G 289

H 296

J 315

READING HINT The *rate*, or speed, that Cindy can type is 34 words per minute.

You can answer this question by solving $\frac{34}{1} = \frac{x}{8.5}$.

For more help with multiplying decimals, see page 284.

7 $5\frac{5}{6} - 2\frac{1}{2} =$ **(5NS2.3)**

A $3\frac{2}{3}$

B $3\frac{1}{3}$

C $2\frac{2}{3}$

D $2\frac{1}{6}$

STRATEGY Find a common denominator for the fractions.

Write each mixed number using the common denominator of 6. Then subtract.

For more help with subtracting mixed numbers, see page 260.

Practice on Your Own

Standard Set 2.0

8 $50{,}594 \div 82 =$ **(5NS2.1)**

F 576

G 617

H 679

J 713

9 Elaine spent $\frac{1}{2}$ hour working on math homework and $\frac{1}{3}$ hour on a reading assignment after school. How much time did she spend doing homework altogether? **(5NS2.3)**

A $\frac{3}{4}$ hour

B $\frac{5}{6}$ hour

C $\frac{2}{3}$ hour

D $\frac{1}{6}$ hour

10 It takes Eduardo $\frac{1}{10}$ hour to ride his bike to Wendy's house and $\frac{1}{5}$ hour to ride from Wendy's house to the mall. How much time does it take him to ride to Wendy's house and then to the mall? **(5NS2.3)**

F $\frac{3}{10}$ hour

G $\frac{1}{15}$ hour

H $\frac{1}{50}$ hour

J $\frac{2}{5}$ hour

11 $4\frac{5}{8} - 3\frac{1}{2} =$ **(5NS2.3)**

A $2\frac{1}{4}$

B $2\frac{1}{8}$

C $1\frac{1}{8}$

D $\frac{7}{8}$

12 Mrs. Wilson bought 4 pounds of birdseed for her feeder. She saved $3.16 by using a store coupon. How much did she save per pound of birdseed? **(5NS2.1)**

F $1.27

G $1.09

H $0.85

J $0.79

13 27.09×0.6 **(5NS2.1)**

A 14.574

B 14.804

C 16.164

D 16.254

14 A carpenter had a board 4.65 meters long. He cut off 1.3 meters. How long was the piece of board that was left? **(5NS2.1)**

F 2.95 meters

G 3.15 meters

H 3.35 meters

J 3.75 meters

15 $3\frac{1}{5} + 4\frac{1}{2} =$ **(5NS2.3)**

A $7\frac{7}{10}$

B $7\frac{2}{3}$

C $7\frac{2}{7}$

D $7\frac{1}{10}$

Practice by Standard: Algebra and Functions

Standard Set 1.0: Students use variables in simple expressions, compute the value of the expression for specific values of the variable, and plot and interpret the results.

DIRECTIONS
Choose the best answer.

QUICK Practice

1 If $b = 5$, what is the value of $3 \times b - 2$? **(5AF1.2)**

A 6

B 10

C 11

D 13

QUICK Review

STRATEGY Substitute 5 for *b* and simplify the resulting expression.

This problem can be solved by simplifying the expression below.

$$3 \times 5 - 2$$

For more help with evaluating algebraic expressions, see page 34.

QUICK Practice

2 Which situation could be described by the expression $h + 1\frac{2}{3}$? **(5AF1.1)**

F Lisa worked *h* hours in her garden yesterday and $1\frac{2}{3}$ fewer hours today.

G Lisa worked $1\frac{2}{3}$ hours in her garden yesterday and *h* fewer hours today.

H Lisa worked *h* hours in her garden yesterday and $1\frac{2}{3}$ more hours today.

J Lisa worked *h* hours in her garden yesterday and $1\frac{2}{3}$ times more hours today.

QUICK Review

STRATEGY The expression shows $1\frac{2}{3}$ being added to some quantity *h*. Look for the choice that represents this expression.

Which situation can be represented by a sum?

For more help with using expressions to describe situations, see page 35.

QUICK Practice

3 What value for *k* makes this equation true? **(5AF1.3)**

$$9 \times 24 = (9 \times 20) + (9 \times k)$$

A 4

B 7

C 11

D 12

QUICK Review

STRATEGY Use backsolving to find which answer choice is the solution. When you backsolve, you substitute each value for the variable to find which choice makes the left side of the equation equal to the right side.

Substitute each answer choice into the equation for *k* and see which one results in a true number sentence.

For more help with the Distributive Property, see page 58.

---

4 The map below shows the location of playground equipment.

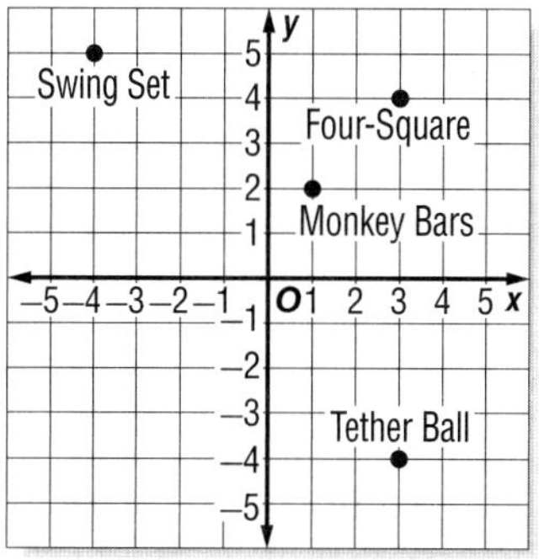

Which ordered pair *best* names the location of the monkey bars? **(5AF1.4)**

F (2, 1) **H** (–1, 2)

G (1, 2) **J** (–2, 1)

STRATEGY Locate the point on the coordinate grid that represents the monkey bars. Then identify the *x*-coordinate and *y*-coordinate of this point.

Remember to list the coordinates of the point as (*x*, *y*).

For more help with naming points on a coordinate grid, see page 378.

---

5 Which equation could have been used to create the table shown below? **(5AF1.5)**

x	–2	–1	1	2
y	–8	–4	4	8

A $y = x + 4$ **C** $y = 4x$

B $x = y + 4$ **D** $x = 4y$

STRATEGY Look for a pattern relating *x* and *y*.

How can you express this as an equation?

For more help with writing equations for a function, see page 450.

Practice on Your Own

Standard Set 1.0

6 If $p = 9$, what is the value of $8p - 5$? **(5AF1.2)**

F 67

G 53

H 31

J 12

7 Which expression represents the sum of a and 10? **(5AF1.2)**

A $a - 10$

B $a + 10$

C $a \div 10$

D $a \times 10$

8 Line n is represented by the equation $y = 2$. Which ordered pair is located on line n? **(5AF1.4)**

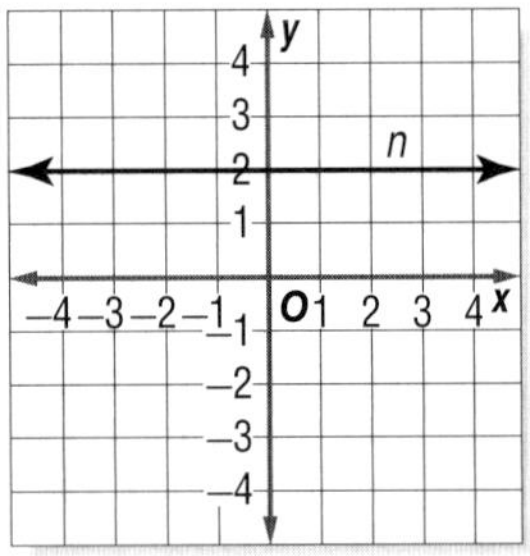

F (−1, 2)

G (0, 0)

H (2, 1)

J (2, 0)

9 If $t = 48$, what is the value of $9 - t$? **(5AF1.2)**

A −57

B −39

C 39

D 57

10 Which table represents values x and y such that $y = x + 6$? **(5AF1.5)**

F

x	y
−2	−8
−1	17

H

x	y
−2	4
−1	5

G

x	y
6	0
2	4

J

x	y
4	−2
3	−3

11 Which equation could have been used to create this function table? **(5AF1.5)**

x	−8	−5	1	7
y	−10	−7	−1	5

A $y = 2x$

B $y = x + 2$

C $y = x - 2$

D $y = x - 1$

12 The map below shows the locations of four different places.

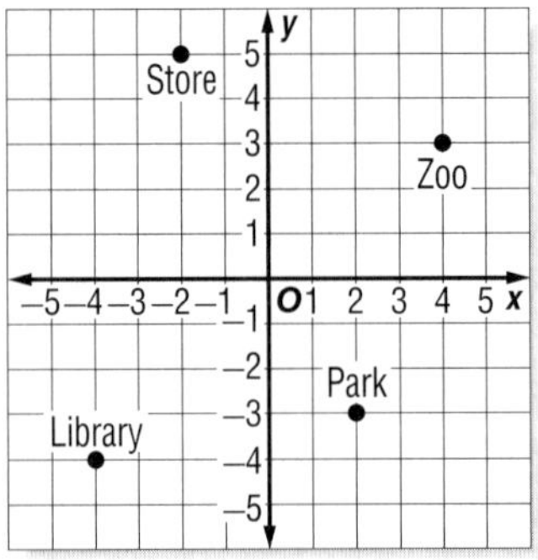

Which place is at the point (4, 3)? **(5AF1.4)**

F Library

G Park

H Store

J Zoo

Practice by Standard: Measurement and Geometry

Standard Set 1.0: Students understand and compute the volumes and areas of simple objects.

DIRECTIONS
Choose the best answer.

QUICK Practice

1 In the figure below, *ABCD* is a parallelogram.

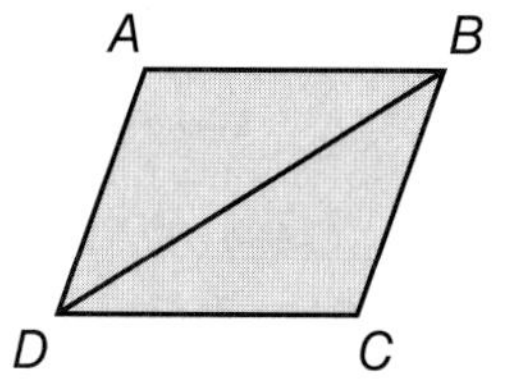

If the area of triangle *ABD* is 15 square centimeters, what is the area of *ABCD*? **(5MG1.1)**

A 15 square centimeters
B 30 square centimeters
C 45 square centimeters
D 60 square centimeters

2 What is the surface area of the cube formed by the net below? **(5MG1.2)**

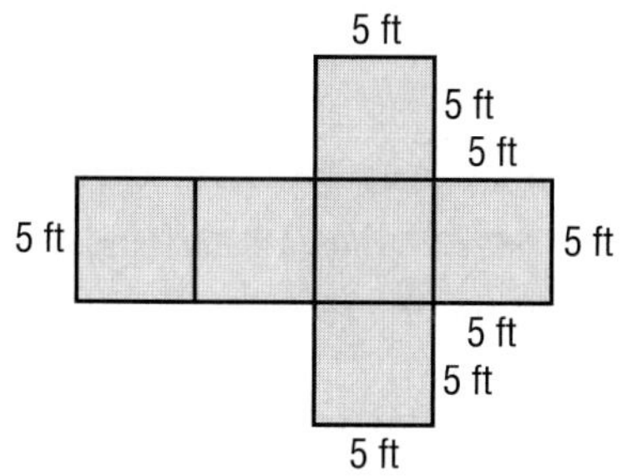

F 25 ft^2 **H** 125 ft^2
G 75 ft^2 **J** 150 ft^2

QUICK Review

READING HINT Recall that a parallelogram can be split into two congruent triangles.

The area of parallelogram *ABCD* is equal to twice the area of triangle *ABD*.

For more help with finding the area of a parallelogram, see page 591.

READING HINT *Surface area* in this problem means the sum of the areas of the six faces of the cube.

What is the area of each face of the cube? How many faces are there?

For more help with finding the surface area of a rectangular prism, see page 618.

QUICK Practice

3 This rectangular prism has a length of 10 millimeters, a height of 5 millimeters, and a width of 4 millimeters. What is the volume? **(5MG1.3)**

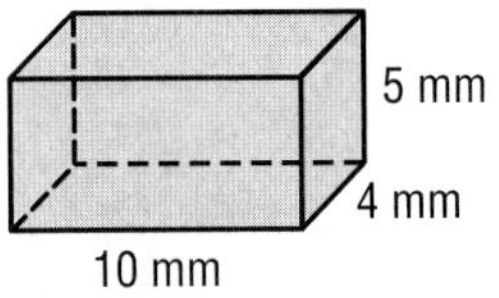

A 19 cubic millimeters

B 56 cubic millimeters

C 200 cubic millimeters

D 220 cubic millimeters

4 Which of the following units would be most appropriate for finding the perimeter of the rectangle shown below? **(5MG1.4)**

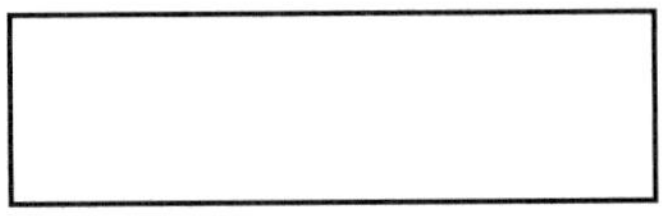

F cubic inches

G millimeters

H square centimeters

J square feet

5 Find the volume of the rectangular prism shown below. **(5MG1.3)**

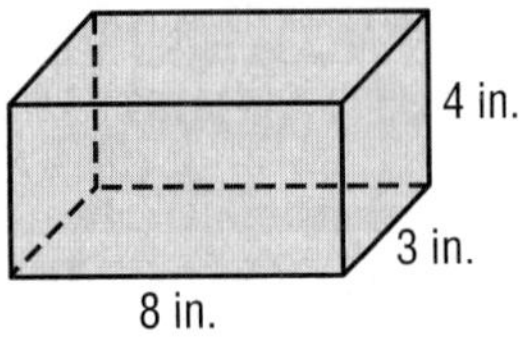

A 15 in^3

B 48 in^3

C 96 in^3

D 192 in^3

QUICK Review

READING HINT The volume of a rectangular prism can be found by using the formula $V = \ell wh$, where ℓ is the length, w is the width, and h is the height.

Replace ℓ with 10, w with 4, and h with 5 in the formula for the volume of a rectangular prism, $V = \ell wh$.

For more help with finding the volume of rectangular prisms, see page 608.

READING HINT Recall the distance around any closed figure is called its *perimeter*.

The perimeter P of a rectangle is the sum of its two lengths and two widths.

For more help with appropriate units of measure for the perimeter of two-dimensional figures, see page 585.

STRATEGY Think: Which answers can you eliminate because they are not reasonable?

Replace ℓ with 8, w with 3, and h with 4 in the formula for the volume of a rectangular prism, $V = \ell wh$.

For more help with finding the volume of rectangular prisms, see page 608.

Practice on Your Own

Standard Set 1.0

6 In the figure below, *HJKL* is a parallelogram. If the area of *HJKL* is 84 square inches, what is the area of triangle *LKH*? **(5MG1.1)**

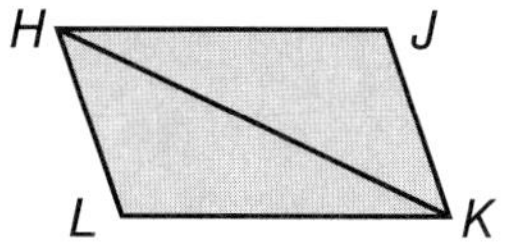

F 21 square inches
G 42 square inches
H 84 square inches
J 168 square inches

7 The rectangular prism below has a length of 7 centimeters, a height of 5 centimeters, and a width of 3 centimeters. What is its volume? **(5MG1.3)**

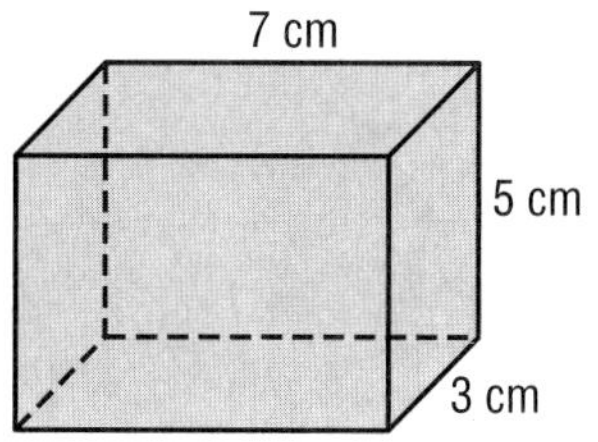

A 88 cubic centimeters
B 105 cubic centimeters
C 120 cubic centimeters
D 142 cubic centimeters

8 Which of the following units would be most appropriate for finding the surface area of a prism? **(5MG1.4)**

F cubic meters
G cubic inches
H square feet
J yards

9 The rectangular prism below has a length of 10 inches, a height of 8 inches, and a width of 4 inches. What is the volume? **(5MG1.3)**

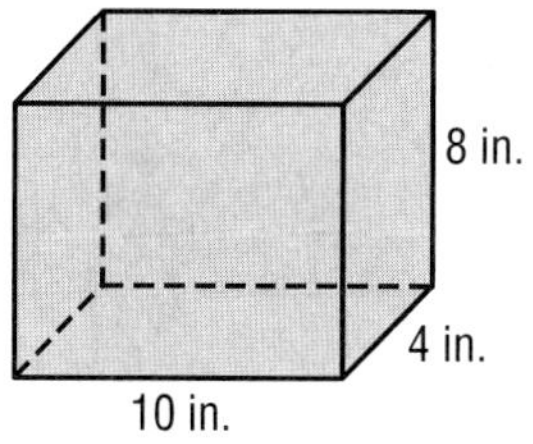

A 22 cubic inches
B 44 cubic inches
C 88 cubic inches
D 320 cubic inches

10 What is the surface area of the rectangular prism formed by the net below? **(5MG1.2)**

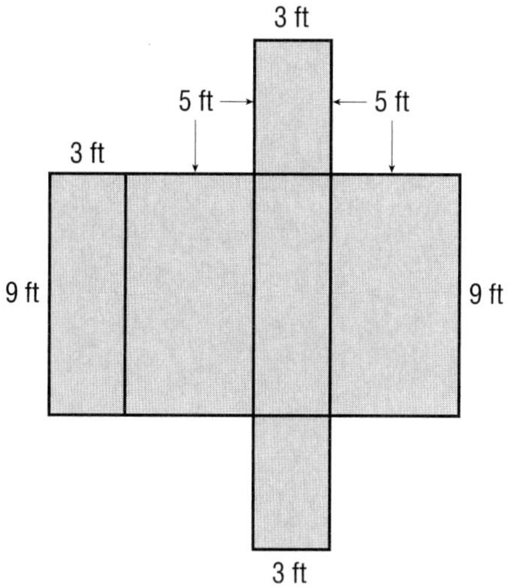

F 174 square feet
G 161 square feet
H 135 square feet
J 108 square feet

Practice by Standard: Measurement and Geometry

Standard Set 2.0: Students identify, describe, and classify the properties of, and the relationships between, plane and solid geometric figures.

DIRECTIONS
Choose the best answer.

QUICK Practice

1 Which is *closest* to the measure of the angle shown below? **(5MG2.1)**

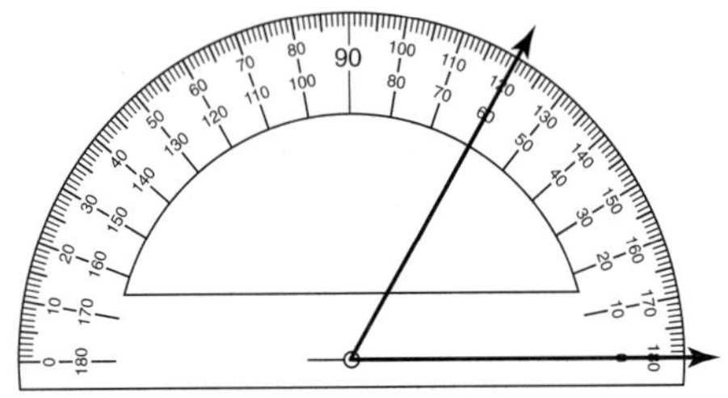

A 60°

B 75°

C 110°

D 120°

QUICK Review

STRATEGY Think: Which answers can you eliminate because they are not reasonable?

The angle measurement should be less than 90°.

For more help with using a protractor to find angle measures, see page 529.

QUICK Practice

2 What is the measure of angle n in the figure below? **(5MG2.2)**

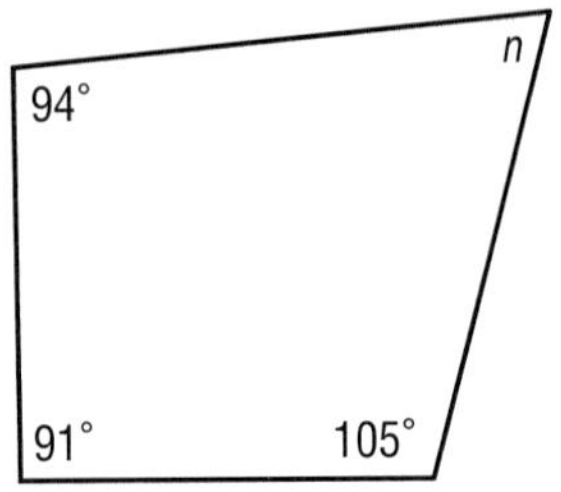

F 160°

G 135°

H 70°

J 55°

QUICK Review

READING HINT The sum of the angles of a quadrilateral is 360°.

This problem can be solved by solving the equation below.

$$n + 94 + 91 + 105 = 360$$

For more help with finding missing angle measures of quadrilaterals, see page 558.

QUICK Practice

3 Which of the following shows the front view of the solid below? **(5MG2.3)**

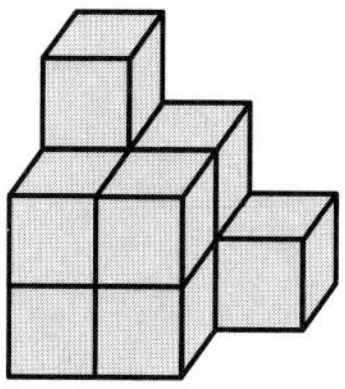

Front

A

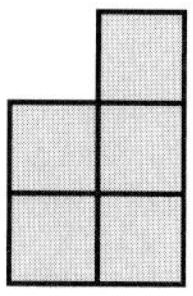

C

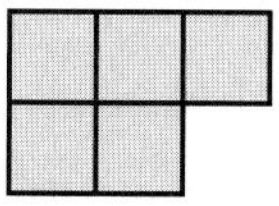

B

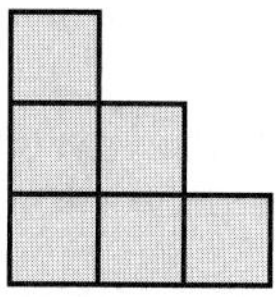

D

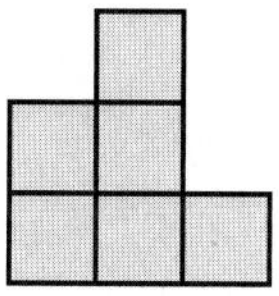

QUICK Review

STRATEGY Try to imagine looking at the solid from the front view.

How many blocks would you see in each stack if you were to look at the solid from the front?

For more help with visualizing two-dimensional views of three-dimensional objects, see page 566.

---

4 Which of the following *best* describes the figure below? **(5MG2.1)**

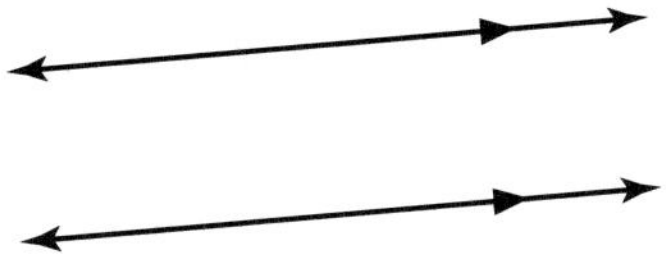

F intersecting lines
G parallel lines
H perpendicular lines
J acute angles

STRATEGY Look at the terms listed. Define the ones that you can and eliminate any choices.

Parallel lines are lines that never intersect.

For more help with identifying parallel lines, see page 541.

---

5 What is the approximate measure of the angle below in degrees? **(5MG2.1)**

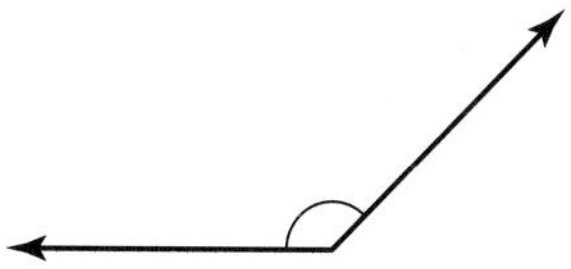

A 75°   **C** 130°
B 100°   **D** 175°

READING HINT Recall that an obtuse angle is any angle that measures greater than 90° but less than 180°.

The angle measurement should be greater than 90°.

For more help with estimating angle measures, see page 536.

Practice on Your Own

Standard Set 2.0

6 What is the measure of angle *c* in the figure below? **(5MG2.2)**

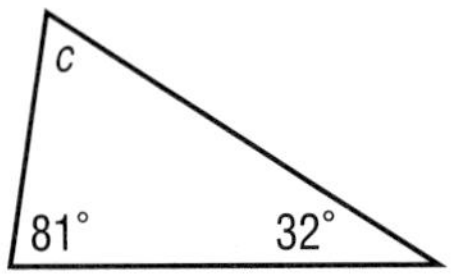

F 157°
G 143°
H 72°
J 67°

7 Kurt made a triangular garden in the corner of his yard. One angle is 40°. What is the measure of the third angle of Kurt's triangle? **(5MG2.2)**

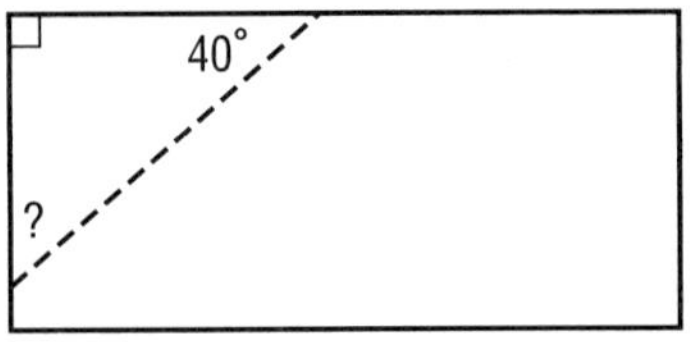

A 50°
B 60°
C 120°
D 140°

8 Which of the following *best* describes the figure below? **(5MG2.1)**

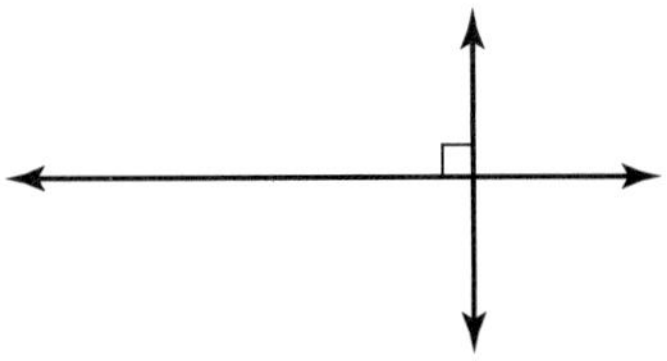

F obtuse angles
G parallel lines
H opposite angles
J perpendicular lines

9 What is the measure of angle *m* in the figure shown below? **(5MG2.2)**

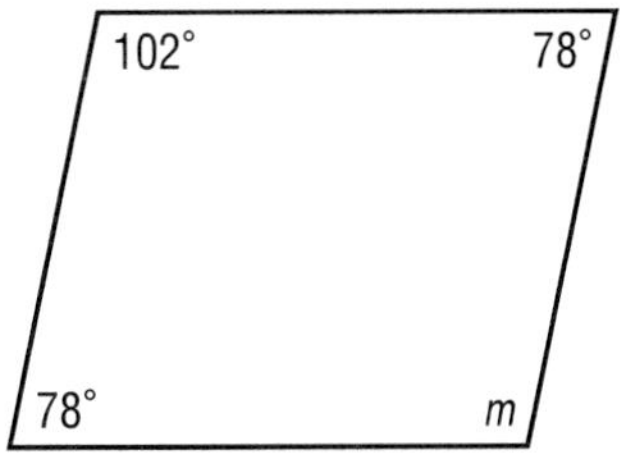

A 102°
B 100°
C 78°
D 12°

10 Triangle *RST* is isosceles. If the measure of ∠*R* is 52° and the measures of ∠*S* and ∠*T* are equal, what is the measure of ∠*T*? **(5MG2.2)**

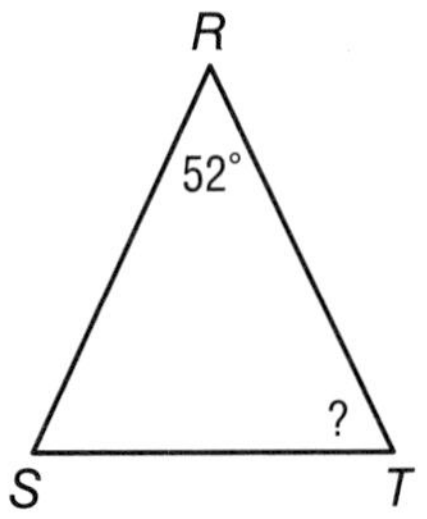

F 64°
G 72°
H 90°
J 128°

11 Which is *closest* to the measure of the angle shown below? **(5MG2.1)**

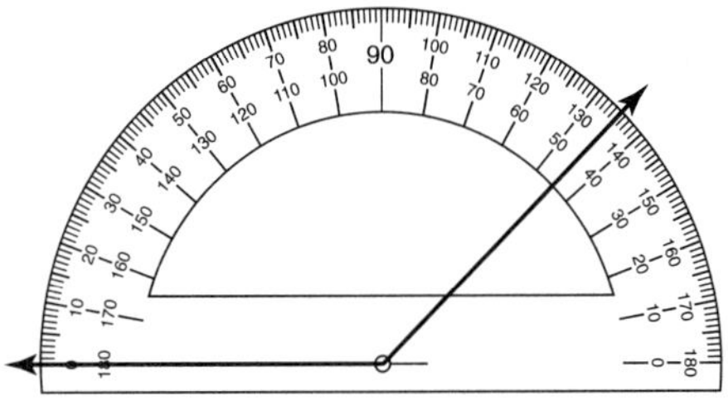

A 45°
B 55°
C 135°
D 145°

Practice by Standard: Statistics, Data Analysis, and Probability

Standard Set 1.0: Students display, analyze, compare, and interpret different data sets, including data sets of different sizes.

DIRECTIONS
Choose the best answer.

QUICK Practice

1 Karen's golf scores over her last five rounds are listed below.

75, 79, 80, 77, 76

What is the median of these numbers? **(5SDAP1.1)**

A 75 **C** 77

B 76 **D** 78

2 The graph shows the cost of renting a jet ski for *x* hours. If Reggie's total cost was $30, for how many hours did he rent the jet ski? **(5SDAP1.4)**

Jet Ski Rental Cost

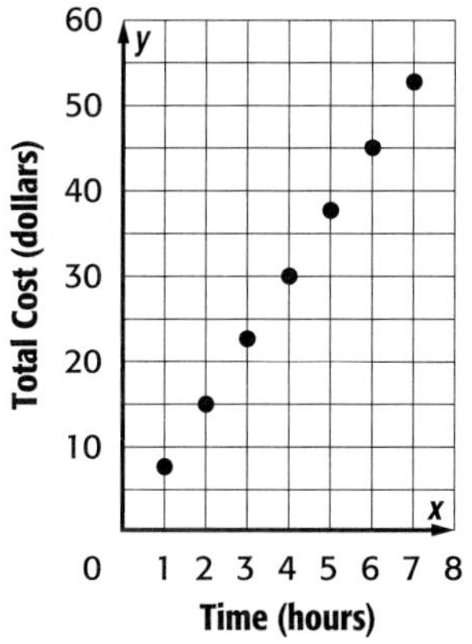

F 3 **H** 5

G 4 **J** 6

QUICK Review

READING HINT The *median* of a data set is the middle number when the data are arranged in order from least to greatest.

Write the golf scores in order from least to greatest to find the median.

For more help with finding the median of a data set, see page 99.

READING HINT An *ordered pair* is a pair of numbers used to locate a point in the coordinate system. The ordered pair is written in this form (*x*-coordinate, *y*-coordinate).

Locate the point on the graph that has a *y*-value of 30. What is the *x*-value of this point?

For more help with interpreting data on a graph, see page 79.

QUICK Practice

3 Which point represents (2, −4) on this graph? **(5SDAP1.5)**

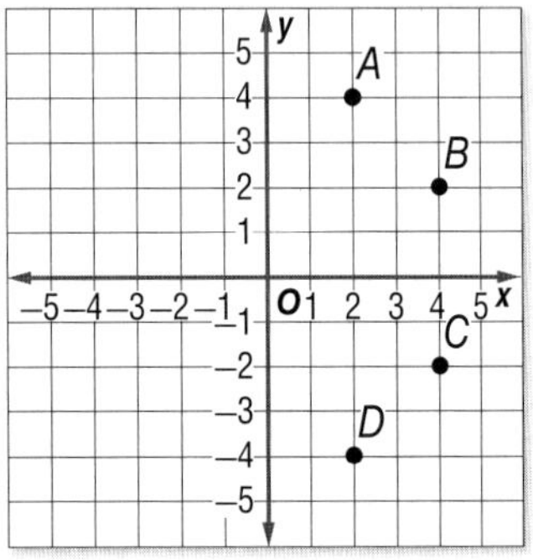

A point *A*

B point *B*

C point *C*

D point *D*

QUICK Review

READING HINT Recall that the *x*-coordinate corresponds to a number on the *x*-axis and the *y*-coordinate corresponds to a number on the *y*-axis.

Locate the point that is 2 units right of the origin and 4 units below the origin.

For more help with identifying the point corresponding to an ordered pair, see page 378.

---

4 Which type of graph would be *best* for displaying the height of a plant over the past several weeks? **(5SDAP1.2)**

F bar graph

G circle graph

H histogram

J line graph

STRATEGY Think: Which answers can you eliminate because they are not reasonable?

Are bar graphs, histograms, or circle graphs appropriate for showing how data change over time?

For more help with choosing appropriate types of graphs, see page 106.

---

5 There are seven fourth-graders and thirteen fifth-graders in the school play. What percent of students in the school play are fifth-graders? **(5SDAP1.3)**

A 72%

B 65%

C 54%

D 35%

READING HINT Percent means *per hundred.*

Solve $\frac{13}{20} = \frac{n}{100}$.

For more help with using percents to represent data, see page 468.

Practice on Your Own

Standard Set 1.0

6 What is the mean of the following set of quiz scores? **(5SDAP1.1)**

8, 9, 7, 6, 10, 9, 7

F 7

G 7.5

H 8

J 8.5

7 The line graph shows the height of a plant after several weeks. What was the height of the plant during week 4? **(5SDAP1.4)**

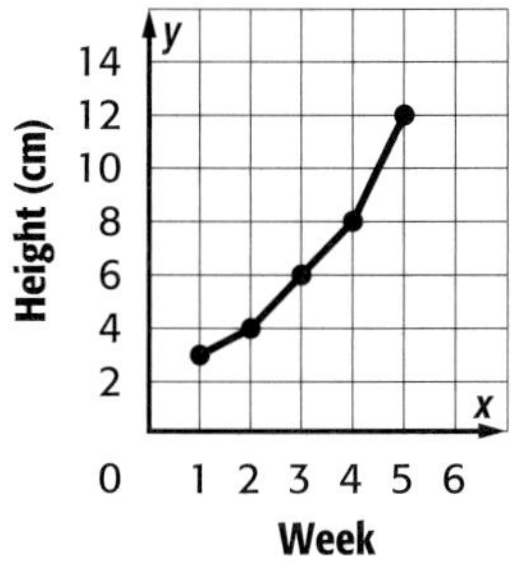

A 12 cm

B 8 cm

C 6 cm

D 4 cm

8 The table below shows the ages of the players on Aaron's soccer team. What is the mode of the data set? **(5SDAP1.1)**

12	12	12	11	9
12	10	9	11	11
10	10	12	12	10

F 9

G 10

H 11

J 12

9 Which type of graph would be best for comparing the parts of a budget to the whole budget? **(5SDAP1.2)**

A bar graph

B circle graph

C histogram

D line graph

10 Which point represents (−3, 5) on this graph? **(5SDAP1.5)**

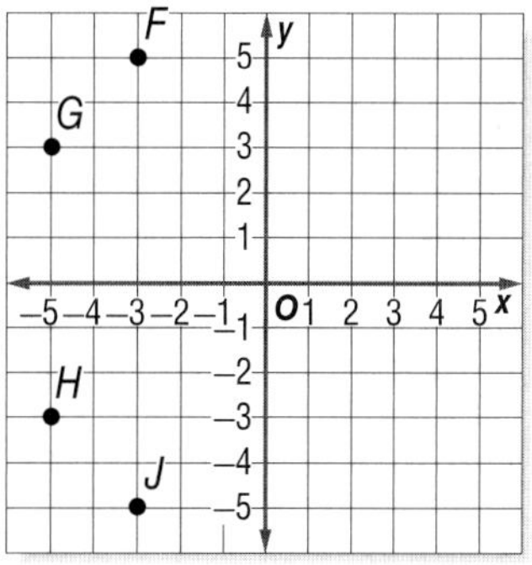

F point *F*

G point *G*

H point *H*

J point *J*

11 Sam kept track of the number of Calories that he burned per minute while running on the treadmill. How long did it take him to burn 60 Calories? **(5SDAP1.5)**

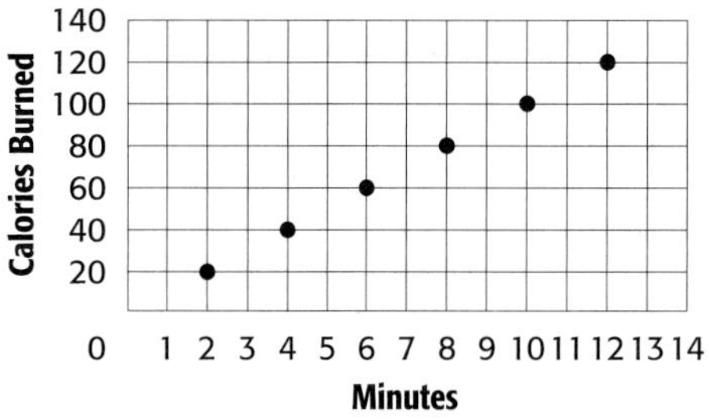

A 4 minutes

B 6 minutes

C 8 minutes

D 10 minutes

Practice by Standard: Mathematical Reasoning

Standard Set 1.0: Students make decisions about how to approach problems.

DIRECTIONS
Choose the best answer.

QUICK Practice

1 Consider the following problem.

> Mandy's room is 14 feet long and 10 feet wide with a ceiling that is 8 feet high. Her parents want to have new carpet installed in the room. The carpeting costs $3.00 per square foot. How much will it cost to have the carpet installed in Mandy's room?

Identify the irrelevant information in the problem. **(5MR1.1, 5MG1.4)**

A the length of Mandy's room
B the width of Mandy's room
C the height of Mandy's room
D the cost of the carpet

QUICK Review

STRATEGY Think: What information do you need to solve the problem? Do not be distracted by extra information.

To find the area of Mandy's room, you need to know the length and the width of the room.

For more help with distinguishing relevant from irrelevant information in a problem situation, see page 104.

QUICK Practice

2 A total of 150 students went on a field trip. Sixty percent of the students brought their own lunches. To mentally find how many students brought their own lunch to the field trip, which of the following could you find first? **(5MR1.2, 5NS1.2)**

F 10% of 60 **H** 150% of 60
G 60% of 10 **J** 10% of 150

QUICK Review

STRATEGY Sometimes it is helpful to break a complex problem into a simpler one. This can involve doing one step of the problem, using smaller numbers, or rounding.

Solve a simpler problem by finding 10% of the number of students who went on the field trip. Then multiply the product by 6.

For more help with using mental math to solve a simpler problem, see page 482.

Practice on Your Own

Standard Set 1.0

3 The total area of California is 424,000 square kilometers. Of that, about 5% is inland water. Which of the following would you do first to find the estimated amount of California that is inland water? **(5MR1.2, 5NS1.1)**

A round 424,000

B find 95% of 424,000

C find 5% of 95

D subtract 5% from 100%

4 The figures below represent the first three terms of a pattern. If the pattern continues, how many squares will be in Figure 6 of the pattern? **(5MR1.1, 5AF1.5)**

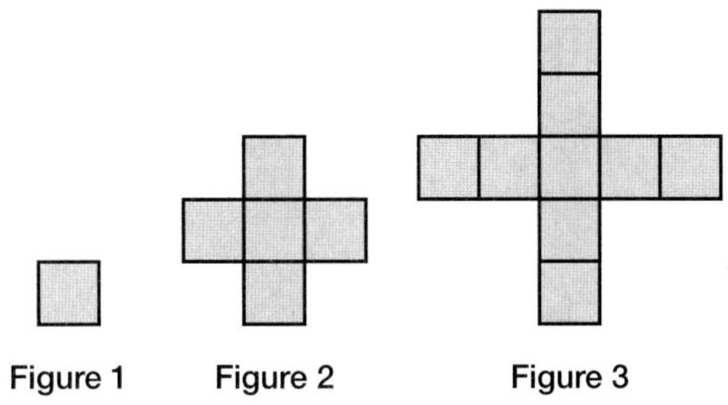

F 17 **H** 24

G 21 **J** 27

5 A total of 29 students are going on a field trip. Each student must pay \$4.65 for transportation and \$5.50 for lunch. About how much money should the teacher collect in all from the students? **(5MR1.2, 5NS1.1)**

A \$225

B \$250

C \$260

D \$300

6 Which equation *best* describes the relationship between *x* and *y* shown in the graph? **(5MR1.1, 5SDAP1.4)**

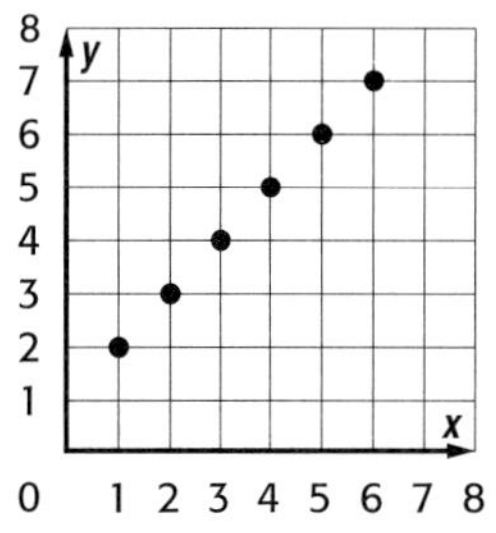

F $y = x + 2$ **H** $y = x - 1$

G $y = x + 1$ **J** $y = x - 2$

7 Consider the following problem.

> There are 450 students and 30 teachers at Pine Villa Elementary School. Eighty percent of the students ride the bus to school. How many students do *not* ride the bus to school?

Identify the irrelevant information in the problem. **(5MR1.1, 5NS1.2)**

A the number of students at Pine Villa Elementary School

B the percent of students who ride the bus to school

C the number of teachers at Pine Villa Elementary School

D the percent of students who do not ride the bus to school

8 If the pattern continues, what will be the next number? **(5MR1.1, 5AF1.5)**

3, 9, 15, ?

F 18 **H** 27

G 21 **J** 45

Practice by Standard: Mathematical Reasoning

Standard Set 2.0: Students use strategies, skills, and concepts in finding solutions.

DIRECTIONS
Choose the best answer.

QUICK Practice

1 The table shows the number of points Kris' football team scored last season.

14	21	24	17	14	21	9	34	15	17

Kris calculated that the mode of the scores was 16. Which of the following shows that his calculation is invalid? **(5MR2.6, 5SDAP1.1)**

A The median is 16, not 17.

B Most scores are above the mode.

C The team never scored 16 points.

D The mean is 17, not 16.

2 Which expression represents the perimeter in inches of the square shown below? **(5MR2.3, 5MG1.4)**

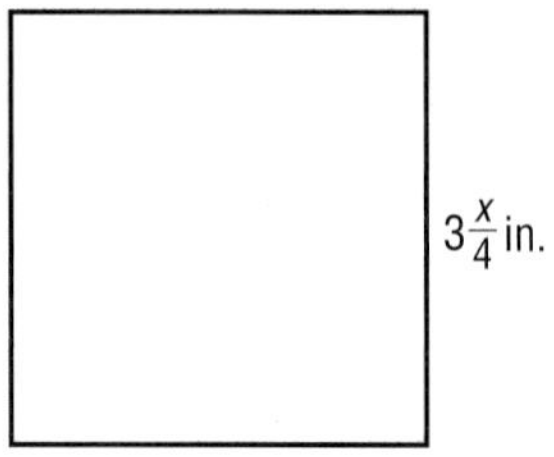

F $3\frac{x}{4} + 3\frac{x}{4}$ **H** $4\left(3\frac{x}{4}\right)$

G $2\left(3\frac{x}{4}\right) + 3\frac{x}{4}$ **J** $4\left(3\frac{x}{4}\right) \times \frac{1}{2}$

QUICK Review

STRATEGY You do not have to calculate the mode in order to answer this problem.

You are looking for a true statement that shows that 16 cannot be the mode. Read through each answer choice, checking for its validity and how it shows that Kris' calculation of the mode cannot be true.

For more help with the mode of a data set, see page 99.

READING HINT The perimeter of a square can be found by using the formula $P = 4s$.

Replace s with $3\frac{x}{4}$ in the formula for the perimeter of a square.

For more help with the perimeter of a square, see page 585.

Practice on Your Own

Standard Set 2.0

3 Which of the following is true concerning the area of the rectangle shown below? **(5MR2.5, 5MG1.4)**

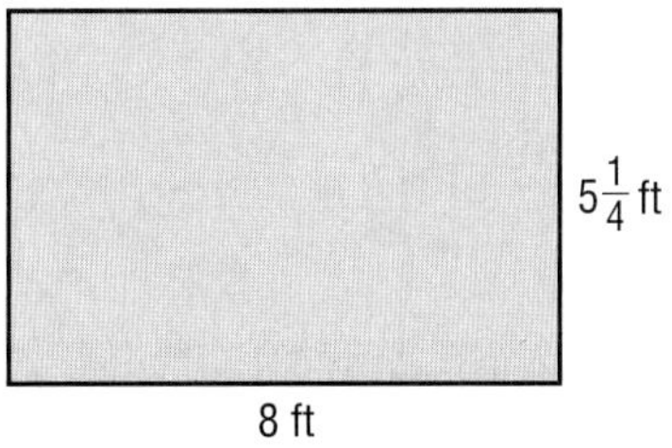

A The exact area is 40 ft^2.

B The approximate area can be found by multiplying 8 by $5\frac{1}{4}$.

C The exact area can be found by multiplying 8 by 5.

D The approximate area can be found by multiplying 8 by 5.

4 Paperback books cost $5.79 including tax at Book Smart. Juliana buys 4 paperback books. She determined the cost of the 4 books is $23.16. Which of the following verifies that her solution is reasonable? **(5MR2.1, 5NS1.1)**

F $5.79 \approx 6$, so $6 \times 4 = 24$

G $5.79 \approx 5$, so $5 \times 4 = 20$

H $23.13 \approx 20$, so $20 \div 4 = 5$

J $23.13 \approx 20$, so $20 \div 5 = 4$

5 Suppose the population of a city was 2,900. Of that, 40% of the people owned dogs. Which of the following could you evaluate first to mentally calculate the number of people who owned dogs? **(5MR2.2, 5NS1.2)**

A 5% of 2,900

B 10% of 2,900

C 60% of 40

D 40% of 60

6 The equation $25 + b = 40$ describes the number of minutes Rebecca spent cleaning her room over two days. Which of the following is true? **(5MR2.4, 5AF1.1)**

F $25 + 40 = 65$, so $b = 65$

G $40 - 25 = 15$, so $b = 15$

H $25 - 40 = -15$, so $b = -15$

J $25 \times 1.6 = 40$, so $b = 1.6$

7 Which expression represents the perimeter in feet of the rectangle shown below? **(5MR2.3, 5MG1.4)**

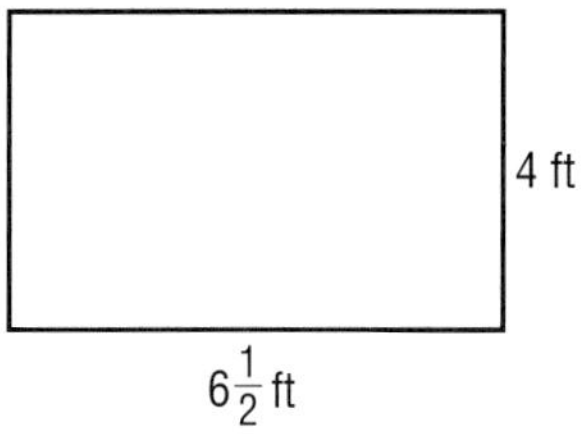

A $13 + 8$

B $6\frac{1}{2} + 8$

C $6\frac{1}{2} + 4x$

D $13 + \frac{4}{x}$

8 For each step that Christian takes, he travels a distance of 3 feet. Let x represent the number of steps that he takes and let y represent the distance traveled. Which of the following equations shows the relationship between x and y? **(5MR2.4, 5AF1.5)**

F $x = 3y$

G $x = y + 3$

H $y = x + 3$

J $y = 3x$

Practice by Standard: Mathematical Reasoning

Standard Set 3.0: Students move beyond a particular problem by generalizing to other situations.

DIRECTIONS
Choose the best answer.

QUICK Practice

1 Luz determined that the next term in the sequence below is 35.

55, 48, 41, 34, 27, …

Which of the following shows that her solution is *not* reasonable?
(5MR3.1, 5AF1.5)

A The terms are increasing.
B The terms are decreasing.
C The terms are multiples of 5.
D The terms are odd numbers.

2 Use the table to make a generalization about the angle measures of quadrilateral *ABCD*.
(5MR3.3, 5MG2.2)

$m\angle A$	$m\angle B$	$m\angle C$	$m\angle D$
99°	81°	99°	81°
40°	146°	116°	58°
65°	95°	80°	120°

F $m\angle A + m\angle B + m\angle C + m\angle D = 360°$
G $m\angle B + m\angle C + m\angle D = 360°$
H $m\angle A + m\angle B = 180°$
J $m\angle A + m\angle B + m\angle C + m\angle D = 180°$

QUICK Review

STRATEGY Think: Which answers can you eliminate because they are not reasonable?

The pattern in the sequence shows that each term is 7 less than the previous term.

For more help with sequences, see page 442.

READING HINT Recall that the sum of the measures of the angles of a quadrilateral is 360°.

Verify that the sum of each set of angles in the table is 360°. Then write an equation representing the sum of the angles of quadrilateral *ABCD*.

For more help with the sum of the angles of quadrilaterals, see page 558.

Practice on Your Own

Standard Set 3.0

3 The difference of $\frac{3}{5}$ and $\frac{1}{5}$ is $\frac{2}{5}$, the difference of $\frac{4}{7}$ and $\frac{2}{7}$ is $\frac{2}{7}$, and the difference of $\frac{7}{11}$ and $\frac{5}{11}$ is $\frac{2}{11}$. Use this pattern to make a generalization about the difference of the fractions $\frac{a}{b}$ and $\frac{c}{b}$. **(5MR3.3, 5AF1.1)**

A $\frac{a}{b} - \frac{c}{b} = \frac{a-c}{b}$

B $\frac{a}{b} - \frac{c}{b} = \frac{a-c}{b^2}$

C $\frac{a}{b} - \frac{c}{b} = \frac{a-c}{b-b}$

D $\frac{a}{b} \div \frac{c}{d} = \frac{ad}{bc}$

4 Ryan wants to save 40% of his paycheck each month. In April, his paycheck was \$320.98. He determines that he should save \$192. Which of the following shows that his solution is *not* reasonable? **(5MR3.1, 5NS1.1)**

F 40% of \$320.98 $\approx \frac{1}{4}$ of \$320, or \$80.00

G 40% of \$320.98 $\approx \frac{1}{2}$ of \$320, or \$160.00

H 40% of \$320.98 $\approx \frac{2}{5}$ of \$320, or \$128.00

J 40% of \$320.98 $\approx \frac{1}{3}$ of \$320, or \$107.00

5 Jessie made 15 key chains in 4 hours. Which of the following is a reasonable calculation for the number of hours it would take her to make 44 key chains? **(5MR3.1, 5NS2.5)**

A 16 hours
B 11 hours
C 10 hours
D 8 hours

6 Nemo draws a diagonal that splits a rectangle into two congruent triangles. Using the formula for the area of a rectangle, which of the following would give the area of each triangle? **(5MR3.2, 5MG1.4)**

F $A = \frac{1}{2}\ell w$
G $A = \ell w^2$
H $A = 2\ell w$
J $A = \ell w + 2\ell w$

7 Jean determined that cost of renting a popcorn machine for 9 hours was \$82.

Number of Hours	Cost (\$)
1	32
3	47
5	62
7	77

Which of the following shows that her solution is *not* reasonable? **(5MR3.1, 5AF1.1)**

A The terms are multiples of 15.

B The terms are decreasing.

C The terms are multiples of 11.

D The terms are increasing by 15.

8 The table gives several possible angle measures for triangle *XYZ*.

$m\angle X$	$m\angle Y$	$m\angle Z$
99°	54°	27°
40°	30°	110°
59°	84°	37°

Use the table to make a generalization about the angle measures of a triangle. **(5MR3.3, 5MG2.2)**

F $m\angle X + m\angle Y + m\angle Z = 360°$

G $m\angle X + m\angle Y - m\angle Z = 180°$

H $m\angle X + m\angle Z = 90°$

J $m\angle X + m\angle Y + m\angle Z = 180°$

Looking Ahead

to the Grade 6 Standards

Let's Look Ahead!

Looking Ahead 1

Length in the Customary System

GET READY to Learn

MAIN IDEA

I will change units of length and measure length in the customary system.

Preparation for Standard 6AF2.1
Convert one unit of measurement to another (e.g., from feet to miles, from centimeters to inches).

New Vocabulary

inch
foot
yard
mile

Hands-On Mini Lab

Step 1 Using string, measure and cut the lengths of your arm and your shoe.

Step 2 Use the strings to find the classroom length in arms and classroom width in shoes. Record the nonstandard measures.

Measure	Nonstandard	Standard
Classroom length	_____ arms	_____ yards
Classroon width	_____ shoes	_____ feet

Step 3 Use a yardstick or tape measure to find the length in yards and width in feet. Record the standard measures.

1. Compare your nonstandard measures with the nonstandard measures of other groups. Are they similar? Why or why not?

2. Compare your standard measures with the standard measures of other groups. Are they similar? Why or why not?

3. Explain the advantages and the disadvantages of using nonstandard measurement and standard measurement.

The most commonly used customary units of length are shown below.

KEY CONCEPT — **Customary Units of Length**

Unit	Model
1 **inch** (in.)	width of a quarter
1 **foot** (ft) = 12 in.	length of a large adult foot
1 **yard** (yd) = 3 ft	length from nose to fingertip
1 **mile** (mi) = 1,760 yd	10 city blocks

Concepts in Motion

Animation
ca.gr5math.com

Rulers are usually separated into eighths of an inch.

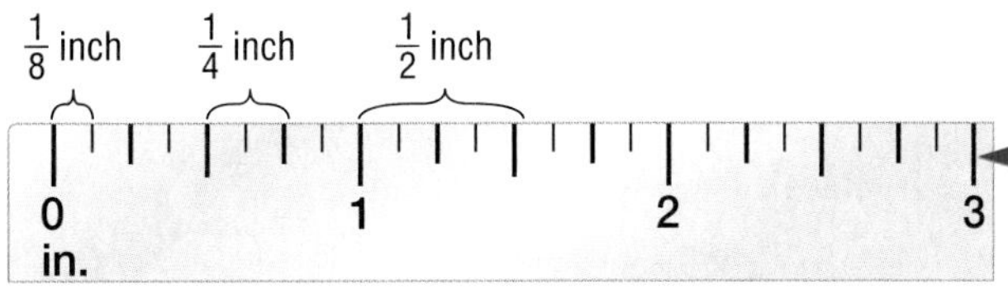

The smallest mark represents $\frac{1}{8}$ inch. The next larger mark represents $\frac{1}{4}$ inch, and the next larger mark represents $\frac{1}{2}$ inch. The longest mark on a ruler represents an inch.

EXAMPLE Draw a Line Segment

1 Draw a line segment measuring $2\frac{3}{8}$ inches.

Draw a line segment from 0 to $2\frac{3}{8}$.

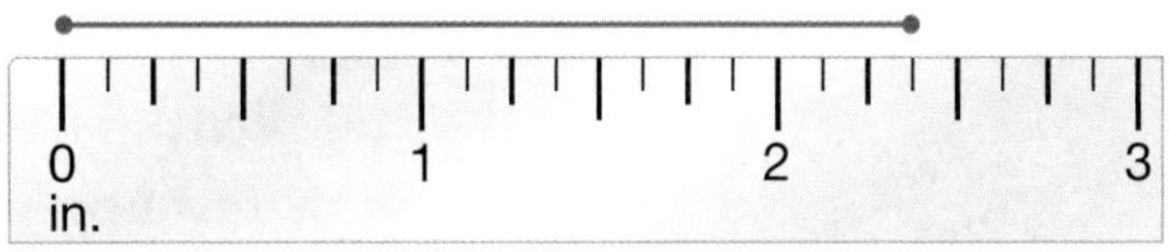

Real-World EXAMPLE Measure Length

2 Measure the key's length to the nearest half, fourth, or eighth inch.

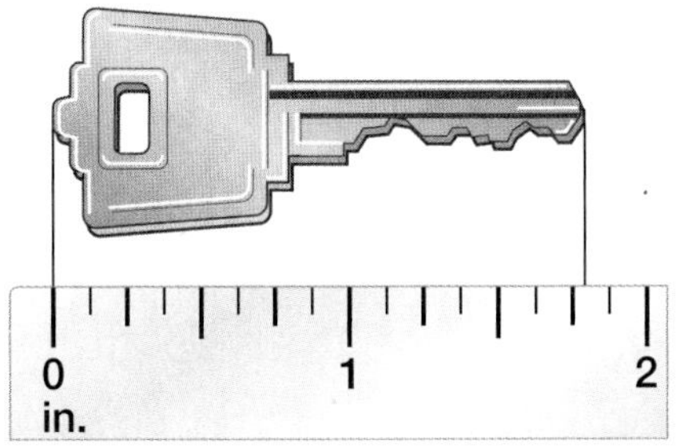

The length of the key is between $1\frac{3}{4}$ inches and $1\frac{7}{8}$ inches. It is closer to $1\frac{3}{4}$ inches.

The length of the key is about $1\frac{3}{4}$ inches.

EXAMPLE Change Larger Units to Smaller Units

3 3 ft = ■ in.

Since 1 foot = 12 inches, multiply 3 by 12.

$3 \times 12 = 36$

So, 3 feet = 36 inches.

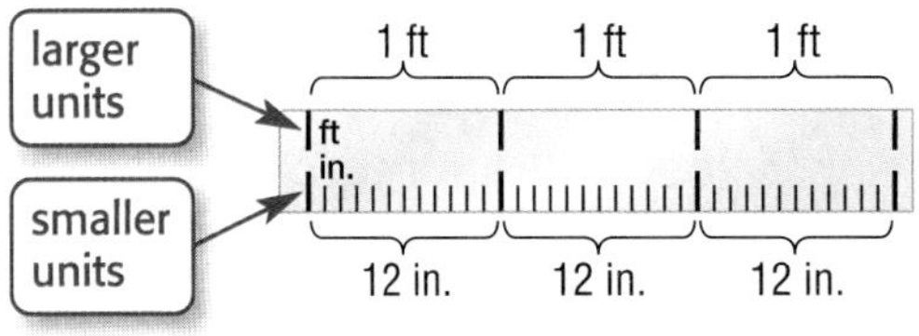

Remember

When changing from larger units to smaller units, there will be a greater number of units. When changing from smaller units to larger units, there will be fewer units.

To change from larger units to smaller units you multiply. Similarly, to change from smaller units to larger units you divide.

EXAMPLE Change Smaller Units to Larger Units

4 **21 ft = ■ yd**

Since 3 feet = 1 yard, divide 21 by 3.

$21 \div 3 = 7$

So, 21 feet = 7 yards.

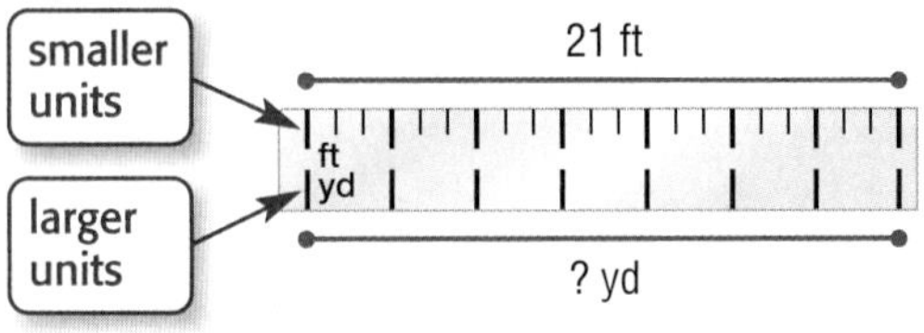

Real-World EXAMPLE

5 **A bookcase is 60 inches tall. The distance between the top of the bookcase and the ceiling is 4 feet. What is the distance in feet between the floor and the ceiling?**

First, find the height of the bookcase in feet.

$60 \div 12 = 5$ Since 12 inches = 1 foot, divide 60 by 12.

Since the bookcase is 5 feet tall and the distance between the top of the bookcase and the ceiling is 4 feet, then the distance between the floor and the ceiling is 5 feet + 4 feet or 9 feet.

Online **Personal Tutor at** ca.gr5math.com

CHECK What You Know

Draw a line segment of each length. See Example 1 (p. 633)

1. $1\frac{1}{4}$ in. **2.** $\frac{5}{8}$ in.

Measure the length of each line segment or object to the nearest half, fourth, or eighth inch. See Example 2 (p. 633)

3.  **4.** 

Complete. See Examples 3, 4 (pp. 633–634)

5. 4 yd = ■ ft **6.** 4 mi = ■ yd **7.** 72 in. = ■ yd **8.** 5,280 ft = ■ mi

9. Brianna's brother is about 25 inches shorter than she is. If Brianna is 5 feet tall, about how tall is her brother in feet? See Example 5 (p. 634)

10. Talk About It Describe how you would change 12 feet to yards.

Practice and Problem Solving

Draw a line segment of each length. See Example 1 (p. 633)

11. $2\frac{1}{2}$ in. **12.** $3\frac{1}{4}$ in. **13.** $\frac{3}{4}$ in. **14.** $1\frac{3}{8}$ in.

Measure the length of each line segment or object to the nearest half, fourth, or eighth inch. See Example 2 (p. 633)

15. 

16. 

17.

18.

19. 

20. 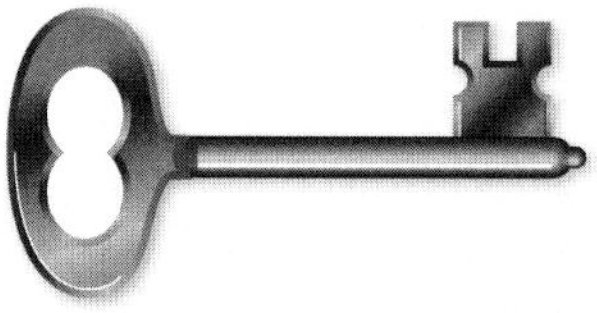

Complete. See Examples 3, 4 (pp. 633–634)

21. 5 yd = ■ in.

22. 6 yd = ■ ft

23. $6\frac{1}{2}$ ft = ■ in.

24. 3.5 mi = ■ ft

25. 48 in. = ■ ft

26. 10 ft = ■ yd

27. 6,160 yd = ■ mi

28. 510 in. = ■ ft

29. The largest telescope in the world is powerful enough to identify a penny that is 5 miles away. How many yards is this?

30. Top Thrill Dragster at Cedar Point in Sandusky, Ohio, is the tallest roller coaster in the United States. It has a height of 420 feet. What is this height in yards?

H.O.T. Problems

31. **OPEN ENDED** Draw a segment that measures between $1\frac{1}{2}$ inches and $2\frac{1}{4}$ inches long. State the measure of the segment to the nearest fourth inch. Then state the measure to the nearest eighth inch.

32. **CHALLENGE** How many sixteenths of an inch are in a foot? How many half inches are in a yard?

REASONING **Determine whether you would measure each length or distance in inches, feet, yards, or miles. Explain your reasoning.**

33. length of a computer monitor

34. distance from your home to school

35. **WRITING IN MATH** Suppose your friend says that 24 feet is equal to 2 inches. Is this reasonable? Explain.

Looking Ahead 2

Capacity and Weight in the Customary System

GET READY to Learn

MAIN IDEA

I will change units of capacity and weight in the customary system.

Preparation for Standard 6AF2.1
Convert one unit of measurement to another (e.g., from feet to miles, from centimeters to inches).

New Vocabulary

- capacity
- fluid ounce
- cup
- pint
- quart
- gallon
- ounce
- pound
- ton

Hands-On Mini Lab

Several different milk containers are shown at the right.

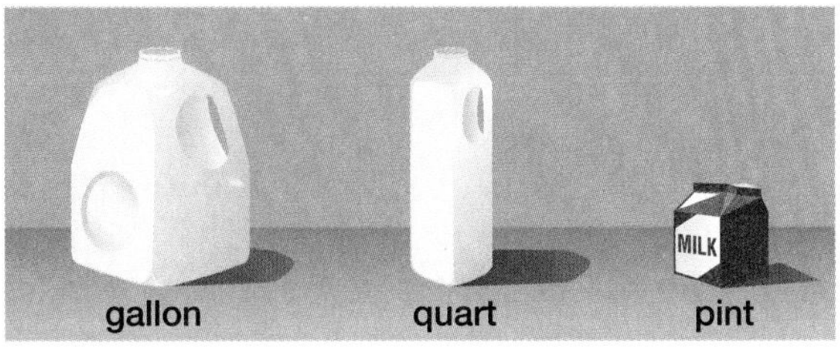

Step 1 Fill the pint container with water. Then pour the water into the quart container. Repeat until the quart container is full. Record the number of pints needed to fill the quart.

Step 2 Fill the quart container with water. Then pour the water into the gallon container. Repeat until the gallon container is full. Record the number of quarts needed to fill the gallon.

Complete.

1. 1 quart = ■ pints

2. 2 quarts = ■ pints

3. 1 gallon = ■ quarts

4. 1 gallon = ■ pints

5. What fractional part of 1 gallon would fit in 1 pint?

6. How many gallons are equal to 12 quarts? Explain.

Capacity refers to the amount that can be held in a container. The most commonly used customary units of capacity are shown.

KEY CONCEPT — Customary Units of Capacity

Unit	Model
1 **fluid ounce** (fl oz)	2 tablespoons of water
1 **cup** (c) = 8 fl oz	coffee cup
1 **pint** (pt) = 2 c	small ice cream container
1 **quart** (qt) = 2 pt	large liquid measuring cup
1 **gallon** (gal) = 4 qt	large plastic jug of milk

As with units of length, to change from larger units to smaller units, multiply. To change from smaller units to larger units, divide.

EXAMPLES Change Units of Capacity

Complete.

1 **3 qt = ■ pt**

You know that there are 2 pints in 1 quart.

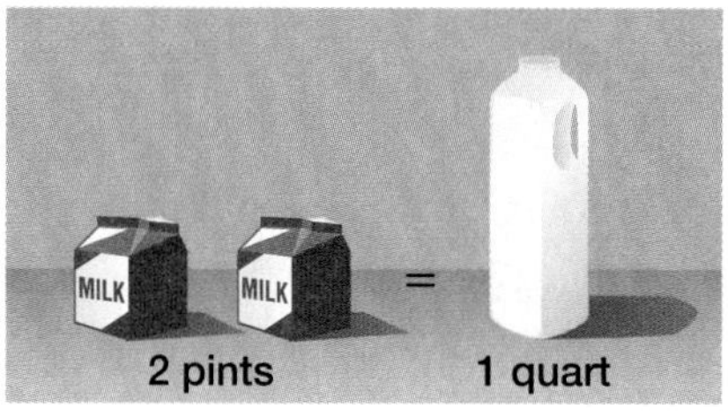

Since you are changing a larger unit to a smaller unit, multiply 3 by 2.

$3 \times 2 = 6$

So, 3 quarts = 6 pints.

2 **64 fl oz = ■ pt**

First, find the number of cups in 64 fluid ounces.

Since 8 fluid ounces = 1 cup, divide 64 by 8.

$64 \div 8 = 8$

So, 64 fluid ounces = 8 cups. Next, find the number of pints in 8 cups.

Since 2 cups = 1 pint, divide 8 by 2.

$8 \div 2 = 4$

So, 64 fluid ounces = 4 pints.

Online Personal Tutor at ca.gr5math.com

Vocabulary Link

Capacity

Everyday Use the maximum amount that can be contained, as in a theater filled to capacity

Math Use amount that can be held in a container

Remember

For Example 2, since 8 fluid ounces = 1 cup and 2 cups = 1 pint, you need to divide twice.
$64 \div 8 = 8$ and $8 \div 2 = 4$.
So, 64 fluid ounces = 4 pints.

The most commonly used customary units of weight are shown.

KEY CONCEPT Customary Units of Weight

Unit	Model
1 **ounce** (oz)	pencil
1 **pound** (lb) = 16 oz	package of notebook paper
1 **ton** (T) = 2,000 lb	small passenger car

EXAMPLES Change Units of Weight

3 A truck weighs 7,000 pounds. How many tons is this?

7,000 lb = ■ T **THINK** 2,000 pounds = 1 ton

$7{,}000 \div 2{,}000 = 3\frac{1}{2}$ Divide to change pounds to tons.

So, 7,000 pounds = $3\frac{1}{2}$ tons.

4 How many 4-ounce party favors can be made with 5 pounds of mixed nuts?

First, find the total number of ounces in 5 pounds.

$5 \times 16 = 80$ Multiply by 16 to change pounds to ounces.

Next, find how many sets of 4 ounces are in 80 ounces.

$80 \text{ oz} \div 4 \text{ oz} = 20$

So, 20 party favors can be made with 5 pounds of mixed nuts.

CHECK What You Know

Complete. See Examples 1, 2 (p. 637)

1. 7 pt = ■ c **2.** 24 qt = ■ gal **3.** 16 pt = ■ gal

4. 5 c = ■ fl oz **5.** 16 pt = ■ qt **6.** 8 c = ■ pt

7. The heaviest land mammal, the African elephant, can weigh more than 7 tons. How many pounds is this? See Example 3 (p. 638)

8. The maximum takeoff weight of an F-15E Strike Eagle is 81,000 pounds. How many tons is this? See Example 3 (p. 638)

9. Miguela bought a 10-pound bag of potatoes. How many people can be served 8 ounces of potatoes? See Example 4 (p. 638)

10. Roman uses 1 cup of milk for his cereal every morning. How many times will he be able to have cereal with milk from 1 quart of milk? See Example 4 (p. 638)

11. Talk About It What operation would you use to change pints to quarts? Explain.

Practice and Problem Solving

Complete. See Examples 1, 2 (p. 637)

12. 5 qt = ■ pt

13. 8 gal = ■ qt

14. 24 fl oz = ■ c

15. 6 pt = ■ c

16. 13 qt = ■ gal

17. 9 gal = ■ pt

18. 24 fl oz = ■ pt

19. 1,500 lb = ■ T

20. 84 oz = ■ lb

21. 4 T = ■ lb

22. The heaviest marine mammal, the blue whale, can weigh more than 143 tons. How many pounds is this? See Example 3 (p. 638)

23. In the United States, the annual consumption of ice cream is 24 pints per person. How many gallons of ice cream is this per person? See Example 3 (p. 638)

24. A pumpkin pie recipe calls for 15 ounces of pumpkin. *About* how many pies can be made with 8 pounds of pumpkin? See Example 4 (p. 638)

25. Vermont produces about 430,000 gallons of maple syrup each year. How many 2-quart containers of maple syrup can be made from 430,000 gallons of syrup? See Example 4 (p. 638)

Choose the better estimate for each measure.

26. cups or quarts?

27. fluid ounces or pints?

H.O.T. Problems

28. **OPEN ENDED** Without looking at their labels, estimate the weight or capacity of three packaged food items in your kitchen. Then compare your estimate to the actual weight or capacity.

29. **CHALLENGE** Create a function table that shows the number of fluid ounces in 1, 2, 3, and 4 cups. Graph the ordered pairs (cups, fluid ounces) on a coordinate plane. Then describe the graph.

30. **WRITING IN ▸MATH** Determine whether 1 cup of sand and 1 cup of cotton balls would have the same capacity, the same weight, both, or neither. Explain your reasoning.

Length in the Metric System

GET READY to Learn

The table shows the deepest points in several oceans.

1. What unit of measure is used?
2. What is the depth of the deepest point?
3. Use the Internet or another source to find the meaning of meter. Then write a sentence explaining how a meter compares to a yard.

Deepest Ocean Points

Ocean	Point	Depth (m)
Pacific	Mariana Trench	10,924
Atlantic	Puerto Rico Trench	8,648
Indian	Java Trench	7,125

Source: geography.about.com

MAIN IDEA

I will use metric units of length.

Preparation for Standard 6AF2.1
Convert one unit of measurement to another (e.g., from feet to miles, from centimeters to inches).

New Vocabulary

meter
metric system
millimeter
centimeter
kilometer

A **meter** is the basic unit of length in the metric system. The **metric system** is a decimal system of weights and measures. The most commonly used metric units of length are shown below.

KEY CONCEPT — **Metric Units of Length**

Unit	Model	Benchmark
1 **millimeter** (mm)	thickness of a dime	1 mm ≈ 0.04 inch
1 **centimeter** (cm)	half the width of a penny	1 cm ≈ 0.4 inch
1 meter (m)	width of a doorway	1 m ≈ 1.1 yards
1 **kilometer** (km)	six city blocks	1 km ≈ 0.6 mile

Vocabulary Link

Milli-
Everyday Use one thousand, as a millennium is one thousand years

Millimeter
Math Use a metric unit of length; one millimeter equals one-thousandth of a meter

The segment below is 1 centimeter or 10 millimeters long. Expressed in customary units, this is about 0.4 inch.

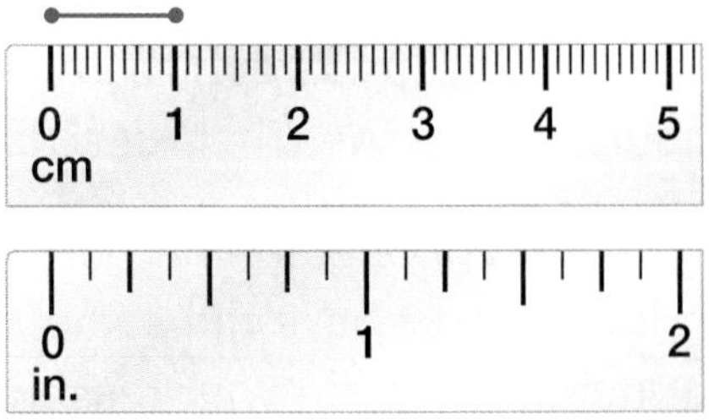

EXAMPLES Use Metric Units of Length

Write the metric unit of length that you would use to measure each of the following.

1 height of a desk

Since the height of a desk is close to the width of a doorway, the meter is an appropriate unit of measure.

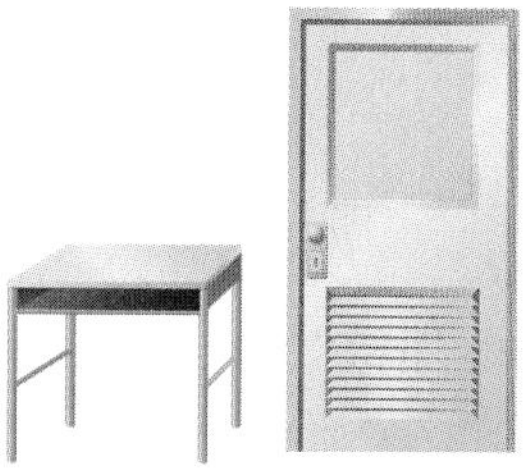

2 distance across Indiana

Since the distance across Indiana is much greater than 6 city blocks, this is measured in kilometers.

3 width of a CD

Since the width of a CD is greater than half the width of a penny and much less than the width of a doorway, the centimeter is an appropriate unit of measure.

Online **Personal Tutor at** ca.gr5math.com

Real-World EXAMPLE Estimate and Measure Length

Remember

To measure metric length, be sure to use the appropriate tools.

4 Estimate the metric length of the honey bee. Then measure to find the actual length.

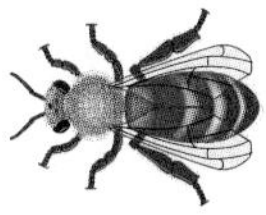

The length of the honey bee appears to be the width of a penny. So, the honey bee is about 2 centimeters.

Use a ruler to measure the actual length of the honey bee.

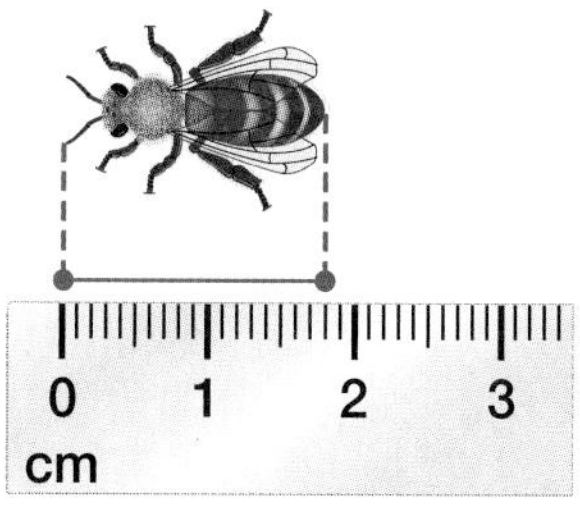

The honey bee is 18 millimeters long. The estimate is close to the actual length of the honey bee.

CHECK What You Know

Write the metric unit of length that you would use to measure each of the following. See Examples 1–3 (p. 641)

1. thickness of a calculator
2. distance from home to school
3. height of a tree
4. width of a computer screen

Estimate the metric length of each figure to the nearest centimeter. Then measure to find the actual length to the nearest millimeter.
See Example 4 (p. 641)

5. 

6. 

7. Talk About It — About how many centimeters is the thickness of a textbook?

Practice and Problem Solving

Write the metric unit of length that you would use to measure each of the following. See Examples 1–3 (p. 641)

8. thickness of a note pad
9. thickness of a watchband
10. length of a trombone
11. width of a dollar bill
12. length of a bracelet
13. length of the Mississippi River
14. distance from Knoxville, Tennessee, to Asheville, North Carolina
15. distance from home plate to first base on a baseball field

Estimate the metric length of each figure to the nearest centimeter. Then measure to find the actual length to the nearest millimeter.
See Example 4 (p. 641)

16. 

17. 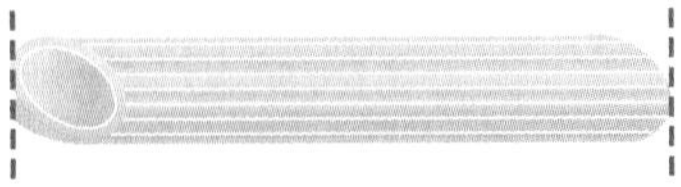

18. 

19. 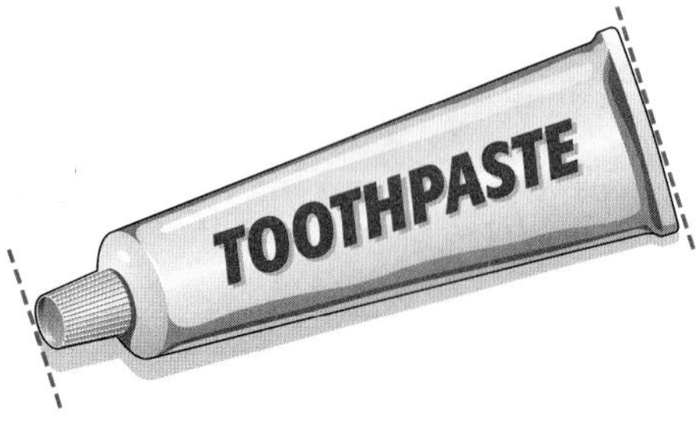

20. Which metric unit of length would be the best to use to describe the height of a 72 story building?

Estimate the metric length of each object. Then measure to find the actual length.

21. student ID card

22. chalkboard

23. eraser on end of pencil

24. width of a cell phone

25. Estimate the metric length and width of your bedroom or classroom. Then use a meterstick to check your measurement.

26. Estimate the distance in centimeters between Los Angeles and Palm Springs on the map. Then use a ruler to check your measurement.

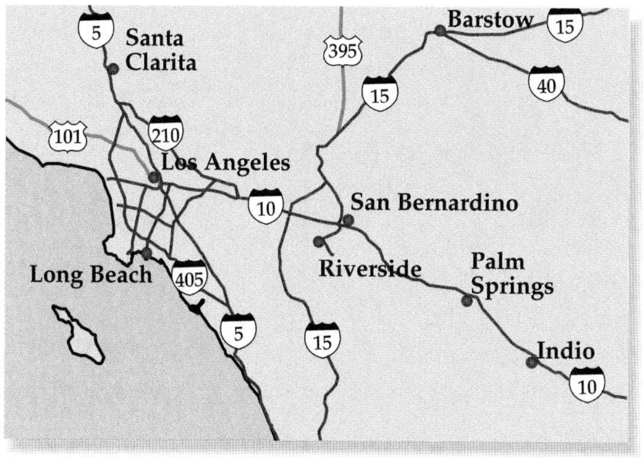

27. Which customary unit of length is comparable to a meter?

28. Is a mile or a foot closer in length to a kilometer?

Find the greater length. Explain your reasoning.

29. 15 millimeters or 3 centimeters

30. 3 feet or 1 meter

31. 1 mile or 2 kilometers

32. 5 centimeters or 1 inch

33. If you were to build a fence around a cattle pasture, would you need to be accurate to the nearest kilometer, to the nearest meter, or to the nearest centimeter? Explain your reasoning.

34. Choose three classmates or three members of your family. (You can include yourself.) Which metric unit of length would you use to measure each person's height? Estimate the combined height of all three people. Then use a measuring device to measure and check the reasonableness of your estimate.

H.O.T. Problems

35. **OPEN ENDED** Give two examples of items that can be measured with a meterstick and two examples of items that cannot reasonably be measured with a meterstick.

36. **CHALLENGE** Order 4.8 mm, 4.8 m, 4.8 cm, 0.48 m, and 0.048 km from greatest to least measurement.

37. **WRITING IN MATH** Identify the four most commonly used metric units of length and describe an object having each length. Use objects that are different from those given in the lesson.

Looking 4 Ahead

Mass and Capacity in the Metric System

GET READY to Learn

Hands-On Mini Lab

Step 1 Place a breath mint on one side of a balance scale and some paper clips on the other side until the scale balances. How many paper clips were used?

Step 2 Read the label on the mints to find the mass in grams of one mint.

Step 3 Find the number of paper clips needed to balance 2 pencils of the same size.

1. How does the number of paper clips needed to balance the roll of breath mints compare to the mass of the roll in grams?
2. Estimate the mass of one paper clip.
3. What is the mass of 1 pencil in grams?

MAIN IDEA

I will use metric units of mass and capacity.

Preparation for Standard 6AF2.1
Convert one unit of measurement to another (e.g., from feet to miles, from centimeters to inches).

New Vocabulary

mass
milligram
gram
kilogram
milliliter
liter

The **mass** of an object is the amount of material it contains.

KEY CONCEPT — Metric Units of Mass

Unit	Model	Benchmark
1 **milligram** (mg)	grain of salt	1 mg ≈ 0.00004 oz
1 **gram** (g)	small paper clip	1 g ≈ 0.04 oz
1 **kilogram** (kg)	six medium apples	1 kg ≈ 2 lb

EXAMPLES Use Metric Units of Mass

Write the metric unit of mass that you would use to measure each of the following. Then estimate the mass.

1 sheet of notebook paper

A sheet of paper has a mass greater than a small paper clip, but less than six medium apples. So, the gram is the appropriate unit.

Since a sheet of paper has slightly more mass than a paper clip, one estimate is about 6 grams.

Math Online Extra Examples at ca.gr5math.com

2 bag of potatoes

A bag of potatoes has a mass greater than six apples. So, the kilogram is the appropriate unit.

Estimate A bag of potatoes contains about 15 potatoes.

One estimate for the mass of a bag of potatoes is about 2 or 3 kilograms.

The most commonly used metric units of capacity are shown below.

Remember

A benchmark is a measurement by which other items can be measured.

KEY CONCEPT — Metric Units of Capacity

Unit	Model	Benchmark
1 **milliliter** (mL)	eyedropper	1 mL ≈ 0.03 fl oz
1 **liter** (L)	small pitcher	1 L ≈ 1 qt

There are 1,000 milliliters in a liter. You can use this information to estimate capacity.

EXAMPLES Use Metric Units of Capacity

Write the metric unit of capacity that you would use to measure each of the following. Then estimate the capacity.

3 goldfish bowl

A goldfish bowl has a capacity greater than a small pitcher. So, the liter is the appropriate unit.

Estimate A goldfish bowl will hold about 2 small pitchers of water.

One estimate for the capacity of a goldfish bowl is about 2 liters.

4 glass of milk

A glass of milk is greater than an eyedropper and less than a small pitcher. So, the milliliter is the appropriate unit.

Estimate There are 1,000 milliliters in a liter. A small pitcher can fill about 4 glasses.

One estimate for the capacity of a glass of milk is about 1,000 ÷ 4 or 250 milliliters.

One kilogram is equal to 1,000 grams. You can use this information to compare metric units.

Real-World EXAMPLE — **Compare Metric Units**

5 **The table shows the average mass of several human organs. Is the combined mass of the lungs more or less than one kilogram?**

Human Organs	Average Mass (g)
Skin	10,886
Right Lung	580
Left Lung	510
Male Heart	315
Female Heart	265
Thyroid	35

Source: *Top 10 of Everything*

Find the total mass.

right lung	580 g
left lung	+ 510 g
total	1,090 g

Since 1 kilogram = 1,000 grams and 1,090 grams is more than 1,000 grams, the combined mass of the lungs is more than one kilogram.

Online **Personal Tutor at** ca.gr5math.com

CHECK What You Know

Write the metric unit of mass or capacity that you would use to measure each of the following. Then estimate the mass or capacity. See Examples 1–4 (pp. 644–645)

1. nickel

2. bucket of water

3. laptop computer

4. juice in a lemon

5. light bulb

6. one-gallon paint can

For Exercises 7–9, use the list of ingredients at the right for a dark chocolate cake. See Example 5 (p. 646)

Dark Chocolate Cake
6 medium eggs
175 grams sugar
280 grams chocolate
100 grams butter
100 grams flour

7. Is the total amount of sugar, chocolate, butter, and flour more or less than one kilogram?

8. Write the quantities of ingredients needed for two cakes.

9. Is the total amount of sugar, chocolate, butter, and flour for two cakes more or less than one kilogram? Explain.

10. Talk About It — If you filled a 150-milliliter beaker with salt, would its mass be 150 milligrams? Explain.

Practice and Problem Solving

Write the metric unit of mass or capacity that you would use to measure each of the following. Then estimate the mass or capacity. See Examples 1–4 (pp. 644–645)

11. granola bar

12. grape

13. large watermelon

14. cow

15. large bowl of punch

16. bathtub

17. chipmunk

18. shoe

19. grain of sugar

20. postage stamp

21. 10 drops of food coloring

22. ink in a ballpoint pen

For Exercises 23 and 24, use the table at the right that shows the mass of ducks. See Example 5 (p. 646)

23. Is the combined mass of a cinnamon teal, cape teal, and marbled teal more or less than one kilogram?

24. Which birds from the table will have a combined mass closest to one kilogram? Explain your reasoning.

Duck Mass

Bird	Average Mass (g)
Cape Teal	409
Cinnamon Teal	440
Hottentot Teal	243
Marbled Teal	308

Source: seaworld.org

25. Your favorite cereal comes in a 1.7-kilogram box or a 39-gram box. Which box is larger? Explain your reasoning.

H.O.T. Problems

26. **OPEN ENDED** Locate and identify an item found at your home that has a capacity of about one liter.

27. **NUMBER SENSE** The mass of a dime is recorded as 4. What metric unit was used to measure the mass? Explain your reasoning.

28. **CHALLENGE** Determine whether the following statement is *true* or *false.* If false, give a counterexample.

Any two items filled to the same capacity will also have the same mass.

29. **WRITING IN MATH** Write a problem about a real-world situation in which you would have to decide which metric unit to use to measure the mass or capacity of an item.

Changing Metric Units

Looking Ahead 5

Concepts in Motion
Interactive Lab
ca.gr5math.com

GET READY to Learn

The table shows the estimated consumption of baked beans per person for several countries. Compare the number of grams and kilograms of baked beans consumed by the countries in the table. Make a conjecture about how to convert from grams to kilograms.

Baked Beans Consumed per Person

Country	g	kg
Ireland	5,600	5.6
United Kingdom	4,800	4.8
United States	2,000	2
Canada	1,200	1.2

Source: *Top 10 of Everything*

MAIN IDEA

I will change units within the metric system.

Preparation for Standard 6AF2.1
Convert one unit of measurement to another (e.g., from feet to miles, from centimeters to inches).

Vocabulary Link

Centi-
Everyday Use one one-hundredth of a dollar, as in 53 cents

Centimeter
Math Use a metric unit of length; one centimeter equals one hundredth of a meter

To change from one unit to another in the metric sytem, you multiply or divide by powers of 10. The chart below shows the relationship between the units in the metric system and the powers of 10.

1,000	100	10	1	0.1	0.01	0.001
thousands	hundreds	tens	ones	tenths	hundredths	thousandths
			•			
kilo	hecto	deka	base unit	deci	centi	milli

Each place value is 10 times the place value to its right.

In Lesson 1, you learned the following methods for changing customary units of measure.

- To change from a larger unit to a smaller unit, multiply.
- To change from a smaller unit to a larger unit, divide.

You can use the same methods for changing metric units of measure.

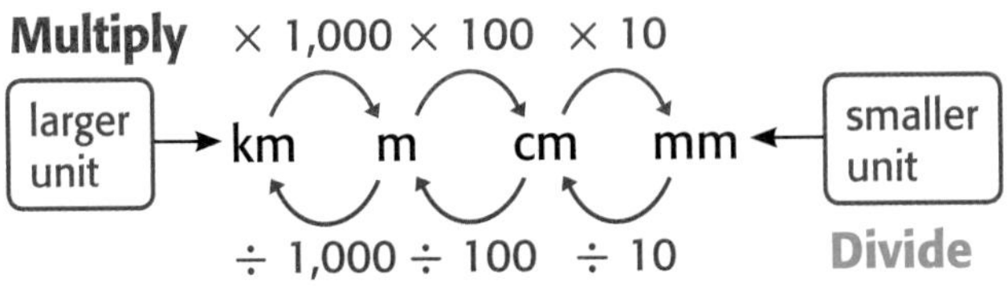

Remember

Since a millimeter is a smaller unit than a centimeter, the number of millimeters needed to equal 26 centimeters should be greater than 26. Since 260 > 26, the answer seems reasonable.

EXAMPLES Change Metric Units

Complete.

1 **■ mm = 26 cm**

Since 1 centimeter = 10 millimeters, multiply 26 by 10.

$26 \times 10 = 260$

So, 260 mm = 26 cm.

2 **135 g = ■ kg**

Since 1,000 grams = 1 kilogram, divide 135 by 1,000.

$135 \div 1{,}000 = 0.135$

So, 135 g = 0.135 kg.

Online **Personal Tutor at** ca.gr5math.com

Real-World EXAMPLE

3 **Will has run 200 meters. How many more kilometers does he need to run in order to finish the running portion of the San Diego International Triathlon?**

San Diego International Triathlon

Swim	Bike	Run
1 km	30 km	10 km

First, change 200 meters to kilometers. You can divide by 1,000. You can also use sequivalent fractions.

$$\frac{1 \text{ km}}{1{,}000 \text{ m}} = \frac{x \text{ km}}{200 \text{ m}} \quad (\div 5 \text{ numerator and denominator})$$

$x = 1 \div 5$ or 0.2

So, 200 meters = 0.2 kilometer.

Subtract to find the number of kilometers Will still needs to run.

$10 - 0.2 = 9.8$ kilometers

Will needs to run 9.8 kilometers.

CHECK What You Know

Complete. See Examples 1, 2 (p. 649)

1. 95 g = ■ mg
2. 5 L = ■ mL
3. ■ mm = 3.8 cm
4. ■ L = 75 mL
5. 205 mg = ■ g
6. 85 mm = ■ cm
7. Booker's family drove 42 kilometers from Brownsville to Harlingen and then another 2,300 meters to his aunt's house. What is the total number of kilometers Booker's family drove? See Example 3 (p. 649)
8. Talk About It Describe how you would change grams to milligrams.

Practice and Problem Solving

Complete. See Examples 1, 2 (p. 649)

9. ■ L = 95 mL
10. ■ g = 1,900 mg
11. 52 mm = ■ cm
12. 354 cm = ■ m
13. ■ mg = 6 g
14. ■ mL = 238 L
15. 4 m = ■ mm
16. 18 L = ■ mL
17. ■ L = 136 mL
18. ■ g = 7 mg
19. 13 g = ■ kg
20. 4 m = ■ km
21. If a rhinoceros has a mass of 3,600 kilograms and a pygmy mouse has a mass of 8 grams, how much more mass does the rhinoceros have than the pygmy mouse? See Example 3 (p. 649)
22. A track is 200 meters long. Isabel wants to run 1 kilometer on this track. How many laps will she have to run? See Example 3 (p. 649)

Order each set of measurements from least to greatest.

23. 4.2 kg, 420 g, 400,000 mg
24. 560 mm, 55 cm, 5.6 km
25. 630 mg, 63 g, 6.3 kg
26. 8.2 km, 8,500 mm, 80 m
27. The table shows the length of the three longest suspension bridges in the United States. If Perez biked over the main span of the Golden Gate Bridge and back, about how many kilometers did he bike?
28. Danielle walked 0.75 kilometer each day for five days. How many meters did she walk in all?

U.S. Suspension Bridges

Bridge	Location	Length of Main Span (m)
Verrazano Narrows	New York	1,298
Golden Gate	San Francisco	1,280
Mackinac Straits	Michigan	1,158

Source: *Top 10 of Everything*

29. At a track meet, Andres raced in the 5,000-meter run, 10,000-meter run, and 400-meter hurdles. How many total kilometers did Andres race at the track meet?

30. Use the Internet or another source to find other metric prefixes for very large and very small units of measure. List three of each type and explain their meaning.

For Exercises 31–33, use the table at the right.

31. List the home runs in order from greatest to least.

32. How much longer was Mickey Mantle's longest home run than his fifth longest home run?

33. Find the mean, median, and mode of the home runs. Which of these measures best represents the data?

Distance of Mickey Mantle's Five Longest Home Runs
192 m
201 m
19,600 cm
22,400 cm
198,000 mm

H.O.T. Problems

34. **OPEN ENDED** Choose a metric measure between 1 and 100. Then write two measures equivalent to that measure.

35. **CHALLENGE** If Tyra has x milligrams of food for her parrot, write an algebraic expression for the amount of kilograms of parrot food she has.

36. **SELECT A TOOL** Rachelle takes a large jug of lemonade to her brother's soccer games. She sells cups of the lemonade to the fans. The jug contains 10 liters of lemonade, and each cup will hold 400 milliliters. Which of the following tools might Rachelle use to determine how many cups to bring with her? Justify your selection(s). Then use the tool(s) to solve the problem.

real objects | paper/pencil | calculator

37. **FIND THE ERROR** Jacinta and Trina are changing 590 centimeters to meters. Who is correct? Explain your reasoning.

Jacinta
$590 \times 100 =$
59,000 m

Trina
$590 \div 100 =$
5.9 m

38. **WRITING IN MATH** Explain the steps you would use to change 7 kiloliters to milliliters.

Student Handbook

Built-In Workbook

Reference

How to Use the Student Handbook

A Student Handbook is the additional skill and reference material found at the end of books. The Student Handbook can help answer these questions.

What If I Need More Practice?

You, or your teacher, may decide that working through some additional problems would be helpful. The **Extra Practice** section provides these problems for each lesson so you have ample opportunity to practice new skills.

What If I Forget a Vocabulary Word?

The **English-Spanish Glossary** provides a list of important, or difficult, words used throughout the textbook. It provides a definition in English and Spanish as well as the page number(s) where the word can be found.

What If I Need to Find Something Quickly?

The **Index** alphabetically lists the subjects covered throughout the entire textbook and the pages on which each subject can be found.

What If I Forget a Formula?

Inside the back cover of your math book is a list of **Formulas and Symbols** that are used in the book.

Extra Practice

Lesson 1-1

Pages 17–20

Tell whether each number is *prime, composite,* or *neither.*

1. 65 **2.** 37 **3.** 26 **4.** 54
5. 155 **6.** 201 **7.** 0 **8.** 93
9. 121 **10.** 29 **11.** 53 **12.** 57

Find the prime factorization of each number.

13. 72 **14.** 88 **15.** 32 **16.** 86
17. 120 **18.** 576 **19.** 68 **20.** 240
21. 24 **22.** 70 **23.** 102 **24.** 121

Lesson 1-2

Pages 21–25

Write each product using an exponent.

1. $4 \times 4 \times 4 \times 4 \times 4$ **2.** $10 \times 10 \times 10$ **3.** 14×14
4. $3 \times 3 \times 3 \times 3$ **5.** $2 \times 2 \times 2$ **6.** $6 \times 6 \times 6 \times 6 \times 6$
7. $8 \times 8 \times 8$ **8.** $7 \times 7 \times 7 \times 7 \times 7 \times 7$ **9.** $9 \times 9 \times 9$

Write each power as a product of the same factor. Then find the value.

10. 9^4 **11.** 2^3 **12.** 3^5 **13.** 4^3
14. 6^5 **15.** 5^4 **16.** 8^3 **17.** 12^2
18. nine cubed **19.** eight to the fourth power
20. six to the fifth power **21.** eleven squared

Write the prime factorization of each number using exponents.

22. 9 **23.** 20 **24.** 18 **25.** 63
26. 44 **27.** 45 **28.** 243 **29.** 175

Lesson 1-3

Pages 27–30

Find the value of each expression.

1. $14 - 5 + 7$ **2.** $12 + 10 - 5 - 6$ **3.** $50 - 6 + 12 + 4$
4. $12 - 2 \times 3$ **5.** $16 + 4 \times 5$ **6.** $5 + 3 \times 4 - 7$
7. $2 \times 3 + 9 \times 2$ **8.** $6 \times 8 + 4 \div 2$ **9.** $7 \times 6 - 14$
10. $8 + 12 \times 4 \div 8$ **11.** $13 - 6 \times 2 + 1$ **12.** $80 \div 10 \times 8$
13. $54 \div (8 - 5)$ **14.** $4^2 + 3^3$ **15.** $(11 - 7) \times 3 - 5$
16. $11 + 4 \times (12 - 7)$ **17.** $6^2 - 7 \times 4$ **18.** $12 + 5^2 - 9$
19. Find two to the fifth power divided by 8 times 2.

Lesson 1-4
Pages 32–33

Use the four-step plan to solve each problem.

1. Sylvia has $102. If she made three purchases of $13, $37, and $29, how much money does she have left?
2. Complete the pattern: 1, 8, 15, 22, ■, ■, ■
3. Sarah is conditioning for track. On the first day, she ran 2 laps. The second day she ran 3 laps. The third day she ran 5 laps, and on the fourth day she ran 8 laps. If this pattern continues, how many laps will she run on the seventh day?
4. The times that a new movie is showing are 9:30 A.M., 11:12 A.M., 12:54 P.M., and 2:36 P.M. What are the next three show times?

Lesson 1-5
Pages 34–38

Evaluate each expression if $m = 2$ and $n = 4$.

1. $m + m$ **2.** $n - m$ **3.** mn **4.** $3m + 5$

5. $2n + 2m$ **6.** $m \cdot 0$ **7.** $64 \div n$ **8.** $12 - m$

9. $5n \div m$ **10.** $6mn$ **11.** $4n - 3$ **12.** $n \div m + 8$

Evaluate each expression if $a = 3$, $b = 4$, and $c = 12$.

13. $a + b$ **14.** $c - a$ **15.** $a + b + c$ **16.** $b - a$

17. $c - a \cdot b$ **18.** $a + 2 \cdot b$ **19.** $b + c \div 2$ **20.** ab

21. $25 + c \div b$ **22.** $c \div a + 10$ **23.** $2b - a$ **24.** $2ab$

Lesson 1-6
Pages 39–43

Copy and complete each function table.

1.

Input (*n*)	*n* − 4	Output
5	■	■
7	■	■
9	■	■

2.

Input (*n*)	3*n*	Output
1	■	■
0	■	■
2	■	■

3.

Input (*n*)	*n* + 7	Output
4	■	■
1	■	■
3	■	■

4.

Input (*n*)	*n* ÷ 4	Output
12	■	■
16	■	■
24	■	■

Find the rule for each function table.

5.

Input (*n*)	Output (■)
1	6
0	5
3	8

6.

Input (*n*)	Output (■)
6	3
0	0
8	4

7.

Input (*n*)	Output (■)
4	20
2	10
6	30

Lesson 1-7

Pages 44–45

Use the *guess and check* strategy to solve Exercises 1–5.

1. David has 5 coins that total \$1.10. What are the coins?
2. Emma is thinking of 3 numbers from 1 through 9 with a product of 30. Find the numbers.
3. Kyle bought pens and markers at an office supply store. Each pen cost \$1.50, and each marker cost \$2.25. If Kyle spent a total of \$9 on 5 writing devices, how many of each did he buy?
4. Tamika has saved \$20 in cash to spend at the mall. If she has 8 bills, how many of each kind of bill does she have?
5. Use the symbols $+$, $-$, $\times$, or $\div$ to make the following sentence true. Use each symbol only once.

$$2 \blacksquare 5 \blacksquare 3 \blacksquare 7 = 14$$

Lesson 1-8

Pages 46–49

Identify the solution of each equation from the list given.

1. $7 + a = 10$; 3, 13, 17
2. $14 + m = 24$; 7, 10, 34
3. $20 = 24 - n$; 2, 3, 4
4. $x + 4 = 19$; 14, 15, 16
5. $23 - p = 7$; 16, 17, 18
6. $11 = w + 6$; 3, 4, 5

Solve each equation mentally.

7. $b + 7 = 12$
8. $s + 10 = 23$
9. $b - 3 = 12$
10. $d + 7 = 19$
11. $23 - q = 9$
12. $21 + p = 45$
13. $17 = 23 - t$
14. $g - 13 = 5$
15. $14 - m = 6$

Lesson 1-9

Pages 52–55

Find the area of each rectangle or square.

1. 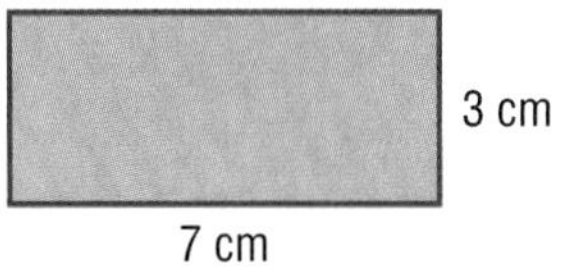

2. 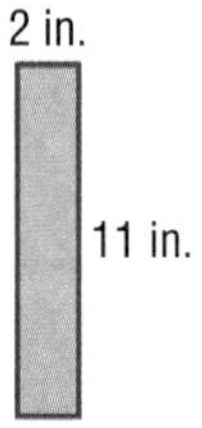

3. 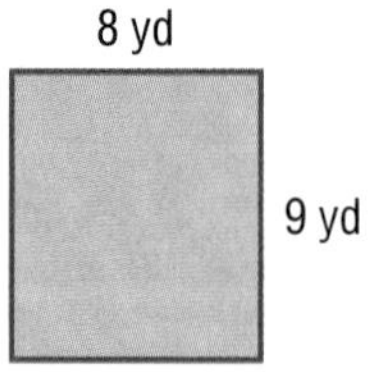

4. 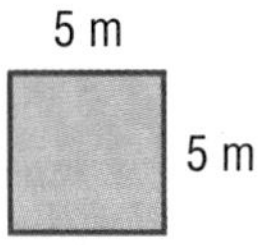

5. 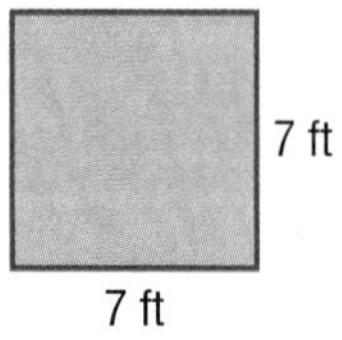

6. 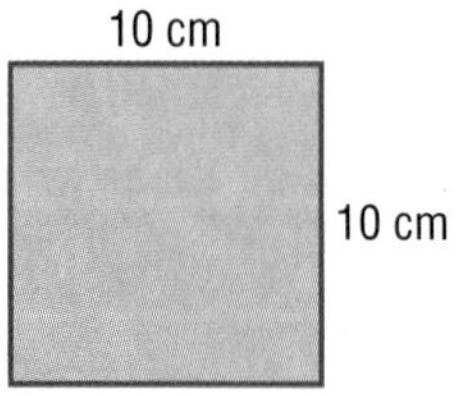

7. Find the area of a rectangle with a length of 18 inches and a width of 21 inches.

Lesson 1-10

Pages 58–61

Find each product mentally. Use the Distributive Property.

1. 5×18 **2.** 9×27 **3.** 8×83

4. 6×34 **5.** 56×3 **6.** 27×8

Rewrite each expression using the Distributive Property. Then evaluate.

7. $(6 + 13) \times 2$ **8.** $(5 + 4) \times 15$

9. $(6 \times 11) + (6 \times 7)$ **10.** $(3 \times 12) + (8 \times 12)$

Lesson 2-1

Pages 73–77

Make a bar graph for each set of data.

1.

Favorite Subject	
Subject	**Frequency**
Math	4
Science	6
History	2
English	8
Phys. Ed.	12

2.

Final Grades	
Subject	**Score**
Math	88
Science	82
History	92
English	94

Make a line graph for each set of data.

3.

Test Scores	
Test	**Score**
1	62
2	75
3	81
4	83
5	78
6	92

4.

Homeroom Absences	
Day	**Absences**
Mon.	3
Tue.	6
Wed.	2
Thur.	1
Fri.	8

Lesson 2-2

Pages 79–82

Use the graph to solve each problem.

1. Give the approximate population in 1960 for:

a. Florida **b.** North Carolina

2. How much greater was the population of Florida than North Carolina in 1980?

3. Which state will have the greater population in 2010?

4. Make a prediction for the population of Florida in 2010.

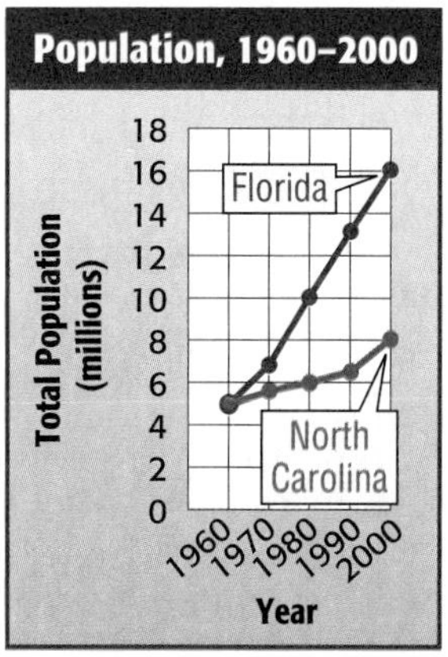

Lesson 2-3

Pages 83–86

1. Display the data in a histogram. What is the least possible score represented in the data?

Test Scores	
Score	**Frequency**
61–70	4
71–80	4
81–90	15
91–100	2

2. Display the data in a histogram. How many buildings have 90 or more stories?

Stories of Various Buildings	
Stories	**Frequency**
70–79	8
80–89	0
90–99	16
100–109	20

Lesson 2-4

Pages 87–91

Make a line plot of each set of data.

1.

Number of Points Scored						
8	10	5	9	12	14	5
6	3	7	0	1	14	16
20	2	5	10	18	0	6

2.

Number of Books Read						
30	25	26	29	18	30	15
15	30	25	16	15	18	11
18	20	20	22	24	17	26

For Exercises 3–6, use the line plot shown.

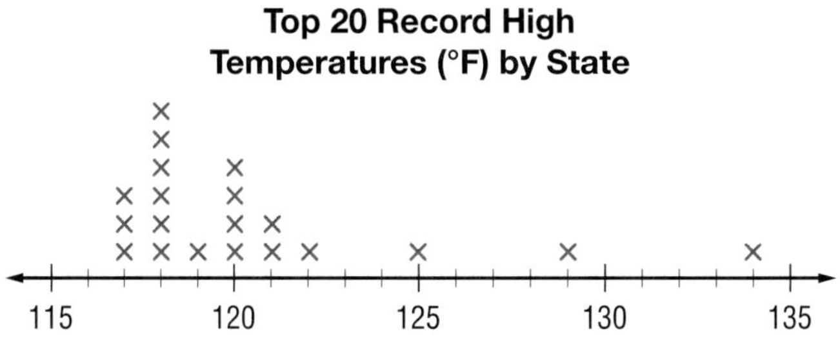

3. How many states have a record high temperature of higher than 120°F?
4. Which temperature is the most common record high temperature?
5. What is the range of the data?
6. Write one or two sentences that analyze the data.

Lesson 2-5

Pages 92–93

Use the *make a table* strategy to solve Exercises 1 and 2.

1. Make a frequency table of the data below. How many more students chose Saturday as their favorite day than Sunday?

Favorite Day of the Week				
Sat.	Sat.	Fri.	Sun.	Fri.
Wed.	Sun.	Fri.	Thurs.	Sat.
Sat.	Sat.	Fri.	Sun.	Thurs.

2. Make a frequency table of the data below. What is the most common number of siblings per student? the least?

Number of Siblings Per Student								
1	0	2	2	3	0	1	2	1
2	2	1	1	4	3	0	2	1
1	2	0	3	3	2	1	0	1
1	1	1	0	0	3	2	2	4

Lesson 2-6

Pages 95–98

Find the mean of the data represented in each model.

1.

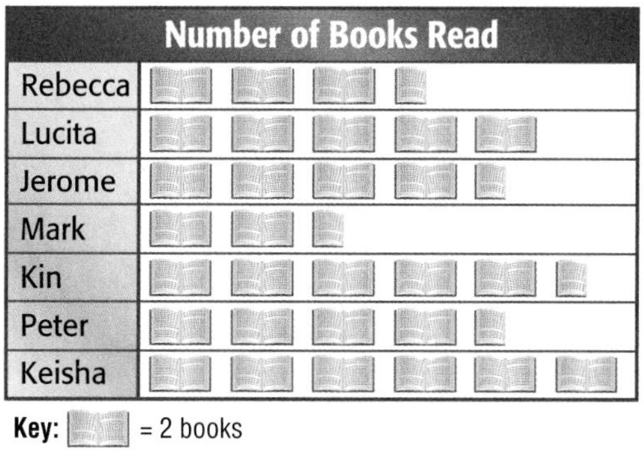

2.

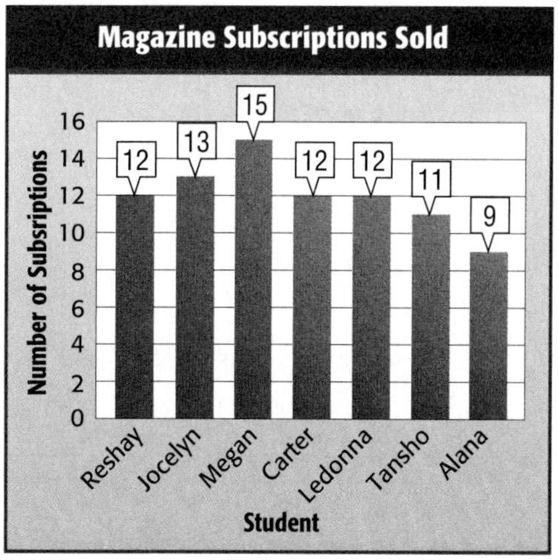

Find the mean for each set of data.

3. Number of birds identified by each student: 1, 5, 9, 1, 2, 4, 8, 2

4. Money raised by each class: \$957, \$562, \$462, \$848, \$721

Lesson 2-7

Pages 99–103

Find the median, mode, and range for each set of data.

1. Number of boxes sold by each student: 16, 12, 20, 15, 12

2. Fliers handed out by each club member: 42, 38, 56, 48, 43, 43

3. Glasses of water drunk by each person: 8, 3, 12, 5, 2, 9, 3

4. Number of people at the library: 85, 75, 93, 82, 73, 78

Lesson 2-8

Pages 104–105

Use any strategy to solve.

For Exercises 1 and 2, use the graph at the right.

1. How many more three-point field goals did Katie Smith make than Crystal Robinson?

2. The number of two-point field goals attempted by Mwadi Mabika is two times the number she actually made. How many two-point field goals did Mabika make?

All-Time Three-Point Field Goal Leaders*

Source: WNBA

3. The Bearcats have 15 players and scored 12 points. The Wolverines have 12 players and scored 14 points. What is the difference in scores?

Lesson 2-9

Pages 106–110

1. Which display makes it easier to determine which type of animal has the most number of endangered species?

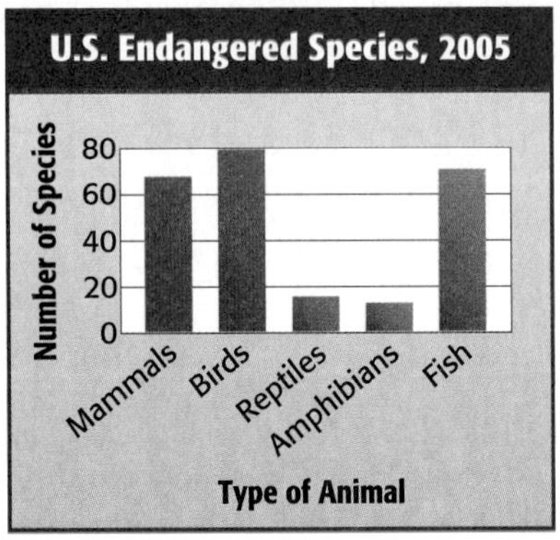

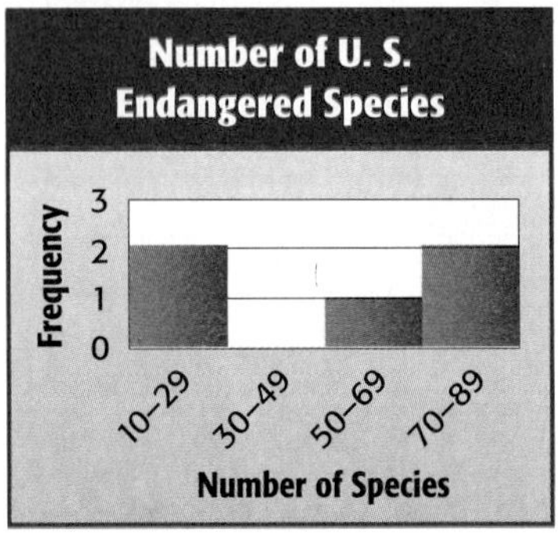

Select an appropriate type of display for data gathered about each situation.

2. gas mileage of different vehicles

3. the number of days of winter with one or more inches of snow

4. the weight of a baby from birth to 18 months of age

Lesson 2-10

Pages 113–117

Write an integer to represent each piece of data.

1. A loss of 15 dollars.

2. It was 9 degrees below zero.

3. 456 feet above sea level.

4. The toy increased in value by $30.

Graph each integer on a number line.

5. −3 **6.** 3 **7.** −1 **8.** −8 **9.** 9 **10.** 10

11. Make a line plot of the data represented in the table below.

Quiz Scores						
5	7	−2	−1	10	5	8
−3	8	−4	7	8	−2	−3
−2	−2	9	−1	7	10	6

Lesson 3-1

Pages 131–134

Write the letter that represents each decimal on the number line below.

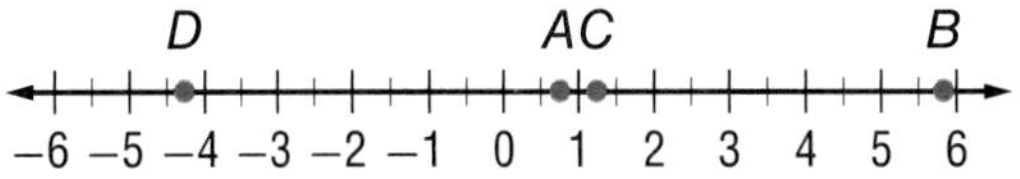

1. 0.8 **2.** 5.9 **3.** −4.2 **4.** 1.34

Graph each decimal in the approximate position on a number line.

5. 0.4 **6.** 9.12 **7.** −2.7 **8.** 5.9

Lesson 3-2

Pages 135–139

Use >, <, or = to compare each pair of numbers.

1. 852,159 ● 847,379
2. 4,793,146 ● 4,792,146
3. 98,657,193 ● 98,657,193
4. 2,576,157 ● 2,576,158
5. 0.03 ● 0.003
6. 6.15 ● 6.151
7. 0.112 ● 0.121
8. 8.007 ● 8.070
9. 6.005 ● 6.0050
10. 0.0345 ● 0.0435

Order each set of decimals from least to greatest.

11. 15.65, 51.65, 51.56, 15.56
12. 2.56, 20.56, 0.09, 25.6
13. 1.235, 1.25, 1.233, 1.23
14. 50.12, 5.012, 5.901, 50.02

Order each set of decimals from greatest to least.

15. 13.66, 13.44, 1.366, 1.633
16. 26.69, 26.09, 26.666, 26.9
17. 1.065, 1.1, 1.165, 1.056
18. 2.014, 2.010, 22.00, 22.14

Lesson 3-3

Pages 141–145

Round each number to the indicated place-value position.

1. 8,325,835; thousand
2. 2,686,444; thousand
3. 39,775,098; ten million
4. 63,348,569; ten million
5. 389,023,569; million
6. 20,747,936; hundred thousand
7. 40,627,031; hundred thousand
8. 1.0049; thousandths
9. 9.25; tenths
10. 67.492; hundredths
11. 4.00098; hundredths
12. 34.065; hundredths
13. 18.999; tenths
14. 74.00065; ten-thousandths

Lesson 3-4

Pages 146–147

Solve. Use the *logical reasoning* strategy.

1. Tonya, Shandra, and Colin are cousins. Tonya is older than Shandra. Colin is younger than Tonya. Shandra is not the youngest. List the cousins from youngest to oldest.

2. Nicolás, Carlie, Kevin, and Greg all have a pet. No two of them have the same pet. Here are some clues. Nicolás is afraid of dogs and frogs. Carlie has a cat. Kevin's pet lives in water. Greg's pet is not a fish. What kind of pet does each person have?

3. Jeff, Pablo, and Renée each had something different for dinner. One had chicken, one had a hamburger, and one had spaghetti. Jeff does not eat meat. Pablo is allergic to tomatoes. Renée had mustard and ketchup on her dinner. What did each person eat?

Lesson 3-5

Pages 149–153

Estimate using rounding.

1. 0.245 + 0.256
2. 2.45698 − 1.26589
3. 0.5962 + 1.2598
4. 0.256 + 0.6589
5. 1.2568 − 0.1569
6. 12.999 + 5.048

Estimate using clustering.

7. 4.5 + 4.95 + 5.2 + 5.49
8. 2.25 + 1.69 + 2.1 + 2.369
9. 12.15 + 11.63 + 12 + 11.89
10. 0.569 + 1.005 + 1.265 + 0.765
11. 9.85 + 10.32 + 10.18 + 9.64
12. 18.32 + 17.92 + 18.04
13. 16.3 + 15.82 + 16.01 + 15.9
14. 0.775 + 0.9 + 1.004 + 1.32

Estimate using front-end estimation.

15. 73.41 + 24.08
16. 88.42 − 63.59
17. 106.08 + 90.83
18. 143.24 − 43.65
19. 64.98 + 52.43
20. 96.51 − 41.32

Lesson 3-6

Pages 154–155

For each problem, determine whether you need an estimate or an exact answer. Then solve it.

1. Allie needs to save $20 to buy the DVD she wants. If she already has $14.65, how much more does she need to save?
2. If 50 students each contribute 3 cans of food for a food drive, how many cans of food will be collected in all?
3. Tasha spent $17.00, $9.85, $5.10, and $12.99 at four stores in the mall. About how much did she spend in all?
4. The average monthly precipitation for Columbus, Ohio, is shown in the table. What is the average yearly precipitation? Round to the nearest tenth.

Average Monthly Precipitation for Columbus, OH (in.)											
Jan.	Feb.	Mar.	Apr.	May	June	July	Aug.	Sept.	Oct.	Nov.	Dec.
2.5	2.2	2.9	3.3	3.9	4.1	4.6	3.7	2.9	2.3	3.2	2.9

Lesson 3-7

Pages 157–161

Find each sum or difference.

1. 0.46 + 0.72
2. 13.7 + 2.6
3. 17.9 + 7.41
4. 0.51 + 0.621
5. 12.56 − 10.21
6. 2.3 − 1.02
7. 1.025 − 0.58
8. 2.35 + 5
9. 20 − 5.98
10. 15.256 + 0.236
11. 3.7 + 1.5 + 0.2
12. 0.23 + 1.2 + 0.36
13. 0.89 − 0.256
14. 25.6 − 2.3
15. 13.5 − 2.84
16. 1.265 + 1.654
17. 24.56 − 24.32
18. 0.256 − 0.255

Lesson 4-1

Pages 175–178

Identify the common factors of each set of numbers.

1. 20, 40 **2.** 8, 28 **3.** 32, 80

4. 9, 54 **5.** 27, 81 **6.** 18, 34, 54

7. 32, 42, 63 **8.** 24, 30, 72 **9.** 15, 21, 36

Find the GCF of each set of numbers.

10. 64 and 32 **11.** 14 and 22 **12.** 12 and 27

13. 17 and 51 **14.** 48 and 60 **15.** 54 and 72

16. 10 and 25 **17.** 12 and 28 **18.** 16 and 24

19. 60 and 75 **20.** 54 and 27 **21.** 14, 28, 42

22. 27, 45, 63 **23.** 12, 18, 30 **24.** 16, 40, 72

Lesson 4-2

Pages 180–181

Use the *make an organized list* strategy to solve Exercises 1–3.

1. The volleyball team is ordering new uniforms. They can choose from 3 styles of shirts and 3 styles of shorts. How many combinations are possible for the complete uniform?

2. Maria is making a scrapbook for her friend's birthday. She has 2 pages with 2 pictures to put on each page. How many different ways can she arrange the pictures?

3. A local restaurant has a 99¢ menu which includes 2 sandwiches, 3 side dishes, and 1 size of soft drink. How many different meals are possible if a meal includes 1 sandwich, 1 side dish, and a drink?

Lesson 4-3

Pages 184–188

Replace each *x* with a number so the fractions are equivalent.

1. $\frac{12}{16} = \frac{x}{4}$ **2.** $\frac{7}{8} = \frac{x}{32}$ **3.** $\frac{3}{4} = \frac{75}{x}$ **4.** $\frac{8}{16} = \frac{x}{2}$

5. $\frac{6}{18} = \frac{1}{x}$ **6.** $\frac{27}{36} = \frac{3}{x}$ **7.** $\frac{1}{4} = \frac{16}{x}$ **8.** $\frac{9}{18} = \frac{x}{2}$

9. $\frac{9}{45} = \frac{x}{15}$ **10.** $\frac{2}{3} = \frac{18}{x}$ **11.** $\frac{24}{32} = \frac{x}{4}$ **12.** $\frac{48}{72} = \frac{6}{x}$

Write each fraction in simplest form. If the fraction is already in simplest form, write *simplest form*.

13. $\frac{50}{100}$ **14.** $\frac{24}{40}$ **15.** $\frac{2}{5}$ **16.** $\frac{8}{24}$ **17.** $\frac{20}{27}$

18. $\frac{4}{10}$ **19.** $\frac{3}{5}$ **20.** $\frac{14}{19}$ **21.** $\frac{9}{12}$ **22.** $\frac{6}{8}$

23. $\frac{15}{18}$ **24.** $\frac{9}{20}$ **25.** $\frac{32}{72}$ **26.** $\frac{36}{60}$ **27.** $\frac{12}{27}$

Lesson 4-4

Pages 189–192

Write each mixed number as an improper fraction. Graph the result on a number line.

1. $3\frac{1}{16}$	**2.** $2\frac{1}{4}$	**3.** $1\frac{3}{8}$	**4.** $1\frac{5}{12}$	**5.** $7\frac{3}{5}$
6. $6\frac{5}{8}$	**7.** $3\frac{1}{3}$	**8.** $1\frac{7}{9}$	**9.** $2\frac{3}{16}$	**10.** $1\frac{2}{3}$
11. $2\frac{3}{4}$	**12.** $1\frac{5}{9}$	**13.** $3\frac{3}{8}$	**14.** $4\frac{1}{5}$	**15.** $6\frac{2}{3}$

Write each improper fraction as a mixed number or a whole number. Graph the result on a number line.

16. $\frac{33}{10}$	**17.** $\frac{105}{25}$	**18.** $\frac{22}{5}$	**19.** $\frac{13}{2}$	**20.** $\frac{29}{6}$
21. $\frac{110}{100}$	**22.** $\frac{21}{8}$	**23.** $\frac{19}{6}$	**24.** $\frac{23}{5}$	**25.** $\frac{90}{50}$
26. $\frac{39}{8}$	**27.** $\frac{13}{4}$	**28.** $\frac{26}{9}$	**29.** $\frac{18}{5}$	**30.** $\frac{11}{11}$

Lesson 4-5

Pages 194–197

Identify the first three common multiples of each set of numbers.

1. 4, 12	**2.** 3, 9	**3.** 2, 5
4. 10, 15	**5.** 4, 12, 16	**6.** 2, 6, 10
7. 3, 8, 12	**8.** 9, 15, 30	**9.** 5, 8, 10

Find the LCM for each set of numbers.

10. 9 and 6	**11.** 4 and 14	**12.** 14 and 49
13. 10 and 45	**14.** 18 and 12	**15.** 12 and 30
16. 5 and 7	**17.** 6 and 15	**18.** 20 and 8
19. 18 and 24	**20.** 11 and 33	**21.** 2, 3, and 6
22. 6, 2, and 22	**23.** 15, 12, and 8	**24.** 15, 24, and 30
25. 12, 18, and 3	**26.** 12, 35, and 10	**27.** 21, 14, and 6

Lesson 4-6

Pages 198–199

Use any strategy to solve.

1. How many phone numbers are possible for one area code if the first three numbers are 423, in that order, and the last four numbers are 0, 1, 5, and 6 in any order?
2. Jacy has $125 in his savings account. He deposits $20 every week and withdraws $25 every four weeks. What will his balance be in 8 weeks?
3. Diego's math scores for his last four tests were 94, 87, 90, and 89. What score does he need on the next test to average a score of 91?

Lesson 4-7

Pages 200–204

Replace each ● with <, >, or = to make a true sentence.

1. $\frac{1}{2}$ ● $\frac{1}{3}$
2. $\frac{2}{3}$ ● $\frac{3}{4}$
3. $\frac{5}{9}$ ● $\frac{4}{5}$
4. $\frac{3}{5}$ ● $\frac{6}{12}$
5. $\frac{12}{23}$ ● $\frac{15}{19}$
6. $\frac{9}{27}$ ● $\frac{13}{39}$
7. $\frac{7}{8}$ ● $\frac{9}{13}$
8. $\frac{5}{9}$ ● $\frac{7}{8}$
9. $\frac{25}{100}$ ● $\frac{3}{8}$
10. $\frac{6}{7}$ ● $\frac{8}{15}$
11. $\frac{5}{9}$ ● $\frac{19}{23}$
12. $\frac{17}{25}$ ● $\frac{68}{100}$
13. $\frac{5}{7}$ ● $\frac{2}{3}$
14. $\frac{9}{36}$ ● $\frac{7}{28}$
15. $\frac{2}{5}$ ● $\frac{2}{6}$
16. $\frac{5}{9}$ ● $\frac{12}{13}$
17. $\frac{3}{5}$ ● $\frac{5}{8}$
18. $\frac{8}{9}$ ● $\frac{3}{4}$
19. $\frac{11}{15}$ ● $\frac{20}{30}$
20. $\frac{15}{24}$ ● $\frac{6}{8}$

Lesson 4-8

Pages 205–208

Write each decimal as a fraction or mixed number in simplest form.

1. 0.5
2. 0.8
3. 0.32
4. 0.875
5. 0.54
6. 0.38
7. 0.744
8. 0.101
9. 0.303
10. 0.486
11. 0.626
12. 0.448
13. 0.074
14. 0.008
15. 9.36
16. 10.18
17. 0.06
18. 0.75
19. 0.48
20. 0.9
21. 0.005
22. 0.4
23. 1.875
24. 5.08
25. 0.46
26. 0.128
27. 0.08
28. 6.96
29. 3.625
30. 0.006
31. 12.05
32. 24.125

Lesson 4-9

Pages 209–212

Write each fraction or mixed number as a decimal.

1. $\frac{3}{16}$
2. $\frac{1}{8}$
3. $\frac{7}{16}$
4. $\frac{14}{25}$
5. $\frac{7}{10}$
6. $\frac{5}{8}$
7. $\frac{11}{20}$
8. $\frac{8}{25}$
9. $\frac{15}{16}$
10. $\frac{1}{10}$
11. $\frac{7}{20}$
12. $\frac{5}{16}$
13. $\frac{9}{10}$
14. $\frac{11}{25}$
15. $\frac{9}{20}$
16. $4\frac{4}{25}$
17. $1\frac{3}{8}$
18. $\frac{7}{16}$
19. $2\frac{3}{10}$
20. $6\frac{3}{5}$
21. $\frac{3}{4}$
22. $3\frac{4}{5}$
23. $2\frac{1}{10}$
24. $\frac{17}{25}$
25. $5\frac{13}{20}$
26. $\frac{37}{50}$
27. $4\frac{9}{25}$
28. $\frac{7}{4}$

Lesson 4-10

Pages 213–217

Use the coordinate plane at the right to name the ordered pair for each point.

1. *E* **2.** *M*

3. *R* **4.** *J*

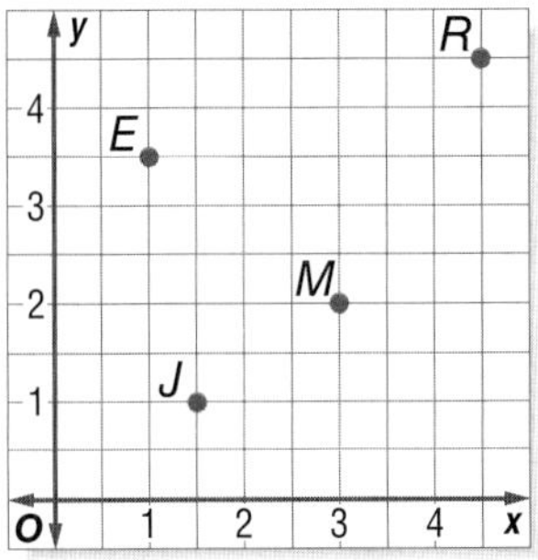

Graph and label each point on a coordinate plane.

5. $H(0, 2)$ **6.** $K(3, 1)$

7. $S(4, 2.5)$ **8.** $Z(1.5, 0)$

For Exercises 9 and 10, use the following information. Tanya is saving \$1.50 each day to buy a new sweater. The table at the right shows this relationship.

Days	Total Saved (\$)
1	1.5
2	3
3	4.5
4	6

9. List this information as ordered pairs (number of days, total amount saved).

10. Graph the ordered pairs. Then describe the graph.

Lesson 5-1

Pages 232–236

Round each number to the nearest half.

1. $\frac{11}{12}$ **2.** $\frac{5}{8}$ **3.** $\frac{2}{5}$ **4.** $\frac{1}{10}$ **5.** $\frac{1}{6}$ **6.** $\frac{2}{3}$

7. $\frac{9}{10}$ **8.** $\frac{1}{8}$ **9.** $\frac{4}{9}$ **10.** $1\frac{1}{8}$ **11.** $\frac{7}{9}$ **12.** $2\frac{4}{5}$

13. $\frac{7}{9}$ **14.** $7\frac{1}{10}$ **15.** $10\frac{2}{3}$ **16.** $\frac{1}{3}$ **17.** $\frac{7}{15}$ **18.** $\frac{5}{7}$

19. $1\frac{2}{7}$ **20.** $9\frac{4}{5}$ **21.** $3\frac{9}{11}$ **22.** $2\frac{3}{7}$ **23.** $7\frac{3}{8}$ **24.** $4\frac{17}{20}$

Lesson 5-2

Pages 237–240

Estimate.

1. $14\frac{1}{10} - 6\frac{4}{5}$ **2.** $8\frac{1}{3} + 2\frac{1}{6}$ **3.** $4\frac{7}{8} + 7\frac{3}{4}$ **4.** $11\frac{11}{12} - 5\frac{1}{4}$

5. $3\frac{2}{5} - 1\frac{1}{4}$ **6.** $4\frac{2}{5} + \frac{5}{6}$ **7.** $4\frac{7}{12} - 1\frac{3}{4}$ **8.** $4\frac{2}{3} + 10\frac{3}{8}$

9. $7\frac{7}{15} - 3\frac{1}{12}$ **10.** $2\frac{1}{16} + 1\frac{1}{3}$ **11.** $18\frac{1}{4} - 12\frac{3}{5}$ **12.** $12\frac{5}{9} + 8\frac{5}{8}$

13. $8\frac{2}{3} - 5\frac{1}{2}$ **14.** $3\frac{1}{8} - 2\frac{1}{5}$ **15.** $9\frac{2}{7} - \frac{1}{3}$ **16.** $11\frac{7}{8} - \frac{5}{6}$

17. $2\frac{2}{5} + 2\frac{1}{4}$ **18.** $8\frac{1}{2} - 7\frac{4}{5}$ **19.** $8\frac{3}{4} + 4\frac{2}{3}$ **20.** $1\frac{1}{8} + 7\frac{1}{10}$

21. $\frac{3}{7} + \frac{8}{9}$ **22.** $5\frac{11}{12} - 3\frac{1}{3}$ **23.** $2\frac{1}{7} + 4\frac{3}{5}$ **24.** $\frac{5}{6} - \frac{1}{4}$

Lesson 5-3

Pages 241–245

Add or subtract. Write in simplest form.

1. $\frac{2}{5}+\frac{2}{5}$	**2.** $\frac{5}{8}+\frac{3}{8}$	**3.** $\frac{9}{11}-\frac{3}{11}$	**4.** $\frac{3}{14}+\frac{5}{14}$
5. $\frac{7}{8}-\frac{3}{8}$	**6.** $\frac{3}{4}-\frac{1}{4}$	**7.** $\frac{5}{7}-\frac{1}{7}$	**8.** $\frac{1}{3}+\frac{2}{3}$
9. $\frac{1}{2}+\frac{1}{2}$	**10.** $\frac{1}{3}-\frac{1}{3}$	**11.** $\frac{8}{9}+\frac{7}{9}$	**12.** $\frac{5}{6}-\frac{3}{6}$
13. $\frac{3}{9}+\frac{8}{9}$	**14.** $\frac{7}{10}+\frac{3}{10}$	**15.** $\frac{6}{13}-\frac{2}{13}$	**16.** $\frac{2}{9}+\frac{8}{9}$
17. $\frac{7}{15}-\frac{4}{15}$	**18.** $\frac{3}{8}+\frac{7}{8}$	**19.** $\frac{11}{20}-\frac{5}{20}$	**20.** $\frac{7}{9}-\frac{2}{9}$
21. $\frac{10}{12}+\frac{7}{12}$	**22.** $\frac{5}{6}+\frac{1}{6}$	**23.** $\frac{5}{8}+\frac{7}{8}$	**24.** $\frac{9}{16}+\frac{5}{16}$

Lesson 5-4

Pages 246–247

Use the *act it out* strategy to solve Exercises 1–4.

1. A sundae bar has 3 flavors of ice cream and 4 toppings. How many different sundaes can be made with one flavor of ice cream and one topping?

2. Paco is coloring the design shown for a poster. How many ways can he color it if he only uses two colors?

3. Rachel uses $7\frac{1}{2}$ inches of string to make a bracelet. She had 4 feet of string, but already used 16 inches for a necklace. Does she have enough string left to make one bracelet for each of her 3 friends? Explain your reasoning.

4. Conner runs on the treadmill for 5 minutes and then walks for 3 minutes. How many sets of this pattern will he complete if he exercises for 45 minutes?

Lesson 5-5

Pages 251–256

Add or subtract. Write in simplest form.

1. $\frac{1}{3}+\frac{1}{2}$	**2.** $\frac{2}{9}+\frac{1}{3}$	**3.** $\frac{1}{2}+\frac{3}{4}$	**4.** $\frac{1}{4}+\frac{3}{12}$
5. $\frac{5}{9}-\frac{1}{3}$	**6.** $\frac{5}{8}-\frac{2}{5}$	**7.** $\frac{3}{4}-\frac{1}{2}$	**8.** $\frac{7}{8}-\frac{3}{16}$
9. $\frac{9}{16}+\frac{3}{4}$	**10.** $\frac{8}{15}+\frac{2}{3}$	**11.** $\frac{5}{14}+\frac{1}{7}$	**12.** $\frac{11}{12}+\frac{7}{8}$
13. $\frac{2}{3}-\frac{1}{6}$	**14.** $\frac{9}{16}-\frac{1}{2}$	**15.** $\frac{5}{8}-\frac{11}{20}$	**16.** $\frac{14}{15}-\frac{2}{9}$
17. $\frac{9}{20}+\frac{2}{15}$	**18.** $\frac{5}{6}+\frac{4}{5}$	**19.** $\frac{13}{20}-\frac{3}{10}$	**20.** $\frac{8}{15}-\frac{1}{3}$
21. $\frac{1}{5}+\frac{2}{3}$	**22.** $\frac{4}{9}-\frac{1}{6}$	**23.** $\frac{1}{3}+\frac{4}{5}$	**24.** $\frac{7}{8}-\frac{5}{12}$

Lesson 5-6

Pages 258–259

Use any strategy to solve.

1. Sunee, Marina, John, and Zack have formed a club that will have a president and a vice-president. Each month, the officers will change until every combination of president and vice-president has been used. For how many months can they have different officers?
2. There were about 300 million people in the U.S. in 2006. This amount is expected to increase by about 2.8 million people each year after 2006. How many years will pass before there are at least 325 million people in the U.S.?
3. Sam, Darren, Monique, and Will all have a different favorite music group. Sam's favorite group is The Collection. Darren does not like The Guys. Monique's favorite does not begin with "The." Will does not listen to Fever or The Wildcats. Find the favorite group of each person.

Lesson 5-7

Pages 260–264

Add or subtract. Write in simplest form.

1. $5\frac{1}{2} + 3\frac{1}{4}$ **2.** $2\frac{2}{3} + 4\frac{1}{9}$ **3.** $7\frac{4}{5} + 9\frac{3}{10}$ **4.** $9\frac{4}{7} - 3\frac{5}{14}$

5. $13\frac{1}{5} - 10$ **6.** $3\frac{3}{4} + 5\frac{5}{8}$ **7.** $3\frac{2}{5} + 7\frac{6}{15}$ **8.** $10\frac{2}{3} + 5\frac{6}{7}$

9. $15\frac{6}{9} - 13\frac{5}{12}$ **10.** $13\frac{7}{12} - 9\frac{1}{4}$ **11.** $5\frac{2}{3} - 3\frac{1}{2}$ **12.** $17\frac{2}{9} + 12\frac{1}{3}$

13. $6\frac{5}{12} + 12\frac{5}{8}$ **14.** $8\frac{3}{5} - 2\frac{1}{5}$ **15.** $23\frac{2}{3} - 4\frac{1}{2}$ **16.** $7\frac{1}{8} + 2\frac{5}{8}$

17. $12\frac{11}{15} - 10\frac{2}{15}$ **18.** $12\frac{1}{3} + 5\frac{1}{6}$ **19.** $2\frac{1}{4} + 3\frac{1}{8}$ **20.** $7\frac{9}{14} - 4\frac{3}{7}$

21. $4\frac{3}{5} - 2\frac{1}{15}$ **22.** $6\frac{1}{8} + 7\frac{3}{4}$ **23.** $5\frac{5}{6} - 2\frac{1}{2}$ **24.** $1\frac{2}{3} + \frac{5}{18}$

Lesson 5-8

Pages 265–269

Subtract. Write in simplest form.

1. $11\frac{2}{3} - 8\frac{11}{12}$ **2.** $3\frac{4}{7} - 1\frac{2}{3}$ **3.** $7\frac{1}{8} - 4\frac{1}{3}$ **4.** $18\frac{1}{9} - 12\frac{2}{5}$

5. $12\frac{3}{10} - 8\frac{3}{4}$ **6.** $43 - 5\frac{1}{5}$ **7.** $8\frac{1}{5} - 4\frac{1}{4}$ **8.** $14\frac{1}{6} - 3\frac{2}{3}$

9. $25\frac{4}{7} - 21$ **10.** $17\frac{3}{9} - 4\frac{3}{5}$ **11.** $18\frac{1}{9} - 1\frac{3}{7}$ **12.** $16\frac{1}{4} - 7\frac{1}{5}$

13. $18\frac{1}{5} - 6\frac{1}{4}$ **14.** $4 - 1\frac{2}{3}$ **15.** $26 - 4\frac{1}{9}$ **16.** $3\frac{1}{2} - 1\frac{3}{4}$

17. $4\frac{3}{8} - 2\frac{5}{6}$ **18.** $18\frac{1}{6} - 10\frac{3}{4}$ **19.** $12\frac{4}{9} - 7\frac{5}{6}$ **20.** $4\frac{1}{15} - 2\frac{3}{5}$

21. $7\frac{1}{14} - 4\frac{3}{7}$ **22.** $12\frac{3}{20} - 7\frac{7}{15}$ **23.** $8\frac{5}{12} - 5\frac{9}{10}$ **24.** $8\frac{1}{5} - 4\frac{2}{3}$

Lesson 6-1

Pages 284–287

Multiply.

1. 0.2×6
2. 0.73×5
3. 0.65×3
4. 9.6×4
5. 12.15×6
6. 0.91×8
7. 0.265×7
8. 2.612×4
9. 0.013×5
10. 0.67×2
11. 9×0.111
12. 1.65×7
13. 9.6×3
14. 4×1.201
15. 6×7.5
16. 0.001×6
17. 5×0.0135
18. 9.2×7
19. 14.1235×4

Write each number in standard form.

20. 3×10^4
21. 2.6×10^6
22. 3.81×10^2
23. 8.4×10^3
24. 6.05×10^5
25. 7.32×10^4

Lesson 6-2

Pages 290–293

Multiply.

1. 9.6×10.5
2. 3.2×0.1
3. 1.5×9.6
4. 5.42×0.21
5. 7.42×0.2
6. 0.001×0.02
7. 9.8×4.62
8. 7.32×9.7
9. 0.008×0.007
10. 0.001×56
11. 4.5×0.2
12. 9.6×2.3
13. 5.63×8.1
14. 10.35×9.1
15. 28.2×3.9

Evaluate each expression if $x = 2.6$, $y = 0.38$, and $z = 1.02$.

16. $xy + z$
17. $y \times 9.4$
18. xyz
19. $z \times 12.34 + y$
20. $yz \times 0.8$
21. $xz - yz$

Lesson 6-3

Pages 294–295

Determine reasonable answers for Exercises 1–5.

1. Mi-Ling wants to buy 2 pairs of jeans for $29.99 each and 2 tops for $15.99 each. Does she need to save up $150, or will $100 be enough?
2. The length of a playground is 88 yards. Which is a more reasonable estimate for the length of the playground in feet: 240 or 270?
3. One hundred fifty students are being honored at an awards banquet. Each student is permitted to bring a maximum of 3 guests. Is it reasonable to set up 40 tables that seat 12 people each? Explain.
4. The data at the right shows the number of bags of popcorn sold by each student in Ms. Taylor's class. Is 1,300 bags a reasonable goal for the class to set for next year's fund-raiser? Explain your reasoning.

Bags of Popcorn Sold

10	250	35	68	102	50	28	18	98
12	75	60	185	11	27	33	87	100

Lesson 6-4

Pages 296–299

Divide. Round to the nearest tenth if necessary.

1. $1.2 \div 6$
2. $23.2 \div 8$
3. $89.4 \div 6$
4. $55.5 \div 15$
5. $128.7 \div 13$
6. $2.583 \div 9$
7. $9.4 \div 47$
8. $33.8 \div 26$
9. $37.8 \div 14$
10. $5.88 \div 4$
11. $3.7 \div 5$
12. $41.4 \div 18$
13. $9.87 \div 3$
14. $8.45 \div 25$
15. $26.5 \div 4$
16. $46.25 \div 8$
17. $19.38 \div 9$
18. $8.5 \div 2$
19. $90.88 \div 14$
20. $23.1 \div 4$
21. $19.5 \div 27$
22. $26.5 \div 19$
23. $46.25 \div 25$
24. $46.25 \div 25$

Lesson 6-5

Pages 303–306

Divide.

1. $18.45 \div 0.5$
2. $5.2 \div 0.08$
3. $0.65 \div 2.6$
4. $12.831 \div 1.3$
5. $5.133 \div 0.87$
6. $24.13 \div 2.54$
7. $35.89 \div 3.7$
8. $32.5 \div 26$
9. $5.88 \div 0.4$
10. $3.7 \div 0.5$
11. $6.72 \div 2.4$
12. $9.87 \div 0.3$
13. $8.45 \div 2.5$
14. $90.88 \div 14.2$
15. $33.6 \div 8.4$
16. $0.1185 \div 7.9$
17. $0.384 \div 9.6$
18. $2.24 \div 0.4$
19. $12.68 \div 3.2$
20. $16.2 \div 0.108$
21. $0.3869 \div 5.3$

Lesson 6-6

Pages 308–309

Use any strategy to solve.

1. The first 5 bells at Watson Middle School ring at 8:50 A.M., 8:54 A.M., 9:34 A.M., 9:38 A.M., and 10:18 A.M. If this pattern continues, when should the next three bells ring?

2. Susan takes her family out to dinner, and the cost of the meal is $43.85. She wants to give the server an 18% tip. How much should she give the server: $4, $6, or $8?

3. Mr. Johnson is rearranging the desks in his classroom. If the desks have to be set up in rows all facing the same direction, how many arrangements are possible for 24 desks?

4. The total enrollment at The Ohio State University for one year was 50,995 students. Which is a more reasonable estimate for the number of freshman students enrolled at the University for that year: 10,500 or 25,500?

Lesson 6-7

Pages 310–313

Estimate each product.

1. $\frac{5}{6} \times 8$
2. $\frac{1}{3} \times 46$
3. $\frac{4}{5}$ of 21
4. $\frac{1}{9} \times 35$
5. $\frac{5}{9}$ of 20
6. $\frac{1}{8} \times 30$
7. $\frac{2}{3} \times \frac{4}{5}$
8. $\frac{1}{6} \times \frac{2}{5}$
9. $\frac{4}{9} \times \frac{3}{7}$
10. $\frac{5}{12} \times \frac{6}{11}$
11. $\frac{3}{8} \times \frac{8}{9}$
12. $\frac{3}{5} \times \frac{5}{12}$
13. $\frac{2}{5} \times \frac{5}{8}$
14. $\frac{4}{5} \times \frac{11}{12}$
15. $\frac{5}{7} \times \frac{7}{8}$
16. $\frac{1}{20} \times \frac{8}{9}$
17. $\frac{9}{11} \times \frac{14}{15}$
18. $\frac{2}{5} \times \frac{18}{19}$
19. $5\frac{3}{7} \times \frac{4}{5}$
20. $2\frac{5}{9} \times \frac{1}{8}$
21. $3\frac{9}{10} \times \frac{15}{16}$
22. $\frac{11}{12} \times 2\frac{1}{3}$
23. $3\frac{14}{15} \times \frac{3}{8}$
24. $\frac{1}{10} \times 3\frac{1}{2}$
25. $9\frac{13}{15} \times \frac{1}{2}$
26. $6\frac{7}{8} \times 2\frac{1}{5}$
27. $7\frac{1}{4} \times 4\frac{3}{4}$
28. $6\frac{2}{3} \times 5\frac{4}{5}$

Lesson 6-8

Pages 316–320

Multiply. Write in simplest form.

1. $\frac{1}{8} \times \frac{1}{9}$
2. $\frac{4}{7} \times 6$
3. $\frac{7}{10} \times 5$
4. $\frac{3}{8} \times 6$
5. $4 \times \frac{5}{9}$
6. $\frac{9}{10} \times \frac{3}{4}$
7. $\frac{8}{9} \times \frac{2}{3}$
8. $\frac{6}{7} \times \frac{4}{5}$
9. $\frac{7}{11} \times \frac{12}{15}$
10. $\frac{8}{13} \times \frac{2}{11}$
11. $\frac{4}{7} \times \frac{2}{9}$
12. $\frac{3}{7} \times \frac{5}{8}$
13. $\frac{5}{6} \times \frac{15}{16}$
14. $\frac{6}{14} \times \frac{12}{18}$
15. $\frac{2}{3} \times \frac{3}{13}$
16. $\frac{4}{9} \times \frac{1}{6}$
17. $\frac{3}{4} \times \frac{5}{6}$
18. $\frac{8}{11} \times \frac{11}{12}$
19. $\frac{5}{6} \times \frac{3}{5}$
20. $\frac{6}{7} \times \frac{7}{21}$
21. $\frac{8}{9} \times \frac{9}{10}$
22. $\frac{7}{9} \times \frac{5}{7}$
23. $\frac{4}{9} \times \frac{24}{25}$
24. $\frac{1}{9} \times \frac{6}{13}$
25. $\frac{5}{9} \times \frac{3}{10}$
26. $\frac{2}{3} \times \frac{7}{8}$
27. $\frac{7}{12} \times \frac{4}{9}$
28. $\frac{11}{15} \times \frac{3}{10}$

Lesson 6-9

Pages 321–324

Multiply. Write in simplest form.

1. $\frac{4}{5} \times 2\frac{3}{4}$
2. $2\frac{3}{10} \times \frac{3}{5}$
3. $8\frac{5}{6} \times \frac{2}{5}$
4. $\frac{3}{4} \times 9\frac{5}{7}$
5. $6\frac{2}{3} \times 7\frac{3}{5}$
6. $7\frac{1}{5} \times 2\frac{4}{7}$
7. $8\frac{3}{4} \times 2\frac{2}{5}$
8. $4\frac{1}{3} \times 2\frac{1}{7}$
9. $4\frac{3}{5} \times 2\frac{1}{2}$
10. $5\frac{5}{6} \times 4\frac{2}{7}$
11. $6\frac{8}{9} \times 3\frac{5}{6}$
12. $2\frac{1}{9} \times 1\frac{1}{2}$
13. $4\frac{7}{15} \times 3\frac{3}{4}$
14. $5\frac{7}{9} \times 6\frac{3}{8}$
15. $1\frac{1}{4} \times 3\frac{2}{3}$
16. $2\frac{3}{5} \times 1\frac{4}{7}$
17. $4\frac{1}{5} \times 12\frac{2}{9}$
18. $3\frac{5}{8} \times 4\frac{1}{2}$
19. $6\frac{1}{2} \times 2\frac{1}{3}$
20. $3\frac{4}{5} \times 2\frac{3}{8}$
21. $5\frac{1}{4} \times 10\frac{3}{7}$
22. $1\frac{5}{9} \times 6\frac{1}{4}$
23. $2\frac{1}{6} \times 1\frac{3}{4}$
24. $3\frac{5}{7} \times 1\frac{1}{2}$
25. $2\frac{3}{5} \times 4\frac{5}{8}$
26. $6\frac{1}{8} \times 5\frac{1}{7}$
27. $2\frac{2}{3} \times 2\frac{1}{4}$
28. $2\frac{1}{2} \times 3\frac{1}{3}$

Lesson 6-10

Pages 327–331

Find the reciprocal of each number.

1. $\frac{12}{13}$ **2.** $\frac{7}{11}$ **3.** 5 **4.** $\frac{1}{4}$ **5.** $\frac{7}{9}$ **6.** $\frac{9}{2}$ **7.** $\frac{1}{5}$

Divide. Write in simplest form.

8. $\frac{2}{3} \div \frac{1}{2}$ **9.** $\frac{3}{5} \div \frac{2}{5}$ **10.** $\frac{7}{10} \div \frac{3}{8}$ **11.** $\frac{5}{9} \div \frac{2}{3}$

12. $4 \div \frac{2}{3}$ **13.** $8 \div \frac{4}{5}$ **14.** $9 \div \frac{5}{9}$ **15.** $\frac{2}{7} \div 7$

16. $\frac{1}{14} \div 7$ **17.** $\frac{2}{13} \div \frac{5}{26}$ **18.** $\frac{4}{7} \div \frac{6}{7}$ **19.** $\frac{7}{8} \div \frac{1}{3}$

20. $15 \div \frac{3}{5}$ **21.** $\frac{9}{14} \div \frac{3}{4}$ **22.** $\frac{8}{9} \div \frac{5}{6}$ **23.** $\frac{4}{9} \div 36$

24. $\frac{15}{16} \div \frac{5}{8}$ **25.** $\frac{3}{5} \div \frac{7}{10}$ **26.** $\frac{5}{9} \div \frac{3}{8}$ **27.** $\frac{5}{6} \div \frac{3}{8}$

Lesson 6-11

Pages 334–337

Divide. Write in simplest form.

1. $\frac{3}{5} \div 1\frac{2}{3}$ **2.** $2\frac{1}{2} \div 1\frac{1}{4}$ **3.** $7 \div 4\frac{9}{10}$ **4.** $1\frac{3}{7} \div 10$

5. $3\frac{3}{5} \div \frac{4}{5}$ **6.** $8\frac{2}{5} \div 4\frac{1}{2}$ **7.** $6\frac{1}{3} \div 2\frac{1}{2}$ **8.** $5\frac{1}{4} \div 2\frac{1}{3}$

9. $4\frac{1}{8} \div 3\frac{2}{3}$ **10.** $2\frac{5}{8} \div \frac{1}{2}$ **11.** $1\frac{5}{6} \div 3\frac{2}{3}$ **12.** $21 \div 5\frac{1}{4}$

13. $12 \div 3\frac{3}{5}$ **14.** $18 \div 2\frac{1}{4}$ **15.** $1\frac{7}{9} \div 2\frac{2}{3}$ **16.** $2\frac{1}{15} \div 3\frac{1}{3}$

17. $1\frac{1}{8} \div 2\frac{2}{3}$ **18.** $5\frac{1}{3} \div 2\frac{1}{2}$ **19.** $1\frac{1}{4} \div 1\frac{7}{8}$ **20.** $2\frac{3}{5} \div 1\frac{7}{10}$

21. $6\frac{3}{4} \div 3\frac{1}{2}$ **22.** $4\frac{1}{2} \div \frac{3}{8}$ **23.** $3\frac{1}{2} \div 1\frac{7}{9}$ **24.** $12\frac{1}{2} \div 5\frac{5}{6}$

25. $8\frac{1}{4} \div 2\frac{3}{4}$ **26.** $2\frac{3}{8} \div 5\frac{3}{7}$ **27.** $4\frac{5}{9} \div 5\frac{1}{3}$ **28.** $3\frac{1}{2} \div 5\frac{1}{4}$

Lesson 7-1

Pages 349–352

Replace each ● with <, >, or = to make a true sentence.

1. −5 ● −55 **2.** 4 ● −66 **3.** −777 ● −77 **4.** −75 ● −75

5. −898 ● −99 **6.** 0 ● 44 **7.** 56 ● −1 **8.** −82 ● −9

9. −6 ● −7 **10.** 90 ● 101 **11.** 4 ● −2,000 **12.** −3 ● 0

13. 8 ● 6 **14.** −5 ● −7 **15.** −2 ● 0 **16.** 3 ● −2

Order each set of integers from least to greatest.

17. 0, 3, −21, 9, −89, 8, −65, −56 **18.** 70, −9, 67, −78, 0, 45, −36, −19

19. 12, 8, −9, −12, 10, 16 **20.** 65, 34, −50, 28, −64, −45

21. −4, 39, −14, 22, −30, 33, −70 **22.** −3, 77, 0, 41, −48, 6, −19

Lesson 7-2

Pages 354–358

Add.

1. $-4 + (-7)$ **2.** $-1 + 0$ **3.** $7 + (-13)$ **4.** $-20 + (+2)$
5. $4 + (-6)$ **6.** $-12 + 9$ **7.** $-12 + (-10)$ **8.** $5 + (-15)$
9. $17 + 9$ **10.** $18 + (-18)$ **11.** $-4 + (-4)$ **12.** $0 + (-9)$
13. $-12 + (-9)$ **14.** $-8 + (+7)$ **15.** $3 + (-6)$ **16.** $-9 + 16$
17. $-5 + (-3)$ **18.** $-5 + 5$ **19.** $-3 + (-3)$ **20.** $-11 + 6$
21. $-10 + 6$ **22.** $-5 + (-9)$ **23.** $18 + (-20)$ **24.** $-4 + (-8)$
25. $2 + (-4)$ **26.** $-3 + (-11)$ **27.** $-17 + 9$ **28.** $-7 + (-4)$

29. Evaluate $a + b$ if $a = 14$ and $b = -5$.

30. Find the value of $m + n$ if $m = -5$ and $n = -6$.

Lesson 7-3

Pages 359–363

Subtract.

1. $7 - (-4)$ **2.** $-4 - (-9)$ **3.** $13 - (-3)$ **4.** $2 - (-5)$
5. $-9 - 5$ **6.** $-11 - (-18)$ **7.** $-4 - (-7)$ **8.** $-6 - (-6)$
9. $-6 - 6$ **10.** $17 - 9$ **11.** $-12 - (-9)$ **12.** $0 - (-4)$
13. $-7 - 0$ **14.** $-12 - (-10)$ **15.** $-2 - (-1)$ **16.** $3 - (-5)$
17. $5 - (-1)$ **18.** $-5 - (-6)$ **19.** $9 - (-1)$ **20.** $1 - 9$
21. $-5 - 1$ **22.** $-1 - 4$ **23.** $0 - (-7)$ **24.** $8 - 13$
25. $8 - (-5)$ **26.** $5 - 8$ **27.** $1 - 6$ **28.** $-8 - (-8)$

29. Find the value of $s - t$ if $s = -4$ and $t = 3$.

30. Find the value of $a - b$ if $a = 6$ and $b = -8$.

Lesson 7-4

Pages 364–367

Multiply.

1. $3 \times (-5)$ **2.** -5×1 **3.** $-8 \times (-4)$ **4.** $6 \times (-3)$
5. -3×2 **6.** $-1 \times (-4)$ **7.** $8 \times (-2)$ **8.** $-5 \times (-7)$
9. $3 \times (-9)$ **10.** -9×4 **11.** $-4 \times (-5)$ **12.** $5 \times (-2)$
13. $-8(3)$ **14.** $-9(-1)$ **15.** $7(-3)$ **16.** $2(3)$
17. $-6(0)$ **18.** $-5(-1)$ **19.** $5(-5)$ **20.** $-2(-3)$
21. $8(-4)$ **22.** $-2(4)$ **23.** $-4(-4)$ **24.** $2(9)$
25. $-2(-12)$ **26.** $7 \times (-4)$ **27.** $-5 \times (-9)$ **28.** -2×11

29. Find the product of 2 and -3.

30. Evaluate qr if $q = -3$ and $r = -3$.

Lesson 7-5

Pages 368–369

For Exercises 1–4, solve using the *work backward* strategy.

1. Mario has \$2.50 left after spending \$4.25 at the arcade and \$5.50 on lunch. How much money did Mario have originally?
2. A number is multiplied by 3, and then 4 is subtracted from the product. Then, 2 is added to the difference. If the result is 16, what is the number?
3. Julia is selling candy bars. In the first week, she sold 23 chocolate bars, 15 peanut butter bars, and 8 caramel bars. If she had 9 candy bars left, how many candy bars did she have at the beginning of the week?
4. Alex finished his homework at 8:15 P.M. He spent 30 minutes working on science, 45 minutes working on math, and 25 minutes working on history. If he worked without taking any breaks, at what time did he begin working on his homework?

Lesson 7-6

Pages 371–375

Divide.

1. $12 \div (-6)$	**2.** $-7 \div (-1)$	**3.** $-4 \div 4$	**4.** $6 \div (-6)$
5. $0 \div (-4)$	**6.** $45 \div (-9)$	**7.** $15 \div (-5)$	**8.** $-6 \div 2$
9. $-28 \div (-7)$	**10.** $20 \div (-2)$	**11.** $-40 \div (-8)$	**12.** $12 \div (-4)$
13. $-18 \div 6$	**14.** $9 \div (-1)$	**15.** $-30 \div 6$	**16.** $-54 \div (-9)$
17. $28 \div (-7)$	**18.** $-24 \div 8$	**19.** $24 \div (-4)$	**20.** $-14 \div 7$
21. $9 \div 3$	**22.** $-18 \div (-6)$	**23.** $-9 \div (-1)$	**24.** $18 \div (-9)$

Lesson 7-7

Pages 376–377

Use any strategy to solve.

1. The sum of three consecutive whole numbers is 45. Find the three numbers.
2. Mr. Vacarro says, "If 2 years are subtracted from my age, the result is 3 times the age of my son." If his son's age is 12, what is Mr. Vacarro's age?
3. When Enrique arrives home from school, he spends 10 minutes eating a snack. Then he studies science, history, and mathematics. He spends 15 minutes on each subject. If he finishes his studies at 5:15 when did he arrive home from school?
4. To attend a class field trip to the bowling alley, each student will have to pay \$6 for transportation and \$4 for bowling. If there are 281 students in the class, how much money will be collected for the field trip?

Lesson 7-8

Pages 378–382

Write the ordered pair that names each point. Then identify the quadrant where each point is located.

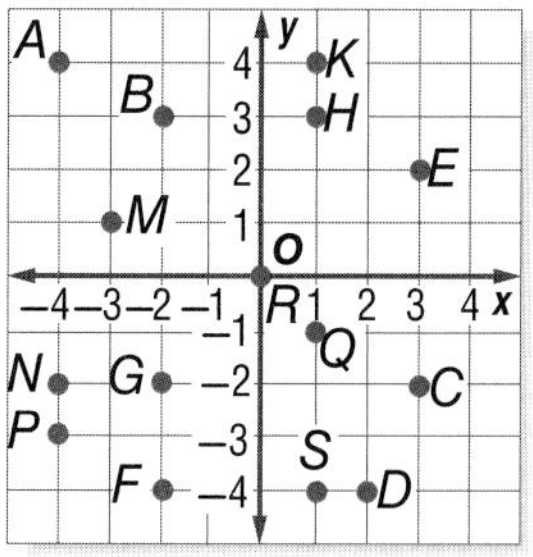

1. *M* **2.** *A* **3.** *D*
4. *E* **5.** *P* **6.** *Q*
7. *B* **8.** *C* **9.** *F*
10. *G* **11.** *N* **12.** *R*
13. *K* **14.** *H* **15.** *S*

Graph and label each point on a coordinate plane.

16. $S(4, -1)$ **17.** $T(-3, -2)$ **18.** $W(2, 1)$ **19.** $Y(-5, 3)$
20. $Z(-1, -3)$ **21.** $U(3, -3)$ **22.** $V(1, 2)$ **23.** $X(-1, 4)$

Lesson 7-9

Pages 385–389

Solve each equation. Check your solution.

1. $x + 4 = 14$ **2.** $b + (-10) = 0$ **3.** $-2 + w = -5$ **4.** $k + (-3) = -5$
5. $6 = -4 + h$ **6.** $-7 + d = -3$ **7.** $9 = m + 11$ **8.** $f + (-9) = -19$
9. $p + 66 = 22$ **10.** $-34 + t = 41$ **11.** $-24 = e + 56$ **12.** $-29 + a = -54$
13. $17 + m = -33$ **14.** $b + (-44) = -34$ **15.** $w + (-39) = 55$ **16.** $6 + a = 13$
17. $-5 = m + 3$ **18.** $w + (-9) = 12$ **19.** $8 = p + 7$ **20.** $-4 + c = -9$
21. $y + 11 = 8$ **22.** $16 = t + 5$ **23.** $-3 + x = 1$ **24.** $14 + c = 6$
25. $-9 = -12 + w$ **26.** $q + 6 = 4$ **27.** $5 + z = 13$ **28.** $9 = h + -5$

Lesson 7-10

Pages 393–396

Solve each equation. Check your solution.

1. $y - 7 = 2$ **2.** $a - 10 = -22$ **3.** $g - 1 = 9$ **4.** $c - 8 = 5$
5. $z - 2 = 7$ **6.** $n - 1 = -87$ **7.** $j - 15 = -22$ **8.** $x - 12 = 45$
9. $y - 65 = -79$ **10.** $q - 16 = -31$ **11.** $q - 6 = 12$ **12.** $j - 18 = -34$
13. $k - 2 = -8$ **14.** $r - 76 = 41$ **15.** $n - 63 = -81$ **16.** $b - 7 = 4$
17. $-5 = g - 3$ **18.** $y - 2 = -6$ **19.** $8 = m - 3$ **20.** $x - 5 = 2$
21. $-6 = p - 8$ **22.** $h - 9 = -6$ **23.** $12 = w - 8$ **24.** $a - 6 = -1$
25. $-11 = t - 5$ **26.** $c - 4 = 8$ **27.** $18 = q - 7$ **28.** $r - 2 = -5$
29. $1 = z - 9$ **30.** $g - 10 = -4$ **31.** $-6 = d - 4$ **32.** $s - 4 = 10$

33. Find the value of c if $c - 5 = -2$.

34. Find the value of t if $4 = t - 7$.

Extra Practice

Lesson 7-11

Pages 398–401

Solve each equation. Use models if necessary.

1. $5x = 30$ **2.** $2w = 18$ **3.** $2a = 7$ **4.** $2d = -28$

5. $-3c = 6$ **6.** $11n = 77$ **7.** $3z = 15$ **8.** $9y = -63$

9. $6m = -54$ **10.** $5f = -75$ **11.** $20p = 5$ **12.** $4x = 16$

13. $4t = -24$ **14.** $7b = 21$ **15.** $19h = 0$ **16.** $22d = -66$

17. $3m = -78$ **18.** $8x = -2$ **19.** $9c = -72$ **20.** $5p = 35$

21. $-5k = 20$ **22.** $33y = 99$ **23.** $6z = -9$ **24.** $6m = -42$

25. $18 = 9x$ **26.** $-5p = 4$ **27.** $-32 = 4r$ **28.** $3w = 27$

29. $-12 = 16a$ **30.** $-4t = 6$ **31.** $16 = -5b$ **32.** $-2c = -13$

33. Solve the equation $3d = 21$.

34. What is the solution of the equation $-4x = 65$?

Lesson 8-1

Pages 413–418

Write each ratio as a fraction in simplest form.

1. 10 girls in a class of 25 students

2. 7 striped ties out of 21 ties

3. 12 golden retrievers out of 20 dogs

4. 8 red marbles in a jar of 32 marbles

5. 6 roses in a bouquet of 21 flowers

6. 21 convertibles out of 75 cars

Write each rate as a unit rate.

7. \$2 for 5 cans of tomato soup

8. \$200 for 40 hours of work

9. 540 parts produced in 18 hours

10. \$2.16 for one dozen cookies

11. 228 words typed in 6 minutes

12. 558 miles in 9 hours

Lesson 8-2

Pages 420–421

Use the *look for a pattern* strategy to solve Exercises 1–3.

1. **Geometry** Draw the next two figures in the pattern below.

2. Mandi is training to run a marathon. She begins by running 3 miles each day for the first week. If she increases her distance by 3 miles each week, how many weeks will it take her to reach 20 miles a day? Explain.

3. Describe the pattern below. Then find the next three numbers in the pattern.

3, 5, 8, 12, 17, 23, ■, ■, ■ . . .

Lesson 8-3

Pages 422–427

For Exercises 1–3, use the ratio tables given to solve each problem.

1. A principal needs 2 chaperones for every 25 students at the school dance. How many chaperones does he need if 225 students are expected to be at the dance?

Chaperones	2		■
Students	25		225

2. Nyoko is having a pizza party. If two large pizzas serve 9 people, how many pizzas should she order to serve 27 guests at the party?

Pizzas	2		■
Guests	9		27

3. Juan can swim 6 laps in 3 minutes. If he swims at the same constant rate, how long will it take him to swim 10 laps?

Laps	6			10
Minutes	3			■

4. A store is having a sale on CDs. Olivia buys 5 CDs and spends $40. If she decides to go back to the sale and buy 2 more CDs, how much will she pay?

Lesson 8-4

Pages 428–432

Determine if each pair of ratios or rates are equivalent. Explain your reasoning.

1. 8 out of 10 boys play a sport; 25 out of 30 boys play a sport
2. $16 for 2 tickets; $40 for 5 tickets
3. 3 teachers for 63 students; 7 teachers for 147 students
4. 15 minutes to read 9 pages; 50 minutes to read 30 pages
5. Lusita earned $85 for 8 hours of baby-sitting. Abigail earned $125 for 11 hours of baby-sitting. Are their earnings equivalent? Explain your reasoning.
6. Miss Ferguson recorded 17 absences in her class during the first 30 days of school. During the last 60 days of school, she recorded 42 absences. Are these attendance rates equivalent? Explain your reasoning.

Lesson 8-5

Pages 434–435

Use any strategy to solve.

1. What is the sum of the first two odd whole numbers (1 and 3)? The first three? The first four? The first forty? The first hundred?
2. Roberto is the first person in the lunch line. Tim is three places in front of Nina and one place behind Roberto. Six places behind Tim is Xavier. In what place in line is Xavier?
3. Kendra baby-sits for her cousin during summer vacation. Her cousin pays her $5 per hour and she works 30 hours per week. How much will Kendra earn during her 9-week summer vacation?

Lesson 8-6

Pages 436–441

Solve.

1. $\frac{15}{21} = \frac{5}{b}$
2. $\frac{22}{25} = \frac{n}{100}$
3. $\frac{24}{48} = \frac{h}{96}$
4. $\frac{9}{27} = \frac{y}{81}$
5. $\frac{4}{7} = \frac{16}{x}$
6. $\frac{4}{6} = \frac{a}{24}$
7. $\frac{6}{14} = \frac{18}{m}$
8. $\frac{3}{7} = \frac{21}{d}$
9. $\frac{4}{10} = \frac{8}{e}$
10. $\frac{9}{10} = \frac{27}{f}$
11. $\frac{a}{3} = \frac{16}{24}$
12. $\frac{5}{9} = \frac{35}{w}$
13. A class survey showed that 8 out of 25 students had plans to travel over spring break. How many students out of the 400 students in the entire school would you expect to be traveling over spring break?

Lesson 8-7

Pages 442–447

Use words and symbols to describe the value of each term as a function of its position. Then find the value of the eleventh term in the sequence.

1.

Position	5	6	7	8	n
Value of Term	15	18	21	24	■

2.

Position	3	4	5	6	n
Value of Term	10	11	12	13	■

3. **Measurement** There are 16 cups in 1 gallon. Make a table and write an algebraic expression relating the number of cups to the number of gallons. Then find the number of cups in 4 gallons.

Lesson 8-8

Pages 450–454

Write an equation to represent the function displayed in each table.

1.

Input, x	0	1	2	3	4
Output, y	0	9	18	27	36

2.

Input, x	1	2	3	4	5
Output, y	2	4	6	8	10

3.

Input, x	4	8	12	16	20
Output, y	1	2	3	4	5

4.

Input, x	6	12	18	24	30
Output, y	1	2	3	4	5

Use the following information for Exercises 5–6.

The average person uses about 12 gallons of water each day for showering.

5. Make a table to show the relationship between the number of gallons g a person uses for showering in days d. Graph the results on a coordinate grid.
6. Write an equation to find g, the number of gallons of water a person uses for showering in d days. How many gallons of water does a person use for showering each week?

Lesson 9-1

Pages 466–470

Write each percent as a fraction or mixed number in simplest form.

1. 13% **2.** 25% **3.** 8% **4.** 105%

5. 60% **6.** 70% **7.** 80% **8.** 45%

Write each fraction or mixed number as a percent.

9. $\frac{77}{100}$ **10.** $\frac{3}{4}$ **11.** $\frac{17}{20}$ **12.** $\frac{3}{25}$

13. $3\frac{3}{10}$ **14.** $\frac{27}{50}$ **15.** $\frac{2}{5}$ **16.** $\frac{3}{50}$

Lesson 9-2

Pages 471–476

1. The table below shows the activities students choose most often as the first thing they do when they get home from school. Sketch a circle graph to display the data.

After-School Activities	
Watch TV	42%
Play video games	20%
Play a sport	8%
Talk on the phone	5%
Have a snack	25%

For Exercises 2–4, use the graph at the right.

2. In which age group are the most Americans?

3. Which age group makes up the smallest portion of the U.S. population?

4. Which two age groups make up exactly half of the total U.S. population?

U.S. Population by Age, 2000

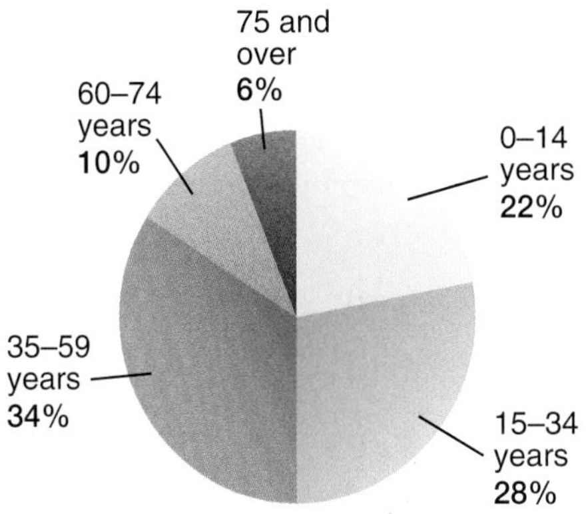

Source: The World Almanac

Lesson 9-3

Pages 477–480

Write each percent as a decimal.

1. 5% **2.** 22% **3.** 50% **4.** 420%

5. 75% **6.** 1% **7.** 100% **8.** 37%

Write each decimal as a percent.

9. 0.02 **10.** 0.2 **11.** 0.04 **12.** 1.02

13. 0.66 **14.** 0.11 **15.** 0.35 **16.** 0.31

Lesson 9-4

Pages 482–483

Use the *solve a simpler problem* strategy to solve Exercises 1–4.

1. Tyler has $70 to spend on clothes. He has chosen 4 items that cost $16.50, $12.99, $24.99, and $19.99. Does he have enough money to buy all four items?
2. Grace wants to tip her hair stylist 20% on a $31 cut and style. About how much money should she tip?
3. A total of 250 students ate lunch in the cafeteria on Friday. Of those students, 80% bought pizza. How many students bought pizza on Friday?
4. The heart rate of a hummingbird is about 1,258 beats per minute. About how many times does a hummingbird's heart beat per second?

Lesson 9-5

Pages 484–488

Estimate each percent.

1. 38% of 150
2. 20% of 75
3. 25% of 70
4. 10% of 90
5. 16% of 30
6. 39% of 40
7. 6% of 86
8. 9% of 29
9. 3% of 46
10. 89% of 47
11. 25% of 48
12. 5% of 420
13. 55% of 134
14. 28% of 4
15. 14% of 40
16. 14% of 14
17. 90% of 140
18. 40% of 45

Lesson 9-6

Pages 492–495

Find the percent of each number.

1. 11% of 48
2. 19% of 50
3. 29% of 500
4. 41% of 50
5. 32% of 300
6. 411% of 50
7. 149% of 60
8. 4% of 50
9. 62% of 200
10. 58% of 100
11. 52% of 400
12. 68% of 30
13. 9% of 25
14. 48% of 1,000
15. 98% of 725
16. 25% of 80
17. 40% of 75
18. 75% of 160
19. 10% of 250
20. 250% of 50
21. 5% of 120
22. Mateo wants to buy new skis. He finds a pair of skis that usually sell for $380. The skis are on sale for 20% off. Find the amount Mateo will save if he buys the skis during this sale.
23. Attendance at a university's baseball games during the 2008 season was 145% of the attendance during the 2007 season. If the total attendance during the 2007 season was 700, find the total attendance during the 2008 season.

Lesson 9-7

Pages 496–497

Use any strategy to solve.

1. School begins at 8:15 A.M. It takes 35 minutes to walk from home. What time should you leave for school?
2. Three workers can make three sails in three days. How many sails can six workers make in twelve days?
3. A number is multiplied by 4. Next, 6 is added to the product. Then, 4 is subtracted from the sum. If the result is 14, what is the number?
4. The total bill at a restaurant for a family of 4 is $48.25. They want to leave a 20% tip. They decide to leave $7.00. Is this estimate reasonable? Explain your reasoning.

Lesson 9-8

Pages 498–503

A set of 30 tickets are placed in a bag. There are 6 baseball tickets, 4 hockey tickets, 4 basketball tickets, 2 football tickets, 3 symphony tickets, 2 opera tickets, 4 ballet tickets, and 5 theater tickets. One ticket is selected without looking. Find each probability. Write each answer as a fraction.

1. *P*(basketball)
2. *P*(sports event)
3. *P*(opera or ballet)
4. *P*(soccer)
5. *P*(*not* symphony)
6. *P*(theater)
7. *P*(basketball or hockey)
8. *P*(*not* a sports event)
9. *P*(*not* opera)

Lesson 9-9

Pages 505–509

For Exercises 1–3, draw a tree diagram to show the sample space for each situation. Tell how many outcomes are possible.

1. tossing a quarter and rolling a number cube
2. a choice of a red, blue, or green sweater with a white, black, or tan skirt
3. a choice of a chicken, ham, turkey, or bologna sandwich with coffee, milk, juice, or soda
4. How many ways can a person choose to watch two television shows from four television shows?

For Exercises 5–7, a coin is tossed three times.

5. How many outcomes are possible?
6. What is *P*(two heads)?
7. What is *P*(*no* heads)?

Lesson 9-10

Pages 512–516

For Exercises 1 and 2, use the following information.
In basketball, Daniel made 12 of his last 18 shots.

1. Find the probability of Daniel making a shot on his next attempt.
2. Suppose Daniel takes 30 shots during his next game. About how many of the shots will he make?

For Exercises 3–6, use the table to predict the number of students out of 1,500 that would be most likely to purchase each type of school apparel.

3. T-Shirt
4. hat
5. jacket
6. denim shirt

School Apparel Most Likely to Purchase

Apparel	Students
Hat	20
T-Shirt	37
Sweatshirt	25
Jacket	12
Denim Shirt	6

Lesson 10-1

Pages 529–532

Use a protractor to find the measure of each angle. Then classify the angle as *acute, obtuse, right,* or *straight.*

1.

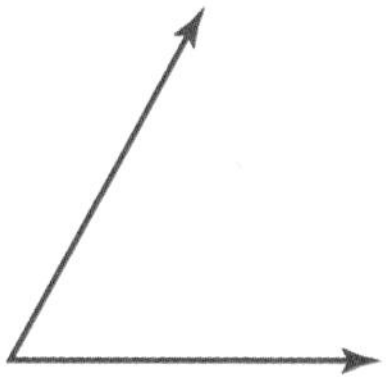

2.

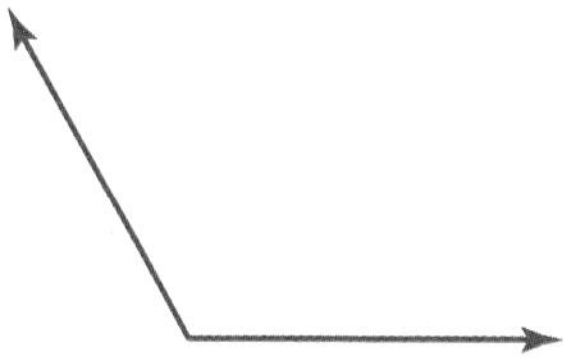

3.

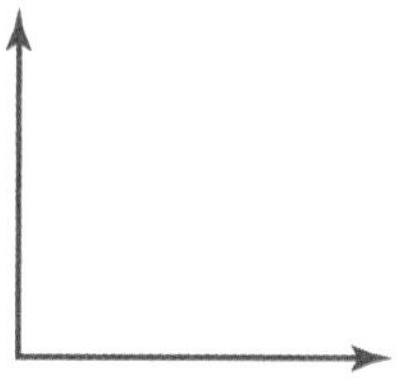

4.

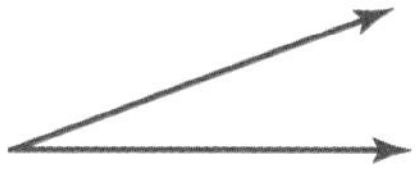

5.

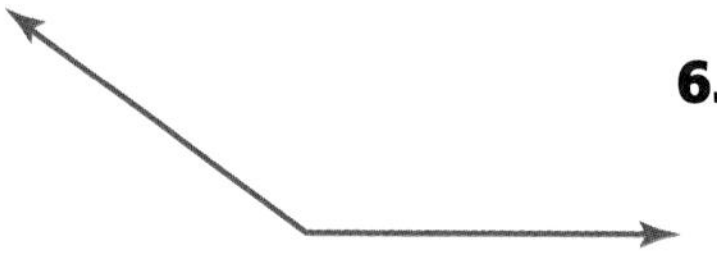

6.

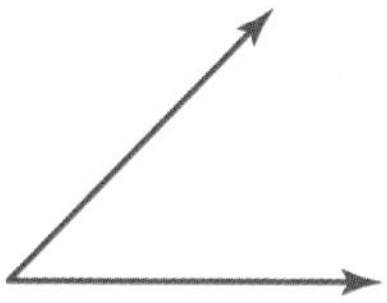

Lesson 10-2

Pages 534–535

Solve Exercises 1–3. Use the *draw a diagram* strategy.

1. Twenty-four cheerleaders are working on a new dance routine. The routine requires groups arranged in triangular formations with each triangle having 3 people in the last row. If all 24 cheerleaders must participate, how many triangles are there?
2. Lucy's mom is making personal size pizzas for a party. Each pizza is 5 inches square. How many pizzas will fit on a baking sheet that is 14 inches by 20 inches if the pizzas are placed 1 inch apart?
3. Jared is designing a flag that is 2 feet wide by 4 feet long. He wants the entire flag to be a checkerboard pattern of squares. If he uses 6 rows and 12 columns to create the checkerboard, what will be the side length of each square?

Lesson 10-3

Pages 536–540

Estimate the measure of each angle.

1. 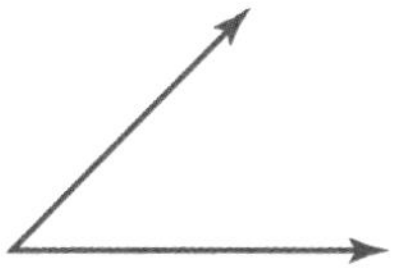

2. 

3. 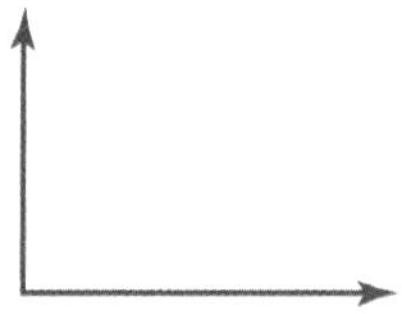

4. 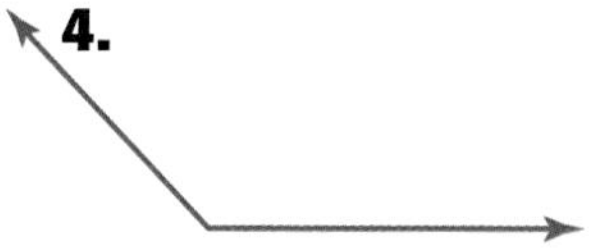

Use a protractor and a straightedge to draw angles having the following measurements.

5. 165°	**6.** 20°	**7.** 90°	**8.** 41°
9. 75°	**10.** 180°	**11.** 30°	**12.** 120°
13. 15°	**14.** 55°	**15.** 100°	**16.** 145°

Lesson 10-4

Pages 541–544

Find the value of *x* in each figure.

1. 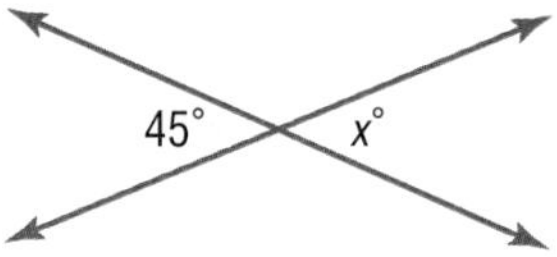

2. 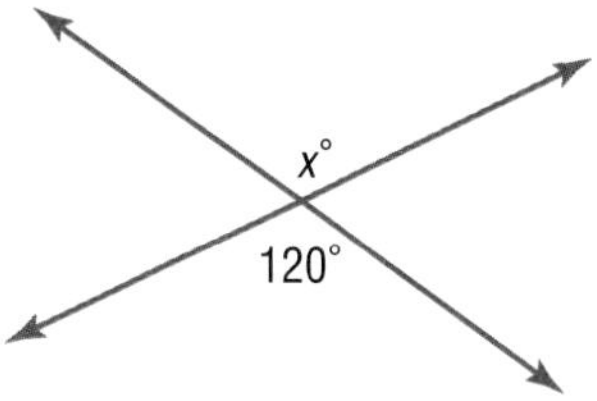

3. 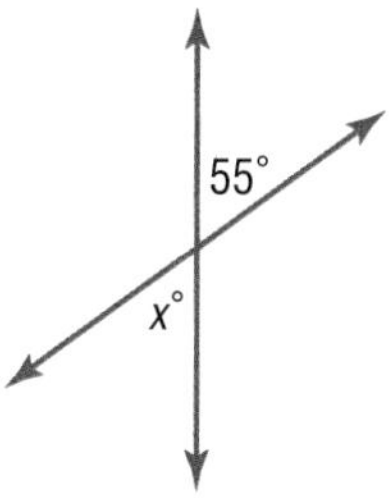

4. **Geometry** Are the lines marked on the trapezoid best described as *parallel, perpendicular,* or *neither*? Explain your reasoning.

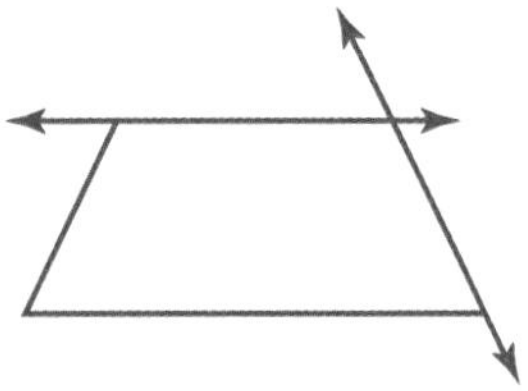

Lesson 10-5

Pages 548–549

Use any strategy to solve.

1. For a bake sale, the students had 144 cookies to sell. By 4:00 P.M., they had sold 36 cookies. By 5:00 P.M., they had sold 72 cookies. At this rate, at what time will they have sold all their cookies?
2. Pedro found $3.00 in change while cleaning his dad's car. He found the same number of quarters and dimes and half as many nickels as quarters. How many of each coin did he find?
3. Mr. Wilson says that $\frac{1}{3}$ of his class has arrived for the day. If 8 students have arrived, how many students are in his class?
4. Corey has eaten $\frac{2}{5}$ of the pizza. If he has eaten 4 pieces, how many pieces were originally in the pizza?

Extra Practice

Lesson 10-6

Pages 551–556

Classify each triangle drawn or having the given angle measures as *acute, right,* or *obtuse*.

1.

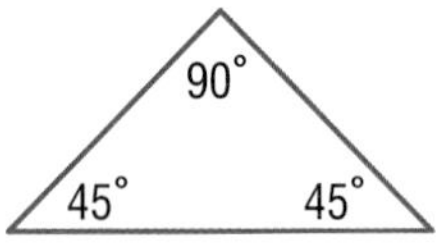

2.

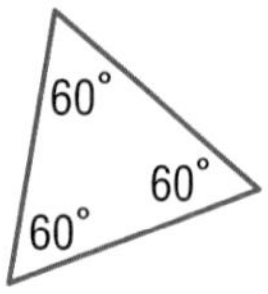

3.

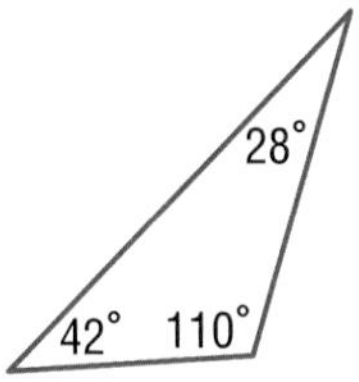

Find the value of *x* in each triangle having the given angle measures.

4.

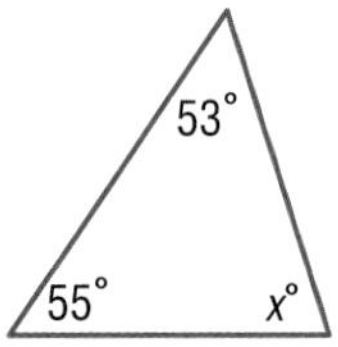

5.

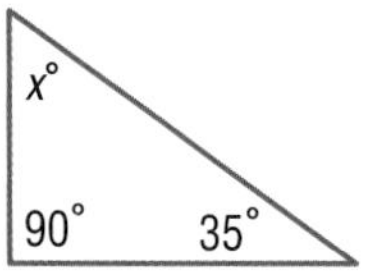

6.

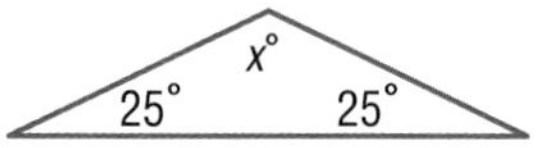

Lesson 10-7

Pages 558–563

Find the value of *x* in each quadrilateral.

1.

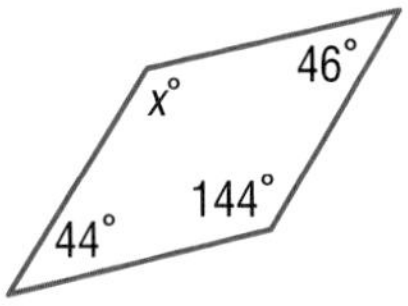

2.

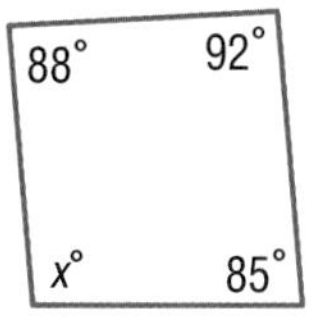

3.

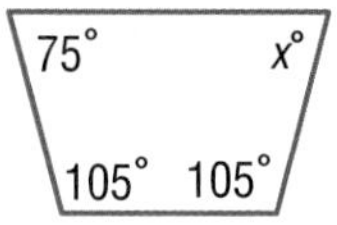

Classify each quadrilateral.

4.

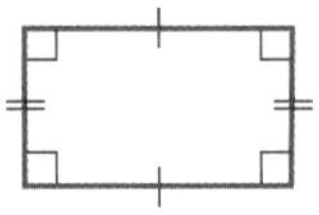

5.

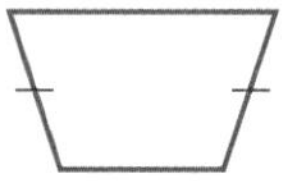

6.

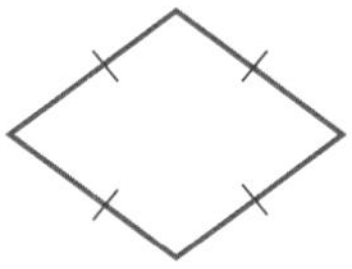

Lesson 10-8

Pages 566–570

1. Draw a top, a side, and a front view of the prism shown.

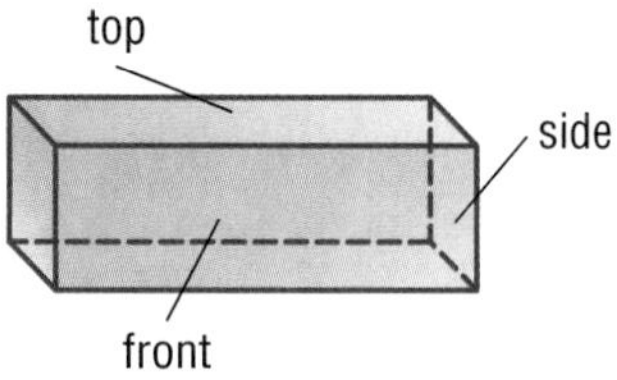

Draw the three-dimensional figure whose top, side, and front views are shown. Use isometric dot paper.

2.

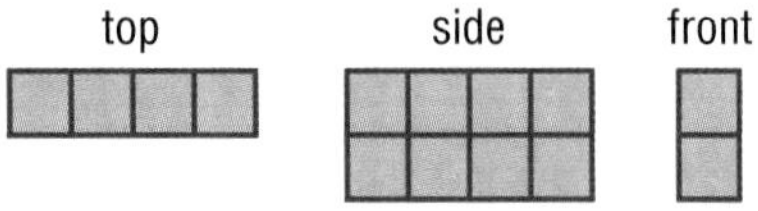

3.

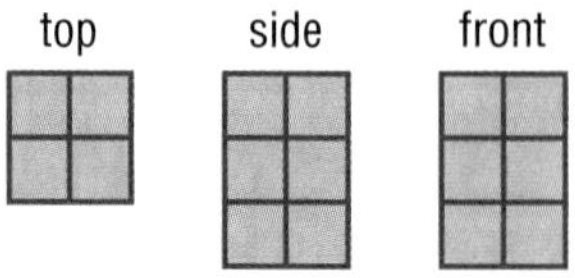

4. Two boxes of pasta are shown. Draw a top, a side, and a front view of the boxes.

Lesson 11-1

Pages 585–589

Find the perimeter of each figure.

1.

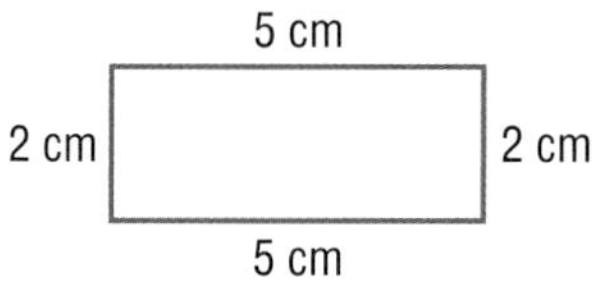

2.

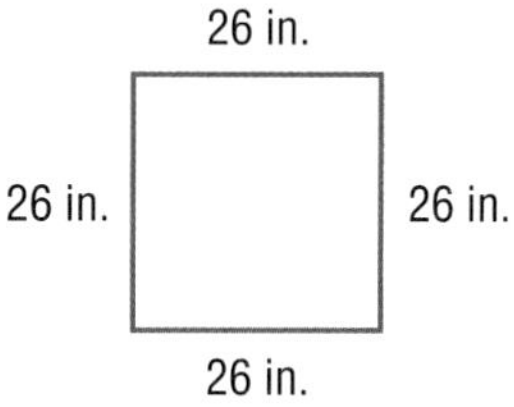

3.

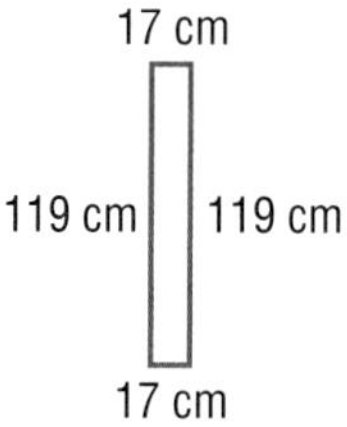

4.

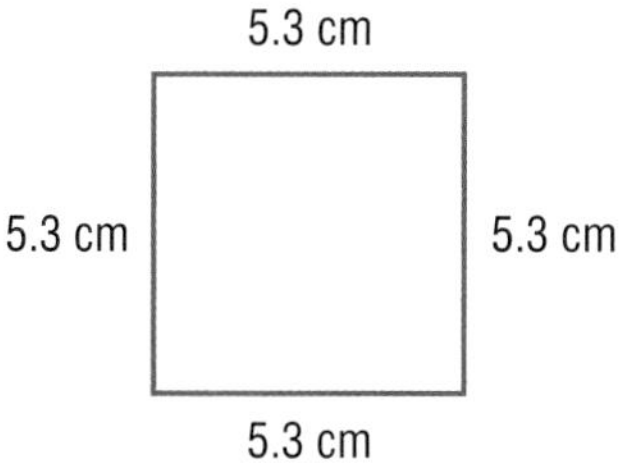

5.

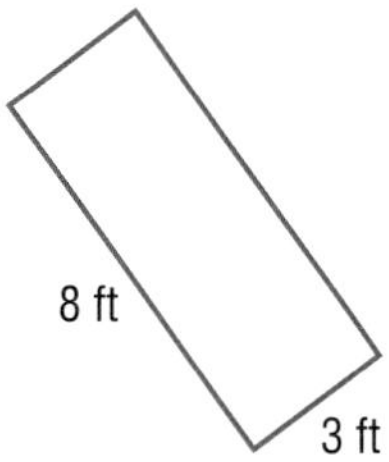

6.

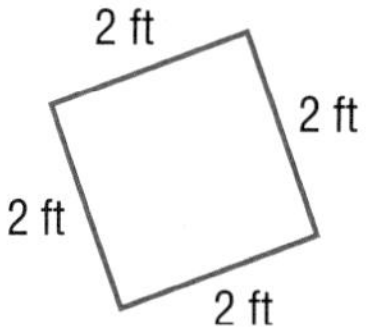

Lesson 11-2

Pages 591–595

Find the area of each parallelogram.

1.

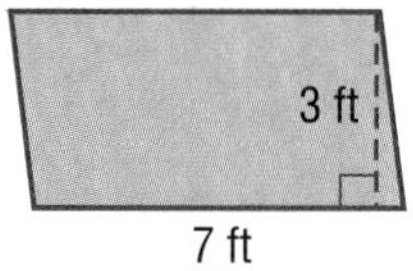

2.

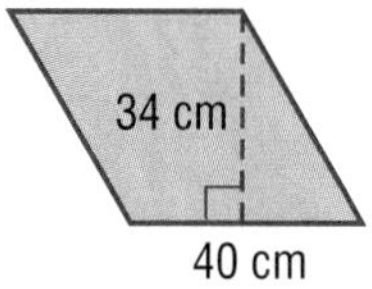

3.

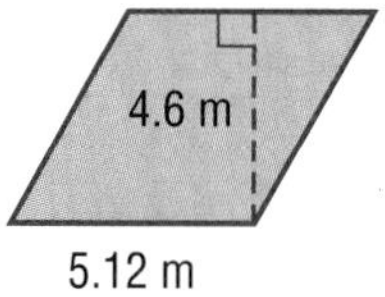

4.

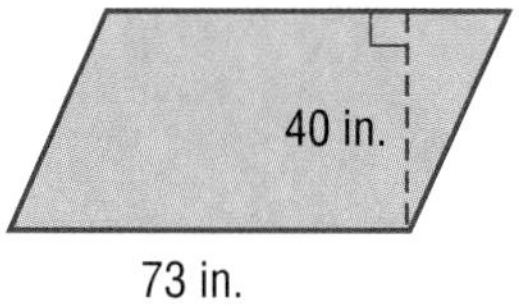

5.

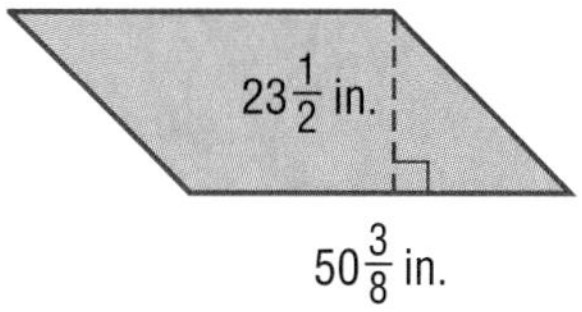

6.

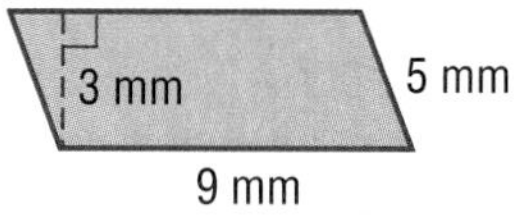

Lesson 11-3

Pages 596–597

Solve Exercises 1–4. Use the *make a model* strategy.

1. A teacher is displaying 24 paintings on the wall to form a collage. Each painting is the same size and shape. If she arranges them in a rectangular shape with the least perimeter possible, how many paintings will be in each row?
2. Latanya has 28 blocks. She wants to use them all to build a pyramid by stacking the blocks in single rows on top of each other. How many rows will there be in the pyramid?
3. A librarian is organizing a seasonal display of books using 4 shelves and 36 books. If each shelf has 2 more books than the previous one, how many books are on each shelf?
4. Mario is planting rows of tulip bulbs in a triangular shape in the center of a flower bed. How many bulbs will he need to buy if the last row has 10 bulbs and each row has 1 more bulb than the row in front of it?

Lesson 11-4

Pages 599–603

Find the area of each triangle.

1.

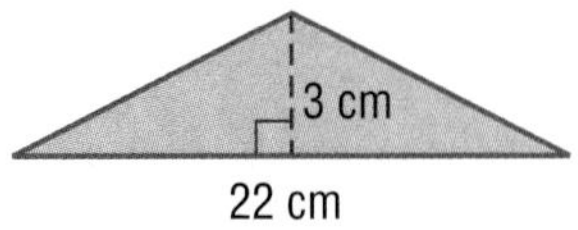

2.

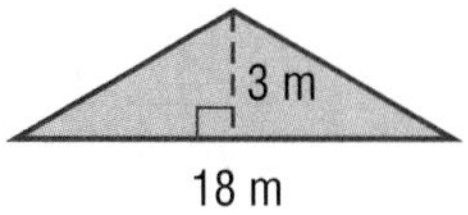

3.

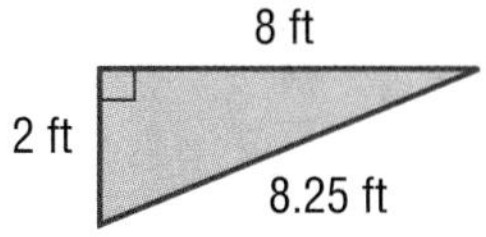

4.

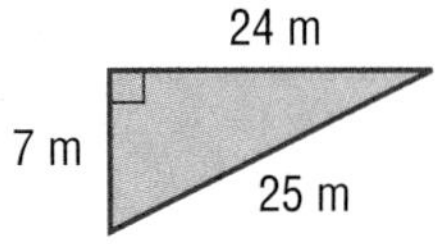

5.

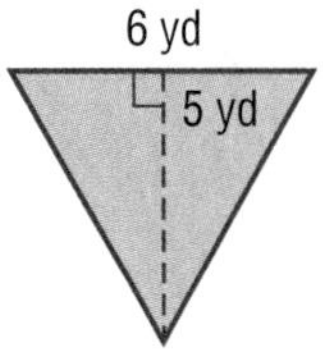

6.

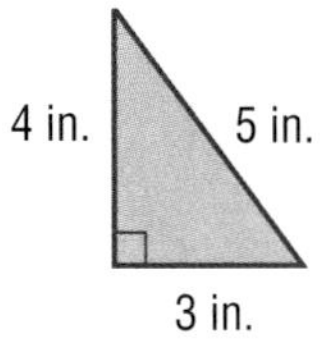

7.

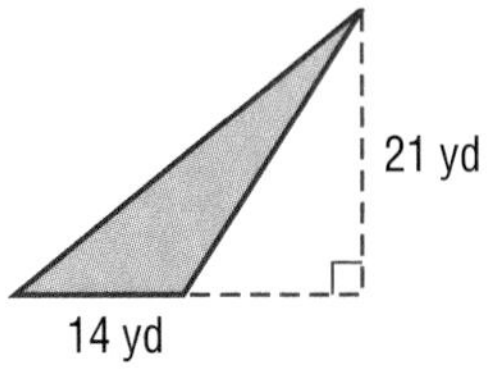

8.

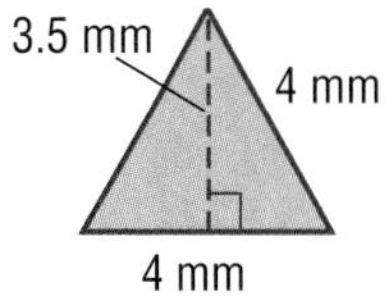

9.

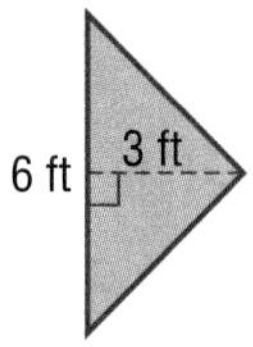

10. base, 4.5 in.
height, 7 in.

11. base, 9 m
height, 7 m

12. base, $13\frac{1}{4}$ cm
height, 16 cm

Lesson 11-5

Pages 606–607

Use any strategy to solve.

1. Mr. Campos is serving a baked ham at 5:00 P.M. The 7-pound ham has to cook for 30 minutes for every pound and then an additional 30 minutes for glazing. What is the latest time he can start baking?
2. Gabriel has a photo that measures 5 inches by 7 inches. If the frame he uses is $\frac{3}{4}$ inches wide, what is the perimeter of the framed picture?
3. A farmer has 6 animals in his barn. Some are cows and some are chickens. When the farmer looks at the animals, he counts 20 legs. How many of each type of animal are there?
4. For a holiday party, strands of lights are hung from the chandelier in the center of a rectangular room to each corner of the room. A strand is also hung from the chandelier to the center of each wall. How many strands of lights are there in all?
5. Paulo's yearly salary is $44,000 and will increase $2,000 per year. Jordan's yearly salary is $34,000 and will increase $3,000 per year. In how many years will Paulo and Jordan have the same yearly salary?

Lesson 11-6

Pages 608–613

Find the volume of each prism.

1.
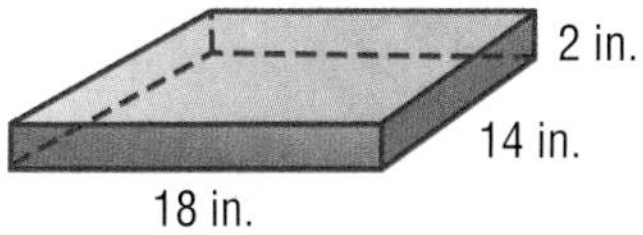

2.
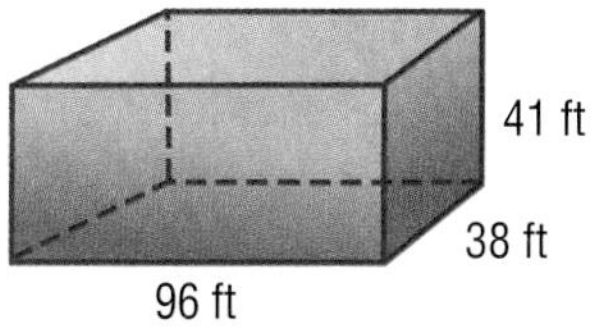

3.
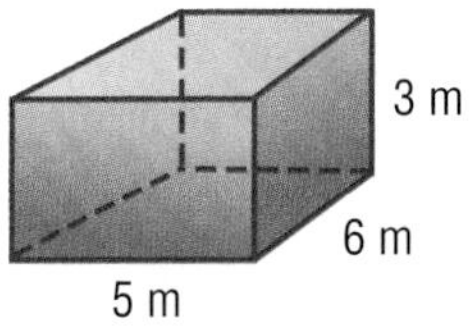

4.
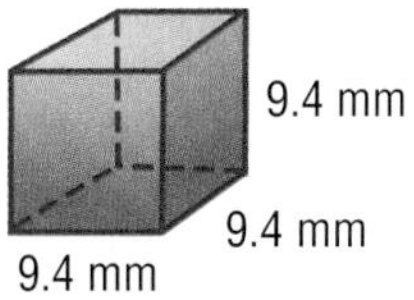

5.
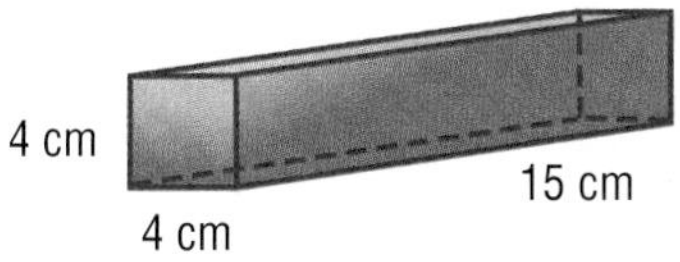

6.
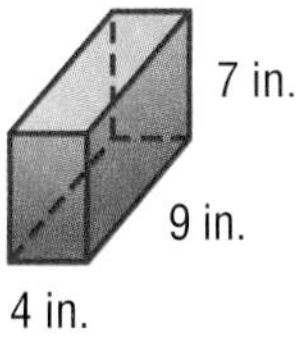

7. A package has a length of $9\frac{2}{3}$ inches, a width of $5\frac{1}{3}$ inches, and a height of 6 inches. Find the volume of the package if the height is increased by 3 inches.

Lesson 11-7

Pages 617–621

Find the surface area of each rectangular prism.

1.
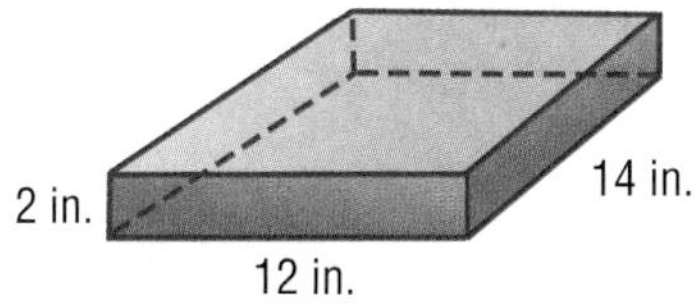

2.
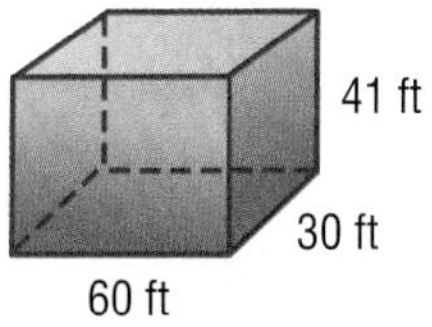

3.
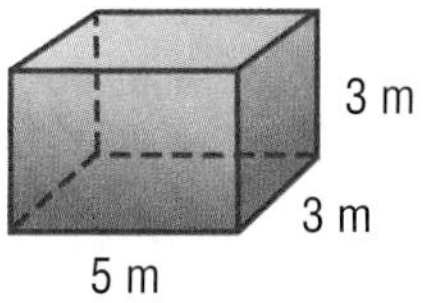

4.
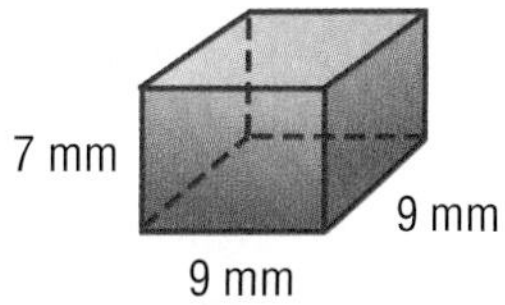

5.
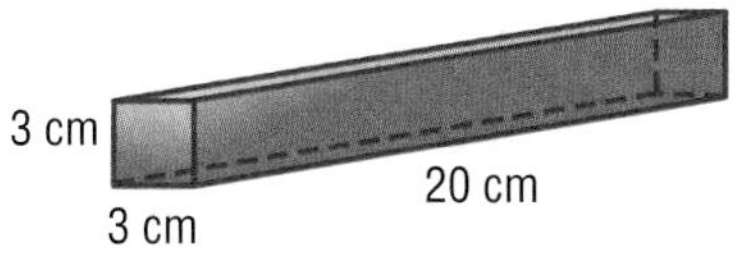

6.
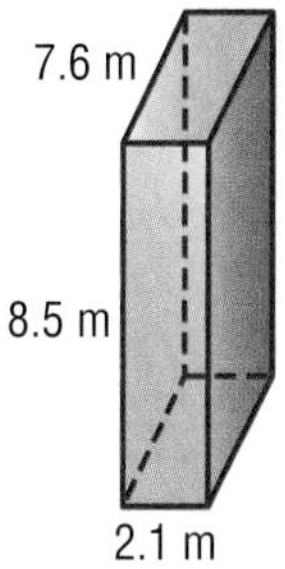

7. Armando is placing a gift inside a box that measures 20.4 centimeters by 16 centimeters by 20 centimeters. What is the surface area of the box?

Glossary/Glosario

Math Online A mathematics multilingual glossary is available at www.math.glencoe.com/multilingual_glossary. The glossary includes the following languages.

Arabic	Cantonese	Korean	Tagalog
Bengali	English	Russian	Urdu
Brazilian Portuguese	Haitian Creole	Spanish	Vietnamese
	Hmong		

Cómo usar el glosario en español:

1. Busca el término en inglés que desees encontrar.
2. El término en español, junto con la definición, se encuentran en la columna de la derecha.

English

A

acute angle (p. 530) An *angle* with a measure greater than 0° and less than 90°.

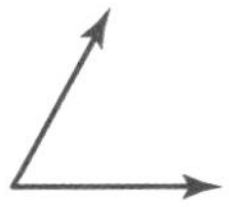

acute triangle (p. 551) A *triangle* with all three *angles* less than 90°.

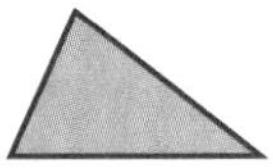

addition An operation on two or more *addends* that results in a *sum*.

$$9 + 3 = 12$$

Addition Property of Equality (p. 394) If you add the same number to each side of an equation, the two sides remain equal.

algebra (p. 34) A branch of mathematics that uses symbols, usually letters, to explore relationships between quantities.

algebraic expression (p. 34) A group of numbers, symbols, and variables that represent an operation or series of operations.

$$3x + 5 \text{ or } y + 5$$

angle (p. 529) Two rays with a common endpoint.

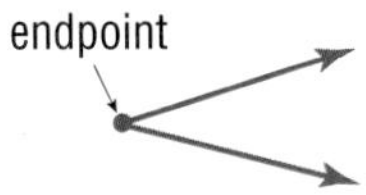

Español

ángulo agudo *Ángulo* que mide más de 0° y menos de 90°.

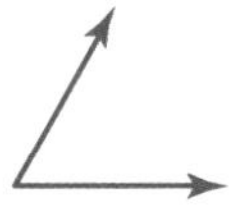

triángulo acutángulo *Triángulo* cuyos tres *ángulos* miden menos de 90°.

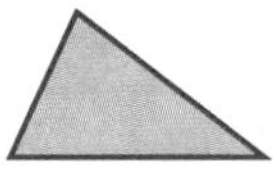

sumar (suma) Operación en dos o más *sumandos* que resulta en una *suma*.

$$9 + 3 = 12$$

propiedad de igualdad de la suma Si sumas el mismo número a ambos lados de la ecuación, los dos lados permanecen iguales.

álgebra Rama de las matemáticas que usa símbolos, generalmente letras para explorar relaciones entre cantidades.

expresión algebraica Grupo de números, símbolos y variables que representan una operación o una serie de operaciones.

$$3x + 5 \text{ o } y + 5$$

ángulo Dos rectas con un extremo común.

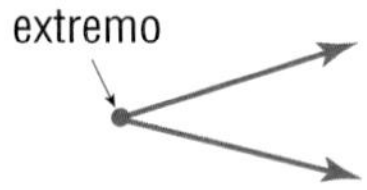

area (p. 52) The number of *square units* needed to cover the inside of a region or plane figure.

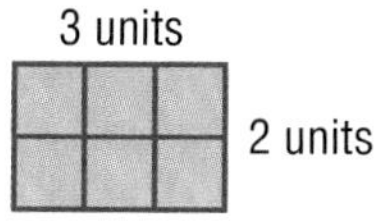

arithmetic sequence (p. 442) A sequence in which each term is found by adding the same number to the previous term.

average (p. 95) The number found by dividing the sum of a group of numbers by the number of addends, sometimes called the *mean*.

axis (p. 213) A horizontal or vertical number line on a graph. Plural is *axes*.

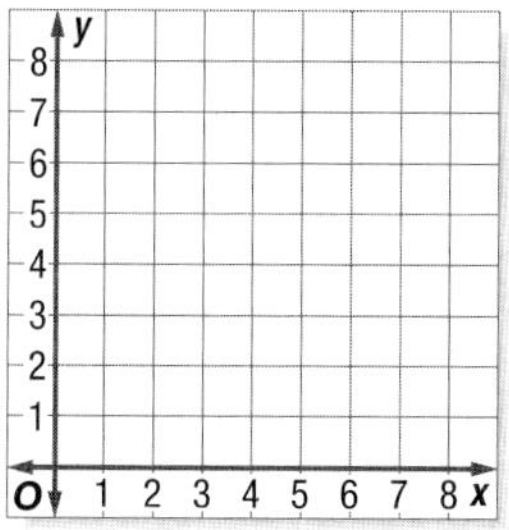

B

bar graph (p. 73) A graph that compares *data* by using bars of different lengths or heights to show the values.

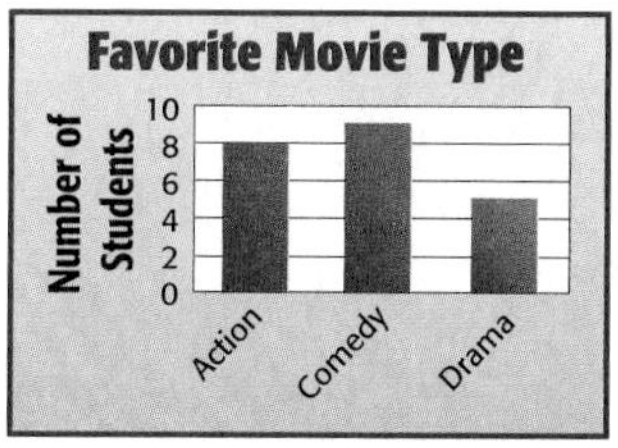

base (p. 592) The side of a plane figure that is used to find its height by drawing a line from the opposite angle.

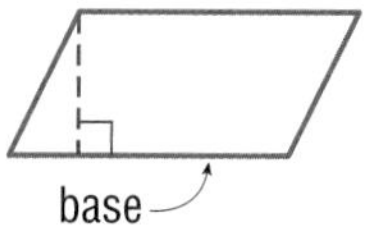

base of a power (p. 21) The number used as the factor.

In 2^5, 2 is the base.

área Número de *unidades cuadradas* necesarias para cubrir el interior de una región o figura plana.

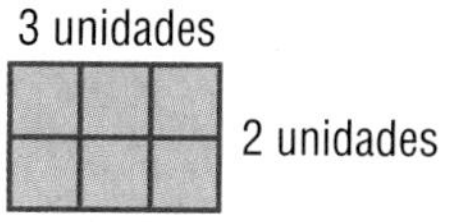

sucesión aritmética Sucesión en la cual cada término se calcula sumando el mismo número al término anterior.

promedio Número que se calcula dividiendo la suma de un grupo de números entre el número de sumandos, algunas veces llamado *media*.

eje Recta numérica horizontal o vertical en una gráfica.

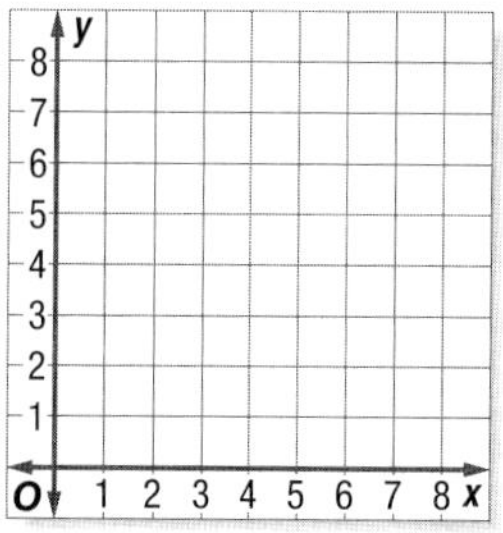

gráfica de barras Gráfica que compara datos usando barras de distintas longitudes o alturas para mostrar los valores.

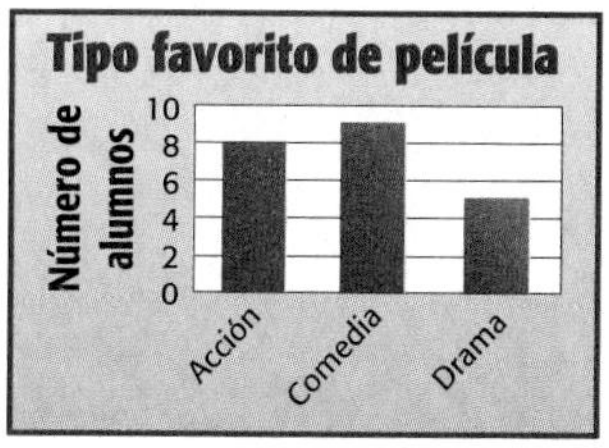

base Lado de una figura plana que se usa para calcular su altura trazando una recta desde el ángulo opuesto.

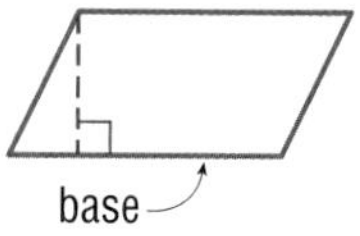

base de una potencia Número que se usa como factor.

En 2^5, 2 es la base.

benchmark (p. 645) A number used as a guide for making an *estimate*.

C

capacity (p. 636) The amount a container can hold, measured in units of dry or liquid measure.

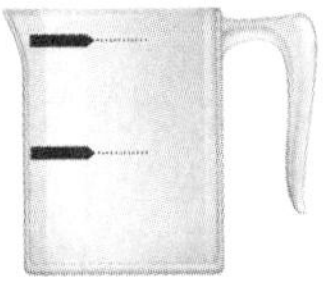

centimeter (cm) (p. 640) A *metric unit* for measuring *length* and *height*.

100 centimeters = 1 meter

circle (p. 488) A *closed figure* in which all points are the same distance from a fixed point, called the *center*.

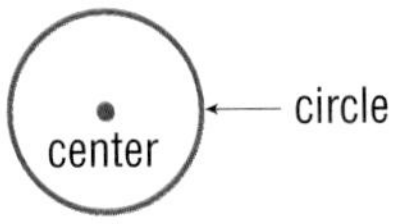

circle graph (p. 471) A graph in the shape of a circle in which *data* are represented by parts of a *circle*.

Books Americans Buy

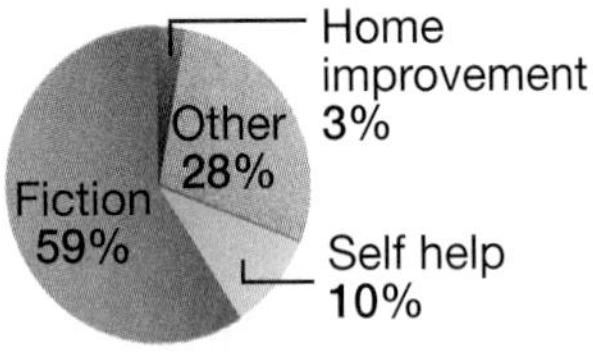

Source: *USA TODAY*

circumference (p. 590) The distance, also known as the length, around a *circle*.

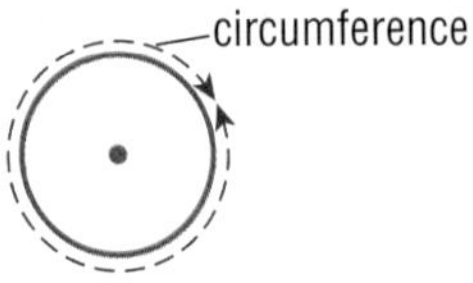

clustering (p. 150) An estimation method in which a group of numbers close in value are rounded to the same number.

coefficient (p. 398) The numerical factor of a term that contains a variable.

punto de referencia Número que se usa como guía para hacer una *estimación*.

capacidad Cantidad que puede contener un envase, medida en unidades de volumen.

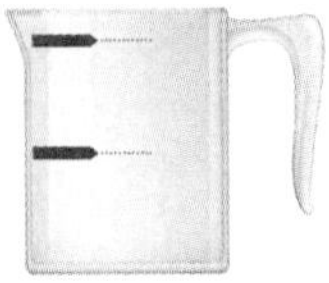

centímetro (cm) *Unidad métrica* de *longitud* y *altura*.

100 centímetros = 1 metro

círculo *Figura cerrada* en la cual todos los puntos están a la misma distancia de un punto fijo llamado el *centro*.

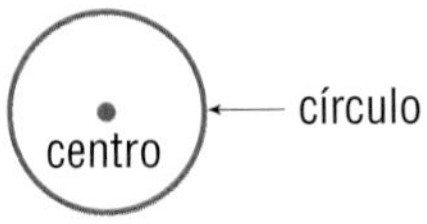

gráfica circular Gráfica con forma de círculo en que los *datos* se representan mediante partes de un *círculo*.

Libros que compran los estadounidenses

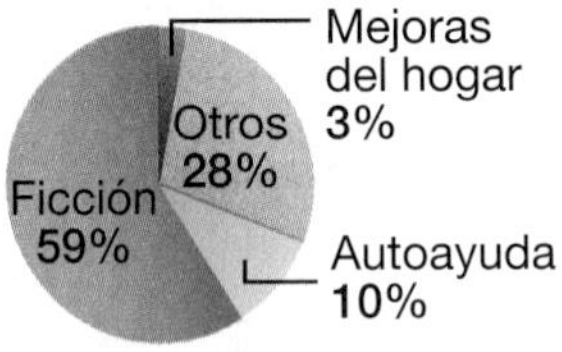

Fuente: *USA TODAY*

circunferencia La distancia alrededor de un *círculo*, también conocida como su longitud.

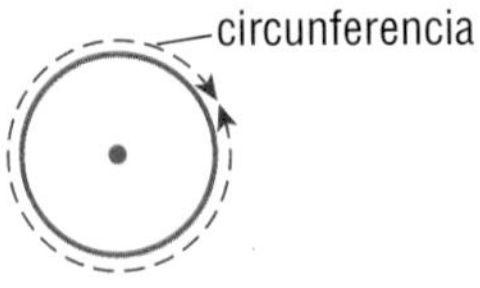

agrupar Método de estimación en el cual se redondea a un mismo número un grupo de números cercanos a un valor.

coeficiente Un factor numérico de un término que contiene una variable.

common denominator (p. 241) The same *denominator* (bottom number) used in two or more *fractions*. In $\frac{1}{4}$ and $\frac{3}{4}$, 4 is the common denominator.

common factor (p. 175) A same *whole number* that is a *factor* of two or more numbers.

3 is a common factor of 6 and 12.

common multiple (p. 194) A same *whole number* that is a *multiple* of two or more numbers.

24 is a common multiple of 6 and 4.

compatible numbers (p. 310) Numbers in a problem or related numbers that are easy to work with mentally.

720 and 90 are compatible numbers for division because $72 \div 9 = 8$.

complementary events (p. 500) Two events in which either one or the other must take place, but they cannot both happen at the same time. The sum of their probabilities is 1.

composite number (p. 17) A whole number that has more than two factors.

12 has the factors 1, 2, 3, 4, 6, and 12.

congruent angles (p. 542) Angles with the same measure.

congruent segments (p. 553) Line segments that have the same length.

coordinate (p. 213) One of two numbers in an *ordered pair*.

The 1 is the number on the *x*-axis, the 5 is on the *y*-axis. A coordinate can be positive or negative.

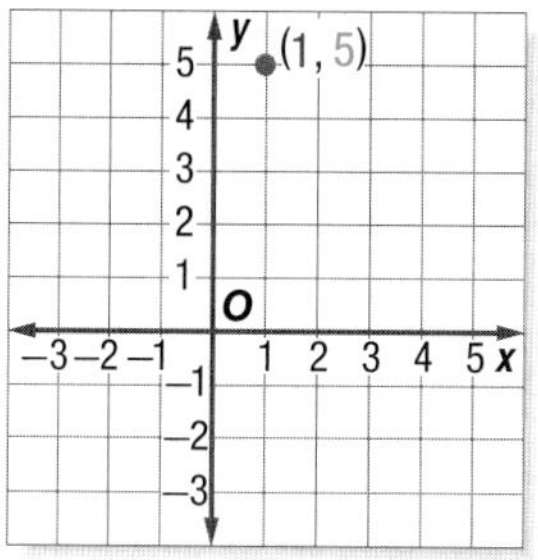

denominador común El mismo *denominador* (número inferior) que se usa en dos o más *fracciones*. En $\frac{1}{4}$ y $\frac{3}{4}$, 4 es el denominador común.

factor común Un mismo *número entero factor* de dos o más números.

3 es factor común de 6 y de 12.

múltiplo común *Número entero múltiplo* de dos o más números.

24 es un múltiplo común de 6 y 4.

números compatibles Números en un problema o números relacionados con los cuales es fácil trabajar mentalmente.

720 y 90 son números compatibles en la división porque $72 \div 9 = 8$.

eventos complementarios Dos eventos en que uno de ellos debe suceder, pero no los dos al mismo tiempo. La suma de sus probabilidades es 1.

número compuesto Número entero que tiene más de dos factores.

12 tiene a los factores 1, 2, 3, 4, 6 y 12.

ángulos congruentes Ángulos con la misma medida.

segmentos congruentes Segmentos de recta que tienen la misma medida.

coordenada Uno de los dos números de un *par ordenado*.

El 1 es el número en el eje *x* y el 5 está en el eje *y*. Una coordenada puede ser positiva o negativa.

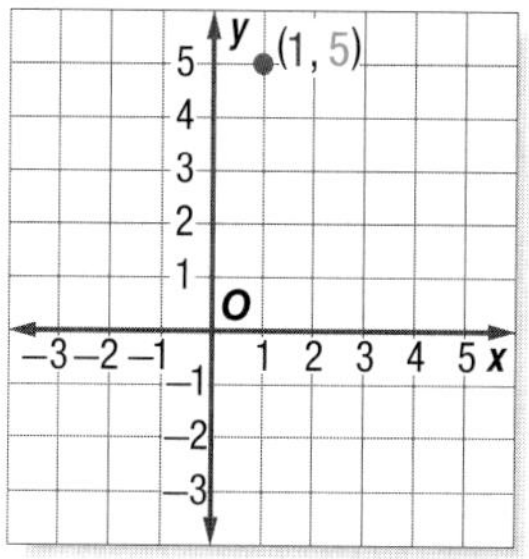

coordinate plane (p. 213) A plane in which a horizontal and a vertical number line intersect at a right angle at the point where each line is zero.

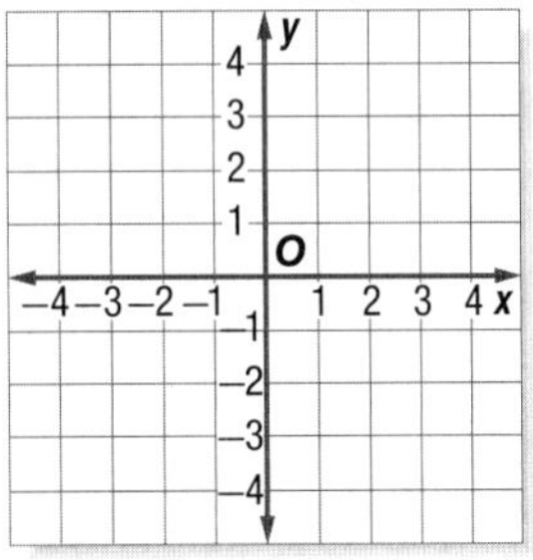

counterexample (p. 178) An example that disproves a statement.

cube (p. 24) A rectangular *prism* with six faces that are congruent squares.

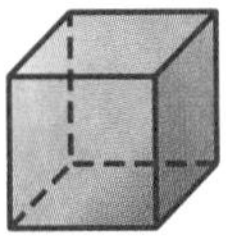

cubed (p. 22) The product in which a number is a factor three times. Two cubed is 8 because 2 × 2 × 2 = 8.

cubic unit (p. 608) A unit for measuring *volume*, such as a cubic inch or a cubic centimeter.

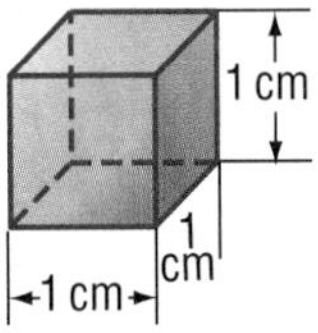

cup (p. 636) A *customary unit* of *capacity* equal to 8 fluid ounces.

customary system (p. 632) The measurement system that includes units such as foot, pound, quart, and degrees Fahrenheit. Also called *standard measurement.*

D

data (p. 73) Numbers of symbols, sometimes collected from a *survey* or experiment, to show information. *Data* is plural. *Datum* is singular.

decimal number (p. 131) A number with one or more digits to the right of the decimal point, such as 8.37 or 0.05.

plano de coordenadas Plano en que una recta numérica horizontal y vertical se intersecan en ángulo recto en el punto donde cada recta es cero.

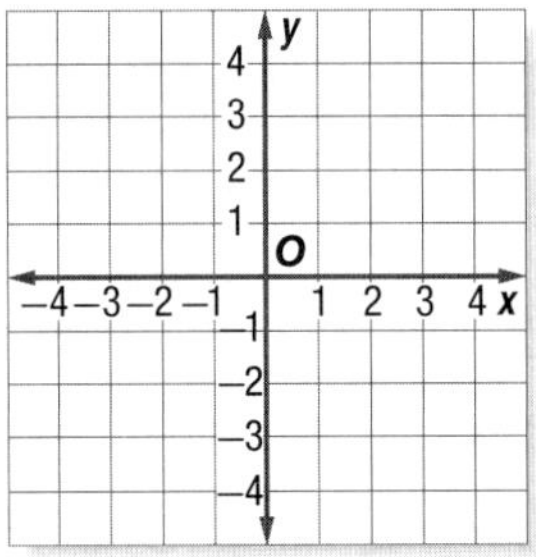

contraejemplo Ejemplo que refuta un enunciado.

cubo *Prisma* rectangular con seis caras que son cuadrados congruentes.

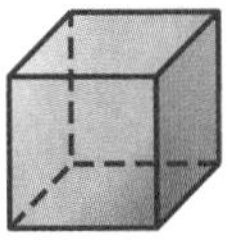

elevado al cubo Producto en el cual un número es factor tres veces. Dos elevado al cubo es 8 porque 2 × 2 × 2 = 8.

unidad cúbica Unidad de *volumen*, como una pulgada cúbica o un centímetro cúbico.

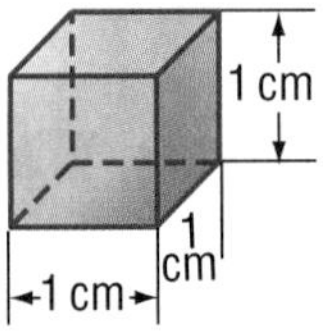

taza *Unidad inglesa* de *capacidad* igual a 8 onzas líquidas.

sistema inglés Sistema de medición que incluye unidades tales como el pie, la libra, el cuarto y los grados Fahrenheit. También llamado *medición estándar*.

datos Números o símbolos que muestran información, a veces reunidos por una encuesta o un experimento.

número decimal Número con uno o más dígitos a la derecha del punto decimal, como 8.37 ó 0.05.

decimal point (p. 131) A period separating the ones and the *tenths* in a decimal number.

0.8

defining the variable (p. 40) Choosing a variable to represent the input when writing a function rule.

degree (°) (p. 529) A unit of measure for temperature. Also, a unit for measuring *angles*.

$1° = \frac{1}{360}$ of a circle

denominator The bottom number in a *fraction*.

In $\frac{5}{6}$, 6 is the denominator.

diameter (p. 590) A *chord* that passes through the *center* of the circle.

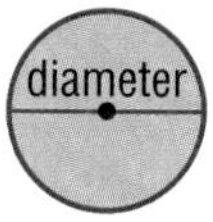

digit A symbol used to write numbers. The ten digits are 0, 1, 2, 3, 4, 5, 6, 7, 8, and 9.

Distributive Property of Multiplication (p. 58) To multiply a *sum* by a number, you can multiply each *addend* by the same number and add the *products*.

$8 \times (9 + 5) = (8 \times 9) + (8 \times 5)$

divide (division) An operation on two numbers in which the first number is split into the same number of equal groups as the second number.

12 ÷ 3 means 12 is divided into 3 equal size groups

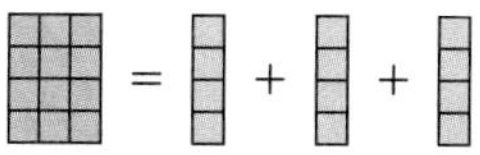

dividend A number that is being divided.

$3\overline{)429}$ 429 is the dividend

divisible Describes a number that can be divided into equal parts and has no remainder.

39 is divisible by 3 with no remainder.

punto decimal Punto que separa las unidades y las *décimas* en un número decimal.

0.8

definir la variable Elegir una variable para representar el valor de entrada al escribir una regla de funciones.

grado (°) Unidad de temperatura. También, unidad para medir *ángulos*.

$1° = \frac{1}{360}$ de un círculo

denominador El número inferior en una *fracción*.

En $\frac{5}{6}$, 6 es el denominador.

diámetro *Cuerda* que pasa por el *centro* de un *círculo*.

dígito Símbolo que se usa para escribir números. Los diez dígitos son 0, 1, 2, 3, 4, 5, 6, 7, 8 y 9.

propiedad distributiva de la multiplicación Para multiplicar una *suma* por un número, puedes multiplicar cada *sumando* por el mismo número y sumar los *productos*.

$8 \times (9 + 5) = (8 \times 9) + (8 \times 5)$

dividir (división) Operación en dos números en que el primer número se separa en tantos grupos iguales como indica el segundo número.

12 ÷ 3 significa que 12 se divide en 3 grupos de igual tamaño.

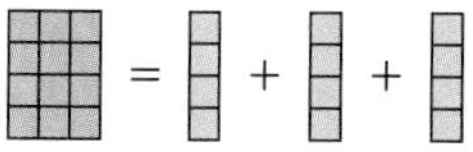

dividendo Número que se divide.

$3\overline{)429}$ 429 es el dividendo

divisible Describe un número que puede dividirse en partes iguales, sin residuo.

39 es divisible entre 3 sin residuo.

divisor The number by which the dividend is being divided.

$3\overline{)19}$ 3 is the divisor

E

edge (p. 566) The *line segment* where two *faces* of a *3-dimensional figure* meet.

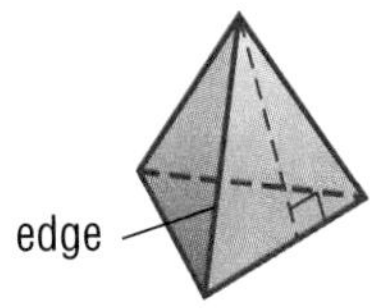

equally likely (p. 499) Having the same chance of occurring.

In a coin toss you are equally likely to flip a head or a tail.

equals sign (p. 46) A symbol of equality, =.

equation (p. 46) A mathematical sentence that contains an equal sign, indicating that the left side of the equal sign has the same value as the right side.

equilateral triangle (p. 553) A *triangle* with three *congruent* sides and three *congruent* angles.

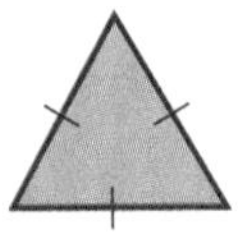

equivalent decimals (p. 136) Decimals that represent the same number.

0.3 and 0.30

equivalent fractions (p. 184) *Fractions* that represent the same number.

$\frac{3}{4} = \frac{6}{8} = \frac{9}{12}$

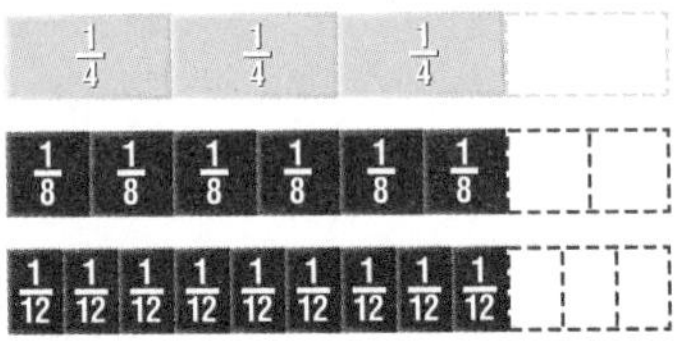

divisor Número entre el que se divide el dividendo.

$3\overline{)19}$ 3 es el divisor

arista Segmento de recta donde concurren dos caras de una *figura tridimensional.*

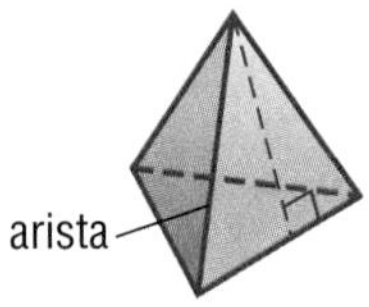

equiprobable Que tienen la misma posibilidad de ocurrir.

Al lanzar una moneda, tienes la misma posibilidad de sacar cara o cruz.

signo de igualdad Símbolo de igual, =.

ecuación Oración matemática que contiene un signo de igualdad, que indica que el lado izquierdo del signo tiene el mismo valor que el lado derecho.

triángulo equilátero *Triángulo* con tres lados *congruentes* y tres ángulos *congruentes*.

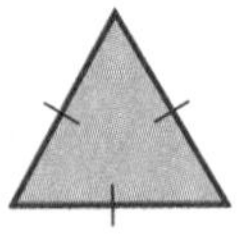

decimales equivalentes Decimales que representan el mismo número.

0.3 y 0.30

fracciones equivalentes *Fracciones* que representan el mismo número.

$\frac{3}{4} = \frac{6}{8} = \frac{9}{12}$

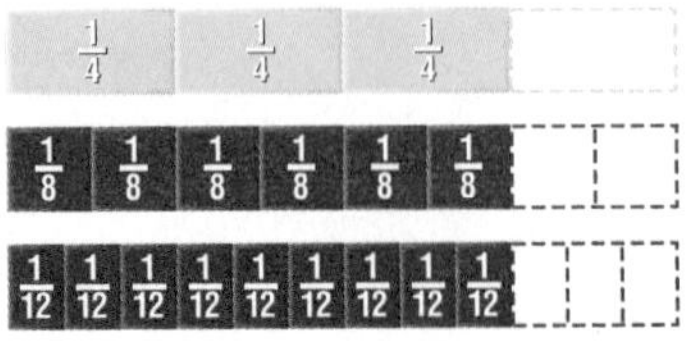

equivalent ratios (p. 422) *Ratios* that can be represented by *equivalent fractions*.

3:5 and 6:10

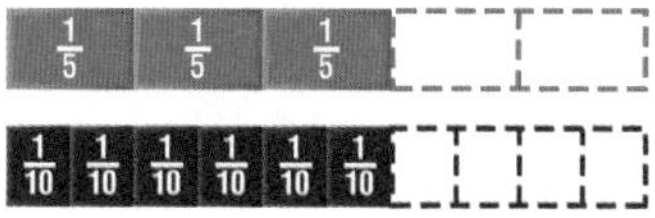

estimate (p. 154) A number close to an exact value. An estimate indicates *about* how much.

47 + 22 (round to 50 + 20)
The estimate is 70.

evaluate (p. 34) To find the *value* of an algebraic *expression* by replacing variables with numbers.

even number A whole number that is divisible by 2.

experimental probability (p. 504) The likelihood of an *event* happening based on experience and observation, rather than on theory.

exponent (p. 21) The number of times a *base* is multiplied by itself.

In 3^2, the exponent is two.

expression (p. 393) A combination of numbers, variables, and operation symbols.

F

face (p. 566) The flat part of a 3-dimensional figure.

A square is a face of a cube.

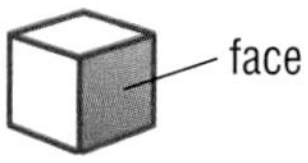

factor (p. 17) A number that divides a whole number evenly. Also a number that is multiplied by another number.

favorable outcomes (p. 498) Desired results in a *probability* experiment.

fluid ounces (p. 636) A *customary unit* of *capacity*.

foot (ft) (p. 632) A *customary unit* for measuring *length*. Plural is *feet*.

1 foot = 12 inches

razones equivalentes *Razones* que se pueden representar mediante *fracciones equivalentes*.

3:5 y 6:10

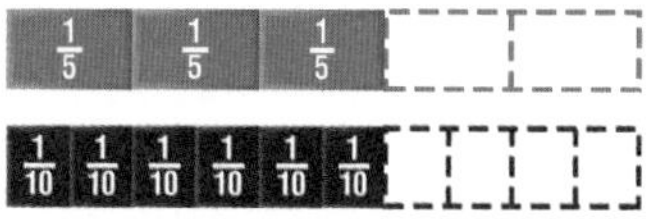

estimación Un número cercano a un valor exacto. Una estimación indica *aproximadamente* cuánto.

47 + 22 se redeondea a 50 + 20
La estimación es 70.

evaluar Calcular el *valor* de una expresión algebraica reemplazando las variables con números.

número par Número entero divisible entre 2.

probabilidad experimental Posibilidad que suceda un *evento* basándose en experiencia y en observación, en vez de teoría.

exponente Número de veces que la *base* se multiplica por sí misma.

En 3^2, el exponente es dos.

expresión Combinación de números, variables y símbolos de operaciones.

cara La parte llana de una figura tridimensional.

Un cuadrado es una cara de un cubo.

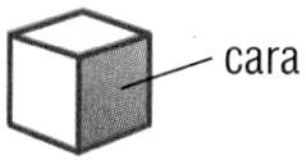

factor Número que divide exactamente a otro número entero. También un número que se multiplica por otro número.

resultados favorables Resultados deseados en un experimento *probabilístico*.

onzas líquidas *Unidad inglesa* de *capacidad*.

pie (pie) *Unidad inglesa* de *longitud*.

1 pie = 12 pulgadas

formula (p. 52) An equation that describes a relationship among two or more quantities.

fraction A number that represents part of a whole or part of a set.

$\frac{1}{2}, \frac{1}{3}, \frac{1}{4}, \frac{3}{4}$

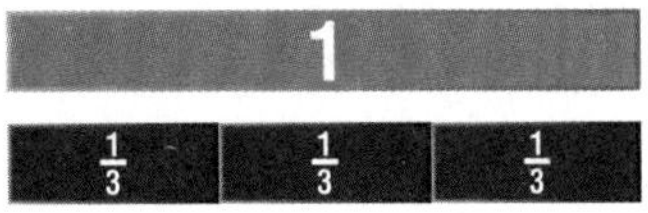

frequency (p. 73) The number of times a result occurs or something happens in a set amount of time or collection of data.

frequency table (p. 92) A table for organizing a set of *data* that shows the number of times each result has occurred.

front-end estimation (p. 150) An estimation method in which the front digits are added or subtracted.

function (p. 39) A relationship in which one quantity depends upon another quantity.

function rule (p. 39) An expression that describes the relationship between each input and output.

function table (p. 39) A table of ordered pairs that is based on a rule.

Rule: $8h = r$	
Input (h)	**Output (r)**
1	8
2	16
3	24
4	32

fórmula Ecuación que describe una relación entre dos o más cantidades.

fracción Número que representa parte de un todo o parte de un conjunto.

$\frac{1}{2}, \frac{1}{3}, \frac{1}{4}, \frac{3}{4}$

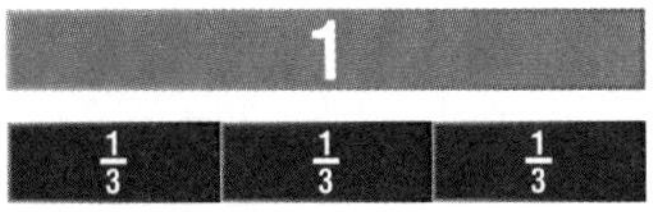

frecuencia Número de veces que ocurre un resultado o sucede algo en un período de tiempo dado o en una colección de datos.

tabla de frecuencias Tabla para organizar un conjunto de *datos* que muestra el número de veces que ha ocurrido cada resultado.

estimación por partes Método de estimación en que se suman o se restan los dígitos iniciales.

función Relación en que una cantidad depende de otra.

regla de funciones Expresión que describe la relación entre cada valor de entrada y cada valor de salida.

tabla de funciones Tabla de pares ordenados que se basa en una regla.

Regla: $8h = r$	
Entrada (h)	**Salida (r)**
1	8
2	16
3	24
4	32

G

gallon (gal) (p. 636) A *customary unit* for measuring *capacity* for liquids.

1 gallon = 4 quarts

gram (g) (p. 644) A *metric unit* for measuring *mass*.

galón (gal) Unidad de *medida inglesa* de *capacidad* de líquidos.

1 galón = 4 cuartos

gramo (g) Una *unidad métrica* para medir *masa*.

graph (pp. 73, 114, 214) **a.** A visual way to display data.

b. To graph an integer on a number line, draw a dot at the location on the number line that corresponds to the integer.

c. Place a point named by an ordered pair on a coordinate grid.

greater than > An inequality relationship showing that the number on the left of the symbol is greater than the number on the right.

5 > 3
5 is greater than 3

Greatest Common Factor (GCF) (p. 175) The largest number that divides evenly into two or more numbers.

The greatest common factor of
12, 18, and 30 is 6.

grid A group of horizontal and vertical lines, that intersect forming squares.

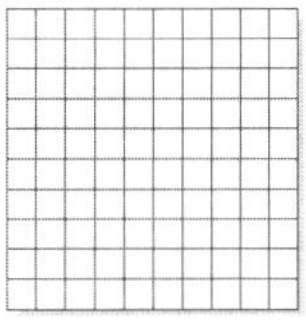

gráfica **a.** Manera visual de representar datos.

b. Para graficar un entero en una recta numérica, traza un punto sobre la recta numérica en la ubicación que corresponde al entero.

c. Coloca el punto indicado por un par ordenado en un cuadriculado de coordenadas.

mayor que > Relación de desigualdad que muestra que el número a la izquierda del símbolo es mayor que el número a la derecha.

5 > 3
5 es mayor que 3

máximo común divisor (MCD) El mayor número que divide exactamente a dos o más números.

El máximo común divisor de
12, 18 y 30 es 6.

cuadriculado Grupo de rectas horizontales y verticales que se intersecan formando cuadrados.

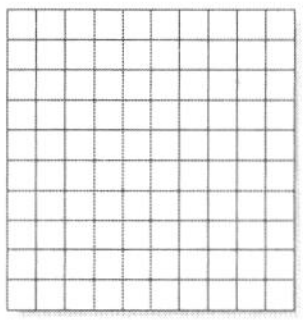

H

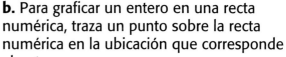

height (p. 592) The length of a perpendicular from a vertex to the base of the perpendicular, or to the opposite side of the triangle.

histogram (p. 83) A *graph* that uses bars to show *frequency* of *data* organized in *intervals*.

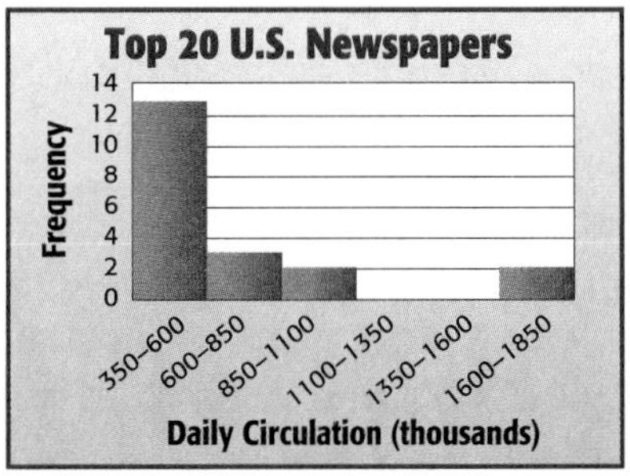

altura Longitud de una perpendicular desde un vértice a la base de la perpendicular o al lado opuesto del triángulo.

histograma *Gráfica* que usa barras para representar *frecuencias* de *datos* organizados en *intervalos*.

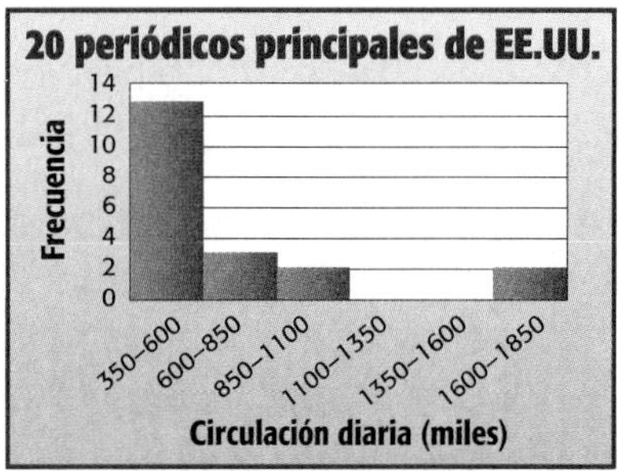

horizontal axis (p. 73) The axis in a coordinate plane that runs left and right (↔). Also known as the *x*-axis.

hundredth (p. 465) A place value position. One of one hundred equal parts.

In the number 0.57, 7 is in the hundredths place.

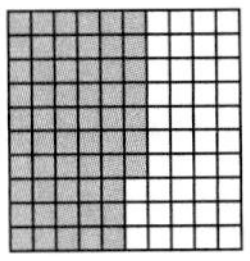

eje horizontal Eje en un plano de coordenadas que va de izquierda a derecha (↔). También conocido como eje *x*.

centésima Valor de posición. Una de cien partes iguales.

En el número 0.57, 7 está en el lugar de las centésimas.

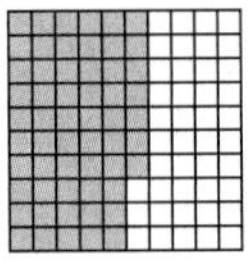

I

impossible (p. 499) An *outcome* or *event* is impossible if it has a *probability* of 0.

It is impossible to choose a yellow tile.

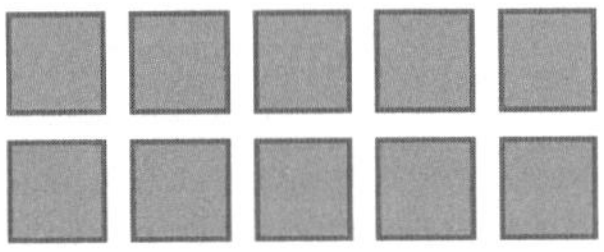

improper fraction (p. 189) A fraction with a numerator that is greater than or equal to the denominator.

$\frac{17}{3}$ or $\frac{5}{5}$

inch (in.) (p. 632) A *customary unit* for measuring *length*. The plural is *inches*.

integer (p. 113) Whole numbers and their opposites, including zero.

$\ldots -3, -2, -1, 0, 1, 2, 3 \ldots$

intersecting lines (p. 541) *Lines* that meet or cross at a *point*.

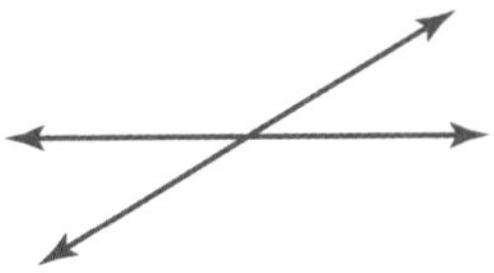

interval (p. 73) The distance between two points or the time between two events.

inverse operations (p. 385) Operations that undo each other. Addition and subtraction are inverse or opposite operations. Multiplication and division are also inverse operations.

imposible Un *resultado* o un *evento* es imposible si tiene una *probabilidad* igual a 0.

Es imposible que elijas un azulejo amarillo.

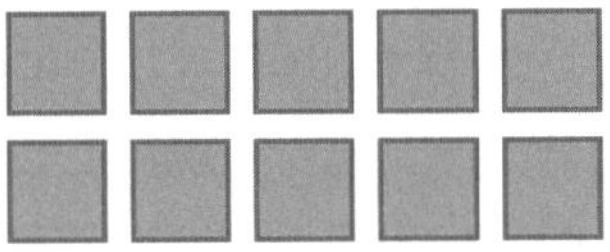

fracción impropia Fracción con un numerador mayor que o igual al denominador.

$\frac{17}{3}$ o $\frac{5}{5}$

pulgada (pulg) *Unidad inglesa* de *longitud*.

entero Los números enteros y sus opuestos, incluyendo el cero.

$\ldots -3, -2, -1, 0, 1, 2, 3 \ldots$

rectas secantes *Rectas* que se intersecan o se cruzan en un *punto*.

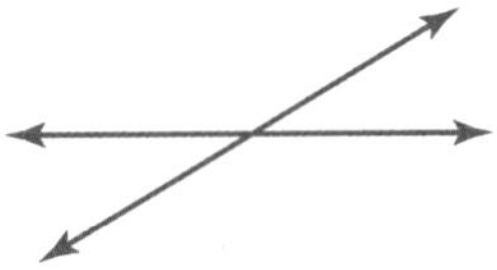

intervalo Distancia entre dos puntos o tiempo entre dos eventos.

operaciones inversas Operaciones que se anulan entre sí. La suma y la resta son operaciones inversas o opuestas. La multiplicación y la división también son operaciones inversas.

isosceles triangle (p. 553) A *triangle* with at least 2 *sides* of the same *length*.

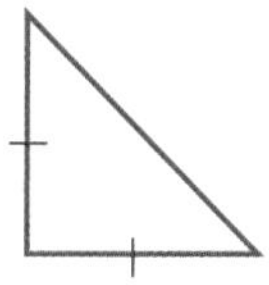

K

kilogram (kg) (p. 644) A *metric unit* for measuring *mass*.

kilometer (km) (p. 640) A *metric unit* for measuring *length*.

L

Least Common Denominator (LCD) (p. 200) The *least common multiple* of the *denominators* of two or more *fractions*, used as a denominator.

$\frac{1}{12}, \frac{1}{6}, \frac{1}{8}$; LCD is 24.

Least Common Multiple (LCM) (p. 194) The smallest *whole number* greater than 0 that is a common *multiple* of each of two or more numbers.

The LCM of 2 and 3 is 6.

length Measurement of the distance between two points.

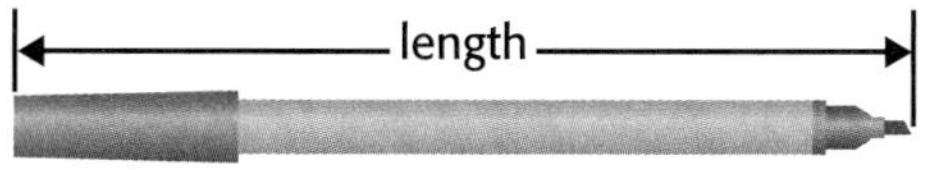

less than $<$ The number on the left side of the symbol is smaller than the number on the right side.

$4 < 7$
4 is smaller than 7

like fractions (p. 241) Fractions that have the same denominator.

$\frac{1}{5}$ and $\frac{2}{5}$

likely (p. 499) An event that will probably happen.

It is likely you will choose a red cube.

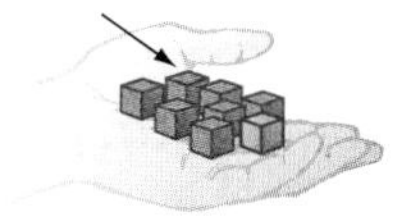

triángulo isósceles *Triángulo* que tiene por lo menos 2 *lados* del mismo largo.

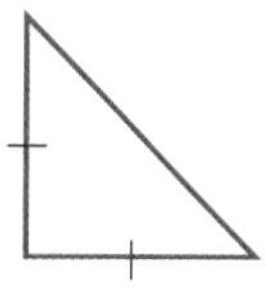

kilogramo (kg) *Unidad métrica* de *masa*.

kilómetro (km) *Unidad métrica* de *longitud*.

mínimo común denominador (mcd) El *mínimo común múltiplo* de los *denominadores* de dos o más *fracciones* que se usa como denominador.

$\frac{1}{12}, \frac{1}{6}, \frac{1}{8}$; el mcd es 24.

mínimo común múltiplo (mcm) El menor *número entero*, mayor que 0, *múltiplo* común de dos o más números.

El mcm de 2 y 3 es 6.

longitud Medida de la distancia entre dos puntos.

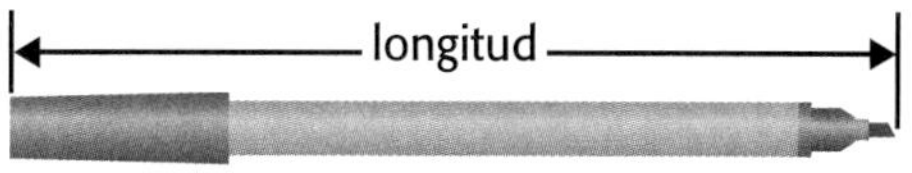

menor que $<$ El número a la izquierda del símbolo es más pequeño que el número a su derecha.

$4 < 7$
4 es menor que 7

fracciones semejantes Fracciones que tienen el mismo denominador.

$\frac{1}{5}$ y $\frac{2}{5}$

posible Un evento que probablemente sucederá.

Es posible que elijas un cubo rojo.

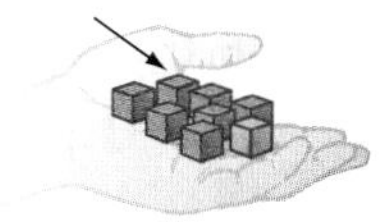

line A set of *points* that form a straight path that goes in opposite directions without ending.

line graph (p. 74) A graph that uses points connected by *line segments* to represent data.

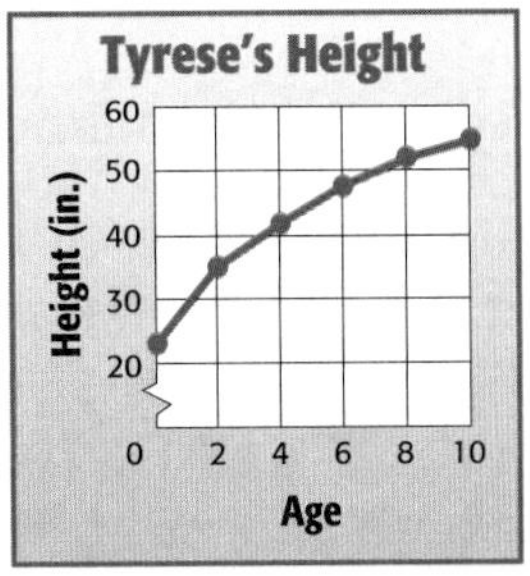

line plot (p. 87) A graph that uses columns of Xs above a *number line* to show frequency of data.

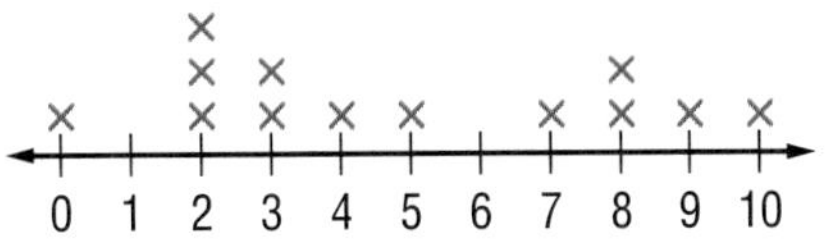

line segment (p. 553) A part of a *line* between two *endpoints*. The length of the line segment can be measured.

linear (p. 382) A graph of a set of ordered pairs that forms a line.

liter (L) (p. 645) A *metric unit* for measuring *volume* or *capacity*.

1 liter = 1,000 milliliters

recta Conjunto de *puntos* que forman una trayectoria recta en direcciones opuestas y sin fin.

gráfica lineal Gráfica que usa puntos unidos por *segmentos de recta* para representar datos.

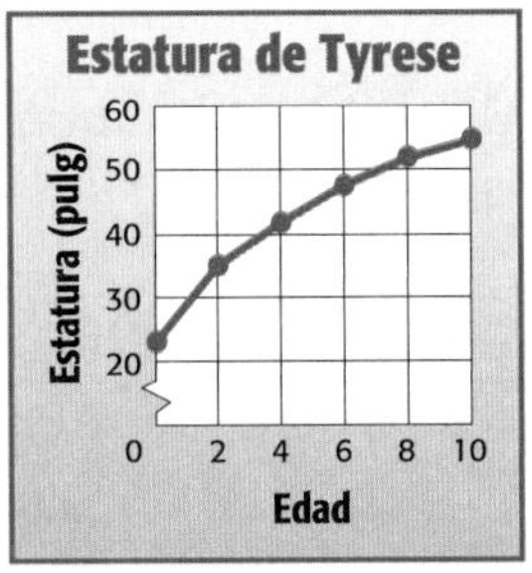

esquema lineal Gráfica que usa columnas de X sobre una *recta numérica* para representar frecuencias de datos.

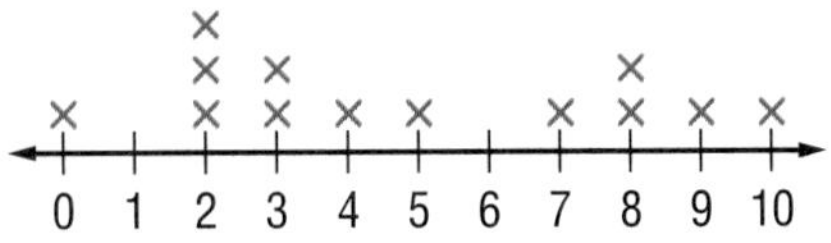

segmento de recta Parte de una *recta* entre dos *extremos*. La longitud de un segmento de recta se puede medir.

lineal Gráfica de un conjunto de pares ordenados que forman una recta.

litro (L) *Unidad métrica* de *volumen* o *capacidad*.

1 litro = 1,000 mililitros

M

mass (p. 644) The amount of matter in an object. Two examples of units of measure would be pound and kilogram.

mean (p. 95) The *quotient* found by adding the numbers in a set of data and dividing this sum by the number of *addends*. A measure of central tendency.

masa Cantidad de material en un objeto. Dos ejemplos de unidades de esta medida son la libra y el kilogramo.

media *Cociente* que se calcula sumando los números en un conjunto de datos y dividiendo esta suma entre el número de *sumandos*. Una medida de tendencia central.

median (p. 99) The middle number in a set of numbers arranged in order from least to greatest. If the set contains an even number of numbers, the median is the *mean* of the two numbers nearest the middle.

3, 4, 6, 8, 9, 9

The median is $7 = \frac{(6 + 8)}{2}$.

metric system (SI) (p. 640) The measurement system based on powers of 10 that includes units such as meter, gram, liter, and degrees Celsius.

mile (mi) (p. 632) A *customary unit* of measure for *distance*.

1 mile = 5,280 feet

milligram (mg) (p. 644) A *metric unit* used to measure *mass*.

1,000 milligrams = 1 gram

milliliter (mL) (p. 645) A *metric unit* used for measuring *capacity*.

1,000 milliliters = 1 liter

millimeter (mm) (p. 640) A *metric unit* used for measuring *length*.

1,000 millimeters = 1 meter

million The name of the number 1,000,000.

mixed number (p. 189) A number that has a *whole number* part and a *fraction* part.

$6\frac{3}{4}$

mode (p. 99) The number(s) that occurs most often in a set of numbers.

7, 4, 7, 10, 7, and 2

The mode is 7.

multiple (multiples) (p. 194) A multiple of a number is the *product* of that number and any whole number.

15 is a multiple of 5 because $3 \times 5 = 15$.

multiplication An operation on two numbers to find their *product*. It can be thought of as repeated *addition*.

4×3 is another way to write the *sum* of four 3s, which is $3 + 3 + 3 + 3$ or 12.

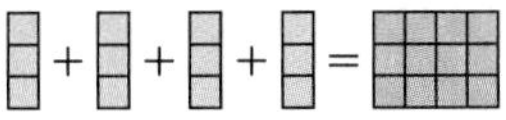

mediana Número central de un conjunto de números ordenados de menor a mayor. Si el conjunto contiene una cantidad par de números, la mediana es la *media* de los dos números centrales.

3, 4, 6, 8, 9, 9

La mediana es $7 = \frac{(6 + 8)}{2}$.

sistema métrico (sm) Sistema de medición que se basa en potencias de 10 el cual incluye unidades como el metro, el gramo, el litro y los grados Celsius.

milla (mi) *Unidad inglesa* de *distancia*.

1 milla = 5,280 pies

miligramo (mg) *Unidad métrica* de *masa*.

1,000 miligramos = 1 gramo

mililitro (mL) *Unidad métrica* de *capacidad*.

1,000 mililitros = 1 litro

milímetro (mm) *Unidad métrica* de *longitud*.

1,000 milímetros = 1 metro

millón El nombre del número 1,000,000.

número mixto Número que tiene una parte *entera* y una parte *fraccionaria*.

$6\frac{3}{4}$

moda Número o números que ocurren con mayor frecuencia en un conjunto de números.

7, 4, 7, 10, 7, y 2

La moda es 7.

múltiplo (múltiplos) Un múltiplo de un número es el *producto* de ese número por cualquier otro número entero.

15 es múltiplo de 5 porque $3 \times 5 = 15$.

multiplicación Operación que se realiza en dos números para calcular su *producto*. También se puede interpretar como una *suma* repetida.

4×3 es otra forma de escribir la *suma* de cuatro veces 3, la cual es $3 + 3 + 3 + 3$ o 12.

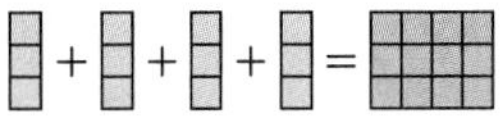

N

negative number (p. 113) Numbers less than zero.

net (p. 616) A flat pattern that can be folded to make a *3-dimensional figure*.

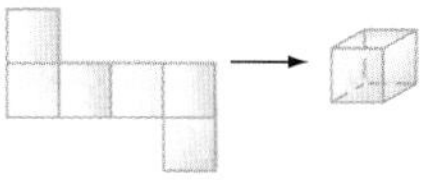

nonlinear (p. 382) A graph of a set of ordered pairs that does not form a line.

number line (p. 88) A line that represents numbers as points.

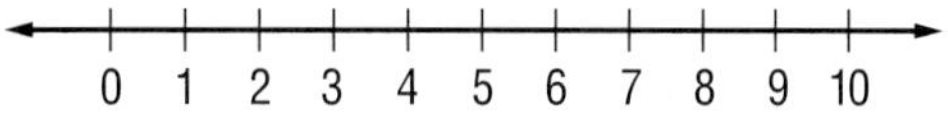

numerator The number above the bar in a *fraction*; the part of the fraction that tells how many of the equal parts are being used.

numerical expression (p. 27) A combination of numbers and operations.

número negativo Números menores que cero.

red Patrón llano que se puede doblar para formar una *figura tridimensional*.

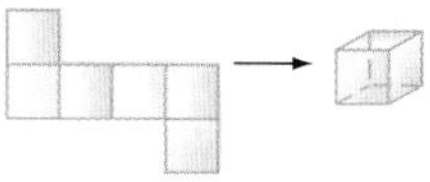

no lineal Gráfica de un conjunto de pares ordenados que no forma una recta.

recta numérica Recta que representa números como puntos.

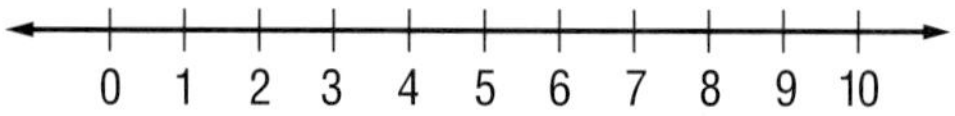

numerador Número que está encima de la barra de *fracción*; la parte de la fracción que indica cuántas partes iguales se están usando.

expresión numérica Combinación de números y operaciones.

O

obtuse angle (p. 530) An *angle* that measures greater than 90° but less than 180°.

obtuse triangle (p. 551) A *triangle* with one *obtuse angle*.

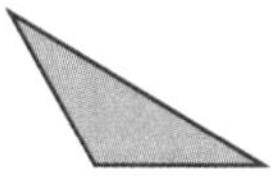

odd number A number that is not divisible by 2; such a number has 1, 3, 5, 7, or 9 in the ones place.

operation A mathematical process such as addition (+), subtraction (–), multiplication (×), division (÷), and raising to a power.

opposite integers (p. 113) Two different integers that are the same distance from 0 on a number line.

5 and –5

ángulo obtuso *Ángulo* que mide más de 90° pero menos de 180°.

triángulo obtusángulo *Triángulo* con un *ángulo obtuso*.

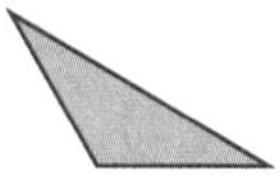

número impar Número que no es divisible entre 2, tal número tiene 1, 3, 5, 7 ó 9 en el lugar de las unidades.

operación Proceso matemático como la suma (+), la resta (–), la multiplicación (×), la división (÷) y la potenciación.

enteros opuestos Dos enteros diferentes que equidistan de 0 en una recta numérica.

5 y –5

order of operations (p. 27) Rules that tell what order to follow when evaluating expressions:

(1) Evaluate within parentheses ().

(2) Do powers and roots.

(3) Multiply or divide left to right.

(4) Add or subtract left to right.

ordered pair (p. 213) A pair of numbers that are the coordinates of a point in a coordinate plane or grid in this order: (horizontal coordinate, vertical coordinate)

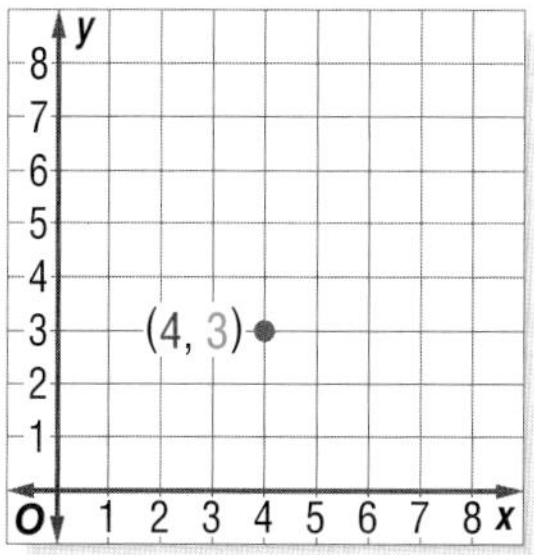

organized data *Data* arranged in a display that is meaningful and assists in the interpretation of the data.

origin (p. 213) The point (0, 0) on a *coordinate graph* where the vertical axis meets the horizontal axis, (0, 0).

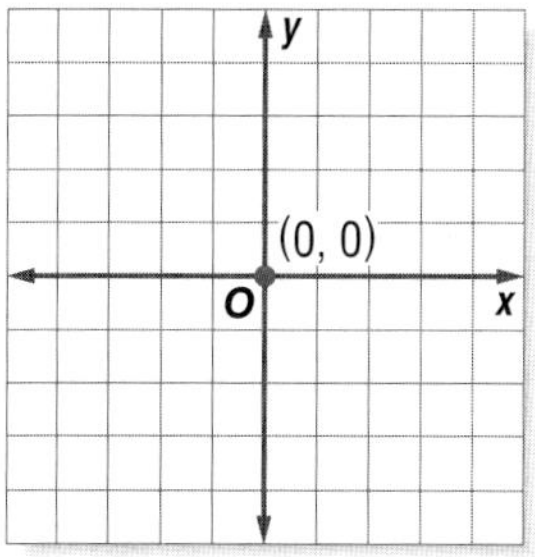

ounce (oz) ounces (p. 637) A *customary unit* for measuring *weight* or *capacity*.

outcome (p. 498) A possible result of an experiment.

outlier (p. 96) A number in a set of data that is much larger or much smaller than most of the other numbers in the set.

orden de las operaciones Reglas que indican qué orden seguir al evaluar una expresión:

(1) Evalúa dentro de los paréntesis ().

(2) Halla las potencias y extrae las raíces.

(3) Multiplica o divide de izquierda a derecha.

(4) Suma o resta de izquierda a derecha.

par ordenado Par de números que son coordenadas de un punto en un plano de coordenadas o un cuadriculado, en este orden (coordenada horizontal, coordenada vertical)

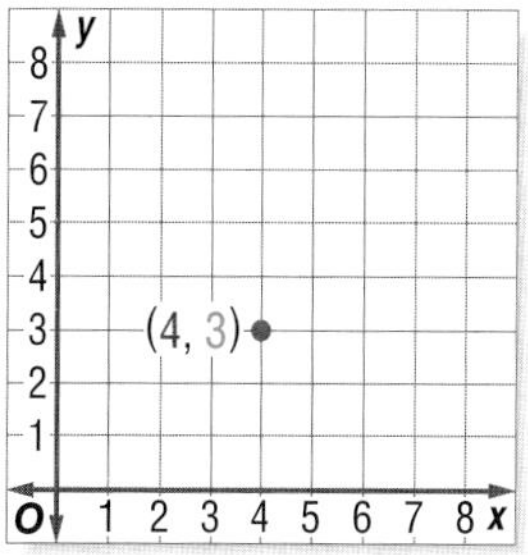

datos organizados *Datos* ordenados en una representación significativa y útil en su interpretación.

origen El punto (0, 0) en una *gráfica de coordenadas* donde el *eje* vertical interseca el eje horizontal, (0, 0).

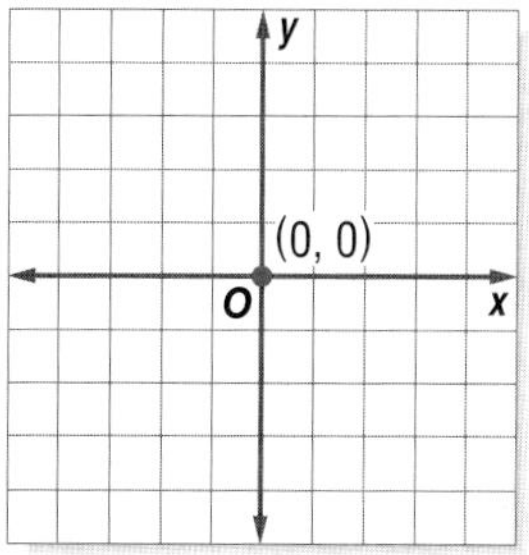

onza (oz) onzas *Unidad inglesa* de *peso* o *capacidad*.

resultado Resultado posible de un experimento.

valor atípico Número en un conjunto de datos que es mucho mayor o mucho menor que la mayoría de los otros números del conjunto.

P

parallel lines (p. 541) Lines that are the same distance apart. Parallel lines do not intersect.

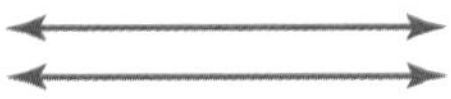

parallelogram (p. 559) A quadrilateral with four sides in which each pair of opposite sides are parallel and equal in length.

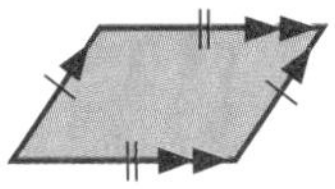

percent (p. 466) A ratio that compares a number to 100.

perimeter (p. 585) The *distance* around a shape or region.

perpendicular lines (p. 541) *Lines* that meet or cross each other to form *right angles*.

pint (pt) (p. 636) A customary *unit* for measuring *capacity*.

1 pint = 2 cups

polygon (p. 566) A closed plane figure formed using line segments that meet only at their endpoints.

population (p. 512) The entire group of items or individuals from which the samples under consideration are taken.

positive number (p. 113) Numbers that are greater than zero.

possible outcomes (p. 498) Any of the results that could occur in an experiment.

pound (lb) (p. 637) A *customary unit* for measuring *weight* or *mass*.

1 pound = 16 ounces

power (p. 22) A number obtained by raising a *base* to an *exponent*.

$5^2 = 25$ 25 is a power of 5.

prime factorization (p. 18) A way of expressing a *composite number* as a product of its *prime factors*.

rectas paralelas Rectas separadas por la misma distancia. Las rectas paralelas no se intersecan.

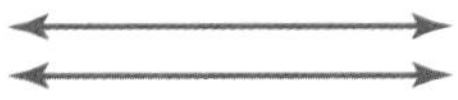

paralelogramo Cuadrilátero de cuatro lados en que cada par de lados opuestos son paralelos y de la misma longitud.

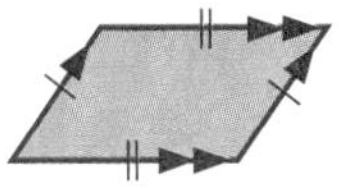

porcentaje Razón que compara un número con 100.

perímetro *Distancia* alrededor de una figura o región.

rectas perpendiculares *Rectas* que se intersecan o cruzan formando *ángulos rectos*.

pinta (pt) *Unidad inglesa* de *capacidad*.

1 pinta = 2 tazas

polígono Figura plana cerrada formada por segmentos de recta que sólo se unen en sus extremos.

población Todo el grupo de cosas o individuos del cual se toman las muestras a considerar.

número positivo Números mayores que cero.

resultados posibles Cualquiera de los resultados que puede ocurrir en un experimento.

libra (lb) *Unidad inglesa* de *peso* o *masa*.

1 libra = 16 onzas

potencia Número que se obtiene elevando una *base* a un *exponente*.

$5^2 = 25$ 25 es una potencia de 5.

factorización prima Una manera de escribir un *número compuesto* como un producto de sus *factores primos*.

prime number (p. 17) A *whole number* with exactly two *factors*, 1 and itself.

7, 13, and 19

prism (p. 566) A *3-dimensional figure* with two *parallel, congruent polygons as bases* and *parallelograms* for *faces.*

probability (p. 498) A number between 0 and 1 that measures the likelihood of an event happening.

product (p. 34) The answer to a multiplication problem. It also refers to expressing a number as the product of its factors.

proper fraction (p. 189) A fraction in which the numerator is less than the denominator.

$\frac{1}{2}$

protractor An instrument marked in degrees, used for measuring or drawing *angles.*

Q

quadrant (p. 378) One of four sections of a *coordinate graph* formed by two *axes.*

quadrilateral (p. 558) A shape that has 4 sides and 4 angles.

square, rectangle, and parallelogram

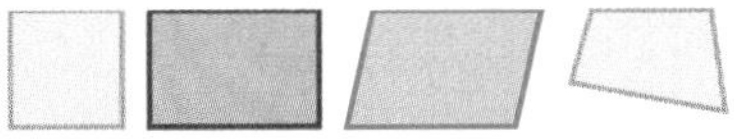

quart (qt) (p. 636) A *customary unit* for measuring *capacity.*

1 quart = 4 cups

quotient The result of a *division* problem.

R

random (p. 499) Outcomes occur at random if each outcome is equally likely to occur.

range (p. 100) The *difference* between the greatest and the least numbers in a set of data.

número primo *Número entero* que tiene exactamente dos *factores*, 1 y sí mismo.

7, 13, y 19

prisma *Figura tridimensional* con dos *polígonos paralelos* y *congruentes como bases* y *paralelogramos* como *caras.*

probabilidad Número entre 0 y 1 que mide la posibilidad de que ocurra un evento.

producto Repuesta a un problema de multiplicación. También se refiere a la expresión de un número como el producto de sus factores.

fracción propia Fracción en que el numerador es menor que el denominador.

$\frac{1}{2}$

transportador Instrumento marcado en grados que se usa para medir o trazar *ángulos.*

cuadrante Una de las cuatro secciones de una *gráfica de coordenadas* formada por dos *ejes.*

cuadrilátero Figura con 4 lados y 4 ángulos.

cuadrado, rectángulo y paralelogramo

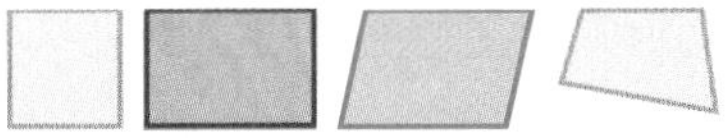

cuarto (ct) *Unidad inglesa* de *capacidad.*

1 cuarto = 4 tazas

cociente El resultado de un problema de *división.*

aleatorio Los resultados ocurren aleatoriamente si cada resultado tiene la misma posibilidad de ocurrir.

rango La *diferencia* entre el mayor y el menor de los números en un conjunto de datos.

rate (p. 414) A *ratio* of two quantities that are measured with different units.

$3.00 for 2 pounds of crackers

ratio (p. 413) A relationship between two quantities that are measured with the same unit.

2 cups of sugar to 5 cups of flour

ratio table (p. 422) A table with columns filled with pairs of numbers that have the same ratio.

rational number (p. 205) A number that can be written as a fraction.

reciprocal (p. 327) A number obtained from a given number by interchanging its numerator and denominator.

The reciprocal of $\frac{3}{5}$ is $\frac{5}{3}$.

rectangle (p. 559) A *quadrilateral* with four *right angles*; opposite *sides* are equal and *parallel*.

rectangular prism (p. 608) A *3-dimensional figure* with six faces that are rectangles.

remainder The number that is left after one whole number is divided by another.

repeating decimal (p. 212) A decimal that repeats in a specific pattern.

0.673673673...

rhombus (p. 559) A *parallelogram* with four *congruent sides*.

right angle (p. 530) An *angle* with a measure of 90°.

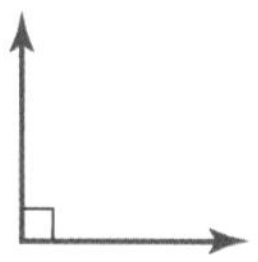

right triangle (p. 551) A *triangle* with one *right angle*.

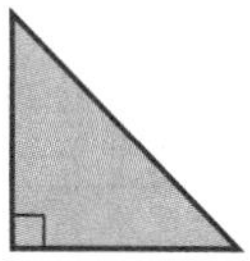

tasa *Razón* de dos cantidades que se miden con distintas unidades.

$3.00 por 2 libras de galletas

razón Relación entre dos cantidades que se miden con la misma unidad.

2 tazas de azúcar a 5 tazas de harina

tabla de razones Tabla con columnas de pares de números que tienen la misma razón.

número racional Número que se puede escribir como fracción.

recíproco Número que se obtiene a partir de un número dado intercambiando su numerador y su denominador.

El recíproco de $\frac{3}{5}$ es $\frac{5}{3}$.

rectángulo *Cuadrilátero* con cuatro *ángulo rectos*; los *lados* opuestos son iguales y *paralelos*.

prisma rectangular *Figura tridimensional* con seis caras rectangulares.

residuo Número que queda después de dividir un número entero entre otro número entero.

decimal periódico Decimal que se repite en un patrón específico.

0.673673673...

rombo *Paralelogramo* con cuatro *lados congruentes*.

ángulo recto *Ángulo* que mide 90°.

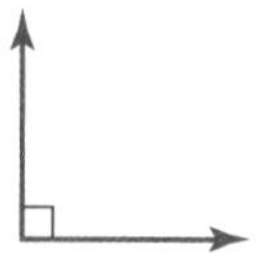

triángulo rectángulo *Triángulo* con un *ángulo recto*.

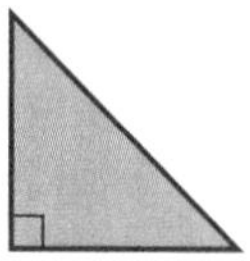

round To change the value of a number to one that is easier to work with. To find the nearest *value* of a number based on a given *place value*.

6.38 rounded to the nearest tenth is 6.4.

S

sample (p. 512) A part of a *population* used in a survey to represent the whole population.

sample space (p. 505) The set of all possible *outcomes* in a *probability* experiment.

scale (p. 73) Equally spaced marks along an axis of a graph.

scalene triangle (p. 553) A *triangle* with no *congruent sides*.

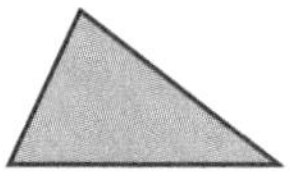

scaling (p. 423) To multiply or divide two related quantities by the same number.

scientific notation (p. 285) Expressing a number as the *product of two factors* where the first *factor* is between 1 and 10 and the second factor is a power of 10.

$$786 = 7.86 \times 10^2$$

sequence (p. 442) A list of numbers in a specific order, such as 0, 1, 2, 3 or 2, 4, 6, 8.

side (p. 529) One of the line segments in a *polygon*. Also one of the rays that form an angle.

simple event (p. 498) A specific outcome or type of outcome.

simplest form (p. 185) A fraction in which the numerator and the denominator have no common factor greater than 1.

$\frac{5}{12}$ is in simplest form because 5 and 12 have no common factor greater than 1.

redondear Cambiar el valor de un número a uno con el cual es más fácil trabajar. Calcular el *valor* más cercano a un número basado en un *valor de posición* dado.

6.38 redondeado a la décima más cercana es 6.4.

muestra Parte de una *población* que se usa en una encuesta para representar a toda la población.

espacio muestral Conjunto de todos los *resultados* posibles en un experimento *probabilístico*.

escala Marcas equiespaciadas a lo largo del eje de una gráfica.

triángulo escaleno *Triángulo* sin *lados congruentes*.

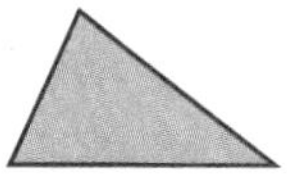

escalamiento Multiplicar por o dividir entre el mismo número dos cantidades relacionadas.

notación científica Escribir un número como el *producto* de *dos factores* donde el primer *factor* está entre 1 y 10 y el segundo factor es una potencia de 10.

$$786 = 7.86 \times 10^2$$

sucesión Lista de números en un orden específico, como 0, 1, 2, 3 ó 2, 4, 6, 8.

lado Uno de los segmentos de *recta* de un *polígono*. También uno de los rayos que forma un ángulo.

evento simple Resultado específico o tipo de resultado.

forma reducida Fracción en que el numerador y el denominador no tienen un factor común mayor que 1.

$\frac{5}{12}$ está en forma reducida porque 5 y 12 no tienen un factor común mayor que 1.

solution (p. 46) The value of a variable that makes an equation true. The solution of $12 = x + 7$ is 5.

solución Valor de una variable que hace verdadera la ecuación. La solución de $12 = x + 7$ es 5.

solve (p. 46) To replace a variable with a value that results in a true sentence.

resolver Despejar una variable y reemplazar este valor en la variable para hacer verdadera la ecuación.

square (p. 559) A rectangle with four *congruent sides*.

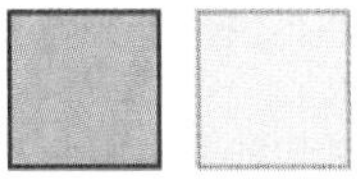

cuadrado Rectángulo con cuatro *lados congruentes*.

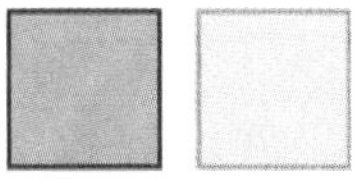

squared (p. 22) The *product* of a number multiplied by itself.

$$5^2 = 5 \times 5 = 25$$

elevado al cuadrado El *producto* de un número multiplicado por sí mismo.

$$5^2 = 5 \times 5 = 25$$

square unit (p. 52) A unit for measuring *area*, such as *square inch* or *square centimeter*.

unidad cuadrada Unidad de *área*, como una *pulgada cuadrada* o un *centímetro cuadrado*.

straight angle (p. 530) An *angle* with a measure of 180°.

ángulo llano *Ángulo* con una medida de 180°.

subtraction (subtract) An operation on two numbers that tells how many are left (*difference*), when some or all are taken away. Subtraction is also used to compare two numbers.

$$14 - 8 = 6$$

restar (resta) Operación que se realiza en dos números y que indica cuántos quedan (*diferencia*), cuando se eliminan algunos o todos. La resta también se usa para comparar dos números.

$$14 - 8 = 6$$

Subtraction Property of Equality (p. 387) If you subtract the same number from each side of an equation, the two sides remain equal.

propiedad de igualdad de la resta Si restas el mismo número de cada lado de una ecuación, los dos lados permanecen iguales.

sum The answer to an addition problem.

suma Respuesta a un problema de suma.

surface area (p. 617) The area of the surface of a *3-dimensional figure*.

área de superficie Área de la superficie de una *figura tridimensional*.

survey (p. 512) A method of collecting data.

encuesta Método para reunir datos.

T

tally mark(s) (p. 92) A mark made to keep track and display data recorded from a survey.

marcas(s) de conteo Marca que se hace para llevar la cuenta y representar datos reunidos en una encuesta.

ten thousandth A place value in a decimal number.

In the decimal 0.7891, the 1 is in the ten thousandths place.

diezmilésima Valor de posición en un número decimal.

En el decimal 0.7891, el 1 está en el lugar de las diezmilésimas.

tenth A place value in a decimal number or one of ten equal parts or $\frac{1}{10}$.
In the decimal 0.78, the 7 is in the tenths place.

terms (p. 442) Each of the quantities that form a series or pattern.

theoretical probability (p. 504) The *likelihood* of an event happening based on theory rather than on experience and observation.

thousandth(s) One of a thousand equal parts or $\frac{1}{1,000}$. Also refers to a place value in a decimal number.
In the decimal 0.789, the 9 is in the thousandth place.

three-dimensional figure (p. 566) A figure that has *length*, *width*, and *height*.

ton (t) (p. 637) A customary unit to measure weight.
1 ton = 2,000 pounds

trapezoid (p. 559) A *quadrilateral* with exactly one pair of *parallel* sides.

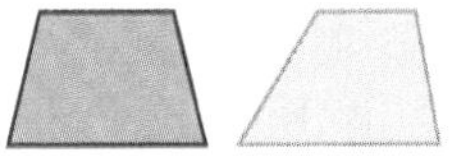

tree diagram (p. 506) **a.** A diagram of all the *possible outcomes* of an event or series of events or experiments.
b. A diagram of all the possible combinations of two or more objects or events being put together.

trial (p. 504) A test or experiment.

triangle (p. 552) A *polygon* with three sides and three angles.

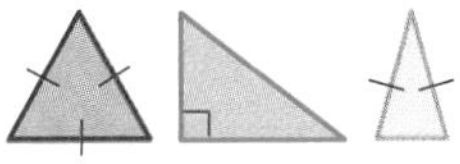

U

unit price (p. 429) The price of a single piece or item.

unit rate (p. 414) A rate in which the value of the second quantity is one.
50 miles per hour

décima Valor de posición en un número decimal o una de diez partes iguales ó $\frac{1}{10}$.
En el decimal 0.78, el 7 está en el lugar de las décimas.

términos Cada una de las cantidades que forman una serie o patrón.

probabilidad teórica La *posibilidad* que suceda un evento basándose en la teoría en vez de la experiencia y la observación.

milésima(s) Una de mil partes iguales ó $\frac{1}{1,000}$. También se refiere a un valor de posición en un número decimal.
En el decimal 0.789, el 9 está en el lugar de las milésimas.

figura tridimensional Figura que tiene *largo, ancho* y *alto.*

tonelada (t) Unidad inglesa de peso
1 tonelada = 2,000 libras

trapecio *Cuadrilátero* con exactamente un par de lados *paralelos.*

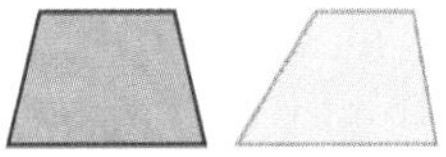

diagrama de árbol **a.** Diagrama de todos los *resultados posibles* de un evento o serie de eventos o experimentos.
b. Diagrama de todas las combinaciones posibles de dos o más objetos o eventos que se están combinando.

ensayo Prueba o experimento.

triángulo *Polígono* con tres lados y tres ángulos.

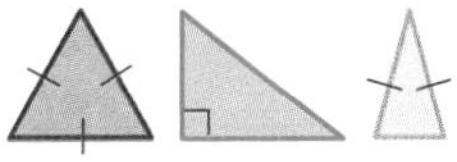

precio unitario El precio de una sola pieza o artículo.

tasa unitaria Tasa en la cual el valor de la segunda cantidad es uno.
50 millas por hora

unlike fractions (p. 251) Fractions with different denominators.

$\frac{2}{5}$ and $\frac{1}{3}$

unlikely (p. 499) An event that is improbable or will probably *not* happen.

It is unlikely you will choose a blue cube.

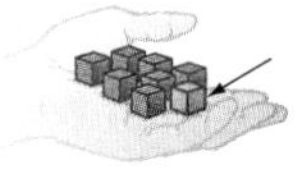

V

value A number amount or the worth of an object.

variable (p. 34) A letter or symbol used to represent an unknown quantity.

vertex (p. 529) The *point* where two rays meet in an *angle*.

vertical angles (p. 542) Nonadjacent angles formed by a pair of lines that intersect.

vertical axis (p. 73) A vertical number line on a graph (↕). Also known as the *y*-axis.

volume (p. 608) The number of cubic units needed to fill a *3-dimensional figure* or solid figure.

W

weight (p. 637) A measurement that tells how heavy an object is.

whole number The numbers 0, 1, 2, 3, 4...

width The measurement of distance from side to side telling how wide.

X

***x*-axis** (p. 213) The horizontal axis (↔) in a coordinate plane.

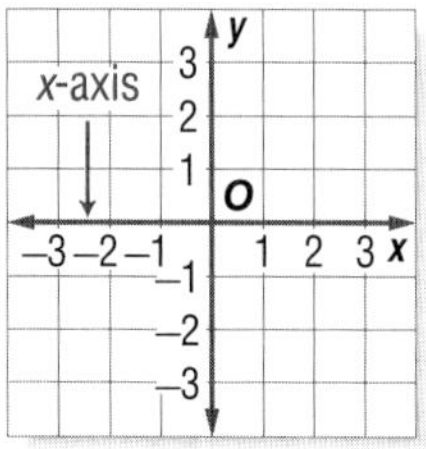

fracciones con distinto denominador Fracciones con diferentes denominadores.

$\frac{2}{5}$ y $\frac{1}{3}$

improbable Evento que es improbable o que es probable que *no* suceda.

Es improbable que elijas un cubo azul.

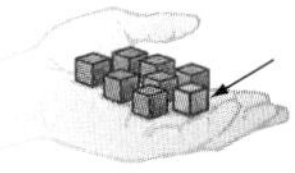

valor Cantidad numérica o lo que vale un objeto.

variable Letra o un símbolo que se usa para representar una cantidad desconocida.

vértice *Punto* donde concurren dos rayos de un *ángulo*.

ángulos opuestos por el vértice Ángulos no adyacentes formados por un par de rectas secantes.

eje vertical Recta numérica vertical en una gráfica (↕). También conocido como eje *y*.

volumen Número de unidades cúbicas necesarias para llenar una *figura tridimensional* o sólida.

peso Medida que indica la pesadez un cuerpo.

número entero Los números 0, 1, 2, 3, 4...

ancho Medida de la distancia de lado a lado y que indica amplitud.

eje *x* Eje horizontal (↔) en un plano de coordenadas.

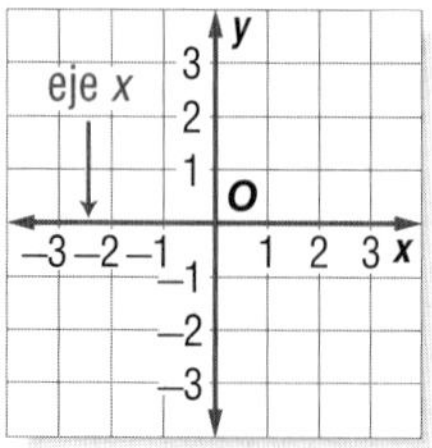

x-coordinate (p. 213) The first part of an ordered pair that indicates how far to the left or the right of the *y*-axis the corresponding point is.

(−1, 2): 1 unit to the left of the *y*-axis

coordenada x Primera parte de un par ordenado que indica la distancia a que está el punto correspondiente a la izquierda o a la derecha del eje *y*.

(−1, 2): 1 unidad a la izquierda del eje *y*

Y

yard (p. 632) A *customary unit* of *length* equal to 3 feet or 36 inches.

yarda *Unidad inglesa* de *longitud* igual a 3 pies ó 36 pulgadas.

y-axis (p. 213) The vertical axis (↕) in a coordinate plane.

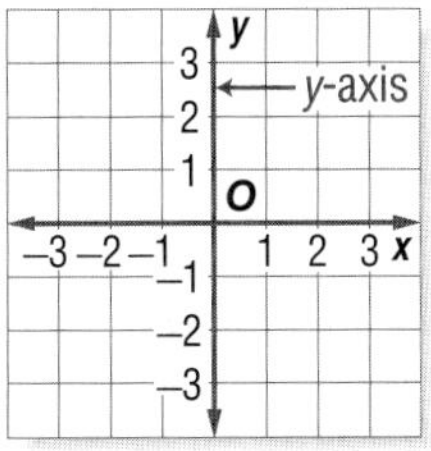

eje y El eje vertical (↕) en un plano de coordenadas.

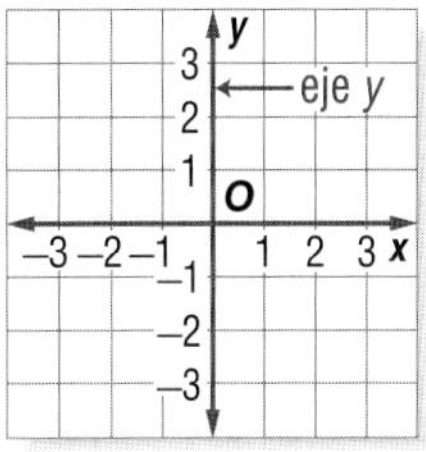

y-coordinate (p. 213) The second part of an ordered pair that indicates how far above or below the *x*-axis the corresponding point is.

(−1, 2): 2 units above the *x*-axis

coordenada y Segunda parte de un par ordenado que indica la distancia a que está el punto correspondiente por encima o por debajo del eje *x*.

(−1, 2): 2 unidades por encima del eje *x*

Z

zero pair (p. 353) The result when one positive counter is paired with one negative counter.

par nulo Resultado cuando se aparea una ficha positiva con una negativa.

Acknowledgements

Art Credits

McGraw-Hill would like to acknowledge the artists and agencies who contributed to illustrating this program: **Cover** Francesco Santalucia represented by Mendola Artists; Articulate Graphics; Kenneth Batelman; Epigraphics, Inc.; Bill Graham represented by Koralik Associates; Annette Lasker; Ralph Voltz.

Photo Credits

iv (cr)courtesy Beatrice Luchin, (bl)courtesy Vik Hovespian, (br)courtesy Donna Long, (others)Aaron Haupt; **v** (bl)courtesy Dinah Zike, (others)Aaron Haupt; **vi** (tl)courtesy Cheryl Avalos, (tc)courtesy William Bokesh, (tr)courtesy Patty Brown, (cl)courtesy David Chamberlain, (c)courtesy Eppie Chung, (cr)courtesy Lisa Cirrcione, (bl)courtesy Carol Cronk, (bc)courtesy Ilene Foster, (br)courtesy Grant Fraser; **vii** (l)courtesy Juvenal Martinez, (tl)courtesy Suzanne Freire, (tcl)courtesy Beth Holguin, (tcr)courtesy Donna Kopenski, (tr)courtesy Kelly Mack, (cl)courtesy John McGuire, (cr)courtesy Donald Price, (r)courtesy Kasey St. James, (bl)courtesy Art Wayman, (bc)courtesy Beverly Wells, (br)courtesy Frances Whitney; **x** Kerrick James Photog/Getty Images; **xii** Miles Ertman/Masterfile; **xiv** George H. H. Huey/CORBIS; **xviii** Robert Landau/CORBIS; **xx** Richard Cummins/CORBIS; **xxiii** Digital Vision/Getty Images; **1** Theo Allofs/CORBIS; **2** Larry Prosor/SuperStock; **3** Getty Images; **4** Reuters/CORBIS; **5** Kerrick James Photog/Getty Images; **6** Boden/Ledingham/Masterfile; **7** Blaine Harrington III/CORBIS; **8** NBAE/Getty Images; **9** Keiji Iwai/SuperStock; **10** Bruce Burkhardt/CORBIS; **11** age fotostock/SuperStock; **12** SuperStock, Inc./SuperStock; **13** Ron & Patty Thomas/Getty Images; **14–15** Donald Miralle/Getty Images; **19** age fotostock/SuperStock; **21** Horizons Companies; **22** Getty Images; **25** (l)Cindy Charles/PhotoEdit, (r)Robert W. Ginn/PhotoEdit; **26** Ed-imaging; **28** CORBIS; **30** (l)David Young-Wolff/PhotoEdit, (r)Tony Freeman/PhotoEdit; **32** Tim Fuller; **34** Myrleen Ferguson Cate/PhotoEdit; **37** Sandy Felsenthal/CORBIS; **39** Joe McDonald/CORBIS; **42** (cr)Wolfgang Kaehler/CORBIS, (bl)Dann Tardif/LWA/Getty Images, (br)Pierre Arsenault/Masterfile; **44** Dana White/PhotoEdit; **45** Maxine Hall/CORBIS; **47** MacDonald Photography/Photo Network Stock/Grant Heilman Photography; **56–57** Franck Jeannin/Alamy; **57** (t)Oleg Moiseyenk/Alamy Images, (b)Getty Images; **59** Michael Murdock; **61** (l)Amos Morgan/Getty Images, (r)The McGraw-Hill Companies Inc.; **70–71** Richard Cummins/SuperStock; **73** Kevin Fleming/CORBIS; **76** age fotostock/SuperStock; **78** Ed-imaging; **79** Getty Images; **80** David Young-Wolff/Photo Edit; **81** Lori Adamski Peek/Getty Images; **84** EyeWire/Getty Images; **87** F. Lukasseck/Masterfile; **88** Tom & Dee Ann McCarthy/CORBIS; **92** Masterfile; **99** Yva Momatiuk/John Eastcott/Minden Pictures; **102** Icon SMI/CORBIS; **104** Paul Barton/CORBIS; **114** Matt Campbell/CORBIS; **116** Georgette Douwma/Photo Researchers; **118–119** Tim Cuff/Alamy Images; **128–129** David Stoecklein/CORBIS; **136** Laura Rauch/AP Images; **138** Jacques M. Chenet/CORBIS; **139** (tl)Michael Newman/PhotoEdit, (tr)David Young-Wolff/PhotoEdit; **140** Ed-imaging; **142** Michael Barley/CORBIS; **143** Scott Tysick/Masterfile; **144** (tr)Tim de Waele/CORBIS, (br)Miles Ertman/Masterfile; **146** Ed-imaging; **150** Blend Images/SuperStock; **154** John Evans; **158** Al Bello/Getty Images; **159** Michael Newman/PhotoEdit; **160** (tr)Gunter Marx Photography/CORBIS, (br)Michael Zagaris/MLB Photos via Getty Images; **162** Melba Photo Agency/Punchstock; **172–173** Anthony Johnson/Getty Images; **179** Ed-imaging; **180** Tim Fuller; **186** John A. Rizzo/Getty Images; **187** Gary Conner/PhotoEdit; **191** Gary Vestal/Getty Images; **196** (l)Karen Tweedy-Holmes/CORBIS, (r)Gary W. Carter/CORBIS; **197** (l)Cleve Bryant/PhotoEdit, (r)Michael Newman/PhotoEdit; **198** John Evans; **201** C Squared Studios/Getty Images; **203** George H. H. Huey/CORBIS; **205** Morrison Photography; **208** (l)PunchStock, (r)Pete Leonard/zefa/CORBIS; **211** Billy E. Barnes/PhotoEdit; **214** Matt Meadows; **218–219** Getty Images; **228** F. Lukasseck/Masterfile; **228–229** Tom Till/Getty Images; **234** (l)Leroy Simon/Visuals Unlimited, (r)Matt Meadows; **235** (l)Mark Burnett, (r)The McGraw-Hill Companies; **237** Bethel Area Chamber of Commerce; **239** SuperStock, Inc./SuperStock; **246** David Young-Wolff/PhotoEdit; **251** C Squared Studios/Getty Images; **253** David Muir/Masterfile; **255** (l)Michelle Pedone/zefa/CORBIS, (r)CORBIS; **257** Ed-imaging; **258** John Evans; **260** Doug Martin; **263** Otto Greule Jr/Getty Images; **267** James Watt/Animals Animals; **268** (l)Ed-imaging, (r)CORBIS; **270** Getty Images; 271 Philip James Corwin/CORBIS; **280** David Tipling/Photographer's Choice/Getty Images; **284** Stephen Marks/Getty Images; **286** Tim Fuller; **290** C Squared Studios/Getty Images; **292** Prisma/SuperStock; **294** CORBIS; **297** Biggie Productions/Getty Images; **299** (l)Simon Watson/Stone/Getty Images, (r)Matthew Donaldson/ImageState; **300** Ed-imaging; **305** Jon Arnold Images/SuperStock; **308** John Evans; **312** photocuisine/CORBIS; **316** CORBIS; **318** Ron Kimball/Ron Kimball Stock; **320** Bob Daemmrich/PhotoEdit; **323** Archivo Iconografico, S.A./CORBIS; **329** Dorling Kindersley/Getty Images; **330** (l)Kevin Peterson/Getty Images, (tr)Bill Ross/CORBIS, (r)Brad Wilson/Getty Images; **332** Everett C. Johnson/eStock Photo; **333** CORBIS; **346–347** Jeremy Woodhouse/Getty Images; **350** (t)NASA/JPL/Malin Space Science Systems, (c)StockTrek/Getty Images, (b)NASA/GSFC; **357** Tom Pidgeon/Getty Images; **362** CORBIS; **366** John Weinstein/Reuters/CORBIS; **368** Michael Newman/PhotoEdit; **372** Akira Matoba/SuperStock; **374** (l)Richard Ross/Getty Images, (r)Ed-imaging; **376** Getty Images; **387** Richard Price/Getty Images; **388** Pierre Tostee/Reuters/CORBIS; **390** (tr)CORBIS; **390–391** SIME s.a.s/eStock Photo; **393** Laura Sifferlin; **395** CORBIS; **396** (l)Michael Newman/PhotoEdit, (r)Myrleen Ferguson Cate/PhotoEdit; **397** Ed-imaging; **398** Laura Sifferlin; **410–411** Robert Landau/CORBIS; **415** Joe McDonald/CORBIS; **418** (l)Big Cheese Photo/SuperStock, (r)First Light; **419** Ed-imaging; **420** David Young-Wolff/PhotoEdit; **423** Chris Hondros/Getty Images; **425** C Squared Studios/Getty Images; **426** Rick Gomez/CORBIS; **428** Getty Images; **431** (t)Daryl Benson/Masterfile, (b)CORBIS; **434** Image Source/Getty Images; **437** Randy Faris/CORBIS; **439** Michael Newman/PhotoEdit; **440** (l)Reza Estakhrian/Taxi/Getty Images, (r)Dann Tardif/LWA/Getty Images; **444** George H. H. Huey/CORBIS; **446** Alack-StockFood Munich/StockFood America; **448–449** Jeff Rotman/Getty Images; **453** Nigel J. Dennis/Photo Researchers, Inc.; **462–463** Zoran Milich/Masterfile; **478** Benn Mitchell/Getty Images; **481** Ed-imaging; **482** Rick Friedman/CORBIS; **486** Stockdisc Classic/Alamy; **495** (tl)CORBIS, (r)MedioImages/Alamy Images; **496** John Evans; **502** (r)Ed-imaging, (tr)George Hall/CORBIS; **503** BananaStock/SuperStock; **508** Doug Martin; **510–511** Ace Stock Limited/Alamy Images; **513** Michael Newman/PhotoEdit; **514** Rayman/Getty Images; **515** (l)RubberBall/Alamy Images, (r)Michael Newman/PhotoEdit; **526–527** Cedar Point; **531** (l)Mark Burnett, (r)Doug Martin; **533** Ed-imaging; **534** Jose Luis Pelaez, Inc./CORBIS; **539** (t)Richard Cummins/CORBIS, (b)Doug Martin; **543** (t)Getty Images, (b)Bryan Mullennix/Getty Images; **548** John Evans; **554** Jan Cook/Botonica/PictureQuest; **555** National Trail Parks And Recreation District; **560** (l)David Pollack/CORBIS, (r)Mark Gibson; **564–565** Robert Harding Picture Library/Alamy Images; **565** (inset)Martin Moos/Lonely Planet Images; **569** David R. Frazier Photolibrary/Alamy Images; **572** Richard Klune/CORBIS; **573** CORBIS; **577** Mark Richards/PhotoEdit; **580–581** Anthony Mercieca/SuperStock; **586** W. Perry Conway/CORBIS; **587** David Pollack/CORBIS; **588** (l)Purestock/SuperStock, (r)Plush Studios/Blend Images/Getty Images; **590** Matt Meadows; **596** The McGraw-Hill Companies; **599** Aaron Haupt; **600** Getty Images; **602** (l)Big Cheese Photo/SuperStock, (r)David Young-Wolff/PhotoEdit; **604** Ed-imaging; **606** Laura Sifferlin; **614–615** Elisabeth Coelfen/Alamy Images; **615** (inset)Roberto Benzi/age fotostock; **618** Denis Scott/CORBIS; **630** Tim Fuller; **631** Tim Fuller; **638** Life Images; **645** Michael Simpson/Getty Images; **647** Kennan Ward/CORBIS; **651** (l)Park Street/PhotoEdit, (r)Dann Tardif/LWA/Getty Images; **652** Eclipse Studios

Index

Index

D

Index

Index

H

I

K

Index

percent-fraction equivalents, 484
perimeter of a rectangle, 586
perimeter of a square, 585
prime and composite, 18
prisms, 566
probability, 498
round decimals, 141
rounding to the nearest half, 232
statistical displays, 107
subtract integers, 359
subtract like fractions, 242
subtraction property of equality, 387
sum of angle measures in a triangle, 552
surface area of a rectangular prism, 617
types of angles, 530
volume of a rectangular prism, 609

Kilogram, 644

Kilometer, 640

L

Labs. *See* Algebra Lab, Geometry Lab, Hands On Mini Lab, Math Lab, Measurement Lab, Statistics Lab

LCD. *See* Least common denominator (LCD)

LCM. *See* Least common multiple (LCM)

Least common denominator (LCD), 200

Least common multiple (LCM), 194, 195

Length (mini lab), 632. *See also* Customary system, Metric system

Like fractions, 241

Linear, 382
functions, 39, 40, 443, 444, 450–452

Line graphs, 74, 79
interpreting, 79

Line plot, 87
analyzing, 88

Line segment, 553

Lines
intersecting, 541
parallel, 541
perpendicular, 541

Liter, 645

Log, 112

M

Making predictions, 512

Manipulatives
adding machine tape, 471
balance scale, 46, 644
base-ten blocks, 296, 302
breath mints, 644
centimeter cubes, 50, 95, 566, 608
centimeter ruler, 585
colored cubes, 504
colored pencils, 189, 314
colored rectangles, 58
compass, 545, 546
counters 353, 364, 371, 383, 385, 392, 398, 434
cube, 616
cups, 383, 385, 392, 398
customary ruler, 32
dot paper, 551
fraction strips, 182
fraction tiles, 228, 242, 244, 249, 265
gallon containers, 636
graph paper, 213–217
grid paper, 50, 241, 557, 583, 591, 598
hole punch, 21
index card, 189
paper bag, 504
paper clips, 413
paper plates, 260, 536
pennies, 32
pint containers, 636
protractor, 529–532, 536–540, 557
quart containers, 636
scissors, 591, 617, 632
square tiles, 17
string, 590, 632
tape measure, 632
tape, 617
water, 636
yard stick, 632

Mass, 644

Mathematics Framework for California Public Schools, Grade 5, xxiv–xxvii

Math Lab
adding and subtracting decimals, 156
dividing by decimals, 302
dividing fractions, 325
equivalent fractions, 182
modeling percents, 465
multiplying decimals by whole numbers, 283
multiplying fractions, 314
percent of a number, 490
rounding fractions, 231
unlike denominators, 249
zero pairs, 353

Math Online. *See* Internet connections

Mean, 95
key concept, 95
mini lab, 95

Measure, nearest half, 233

Measurement, 25, 35, 37, 38, 54, 61, 67, 77, 191, 203, 207, 211, 216, 224, 234, 235, 238, 244, 245, 248, 254, 256, 259, 263, 264, 267, 273, 276, 277, 286, 287, 292, 307, 309, 312, 313, 320, 322, 323, 329, 334, 336, 337, 339, 343, 444, 445, 446, 595, 603, 613, 621, *See also* Customary system, Measurement Lab, Metric system
angles, 529
area, 571, 573
circumference, 590
lab, 583, 590, 598, 622
perimeter, 583, 585, 586
volume, 608, 609

Measurement Lab
area and perimeter, 583
area of triangles, 598
circumference, 590
selecting formulas and units, 622

Measuring angles, 529

Median, 99

Mental math. *See also* Number sense, Remember
comparing fractions, 102
percent-fraction equivalents, 484
remember, 202, 599
solving equations, 47, 48
solving percents, 485
using the Distributive Property, 59, 60

Index

N

O

P

Powers, 22

Predictions, 512

Prerequisite Skills
Are You Ready for Chapter, 16, 72, 130, 174, 230, 282, 348, 412, 464, 528, 582
Get Ready to Learn, 17, 21, 27, 34, 39, 46, 52, 58, 73, 79, 83, 87, 95, 99, 106, 113, 131, 135, 141, 149, 157, 175, 184, 189, 194, 200, 205, 209, 213, 232, 237, 241, 251, 260, 265, 284, 290, 296, 303, 310, 316, 321, 327, 349, 354, 359, 364, 371, 385, 393, 398, 413, 422, 428, 436, 442, 450, 466, 471, 477, 484, 492, 498, 505, 512, 529, 536, 541, 551, 558, 566, 585, 591, 599, 608, 617, 632, 636, 640, 644, 648

Prime factorization, 18, 21, 23, 26
exponents, 23

Prime factors, 17

Prime number, 17

Prism, 566. *See also* Rectangular prism

Probability, 498
complement, 500
experimental, 504
finding, 499
outcomes, 498
sample space, 505
simple event, 498
theoretical, 504
tree diagrams, 506
using a mathematical model to describe, 498, 499, 501, 505, 506
using a physical model to describe, 504

Problem-solving. *See* Problem-Solving Investigation/Strategy

Problem-Solving in
art, 118, 564
geography, 218, 390
history, 56, 332
science, 162, 270, 448, 510, 614

Problem-Solving Investigation/Strategy
act it out, 246
choose the best strategy, 198, 258, 308, 376, 434, 496, 548, 606
draw a diagram, 534
extra or missing information, 104
guess and check, 44
look for a pattern, 420
make a model, 596
make an organized list, 180
make a table, 92
reasonable answers, 294
solve a simpler problem, 482
use estimation, 154
use logical reasoning, 146
work backward, 368

Problem-Solving Plan
Four Steps, the, 32
using, 33

Product, 22
estimation, 310
exponents, 22
factor, 22

Product of prime factors, 21

Proof
of the Distributive Property, 58
of the formula for the area of a parallelogram, 591
of the formula for the area of rectangle, 52
of the formula for the area of a square, 53
of the formula for the area of a triangle, 598
of the formula for the circumference of a circle, 590
of the formula for the perimeter of a rectangle, 586
of the formula for the perimeter of a square, 585
of the formula for the surface area of a rectangular prism, 617
of the formula for the volume of a rectangular prism, 608
that the sum of the angle measures in a quadrilateral is 360°, 557
that the sum of the angle measures in a triangle is 180°, 550

Proper fractions, 189

Protractor, 529–532, 536–540, 557

Q

Quadrants, 378

Quadrilaterals, 558
angles, 557, 558
mini lab, 558

Quantitative reasoning. *See* Number Sense

Quick Check, 16, 72, 130, 174, 230, 282, 348, 412, 464, 528, 582

R

Random, 499

Range, 100

Rates, 414

Rating scales, 111

Ratios, 184, 413
See also Fractions
equivalent, 422, 423
mini lab, 413
rates, 414
simplest form, 413
unit rates, 414, 415

Ratio tables, 422

Rational number, 205. *See also* Decimals, Fractions, Percents

Reading Math
approximation symbol, 157
arcs, 545
area measurement, 592
congruency symbol, 542
congruent angles, 559
division, 95
inequality symbols, 349
greater than, 135
less than, 135

Index

infinite, 18
lines, 541
naming angles, 530
outcomes, 506
perimeter, 590
positive and negative signs, 113
probability, 499
probability notation, 506
segments, 553
straightedge, 537
trials, 504
units, 50
volume measurement, 609

Real-World Problem Solving
animals, 116
architecture, 569
baseball, 81, 431
books, 508
fish, 24, 612
flags, 531
food, 620
football, 400
geography, 144, 203, 255, 330, 381
health, 286
insects, 417
measurement, 268
music, 323
nature, 98
school, 494
science, 19, 196, 211
sports, 152
statistics, 244
volunteering, 515
weather, 76, 351

Reasonableness, Check for. *See* Check for Reasonableness

Reasoning. *See* H.O.T. Problems

Reciprocals, 327

Rectangle, 559
area, 52
drawing, 562, 557
identifying, 559, 565
increase side lengths, 583
measuring, 557, 561
perimeter, 583, 584, 586, 624

Rectangular prism, 566, 608
nets, 616
surface area, 617
volume, 20, 609

Related measurement units, 444–446, 632–639, 644–647, 648–651

Remember
angles, 546
area of squares, 584
area units, 52
bar graphs, 74
benchmarks, 645
bias, 112
changing metric units, 649
changing units, 634
check by adding, 360
check for accuracy, 28, 114
check for reasonableness, 136
check your answer, 132, 158, 185, 266, 297, 423, 424, 567, 586, 618
checking solutions, 386, 399
circle graphs, 473
clustering, 150
comparing mixed numbers, 201
converting measures, 637
coordinate plane, 213
data, 96
decimal fraction equivalencies, 206, 209
decimal models, 289
decimals as percents, 478
displays, 107
estimating, 261
estimating area, 600
estimating differences, 252
estimation, 149
evaluating algebraic expressions, 444
evaluating expressions, 253
exponents, 22
expressions, 393
factoring, 195
finding the mean, 491
fractions as decimals, 210
graphing decimals, 214
graphing points, 379
guess and check, 47
line plots, 87
measuring angles, 537
mental math, 202, 599
metric length, 641
mode, 100
modeling percents, 465
multiplication, 35
multiplying negative integers, 365
number lines, 88, 190
ordering integers, 349
percents, 467, 493
percents as decimals, 477
prime factorization, 18
range, 100
ratio tables, 633
ratios, 437
reasonable answers, 467
reciprocal, 328
rounding, 142, 233, 238, 304
rounding fractions, 311
signs, 355
simplifying fractions, 413, 472
solving equations, 500, 513
solving mentally, 485
subtracting integers, 361
surveys, 512
triangles, 552
unit rates, 414, 429
whole numbers, 451
work backward, 372
zero pairs, 360, 384

Renaming mixed numbers, 265

Representing decimals, 131

Review. *See* Extra Practice, Prerequisite Skills, Spiral Review, Study Guide and Review

Review Vocabulary
equation, 383
factor, 317
function, 443
least common denominator (LCD), 252
mixed number, 232
multiple of a number, 310
opposites, 359
power, 303
prime factorization, 176
prime number, 176
quotient, 296
simplest form, 243

Rhombus, 559

Right angle, 530

Right triangle, 551

Index

Unit rates, 414, 429
Units, 622, *See also* Area, Perimeter, Volume
Unlike denominators, 249
Unlike fractions, 251
addition, 251
subtraction, 252

V

Variable, 34, 46
defining, 40
vocabulary link, 34
Venn diagrams, 175
Verbal model
for problem solving, 242
Vertex
of an angle, 529
of a prism, 566
Vertical angles, 542
Vertical axis, 73
Vocabulary Check, 62, 120, 164, 220, 272, 338, 402, 455, 517, 571, 623
Vocabulary Link
annex, 136, 285
capacity, 637
centi-, 648
centimeter, 648
complement, 500
complementary events, 500
decibel, 131
decimal, 131
distribute, 59
distributive, 59
equivalent, 184
horizon, 83
horizontal, 83
milli-, 640
millimeter, 640
quadrant, 378
quadruplet, 378
variable, 34
Vocabulary Review. *See* Internet connections
Volume, 608
measuring systems, 609
rectangular prism, 21, 608, 609

W

Which One Doesn't Belong? *See* H.O.T. Problems
Whole numbers
comparing, 135
converting to improper fractions, 265–269
decimals, multiplying, 283
multiplication, 317
number lines, 141
rounding, 141
Write decimals as fractions, 205
Writing formulas, 50
Writing in Math, 3, 5, 7, 9, 11, 13, 20, 25, 30, 31, 33, 38, 43, 45, 49, 55, 61, 67, 77, 82, 86, 91, 93, 94, 98, 103, 105, 110, 117, 125, 134, 139, 145, 147, 148, 153, 155, 161, 169, 178, 181, 188, 192, 193, 197, 199, 204, 208, 212, 217, 225, 236, 240, 245, 247, 248, 256, 259, 264, 269, 277, 287, 293, 295, 297, 306, 307, 309, 313, 319, 324, 337, 343, 352, 357, 363, 367, 369, 370, 375, 377, 382, 389, 396, 401, 407, 418, 421, 427, 432, 433, 435, 440, 447, 449, 454, 459, 470, 475, 480, 483, 487, 489, 495, 497, 503, 509, 511, 515, 523, 532, 535, 539, 544, 547, 549, 556, 563, 570, 577, 589, 595, 597, 603, 605, 607, 613, 615, 621, 627, 635, 639, 643, 647, 651

X

***x*-axis,** 213
***x*-coordinate,** 213

Y

***y*-axis,** 213
***y*-coordinate,** 213

Z

Zero pairs, 353
math lab, 353
Zeros, 136, 158, 285

Symbols

Number and Operations		Geometry and Measurement	
$+$	plus or positive	$\cong$	is congruent to
$-$	minus or negative	$^\circ$	degree(s)
$a \cdot b$ $a \times b$ ab or $a(b)$	a times b	$\overleftrightarrow{AB}$	line AB
$\div$	divided by	$\overline{AB}$	line segment AB
$=$	is equal to	∟	right angle
$>$	is greater than	$\perp$	is perpendicular to
$<$	is less than	$\parallel$	is parallel to
$\approx$	is approximately equal to	$\angle A$	angle A
%	percent	$m\angle A$	measure of angle A
$a:b$	the ratio of a to b, or $\frac{a}{b}$	(a, b)	ordered pair with x-coordinate a and y-coordinate b
$0.7\overline{5}$	repeating decimal 0.75555...	O	origin

Algebra and Functions		Probability and Statistics	
a^n	a to the nth power	$P(A)$	probability of event A